SOURCES AND ANALOGUES OF THE CANTERBURY TALES

Volume II

ROBERT M. CORREALE
General Editor

MARY HAMEL
Associate General Editor

D. S. BREWER

First published 2005
D. S. Brewer, Cambridge
Reprinted in paperback 2009

ISBN 978-184384-190-6

D. S. Brewer is an imprint of Boydell & Brewer Ltd
PO Box 9, Woodbridge, Suffolk IP12 3DF, UK
and of Boydell & Brewer Inc.
668 Mt Hope Avenue, Rochester, NY 14620, USA
website: www.boydellandbrewer.com

A catalogue record for this book is available
from the British Library

Library of Congress Catalog Card Number: 2001037783

This publication is printed on acid-free paper

Printed in Great Britain by
CPI Antony Rowe, Chippenham and Eastbourne

Contents

Foreword

This volume has its origin some thirty or more years ago, when one of the objects of setting up D. S. Brewer Ltd was to publish an updated version of the much-valued *Sources and Analogues to the* Canterbury Tales, edited by Bryan and Dempster, which was by then in need of revision, expansion, and some translation. Since then the value of studying sources and analogues in relation to a text – quite beyond the simple identification of a real or possible source – has been ever more appreciated, while at the same time the bulk of the material available has greatly increased.

After some false starts, the project was taken up by the New Chaucer Society, who asked Professor Robert Correale to serve as General Editor. Delays continued, perhaps inevitable on such a complex and large volume; and some involved felt a more suitable publisher might be found, but on being approached, all in their wisdom declined. The book subsequently fell into some abeyance, until at the Paris Congress of the New Chaucer Society, in 1994, Professor Gila Aloni, then recently awarded her doctorate by the University of Paris IV (Sorbonne), galvanised editors, contributors, and project alike with her enthusiasm. Professor Derek Pearsall agreed to act as Chair of a new committee, and Professor Correale and others were approached again, with Professor Mary Hamel kindly agreeing to act as Associate General Editor. Some scholars, whose work had been started and completed, agreed to re-activate and revise their contributions; others, new to the project, were recruited.

The whole project obviously owes an enormous debt to the contributors, and especially to the principal editors; they have worked selflessly for many years, often carrying a heavy teaching load, and sometimes hindered by ill-health. It is right here also to acknowledge with gratitude the support of their universities (particularly for the American contributors) for an otherwise unfunded project. Many other individuals, indeed too many to name here, have also generously contributed their time and learning; but I would particularly like to thank Professor Jill Mann for her help at a late stage in the project's development.

It gives me great pleasure to see the volume finally in production.

Derek Brewer
Cambridge, 2004

Preface

This second volume of *Sources and Analogues of The Canterbury Tales* completes the project, sponsored by the New Chaucer Society, to revise and expand the collection of Chaucer's sources published by Bryan and Dempster in 1941.[1] Appearing here for the first time in any such collection are investigations of the sources and analogues of *The General Prologue* and analogues to Chaucer's *Retraction.* The other chapters cover the remaining tales not included in Volume 1 – those of the Knight, Miller, Man of Law, Wife of Bath, Summoner, Merchant, Physician, Shipman, Prioress, Sir Thopas, Canon's Yeoman, and Manciple.

In addition to the new first-time chapters, readers will find several other significant differences between the source materials printed here and those in Bryan and Dempster. A new and greatly extended discussion of *The Knight's Tale* includes not only a summary of the *Teseida*, but also all the relevant passages from it and from Chaucer's other principal sources in Statius and Boethius. Other additions include one major and six "minor" sources of *The Wife of Bath's Prologue,* the sources of the prologues to the tales of the Man of Law, Summoner, and Prioress, and a number of new analogues, especially to *The Prioress's Tale* and *The Canon Yeoman's Tale.* Three new stories from *The Decameron* have also been added, two identified as analogues to *The Merchant's Tale* and one as an analogue to *The Shipman's Tale,* providing further evidence of the belief among many contemporary scholars that Boccaccio's work was an important influence on the development of *The Canterbury Tales.* At the same time, many analogues in Bryan and Dempster have been dropped by individual contributors because they are too distant in time or place from Chaucer's work, or are lacking in word-for-word correspondences, or differ substantially in narrative structure or other plot motifs. One example of such pruning occurs in the chapter on *The Miller's Tale,* where only one of the four analogues found in the earlier volume, the Flemish fabliau, is judged to be closest to Chaucer's tale, close enough even to be considered its "near source."

The format and purpose remain the same as in the first volume. Each chapter contains a review of the research done over the past sixty years on such matters

[1] W. F. Bryan and Germaine Dempster, eds. *Sources and Analogues of Chaucer's Canterbury Tales* (1941; rpt. Humanities Press, 1958). Additional analogues are printed and discussed by Larry D. Benson and Theodore M. Andersson, eds. in *The Literary Context of Chaucer's Fabliaux* (Indianapolis, IN, and New York, 1971).

as the origin of Chaucer's sources, their transmission down to his time, and evidence of his indebtedness to them. The arrangement of chapters again follows the order of the tales in *The Riverside Chaucer.* Modern English translations are provided for all foreign language sources, generally on facing pages for lengthy texts, but also immediately following shorter passages in chapters like *The General Prologue and Retraction* and elsewhere where brief excerpts are quoted. The individual contributors have made the decisions about what texts to include, whether to reproduce them from printed editions or re-edit them from original manuscripts according to current editorial practice, and whether to use their own translations or those of others. Some well-known sources (in *The Knight's Tale*, *The Man of Law's Tale*, *The Wife of Bath's Prologue*) have been newly edited from surviving texts similar to those Chaucer presumably knew and used.

Our primary purpose has been, as it was for Bryan and Dempster (p.viii), to describe, within the boundaries of our present knowledge, all the important known written *literary* sources and analogues of *The Canterbury Tales,* and to present them as accurately and as attractively as possible, leaving questions of how Chaucer used them for his own artistic purposes to be answered by others. At the same time, contributors have not been unaware of, or insensitive to, the changes that have occurred in the field of source-study over the past several decades. In their opening essays several have mentioned, or alluded to, ways that non-literary sources – such as memory, manuscript production and illumination, and iconography – have influenced the creation of the *Tales*. In years to come, increased interest in these and similar kinds of "sources" by Chaucerians may very likely play a more important role in shaping the contours of the successor to this volume and future collections of the sources and analogues of Chaucer's work.

The general editors are grateful to the many people who have aided us in various ways during the production of this second volume. We are indebted to the contributors who gave generously of their time and expertise to write on the individual tales, and to their colleges and universities for the financial aid and other assistance they have received. The editors also express their thanks and appreciation to the many scholars whose learning and assistance the contributors themselves have acknowledged in their individual chapters. We also thank the members of the editorial board for their insights and advice, and our many colleagues in the New Chaucer Society who offered moral support and encouragement over the years.

We owe a special debt of gratitude to Professor Jill Mann for her help in correcting and improving translations in Volume I. She has also carefully vetted every chapter in the present volume, has again offered invaluable assistance with many translations, and has helped us to avoid various kinds of errors.

The English department at Wright State University has continued to support our efforts, and we thank Dr. Henry Limouze, department chair, and his excellent secretarial staff – Leanne Moeller, Jennifer Sheets and Lynn Morgan – for their many personal and professional kindnesses. Three former WSU administrators,

the late Dean Eugene Cantelupe and former department chairs Peter Bracher and Lawrence Hussman, also provided encouragement and financial help during the early stages of the project. Bert Nagy, Christopher Correale and the staff at the WSU CaTS help desk provided timely assistance with computer problems, as did Jan Barbour with photocopying.

We are especially happy to acknowledge our gratitude to the editors and staff at Boydell & Brewer, in particular to Caroline Palmer, editorial director, for her good sense, sound advice, and encouragement during all the time she has worked with us in preparing these two volumes. Our thanks also go to Pam Cope, copy-editor and designer; Ken Shiplee, typesetter; and Vanda Andrews in production – whose talents and just plain hard work have contributed enormously to the successful completion of these books.

Finally, I am grateful to my wife Jeanne for giving so much of her time and energy to help us in a number of important areas, particularly by carefully reading and checking all texts and notes for accuracy. And much more importantly I am grateful for her love and support, her many personal sacrifices, and her constant encouragement in the face of difficulties during all the years we have worked together on this project.

Acknowledgements

The editors, contributors and publishers are grateful to all the institutions and journals listed below for permission to reprint, or to quote from, the materials for which they hold copyright. Every effort has been made to trace the copyright holders; apologies are offered for any omission in this regard, and the publishers will be pleased to add any necessary acknowledgement in subsequent editions.

General Prologue

Guillaume de Lorris and Jean de Meun, *The Romance of the Rose*, Oxford World's Classics, trans. and ed. Frances Horgan (New York, 1994). Reprinted by permission of Oxford University Press.

John Gower, *Vox Clamantis*, trans. E. W. Stockton, *The Major Latin Works of John Gower* (Seattle, 1962). Reprinted by permission of the University of Washington Press.

John Gower, *Mirour de l'Omme* (The Mirror of Mankind), trans. William Burton Wilson, rev. Nancy Wilson Van Baak (East Lansing, MI, 1992). Reprinted by permission of Michigan State University Press.

Knight's Tale

Giovanni Boccaccio, *Teseida*, from Biblioteca Marciana, Venice, MS it. IX, 61, fols 3^{r}–64^{r} (selections). By permission of the Biblioteca Marciana.

P. Papinius Statius, *Thebais*, eds. Alfred Klotz and Thomas C. Klinnert (München-Leipzig, 2001; reprint of the 2nd edn, Leipzig, 1973), book 1: 7–14, 171–85; book 4: 455–68, 494–99; book 6: 35–6, 54–65, 98–106, 110–13, 495–506; book 7: 34–61, 178–80; book 9: 606–36; book 11: 530–6, 539–40; book 12: 519–22, 702–5. Reprinted by permission of K. G. Saur Verlag, München-Leipzig.

Boethius, *Consolation of Philosophy*, trans. W. V. Cooper, The Temple Classics, ed. Israel Gollancz (London, 1902), 1 met. 5; 2 met. 8; 3 met. 9; 4 met. 6; selections from: 2 pr. 5; 3 pr. 2; 3 pr. 10; 3 met. 12; 4 pr. 6. Reprinted by permission of Everyman Publishers Plc., London.

Man of Law's Tale

Lotario Dei Segni (Pope Innocent III), *De Miseria Condicionis Humane*, ed. and trans. Robert Enzer Lewis (Athens, GA, 1978), pp. 114–15; 128–31; 166–9; 170–1. Reprinted by permission of the University of Georgia Press.

Nicholas Trevet, *Les Cronicles*, from BN ms français 9687, fols. 62v–69r; by permission of the Bibliothèque Nationale de France.

Wife of Bath's Prologue

Theophrastus, *Liber de Nuptiis*, from *Jankyn's Book of Wikked Wyves, 1: The Primary Texts (JBWW1)*, ed. and trans. Ralph Hanna and Traugott Lawler, The Chaucer Library (Athens and London: University of Georgia Press, 1997), pp. 121–47; 149–55. Reprinted by permission of the University of Georgia Press.

Le Roman de la Rose, CFMA, ed. Félix LeCoy (Paris, 1965–70), vols 1–3 lines 7379–80; 8549–70; 8999–9008; 9161–80; 9929–33; 9950; 12731–9; 12771–81; 12902–18; 13007–14; 13120–2; 13422–6; 13492–8; 13559–62; 13667–78; 14351–5; 14363; 14448–82; 18106–07. Reprinted by permission of Éditions Honoré Champion, Paris.

Valerius Maximus, *Facta et Dicta Memorabilia*, ed. John Briscoe (Stuttgart and Leipzig, 1998), vol. 1, Book VI, Chapter 3, "De Severitate."

Wife of Bath's Tale

Oxford, Bodleian Library, MS. Fairfax 3 [c. 1399], fols 16a–18c. Oxford, Bodleian Library, MS. Rawlinson C. 86 (c.1500), fols 128v–140r. London, British Library, MS. Additional 27879 (c. 1650), pp. 46–52. The editors express their gratitude to the Bodleian Library and the British Library.

Summoner's Tale

Nouveau Recueil Complet des Fabliaux (NRCF) X, ed. W. Noomen (Van Gorcum, Assen, 1998), pp. 295–303. Reprinted by permission of the publisher.

The Literary Context of Chaucer's Fabliaux, ed. Larry D. Benson and Theodore M. Andersson (Indianapolis, IN, and New York, 1971), pp. 345, 347–9, 351–3, 355, 357, 359. Reprinted by permission.

Merchant's Tale

Albertano of Brescia, *The Book of Consolation and Advice*, trans. C. W. Marx from *Women Defamed and Women Defended: An Anthology of Medieval Texts*, ed. Alcuin Blamires (Oxford, 1992), pp. 240–1. By permission of Oxford University Press.

Boccaccio, 'Day II, 10' and 'Day VII, 9', from *Decameron*, ed. Vittore Branca (Turin, 1980), pp. 303–14 and 861–75.

Boccaccio, *La comedia delle ninfe fiorentine*, XXXII, pp. 772–6, from the edition by Antonio Enzo Quaglio in *Tutte le opera di Giovanni Boccaccio*, ed. Vittore Branca (Milan, 1964).

Manuale ad usum percelebris ecclesie Sarisburiensis, ed. A. Jefferies Collins (London: The Henry Bradshaw Society, 1960), p. 54. By kind permission of the Society.

Physician's Tale

Titus Livius, *Ab urbe condita*, III. 44–48; 58. Reprinted by permission of the publishers and Trustees of the Loeb Classical Library from LIVY: AB URBE CONDITA VOLUME II, Loeb Classical Library Volume L 133, translated by B.O. Foster (Cambridge, MA and London, 1922). The Loeb Classical Library ® is a registered trademark of the President and Fellows of Harvard College.

Guillaume de Lorris and Jean de Meun, *The Romance of the Rose*, ll. 5589–5658, edited and translated by Frances Horgan, Oxford World's Classics (Oxford, 1994), pp. 86–7. Reprinted by permission of Oxford University Press.

Shipman's Tale

Boccaccio, *Tutte Le Opere di Giovanni Boccaccio*, ed. Vittore Branca, 10 vols (Verona, 1964–2000), IV. 670–3, 5–18; 674,6–680,47.

Prioress's Tale

NA1. Alfonso El Sabio, *Songs of Holy Mary*, translated by Kathleen Culp-Hill (Tempe, 2000), pp. 1–12. Reprinted by permission of the translator.

NA3. *De quodom puero qui solebat psallere alma redemptoris mater* (from Balliol College MS 228 fol. 290r, col. 1); text and translation reprinted by permission of Balliol College Library, Oxford University.

NA4. *Gaude Maria reponsorium puer cantans occiditur pro quo Salve sancta parens celitus decantatur* (from Trinity College Dublin, MS 167, chapter 107, fol. 36v, col. 1); text and translation reprinted by permission of the Board of Trinity College Dublin.

NA5. *Monachus cantans responsorium Gaude Maria a judeo occisus per beatam virginem est resuscitatus* (from Trinity College Dublin, MS 167, chapter 254, fol. 69v, col. 2); text and translation reprinted by permission of the Board of Trinity College Dublin.

C10. "The Story of the *Alma redemptoris mater*," translated with annotatations by A. C. Rigg. Reprinted from *Geoffrey Chaucer, The Canterbury Tales: Nine Tales and the General Prologue*, ed. V. A. Kolve and Glending Olson (New York, 1989), pp. 418–23. Reprinted by permission of A. C. Rigg.

Canon's Yeoman's Tale

Bodleian MS Ashmole 1487, fols 182–6. The editors express their gratitude to the Bodleian Library.

Anthony Bonner, trans., *Selected Works of Ramon Llull* (Princeton, 1985). Copyright 1985 by Princeton University Press. Reprinted by permission of Princeton University Press.

J. R. Partington, "Albertus Magnus on Alchemy," *Ambix* 1 (1937), p.16. Reprinted by permission of The Society for the History of Alchemy and Chemistry.

H. G. Richardson, "Year Books and Plea Rolls as Sources of Historical Information," *Transactions of the Royal Historical Society*, fourth series, vol. 5 (1922), p. 39. Reprinted by permission of The Royal Historical Society.

Thomas Norton's Ordinal of Alchemy, ed. John Reidy, EETS OS 272 (London, 1975), pp. 14, 26–7, 38, lines 323–36, 757–78, 1151–66. Reprinted by permission of The Council of the Early English Text Society.

Robert Belle Burke, trans., *The Opus Maius of Roger Bacon*, vol 2, pp. 626–7. Copyright 1928 by University of Pennsylvania Press. Reprinted by courtesy of the publisher.

The Romance of the Rose, ed. and trans. Frances Horgan, Oxford World's Classics (Oxford, 1994), pp. 272–3, lines 16035–118. Reprinted by permission of Oxford University Press.

Manciple's Tale

Guillaume de Machaut, *Le Livre dou Voir Dit* (The Book of the True Poem), ed. Daniel Leech-Wilkinson; trans. R. Barton Palmer (New York: Garland, 1998). Reprinted by permission of the publisher.

Ovid, *Metamorphoses* 9. 134–41. Reprinted by permission of the publishers and Trustees of the Loeb Classical Library from OVID: METAMORPHOSES VOLUME IV, Loeb Classical Library Volume L 043, translated by Frank J. Miller, revised by G. P. Goold (Cambridge, Mass., 1916, 1984). The Loeb Classical Library ® is a registered trademark of the President and Fellows of Harvard College.

Chaucer's Retraction

Bede, *Retractatio in Actus Apolostorum*, ed. M.L. W. Laistner, The Medieval Academy of America Publication 35 (1939; rpt New York, 1970). Reprinted by permission of the Medieval Academy.

Ovid, *Tristia.* Reprinted by permission of the publishers and the Trustees of the Loeb Classical Library from OVID: VOLUME VI, Loeb Classical Library ® Volume L 151, translated by A. L. Wheeler, revised 1988 by G. P. Goold (Cambridge, Mass., 1924, 1988), pp. 79, 201, 255,and 257 The Loeb Classical Library ® is a registered trademark of the President and Fellows of Harvard College.

Apollonaris Sidonius, *Letter, IX.xvi.* Reprinted by permission of the publishers and the Trustees of the Loeb Classical Library from SIDONIUS: VOLUME II, Loeb Classical Library ® Volume L 296, translated by W. B. Anderson, pp. 602–605 (Cambridge, Mass., 1936). The Loeb Classical Library ® is a registered trademark of the President and Fellows of Harvard College.

Guibert de Nogent, *Autobiographie*, from Paul J. Archambault, trans., *A Monk's Confession: The Memoirs of Guibert of Nogent* (University Park, PA, 1996), pp. 58, 59, 60. Copyright 1996 by The Pennsylvania State University. Reproduced by permission of the publisher.

Hartmann von Aue, *Gregorius*, ed. Hermann Paul, 13th ed. (Tübingen. 1984), pp. 20–3, lines 1–16, 35–42. Reprinted by permission of the publisher.

Rudolf van Ems, *Barlaam und Josaphat*, ed. Franz Pfeiffer (Berlin, 1965), pp. 5, 404–5, lines 150–6, 16105–14, 16129–43. Reprinted by permission of the publisher.

Denis Piramus, *La Vie Seint Edmund le rei, Poème anglo-normand du XIIe siècle*, ed. Hilding Kjellman (Geneva, 1974), pp. 3–4, lines 1–8, 13–21. Reprinted by permission of the publisher.

Francesco Petrarch, *Canzioniere "Poem I."* Reprinted by permission of the publisher from *Petrarch's Lyric Poems: the Rime Sparse and Other Lyrics*, translated and edited by Robert M. Durling (Cambridge, Mass., 1976), pp. 36–37. Copyright © 1976 by Robert M. Durling.

Bede, *Ecclesiastical History of The English People*, edited and translated by Bertram Colgrave and R. A. B. Mynors (Oxford, 1991), pp. 566–71. Reprinted by permission of Oxford University Press.

The General Prologue

ROBERT R. RAYMO

Chaucer was familiar with many of the framed story-collections circulating in the medieval west and he absorbed and occasionally followed their innovations, but Boccaccio's *Decameron* was the only one to exert a decisive influence upon him in the composition of *The Canterbury Tales.* How thoroughly he knew it, when and where he became acquainted with it, and in what form are still matters of conjecture. Nevertheless, his debt to the *Decameron* for the overarching structure and plan of the Tales as well as for crucial aspects of narrative technique and content is well established and represents the broad consensus of modern scholarship.[1] The parallels between the *General Prologue* and Boccaccio's *Introduzione* are also striking. Both groups of people meet by chance, agree to go off together the following morning and to divert one another with stories under the direction of a master of ceremonies. Both authors, moreover, defend their literary autonomy by the use of similar authenticating devices (Chaucer in the *General Prologue*, Boccaccio in his *Conclusione Dell'Autore*) and see their tales as offering both profit and pleasure.

These similarities, however, are of a general nature. For a precise source of the *General Prologue*, Helen Cooper proposes the A-text of *Piers Plowman* as having the "strongest claim to being his direct model":

> [It] opens with a prologue that contains a spring setting followed by an estates satire, of the people working (or not) in the 'field of folk' that is an epitome of late fourteenth-century England. They include ideal ploughmen, merchants who appear to be thriving, priests who run off to London chantries to sing for silver, friars who dress in fine copes and give absolution in return for cash, a venal pardoner, rich sergeants-at-law, and a group of assorted burgesses, mostly clothworkers, ending, as does Chaucer's list of guildsmen, with cooks. The Prologue and the other Sections of the A-text provide analogues to some

For research assistance and other kinds of help in the preparation of this chapter, I am grateful to the following: Robert Correale, Paul Gans, Kevin Petersen, Nancy Regalado, Judith Sands, Ruth Sternglantz, Kathryn Talarico, George Thompson, and, above all, my wife, Judith Glazer Raymo.

1 Helen Cooper makes the case in her essay on "The Frame" in vol. 1 of *Sources and Analogues of the Canterbury Tales*, ed. Robert M. Correale and Mary Hamel (Cambridge, 2002), pp. 7–18. See also *The Decameron and the Canterbury Tales: New Essays on an Old Question*, ed. I. M. Koff and B. D. Schildgen (Madison, WI, 2000); and N. S. Thompson, *Chaucer, Boccaccio and the Debate of Love: A Comparative Study of the Decameron and The Canterbury Tales* (Oxford, 1966). Quotations from the *Decameron* are taken from the edition of V. Branca (Florence, 1976).

sixteen of Chaucer's pilgrims, including such unusual inhabitants of estates satire as cooks and pardoners, and there is a generous coincidence of detail.[2]

Professor Cooper's argument for the influence of *Piers Plowman* – and in particular the A-text of the poem[3] – is strong and persuasive. The appearance of the tale-telling pilgrims among the estates may have given Chaucer the "hint" for the framing fiction he required to launch his diverse story-collection, or it may have germinated an idea he had originally received from the *Decameron.* (*The Legend of Good Women* suggests that he was actively searching for a suitable frame for a story-collection.) The scene of the pilgrims at the Tabard Inn may have been inspired by the reference to cooks and taverners at the end of Langland's *Prologue*. Chaucer's sympathetic portraits of the Clerk and the Plowman, and his satirical portraits of the Pardoner and Friar are certainly indebted to Langland, as are other details contained in the portraits of the Monk, Merchant, Sergeant, Doctor, Miller and Summoner. Some of these details appear to have been drawn from passus of the B-text, an indication of Chaucer's continuing interest in the work.

The *General Prologue* was also directly influenced by the *Romance of the Rose*, notably in the portraits of the Squire, Prioress, and Friar, and, to a lesser extent, in those of the Sergeant and Summoner. His portrait of the Host is partially based on the character of Deduit. The narrator's justification for using indelicate language derives from Jean de Meun's defense against the charge of obscenity, although it may also recall a similar statement in the *Decameron*. The rhetorical and structural influence of the *Rose* on the *General Prologue* can be seen in Chaucer's use of an elaborate description of the springtime setting, the introduction of an author – or compiler as Chaucer would have it – as a character within the narrative, the invention of a character to forward the action of the narrative, and the suspension of the narrative to present a series of formal portraits. In addition, the portraits reflect Chaucer's wide range of reading, encompassing courtly and popular literature, the bible and biblical commentaries, standard chivalric and military manuals, agricultural and estates management treatises, medica, and pseudo-scientific physiognomies, especially the *Secretum Secretorum*, a compendium of practical advice on human behavior enormously popular from the twelfth century onwards.[4]

Moreover, Chaucer's portraits are so structured sequentially and in detail as to reflect, as Jill Mann has brilliantly demonstrated, their indebtedness to a vast body of satirical literature in the estates tradition.[5] Chaucer made extensive use

2 Helen Cooper, *The Canterbury Tales*, The Oxford Guides to Chaucer (Oxford University Press, 1966), pp. 30–1. "Even without these similarities," she continues, "it would be likely that Chaucer knew Langland's work . . . probably written on Cornhill within a mile of the house at Aldgate where Chaucer wrote many of his own poems; and it was widely disseminated in the south-east well before Chaucer began work on the Tales" (p. 31).

3 See "Langland's and Chaucer's Prologues," *The Yearbook of Langland Studies* 1 (1987): 74.

4 See Douglas Wurtele, "Another Look at an Old 'Science': Chaucer's Pilgrims and Physiognomy," *From Arabye to Engelond: Medieval Studies in Honour of Mahmoud Manzalaoui*, ed. A. E. Christa Canitz and Gernot R. Wieland (Ottawa, 1999), pp. 93–111. On the influence of the *Secretum*, see Judith Ferster, *Fictions of Advice* (Philadelphia, 1966).

5 Jill Mann, *Chaucer and Medieval Estates Satire* (Cambridge, 1973).

of this material, drawing chiefly from native sources, including, in addition to *Piers Plowman*, Gower's *Mirour de l'Omme* and *Vox Clamantis*, *The Simonie*, *Speculum Stultorum*, *Wynnere and Wastoure* and *The Parliament of the Three Ages*. He supplemented these with such continental satires as the *Romans de Carité*, perhaps *Les Lamentations de Matheolus*, and various Golidardica, though some of these are also of Anglo-Latin provenance. Among the non-satirical works dealing with estates he apparently was familiar with the *Libellus De Ludo Schachorum* of Jacobus de Cessolis in the French version of Jehan de Vignay, hereafter referred to as the *Chessbook,* and, again from native sources, the popular handbooks for preachers known as *Communiloquium*, *Fasciculus Morum* and *Summa Predicantium*; the confessional manual *Memoriale Presbiterorum*; and possibly John of Salisbury's *Policraticus* and *Entheticus ad Policraticum*.

Estates literature was based on the notion that society is composed of three orders – those who fight (bellatores), those who pray (oratores), and those who labor (laboratores). Chaucer reflects this scheme as do Langland and Gower: Chaucer in the portraits of the Knight, Parson and Plowman; Langland – somewhat eccentrically – by those who put themselves to the plough, those who put themselves to Pride (the knightly class), and those who put themselves to prayers and penances such as good anchorites and hermits (A-text Prologue, lines 20–30); and Gower tersely in the *Vox Clamantis*: "There are the cleric, the knight, and the peasant, the three carrying on three [different] things. The one teaches, the other fights, and the third tills the fields."[6] Within this framework the estates were divided into clergy and laity and classified hierarchically. Thus, again in the *Vox Clamantis*, Gower, intending to show the corruption of all estates, dutifully reviews the clergy from the Court of Rome down to the monks and friars, and then the laity, from the rulers (i.e. kings and emperors) to shepherds and herdsmen.[7] The same procedure is followed in other estates satires (e.g. *The Simonie)* and non-satirical works in the estates tradition (e.g. the *Chessbook* and sermon collections of Jacques de Vitry, Humbert de Romans and Gilbert of Tournai). Chaucer boldly rehandles the tradition, generally preserving hierarchy, but eliminating the *principes* of the church and state, and, in imitation of John of Wales' *Communiloquium*,[8] starting with the laity (Knight, Squire, Yeoman) instead of the clergy (Prioress, Monk, Friar). Between the Franklin and the Ploughman he introduces a group of craftsmen – from the Guildsmen to the Wife of Bath – whose selection and sequence reflect the influence of Hugh of St Victor's *Didascalicon* where the mechanical arts are classified into seven categories corresponding to the seven liberal arts: (1) textile and leather work; (2) weaponry and manufacture in wood, stone and metal;

[6] *The Major Latin Works of John Gower*, trans. E. W. Stockton (Seattle, 1962), p. 116, translating "Sunt Clerus, Miles, Cultor, tres trina gerentes; Hic docet, hic pugnat, alter et arva colit." For the *Vox Clamantis* see *The Complete Works of John Gower*, ed. G. C. Macaulay, vol. 4 (Oxford, 1902), Book 3, chapter 1, lines 1–2. All quotations from the *Vox* are taken from this edition. For Langland see *Piers Plowman: A Parallel-Text Edition of the A, B, C and Z Versions*, ed. A. V. C. Schmidt (London and New York, 1995), from which all quotations are taken.

[7] Gower, *ibid.*, Books 3 and 4 (Clergy), 5 and 6 (Laity).

[8] See Jenny Swanson, *John of Wales*: *A Study of the Works and Ideas of a Thirteenth-Century Friar* (Cambridge, 1989), pp. 63–141.

(3) navigation and trade; (4) agriculture; (5) hunting; (6) medicine, and (7) theatrics.[9] Chaucer's Guildsmen (apart from the carpenter) and Wife of Bath represent the first group. The carpenter and Shipman represent the second and third groups. The fifth category, hunting, was divided into gaming, fowling and fishing, and included the offices of "bakers, butchers, cooks, and tavern keepers."[10] The classification of medicine after navigation accounts for the placement of the Physician after the Shipman, for Chaucer, like Petrarch, thought of physicians as *operarii.* The Wife of Bath, though a member of the cloth industry, comes last in the category of craftsmen because women occupied a place after men within any given estate or within the estates tradition generally. For a variety of reasons, the Plowman, representing agriculture, the fourth category, is coupled with the Parson, out of sequence. The final group of pilgrims, the Summoner and Pardoner, are, as Professor Cooper aptly describes them, "social and moral misfits in almost every sense with no obvious place in the class hierarchy."[11]

Owing to limitations of space I address only primary sources and analogues in this essay. Additional material will be found in the works of Andrew, Bowden, and Mann cited in the notes as well as in the annotations of *The Riverside Chaucer* (third edition).

Springtime Setting

The description of spring is a literary convention whose traditional details are paralleled in numerous works from classical antiquity to the fourteenth century. Chaucer may have derived the idea of beginning his narrative with this topos from the dream-vision genre as, for example, the description of a May morning in the *Roman de la Rose* (lines 45–80), which contains many of the commonplaces of descriptions of springtime,[12] but his description is chiefly indebted to the following passage from Guido delle Colonne's *Historia Destructionis Troiae,* a work he knew well and from which he borrowed both these expressions and ideas: the movement of the zodiac – the time is in the Ram, and it is

9 Hugh of St Victor, *Didascalicon*, PL 176, cols 760–3. Later commentators omitted the category of theatrics and divided weaponry from other forms of manufacture.

10 *Didascalicon*, col. 762: "Venatio igitur continet omnia pistorum laniorum, cocorum, cauponumque officia."

11 Helen Cooper, *The Canterbury Tales*, p. 32; Chaucer may also have taken a hint from the *Memoriale Presbiterorum*, which relegates Pardoners to its penultimate chapter on restitution, followed only by those who obtain benefices illicitly and exploit their income. See M. Haren, *Sin and Society in Fourteenth-Century England: A Study of the Memoriale Presbiterorum* (Oxford, 2000), pp. 174–5.

12 For a review of the many sources and analogues that have been proposed since Skeat see M. Andrew, *A Variorum Edition of The Works of Geoffrey Chaucer. Volume II: The Canterbury Tales, The General Prologue*, Part One B Explanatory Notes (Norman, OK, and London, 1993), pp. 3–7. Spring openings in the dream vision genre may also be found in *Wynnere and Wastoure*, lines 35–44; *The Parlement of the Thre Ages*, lines 1–20 (T. Turville-Petre, ed., *Alliterative Poetry of the Middle Ages* [Washington, D.C., 1989], pp. 42–3, 70); and *Death and Life*, lines 22–36 (ed. J. H. Hanford and J. M. Steadman in *Studies in Philology* 15 [1918]: 261–2). For a general study of the genre see R. Tuve, *Seasons and Months* (Paris, 1933; rpt. Cambridge, 1974). Judith M. Davidoff, *Beginning Well* (Rutherford, NJ, and London, 1988), pp. 129–30, suggests the influence of the *Chansons d'aventure* on this passage, but the evidence is slight and late. Chaucer's lines (especially 5–6) look back to *The Book of the Duchess*, lines 291–320, 398–404, and *The Legend of Good Women*, lines 171–4.

nearly mid April – the maturing (i.e., young) sun, the softly blowing zephyrs, the flower-imagery, the moisture bringing life to plants, the renewal of nature enticing mortals to travel, and the correlative structure of *when/then.*

> Tempus erat quod sol maturans sub o(b)liquo zodiaci circulo cursum suum sub signo iam intrauerat arietis, in quo noctium spatio equato diebus celebratur equinoctium primi ueris, tunc cum incipit tempus blandiri mortalibus in aeris serenitate intentis, tunc cum dissolutis niuibus molliter flantes zephiri crispant aquas, tunc cum fontes in ampullulas tenues scaturizant, tunc cum ad summitates arborum et ramorum humiditates ex terre gremio exhalantes extolluntur in eis, quare insultant semina, crescunt segetes, uirent prata uariorum colorum floribus illustrata, tunc cum induuntur renouatis frondibus arbores circumquaque, tunc cum ornatur terra graminibus, cantant volucres et in dulcis armonie modulamine citarizant. Tunc quasi medium mensis Aprilis effluxerat, cum mare, ceruicosa fluctuatione laxata, iam undas equaverat factum equor. Tunc predicti reges Iason et Hercules cum eorum navibus portum intrant (Variants: partirent, exeunt).[13]
>
> [It was the time when the aging [sic] sun in its oblique circle of the zodiac had already entered into the sign of Aries, in which the equal length of nights and days is celebrated in the equinox of spring; when the weather begins to entice eager mortals into the pleasant air; when the ice has melted, and the breezes ripple the flowing streams; when the springs gush forth in fragile bubbles; when moistures exhaled from the bosom of the earth are raised up to the tops of the trees and branches, for which reason the seeds sprout, the crops grow, and the meadows bloom, embellished with flowers of various colors; when the trees on every side are decked with renewed leaves; when earth is adorned with grass, and the birds sing and twitter in music of sweet harmony. Then almost the middle of the month of April had passed when the sea, made calm after its fierce heaving had subsided, had already calmed the waves. Then the aforesaid kings, Jason and Hercules, left port with their ships.][14]

Chaucer's description was also influenced by Virgil's praise of the fecundity and beneficence of Spring in the *Georgics* (2.323–35), particularly Virgil's use of sexual metaphors to express the regenerative powers of Spring and his reference to the invigorating effect of Zephirus on the entire countryside:

> Ver adeo frondi nemorum, ver utile silvis;
> Vere tument terrae et genitalia semina poscunt.
> tum pater omnipotens fecundis imbribus Aether
> coniugis in gremium laetae descendit, et omnis
> magnus alit magno commixtus corpore fetus.

[13] Guido de Columnis, *Historia Destructionis Troiae,* ed. N. E. Griffin (Cambridge, 1936), pp. 34–5. Chaucer rearranges the details, following the hexameral order of creation in Gen. 1, and in lines 5–7 he introduces an allusion to the influence of Zephyrus on plant life that recalls Boethius, *Consolation of Philosophy* (1. m. 2, lines 19–20 echoing Ovid, *Met.* 1. 107–8). See J. C. Nitzsche, "Creation in Genesis and Nature in Chaucer's 'General Prologue' 1–18," *Papers on Language and Literature* 14 (1978): 461–3; and M. Andrew, "Chaucer's *General Prologue* to the Canterbury Tales," *Explicator* 43 (1984): 5–6, who suggests that the word *inspired* (6) is a "deliberate echo" of Gen. 2.7. For other instances of its use, see C. Wilcockson, "The Opening Lines of Chaucer's General Prologue to *The Canterbury Tales*," *Review of English Studies* 50 (1999): 347 n. 2.

[14] Guido delle Colonne, *Historia Destructionis Troiae*, trans. M. F. Meek (Bloomington, IN, and London, 1974), pp. 33–4. Meek's translation correctly follows the Latin variant.

Avia tum resonant avibus virgulta canoris,
Et Venerem certis repetunt armenta diebus;
parturit almus ager Zephyrique tepentibus auris
laxant arva sinus; superat tener omnibus umor,
inque novos soles audent se gramina tuto
credere, nec metuit surgentis pampinus Austros
aut actum caelo magnis Aquilonibus imbrem,
sed trudit gemmas et frondes explicat omnis.

[Spring it is that clothes the glades and forests with leaves, in spring the soil swells and craves the vital seed. Then does Heaven, sovereign Father, descend in fruitful showers into the womb of his joyful consort and, mightily mingling with her mighty frame, gives life to every embryo within. Then secluded thickets echo with melodious birdsong, and at the trysting hour the herds renew their loves; the bounteous earth prepares to give birth, and the meadows ungirdle to the zephyr's balmy breeze, the tender moisture avails for all. The grass safely dares to face the nascent suns, nor does the vine tendril fear the South Wind's rising or showers launched from the skies by the blustering North, but puts forth buds and unfurls its every leaf.][15]

The linkage of spring and pilgrimage as a framing device for the ensuing narrative may have been influenced by the opening lines of Adenet le Roi's thirteenth-century romance *Berte as grans piés*:

A l'issue d'avrill, un tans douç et joli,
Que herbeletes pongnent et pre sont raverdi
Et arbrissel desirent qu'il fussent parflori,
Tout droit en cel termine que je ici vous di,
A Paris la cité estoie un venredi;
Pour ce qu'il ert devenres, en mon cuer m'assenti
K'a Saint Denis iroie por priier Dieu merci.
A un moine courtois, c'on nonmoit Savari,
M'acointai telement, Damedieu en graci,
Que le livre as estoires me moustre et g'i vi
L'estoire de Bertain et Pepin aussi.[16]

[At the end of April, a sweet and pretty time, when the grasses shoot up and the meadows are in flower and shrubs are eager to bloom, in that very time that I am here describing, I was in the city of Paris one Friday; because it was Friday I decided that I would go to St Denis to pray for God's mercy. I made

15 Virgil, *Georgics*, ed. and trans. H. R. Fairclough, revised G. P. Goold (Cambridge, MA, 1999), pp. 158–9. *The Pervigilium Veneris*, an anonymous second-century Latin poem, also describes the spring in terms of sexual union and provides several verbal parallels to Chaucer's lines 1–6 and 9. The phrase "droghte of March" (2) comes from Walter of Henley's book on husbandry (see below, note 152) and the phrase "sweete breeth" echoes the *Consolation of Philosophy* (2. m. 3, line 5). See E. E. Hankins, "Chaucer and the Pervigilium Veneris," *Modern Language Notes* 49 (1934): 80–3; A. C. Cook, "Chaucerian Papers – I," *Transactions of the Connecticut Academy of Arts and Sciences* 23 (1919): 10, 17; O. G. Hill, "Chaucer's 'Englished' Georgics," *Medieval Perspectives* 4–5 (1989–90): 71–3; and J. Chance, "Chaucer's Zephyrus," in *The Mythographic Art*, ed. J. Chance (Gainesville, FL, 1990), pp. 177–98.

16 Adenet le Roi, *Berte as Grans Piés*, ed. Albert Henry (Geneva, 1982), p. 57; the analogue was first identified by J. A. Rea, "An Old French Analogue to the General Prologue 1–18," *Philological Quarterly* 46 (1967): 128–30. Berchorius in his encyclopedic *Reductorium Morale* also links Spring and pilgrimage, as B. F. Huppé notes (*A Reading of the Canterbury Tales* [Buffalo, NY, 1964], p. 17).

the acquaintance of a courteous monk named Savari (thanks be to the Lord) who showed me a book of stories, and there I saw the story of Bertain and Pepin.]

The Knight

The Knight is a model of Christian chivalry, who is devoted to its ideals and fulfills them in practice. He is a veteran of the crusades, a fierce fighter, whose bravery and martial skill have enabled him to win an outstanding reputation. Yet he is devoid of pride, a fault of which medieval knights were often accused. His modest behavior, refined manners, and unostentatious appearance are indices of a moral excellence matching his physical prowess. He is repeatedly described as "worthy" (43, 47, 64, 68). The narrator refers to him with admiration as a "verray, parfit gentil knyght" (72).

Chaucer's portrait celebrates the ideals of medieval chivalry set forth in Ramon Llull's *Le Libre De l'Orde De Cavalleria* (1275–6), which was immensely popular throughout the later Middle Ages, particularly in an anonymous French version, *Livre De L'Ordre De Chevalerie*, which William Caxton turned into English as *The Book of the Ordre of Chyvalry* in 1484. "The Order of Chivalry" purports to instruct aspirants to knighthood in its exacting duties and to have been written by a wise old knight (now retired) whose long and distinguished career and virtuous character exhibit the essential features on which Chaucer modeled his portrait.

> Ung sage chevalier – qui longuement avoit maintenu l'ordre de chevalerie et qui par la noblesse et force de son hault courage et sagesse et en aventurant son corps avoit maintenu guerres, joustes et tournoiz, et en maintes batailles avoit en moult de nobles et glorieuses victoires. . . . Office de chevalier est maintenir et deffendre la sainte foy catholicque. . . . Donc, tout aussy comme Nostre Seigneur Dieu a esleu les clers pour maintenir la sainte foy catholique avec escriptures et raisons contre les mescreans, aussy Dieu de gloire a esleu chevaliers pour ce que, par force d'armes, ilz vainquent et sourmontent les mescreans, qui chascun jour font leur povoir de destruire sainte Eglise. . . . Office de chevalier est maintenir et deffendre son seigneur terrien. . . . Courtoisie et chevalerie se concordent, car vilenie et laides parolles sont contre la noblesse de chevalerie. Priveté et acointance de bonne gent, loyaulté, verité, hardiesse, largesse, honnesteté, humilité, pitié et les aultres choses semblables a cestes appartiennent a chevalerie. . . . Chevalerie et hardiesse ne se pevent accorder sans sens et discrecion. . . . Car nulles gens ne mettent leurs corps en tant de perilz comme chevaliers font, quelle chose doncquez est plus neccessaire a chevalier que prudence? . . . Election ne cheval ne armes ne seigneurie ne suffisent mye encore au hault honneur qui affiert a chevalier, aincois convient que on luy donne escuyer et garson qui le servent et prennent garde de ses chevaulx.[17]

[17] Ramon Llull, *Livre de L'Orde de Chevalerie*, ed. V. Minervini (Bari, 1972), pp. 75, 97–8, 102, 172, 110, 159, 91; my translation. For the Spanish original, see Ramon Llull, *Libre de l'Orde de Cavalleria*, ed. M. Giustà (Barcelona, 1980). For the topos *fortitudo et sapientia* see E. Curtius, *European Literature and the Latin Middle Ages* (New York, 1953), pp. 167–75.

[A wise knight who long had kept the order of chivalry and who by the nobility and strength of his high courage and wisdom and in adventuring his body had engaged in wars, jousts and tournaments, and in many battles had achieved many noble and glorious victories. . . . The office of a knyght is to maintain and defend the holy catholic faith. . . . Just as our Lord God chose the clergy to maintain the holy catholic faith with scripture and reason against the infidels, so the God of Glory chose knights in order that by force of arms they may vanquish and overcome the infidels who do all in their power daily to destroy holy church. . . . the office of a knight is to maintain and defend his earthly lord. . . .Courtesy and chivalry are in accord, for villainy and foul words are against the noble order of chivalry. The familiarity and acquaintance of good people, loyalty, truth, courage, generosity, decency, humility, pity, and other virtues like to these belong to chivalry. . . . Chivalry and courage cannot be in harmony without sense and discretion. . . . Because no other persons place their lives in such perils as do knights, what is then more needful to a knight than prudence? . . . Neither appointment, nor a horse, nor arms, nor a lordship suffices for the high honor of a knight; rather he must be given a squire and a boy to serve him and look after his horses.]

The Knight's dedication to the ideals of knighthood and his gentle manners resemble the characterization of Gauchier de Chatillon in *Le Dit du Connestable de France* by the Hainault poet Watriquet de Couvin:

17 Car li preudons estoit parfais
En honneur par diz et par fais,
19 Courtois et de tres grant vaillance;
. . .
30 Prouesce faisoit esveillier,
Courtoisie, honneur, et largesce
Et loiauté, qui de noblesce
33 Toutes les autres vertus passe.
. . .
42 Tant fust plains de courouz ne d'ire
Onques n'issi hors de sa bouche
Vilains mos; maniere avoit douche,
45 Plus que dame ne damoisele.[18]

[For the worthy knight was perfectly honorable in word and deed, courteous, and very brave. He made prowess awaken courtesy, honor, generosity, and loyalty which surpasses all the other virtues in nobility. However angry or wrathful he may have been, he never uttered a villainous word; he had a sweet manner, more so than a lady or damsel.]

The centerpiece of the Knight's portrait, which has been described as a "chivalric biography compressed to its essentials," is a long list of the knight's campaigns and battles (51–66) which may have been suggested by a similar catalogue in Guillaume de Machaut's *Le Dit Dou Lyon*. In times past, we are

[18] Watriquet de Couvin, *Le Dit du Connestable de France. Dits de Watriquet de Couvin*, ed. A. Scheler (Brussels, 1868), p. 44. This parallel was first observed by W. H. Schofield, *Chivalry in English Literature* (Cambridge, 1912), pp. 30–3. On the chivalric virtues see G. Mathew, *The Court of Richard II* (London, 1968), pp. 114–28, and M. Keen, *Chivalry* (New Haven, CT, 1984), pp. 4–15.

told, knights who were eager to serve their ladies rushed off to do battle in foreign lands:

> Car s'il sceüssent une armee
> Ou une guerre en Alemaingne,
> En Osteriche ou en Beháingne,
> En Hongrie ou en Danemarche
> Ou en aucun estrange marche,
> En Pruce, en Pouleinne, en Cracoe,
> En Tartarie ou en Letoe,
> En Lifflant ou en Lombardie,
> En Atenes ou en Rommenie,
> Ou en France ou en Angleterre,
> II y alassent honneur querre;
> Puis s'en raloient en Grenade,
> L'une heure sain, l'autre malade,
> L'une heure a cheval, l'autre a pié.[19]

> [For if they knew of an expedition or a war in Germany, Austria, Bohemia, Hungary, Denmark, or some other foreign country, in Prussia, Poland, Cracovia, Tartary, Lithuania, Livonia, Lombardy, Athens, Romania, France or England, they went there to win honor; then they went off to Granada, one hour healthy, the other ill, one hour on horseback, the other on foot.]

Chivalric biographies have affinities with the German and Dutch genre of *Ehrenreden,* short, encomiastic poems about knights who had undertaken distant journeys to prove their courage. *Ehrenreden* were written by heralds and promoted the chivalric ideal. Prussia was the most frequent destination of the fourteenth-century knights who were eulogized in these poems. Heralds memorialized their exploits, and it was they who decided which knights deserved to sit at the Table of Honor (*Ehrentisch*) at the ceremonies instituted by the Order of Teutonic Knights. Chaucer's knight was among those so honored: "Ful ofte tyme he hadde the boord bigonne/ Aboven alle nacions in Pruce" (52–3). Wim van Anrooij maintains that Chaucer may have become familiar with this continental genre through his father-in-law, Sir Payne Roet, or the Chandos Herald, a native of Hainault.[20]

19 Guillaume de Machaut, *Oeuvres*, ed. E. Hoepffner, vol. 2 (Paris, 1911), pp. 209–10; D. Brewer, "Chaucer's Knight as Hero, and Machaut's *Prise d'Alexandrie*," *Heroes and Heroines in Medieval English Literature*, ed. L. Carruthers (Woodbridge, 1994), p. 83.

20 Wim Van Anrooij, "Heralds, Knights and Travelling," *Medieval Dutch Literature in its European Context*, ed. E. Kooper (Cambridge, 1994), pp. 53–6; R. Barber, *The Knight and Chivalry* (Woodbridge, 1995), pp. 297–317; M. Keen, *Chivalry*, pp. 171–4; "Chaucer and Chivalry Re-visited," *Armies, Chivalry and Warfare in Medieval Britain and France*, ed. M. Strickland (Stamford, 1996), p. 9; and "Chaucer's Knight, the English Aristocracy and the Crusade," *English Court Culture in the Later Middle Ages*, ed. V. J. Scattergood and J. W. Sherborne (New York, 1963), pp. 58–61; W. Paravicini, "Die Preussenreisen des europäischen Adels," *Historische Zeitschrift* 232 (1981): 25–38; A. S. Cook, "Beginning the Board in Prussia," *Journal of English and Germanic Philology* 14 (1915): 375–88; and A. Luttrell, "Chaucer's Knight and the Mediterranean," *Library of Mediterranean History* 1 (1994): 127–60.

The Squire

The Squire is a "lovyere and a lusty bacheler" (80) with all the attributes needed to win his lady. He is young, handsome, strong, athletic, stylish, and courtly. His social accomplishments are constructed from the God of Love's advice to the young twenty-year-old lover in the *Roman de la Rose*:

Après ce te doit sovenir
D'envoiseüre maintenir.
A joie e a deduit t'atorne:
Amor n'a cure d'ome morne;
. . .
Se tu sez nul bel deduit faire
Par quoi tu puisses as genz plaire,
Je te comant que tu le faces:
Chascuns doit faire en toutes places
Ce qu'il set qui miauz li avient,
Car los e pris e grace en vient.
Se tu te senz viste e legier,
Ne fai pas de saillir dangier;
Et se tu es bien a cheval,
Tu doiz poindre amont e aval;
Et se tu sez lances brisier,
Tu t'en puez faire mout prisier;
Et s'as armes es acesmez,
Par ce seras dis tanz amez.
Se tu as la voiz clere e saine,
Tu ne doiz mie querre essoine
De chanter, se l'en t'en semont,
Car biaus chanters abelist mont.
Si avient bien a bacheler
Que il sache de vieler,
De fleüter e de dancier:
Par ce se puet mout avancier.[21]

[Besides this, you must always remember to be blithe. Prepare yourself for joy and pleasure, for Love cares nothing for gloomy men. . . . If you know how to do something entertaining that will bring pleasure to others, I order you to do it. Everyone must always do what he knows suits him best, for as a result he will be praised and esteemed and favoured. If you know yourself to be agile and athletic, do not make difficulties about jumping, and if you are an accomplished horseman, you should gallop up hill and down dale. If you are good at breaking lances, you can win great renown, and if you are skillful in arms, the love men have for you will be increased tenfold. If your voice is clear and pure, you should never excuse yourself from singing, if you are asked, for good singing is

[21] Guillaume de Lorris and Jean de Meun, *Le Roman de la Rose*, ed. E. Langlois, vol. 2 (Paris, 1920), pp. 112–13. All quotations from the *Roman* are taken from this edition (5 vols, 1914–24). Langlois seems closer than Lecoy (see below) to the version of the text with which Chaucer was familiar. The lines of these two editions do not match although based on the same manuscript (Paris, Bibliothèque Nationale, fr. 1573) extensively corrected.

a great enhancement. Also, a young man ought to learn how to play on the viol and the citole [the reading of Lecoy; Langlois reads "fleüter" "to flute," as above], and how to dance, for in this way he will win great advancement.][22]

The Squire looks like and has some of the traits of Deduit in the *Roman de la Rose*:

801 Deduiz fu biaus e lons e droiz:
Jamais entre gent ne vendroiz
803 Ou vos veiez nul plus bel ome.
. . .
809 Cheveus ot blonz, recercelez;
. . .
812 Il resembloit une pointure,
Tant estoit biaus e acesmez,
E de toz membres bien formez.
815 Remuanz fu e preuz e vistes:
Plus legier ome ne veïstes.

[Pleasure was handsome, straight, and tall: never in any company would you find a better-looking man. . . . His hair was blond and curly. . . . He was so handsome and elegant and had such shapely limbs that he looked like a painting. He was lively, spirited, and agile, the nimblest man you have ever seen . . . (Horgan, p. 14)][23]

Although the moralists and satirists cited by Mann (pp. 118–19) disapprove of luxurious dress, Chaucer seems rather to support the view of *The Book of Chivalry* that such dress is appropriate to the Squire's age and status.[24] His embroidered costume is adapted from the attire of the God of Love in the *Roman,* who urges the dreamer to dress elegantly.

22 Guillaume de Lorris and Jean de Meun, *The Romance of the Rose*, trans. Frances Horgan (Oxford, 1994), pp. 33–4. All translations of the *Roman* are taken from this work. Horgan based her translation on the edition of F. Lecoy, 3 vols (Paris, 1965–75). Significantly, the *Romaunt of the Rose* (B 2325–8) adds four lines not in the French that are also reminiscent of the Squire's behavior in love: "Among eke, for thy lady sake,/ Songes and compleyntes that thou make,/ For that wole meven in hir herte,/ Whanne they redden of thy smerte."

23 Mann (pp. 119–20) notes a resemblance between the Squire's portrait and that of the bachelor in Jehan Le Fèvre, *Les Lamentations de Matheolus et le Livre de Leesce*, ed. A. G. Van Hamel, vol. 1 (Paris, 1892), p. 54, lines 259–64. In its mixture of adventure and romance, it may also recall the allegorical figure of youth in *The Parlement of the Thre Ages*. Both the Squire and Youth display the same exuberant energy in their vigorous physical activity and their pleasure in the games and pastimes of the court. And both pursue a military career motivated by love of a lady. The Squire's curly locks which give the impression that they were "leyd in presse" (81) come from St Jerome's *Letter to Eustochium* (22.28), warning her against the attentions of foppish presbyters whose "hair is curled with the trace of a thong" ("Crines calamistri vestigio rotantur"). See St Jerome, *Select Letters*, trans. F. A. Wright (Cambridge, 1933), p. 118.

24 Geoffroi de Charny, *The Book of Chivalry*, ed. and trans. R. W. Kaeuper and E. Kennedy (Philadelphia, 1996), pp. 190–1: "But there is no reason why it should not and cannot be fitting for young men in all circumstances, whether at home or on the field, to be dressed decently, neatly, elegantly, with due restraint and with attractive things of low cost and often replaced; for it is right that people should behave, each according to their years, provided so much be not devoted to adornment of the body that the more important things remain undone, that is to say, great and good deeds. And if anyone is thus elegantly dressed and in good fashion, as befits a young man, it should not be done through pride. . . ."

Mais de sa robe devisier
Crien durement qu'encombrez soie;
Qu'il n'avoit pas robe de soie,
Ainz avoit robe de floretes,
Faites par fine amoretes.
. . .
Flors i'avoit de maintes guises,
Qui furent par grant sen assises.
Nule flor en esté ne naist
Qui n'i fust, nes flor de genest,
Ne violete ne parvenche,
Ne flor jaune n'inde ne blanche.
S'i ot par leus entremellees
Fueilles de roses granz e lees.

[I am very much afraid that I shall find it difficult to describe his robe, for it was made not of silk but rather of tiny flowers, and fashioned by courtly loves. . . . There were flowers of many different kinds, most skillfully arranged. No summer flower was absent, not broom nor violet nor periwinkle, not yellow nor indigo nor white, while intertwined in place were great, broad rose-leaves. (Horgan, p. 15)][25]

E qui d'orgeuil est entechiez,
Il ne puet son cuer apleier
A servir ne a soupleier:
Orguilleus fait tot le contraire
De ce que fins amanz doit faire.
Mais qui d'amors se viaut pener,
Il se doit cointement mener:
On qui porchace druerie
Ne vaut neient senz cointerie.
Cointerie n'est pas orguiauz:
Qui est cointes il en vaut miauz,
Por quoi il soit d'orgueil vuidiez,
Qu'il ne soit fos n'outrecuidiez.
Moine toi bel, selonc ta rente,
Et de robe e de chaucemente:
Bele robe e bel garnement
Amendent ome durement.
. . .
Mais au plus bel te doiz deduire
Que tu porras senz toi destruire:
. . .
Cous tes manches, tes cheveus pigne.

[A man tainted with pride is incapable of subduing his heart to serve and beg. The proud man does precisely the opposite of what the true lover should do. But he who wishes to toil in the service of love should bear himself with elegance. It is useless for a man who lacks elegance to aspire to love. Elegance is

[25] On the Squire's costume as the height of fashion, as well as its social implications and its mythological associations with Pan, see Laura Hodges, *Chaucer and Costume: The Secular Pilgrims in the General Prologue* (Cambridge, 2000), pp. 59–70.

not pride, for the elegant man is all the more worthy for being free from pride and foolish presumption. Provide yourself, as far as your income will permit, with fine clothes and shoes, for fine clothes and garments improve a man wonderfully. . . . You should live as elegantly as possible, without ruining yourself. . . . Lace up your sleeves and comb your hair. . . . (Horgan, p. 33)]

The Squire displays the social graces of a young lover and fulfills the duties of an aspirant to knighthood. As required by the precepts of "The Order of Chivalry," he travels with his father on the pilgrimage after receiving military training and instruction in courtesy and service.

> [La science et l'escolle de l'ordre de chevalerie est que le chevalier face son filz aprendre a chevaucher en sa jennesse. . . . Et convient que il serve avant et il soit aincois subject que seigneur, car aultrement ne cognoistroit il pas la noblesse de la seigneurie quant il seroit chevalier. Et pour ce tout chevalier doit son filz mettre en service d'aultre chevalier pour ce que il aprengne a tailler sur table et a servir et a armer et a adouber chevalier en sa jennesse.][26]

> [The teaching and instruction of the order of chivalry is that the knight make his son learn to ride in his youth. . . . And he must first serve and be a subject before he is a lord. For otherwise he would never know the high estate of lordship when he becomes a knight. And therefore every knight should put his son into service with another lord in his youth to learn to carve at table, serve, arm and dub a knight.]

The Yeoman

The close relationship of the military group – knight, squire, yeoman – parallels the composition of Wastoure's army into "sadde men of armes,/ Bolde sqwyeres of blode, bowmen many";[27] and the same succession of knight, squire, and yeoman in Ralph Higden's *Polychronicon*.[28] In the Yeoman's portrait, Chaucer, like his contemporaries, is also acknowledging the growing importance of the role of archers in the Hundred Years War "until longbowmen constituted almost the entire infantry force, and, by the early 15th century, the normal ratio of archers to knights was at least three to one."[29] The Yeoman appropriately bears an array of battle weapons: for offense a "myghty bowe" (108) with a sheaf of peacock-fletched arrows (104–5) and for defense a

26 Llull (Minervini), p. 93. Cf. also E. P. Kuhl and H. J. Webb, "Chaucer's Squire," *ELH* 6 (1939): 282–4.

27 Wynnere and Wastoure, lines 193–4 (ed. Turville-Petre, *Alliterative Poetry*, p. 51).

28 Ralph Higden, *Polychronicon*, ed. C. Babington, Rolls Series 41 (London, 1857), vol. 2, Book 1, chapter 60, p. 170. See also "A Gest of Robyn Hode," in *English and Scottish Popular Ballads*, ed. H. C. Sargent and G. L. Kittredge (Boston, 1965), p. 258, lines 317–20; and the fifteenth-century political poem, based on estates literature, "The Descryvying of Mannes Membres," in *Twenty-six Political and Other Poems*, ed. J. Kail, EETS OS 124 (London, 1904), p. 65, lines 33–8.

29 Matthew Strickland, "Archers," *The Oxford Companion to Military History*, ed. R. Holmes (Oxford, 2001), p. 69. See also Andrew Ayton, "English Armies in the Fourteenth Century," *Arms, Armies, and Fortifications in the Hundred Years War*, ed. A. Curry and M. Hughes (Woodbridge, 1994), p. 33.

buckler, sword, and dagger for use in close combat (112–13).[30] The arms are a tribute to his martial courage and skill.

Archers were not recruited from the nobility; Chaucer's yeoman is a countryman – a forester by profession, perhaps a gamekeeper. The details of the Yeoman's rustic appearance, soldierly posture, and professional efficiency, in striking contrast to the noble manners, preoccupations, and dress of the Squire, suggest that his portrait is likely to have emerged from classical discussions of the suitability of countrymen for military service, a topos that underlies and reinforces the contrast with the Squire. In the *Epitoma Rei Militaris,* the most popular handbook of military science in Chaucer's day, Vegetius argues that rustics are preferable to recruits from the city:

> [De qua parte numquam credo potuisse dubitari aptiorem armis rusticam plebem, quae sub diuo et in labore nutritur, solis patiens, umbrae neglegens, balnearum nescia, deliciarum ignara, simplicis animi, paruo contenta, duratis ad omnem laborum tolerantiam membris, cui gestare ferrum, fossam ducere, onus ferre consuetudo de rure est.][31]
>
> [On this point I think it beyond doubt that the countryman is better suited for military service, the countryman who is nurtured by hard work in the open air, able to endure the heat of the sun [hence the Yeoman's "broun visage" (109)], indifferent to shade, unaccustomed to the baths, knowing nothing of luxuries, of a simple spirit, content with little, whose limbs are hardened to bear every kind of work, and who is accustomed as a countryman to handle iron, dig a ditch, or carry a heavy burden.]

Later, Vegetius mentions the crafts from which military recruits should be selected or rejected:

> [Piscatores aucupes dulciarios linteones omnesque, qui aliquid tractasse uidebuntur ad gynaecea pertinens, longe arbitror pellendos a castris; fabros ferrarios carpentarios, maccellarios et ceruorum aprorumque uenatores conuenit sociare militiae.][32]
>
> [Fishermen, fowlers, confectioners, linen-weavers, and all who seem to engage in activities pertaining to women, I think, should be far removed from the camp; masons, blacksmiths, carpenters, butchers, and hunters of stags and boars are suitable to join the military.]

[30] Strickland, p. 69: "Some archers wore virtually no defensive equipment and were even barefoot, carrying perhaps a small buckler, as well as a sword, dagger, or lead maul." Clive Bartlett, *English Longbowmen 1330–1515* (London, 1997), p. 18: "For arms the archer had a dagger, some type of sword and a small, round shield known as the buckler."

[31] P. Flavius Vegetius Renatus, *Epitoma Rei Militaris*, ed. O. Önnerfors (Stuttgart, 1995), Book 1, chapter 3, p. 11. This passage reappears almost verbatim in John of Salisbury's *Policraticus* (6.2.593 G) and John of Wales' *Communiloquium* (1.9.4.). See *Ioannis Saresberiensis Episcopi Carnotensis Policratici sive De Nugis Curialium Et Vestigiis Philosphorum Libri VIII*, ed. C. C. I. Webb, vol. 2 (Oxford, 1909), pp. 9–10; and John of Wales, *Communiloquium* (Paris, 1550), Part I, Dist C, fol. 39. Vegetius reflects the attitude of earlier agriculturists. See Marcus Porcius Cato, *On Agriculture*, trans. W. D. Hooper, rev. H. B. Ash (Cambridge, 1935), praefatio, p. 2; and Lucius Junius Moderatus Columella, *On Agriculture I-IV*, ed. and trans. H. B. Ash (Cambridge, 1941), Book 1, preface 17, pp. 14–15.

[32] *Epitoma*, Book 1, chapter 7, pp. 17–18. This list was frequently quoted and adapted by medieval writers on warfare. See P. Richardot, *Végèce et la Culture Militaire au Moyen Âge (Ve–XVe siècles)* (Paris, 1998), pp. 105–7.

With his expertise in "wodecrafte" (110), skill in matters pertaining to the chase, the Yeoman certainly falls within the category of the stag – and boar – hunters who are singled out for Vegetius's approval. Woodcraft is a skill which he shares with the unidentified "wyze" who brittles the boar in *Gawain and the Green Knight* (1605–6). His green coat, hood, and baldric, as well as other accoutrements (bow and arrows, horn, dagger, sword), are suitable for both an archer and a yeoman-forester. The St Christopher medal is worn for protection against sudden death and injury; it has no particular association with archers or foresters.[33]

The Prioress

The Prioress is portrayed as a courtly romance heroine. She has the elements of ideal feminine beauty: a well-proportioned nose, gray eyes, a soft, small, red mouth, a broad, fair forehead, a statuesque (perhaps overly statuesque) figure. Her appearance is stylish, but not inappropriate: a pleated wimple, a fine cloak, a pair of coral beads with a gold brooch inscribed *Amor vincit omnia.* She studiously imitates the manners of the court, observing the forms of good breeding, behaving with proper dignity, smiling unaffectedly, speaking French ("After the scole of Stratford atte Bowe" [125]). Her delicate sensibility is moved to compassion for a trapped mouse or the suffering of her pet dogs whom she feeds on "rosted flessh, or milk, and wastel-breed" (147). When she swears – out of anger? – she swears by the courtly St Loy (120). Her name in religion, Eglentyne, is also drawn from the world of courtly secular romance.[34]

Her portrait is heavily indebted to the *Roman de la Rose.* To begin with, her impeccable table manners are taken directly from La Vieille's advice to women on the ways to attract men:

13385 Si rafiert bien qu'el seit a table
De contenance couvenable;
. . .
13408 E bien se gart qu'ele ne mueille
Ses deiz es broez jusqu'aus jointes,
13410 Ne qu'el n'ait pas les les levres ointes

[33] See Hodges, pp. 137–41. R. Almond, *Medieval Hunting* (Stroud, 2003), p. 98, observes: "green was the livery colour not only of professional hunt servants but also of the employed forestry officials, the so-called Yeomen of the Forest." On the use of the medal, see I. B. Jones, "Popular Medical Knowledge in Fourteenth-Century English Literature," *Bulletin of the Institute of the History of Medicine* 5 (1937): 441.

[34] J. L. Lowes, "The Prioress's Oath," *Romanic Review* 5 (1914): 368–85; Andrew, pp. 126–30; and R. Rex, *The Sins of Madame Eglentyne and Other Essays on Chaucer* (Newark, NJ, 1995), pp. 108–10. On the name Eglentyne and its romantic associations see the comments of Muriel Bowden, *A Commentary on the General Prologue to the Canterbury Tales* (London, 1986), p. 94, and Andrew, pp. 131–2. For an opposing view see J. A. Dane, "The Prioress and her Romanzen," *Chaucer Review* 24 (1990): 219–22. H. L. Frank, "Chaucer's Prioress and the Blessed Virgin," *Chaucer Review* 13 (1979): 347–8, quotes a chanson by Gautier de Coinci calling the Virgin "fleur de esglentier" ["blossom of eglentine"]. See also G. L. Engelhart, "The Ecclesiastical Pilgrims of The Canterbury Tales: A Study in Ethology," *Mediaeval Studies* 37 (1975): 294, who suggests an allusion to the *esglentiers* which hedge the rose where Dangiers lurks in *Roman de la Rose*.

De soupes, d'auz ne de char grasse,
Ne que trop de morseaus n'entasse,
Ne trop gros nes mete en sa bouche.
Dou bout des deiz le morsel touche
Qu'el devra moillier en la sausse,
Seit vert ou cameline ou jausse,
E sagement port sa bouchiee,
Que seur son piz goute n' en chiee
De soupe, de saveur, de peivre.
Et si gentement redeit beivre
Que seur sei n' en espande goute,
Car pour trop rude ou pour trop gloute
L'en pourrait bien aucuns tenir
Qui ce li verrait avenir;
E gart que ja hanap ne touche
Tant come ele ait morsel en bouche.
Si deit si bien sa bouche terdre
Qu'el n'i laist nule graisse aerdre,
Au meins en la levre deseure,
Car, quant graisse en cele demeure,
Ou vin en perent les mailletes,
Qui ne sont ne beles ne netes.

[She ought also to behave properly at the table. . . . She must be very careful not to dip her fingers in the sauce up to the knuckles, nor to smear her lips with soup or garlic or fat meat, nor to take too many pieces or too large a piece and put them into her mouth. She must hold the morsel with the tips of her fingers and dip it into the sauce, whether it be thick, thin, or clear, then convey the mouthful with care, so that no drop of soup or sauce or pepper falls on to her chest. When drinking, she should exercise such care that not a drop is spilled upon her, for anyone who saw that happen might think her very rude and coarse. And she must be sure never to touch her goblet when there is anything in her mouth. Let her wipe her mouth so clean that no grease is allowed to remain upon it, at least not upon her upper lip, for when grease is left on the upper lip, globules appear in the wine, which is neither pretty nor nice. (Horgan, pp. 206–7)][35]

Before her instruction in table etiquette, La Vieille advises women to acquire graces if they lack them, to behave haughtily to their lovers to ensure their service, to be friendly, to avoid quarrels, to show off their beauty to best

[35] The passage expands *Ars Amatoria* III.755–6. For other examples of table etiquette poems, see S. Glixelli, "Les Contenances de Table," *Romania* 47 (1921): 1–40, and Andrew, p. 141. U. C. Knoepflmacher, "Irony through Scriptural Allusion. A Note on Chaucer's Prioresse," *Chaucer Review* 4 (1970): 180–3, connects her table manners to Matt. 23.25–6. B. R. Ragen, "Chaucer, Jean de Meun, and Proverbs 30:20," *Notes and Queries* 233 (1988): 295–6, suggests a source in this passage from Proverbs, as does D. Loney, "Chaucer's Prioress and Agur's Adulterous Woman," *Chaucer Review* 27 (1992): 107–8. Rex, pp. 116–18, believes the Prioress's "seemly" behavior carries negative connotations (see also Andrew, p. 134). J. Nicholls, *The Matter of Courtesy: Medieval Courtesy Books and the Gawain-Poet* (Cambridge, 1985), pp. 22–44, especially pp. 31–8, argues that the Prioress could have gained a knowledge of polite behavior at table from the precepts of her convent's customary books. Cf. also Mary T. Brentano, *Relationship of the Latin Facetus Literature to the Medieval English Courtesy Poems* (Lawrence, KS, 1935).

advantage, to laugh with discretion and decorum, keeping their lips closed, and to develop the ability to weep readily:

13273 S' el n'a graces, si les aquiere,
E seit toujourz vers ceus plus fiere
13275 Qui plus, pour s'amour deservir,
Se peneront de li servir.
E de ceus acuillir s'efforce
Qui de s' amour ne feront force.
Sache de jeus e de chançons
13280 E fuie noises e tençons.
S'el n'est bele, si se cointeit,
La plus laide atour plus cointe ait.
. . .
13313 S'ele a beau col e gorge blanche,
Gart que cil qui sa robe trenche
Si trés bien la li escolete
Que la char pere blanche e nete
Demi pié darriers e devant,
13318 S'en iert assez plus decevant.
. . .
13357 Ja ses levres par ris ne s'euvrent,
Mais repoignent les denz e cueuvrent.
Fame deit rire a bouche close.
. . .
13367 Au plourer rafiert il maniere;
Mais chascune est assez maniere
De bien plourer en quelque place;
13370 Car, ja seit ce qu'en ne leur face
Ne griés ne hontes ne molestes,
Toujourz ont eus les lermes prestes,
Toutes pleurent e plourer seulent
En tel guise come eles veulent.

[If she has no graces, let her acquire them and always behave more cruelly towards those who will strive all the harder to serve her in order to win her love, while exerting herself to welcome those who do not care about it. She should be familiar with games and songs, but avoid quarrels and strife. If she is not beautiful, she should enhance her appearance; the ugliest should be the most elegantly attired. . . . If her neck and throat are fair and white, let her see to it that her dressmaker cuts the neck so low that half a foot of fine white flesh is visible front and back; in this way she will deceive men more easily. . . . When she laughs, she must never open her mouth but hide her teeth and conceal them. A woman should laugh with her mouth closed. . . . There is also a proper way to weep, but every woman has the skill to weep properly wherever she may be. Even when no one has caused them any trouble or shame or annoyance, they still have tears at the ready: they all weep in whatever way they like, and make a habit of it. (Horgan, pp. 204–6)][36]

[36] C. Wilcockson, "A Note on Chaucer's Prioress and her Literary Kinship with the Wife of Bath," *Medium Aevum* 61 (1992): 92–6, analyzes this passage (which is based on *Ars Amatoria* III. 281–4, 291–2, 315) as the source of the Prioress's portrait.

Following La Vieille's advice, the Prioress smiles with restraint, observes proper table manners, strives to be agreeable and to be held worthy of respect, weeps readily, sings, and enhances her personal appearance through careful attention to her clothes and adornment and the display of her broad forehead.[37] She adds to her courtly charm by speaking French, albeit provincial French, a subject of sardonic humor,[38] and keeps lap dogs after the fashion of high-born ladies. The attentive lover in the *Confessio amantis* tactfully plays with his lady's "litel hound."[39] Her marks of personal beauty, although conventional, bear a close resemblance to the description of Lady Idleness in lines 529, 532–3, 537 of the *Roman de la Rose*: "Front reluisant . . . Le nés ot bien fait a droiture, E les iaux vairs come uns faucons . . . La bouche petite e grossete." [Her forehead radiant . . . her nose straight and well-formed, and her eyes as bright [*Romaunt of the Rose* A. 546 "grey"] as a falcon's . . . a little, full-lipped mouth.) The characters Joy, Franchise, and Pleasant Thought have several similar attributes (lines 844, 846–52, 1195–6, 2655–7).[40]

[37] Wilcockson, p. 94, suggests that "demi pié" (13311) may account for the Prioress's span-broad forehead, a feature that has given rise to considerable critical comment. The physiognomies take it as evidence of a foolish and irresponsible person. See T. B. Clark, "Forehead of Chaucer's Prioress," *Philological Quarterly* 9 (1930): 312–13; and Rex, p. 124, who relates the Prioress's forehead to the "harlot's brow" of Jer. 3.3. C. W. and P. Cunnington, *Handbook of English Medieval Costume* (Philadelphia, 1952), p. 97, observe that "shaved front hair, to produce a broad, high forehead, was a new mode (1370–1480)." A broad forehead, even if artificially achieved, was a considerable mark of beauty from the time of Maximianus (*Elegiae* I.95) onwards. In Boccaccio's *Teseida* Emilia's forehead is described as "ampia e spaziosa" (XII.55). The confessor of *Confessio Amantis* (Book 6, lines 769–70) admires the beauty of a woman whose forehead is "large and plein/ Withoute fronce of eny grein." *Ancrene Wisse*, ed. J. R. R. Tolkien and N. R. Ker, EETS OS 249 (London, 1962), p. 103, warns against excessive care about adornment, particularly the coloring and pleating of clothes, as a sign of pride.

[38] The Anglo-Norman dialect was a familiar butt of humor. Cf. *Piers Plowman* B.V.235: "And I ken no Frenssh, in feiþ, but of þe ferþest ende of Northfolk," a line which may have suggested to Chaucer that there was still some mileage to be had from this hoary jest. See I. Short, "On bilingualism in Anglo-Norman England," *Romance Philology* 33 (1980): 467–79, on the disdain for provincial French going back to Walter Map and Giraldus Cambrensis, and W. Rothwell, "Chaucer and Stratford Atte Bowe," *Bulletin of the John Rylands Library* 74 (1992): 2–28, on the cultural position of Anglo-Norman in the fourteenth century. The Prioress doubtless spoke French, however un-Parisian, as a mark of gentility. R. Parsons, "Anglo-Norman Books of Courtesy and Nurture," *PMLA* 44 (1929): 399, cites a version of *Urbanus* containing this admonition (lines 49–52): "Seez debonair e curteise/ Et ke tu saches bien parler fraunceys,/ Car molt est langage alosé/ De gentil home, et mout amé." For a review of the scholarship see Andrew, pp. 134–7. W. Rothwell, "Stratford Atte Bowe Revisited," *Chaucer Review* 36 (2001): 201, regards Chaucer's mildly derogatory remark "solely as an indication of her insular horizon."

[39] *CA*, Book 4, lines 1188–9: "forto feigne som desport/ I pleie with hire litel hound." The story of a lady who was reproved for feeding her dogs on milk and meat while people were starving is told in *The Book of the Knight of La Tour-Landry*, ed. T. Wright, EETS OS 33 (London, 1868), pp. 28–9. See also the Anglo-Norman satire "The Lady and her Dogs," *Reliquiae Antiquae*, ed. T. Wright and J. O. Halliwell (London, 1841), vol. 1, pp. 155–6. Keeping pets and feeding them as she does, the Prioress clearly abuses Benedictine regulations and violates received concepts of compassion and charity. See J. M. Steadman, "The Prioress' Dogs and Benedictine Discipline," *Modern Philology* 54 (1956): 1–6, and R. D. Simons, "The Prioress's Disobedience of the Benedictine Rule," *Journal of the College Language Association* 12 (1968): 80–1. Rex, pp. 100–5, 113–16, cites denunciations by Wyclif and Bromyard of the feeding of dogs on lavish food, which he interprets as a sign of dietary laxity. G. R. Owst, *Literature and Pulpit in Medieval England* (Oxford, 1961), pp. 327–8, also notes complaints against the wealthy for providing extravagantly for their lapdogs. Cf. Andrew, pp. 150–3.

[40] D. S. Brewer, "The Ideal of Feminine Beauty in Medieval Literature, Especially 'Harley Lyrics', Chaucer, and Some Elizabethans," *Modern Language Review* 50 (1955): 257–69; W. C. Curry, *The Middle English Ideal of Personal Beauty as Found in the Metrical Romances, Chronicles, and Legends*

The interest of nuns in fine clothes is a satirical topos,[41] but the Prioress's "ful fetys" cloak (157), which so captivates the narrator, may owe something to La Vieille's instructions on dress:

13529 Mais bien se seit anceis miree,
Saveir s'ele est bien atiree.
Et quant a point se sentira,
Et par les rues s'en ira,
13533 Si seit de beles aleüres.
. . .
13555 E s'ele est teus que mantel port,
Si le deit porter de tel port
Qu'il trop la veüe n'encombre
13558 Dou bel cors a cui il fait ombre.
. . .
13568 Et li souviegne de la roe
Que li paons fait de sa queue;
Face ausinc dou mantel la seue.

[But first she [a woman] should inspect her reflection carefully to see if she is properly attired. When she feels she is ready and goes out into the streets, she must carry herself well. . . . If she wears a mantle, she must wear it in such a way that it does not hinder people too much from seeing the lovely body it covers. . . . She should have in mind the way a peacock makes his tail into a wheel and do the same thing with her mantle. (Horgan, pp. 208–9)].[42]

The coral beads worn by the Prioress were a fashionable and costly ornament. In the Bodleian Library MS E Musaeo 65 (fol. 95) version, Constrained Abstinence, the companion of False Seeming, also wears coral beads. Coral was believed to have apotropaic power to ward off demons, as Thomas of Cantimpré explained in *De Naturis Rerum*: "Demonibus terribilis est, et hoc forte quia frequenter modum crucis habet" [Demons are terrified of it, and perhaps for this reason it often has the form of a cross]. The complement of an ostentatious gold brooch to the beads highlights the Prioress's worldliness.[43] The motto inscribed on it, "Amor vincit omnia," (from Virgil's *Eclogues*, 10.69) signifies profane

of the XIII, XIV, and XV Centuries (Baltimore, 1916), pp. 42–4, 63–5, 66–7, 101–3; A. M. Colby, *The Portrait in Twelfth Century Literature* (Geneva, 1965), pp. 37, 48–51; A. K. Moore, "The Eyen Greye of Chaucer's Prioress," *Philological Quarterly* 26 (1947): 307–12; and Rex, pp. 54–68 and notes, who argues that the grayness of her eyes refers simply to their brightness. K. S. Kiernan, "The Art of Descending Catalogue, and a Fresh Look at Alisoun," *Chaucer Review* 10 (1975): 8–10, and G. S. Daichman, *Wayward Nuns in Medieval Literature* (Syracuse, 1986), pp. 147–8, suggest the influence of Geoffrey of Vinsauf's model "descriptio pulchritudinis" on the portrait. Cf. Andrew, p. 157. The lines above are cited from Horgan, pp. 10, 14, 18, 41, respectively, and Geoffrey Chaucer, *The Romaunt of the Rose*, ed. C. Dahlberg (Norman, OK, 1999), p. 92 and note. It is worth noting that *Romaunt* A 546, 822, and 862 translate *iauz vairs* as "yen greye."

41 Mann, pp. 129–30; Daichman, pp. 151–6.

42 The passage is based on *Ars Amatoria* III. 297–306.

43 J. B. Friedman, "The Prioress's Beads of 'Small Coral,'" *Medium Aevum* 39 (1970): 304 n. 1. See also RR 12044–51; Horgan, pp. 185–6; Thomas of Cantimpré, *De Naturis Rerum*, as quoted from British Library MS Royal 12 F vi, fol. 103r by J. R. Friedman, p. 302. Nuns are forbidden to wear a ring or brooch in the *Ancrene Wisse*, p. 215. A nun longs for a brooch in the twelfth-century "Planctus Monialis" edited by P. Dronke, *Medieval Latin and the Rise of the European Love Lyric*, vol. 2, 2nd edn (Oxford, 1996), p. 357, line 19.

love, the same sense in which it is employed in the *Roman* as part of Courtesy's appeal to Fair Welcome to yield the rose: ("Amours vaint toutes choses ... Amours vaint tout," lines 21327, 21332). The application of the motto to sacred love by the Church underlies the deliberate ambiguity which concludes the portrait.[44]

Descriptions of ideal feminine beauty invariably include the trait of gaiety exhibited by the Prioress (137–41). Her cheerful manner complements the elegance of her behavior at table (127–35), the kind of deportment one is advised to adopt in courtesy books such as *De moribus in mensa servandis*, *La Contenance de Table* and Bonvesin de la Riva's *De Quinquagenta Curialitatibus ad Mensam*.[45] But we hear little of her inner life. The stock phrase "simple and coy," applied to ladies in French love poetry and occasionally in Marian lyrics, Chaucer slyly transfers to the Prioress's smile, perhaps remembering the ironical use of the phrase to describe the facial expression of False Seeming in the *Roman de la Rose* ("chiere simple e queie," 12003). Her "conscience" is confined to her solicitude for animals – an ironic detail adapted from a twelfth-century satirical allegory, *Speculum Stultorum,* to which Chaucer alludes under its alternate title "Daun Burnel the Asse" in *The Nun's Priest's Tale*. Writing about spiritual shepherds, its author Nigel de Longchamps notes: "Plus cane percusso dolet anxius aut ave laesa/ Quam si decedat clericus unus ei." ("A cudgeled dog or a wounded bird grieves him more than the death of a single cleric.")[46]

[44] Cf. J. Finlayson, "Chaucer's Prioress and Amor Vincit Omnia," *Studia Neophilologica* 60 (1988): 171–4. E. C. Jacobs, "Further Biblical Allusions for Chaucer's Prioress," *Chaucer Review* 15 (1980): 151–4, draws attention to two passages admonishing women against the use of gold ornaments: 1 Pet. 3.3–4 and 1 Tim. 2.9–10 and to two Pauline passages (1 Cor. 13.1–13, Col. 3.12–14) which the Prioress's brooch is said to parody. For an alternative view of the significance of the brooch and motto, see L. F. Hodges, "Chaucer's Costume Rhetoric in his Portrait of the Prioress," unpublished dissertation (Rice University, 1985), pp. 207–13. For the appropriation of the motto by the church see J. L. Lowes, *Convention and Revolt in Poetry* (Boston and New York, 1919), p. 66.

[45] On the sexual and romantic implications of the terms *desport*, *plesaunt*, *amiable* used to describe the Prioress's cheerful manner, see Wilcockson, p. 94 and nn. 6, 7, and on the phrase *cheere of court*, see Rothwell, p. 12. *Ars Amatoria* III. 501–2, 513–17 (J. H. Mozley, trans.; rev. G. P. Goold [Cambridge, MA, 1985], p. 155) urges ladies to behave pleasantly: "It is beauty's task to hold mad moods in check. . . . Look at one who is looking at you; return a pleasant smile; if he beckons, acknowledge and return his nod. Tis after such prelude that young Cupid, abandoning the foils, draws the sharp arrows from his quiver. Melancholy women too I hate . . ." The advice from the courtesy books can be found in F. Novati, *Carmina Medii Aevi* (Florence, 1883), p. 49, line 20: "in vultu sit hilaris"; Glixelli, p. 32: "Ains fais grande chiere et grant joye"; and Bonvesin de la Riva, *I Volgari*, ed. A. M. Gökçen (New York, 1996), p. 182, lines 21–2: "sta conzamente al desco/cortes, adorno, allegro e confortoso e fresco." Bonvesin's advice is addressed to men.

[46] J. L. Lowes, "Simple and Coy: A Note on Fourteenth Century Poetic Diction," *Anglia* 33 (1910): 440–51, and Frank, pp. 347–8. *Romaunt* C 7321 translates "simple e queie" as "chere of simplenesse." For Longchamps, see *Speculum Stultorum*, ed. J. H. Mozley and R. R. Raymo (Berkeley and Los Angeles, 1960), p. 93, lines 2797–8. Mention should perhaps be made here of H. A. Kelly, "A Neo-Revisionist Look at Chaucer's Nuns," *Chaucer Review* 31 (1996): 127, who suggests (without supporting evidence) "some influence from the prosopographical genre of *De Viris Illustribus* which Boccaccio developed . . . in the *De Casibus Virorum Illustrorum* featuring cautionary thumbnail sketches . . . Many of the character descriptions of the General Prologue resemble the portraits of Chaucer's tragic protagonists in their prosperity phase." Though many autobiographical characterizations of Ovid's epistles bear generically on all of the portraits in the General Prologue, "the female speakers of the thirteen single *heroides* make them particularly relevant to the Prioress, specially in the light of his adaptation of these epistles to yet another genre, the *vita sanctorum*, in the Legend of Good Women."

The Monk

The Monk's portrait is composed of the stereotypical features of anti-monastic satire. He is prosperous and worldly with a lordly air and luxurious tastes in food, dress, and adornment. He passionately pursues the aristocratic sport of hunting, assembling a stable of fine horses and fleet greyhounds to engage in the chase (166–8, 190–2, 203). He is an administrator of a subordinate monastery ("kepere of the celle" [172]), an office which he exploits in order to support his affluent way of life. He openly and defiantly rejects the injunctions of the monastic rule to manual labor, study, and claustration (173–88). His portrait is heavily indebted in detail, imagery, and vocabulary to Gower's denunciation in the *Mirour de l'Omme* of corrupt monks (and ecclesiastics generally) who betray their religious ideals and neglect their duties in order to live worldly lives:

20953 Cil moigne n' est pas bon claustral
Q'est fait gardein ou seneschal
D' ascun office q'est forein;
Car lors luy falt selle et chival
20957 Pour courre les paiis aval,
Si fait despense au large mein;
Il prent vers soy le meulx de grein,
Et laist as autres comme vilein
Le paille, et ensi seignoral
Devient le moigne nyce et vein:
De vuide grange et ventre plein
20964 N'ert pas l'acompte bien egal.[47]

[A monk is not suited for cloister life if he is made overseer or steward in any outside office; for in that case he has to have a horse and saddle to ride over the countryside, and he spends money generously. He takes for himself the best grain, leaving the chaff for others, such as the peasants. Thus the foolish, vain monk becomes lordly. The account of empty barn and full belly is not a balanced one. (Wilson, p. 280)]

21037 Trop erre encontre le decré
Le moigne qui quiert propreté
Mais il du propre ad nepourqant
Les grandes soummes amassé,
Dont il son lucre ad pourchacié
21042 Du siecle, ensi come fait marchant,
Et pour delit tient plus avant
A la rivere oiseals volant,
La faulcon et l'ostour mué,
Les leverers auci courant
Et les grantz chivals sojournant,
21048 Ne falt que femme mariée.

[47] John Gower, *Mirour de l'omme* in *The Complete Works of John Gower*, ed. G. C. Macaulay, vol. 1 (Oxford, 1902). All quotations from the *Mirour* are taken from this edition. Where indicated, translations from the *Mirour* are taken from John Gower, *Mirour de l'omme* (The Mirror of Mankind), trans. W. W. Wilson, rev. Nancy Wilson Van Baak (East Lansing, MI, 1992).

[The monk who seeks property errs greatly against the rule, but nonetheless he amasses great sums for himself, whereby he procures his gain from the world just as a merchant does. And, moreover, for his delight he has flying birds at the river – a falcon and a moulted goshawk, also running greyhounds and great steeds all ready to go. Only a wife is lacking. (Wilson, p. 281)]

20845 Saint Augustin en sa leçoun
Dist, tout ensi comme le piscoun
En l'eaue vit tantsoulement,
20848 Tout autrecy Religioun
Prendra sa conversacioun
Solonc la reule du covent
El cloistre tout obedient:
20852 Car s'il vit seculierement,
Lors change la condicioun
Del ordre qu'il primerement
Resceut, dont pert au finement
20856 Loer de sa professioun.

[Saint Augustine in his teaching says that just as a fish lives only in water, so the religious shall take up his way of life very obediently in the cloister, according to the rule of the community. For if he lives in the world, then he changes the conditions of the order that he first accepted, so that in the end he loses the reward of his calling. (Wilson, p. 279)]

20995 Mais nostre moigne au present jour
Quiert en sa guise bell atour
Au corps, et l'alme desfigure:
Combien q'il porte de dolour
La frocque, il ad du vein honour
21000 La cote fourré de pellure.

[But our monk nowadays seeks fine attire for his body and debases his soul. Although he wears the frock of sorrow, he has the fur-lined cloak of vain honors. (Wilson, pp. 280–1)]

21014 Cil moigne puet avoir esmay
Qui pour le mond se fait jolys,
Ne quiert la haire ainz quiert le say
Tout le plus fin a son essay,
21018 Ove la fourrure vair et gris,
Car il desdeigne le berbis.
L'aimal d'argent n'ert pas oubliz,
Ainz fait le moustre et pent tout gay
21022 Au chaperon devant le pis.

[A monk can have disquiet if he beautifies himself for the world. He seeks for his use not the hair shirt, but rather the finest woolen materials, together with furs vair and gray, for he disdains sheep's fleece. Enameled silver jewelry is not forgotten; it makes a show and hangs gaily from his hood in front of his breast. (Wilson, p. 281)]

20857 Solonc la primere ordinance
Ly moigne contre la plesance

Du char s' estoiont professez,
Et d'aspre vie la penance
Suffriront; mais celle observance
20862 Ore ont des toutez partz laissez:
Car gule gart tous les entrez
Qe faim et soif n'y sont entrez
Pour amegrir la crasse pance;
Si ont des pelliçouns changez
Les mals du froid et estrangez,
20868 Qe point ne vuillont s'aqueintance.

[According to the first rule, the monks, having professed themselves against the pleasures of the flesh, then take on the penance of hard life; but nowadays they have neglected everywhere the observance of this. Gluttony guards all the entrances, so that hunger and thirst have not come in to thin down their fat bellies. With furred cloaks they have eliminated the hurt of cold and removed it so far that they do not know it at all. (Wilson, p. 279)]

Gower returns to the attack in Book 4 of *Vox Clamantis*, employing the same fish out of water image to excoriate well-dressed monks who manage to live out of the cloister (chapter 5, lines 276–82, 297–303). Fat monks, moreover, make gluttony their only labor and study (chapter 2, lines 67–8, 71–2, 75–6). Chaucer's description of the monk's eyes (201–2) to indicate his propensity to wrath and lechery is also adapted from the *Vox Clamantis* (chapter 3, line 176): "Lumina commota lenius igne micant" ["The rolling eyes flash brighter than fire" (Stockton, p. 169)].

Additional details indicative of monastic ease and comfort are drawn from *The Simonie* and *Romans de Carité*. Both reprove monks who wear furs and fine shoes. And the *Romans de Carité* (ironically) and *Vox Clamantis* condemn monks, like Chaucer's, who reject the rule of St Maurus and St Benedict and hold "after the newe world the space."[48] Hunting clerics were also a familiar target of medieval satirists, sermonists and reformers.[49] Langland's parson, Sleuþe, for example, is an avid hunter (B.V. 418–20); and in *Vox Clamantis* (Book 3, chapter 18) Gower paints a mordantly satirical picture of a curate riding to the chase with the barking of dogs ringing in his ears as loudly as the "chapel belle" mentioned in the Monk's portrait (171).

1493 Est sibi crassus equs, restatque sciencia macra,
Sella decora que mens feda perornat eum.
Ad latus et cornu sufflans gerit, unde redundat
Mons, nemus, unde lepus visa pericla fugit;

[48] See *The Simonie*: *A Parallel-Text Edition*, ed. D. Embree and E. Urquhart (Heidelberg, 1991), pp. 73–4, lines 145–56; Renclus de Moiliens, *Li Romans de Carité et Miserere*, ed. A. G. Van Hamel (Paris, 1885), p. 74, stanza 139, lines 6–10; p. 78, stanza 146, lines 1–7, 10–12; *Vox Clamantis*, Book 4, chapter 7, p. 175, lines 337–42. For Chaucer's statement that "hunters ben nat hooly men" (178), deriving from Pseudo-Jerome's commentary on Psalm 90, see O. F. Emerson, "Some of Chaucer's Lines on the Monk," *Modern Philology* 1 (1904): 104–10. R. B. White, Jr., "Chaucer's Daun Piers and the Rule of St Benedict: The Failure of an Ideal," *Journal of English and Germanic Philology* 70 (1971): 13–30, documents the Monk's defiance of the Rule.

[49] See Mann, pp. 24–7, 221–2; Owst, pp. 260, 264, 269–70, 278–9, 352–3. On the actual practice of hunting by monks, see Almond, pp. 131–2.

Oris in ecclesia set vox sua muta quiescit,
1498 Ne fugat a viciis sordida corda gregis.
. . .
1505 Vix sibi festa dies sacra vel ieiunia tollunt,
Quin nemus in canibus circuit ipse suis:
Clamor in ore canum, dum vociferantur in unum,
Est sibi campana, psallitur unde deo.
Stat sibi missa breuis, deuocio longaque campis,
Quo sibi cantores deputat esse canes:
Sic lepus et vulpis sunt quos magis ipse requirit;
1512 Dum sonat ore deum, stat sibi mente lepus.

[He has a fat horse, while his learning remains meagre. An elegant saddle and a lowly mind are his ornaments. He blows upon a horn he carries at his side, and mountains and meadows re-echo from it; the hare flees the dangers evident from it. But his voice keeps quiet in church, lest it should drive the base hearts of his flocks away from vice. . . . Holy days of feasting or fasting are hardly over but that he is circling the meadow in the midst of his dogs. To him the noise of the dogs as they bark together is a church bell on which hymns are played to God. His mass is short but long are his devotions in the fields, where he appoints his dogs as cantors. The hare and the fox are what he wants most; as he speaks of God his mind is still on the hare. (Stockton, pp. 149–50)]

Chaucer's Monk was qualified to be an abbot (167), and judging by *The Simonie* (lines 121–3), his love of "venerie" would have made him a fit companion of other abbots and priors. In short, his life of shameless self-indulgence, love of hunting, and scornful disregard of the rule in matters of labor, study and claustration show him to be an acedious monk. And his physical appearance – bald, oily, fat, ruddy(?) complexion and rolling, gleaming eyes – is one that the physiognomies would characterize as belonging to an indiscreet, foolish, proud, lecherous, shameless, slothful and disobedient man.[50]

The Friar

The portrait of the Friar, the longest of the *General Prologue*, incorporates many of the favorite themes of antimendicant satire. His genial, pleasure-loving manner, talent for singing and skill in "daliaunce and fair langage" (211) are the instruments of his hypocrisy. He haunts taverns, prefers the company of the rich to the poor, and is courteous and humble only where money is to be made

[50] See *Secretum Secretorum*, ed. M. A. Manzalaoui, EETS OS 276 (Oxford, 1977), p. 112 (Ashmole version); and *Three Prose Versions of the Secreta Secretorum*, ed. R. Steele, Part 1, EETS ES 74 (London, 1898), pp. 115, 223. The Monk's rejection of work, study, and claustration are characteristics of *acedia*. See Cassian, *De Coenobiorum Institutis*, PL 49, cols 366, 368–9. Cf. also J. E. Grennen, "Chaucerian Portraiture: Medicine and the Monk," *Neuphilologische Mitteilungen* 69 (1968): 569–74, and "Chaucer's Monk: Baldness, Venery, and Enbonpoint," *American Notes and Queries* 6 (1968): 83–5, on the bawdy pun "venerie" and the association of the Monk's baldness with sexual acts. The hare which the Monk chases is also a traditional symbol of lechery. See E. Reiss, "The Symbolic Surface of the Canterbury Tales: The Monk's Portrait. Part I," *Chaucer Review* 2 (1968): 257 and n. 6.

(215–17; 240–50). His motivation is not to minister to the poor or preach the gospel, but to amass wealth, chiefly by abusing the sacrament of penance, but also by begging (even wheedling money from a shoeless widow), being helpful in "love-dayes," and brokering marriages (212–13). He is pleasure-loving, and he has a special affinity for women of all kinds: young women (213), "worthy wommen of the toun" (217), barmaids (241), and "faire wyves" to whom he makes gifts of knives and pins (234). His expensive attire is in keeping with his sense of self-importance (259–63).

Much of this material is from stock, filtered down from the Latin polemical treatises of William of St Amour's *De Periculis novissorum temporum* (1254) and Richard Fitzralph's *Defensio Curatorum* (1357), and it parallels many of the charges leveled at friars in the *Memoriale Presbiterorum*, the *Omne Bonum*, and various Lollard texts.[51] But the portrait of Brother Huberd is also closely modeled on the allegorical figure of False Seeming in the *Roman de la Rose.* False Seeming associates himself with the mendicants. Like the Friar, he confesses and courts the rich and neglects and scorns the poor, engages in match-making and brokerage, likes to be addressed as master, boasts that his "purchas" is better than his "rente", behaves in a proud and overbearing manner, regards himself as superior to the parish priest, and indulges in excesses of food and finery. His motivation is only to accumulate "great piles and heaps of treasure":

11232 C'est veirs, mais je sui ypocrites.
Tu vas preeschant astenance.
Veire veir, mais j'emple ma pance
11235 De trés bons morseaus e de vins
Teus come il afiert a devins.
Tu vas preeschant povreté
Veire, riches a poeté.
Mais, combien que povres me feigne,
11240 Nul povre je ne contredeigne.
J'ameraie meauz l'acointance
Cent mile tanz dou rei de France
Que d'un povre, par nostre dame!
11244 Tout eüst il ausinc bone ame.
...
11261 E s'aucuns vient qui me repreigne
Pour quei dou povre me restreigne,
Savez vous coment j'en eschape?

[51] For a comprehensive survey of this literature, both Latin and vernacular, see P. R. Szittya, *The Antifraternal Tradition in Medieval Literature* (Princeton, 1986), especially pp. 183–287, for the English literary tradition. See also W. Scase, *Piers Plowman and the New Anticlericalism* (Cambridge, 1989), *passim*; M. J. Haren, "Friars as Confessors: The Canonist Background to the Fourteenth Century Controversy," *Peritia* 3 (1984): 503–16, on the conflict between the friars and parish priests on this issue; M. Aston, "'Caim's Castles': Poverty, Politics, and Disendowment," *The Church, Politics, and Patronage in the Fifteenth Century*, ed. R. B. Dobson (Gloucester, Eng., and New York, 1984), pp. 45–81, especially for Wycliffite attitudes toward begging and almsgiving; and A. Williams, "Chaucer and the Friars," *Speculum* 28 (1953): 499–513, for parallels to the works of William of St Amour and Richard Fitzralph. The charges against friars ultimately stem from Matt. 23 and 2 Timothy 3.

Je faz entendant par ma chape
Que li riches est entechiez
Plus que li povres de pechiez,
S' a greigneur mestier de conseil
Pour c'i vois, pour ce le conseil.
…
De labourer n' ai je que faire:
Trop a grant peine en labourer.
J'aim meauz devant les genz ourer
E afubler ma renardie
Dou mantel de papelardie.
…
Par ma lobe entas e amasse
Grant tresor en tas e en masse,
Qui ne peut pour riens afonder;
Car, se j'en faz palais fonder,
E acomplis touz mes deliz
De compaignies ou de liz,
De tables pleines d'entremès,
Car ne vueil autre vie mais,
Recreist mes argenz e mes ors;
Car ainz que seit vuiz mes tresors
Denier me vienent a resours.
Ne faz je bien tomber mes ours?
En aquerre est toute m' entente
Meauz vaut mes pourchaz que ma rente.
S'en me devait tuer ou batre
Si me vueil je par tout embatre;
Si ne querraie ja cessier
Ou d' empereeurs confessier
Ou reis, ou dus, ou bers, ou contes,
Mais de povres genz est ce hontes:
Je n'aim pas tel confession
Se n'est pour autre occasion,
Je n'ai cure de povres genz:
Leur estaz n'est ne beaus ne genz.
…
E pour le sauvement des ames,
J' enquier des seigneurs e des dames,
E de trestoutes leur maisnies
Les proprietez e les vies,
E leur faz creire e met es testes
Que leur prestre curé sont bestes
Envers mei e mes compaignons.
…
S'il font euvres qui bones seient,
C'est pour ce que les genz les veient.
Leur philateres eslargissent,
E leur fimbries agrandissent,
E des sieges aiment aus tables
Les plus hauz, les plus enourables,

E les prumiers des sinagogues,
Con fiers e orguilleus e rogues;
E aiment que l' en les salue
Quant il trespassent par la rue;
11633 E veulent estre apelé maistre.
. . .
11679 Si m' entremet de courretages,
Je faz pais, je joing marriages,
Seur mei preing execucions
11682 E vois en procuracions.

["That is true, but I am a hypocrite." "You preach abstinence." "True indeed, but I fill my belly with rich food and wine, as a theologian should." "You preach poverty." "Indeed, though I am abundantly wealthy. But however much I pretend to be poor, I have no regard for poor men. By Our Lady, I would infinitely rather have the acquaintance of the King of France than of a poor man, even though his soul were just as good. . . . And if anyone rebukes me for avoiding the poor man, do you know how I get out of it? I suggest by the cloak I wear that the rich man is more stained with sin than the poor, and so has greater need of counsel, and that is why I go to him and counsel him. . . . I have nothing to do with work; working costs too much effort. I prefer to pray where people can see me, and hide my duplicity beneath a cloak of religious hypocrisy. . . . Through my trickery I accumulate and amass great piles and heaps of treasure that nothing can undermine; for if I use it to build palaces and obtain all the delights that company and bed and tables loaded with delicacies can supply (for I no longer want any other kind of life), then in the meantime my silver and gold increase, for before my treasury is empty, I acquire money in abundance. Do I not make my bears dance well? I concentrate all my effort on gain, and this quest is worth more than my revenues. Were I to be killed or beaten for it, I would still penetrate every place, and never seek to resign my post as confessor of emperors, kings, dukes, barons, or counts. But it is shameful to be the confessor of poor people, nor do I like such confessions. Unless there is some other reason for it, I care nothing for the poor; their estate is neither fair nor noble. . . . For the salvation of their souls, I make enquiries about the property and the lives of the lords and ladies and all their household, and I instill in them the belief that their parish priests are animals in comparison with me and my companions. . . . If they do good works, it is in order to be seen doing them. They make their phylacteries broad and their fringes long, and they love the highest and most honorable places at table and the best seats in the synagogue, for they are proud and haughty and overbearing. They like to be greeted as they go about in the streets and to be addressed as master. . . . I am also involved in brokerage, I effect reconciliations and arrange marriages. I undertake the duties of executor and procurator." (Horgan, pp. 172–3, 177–80)]

Later, addressing Evil Tongue, False Seeming again extols his power of confession and reiterates his superiority to the parish priest:

12336 Confès sereiz en cete place,
E ce pechié, senz plus, direiz;
De cetui vous repentireiz,
Car je sui d'ordre e si sui prestres,

De confessier li plus hauz maistres
Qui seit, tant con li mondes dure;
J'ai de tout le monde la cure;
Ce n'ot onques prestres curez,
Tout fust a s'iglise jurez;
E si ai, par la haute dame!
Cent tanz plus pitié de vostre ame
Que voz prestres parrochiaus,
Ja tant n'iert vostre especiaus.

[You must make your confession here, and tell your sin without more ado, and you must repent of it, for I am from an order and am a priest, the greatest master of the art of confession throughout the world. I have charge of all the world, which no parish priest, however devoted to his church, ever had. And by Our Lady, I have one hundred times more pity for your soul than your parish priest, however good a friend he may be. (Horgan, p. 190)]

Additional details are taken from the criticisms directed against friars in the *Mirour de l'Omme*. There we find two limiters, Friar Hypocrisy and Friar Flattery, who visit the houses of the rich and dispense easy absolution ("without pain and without punishment") in return for large stipends. Their only care is for money, and they force even the poor to contribute to their coffers. They are shameless womanizers, deceitful in word and deed, and overbearing in their pride:

Ly confessour, ly limitantz,
Chascun de s'aquointance ad tant
Pour confesser et pour aprendre,
Que ce leur fait eslire et prendre
Tout la plus belle et la plus tendre,
Car d'autre ne sont desirantz.
. . .
Ils ont corage mondial;
Ils ont la langue liberal,
Dont la mençonge serra peinte,
Ils ont parole belle et queinte
Dont font deceipte a lour acqueinte.
. . .
Deux freres sont de la partie,
Qui vont ensemble sanz partie
Les paiis pour environner;
Et l'un et l'autre ades se plie
Au fin que bien leur multeplie
Du siecle; dont sont mençonger
Pour blandir et pour losenger
Et pour les pecchés avancer:
L'un ad noun frere Ypocresie,
Qui doit ma dame confesser,
Mais l'autre la doit relesser,
Si ad noun frere Flaterie.
Ipocresie vient au lit,
Et est pour confessour eslit

21255 Pour ce qu'il semble debonnaire;
Et qant ma dame ad trestout dit,
Lors Flaterie la blandist,
Qui point ne parle du contraire,
Car ce n' est pas de son affaire,
21260 Q'il quiert contricioun attraire
De nul ou nulle, ainz pour profit
Assolt sanz autre paine faire;
Et ensi gaigne le doaire
De sa viande et son habit.
21265 Le frere qui son lucre avente
Dist a ma dame que jovente
Du femme doit molt excuser
La freleté de son entente;
Dont il sovent plus entalente
21270 La pecché faire que laisser,
Qant pour si poy voet relaisser.
. . .
21277 Ipocresie tielement
Du dame et seignour ensement
Quiert avoir la confessioun;
Mais Flaterie nequedent
21281 Par l'ordinance du covent
En dorra l'absolucioun,
Car il ad despensacioun
Solonc recompensacioun,
Que vient du bource au riche gent,
Qu'il puet donner remissioun
Sanz paine et sanz punicioun,
21288 Pour plus gaigner de leur argent.
. . .
21313 Frere Ipocrite, u qu'il vendra,
D'onesteté tout parlera
Pour soy coverir de sa parole,
Dont il les oills avoeglera
De ces maritz, qant tretera
21318 Les femmes quelles il affole.
. . .
21373 O comme le frere se contient,
Qant il au povre maison vient!
O comme le sciet bien sermonner!
Maisque la dame ait poy ou nient,
Ja meinz pour ce ne s'en abstient
Clamer, prier et conjurer;
La maile prent s'il n'ait denier,
Voir un soul oef pour le soupier,
21381 Ascune chose avoir covient.
. . .
21493 En halt estat humilier
Se doit om, mais contrarier
Le frere voet, qant en escole

De sa logique puet monter
En halt divin et noun porter
21498 Du mestre, dont sa fame vole.

[Confessors and limiters have so many women to confess and advise that they choose and take the most beautiful and most tender, for they desire no other. . . . They have a worldly spirit. They have a free tongue, with which lies will be painted. They have pretty and clever words, with which they will deceive their acquaintances. . . . Friars go in pairs, and they stay together without separating. They go about the countryside, and both of them bend their efforts to multiplying their worldly goods. They lie in order to blandish and to flatter and to encourage sins. One is called Friar Hypocrisy, who is to confess my lady; and the other is called Friar Flattery, and he is to absolve her. Hypocrisy comes to her bed and is chosen as a confessor because he seems to be kindly. And when the lady has told everything, Flattery blandishes her, and says nothing of transgressions (for that is not his business). He does not seek to get anyone's contrition but gives absolution for profit without imposing any penance; and thus he earns the endowment of his food and clothing. The friar who goes after his lucre tells the lady that a woman's youth excuses much of the frailty of her intent. Thus he often induces her to sin more rather than to give up sinning, since he is willing to give her such easy absolution. . . . Hypocrisy wants to get the confession of both lord and lady; but Flattery (by command of the order) will give them absolution, for he has the dispensation in accordance with the compensation that comes from the purse of rich people, so that he can give remission without pain and without punishment, in order to earn more of their money. . . . Friar Hypocrite talks a great deal about honesty wherever he goes, in order to cover himself by his words, wherefore he blinds the eyes of the husbands when he is dealing with wives whom he has made wanton. . . . Oh, how the friar conducts himself when he comes to a poor house! Oh, how he knows how to give a sermon! Even if the lady has little or nothing, nevertheless he does not abstain from crying out, imploring, and entreating. He takes a halfpenny if she does not have a penny – or even a single egg for supper. He has to get something. . . . A man in high estate ought to humble himself, but the friar wishes the contrary when, through his knowledge of logic, he succeeds in mounting to lofty theology and bears the title of Master, which makes his fame widespread. (Wilson, pp. 126, 284–7)]

Like Fraud, the Friar visits taverns to "fatten his purse" from the ladies (26081–5). The same charge was brought against the Carmelite friars in the interpolated version of the *Speculum Stultorum* (p. 188): "His magis interne mulieres atque taberne/ Et mendicare quam sacra verba dare." ("They are more intimate with women and taverns and begging than with preaching the Gospel.") The denunciation of friars in the *Vox Clamantis* repeats many of these criticisms. They are charged with neglecting the poor, pursuing wealth and violating their vow of poverty, courting the rich, and seducing women. They are also charged with busying themselves with worldly affairs for personal gain.[52]

Piers Plowman is also fiercely antifraternal. One of Langland's chief complaints against the friars is their corruption of the confessional, which in the

[52] See *Vox Clamantis*, Book 4, chapter 16, p. 186, lines 721–2, 743–5; chapter 17, p. 187, lines 779–80; chapter 18, pp. 189, 190, lines 833–6, 863–4.

following lines he takes as a sign of the degeneracy of the Church. An amenable friar is prepared to hear the confession of Lady Meed and to bestow absolution for "a sem of whete":

	Þanne com þere a confessour ycopid* as a frere;	wearing a cope
	To Mede þe maiden mekeliche he loutide*,	bowed low
	And seide* ful softely, in shrifte* as it were,	spoke/ in confession
	'þeiȝ* lerid and lewide hadde leiȝe* be þe ichone,	Though/ had lain
	And þeiȝ Falshed hadde folewid þe þis fiftene wynter,	
	I shal assoile* þe myself for a sem* of whete,	absolve/ load
	And ek* be þi baudekyn*, and bere wel þin arnde*	also/ little bawd/ message
	Among clerkis and kniȝtes, Consience to felle'.	
	Þanne Mede for hire mysdedis to þat man knelide,	
	And shrof* hire of hire shrewidnesse*-shameles, I trowe;	confessed/ wickedness
	Tolde hym a tale and toke* hym a noble*	gave/ noble (coin)
	For to be hire bedeman* and hire baude aftir. (A.III)	messenger

In return for her generous support the Friars will forgive her "freletee of flesh":

51	'Wiste I* þat,' quod þat womman, 'I wolde noȝt spare*	If I knew/ hold back
	For to be youre frend, frere, and faile* yow neuere	would fail
	While ye loue* lordes þat lecherie haunten,*	love/ indulge in
	And lakkeþ* noȝt ladies þat louen wel þe same.	disparage, vilify
	It is a freletee* of flessh – ye fynden it in bokes –	frailty
56	And a cours of kynde*, wherof we comen alle.' (B.III)	natural process

Langland notes the popularity of private boudoir-confessions which had led to the rivalry between friars and parish priests:

139	And siþen þei blosmede abrood in boure* to here shriftes.	bedroom
	And now is fallen þerof a fruyt – þat folk han wel leuere*	prefer
	Shewen hire shriftes to hem þan shryve hem to hir persons*.	parish priests
	And now persons han parceyued þat freres parte* wiþ hem,	share (the profits)
	Thise possessioners* preche and depraue* freres;	beneficed priests/ revile
144	And freres fyndeþ hem in defaute*, as folk bereþ witnesse. (B.V)	in fault, error

A friar's visit to a private house results in an unwanted pregnancy:

344	'I knew swich oon ones*, noȝt eighte wynter passed,	once
	Coom in þus ycoped at a court þere I dwelde,	
	And was my lordes leche* – and my ladies boþe.	physician
	And at þe laste þis lymytour*, þo* my lord was oute,	licensed friar/ when
348	He saluede* so oure wommen til some were wiþ childe!' (B.XX)	treated

Langland also protests against the involvement of "Religioun" (not specifically friars) in love-days and other secular business (A.XI.211–13).

Regarding Brother Huberd's musical talents (235–7, 266–8), Mann notes (p. 45) a satirical parallel in the *Decameron* (7.3) where a friar begins to "compose songs, sonnets and ballades, sing, and do many other things of a similar nature." ("a fare delle canzoni e de' sonetti e delle ballate, e a cantare e tutto pieno d'altre cose a queste simili"). Wyclif accuses friars of occupying themselves on holidays with "veyn songis and knackynge and harpynge, gyternynge &

daunsynge & oþere veyn triflis to geten þe stynkyng loue of damyselis, and stere hem to worldely vanyte and synnes." He also deplores the friars' practice of using trinkets to ingratiate themselves with the ladies.[53]

The Friar's affected lisp is revealed near the end of the portrait. It is another instrument of his hypocrisy, and it epitomizes the character of a corrupt ecclesiastic who utterly undermines the ideals of mendicancy. Gower, in *Vox Clamantis* (Book 5, chapter 6, line 376), describes a woman "whose cunning tongue charms with its lispings" ("Et placet in blesis subdola lingua suis"), echoing Ovid's advice to the lover to affect a lisp because women take readily to the habit (*Ars Amatoria* I.598, III.293–6). But lisping was viewed by St. Jerome in his letter to Eustochium as foppish (delicata), and denounced by the author of *Ancrene Wisse* as a sign of pride.[54]

The criticism of friars for their luxurious dress was a commonplace of the satirical tradition. Special notice was taken of their copes, which were worn to impress the faithful with their status and importance. Chaucer makes it clear that the Friar's cope was particularly splendid. Boccaccio contrasts the copes worn by the founders of the mendicant orders and the present-day friars:

> Dove dagl' inventori de' frati [le cappe] furono ordinate strette e misere e di grossi panni . . . essi oggi le fanno larghe e doppie e lucide e di finissimi panni, e quelle in forma hanno recate leggiadra e pontificale, in tanto che paoneggiar con esse nelle chiese e nelle piazze . . . non si vergognano. (3.7)
>
> [Whereas the founders of the friars stipulated that their copes be tight, poor, and of coarse cloth, today they are made wide, doubly thick, elegant and of the finest cloths, and in a graceful and pontifical style so that they can go about in churches and squares without shame.]

> Né San Domenico né San Francesco, senza aver quatro cappe per uno, non di tintillani né d'altri panni gentili ma di lana grossa fatti e di natural colore, a cacciare il freddo e non a apparere si vestissero. (7.3)
>
> [Neither Saint Dominic nor Saint Francis had four copes each. They were not dyed or made of fine cloths, but of coarse wool in a natural color, to ward off the cold and not to appear decked out in finery.]

Langland sardonically observes that friars construed the gospel as they pleased for "coueitise of copis" (A. Pr. 55–8), and followed Antichrist because he gave them copes (B.XX.57).[55]

[53] *The English Works of Wyclif*, ed. F. D. Matthew, EETS OS 74 (London, 1880), pp. 9, 12 ("Of the Leaven of Pharisees"). The practice is also mentioned in lines 37–40 of the contemporary antifraternal poem, "Preste, ne monke, ne ȝit chanoun." See *Historical Poems of the XIVth and XVth Centuries*, ed. R. H. Robbins (New York, 1959), p. 158. A squib from British Library MS Harley 3362, fol. 47r reads: "Fratres cum knyvis goth about and swyvet mennis wyvis." Brother Huberd derives his name from the corrupt clerics in the Old French *Roman de Renart* and other poems in the Renart tradition. See C. Muscatine, "The Name of Chaucer's Friar," *Modern Language Notes* 70 (1955): 169–72.

[54] Jerome, *Letters*, 22.29, pp. 124–5, and *Ancrene Wisse*, p. 103. According to *Certeyne Rewles of Phisnomy* (*Secretum Secretorum*, ed. Manzalaoui, p. 14), lisping "shewes a right wicked and deceytus man." In his treatise on the French language (*Le Tretiz*, ed. W. Rothwell [London, 1990], p. 28, lines 1089–92), Walter de Bibbesworth voices his strong disapproval of the practice.

[55] In the *Protectorium Pauperis* (c. 1380) Richard Maidstone disputes the teaching of the Wycliffite John Ashwardby that "no one should give alms to a friar who perhaps has a cope better than all his possessions." See A. Williams, "Two Notes on Chaucer's Friars," *Modern Philology* 54 (1956):

The Merchant

The Merchant is preoccupied with his public image. He sports a fashionable beard and sits high on his horse. He is well dressed in motley with stylish buckled boots and a "Flaundryssh" beaver hat. His appearance is intended to convey a sense of his superior social status and prosperity (270–3). He projects an image of sober respectability with the outlook of a hard-headed business man engrossed in money-making and advocating a mercantile policy protective of his trade routes. Judging by his desire to see the shipping lanes be kept open "Bitwixe Middleburgh and Orewelle" (274–7), he is a wool merchant and a member of either the Merchants of the Staple or the Merchant Adventurers. In a brief portrait Chaucer twice describes him as "worthy," but engaged in dubious business practices that were often associated with illegal money exchange and usury. He is in debt, but he discreetly keeps it to himself, recognizing the need to maintain good credit and his professional reputation (279–83).

Chaucer is working here within the general tradition of anti-merchant satire. The association of trade with fraud, usury, and avarice is commonplace.[56] In the *Speculum Stultorum*, Burnellus the ass meets a dishonest merchant who calls Guile his mother, Trickster his father, Gluttony his sister, and Deceit his wife. A similarly disreputable family makes its appearance at the opening of Gower's long diatribe against merchants in the *Vox Clamantis*.[57] In *Piers Plowman*, "Coveytise" relies on guile to sell his wares at market, and, although he engages in a different form of transaction from Chaucer's Merchant, he freely admits to usury through "eschaunges and chevysaunces" (B.V.243–6).

Chaucer does not seem to have followed a single model for his portrait, but much of the material in it is paralleled in the *Mirour de l'Omme*, which describes the dishonest dealings of a wool merchant called Fraud, who is engaged in "eschange, usure et chevisance" and talks incessantly about his profits:

> Si Triche est en son drap vendant
> As deux deceiptes entendant,
> Il est enquore au double plus
> En son office deceivant,
> Qant il des leines est marchant:
> Car lors est Triche a son dessus.
> ...
> Triche ad sa cause trop mondeine,
> Car l'autry prou toutdis desdeigne
> Et quiert son propre lucre ades:
> Mais il ad trop soubtile aleine
> Qant il l'estaple de la leine

118–19. Chaucer's lines may echo Matt. 23.5. Cf. Szittya, pp. 204, 298–9. Laura Hodges, "Chaucer's Friar: 'Typet' and 'Semycope,'" *Chaucer Review* 34 (2000): 329, argues that Chaucer depicts the Friar as "openly flaunting his character in a cloak made of cloth too good to suit his vows of poverty, and fashioned in an unsuitable length and width." See also Mann, pp. 43–4.

56 Mann, pp. 99–101; Owst, pp. 352–60; Bowden, pp. 148–50.

57 *Speculum Stultorum*, lines 785–8; *Vox Clamantis*, Book 5, chapter 12, lines 703–10.

Governe, car de son encress
Lors trete et parle asses du pres:
. . .
O leine, dame de noblesce,
Tu es des marchantz la duesse.
. . .
O belle, O blanche, O bien delie,
L'amour de toy tant point et lie,
Que ne se porront deslier
Les cuers qui font la marchandie
De toy; ainz mainte tricherie
Et maint engin font compasser
Comment te porront amasser:
Et puis te font la mer passer,
Comme celle q'es de leur navie
La droite dame, et pour gaigner
Les gens te vienont bargainer
Par covoitise et par envie.
Eschange, usure et chevisance
O laine, soubz ta governance
Vont en ta noble Court servir;
Et Triche y fait lour pourvoiance,
Qui d'Avarice l'aquointance
Attrait, et pour le gaign tenir
Il fait les brocours retenir.
Mais quique s' en voet abstenir
Du fraude, Triche ades l'avance,
Si q' en les laines maintenir
Je voi plusours descontenir
Du loyalte la viele usance.

[If Fraud is an expert in his double deceit when he sells his piece-goods [as a Draper], he is even twice as deceiving when he buys and sells wool. Then he is the epitome of Fraud. . . . Fraud is very worldly in his way, for he always disdains others' profits and continually seeks his own lucre. But he has a very keen nose when he checks the staple of the wool, for he is now dealing with and talking about his own profit [and his loans]. . . . O wool, noble lady, you are the goddess of the merchants. . . . O beautiful, white, delicate Wool, love of you pierces and binds the hearts of those who trade in you so that they cannot unbind themselves. On the contrary, they contrive all kinds of trickery and conspiracy in order to collect great quantities of you. And then they take you overseas as if you were the mistress of their ships. And, in order to get you, the people come to bargain in covetousness and envy. Foreign exchange, usury, and bargaining go under your rule to serve in your noble court, O Wool; and Fraud is their supplier there. And Fraud becomes acquainted with Avarice, and he engages agents in order to get profits. But though some abstain from Fraud, Fraud always increases, so that, in keeping wool going, I see many who cease to observe the old-fashioned usages of honesty. (Wilson, pp. 332–3, as corrected)]

John Bromyard in his *Summa Praedicantium* also notes the predilection of merchants to talk expansively of their own gains, as does Thomas Wimbledon

who remarks that priests have adopted the same practice, speaking "unhonestly as cherlis, oþer of wynnynge as marchaundis."[58] Governed by Fraud, Gower's merchants also conceal the debts they have incurred through their business dealings, and even go on pilgrimages to escape their creditors:

25813 Jadis qant les marchantz parloiont
De vingt et Cent, lors habondoiont
De richesce et de soufficance,
Lors de lour propres biens vivoiont,
Et loyalment se contenoiont
25818 Sanz faire a nully decevance:
Mais ils font ore lour parlance
De mainte Mill; et sanz doubtance
25821 Des tieus y ad que s'il paioiont
Leur debtes, lors sanz chevisance
Ils n' ont quoy propre a la montance
D'un florin, dont paier porroiont.
. . .
25849 L'en voit ascuns de tiele enprise
Qui par deceipte et par queintise
Al oill passont tout lour voisin;
Mais ce n' est pas honeste guise,
Qant puis s' en fuiont au franchise
De saint Piere ou de saint Martin,
25855 Q'attendre n'osent en la fin
Deinz la Cité, mais au chemin
Se mettont vers la sainte eglise.
Maldit soient tiel pelerin,
Q'ensi vienont au lieu divin
25860 Pour faire au deable sacrefise.

[When merchants of old talked of twenty or a hundred, they had plenty and abundance of wealth, and lived from their own means, conducting themselves honestly without deceiving anyone. But now they parley about many thousands; and no doubt there are some who, if they paid their debts, would not have left any more than a florin with which to pay. . . . Some of this sort are seen, who in deceit and cunning pass their eye over all their neighbors. But it is no honest way when they flee to the sanctuary of Saint Peter or of Saint Martin because finally they dare not wait in the city but set out towards a holy church. Accursed be such pilgrims, who thus come into holy places to make sacrifice to the devil! (Wilson, p. 339)]

The Merchant's motley attire may allude to Ezechiel 27.24. His outfit, however, is appropriate to his social standing, and, together with his solemn manner, reserve, and dignity, reflects the concern of merchant guilds that their members keep up appearances and exhibit a semblance of respectability.[59]

58 John Bromyard, *Summa Praedicantium* (Venice, 1586), p. 448; Wimbledon's Sermon: *Redde Rationem Villicationis Tue: A Middle English Sermon of the Fourteenth Century*, ed. I. K. Knight (Pittsburgh, 1967), p. 78.

59 G. Stillwell, "Chaucer's 'Sad' Merchant," *Review of English Studies* 20 (1944): 14–18; Hodges, pp. 75–87; Bowden, pp. 150–1.

The Clerk

The Clerk is an Oxford logician dedicated to his studies. He is poor, threadbare, lean. Although he has yet to acquire a benefice, he refuses to accept secular employment. Whatever support he receives from his friends he spends on books and learning (304–8). Chaucer has taken details of the Clerk's portrait from several sources. In *Piers Plowman* Dame Study, who is described as "lene . . . of lich and of louz chere" (A.XI.2), rails at those who, unlike the Clerk, misuse language and learning (5–136). She directs the dreamer seeking Do-Well to Clergy, that is, to learning by an allegorical route that epitomizes the character of the Clerk:

'Axe* þe heiȝe wey,' quaþ* heo*, 'from henis* to Suffre- ask/ said/ she/ hence
Boþe-wele-and-wo, ȝif* þat þou wile lerne; if
And rid forþ be* ricchesse, ac* reste þou not þereinne, by /but
For ȝif þou couplist* þe with hym, to Clergie comist þou neuere. join
And ek þe longe launde þat Leccherie hatte* – is called
Leue hym on þi left half* a large myle or more, side
Til þou come to a court, Kepe-wel-þi-tunge –
Fro lesinges* and liþer speche* and likerous* drinkes. lies/ evil talk/ pleasant
Þanne shalt þou se Sobirte and Simplite-of-speche,
Þat iche wiȝt* be in wille his wyt* þe to shewen; person/ wisdom
So shalt þou come to Clergie, þat can* many þinges.' (A.XI) knows

And it was Dame Study who introduced Clergy to Aristotelian logic: "Aristotel and oþere mo to arguen I tauȝte." (131) Langland's conception of study as a moral discipline, which Chaucer reflects, can be traced to Hugh of St. Victor and John of Salisbury.[60] Gower echoes the same idea in Book 3, chapter 28, of the *Vox Clamantis* (lines 2049–60), and in the *Mirour de l'Omme*:

Clercs qui sert deinz la dieu mesoun
Doit estre honneste par resoun;
Car l'escripture ensi devise,
Disant par droit comparisoun
En resemblance ly clergeoun
Fenestre sont du sainte eglise.
Car la fenestre y est assisse
Pour esclarcir deinz la pourprise,
Dont tous voient cils environ;
Et ly clergons en tiele guise
As autres doit donner aprise
D'oneste conversacioun.

[A cleric who serves in God's house must, by reason, be honorable; for the Scripture requires this, saying that, properly speaking, the students are like

[60] Hugh of St. Victor, *Didascalicon*, ed. C. H. Buttimer (Washington, D.C., 1939), Book 3, chapter 13, p. 61; John of Salisbury, *Metalogicon*, ed. C. C. I. Webb (Oxford, 1929), Prologus, p. 4. The *Sermones nulli parcentes*, cited by Mann (p. 75), also urges scholars to "excel in virtues, always teaching and learning how to please God." See T. von Karajan, "Buch der Rügen," *Zeitschrift für Deutsches Altertum* 2 (1842): 29.

windows of Holy Church. For a window is placed to enlighten the interior of an enclosure, in order that everyone can see round about; and the student similarly should give teaching to others in the honorable way of living. (Wilson, p. 278)]

The Clerk's taciturnity (which irks the Host, 840–1) is a proverbial manifestation of wisdom as exemplified in *Proverbs* 10.17 and 17.28. It may have been inspired by an anecdote about a philosopher in the *Consolation of Philosophy* (2. Pr. 7, lines 75–7) which is recalled to rebuke the dreamer in *Piers Plowman* (B.XI.417): "Philosophus esses si tacuisses" ["You would have been a philosopher if you had remained silent"].

Mann observes that poverty is the commonest feature of the Clerk's estate in medieval literature. For some writers it was a "necessary condition for scholarship."[61] That is why Dame Study orders the dreamer to ride by riches. Poverty is a key of knowledge according to John of Salisbury, who regards wealth and learning as incompatible: "Nulla libris erit apta manus ferrugine tincta, Nec nummata queunt corda vacare libris./ Non est eiusdem nummos librosque probare" ["No hand dyed with iron-rust will be fitted for books, And moneyed hearts cannot take their leisure on books:/ It does not belong to the same man to appreciate both coin and books"[62]].

One reason for the poverty of Chaucer's Clerk is his passion for acquiring books: "But al that he myghte of his freendes hente,/ On bookes and on lernynge he it spente." (299–300). The *Philobiblon* of Richard de Bury offers a striking analogy:

> terrenis aliis abdicatis ab animo, acquirendorum librorum solummodo flagraremus affectu. . . . nullam videlicet debere caristiam hominem impedire ab emptione librorum. . . . Quicquid vera poterant [paupertatis evangelicae professores] a famescente ventre furari, vel corpori semitecto surripere, illud lucrum praecipuum arbitrantes, vel emendis vel edendis codices adscripserunt.
>
> [We have resigned all thoughts of other earthly things, and have given ourselves up to a passion for acquiring books. . . . No dearness of price ought to hinder a man from the buying of books. . . . And whatever they [the early churchmen] could steal from their famishing belly, or intercept from their half-covered body, they thought it the highest gain to spend in buying or correcting books.]

And, like the Clerk, Richard also revered Aristotle, calling him the *princeps philosophorum* ("prince of philosophers").[63]

For the Clerk's emaciated appearance, J. A. Alford points to allegorical representations of Dialectic, a thin, pale female figure in Martianus Capella's *The*

[61] Mann, p. 79.

[62] John of Salisbury, *Entheticus Major and Minor*, ed. J. van Laarhoven, vol. 1 (Leiden, 1987), pp. 246–7, lines 269–71, 281–2. The theme is repeated in *Metalogicon* 4.10.

[63] Richard de Bury, *Philobiblon*, ed. and trans. E. C. Thomas (New York, 1889), pp. 7, 20, 49–50; 158, 169, 187–8; 18.

Marriage of Philology and Mercury and in Alan of Lille's *Anticlaudianus*,[64] the former certainly known to Chaucer. There is a closer analogue, however, in John of Hauville's picture of the ragged scholar who is also a philosopher and a logician:

Vacui furit aspera ventris
Incola longa fames, forme populatur honorem
Exhauritque genas . . .
. . .
Quem scopulum mentis – scopolo quid durius? – illa
Horrida non flectat logicorum turba? rigorem
Quis non excuciat et toto pectore dulces
Derivet lacrimas, quociens occurrit honesta
Philosophi fortuna minor? defringitur evo,
Qua latitat, vestis; etatis fimbria longe
Est, non artificis . . .

[Long and bitter hunger rages within the empty stomach, laying waste to the beauty of the figure, emaciating the cheeks . . . Who is there so rock-hard of mind – what is harder than rock? – that is not moved by this ragged horde of logicians? Who does not expel severity and shed tender, heartfelt tears as often as he sees the philosopher's misfortune? The cloak which covers him is made threadbare by time. The fringe comes far more from age than from craft.][65]

The hollow look of the Clerk is viewed by the physiognomies as a strong indication of character. The Ashmole version says: "Who hath a sclender face, he is bifore-seen in his werkes and sotill of intellect. Who hath a sotill face, he is of many thoughtis." The *Governaunce of Princes* takes it as a sign of "study and besynes." The financial support the Clerk receives from his friends is analogous to Will's acknowledgement in *Piers Plowman* that his father and friends paid for his schooling (C.V.35–6), a practice also referred to in the *Physionomy* by John Metham: "scolerys the quiche stody in unyversyteys at her frendys fyndyng."[66]

The Clerk's commitment to teaching and learning embodied in the last line of the portrait recalls a passage from John of Salisbury's attack on the Epicureans in the *Policraticus*, Book 7, chapter 15: "Rarius est caritatis aut humilitatis pede

[64] J. A. Alford, "The Wife of Bath Versus the Clerk of Oxford: What their Rivalry Means," *Chaucer Review* 21 (1986): 108–32; Martianus Capella, *De Nuptiis Philologiae et Mercurii*, ed. J. Willis (Leipzig, 1983), Book 4, sections 328–9, 332, pp. 106–8; Alain de Lille, *Anticlaudianus*, ed. R. Bossuat (Paris: J. Vrin, 1955), Book 3, p. 89, lines 9–13. For the topos "thinness," see Caelius Aurelianus (*On Acute Diseases and on Chronic Diseases*, ed. and trans. I. E. Drabkin [Chicago, 1950], pp. 1000–01) who observes that "studious persons generally have thin bodies because they are continually sharpening their minds with thought and discussion."

[65] Johannes de Hauvilla, *Architrenius*, ed. and trans. W. Wetherbee (Cambridge, 1994), Book 3, pp. 60–3, chapter 1, lines 13–15; chapter 3, lines 35–41. A clerk complains of his threadbare cloak in the Goliardic poem *Exul ego clericus* (*The Goliard Poets*, trans. G. F. Whicher [New York, 1949], pp. 224–5, lines 9–12). See also Mann, pp. 80–1. Cf. Pliny the Younger's *Letters*, Book 7, 25: "You will find that, as in the army, so, in literature, the best scholars are often concealed under the most uncouth appearances."

[66] *Secretum Secretorum* (ed. Manzalaoui), p. 108; *Secreta Secretorum* (ed. Steele), p. 228; *The Works of John Metham*, ed. H. Craig, EETS OS 132 (London, 1916), p. 135, lines 31–3. See also F. Somerset, *Clerical Discourse and Lay Audience in Late Medieval England* (Cambridge, 1998), pp. 25–6 and n. 11.

sapientiae vias scrutetur ut doceatur aut doceat" ["A person rarely follows the paths of wisdom in charity and humility that he may be taught himself or teach (others)"].The formula "docere, doceri" also appears – with added emphasis on the pleasure of learning – in Seneca's *Epistle to Lucilius* (6.4): "gaudeo discere ut doceam" ["I am glad to learn in order that I may teach"]. And Augustine associates the phrase with Dialectic, which is peculiarly appropriate to the Clerk, a long-time student of logic and a devotee of Aristotle:

> Haec docet docere, haec docet discere; in hac se ipsa ratio demonstrat, atque aperit quae sit, quid velit, quid valeat. Scit scire; sola scientes facere non solum vult, sed etiam potest.
>
> [Dialectic teaches how to teach, Dialectic teaches how to learn. In Dialectic reason discloses itself and reveals who it is, what it wants, and what it can do. Dialectic knows how to know; it alone has the will and the power to make men knowledgeable.][67]

The Sergeant at Law

The Sergeant at Law is a high-ranking member of the bar. By virtue of his knowledge and prestige he maintains a large and lucrative practice.[68] The portrait emphasizes his professional expertise – his learning, impeccable draughtsmanship, and experience – and his forceful presence. He is characterized as prudent, industrious, and wise, but these qualities may be more apparent than real (312–14, 316–22).

The wealth of lawyers as evidence of their greed was a common target of medieval satire.[69] The *Roman de la Rose* typically complains of their insatiable desire for more clients as doctors crave more patients:

> Avocat e fisicien
> Sont tuit lié de cet lien;
> S'il pour deniers science vendent,
> Trestuit a cete hart se pendent.
> Tant ont le gaaing douz e sade
> Que cist voudrait, pour une malade
> Qu'il a, qu'il en eüst seissante,
> E cil pour une cause trente,
> Veire deus cenz, veire deus mile,
> Tant les art couveitise e guile.
>
> [Lawyers and physicians are all bound with these bonds, all hanged with this rope, if they sell their knowledge for money. They find gain so sweet and desirable and are so fired with covetousness and trickery that the one would like to have sixty patients for every one he has, and the other thirty cases, or indeed two hundred or two thousand. (Horgan, p. 78)]

[67] Augustine, *De Ordine*, Book 2, chapter 13 (PL 32, col. 1013).

[68] J. H. Baker, *The Order of Sergeants at Law* (London, 1984), pp. 25–6: "When Chaucer said of his serjeant that he had many fees and robes, he meant that he was retained permanently by many clients for annuities of money and robes."

[69] Mann, p. 89. Cf. J. A. Yunck, *The Lineage of Lady Meed* (Notre Dame, IN, 1963), pp. 153–9, 205–11.

Sergeants appear for the first time in English literature in *Piers Plowman*, their reputation for acquisitiveness already established (B. Pr. 212–16). They were particularly vulnerable to charges of greed and venality because they earned much more than other lawyers, and, like lawyers generally and even justices, they engaged in land speculation for their personal profit.[70] Chaucer's Sergeant is a flagrant offender in this regard (318–20). In the *Miroir de l'Omme* Gower launches a bitter attack on the venality of sergeants which includes a protest against their extensive investment in real estate:

Et puis apres qant l' apprentis
Un certain temps ara complis,
Dont au pleder soit sufficant,
Lors quiert q'il ait la coife assis
Dessur le chief, et pour son pris
Le noun voet porter de sergant.
Mais s'il ad esté pardevant
En une chose covoitant,
Des Mill lors serra plus espris;
Car lors devient si fameillant,
Ne luy souffist un remenant,
Ainz tout devoure le paiis.
Mais ils ont une acoustummance,
Qant l'aprentis ensi s'avance
A cell estat du sergantie,
Luy falt donner une pitance
Del orr, q'ad grant signefiance:
Car l'orr qu'il donne signefie
Q'il doit apres toute sa vie
Reprendre l'orr a sa partie;
Mais ce serra grande habondance,
Qant pour donner la soule mie
Prent tout le pain, dont ne tient mie
Le pois ovel en la balance.
. . .
La main ont toutdis estendu,
Maisq'ils del orr soient certain,
Ou soit de pres ou de longtain,
Chascun serra le bienvenu.
. . .
L'en porra dire as gens du loy,
Comme dist Jacob, ce semble a moy,
Q'en son baston Jordan passoit,
Mais deinz brief temps a grant desroy,
Tout plein des biens ove beau conroy,
Riche et manant y revenoit:
Ensi ly pledour orendroit

[70] Baker, p. 35. Cf. J. Fortescue, *De Laudibus Legum Anglie*, ed. and trans. S. B. Chrimes (Cambridge, 1942), pp. 124–5: "Non est advocatus in universo mundo qui racione officii sui tantum lucratur ut serviens huiusmodi" ["Nor is there any advocate in the whole world who enriches himself by reason of his office as much as the serjeant"]; Mann, p. 88.

Combien q'il povre au primer soit,
Bien tost apres avera du quoy
Si largement, que tout q'il voit
Luy semble a estre trop estroit
De pourchacer soulein a soy.
O vous q'ensi tout devouretz,
Ce que dist Isaïe orretz:
'Way vous,' ce dist, 'o fole gent,
Mesoun as mesouns adjoustetz,
Et champ as champs y assembletz;
Vo covoitise au tout s'extent,
Comme cil qui volt souleinement
Avoir la terre proprement.'

[When the apprentice has worked for a certain time so that he is competent at pleading, then he seeks to have the lawyer's cap placed on his head and, as his reward, he bears the name of sergeant-at-law. But if he previously coveted one thing, now he will covet a thousand. He becomes so hungry that a remnant suffices not for him; he devours, rather, the entire country. They have a custom when the apprentice advances to the estate of sergeant, [he must give] a pittance of gold. This has great significance, for the gold [that he gives] signifies that forever after, for all his life, he must take gold on his side. But it will be in great abundance, for he takes the whole loaf [in return for giving] a single crumb, so he does not maintain at all an even weight in the balance. . . . They always have their hands stretched out; everyone will be welcomed from far and near, provided they be assured of gold. . . . One might say of the men of law, as Jacob said (it seems to me) that with his staff he passed over the Jordan, but within a short time, with great tumult, he came back all loaded with wealth and fine equipage, rich and powerful. Likewise, nowadays the lawyer – however poor he may be at first – will have very soon thereafter so much wealth that everything he sees appears too limited for him to purchase for himself alone. O you who thus devour everything, hear what Isaiah said: "Woe unto you, O foolish people, who add house to house and join field to field." Your covetousness extends to everything, like the man who wants personally to have the land for himself alone. (Wilson, pp. 319–21, as corrected)]

The charge is repeated in *Vox Clamantis* (Book 6, chapter 2, lines 105–6, 133–4, 141–2). Wycliff, too, denounces land-hungry lawyers twice. In "þre þingis" he criticizes "false men of lawe" who "geten hem gold & purchasen rentis & londis of lordis & distroien verrey heieris, & þis distroieþ moche oure lond for hou schulde riȝt be among suche men, þat þis day han but here penye and anoon purchasen rentis & londis to be peris wiþ knyttis or barons."[71] And in "Of Servants and Lords" he condemns "men of lawe" who "meyntenen wrong for money & fees & robis. . . . bi here coueitise and falsenesse þei purchasen londis & rentis ynowe." Chaucer, it may be noted, also collocates "fees and robes" and employs the term "purchasyng" with the same negative connotation.[72]

71 *English Works of Wyclif*, pp. 182–3.

72 *Ibid.*, pp. 234, 237. On the unfavorable connotation of the word *purchasour*, see Mann, pp. 88–9, and N. L. Ramsay, "The English Legal Profession c.1340–1450," unpublished dissertation (Cambridge University, 1985), p. 19; and R. Myles, *Chaucerian Realism* (Cambridge, 1994), p. 102.

The Sergeant is modestly attired for travel, unlike Langland's sergeants who are identified by their silken coifs in the field full of folk (A. Pr. 84). "The medley coat [a rayed long robe]," Laura Hodges comments, "announces the Sergeant's professional status, while the silken girdle speaks delicately of his social and financial status."[73]

The Franklin

The Franklin, a "worthy vavasour" (360), is an elderly member of the country gentry, who loves food, maintains a fine table, and is notable for his generous hospitality: "Seint Julian he was in his contree" (340). He is modeled on the vavassors of medieval romances, especially those of Chretien de Troyes, who are depicted as decent elderly gentlemen unstintedly hospitable.[74] The vavassor in *Yvain* generously entertains the Knight and provides him lodging:

777 La nuit ot, ce poez savoir,
tel oste come il vost avoir;
car plus de bien et plus d'enor,
trueve il assez el vavasor
781 que ne vos ai conté et dit;
...
787 des qu'il s'atorne a grant bonté
Ja n'iert tot dit ne tot conté
que leingue ne puet pas retreire
790 tant d'enor con prodon fet faire.[75]

[That night, you can be sure, he found the host he sought, for he received more favour and respect from the vavasour than I've recounted to you. . . . When a man devotes himself to true goodness, his full worth can never be told, for no tongue can rehearse all the goodness a noble man can do.][76]

Enide's father in *Erec et Enide* is similarly characterized, and, like Chaucer's Franklin, is a gracious host with a highly competent cook.[77]

Mann finds evidence of gluttony satire in the account of the Franklin's diet. His preferences for birds, fish, spicy sauces, baked meat (343–52), a morning "sop in wine" (334), and other "deyntees" (346) are familiar from other portrayals

[73] Hodges, p. 122.

[74] For evidence that Chaucer read Chrétien de Troyes, see P. J. Frankis, "Chaucer's 'Vavasour' and Chrétien de Troyes and Romance," *Notes and Queries* 213 (1968): 46–7, and D. S. Brewer, "Chaucer and Chrétien de Troyes," in *Chaucer and Middle English Studies in Honour of Rossell Hope Robbins*, ed. B. Rowland (London, 1974), pp. 255–9. See also R. J. Pearcy, "Chaucer's Franklin and the Literary Vavasour," *Chaucer Review* 8 (1973): 33–79, who discusses other characteristics of the vavasour and his relationship with knights.

[75] Chrétien de Troyes, *Des Romans*, ed. M. Roques, vol. 4: *Le Chevalier au Lion* (Yvain) (Paris, 1955), pp. 24–5.

[76] Chrétien de Troyes, *Arthurian Romances*, trans. W. W. Kibler (Harmondsworth, 1991), p. 304.

[77] See Chrétien de Troyes, *Des Romans*, ed. M. Roques, vol. 1, pp. 12–13, lines 373–8, 381–9; p. 16, lines 488–92.

of gluttony in *Renart Le Contrefait*, *Wynnere and Wastoure*, Guiot de Provin's *Bible*, and Gower's *Mirour de l'Omme*.[78] Gower's portrayals of "Voracity" and "Delicacy," Gluttony's daughters, provide close analogues to Chaucer:

7746 Ne luy souffist un soul capoun,
Ainçois le boef ove le moltoun,
La grosse luce et le salmoun,
7749 A son avis tout mangeroit.
. . .
7801 De ceste file [Delicacie] ly norris
Des autres est ly plus cheris,
Qui servent Gloutenie au main;
7804 Primer le pain dont ert servis
Falt buleter par tieu devis,
Qe tout le plus meillour du grain
7807 Ert la substance de son pain.
. . .
7813 Ne vuil les nouns del tout celer
Des vins q'il ad deinz son celer
Le Gernache et la Malveisie,
Et le Clarré de l'espicer,
Dont il se puet plus enticer
7818 A demener sa gloutenie.
. . .
7825 Si nous parlons de sa cusine,
Celle est a Jupiter cousine,
Q'estoit jadys dieus de delice,
Car n'est domeste ne ferine
Du bestial ne d'oiseline
7830 Qe n'est tout prest deinz cel office:
La sont perdis, la sont perdice,
La sont lamprey, la sont crevice,
Pour mettre gule en la saisine
De governer tout autre vice;
7835 Car pour voir dire elle est norrice,
Vers quelle pecché plus s'acline.
Ly delicat ne tient petit
Pour exciter son appetit;
Diverses salses quiert avoir
7840 Et a son rost et a son quit,
Dont plus mangut a son delit.

[A single capon does not suffice for him [Gluttony served by Voracity]; he still wants beef and mutton, a large pike and a salmon – he would like to eat everything. . . . The nourishment of this daughter [Delicacy] is costlier than that of the others who serve Gluttony. First the bread with which she is served is made from flour bolted in such a way that the best part of the wheat forms the substance of her bread. . . . Nor do I wish to conceal the names of the wines in her cellar: vernage, malmsey, and spiced claret, with which she can

78 Mann, pp. 153–4; Bowden, pp. 175–6; see also *Roman de la Rose*, lines 11710–13 and 21553–61.

be more enticed to stimulate her gluttony. . . . If we talk of her cooking, she is to the cousin of Jupiter, who formerly was the god of pleasure. There is neither tame nor wild beast nor bird that is not ready in her kitchen. There are partridges, cock and hen, lampreys, crayfish, all to put gluttony in command to rule all other vices, for, to tell the truth, she is the nurse toward whom sin most inclines itself. The delicate person does not mind exciting his appetite; divers[e] sauces he wants to have for both his roasts and his boiled meat so that he may eat them to his greater delight. (Wilson, pp. 107–8)]

The morning "sop in wine" enjoyed by the Franklin is also taken by the "ladies of the bourgeoisie": "Et en gernache au matinez/ Font souppes de la tendre mie." (7907–8) ["And in the morning from vernage wine they make sops of the soft bread." (Wilson, p. 109, as corrected)].

The characterization of the Franklin as Epicurus's son (335–8) is ultimately based on the *Consolation of Philosophy* (3. pr. 2, lines 48–51), but Chaucer's wording seems closer to Gower's lines in the *Mirour*:

9529 Trop fuist du Foldelit apris
Uns philosophes de jadys
Qui Epicurus noun avoit:
Car ce fuist cil q'a son avis
Disoit que ly charnels delitz
9534 Soverain des autres biens estoit.

[A philosopher of olden days was well taught by Wantonness, and his name was Epicurus. For he said that in his opinion carnal delight was the sovereign of all other good things (Wilson, p. 131)].

The Franklin has the character of a man of sanguine complexion (333) whose qualities are delineated in *The Governaunce of Prynces*: "The sangyne by kynde sholde lowe Ioye and laghynge, and company of women, and moche Slepe and syngynge: he shal be hardy y-nowe, of good will and wythout malice . . . he shal haue a good stomake, good dygescion, and good delyueraunce . . . he shall be fre and lyberall."[79]

The portrait lists the public offices that the Franklin has occupied: member of parliament (356), sheriff (359), justice of the peace (355), and auditor (359). Mann notes their occasional appearance in estates satire, and aptly comments that "they are presented merely as evidence for his status as a 'worthy vavasour,' "(pp. 158–9) – that is, the status of a wealthy landholder who enjoys some degree of political prominence in his community and lays claim to gentility. The brief description of the Franklin's dress that concludes the portrait – an anelace together with a white silk gipser and girdle – is sufficient, as Laura Hodges shows (pp. 141–8), to mark him as a man of taste and authority.[80]

[79] *Secreta Secretorum* (ed. Steele), pp. 219–20.

[80] See H. Specht, *Chaucer's Franklin in the Canterbury Tales: The Social and Literary Background of a Chaucerian Character* (Copenhagen, 1981), pp. 37–117. Chaucer may also have taken a hint from the depiction of Medill Elde (*Parlement of the Three Ages*, p. 76, lines 148–51), who is sixty and also a rich landowner who holds manorial courts presided over by auditors and clerks. It may be worthy of note that the Franklin is attired in the expensive belt and silk purse recommended to the young lover in the *Roman de la Rose* (lines 2155–6): "De ganz, d'aumosniere de soie/ E de ceinture te cointoie."

The Guildsmen

The guildsmen are five burgesses of different trades whose social pretensions and aldermanic ambitions are held up to gentle ridicule. They are treated as a group, without individualizing traits, and nothing more is heard of them on the pilgrimage. They are dressed alike in the livery of a parish guild (364) enhanced by their newly acquired "geere" of silver-mounted knives, girdles, and pouches. Their array, Mann observes, "testifies to their sense of their own status."[81] Wealth largely determined rank in the medieval city,[82] and the Guildsmen have sufficient income to justify their pretentious costumes and to sustain their aspirations for public office (369–73). Their wives, who support them because they wish to be called "Madame" and lead processions at the vigils (374–8), recall the vainglorious wives of Theophrastus's *Liber de Nuptiis* (excerpted in St Jerome's *Adversus Jovinianum*), who demand to be called "lady" (domina vocanda),[83] and the depiction of "Vainglory" in Gower's *Mirour de l'Omme*:

1203 C'est une dame trop mondeine:
Car pour la vanite du monde
Son corps ove tout dont elle abonde
Despent et gaste en gloire veine:
Tout se travaille et tout se peine
Pour estre appellé cheventeine,
1209 Du quoy son vein honour rebonde.

[She is a very worldly lady. For the sake of worldly vanity she spends and wastes her body and all her wealth in vainglory. She devotes all her labor and effort to be called "mistress," from which springs her empty honor.]

The Wife of Bath, who has the same social status as the Guildsmen's wives, would also like to be addressed as "Dame Alys" (*WBP* 320).[84] Their desire for social compliment and for precedence at processions effectively trivializes the political ambitions of their husbands as well as the purposes of lay piety and charity parish guilds were intended to serve. Behind the portrait is a larger concern with the misuse and waste of wealth by the well-to-do urban middle class. Estates satires often couple them with merchants to excoriate their avarice, fraud, and usury,[85] but Chaucer ignores these charges and concentrates on their bourgeois pretensions to gentle status.

81 Mann, p. 105; Hodges, pp. 135–6. F. W. Fairholt, *Satirical Songs and Poems on Costume from the 13th to the 19th Century* (London, 1849), pp. 49–51, prints a poem entitled "The Baselard," about a pretentious young man wearing a knife and silver cross-bar or guard and a sharp blade who meets a carter and is beaten.

82 E. M. Carus-Wilson, "Towns and Trade," in *Medieval England*, ed. A. L. Poole (Oxford, 1958), p. 251.

83 *Jankyn's Book of Wikked Wyves, Volume 1: The Primary Texts*, ed. R. Hanna and T. Lawler (Athens, GA, and London, 1997), p. 153. The title was open to the wives of guild and municipal aldermen.

84 B. R. McRee, "Charity and Gild Society in Late Medieval England," *Journal of British Studies* 32 (1993): 196–225.

85 Mann, pp. 103–4.

The Cook

The Cook accompanies the Guildsmen on the pilgrimage for semblance of affluence and gentility.[86] He was created for low comedy. The clash between him and the Host follows from their rivalry as tradesmen. In retaliation for the Host's scathing comments about his unsavory shop the Cook promises to tell a tale about a "hostileer" (4360) before the end of the pilgrimage. He also comes under criticism from the Manciple, who may be among his unhappy clients. These animosities, together with those of the Miller and the Reeve and the Friar and the Summoner, are not "traditional," but are invented by Chaucer to advance his narrative program.[87] For the rivalry between the Cook and the Host he may have received a suggestion from the A-text of Langland's *Prologue* where cooks are seen vying with taverners for custom:

104 Cookis and here knaues* crieþ 'Hote pyes, hote! servants
Goode gees* and gris*; Go we dyne, go we!' geese/ pork
Tauernes* to hem tolde þe same: Taverners
'Whit wyn of Osay*, and wyn of Gascoyne*, Alsace/ Gascony
108 Of þe Ryn* and of þe Rochel*, þe rost to defie*!' Rhine/ Rochelle/ digest

The Cook is a master chef, and his portrait emphasizes his technical proficiency and the fine dishes he prepares for his clients (379–87). In Book 4 of the *Vox Clamantis* (chapter 2, lines 69–70) the cook who labors energetically in the monastic kitchen, preparing daily feasts, displays similar skills:

"Nunc cocus ecce coquit, assat, gelat atque resoluit,
Et terit et stringit, colat et acta probat."

["See how the cook bakes and roasts, freezes and melts, grinds and presses, strains and tests his achievement." (Stockton, p. 167)]

Another monastic cook carefully attends to his seasonings:

Crocum, garyophyllum, piper, et cyminum,
Cocus terit, conficit, onerat catinum.[88]

[The cook grinds the saffron, Indian spice, pepper, and cumin, prepares the mixture, and fills the pot.]

As Mann has pointed out (pp. 153–5, 168), with particular reference to the Franklin's portrait, details of food preparation are easily associated with gluttony satire. In a *sermo ad status* addressed to merchants and moneychangers, Jacques de Vitry takes us into a tavern kitchen presided over by Gluttony

[86] See Martha Carlin, "Fast Food and Urban Living Standards in Medieval England," *Food and Eating in Medieval Europe*, ed. M. Carlin and J. T. Rosenthal (London and Rio Grande, OH, 1998), pp. 34–8, and P. Lisca, "Chaucer's Guildsmen and their Cook," *Modern Language Notes* 70 (1955): 321–4, on the hiring of caterers for the journey by the rich and the burgeoning efforts of the nouveaux riches to acquire respectability.

[87] The misconception that the host and the cook are "traditional" enemies appears to have originated with F. Tupper, "The Canterbury Pilgrims," *Journal of English and Germanic Philology* 14 (1915): 256–70.

[88] [De Mauro et Zoilo], *The Latin Poems commonly attributed to Walter Mapes*, ed. T. Wright, Camden Society 16 (London, 1841), p. 248, lines 165–6.

("Gastrimargia"), the sister of Drunkenness ("Ebrietas"): "Some of the servants roast the meat; others mix the sauces; others stuff the chickens and eggs; others attend to the meat pies and others to the fritters; others toil with great zeal to prepare the rolls of bread, cheese rolls or twists; others ceaselessly carry different kinds of wine in great flagons."[89] Pope Innocent III, in a passage quoted by Chaucer in the *Pardoner's Tale* (538–9), also invokes the scene of a busy kitchen: "Alius contundit et colat, alius confundit et conficit, substanciam vertit in accidens, naturam mutat in artem" ["One grinds and strains, another mixes and prepares, turns substance into accident, changes nature into art"].[90]

The special dishes prepared by the Cook for wealthy clients are the emblems of medieval *haute cuisine.* "Blankmanger," consisting basically of white chicken meat, rice, sugar, and almond milk, was the international favorite of the well-to-do. Recipes for this and other culinary delights fill the pages of contemporary cookbooks.[91] The Cook's preference for London ale (382) hints at his later drunkenness on the pilgrimage: cooks were proverbially characterized as drunkards in the Middle Ages.[92]

Afflicted with an unsightly mormal, or ulcer, on his shin (386–7), the Cook suffers from a disease known as "malum mortuum" which may have been brought on by intemperance or perhaps by unclean or licentious habits.[93] Lanfranc describes the malady and its causes:

> Icchinge & scabbe comeþ of salt humouris, and a mannys kynde haþ abhominacioun þerof, & putteþ hem out of þe skyn, & þis falliþ ofte of salt metis and scharpe metis and of wijn þat is strong; & it falliþ ofte to hem þat wakith and traveiliþ & usiþ no baþing and weriþ no lynnen cloþis, & þis is oon of þe siknes þat is contagious . . .[94]

89 Jacques de Vitry, *Sermones Vulgares*, Paris, Bibliothèque Nationale MS Latin 17509, *Sermo LVI: Ad mercatores et campsores*, fol. 114b: " In hoc foro gulositatis ebrietas habet tabernam, soror ejus gastrimargia coquinam. Quidam autem ex ministiris carnes assant; alii salsamenta distemperant; alii pullos et ova farciunt; alii artocreis et alii frixariis intendunt; alii pastillis et caseatis seu tortis praeparandis cum magno studio laborant; alii vinorum diversa genera in magnis amphoris portare non cessant."

90 Lotario Dei Segni (Pope Innocent III), *De Miseria Condicionis Humane*, ed. R. E. Lewis (Athens, GA, 1978), Part 2, chapter 17, pp. 164–5. These catalogues of the different genres of cookery are reminiscent of William Fitzstephen's description of the public cook-shop on the river bank in London. See *Descriptio Nobillissimae Civitatis Londoniae*, in John Stow, *A Survey of London* (Oxford, 1908), p. 222.

91 See C. B. Hieatt, "'To boille the chiknes with the marybones': Hodge's Kitchen Revisited," *Chaucerian Problems and Perspectives*, ed. E. Vasta and Z. P. Thundy (Notre Dame, IN, 1979), pp. 151–3, 155–7, 163 n. 33; and her "Sorting through the Titles of Medieval Dishes," *Food in the Middle Ages*, ed. M. W. Adamson (New York, 2002), pp. 25–43; T. Scully, *The Art of Cooking in the Middle Ages* (Woodbridge, 1995), pp. 207–11, 214, 216. See also *Two Fifteenth-Century Cookery-Books*, ed. T. Austin, EETS OS 91 (London, 1888), pp. 14, 19, 21, 23, 50, 55, 85, 114; *Curye on Inglysch*, ed. C. B. Hieatt and S. Butler, EETS SS 8 (London, 1985), pp. 62–8, 71, 75, 106–8, 143; *An Ordinance of Pottage*, ed. C. B. Hieatt (London, 1988), p. 170; *Libellus de Arte Coquinaria*, ed. and trans. R. Grewe and C. B. Hieatt (Tempe, AZ, 2001), pp. 104–5; and C. Hieatt, B. Hosington and S. Butler, *Pleyn Delit* (Toronto, 1996), pp. 63, 64, 105, 108, 109, 111.

92 Joseph Strutt, *The Sports and Pastimes of the People of England: A New Edition of William Hone* (London, 1830), p. 22.

93 W. C. Curry, "Two Notes on Chaucer," *Modern Language Notes* 36 (1921): 274–6, and *Chaucer and the Mediaeval Sciences*, revised and enlarged edition (New York, 1960), pp. 50–1.

94 *Lanfrank's Science of Cirurgie*, ed. R. von Fleischhacker, EETS OS 102 (London, 1894), p. 191.

In short, the portrait is stereotypical of the general reputation of cooks as habitually unclean, promoters of gluttony, and given to excesses of drink. By contrast, Platina (Bartolomeo Sacchi) describes the qualities of an ideal cook, cleanliness among them, in *De honesta voluptate et valetudine* (c. 1460):

> De coquo. Coquum habeat arte et longa experientia doctum, patientem laboris, et qui laudari in ea re maxime cupiat. Careat is omni squalore et spurcitia: cognoscat apposite carnium, piscium, olerum vim et naturam ut quid assum quid elixum quid frictum fieri debeat deprehendat.
>
> [On the cook. One should have a trained cook with skill and long experience, patient with his work and wanting especially to be praised for it. He should lack all filth and dirt and know in a suitable way the force and nature of meats, fish and vegetables so that he may understand what ought to be roasted, boiled, or fried.][95]

The Shipman

The Shipman is depicted as a master mariner whose long career was spent chiefly in the import trade of wine, which dominated English maritime commerce at this time,[96] but also by implication with some engagement in piracy as well (407–9). He is suitably attired in a knee-length falding gown (391) as protection against the elements and for ease of movement. He is an expert navigator (401–4). Vegetius describes good seamanship in similar terms:

> Nauticorum gubernatorumque sollertia est loca, in quibus nauigatur, portusque cognoscere, ut infesta prominentibus vel latentibus scopulis, uadosa ac sicca uitentur; tanto enim securitas maior est, quanto mare altius fuerit.[97]
>
> [It is the responsibility of sailors and pilots to know the places in which they are to sail, and the harbors so that the shoals, infested with protruding or hidden rocks, and the sandbanks may be avoided. The deeper the sea, the greater the safety.]

The Shipman is well aware of the dangers of the sea (406), and, although he is brave, he is also prudent, as the *Chessbook* advises:

> and therfore ought be in them strengthe force and corage and ought to considere the peryls that might falle. . . . And hit apperteyneth well that a man of good and hardy corage be sette in that office in suche wyse that he haue ferme and seure mynde ayenst the paryls that oftetymes happen in the see. . . .[98]

Yet despite his admirable seamanship and courage he exhibits the vicious traits commonly imputed to his trade. He is dishonest and without scruple (398).

95 Platina, *On Right Pleasure and Good Health: A Critical Edition and Translation of De Honesta Voluptate et Valetudine* by M. E. Milham (Tempe, 1998), Book 1, chapter 11, p. 118.

96 G. Hutchinson, *Medieval Ships and Shipping* (London, 1994), p. 89.

97 *Epitoma Rei Militaris*, Book 4, chapter 43, p. 254.

98 *Caxton's Game and Playe of the Chesse*, introduction by W. E. A. Axon (London, 1883), Book 3, chapter 2, p. 91; C. S. Fuller, "A Critical Edition of *Le Jeu des Eschés, Moralisé*," unpublished dissertation (Catholic University of America, 1974), chapter 10, p. 223.

He regularly pilfers wine from chapmen and, perhaps piratically, murders the victims of his combats at sea (396–400). His grisly character is confirmed by the menacing detail of the dagger hanging under his arm from a baldric to facilitate "easy access."[99]

Mann (p. 171) cites an estate poem accusing sailors of "fraud" ("dolus"). In the confessional manual *Memoriale Presbiterorum*, however, there is a more graphic description of the malpractices of shipmen, a description that bears a close resemblance to the unsavory details of Chaucer's portrait:

> Tu confessor, si contingat te audire aliquem nautam in confessione, necesse habebis caute et studiose te habere in inquirendo; quia scire debes quod vix sufficit calamus scribere peccata quibus involvuntur. Tanta est enim illorum malicia quod omnium hominum aliorum peccata excedit. . . . Item non solum occidunt clericos et laicos dum sunt in terra, sed eciam, quando sunt in mari, piraticam exercent pravitatem, rapiendo bona aliorum et potissime mercatorum mare transeuncium, et eos crudeliter interficiunt.[100]

> [Confessor, if it befalls you to hear any sailor in confession, you will have of necessity to conduct yourself cautiously and zealously in making inquiry, because you ought to know that the pen scarcely suffices to write the sins in which they are involved. For so great is their malice that it exceeds the sins of all other men. . . . Item, not only do they kill clerks and laymen while they are on land, but also, when they are at sea, they practise the depravity of piracy, plundering the goods of others, and especially of merchants crossing the sea, and cruelly do they slay them.]

The Physician

The Physician who is also a surgeon is portrayed as a highly skilled practitioner. He knows all the major medical authorities, he is well versed in astronomy, and he is an expert diagnostician – in short, "a verray, parfit praktisour" (422). His practice is lucrative (as his costly and elegant attire attests) and of long standing (442). He is manifestly greedy as well as stingy (441) and colludes with apothecaries for their mutual benefit (425–8).

The portrait reflects many of the qualities of an ideal physician. The *Chessbook* states that a physician ought to know "the mesures of the houres and dayes and of the cours of astronomye" and to "enquere the cause of theyr [the patients] seknessis and the syngnes and tokens of theyr maladyes as is rehercid in the bookes of the auctours by ryght grete diligence and specially in the bookes of ypocras galyene and of Auycene."[101] Guy de Chauliac declares in the *Cyrurgie* that the first "condicioun" required of a surgeon is that he be a "lettred

[99] Hodges, p. 158. See also A. Breeze, "An Irish Etymology for Chaucer's Falding (Coarse Woolen Cloth)," *Chaucer Review* 35 (2000): 112–14. M. R. Stobie, "Chaucer's Shipman and the Wine," *PMLA* 64 (1949): 568–9, argues that the Shipman is merely helping himself to "courtesy wine."

[100] M. Haren, "The Interrogatories for Officials, Lawyers and Secular Estates of the *Memoriale Presbiterorum*," in *Handling Sin: Confession in the Middle Ages*, ed. P. Biller and A. Minnis (York, 1998), pp. 150–1.

[101] *Game and Playe of the Chesse*, Book 3, chapter 5, pp. 119–20; Jehan de Vignay, *Le Jeu*, chapter 13, p. 44.

man," and John of Arderne, Chaucer's contemporary, lists studiousness among the qualities required of a good physician: "for the excercyse of bokes worshippeþ a leche. For why; he shal boþ byholden and he shal be more wise."[102] Chaucer firmly establishes the Physician's academic credentials. The list of medical authorities he is familiar with (429–34) emphasizes the comprehensiveness of his learning. It is much longer than the lists found in the *Chessbook*, the *Roman de la Rose* (15959–61) or Dante's *Inferno* (4.139, 143–4). Writers of medical textbooks, such as Guy de Chauliac, John of Arderne, John of Mirfield, and John of Gaddesden, also give extensive lists of authorities, but none of them duplicates Chaucer's, whose list "contains just those names that an educated doctor of his day would have cited."[103] In addition to his learning, the physician possesses the qualities of sobriety and moderation (435–7) recommended in John of Arderne's model of a good physician:

> And aboue al þise it profiteth to hym that he be founden euermore sobre; for dronkennez destroyeth al vertu and bringith it to not, as seith a wise man, 'Ebrietas frangit quicquid sapiencia tangit': 'Dronkenes breketh what-so wisdom toucheth.' Be he content in strange places of metes and drinkes þer y-founden, vsing mesure in al thingis. For the wise man seith, 'Sicut ad omne quod est mensuram ponere prodest, Sic sine mensura deperit omne quod est': 'As it profiteth to putte mesure to al thing that is, So without mesure perissheþ all þing þat is.' (p. 4).

Mann (p. 252) suggests that the vocabulary of Chaucer's lines comes directly from the *Mirour de l'Omme* (16249–54), where "Nourishment" (Measure's third daughter) combats "Superfluity" (Measure's first daughter) and "Diet" points the way to good health (pp. 252–3, n. 41). Langland also advocates a temperate diet to Piers' "servants" with a warning against "Sire Surfet" (A.VII.241–51).

Chaucer's physician excels as a diagnostician, basing his procedures on a combination of lunar astrology and Galenic humoral theory with the use of talismanic figures whenever necessary (414–21). It is because of his competence in astrological medicine that he deserves to be called a "parfit praktisour." The perfect physician is described in Peter of Albano's translation (c.1310) of the *Libellus de medicorum astrologia* attributed to Hippocrates: "Ypocras, who was a physician and a most worthy master, asked, 'What manner of physician is he who does not know astronomy [medicus non astroniam ignorat]? No one ought to place himself in the hands of any physician who is less than perfect." Laurel Braswell believes this description is deliberately echoed in Chaucer's portrait of the Doctor of Physic, a physician so well "grounded in astronomye" (non astroniam ignorat) as to be able to apply it judicially to medicine.[104]

102 *Cyrurgie of Guy de Chauliac*, I (Text), ed. M. S. Ogden, EETS OS 265 (London, 1971), p. 12. *John Arderne: Treatises of Fistula in Ano, Haemorrhoids, and Clysters*, ed. D'A. Power, EETS OS 139 (London, 1910), p. 4. Elaine E. Whitaker, "John of Arderne and Chaucer's Physician," *American Notes and Queries* 8 (1995): 3–8, argues for a close connection between the two practitioners.

103 Rossell H. Robbins, "The Physician's Authorities," *Studies in Language and Literature in Honour of Margaret Schlauch*, ed. M. Brahmer, S. Helsztynski, and J. Krzyzanowski (Warsaw, 1966), p. 341.

104 Laurel Braswell, "The Moon and Medicine in Chaucer's Time," *Studies in the Age of Chaucer* 8 (1986): 146–7. "Astroniam" should perhaps be emended to "astronomiam," but it is possibly a

Having determined the cause of the ailment, the physician prescribes a remedy (boote) to be prepared by apothecaries only at a time that is astrologically favorable to the patient. The lunar medicine practiced by Chaucer's physician, including the precise, complex, and prolonged astrological calculations, the employment of images, the application of humoral theory, and the determination of the proper times for treatment, is state of the art and is fully explained in canons 11 and 12 of the *Kalendarium,* written in 1386 by the Oxford friar Nicholas of Lynn and dedicated to John of Gaunt.[105] Chaucer was familiar with this work and planned to use it, as he himself states, in the third part of the *Astrolabe.*[106]

> Et si medicus ista respicere neclexerit dando medicinam, ab effectu curacionis necessario multociens privabitur, quia virtus celi contrarium operabitur. Ut siquis Expulsivam confortare affectat dando medicinam laxativam, virtus celi interdum per influenciam lune operabitur ad Retentivam fortificandum, et ita in aliis. Propter quod siquis medicorum velit sua arte confortare Retentivam, eligat tempus quo luna fuerit in signo frigido et sicco, secundum in Tauro vel Virgine. Respiciat eciam quod ascendens sit signum euisdem complexionis. Necnon pro utiliori, fiat confeccio talis medicine in simili constellacione, eo quod tanto efficacius et melius operabitur pro virtute quam recipit tempore confeccionis ex influencia supercelesti. Nam secundum dicit Thebyth, ymagines et sculpture fiunt in lapidibus ut virtutem Geminarum ex celi influencia recipiant. Virtutem autem non habent nisi ex aspectu planetarum in tempore quo artificiantur, eo quod materia illarum ymaginum siccea est et terrea seu metallina, que nullam talem virtutem ipsis sculpturis imprimere potest. Set istam quam habent virtus supercelestis eisdem administrat. Et sic est de confeccionibus quibuscumque a medicis compositis. . . . Sentencialiter autem sciendum est quod tempus electum ad dandum medicinam dum luna et dominus ascendens sunt liberi a malo et non impediti ab eo, et decima domus est bene disposita; et summe cavendum est dare medicinam dum luna est in malo aspectu cum Saturno vel Marte, et summe eligendum est quando luna est in Piscibus cum paribus non impedita. Si autem luna in principio egritudinis fuerit in signo mobili, ipsa egritudo cito mutabilis est; si in signo stabili, permanens est; in mediocri vero, mediocris est.
>
> Siquis autem habuerit almanak et magis ad unitatem accedere voluerit, ad horam inicii egritudinis planetas omnes adequare debet, eosque equatos, in domibus adequatis constituere; quo facto, ad septem adminus respicere debet: primo scilicet locum lune in figura; secundo ascenciones et dominum eius; tercio medium celi, que est decima domus; quarto angulum terre, que est quarta domus et dominum eius; quinto sextam domum et dominum eius; sexto octavam domum et dominum eius; septimo nativitatem pacientis et dominum eius. Quo ad primum si malus fuerit in ascencione et dominus eius malus vel aspectu malivolo aliqua fortuna aspiciatur, et conjunctus fuerit alicui malo

phonetic reduction. Cf. *MED* "*astronomie*" n. (1) with variants "astrony" and "astromye" and *OED* "astronomien" with variant "astromyen".

105 *The Kalendarium of Nicholas of Lynn*, ed. Sigmund Eisner (Athens, GA, 1980), pp. 206–23.

106 *A Treatise on the Astrolabe*, Prologue, p. 1095, lines 84–6, and note. C. D. Benson, "The Astrological Medicine of Chaucer's Physician and Nicholas of Lynn's *Kalendarium*," *American Notes and Queries* 22 (1984): 64, suggests that Chaucer's knowledge of lunar medicine came from the *Kalendarium* or a similar work.

sive soli sit conjunctus, quia sol per conjunccionem significat malum licet per aspectum significat bonum, ipse paciens sibimet nocebit. Si vero ibi fuerit bonus, dicat bonum econtra. Et causa huius rei est quia illa pars celi que vocatur ascendens habet aspectum ad pacientem. Et similiter si in decima domo fuerit bonus vel dominus eius bonus, bene proficiet sibi medicus. Si vero tibi fuerit malus tunc, ledetur paciens a medico et causa est hec: Pars celi respicit medicum et operationes eius.

[And if the physician should neglect to look at these things [the signs of the moon] when giving medicine, he will be deprived very often of the effect necessary for a cure, because the power of heaven will work to the contrary. Thus, if anyone tries to help expulsion by giving a laxative medicine, the power of heaven occasionally will operate through the influence of the moon to strengthen the retentive power, and the same is true for other [powers]. For that reason, if any physician wishes by his art to improve retention, he should choose a time when the moon is in a cold and dry sign, such as Taurus or Virgo. Let him take care, also, that the ascending sign should be of the same complexion. In addition, to make it more useful, let the preparation of such medicine take place in a similar constellation, the reason being that it will work more efficaciously and better because of the power it receives at the time of preparation from the heavenly influence. For, as Thebith says, images and sculptures are made in stones so that they might receive the worth of precious stones from the influence of heaven. However, they do not have the power except from the aspect of the planets at the time when they were sculpted, the reason being that the substance of these images is dry and made of earth or metal, which is not able to stamp any such power on these sculptures. But the supercelestial power gives them the power they possess. And the same applies to whatever mixtures are compounded by physicians. . . . To sum up, then, it should be known that the choice time for giving medicine is [the time] when the moon and the ascendant lord are free from evil and not impeded by it, and the tenth house is well disposed; and one must above all beware of giving medicine while the moon is in a bad aspect with Saturn or Mars, and one must above all choose [the time] when the moon is in Pisces and not impeded by equals. If, however, the moon at the start of the sickness should be in a moving sign, the sickness is quickly changeable; if in a stable sign, it is permanent; while if in an average sign, it is average.

If, however, one has an almanac and wants to get closer to the truth, one should correlate all the planets at the hour of the beginning of the illness, and when they are correlated, locate them in the appropriate houses; and when he has done this he should study at least seven: first, namely, the place of the moon in the figure; second the ascendant and its lord; third the middle of the sky, which is the tenth house; fourth the angle of the earth, which is the fourth house and its lord; fifth the sixth house and its lord; sixth the eighth house and its lord; seventh the birthday of the patient and his lord. If for [the patient] at the beginning a bad [lord] should have been ascendant, and his lord [now] bad or seen by some chance with an evil aspect, and should be in conjunction with something evil or with the sun, because the sun through conjunction signifies evil although through its aspect it signifies good, the patient will do himself harm. But if [the lord] were there good, let him on the contrary indicate good. And the reason for this is that the part of the sky which is called the ascendant has a relation to the patient. And similarly if in the tenth house [the ascendant] was good or its lord good, the doctor will perform well for him. But if it were

bad there, then the patient would be hurt by the doctor, and the reason is this: a part of the sky is related to the doctor and his operations.][107]

The satirical features of the portrait are stereotypical. Chaucer gives the physician the customary vices of greed and tight-fistedness (441–4). The *Roman de la Rose*, as we have seen in the portrait of the Sergeant at Law, couples doctors and lawyers in their insatiable desire for wealth. They cannot have too many patients or clients. The same charge is found in Gower's *Mirour* (24289–91): "Phisicien d'enfermeté/ Ly mires de la gent blescé,/ Sont leez, q'ensi gaigner porront" ["Physicians are glad of sickness and surgeons of hurt people, when they can thus earn something"]. and in Bromyard: "mali medic[i]. . . . de multorum letantur infirmitate" ["evil physicians rejoice when many people are ill"].[108] Chaucer echoes this idea when he observes that the Physician profited handsomely from the plague. He is never directly accused of greed, but presumably he "loved gold" for itself as well as for its medicinal properties. The use of gold in remedies defines the social and economic level of his patients and points to a lucrative practice. Costly medicines were dispensed only to the rich; the poor had to make do with inexpensive drugs.[109] The Physician's stinginess is typical, as *Matheolus* explains: "Chascuns a paour qu'il ne perde,/ Et pour ce pleurent leur despense,/ Tristes, pensis et en offense;/ Car avarice les rebourse,/ Qui ne leur lait ouvrir leur bourse." ("Each is afraid to lose money, and therefore they lament spending it, sad, full of care, and mortified, for avarice restrains them and doesn't allow them to open their purses.")[110]

Connivance between doctors and apothecaries is a frequent complaint of medieval satire. Their old "friendship" (428) is noted by Gower in the *Mirour* under the rubric of fraud:

25633 Phisicien de son affaire
En les Cités u q'il repaire
Toutdis se trait a l'aquointance
De l' espiecer ipotecaire;
Et lors font tiele chose faire
25638 Dont mainte vie ert en balance.
. . .
25645 Phisique et Triche l'Espiecer
Bien se scievont entracorder;
Car l'un ton ventre vuidera
Asses plus que ne fuist mestier,
Et l'autre savra bien vuider
25650 Ta bource . . .

[The physician, [for the sake of his business, in whatever city he goes to, always cultivates the acquaintance of the apothecary or spicer – and they have

[107] *Kalendarium*, pp. 210–11, 216–19.

[108] Wilson, p. 318; John Bromyard, *Summa Praedicantium* (Venice, 1586), p. 385.

[109] Faye M. Getz, *Healing and Society in Medieval England: A Middle English Translation of the Pharmaceutical Writings of Gilbert Anglicus* (Madison, 1991). Expensive recipes containing gold are given on pp. 38, 43, 47, 146 (heart), 148 (heart), 152, 174, 176, 238. John of Arderne also favored gold-based drugs (Whitaker, p. 4).

[110] Matheolus, p. 286, lines 602–6.

things made up from which many a life will hang in the balance]. . . . The physician and Fraud the apothecary know how to get along together; the one empties your belly more than necessary, and the other knows how to empty your purse (Wilson, p. 337, as corrected)].[111]

Luxurious attire (439–40) as a sign of wealth is another characteristic complaint against doctors. Langland paints a similar picture of "Fisik" with "his furrid hoodes . . ./ And his cloke of Calabre wit þe knoppis of golde" (A.VII.252–3).

The physician's learning (which has given him an encyclopedic knowledge of medicine) does not extend to the Bible (438). The proverb "Ubi tres medici, duo athei" ["Where there are three doctors, there are two atheists"] reflects the general belief that doctors were inclined to skepticism. It also echoes John of Salisbury's derogatory charge against doctors in the *Policraticus*: "At physici dum naturae nimium auctoritatis attribuunt, in auctorem naturae adversando fidei plerumque impingunt" ["Physicians, in their opposition to faith, attribute too much to nature and often come into conflict with the author of nature"].[112]

The Wife of Bath

The Wife of Bath is portrayed as a rich widow with an insatiable interest in sex. She is proud, aggressive, independent, domineering, and sensual. Her care for clothes, her many marriages and affairs, her demand for precedence at the offertory of the mass, and her love of pilgrimages are all consistent with the traits of her character. She is a clothmaker by trade, an occupation which establishes her status in the social hierarchy and earns her a place among the pilgrims who are representative of the *artes mechanicae*. Her portrait is compounded of various sources and evolved over several stages. Portions of it were written, or possibly rewritten, as a prelude to her *Prologue* and *Tale*. The basic conception of her character comes from La Vieille in the *Roman de la Rose*. The old harridan speaks of the extensive sexual experience which has made her "wise in love's ways" (12802–6). She knows "all the old dance" and boasts of "other company" in youth (3936, 12781).

The description of the Wife's traditional office of clothmaking and her expensive Sunday clothes associate her with the Valiant Woman (mulier fortis) of *Proverbs* 31, "a capable business woman who lives in a mercantile world of

[111] John of Gaddesden specifically forbids a physician to be in partnership with an apothecary (H. P. Cholmeley, *John of Gaddesden and the Rosa Medicinae* [Oxford, 1912], pp. 105–6). See also Mann, pp. 95–6.

[112] W. G. Smith and J. E. Heseltine, *The Oxford Dictionary of English Proverbs*, 2nd edn rev. P. Harvey (Oxford, 1948), p. 498; H. Walther, *Lateinische Sprichwörter und Sentenzen des Mittelalters*, vol. 2, Part 5 (Göttingen, 1967), p. 445, no. 32070b; *Policraticus*, Book 2, chapter 29, p. 167. The *Florarium Bartholomaei* by Johannes de Mirfield, Chaucer's contemporary, observes that physicians are rarely good Christians because "by their works they show themselves to be disciples not of Christ, but of Avicenna and Galen" (P. H.-S. Hartley and H. R. Aldridge, *Johannes de Mirfield: His Life and Works* [Cambridge, 1936], pp. 132–3).

product, payment, and exchange."[113] The biblical woman, like the Wife, is an accomplished and successful clothmaker:

> Quaesivit lanam et linum et operata est consilio manuum suarum. . . . Accinxit fortitudine lumbos suos et roboravit brachium suum. Gustavit quia bona est negotiatio eius. . . . Manum suum misit ad fortia et digiti eius adprehenderunt fusum. . . . Sindonem fecit et vendidit et cingulum tradidit Chananeo. (13, 17–18, 19, 24)
>
> [She hath sought wool and flax, and hath wrought by the counsel of her hands. . . . She hath girded her loins with strength, and hath strengthened her arm. She hath tasted and seen that her traffic is good. . . . She hath put out her hand to strong things: and her fingers have taken hold of the spindle. . . . She made fine linen, and sold it, and delivered a girdle to the Chanaanite [i.e., merchant].]

Her finery proclaims her social position and material success, as does the Wife's coverchiefs of *fine* texture (453), new shoes, and stockings of *fine* red scarlet (456):[114]

> Stragulam vestem fecit sibi byssus et purpura indumentum eius. . . . Fortitudo et decor indumentum eius et ridebit in die novissimo. (22, 25)
>
> [She hath made for herself clothing of tapestry: fine linen, and purple is her covering. . . . Strength and beauty are her clothing [i.e., of good quality and elegant] and she shall laugh in the latter day.]

On the image of the Valiant Woman, as Paule Mertens-Fonck has argued persuasively, Chaucer "superimposed" the image of the Adulterous Woman of Proverbs 7, a text which, as Owst first pointed out, became "the authoritative ground and substance" of the sermonists' attacks against women.[115] Like the Adulterous Woman of Proverbs 7 (7, 10–13, 18–19) Alice is talkative, wandering, deceitful, and makes advances to young Jankyn in her husband's absence. Her "impudent" or wanton look and harlot's attire inspired Chaucer to picture

[113] F. M. Biscoglio, *The Wives of the Canterbury Tales and the Tradition of the Valiant Woman of Proverbs 31: 10–31* (San Francisco, 1992), p. 75. See also J. L. Boren, "Alysoun of Bath and the Vulgate 'Perfect Wife,' " *Neuphilologische Mitteilungen* 76 (1975): 247–56. Biblical quotations are taken from *Biblia Sacra Iuxta Vulgatam Versionem*, ed. R. Weber, vol. 2 (Stuttgart, 1969) and translations from *The Holy Bible Translated from the Latin Vulgate* (New York, 1944).

[114] Hodges, pp. 162–3: "The earlier description [of her Sunday clothes] portrays the proud and successful 'capitalist entrepreneur', skillful enough in her cloth-making and merchandizing to surpass those of Ypres and Gaunt. . . . while the second description [of her traveling outfit] pictures the seasoned traveler, the practical cloth-maker, careful to protect and defend herself and her clothing from the elements and soil of the road . . .".

[115] P. Mertens-Fonck, "Tradition and Feminism in Middle English Literature: Source-hunting in the Wife of Bath's Portrait and in The Owl and the Nightingale," *Multiple Worlds, Multiple Words: Essays in Honour of Irene Simon*, ed. H. Maes-Jelinek, P. Michel, and P. Michel-Michot (Liège, 1988), pp. 177–82; Owst, pp. 385–6. H. P. Weissman, "Antifeminism and Chaucer's Characterization of Women," *Geoffrey Chaucer: A Collection of Original Articles*, ed. G. D. Economou (New York, 1975), p. 105, argues that Chaucer's portrait is "a very nearly systematic parody" of the Valiant Woman. In Proverbs 7.5 the Adulterous Woman is described as "mulier extranea." She is possibly to be identified with the "mulier aliena et extranea" of 2.16 or the "mulier mala" of 6.24. B. Rowland ("Chaucer's Working Wyf: The Unraveling of a Yarn Spinner," *Chaucer in the Eighties*, ed. J. N. Wasserman and R. J. Blanch [Syracuse, 1986], pp. 141–2) traces the Wife's ancestry back to Eve. Alford, pp. 120–2, argues that the Wife is derived from personifications of Rhetoric as a traditional rival of Logic or Dialectic here represented by the Clerk.

the Wife as bold-faced (458) and wearing eye-catching red stockings and an outlandish headdress (453–5). For the idea of merging the characterizations of the two types of women Chaucer took a hint from the *Vox Clamantis* (Book 5, chapter 6), where the ideal wife is described in terms that closely paraphrase *Proverbs* 31.10–31:

De muliere bona bona singula progrediuntur,
Cuius honestus amor prebet amoris opem:
Preualet argento mulier bona, preualet auro,
Condignum precii nilque valebit ei;
Lingua referre nequit aut scribere penna valorem
Eius, quam bonitas plena decore notat.
Nobilis in portis reverendus vir sedet eius,
Hospiciumque suum continet omne bonum:
Vestibus ornantur famuli, quas ordine duplo
Eius in activis fert operosa manus:
Ocia nulla suos temptant discurrere sensus,
Quos muliebris ope servat ubique pudor.
Sic laudanda bona meritis est laude perhenni,
Quam mala lingua loquax demere nulla potest.

[All good things come from a good woman, whose chaste love provides love's riches. A good woman is worth more than silver or gold; no fit value can be set upon her. Tongue cannot recite nor pen describe the worth of her whom utter goodness distinguishes [with beauty]. Her noble husband dwells revered within his gates, and her household contains all that is good. Her servants are fitted out with garments which her hand, busy in its activities, fashions of double strength. No idleness [tempts her thoughts to wander]; womanly modesty effectively protects them at all times. For her merits, such a good woman should receive everlasting praise which no wicked, gossiping tongue can take away. (Stockton, pp. 202–3, as corrected)]

In the same chapter, Gower contrasts this "good" woman with the "bad" woman, partially drawn from *Proverbs* 7. Like the Adulterous Woman, she appears in public showily dressed to attract men and deceive her husband:

Mille modis fallit, subtiles milleque tendit
Insidias, unus ut capiatur homo.
Femina talis enim gemmis radiantibus, auro,
Vestibus, ut possit fallere, compta venit:
Aptantur vestes, restringitur orta mamilla,
Dilatat collum pectoris ordo suum;
Crinibus et velis tinctis caput ornat, et eius
Aurea cum gemmis pompa decorat opus:
. . .
Non erit huius opus lanam mollire trahendo,
Set magis ut possit prendere compta viros:
Se quoque dat populo mulier speciosa videndam;
Quem trahit e multis forsitan unus erit.
. . .
Ve cui stulta comes sociali federe nupsit!
Non erit illius absque dolore thorus:

Federa seruasset, si non formosa fuisset,
Sponsa, que multociens res docet ista patens.
Quam Venus inspirat servat custodia nulla,
434 Ad fatuam nullus limes agendus erit.

[She deceives in a thousand ways and sets a thousand snares in order to catch one man. Such a woman comes adorned with radiant jewels, gold and finery so that she can deceive. Her clothes are well arranged, her rising breast is bound up, and the pattern of her bosom extends her neckline. She adorns her head with tinted hair and veils, and the golden splendor of gems decorates her handiwork. . . . It is not her task to soften wool by spinning it, but to be able to catch men when she is all decked out. A showy woman lets herself be seen by people; perhaps there will be one out of many whom she can allure. . . . Woe unto the man whom a foolish mate has married in conjugal union! His bed will not lack sorrow. The bride would have preserved the marriage contract, had she not been beautiful and the facts often show this clearly. No watchfulness protects her whom Venus incites, no boundary can be set for the foolish woman. (Stockton, pp. 203–5)]

Women's headdresses were a frequent object of medieval satire and were often equated with pride and quarrelsomeness.[116] The proud and combative nature of the Wife shows in much of her behavior, but especially in her determination to be first at the offering at Mass (449–52). This trait in women is criticized in Book 2 of *Matheolus*, a text that Chaucer used again in the Wife's *Prologue*:

1431 S'il y a une coustumiere
De seoir au moustier premiere
Ou d'aler devant a l'offrande,
Il convient qu'ele soit bien grande,
1435 Se son fait vouloit frequenter
Sans rioter ne tourmenter
Souvent grans batailles en sourdent;
Celles qui d' envie se bourdent
Ne veulent pas ainsi souffrir
1440 Que premiere deüst offrir.
. . .
1449 Il n' est femme qui soit en vie
Qui sur pareille n' ait envie.
1451 A ce nature les encline.

[If a woman is accustomed to have the first seat in the church or is used to go first during the Offertory procession, it is necessary that she be a prominent

[116] Mann, pp. 124–5; Hodges, pp. 163–7; Elaine E. Whitaker, "Chaucer's Wife of Bath and her Ten Pound Coverchiefs," *Publications of the Arkansas Philological Association* 15 (1989): 27–8, 30; "The Abuse of Women," ed. R. H. Robbins, *Secular Lyrics of the XIVth and XVth Centuries* (Oxford, 1952), p. 36, no. 38, lines 37–40. J. F. Plummer, "The Wife of Bath's Hat as Sexual Metaphor," *English Language Notes* 18 (1980): 89–90, suggests that in describing the hat as broad as a buckler or a targe Chaucer is referring to the "commonplace" metaphor of a small shield as a *mons veneris* and implying that the Wife is "sexually aggressive." Satirists and moralists notwithstanding, ornate and "heavy" headdresses were stylish in the 1380s. See Hodges, pp. 169–71, and D. E. Wretlind, "The Wife of Bath's Hat," *Modern Language Notes* 63 (1948): 381–2. H. P. Weissman, "The Pardoner's Vernicle, The Wife's Coverchiefs, and Saint Paul," *The Chaucer Newsletter* 1 (1979): 10–12, finds an echo of 1 Cor. 11:3–13, 15.

lady, especially if she wants to continue doing so without causing a disturbance. Often great strife stems from that; for those who are envious do not want to allow her to go to the offering first. . . . There is not a woman alive who does not envy her peers; nature inclines them to this.][117]

In the *Miroir de Mariage* Eustace Deschamps writes scornfully of the "most important lady" who "goes before the others to the offering" ("va la plus grande/ Devant les aultres a l'offrande"). The Knight of La Tour-Landry urges his daughters to model their behavior after women of humility – the Virgin Mary being the supreme example – rather than women of "great pride" who are envious "whiche shalle goo furst up on the offerande, forto have most of the vayne glorie of the worlde." In *Le Livre des Trois Vertus* Christine de Pizan criticizes women who "make a charade of getting in front of each other on their way to the Offering and often come to blows in the church itself, saying and doing flagrantly insulting things."[118]

The Wife has taken sundry pilgrimages to Jerusalem, Rome, Boulogne, Galicia, and Cologne (463–6) more for pleasure than devotion, as she is later to confess in the Prologue to her tale (551–9). *Matheolus* castigates women for their love of pilgrimages to distant shrines, especially by those who "find new ways to obey Venus." The satirical *De Conjuge non Ducenda* makes a similar charge, and in *Le Livre des Trois Vertus* Christine de Pizan also rebukes the woman who goes on pilgrimages for the wrong reason.[119] The Wife's knowledge of the "remedies of love" (475) may also incorporate an oblique reference to her fondness for pilgrimages. If the phrase alludes to Ovid's *Remedia Amoris* (213–18), disappointed lovers are there advised to seek distraction in long voyages. But the Wife goes on pilgrimage not to overcome love, but "to remedy [that is, satisfy] her need for love."[120]

The Wife's physical features give further evidence of her character and disposition. According to the physiognomies, large hips signify "excessive virility." A florid complexion and raucous voice, together with other details that come to

[117] Z. P. Thundy, "Matheolus, Chaucer, and the Wife of Bath," *Chaucerian Problems and Perspectives: Essays Presented to Paul E. Beichner*, ed. E. Vasta and Z. P. Thundy (Notre Dame, IN, and London, 1979), p. 47; R. L. Hoffman, "The Wife of Bath's Uncharitable Offerings," *English Language Notes* 11 (1974): 165–7; Mann, pp. 122–3, 266–7.

[118] Eustace Deschamps, *Oeuvres Complètes*, ed. G. Raynaud, vol. 9 (Paris, 1894), p. 110, lines 3289–90; *La Tour-Landry*, p. 150; Christine de Pizan, *Le Livre des Trois Vertus*, ed. C. Willard (Paris, 1989), p. 161.

[119] *La Tour-Landry*, p. 50: "Alle thei that gone on pilgrimage to a place for foule plesaunce more thanne deuocion of the place that thei go to, and couerithe thaire goinge with seruice of God, fowlithe and scornithe God and oure lady . . .". But pilgrimage may suit the Wife by nature. Venus (whose seal she bears) is favorable to pilgrimages under certain circumstances. See F. Tupper, "Saint Venus and the Canterbury Pilgrims," *The Nation* 97 (1913): 354, and Curry, p. 99, quoting J. F. Helvetius, *Microscopium Physiognomiae Medicum* (Amsterdam, 1676), p. 91: "They like to wander and sojourn in foreign lands . . .". See also *Matheolus*, Book 2, p. 73, lines 1004–7, 1020–1; Mann, pp. 123–4; *The Latin Poems commonly attributed to Walter Mapes*, p. 81, lines 97–100; Christine de Pizan, *Le Livre des Trois Vertus*, p. 182. The subject is discussed by S. S. Morrison, *Women Pilgrims in Late Medieval England: Private Piety as Public Performance* (London, 2000), pp. 112–19.

[120] H. A. Kelly, *Love and Marriage in the Age of Chaucer* (Ithaca, NY, and London, 1975), p. 73 n. 4. *MED* (remedy 1(d)) also identifies the phrase with the *Remedia Amoris*, but is unsure of its meaning, offering two possible definitions: "means of relief for lovers" and "means of contraception or abortion." The emphasis on travel throughout the portrait, I submit, favors the former. For a review of the different interpretations of "remedies of love," see Andrew, pp. 428–30.

light in the *Prologue*, are "signs of a voluptuous and passionate woman" ("Signa mulieris calidae et quae libenter coit") who bears a remarkable likeness to the Wife:

> Audax in lingua; in loquendo vox subtilis et alta; in animo superba . . . boni coloris in facie; recta in hasta; . . . ebriosa; cantat libenter; circuit loca, et delectatur ornatibus suis si ea potest habere.
>
> [She is bold in speech, having a keen, high-pitched voice, proud in mind, red of face, erect in carriage, given to drink; she loves to sing, wanders much and delights in adorning herself as much as possible.][121]

Gap teeth are decidedly unflattering, but they may also indicate that the Wife is "envious, irreverent, luxurious by nature, bold, deceitful, faithless, and suspicious."[122]

The Parson

The Parson is a "good man," an educated priest, who, though poor, is rich in "hooly thoght and werk" (478–9). He fulfills his duties with great diligence and devotion, attending to the spiritual needs of his parishioners, preaching "Cristes gospel" (481), and setting a "noble ensample" (496) of piety and virtue. He receives one of the highest encomia of the pilgrimage (524). The portrait of his extraordinary holiness is developed in terms of the biblical parable of the sheep and the shepherd (John 10.11–14), and supported by echoes of numerous other biblical passages.[123] The image of rusted gold (500) from Lamentations 4.1 is applied to corrupt priests in Gregory the Great's *Pastoral Care* (2.7), and this image and the reference to such clerics in the phrase "shiten shepherde" are paralleled in, and probably taken from, the *Romans de Carité*.[124]

Although the lines (483–90, 515–26) that describe the Parson as the ideal priest also resonate with biblical injunctions to patience, kindness, and humility (e.g., 1 Cor. 13.4–7 and 2 Tim. 2.4–5), they seem rather to have been shaped by

[121] Curry, *New Light*, p. 108, and his article, "More about Chaucer's Wife of Bath," *PMLA* 37 (1923): 44 n. 34, where he quotes M. Agnellus Blondus, *De Cognitione Hominis per Aspectum* (Rome, 1544), p. xv: "Ac protensa coxendicorum ossa virilitatis signum ni mollis caro contingit," and R. Goclenius, *Physiognomica et Chiromantica specialia* (Hamburg, 1661), p. 93: "Coxarum ossa duriter eminentia, & exterius apparentia, virilitatem monstrant." See also Curry, *New Light*, p. 109, and his article, as above, p. 45 n. 36, quoting Michael Scotus, *Liber physiognomiae et procreationis* (Venice, 1477), chapter 4. C. P. Biggam, "Aspects of Chaucer's Adjectives of Hue," *Chaucer Review* 28 (1993): 48, notes the Wife's red face as a sign of sensuality.

[122] Curry, *New Light*, p. 109, and his article as above, p. 46 n. 38, quoting L. B. Porta, *De Humana Physiognomia* (Hanover, 1593), p. 225: "Cuius dentes acuti, longi, rari et fortes in opere significant hominem invidum, impium, gulosum, audacem, falsum, infidelem, et suspiciosum." Cf. also A. J. Barnouw, "The Prente of Seinte Venus Seel," *The Nation* 103 (1916): 540, who draws attention to the primitive belief that gap-toothed women were predestined "for the office of love"; and Colby, p. 53.

[123] In lines 478–9 (Prov. 13.7, Jas. 2.5, 2 Cor. 8.9, Apoc. 2.9); lines 497–8 and 523 (Matt. 5.19, Acts 1.1); line 490 (Matt. 6. 25–6, 31–3); lines 521–3 (Tit. 1.13); lines 512–13 (Matt. 7.15); lines 521–3 (Matt. 18.15).

[124] *Romans de Carité*, p. 34, stanza 62, line 10, and p. 38, stanza 71, lines 9–11. Cf. *Vox Clamantis*, Book 3, chapter 12, line 1063: "In this way the sheep becomes tainted with the shepherd's stains" (Stockton, p. 140).

the requirements of character and conduct laid down for the priesthood by Gregory the Great in his *Pastoral Care*, a text Chaucer (like Gower and Langland) knew well. Gregory's emphasis on a combination of gentleness and firmness and the priestly duty to set an example to his parishioners are particularly prominent features of the Parson's portrait:

> Ille igitur, ille modis omnibus debet ad exemplum vivendi pertrahi, qui cunctis carnis passionibus moriens jam spiritaliter vivit, qui prospera mundi postposuit, qui nulla adversa pertimescit, qui sola interna desiderat. . . . Qui ad aliena cupienda non ducitur, sed propria largitur. Qui per pietatis viscera citius ad ignoscendum flectitur, sed nunquam plus quam deceat ignoscens, ab arce rectitudinis inclinatur. . . . Qui ita se imitabilem caeteris in cunctis quae agit insinuat, ut inter eos non habeat quod saltem de transactis erubescat. . . . Nam sunt nonnulli, qui eximia virtutum dona percipiunt, et pro exercitatione caeterorum magnis muneribus exaltantur, qui . . . doctrinae dapibus referti, patientiae longanimitate humiles, auctoritatis fortitudine erecti, pietatis gratia benigni, justitiae severitate districti sunt. . . . Si rector operatione praecipuus, ut vitae viam subditis vivendo denuntiet, et grex qui pastoris vocem moresque sequitur, per exempla melius quam per verba gradiatur. . . . bonis in nullo se praeferat, et cum pravorum culpa exigit, potestatem protinus sui prioratus agnoscat quatenus et honore suppresso aequalem se subditis bene viventibus deputet, et erga perversos jura rectitudinis exercere non formidet. . . . Nunc sicut in libris Moralibus jam diximus disciplina vel misericordia multum destituitur, si una sine altera teneatur. Sed erga subditos suos inesse rectoribus debet et juste consulens misericordia, et pie saeviens disciplina. . . . Hinc David ait: Virga tua et baculus tuus, ipsa me consolata sunt. Virga enim percutimur baculo sustentamur.[125]
>
> [He, therefore – indeed, he precisely – must devote himself entirely to setting an ideal of living. He must die to all passions of the flesh and by now lead a spiritual life. He must have put aside worldly prosperity; he must fear no adversity, desire only what is interior. . . . He is not led to covet the goods of others, but is bounteous in giving of his own. He is quickly moved by a compassionate heart to forgive, yet never so diverted from perfect rectitude as to forgive beyond what is proper. . . . In all that he does he sets an example so inspiring to all others that in their regard he has no cause to be ashamed of his past. . . . There are those who are gifted with virtues in a high degree and who are exalted by great endowments for the training of others; men who are . . . replete with feasts of knowledge, humble in their long suffering patience, erect in the fortitude of authority, gentle in the grace of loving-kindness, strict and unbending in justice. . . . The ruler [i.e., the priest or spiritual ruler] should be exemplary in his conduct that by his manner of life he may show the way of life to his subjects, and that the flock, following the teaching and conduct of its shepherd, may proceed the better through example rather than words. . . . He must not set himself over the good in any way, and when the sins of the wicked demand it, he must assert the power of his supremacy at once. Thus, waiving aside his rank, he regards himself the equal of his subjects who lead good lives, but does not shrink from exercising the laws of rectitude against the perverse. . . . We have said in the *Books on Morals*

[125] *Cura Pastoralis*, Part 1, chapters 10, 5 (PL 77, col. 23, 18); Part 2, chapters 3, 6 (PL 77, col. 28, 34, 38).

> [*Moralia* 20.5.14] that either discipline or compassion is greatly wanting if one is exercised independently of the other. But rulers in their relations with subjects should be animated by [mercy justly caring and by justice mercifully chastising]. . . . Wherefore, David says, Thy rod and Thy staff have comforted me (Psalm 22.4). It is with a rod that we are smitten, but we are supported by a staff.][126]

The Parson fulfills his sacerdotal obligation to instruct his parishioners in the tenets of the faith (480–2). A Middle English sermon describes the estate of priesthood in words remarkably similar to Chaucer's: "Prestes shuld principally entermet to lern þe lawe of Criste and lawfully to teche itt"; and the emphasis on preaching in the opening lines of the Parson's portrait parallels the position it occupies in *Jack Upland*'s definition of the duties of the office: "to preche þe gospel truli and to preye in herte devoutli, to mynistre þe sacramentis freli, to studie in Goddis lawe oonli, and to be trewe ensaumpleris of holi mennis lijf continuli, in doynge and in suffringe."[127] The zeal with which the Parson visits his far-flung parishioners (491–5) resembles a similar detail in the account of Aidan in Bede's *Ecclesiastical History*: "Discurrere per cuncta et urbana et rustica loca non equorum dorso sed pedum incessu vectus . . . solebat" ["He was accustomed to travel through all places both in town and country not on horseback, but on foot"].[128]

The Parson's reluctance to curse for tithes (486) and his contribution of financial assistance to the poor of his diocese (in keeping with Gregory's injunctions) (487–9) are often thought to reflect Wycliffite sympathy.[129] But similar views are found in non-Wycliffite commentators. In *Handlyng Synne*, Robert Mannyng criticizes priests who lightly resort to excommunication, urging them to the more charitable course of action practiced by the Parson:

10889 þe prest wote* neure what he menes* knows/ means
þat for lytel* curseþ* hys parysshenes. small (offenses)/ excommunicates
. . .
10897 þe lord boghte þe shepe ful dere
Lese* hem nat þan so lyghtly here. lose
þogh þey outrage* and do folye, commit sin
10900 He shal nat sle* hem wyþ felonye*. destroy/ ruthlessly
He shal hem chastyse wyþ lewed* speche, ordinary, unpolished

126 St. Gregory the Great, *Pastoral Care*, trans. H. Davis (Westminster, 1950), pp. 38–9, 29, 48, 59–60, 66–7 (as corrected). Gregory's works, particularly *Pastoral Care*, provided a rich quarry of aphorisms on the priestly ideal. A cento of Latin tags from Gregory in a York priest's commonplace book that epitomizes the Parson's qualities is cited in R. M. Haines, *Ecclesia Anglicana: Studies in the English Church of the Later Middle Ages* (Toronto, 1989), p. 175, and translated in *Pastors and the Care of Souls in Medieval England*, ed. J. Shinners and W. J. Dohar (Notre Dame, IN, 1998), pp. 15–16. The Latin text is printed from Bodleian Library MS Wood Empt. 20, fols 56v–57r (late 1470s). A similar version is printed from Bodleian Library MS Bodley 54, fol. 155v (Haines, p. 317 n. 90). A third copy is in Jesus College Library, Cambridge, MS 4, fol. 187r.

127 *Middle English Sermons*, ed. W. O. Ross, EETS OS 209 (Oxford, 1960), p. 224; *Jack Upland; Friar Daw's Reply; and, Upland's Rejoinder*, ed. P. L. Hayworth (Oxford, 1968), p. 54. A Lollard sermon also emphasizes the duty of preaching by priests. See *Lollard Sermons*, ed. G. Cigman, EETS OS 294 (Oxford, 1989), p. 4.

128 Bede, *Opera Historica*, trans. J. E. King, vol. 1 (Cambridge, 1979), p. 347.

129 Mann, p. 59.

Wyþ smale baytynges* & nat wyþ wreche*. harassments/ banishment
As þe gode shepherd kepeþ hys shepe,
So shal þe prest hys parysshenes kepe.
þere* shepe goun* wrong bysyde* þe paþe, where/ go/ off
þe shepherd cryeþ for drede* of skaþe*. fear/ harm
And ȝyf* þey wyl nat at his crye if
Turne aȝen* to here pasture nye*, again/ nearby
þan sytteþ he on hys hounde
And bayteþ* hem a wel gode stounde*, entices/ time
And bryngeþ hem to here pasture weyl*, safely
Ne slep he ȝyt* none neure adeyl*. gets/ never a bit
Wyþ þese prestes hyt shuld fare so
Whan here paryshennes oght mysdo*, commit any sin
Wyþ feyre* techyng & gode spelles* gentle/ sermons
And stoutly* whan þey wyl nat elles, boldly
And wyþ ordynaryys* of holy cherche, bishops
Tyl þat þey wyl ryghtly werche*, act
Nat wyþ cursyng* þat ys slaghter* euyl*, excommunication/ spiritual slaying/ evil
So sone betake* hem to þe deuyl. consign
Have to hem swych* charyte such
As þow wldest* god had* to þe.[130] would/ have

In the *Mirour de l'Omme*, Gower observes that the good parish priests of old made substantial contributions to poor relief:

Les bons curetz du temps jadis,
Qui benefice avoient pris
Du sainte eglise, deviseront
En trois parties, come je lis,
Leur biens, siq' au primer divis
A leur altier part en donneront,
Et de la part seconde aideront,
Vestiront et sauf herbergeront
De leur paroche les mendis;
La tierce part pour soy garderont:
D'oneste vie ils essampleront
Et leur voisins et leur soubgitz.

[Good parish priests of olden days who had taken a benefice of Holy Church divided (as I have read) their wealth into three parts. First, they gave a part to the altar; with the second part, they aided, clothed, and sheltered the poor of their parish; the third they kept for themselves. They gave an example of honorable life to their neighbors and their subjects. (Wilson, p. 273)]

Jill Mann instances numerous complaints against bad priests in the satirical literature – absenteeism, neglect of visitation duties, misuse of parish income, lack of charity, general indifference to, and alienation from, parishioners (pp. 56, 58–66). Employing a series of negatives, Chaucer makes it pellucidly

[130] Robert Mannyng of Brunne, *Handlyng Synne*, ed. I. Sullens (Binghamton, NY, 1983), p. 271. In the *Confessio Amantis* (Prologue, lines 250–74), Gower also laments the combative stance of the church on the subject of tithes. Cf. Mann, p. 61.

clear that his Parson is guilty of none of these abuses. He is actuated by the biblical and Gregorian ideals of his office. By a latent contrast between what the Parson does and what other priests do not do, Chaucer undoubtedly, if indirectly, exposes the corruption and misconduct of the secular clergy.

The Plowman

The Parson is accompanied on the pilgrimage by his brother the Plowman who is not an employee, but a husbandman in possession of a plough-team and a "more or less substantial holding of land."[131] The genealogical detail is of interest since it places the Plowman among the wealthiest members of the village community. It is from this level of the peasantry that many of the clergy of the period came.[132] The Parson would presumably be among them.

The Plowman is linked to the Parson not only in brotherhood, but also in his strict observance of the tenets of Christianity and of the obligations of his office. He is an emblem of the good Christian, loving God and his neighbor in fulfillment of the two precepts of the Law (Matt. 22.36–40). He is also an emblem of human labor, faithfully working for his lord, for the Church to which he pays his tithes in full, and, without recompense, for the poor. He is content with his lot (532), and gives no indication of social unrest or complaint. He follows the *Reule of Lif* enjoined by John Wyclif:

> If þou be a laborer, lyve in mekenesse, and trewly and wylfully do þi labour. . . . And in alle þyngis bewar of grucchyng aȝens God and his visitacion, in gret labour and long, and gret sikenesse, and oþer adversities, and bewar of wraþe, of cursyng and waryng or banning, of man or of best. And ever kepe pacience and mekenesse and charite boþe to God and man.[133]

Chaucer may have modeled his character on *Piers Plowman*, so close is the resemblance both verbally and in detail.[134] Both countrymen are depicted as good-hearted, honest, unselfish laborers. A series of quotations from the A and B texts parallel Chaucer's portrait (*GP*, 529–41).

> With hym ther was a Plowman, was his brother,
> That hadde ylad of dong ful many a fother; (*GP*, 529–30)

> Lawe shal ben a labourer and lede afeld donge. (A.IV.130)

> A trewe swynkere and a good was he,
> Lyvynge in pees and parfit charitee. (*GP*, 531–2)

131 R. H. Hilton, *The English Peasantry in the Later Middle Ages* (Oxford, 1975), p. 21.

132 R. N. Swanson, "Chaucer's Parson and Other Priests," *Studies in the Age of Chaucer* 11 (1991): 52.

133 John Wyclif, *Select English Works*, ed. T. Arnold, vol. 3 (Oxford, 1871), p. 207. The Plowman also follows the earlier admonitions in *Game and Playe of the Chesse*, Book 3, chapter 1, pp. 77–8; Jehan de Vignay, *Le Jeu*, chapter 9, p. 12. See also *Middle English Sermons*, p. 224.

134 N. Coghill, "Two Notes on Piers Plowman," *Medium Aevum* 4 (1935): 92–4. Coghill used the B-Text exclusively to identify the parallel passages. I have used the A-Text where it is available to the same purpose. Bowden, pp. 220–1, argues for the influence of the *Seneschauchie* and *Chessbook* on the description of the Plowman.

The Commune contreued* of* Kynde Wit craftes*,	devised/ with/ crafts
And for profit of al þe peple plowmen ordeyned*	appointed
To tilie* and to trauaille* as trewe lif askeþ. (B Pr. 118–20)	till/ toil
I weue* and I wynde* and do what Truþe hoteþ (B. V.548)	weave/ wind yarn
Ac þere arn* seuene sistris þat seruen Treuþe euere*	are/ always
And ben porteris* of þe posternis* þat to þe place longiþ*.	porters/ posterns (gates)/ belong
þat on* hattiþ* Abstinence, and Humylite anoþer;	one/ is called
Charite and Chastite beþ* hise chief maidenes;	are
Pacience and Pees mekil* peple þei helpen;	many
Largenesse* þe lady let in ful manye. (A.VI.107–12)	Generosity
Ac Treuþe shal teche ȝow* his tem* for to dryue (A.VII.126)	you/ team
God loved he best with al his hoole herte	
At alle tymes, thogh him gamed or smerte,	
And thanne his neighebor right as hymselve. (*GP*, 533–5)	
Ac if ȝe wilneþ* to wende, þis is þe weye þider:*	wish/ thither
Ȝe mote* go þoruȝ* Meknesse, boþe men and wyues,	must/ through
Tyl ȝe come into Consience, þat Crist wyte* þe soþe,*	knows/ truth
þat ȝe loue hym leuere* þanne þe lif in ȝoure hertis,	more dearly
And þanne ȝoure neiȝebours next. . . . (A.VI.47–51)	
He wolde thresshe*, and therto dyke and delve,	thresh corn
For Cristes sake, for every povre wight,	
Withouten hire, if it lay in his myght. (*GP*, 536–8)	
I dyke and I delue, I do þat he hoteth*;	bids, orders
Some tyme I sowe and some tyme I þresshe (B.V.545–6)	
Idyked and idolven, ido þat he hiȝte* (A.VI.33)	bade, ordered
'Nay, be þe peril of my soule!' quaþ* Piers, and gan to swere,	said
'I nolde fonge* a ferþing*, for Seint Thomas shryne!	would not take/ farthing
Treuþe wolde loue me þe wers a long tyme aftir!' (A.VI.44–6)	
His tithes payde he ful faire and wel,	
Bothe of his propre swynk and his catel. (*GP*, 539–40)	
þe kirke* shal haue my caroyn*, and kepe my bones,	church/ corpse
For of my corn* and my catel he crauide* þe tiþe*.	grain/ demanded/ tithe
I payede it hym prestly*, for peril of my soule. (A.VII.83–5)	promptly

It has been noted that Piers "manures his fields with dung carried on a cart drawn by a mare [A.VII.271–2] – the mare that Chaucer's Ploughman rides (541)." The mare and the tabard he wears are traditional symbols of his lowly station.[135]

Chaucer and Langland were not alone in honoring ploughmen. A Welsh contemporary, Iolo Goch, pays tribute to "The Ploughman" (*Cywyddy Llafurwr*)

[135] J. A. W. Bennett, "Chaucer's Contemporary," *Piers Plowman: Critical Approaches*, ed. S. S. Hussey (London, 1969), p. 318. Mann, p. 72. O. G. Hill, *The Manor, the Plowman, and the Shepherd* (Selinsgrove, 1993), p. 77, detects in line 530 an echo of Virgil's *Georgics* 1. 79–80. See also Hodges, pp. 218–24.

who also pays his tithes and works hard for the good of society – a humble, peaceful, generous, and patient husbandman, who will receive his just reward in the afterlife.[136]

Finally, mention should be made of Paul Hardwick's suggestion that the Plowman may be associated with Chaucer himself. He alludes to a topos descending from Isidore of Seville that represents the act of ploughing a field with oxen and seeding it as a metaphor for writing. Ernst Curtius traces its use from Prudentius through Carolingian poetry.[137]

The Miller

Chaucer follows popular tradition in portraying the Miller as greedy and dishonest, traits commonly attributed to millers as a class in medieval literature.[138] George Fenwick Jones draws examples mainly from late German and English literature, but there is no reason to think that they initiated the tradition or that it expressed anything other than a universal view of their character. The author of *Devil's Net*, a fifteenth-century poem from Switzerland cited by Jones, says of millers: "Ich waisz kain fromen uf der erden" ["I know no honest one in the world"]. "A thombe of gold" (563) is a proverbial expression of their greed, and millers in literature commonly have red beards as a sign of their deceitful nature, the Miller's being as broad as a spade and as red as a sow or fox (552–3). Jones quotes a medieval proverb: "Sub barba rufa est cor cum trufa" ["Under a red beard is a deceitful heart"].[139] The prejudice against redheads as untrustworthy was old and widespread, appearing, for example, in works as diverse as *Ruodlieb*, *The Proverbs of Alfred*, and James Yonge's version of the *Secreta Secretorum*, which views "rede men" as "Parceuynge and trechurus, and full of queyntise, i-lykenyd to Foxis."[140]

The Miller's physical features (545–59) are decidedly unsightly, even repellent. His abnormally large mouth, broad red beard, and wart atop his nose with its wide, black nostrils, are common attributes of "ideal ugliness."[141] According to the physiognomies, these, and other details of his stocky build, mark him as a man "easily angered, shameless, loquacious, and apt to stir up strife"; the Ashmole

[136] Iolo Goch, *Poems*, trans. Dafydd Johnston (Llandysul, 1993), p. 114, lines 1–24; and A. Breeze, "A Welsh Addition to the Piers Plowman Group?," *Notes and Queries* 238 (1993): 142–51. The thirteenth-century writer Wernher der Gartenere also provides a model of the good peasant in *Helmbrecht*, ed. U. Seelbach, trans. L. B. Parshall (New York and London, 1987), p. 18.

[137] P. Hardwick, "Chaucer the Poet as Ploughman," *Chaucer Review* 33 (1998): 152; Curtius, pp. 313–14.

[138] G. F. Jones, "Chaucer and the Medieval Miller," *Modern Language Quarterly* 16 (1955): 8–15, and "Christis Kirk, Peblis to the Play, and the German Peasant-Brawl," *PMLA* 68 (1953): 1101–25.

[139] Jones, *Ibid.* (1955), pp. 4–5, 12; and B. J. Whiting, *Proverbs, Sentences and Proverbial Phrases* (Cambridge, 1968), W559.

[140] On medieval prejudice against redheads see R. Mellinkoff, *Outcasts: Signs of Otherness in Northern European Art of the Late Middle Ages*, vol. 1 (Berkeley, 1993), pp. 147–59; *The Ruodlieb*, ed. and trans. C. O. Grocock (Chicago, 1985), p. 90, lines 451–4; *An Old English Miscellany*, ed. R. Morris, EETS OS 49 (London, 1872), p. 138, lines 702–5; *Secreta Secretorum*, ed. Steele, p. 229. The dishonest innkeeper of the Goliardic *Hospes Erat* is also redheaded. See also Biggam, p. 50, who judges that the Miller's red beard denotes sensuality.

[141] Mellinkoff, pp. 169–78; Colby, pp. 73, 78, 81; Jones (1953), 1117; Biggam, p. 48.

version of the *Secreta Secretorum* interprets a wide mouth as an indicator of a man who is “glotenous and bold,” “batellous and hardy,” the wide nostrils of a man who is “wrothfull.”[142] The comparison with animals – the resemblance of the color of the beard to a sow or fox, the apelike appearance – suggests cunning, thievery, and lasciviousness. The arms he carries – millers rarely carry arms – are emblematic of the combativeness of millers in general, and perhaps, too, of their propensity for social climbing, at least in the fabliau tradition.[143]

The direct characterization of the Miller as a loudmouth, a teller of indecent stories, and a low, popular entertainer (560–1) parallels a passage from the Passus X of the B-text of *Piers Plowman* denouncing common minstrels:

Harlotes* for hir harlotrie may haue of hir goodes,	buffoons
And iaperis* and iogelours and iangleris* of gestes;*	jesters/ tellers/ tales
Ac he þat haþ Holy Writ ay in his mouþe	
And kan telle of Tobye* and of þe twelue Apostles	Tobias
Or prechen of þe penaunce* þat Pilat wroȝte*	suffering/ caused
To Iesu þe gentile, þat Iewes todrowe* –	drew asunder, tortured
Litel is he loued [or lete* by] þat swich a lesson sheweþ,	esteemed, well regarded
Or daunted* or drawe forþ* – I do* it on god hymselue!	flattered/ promoted/ call to witness
But þoo þat feynen* hem foolis, and wiþ faityng* libbeþ*,	pose as/ fraud/ live
Ayein* þe lawe of Oure Lord, and lyen on* hemselue,	against/ lie about
Spitten and spuen* and speke foule wordes,	spew up
Drynken and dreuelen* and do* men for to gape,	slobber/ make
Likne* men and lye on* hem þat leneþ* hem no yiftes –	Compare (unfavorably)/ slander/ give
Thei konne na moore mynstralcie ne musik men to glade	
Than Munde þe Millere of *Multa fecit deus*.	
Ne were* hir vile harlotrye, haue God my trouþe,	Were it not for
Sholde neuere kyng ne knyȝt ne canon of Saint Poules	
Ȝyue hem to hir yeresȝyue* þe worþ of a grote!	New Year’s gift
Ac murþe and mynstralcie amonges men is nouþe*	now
Lecherie* and losengerye* and losels* tales –	debauchery/ flattery/ rogues’
Glotonye and grete oþes, þis [game*] þey louyeþ.	amusement

In both works the words “harlotrie/harlotries” and “Iangleris/janglere” appear in proximity and are significantly associated with millers. Chaucer’s use of the word “janglere” carries with it the implication of a teller of malicious tales, a sense derived from the *Roman de la Rose* to describe Male Bouche, a slanderer (jangleor, 3530), and well in accord with the character of the Miller as it is later revealed in his prologue and tale.[144] The term “goliardeys” (560) may derive from a character called “a goliardeis, a gloton of wordes” in Langland’s *Prologue* (B.139).

The Miller’s white coat may be appropriate to his occupation, but his blue

[142] Curry, pp. 81, 85–6; *Secretum Secretorum*, ed. Manzalaoui, p. 105.

[143] B. Rowland, “Aspects of Chaucer’s Use of Animals,” *Archiv für das Studium der neueren Sprachen und Literaturen* 201 (1964): 111; Jones (1955), p. 7.

[144] W. A. Quinn, “Chaucer’s Janglerye,” *Viator* 18 (1987): 309–13. Cf. also the use of the phrase “felonesses jangles” in the *Roman de la Rose* (11433). Male Bouche also plays the bagpipes (3898–9). See also Mann, p. 161.

hood is socially presumptuous and is a commonplace detail in the satire on the clothing of peasants. He leads the pilgrims out of Southwerk playing the bagpipes as a culminating symbol of his gluttony and lechery (565–6).[145]

The Manciple

The Manciple, a provisioner for one of the Inns of Court, is drawn after the character of the faithless servant. In the *Memoriale Presbiterorum* the confessor is directed to interrogate servants (whose honesty was always under suspicion) as follows:

> 'Iurasti vel fidem dedisti ad serviendum fideliter domino tuo?' et si dicat quod sic, inquiras sic: 'Fecisti unquam fraudem in servicio tuo?' quod sit multis modis, prout quilibet discretus per se novit de facto explicare.
>
> ['Did you ever swear or give faith to your Lord to serve faithfully?' and if the answer be yes, inquire as follows: 'Did you ever commit fraud in your service?' – which occurs in many ways, as any man of discretion himself knows to explain from experience.][146]

The Manciple's fraud (like the Reeve's deception of his master) goes undetected by the clever lawyers who employ him, a dozen of them worthy of the best stewardships in England. His ability to outwit them earns the narrator's grudging admiration (573–5).

There is no direct source for Chaucer's portrait. The appearance of manciples in medieval literature is a rare occurrence. They are fleetingly mentioned among the manorial officials, lawyers, and provisioners who are guests at the marriage of Lady Meed in *Piers Plowman* (B.II):

> 57 To marien þis mayde was many man assembled,
> . . .
> 59 As sisours* and somonours, sherreues* and hire clerkes, assizers/ sherrifs
> Bedelles* and baillifs and brocours of chaffare*, beadles/ brokers of trade
> Forgoers* and vitaillers* and vokettes* of þe Arches; harbingers/ victuallers/ advocates
> 62 I kan noȝt rekene* þe route* þat ran aboute Mede. number/ throng

Chaucer similarly couples manorial officials and provisioners in the juxtaposed portraits of the Manciple and the Reeve.

The portrait of the Manciple with his shady business dealings recalls the parable of the Unjust Steward (Luke 16.1–8). The Manciple, like the biblical steward, is an "example for others, wise in his dishonesty, commended in particular for his attention to accounts. . . . [Chaucer] created the essentially ironic

[145] P. Cunningham and C. Lucas, *Occupational Costume in England from the Eleventh Century to 1914* (London, 1967), pp. 122–3; Jones (1955), p. 7, (1953), pp. 1110–11, and "Sartorial Symbols in Medieval Literature," *Medium Aevum* 25 (1956): 68; Hodges, pp. 212–13, who argues that the combination of blue and white parodies the "most commonly worn colors of the additional surcoats of the Order of the Garter." On the Miller's bagpipes, see E. A Block, "Chaucer's Millers and their Bagpipes," *Speculum* 29 (1954): 239–43, who also draws attention to the symbolic use of bagpipes in the paintings of Hieronymus Bosch and Peter Bruegel the Elder.

[146] Haren, "Interrogatories," pp. 148–9.

persona of the Manciple, who is the Steward's counterpart, crafty in his accounts for his own gain, not his master's."[147]

The Reeve

The Reeve, who comes from Bawdeswell in Norfolk, is a slender, choleric man who shrewdly oversees his lord's demesne and its villeins. He is an experienced husbandman,[148] and his managerial functions go beyond those usually assigned to reeves. He appears to exercise the duties of a bailiff or even to some extent a steward. He clearly exploits his position to enrich himself at the expense of his young lord and to oppress his subjects (593–612). His dishonesty and avarice typify the abuses associated with manorial officials. In the *Memoriale Presbiterorum* the confessor is advised with respect to seneschals and bailiffs:

> debes insistere viriliter ad eruendam veritatem; quia tales cavillosi sunt valde, et omnino avaricie et falsitati dediti, et ceca cupiditate ducti . . . nec curant de Deo, vel de sancta ecclesia, vel eius ministris, sed tantummodo de lucris et muneribus consequendis.
>
> [You must strive manfully to extract the truth, because such people are exceedingly cavilling and altogether given to avarice and falsity and led by blind greed . . . nor do they care for God or for holy Church or its ministers, but only for securing profits and rewards.][149]

Moreover, bailiffs and other servants of magnates who are ["deputed to lay out household expenses or other necessary expenses consume the goods of their lords in superfluous expenditure. . . . Wherefore they often write in their accounts that they expended more on the affairs of their lords than they did and sometimes they say that they bought provisions or other necessities for thirty, when in truth they paid for them no more than twenty, and thus they retain part of the price for themselves, committing deceit, fraud and theft. Such bailiffs and servants enriched of such mammon of iniquity, more than anyone else enjoy revenues and possessions nowadays."]

> Alii ministri magnatum ad faciendum expensas domus vel alias expensas necessarias deputati, bona dominorum suorum consumunt superflue. . . . Unde multociens scribunt in compotis suis quod plus expendiderunt circa negocia dominorum suorum quam fecerunt et quandoque dicunt se emisse cibaria vel res alias necessarias pro triginta, pro quibus in veritate non solverunt nisi viginti, et sic partem illius precii sibi ipsis retinent, dolum, fraudem et

[147] J. C. Hirsh, "The Politics of Spirituality: The Second Nun and the Manciple," *Chaucer Review* 12 (1977–78): 138–9.

[148] The Reeve was experienced in both arable and pastoral husbandry. Cf. M. S. Campbell, "Livestock of Chaucer's Reeve: Fact or Fiction?" in *The Salt of Common Life: Individuality and Choice in the Medieval Towns, Countryside, and Church. Essays Presented to J. Ambrose Raftis*, ed. E. B. De Windt (Kalamazoo, MI, 1995), pp. 271–305.

[149] Haren, "Interrogatories," pp. 134–5.

periurium committendo. Tales ballivi et ministri de tali mammona inequitatis ditati redditibus et possessionibus gaudent pre ceteris hiis diebus.[150]

Reeves are proverbally thieves: "Thefe is reve"; they are among the "great thieves" denounced by the *Ayenbite of Inwyt*[151] and their ill repute is reflected in *Piers Plowman* where "Reynald þe Reue of Rutland Sokene" acts as a signatory to the marriage contract of Lady Meed (B.II.111). Although a new reeve is bound by an official charge to be faithful to his lord in the discharge of all expenses, nevertheless Walter of Henley, aware of their notorious reputation for fraudulent transactions and record-keeping, prudently advises a careful audit of manorial accounts.[152] The Reeve fits the evil stereotype, but, like the Manciple, he is far too shrewd to be caught out by accountants (594). Moreover, his dishonesty conforms to the unsavory reputation of Norfolk people as crafty, treacherous, and grasping.[153] He is ruled by Covetousness who in the *Roman de la Rose* (180–2) instigates people "to take the property of others, to steal, to carry off, to defraud, to misaccount, and to mistally" ["l'autrui prendre,/ Rober, tolir e bareter,/ E bescochier e mesconter"].

The description of the choleric man in James Yonge's version of the *Secreta Secretorum* delineates aspects of the Reeve's character (more fully explored in the tales) and accounts for his slender body and thin legs:

> The colerike by kynde he sholde be lene of body, his body is hote and drye, and he shalbe sumwhat rogh . . . of sharp witte, wyse and of good memorie, a grette entremyttere, full-large and foolehardy, delyuer of body, hasty of worde and of answere; he louyth hasty wengeaunce; Desyrous of company of women moore than hym nedyth. . . . Tho men whyche haue smale legges and synnowy bene luchrus.[154]

A man of choleric disposition is easily moved to anger which is aggravated in old age by the "noxious vapors produced in impaired digestion", as Carol A. Everest has shown, citing Roger Bacon, who regarded "wrath and disquietude of spirit" ("ira et inquietatio animi") as characteristic of age and attributes them to "melancholic fumes rising to the brain" ("ex fumis melancolicis ascendentibus ad cerebrum"). It is little wonder that the Reeve's hot temper inspires terror in his underservants, who fear him like the death (605).[155] On the other hand, a

150 M. J. Haren, "Social Ideas in the Pastoral Literature of Fourteenth-Century England," *Religious Beliefs and Ecclesiastical Careers in Late Medieval England*, ed. C. Harper-Bill (Woodbridge, 1991), p. 53; and "A Study of the *Memoriale Presbiterorum*, a Fourteenth-Century Confessional Manual for Parish Priests," unpublished dissertation (Oxford University, 1953), Part 2, pp. 234–5.

151 Cf. Whiting W436: "There child is kynge and clerke bysshop/ And chorle reve all is greve"; Dan Michel, *Ayenbite of Inwyt*, ed. R. Morris, EETS OS 23 (London, 1866), p. 37.

152 See *The Court Baron*, ed. F. C. Maitland and W. P. Baildon, Selden Society Publications 4 (London, 1891), p. 103; D. Oschinsky, *Walter of Henley and Other Treatises on Estates Management and Accounting* (Oxford, 1971), p. 340; Bowden, pp. 250–2.

153 A. J. Fletcher, "Chaucer's Norfolk Reeve," *Medium Aevum* 52 (1983): 100–3; Mann, p. 166; Campbell, pp. 304–5. In his *Physiognomy* (p. 131) John Metham describes Norfolk people as "dysseyuabyl and fals off here behestys, passing enuyus and fulle off malyce and euer onstedffaste, ontrw, and ful off lesyngys."

154 *Secreta Secretorum*, ed. Steele, pp. 220, 226.

155 C. A. Everest, "Sex and Old Age in Chaucer's Reeve's Prologue," *Chaucer Review* 31 (1996): 109.

collection of Anglo-Saxon ordinances on the duties of a reeve ("Be gescead gerafan") gives the following admonition:

> Symle he sceal his hyrmen scyrpan mid manunge to hlafordes neode and him eac leanian be þam þe hy earnian. Ne laete he naefre his hyrmen hyne oferwealdan, ac wille he aelcne mid hlafordes creafte and mid folcrihte. Selre him his aefre of folgoþe þonne on, gyf hine magan wyldan þa þe he scolde wealdan. Ne biþ hit hlaforde raed þaet he þaet þafige.
>
> [He should ever stimulate his servants by an admonition (to observe) their lord's desire; and moreover should pay them according to what they deserve. He should never let his servants get the upper hand of him, but let him wish (to direct) each one, with a lord's authority and according to folk-right. Far better were it for him to be always out of office rather than in it, if they whom he should rule come to rule him. It will not be prudent for his lord to permit this.][156]

Other details of his appearance are introduced to define his social and financial status. He is expensively attired in a long surcoat of fine blue cloth characteristic of the upper classes. Yet the length of the surcoat is old-fashioned,[157] and the way in which he wears it betrays his humble status (621). He is, however, clean-shaven, and his hair is stylishly cropped, attributes commonly seen only on the high born. But the horse he rides ("a full good stot" [615]), an agricultural laboring animal, is a standard peasant's mount, and his "rusty blade" (618) plays on the comic literary motif of the peasant displaying rusty, that is, unused arms. The portrait appears to initiate a minor English tradition of the rich (609), upstart reeve who figures in Lydgate's *A Mumming at Hertford* (c. 1426), the *Tournament of Tottenham* (c. 1450), and *John the Reeve* (c. 1500–50).[158]

The Summoner

The Summoner and the Pardoner are the archvillains of the pilgrimage. They ride together singing a duet (672). The scabrous Summoner is a minor official of the archdeacon's court whose repulsive facial features betray his depraved moral state.[159] His disfiguring disease, probably a form of leprosy called alopicia, comes from his own lechery (626) and is aggravated by his indulgence in strong food and drink (623–5, 627–35). The Summoner's malady and its facial manifestations – fiery redness, pustules, swollen eyelids, thinness of the beard, black, scabby brows – are described by a host of medical authorities, many of whom Chaucer mentions elsewhere in his work and with whom he appears to have been familiar. They attribute the disease to lechery and a diet

[156] W. Cunningham, *The Growth of English Industry and Commerce during the Early and Middle Ages*, 4th ed., vol. 1 (Cambridge, 1905), pp. 572, 574.

[157] H. S. Houghton, " 'Degree' and 'Array' in Chaucer's Portrait of the Reeve," unpublished dissertation (University of York, 1975), pp. 201–6, 212–13, 241–80; Hodges, pp. 230–1, who suggests that the rusted blade signifies that the Reeve is untrustworthy.

[158] Houghton, pp. 231–40, 193–9, 147–8, 289–308.

[159] Mann, pp. 137–9, relates the Summoner's scabby face to a rhetorical tradition that is intended to disgust the reader.

adversely affecting the humors in the blood.[160] Bartholomaeus Anglicus advises that it is consequent of "fleischely lygynge by a womman sone aftir þat a leprous man haþ ilaye by here. . . . And sometyme of hote metis, as of longe use of stronge peper and of garlike, and oþer suche; and somtyme . . . of unclene wyn and corrupt" ("Accidit etiam ex accessu et coitu mulieris statim a leproso praecognitae . . . Aliquando accidit ex cibis nimis calidis, ut ex nimis diurno usu fortis alliatae, piperate et huiusmodi . . . et vino impuro et corrupto"). The Summoner treats the disease with the recommended remedies. Lanfranc prescribes, inter alia, "litargiri, auripigmenti, sulphuris viui, viridis eris ana . . . olio tartarino . . . argenti viui ana."[161] Guy de Chauliac's cure for *gutta rosacea* has a longer list of ingredients that includes "quyk siluer . . . sulphre . . . alume . . . oyle of tartir." He quotes other recipes that call for "ceruse" and "boreys." And he advises the patient to "eschewe fro alle spices and fro scharpe thinges, as from garlik, from oynouns . . . and fro leccherie and fro alle excessyf hete."[162] Garlic, leeks, and onions were widely regarded as aphrodisiacs which promote lechery. The Summoner's inordinate fondness for them to the detriment of his health recalls the backsliding Hebrews of Numbers 11.5, who look back wistfully to the foods they had enjoyed in Egypt.[163] The physiognomies also take notice of the facial features that mar the Summoner's appearance. The Ashmole version of *Secreta Secretorum* takes a fiery-red face as evidence that one is "vnstable and suffreth manyacy." Swollen eyelids are also meaningful: "The lidde, and þat þat sheweth, and þat þat lieth undre the eye, more swollen þan full aboue, sheweth vpon þe slomeryssh man and a violent."[164] When the narrator says the Summoner is "saucefleem" or "salt plegm," he refers to a condition resulting from an unnatural mixture of phlegm and yellow choler and characterized by an excess of heat which is not helped by his diet.[165]

160 See Curry, pp. 41–4, 45–6, and B. L. Grigsby, *Pestilence in Medieval and Early Modern English Literature* (New York and London, 2004), pp. 85–8. G. B. Pace, "Physiognomy and Chaucer's Summoner and Alison," *Traditio* 18 (1962): 418, cites John Metham's *Physiognomy*: "Blake browys, thei sygnyfye gret dysposycion to lechery." Jordan of Turre, as quoted in *A Source Book on Medieval Science*, ed. E. Grant (Cambridge, 1974), pp. 154–5, describes the symptoms of leprosy as thin, fine hair, lumpiness of skin on the head, and lack of hair on the eyebrows.

161 Bartholomaeus Anglicus, *De Proprietatibus Rerum* (Frankfurt, 1601), Book 7, chapter 64, p. 354; *On the Properties of Things: John Trevisa's Translation of Bartholomaeus Anglicus, De Proprietatibus Rerum*, vol. 1 (Oxford, 1975), p. 426. Gilbertus Anglicus asserts that leprosy is brought on by melancholic foods such as strong wine and garlic (Grant, p. 754); *Lanfranks Science of Cirurgie*, pp. 190–1 and notes. Pauline Aiken, "The Summoner's Malady," *Studies in Philology* 3 (1936): 40–4, attributes the source of Chaucer's description of the disease to Vincent of Beauvais' account (*Speculum Doctrinale*, 15: 33–4) of the symptoms of scabies from an excess of salt phlegm.

162 *Cyrurgie of Guy de Chauliac*, pp. 435–6.

163 R. E. Kaske, "The Summoner's Garleek, Onyons, and eek Lekes," *Modern Language Notes* 74 (1959): 481–4. The text was interpreted as a sign of spiritual depravity among worldly clerics, as in *Vox Clamantis*, Book 3 , chapter 2, lines 85–8. C. C. Wood, "The Source of Chaucer's Summoner's 'Garleek, Onyons, and eek Lekes,'" *Chaucer Review* 5 (1971): 240–6, notes that Gower was indebted for these lines to Peter Riga's *Aurora*, a work which Chaucer also knew and used in the *Book of the Duchess*.

164 *Secretum Secretorum*, ed. Manzalaoui, pp. 91, 95.

165 L. Braswell-Means, "A New Look at an Old Patient: Chaucer's Summoner and Medieval Physiognomia," *Chaucer Review* 25 (1991): 271. An anonymous Middle English poem, "Of the iiij Complexions," describes the traits of the choleric that are also applicable to the Summoner. See *Cambridge Middle English Lyrics*, ed. H. A. Person (New York, 1969), p. 51, lines 21–7.

The Summoner's bouts of drunkenness which end in his spouting Latin legal jargon like a jay (636–43) have been likened to satirical accounts of birds trained to speak volubly but incomprehensively.[166]

Satirists criticized consistory courts and their officials for their hypocrisy, corruption, and intimidating behavior, especially toward the poor. *The Simonie* deplores their venality and acceptance of bribes, and the poem, *A Satire on the Consistory Courts*, bitterly expresses its hatred of court officials, especially summoners who make false accusations (mysmotinde) and exact payment through trickery (colle) in each parish.[167]

Langland (B.II, III, IV) directs a scathing attack against summoners who attend the marriage of Lady Meed, praise her profusely, and remain her loyal followers:

169	Ac þanne swoor* Symonye and Cyuylle boþe	swore
	That somonours sholde be sadeled* and seruen hem echone.	saddled
	'And late* apparaille þe prouisours in palfreyes wise*;	let/ like horses
	Sire Symonye hymself shal sitte vpon hir bakkes.	
173	Denes* and souþdenes,* draw yow togideres;	Deans/ sub-deans
	Erchedekenes* and officials* and alle youre registrers*,	Archdeacons/ presiding officers/ registrars
	Lat sadle* hem wiþ siluer oure synne to suffre* –	be saddled/ permit
	As deuoutrye* and diuorses* and derne* usurie –	adultery/ annulments/ clandestine
177	To bere bisshopes aboute abrood* in visitynge.' (B.II)	abroad
134	'Sisours and somonours, swiche men hire preiseþ*,	prize, value
	Sherreues of shires were shent* if she nere –	would be ruined
	For she dooþ* men lese* hire lond and hire lif boþe.	makes/ lose
	She leteþ passe* prisoners and paieþ* for hem ofte,	go free/ pays
	And gyueþ þe gailers gold and grotes togidres	
139	To vnfettre þe Fals – fle* where hym likeþ*;	flee/ pleases
	And takeþ Trewþe bi þe top* and tieþ hym faste*,	hair/ firmly
	And hangeþ hym for hatrede þat harm[e]de* neuere.	did harm
	To be cursed* in consistorie she counteþ noȝt a russhe,*	condemned/ "cares nothing"
	For she copeþ* the commissarie and coteþ* his clerkes.	provides copes for/ provides coats for
144	She is assoiled* as soone as hireself likeþ.' (B.III)	absolved

[166] Mann, pp. 142–3 and notes 76–8, particularly the citations of *The Simonie*, *Wynnere and Wastoure*, and *Matheolus*. Chaucer may have recalled a passage from the *Apocalypsis Goliae Episcopi*, perhaps the single most popular satire of the Middle Ages, employing the image of birds to ridicule the chatter of intoxicated monks: "Quisque de monacho fit demoniacus, et cuique monacho congarrit monachus/ ut pica picae ut psittaco psittacus, cui dat ingenium magister stomacus." ["Each is transformed from a monk to a demon, each jabbers at the other, like a magpie to a magpie or a parrot to a parrot, with a wit provided by their master the stomach."] *The Latin Poems commonly attributed to Walter Mapes*, p. 18, lines 381–4. The idea of speaking Latin when intoxicated was proverbial. See H. B. Hinckley, "Chauceriana. The Canterbury Tales," *Modern Philology* 14 (1916): 317, and *Mirour*, lines 8149–52.

[167] Bowden, pp. 269–72; Mann, pp. 139–41; L. A. Haselmayer, "The Apparitor and Chaucer's Summoner," *Speculum* 12 (1937): 54–6; *The Simonie*, p. 68, lines 49–53; *Historical Poems of the XIVth and XVth Centuries*, ed. R. H. Robbins (New York, 1959), p. 26, lines 37–42. Gower also inveighs against court officials who "put sins on sale" in *Mirour de l'Omme*, lines 20091–109. The *Speculum Vitae*, written by William Nassington about 1384, accuses sommoners and beadles of rapine, the third branch of avarice: "Sompnoures and bedilles þat beþ mynistres to þis lawe, þat procureþ to do men be accused & in oþer wyses greueþ men by colour of her offices to have of her good, & so robbeth þe peple." *A Myrour to Lewde Men and Wymmen: A prose version of the Speculum Vitae*, ed. V. Nelson (Heidelberg, 1981), p. 135.

Mede mornede* þo*, and made heuy chere, grieved/ then
166 For þe mooste commune of þat court called hire an hore*. whore
Ac a sisour and a somonour sued* her faste*. (B.IV) attended on/ closely

Chaucer's Summoner is similarly a client of Lady Meed, as open to bribes as any official of the ecclesiastical court, and for a small consideration he will overlook charges of sexual misconduct (649–51). Like Lady Meed, he is dismissive of the archdeacon's curse, and he is prepared to teach "a good felawe" to disregard it provided he empties his purse (653–9). His crude reference in "Purs is the ercedekenes helle," may have been taken from Gower's fierce criticism of the malpractice of deans in the *Mirour de l'Omme* (lines 20197–9), an image Gower reused in his comments on corrupt priests in the *Vox Clamantis* (Book 3, chapter 3, lines 191–4).

Langland emphasizes the simoniacal character of the summoner's activities, but Chaucer deals with the subject indirectly by afflicting his Summoner with leprosy, which had a symbolic association with simony going back to the biblical account of Gehazi (4 Kings 5.20–7). Wyclif made use of this tradition in his *Tractatus de Simonia*:

> Lepra, inquam, secundum sanctos signat mistice symonem, quia sicut nullus morbus est isto infectivior, ad solvendam continuitatem et formam deformancior, vel ad cohabitandum ex fetore vel voce horribilior, sic est heresis symoniaca.[168]
>
> [The leper, I say, according to the sacred writers allegorically signifies Simon [Acts 8.9–24], for just as no disease is more infectious than it, more destructive, and more disfiguring of lasting beauty, or more horrible to live with by virtue of its stench and sound, so is the heresy of simony.]

The Summoner's portrait recalls the character of False Seeming in the *Roman de la Rose*, who, together with other servants of Antichrist, performs the functions in part of a summoner and in part of an inquisitor among the many roles he assumes as a shape-shifting and hypocritical friar. And the accused must defend himself with a bribe of wine and food, precisely the sort of bribe which would appeal to the Summoner with his voracious appetite and his willingness to overlook a sexual transgression for a "quart of wyn":

11723 S'il i a chastel ne cité
Ou bougre seient recité,
Neïs s'il ierent de Melan,
Car ausinc les en blasme l'en,
Ou se nus on outre mesure
11728 Vent a terme ou preste a usure,
Tant est d' aquerre curieus,
Ou s'il est trop luxurieus,
Ou lierres ou symoniaus,

[168] John Wyclif, *Tractatus de Simonia*, ed. Herzberg-Frankel and M. H. Dziewicki (London, 1898), p. 61. See also T. A. McVeigh, "Chaucer's Portraits of the Pardoner and Summoner and Wyclif's *Tractatus de Simonia*," *Classical Folia* 29 (1975): 54–8. On the traditional association of Gehazi with leprosy and simony, see R. K. Emmerson and R. B. Herzman, *The Apocalyptic Imagination in Medieval Literature* (Philadelphia, 1992), pp. 177–81.

Seit prevoz, seit oficiaus,
11733 Ou prelaz de jolie vie,
Ou prestres qui tiegne s' amie,
Ou vieilles putains ostelieres,
Ou maquerel, ou bordelieres,
Ou repris de quelconques vice
11738 Don l'en deie faire joustice;
Par trestouz les sainz que l'en preie!
S'il ne se defent de lampreie,
De luz, de saumon ou d'anguile,
S' en le peut trouver en la vile,
Ou de tartes, ou de flaons,
11744 Ou de fourmages en glaons,
. . .
11752 Il avra de corde une longe
A quei l'en le menra bruler,
. . .
11756 Ou sera pris e mis en tour
. . .
11759 Ou sera puniz dou mesfait,
Plus, espeir, qu'il n'avra mesfait.
. . .
11767 Mais qu'il eüst laienz assez
Des biens temporeus amassez,
. . .
11775 E gitast en granz mangoneaus
Vins en bariz ou en toneaus,
Ou granz sas de centaine livre,
11778 Tost se pourrait voeir delivre.

[If heretics are reported in any castle or city, even if they come from Milan, for the Milanese also are tainted with this heresy; if anyone is so anxious for gain that he makes unreasonable terms when selling on credit or lending at interest; if anyone, even a provost or official, is also a lecher, a thief or a simonist, a jolly living prelate, a priest who keeps a mistress, an old whore who has a house, a pimp or a brothelkeeper, or charged with some other vice for which he should be brought before the courts, then, by all the saints we pray to, unless he defend himself with lamprey, pike, salmon, or eel (if they can be found in the town), with tarts, flans, cheeses in their trays . . . he will be tethered with a rope and led off to be burned . . . or else he will be captured and imprisoned in a tower . . . or else, perhaps, he will be punished more severely for his crime than he deserves. . . . Provided that he had amassed there enough of his world's goods . . . provided he used great mangonals to hurl wine in barrels and casks and huge sacks containing a hundred pounds, he would soon find himself free. (Horgan, p. 181)]

The Summoner appears on the pilgrimage crowned with a garland of flowers and bearing a loaf of bread or cake in the form of a shield. The former is perhaps a mock parody of the chaplet of flowers the lover is advised to wear in the *Roman de la Rose* (2161–3), and the intention of this detail may be to introduce the relationship of the Summoner and the Pardoner. They sing a love duet, and the Summoner's accompaniment of the Pardoner with a "stif burdoun" (673)

has been seen as a sexual pun also derived ftom the *Roman de la Rose* (21353–6): "E port o mei, par grant effort,/ Escharpe e bourdon reide e fort/ Tel qu'il n'a mestier de ferrer/ Pour journeier ne pour errer." ["I had laboriously brought with me my scrip and my staff that was so stiff and strong that it needed no ferule when going on journeys."][169] Within the portrait there are suggestions of the Summoner's sexual impropriety; the threefold repetition of the term "purse" (656–8) is one such, and the line, "Ful prively a finch eek koude he pulle" (652), which connotes illicit sexual intercourse in other literary uses of the phrase and perhaps also hints at his relationship with the Pardoner.[170]

The Pardoner

The Pardoner sells indulgences (which he claims to have brought "al hoot from Rome," 671, 687) on behalf of his sponsor the charity Hospital of St Mary Roncevall. They are of doubtful authenticity. He is a shameless scoundrel, employing sham relics and the opportunities afforded by the pulpit to defraud ignorant rustics and their parsons (692–706).

Piers Plowman has several references to dishonest pardoners. The description in the *Prologue* of a false pardoner who colludes with a parish priest to share the proceeds of his preaching may have influenced Chaucer's portrait. Both pardoners are highly successful preachers, but Chaucer's parish priest, unlike Langland's, is no party to the Pardoner's deception: he is as much the Pardoner's dupe as his parishioners:

þere prechide a pardoner as* he a prest were:	as if
Brouȝte forþ a bulle* wiþ bisshopis selis*,	bull(papal edict)/ seals
And seide þat hymself miȝte assoile hem alle	
Of falsnesse of fastyng*, of auowes* broken.	breaches of fasting/ vows
Lewide* men leuide* hym wel and likide his wordis;	ignorant/ believed
Comen up knelynge to kissen his bulle.	
He bunchide* hem wiþ his breuet* and bleride here eiȝen*,	tapped/ letter of indulgence/ blinded their eyes
And rauȝte* wiþ his rageman* ryngis and brochis*.	got/ legal document (bull)/ brooches
þus ȝe gyven ȝoure gold glotonis to helpe,	
And leniþ* it loselis þat leccherie haunten!*	bestow on/ indulge in
Were þe bisshop yblissid* and worþ* boþe hise eris*,	holy/ worth/ ears
His sel* shulde not be sent to disseyve þe peple.	seal

[169] Horgan, p. 329. See also Hodges, pp. 148–50; B. D. H. Miller, "Chaucer's General Prologue, A 673: Further Evidence," *Notes and Queries* 205 (1960): 404–6; P. F. Baum, "Chaucer's Puns," *PMLA* 71 (1956): 232. Line 672 may contain an echo of Canticles 2:10, 4:7–8.

[170] A. C. Cawley, "Chaucer's Summoner, the Friar's Summoner, and the Friar's Tale," *Proceedings of the Leeds Philosophical and Literary Society* 8 (1957): 173–4; G. L. Kittredge, "Chauceriana," *Modern Philology* 7 (1910): 475–7. The grotesque shield may reflect the Summoner's desperate search for a cure to his disease. G. A. Renn, "Chaucer's Canterbury Tales," *Explicator* 43 (1985): 8–9, has suggested that the bread parodies the folk belief in the efficacy of the consecrated host for relieving ailments. John Fleming ("Chaucer and the Visual Arts of his Time," *New Perspectives in Chaucer Criticism*, ed. D. M. Rose [Norman, OK, 1981], p. 135) believes that Chaucer adapted the image from the "alimentary weapons" used to bribe summoners in the *Roman* (see above, lines 11739ff). On the use of the terms *burdoun, fynche, privily and purse*, see Myles, pp. 125–6.

It is not be* þe bisshop þat þe boy* prechiþ – by the leave of/ rogue
Ac þe parissh prest and þe pardoner parte* þe silver divide
þat þe pore peple of þe parissh shulde have ȝif þei ne were.* if it were not for them
(A Pr.)

A second pardoner called Piers witnesses Lady Meed's wedding contract (A.II.73), and a third joins the pilgrimage to truth in the B-text: "'Bi Seint Poul!' quod a pardoner, 'paraventure I be noȝt knowe þere; I wol go fecche my box wiþ my breuettes and a bulle with bisshopes lettres.'" (V.639–40). What all three have in common with Chaucer's Pardoner is their desire for gain.

The clerical use of false relics is a familiar topic of medieval satire.[171] The association of pardoners with false relics is made, possibly for the first time, in the *Fasciculus Morum,* a widely read Latin handbook for preachers written by an anonymous English Franciscan in the early fourteenth-century. Pardoners here are compared to the faithful who attempt to conceal their sins. The false relics are said to be "bones from a farm animal" which Chaucer could easily have converted to "pigges bones":

> Est ergo sciendum quod tales sic peccata sua palliantes assimilantur istis falsis quaestionariis qui ostendendo reliquias suas ostendunt illas in aliquo vase deaurato et lapidibus preciosis perornato, ac eciam in pannis aureis et cericis involutas, ut saltem sic preciose appareant hominibus. Que tamen, ut frequenter, si detegerentur aperte, non invenies nisi ossa alicuius iumenti de fovea extracta, fetida et arida ac omni abhominacione digna.
>
> [We should thus know that people who veil their sins in this fashion are like these false pardoners, who show their relics in some golden vessel that is decorated with precious gems, or else wrapped in cloths of gold and silk, so that they may look truly precious before the people. But as it often happens, when they open them up, you will find nothing but the bones from a farm animal that have been pulled out of a ditch, stinking and dried up and worthy of every abomination.][172]

Perhaps the closest analogue to Chaucer's account of the professional activities of the Pardoner is to be found in the *Memoriale Presbiterorum*. Here, too, pardoners collect for hospitals, cheat both the clergy and the people, and exhibit a religious object – in both cases, a cross (possibly a fake reliquary) – to elicit alms:

> Questores dicuntur a quaerendo, eo quod mittuntur ad querendum elemosinas fidelium in usus hospitalium et miserabilium personarum degencium in eisdem. . . . Et isti questores plerumque varia bona per dolum et fraudem, animos audiencium et sibi bona conferencium, subsidia caritatis, excaecando, illicite adquirunt. Quidam autem ipsorum veri sunt nuncii locorum a quibus

[171] Mann, pp. 150–2; Bowden, pp. 279–80.

[172] *Fasciculus Morum: A Fourteenth-Century Preacher's Handbook*, ed. and trans. S. Wenzel (University Park, PA, and London, 1989), pp. 476–7. Another Franciscan canonist Hugo de Novocastro (fl. c. 1320) protested against the use of false relics by pardoners. See T. P. Dunning, *Piers Plowman: An Interpretation of the A Text*, rev. and ed. T. P. Dolan (Oxford, 1980), p. 18. Passing references to pardoners with false relics are found in *Middle English Sermons*, p. 125, and *English Works of Wyclif*, p. 154. See also A. L. Kellogg and L. A. Haselmayer, "Chaucer's Satire of the Pardoner," *PMLA* 66 (1951): 275 n. 149. Lines 696–8 refer to Matt. 14:29–31.

mittuntur, habentes veras literas, tam apostolicas quam aliorum ordinariorum, certas et veras indulgencias continentes. Et istorum quidam multociens fraudem in officio suo committunt. Ecce enim quod quandoque non solvunt hospitalibus vel aliis locis quorum sunt nuncii partem vicesimam elemosinarum et bonorum, ad opus eorundem collectorum. Set ipsa consumunt expendendo voluptuose, luxoriose viventes, et inhonestam ac suspectam familiam nonnunquam secum ducunt. . . . Quidam autem questores sunt funditus falsi, quia nec mittuntur ab aliquo, nec auctoritatem habent elemosinas querendi, Ecce enim quod tales fingunt se habere litteras tam apostolicas quam alias certas litteras, indulgencias continentes, que omnino sunt falsae tam in dictamine quam in sigillis. Habent enim scriptores ad vota qui scribunt literas falsas sub nominibus ordinariorum qui indulgencias de iure concedere possunt, et multociens fabricant sigilla falsa et adulterina, quibus questores tamquam falsarii palam utuntur, et sic decipiendo et circumveniendo tam clericos quam laicos, multa bona sibi fallaciter adquirunt. . . . Quidam autem sunt questores . . . exponunt populo ostensa cruce, syndone velata, multas indulgencias falsas, mendacia varia predicando, et sic collectis elemosinis, bona intencione sibi collatis, conferentes fallaciter decipiunt.[173]

[Questors [pardoners] are so called from seeking (quaerendo) because they are sent to seek the alms of the faithful for the support of hospitals and their wretched patients. . . . They often illicitly acquire goods of various kinds by guile and fraud, blinding the minds of those who attend them and who contribute the goods and aids of charity to them. Some of them actually represent the houses which send them out and have trustworthy credentials, apostolic as well as of other ordinaries, containing genuine and true indulgences. Yet some of them too frequently commit fraud through their office. For behold! sometimes they do not remit to the hospitals or other places that sent them even the twentieth part of the alms and goods they have received for the support of these same agencies. Rather they consume them themselves, spending on sensual pleasures and living licentiously, and they sometimes conduct with them a dishonorable and suspect company. . . . Some questors, however, are utterly false because they have not been sent by anyone, nor have they the authority to seek alms. For behold! they arrange to have in their possession apostolic and other [supposedly] trustworthy credentials, containing indulgences which are completely false both in their composition and seals. For they have scribes at their service who write out false credentials in the names of ordinaries who can lawfully assent to indulgences and very often they fabricate false and counterfeit seals which questors, like forgers, use openly, and thus, deceiving and defrauding both clerics and laymen, falsely acquire many goods for themselves. There are some questors [who], holding up a cross wrapped in a corporal cloth, offer the people many false indulgences, preaching various lies, and thus, with the alms collected, which have been bestowed on them with good intentions, they falsely deceive the donors.]

Chaucer and Langland portray their pardoners as lechers. Chaucer's has the glaring eyes of a hare (684) and the thin voice of a goat (688), both symbols of

[173] Haren, "A Study," Part 2, pp. 263–5, and *Sin and Society*, pp. 174–7. The *Memoriale* was written in 1344 by William Doune. On the Pardoner as a simoniac see L. Patterson, "Chaucer's Pardoner on the Couch: Psyche and Clio in Medieval Literary Studies," *Speculum* 76 (2001): 664–6.

lust.[174] Although his sexual orientation is still an open question, the details of his physical appearance – long, fine hair, high voice, beardlessness – suggest effeminacy widely regarded as a consequence of licentiousness. Richard Firth Green illustrates the putative connection between lechery and effeminacy from the exemplary legends of Samson, Mars, Paris, and Sardanapalus. Vincent of Beauvais writes of Sardanapalus:

> Qualiter autem luxuria emolliat, et resolvat animum virilem et regimen, patet per Sardanapalum. . . . Hic inter mulieres conversabatur omni muliere mollior, in operibus muliebribus gestu et habitu.
>
> [Now how lechery softens and relaxes a manly spirit and discipline is shown by Sardanapalus. . . . This man from being amongst women became softer then any woman and was converted to female ways of acting and dressing.][175]

The physiognomists provide additional testimony to this idea. James Yonge warns that "The foly company of women destrueth the body. . . . And doghty men and hardy hit makyth lyke women." Johannes de Caritate advises that, "oftyn carnal comyxtyon is destrucion of þe body and schortyng of þe lyfe. . . . and it gendryth womannys condycionys."[176] Their comments on physical details confirm these observations. According to *The Governaunce of Prynces*, a man with a high, small voice has "lytill of manhode, and i-likenyd to women"; in the Ashmole version, soft, thin hair "sheweth womans witte," but it has still deeper significance, shedding light on other aspects of the Pardoner's character: "The thynner þe heeres ben, the more gileful, sharp, ferefull, and of wynnyng covetous, it sheweth."[177]

Explanation and Apology (715–46)

Following the portraits, the poet-pilgrim offers a long apology for the unseemly language his audience is about to hear. His exculpatory explanation is that he is obliged as a true reporter to maintain authenticity despite the breach of social decorum (731–9), and he appeals to the combined authority of Christ and Plato for the right to do so. "Crist spak hymself ful brode in hooly writ/ And wel ye woot no vileynye is it./ Eek Plato seith, whoso kan hym rede,/ The wordes moote be cosyn to the dede." (739–42). Here Chaucer casts the narrator in the distinctive literary role of a *compilator* who bears no responsibility for the content of his work, merely functioning as a reporter of what others have said or

174 B. Rowland, *Animals with Human Faces* (Knoxville, TN, 1973), pp. 80–6, 91–2, and "Animal Imagery and the Pardoner's Abnormality," *Neophilologus* 48 (1964): 57–8. E. C. Schweitzer, Jr., "Chaucer's Pardoner and the Hare," *English Language Notes* 4 (1967): 247–50, detects an echo of Terence's *Eunuchus* III.1.35–6 with its possible suggestion of sexual abnormality.

175 R. F. Green, "The Sexual Normality of Chaucer's Pardoner," *Mediaevalia* 8 (1985 for 1982): 355, 358 n. 18. The quotation from Vincent of Beauvais is from the *Speculum Morale*, III.3.9.

176 *Secreta Secretorum*, ed. Steele, p. 139; *Secretum Secretorum*, ed. Manzalaoui, p. 135.

177 *Secreta Secretorum*, ed. Steele, pp. 231; *Secretum Secretorum*, ed. Manzalaoui, p. 92. Mann (pp. 147–8) traces the details of the Pardoner's carefully combed hair and smooth face to the satiric tradition on foppery. In *The Simonie* (p. 86, line 279), a squire rides with his hood off, like the Pardoner. Cf. also Bowden, pp. 275–6.

done, adding little or nothing to his sources.[178] Disclaiming authorship in the guise of his first-person narrator shields Chaucer from the charge of "vileynye" (726) while at the same time reinforcing his literary autonomy. Boccacio resorts to a similar strategy in the *Decameron.* In an effort to shift moral responsibility from himself to his fictional characters, he claims that as a transcriber of their stories he could not have written otherwise: "Ma io non pote' né doveva scrivere se non le raccontate." ["But I could not and should not have written them if they [the ladies] had not recounted them."][179]

Chaucer's apology has been strongly influenced by Jean de Meun's defense against the charge of obscenity:

Si vous pris, seigneur amoureus,
Par les jeus d'Amours savoreus,
Que, se vous i trouvez paroles
Semblanz trop baudes ou trop foles,
Par quei saillent li mesdisant,
Qui de nous aillent mesdisant,
Des choses a dire ou des dites,
Que courteisement les desdites;
E quant vous les avreiz des diz
Repris, retardez ou desdiz,
Se mi dit sont de tel maniere
Qu'il seit dreiz que pardon en quiere,
Pri vous que le me pardoigniez,
E de par mei leur respoigniez
Que ce requerait la matire,
Qui vers teus paroles me tire
Par les proprietez de sei;
Et pour ce teus paroles ai;
Car chose est dreituriere e juste,
Selonc l'auctorité Saluste,
Qui nous dit par sentence voire:
"Tout ne seit il semblable gloire
De celui qui la chose fait
Et de l'escrivain qui le fait
Veaut metre proprement en livre,
Pour meauz la verité descrivre,
Si n'est ce pas chose legiere
Ainz est mout fort de grant maniere,
Metre bien les faiz en escrit;
Car, quiconques la chose escrit,
Se dou veir ne vous veaut embler,
Li diz deit le fait resembler;
Car les voiz aus choses veisines
Deivent estre a leur faiz cousines."
Si me couvient ainsinc paler,
Se par le dreit m'en vueil aler.

178 A. J. Minnis, *Medieval Theory of Authorship*, 2nd edn (Philadelphia, 1984), pp. 94–117, 191–210.
179 *Decameron*, *Conclusione*, p. 719.

[I beg you, sir lovers, by the delectable games of love, that if you find any words that seem to be too bold or shameless, such as will make the scandalmongers leap to their feet and criticize the things we have said or are about to say, you will courteously contradict them. And when you have rebuked them for what they say, or stopped or contradicted them, if my words are such that I should ask pardon for them, I beg you to pardon me and to reply on my behalf that they were called for by my subject, whose intrinsic properties drew me to such language; that is why I use these words. And this is quite right, and in accordance with the authority of Sallust, who gives it as his true opinion that "although glory is not equally divided between the man who does something and the writer who tries to find an appropriate way of putting the deed into a book, so as to describe it as accurately as possible, nevertheless it is not easy, but on the contrary extremely difficult, to give a good written account of deeds. Whoever does the writing, if he is not to deprive us of the truth, his words must echo the deed, for when words rub shoulders with things, they should be cousins of the deeds." And so I must speak in this way if I want to proceed correctly. (Horgan, pp. 234–5)]

Chaucer alters the passage, dropping the quotation from Sallust's *Bellum Catilinae* and substituting references to Christ and Plato. The dictum attributed to Plato in line 742 *(RR* 15191–2) is taken from the *Consolation of Philosophy* (3 Pr. 12, lines 11–12). The allusion to Christ (739–40) refers to the plain and forthright speech of the parables.[180] Although the juxtaposition of Christ and Plato does not appear in the *Roman de la Rose*, it may well have been influenced by the appeal to the authority of God and Plato in Reason's disquisition on the propriety of her use of "unglossed" language for the male genitalia:

7078 Par son gré sui je coustumiere
De parler proprement des choses
Quant il me plaist, sanz metre gloses.
E quant me reveauz oposer,
7082 Tu, qui me requiers de gloser.
Veauz oposer! Anceis m'oposes
Que, tout ait Deus faites les choses,
Au meins ne fist il pas le non,
7086 Ci te respon: espeir, que non,
Au meins celui qu'eles ont ores;
. . .
7091 Mais il vost que nons leur trouvasse
A mon plaisir e les nomasse
Proprement e comunement,
Pour creistre nostre entendement;
7095 Et la parole me dona
Ou mout trés precieus don a.
Et ce que ci t'ai recité
Peuz trouver en auctorité,
Car Platons lisait en s'escole

[180] Sallust, *Bellum Catilinae*, trans. J. C. Rolfe (Cambridge, 1995), III, p. 6: "Festa dictis exaequanda sunt." For a discussion of the sources of this paragraph see P. B. Taylor, "Chaucer's *Cosyn to the Dede*," *Speculum* 57 (1982): 315–27. The biblical allusion is perhaps to Matt. 13: 10–13.

Que donee nous fu parole
Pour faire noz vouleirs entendre,
Pour enseignier e pour aprendre.
Cete sentence ci rimee
Trouveras escrite en Timee
De Platon, qui ne fu pas nices.

[It is by his (God's) will that I am accustomed to call things by their names when I want to, without glossing them. And when in your turn you wish to raise an objection and require me to supply a gloss – raise an objection do I say? – rather you do in fact object that although God made things, at least he did not make their names – this is my reply: perhaps he did not, or at least not the names they now have . . . but he wanted me to find proper and common names for them as it pleased me, in order to increase our understanding, and he gave me speech, a most precious gift. And you may find authority for what I have told you, for Plato taught in his school that speech was given to us to make our wishes understood, to teach, and to learn. You will find this idea, here expressed in verse, in the *Timaeus* of Plato, who was not stupid. (Horgan, p. 108)]

A. J. Minnis relates Reason's argument to the late scholastic distinction between "proper" and "improper" speech, the former literal and direct, the latter figurative and oblique.[181] The coupling of Christ and Plato is interpreted as a reflection of the larger tradition of 'classicising' Scriptural exegesis in fourteenth-century England:

Quite apart from the theology, these 'classicising' commentaries [Holcot on Wisdom and Ecclesiastes, Lathbury on Lamentations, and Ringstead on Proverbs] were of interest to practicing poets because they contained many extracts from pagan writers, both philosophers and poets. . . . The 'classicising' commentaries are major repositories of scholastic literary theory. To obtain examples of this theory in practice, Chaucer and his contemporaries need have read no further than the prologues. In the prologues and in the commentaries themselves, they would have found *auctoritates* being employed in the elucidation of pre-Christian ideas and mores, and the expertise of pagan sages constantly being drawn on in the interests of Christian learning. These are aspects of a general 'coming together' of sacred and profane auctores in the minds and treatises of late-medieval academics.[182]

For his failure to rank the pilgrims in their proper social order, the narrator offers a second apology in the form of a modesty-topos, a familiar rhetorical device to win the sympathy of the audience (743–6). Ernst Curtius cites many different formulas of self-disparagement from Cicero onwards. Chaucer's statement bears a resemblance to that of Bernard Silvestris in *De Mundi Universitate*: "Siquidem de mundi universitate tractatus suapte natura difficilis, sed et *sensu tardiore* conpositus, sicut aures sic oculos arguti iudicis reformidat." [Since a treatise on the whole universe is in and of itself difficult –

181 A. Minnis, *Magister Amoris* (Oxford, 2001), pp. 19–40. For the relevant documents see *Medieval Literary Theory and Criticism c.1100–c.1375*, ed. A. J. Minnis and A. B. Scott, rev. edn (Oxford, 1991), pp. 205–6, 212–13, 239–43, 250–66.

182 Minnis, *Medieval Theory*, pp. 165–6.

and this the work of a *slow wit* – it fears to be seen and heard by a perceptive judge.][183]

For E. T. Donaldson the persona of the pilgrim-poet, viewed in a larger perspective, belongs:

> to a very old – and very new – tradition of the fallible first person singular. . . . In his own century he is related to Long Will of *Piers Plowman,* a more explicit seeker after the good, but just as unswerving in his inability correctly to evaluate what he sees. Another kinsman is the protagonist of the *Pearl,* mankind whose heart is set on a transitory good that has been lost – who, for very natural reasons, confuses earthly with spiritual values. Not entirely unrelated is the protagonist of Gower's *Confessio amantis*, an old man seeking for an impossible earthly love that seems to him the only good. And in more subtle fashion there is the teller of Chaucer's story of *Troilus and Cressida*, who while not a true protagonist, performs some of the same functions . . . Finally, of course, there is Dante of the Divine Comedy, the most exalted member of the family and perhaps the immediate original of these other first person pilgrims.[184]

The Host and his Proposal (747–821)

The narrative resumes with the introduction of a jovial host (later named Herry Bailly, I, 4358), a shrewd innkeeper who knows how to please his guests with cheerful hospitality, fine food, and strong wine (747–50). His portrait in the first instance is drawn after the idealized stereotype of "taverners, hostelers, and sellars of vitaylle" depicted in the *Chessbook*:

> Hit apperteyneth to them for to seke and enquyre for good wyns and good vitayll for to gyve and selle to the byers and to them that they herberowe. . . . The hostelers ought to be well bespoken and courtoys of wordes to them that they receyue in to their loggynge. For fayr speche & Ioyous chiere & debonayr cause men to gyve the hostelyer a good name.[185]

The *Summa Praedicantium* by John Bromyard pictures innkeepers in rather more vivid and realistic terms. Like the Host they are courteous and sociable, but with an eye to profit:

> Illi enim hospitiarii in multis partibus hilariter occurrunt peregrinis, et eos ad hospitia sua diligenter invitant et trahunt, et multa eis delicata promittunt.

[183] Curtius, pp. 83–5. Bernardus Silvestris, *De Mundi Universitate*, ed. C. S. Barack and J. Wrobel (Frankfurt, 1964), p. 5. For additional instances of the modesty formula see M. Stevens, "The Performing Self in Twelfth-Century Culture," *Viator* 9 (1978): 198–202. See also Cicero, *De Academicis* 1.8.31: "sensus omnes hebetes et tardos," and Terence, *Heauton Timorumenos* 4.5.28: "tardus es." Lawrence Minot's unadorned expression of modesty is also reminiscent of Chaucer: "Help me, God, my wit es thin," *The Poems of Laurence Minot 1333–1352*, ed. R. H. Osberg (Kalamazoo, MI, 1996), no. 7, p. 51, line 19.

[184] E. T. Donaldson, *Speaking of Chaucer* (New York, 1970), pp. 8–9.

[185] *Game and Playe of the Chesse*, Book 3, chapter 6, pp. 129, 133; Jehan de Vignay, *Le Jeu*, chapter 14, pp. 251, 255. The stereotype appears to originate with John of Salisbury's *Entheticus*, pp. 204–5, lines 1543–6.

> Pulchre loquuntur, comedentes et bibentes, ridentes et ludentes cum eis usque veniatur ad computum, in quo aliqui illorum nihil dimittunt quod habere possunt.[186]

A Middle English homilist rendered the passage as follows:

> We see well that osteleres in many places thei will renne gladdely aȝeyns pilgryms to prey hem to com to ther Innes, and draweth hem by the honde, and behoteth hem many delycate thinges. Fayre thei speke with hem, and eteth and drynketh with hem, and lawyȝth and makes gret chere, unto that thei shall come to acounte, in the wiche acounte thei will nowthe forȝeve. . . .[187]

The Host is a large man with prominent eyes ("eyen stepe"), an assertive manner, and a domineering personality. His physical attributes are those of quasi-heroic figures such as Seraphe in the *History of the Holy Grail* – "a large man . . . with grete stepe eyen" – and Achilles in the *Gest Historiale of the Destruction of Troy* – "a large man" with "ene out stepe."[188] The narrator is impressed by his imposing presence and hospitality despite his overbearing nature and elevates his professional status, deeming him suited to occupy the prestigious office of marshall (751–7).

In addition to didactic and homiletic traditions, the portrait draws on the character of Deduit, the lord of the garden and the master of revels, in the *Roman de la Rose*. Deduit is called "Sir Myrthe" in Fragment A (733) of the *Romaunt of the Rose*, the English translation attributed to Chaucer. The Host is conspicuously merry, and the words *myrthe*, *myrie*, *chiere*, *pleye(n)*, *confort*, *ese*, and *disport* occur fourteen times in the description of him and his first address to the pilgrims (747–83). Peter Brown notes how much he and Mirth have in common:

> In their different spheres, they are presiding spirits; each promotes in his own way the comforting and solacing virtues of communal recreation; both have a commanding presence and a controlling function in relation to their immediate social group; each is inventive or innovative: Mirth in building the garden and encouraging its festivities and rituals, Harry Bailly in deploying the arts of hospitality and in devising the story-telling game.[189]

The game the Host devises takes the form of a contest calling for each of the pilgrims to tell two stories on the way to Canterbury and two on the way back. He proposes to accompany them as a guide and to conduct and judge the contest, the winner to receive a free supper at the Tabard Inn at the expense of the company. The game is intended to divert the pilgrims on their journey, but in monetary terms it works entirely to the advantage of the Host (790–806). Helen Cooper attributes the source of the Host's proposal to the practice of the

[186] Owst, pp. 31–2 n. 3. The passage is based on "Hospes Erat" by the Goliardic poet Hugh Primas (*The Golardic Poets*, pp. 76–9).

[187] *Ibid.*, p. 31, and *Middle English Sermons*, p. 85, lines 26–9. For further attacks on greedy innkeepers see Matfre Ermengaud, *Le Breviari D'Amor*, ed. G. Azais, vol. 2 (Beziers, 1881), lines 18302–425, and *La Borjos Borjon* in T.Wright, *Anecdota Literaria* (London, 1854), pp. 57–9.

[188] *The History of the Holy Grail*, ed. F. J. Furnivall, EETS ES 20 (London, 1874), p. 137, lines 647–51; *The "Gest Hystoriale" of the Destruction of Troy*, ed. G. A. Panton and D. Donaldson, EETS OS 39 (London, 1869), p. 122, lines 3755–9.

[189] P. Brown, *Chaucer at Work: The Making of the Canterbury Tales* (London, 1994), p. 44.

London Puy, a literary as well as a social and religious fraternity comprising merchants, clerks, and civic officials, which gave a prize of a silver crown and a free supper to the member who composed the best *chant royal* for its annual feast in honor of Christ and his mother.[190] Founded in the 1270s under the inspiration of the Arras Puy, it appears to have expired in the early fourteenth century, certainly by 1321. With no purpose-built hall for its meetings, it may have assembled at The Tumbling Bear, the largest tavern on Cheapside.[191] Although the London Puy had a relatively short life, Professor Cooper demonstrates its relevance to the Canterbury pilgrimage: "Canterbury pilgrims form a looser fraternity, but of a not dissimilar kind: they agree to associate as a compaignye gathered for a mixture of literary and pious purposes; they are headed by a temporary lord who will judge their poetry, and who endeavours to maintain good will (III.1288); and the climax of their association will be a prize supper" (p. 21). It may be relevant to add that some French puys bestowed prizes for submissions on secular as well as Marian themes in a variety of poetic forms and were made up of a larger cross-section of the community, both lay and religious, than the London Puy. In 1388, about the time Chaucer was writing the *General Prologue*, a puy was established at Amiens for the best *chant royal* with the winner to be awarded a silver crown as at London. Its contestants were lawyers, prosecutors, canons, priests, mercers, tanners, goldsmiths, tavern-keepers, and other merchants, and its judges were selected for their knowledge of poetic rather than musical matters. Professional poets also entered these competitions. Jean Froissart (whom Chaucer certainly knew from his long residence at the court of Edward III) won prizes at Valenciennes, Abbeville, Lille, and Tournai. He contributed a *sotte* to the competition at Lille which by the third quarter of the fourteenth century accepted secular poems on love. The practices of the French puys may have encouraged Chaucer to diversify his characters socially and professionally beyond the literary conventions of estates satire and to vary the metrical forms of the tales.[192]

The Host's criterion for judging the tales ("best sentence and moost solace") echoes Horace's *Ars Poetica* (333–4): "Aut prodesse volunt aut delectare poetae/ aut simul et jucunda et idonea dicere vitae." ("Poets wish either to benefit or to delight or to say what is simultaneously pleasing and applicable

[190] H. Cooper, "The Frame," *Sources and Analogues of the Canterbury Tales*, vol. 1, ed. R. M. Correale and M. Hamel, pp. 18–21. Prize dinners were not exclusive to the Puys. In the *Decameron* (6.6) the prize of a free supper is bestowed on Michele Scalza and seven of his companions for proving that the Baronci were the oldest and noblest family in Florence and the whole world. On the French Puys which flourished throughout the fourteenth century, particularly in northern France, see G. Gros, *Le Poète, la Vierge et le Prince du Puy* (Paris, 1992); C. Vincent, *Les Confréries Médiévales dans le Royaume de France XIIIe–XVe siècle* (Paris, 1944) and *Des Charités bien ordonnées: Les confréries normandes de la fin du XIIIe siècle au debut du XVIe siècle* (Paris, 1988), pp. 213–15, 215–17; N. Wilkins, *The Lyric Art of Medieval France* (Fulbourn, 1988); R. Brusegan, "Culte de la Vierge et origine des pays et confréries en France au moyen âge," *Revue des Langues Romanes* 95 (1991): 31–58.

[191] A. E. Sutton, "Merchants, Music and Social Harmony: The London Puy and its French and London Contexts, circa 1300," *The London Journal* 17 (1992): 1–17; and "The Tumbling Bear and its Patrons: A Venue for the London Puy and Mercery," *London and Europe in the Later Middle Ages*, ed. J. Boffey and P. King (London, 1995), pp. 85–110.

[192] D. Poirion, *Le Poète et le Prince* (Geneva, 1978), p. 39. See also Wilkins, pp 13–14; E. C. Teviotdale, "Puy," *New Grove Dictionary of Music and Musicians* 15 (1980), p. 481, and Gros, p. 46.

to life.") The dictum became a commonplace of medieval literary theory, and authors often chose to express their aims in terms of it. "The intention of poets," remarks Jean de Meun, "is solely to edify and please" ("Profiz a delectacion,/ C'est toute leur entencion" 15241–2). Boccacio offers the ladies who read his stories "pleasure" (*diletto*) and "useful advice" (*utile consiglio*).[193] John Gower promises to "go the middel weie" in the *Confessio Amantis*: "And wryte a bok between the tweie,/ Somwhat of lust, somwhat of lore" (17–18).

For the curious choice of an innkeeper to lead the pilgrimage, Chaucer appears to have turned again to the *Chessbook* and taken a clue from its advice to hostelers:

> Also for as moche as many paryls and aduentures may happen on the wayes and passages to hem that herberowed within their Innes therfore they [hostelers] ought to accompanye them whan they departe and enseigne them the wayes and telle to them the paryls to thende that they may surely go theyr viage and Iourney.[194]

The Start of the Pilgrimage (822–58)

The following morning the Host, briskly assuming his roles as director of the pilgrimage and games-master, rouses the company and at St Thomas Watering has them draw lots to determine who will tell the first story. The cut conveniently falls to the knight who cheerfully agrees to abide by the draw. "The casting or drawing of lots," Michael Olmert observes, "has the longest pedigree of all the games of chance known in the Middle Ages."[195] Its literary antecedents as a narrative device go back to Homer and Herodotus. Chaucer knew the tradition well. He employs this device again in the *Pardoner's Tale* (793–804), having found it perhaps in *The Play of Saint Anthony*, a close analogue, where the robbers draw straws to see who will return to town for food and drink: "Facciamo alle buschette chi debbe ire" ["Let us draw straws to see who should go"].[196]

[193] C. L. Wrenn, "Chaucer's Knowledge of Horace," *Modern Language Review* 18 (1923): 286–92, proves that he was directly acquainted with the *Epistola ad Pisones de Arte Poetica* and with at least one, and perhaps two, of the odes. For Boccaccio, see *Decameron*, Proemio 14, p. 5.

[194] *Game and Playe of the Chesse*, Book 3, chapter 6, p. 134; Jehan de Vignay, *Le Jeu*, chapter 14, p. 255.

[195] M. Olmert, "Chaucer's Little Lotteries: The Literary Use of a Medieval Game," *Arete* 2 (1984): 171.

[196] M. Hamel, "The Pardoner's Prologue and Tale," *Sources and Analogues of the Canterbury Tales*, vol. 1, ed. R. M. Correale and M. Hamel, pp. 300–1, line 138. There is a further allusion to the casting of lots adapted from Ovid's *Metamorphoses* (8.171) in Chaucer's *The Legend of Ariadne* (*LGW* 6.1933–7): "tertia sors annis domuit repetita novenis" ["The lottery, repeated every nine years, mastered him [Theseus] on the third draw"]. Ludic activity is often associated with medieval taverns. See A. Cowell, *At Play in the Tavern* (Ann Arbor, 1999), pp. 111–79; Owst, p. 430. In Jean Bodel's *Le Jeu de Saint Nicolas*, lines 290–1, a tavern regular who is a thief invites a gullible visitor to engage in a lottery. The implication is that he is capable of the same sleight of hand as is suspected of the Host. The formulaic phrase "be aventure, or sort, or cas" (844) echoes the *Consolation of Philosophy* (5. Pr. 1, lines 34–5).

The Knight's Tale*

WILLIAM E. COLEMAN

Whilom, as olde stories tellen us (*KnT* I, 859)

Several books occupied Chaucer's desk while he was composing *The Knight's Tale*: Boccaccio's *Teseida*,[1] Statius's *Thebaid*, and Boethius's *De consolatione philosophiae* (in Latin and in Chaucer's own translation, the *Boece*). In Chaucer's mind's eye, if not also on his desk, were Virgil's *Aeneid*, Ovid's *Metamorphoses*, the Vulgate Bible, Dante's *Commedia*, and perhaps the *Roman de la Rose* and the *Roman de Thèbes*.

Boccaccio's Teseida

The most important book on that very crowded desk was the *Teseida*. Boccaccio composed the *Teseida* c. 1340 in response to Dante's observation in the *De vulgari eloquentia* that a vernacular work on the theme of arms still

* This chapter is dedicated to the memory of Prof. Vittore Branca and Prof. Robert A. Pratt.

[1] The title of Boccaccio's work is *Teseida*. Like Boccaccio's *Decameron*, the title is considered masculine, but it lacks the masculine article *il*. See G. Vandelli, "Un Autografo della *Teseide*," *Studi di Filologia Italiana* 2 (1929): 19–20.

remained to be written.[2] The poem consists of 1238 octaves, totaling 9904 lines, or about the same number of lines as in the *Aeneid*.[3] Boccaccio envisioned the *Teseida* as a demonstration piece to show that a classical epic could be written in a modern language and, with its ottava rima structure, that it could be cast in a contemporary poetic idiom.

From the time that Chaucer acquired his copy of Boccaccio's poem, the *Teseida* was a major presence in his work. Chaucer seems to have thoroughly digested the *Teseida* over a long period of careful reading. Its influence is clear in the *Parliament of Fowls*, *Troilus and Criseyde*, *The Franklin's Tale*, *Anelida and Arcite*, the *Legend of Good Women*, and perhaps the *House of Fame*,[4] but its most extended use occurs in *The Knight's Tale*. In constructing *The Knight's Tale*, Chaucer borrows from all twelve books of the *Teseida*. All told, the *Teseida* was Chaucer's source for some 1805 (of 2250) lines, that is, for 80% of *The Knight's Tale*. In adapting the *Teseida*, however, Chaucer did not merely follow the outline of Boccaccio's tale.[5] As Tables 1 and 2 in the Appendix below demonstrate, *The Knight's Tale* is an abridgment, revision, and re-arrangement of the *Teseida*.[6]

The narrative circumstances of *The Knight's Tale*, as one of a series of stories told during a limited period of time and as part of a competition, required that the *Teseida* be shortened. In its present form, *The Knight's Tale* is Chaucer's longest poem after *Troilus and Criseyde*. If the Knight had proposed a narrative approaching the length of the *Teseida*, however, he might well have merited a response similar to the Franklin's polite interruption of *The Squire's Tale* or to Herry Bailly's less courteous interruption of *The Tale of Sir Thopas*.

2 In the *De vulgari eloquentia* (2.2) Dante remarks that the three proper subjects of vernacular poetry are "armorum probitas, amoris accensio, et directio voluntatis" [valor in arms, love's enkindling, and moral rectitude]. Cino da Pistoia had written of love, while Dante himself had made rectitude the subject of his *Commedia*, but he had not yet found any Italian poet who had written of arms ("arma vero nullum latium adhuc invenio poetasse"). That the *Teseida* was composed in response to Dante's challenge is made clear at the end of the work, where Boccaccio addresses his book, saying that it is the first literary work in the Italian vernacular ("nel volgar lazio") to treat of the affairs of Mars (12.84.7–8).

3 In *Before the Knight's Tale: Imitation of Classical Epic in Boccaccio's* Teseida (Philadelphia: U Pennsylvania P, 1988), David Anderson points out that the text in medieval copies of the *Aeneid* was inconsistent and therefore one can say only that, in designing the *Teseida*, Boccaccio approximated the length of the *Aeneid* (p. 142).

4 For indications of the presence of the *Teseida* in these works, see the notes in *The Riverside Chaucer*.

5 Table 1, below, cites the following lines from *The Knight's Tale* as having a direct or a general source in the *Teseida*: I, 865–83, 893–1274, 1281–98, 1361–1448, 1451–79, 1488–96, 1542–9, 1623–6, 1638–41, 1668–1741, 1812–69, 1885–2050, 2056–9, 2062–8, 2102–2206, 2209–2437, 2491–2531, 2537–79, 2581–2739, 2743–2964, 2967–3102. Only a portion of these lines are Chaucer's direct translations. H. L. Ward identified 272 translated lines in his marginal notes to the Chaucer Society's, *A Six-Text Print of Chaucer's Canterbury Tales*, ed. F. J. Furnivall, 1868–79. These were the basis for the table of correspondences in W. W. Skeat, ed., *The Works of Geoffrey Chaucer*, 2nd edn (Oxford: Clarendon, 1900), vol. 5: notes to *The Canterbury Tales*, p. 60. See also Hubertis M. Cummings, *The Indebtedness of Chaucer's Works to the Italian Works of Boccaccio: A Review and Summary* (1914; rpt. New York: Haskell House, 1965), pp. 123ff.

6 For a study of the various ways that Chaucer used the *Teseida* in his works, see Robert Pratt's article on *The Knight's Tale* in Bryan and Dempster (pp. 82–105) and his "Chaucer's Use of the *Teseida*," *PMLA* 62 (1947): 598–621. For a detailed study of Chaucer's use of Book 7 of the *Teseida*, see Piero Boitani, *Chaucer and Boccaccio*, Medium Ævum Monographs n.s. 8 (Oxford: Society for the Study of Mediæval Languages and Literature, 1977).

Beyond the question of the narrative situation is the more important issue of Chaucer's thematic intentions in *The Knight's Tale*. In the *Teseida* the death of Arcita is viewed as an example of the random misfortunes that afflict humanity. While acknowledging that Arcite's death was a human misfortune, *The Knight's Tale*, quoting the *Consolation of Philosophy*, also views it in the context of divine providence. Chaucer shortens, rewrites, and restructures the *Teseida* with this Boethian theme in mind.[7] He accomplishes this by summarizing, by limiting the locales of the story, by reducing its epic elements, and by omitting many of Boccaccio's characters while recasting the others so as to eliminate many of their individual traits.

Summary: Although the *Teseida* is Chaucer's major source, he used material from only about half of Boccaccio's narrative in creating *The Knight's Tale*.[8] The most extreme example of Chaucer's abridgement is his treatment of Book 1 of the *Teseida*. At the beginning of the tale, a quotation from Statius's *Thebaid* introduces Chaucer's readers to the Theban war and to the Argive widows who have come to Athens to plead for Theseus's help. For the reader familiar with the *Thebaid* and the legend of the war against Thebes, this serves to establish the literary/historical context of *The Knight's Tale*. In a mere eight lines (I, 877–84), Chaucer then summarizes the 1104 lines of the first book of the *Teseida*, which relate the story of Theseus's conquest of the Amazons and his marriage to the Amazon queen, Ypolita.

The second book of the *Teseida* spends 99 stanzas (792 lines) in describing Theseus's encounter with the Theban women, his conquest of Thebes, the burial of the Argive warriors, and Theseus's return to Athens with the two captive princes. Chaucer preserves all these events, but narrates them in only 140 lines (I, 893–1032), or about a sixth of Boccaccio's text. Chaucer's technique is to concentrate on those dramatic events that are necessary to his story and then to summarize the rest of Boccaccio's narrative. Thus his major borrowing from Book 2 is his representation of the dialogue between Theseus and the Theban women (I, 893–974), which caused Theseus to leap from his horse "With herte pitous" (I, 953). Chaucer summarizes the rest of Book 2 in 53 lines that describe Theseus's war with Creon (I, 975–90), the burial of the Argive soldiers (I, 991–9), and the discovery and imprisonment of Palamon and Arcite (I, 1005–32). In his treatment of Books 3–6, 8–10, and 12 of the *Teseida*, Chaucer continues this technique of concentrating on crucial dramatic elements, summarizing events necessary for his narration, and excluding other unrelated details.

While Chaucer often drastically abridges Books 1–6, 8–10, and 12 of the *Teseida*, he borrows extensively from the remaining two. His most extended use of the *Teseida* occurs in Book 7, where he uses some 105 (of 145) stanzas for his extended description of the amphitheater, the oratories of Venus and Mars,[9]

[7] Pratt, "Chaucer's Use of the *Teseida*," p. 615; William E. Coleman, "The *Knight's Tale*: A Search for the Ordered Universe," M.A. thesis, Univ. of Virginia, 1966.

[8] Table 2 indicates that Chaucer used some 695 of the 1238 octaves (or 56%) of the *Teseida*. Many of these borrowings are general in nature, however. As for specific borrowings (indicated in italics in Table 2), he used only 185 octaves (or 15%) of the *Teseida*.

[9] The *Teseida* does not contain a description of a temple of Diana. Chaucer's description of the temple is based on details from Ovid's *Metamorphoses*. See Table 1.

the prayers of Palamon, Emily, and Arcite, and the pageantry on the day of the combat.[10] He then uses 30 (of 91) stanzas of Book 11 to describe the funeral of Arcite (I, 2809–2962).

Locales: Chaucer narrows the scope of the *Teseida* by limiting the events of the story to Thebes and to Athens. Boccaccio spends almost half of Book 4 of the *Teseida* in describing Arcita's exile from Athens and his wanderings to Thebes, Corinth, Mycenae, and Aegina.[11] Chaucer makes this material into a description of the effects of Arcite's lovesickness, transforming him so that he is unrecognizable when he returns to Athens (I, 1355–1413). In Athens itself, Chaucer limits the locations associated with the story. The *Teseida* describes events at Theseus's palace, in the grove outside the city, in the amphitheater, and in temples within the city. In addition, personified prayers are sent from the temples in Athens to the gods in their dwelling places: to Mars in Thrace and to Venus on Mount Cithaeron. *The Knight's Tale* presents the same events, but concentrated in two places: the palace of Theseus and the grove outside the city. Besides being the place where Palamon and Arcite meet and fight, the grove is also the site of the amphitheater – which itself houses the oratories of Mars, Venus, and Diana – and, eventually, of Arcite's funeral pyre.

Epic elements: One important component in Chaucer's reworking of the *Teseida* is his elimination or drastic reduction of the epic elements in Boccaccio's story. All but disappeared are the rhetoric and the allusions to classical myth that characterize both the *Teseida* and the Latin epics which it imitates, the *Aeneid* and the *Thebaid*. Chaucer's rhetoric in *The Knight's Tale* is much less florid, and his classical allusions are largely limited to the descriptions of the three oratories and of the prayers to Venus, Diana, and Mars. Chaucer also limits another example of epic machinery, the catalogue. Boccaccio's catalogue of the twenty-two heroes arriving in Athens to participate in the lists occupies 51 stanzas – 408 lines – of the *Teseida*.[12] In *The Knight's Tale*, Chaucer chooses two heroes, "Lygurge of Trace" and "Emetreus of Inde," to represent the assembled champions, taking 57 lines to describe them and their entourages (I, 2129–54, 2156–86). The description of Lygurge and Emetreus is patched together from Boccaccio's description of various champions[13] plus Chaucer's addition of certain astrological details related to the Boethian themes of fate and providence.[14]

Characterization: A final point of difference between the *Teseida* and *The Knight's Tale* is Chaucer's reworking of character. After first reducing the cast of characters, he then deprives all the minor characters except Egeus of their

[10] The borrowings, which occur in a 700-line section of *The Knight's Tale* (I, 1885–2593), demonstrate Chaucer's thorough digestion and reworking of Book 7 of the *Teseida*.

[11] *Teseida* 4.1–38.

[12] *Teseida* 6.14–64.

[13] The details which Chaucer uses in describing Lygurge and Emetreus are based on Boccaccio's descriptions of several heroes: Ligurgo, Pelleo, Agamenone, Nestore, Evandro, and Peritoo.

[14] Pratt ("Chaucer's Use of the *Teseida*," p. 619 and n. 77, quoting Walter Clyde Curry's *Chaucer and the Medieval Sciences* [New York, 1926], pp. 119–63), suggests that the details which Chaucer added to his portraits of Lygurge and Emetreus are related to Chaucer's emphasis on astrological influences, plus the Boethian themes of fate and providence in *The Knight's Tale*.

speaking roles, dispenses with Emily's first betrothed (Acate), and makes Palamon's servant (Panfilo) and his physician (Alimeto) nameless. As for the major characters of the story – Theseus, Palamon, Arcite, and Emily – Chaucer presents them as less complex, less rounded than their counterparts in the *Teseida.* Theseus is transformed into a sort of philosopher-monarch who acts the role of master of ceremonies.[15] While Boccaccio spends much poetic effort in creating a psychological portrait of his two heroes' hopeless, romantic anguish, Chaucer characterizes the two in a similar way, but with less detail. The coy and flirtatious Emilia of the *Teseida* loses much of her voice and personality in *The Knight's Tale.* Deprived of the dialogue Boccaccio composed for her, Emily speaks just two sentences invented by Chaucer (I, 2362–4).

Statius's Thebaid

The second important work on Chaucer's desk while he was composing *The Knight's Tale* was Statius's *Thebaid.* After Ovid and Boethius, the first-century imperial court poet Publius Papinius Statius (48–96) was the Latin author whom Chaucer knew best and most often quoted. "The nature and extent of his borrowings from the *Thebaid,*" as Boyd Wise has noted, "show an intimate acquaintance extending over almost the entire period of his activity."[16] Composed between 79 and 92, the *Thebaid* relates the tale of the fraternal strife between the two sons of Oedipus, Eteocles and Polynices, the subsequent incursion by the seven armed forces from Argos, the tyranny of Creon, and Theseus's eventual invasion and defeat of Thebes.

The *Thebaid* enjoyed great popularity during the Middle Ages since it was the primary source for the legend of Thebes. In addition to Boccaccio's *Teseida*, the *Thebaid* provided the materials for several long poems, among them the anonymous mid-twelfth-century *Roman de Thèbes* and John Lydgate's early fifteenth-century *Siege of Thebes*. Another attraction for medieval readers was Statius's rich, complex, allusive literary style, for which Dante called him "lo dolce poeta" [the sweet poet].[17]

A particular reason for the medieval interest in Statius was the legend of his conversion to Christianity. Dante has him relate this story in canto 22 of the *Purgatorio* near the summit of the Mount of Purgatory where the poet has finished his penance and is preparing to journey to paradise. (Statius is thus the only writer from classical antiquity who would eventually earn a place among the blessed in the Christian afterlife.) When the three poets meet, Statius describes himself as having been converted both to poetry and to religion as a result of reading Virgil's Fourth Eclogue, the so-called messianic eclogue. Statius acknowledges his debt to Virgil, telling him: "Per te poeta fui, per te

[15] Pratt, "Chaucer's Use of the *Teseida,*" p. 615.

[16] Boyd A. Wise, *The Influence of Statius upon Chaucer* (Baltimore, 1911; rpt. New York: Phaeton, 1967), p. 141.

[17] *Convivio* 4.25.6.

cristiano."[18] (On your account was I a poet, on your account a Christian.) Statius then says that he was baptized by the time he had brought the Argive army to the rivers of Thebes – that is, when he had written the seventh book of the *Thebaid*. Thereafter, as a result of the persecutions under the Emperor Domitian (81–96), Statius says that he lived as a hidden Christian.[19]

Most medieval copies of the *Thebaid* included the glosses of the late fourth-century commentator Lactantius Placidus.[20] Boccaccio owned a copy of the *Thebaid* with the glosses of Lactantius,[21] and Statius's epic served Boccaccio as his major rhetorical and thematic source for the *Teseida*.[22] Although no books that belonged to Chaucer have been identified, he certainly would have owned or at least have had extended access to a copy of the *Thebaid* – and very likely a glossed copy[23] – because the presence of Statius's epic is evident from the first lines of *The Knight's Tale*. While neglecting to acknowledge Boccaccio, Chaucer twice cites Statius in *The Knight's Tale*. In addition to selecting a quotation from the *Thebaid* as the epigram for *The Knight's Tale*,[24] Chaucer recommends "Stace of Thebes" (I, 2294) as a source of further information for anyone interested in the details of Emily's ritual at the temple of Diana.

The *Thebaid* has another type of presence in *The Knight's Tale* since it was the inspiration for much of Boccaccio's *Teseida*. Chaucer certainly recognized that the *Thebaid* was itself the prime source of his own main source, the *Teseida*. At certain points in *The Knight's Tale* – his description of Arcite's funeral, for example – he seems to be calling attention to this fact when he alternately draws on both the *Thebaid* and the *Teseida*, balancing the one against the other.[25] When he cites Statius as a source for his description of Emily at the temple of Diana (I, 2271–2364), he is enjoying a literary joke of another sort because the passage is actually – and rather closely – based on

[18] *Purgatorio* 22.73.

[19] *Purgatorio* 22.88–90.

[20] The critical edition is Lactantius Placidus, *In Statii Thebaida commentum. Anonymi in Statii Achilleida commentum, Fulgentii ut fingitur Planciadis super Thebaiden commentariolum*, vol. 1, ed. R. D. Sweeney, Scholia in Statium (Stuttgart: Teubner, 1997).

[21] See n. 72, below.

[22] For the sources of the *Teseida* see Umberto Limentani, ed., *Tutte le opere di Giovanni Boccaccio*, ed. Vittore Branca, 2 (Milan: Mondadori, 1964), pp. 887–99; Piero Boitani, "Table of the Sources, Influences, and Reminiscences in the *Teseida*," *Chaucer and Boccaccio*, pp. 61–71.

[23] See Wise, *The Influence of Statius upon Chaucer*, pp. 46–54, 78–115; and Paul M. Clogan, "Chaucer's Use of the *Thebaid*," *English Miscellany* 18 (1967): 8–15, 25–31.

[24] *Thebaid* 12.519–20: see text and translation in selections from Statius, below. The epigram introduces a description of Theseus returning in triumph from Scythia after having vanquished the Amazons. The same epigram also occurs in *Anelida and Arcite*, which is loosely based on the *Teseida*. The epigram does not appear in all the copies of *The Canterbury Tales*, but it is to be found in the authoritative Ellesmere and Hengwrt MSS; this suggests that it is not a later scribal interpolation, but that Chaucer intended the quotation from Statius to head *The Knight's Tale*. A thematic reason also argues for the authenticity of the quotation. These lines precede Statius's description of the Theban widows who stop Theseus's carriage in order to ask him to avenge their dead husbands and to make war on the tyrant Creon. David Anderson points out that Chaucer's quoting the epigram "acknowledges the source for the opening 145 verses [of *The Knight's Tale*], which are based directly on *Thebaid* 12.519ff and Boccaccio's earlier vernacularization of the same scenes in *Teseida* 2.19ff" (*Before the Knight's Tale*, p. 101). The epigram also provides a reference about the conquest of the Amazons for an audience which would not know the story in Boccaccio's contemporary Italian (*Teseida* 1–2.18), but which could be expected to know it in Statius.

[25] See Table 1, lines 2853–2938.

Boccaccio.[26] Boccaccio's description of Emilia's sacrifice at the temple of Diana was itself taken from a much shorter and rather different scene in Statius where Manto, the daughter of the seer Tiresias, is helping her father summon spirits from the underworld in order to hear their predictions about the impending war between Thebes and Argos.[27] By citing Statius (the remote source for the passage), Chaucer is making the point that Statius is available in two forms in *The Knight's Tale*: directly and at second-hand via the *Teseida*.

Statius is the source of 214 lines in *The Knight's Tale*.[28] He is the primary source of only 22 lines[29] and a remote source (via Boccaccio) of 132 lines.[30] An additional 60 lines of *The Knight's Tale* have a double source: both Statius and Boccaccio.[31] Statius's contribution to the tale is, therefore, significantly smaller than Boccaccio's. But Statius served Chaucer both as a model and as a presence in his construction of *The Knight's Tale*. David Anderson has made the case that, in addition to the lines that the epic supplied and the incidents that it inspired, the *Thebaid* provided Chaucer with a rationale for revising the *Teseida*. "Chaucer's changes in the *Teseida*," he argues, "are governed by a program of open imitation of the *Thebaid*"[32] and of other works of Statius. These Statius-inspired revisions include Chaucer's structural divisions of *The Knight's Tale*[33] and his telescoping of the beginning of the *Teseida*.[34]

Statius also provided the basis for several instances where Chaucer revised events or characterizations in the *Teseida*. Theseus's conduct with the Theban women at the temple of Clemence (I, 893–974), for example, is a scene adapted from the *Teseida*,[35] but modified by Statius's description of the temple of Clementia.[36] The meeting of Palamon and Arcite in the grove (I, 1421–1622),

26 *Teseida* 7.70–92.

27 *Thebaid* 4.463–8.

28 See Table 1. Boyd A. Wise made a more extensive argument for the presence of Statius in *The Knight's Tale*, but many of these readings consist of general resemblances between the two texts. See *The Influence of Statius upon Chaucer*, pp. 46–115. See also Paul M. Clogan, "Chaucer's Use of the *Thebaid*," pp. 9–11. For Statius's influence on Chaucer's portrait of Theseus see Walter Scheps, "Chaucer's Theseus and *The Knight's Tale*," *Leeds Studies in English* 9 (1976–77): 19–34.

29 *KnT* I, epigram, 1331, 1546, 1638–48, 1660, 1987, 2022–3, 2027–30.

30 *KnT* I, 1967–2050, 2017, 2293–4, 2297–2330, 2684, 2853–2962 (especially 2921–3, 2925–7, 2933–8).

31 *KnT* I, 1985, 1995–2028, 2129–52, 2327.

32 Anderson, *Before the Knight's Tale*, p. 212.

33 Anderson (*ibid*., p. 193) proposes that the three-part division of *The Knight's Tale* in the Hengwrt MS and the four-part division of the *Tale* in the Ellesmere MS were suggested by Statius's *Achilleid*, a work in one book plus a fragment of a second. One academic question current in fourteenth-century Italy – a question of which Chaucer may have been aware – was whether the *Achilleid* was incomplete (as Dante argued) or complete (as Petrarch argued). For those who believed it was a complete work, the *Achilleid* was understood to be "Statius minor," an example of a shorter epic. It also functioned as a school text and was often divided into four or five chapters.

34 The epigram from Statius (*Thebaid* 12.519–20) quoted at the beginning of *The Knight's Tale* refers briefly to Theseus's return from Scythia after defeating the Amazons. Since Statius provides no other information about the siege, Boccaccio, drawing on the Argonauts' siege of the Lemnian women (*Thebaid* 5), invents the descriptions of Theseus's voyage to Scythia and his siege and defeat of the Amazons. Chaucer's quotation from *Thebaid* 12 thus serves to announce and to justify his trimming of Boccaccio's long description of the voyage to Amazonia (*Teseida* 1–2:18). See Anderson, *Before the Knight's Tale*, pp. 201–3. Like Statius's brief description of the proud, unbowed Amazon captives in Theseus's triumphal march (*Thebaid* 12.529–31), Chaucer summarizes Theseus's Scythian adventure in a brief *occupatio* (I, 866–71).

35 *Teseida* 2.10–49.

36 *Thebaid* 12.481–518. See Anderson, *Before the Knight's Tale*, pp. 160–6, 200–3; David Anderson,

which telescopes the events in two books of the *Teseida*,[37] is modified with reference to the theme of fraternal strife from the first book of the *Thebaid*.[38] Chaucer's presentation of Emily as a two-dimensional character who lacks much of the interesting detail in Boccaccio's portrait of Emilia may be a means for him to emphasize Statius's observation that political conflict often exacts an enormous sacrifice for a disproportionately small reward.[39] A final instance of Chaucer's use of the *Thebaid* as a basis for revising the *Teseida* is his consistent attention to the genealogy of Palamon and Arcite as kinsmen and members of the royal family of Thebes – a process that serves to emphasize the Statian theme of fraternal strife.[40] The *Thebaid* and the *Teseida*, in this view, had a complex relationship in the genesis of *The Knight's Tale*. While Chaucer depended to a far greater degree on the *Teseida*, his use of Boccaccio was always mediated and tempered by the presence of Statius.

Boethius's Consolation of Philosophy

In addition to Boccaccio and Statius, the most prominent other source that contributed to the fashioning of *The Knight's Tale* is the *De consolatione philosophiae* (*Consolation of Philosophy*) by Anicius Manlius Severinus Boethius (c. 480 – c. 525).[41] Composed in prison while Boethius was awaiting execution at the order of the Ostrogothic king Theodoric, the *Consolation* became a philosophical and spiritual classic that was widely read and often translated in the Middle Ages.[42] Because of his theological writings and because his death was ordered by an Arian king who accused him of loyalty to the orthodox emperor Justin, Boethius was considered to be a Christian martyr. He is buried in Pavia in the crypt of the church of San Pietro in Ciel d'Oro, a fact noted by Dante in canto 10 of the *Paradiso*.[43]

"The Fourth Temple of *The Knight's Tale*: Athenian Clemency and Chaucer's Theseus," in John V. Fleming and Thomas J. Heffernan, eds, *Studies in the Age of Chaucer, Proceedings, No. 2, 1987. Papers presented at the Fifth International Congress of the New Chaucer Society, 1986, Philadelphia* (Knoxville, TN: New Chaucer Society, 1987), pp. 113–25.

37 *Teseida* 4.79–5.63.

38 Anderson, *Before the Knight's Tale*, pp. 204–5. See David Anderson, "Theban Genealogy in *The Knight's Tale*," *Chaucer Review* 21 (1987): 311–20.

39 *Thebaid* 1.151. "Pugna est de paupere regno" [The conflict concerns a trifling kingdom]. See Anderson, *Before the Knight's Tale*, pp. 206–7.

40 Anderson, *Ibid.*, pp. 209–12.

41 A Latin edition of the *De consolatione* with an English translation is available on the internet at http://etext.lib.virginia.edu/latin/boethius/consolatio.htm

42 In addition to the Old English version commissioned by King Alfred (†899), the *Consolation* exists in an Old High German version by Notker Labeo of St. Gall (†1022) and in several medieval French translations, including one by Jean de Meun (†1305). Chaucer's version, the *Boece*, dates from c. 1380 and was made with the aid of Jean de Meun's translation. See A. J. Minnis, ed., *The Medieval Boethius: Studies in the Vernacular Translation of* De Consolatione Philosophiae (Cambridge: D. S. Brewer, 1987) and *Chaucer's* Boece *and the Medieval Tradition of Boethius* (Cambridge: D. S. Brewer, 1993).

43 In Canto 10 of the *Paradiso* (125–9), Dante refers to Boetius as: "l'anima santa che 'l mondo fallace/ fa manifesto a chi di lei ben ode./ Lo corpo ond'ella fu cacciata giace/ giuso in Cieldauro; ed essa da martiro/ e da esilio venne a questa pace." [. . . the blessed soul who reveals the deceitful world to whoever listens well to it. The body from which it was expelled reposes down in Ciel d'Oro, and it has come from martyrdom and from exile to this peace.]

Boethius contributed only 87 lines to *The Knight's Tale*,[44] but his work transformed the themes of Chaucer's story. The major borrowings from Boethius occur in three speeches. The first speech, which is based on prose selections in Books 2, 3, and 4 of the *Consolation*, is Arcite's unsuccessful attempt at consoling Palamon before leaving Athens (I, 1251–67). This is followed by Palamon's statement of despair (I, 1303–27), which Chaucer adapted from a meter in Book 1. The last and best known borrowing from Boethius is Theseus's "faire cheyne of love" speech to Palamon and Emily, which describes the operations of divine providence (I, 2987–3016). Patched together from various meters in Books 1 through 4 and from prose pieces in Books 3 and 4, the speech serves as an apt demonstration of Chaucer's thorough assimilation and distillation of Boethius's thought.

Chaucer had Boethius's *De consolatione* in two versions: in the Latin original and in his own translation of the work, the *Boece*,[45] which is generally dated about 1380 and which also includes glosses derived from Nicholas Trevet's commentary on the *De consolatione*.[46] Chaucer seems to have used the *Boece* as his prime source for the Boethian materials in *The Knight's Tale*.[47] But just as the *Thebaid* served Chaucer as a corrective and control for his use of the *Teseida*, the *De consolatione* served the same purposes in his use of the *Boece*.

Other sources

This same process of recycling a translation, but with reference to its original version, also seems to be at work in the few lines of the *Romaunt of the Rose* that Chaucer used as the source of readings in *The Knight's Tale*.[48] While Chaucer used the *Romaunt* in three instances, he seems to have used the *Roman de la Rose* only once.[49]

Chaucer made use of several other classical and medieval sources in constructing *The Knight's Tale*. Since the temple of Diana has no source in the *Teseida*, Chaucer imagined the building himself, decorating it with scenes from Ovid (I, 2062–8, 2070–2). When he was formulating a few philosophical observations during the *Tale*, Chaucer had recourse to both testaments of the Vulgate

44 *KnT* I, 1163–4, 1251–9, 1261–7, 1303–27, 1663–72, 2987–3016, 3035–8. For Chaucer's use of Boethius, see Bernard L. Jefferson, *Chaucer and the Consolation of Philosophy of Boethius* (1917; rpt. New York: Haskell House, 1965); and *The Riverside Chaucer*, p. 827.

45 Because Chaucer used the French translation of Boethius by Jean de Meun as an aid in preparing the *Boece*, it would be more correct to say that he had the *De consolatione* in three versions.

46 Since these glosses are woven into the text of Chaucer's translation, thus adding to its length, the Latin original and the Middle English version have a different line numbering.

47 Because it is available to scholars in the standard editions of the works of Chaucer, such as *The Riverside Chaucer*, the selections from the *Boece* which served Chaucer for *The Knight's Tale* are not reproduced in this chapter. However, the Latin selections below include the line numbering both for the *De consolatione* and for the *Boece*.

48 Alfred David points out that Chaucer continues this composition habit elsewhere, using *Anelida and Arcite* as a source for *The Squire's Tale*. See "Recycling *Anelida and Arcite*: Chaucer as a Source for Chaucer," in Paul Strohm and Thomas J. Heffernan, eds, *Studies in the Age of Chaucer, Proceedings, No. 1, 1984: Reconstructing Chaucer* (Knoxville, TN: New Chaucer Society, 1985), pp. 105–15.

49 I, 1606, 1940, 2236. Lines I, 1197–1200 are from the *Roman de la Rose*, however, and are not mediated through the *Romaunt*. The *Roman* is also the ultimate source of several lines: I, 1925–35, 2209–70.

Bible (I, 1260, 1307–9, 1422). The twelfth-century *Roman de Thèbes* is the probable source of some lines concerning the war with Thebes (I, 938, 949–50, 952, 957).

As for the writers of his own century, Chaucer borrowed from other works by Boccaccio and also from Dante. "Philostrate" (I, 1428), the pseudonym which Arcite used on his return to Athens, came from the title of Boccaccio's *Filostrato* – the work on which Chaucer had based *Troilus and Criseyde*. The *Filostrato* and Boccaccio's *Genealogia deorum gentilium* may also have served Chaucer for the adornment of the temple of Diana (I, 2070–2). After Boccaccio, Dante was Chaucer's most important contemporary presence in *The Knight's Tale*. The *Purgatorio* and the *Paradiso* supplied Chaucer with brief descriptions of the sunrise and its effects, and the *Inferno* was the source of a discussion about divine "destinee" that Chaucer uses to explain why Theseus chose to go hunting on the very day and in the very place where he would discover Arcite and Palamon in battle (I, 1493, 1501, 1663–72). Although Dante is the source of only a few lines in *The Knight's Tale*, his *Commedia* supplied Chaucer with an important narrative model. Like Statius, Dante provided a pattern and served as a standard in the creation of *The Knight's Tale*.[50]

Chaucer's copies of his sources

Copies of Statius's *Thebaid* and of Boethius's *De consolatione philosophiae* would have been available to Chaucer during his formative years in England and also during his later visits to Flanders, France, and Italy. Chaucer's use of the *Thebaid* was most often second-hand (via the *Teseida*) and he presents much of the *Consolation* in the form of synopsis. At those points where Chaucer follows Statius and Boethius more closely, *The Knight's Tale* does not appear to have been based on a variant text. Therefore, it has been possible to depend on the standard editions of Statius and of Boethius for the selections from these works printed below.

The *Teseida*, however, presents a different set of circumstances. In the prologue to *The Legend of Good Women*, Alceste refers to Chaucer's tale of the love of Palamon and Arcite of Thebes, remarking that "the storye ys knowen lyte."[51] The remark could merely be an echo of Boccaccio's statement at the beginning of the *Teseida* that he would be telling an old, unknown story which had never served as a theme for any Latin poet.[52] It could also be an admission that, in choosing to tell a tale based on the *Teseida*, Chaucer was not borrowing from one of the well known classical and medieval narratives that usually provided the raw material for his tales. Almost as if to compensate for the neglect that the tale is supposed to have suffered in the past, Chaucer used the

[50] See Howard H. Schless, *Chaucer and Dante: A Revaluation* (Norman, OK: Pilgrim Books, 1984), pp. 171–8. In *Chaucer Reads The Divine Comedy* (Stanford, 1989), Karla Taylor argues that, while Dante provided Chaucer with a backdrop for establishing a poetic vision, Chaucer's vision in many ways differs from Dante's.

[51] *LGW Prol* F 421, G 409.

[52] *Teseida* I.2.2–5.

Teseida to an extraordinary degree in *The Knight's Tale*, adapting, translating, paraphrasing, and conflating incidents from every part of Boccaccio's story. Chaucer used the tale so thoroughly that we have the basis for understanding that his manuscript copy of the *Teseida* varied significantly from the autograph copy of the work that Boccaccio copied c. 1350.

Possible sources for Chaucer's copy of the *Teseida*: Chaucer and his family had contacts with Italians in London, who could have been the source of Italian literary manuscripts.[53] But his two journeys to Italy in the 1370s[54] provided him with the best opportunity to acquire his manuscripts of the works of Boccaccio (and Dante and Petrarch).[55] In the winter and spring of 1372–73 he was part of a commission sent to Genoa in order to discuss a treaty proposing special trading privileges for Genoese merchants in the port of London. Chaucer subsequently continued on alone to Florence (via Pisa) on "the king's secret business"[56] – most likely a matter concerning one of Edward III's many loans from the Italian bankers. Chaucer could have obtained his *Teseida* in Florence, which was an important center for the copying of works by Boccaccio,[57] but his second journey to Italy provided him with more time and a better opportunity to acquire his copy of Boccaccio's story.

During the summer of 1378 he spent about six weeks in Lombardy, where he had been sent to confer with the English mercenary, John Hawkwood, who was then in service with the two Visconti dukes, Bernabò in Milan and his brother Galeazzo II in Pavia.[58] Pavia, twenty-two miles to the south of Milan, would have had a particular interest for Chaucer. The church of San Pietro "in Ciel d'Oro," a few minutes' walk from the Visconti palace, contained the tombs of two of his heavenly patrons, Boethius and St. Augustine, and of his first earthly patron, prince Lionel of Clarence, who had died shortly after his marriage to Violante Visconti in the summer of 1368.[59]

An additional attraction of Pavia for Chaucer would have been the library in the ducal palace, which housed one of the greatest manuscript collections in

53 Vincent B. Redstone and Lillian J. Redstone, "The Heyrons of London: A Study in the Social Origins of Geoffrey Chaucer," *Speculum* 12 (1937): 182–95; and Wendy Childs, "Anglo-Italian Contacts in the Fourteenth Century," in *Chaucer and the Italian Trecento*, ed. Piero Boitani (New York: Cambridge UP, 1983), pp. 65–86.

54 Another Italian journey has been suggested: to Milan in 1368 to join the entourage of Lionel, Duke of Clarence shortly after the Duke's marriage to Violante Visconti. The archival evidence for this is scanty and the journey is unlikely, however. See Edith Rickert, "Chaucer Abroad in 1368," *Modern Philology* 25 (1928): 511–12, and Margaret Galway, "Chaucer's Journeys in 1368," *Times Literary Supplement*, 4 April 1958, p. 183.

55 See George B. Parks, *The English Traveler to Italy*, I, *The Middle Ages* (Stanford, CA, 1954), *passim*; Howard Schless, "Transformations: Chaucer's Use of Italian," in D. S. Brewer, ed., *Geoffrey Chaucer* (London: Bell, 1974), pp. 184–223.

56 See Martin C. Crow and Clair C. Olson, eds, *Chaucer Life-Records* (Oxford: Clarendon, 1966), pp. 32–40.

57 Most of the copies of Boccaccio's *Teseida* which can be identified by location or by scribe were made in Florence. See Edvige Agostinelli, "A Catalogue of the Manuscripts of *Il Teseida*," *Studi sul Boccaccio* 15 (1985–86): 5.

58 Galeazzo II died on 4 August 1378, during the time that Chaucer was in Lombardy, and was succeeded by his son Gian Galeazzo Visconti. For the documents concerning Chaucer's journey to Lombardy, see Crow and Olson, *Chaucer Life-Records*, pp. 53–61.

59 Rodney Delasanta, "Notes: Chaucer, Pavia, and the Ciel d'Oro," *Medium Aevum* 54 (1985): 117–21.

Europe.[60] The ducal library had received Petrarch's manuscripts after his death in 1374, and it was known to contain copies of the works of Dante, Petrarch, and Boccaccio.[61] The Visconti dukes, who were unusually generous in allowing copies of their manuscripts to be made, might have been particularly inclined toward generosity in dealing with a book-loving English emissary who, as a young man, had been connected with the household of the late prince Lionel.[62] The Visconti Library at Pavia had two copies of the *Teseida* in the late fourteenth century, both of which have subsequently and unfortunately disappeared. I have suggested elsewhere that one of these, MS 881, was the basis of Chaucer's copy of the *Teseida*.[63]

One other argument in favor of Chaucer's having obtained his copy of the *Teseida* in Lombardy in 1378 is that his writings begin to show the influence of Boccaccio's story only after his return from this second trip to Italy. During the following decade, beginning with *Anelida and Arcite* and the *Parliament of Fowls*, continuing with *Troilus and Criseyde*, and culminating in *The Knight's Tale*, the *Teseida* became a consistently stronger presence in Chaucer's literary work.

Faced with this clear evidence of Chaucer's continued interest in the *Teseida*, the source scholar must then deal with the question, what form of Boccaccio's epic did Chaucer know? Did he have a copy of the work in the form that Boccaccio composed it, or did he have a copy with the variants, additions, and omissions that manuscripts customarily accumulate during the process of replication and transmission? This issue is a crucial one for source scholarship, for only by understanding the form of a literary source that was on a writer's desk can we judge how the writer depended on, deviated from, and transformed his source.

The text of Chaucer's *Teseida*: The question of what Chaucer's manuscript copy of the *Teseida* contained or what it lacked, is a difficult one, however. One way of dealing with that question is to do a close reading of *The Knight's Tale* to determine whether any traces of Chaucer's personal copy of the *Teseida* are evident in it. That process is complicated by the peculiar history of the text of the *Teseida*.

60 The collection, begun by Galeazzo II about 1365, was largely assembled during the late fourteenth century. An inventory made in 1426 lists 988 volumes in Latin, French and Italian. See Elisabeth Pellegrin, *La bibliothèque des Visconti et des Sforza, ducs de Milan au XVe siècle* (Paris: CNRS, 1955) and *Supplement*, Société internationale de bibliophilie (Florence: Olschki, 1969), and Robert A. Pratt, "Chaucer and the Visconti Libraries," *English Literary History* 6 (1939): 191–9.

61 The library had 8 MSS of Dante's works, 26 MSS of Petrarch's works, and 12 MSS of Boccaccio's works. The Boccaccio manuscripts, with their inventory numbers, are the *Amorosa visione* (859), the *Rime* (859), the *Caccia di Diana* (859), the *Decameron* (870), "*Res vulgares*" (296, probably a second copy of the *Decameron*), *De casibus virorum illustrium* (383), *De claris mulieribus* (381), *De genealogia deorum* (384), *De montibus, silvis, fontibus. . .* (382), the *Filostrato* (800), and the *Teseida* (881, 935). A letter of Boccaccio's could be found in a collection of letters to Petrarch (392). In the 1426 library inventory, all of the Boccaccio MSS were attributed to their author except the *Filostrato* and the two copies of the *Teseida*. See Elisabeth Pellegrin, *La bibliothèque des Visconti*, p. 11, inventory A, and index 4.

62 Pratt, "Chaucer and the Visconti Libraries," pp. 197–9.

63 See William Coleman, "Chaucer, the *Teseida*, and the Visconti Library at Pavia: A Hypothesis," *Medium Aevum* 51 (1982): 92–101.

Since the time of Thomas Tyrwhitt,[64] Chaucer editors have recognized Boccaccio's *Teseida* as the source of *The Knight's Tale*. Nineteenth-century editors, in particular W. W. Skeat,[65] provided general indications of the relationship. But extended, close study was not possible because, beginning with the two fifteenth-century printings, the *Teseida* was available only in unreliable editions.[66] Complaining about the untrustworthy text of the *Teseida*, an eighteenth-century philologist, Anton Maria Salvini, lamented: "chi cita la stampata, che pure è Opera grande, non cita Boccaccio, ma un fantasma" [whoever quotes the printed edition – even though it is a great work – is not quoting Boccaccio, but a phantasm].[67] Salvini's objection about the *Teseida* was valid until the late 1920s, when an autograph copy of the *Teseida* was identified, purchased by the Italian government, and subsequently deposited in the Laurentian Library (Biblioteca Medicea-Laurenziana) in Florence.[68]

Laurentian Library autograph: Boccaccio first composed and circulated the *Teseida* between 1338 and 1341.[69] The Laurentian Library autograph (*Aut*) was copied several years later, in the late 1340s or early 1350s.[70] Boccaccio was in the habit of making subsequent copies of his works – often producing a variant version in the process[71] – so the existence of a later autograph copy of the *Teseida* is not unusual.

The *Teseida* autograph is a complex text including the poem plus eight types

64 *The Canterbury Tales of Chaucer*, 5 vols (London: T. Payne, 1775–78).

65 *The Works of Geoffrey Chaucer*, 2nd edn (Oxford: Clarendon, 1900): vol. 5, Notes, p. 60.

66 The incunabula editions were printed in Ferrara (Agostino Carnerio, 1475) and in Naples (Francesco del Tuppo, c. 1490). The Ferrara edition is based on a MS (Milan, Biblioteca Ambrosiana, Cod. D, 524 inf.) that is a textual composite from the *alpha* and the *beta* families, while the Naples edition is based on a MS of the *alpha-zeta* group, with many corrupt readings. The Ferrara edition subsequently supplied many erroneous readings to the edition of Gaetano di Pofi (Lecco, 1528) and the prose translation by Nicolao Granucci (Lucca, 1575). The *Teseida* was not re-edited until the nineteenth-century. The nineteenth-century editions were based on different MSS, but these were defective in other ways. The edition by Guglielmo Camposampiero (1819; rpt. 1821) is based on perhaps the most corrupt MS of the *Teseida*, but this MS, interestingly enough, is the one presented below as the extant copy most closely related to Chaucer's own copy of the *Teseida*. The edition of Ignazio Moutier (1831) is based on several Florentine MSS; although his edition contains many errors, it represents an improvement in the published text of the *Teseida* and was subsequently used in the editions of 1837 (Milan: Giovanni Silvestri) and 1838 (Venice: Giuseppe Antonelli). For further information about these editions and their manuscript sources, see Salvatore Battaglia's introduction to Giovanni Boccaccio, *Teseida*, Edizione critica (Florence: Sansoni, 1938), pp. xxxvi–xlii.

67 Cited in Giovanni Maria Mazuchelli, *Gli scrittori d'Italia* (Brescia, 1762), 2.3.1362 n. 272.

68 For descriptions of the MS (Cod. Acquisti e Doni 325), see G. Vandelli, "Un autografo della *Teseide*," 5–76; Salvatore Battaglia, ed., *Teseida*, pp. xi–xv; VIII° Congresso Internazionale di Studi Romanzi, *Mostra di codici romanzi delle Biblioteche Fiorentine* (Florence, 1956), pp. 44–5; *Mostra del 650° anniversario della nascita di Giovanni Boccaccio* (Florence, 1963), pp. 10–11; VI° Centenario della Morte di Giovanni Boccaccio, *Mostra di manoscritti, documenti e edizioni, Firenze, Biblioteca Medicea Laurenziana, 22 maggio – 31 agosto 1975*, I, Manoscritti e Documenti (Certaldo: Comitato Promotore, 1975), pp. 32–3; Biblioteca Medicea Laurenziana, *Mostra di Autografi Laurenziani* (Florence, 1979), no. 2, p. 5; Agostinelli, "A Catalogue of the Manuscripts of *Il Teseida*," pp. 17–19.

69 Vittore Branca dates the composition of the poem before Boccaccio's return from Naples to Florence in 1341: *Giovanni Boccaccio: profilo biografico*, 2nd edn (Florence: Sansoni, 1992), pp. 48–9.

70 A. C. de la Mare, *The Handwriting of Italian Humanists*, I (Oxford, 1973), p. 27.

71 Among the variant versions of his work that Boccaccio circulated is the autograph of the *Decameron* (Berlin, Staatsbibliothek, Cod. Hamilton 90), which he copied c. 1370–71, or about twenty years after the original composition of the work. Although the manuscript has some minor variants from the rest of the *Decameron* MS corpus, it cannot be considered an alternate edition. Interesting, however, is the

of access to the poem: by means of glosses, marginal parafs, illustrations, sub-linear punctuation, a prose preface, rubrics, introductory sonnets, and decorated initials. These aids explain the poem, point out its divisions, summarize its contents, and even indicate how it is to be pronounced.

The glosses in the autograph reflect the medieval habit, when copying manuscripts of the Latin classics, of including later commentaries on the work. When he was composing the *Teseida*, Boccaccio had on his own desk a twelfth-century MS of Statius's *Thebaid* with the late classical commentary by Lactantius Placidus.[72] In composing his auto-commentary for the *Teseida*, Boccaccio was creating his epic in the form in which his age understood the genre, making an "instant classic"[73] of it in the process. His interlinear and marginal glosses – about 1320 in number – are of varying length, from one to over 5200 words.[74] The commentary provides information about classical myth, literature, and history, defines technical terms and poetic phrases, discusses the poet's own feelings for his beloved lady, and (in Book 7) provides two extended allegorical readings connected with the temples of Mars and Venus.

A program of 100 parafs – paragraph signs that, like the pointing hands in the margins of many manuscripts, indicate the octaves that the poet considers crucial to the argument of his poem – appear throughout Boccaccio's autograph manuscript.[75] These indicate a theme of love and war, represented in the poem by the two young knights and their patron deities, Mars and Venus.[76] Boccaccio also conceived of a program of 59 illustrations, spread through the text of the poem. Only one of these illustrations, a damaged and obscured representation of the author presenting his work to a lady, appears in the manuscript; it is also uncertain that the drawing is by Boccaccio. However, the spaces in the autograph where the other 58 drawings should have appeared indicate those places in the poem that Boccaccio chose for illustration either because of their narrative or their thematic value.

A notational system of sub-linear dots in the autograph manuscript indicates

fact that Boccaccio's making a copy of the *Decameron* in the last few years of his life disproves the common tale that, after a spiritual crisis in the mid-1360s, he abandoned his interest in secular literature.

72 The MS, now at the Biblioteca Medicea Laurenziana, Florence (Plut. 38.6), was part of the "Parva Libreria" at the Augustinian church of Santo Spirito in Florence, to which Boccaccio willed his books. Four missing folios have been supplied in Boccaccio's hand. See Anderson, *Before the Knight's Tale*, pp. 38–50 and notes. For the critical edition of Lactantius Placidus, see n. 20, above.

73 Robert Hollander, "The Validity of Boccaccio's Self-Exegesis in his *Teseida*," *Medievalia et Humanistica: Studies in Medieval and Renaissance Culture*, n.s. 8: Transformation and Continuity, ed. Paul M. Clogan (Cambridge, 1977), p. 164.

74 The exact number of glosses that Boccaccio composed for the *Teseida* autograph is not certain because of the loss of a folio (137a) in the MS. Modern editors have supplied two glosses from other MSS, but the authoritative Naples MS (described below) contains 18 glosses in this portion of the text. While examining the autograph in January 2003 for our forthcoming "old-spelling" edition, Edvige Agostinelli and I discovered eight additional glosses which do not appear in the modern editions. At best, one can say only that when Boccaccio copied the autograph it contained approximately 1320 glosses.

75 Parafs also appear in most MSS of *The Knight's Tale*. See Joel Fredell, "The Lowly Paraf: Transmitting Manuscript Design in *The Canterbury Tales*," *Studies in the Age of Chaucer* 22 (2000): 213–80.

76 Personal communication from Joel Fredell. See also Fredell, "The Lowly Paraf," pp. 225 n. 27, 231 n.. 44.

how the spoken text is to be elided. The system serves to keep the text as both a reading version and a performance version.[77] A prose preface, addressed to an idealized lady, Fiammetta,[78] explains that the work is also an allegory about unrequited love that she alone will be able to understand. Fifteen sonnets – one at the beginning and two at the end of the poem plus one at the beginning of each book – summarize the contents of the work, discuss the author's intentions, and report the formal title of the work. A program of some 200 rubrics divides the poem into thematically grouped sections.[79] A system of colored and decorated initials (from 2 to 8 lines in height) subordinates the divisions within each book.

In 1938 Salvatore Battaglia produced an edition of the autograph of the *Teseida* that was sponsored by the Accademia della Crusca. Battaglia's concern, after six centuries of confusion, was to establish a reliable text of the *Teseida*. Following the editorial conventions of his time, Battaglia normalized Boccaccio's fourteenth-century Tuscan spelling and omitted discussion of the parafs, the illustrations, the sub-linear punctuation, and the decorated initials. Battaglia's edition has been the basis for all subsequent editions of the *Teseida*.[80]

Girolomini Library manuscript: In addition to the autograph, Edvige Agostinelli and I have identified another authoritative redaction of the *Teseida*. This manuscript, at the Biblioteca Nazionale dei Girolomini in Naples and indicated hereafter as *NO*,[81] is not in Boccaccio's hand; rather, it was copied c. 1450, some seventy-five years after his death. A transcription of another, missing autograph copy (which can be designated as NO^{I}), the Girolomini Library copy has 1093 glosses (8% of which are unique), 99 parafs (13 of which refer to different points in the text from the parafs in *Aut*), and provision for 57 illustrations (18 of which are positioned elsewhere in the text than in *Aut*). It lacks the sub-linear punctuation of Boccaccio's autograph.

Aut and *NO* represent Boccaccio's ultimate ideas about the *Teseida*. Rather than arguing for an evolution of the text, with the longer collection of glosses in *Aut* representing Boccaccio's final thoughts about the *Teseida*, I would describe

77 For a discussion of how these function, see Vandelli, "Un autografo della *Teseide*," pp. 38–42.

78 Several nineteenth-century writers proposed that Fiammetta was an historical figure, Maria d'Aquino, supposedly a natural daughter of King Robert of Anjou. The woman is an invention, however: Boccaccio's version of the idealized lady of *dolce stil novo* poetry. See Vittore Branca, *Giovanni Boccaccio: profilo biografico* (Florence: Sansoni, 1977), p. 28 and Anderson, *Before the Knight's Tale*, pp. 197–8.

79 The rubrics are of two types: 27 divisional rubrics which mark the beginning and end of each book and 174 narrational rubrics, which introduce the narrative units within each book.

80 Editions to date after Battaglia are: Aurelio Roncaglia, ed., *Teseida delle Nozze d'Emilia* by Giovanni Boccaccio, Scrittori d'Italia, no. 185 (Bari, 1941); Alberto Limentani, ed., *Teseida delle Nozze d'Emilia*, 2, *Tutte le Opere di Giovanni Boccaccio*, ed. Vittore Branca (Milan, 1964); Mario Marti, ed., *Filostrato, Teseida, Chiose al Teseida*, 2, *Opere Minori in Volgare* by Giovanni Boccaccio (Milan, 1970). Battaglia's edition (Florence, 1938) provides a sound philological basis for the text which is still valid, even though some 35 additional MSS unknown to Battaglia have been identified. Roncaglia's edition suggests some minor editorial changes to Battaglia's text. Limentani's edition, besides offering additional editorial changes, provides an excellent study of the sources of the *Teseida*, plus notes, bibliography, and indices. Marti's edition does not add to our understanding of the text or the sources of the *Teseida*.

81 See Agostinelli, "A Catalogue of the Manuscripts of *Il Teseida*," pp. 45–7. Battaglia points out (ch. 4) that *Aut* combines readings from the *alpha* and *beta* families of the *Teseida* MSS, while favoring the *alpha* readings; *NO* also combines readings from both families, but favors the *beta* readings.

Aut and *NO* as two different and equally valuable settings or redactions of the text. These two redactions of the *Teseida* are independent of the genealogy of the other MSS. No extant MS descends from the autograph,[82] and *NO* is the only witness to Boccaccio's other, lost autograph of the *Teseida*.[83]

The other 65 *Teseida* manuscripts that have been identified to date more than double the number described in Battaglia's edition; 54 of these are complete copies of Boccaccio's poem.[84] Six of these 54 manuscripts can be omitted from this discussion since they are composites or hybrids, the products of fifteenth-century editors who tried to reconcile variant readings in different texts.[85] Because these re-workings of the text were created during the century after Chaucer, they are irrelevant to an examination of a discussion of the manuscript that Chaucer owned. The remaining 47 MSS are the product of the first redaction of the poem (c. 1340).

Even though the number of known MSS is much greater than the 28 which Battaglia knew, Battaglia's system for classifying the Teseida MSS is still generally valid.[86] The 47 manuscripts of the first redaction occur in three families: *alpha* (37 MSS plus three composite MSS), *beta* (six MSS), and *gamma* (one MS).[87] The textual scholarship since Battaglia has produced great advances

[82] Battaglia lists some 23 variants where the extant MSS all agree against the autograph and several other places where the text in the autograph needs minor emendation (pp. lxxxviii–xcix). The variants and the mistranscriptions are the product of Boccaccio-as-scribe.

[83] Agostinelli and I are preparing a critical edition of *Aut* that will preserve the spelling and other characteristics of the MS. The edition, to be published by the Società Internazionale per lo Studio del Medioevo Latino (SISMEL: Franceschini Foundation, Florence), will reproduce the original spelling, parafs, decorated initials, illustration-spaces and sub-linear punctuation of *Aut*.

[84] The 67 MSS of the *Teseida* identified to date are listed below in the "Manuscripts" section of the Appendix. See Agostinelli's descriptions of these in "A Catalogue of the Manuscripts of *Il Teseida*," pp. 1–83; Vittore Branca, *Tradizione dell'opere di Giovanni Boccaccio*, 1 (Rome: Edizioni di Storia e Letteratura, 1958) and 2 (1991), pp. 41–4; and William Coleman, *Watermarks in the Manuscripts of Boccaccio's Il Teseida: A Catalogue, Codicological Study, and Album*, Biblioteca di Bibliografia Italiana CXLIX (Florence: Olschki, 1997). MS *SanF* is briefly described in *Giovanni Boccaccio, Theseid of the Nuptials of Emilia* trans. and ed. Vincenzo Traversa, Currents in Comparative Romance Languages and Literatures 116 (New York: Peter Lang, 2002), pp. 35–6. The following discussion omits one MS inaccessible in a private collection (Utopia), seven fragments (Ar L^5 FM M^7 Lo Pa^2 V^5), one commentary (Pr^1), and three eighteenth-century transcriptions of Vz (Pa Pa^1 Vz^1).

[85] Five of these MSS (MA CaM Ch V^3 and V^4) represent a composite and arbitrary edition with commentary produced in the 1430s by Pietro Andrea de' Bassi. De' Bassi's autograph was the source of the *editio princeps* of the *Teseida* (Ferrara, 1475), which itself was the basis of the editions of the *Teseida* published until the early nineteenth-century. The sixth MS is L^6.

[86] For Battaglia's proposed outline of the *Teseida* MS genealogy, see pp. lxxix–xcix. The best English summary is in Pratt's discussion of *The Knight's Tale* in Bryan and Dempster, pp. 83–5. Battaglia's model needs to be modified in two instances, however. One is his identification of only two families: *alpha* and *beta*. Gianfranco Contini (Review of Giovanni Boccaccio, *Teseida*, ed. Salvatore Battaglia, *Giornale storico della letteratura italiana* 112 [1938]: 87) pointed out that a single MS (P^2), which Battaglia is at pains to place in the *beta* family, actually represents another family, here indicated by *gamma*. A second issue is Battaglia's division of the *alpha* family into two groups, *kappa* and *zeta*, on the basis of a missing octave (9.47) that supposedly identifies the MSS of the *zeta* group. While it is clear that the two MS groups are discrete, they are more closely related since the *kappa* group also lacks octave 9.47. An additional issue is the redactions of the poem, that is, that the *Teseida* was created in three stages: a first version which included the *alpha*, *beta*, and *gamma* families, plus second and third versions represented by *NO* and *Aut*. See the discussion and diagram, "Redactions of the *Teseida*," in the Appendix below.

[87] For the MSS in each of these families and sub-groups, see "Manuscripts of the *Teseida*," in the Appendix below.

in our knowledge about the history of Boccaccio's works.[88] This, in turn, puts us in a much clearer position to discuss the "location" of Chaucer's copy of the *Teseida*, that is, whether his copy of the *Teseida* was related to the first redaction of c. 1340, to the autograph version of c. 1350 (*Aut*), or to the other authoritative version of the text represented by *NO*.

The question is important because source study done on *The Knight's Tale* to date has been based on the modern editions of the Laurentian Library MS. As such, this research implies that the *Teseida* on Chaucer's desk was a copy or a close relative of *Aut*.[89] A comparison of *Aut* and *NO* with Chaucer's text, however, has suggested that Chaucer was translating from a variant text of the *Teseida*. Five instances of Chaucer's unusual renderings of Boccaccio will demonstrate this contention.

(1) The first instance concerns Chaucer's version of the name of one of his heroes. While the autograph and *NO* call the young man "Palemone," Chaucer's name for the young Theban prince is "Palamon." It might be suggested that the name change was Chaucer's invention, but 32 of the "first redaction" MSS of the *Teseida* spell the name "Palamone" instead of "Palemone." One can therefore suppose that Chaucer was merely rendering the name as it appeared in his MS copy, which was a variant text of the *Teseida*.

(2) A second example concerns Boccaccio's Palemone at the temple of Venus. His prayer includes the following avowal:

> Io non poria con parole *l'affecto*
> mostrar ch'io ò nè dir quanto io sento (7.45.1–2)

> [I could not show with words the *affection* which I have, nor speak how much I feel.]

Chaucer renders these lines:

> Allas! I ne have no langage to telle
> Th'*effectes* ne the tormentz of myn helle; (I, 2227–8)

Clearly, Chaucer's copy of the *Teseida* read "effetto" at 7.45.1. In fact, the reading is "effetto" in 46 of the 59 MSS where the line occurs.

Three passages from Chaucer's other works also appear to be based on variant readings in his copy of the *Teseida*.

(3) In the *Teseida,* Boccaccio states that Arcita returned to Athens in disguise, entered into the service of Theseus, and hoped ("et isperava," 4.63.2) that he might at least have the opportunity to see Emilia. Chaucer adapts this line as "He was despeyred," when describing Aurelius's unrequited love for Dorigen in *The Franklin's Tale* (V, 943). The change from Arcita's hope to Aurelius's despair may well have resulted from the common Italian representation of the

[88] Vittore Branca's *Tradizione dell'opere di Giovanni Boccaccio*, 1 (Rome: Edizioni di Storia e Letteratura, 1958) and 2 (1991) have listed all extant MS copies of the *Teseida* plus untraceable copies from wills and inventories.

[89] In *Chaucer and Boccaccio* (p. 113) Boitani pointed out that, while Chaucer may well have had a MS quite different from the autograph of the *Teseida*, there was no means at the time (1977) to find out about Chaucer's copy. So source study – for the moment, at least – would have to be based on the autograph.

phrase, "ed isperava," that Chaucer could easily have misunderstood as "e disperava" [and he despaired].[90]

(4) A line in the *Teseida* describes a journey through a garden, which includes the phrase: "et fonti *vide* chiare" [and *she saw* clear fountains, 7.51.6]. In the *Parliament of Fowls* Chaucer renders this line as "And colde welle-stremes, *nothyng dede*" (*PF*, 187) then invents a few additional lines of poetry to describe how the fountain was not dead, but alive with various kinds of fishes. The best explanation for this reading is that Chaucer's *Teseida* at this point read "e fonti *vive* chiare" [and clear *living* fountains] – a variant that does in fact occur in about a third of the manuscripts.[91]

(5) Shortly afterwards, the *Parliament of Fowls* describes "*Wille*," the daughter of Cupid, tempering her father's arrowheads in a well (*PF*, 214–15). The description is borrowed from Boccaccio's portrayal of the temple of Venus and its inhabitants. But the name of Cupid's daughter both in Boccaccio's poem (7.54.4) and in his gloss to the *Teseida*[92] is *Voluttà*, that is, "Voluptuousness." In all the extant MSS of the *Teseida* except the autograph, however, the name of Cupid's daughter is *Volontà,* which clearly is the source of Chaucer's "Wille."[93]

One might make the case that Chaucer had a good text, but his mastery of Italian was faulty. Both text and diplomacy argue against this assumption, however. Chaucer's renderings of the Italian, particularly in the seventh book of the *Teseida*, which he used so thoroughly, indicate that he had a sophisticated knowledge of Italian. In addition, Edward III would not have sent an emissary to Italy on the king's secret business if the man's Italian was less than excellent.

The manuscript evidence from these few examples thus suggests that Chaucer's copy of the *Teseida* contained readings that varied from those in *Aut* and *NO*.[94] The question then remains, to what degree did Chaucer's *Teseida* MS differ from these two authoritative MSS? The question is difficult since the 47 MSS in the first redaction of the *Teseida* contain a great range of variants, both in the "decoration" and in the text of the poem.

The decoration of the poem consists of the eight levels of access, described above,[95] which Boccaccio created to explain and summarize the poem, to point out its divisions, to indicate its significant themes, and to aid in reading the text.

[90] F. N. Robinson cites E. H. Wilkins and J. L. Lowes for this suggestion; see Robinson, *The Works of Geoffrey Chaucer*, 2nd edn (Boston: Houghton Mifflin, 1957), p. 723.

[91] William E. Coleman, "Giovanni Boccaccio, *Il Teseida*," pp. 53–5 in David Anderson, ed., *Sixty Bokes Olde and Newe*: *Manuscripts and Early Printed Books from Libraries in and near Philadelphia Illustrating Chaucer's Sources, his Works and their Influence* (Knoxville, TN: New Chaucer Society, 1986).

[92] The description of Voluttà occurs as part of Boccaccio's long gloss to 7.50.1 devoted to the description and interpretation of the temple of Venus. The section concerning Voluttà repeats her name four times. See *Teseida*, ed. Alberto Limentani, p. 464.

[93] In the autograph itself, Boccaccio first wrote Volontà then erased the name and substituted Voluttà. Robinson (p. 794) cites Kemp Malone's argument that "Voluttà" could be translated as "Wille"; however, the predominance of "Volontà" in the *Teseida* MSS indicates that this would have been the form in Chaucer's copy. See Coleman, "Giovanni Boccaccio, *Il Teseida*," pp. 55–6.

[94] In these seven citations, *NO* has two readings that differ from *Aut*: "Volontà" at 7.54.4 (a variant common to all the MSS except *Aut*) and "frondi verde" (green boughs) at 7.51.6. This last reading is unique among the MSS.

[95] These are the preface, introductory sonnets, glosses, rubrics, decorated initials, illustration program, parafs, and underdotting. See discussion above, "Laurentian Library Autograph."

None of these 47 MSS has the parafs, the illustration program, and the underdotting. All the extant copies of the *Teseida* have at least some capitalized initials, but none has the same capitalization as *Aut* and *NO*. Nine MSS lack Boccaccio's prose preface and five also lack the introductory sonnets to the *Teseida*. Only about half the MSS reproduce Boccaccio's rubric program. Seven MSS have no rubrics at all, however, while 16 have only occasional rubrics. All the MSS have the introductory sonnets to Books 2–12 of the *Teseida*, but 22 lack the two concluding sonnets.[96]

Boccaccio's commentary on the *Teseida* occurs in all three families of the first redaction, but in an abbreviated form. Five of the 40 *alpha* family MSS contain glosses,[97] while three of the six *beta* family MSS[98] and the single *gamma* family MS[99] are glossed. Not only do these MSS have fewer glosses than *Aut* and *NO*, but the number differs in each MS. The number in the nine glossed MSS from the first redaction ranges from 54 to 213. When sorted out, this totals 310 different glosses that subsequently appear in Boccaccio's autograph. The first redaction of the commentary thus consists of fewer than one-quarter the number of glosses in the autograph. Each family of the first-redaction MSS also contains a few additional glosses.[100]

For the sake of convenience, we could designate this collection of glosses from the first redaction as the "short" commentary. But since each of the nine manuscripts contains unique, authentic readings, one could just as well describe the short commentary as a collection of nine variant, authentic texts. This combination of common and unique glosses suggests that the first redaction of the *Teseida* may not descend from a single manuscript, but from a continuing process of textual composition on Boccaccio's part in which he was accumulating material that would eventually be used in *Aut*.[101]

96 In addition, the missing Visconti Library *Teseida* lacked the two concluding sonnets.

97 These occur only in the *zeta* sub-group of the *alpha* MSS. The glossed MSS are Ai L^7 M^4 R^2 and RL. Although Battaglia examined both L^7 and M^4, he erred in stating that no *alpha* MS contains the commentary (p. lxxiii). This, in turn, misled Robert A. Pratt, who concluded that Chaucer had an *alpha* MS and that his copy would therefore have lacked the commentary. See his "Conjectures Regarding Chaucer's Manuscript of the *Teseida*," *Studies in Philology* 42 (1945): 745–63. An *alpha* MS, *SanF*, dated 13 February 1462, contains 225 fifteenth-century glosses which are unrelated to Boccaccio's commentary.

98 The glossed *beta* MSS are L^1 A and MT.

99 The *gamma* family is an incomplete witness. Its single representative P^2 was copied in the late 1390s and the early 1400s by scribes using different exemplars. MS P^2 is a *gamma* text only from the prologue to Book 7.93.4; after that point, the poem is copied by different hands. The remainder of the MS is an *alpha-zeta* text with a few *alpha* glosses. In calculating the "common" glosses in the first redaction, two figures were used: the *alpha* + *beta* + *gamma* MSS to 7.91.4 (the last *gamma* gloss) and the *alpha* + *beta* MSS afterwards.

100 An *alpha* gloss at 1.24.6 identifies Cupido as "amore" [RL]; a *gamma* gloss at 4.17.3 identifies Agenore as a "re" (king); and a beta gloss at 11.19.3–4 explains that a "velo" (veil) on the face of the earth is an "ombra" (cloud). These glosses may well be authentic. The alpha family MSS also contain five erotic glosses – transcribed in n. 135, below – that were the product of a fourteenth-century Tuscan scribe other than Boccaccio.

101 The late, lamented Giorgio Padoan pointed out that Boccaccio was constantly revising his text, as is evidenced by the multiple authoritative versions of his works. He argued that Boccaccio scholars should think, not of an "original" version from which all subsequent copies descend, but rather of a "fan" (ventaglio) of autographs of a work which surround the stemma of a single redaction: see "Trasmissione manoscritta e varianti d'autore: Apparenti anomalie in opere del Boccaccio," *Studi sul Boccaccio* 11 (1979): 3.

The second and third redactions of the poem – represented by MSS *NO* and *Aut* – exemplify a different method of composition. In their present state, both these manuscripts share a common number of 993 glosses. In addition, each manuscript has a number of glosses that are particular to it: 314 in the autograph and 99 in *NO*. This same system of a core of common examples plus a number of unique examples also occurs in the drawing program and the program of marginal paragraph signs in the two MSS.

The three redactions of the *Teseida* represent two different composition processes. The first redaction of the *Teseida* can be regarded as an evolutionary accumulation of materials working toward the establishment of a text. The second and third redactions of the poem can, on the other hand, be regarded as variant settings of an already established text.

Chaucer's copy of the Teseida

In addition to these variants in the decoration of the *Teseida*, the MS copies of the poem also present significant textual variety. All the MSS of the first redaction contain lacunae or gaps in the text, some of which are common to manuscript families or groups.[102] Most MSS contain their own particular gaps, several MSS have transposed or reordered text, and some contain added, unauthoritative text. In addition, every MS contains readings – sometimes several hundred readings – that vary from those in *Aut* and *NO*.

The challenge for Chaucerian source scholars is to try to determine what Chaucer's copy might – and might not – have contained, to discover whether it was similar to the two authoritative MSS (*Aut* and *NO*) or to one of the 47 copies in the first redaction of the *Teseida*, with their omissions, additions, and variants. Barring the highly unlikely discovery of the manuscript that Chaucer had on his desk while composing *The Knight's Tale*, the Chaucer Library edition of the *Teseida*, which Agostinelli and I have been preparing, will seek to provide the closest approximation of that copy.[103] During the past several years, our collation of the poem[104] and the glosses in the extant *Teseida* MSS has produced a list of several thousand variants. In addition, we have noted the gaps and the additions in the poem and the rubrics, and studied descriptions of

[102] All *alpha* MSS lack octaves 3.69 and 9.47; all *beta* MSS lack 2.29.7–8 + .30.1–6. The single *gamma* MS contains no gaps up to 7.93.4, after which other MSS from the *alpha-zeta* group, with gaps typical of that group, were used to complete the text. The only lacuna in *NO* is the fused stanza at 2.29–30, which is characteristic of the *beta* family; this suggests that the *beta* gap is an authentic variant created by Boccaccio. The only other MSS without textual lacunae are six fifteenth-century texts – MA CaM Ch V^3 V^4 and L^6 – that were produced by collating MSS from the *alpha* and the *beta* families. As noted above, however, these "mixed texts" are omitted from consideration because they were produced in the century after Chaucer.

[103] The Chaucer Library series, a project sponsored by the Modern Language Association and the Medieval Academy of America, provides editions of the complete texts of source works used by Chaucer.

[104] The number of lines is those listed in Robert Pratt's chapter on *The Knight's Tale* in Bryan and Dempster (p. 92). Pratt cited 195 octaves of the *Teseida* used by Chaucer in *The Knight's Tale*, *Anelida and Arcite*, *The Franklin's Tale*, *The Parliament of Fowls*, and *Troilus and Criseyde*. In preparation for the Chaucer Library edition of the *Teseida*, these 195 octaves have been collated in all extant MSS except two copies in private collections.

missing MSS from published medieval and Renaissance wills and inventories. These variants were weighed against the comparable text in Chaucer in order to identify the *Teseida* MS or MSS that most closely resemble Chaucer's Italian original.

One fact that has complicated our work is that most of the surviving *Teseida* MSS are fifteenth-century copies of the work[105] and thus did not circulate during Chaucer's century. Since the copying of manuscripts results in the inevitable accumulation of variants and corruptions, later manuscripts differ from their earlier exemplars. Thus a gap or a corrupt reading in a fifteenth-century text may not have been present in its fourteenth-century antecedent. Of the copies made before 1390, when Chaucer would have had his own *Teseida* in hand, only the autograph and two other *Teseida* MSS survive.[106] It is doubtful, therefore, that Chaucer saw any of the surviving copies of the *Teseida*. Keeping these various issues in mind, one can proceed to look at the evidence in the MSS in order to arrive at an idea of the shape and contents of Chaucer's copy.

Missing text: One consideration in our examining the *Teseida* corpus was gaps in certain MSS where Chaucer would have needed the missing text. But since individual MSS from all parts of the *alpha*, *beta*, and *gamma* families lack octaves that were necessary for Chaucer,[107] it was not possible to eliminate any family from consideration. Of the sub-divisions of each family, only *zeta-zeta* is missing needed text and therefore might be excluded.[108]

"Unused" text: Besides the question of gaps where Chaucer needed the text, we also considered the question of text that Chaucer did not use: the prose preface to the *Teseida*, for example, which is missing in nine MSS.[109] Here, of course, one has to exercise a certain caution. Chaucer was the medieval English writer who most often used his sources in unconventional ways. One must take particular care in studying his works in order to infer information about the contents of his copy of the works of another author whom he used as a source. So the fact that Chaucer did not use the preface to the *Teseida*, with its exposition

105 For dating see Appendix 5: "Typology of the *Teseida* MSS" in Coleman, *Watermarks in the Manuscripts of Il Teseida*, pp. 158–60.

106 These two MSS are Cn (second half of the fourteenth century) and L^2 (late fourteenth century). The first dated *Teseida* MS, Ai, which was copied in 1394, has a fragmentary version of the glosses and many readings which would not have been in Chaucer's MS. Battaglia incorrectly dated several MSS as being produced in the late fourteenth century; this dating misled Pratt ("Conjectures," p. 761 n. 88), who suggested that many copies which circulated in Italy during Chaucer's visits were still extant.

107 The deficient MSS are to be found in both divisions of the *alpha* family: in *zeta*, 5 (of 31) MSS: L^8 (10.102: *KnT* I, 2771–4), M^4 P^2 Re and RL (11.8: *KnT* I, 2827–30); and in *kappa*, 2 (of 6) MSS: L^2 and R^4 (7.32–3: *KnT* I, 1992–8). In the *beta* family, 4 (of 6) MSS lack needed text: L^4 A MT Pr (11.55.2–7: *KnT* I, 2948). P^2, the single *gamma* family MS, does not lack any needed text, but the *gamma* text is incomplete, ending at 7.94.3.

108 A sub-group of *alpha-zeta*, the five *zeta-zeta* MSS (L^8 P^1 Pn RN and V^2) lack 8.124–7 (*KnT* I, 2680–3). Pratt (in Bryan and Dempster, pp. 86–7) argued for excluding the *alpha- kappa* MSS based on the missing *Teseida* 8.5; however, the octave is not missing in *Vz*, an *alpha-zeta* MS which was not catalogued by Battaglia and therefore unknown to Pratt.

109 In addition, MS 881 in the Visconti library at Pavia in the late 14th century also lacked the preface. See Coleman, "Visconti Library," p. 94.

of the Fiammetta story that underlies the poem,[110] cannot be used to conclude that it was necessarily missing from his MS. But if his copy had the preface, which contains material that he would have found interesting, it is noteworthy that Chaucer neglected to use it in some way.

It is also to be noted that five MSS lack the two introductory sonnets and begin at Book 1.1, where Chaucer starts using the text.[111] Five other MSS end at 12.83, where Chaucer stops using the *Teseida*.[112] These five MSS lack 12.84–6 (the octaves that return to the Fiammetta story as the allegorical frame for the tale, present a discussion of the author's poetics, and identify the work as the first attempt at an epic in Italian) plus the two concluding sonnets to the *Teseida* (where the poem is formally named). Again, one can only wonder why Chaucer would have neglected to use such interesting material in some manner if it were to be found in his MS copy. It is also noteworthy that Chaucer would have invented a name for his adaptation of the *Teseida*, calling it "al the love of Palamon and Arcite/ Of Thebes" in the Prologue to the *Legend of Good Women*.[113] This would not have been necessary if his MS copy already contained Boccaccio's two concluding sonnets in which the author begs the muses to supply a name to his poem and the muses' reply, naming the poem and promising it "in ongni etate fama immensa" [huge fame in every age].[114]

The unacknowledged source: Another oddity about Chaucer's use of the *Teseida* is that, while he acknowledges Dante "the grete poete of Ytaille" (VII, 2460) as the source of the Ugolino story in *The Monk's Tale* and "Fraunceys Petrak, the lauriat poete" (IV, 31) as the source of the Clerk's tale of Griselda, he makes no reference to his even greater debt to Boccaccio and, in particular, to the *Teseida*. Chaucer was not averse to fabricating an author when the narrative circumstances required; his invented sources, "Lollius" in *Troilus and Criseyde* and "Corynne" in *Anelida and Arcite*, attest to this fact. But Chaucer neither names a source nor invents the name for a source of *The Knight's Tale*. Instead, he alludes to "olde stories" as a general source (I, 859)[115] and to Statius as a source of further information about a minor detail of the story (I, 2294). While a sort of medieval "anxiety of influence" about Chaucer's use of

[110] The one possible influence of the preface is Boccaccio's "solo il bomere aiutato da molti ingegni fende la terra" [a plow can furrow the earth only if it is aided by much inventiveness] as a source of Chaucer's "I have, God woot, a large feeld to ere,/ And wayke been the oxen in my plough" (I, 886–7), but this metaphor has a long history in classical and medieval sources.

[111] A M^4 RL T V^2 plus Visconti Library MS 881 (1426 inventory).

[112] P^2 R^5 Ph Vz plus Visconti Library MS 881 (1426 inventory).

[113] *LGW Prol* F 420–1, G 408–9.

[114] 2 Concl. Son. 14. The most common titles for the work are Boccaccio's own: *Teseida* and *Teseida di* [or *delle*] *nozze d'Emilia* [Theseid of the Espousals of Emilia]. About a quarter of the manuscripts contain variant titles, the most common of which is *Teseo* [Theseus] or *Il libro di Teseo* [The Book of Theseus]. Some other variant titles are the Latin *Liber Theseidus* [The Theseid Book] and *Il Teseida delle nozze della reina Ipolita* [The Theseid of the Espousals of Queen Ipolita]. Two MSS contain interesting variant titles: "Libro chiamato di Texeo: trata delo innamoramento de Arzita et Palimone che loro ebeno ad Emilia" [Book called Theseus; it deals with the love which Arcita and Palemone had for Emilia] and "Il Teseida d'amore" [The Theseid of Love]. Agostinelli's catalogue of the *Teseida* MSS lists the various titles.

[115] Elsewhere he refers to ancient or classical sources: "the olde clerkes sawe" (I, 1163, referring to Boethius, who is then quoted) and "as olde bookes sayn" (I, 1198, 1463).

Boccaccio has been proposed,[116] one can suggest another reason. Both *Aut* and *NO* lack an author's name, and Boccaccio is named as author in only about half of the complete copies of the *Teseida* that have been identified to date. Chaucer may not have cited Boccaccio as the author of the work on which he based *The Knight's Tale* because his copy lacked an author's name.

This is not to imply, of course, that Chaucer was ignorant of Boccaccio's name or of his literary fame. When Chaucer was in Florence early in 1373, Boccaccio, who was living some twenty miles away in Certaldo, was revered as one of the great literary figures of his time. That spring, a proposal was circulating in Florence to invite Boccaccio to present a series of Dante lectures; he was eventually commissioned to deliver these lectures that fall at the church of Santo Stefano in Badia. One can assume that this project was a topic of conversation in the circles that Chaucer frequented while in Florence.[117] When he was in Lombardy in 1378, the fame of Boccaccio, who had died three years before, would have been even greater. The Visconti collections in Milan and Pavia, which were among the greatest in Italy, would have been particularly attractive objects of Chaucer's interest because these libraries contained copies of the works of Dante, Petrarch, and Boccaccio. Although he would certainly have known about Boccaccio, Chaucer might have been using one of the many anonymous copies of the *Teseida* and therefore would have been ignorant that Boccaccio was the author of the work.

While one must be cautious about making inferences based on material that Chaucer did not use, the variant readings in the *Teseida* MSS can provide surer evidence for the contents of Chaucer's MS. These variants can be characterized as "negative" and "positive." A variant is negative if it cannot have produced a reading in Chaucer. Thus, Chaucer's description of the door of the temple of Mars as being constructed "of adamant eterne" is clearly based on the critical reading "d'etterno adamante" [of eternal adamant/diamond].[118] The variants of the line – "di duro diamante" [of hard diamond], "d'ornate diamante" [bedecked with diamond], "di ferro e diamante" [of iron and diamond], and "di diamante serrate" [shut tight with diamond] – are all interesting, but none of them could have produced Chaucer's line. So for the purposes of this edition in this volume, these would be "negative" variants since they could not have been in Chaucer's copy of the *Teseida*. All of the extant *Teseida* MSS contain between one and thirty of these negative variant readings.

On the other hand, all the MSS also contain one or more "positive" variants that explain those points where Chaucer's text diverges from a reading in Boccaccio. Previous discussion dealt with five examples of these positive variants – from the spelling of Palamon's name in *The Knight's Tale* to the source of "Wille" in the *Parliament of Fowls* – where Chaucer's usage was most likely inspired by a defective or variant reading in his copy of the *Teseida*. Positive readings of this sort, which are discussed below in the notes to the edition, range

116 Donald R. Howard, *Chaucer: His Life, his Works, his World* (New York: Fawcett Columbine, 1987), pp. 189–91.

117 David Wallace, *Chaucer and the Early Writings of Boccaccio*, Chaucer Studies 12 (Cambridge: D. S. Brewer, 1985), p. 5.

118 *KnT* I, 1990; *Teseida* 7.32.7.

from one to six in all the MSS except one: a fifteenth-century copy of the *Teseida* in the Biblioteca Marciana in Venice, which contains 21 positive variants and has been chosen as the base text edited below.

Boccaccio's commentary: Besides examining the variant readings in the poem, we also collated the three versions of Boccaccio's glosses in the eleven MSS that contain his commentary. This multiplicity of commentaries presents an interesting problem for Chaucer scholars. Previous studies of the question whether Chaucer's copy of the *Teseida* contained Boccaccio's commentary assumed that Boccaccio created a single commentary on the *Teseida.* It now seems that Boccaccio's commentary was a work-in-progress during the 1340s and early 1350s and that it exists in three versions: a short form (totaling 310 different glosses, but occurring in nine MSS that range from 54 to 213 glosses), an intermediate form (MS *NO*, with 1092 glosses), and a long form (one MS, the autograph, with some 1320 glosses). The question now becomes whether Chaucer might have had a manuscript with one of eleven forms of Boccaccio's commentary.[119]

The task is not so daunting as it might seem, however, since the arguments that have been made in favor or against the commentary hinge on only a few glosses. Some sixty years ago, Robert A. Pratt made the case against Chaucer having a *Teseida* MS with Boccaccio's commentary. Pratt first discussed several glosses that might have contributed to Chaucer's understanding and use of Boccaccio's poem, but indicated in each case that the information was available to Chaucer in other literary sources known to him or in the common knowledge of his time.[120] Pratt also pointed out some errors on Chaucer's part that would not have occurred if he had the benefit of Boccaccio's glosses.[121] In the *House of Fame*, for example, Chaucer incorrectly assumes that Marcia (Marsyas) was a woman, but the gloss would have made it clear that he was a man.[122] In *Troilus and Criseyde* Chaucer's description of the death of Troilus is borrowed from Boccaccio's portrayal of Arcita's soul ascending toward the "concavity" of the heavenly spheres while leaving the earth's "convex" elements behind. Chaucer's presentation of the episode suggests that his MS lacked Boccaccio's gloss, which clarifies Boccaccio's allusion.[123] In *The Knight's Tale*, Chaucer borrows a line from the *Teseida* where the temple of Mars is characterized as a place where one sees "l'impeti dementi," that is,

119 See William E. Coleman, "Chaucer's MS and Boccaccio's Commentaries on *Il Teseida*," *The Chaucer Newsletter* 9:2 (Fall 1987): 1, 6.

120 Pratt, "Conjectures Regarding Chaucer's Manuscript of the *Teseida*," pp. 746–55.

121 Pratt, *Ibid.*, pp. 755–9.

122 "And Marcia that loste her skyn" (*HF*, 1229). Boccaccio's gloss to *Teseida* 11.62.7 describes the musical contest between Apollo and the satyr Marsyas; after Apollo defeated and then flayed him, the gods then changed Marsyas into a river. The gloss is present in all three versions of Boccaccio's commentary.

123 Boccaccio describes Arcita's soul ascending "ver la concavità del cielo octavo,/ degli elementi i convexi lasciando" [toward the concavity of the eighth heaven, leaving the convex elements behind] (*Teseida* 11.1.4–5). Chaucer describes the soul of Troilus rising "Up to the holughnesse of the eighthe spere,/ In convers letyng everich element" (*TC* 5.1809–10). While Chaucer clearly had the critical reading of the first line, his MS must have had a variant reading at the second line. (In fact, the line is corrupt in about half the extant MSS.) The gloss to *Teseida* 11.1.4–5, which describes the distinction between concave and convex surfaces, occurs in all three versions of the commentary, however.

"demented assaults" in one translation or "mad impulses" in another.[124] He rather skillfully renders this as "a rage and swich a veze" (I, 1985). If he had the gloss to this line, however, he would have known that Boccaccio actually meant the "impeti" to be allegorical figures.[125] He most likely would have then included them in his list of other such figures associated with the temple of Mars, which follows soon after this line (I, 1995–2030). In his description of the temple of Diana in *The Knight's Tale*, Chaucer depends on an ambiguity in the text of the *Teseida* and describes the transformation of Callisto and Arcas into stars, asserting that Callisto eventually became the North Star. Boccaccio's commentary states that they became constellations and adds that the North Star was part of Arcas's constellation.[126] In describing the paintings on the wall of the temple of Venus in the *Parliament of Fowls*, Chaucer, borrowing a few lines from the *Teseida*, describes Atalanta, "And many a mayde of which the name I wante" (287). If Chaucer's MS had Boccaccio's commentary, where these names are supplied, he would not have had to plead ignorance of them in his own story.[127]

Pratt's conclusion that Chaucer's copy of the *Teseida* lacked Boccaccio's commentary was subsequently challenged by P. Boitani, who maintained that Chaucer must have had Boccaccio's glosses, because two points in Chaucer's text showed evidence of his use of the glosses. The first concerns Boccaccio's depiction of the funeral procession for Arcita, which included horses whose riders displayed the dead knight's arms, ancestral heirlooms, quivers with bows and arrows, and his most splendid robes. In Chaucer's text this becomes a description of three riders who display Arcite's arms, shield, spear, and his "bowe Turkeys" with a burnished gold quiver and mounting.[128] Among Chaucer's additions to Boccaccio's description is his specifying that Arcite owned a Turkish bow.

Chaucer would have been familiar with the Turkish bow since he had already correctly translated "arc Turquois" in the *Roman de la Rose* as "Turke bowes."[129] Boitani argued, however, that Chaucer arrived at his description of the Turkish bow by misreading and mistranslating Boccaccio. In the poem Boccaccio describes "faretre e archi con saette" [quivers and bows with arrows]. Since *faretre* is the less common word for quivers, Boccaccio supplies the more

[124] *Teseida* 7.33.3. See *Chaucer's Boccaccio:* Sources of *Troilus* and the *Knight's* and *Franklin's Tales*, ed and trans. N. R. Havely (Cambridge and Totowa, NJ: D. S. Brewer / Roman and Littlefield, 1980), p. 126; *The Book of Theseus: Teseida delle Nozze d'Emilia by Giovanni Boccaccio*, trans. Bernadette Marie McCoy. Medieval Text Association (Sea Cliff, NY: Teesdale, 1974), p. 173.

[125] See gloss to *Teseida* 7.30.1. The gloss occurs in all three versions of Boccaccio's commentary.

[126] Boccaccio's gloss to *Teseida* 7.50.1 occurs in all three versions of Boccaccio's commentary. The gloss makes clear that Callisto and her son Arcas were transformed into the constellations Ursa major and Ursa minor, and that the North Star is to be found in the tail of Arcas/Ursa minor. Chaucer bases his description of the two on his misreading of Ovid's account of the transformation of the two into "vicina . . . sidera" (*Metamorphoses* 2.507), which could be translated as either "nearby constellations" or "nearby stars." Opting to describe the two as stars, Chaucer then mistakenly describes Callisto as the lode (or North) star.

[127] See Boccaccio, *Teseida* 7.61.4–8 and gloss to 7.50.1. The gloss occurs in all three versions of the commentary.

[128] *Teseida* 11.35; *KnT* I, 2889–96; see Boitani, pp. 195–6.

[129] *Roman de la Rose*, 909; *Romaunt of the Rose*, 923.

common word, *turcassi*, in a gloss.[130] Boitani supposed that Chaucer misread the gloss *turcassi* in his MS, applying it to bows (*archi*) instead of to quivers (*faretre*). In addition, he supposed that Chaucer mistranslated it to mean "Turkish."

This argument is problematic because it assumes that Chaucer would not have known the common word for quivers (*turcassi*), which occurs five times in the *Teseida* and is never glossed.[131] Even though *faretre* is the less common word and is usually glossed when it appears in the *Teseida*,[132] Chaucer would have understood it, too, since it is a cognate of the Latin *pharatrae*, which appears throughout the *Thebaid.* It seems more likely that Chaucer understood the meaning of both *turcassi* and *faretre* whenever he read them in the *Teseida* and that he did not need Boccaccio's gloss for his two translations of *faretre.*[133]

As for the suggestion that Chaucer confused the plural noun *turcassi* (quivers) with the plural adjective for "Turkish" (*turchi*), this is unfounded speculation. Additional evidence against the *archi/turcassi* argument is provided by the *Teseida* MSS where the commentary occurs. The gloss in question (11.35.7) occurs only in *Aut* and in *NO*, the two authoritative but isolated MSS in the *Teseida* genealogy that have no textual relationship with any of the other 65 MSS. It does not occur in any of the nine *Teseida* MSS with the short version of the commentary. The easiest explanation seems to be that, in translating *archi*, Chaucer remembered the "Turke bowes" from his *Romaunt* and fixed on the phrase, which also served his needs as a rhyme for "harneys" in the following line (*KnT*, 2896).

A second argument for Chaucer's having Boccaccio's glosses is his four uses of "as was tho the gyse" that parallel three descriptions of ancient customs in the *Teseida.*[134] These glosses occur in all three versions of the commentary. In each instance, however, it is quite clear that ancient customs are the subject of the narrative; furthermore, the glosses provide additional detail about the ancient customs, none of which is to be found in Chaucer's text. The glosses on the ancient customs can be just as well used to argue against Chaucer having had them in his MS copy.

While the argument that Chaucer knew Boccaccio's glosses is unconvincing, the commentary in the *alpha* family MSS of the short text raises another interesting question. In addition to Boccaccio's glosses, the commentary in the *alpha* MSS includes several rude, erotic, bordering-on-the-obscene glosses. The products of a late fourteenth- or early fifteenth-century scribe who is most likely

[130] *Teseida* 11.35.7 and gloss.

[131] The five unglossed occurrences of *turcasso* in the *Teseida* are 1.48.3; 5.79.5; 6.16.5; 9.72.3; and 11.56.4. Another indication that *turcasso* is the more common word for quiver is that Boccaccio uses it (and not *faretra*) in a gloss describing Diana's hunting equipment (7.80.3).

[132] The word *faretra/-e* appears four times in the poem: 7.81.2; 7.88.7; 7.90.2; 11.35.7. Boccaccio glosses all instances of *faretra* except 7.90.2, but the word is glossed in two previous, nearby octaves.

[133] "caas": *KnT* I, 2358 (based on *Teseida* 7.90.2) and *KnT* I, 2896 (based on *Teseida* 11.35.7).

[134] *Teseida* 2.78–80 and *KnT* I, 993; *Teseida* 7.71.2 and *KnT* I, 2279 ("as was the gyse"); *Teseida* 11.40.6–7 and *KnT* I, 2911 ("as was that tyme the gyse") and 2941 ("as was the gyse"). See Boitani, pp. 193–4.

not Boccaccio, these glosses (which can be read in a discreet footnote[135]) undercut and burlesque Boccaccio's genteel narrative. If, as is argued below, Chaucer's copy of the *Teseida* was from the *alpha* family, his MS would have contained these same erotic glosses if it were a glossed text. It seems curious that Chaucer would not have responded to them in some way if they were to be found in his MS.

The real issue in this discussion is not so much whether Chaucer might have used the few glosses cited to argue that he had a MS with glosses; rather, the question is why, if he had Boccaccio's commentary, would Chaucer have made such little use of it?[136] The two major set pieces in the commentary are the allegorical readings of the temples in Book 7 of the *Teseida*,[137] where Boccaccio devotes some 1300 words to the temple of Mars and some 5200 words to the temple of Venus. These enormous glosses occur in all the MSS with the commentary – not only the two authoritative MSS, but also the MSS with the *alpha*, *beta*, and *gamma* versions of the short text. Yet no part of these extended glosses can be attributed as a source for Chaucer. All versions of the glosses contain mythological references and explanations of Boccaccio's Italian that could have improved Chaucer's understanding and his use of the *Teseida* and prevented errors in his text (concerning the gender of Marsyas, the convexity of the earth, whether Callisto and Arcas were stars or constellations, and the like). The most prudent conclusion regarding the question of Boccaccio's glosses is

135 The five erotic glosses, with their manuscript sigla in brackets, are:

10.40.5, continuing a gloss that quotes the dying Arcita's wish that he had been able to marry Emilia and that they had remained together for three days as man and wife: "acciò che avessi sentito di quella dolcitudine che piace così ai frati" [so that he might have felt that sweetness which is so pleasing to the friars] [L^7 M^4 RL];

10.40.7, where the dying Arcita laments that he had not been able to have been married to Emilia even briefly, so that she would have allowed him entry into her "places." "*Loughi*. Cioè donde si cava il mele." [*Places*. That is, where the honey is scooped out.] [L^7 M^4 RL];

12.43.7, where Teseo encourages Emilia to renounce the service of Diana: "Non pareva a Teseo che la grandissima belleza di Emilia si dovesse perdere per andare seguitando Diana per boschi conservando castità. Ma più tosto maritarla acciò ch' ella non si perdesse il tempo et che ella postesse fare lavorare il suo giardino" [It seemed to Theseus that Emilia's very great beauty ought not be lost by following Diana through the woods, preserving her chastity. But rather he should arrange for her to wed so that she would not lose time and so that she might have [someone] work her garden.] [L^7 M^4 RL];

12.77.4, which states that Palemone and Emilia seven times enkindled the fires of love during their wedding night: "Dice che sette volte toccò il giglio dove più giova alla femina e credesi che quella notte ne cavassi gran quantità di zucchero e di mele." [It means that seven times he touched the lily where it does most good for a woman, and one can believe that that night he scooped out a great deal of sugar and honey from it.] [L^7 M^4 RL];

12.79.5–8, which refers to the Greek kings joking with Palemone the morning after his wedding: "La mattina li re greci e gli altri signori ogniuno domandav' a Palamone motteggiando con lui di diverse cose: 'Sì com' era rompesi quel pannicello?' 'Pianse ella come camminasti a la tua scorticata?' 'Scharicasti tu dentro?' 'Trovera' ve ne tu per un' altra volta?' 'A chui ne giovò più?' 'Farai ch' io abbi un pezuolo di quel migliaccio?' 'Serbera' mi il chuoio?' [That morning the Greek kings and the other lords were each questioning Palamone, joking with him about various things: "So how was it to break that little cloth?" "Did she cry out as you kept up skinning her?" "Did you unload inside?" "Will you come up with enough for a second time?" "Who got the most out of it?" "Will you let me have a piece of that sweet-cake?" "Will you save the best part [lit., "skin"] for me?"] [L^7 M^4 RL].

See Coleman, "Chaucer's MS and Boccaccio's Commentaries," p. 6.

136 After surveying the possible influences of Boccaccio's commentary on Chaucer's text, Pratt noted that "the amazing thing is not the presence of these parallels, but their paucity" ("Conjectures," p. 755).

137 *Teseida* 7.30, 7.50.

that the case is not proved. The evidence suggests, however, that Chaucer's *Teseida* was a product of the first redaction of the work and that it was related, not to one of the nine MSS with Boccaccio's glosses, but rather to one of the 38 MSS without them.

Marciana Library manuscript

One of these first-redaction MSS without Boccaccio's commentary is an early fifteenth-century copy of the *Teseida* at the Biblioteca Marciana (St Mark's Library) in Venice.[138] The MS, which is edited below, has 21 positive variant readings – positive, that is, in the sense that they can account for corresponding readings in Chaucer. These positive variants from this Venice MS, hereafter referred to as *Vz*, are unique among the *Teseida* MSS and are indicated with an asterisk in the notes to the edition.[139] The following selection indicates how these variants in *Vz* can explain readings where Chaucer seems to be deviating from the corresponding text in the standard editions of the *Teseida*.

(1) In the autograph, Boccaccio describes Theseus, after his return from the conflict with the Amazons, as not even having time to fold up his battle standards (*l'ensengne*) before he had to go off to lay siege to Thebes.[140] Chaucer would seem to be adding to the narrative when he describes Theseus's battle flag as being "Of gold ful riche" (I, 979). Since Chaucer often chooses to make more concrete a detail in Boccaccio, one might conclude that this is another example of his poetic practice. A unique variant in *Vz*, however, describes Theseus's battle insignia as rich (*le ricche insengnie*), a reading that presumably inspired Chaucer's description of the opulent standard.

(2) When Arcita secretly returns from exile and joins the service of Teseo, Boccaccio describes Teseo as placing all his confidence (*in tutto suo segreto*) in his new servant.[141] In *The Knight's Tale*, however, Theseus appoints Arcite as squire of his chamber (I, 1440). A unique variant of this line in *Vz* describes Teseo as awarding Arcita a title, making Arcita his sergeant in charge of everything (*in tutto suo sergiente*). This variant in *Vz* would explain Arcite's promotion to squire in Chaucer.

(3) In adapting Boccaccio's description of Teseo's hunt just prior to his discovery of the two young knights dueling over Emilia, Chaucer typically narrows his cast of characters. While Boccaccio describes Teseo as being accompanied by a troop of companions, Chaucer describes only three hunters: Theseus, Ypolita, and Emily. In the standard reading, some of Teseo's companions are calling to each other, while others are calling to their dogs (*alcun compagni e alcun chan chiamando*).[142] A unique variant of this line in *Vz* describes his companions as delighting in their hunting and hawking (*cacciando al lor diletto e*

138 Cod. marciano it. IX, 61 (=6304).

139 The unique "positive" variants in Vz are: *Tesdida* 2.26.2; 2.27.3; 2.50.1; 2.50.2; 4.59.5; 5.77.8; 7.12.2; 7.31.6; 7.45.1; 7.45.2; 7.48.1; 7.50.2; 7.50.3; 7.108.1; 8.124.6; 9.rub. bk.; 11.28.1; 11.35.1; 12.4.1; 12.7.7; and 12.7.8.

140 *Teseida* 2.50.1–2.

141 *Teseida* 4.59.5.

142 *Teseida* 5.77.8.

ucciellando). This variant would have produced Chaucer's description of Theseus's love of hunting: "For in his huntyng hath he swich delit" (I, 1679).

(4) The night before the contest in Athens, Palamone goes to the temple of Venus, offering the goddess his eternal devotion if she will help him in winning Emilia. In Boccaccio's autograph, the young man promises Venus that her temples will always be honored by him (*sempre honorati/ da me*)[143] if she grants him his wish. In other MSS, he pledges that her temples will be forever adorned (*ornati*) by him. A unique reading in *Vz*, which reports Palamone as promising Venus that her temples will always be worshiped (*orati*) by him, is the best source for Palamon's prayer to Venus: "Thy temple wol I worshipe everemo" (I, 2251).

(5) On the day of the contest in Athens, Teseo exits from the palace and is described as being quite magnificent (*magnifico molto*) in the presence of all the people.[144] Chaucer, on the other hand, states that Theseus was put on display – "was at a wyndow set" (I, 2528) – so that all could admire him. A unique variant in *Vz*, which describes Teseo as being notably conspicuous (*manifesto molto*) before all the people, can explain Chaucer's description of this unusual manner of displaying Theseus.

(6) Two lines from Teseo's speech to Palemone and Emilia in the last book of the *Teseida* describe the effects of the passage of time, with ancient (*perenni*) rivers drying up and other, new ones (*altri nuovi*) springing up from the dry riverbeds.[145] Unique variant readings in *Vz* describe rivers that are full almost to overflowing (*pieni*), but that run dry and are replaced by high mounts (*alti monti*). These are the best sources for Chaucer's rendering of this passage, which describes the "brode ryver" that dries up and the "grete tounes" (3024–5) that shrink and disappear.

(7) A final argument in favor of the authority of *Vz* is based on two lines from the *Teseida* that describe the temple of Venus, above which sparrows were flying and doves were cooing.[146] Unique variant readings in *Vz* transform this into a description of an enchanted garden, without sparrows, where the doves perch on the temple and coo.[147] This reading in *Vz* could have produced Chaucer's line in the *Parliament of Fowls* that omits both the sparrows and the cooing: "And on the temple, of dowves white and fayre/ Saw I syttynge many an hundred peyre" (*PF* 237–8).

Besides its striking textual variants like these, MS *Vz* has three other characteristics that support the argument that it is closely related to Chaucer's copy of the *Teseida*. These are its rubrics, its gaps, and its northern Italian accent.

Rubrics: An interesting curiosity that supports the case for the authority of *Vz* concerns its rubrics. Although only about half the MSS contain Boccaccio's program of some 200 rubrics, most of the remaining MSS contain at least the

[143] *Teseida* 7.48.1–2.
[144] *Teseida* 7.100.1.
[145] *Teseida* 12.7.7–8.
[146] "vide volitare/ passere molt? et colombi rucchare" [she saw many sparrows flying and doves cooing], *Teseida* 7.57.7–8.
[147] "vidde olitar' e/ posarsi molte colonb' e rugghiare" [she saw [word?] and many doves perch and coo)]. See note to *Teseida* 7.57.7.

rubrics announcing the beginning and end of the books. MS *Vz* contains just three of Boccaccio's rubrics: one that indicates a division between two books, and two others that introduce narrative events. These narrative rubrics describe the *infernale furia* (infernal fury) that frightens Arcita's horse and eventually causes his death (rub. 9.1) and the epitaph for Arcite's funeral urn (rub. 11.91). One rubric, the discussion of the fury, is the single instance where Chaucer uses a rubric from the *Teseida* as the source of text in *The Knight's Tale.*[148] Again, it is interesting to note that *Vz* uniquely contains just two narrative rubrics and that one of these is the only rubric that Chaucer turns into a line in *The Knight's Tale*.

Missing text and attribution: While keeping in the mind the caution that Chaucer's failure to use material in a source cannot prove that the text was missing in his MS copy, it is notable that MS *Vz* is also one of five copies that end at 12.83, where Chaucer stopped using the *Teseida.*[149] While MS *Vz* also lacks several other octaves,[150] it has all the text that Chaucer used to construct *The Knight's Tale*. *Vz* is one of 37 complete copies of the *Teseida* that lack Boccaccio's commentary.[151] Besides lacking glosses, it has a peculiar title (*Teseo*: Theseus) and it lacks an attribution to Boccaccio. As the discussion above suggested, all of these qualities could have characterized Chaucer's copy of the *Teseida*.

***Vz* as a northern text:** Almost all the *Teseida* MSS were either copied in Tuscany or retain Boccaccio's Tuscan language forms. Although MS *Vz* was copied c. 1430,[152] its text is a product of the last decades of the fourteenth century or the beginning of the fifteenth century. While still basically Tuscan, it has many northern Italian linguistic forms.[153] These northernisms in MS *Vz* could be used to support the argument that Chaucer obtained his copy of the *Teseida* when he was visiting the Visconti dukes in Lombardy.

The "problem" with *Vz*: Although MS *Vz* has the greatest number by far of positive variants that are likely sources for readings in Chaucer, it is also a problematic text. The MS is part of the *alpha* family's *kappa* group, which Salvatore Battaglia described as the most corrupt and error-filled group in the whole *Teseida* manuscript corpus.[154] The MS contains a significant number of corruptions that require emendations in this edition.[155] Since MS *Vz* was copied some

148 *KnT* I, 2684: "a furie infernal"; see notes to *Teseida* for discussion of rubric 9.1.

149 See note 112 above.

150 The complete list of lacunae in *Vz* is: 1.15, 110.5,6,8; 2.36; 3.45–7, 69; 4.son.10; 5.93; 7.7.6, 125.3, 126, 134.6; 8.25.4, 44, 55.1b, 57.2; 9.son.9–11; 9.44, 47; 10.50, 51.6; 11.19.8, 69.4–8; 12.son.14; 12.27.7, 79.8, 84–6; 2 concl. sons. The MS also lacks a folio containing 12.58–77.5.

151 *Vz* is a member of the *alpha-kappa* group, none of whose MSS contain any glosses.

152 The text is datable from its hand and from the watermarks in the MS paper. See Agostinelli, *Catalogue*, pp. 63–4; Coleman, *Watermarks in the Manuscripts of Boccaccio's Il Teseida*, pp. 135–6.

153 These are indicated in the textual notes to the edition. For indications of spelling changes and dialectal variants in late fourteenth-century and early fifteenth-century texts, see Paola Manni, "Ricerche sui tratti fonetici e morfologici del fiorentino quattrocentesco," *Studi di Grammatica Italiana* 8 (1979): 115–71.

154 Battaglia (p. lv) noted that the *alpha-kappa* MSS contain a series of errors that isolate it from the rest of the *Teseida* MSS.

155 There are 89 instances listed among the variants and emendations where the text in *Vz* has to be corrected because of a misspelled, unintelligible, or ungrammatical word. At least half of these are due to copying errors of the scribe of *Vz*. Eighteen of the emendations were required because of readings in *The Knight's Tale*: 2.26.3; 2.98.8; 7.24.1; 7.30.1; 7.32.7; 7.34.1; 7.43.3; 7.46.3; 7.50.7; 7.56.5; 7.71.2;

fifty years after Chaucer's second journey to Italy, these variants can be considered to be corruptions that accumulated in the generations of the text that were copied up to the production of *Vz*. Most of the defects of MS *Vz* can be supplied from the other five MSS of the *alpha-kappa* family.[156]

In short, none of the extant MSS of the *Teseida* satisfies all the qualifications discussed above for the copy of the *Teseida* that occupied Chaucer's desk when he was composing *The Knight's Tale*. MS *Vz* is therefore not to be considered as an exact representation of Chaucer's copy of the *Teseida*.[157] Rather, it is to be understood as the closest approximation of that copy that one can make based on bibliographical and manuscript evidence available at present. MS *Vz* confronts us with a variety of textual problems. It contains more variant readings than any other MS copy of the *Teseida* and it is the MS that most differs from Boccaccio's splendid autograph copy of the work. In the end, though, it provides us with a clearer understanding and appreciation of Chaucer's achievement in transforming what must have been a sow's ear of a source manuscript into the splendid silk purse of *The Knight's Tale*.

Edition of MS Vz

Variants: *Vz* contains more substantive variant readings than any other *Teseida* MS. This edition of 173 stanzas comprises only 14% – or one-seventh – of the *Teseida*. Yet these 173 stanzas contain 600 readings where *Vz* varies substantially from the two authoritative *Teseida* MSS: *Aut* and *NO*. About half of these substantive variants in *Vz* also occur in one or more of the *alpha-kappa* MSS, while the other half of the variants are unique to *Vz*. The variants cited in the text below compare readings in *Vz* with those in *Aut*, *NO*, and the five other *alpha-kappa* MSS.[158] Readings from the other MSS are cited only when they have some interest in terms of Chaucer's translation and adaptation of the *Teseida*.

Among the variants cited below are thirty proper names and proper adjectives. Salvatore Battaglia noted in his edition of the *Teseida* autograph that the mythological names have been violently altered in the five *alpha-kappa* MSS that he knew.[159] Many proper names and adjectives are even further corrupted in

7.71.5; 7.72.5; 7.77.1; 7.80.3; 7.98.4; 11.38.1; 11.51.1. In a few instances where a proper name appears in a variant form but Chaucer would have known the name from classical sources, the name is not emended; see 1.6.2; 2.28.5; 2.29.2; 2.88.3. Note that, despite the errors of MS *Vz*, Guglielmo Camposampiero used it as the basis of his edition of the *Teseida* (Milan: Silvestri, 1819, 1821).

156 See the notes to the edition below. In "Conjectures," Pratt disqualified the *alpha-kappa* MSS because of a corrupt reading which, according to Battaglia, was characteristic of the group (*Teseida* 9.8.2; Battaglia p. lx). Even this reading can be found in one *alpha-kappa* MS, however.

157 One other "problem" with *Vz* is that it contains Boccaccio's prose preface, which may well have been missing in Chaucer's MS. If Chaucer's copy lacked Boccaccio's preface, then *Vz* could not have been a direct descendent of Chaucer's *Teseida*. The missing Visconti Library MS 881, which I have suggested as the basis of Chaucer's copy, is the only known MS to begin at *Teseida* 1.1 (where Chaucer begins to use the *Teseida*) and to end at 12.83 (where Chaucer ceases to use the *Teseida*).

158 Three of the MSS – L^2 R^1 and R^4 – are composites; that is, they are *alpha-kappa* only in part. In the variants and emendations, only the *alpha-kappa* sections of these MSS are cited.

159 See p. lxi.

the sixth *alpha-kappa* MS, *Vz*. In *The Knight's Tale*, Chaucer often omitted the obscure mythological names found in the *Teseida*. This is not unexpected since, in creating *The Knight's Tale*, he summarized and omitted much of the *Teseida*. Some names might have been omitted, however, if they were corrupted or unintelligible in his copy of the work.

Emendations: The edition in this volume contains eighty-nine emendations, which are reproduced below in brackets. These emendations substitute for misspelled, unintelligible, or ungrammatical words in *Vz*, or are made necessary because of a reading in *The Knight's Tale*. More than half of these emendations were required because of scribal spelling errors in *Vz*. These misspellings, which are unique to *Vz*, are indicated by asterisks in the list of variants and emendations. The non-professional copyist of *Vz* usually misspells by "attraction"; that is, he errs by repeating a letter he has copied in a previous word or syllable or by anticipating a letter that he will be copying in a subsequent word or syllable.[160] When the misspelled words occur elsewhere in different contexts in MS *Vz*, where they are not subject to spelling errors by attraction, the scribe copies them correctly. The other *alpha-kappa* texts supplied almost all emendations. When a word could not be emended with reference to the *alpha-kappa* MSS because the reading in *Vz* is unique, the editors made the emendation, keeping in mind the usage of the *Vz* scribe.

Substantives and accidentals: Because Vz contains more variants than any other *Teseida* MS, a list that also included all accidental variants would overwhelm the edition. Except for two cases – the proper names and the scribal misspellings – the list omits accidental variants. The variant proper names provide information about the transformations that mythological names often underwent in fifteenth-century Italian vernacular MSS. This subject is of particular interest because of Chaucer's general neglect of much of Boccaccio's mythological references in the *Teseida*. As for the scribal spelling errors, the accidental variants are included in order to demonstrate the contention about the scribe's errant spelling habits.

In the list of variants, the abbreviation *lac* indicates that the line is missing in the MS, *om* indicates that the word is omitted from the line, and *var* indicates that the line is completely variant.

Translation

Like most surviving copies of the *Teseida*, MS *Vz* preserves the occasionally obscure text while lacking the visual aids (the parafs and illustrations), the textual aids (the prose glosses and rubrics), and the linguistic aids (the underdotting to indicate elision) that Boccaccio designed to clarify and explain the poem. In addition, MS *Vz* presents even more serious challenges. Like the other MSS of the *alpha-kappa* family, it contains several hundred variant readings. It

[160] Thus, in 2.31.5 the scribe was supposed to copy "alla pallude" but, once having copied "alla," he then produced the erroneous "pallade." In 5.13.1 he copied the first two syllables of "Tesifon," then repeated the "s" of the second syllable, producing "Tesison." At 7.25.6, instead of copying "Vulcano," his eye jumped ahead to the end of the word and he copied "Vuncano."

also contains many corrupted proper names and place names, most of which appear not to be due to the careless spelling of the scribe of *Vz*. (The names in MS *Vz* and its family are so problematic, that one wonders whether Chaucer makes a point of citing Statius as his source because he must have had to use the *Thebaid* so often in order to understand the name and place readings in his copy of the *Teseida*.) Another challenge is the language: MS *Vz* presents a substantially Tuscan text with many northern readings, several Latinate hypercorrections, and late-fourteenth-/early-fifteenth-century spelling. In addition, and unlike Boccaccio's autograph, the text in *Vz* is elided.

The translation is designed for the reader who is interested in studying Chaucer's use of the Italian original in *The Knight's Tale*. It is literal without, we hope, being difficult to understand. Words added in brackets are sometimes necessary to make sense of a line. While perhaps at times excessive, punctuation is used to support the meaning of the text; a "literary" translation would not always require the same kind of punctuation as occurs here.

While Boccaccio's narrative often consists of extended periodic sentences, the translation generally renders them into shorter English sentences. To give some sense of Boccaccio's language, however, the prose translation often contains sentence fragments or sentences beginning with a coordinating conjunction. The Italian text follows Italian punctuation practice, while the English translation follows Anglophone conventions. When feasible and the word-choice allows it, we have translated lines so as to show a "Chaucerian" reading. When Chaucer seems to have misread the poem, this is pointed out in the notes.

In preparing our work, we have consulted two English translations of the *Teseida*, Bernadette McCoy's rendering of the complete text (1974)[161] and Nicholas Havely's excellent translation of the part of the text used by Chaucer (1980), both of which are based on Limentani's edition of Boccaccio's autograph (1964). As for the proper names, we follow Robert Pratt's habit in Bryan and Dempster and leave them in the original. The gods' names and the place names are translated into English, unless an Italianate form will help in source study.

Many of the obscure classical names occur in corrupt form in MS *Vz*. These are generally not emended, for several reasons. First, since few of the misspellings can be attributed to the scribe of *Vz*, they cannot be regarded as fifteenth-century corruptions of the text. Second, many of the passages Chaucer was using have a "shadow source" in the *Thebaid*, which Chaucer could have used to supply a correct form of the name. (These parallel passages from the *Thebaid* are indicated in the summary table.) Third, many names in the *Teseida* do not reappear in *The Knight's Tale*; this may reflect Chaucer's different aesthetic intentions, but it could also indicate that he did not use a name because it was corrupt or unintelligible in his MS. Therefore, it would be misleading for source scholars if the names were all emended in the edition and the translation. As a readers' aid, the names in the text are given their correct English form in the

[161] The translation is sometimes problematic; however, it is for the moment the only published English rendition of the complete text of the *Teseida* autograph. Vincenzo Traversa's edition (2002) also contains a translation of the entire poem, but this is based on a single *alpha-zeta* MS with many readings that differ significantly from the text in *Aut* and *NO*.

footnotes. When the name in *Vz* varies from the name in the autograph, the footnote version appears in italics. Anyone wishing to consult different forms of the name can check the list of variants.

In *The Knight's Tale*, Chaucer quotes from each of the twelve books of the *Teseida*. We have edited and translated the 173 stanzas of the poem that Chaucer most closely follows. The rest of the work is provided in summary form, in square brackets.[162] Although only three of Boccaccio's rubrics appear in MS *Vz*, his rubric system in *Aut* provides logical divisions for the poem; therefore, the textual summary has been organized into sections that generally correspond to these rubric divisions.

APPENDIX

Three Redactions of the Teseida

The *Teseida* was produced in three redactions, the first beginning in the early 1340s and the second and third in the late 1340s and early 1350s. The MSS of the first redaction are not descended from a single, lost autograph because the *alpha*, *beta*, and *gamma* families each contain unique readings that are also authoritative (since they appear in the autograph). The first redaction should thus be understood as a process of composition whereby Boccaccio produced a series of authoritative, related versions of the text. During this period the poem achieved its final form, but Boccaccio continued to accumulate the material for the glosses. Boccaccio's concept of the *Teseida* at this point seems not to have included a provision for illustrations, parafs, and underdotted vowels for the sake of elision.

In the representation of the first redaction below, the number of MSS in each family or sub-group is indicated in parentheses. The sub-groups of *alpha* also contain three composite MSS, which are described below in the list of MSS. The existence of these additional composite texts is indicated by a plus sign.

The second and third redactions represent the *Teseida* in its final stage of composition, with fully developed, but variant, programs of parafs, illustrations, and underdotting. The two redactions are represented together because it is not certain which was produced first. In addition, it does not seem that one or the other is a "best text" that represents Boccaccio's ultimate ideas about the *Teseida*. The most useful way of understanding the two MSS is to describe them, instead, as two alternate – and equally valuable – settings of the *Teseida*. In the representation below, MS NO^{I} represents the missing autograph exemplar from which MS *NO* is descended.

[162] The summaries omit the 15 octaves, 2 sonnets, and 23 lines of the poem which are missing in MS *Vz*. These lacunae in *Vz* are: **1**.15; 110.5, 6, 8; **2**.36; **3**.45–7; 69; **4**.son.10; **5**.93; **7**.7.6; 125.3; 126; 134.6; **8**.25.4; 44; 55.1b; 57.2; **9**.son.9–11; 44; 47; **10**.50; 51.6; **11**.19.8; 69.4–8; **12**.son.14; 27.7; 79.8; 84–6; 2 concluding sonnets.

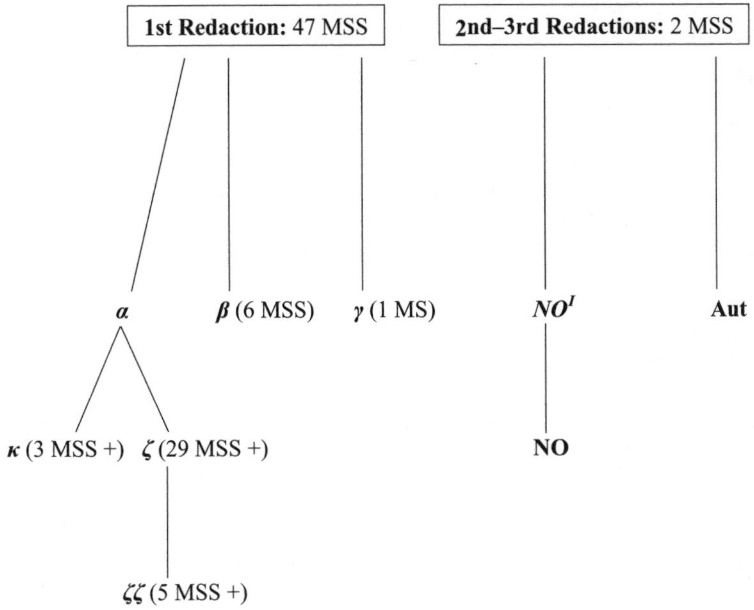

Manuscripts of the Teseida

The list below includes 66 MSS plus one incunabulum (which is the only witness to a missing MS).[163] For a description of the MSS, see Agostinelli and Branca.[164] Eleven of the MSS, identified by an asterisk, contain some version of Boccaccio's glosses on the *Teseida*. Besides the two authoritative MSS (*Aut* and *NO*), 44 other MSS can be assigned to one of the three MS families (alpha, beta, gamma). Several additional MSS are composites (with part of the text copied from a MS in one family and part from a MS in another) or mixed texts (hybrids created by amalgamating texts from two families). The list also includes three manuscript fragments, three copies of the preface to the *Teseida* (from later prose miscellanies), a commentary on the *Teseida*, and two MSS that are unavailable in private collections.

1. *Authoritative MSS*

*** Aut Laur**	Florence. *Biblioteca Medicea Laurenziana.* Cod. Acquisti e Doni 325
*** NO**	Naples. *Biblioteca Oratoriana del Monumento Nazionale dei Girolomini*. Cod. CF.2.6 (Pil. X.36)

163 Naples: Francesco del Tuppo, c. 1490. A second incunabulum (Ferrara: Agostino Carnerio, 1475), which was derived from a single MS that is still extant (MA), is not included in the list.

164 Agostinelli, "A Catalogue of the Manuscripts of *Il Teseida*," pp. 1–83; Branca, *Tradizione delle opere di Giovanni Boccaccio* 2, pp. 41–3. Vincenzo Traversa provides an abbreviated description of MS *SanF* in *Giovanni Boccaccio, Theseid of the Nuptials of Emily*, pp. 35–6.

2. *MS Stemma*

a. ***ALPHA***

Kappa

S Florence. *Biblioteca Medicea Laurenziana*. Cod. Strozziano 179
M[6] Florence. *Biblioteca Nazionale Centrale*. Cod. II, IV, 72 (Santa Maria Novella 196)
Vz Venice. *Biblioteca Marciana*. Cod. marciano it. IX, 61 (6304; Farsetti 203)

composite

L[2] Florence. *Biblioteca Medicea Laurenziana*. Cod. Pluteo XLIV, 25 [prologue – 9.31.7a]
R[1] Florence. *Biblioteca Riccardiana*. Cod. 1055 (O.II.37) [bks. 1–7.59.4]
R[4] Florence. *Biblioteca Riccardiana*. Cod. 1058 [bks. 3–12]

Zeta

* **Ai** Aix. *Bibliothèque Méjanes*. Cod. 180 (921 – R.197)
Bg Bergamo. *Biblioteca Civica "Angelo Mai."* Cod. MA 364 (Delta. VII. 4)
Cn Cortona. *Biblioteca dell'Accademia Etrusca*. Cod. 89
L[1] Florence. *Biblioteca Medicea Laurenziana*. Cod. Pluteo XC super, 91
L[3] Florence. *Biblioteca Medicea Laurenziana*. Cod. Pluteo XC super, 92
* **L**[7] Florence. *Biblioteca Medicea Laurenziana*. Cod. Rediano 150 (159)
M[2] Florence. *Biblioteca Nazionale Centrale*. Cod. II, II, 25 (Magliabechiano VII, 1323)
M[3] Florence. *Biblioteca Nazionale Centrale*. Cod. II, II, 26 (Magliabechiano VII, 109)
* **M**[4] Florence. *Biblioteca Nazionale Centrale*. Cod. II, II, 27 (Magliabechiano VII, 110)
M[5] Florence. *Biblioteca Nazionale Centrale*. Cod. II, II, 56 (Magliabechiano VII, 786; VI, 169; XXV, 571)
F Florence. *Biblioteca Nazionale Centrale*. Cod. Nuovi Acquisti 983 (Bargagli Petrucci III, 98)
P[3] Florence. *Biblioteca Nazionale Centrale*. Cod. Palatino 353 (365; E, 5, 5, 34)
* **R**[2] Florence. *Biblioteca Riccardiana*. Cod. 1056
R[3] Florence. *Biblioteca Riccardiana*. Cod. 1057
R[5] Florence. *Biblioteca Riccardiana*. Cod. 2733 (O.III.16)
Ma Madrid. *Biblioteca Nacional*. Cod. 10271 (Ii, 22; Osuna 34)
MA[1] Milan. *Biblioteca Ambrosiana*. Cod. D, 524 inf.
Pr[2] Paris. *Bibliothèque Nationale de France*. Cod. Ital. 582 (7779)
Pr[3] Paris. *Bibliothèque Nationale de France*. Cod. Ital. 583 (7780)
Ph Philadelphia. *University of Pennsylvania Library*. Cod. Ital. 12
Re Reggio Emilia. *Biblioteca Municipale "A. Panizzi"*. Cod. Turri F, 13 (45)
* **RL** Rome. *Biblioteca dell'Accademia dei Lincei (Biblioteca Corsiniana)*. Cod. 44.B.12 (Rossiano CLXXVI)
RL[1] Rome. *Biblioteca dell'Accademia dei Lincei (Biblioteca Corsiniana)*. Cod. 44.F.18 (Rossiano LV)

SanF San Francisco. *Library of Vincenzo Traversa.*
Si Siena. *Biblioteca Comunale degli Intronati.* Cod. I. II. 42 [bks. 1–6]
T Treviso. *Biblioteca Comunale*. Cod. 340
V[1] Vatican City. *Biblioteca Apostolica Vaticana.* Cod. Chigiano L, VI, 224 (398 A.-2303)
VzQ Venice. *Biblioteca Querini Stampalia*. Cod. 737 (C. VI. Cod. II; I.3)
N Incunabulum: Naples: Francesco del Tuppo, c. 1490.

composite

L[2] Florence. *Biblioteca Medicea Laurenziana*. Cod. Pluteo XLIV, 25 [9.31.7b-12.86]
P[2] Florence. *Biblioteca Nazionale Centrale*. Cod. Palatino 352 (222; E, 5, 4, 48) [Books 7.93.5–12.83]
R[1] Florence. *Biblioteca Riccardiana*. Cod. 1055 (O.II.37) [Books. 7.93.5–12.26]

zeta zeta

L[8] Florence. *Biblioteca Medicea Laurenziana*. Cod. Antinori 140 (A, 2, 64)
P[1] Florence. *Biblioteca Nazionale Centrale*. Cod. Palatino 351 (189; E, 5, 4, 53)
Pn Florence. *Biblioteca Nazionale Centrale*. Cod. Panciatichiano 15 (34; III, 17)
RN Rome. *Biblioteca Nazionale Centrale Vittorio Emanuele*. Cod. San Pantaleo 11 (104)
V[2] Vatican City. *Biblioteca Apostolica Vaticana.* Cod. Chigiano L. VII, 263 (398 B.-2304)

composite

R[4] Florence.*Biblioteca Riccardiana*. Cod. 1058 [bks. 1–2]

b. ***BETA***

* **L**[4] Florence. *Biblioteca Medicea Laurenziana.* Cod. Pluteo XC super, 140
* **A** Florence. *Biblioteca Medicea Laurenziana.* Cod. Ashburnhamiano 963
M[1] Florence. *Biblioteca Nazionale Centrale*. Cod. II, I, 157
G Genoa. *Biblioteca Universitaria*. Cod. A.IX.30 (Gaslini)
* **MT** Milan. *Biblioteca Trivulziana.* Cod. 1017
Pr Paris. *Bibliothèque Nationale de France.* Cod. Ital. 580 (7758)

c. ***GAMMA***

* **P**[2] Florence. *Biblioteca Nazionale Centrale*. Cod. Palatino 352 (222; E, 5, 4, 48) [bks. 1–7.93.4]

3. *Mixed Texts*

a. **L**[6] Florence. *Biblioteca Medicea Laurenziana.* Cod. Ashburnhamiano 542 (474)

b. *DeBassi*

MA Milan. *Biblioteca Ambrosiana*. Cod. D, 524 inf.
CaM Cambridge, Mass. *Houghton Library, Harvard University*. Cod. Typ. 227 H
Ch Chicago. *University of Chicago Library*. Cod. 541 (Phillipps 16259)
V[3] Vatican City. *Biblioteca Apostolica Vaticana* Cod. Vaticano lat. 10656
V[4] Vatican City. *Biblioteca Apostolica Vaticana*. Cod. Urbinate lat. 691

c. *Camposampiero*

Pa Padua. *Biblioteca Universitaria*. Cod. 84 (fols. 1–178)
Pa[1] Padua. *Biblioteca Universitaria*. Cod. 84 (fols. 180–297) [bks. 1–7]
Vz[1] Venice. *Biblioteca Marciana*. Cod. marciano it. IX, 62 (6305: Farsetti 204)

4. *Fragments*

L[5] Florence. *Biblioteca Medicea Laurenziana*. Cod. Pluteo XLII, 28
M[7] Florence. *Biblioteca Nazionale Centrale*. Cod. II, II, 82 (Magliabechiano VIII, 1374; VIII, 1386)
Lo London. *Library of Brian Lawn*. Cod. 18, fasc. 42

5. *Prefaces*

Ar Arezzo. *Biblioteca Consorziale (Biblioteca della Fraternita dei Laici)*. Cod. 162
FM Florence. *Biblioteca Marucelliana*. Cod. A. LXXIV
V[5] Vatican City. *Biblioteca Apostolica Vaticana*. Cod. Boncompagni E, 1 (Archivio Boncompagni E, 1)

6. *Commentary*

Pr[1] Paris. *Bibliothèque Nationale de France*. Cod. Ital. 581 (77582)

7. *Unavailable MSS in Private Collections*

Pa[2] Studio "Albertino Mussato." See Branca. *Tradizione* II, p. 42. (15th cent., partial copy)
Utopia See Kristeller. *Iter italicum*, V (Brill: Leiden, 1990), p. 460. (MS dated 1458)[165]

[165] I wish to acknowledge a grant from the Research Foundation of the City University of New York that provided support during the time that this chapter was written.

Tables

Although the tables below are a testament to more than a century of source scholarship on *The Knight's Tale*, they are not a final and absolute statement. Chaucer so thoroughly assimilated his sources that, while many lines of *The Knight's Tale* suggest, echo, or resemble a phrase in Boccaccio, Statius or Boethius, their source cannot absolutely be identified.

Table 1 identifies the sources of *The Knight's Tale* as they occur in the poem. Tables 2, 3 and 4 then survey the most important of these sources: Boccaccio's *Teseida*, Chaucer's *Boece* (and the *Consolation of Philosophy*), and Statius's *Thebaid*.

The abbreviations below identify the sources that appear in the tables. Editions of the *Roman de la Rose* and the *Roman de Thèbes* are specified because the line numbering differs in the various versions. R3 indicates that the citation of the line in the *Riverside* edition provides useful information about the source.

Bocc = Giovanni Boccaccio
Gen = *De Genealogia deorum gentilium*
Fil = *Filostrato*

Boece = Geoffrey Chaucer, trans., *Boece*. When Chaucer's source is both the *Boece* and Boethius's *De consolatione philosophiae*, the citation from Boethius appears in parentheses.

Dante = Dante Alighieri, *Divina Commedia*: *Inferno, Purgatorio, Paradiso*.

Fil = Giovanni Boccaccio, *Filostrato*.

Macr. *Comm* = Ambrosius Aurelius Theodosius Macrobius, *Commentarium in Ciceronis Somnium Scipionis*.

Ovid = Publius Ovidius Naso
Met = *Metamorphoses*
Her = *Heroides*

RR = Guillaume de Lorris and Jean de Meun, *Le Roman de la Rose*, ed. Felix Lecoy, Les classiques français du moyen âge, vols 92, 95, 98 (Paris: Champion, 1966–1970).

Rom = Geoffrey Chaucer, trans., *The Romaunt of the Rose*.

Tes = Giovanni Boccaccio, *Teseida delle nozze d'Emilia* [*Teseo*].

Theb = P. Papinius Statius, *Thebais*.

Thèbes = *Le Roman de Thèbes*, ed. Guy Raynaud de Lage, Les classiques français du moyen âge, vols 94, 96 (Paris: Champion 1966, 1967).

Vulg = *Biblia Sacra iuxta vulgatam versionem*

The following source studies of *The Knight's Tale* have been consulted in compiling the tables:

J. A. W. Bennett, ed., *The Knight's Tale*, 2nd edn rev. (London: Harrap, 1958; rpt. 1976).

———. "The Knight's Tale: A Commentary, Parts 1–4" (Cambridge, 1976), mimeograph copy.

Piero Boitani, *Chaucer and Boccaccio*, Medium Aevum Monographs, n.s. 8 (Oxford: Society for the Study of Mediaeval Languages and Literature, 1977).

Geoffrey Chaucer, *The Works of Geoffrey Chaucer*, ed. F. N. Robinson, 2nd edn (Boston: Houghton-Mifflin, 1957).

Vincent DiMarco, Notes to the *Knight's Tale. The Riverside Chaucer*, ed. Larry D. Benson (Boston: Houghton-Mifflin, 1987).

Robert A. Pratt, "Knight's Tale," in *Sources and Analogues of Chaucer's Canterbury Tales*, ed. W. F. Bryan and Germaine Dempster (1941; rpt. Atlantic Highlands, NJ: Humanities Press, 1958).

If the cited text in any of the following sources appears in this chapter of *Sources and Analogues*, the citation is italicized. Boldface entries in tables 1 and 2 are the *Teseida* source summaries prepared in the editions by W. W. Skeat (1894; 1900).

Table 1: Sources of The Knight's Tale

Knight's Tale	*Literary source*
motto:	
Iamque domos	Theb *12.519–20*
865–83	**Tes 1;2**
893–1027	**Tes 2. 2–5, 25–95**
894–8, 900–4	Tes *2.25*
899, 905–8, 911	Tes *2.26*
917	Tes *2.27*
923, 932	Tes *2.28*
924	Caytyves as it is wel seene: Thèbes 10028 ". . . chetives que vez ci"
931–47	Tes *2.29–31*
938	olde Creon: Thèbes 5416, 10076 Creon "li viex"
949–50, 952, 957	Theseus's encounter with the Argive women: Thèbes 10016–20.
965–6, 978–84	Tes *2.50*
971–2	Tes *1.128*
987–8	Tes 2.54–73
1005–17, 1020–32	Tes 2.85–9, 95–9
1018–19	Tes 1.5
1030–1274	**Tes 3.1–11, 14–20, 47, 51–4, 75**
1049, 1053–5	Tes *3.9–10*
1051–2	Tes *3.8.4–8*
1075–6	Tes *3.11*
1129–32, 1169–70, 1172–6	Tes *5.51*, 52–4
1163–4	Boece *3.m 12*.52–5 (*47–8*)
1194–1208	Tes 3.50–2
1198–1200	Theseus and Pirithous's story: RR 8118–24
1209–18	Tes *3.53–4*
1251–4	Boece *4.pr 6*.214–24 (*29–31*)
1255–9	Boece *2.pr 5*.90–5, 171–3 (*18–33*); *3.pr 2*.25–8 (*5*)
1260	*Vulg*: Romans 8.26.
1261–7	Boece *3.pr 2*.83–8 (*13*)
1281–98	Tes 3.77–9

Knight's Tale	*Literary source*
1303–27	Boece *1.m 5*
1307–9	*Vulg*: Eccl 3.18–20. (cf. R3)
1331	Theb *12.704*
1361–1448	**Tes 4.26–9, 59**
1363–4	Tes *4. 27–8*
1370–1	Tes *4. 28.7–8, 29.1; 37*
1391–2	Tes *4.37*
1399–1407	Tes *4.38*
1408–10	Tes *4.22–3*
1422	Vulg: Jos 9.21
1428	"Philostrate" defined: Bocc. Fil, title
1439–40, 1448	Tes *4.59*
1451–79	**Tes 5.1–3, 24–7, 33**
1467	Tes 5.29
1468	Tes 5.46
1488–96	conflation of Tes *4.73–4*; 4.79–81,*82–9*; 5.29–36
1493	Phoebus: Dante, Purg.1.20; Tes 3.5; *4.73*
1501	Dante, Purg.12.20; Par.22.26
1542–9	Tes 4.81.1–5
1545–65	**Tes 4.13, 14, 31, *85, 84*, 17, *82***
1546	Cadme and Amphioun: Theb *1.7–14, 171–85*
1553–4	Tes *4.85–6*
1557–8	Penteo/Philostrate: Tes *4.84.8*
1564–5	Tes *4.82.5–6*
1606–7	Rom 3432–4 (no correspondent in RR)
1623–6	Tes *5.13.7–8* (cf. R3)
1638–41	**Tes 7.106, 119**
1638–48	Theb *4.494–9*
1660	Cf. Theb *11.530–6, 539–40*
1663–72	Boece 4.pr 6; Dante, Inf.7.61–96. (cf. R3)
1668–9	Tes 5.77.1–5
1668–1739	**Tes 5.77–91**
1678–80	Tes *5.77.6–8*
1708, 1710–11	Tes *5.83*
1714–41	Tes *5.84–5*; 86–90
1812–60	**Tes 5.92–8**
1814	Tes 5.92.1–2
1829–69	Tes *5.95–8*
1829–32	Tes *5.96*
1835	Tes *5.95.7–8*
1850–3	Tes *5.97*
1859, 1856–61	Tes *5.98*
1885–1901	**Tes *7.108–10***
1891–2	Tes *7.110.8*
1902–2050	**Tes 7.50–66, *29–37*, 38**
1918–66	temple of Venus: Tes *7.50*, 51–4, *55–7*, 58–60, *61*, 62–6
1920–4	Tes 7.59
1925–35	Personifications: Tes 7.54, *55–6*, based on RR 573–92
1925	Tes *7.56.7*
1931	musical instruments and dancing: Tes 7.53.1, *57.3*
1932	Lust: Tes *7.55.7*
	Array: Tes *7.56.6, 57.4–5*
1936–7	Tes *7.50.2–5*
1940	Idleness, porter of garden of love: Rom 593

Knight's Tale	*Literary source*
1942–6	victims of love, including Hercules: Tes 7.62
1967–2050	temple of Mars: Tes *7.29–37*, 38; ultimate source is Theb *7.34–59*
1971–2, 1974	Tes *29.3–8*
1973	Tes *7.30*
1976	Tes *7.31.8*
1978	Tes *31.6,8*
1982	Tes *7.32.2*
1983–4	Tes *7.32.6*
1985	Theb *7.47* or Tes *7.33.3* (cf. R3)
1987	northren light: Theb *7.45* (cf. R3)
1990–2	Tes *7.32.7–8*
1994	Tes *7.32.3*
1995–2028	Tes *7.33–5*; Theb *7.48–53*
1997	Tes *7.33.7*
1998	Tes *7.33.8*
1999–2003	Tes *7.34–5*
2008	Tes *7.35.1–3*
2012–20	Tes *7.36–7*
2017	Tes *7.37.1*, based on Theb *7.57* (*bellatricesque carinae*: and ships of war)
2022–3	Theb *7.58–9*, a better source than Tes *7.37.2*
2027–8	Theb *7.55–7*, a better source than Tes *7.36* (cf. R3)
2029–30	Macr. Comm. I.10.
2049	soutil pencel: Tes *7.36.1–2*
2056–9	Calistopee . . . bere . . . loode-sterre: Tes *7.61.3–4*
2062–4	Dane: Ovid. *Met.*1.548–52; see notes to Tes 3.16.3
2065–8	story of "Attheon": Ovid. *Met.* 3.138–252: allusions to story: Thèbes 9128–30; Tes.5.57.6 and *7.79.4–5* (cf. R3)
2070–2	"Atthalante," "Meleagre" and the wild boar of Calidonia: Ovid. *Met.*8.260–541 and *Her.*4.99–100, 6.122; Bocc. *Gen.* 9:15, 19
2102–2206	**Tes 6.71, 14–22, 65–70, 8**
2129–52	Lygurge: Tes *6.14*; Theb *6.35–6*; *7.180*; Tes *6.21–2*; *35–6*
2138–9	Tes *6.21–2*
2141–2	gilded claws Tes *6.22*, *36*
2157	bayhorse: Tes 6.16
2175	laurel garland: Tes 6.41
2182; 2190–6	Tes *6.65*
2197–2208	Tes *6.70*, *7.99*
2203	love talk: Tes *6.70.2*
2204–5	animals: Tes *7.99*
2206–7	narrator's voice: Tes *6.69*
2222–95	**Tes 7.43–9, 68–93, 23–41, 67, 95–9, 7–13, 131–2, 14, 100–2, 113–18, 19**
2209–70	Tes 7.42, *43*, 44, *45–9*: (cf. RR 21053–78: Pygmalion's prayer to Venus)
2227–32	Tes *7.45.1–4*
2236	Venus's war against chastity: Rom 3698–9
2238–41	Tes *7.46.1–3*
2242–3	possessioun of Emelye: Tes *7.45.7–8*
2244–7	Tes *7.47.1–4*
2251–3	Tes *7.48.1–5*
2254–6	Tes *7.49.1–3*
2257–8	Tes *7.49.6–8*
2271–2366	**Tes 7. 70–93**

Knight's Tale	*Literary source*
2273–94	Tes 7. 71–6
2275, 2277–9	Tes *7.71*
2281	smokynge the temple: Tes *7.72.1*; see note
2283, 2289	Tes *7.72*
2290–2	Tes *7.74*
2293–4	Stace of Thebes: Tes *7.75–6* (modeled on Theb *4. 455–68*), but Chaucer cites Statius as the source.
2295	Tes *7.75.1*
2297–2330	Tes *7.77*, *79–81*, *84–7*, modeled on Theb *9.607–35*
2297–9	Tes *7.77.1–2*
2300–3	Tes. *7.79.3–8*
2304	chaste goddesse: Tes *7.79.2*
2307–10	Tes *7.81.1–4*
2313	Tes *7.80.2–3*
2320–1	Tes *7.84.6–8*
2323	Tes *7.83.1*
2323–5	Tes *7.85.1–2*
2327	Tes 7.78.5; cf. Theb *9.635–6*
2331–8	Tes *7.91*
2339–40	Tes *7. 92.1–3* (cf. R3)
2348–57	Tes *7.88.7–8; 89*
2349–52	Tes *7. 85.1–6*
2358	Tes *7.90*
2365	Tes *7.93.1*
2367–2437	Tes *7. 23–8; 39–40*
2368–72	Tes *7.23*
2373–4	Tes *7.24.1–2*
2383–90	Tes *7.25.4–6* (cf. R3)
2394–5	Tes *7.26.2–3*
2406	Tes *7.27.8*
2407–18	Tes *7.28* (cf. R3)
2422–4	Tes *7.39–5-8*
2425–33	Tes *7.40*
2435	Tes *7.41.1–2*
2438–41	Tes *7.67*
2491	Tes 7.94
2492–2527	Tes *7.96–9*
2506–7	Tes *7.97.1–3*
2514–15	Tes *7.98.3–8*
2523–5	Tes *7.96.1–3*
2528–31	Tes *7.100.1–3*
2537–65	Tes 7.1–11, *12*, 13, *14*
2543–60	Tes *7.12*
2561–4	Tes *7.14.1–6*
2566–79	Tes *7.113*
2581–3	Tes *7.114.7–8*
2587–93	Tes *7.19.1–7*
2600–83	**Tes 8.2–131**
2626–8	"tiger" simile: Tes 8.26.1–5 (cf. R3)
2630–2	"lion" simile: Tes 7.115
2657	Tes 7.13
2680–3	Tes *8.124–26*, 127–8
2684	infernal fury: Tes *rubric 9.1*; 9.4 (based on Theb *6.495–506*)
2684–2734	**Tes 9.4–61**

Knight's Tale	*Literary source*
2686–91	Tes *9.7–8.1–4*
2694–9	Tes *9.48–9*
2735–9	**Tes 12.80, 83**
2743–2808	**Tes 10.12–113**
2768–9	Tes *10.65.1,3–4*
2771–4	Tes *10.102*
2775–6	Tes *10.104.1–3*
2781	Tes *10.66*
2786	Jupiter: Tes 10.85.7–8
2798–2809	Tes 10.111, *112–13*
2798–2806	Tes *10.112*
2800	Tes 10.64.1–3
2803–5	Tes *10.112.4–6*
2808–9	Tes *10.113.7–8*
2809–10	Tes *11.6.2–3*; ultimate source is *Vulg*: 2 Cor 5.1
2809–2962	**Tes 11.1–67**
2827–30	Tes *11.8*
2831–3	Tes *7.1–3*
2837	Tes *11.9.1*
2839–42	Tes *11.10–11*
2853–2962	Tes.11.13–67, based on Theb 6
2843–6	Tes *12.6.1–3*
2853–81	Tes *11.13–16*, 17
2853–64	Tes *11.13*
2865–9	Tes *11.14*
2870–3, 2875	Tes *11.15*
2879–81	Tes *11.16*, 17
2881–6	Tes *11.30–1*
2889–93, 2895	Tes *11.35*
2887–8	Tes 11.36.1–2
2899–2900	Tes *11.38.1–2*
2901, 2907–8	Tes *11.37*
2905–6, 2909–12	Tes *11.40*
2913	Tes *11.18.1*
2913–17	Tes. *26*
2915–17	Tes *11.19.1–3*
2918	Tes *11.27*
2919–64	Innarabil: Tes *11.28.1* and note
2921–3	Tes *11.22–24*, based on Theb *6.98–106*
2925	gods: Tes *11.20*
2925–7	Tes *11.25*, based on Theb *6.110–3*
2929–30	Tes *11.21–4-6*
2933–8	Tes *11.27–28*, based on Theb *6.56–65*
2936	Tes *11.29.2*
2939–66	Tes 11.41–50, *51*, 52, *53–5*, 56–68
2941–2	Tes 11.44.1–2
2943	Tes 11.43.3–4; 46.2–5
2944	Tes 11.41–3
2945	Tes 11.48
2946	Tes 11.49.1–4
2947	Tes 11.56.1–6
2948	Tes *11.55.1–2*
2949–50	Tes *11.51.1–4*
2952–5	Tes *11.53–4*

Knight's Tale	*Literary source*
2958–9	Tes 11.57–8
2960	Tes 11.59–68
2967–3102	**Tes 12.3–19, 69–83**
2967–9	Tes *12.3*
2975	Tes *12.4.1*
2975–82; 2985–6	Tes *12.4–5*
2987–3016	Boece *1.m 5*; *2.m 8*; *3.m 9*; 3.pr 10; 4.pr 6; *4.m 6*
2988–93	Boece *2.m 8*
2994–3015	Boece *4.pr 6*.42–47 (*7*)
3001–2	Tes *12.11*
3005–10	Boece *3.pr 10*.25–30 (*5*)
3011–16	Boece *4.pr 6*.149–65 (*18*); *4.m 6*
3017, 3019–25	Tes *12.7*
3027–30	Tes *12.8*
3031–4	Tes *12.10*
3035–8	Boece *4.m 6.47–54*; *3.m 9.41*
3041–5	Tes *12.11*
3047–9	Tes *12.9, 12*
3055–60	Tes *12.12*
3059–60	Tes 12.14–15

Table 2: The Teseida *in* The Knight's Tale

Teseida	*Knight's Tale*	*Teseida*	*Knight's Tale*
1; 2	**865–83**	*4.37*	1391–2
1.5	1018–19	*4.38*	1399–1407
1.128	971–2	*4.59*	1439–40, 1448
2.2–5, 25–95	**893–1027**	4.*73*–4, 79–81, 82–9; 5.29–36	1488–96
2.25	894–8, 900–4	*4.81.1–5*	1542–9
2.26	899, 905–8, 911	*4.82.5–6*	1564–5
2.27	917	*4.84.8*	1557–8
2.28	923, 932	4.*85*–6	1553–4
2.29–31	931–47	**5.1–3, 24–7, 33**	**1451–79**
2.50	965–6, 978–84	*5.13.7–8*	1623–6
2.54–73	987–8	5.29	1467
2.85–9, 95–9	1005–17, 1020–32	5.46	1468
3.1–11, 14–20, 47, 51–4, 75	**1030–1274**	5.*51*, 52–4	1172–6
3.8.4–8	1051–2	5.57.6	2065–8
3.9–10	1049, 1053–5	**5.77–91**	**1668–1739**
3.11	1075–6	*5.77.1–5*	1668–9
3.16.3	2062–4	*5.77.6–8*	1678–80
3.50–2	1194–1208	*5.83*	1708, 1710–11
3.53–4	1209–18	5.84–5; 86–90	1714–41
3.77–9	1281–98	**5.92–8**	**1812–60**
4.13, 14, 31, *85*, *84*, 17, *82*	**1545–65**	5.92.1–2	1814
4.22–3	1408–10	*5.95–8*	1829–69
4.26–9, 59	**1361–1448**	*5.95.7–8*	1835
4.27–8	1363–4	*5.96*	1829–32
4.28.7–8, 29.1; *37*	1370–1	*5.97*	1850–3
		5.98	1859, 1856–61

Teseida	*Knight's Tale*
6.*14*, 21–2, 35–6	2129–52
6.16	2157
6.21–2	2138–9
6.22, 36	2141–2
6.41	2175
6.65	2182, 2190–6
6.69	2206–7
6.*70*; 7.99	2197–2208
6.70.2	2203
6.71, 14–22, 65–70, 8	**2102–2206**
7.1–11, 12, 13, 14	2537–65
7.1–3	2831–3
7.12	2543–60
7.13	2657
7.14.1–6	2561–4
7.19.1–7	2587–93
7.*23–8*, 39–40	2367–2437
7.23	2368–72
7.24.1–2	2373–4
7.25.4–6	2383–90
7.26.2–3	2394–5
7.27.8	2406
7.28	2407–18
7.29–37	1967–2050
7.29.3,8	1971–2, 1974
7.30	1973
7.31.6, 8	1976
7.32.2	1982
7.32.3	1994
7.32.6	1983–4
7.32.7–8	1990–2
7.33–5	1995–2028
7.33.3	1985
7.33.7	1997
7.33.8	1998
7.34–5	1999–2003
7.35.1–3	2008
7.36–7	2012–20
7.36	2027–8
7.36.1–2	2049
7.37.1	2017
7.37.2	2022–3
7.39.5–8	2422–4
7.40	2425–33
7.41.1–2	2435
7.42, *43*, 44, 45–9	2209–70
7.7–14, 23–41, 43–9, 67–93, 95–9, 100–2, 113–19, 131–2	**2222–95**
7.45.1–4	2227–32
7.45.7–8	2242–3
7.46.1–3	2238–41
7.47.1–4	2244–7
7.48.1–5	2251–3
7.49.1–3	2254–6
7.49.6–8	2257–8
7.50–66, 29–37, 38	**1902–2050**
7.50, 51–4, 55–7, 58–60, 61, 62–6	1918–66
7.50.2–5	1936–7
7.54, *55–6*	1925–35
7.55.7; 56.6; 57.4–5	1932
7.56.7	1925
7.59	1920–4
7.61.3–4	2056–9
7.62	1942–6
7.67	2438–41
7.70–93	**2271–2366**
7.71–6	2273–94
7.71	2275, 2277–9
7.72	2281, 2283, 2289
7.74	2290–2
7.75.1, 76.7–8	2295–6
7.75–6	2293–4: Chaucer cites Statius as source
7.*77*, 79–81, 84–7	2297–2330
7.77.1–2	2297–9
7.78.5	2327
7.79.2	2304
7.79.3–8	2300–3
7.79.4–5	2065–8
7.80.2–3	2313
7.81.1–4	2307–10
7.83.1	2323
7.84.6–8	2320–1
7.85.1–2	2323–5
7.85.1–6	2349–52
7.88.7–8; 89	2348–57
7.90	2358
7.91	2331–8
7.92.1–3	2339–40
7.93.1	2365
7.94	2491
7.96–9	2492–2527
7.96.1–3	2523–5
7.97.1–3	2506–7
7.98.3–4	2514–5
7.99	2204–5
7.100.1–3	2528–31
7.106, 119	**1638–41**
7.108–10	**1885–1901**
7.110.8	1891–2
7.113	2566–79
7.114.7–8	2581–3
7.115	2630–2
8.2–131	**2600–83**
8.26.1–5	2626–8

Teseida	*Knight's Tale*
8.*124–6*, 127–8	2680–3
9.1 rubric	2684
9.4–61	**2684–2734**
9.7–8.1–4	2686–91
9.48–9	2694–9
10.12–113	**2743–2808**
10.64.1–3	2800
10.65.1,3–4	2768–9
10.66	2781
10.85.7–8	2786
10.102	2771–4
10.104.1–3	2775–6
10.111, *112*–13	2798–2809
10.112	2798–2806
10.112.4–6	2803–5
10.113.7–8	2808–9
11.1–67	**2809–2962**
11.6.2–3	2809–10
11.7.1–3	2831–3
11.8	2827–30
11.9.1	2837
11.10–11	2839–42
11.*13–16*, 17	2853–81
11.*13*	2853–64
11.*14*	2865–9
11.*15*	2870–3, 2875
11.*16*, 17	2879–81
11.18.1	2913
11.19.1–3	2915–17
11.20	2925
11.21.4–6	2929–30
11.22–4	2921–3
11.25	2925–7
11.26	2913–17
11.27–8	2933–8
11.27	2918
11.28.1	2919–64; see note
11.29.2	2936
11.30–1	2881–6
11.35	2889–93, 2895
11.36.1–2	2887–8
11.37	2901, 2907–8
11.38.1–2	2899–2900
11.40	2905–6, 2909–12
11.41–3	2944
11.41–50, 51, 52, 53–5, 56–8	2939–66
11.43.3–4; 46.2–5	2943
11.44.1–2	2941–2
11.48	2945
11.49.1–4	2946
11.51.1–4	2949–50
11.53–4	2952–5
11.55.1–2	2948
11.56.1–6	2947
11.57–8	2958–9
11.59–8	2960
12.3–19, 69–83	**2967–3102**
12.3	2967–9
12.4–5	2975–82, 2985–6
12.4.1	2975
12.6.1–3	2843–6
12.7	3017, 3019–25
12.8	3027–30
12.9	3047–9
12.10	3031–4
12.11	3001–2; 3041–5
12.12	3047–9, 3055–60
12.14–15	3059–60
12.19	3068, 3070–2
12.80, 83	**2735–9**

Table 3: The Thebaid *in* The Knight's Tale

Just as he had two versions of Boethius – the Latin original and the *Boece* – Chaucer had two versions of the Troy materials: Statius's *Thebaid* and Boccaccio's *Teseida*. In both cases, he based *The Knight's Tale* on the modern version (the *Boece* and the *Teseida*) while using the older materials (the *De consolatione philosophiae* and the *Thebaid*) largely as secondary sources. The list below indicates 20 instances where a reading in *The Knight's Tale* shows the influence of the *Thebaid*. In six of these, the *Thebaid* served as Chaucer's primary source. In another two, the *Thebaid* seems to be a better source than the *Teseida* although either could have produced the readings in question. In the remaining 14, the *Teseida* was his primary source, but the *Thebaid* served as a secondary source. In these instances,

Chaucer used the *Thebaid* "through" the *Teseida*. In the table below, the symbol → links the citation from the *Thebaid* with its equivalent line in the *Teseida*. When the *Thebaid* text appears in this chapter, the line number is cited in italics.

Thebaid	*Knight's Tale*
Theb *1.7–14, 171–85*	1546
Theb *4. 455–68* → Tes 7.75–6 [Chaucer cites "Stace of Thebes" as his source] 2293–4	
Theb *4.494–9*	1638–48
Theb 6 → Tes.11.13–67	2853–2962
Theb *6.35–6; 7.180* → Tes 6.14, 21–2, 35–6 [Lygurge]	2129–52
Theb *6.56–65* → Tes 11.27–8	2933–8
Theb *6.98–106* → Tes 11.22–4 2921–3	
Theb *6.110–3* → Tes 11.25	2925–7
Theb *6.495–506* → Tes rubric 9.1; 9.4	2684
Theb *7.34–59* → Tes 7.29–37, 38	1967–2050
Theb *7.45*	1987
Theb *7.57* → Tes 7.37.1	2017
Theb *7.55–7* [a better source than Tes 7.36]	2027–8
Theb *7.58–9* [a better source than Tes 7.37.2]	2022–3
Theb *7.180* [see 6.36, above]	
Theb *9.607–35* → Tes 7.77, 79–81, 84–7	2297–2330
Theb *9.635–6* → Tes 7.78.5	2327
Theb *11.530–6, 539–40*	1660
Theb *12.519–20*	motto: *Iamque domos*
Theb *12.704*	1331

Table 4: Boethius in The Knight's Tale

The *Boece*, Chaucer's own translation of the *De consolatione philosophiae*, is his primary source for the Boethian material in *The Knight's Tale*. Boethius's Latin original was, however, a continued presence in Chaucer's creative mind during the composition of *The Knight's Tale*. Chaucer assimilated his source so thoroughly that some lines in *The Knight's Tale* are based on readings from various parts of the *Boece*. When lines in Chaucer originate from more than one part of Boethius's text, the first citation in this appendix is followed by the citations from elsewhere in the source. When the appendix cites specific lines from the *Boece*, the equivalent lines or section numbers in Boethius's Latin text appear in parentheses. The text of the *Boece* is available in modern editions of the works of Chaucer, including *The Riverside Chaucer*. Except for a few longer prose pieces, the selections from the *De consolatione philosophiae* are to be found in this chapter. These are identified by line numbers in italics.

Boece/De consolatione philosophiae	*Knight's Tale*
Book I	
1.m 5	1303–27
1.m 5 + 2.m 8; *3.m 9*; 3.pr 10; 4.pr 6; *4.m 6*	2987–3016

Boece/De consolatione philosophiae	*Knight's Tale*
Book II	
2.pr 5.90–5, 171–3 (*18, 33*) + *3.pr 2*.25–8 (*5*)	1255–9
2.m 8 + *1.m 5*; *3.m 9*; 3.pr 10; 4.pr 6; *4.m 6*	2987–3016
2.m 8	2988–93
Book III	
3.pr 2.25–8 (*5*) + *2.pr 5*.90–5, 171–3 (*18, 33*)	1255–9
3.pr 2.83–8 (*13*)	1261–7
3.m 9.41(*23*) + *4.m 6*.47–54 (*40–4*)	3035–8
3.m 9; 3.pr 10 + *1.m 5*; *2.m 8*; 4.pr 6, *4.m 6*	2987–3016
3.pr 10.25–30 (*5*)	3005–10
3.m 12.52–5 (*47–8*)	1163–4
Book IV	
4.pr 6	1663–72
4.pr 6.42–47 (*7*)	2994–3015
4.pr 6.149–65 (*18*); 4.*m 6*	3011–16
4.pr 6.214–24 (*29–31*)	1251–4
4. pr 6; *4.m 6* + *1.m 5*; *2.m 8*; *3.m 9*; 3.pr 10	2987–3016
4 m 6.47–54 (*40–4*) + *3.m 9*.41 (*23*)	3035–8

I

Il Libro Chiamato *Teseo*[1]

(edited by William E. Coleman and Edvige Agostinelli[2]
from MS Venice, Biblioteca Marciana, Cod. marciano it. IX, 61 [=6304],
fols 3r-64r [selections], by courtesy of the Biblioteca Marciana, Venice)

Preface: [*Although the poet no longer enjoys his lady Fiammetta's favor, he consoles himself by thinking of her and resolves to remain in her service. Remembering her pleasure in stories of love, he has decided to create for her a vernacular version of an ancient love story that he has discovered. The story of the two lovers and the young woman echoes the poet's relationship with his former beloved; he has added certain details to the story in order to conceal their relationship. The story is an allegorical narrative; he summarizes its contents. If she understands the argument of the poem, this might rekindle her love for the him. Although this might not happen, he prays that she will accept the book as a gift and hopes that it will have the desired effect.*]

Book 1

[*Introductory sonnet to the book, summarizing the tale. Introductory sonnet to book 1.*]

[(1–4) *The poet invokes the Muses, plus Mars and Venus, who are the patron gods of the poem, and also his beloved lady.*]

fol. 3^r 5. E questo con assai chiara ragione [1018–19[3]
conprenderete, udendo ragionare
d'Arcita i fatti e sì di Palamone,
di real sangue nati, come apare,
ed amenduni tebani, ed a quistione,
parenti essendo, per superchio amare
Emilia bella, vennero, amanzona;
donde l'un d'essi perdè la persona.

5. And you will understand this quite clearly enough when you hear tell of the deeds of Arcita and likewise those of Palamone – born of royal blood, as will be

[1] For title, see colophon, after 12.83, below. The title, *Teseo* (Theseus), occurs three other times in the text: in a rubric that bridges the prologue and the poem and at the beginning and end of book 8. *Vz* is one of 19 manuscript copies that entitle the work *Teseo*: L^2 (scribe A), L^8 L^6 S M^3 M^6 P^1 Pn R^1 R^4 MA^1 Pr Pr^1 Re RL RL^1 V^2 Vz VzQ.

[2] The edition is based on the model for editing medieval Italian texts proposed in Arrigo Castellani, *La prosa italiana delle origini*, 2 vols (Bologna: Pàtron, 1982). While the edition follows modern conventions for punctuation, capitalization, and diacritical marks, the spelling is not normalized. The editors would like to thank Prof. Paola Manni (Facoltà di Lettere e Lingue, Università degli Studi di Firenze) for her invaluable and generous advice concerning the dialectal and linguistic questions presented by this text.

[3] Bracketed numbers identify lines in *The Knight's Tale* whose source is the *Teseo* text.

seen, and both of them Thebans. And even though they were relatives, they came into conflict on account of their excessive love for beautiful Emilia the Amazon; as a result, one lost his life.

[(6–14; 16–17) *On hearing that the Amazon women have killed their men and elected Ipolita their queen, Teseo,*[4] *the duke of Athens, determined to invade Istizia,*[5] *the Amazon kingdom.* (18–20) *Teseo and his men sailed off to confront the women.* (21–2) *Rumor informed Ipolita about the advancing Athenians.* (23–36) *Ipolita gave a speech to encourage her followers to fortify her cities; they offered themselves to her service.* (37–40) *Ipolita armed her country against the Athenians.* (40–3) *Teseo arrived with his troops and determined a landing site.* (44–6) *Teseo sent ambassadors to Ipolita, who rejected their proposals.* (47–56) *When Teseo's men attempted to go ashore, the Amazons drove them back.* (57–68) *In response, Teseo first prayed to Mars then went ashore himself.* (69–78) *The Athenians battled the Amazons on the seashore and drove them back into their city.* (79–84) *The Athenians pitched camp outside the Amazon city.* (85–90) *Awaiting the siege, Ipolita encouraged her women, set her city in order, and made offerings to the gods.* (91–5) *Teseo besieged the city for several months; he devised a plan to tunnel into the city.* (95–8) *Frightened at this prospect, Ipolita had stouter walls erected, then sent him a letter.* (99–108) *Ipolita berated Teseo for besieging her city, warned him that his excavations would fail, and ordered him to leave her kingdom.* (109–10.1–4, 7; 111–13) *Teseo replied to Ipolita and her women that they would be harmed if he stormed the city.* (114–15) *Teseo's reply caused Ipolita great sadness.* (116–22) *After she consulted with her advisors, Ipolita determined that the Amazons should surrender.* (123–6) *Ipolita sent two aides to Teseo in order to seek peace; impressed with Ipolita's virtues, he determined to marry her.* (127) *Teseo and the Greeks peacefully occupied the Amazon city.*]

fol. 9r 128. Incontro venne, sopr'un gran destriere, [971–2
al suo Teseo Ipolita reina;
più bella assai che rosa di verziere
co· llei veniva una chiara fantina,
Emilia chiamata, al mio parere,
d'Ipolita sorella piccolina;
e dopo loro molt' altre ne venieno,
ornate e belle quant' elle potieno

5 2 **ragionare** L^2 S M^6 R^1; raccontare Aut NO, *alpha*, *beta*, *gamma*. (cf. Battaglia, ed. *Teseida*, p. lv). 3 **sì di** del buon Aut NO L^2 S M^6 R^1. **Palamone** *alpha-kappa* [Vz, L^2, S, M^6, R^1] + *alpha-zeta* [L^3 Ai Bg Cn L^7 M^2 M^3 M^4 F P^3 R^3 Ma Pr^2 Pr^3 Re RL RL^1 RN SanF T V^1 VzQ] + *alpha- zeta zeta* [Pn, V^2] + *beta* [A M^1 G MT Pr] + *de Bassi* [V^3] + *composite* [L^6]; Palemone [Aut, NO] + *alpha-zeta* [R^5 M^5 Ma^1 Ph Si] + *alpha-zeta zeta* [L^8 M^7] + *beta* [L^4] + *gamma* [P^2] + *de Bassi* [MA CaM Ch V^4]. R^4, which is an *alpha-zeta* text in books. 1–2 and an *alpha-kappa* text in books. 3–12 uses "Palamone" throughout. 7 **amanzona** NO L^2 S M^6 R^1; amazona Aut.

[4] Theseus. Geographical names and well known classical names (Athens, Thebes, Creon, Hercules) appear in English in the translation and summary. Italian personal names are left in their original form, but translated in the footnotes.

[5] *Scithia*. This is one of several names that appear in a different form in *Vz* and the other *alpha-kappa* MSS from the version in *Aut* and *NO*. When a variant form of a name in *Vz* does not require emendation because Chaucer did not make use of the name, it is transcribed as it appears in the MS. The proper English form of the variant name is provided in the note, in italics. Note that various sources known to Chaucer identify Scythia as the Amazon kingdom. See, for example, *Thebaid* 5.144; 12.592.

128. Mounted on a great steed, Queen Ipolita, came out to meet her Teseo. With her came a fair maiden named Emilia, more beautiful than a garden rose. She was, it seems to me, Ipolita's young sister. And after them came many more, as adorned and beautiful as they could be.

Book 2

[*Introductory sonnet to book 2*]

[(1–9) *Teseo decided to leave Istizia and return to Athens with Ipolita and Emilia.* (10–14, 16–17) *The author will digress from his story in order to explain the reason for Teseo's quarrel with Creon. After the civil war had devastated Thebes and the sons of Oedipus had died, Creon invaded the kingdom, took the throne by force, and forbade the burial of the dead warriors, leaving their bodies to the wild animals. The women of Argos traveled to Athens to seek the help of Teseo. Declining the Athenians' kind offer of hospitality, they camped in the temple of Clemency while awaiting the arrival of Teseo, whom they would beg to avenge the cruelty of Creon.* (18–24) *Teseo was returning to Athens in triumph with his retinue. The Athenians had decorated the city for his arrival, including royal robes and a triumphal chariot for Teseo. When Teseo moved in procession through the city, vast throngs of joyful citizens greeted him.*]

fol. 11^r 25. E mentre ch' egli in cotal guisa giva, [894–8, 900–4
per aventura dinanzi al piatoso
tenpio passò, nel qual era l'achiva
turba di donne inn abito doglioso;
le quali udendo che quivi veniva,
su ssi levaron con atto furioso:
con alte grida, pianto e gran romore
pararsi inanzi al carro del singnore.

25. And while he was proceeding in such a style, by chance he passed in front of the sacred temple where there was the crowd of Argive women in their mourning clothes. Hearing who was coming there, they roused themselves in a frenzy. With loud cries, weeping, and great clamor they placed themselves before the ruler's chariot.

26. "Chi son costoro [ch' a'] nostri lieti aventi [899, 905–8, 911
con grida isparte, battendosi il petto
de' gua' lor pieni, [in atri] vestimenti
tutte piangendo, come se 'n dispetto
avesson di mia groria, e ll'altre gienti
sì ccom' i' veggio, cagion di diletto?"
Disse Teseo: "Chè fatte questo?" istando;
a cchui una rispuose lagrimando:

128 1 **gran** L^2 S M^6 R^1; bel Aut NO. 3 **più** L^2 S M^6 R^1; e più Aut NO. **assai** S R^1; *om* Aut L^2 M^6. 8 **elle** M^6; più Aut NO L^2 S R^1.

25 2 **dinanzi** *alpha*; davanti Aut NO *beta*, *gamma*. (cf. Battaglia, p. xlviii). 5 **le quali** NO *alpha- beta- gamma*; la qual Aut. (cf. Battaglia, p. xciii) **quivi** NO L^2 S M^6 R^1 + 3 MSS; quindi Aut.

26. "Who are these at our happy celebrations with broken cries, beating their breasts over their profound troubles, all of them wailing in their black garments – as if they held my glory in contempt? For the rest of the people, as far as I can see, it is a reason for delight." Teseo said, "Why are you doing this?" as he stood. A weeping woman replied:

27. "Singnor, nonn amirar l'abito tristo [917
che inanzi a tte è qui dispettuose,
né creder dispiaciere del tuo aquisto,
né d'alcun tuo onore esser crucciose;
ben che d'averti in cotal groria visto
per nostri danni ne faccia animose
a piangier più che non facemo forse,
essendo pur dal primo dolor morse."

27. "My lord, do not wonder [whether] the sad clothing here in front of you here is disrespectful, nor should you believe that anyone is troubled by your achievement, nor that anyone is resentful of your rank; but rather having seen you in such glory impelled us to weep perhaps even more for our injuries than we did when first struck by grief."

28. "Dunque chi ssiete?" disse a llor Teseo, [923, 932
"e perché ssì nella piuvica festa
sole piangiete?" Allora si feo
Evaneus, ch' è di parlar maesta
e disse: "Sposa fu' di Canpaneo,
e qualunqu' altra ancor vedi in questa
turba, di re fu madre, figlia o suora;
e aprirotti tutto che m'acora.

***26.2** The reading "broken cries" (grida isparte) is a textual variant that appears uniquely in *Vz*. In Boccaccio's autograph MS (*Aut*) the reading is "disheveled hair" (crini sparti). When Theseus addresses the Theban women (I, 905–11), he repeats all the details of *Teseida* 2.26 except the description of their hair, and he makes much of their weeping. This unique variant reading is a better source for Chaucer's version of Boccaccio's description. MS *Vz* contains 21 such textual variants, and many more variants of this type occur in *Vz* than in any other copy of the *Teseida*; 15 of the 21 are unique to *Vz*. An asterisk before a note identifies the unique variants in *Vz* that are better sources for readings in *The Knight's Tale* than their counterparts in *Aut*.

***27.3** In *Vz* a Theban woman tells Theseus that none of her companions is "troubled by" or "unhappy at" dispiaciere) his conquest of the Amazons. In *Aut*, she tells him that none "weep at" (pianger) his achievement. In *KnT*, the woman assures him that his glory and honor do not vex ("greveth" I, 917) the women. The unique variant reading in *Vz* is a slightly better source for Chaucer's line.

26 1[**ch'a**] Aut NO L[2] S M[6] R[4]; che Vz R[1]. 2 **grida isparte** crini sparti Aut NO L[2] S M[6]. 3 **gua' lor** L[2] S M[6] R[1]; squalor Aut NO; dolor M[3] P[3] Pr[2] Si V[1].[**in atri**] Aut NO L[2] S; i' vego i Vz; in tristi R[1] L[8]; amari M[6]; i· neri RL[1]; in bruni 3 MSS; in altri 6 MSS. (cf. *KnT* I, 911: " in blak"). 7 **Chè fatte questo** stupefatto Aut NO.

27 3 **dispiaciere** pianger Aut NO L[2] S M[6] R[1].

28 3 **allora** *add* oltre Aut NO L[2] S M[6] R[1]. 4 **Evaneus** Evannès Aut NO; Evanès L[2] S R[1]. **ch' è di parlar** più che nesssuna altra Aut NO L[2] S M[6] R[1]. 5 **Canpaneo** Campaneo Aut L[2] (2.11.5); Campanneo S; Chanpaneo NO; R[1] · Chaucer takes the name Cappaneus (1.932) from Statius, who refers to Capaneus in eleven books of the *Thebaid*. 7 **fu** L[2] S M[6] R[1]; *add* moglie o Aut NO. **tutto che m'** che ci Aut NO; tutto ciò che ci L[2] S R[1].

28. "Who are you then?" said Teseo to them, "and why are you alone weeping like this at a public festival?" Then the sorrowful Evaneus[6] presented herself in order to speak and said: "I was wife of Canpaneus,[7] and whomever else you see in this crowd was the mother, daughter or sister of a king. And I shall reveal to you all that grieves me:

29. "Lo perfido nimico del tiranno +[8] [931–47
figliuol di 'Dippo: contro ad Apolicie
suo inniquo fratello, a fiero inganno
del rengnio, artemini lor felicie
e ferrato tirò a suo gran danno,
che a maggiore assai che nun si dicie,
davante a Tebe con tristissime sorte,
e altri molti assai tolse con morte.

29. "That treacherous enemy of 'Dippo's[9] tyrant son: happy and iron-willed, he brought their Artemines[10] against his unjust brother Apolicie[11] to proud betrayal of the kingdom, to his great harm at Thebes – even greater than anyone can say – with a most sad destiny. And he took very many others away by death.

30. "E dove noi, invano, aspettavamo
con bello honore vederti ritornare
a nostre terre e agual ti veggiamo,
ma il tuo onorato trionfare;
nell'abito dolente in che no' siamo
a soppelligli ci conviene andare;
ma quel crudel singniore il qual a preso
il rengnio dopo lor ciò ci a conteso.

30.8 *lor*: them, i.e., the two sons of Oedipus.

29 1 **nimico** L^2 S M^6 R^1; nequitia Aut NO. 2 **'Dippo** L^2 S; Edippo Aut NO; Dipo M^6; Eippo R^1 (+ **Edipo** 4.16.2; **Dippo** 5.59.2; **Edippo** 10.97.7) Other forms of the name in *Vz* are **'Dipo** (4.16.2; 5.59.2; 10.97.7) and **Edopo** (5.13.2). Statius refers to Oedipodes in seven books of the *Thebaid*. **Apolicie** Appolicie L^2 S; Polinice Aut NO S (2.11.7) L^2 (2.11.7) R1 (2.11.7); Pollonicie M^6; Poluce R^1 (2.11.7). Statius refers to Polynices in ten books of the *Thebaid*. 3 **inniquo** unico Aut NO L^2 S M^6 R^1; nimico Bg; inimico Si. 4 **artemini** M^4 Argivi Aut NO; Arcivi S R^1; Arhivi M^6; Artimi L^2 . 5 **e ferrato** exercito Aut NO L^2 S M^6 R^1. 7 **con tristissime** dove trista Aut; dove con triste L^2 S M^6 R^1; *lac* NO. 8 **e altri molti assai tolse** ciascuno alto baron tolto a Aut L^2 SM^6 R^1; *lac* NO.

30 1 **aspettavamo** speravamo Aut L^2 S M^6 R^1; *lac* NO. 2 **bello** quello Aut L^2 S M^6 R^1. **vederti** M^6; vederli Aut R^1; vererci L^2 S; *lac* NO. 3 **nostre** L^2 S M^6 R^1; lor Aut; *lac* NO. 4 **ma il tuo onorato** L^2 S M^6 R^1; nella tua laurato Aut; *lac* NO. 7 **quel crudel singniore il qual** l'aspra tyrapnia di que' Aut NO; l'aspro signore il qual L^2 S M^6 R^1. 8 **dopo** L^2 S M^6 R^1; dietro Aut NO. **conteso** L^2 S M^6 R^1; difeso Aut; hoffeso NO.

[6] *Evadne*

[7] *Capaneus*

[8] The + symbol indicates that, in addition to the present octave of the *Teseo*, subsequent octaves or other parts of the text serve as the source of the lines in *The Knight's Tale*. Consult Appendix, tables 1 and 2, to identify these additional octaves.

[9] *Oedipus*

[10] *Argives*

[11] *Polynices*

30. "And in the place where we waited in vain to see you revisit our lands with noble honor, so we imagine you just the same – but with your honor triumphing. In the mourning clothes that we are wearing, we have to go bury them; but that cruel lord who seized the kingdom after them has hindered us from doing this.

31. "Il perfido Creonte a chui più dura
odio c' a' morti non fecie la vita,
a' greci morti niega sepoltura
– non fu ma' crudeltà maggiore udita! –
e di que' ll'onbre alla [pallude] scura
di Stigia ci ritiene; onde 'nfinita
doglia ci asale tra gli altri nostri mali,
sentendogli mangiare agli animali."

31. "Treacherous Creon, whose hatred outlives the dead, is denying burial to the dead Greeks – never was there heard worse cruelty than this! – and he detains the shades of these men there at the dark swamp of Styx. As a result, infinite pain – in addition to our other ills – overcomes us when we hear about animals devouring them."

[(32–5) *The Argive women described their arrival in Athens and begged Teseo's help.* (37–9) *Their story affected the Athenian lords, and Teseo promised to help them.* (40–3) *Teseo left Ipolita and Emilia in Athens.* (44–8) *He ordered his men to battle, and his men shouted out their support of his new enterprise.* (49) *He left Athens.*]

fol. 12^r 50. Le ricche insengnie, c'ancor ripiegate [965–6, 978–84
nonn eran, si rizaro prestamente;
e' cavalieri co· lle schiere ordinate,
dietro alla sua ciascun arditamente,
ne givan, e lle donne sconsolate
lor proccieden, di ciò molto contente;
e poi dopo alcun giorno furo a Tebe,
e fermar canpo in su lle triste grebe.

50. The rich standards, which were not yet folded, were quickly raised; and the knights rode out in orderly ranks, each one bravely behind the other, and the disconsolate women followed along with them, quite happy in doing so; and a few days later they were at Thebes, and set up camp in that sad earth.

***50.1** Theseus' battle standards are "rich" ("ricche"), a unique variant in *Vz*. It could well have inspired Chaucer's description of Theseus' pennon "of gold ful riche" (*KnT* I, 979).

***50.2** The unique *Vz* variant "prestamente" (quickly) appears to be the source of Chaucer's "And right anoon, withouten moore abood" (*KnT* I, 965).

31 3 **morti** L^2 S M^6 R^1 + 12 MSS; corpi Aut NO. 4 **non fu ma' crudeltà maggiore** crudeltà credo non mai più Aut NO; crudeltà più dura non credo mai L^2 S; né crudeltà più dura mai M^6; crudeltà dura non lo mai R^1. *5 [**pallude**] M^6; pallade Vz; palude NO L^2 S R^1; padule Aut. 6 **ci** *alpha*; *om* Aut NO, *beta*, *gamma*. (cf. Battaglia, p. xlviii).

50 1 **ricche** *om* Aut NO L^2 S M^6 R^1. 2 **prestamente** di presente Aut NO L^2 S M^6 R^1. 4 **arditamente** acconciamente Aut NO L^2 S M^6 R^1. 6 **proccieden** L^2 S M^6 R^1; precedean Aut NO. 7 **poi** *om* Aut NO L^2 S M^6 R^1. **furo** giunsero Aut NO L^2 S M^6 R^1.

[(51–3) *In Thebes, Teseo challenged Creon, who sent an arrogant reply. The Athenians and the Thebans prepared to meet in battle.* (54–73) *In the battle, Creon was killed and his forces were routed.* (74–7) *Teseo had Creon buried and he allowed the Argive women to burn the bodies of their dead and perform the appropriate funeral rituals. He then turned the city over to them.* (78–84) *After burning the bodies of their men, the women torched Thebes and returned to Argos.*]

fol. 14r 85. Mentre che Grec' i lor givan ciercando, + [1005–17, 1020–32
e rovistando il canpo sanguinoso,
e' corpi sottosopra rovesciando,
per aventura in caso assai dubbioso
due giovani fediti dolorando
quivi trovaro, sanz' alcun riposo;
e ciaschedun la morte domandava,
tanto dolor del lor mal gli gravava.

85. While the Greeks were going around in search of their dead, ransacking the bloodstained field and turning over the bodies, by chance they found two wounded young men there. They were in a dangerous state, suffering constant agony; and so greatly did the pain of their injuries torment them that each one begged to die.

86. E' nonn eran da llor quasi lontani,
armati tutti ancora, e a giaciere;
i qua', come choloro a le cui mani
pervenne· prima, udendo dolere,
li veder si pensar che de' sovrani
esser vedieno; e cciò fecie vedere
le lucienti armi e lloro altiero aspetto
che dio nell'ira loro facie dispetto.

86. They were not far from each other, still fully armed, lying on the ground; when those who first touched them heard them cry out in pain and saw them, they thought they must be royalty. This was apparent in their shining armor and in their disdainful expression that, in their wrath, seemed even to hold God in contempt.

87. E' s'apressaro a llor e umilmente,
quaṣi già cierti di lor condizione,
né disarmagli, come l'altra giente,
né mai avea fatta contenzione
con esso loro; e poi beningniamente
recatosegli in braccio, e co· rragione
gli ripigliaro del disperar loro;
e menagli a Teseo sanza dimoro.

85 3 **rovesciando** L² S; rivoltando Aut NO M⁶ R¹.

86 1 **lor quasi** L² S M⁶ R¹; ssé guari Aut NO; quasi 16 MSS. 4 **udendo** L² S M⁶; *add* lor Aut NO R¹. 6 **vedieno** R¹; doveano Aut NO L² S M⁶.

87 4 **ne mai avea fatta contenzione** L² S M⁶ R¹; nemica avevan facta et cui in prigione Aut NO. 5 **con esso loro** avevan messi Aut NO L² S R¹; onde che quegli M⁶.

87. And they respectfully approached them, since they were fairly certain of their rank, nor did they disarm them as they did everyone else. (Nor was there ever any disagreement about this among them.) And then they gently gathered them up in their arms and, by reasoning with them, diverted them from their despair; and they brought them to Teseo without delay.

88. I qua' Teseo come gli ebbe veduti,
da tal far gli privò, lor domandando
se del sangue cadino e' fosson suti.
E l'un di loro, altiero di suo adimando,
rispuose: "In casa sua nati e cresciuti
fumo; de' suo nipoti siamo; e quando
Creonte contra tte l'armi prese,
fumo co· llui e nostri a suo difese."

88. As soon as Teseo saw them, he stripped them of their rank, asking them whether they were of the Cadine[12] blood. And one of them, scornful of his question, replied: "We were born and grew up in his house; we are grandsons of his, and when Creon took up arms against you, we were with him and our own men in his defense."

89. Ben conobbe Teseo nel dir lo sdegnio
real c'avie' costoro, ma non seguio
però l'effetto a cotal ira dengnio;
ma 'nverso loro diventò più pio
e, ssì come de' suoi, con ongni ingengnio,
fé ssì che tutte lor piaghe guario;
e poi cogli altri in prigion gli ritenne,
lor riserbando al trionfio solenne.

89. Teseo was well aware of the royal scorn that they had in their speech, but a consequence worthy of such anger did not follow; instead he became more merciful towards them and, as if they were his own kinsmen, with every skill, he saw to it that all their wounds would heal; and then he held them in prison with the others, keeping them for the solemn triumphal march.

[(90–4) *Returning to Athens with Palamone and Arcita as his prisoners, Teseo went to the temple of Mars.*]

fol. 14^v 95. Quivi fé dare l'arme c'a Creonte
avie nel canpo per forza spogliate,

88 2 **da tal far gli privò** d'alto affar li stimò Aut NO L^2 S M^6 R^1. 3 **cadino** di Cadmo Aut; di Chadino NO M^6; di che L^2 S Elsewhere *Vz* distorts the name to "candide" (2.72.7) before eventually reporting it as Cadino (4.14.2, 5.57.2), the *alpha-kappa* form. Cadmus is named at the beginning of the *Thebaid* (1.6) and in nine other books. 7 **l'** Pr^3 RL^1 MT V; *add* empie Aut NO L^2 S M^6 R^1. 8 **e** co' Aut NO L^2 S M^6 R^1.

89 5 **sì come de'** *alpha*; co'medici Aut NO *beta*, *gamma*. (cf. Battaglia, p. xlviii, lxxx).

12 of Cadmus, Cadmean.

e a Marte l'oferse, e alla fronte
co· man le fronde di Peneo levate
di' simigliante, e con parole pronte
delle vittorie da llui aquistate
grazie rendendo a Marte copiose,
offerendogli e le [ultime] e piatose.

95. There he had the arms that he had forcefully stripped from Creon on the battlefield handed over and he offered them to Mars; and, having lifted the leaves of Peneus with his hand to his brow, he presented them in like manner and with prompt words about the victories won by him, giving lavish thanks to Mars, offering him both final and devout prayers.

96. Quindi uscì poi, e al suo palagio
tornò, aconpangniato dal suo padre;
quindi prendendo festa, giuoco ed agio,
alla reina le cose leggiadre
narrava c' avie fatte e 'l suo disagio,
spesso assalito dalle lucie ladre
di quella donna, che 'l mirava fiso;
per ch'essere gli parea in paradiso.

96. Then he left and returned to his palace accompanied by his father; then feasting, gaming, and relaxing, he told the queen pleasant stories about his deeds and his trials, often assailed by the "thieving lights" of that woman on whom his gaze was fixed; because of this he felt he was in paradise.

97. Riposat' i più giorni in lieta vita,
il buon Teseo si fé innanzi venire
il teban Palamone e 'l bello Arcitra
e ciaschedun vidde molto da gradire
e nell'aspetto di senbianza ardita;
per che pensò vole· gli far morire,
dubitando che sse lasciar gli andasse,
che forse anco· non molto gli giovasse.

97. Having rested for a few days of carefree living, noble Teseo had the Theban Palamone and the handsome Arcitra brought before him and he saw that there was much to appreciate in each one and that they seemed courageous in appearance. On

95.4 *le fronde di Peneo*: the leaves of Peneus, i.e., laurel leaves.

95.8 *piatose* is a substantive.

96.6 *lucie ladre*: thieving lights, i.e., the eyes that seduce and cause one to fall in love.

95 2 **per forza spogliate** L^2 S M^6 R^1; theban dispogliate Aut NO *alpha*, *beta*, *gamma*. (cf. Battaglia, p. lvi). 4 **Peneo** Pennea Aut NO; Penneo L^2 S; Penteo M^6; *lac* R^1. *8 e le [ultime] S M^6 L^1; e le utime Vz; e le hultime L^2 S; vittime Aut NO R^1. **e piatose** L^2 S M^6 R^1; piatose Aut NO.

96 1 **suo** L^2 S M^6 R^1; mastro Aut NO. 3 **quindi** M^6 CaM Cn L^1 R^3; quivi Aut NO L^2 S R^1.

97 3 **Arcitra** L^2 S; Arcita Aut NO M^6 R^1. Even though the end-rhyme requires Arcita, the spelling is uncorrected since it is an *alpha-kappa* variant. 6 **vol egli far** di farli ambo Aut NO L^{2}S M^6 R^1. 8 **giovasse** noiasse Aut NO L^2 S M^6 R^1.

account of this he considered that he might want to have them executed, fearing that if he should let them go free, it still might not be of much benefit to him.

98. Po' fra ssé disse: "I' fare' gran peccato,
nullo di loro non 'sendo traditore";
e fra ssé stesso fu diliberato
di tenegl' i· prigion per lo migliore;
e tosto al prigioniere à comandato
che ben gli guardi e faccia loro onore.
Così da llui Arcitra e Palamone
[dannati furo ad etterna] prigione.

98. Then he said to himself: "I would make a great mistake, since neither of them is a traitor"; and he determined that the best course would be to keep them in prison, and soon he ordered the jailer to guard them well and to respect them. So Arcitra and Palamone were condemned to eternal prison by him.

99. Gli prigion furon tutti carcierati
e dati in guardia a cchi 'l sapè ben fare;
e questi due furon riserbati
per fargli alquanto più ad agio stare,
perché di real sangue egli eran nati;
e fegli dentro al palagio abitare
inn una riccha zanbra li tenere,
facciendogli servire a llor piaciere.

99. The prisoners were all jailed and given in custody to someone who well know what to do. And these two were secluded so as to let them be a bit more comfortable because they were born of royal blood. And he had them live within the palace, kept there in a rich room, having them served at their pleasure.

Book 3

[*Introductory sonnet to book 3*]
[(1–2) *After Juno's anger over the destruction of Thebes had cooled, Mars returned to his homeland. Cupid is invoked as the deity who will regulate book 3.* (3–4) *Palamone and Arcita suffered almost a year in prison until Venus determined that she would give them something else to sigh over.* (5) *In the springtime* (6–7) *the planets were aligned under the influence of Venus, the birds sang, and the two young prisoners began to think of love.*]

fol 15ʳ 8. Quando la bella Emilia giovinetta,
a ciò tirata da propria natura

98 7 **Arcitra** L² S; Arcita Aut NO M⁶ R¹. Like 2.97.3, on the same MS page, the name is an *alpha-kappa* variant. It is spelled Arcita elsewhere in *Vz*. 8 [**dannati furo ad etterna**] Aut NO L² S M⁶ R¹; partir gli fe e mettere in Vz (cf. *KnT* I, 1023–4)

99 7 **in una riccha** et così in una Aut NO; e feci egli in una L² S M⁶ R¹. **Li** *om* Aut NO L² S M⁶.

non che d'amare altrui fosse costretta,
ongni mattina veniva ad un'ora [1051–2
inn uno giardino tutta soletta
c'allato alla suo camera dimora
entrava, in giuba, iscalze e gie cantando
amorose canzone, sé dilettando.

8. When lovely young Emilia – drawn to this by her own nature and not because she was obligated by love for someone else – came all alone into a garden that lay outside her bed-chamber every morning at a set time, she walked around in a tunic, barefoot, singing love songs, amusing herself.

9. E questa vita più giorni tenendo + [1049, 1053–5
la giovinetta senplicietta e bella,
co· lla candida man talor cogliendo
d'in sulla spina la rosa novella,
e poi con quella più fior congiungnendo
al biondo capo facie grillandella;
avenne nuova cosa una mattina
per la belleza di quella fantina.

9. And keeping this custom for many days, the lovely, unaffected young girl, at times plucking a rosebud from the thorns with her white hand and then weaving it with other flowers, made a garland for her blond head; one morning something unexpected happened on account of the beauty of that young maiden.

10. Ella si fu un bel mattin levata
co' biondi crini avolti alla sua testa
e sciese nel giardino, com' era usata;
quivi cantava e facieva gran festa,
co· molti fiori, in su l'erbetta asettata;
facieva grillandetta lieta e questa
senpre cantando be' versi d'amore
con angielica vocie e lieto core.

10. She got up one fine morning with her blond hair wrapped around her head and went down into the garden, as was her custom; she was singing there and making merry, seated on the grass among many flowers. She was joyfully making a garland, and she was all the while singing beautiful love songs with an angelic voice and joyous heart.

8.4 *veniva ad un' ora*: Boccaccio's "venuta l'aurora" ("when the sunrise came") would have been a better source for Chaucer's "at the sonne upriste" [*KnT* I, 1051]. But the phrase in *Vz* is a characteristic *alpha* reading (Battaglia, p.xlviii) and it could have produced Chaucer's line, so it is not emended.

8 2 **a ciò tirata da propria natura** Aut NO L^2 S M^6 R^1 Vz. An 18th century hand has substituted "per lo puro piacer della fresca ora." 3 **amare altrui** NO L^2 S R^1; amore alcun Aut NO M^6 R^4. 4 **ad un ora** *alpha*; venuta l'aurora Aut NO *beta, gamma.* (cf. Battaglia, p. xlviii) 5 **tutta** se n'entrava Aut NO M^6R^4; tutta sola L^2 S R^1. 7 **entrava** L^2 S R^1; faceva Aut NO M^6; per quello R^4. **iscalza** L^2 S M^6; e scalza Aut NO R^1 R^4. 8 **dilettando** diportando Aut NO L^2 S M^6 R^1 R^4.

10 6 **grillandetta** L^2 S; sua ghirlanda Aut NO M^6 R^4; sua ghirlandetta R^1. **questa** presta Aut NO L^2 S M^6 R^1 R^4.

11. Al suon di quella vocie graziosa [1075–6
Arcita si levò, ch'era in prigione
allato al giardino amorosa,
sanza niente dire a Palamone;
allora una finestra disiosa
aprì per meglio udir quelle canzone,
e per vedere ancor chi llà cantasse,
tra' ferri il capo fuori alquanto trasse.

11. At the sound of that charming voice, Arcita, who was in prison next to the love garden, arose without saying anything to Palamone; then he longingly opened a window in order to better hear those songs; and, even more, in order to see who was singing there, he stuck his head out a bit through the bars.

[(12–44) *First Arcita, then Palamone said he believed Emilia to be Venus; both confessed themselves to be wounded by Cupid. Emilia saw them and withdrew, but out of vanity returned each morning to sing songs while pretending not to notice them. The two men suffered the pangs of love sickness, then they finally learned Emilia's name. At the end of the summer, the two lovers lost the sight that most pleased them when Emilia no longer entered the garden.* (48) *Teseo's visitor Periton*[13] *asked to see the prisoners.* (49) *The appearance and character of Palamone are described.* (50–2) *Periton recognized Arcita, and asked for his release.*]

fol 17^r 53. Teseo rispuose: "Dolcie amico caro, + [1209–18
ciò che ttu mi domandi sarà fatto,
ma odi come, non ti sia discaro.
I' 'l trarrò di prigione a questo patto,
che nel mio rengnio non faccia riparo,
né cci venga giamai in nessun atto;
ch' i' l'ò disfatto e tenuto [in] pregione,
perc', adirato di lui, ò ssospeccione.

53. Teseo replied: "Dear, kind friend, what you ask of me will be done, but listen to [the way] how: I hope this is not unpleasant for you. I will release him from prison under this condition: that he will never take refuge in my kingdom, nor that

11.3 *giardino amorosa* is an agreement error needed for the sake of the rhyme. See Boccaccio's variant of the same type in the same stanza of MS Aut: *voce grazioso* (3.11.1).

16.3 *Teseida* 3.16, which is not included in the edition, contains the only reference to Daphne in the poem. At *KnT* I, 2062–4, Chaucer refers to the Daphne and Apollo myth (Ovid. Met.1.548–52), emphasizing that he is discussing Dane (i.e. Daphne) and not the goddess Diana. While the young woman's name is spelled Danne in Boccaccio's autograph MS, three *alpha-kappa* MSS – L^2 S and M^6 – use Chaucer's spelling: Dane. MS *Vz* contains a variant reading, *donne*, which will be emended to Dane in the Chaucer Library edition.

11 3 **allato** *add* allato Aut NO L^2 S M^6 R^1 R^4. 5 **allora** et Aut NO S M^6; a L^2 R^1; e a R^4.

53 4 **a** M^6 R^1; con Aut NO L^2 S R^4. 5 **non** L^2 S M^6 R^1 R^4; e' non Aut NO. 6 **in** M^6 R^1; per Aut NO L^2 S R^4. 7 **[in]** Aut NO L^2 S M^6 R^1 R^4; *om* Vz. 8 **adirato** a diritto L^2 S R^1; a dritto Aut R^4 M^6; a dorete NO.

[13] *Pirithous*

he will ever come here under any circumstance. For I have subdued and imprisoned him because I am angry at him [and] have misgivings [about him].

54. "Sei i ciel prendo i' gli farò tagliare
la testa sanza fallo immantanente;
però, se vuole tal patto pigliare,
vada dove gli piace incontanente
per lo tuo amore, che llo mi fa fare;
ché altrimenti mai al suo vivente
uscito non saria di pregionia,
be· llo ti giuro per la fede mia."

54. "If I should capture him here, I will have his head cut off immediately without delay; so if he wants to accept such an condition, let him at once go wherever he pleases on account of my affection for you, which makes me do this. Except for this he never would have left prison while he was alive – I swear this to you on my faith."

[(55–68, 70–3) *Arcita considered remaining in prison in order to continue to see Emilia, but Periton persuaded him to leave. Arcita thanked Teseo and Periton, accepted gifts, and prepared to exit the prison.* (74–5) *Arcita took his leave of Palamone, trying to console him by telling Palamone that he, at least, will continue to enjoy the sight of Emilia.* (77–9) *Palamone bewailed his situation, telling Arcita that his freedom would distract him from his pain; on the other hand, Arcita, in prison, would be consumed by the pain of hopelessly seeing Emilia.* (80–5) *After much weeping, Arcita prepared to leave a wretchedly unhappy Palamone behind. Arcita was desperate to remain in Athens. Periton tried to comfort him, then took his leave. Arcita tried to console Palamone, but Palamone reminded Arcita that his freedom to travel would lighten his pain. They wept and embraced, and Arcita departed. As he was leaving, Arcita prayed to see Emilia. She appeared on a balcony and he sorrowfully rode from Athens.*]

Book 4

[*Introductory sonnet.*4.1–9, 11–14]

[(1–11) *After leaving Athens, Arcita, who now called himself Penteo, berated Love because of his unhappy circumstances.* (12–17) *Arcita / Penteo journeyed to Boetia*[14] *and visited the ruins of Thebes, lamenting its destruction.* (18–21) *He traveled to Corinth and then to Mycenae, where he stayed with King Menelaus.* (22–30) *About a year later, much changed in appearance, he went to the island of Aegina, where he would serve King Peleo.*[15]]

54 3 **tal** R[1]; cotal Aut NO L[2] S M[6] R[4]. 4 **incontanente** di presente Aut NO M[6] R[1] R[4]; immantanente L[2] S. 5 **fare** L[2] S R[1]; lasciare Aut NO M[6] R[4].

[14] Boeotia.
[15] Peleus.

fol. 20^{r} 22. Quivi in maniera di pover valletto, + [1408–10
non degli suoi maggiore ma conpangnone,
al servigio del re sanza sospetto
fu ricievuto e messo in comessione;
e ubidendo acciò che gli era detto,
si fece a modo che umil garzone,
acciò che e' potesse ivi durare,
fin che fortuna il volesse atare.

22. There like a poor servant, not his men's superior but their companion, he was received into the king's service without any question and assigned his duties; and obeying what he was told to do, he played the part of a humble servant, so that he might stay there until such time as fortune might wish to help him.

23. Quivi con seco sovente piangiea
la sua fortuna e lla suo trista vita,
e spesse volte con sospiri diciea:
"O doloroso più che alcuno Arcita!
Sè fatto fante là dove solea
esser tuo casa di fanti fornita;
così fortuna insieme e povertate
t'à cconcio per voler tuo libertate."

23. Alone there he often wept over his fortune and his sad life, and many times he said with sighs: "O sadder than anyone is Arcita! You have become a domestic when your own house was usually furnished with domestics; so fortune together with poverty has reduced you [to this state] for wanting your freedom."

[(24–6) *Arcita / Penteo continued to lament his misfortune and his loss of noble rank. Love sickness tormented his heart and transformed his appearance.*]

27. Egli era tutto quanto divenuto + [1363–4
sì magro, che assai agievolmente
ciascun su' osso si facie veduto;
né credo ch' Essicome altrimente
fosse nel viso che egli è paruto
nel tenpo della sua fama dolente;
né solamente inpalidito n'era
ma lla suo pelle parea quasi nera.

22.6 While *Aut* describes Arcita acting the role of a base ("*vil*") servant, a variant in *Vz* describes him as a humble ("*umil*") servant. The variant is a better source of Chaucer's description of Arcita playing the part of a "povre laborer" (*KnT* I, 1409).

22 6 **umil** M^6 $R^{4;}$ un vil Aut NO L^2 S R^1. 8 **il** NO L^2 M^6; li Aut; lui R^1; lo R^4.

23 4 **alcuno** altro et tristo Aut NO L^2 S M^6 R^1 R^4. 6 **fornita** NO L^2 S M^6 R^1; guarnita Aut R^4. 8 **per** M^6; et il Aut NO L^2 S R^1 R^4.

27 4 **Essicome** Erisitone Aut; Erisichone NO; Christone L^2; Eristone S; Ericonne M^6; Ereseon (?) R^1; (E)risitone R^4. 7 **né** R^1; et non pur Aut NO R^4; et non L^2 S; et non più M^6.

27. He had become so thin that each of his bones could quite easily be seen; nor do I believe that the face of Essicome[16] appeared any different at the time of his hunger pangs; nor was he merely pallid, but his skin seemed almost black.

28. E nella testa appena si vedieno
gli occhi dolenti; e lle guancie, lanute
di folto pelo e nuovo, le pareno;
e lle suo ciglia pilose e agute
a riguardare orribile il facieno;
le chiome tutte rigide e arsute;
e ssì era del tutto trasmutato, + [1370–1
che nullo no ll'arie raffigurato.

28. And his mournful eyes could hardly be seen in his head; and his cheeks appeared thick with new, wooly growth; and he made his brows appear thick, sharp, and fearful; his hair rigid and bushy; and he was so completely changed that no one would have recognized him.

[(29) *Even his voice had changed, and his strength was gone.* (30) *Whenever an Athenian boat arrived, he inquired about Emilia.* (31–6) *Once when he felt he would soon die, he went down to the shore and was refreshed by the wind coming from Athens. A small boat arrived from Athens and he was invited to return to that city. When he asked about Emilia, he was told that she was as beautiful as ever, even though her fiancé Acate*[17] *had died.*]

fol. 20^v 37. E' si sentiva sì venuto meno, [1391–2
c' appena si poteva sostenere;
onde, se queste pene che 'l tenieno
non mitigasson d'Emilia vedere,
assai in brieve tenpo ucciderieno;
però diliberò pur di volere
in ongni modo ritornare a 'ttene
per dare etterno spasso alle suo pene,

37.8 In *The Knight's Tale* Arcite dreams of Mercury, who tells him to return to Athens because "Ther is thee shapen of thy wo an ende" (I,1392). The inspiration could be the phrase from *Aut*, where Arcita/Penteo decides to return to Athens in order to alleviate or to finish (*ad alleggiare o ad finir*) his troubles. In *Vz*, however, a variant line describes him as deciding to return to Athens in order to give eternal latitude (*per dare etterno spasso*) to his troubles. The unique variant *spasso* has various imprecise meanings: leeway, latitude, range, scope, room. Either of these two ambiguous phrases may have been the source of the equally ambiguous promise that Chaucer puts into Mercury's mouth.

28 3 **le** non Aut NO L^2 S M^6 R^4.
37 3 **se queste** se a quelle Aut NO; se quelle L^2 S M^6 R^1**;** so quelle R^4. 3–4 **tenieno non mitigasson** L^2 S R^1; coceno nol medicasse Aut NO M^6 R^4. 5 **tenpo** lui Aut NO L^2 S M^6 R^1 R^4. 6 **però** L^2 S R^1; per che Aut NO M^6 R^4. 8 **per dare etterno spasso alle** ad alleggiare o ad finir Aut NO M^6 R^4; a finir o aleggiare L^2 S; o finir o aleggiare R^1.

[16] *Erysichthon*
[17] Achates

37. He felt so faint that he could hardly hold himself up; hence, if seeing Emilia did not ease these pains that he had, they would kill him in time soon enough. Therefore he determined that he still wished in any case to return to Athens in order to give eternal scope to his pains.

38. e fra ssé dicie: "I' son sì trasmutato [1399–1407
di quel che di sole', che conosciuto
i' non sarò, e sarò consolato,
me ristorando del mal c'ò avuto,
veggiendo quello aspetto ove fu nato
quel disio che mi tiene e à tenuto;
e s'a· servigio di Teseo potessi
esser, non so che poscia mi volessi."

38. And he said to himself: "I am so changed from what I used to be, that I shall not be recognized, and I will be comforted, recovering myself from the trouble that I had, seeing that sight where that desire that grips me and has gripped me was born; and if I could be in service to Teseo, I do not know what else I might want."

[(39–58) *Arcita / Penteo was willing to risk death in order to see Emilia.* (40–1) *He came to Athens disguised as a poor servant.* (42–8) *Having prayed to Apollo that he not be recognized, he received a sign that his prayer had been answered.* (49–58) *He became a servant of Teseo and regained his strength. At a feast he was delighted to see Emilia. She alone recognized him, but remained silent.*]

fol. 21^v 59. Incominciò il nobile Penteo, [1439–40, 1448
amaestrato da fervente amore,
sì a servir sollecito Teseo
e da ciascun degli altri per suo onore,
ch' egli in tutto suo sergiente il feo,
amando lui più c' altro servidore;
e simile l'amava la reina
del buono amore, e anche la fantina.

59. Noble Penteo, taught by fervent love, began to serve Teseo and each of the others according to their rank with such care, that he made him his sergeant in charge of everything, loving him more than any other servant; and so too did the queen hold him in great affection, and so did the maiden.

***59.5** While Boccaccio's autograph describes Teseo as placing all his confidence (*segreto*) in Arcita a unique variant line in *Vz* describes Teseo's appointing Arcita as his sergeant in charge of everything (*in tutto suo sergiente*). In *The Knight's Tale*, Theseus appoints Arcite squire of his chamber (I, 1440). Because it specifies a title for Arcita, *Vz* is a better source for Chaucer.

38 3 **e sarò** et vivrò Aut NO L^2 S M^6 R^1 R^4. 5 **quello** il bello Aut NO L^2 S M^6 R^1 R^4. 6 **quel** il Aut NO L^2 S M^6 R^1 R^4. 8 **poscia** poi più Aut NO L^2 S R^1 R^4; più poi M^6. **volessi** chiedessi Aut NO L^2 S M^6 R^1, R^4.

59 4 **da ciascun** ad ogni Aut NO L^2 S M^6; ogni R^1; o ciascuno R^4. 5 **sergiente** segreto Aut NO L^2 S M^6 R^1 R^4. 8 **anche** ancor Aut NO L^2 S M^6 R^1 R^4.

[(60–72) *Arcita / Penteo continued to love Emilia, but kept his love and his identity hidden. When he stared longingly at Emilia, she pretended not to notice him. He made merry and entered competitions, but suffered because he thought Emilia did not know he was performing for her. To hide his grief, he often traveled to a grove about three miles outside the city in order to lament about love. He often slept there until dawn.*]

fol. 22v 73. Allor, sentendo cantar Filomena + [1488–96
che ssi fa lieta del morto Chereo,
si riza Apollo con vista serena;
mirando un poco, lauldava Penteo
la man di Giove d'ongni grazia piena,
che llavoro sì grande e bello feo;
poi ad Emilia il suo pensier voltava,
veggiendo Cieterea che ssi levava.

73. Then hearing the singing of Philomena,[18] who rejoiced over dead Chereo,[19] Apollo rose up with a serene appearance; gazing in awe for a moment, Penteo praised the hand of Jove, full of every grace, that produced so great and fine a work; then he turned his thoughts to Emilia, seeing that Citerea[20] was rising.

[(74–8) *At sunrise he would beg Apollo and Venus to inspire Emilia to love him. After singing his song, he would return to serve Teseo in Athens.* (79–80) *Because he made little progress in love, he one morning lamented his various misfortunes.*]

fol. 23r 81. "Di real sangue, lasso!, ingienerato, [1542–9
venni nel mondo e d'ongni buon ostello,
e con gran cura e richeza allevato,
nella città di Bacco tapinello
ivi con gioia, ivi con grande stato
sanza pensare il tuo operar fello;
po' per altro peccato, e non per mio,
lasciai il rengnio e 'l mio sangue pio.

81. "Born of royal blood, alas!, I came into the world and dwelling place of every good. And with great care and riches I was raised, poor fellow, in the city of

73.2 The name Chereo (Aut: Thereo) has been corrupted in *Vz*. Chaucer would, however, have known the story of Tereus and Philomela / -mena in Ovid (*Met.* 6.424 ff), the *Ovide Moralisé*, and other French versions that were Chaucer's sources for the Philomela legend in the *Legend of Good Women*. (See notes to *Riverside* Edition.)

73 2 **Chereo** (and 4.54.2) S L² M⁶; Thereo Aut NO R¹ R⁴. 3 **Apollo** R⁴; e 'l polo Aut NO; al polo L² S; a polo R¹; al popol M⁶. 4 **poco** R¹; pezzo Aut NO L² S M⁶ R⁴.

81 2 **buon** pena Aut NO L² S M⁶ R¹ R⁴. 3 **cura e** L² S R¹; cura in Aut NO M⁶ R⁴. 5 **ivi** L² S R¹; vissi e Aut R⁴; vissi NO M⁶. **ivi con** tenni Aut NO M⁶; venni L², S, R⁴. 7 **altro** l'altrui Aut NO; altrui L² S M⁶ R¹ R⁴. **e** L², S, R¹; *om* Aut NO M⁶ R⁴. 8 **lasciai** la gioia e Aut NO L² S M⁶ R¹ R⁴. **pio** [*corrected to* perio *in an 18th century hand*]; perio Aut NO L² S M⁶ R¹ R⁴.

18 also called Philomela.

19 *Tereus*.

20 Cytherea.

Bacchus – with joy there, with great rank there, without any thought of your malevolent conduct. Then, on account of the sin [of] another, and not because of my own, I left the kingdom and my worthy lineage.

82. "E fu' del canpo per morte doglioso
tolto, ferito, e recato a Teseo,
il quale, come singnor poderoso,
come gli piacque, in pregion mi feo;
quivi, per farmi peggio, l'amoroso [1564–5
dardo m'entrò nel cor, focoso e reo,
per la belleza d'Emilia piaciente,
che mai di me non si curò niente.

82. "And I was picked up wounded on the grievous death-field and brought to Teseo who, like a mighty lord, had me imprisoned as it pleased him; there, to make it even worse for me, the love dart – fiery and wicked – entered my heart on account of the beauty of the charming Emilia who has never given a care for me."

[(83) *He remembered Periton's request that he be freed and Teseo's command that he leave Athens.*]

84. "Ch' i' [mi] trovai povero pellegrino
del rengnio mio caccciato, per amore
d'ir sospirando a guisa di tapino;
e là dov' altra volta fu' singnore,
servo divenni per quello gran dichino
della fortuna; e non potendo il core
più sofferire, da Pelleo fè partita,
Penteo essendo tornato d'Arcita. [1557–8

84. "Because I found myself a poor pilgrim driven out of my kingdom, for the sake of love going about sighing [and] disguised like a poor wretch. Whereas at another time I was a lord, I have become a servant on account of that great reversal of fortune; and since my heart could no longer bear it, I departed from Pelleo, coming back as Penteo [instead] of Arcita.

85. "E ssì di lei mi strinse la belleza, [1553–4
che di Teseo cacciai ongni paura;
quivi mi missi per la mia matteza
e ritornaci con mente sicura,
essendo suo nimico; alla sua alteza
divenni servidore con somma cura,
sicché vedela potessi sovente,
po'ch' è donna di me veraciemente."

85.4 ritornaci = ritornaici.

82 1 **morto** NO S R^4; morte Aut L^2; lasso M6.
*84 1 **[mi]** Aut NO L^2 S M^6 R^1 R^4; ti Vz. **povero** M^6 R^1; povero et Aut NO L^2 S R^4. 5 **quello** lo Aut NO L^2 S M^6 R^1 R^4.

85. "Her beauty so seized me, that I cast aside all fear of Teseo. On account of my [love] madness there, I set out and I returned here sound of mind, as his enemy. With great discretion I became his highness' servant so that I might be able to see her often, since she truly is my lady."

[(86) *He lamented that Emilia cared nothing for his sufferings and that cruel Fortune continued to torture him.* (87–91) *Fortune has kept his name secret and has made him gentler, but this would mean nothing if Emilia did not love him. Panfilo, one of Palamone's servants, overheard the lament of Arcita / Penteo, recognized him, and returned to Palamone in prison in order to report this information. Unaware of this, Arcita / Penteo returned to Athens, spoke pleasantly with Teseo, and took his leave, hoping to catch a glimpse of Emilia.*]

85 1 **di lei mi** d'Emilia Aut NO L^2 S M^6 R^1 R^4 2 **ongni** via la Aut NO L^2 S M^6 R^1 R^4. 4 **e** ad Aut NO L^2 S M^6 R^1 R^4. 7 **vedela potessi** io Emilia vedessi Aut NO L^2 S M^6 R^1 R^4.
8 **po'** cholei Aut NO L^2 S M^6 R^1 R^4.

Book 5

[*Introductory sonnet to book 5*]

[(1–8) *Palamone languished alone in prison; jealousy made him fear that Emilia might have been responsible for Arcita's release from leaving prison.* (3–12) *Panfilo informed Palamone that Penteo was Arcita, saying that he had seen him, greatly changed, in the grove. Palamone first warned Panfilo to be silent about Arcita in order to protect him.* (9–12) *Then, beginning to consider Arcita as his rival, he started to think of escaping from prison.*]

fol. 24^r 13. E così come [Tesifon], chiamata
dal cielo Edopo nella oscura parte
[dov'] egli lunga notte avie menata,
a duo frategli, dengnia con su arte,
mise l'arsura, così nell'entrata
con quel vapor che suo voler comparte,
d'Emilia avendo, dì ciò: "Singnioria [1623–6
né amore sta ben con conpangnia."

13. And just as Tesifon, after she was summoned from heaven [by] Edopo[21] in that hidden place where he had passed the long night, enflamed the two brothers

*13 1 [**Tesifon**] R^1; Tesison Vz; Thesifon L^2 S; Tesiphone Aut R^4; Tesifone NO; esso si fa ssé M^6. 2 **cielo** L^2 S R^1 R^4 ciecho Aut NO M^6. **Edopo** Edippo Aut NO R^4; Edipo L^2 S; Idipo M^6; Dopo R^1. (See 2.29.2, above.) *3 [**dov'**] Aut NO L^2 S M^6 R^4; dav' Vz. 4 **dengnia** del rengno Aut NO L^2 S M^6 R^4. 5 **nell'** a llui Aut NO L^2 S M^6 R^1 R^4. 6 **vapor** velen Aut NO L^2 S M^6 R^1 R^4. 7 **dì ciò** dicendo Aut NO L^2 S M^6 R^1; e dise R^4.

[21] *Oedipus.*

with her worthy skill: so too, once she had taken possession of him with that confusion that his wish for possessing Emilia confers, he said the following: "[Neither] lordship nor love will endure a partnership very well."

[(14–23) *Once Palamone determined to escape from prison, Panfilo formulated a plan. Palamone would feign sickness. Alimeto, a Theban physician who had recently arrived in Athens, would be called. Palamone would exchange clothing with Alimeto, and Alimeto with Panfilo. They would exit the prison, leaving Panfilo behind, and Palamone would go to meet Arcita in the grove.* (24–6) *When the preparations were completed and Panfilo had made the guards drunk with wine, the plan was carried out. Palamone and Alimeto left the prison, leaving instructions that the prisoner was not to be disturbed.* (27–8) *After sleeping at an inn, the next morning Palamone armed himself and went to the grove where Arcita was sleeping.* (29) *The hour was still and the moon, almost full, had reached the zenith.* (30–1) *Palamone prayed to the moon, identifying himself as a lover, and begging her to light his steps and to protect him.* (33–6) *Seeing Arcita asleep, he recognized him and stood beside him, telling himself that they would soon determine who would have Emilia.* (37–45) *When Arcita awoke, they greeted each other. Palamone declared his love for Emilia and asked Arcita to cede her to him; Arcita made the same request of Palamone. Palamone insisted that they would have to fight. Arcita argued that each should pursue Emilia in his own way, letting Fortune grant her to one of them.* (46) *Arcita tried to convince Palamone of the futility of their combat for Emilia, since they both would be executed if they were captured by Teseo.* (47–50) *Arcita suggested that they should reconsider, since there might be another way to resolve their difficulty. Palemone insisted that they fight. Arcita replied that Teseo would not grant her to the survivor. Then he raised the subject of the absurdity of their trying to come to an agreement over who would have the right to love Emilia.*]

fol. 26r 51. "E sse di qui con fé ti prometessi [1172–6
di non mirarla, credi tu che ffare
con tutto mio ingiengnio io il potessi?
Cierto più tosto sanza mai mangiare
credere vivere che di miralla istessi;
e amor non si può così lasciare
come tu credi; e poch' ama chi posa,
per promessa, d'amore alcuna cosa."

51. "And even if I should at this point promise on my word not to desire her, do you think that I might be able to do so with all my strength? Indeed, I believe that I could sooner live without eating than [without] marveling at her. Love is not something that can just be cast off, as you believe; and little does he love who, for the sake of a promise, puts aside anything related to love."

[(52–3) *Arcita said they were foolish to fight over something that they could not possess and urged Palamone to leave before they were discovered and arrested.*

51 1 **di** io Aut NO L² S M⁶ R¹ R⁴. 2 **mirarla** amarla Aut NO L² S M⁶ R¹ R⁴. 5 **miralla** L² S R¹; amarla Aut NO M⁶ R⁴. 6 **lasciare** L² S R¹; chacciare Aut NO M⁶ R⁴. 8 **promessa** . . . **alcuna** inpromessa amare una Aut NO L² S M⁶ R¹ R⁴.

Palamone insisted that they must fight. (54–6) *Palamone urges Arcita to fight, while Arcita laments that Fortune, not love, has destined them to fight.* (57) *Arcita described the various forms of hatred that had plagued the Theban royal line, including Acheon,*[22] *who was dismembered by his dogs.* (58–63) *and lamented that they would be the last royal Thebans to kill each other. They mounted their horses, while Arcita blamed Palamone for wanting to battle instead of trying to negotiate a peace.* (64–76) *They violently charged at each other. Arcita struck Palamone, who appeared to be dead. Arcita bewailed his companion, blaming himself for ever having loved. Palamone recovered, discounting Arcita's pity and insisting that they continue their battle. Each beseeched the gods; they fought each other fiercely, but no one had an advantage.*]

fol. 27^r 77. Ma ccome noi veggiamo venire inn ora [1668–9
cosa che in mill'anni nonn aviene,
così avenne veramente allora
che Tteseo con Emilia d'Attene
uscì co· molti in conpangnia di fora,
e qual di loro ucciello e qual can tene, [1678–80
e nel boschetto entraro, alcun cornando,
cacciando al lor diletto e ucciellando.

77. But just as we see something occur in a moment that has not happened in a thousand years, so it truly happened then that Teseo, along with Emilia, came out from Athens with a company of many. Some of them had birds and some of them, dogs. They entered the wood, some sounding horns, delighting in their hunting and hawking.

[(78–82) *When the two combatants recognized Emilia, they fought more ferociously. She called on Teseo, who rode up to the two young men.*]

fol. 27^v 83. Po' disse loro: "O cavalieri, se Marte [1708, 1710–11
doni vettoria a cchui la disia,
ciascun di voi si traggha d'una parte;
s'egli è in voi nessuna cortesia,
mi dite chi vo' siete e cchi tal parte
v'inducie alla battaglia tanto ria,
secondo che mostrate nel ferire
nell'un nell'altro cura di morire."

***77.8** *cacciando al lor diletto e ucciellando* ("delighting in their hunting and hawking"): This unique variant in *Vz* is a much better source of Chaucer's "For in his huntyng hath he swich delit" (*KnT* I, 1679) than the reading in *Aut* and in the other *alpha-kappa* MSS (*alcun compangni et alcun chan chiamando*: "some calling to their companions and some calling their dogs").

77 8 **cacciando al lor diletto e ucciellando** alcun compangni et alcun chan chiamando Aut NO L^2 S R^1 R^4.

83 4 **nessuna** alcuna Aut NO R^4; niuna L^2 S M^6 R^1. 5 **chi tal** chi in tal Aut NO L^2 S M^6 R^1 R^4. 7 **che** L^2 S M^6 R^1 R^4; ne Aut NO. 8 **nell'un nell'altro cura di** che fate l'uno ad l'altro da Aut NO; che fate 'uno ver l'altro da L^2 S M^6 R^1 R^4.

[22] *Actaeon.*

83. Then he said to them: "O knights, if Mars should give victory to whoever might desire it, let each of you step aside. If there is any courtesy in you, tell me who you are and who impels you [in] a place like this to such cruel combat by which you show, in the way that you wound each other, that neither of you has any concern about dying."

[(84–5) *The two separated and identified themselves as rivals in love. Teseo said he would not permit them to continue fighting; because of their noble cause and their valor, he did not wish them to be harmed.* (86–90) *After Arcita and Palamone had named themselves, Teseo was first angry with them, then demanded to know the object of their love. Palamone explained their story, saying he deserved to die for having fled from Teseo's prison.* (91) *Teseo said that they would not die, although he could not be blamed for executing them.* (92) *Remembering his own youthful misdeeds for the sake of love and the pardon he received for them, Teseo promised to pardon the two young men.* (94) *Teseo then explained that his first intention had been to give Emilia to his cousin Acate, but Acate then died.*]

fol. 28^r 95. "Dunque conviene a me pensar d'altrui, + [1829–69
perché l'età di lei omai richiede,
in ciò non so pensare ben bene chui
i' la mi dea, che con più ferma fede
l'ami 'd onori quanto l'un di voi,
se voi l'amate come il mio cuor crede;
perc' aver non la può di voi ciascuno [1835
sicché conviene ch' ella rimanga all'uno.

95. "Therefore it is appropriate of me to think of others, because her age now requires it. As for this, I cannot imagine anyone to whom I might give her, who would love and honor her with a steadier faith than one of you, if you love her as my heart would lead me to believe. Since both of you cannot have her, it is therefore fitting that she stay with one.

96. "All'un di voi sarà bene investita, [1829–32
però che siete di sangue reale
e di nobile affare e d'alta vita;
ed ella anch' è simil' e altrettale,
ed è sorella alla reina ardita
che mecho è stata serva inperiale;
per la qualcosa isdengniar non dovete
per moglie lei, s'averla potete.

96. "She would be well bestowed on one of you, since you are of royal blood and of noble rank and of distinguished conduct. And she too is alike and in the same degree, and she is sister to the valorous queen who has been a servant of the empire along with me; on this account you ought not be averse to having her for wife – if to have her you are able.

95 3 **in ciò** L^2 S R^1 R^4; né io Aut NO M^6. **chui** R^1 R^4; ad chui Aut NO S M^6; in cui L^2. 5 **quanto** che farà Aut NO L^2 S R^1 R^4; come M^6. 6 **voi** R^4; sì Aut NO L^2 S M^6 R^1. 7 **perc'** ma Aut NO L^2 S R^1 R^4; e non M^6. 8 **sicchè** però Aut NO L^2 S M^6 R^1 R^4.

96 3 **nobile** . . . **alta** L^2 S R^1 R^4; alto . . . nobile Aut NO M^6. 4 **anch'** L^2 S R^1 R^4; *om* Aut NO M^6.

97. "Ma per ciessar da voi ongni quistione, [1850–3
coll'arme indosso vi convien provare
nel modo ch' i' dirò: a Palamone
ciento conpangni farà di trovare
dall'una parte con sua lezione,
e similmente a tte converrà fare;
poi a battaglia nel teantro nostro
sarete insieme col seguito vostro.

97. "But to make an end to all dispute between you, it is only proper that you put yourselves to the proof, with armor on, in a way that I shall explain. As for Palamone, he will undertake to find a hundred companions of his choice on one side, and it will be to your advantage to do the same. Then you will [assemble] for battle in our amphitheater together with your followers.

98. "Chi l'altra parte caccierà di fuore [1859, 1856–61
per forza d'arme, marito le fia;
l'altro, di lei fie privo dell' onore;
a quel giudicio converrà che stia
che lla donna vorrà, a cchui valore
conmesso da quest' ora innanzi sia;
e termine vi sia acciò donato
un anno intero." E così fu ordinato.

98. "Whoever drives out the other group by force of arms will become her husband; the other will be deprived of the honor of her. He will be subject to whatever judgment is willed by that lady, on whose mercy he will depend from that hour onward. And the time allotted to you for this will be one full year." And so it was ordered.

[(99–102) *The two men gratefully accepted these conditions. Emilia looked at them with great compassion. Teseo reminded Emilia about the power of love and about her eventual betrothal; embarrassed, she did not reply.* (103–5) *Teseo brought the two young men back to Athens, with Emilia between them. In his palace they would be healed of their injuries. He restored their former wealth and possessions to them.*]

Book 6

[*Introductory sonnet to book 6*]

[(1–5) *The two young Thebans were victims of cruel fortune; human wisdom cannot explain the workings of fortune.* (6–12) *Once they were reconciled to Teseo, Palamone and Arcita renewed their loving friendship. They enjoyed their wealth,*

97 3 **a** che Aut NO L² S M⁶ R¹ R⁴. 5 **dall'una parte con** quali e' potrà ad Aut NO L² S R¹ R⁴; qual e'vorrà a M⁶.

98 3 **fie** *om* Aut NO L² S M⁶ R¹ R⁴. 8 **ordinato** L² S R¹ R⁴; fermato Aut NO M⁶.

entertained and hunted, held jousts, and tried to please Emilia. In preparing for the coming contest between them, they were willing to win or to die. Each cultivated friends and made preparations. (13) *When the day for the contest approached, each invited his friends to participate; Athens was thronged with crowds.*]

fol. 29v 14. Il primo venne, ancora lagrimoso [2129–52
per la morte d'Aphelte, a ner vestito,
il re Lagorgo, forte e poderoso,
di senno grande e di coraggio ardito;
e menò seco popolo valoroso
del rengnio suo tutto il più fiorito,
e ad Arcita s'oferse inn aiuto,
il qual fu caramente ricievuto.

14. The first to come, still mourning for the death of Afelte[23] [and] dressed in black [was] King Lagorgo,[24] strong and powerful, of great wisdom and intrepid courage. And with him he brought a valiant company, the flower of his whole kingdom, he offered himself in aid to Arcita and was warmly received.

[(15) *King Pelleo*[25] *came; young, valorous, and a great leader, he had a bright countenance.* (16) *Pelleo rode a sorrel-colored charger. He carried a richly designed quiver and a sturdy bow.* (17–19) *He had blond curls and was arrayed in gold and precious stones, carried splendid arms and was much admired. Many nobles came with him in the hope of winning honor.* (20) *King Niso*[26] *came, in shining armor and with a company of men.*]

21. Po' su un carro, da quattro gran tori + [2138–9
tirato, di Tenaria, Agamennone
vi venne aconpangnato da plusori,
armato tutto a guisa di barone,
mostrandosi già dengnio degli onori
ch' ebe da' Greci nella 'struzione
a Troia fatta: nel senbiante arguto,
con nera barba, grande e ben nenbruto.

14.3 Chaucer fashioned his description of "Lygurge . . . the grete kyng of Trace" (*KnT* I, 2129) from two figures in Statius: Lycurgus, king of Nemea and father of Opheltes (*Thebaid.* 4.749; 5.39, 638, 647, 653, 696, 702, 715; 6.130) and Lycurgus, king of Thrace (*Theb.* 4.386; 7.180). (See notes to the *Riverside* edition.)

14 2 **Aphelte** Ophelte Aut; Oferte NO [cf. 11.18.2]; Phelte L² S R¹ R⁴; Fleta M⁶. (For Opheltes, see *Thebaid* 4.729.) 3 **Lagorgo** Ligurgho Aut; Lighurgho NO; Lugurgo L² S; Ligurgo M⁶ R¹ R⁴. (See note.) 6 **tutto** pure Aut NO L² S M⁶ R¹ R⁴. 8 **il qual fu caramente ricievuto** per chui era di Nemea venuto Aut NO L² S M⁶ R⁴; *om* R¹.

21 1 **Po' su** Sopra Aut NO L² S M⁶ R¹ R⁴. 2 **Tenaria** M6; Threnarea Aut; Trenarea NO; Tenereaia L²; Tenaraia S; Teneraia R¹; Trinaria R⁴. 6 **'struzione** L² S R¹ R⁴; obsidione Aut NO M⁶.

23 *Opheltes.*

24 *Lycurgus.*

25 Peleus.

26 Nisus.

21. Then on a carriage drawn by four great bulls of Tenaria,[27] Agamennone[28] came there accompanied by many, completely armed, in the manner of a baron, showing himself by now worthy of the honors that he had from the Greeks for the "lesson" given to Troy: with his striking appearance, black beard, imposing and well-limbed.

fol. 30^r 22. Non armi chiare, non mantel lodato, + [2141–2
non pettinati crini, non ornamenti
d'or' o di pietre aveva, [ma] legato
d'orso un velluto co· chuoi lucienti
unghioni al collo, il qual d'ongni lato
ricoprie· l'armi tutte rugginenti;
e chiunque quel vedeva d'esso:
"E' vincierà con qualunque fie messo."

22. He did not have shining armor, nor an illustrious cloak, nor combed hair, nor ornaments of gold or precious stones, but a shaggy bear[skin] with shining, leathery claws, tied to the neck. On every side it covered all his rusty armor. And whoever saw him [said] of him: "Whoever's side he's on will win."

[(23–6) *After him came Menellao,*[29] *Castore and Policie.*[30] (27–9) *Eromio*[31] *came dressed in a lion skin and riding a great horse. A large group, including Chupidonio,*[32] *accompanied him.* (30–4) *Nestore*[33] *came, armed with silver-plated iron.* (35) *Evandro*[34] *arrived with many of his barons.*]

fol. 30^v 36. Egli era in sun il tesalico destriere;
co' suoi insieme giva baldanzoso,
ed era armato d'armi forte e fiere,
e per mantel un chuoio d'orso piloso
libistrico, lle chu' unghie già ciere
sott' oro eran coverte luminoso,
e de' suo molti avien tal copritura,
e di leone alcuno la pelle dura.

22.4–5 The critical reading in Aut and NO describes Agamemnon as wearing "d'orso un velluto chuoio con rilucenti/ unghioni" (a shaggy bearskin with shining claws). The reading in Vz contorts the sense, but did not influence Chaucer's text, so it is not emended.

22 1 **lodato** dorato Aut NO L^2 S M^6 R^1 R^4. *.3 **[ma]** Aut NO L^2 S R^1 R^4; me Vz; avie M^6. 7 **quel** S; il Aut NO L^2 M^6 R^1 R^4. v**edeva** vedea diceva Aut NO L^2 S M^6 R^1 R^4. 8 **E'** Que' Aut NO L^2 S M^6 R^1 R^4. **qualunque** chui questi Aut NO; chiunque S R^4; conunque L^2; colui . . . chui M^6; cui R^1.

27 *Trenarea.*
28 Agamemnon.
29 *Menelaus.*
30 Castor and *Pollux.*
31 *Cromis.*
32 *Hippodam.*
33 Nestor.
34 Evander.

36. He was up on the Thesalian steed. He moved around self confidently with his men, and he was armed with strong and fierce weapons, and for his mantel [he wore] a skin of hairy Libistrican bear, whose once-pallid claws were covered under luminous gold. And many of his men had similar attire, and some [wore] sturdy lion skin.

[(37–40) *His company had unpolished armor and some wore boar skins. He carried a shield with elaborate decoration; although he did not appear handsome, all admired him.* (41) *Periton*[35] *came; he was handsome, blond, and crowned with laurel.* (42–3) *He rode a huge stallion, and Teseo came from the palace to greet him. Most of the city came out to see him, accompanied by Teseo on their way to the palace.* (44) *Ulisse*[36] *and Diomede*[37] *came.* (45) *A "great baron"*[38] *and Siccheo*[39] *came.* (46–50) *Minosso,*[40] *the King of Crete came with Radamante and Serpidone,*[41] *who bore a decorated shield; the Athenians thronged to see the Bistonian came.* (52–4) *Ida the Pisean came.* (55–7) A*rmato*[42] *also came, riding on a great horse, and accompanied by a troop of men.* (58–60) *Many others came from lands ruled by Arcita and Palamone.* (61–4) *Sad circumstances prevented some heroes from coming; the others who did come were there to display their nobility and to win fame.*]

fol. 32^r 65. Quanti vi fu di possenti singniori, [2182, 2190–6
re, duchi, prenzi e altri d'onor dengnio,
e qual si fosse piccolo o maggiori,
che di Teseo venisse ancor nel rengnio,
e' fur co· sommi e lietissimi honori
ricievuto, ciascun con tutto ingiengnio;
e per sé prima gli onorò Egieo,
e po' co· lieto volto fé Teseo.

36.4–5 *orso piloso libistrico* (hairy Libistrican bear): Boccaccio's *De montibus, silvis, etc.* describes Libistris as a forest either in Thesalia or in Bistonia that is noted for its many animals, and in particular for its huge and powerful bears: "ursos . . . prægrandes . . . et validos" (Venice: Vindelinus de Spira, 1472 s.v. "De Silvis").

36.5 *già ciere* (once-pallid): before receiving their decorative gold-covering, the nails of the bearskin were originally – and uniquely – pallid in *Vz*. They were originally black (*nere*) in the other MSS. Chaucer's concern, however, is their present gilded and shining state, so the line requires no emendation.

41–55 Many names from these 15 stanzas occur in variant or garbled form. Some names appear in the poem as allusions that *Aut* identifies in a gloss or rubric. Since Chaucer does not use them, the names are not emended. The correct forms of the names appear below in the footnotes.

36 2 **giva** andando Aut NO L^2 S M^6 R^1 R^4. 5 **ciere** nere Aut NO L^2 S M^6 R^1 R^4. 6 **coverte** nascose Aut NO L^2 S M^6 R^1 R^4.

[35] *Pirithous*.
[36] Ulysses.
[37] Diomedes.
[38] *Pingmaleone*.
[39] Sichaeus.
[40] *Minos*.
[41] *Sarpedon*.
[42] *Admetus*.

65. However many powerful lords, kings, dukes, princes and others worthy of honor were there, whether minor or grand, who continued to come into the kingdom of Teseo, these were received with the highest and most agreeable honors, each one with all diligence. And first Egeo[43] himself honored them and then Teseo did so with a joyful expression.

[(66–8) *Ipolita and Emilia graciously received the visitors. No one considered it foolish that Arcita and Palamone would try to win such a treasure.*]

69. Se gli altri regi furono honorati [2206–7
da Palamone e dal nobile Arcita,
non cal ch'i' narri, ché huomini nati
non si crede che mai in questa vita
fosson serviti o tanti lauldati
veduti come questi, a chu' fornita
er' ongni cosa larga e con disire,
tanto ch'i' no 'l potre' giamai ridire.

69. As for [the way] the other kings were honored by Palamone and by noble Arcita, it does not matter how I tell [my story]: since no man born in this life would ever believe how they were served or how so many seemed [to be] praised as these were. Every important thing was provided for them, and with pleasure. Such [was all this] that I would not ever be able to describe it again.

70. Altri conviti e doni a regi dengni [2197–2208
s'usava quivi, e sol d'amor parlare, [2203
quivi si biasimava tutti i sdengni;
giovinil giuochi e sovente armeggiare
il più del tenpo occupavan gl'ingiengni,
e ne' giardini con donne fessteggiare.
Lieti v'erono i grandi e i minori;
facien grillande di rose e di fiori.

70. Other sorts of banquets and gifts fit for a king were the rule there, and speaking only of love. There every type of animosity was condemned; youthful games and frequent jousting tested their skill most their time, and celebrating with the ladies in the gardens. The great and the small were joyful there; they made garlands of roses and of flowers.

65 1 **Quanti vi** Qualunque Aut NO M⁶; Quantunque L² S R¹ R⁴. 4 **ancor** L² S M⁶ R¹R⁴; allor Aut NO. 8 **volto fé** viso il buon Aut NO L² S M⁶ R⁴; volto il buon R¹.

69 1 **altri** S; alti Aut NO M⁶ R¹ R⁴; *om* L². 2 **nobile** gentile Aut NO L² S M⁶ R¹ R⁴. 5 **serviti o tanti lauldati** co' servigi lieti et grati Aut NO L² S M⁶ R¹ R⁴. 6 **chu'** qua Aut NO L² S M⁶ R⁴; quale R¹. 7 **cosa larga e con disire** voglia sol che essi dire Aut NO L² S M⁶ R¹ R⁴; ogni mestieri con sembianza lieta M⁶. 8 **tanto ch'i' no 'l potre giamai ridire** volesser ciò che non potean sentire Aut NO L² S M⁶ R¹ R⁴.

70 1 **altri** alti Aut NO L² S M⁶ R¹ R⁴. 3 **tutti** et Aut; egli NO L² S R¹ R⁴; *om* M⁶. 6 **e ne'** o in Aut NO L² S M⁶ R¹ R⁴. 8 **facien grillande di rose e di fiori** et adagiati da' fini amadori Aut NO L² S M⁶ R¹ R⁴.

[43] Aegeus.

[(71) *Teseo considered it a great honor that so many noble guests had gathered in his city.*]

Book 7

[*Introductory sonnet to book 7*]

[(1–7.5,7–8; 8–11) *Teseo brought the nobles and the citizens to the amphitheater. He stated his dismay at the number of visitors who had arrived. His intention was that the contest be a palestral game, not a battle, and that love, not hatred, should be its theme. One hundred men would be named for each side.*]

fol. 33r 12. "Acciò che odio fra vo' non nasciesse, + [2543–60; 2537–65
le lancie in mano niente porterete;
sol con i spade o maze alle riprese
forze di voi contenti proverete;
e lle lor pene porti chi volesse,
e altro no: di questo assai avete;
e quel che ne farà arà vettoria
sopra la donna, il pregio e l'alta gloria."

12. "So that no hatred should be born among you, you may carry no lances in your hands. Only with swords or maces may you test your stamina as it pleases you, and whoever wants to [do this] should put up with the pain; who doesn't should not. You have enough of this type [of weapons]. And whoever uses them will be victorious in regard to the woman, will have prestige, and will have high glory.

[(13) *Teseo said that, as judge, he would not participate in these games dedicated to Mars. He counseled the participants to conduct themselves well.*]

14. De' nobili e de'popilli il romore [2561–64
toccò le stelle, sì fu alto e forte:
"Gl'iddii," diciendo, "salvi tal singniore
che tra gli amanti fuggie la rie morte,
e con piatoso e grazioso amore
dere' contasti men gravose sorte."
E in quel loco sanza dipartirsi,
i cento e cento elessero e si girsi.

***12.2** *Aut* and the other *alpha-zeta* MSS describe Teseo ordering the combatants to leave only the most harmful (*più nocive lascerete*) of their lances outside the arena. A unique variant in *Vz* has him order them not to carry any lances at all in their hands (*in mano niente porterete*). This variant line could be a source of Chaucer's catalogue of the weapons forbidden in the combat (*KnT* I, 2544, 2546) and his command that no one may draw a short sword or even "bere it by his syde" (*KnT* I, 2547).

12 2 **in mano niente porterete** più nocive lascerete Aut NO L² S M⁶ R¹ R⁴. 3 **o** R⁴; o con Aut NO; e L² S R¹; e con M⁶. **alle riprese** l'expresse Aut NO; le riprese L² S R⁴; e le riprese R¹; spesse M⁶. 6 **e** ma Aut NO L² S M⁶ R¹ R⁴. 7**che ne farà arà** S R⁴; ad chui il bene ovrar Aut NO; come farà e avrà L²; che l'arà avrà R¹; chui ben operrà M⁶. 8 **sopra la donna il pregio** S R⁴; darà s'avrà et la donna Aut NO; avrà sopra la donna onore M⁶; s'avrà la donna L² R¹. **e l'alta** et la Aut L² S R¹ R⁴; e M⁶; con NO.

14. The noise of the common people and of the nobles touched the stars, so loud and strong was it: “May the gods,” they said, “preserve such a lord who would protect lovers from a bitter death, and through his kind and gracious love would bring quarrels to less grievous conclusions!” And in that place, without leaving, they chose the [companies of] a hundred and a hundred and they assembled them.

[(15–18) *One hundred men enrolled on Arcita’s side, and another hundred on Palamone’s side.*]

fol. 33^{v} 19. E similmente fecie Palamone; [2587–93
di francha giente si trovar sì pari,
ched e’ non v’erà di varazione;
e crediesi che non ne fosse guari
rimasi al mondo di tal condizione,
così gientili e di prodeza pari,
qual era quivi l’uno e ll’altro ciento:
di che Teseo fu assai contento.

19. And Palamone did likewise. Here were to be found honest men so much alike that there was no difference between them; and one can believe that there were hardly any of that type left in the world – so well-mannered and equal in talents – as were in the [group of] the one and the other hundred: Teseo was very pleased about this.

[(20–1) *Teseo led the men through the city. The men were courteous with their opponents.* (22) *Palamone and Arcita each went to the temples of the gods, to ask their help in the contest.*]

23. Ma pure Arcita ne’ tenpi di Marte + [2368–72; 2367–2437
poscia ch’egli ebbe gli altri vicitati
e dato fuoco e inciienso in ongni parte,
si ritornò a quegli aluminati
vie, più che gli altri ancora e con più arte
e di licori sommi e onorati,
col cor divoto tale orazione
a Marte fecie con gran divozione:

23. But Arcita, too, after he had visited the others and had lit fires and burned incense everywhere, he returned to the temples of Mars, to those light-filled places. And there, even more so and with greater art and the finest and most renowned liquors, he made this plea to Mars with a pious heart [and] with great devotion:

14 3 **salvi** L^2 S R^1 R^4; servin Aut NO M^6. 4 **tra gli amanti** delli amici suoi Aut NO M^6 R^1; degli amici L^2 S R^4. **rie** L^2 S M^6 R^4; *om* Aut NO R^1. 8 **si girsi** partirsi Aut NO L^2 S M^6 R^1 R^4.

19 1 **E similmente** Il simil Aut NO L^2 S M^6 R^4; e simil R^1. **fecie** *add* anchora Aut NO L^2 S M^6 R^1 R^4. 2 **di francha giente** et di buoni huomin Aut NO L^2 S M^6 R^1 R^4. 3 **di** R^1 R^4; *om* Aut NO L^2 S M^6. 6 **di** L^2 S R^1 R^4; per Aut NO M^6.

23 4 **a** NO L^2 S R^1 R^4; et Aut M^6. 5 **vie** *om* Aut NO L^2 S M^6 R^1 R^4. **gli** L^2 S R^1 R^4; *om* Aut NO M^6. **ancora** assai Aut NO L^2 S M^6 R^1 R^4. **arte** L^2 S R^1 R^4 solenne arte Aut NO; solepnitate M^6. 6 **sommi e onorati** sommissimi rorati Aut; sommissimi in rorati NO; sommissimi onorati L^2 S M^6 R^4; soavissimi onorati R^1.

24. "O [forte] ideo che ne' rengni nevosi [2373–4
conservi senpre tuo sagreti cose,
ne' luoghi a' sol nimici e tenebrosi,
de' tuoi ingiengni pieni per qua' rose
d'ardi· le fronti furon a' 'rgogliosi:
fedele Terra allor c'ongniun ripuose
di morte freddo su per le pruove
fatte da tte e dal tuo padre Giove,

24. "O strong god, who forever keeps your sacred possessions in the snowy realms, in places that are unfriendly to the sun and somber: on account of your full powers of boldness, by which the effrontery of the proud was ground down. The loyal earth [was] where each one lay cold in death due to the efforts made by you and your father Jove.

25. "e, per alto valore, la mia etade
e lle mie forze meritan ched io
de' tuo sie detto, per quella piatade
ch' ebe Nelpluno allor che con disio [2383–90
di Cieterea usavi la biltade,
rinchiuso da [Vulcano], e d'ongn' idio
fatto palese, umilmente ti priego
c'agli mie prieghi tu non faccia niego.

25. "And, on account of high merit, [both] my age and my powers warrant that I might be considered one of your own. For the sake of that pity that Nelpluno[44] once had when, with ardor, you were enjoying the beauty of Cytheraea [and you were] trapped by Vulcan and exhibited to every god: I humbly beg you that you do not deny my prayers.

26. "I' son come tu vedi, giovinetto,
e per nuova belleza tanto Amore [2394–5
sotto sua singnioria mi tien sì stretto,
che lle mie forze e tutto mie valore
convien ch' i' mostri, sed i' vo' diletto
sentir di ciò che più disia il core;
e sanza te i' son poco possente,
anzi più tosto non posso niente.

24 1 [**forte**] Aut NO L^2 S M^6 R^1 R^4; Marte Vz (cf. *KnT* I, 2373: stronge) . 2 **conservi senpre tuo' sagreti cose** bistonii servi le tue sacre chase Aut NO L^2 S M^6 R^1 R^4. 6 **ripuose** rimase Aut NO L^2 S M^6 R^1 R^4. 7 **su** in sul suol Aut NO L^2 S M^6 R^1 R^4.

25 1 **e . . .valore** L^2; se . . . voler Aut NO S R^1 R^4; che voler M^6. 4 **Nelpluno** Neptunno Aut S L^2; Neturno NO; Netunno R^4; Netturno M^6; Nepruno R^1. *Vz* also spells the name Noturno (6.42.6). *.6 [**Vulcano**] S L^2 R^4; Vuncano Vz; Ulgano R^1; alchun M^6; Vulchano Aut; Vulghano NO; Vulgano R^1. MS *Vz* also spells the name Vlcano (7.43.2; 8.4.3 9.2; 9.73.5) and Ulgan (11.57.2; 11.61.4). **e** L^2 S; ad Aut NO; *om* M^6 R^1 R^4.

26 3 **ì stretto** distrecto Aut NO L^2 S; constretto R^4; stretto M^6 R^1. 5 **ch'i' mostri** ovrarmi Aut NO L^2 S R^1; ad operar M^6; obliare R^4.

44 *Neptune.*

26. I am, as you can see, a young man and, for the sake of extraordinary beauty, Love keeps me so tightly under its mastery, that it is necessary for me to show my strength and all my courage, if I wish to feel the delight of that which my heart most desires. And without you I am capable of little; in fact, I can [do] nothing at all.

27. "Dunque m'aiuta per quel sommo foco
che t'arse già siccome me ard' ora,
e nel presente mio paternal gioco
co· lle tuo forze e nel pungner m'onora;
cierto sì fatto dono non mi fia poco,
ma sommo bene; [adunque] qui lavora;
s'i' son di questa punga vincitore,
io il diletto e ttu abbia l'onore. [2406

27. "Therefore help me for the sake of that lofty fire that inflamed you as it now inflames me; both in my present family conflict and in the battle honor me with your strength. Indeed, a gift thus granted would be no small thing for me, but rather the highest good. Therefore do your work here. If am to be the winner of this conflict, I shall have the joy and you, the honor.

28. "I tenpi tuoi eterni s'oneranno [2407–18
dell'armi del mie vento conpangnione,
e ancora le mie vi penderanno,
e fievi disengniata la cagione;
etterni fuochi senpre v'arderanno,
e la barba e' mie crini, che ofensione
di ferro non sentiron, ti prometto,
se mi fa' vincitor com' i'ò detto."

28. "Your eternal temples will be adorned with the arms of my conquered companion and my own will hang there and an account of it will be inscribed there. Eternal fires will always burn there, and I promise you my beard and hair, which have yet to suffer the indignity of steel, if you make me the victor in the manner that I have said."

fol. 34r 29. Era allora forse Marte in esercizio + [1967–2050
di chiara far la parte rugginosa
del grande suo orribile ispizio, [1971–2, 1974
quando d'Arcita l'Orazion piatosa
pervenne lì per fare il dengno ufizio,
tutt' una nell'aspetto lagrimosa;
la qual vi venne di spavento muta,
con di Marte la cosa ebbe veduta

28.6–7 *ofensione di ferro*: Boccaccio's gloss explains that Arcite's hair and beard have not suffered the "indignity of steel" because they were uncut and untrimmed. In having Arcite describe his beard and hair "That nevere yet ne felte offensioun/ Of rasour nor of shere . . ." (*KnT* I, 2416–17), Chaucer translates the poem closely, but his language shows no influence of the gloss.

27 1 **quel sommo** lo santo Aut NO L² S M⁶ R¹ R⁴. 4 **e** *om* Aut NO L² S M⁶ R¹ R⁴. *6 **[adunque]** Aut NO L² S M⁶ R⁴; adunqui Vz; adunche R¹. 8 **tu** tu n' Aut NO L² S M⁶ R¹ R⁴.

29. Mars was perhaps then in process of illuminating the rusty part of his great, horrible dwelling, when Arcita's pious Prayer arrived there to complete her worthy task, completely tearful in appearance. She arrived there speechless with terror, since she had seen Mars's possessions

30. ne' campi [trazi] sotto i cieli eberni, [1973
da tenpesta continoui gittati,
dove schiere di nube senpiterni
da' venti or qua or là trasmutati
in vari luoghi ne' guazosi verni,
e d'aqua gli occhi e per freddo agroppati
gittati sono, e neve tuttavia
che 'n ghiaccio a mano sidero cria;

30. in the Thracian fields under winter skies, assailed by constant storms, where banks of eternal clouds transformed by winds in varied places here and there into wintry downpours and globes of water contracted by the cold are tumbled about, and snow everywhere that gradually turns into crystal ice.

31. e una selva steril da' rabusti
[cierri], dov' era, folti ed alti [molti]
nodosi ed aspri, rigidi, vedusti,
che d'onbra etterna ricuoprono [i] volti
del tristo suolo, e tra [gl'] antichi frusti
da ben mille vì fu senpre ravolti [1976
vi si sentia grandissimo romore,
né v'era bestia ancor né pastore:

30. Much of this language is obscure, with words elided and run together. Without punctuation, it can be impenetrable. This could explain Chaucer's use of only the most accessible parts and his neglect of much of the classical allusion in the section.

31.5 *frusti* would normally require an emendation because it seems to be a corruption of *fusti* and because it has other meanings; however, its occurrence in the alpha kappa MSS and in several others suggests that *frusti* was a variant form of *fusti*.

***31.6** *Aut* describes a mighty sound twisting about the aged tree trunks due to the efforts of about a thousand furies (*di ben mille furor*). A unique variant in *Vz* describes the same sound, adding that about a thousand trees were all twisted together in that spot (*da ben mille vì fu*). This variant reading could well be the source of Chaucer's neglect of the thousand furies and his emphasis on the tree trunks as "stubbes sharpe and hidouse to biholde" (*KnT* I, 1978).

29 3 **suo** NO M^6 R^1; *add* et Aut L^2 S R^4. 5 **dengno** dato Aut NO L^2 M^6; *erasure* S; detto R^1 R^4. 6 **tutt' una** tututta Aut NO; tutt'era M^6; tutto L^2 R^4; tutta S R^1. 7 **vi venne** venne L^2 S R^1 R^4; pervienne M^6; divenne Aut NO. 8 **cosa** M^6; chasa Aut NO L^2 S R^1 R^4.

30 1 **[trazi]** NO L^2 S R^1 R^4; ozii Vz; tratii Aut; v'eran M^6 + 2 MSS; (cf. *KnT* I, 1972: "Trace") 6 **gli occhi e** globi Aut NO L^2 S M^6 R^4; gli abbia R^1. 8 **a mano sidero** ad mano ad man sindura et Aut NO L^2 S; in mano si dì R^1; si dì R^4; a mano a mano aver M^6.

31 2 **[cierri** M^6**]**; cierti Vz P^1; certi L^2 S; cerri NO Aut R^1 R^4. The M^6 reading follows the spelling typical of the Vz scribe. * **[molti]** *Ed*; monti Vz; molto: Aut NO L^2 S M^6 R^1 R^4. 3 **rigidi** *add* et Aut NO L^2 S M^6 R^1 R^4. *4 **[i]** *Ed*; il Vz Aut NO R^1 R^4 L^2 S M^6. **volti** volto Aut NO R^1 R^4 L^2 S M^6. *5 **[gl']** S; g' Vz; gli Aut NO L^2 M^6 R^1 R^4. **frusti** L^2 S M^6 R^1 R^4 + 4 MSS; fusti Aut NO; fusta M^6. 6 **vì fu** furor Aut NO L^2 R^4; furie M^6; furon S R^1. **ravolti** ravolto Aut NO; L^2 S M^6 R^1 R^4. 8 **ancor** L^2 S R^1 R^4; alcuna Aut NO; in essa M^6.

31. And where it stood [was] a barren forest of hardy turkey oaks – dense and quite tall, knotty and rough, stiff, ancient – that covered the surfaces of the sad ground with eternal shade. And amidst the age-old trunks – almost a thousand of them were all twisted together there – a tremendous noise could be heard. No animal was there any more, nor any herdsman.

32. in questa vide la cha del suo idio
armipotenti; quest', edificata [1982
tutta d'acciaio, isplundì del pulio, [1994
la qual era dal sole rinvenbrata
la lucie c' aborea il luogo rio;
tutta di ferro era la stretta entrata, [1983–4
e lle port' eranno [d'etterno adamante] [1990–2
ferrate d'ongni parte tutte quante.

32. In this [place] she saw the home of its god [who was] powerful in arms; constructed entirely of steel, it shone in its luster. It reflected the sunlight, which detested that foul place. The narrow entrance was of iron and the doors were reinforced everywhere with eternal adamant.

33. E lle colonne di ferro costei + [1995–2028
vidde che quel 'dificio sostenieno;
e ll'[Inpetti dementi] parve a llei [1985
veder, che fieri della porta uscieno;
il cieco Peccator e ongni Omei
similemente quivi si vedieno;
viddevi l'[Ire] rosse come fuoco [1997
per le Paure palide in quel loco. [1998

33. And she saw the pillars of iron that supported that building. She thought she saw mad Onslaughts that proudly rush out of doors; the blind Wrongdoer and every Distress she likewise saw there; she saw Angers there, red as fire, on account of the pallid Fears in that place.

34. E cogli [occulti] ferri i Tradimenti + [1999–2003
vidde, e le 'nvidie con giusta apparenza;
lì Discordia sedea e sanguinenti

32.7 Because Chaucer describes the doors of the temple of Mars as being constructed "of adamant eterne" (*KnT* I, 1990) this required an emendation of *Vz*, which describes them as being constructed of hard diamond (*duro diamante*). *Vz* is one of 16 MSS that have the reading *diamante* instead of *adamante*.

32 4 **la** S; dal Aut NO M^6 R^1 R^4; *lac* L^2. 7 [**d'etterno**] Aut NO M^6; a duro Vz; di duro S; d'intorno R^1. [**adamante**] Aut NO M^6 R^1; diamante Vz S (cf. *KnT* I, 1990: "of adamant eterne").

33 2 **quel** l' Aut NO S M^6 R^1 R^4; *lac* L^2. 3 **e** lì Aut NO S M^6 R^1 R^4; *lac* L^2. [**Inpetti**] *Ed*; Inpetto Vz; Impiti M^6; Ipenti S; Impeti Aut; Inpiti NO; inpedite R^1; *om* L^2 R^4. The emendation preserves the characteristic spelling of Vz. [**dementi**] Aut NO S; dimonti Vz + 6 MSS; *om* L^2 R^4; de marti M^6; mente R^1. 4 **che** che fier Aut NO S M^6 R^1 R^4; *lac* L^2. **fieri** + 9 MSS; fieri fuor Aut NO S R^1; fier fuor M^6; *lac* L^2. 5 **il** S; et il Aut NO M^6 R^1 R^4; *lac* L^2. 7 [**Ire**] Aut NO S M^6 R^1; ore Vz; *lac* L^2; *om* R^4. 8 **per** S; e Aut NO M^6 R^1 R^4; *lac* L^2.

ferri avie in mano, ed ongni Diferenza;
e tutti i lochi vi parie· ripenti
d'aspri Minacci e di Crudel Sintenzia;
e mezo loco la Vertù tristissima
sediè, di degne lode poverissima.

34. And Betrayals with their hidden weapons she saw, and Envies with their expressions of sincerity. Strife was seated there and had bloody weapons in hand, and every Dispute. And it seemed that every place was subject to harsh Threats and Cruel Judgments; and in the middle sat wretched Goodness, bereft of worthy praise.

35. Viddevi ancora [l'allegro] Furore, [2008
e oltre a cciò con volto sanguinoso
la Morte armata vidde e lo Stipore;
e ongni altare quiv' era copioso
di sangue, sol nelle battaglie fore
de' corpi umani cacciato; luminoso
era ciascun di fuoco colto a terra
ars' e disfatte per la trista guerra.

35. She also saw joyful Madness there, and in addition to this she saw armed Death, with its bloody face, and Amazement. Every altar there was overflowing with blood, but only that shed in battle by human bodies; each one was lit with fire gathered from land burned and devastated by sad war.

36. Ed era il tenpio tutto istoriato + [2027–8, 2049, 2012–20
da sottil mano di sopra e dintorno,
che ciò che prima vidde disengniato
eran le prede, di notte e di giorno
tolto alle terre; e qualunque isforzato
fu, era quivi inn abito musorno;
vedendosi le gienti incatenate,
porte di ferro e forteze ispezate.

36. The whole temple, above and within, was decorated by a keen hand with scenes of past events. What she first saw depicted were spoils taken day and night from different lands, and anyone who ever suffered violence was there in somber garb. People could be seen in chains, iron gates and citadels shattered.

34.5 ripenti = rep-

34 1 [**occulti**] Aut NO L^2 S M^6 R^1; aghuti Vz R^4 (cf. *KnT* I, 1999: "under the cloke") 2 **'nvidie** S M^6; 'nsidie Aut NO L^2 R1 R^4. 6 **Sintenzia** L^2 S M^6; Intenza Aut NO R^1 R^4. 7 **e** M^6 R^4 e 'n Aut NO L^2 S R^1. **mezzo** *add* il Aut NO M^6 R^1; *add* del L^2 S R^4.

35 1 [**l'allegro**] Aut NO L^2 S M^6 R^1 R^4. (In Vz the original has been erased, with "festante il" supplied in a later hand.) 6 **cacciato** M^6; *add* et Aut L^2 S R^1 R^4; *add* il NO. 7 **colto** S; tolto Aut NO M^6 R^1 R^4; avolte L^2. 8 **la trista guerra** le triste guerre Aut NO L^2 S M^6 R^1 R^4.

36.2 **mano** L^2 S M^6 R^4; *add* et Aut NO R^1. 3 **che** et Aut NO L^2 S M^6 R^1 R^4.

37. Vedev' ancor le navi [bellatriti], [2017
involti carri e li volti guastati [2022–3
con miseri pianti e infelliti,
e ongni forza cogli aspetti 'lati;
ongni fedita ancor si vidde liti,
e' sangui co· lla terra mescolati;
e 'n ongni loco coll'aspetto fiero
si vidde Marte torbido ed altero.

37. She also saw warlike ships there, chariots turned upside down and broken faces with woeful and sorrowful cries, and all types of Oppression, with wild expressions; even every type of wound was to be seen there, and blood was soaking the earth. And from everywhere could be seen grim, disdainful Mars with his cruel appearance.

[(38) *Vulcan had constructed Mars's temple; Mars knew what the Prayer's request would be, so he received her.*]

fol. 34v 39. Udita adunque questa di lontano
d'Arcita mandata humilemente,
sanza più stare sen gi' a mano a mano
là dov' era chiamato ocultamente;
né prima i tenpi il loro idio sovrano [2422–4
sentiro che tremero di presente;
rughiaron tutte ad un'ora le porte:
di che Arcita in sé temette forte.

39. Then having listened to this [Prayer] humbly sent from afar by Arcita, [Mars] set off without delay for the place where he had been secretly summoned. Just as soon as the temples sensed that their sovereign god was present, they trembled. The doors resounded all at once; at that, Arcita felt stricken with fear.

40. Gli fuochi diero lume vie più chiaro [2425–33
e diè la terra mirabile odore,
e funiferi 'nciensi si tiraro
a la 'magine lì posta ad onore

37.1 The great majority of MSS, the *alpha-kappa* group included, have the correct reading *bellatrici* (warlike). Of the 54 *Teseida* MSS where the line appears, only three have *ballatrici* (dancing), which would have produced Chaucer's "shippes hoppesteres" (*KnT* I, 2017). This suggests three possibilities: (1) Chaucer's MS read *ballatrici*; (2) Chaucer's MS read *bellatrici*, but he made the easy mistake of confusing *e* for *a* and understood it as *ballatrici*; (3) Chaucer's MS read *bellatrici*, but he opted to describe the ships as dancing (*ballatrici*). Chaucer would certainly have been familiar with Boccaccio's source for this passage: Statius' depiction of the temple of Mars in bk 7 of the *Thebaid* (45–60), which includes a reference to shattered warships (fragmina . . . bellatricesque carinae 7.57).

37.1, 3, 5 *bellatriti*, *infeliti*, *liti*: The scribe of *Vz* has varied the spelling so that lines 1–6 will have the same end-rhyme.

*37.1 [**bellatriti**] *Ed*; bellacriti Vz; bellatrici Aut NO L² S M⁶ R¹ R⁴; ballatrici Bg RN VzQ. 3 **con** et i Aut NO L² S M⁶ R¹ R⁴.
39 7 **rughiaron** et rugghiar Aut NO L² S M⁶ R¹ R⁴.

di Marte, le chui armi rinsonaro
tutte ismosse con dolcie romore;
e sengni fecie al mirante Arcita
della sua orazione asauldita.

40. The flames gave a much brighter light and the earth a wonderful fragrance, and the burners sent incense toward the image placed there in honor of Mars, whose arms, all striking together, resounded with sweet music. These served as signs to the awestruck Arcita that his prayer had been heard.

41. Dunque contento il giovinetto stette [2435
con isperanza di vettoria avere;
né la qual notte di quel tenpo usciette,
anzi la spese tutta in prerere,
e più sengniali in quella ricievette
che afermaro più le cose vere;
ma po' che [gli] aparve il nuovo giorno,
feciesi armare il giovinetto adorno.

41. The young man thus rested content with the thought of achieving victory; nor did he leave the temple that night, but rather spent it completely in praying. He received further signs that night, which even more affirmed these things to be true. But once the new day appeared to him, the young man had himself adorned with armor.

[(42) *After praying at all the other temples in Athens, Palamone went to the temple of Venus.*]

43. E fé divota cotale orazione: + [2209–70
"O bella idea del grande [Vulcano] isposa,
per chu' s'allegra el monte [Citerone],
io ti priego che mi sia piatosa
per quello amore che portasti ad Adone;
e lla mia voglia per te amorosa
contenta, e fa la man destra possente
doman, per modo ch' i' ne sia godente.

43. And he devoutly made the following prayer: "O beautiful goddess, spouse of great Vulcan, because of whom mount Cithaeron is made happy, I beg you that you

43.3 This is the single occurrence in the edition of "el" as a masculine article. The substitution of "el" for "il" is a characteristic northern Italian usage.

40 6 **ismosse** in sé mosse Aut NO L² S M⁶ R¹ R⁴. 7 **fecie** dieron Aut NO L² S M⁶ R¹ R⁴. 8 **della** L² S R⁴; che la Aut NO M⁶ R¹. **asaldita** era exaudita Aut NO M⁶ R¹; essere essaudita L² S R⁴.

41 3 **la qual** quella Aut NO L² S M⁶ R¹ R⁴. 6 **che** L² S R⁴; *add* gli Aut NO M⁶ R¹. 7 **che [gli]** NO Aut L² S M⁶ R¹ R⁴; ched egli Vz.

*43. 2 **[Vulcano]** L² S R⁴; Vlcano Vz; Vulgano M⁶ R¹; Vulchano Aut; Vulghano NO. *3 **[Citerone]** R¹ R⁴; Echerone Vz; Cieterone M⁶; Cytherone Aut NO (cf. *KnT* I, 2223: Citheron) The scribe copies the name correctly at 7.50.3. 4 **io** de i' Aut NO L² S R¹ R⁴; dengnia M⁶. 7 **man** mia Aut NO L² S R¹ R⁴; sia M⁶.

take pity on me for the sake of that love that you had for Adonis. Satisfy my desire made into love by you, and strengthen my right hand tomorrow, so that I might be exultant in it."

[(44) *Palamone said that no one knew how much he yearned for Emilia; Venus alone knew how much Love had made him suffer.*]

45. "I' non porria con parole l'effetto [2227–32
del mio dolor mostrar quant' io ne sento;
tu sola il conosci e al difetto
puoi donare lieto contentamento;
il mio penare ritornerà in diletto;
tu ssai ciò ch' i' dico qui atento;
[tanto ti priego ciò che 'l cor disia: [2242–3
mi dia] possessione d'Emilia donna mia

45. "I could not show with words the effect of my pain – how much of it I feel. You alone know it and, once it is taken away, you can grant joyous contentment. My pain will turn into delight. You know what, respectfully, I am saying here. I am just asking for what my heart desires: that you might give me possession of my lady Emilia.

46. "I' non ti chieggio inn arme aver vettoria [2238–41
per li tenpi di Marte d'armi hornare;
i' non ti cheggio di [portarne] gloria
di que' domane contra gli qua' provare
mi converrà, né cierto che memoria
lontana duri del mio operare;
i' cierco Emilia sola la qual puoi
donare a me se donar la mi vuoi.

46. "I do not ask you for victory in arms in order to adorn the temples of Mars with armor. I do not ask you to take glory away from those against whom I shall be required to test [myself] tomorrow, nor, of course, that any deed of mine be preserved in lasting memory. I seek Emilia alone, whom you have the power to give me if you wish to give her to me.

***45.1** *efetto*, the reading in 46 MSS, must also have been in Chaucer's copy, since he describes "effectes" (*KnT* I, 2228). The reading *affetto* (affection) occurs only in *Aut* and nine other MSS: L^3 L^7 M^3 P^1 P^2 Pn R^3 MA^1 and SanF.

***45.2** Continuing the statement from the previous line, Palamone, in *Vz*, says that he cannot express the effects of his pain (*del mio dolor*). Palamon's prayer to Venus that describes "the tormentz of myn helle" and the "harmes that I feele" (*KnT*, I, 2228, 2232), could be based on this unique variant.

45. 1 **efetto** NO L^2 S M^6 R^1 R^4; affetto Aut. 2 **del mio dolor mostrar quant' io ne** S; mostrar ch'io ò né dir quanto io Aut NO L^2 M^6 R^1; mostrar di quanto io R^4. 3 **il** L^2 R^4 *add* ti Aut NO S M^6; vi R^1. 4 **donare lieto** dea dar lontan Aut NO L^2 S M^6 R^1 R^4. 5 **il** e 'l Aut NO L^2 S M^6 R^1 R^4. 6 **tu sai ciò** se L^2 S R^4; tu fai ciò di Aut NO; se ttu farai o ddea M^6; se tu fai qui di ciò R^1. **ch' i' dico qui** R^4; che io qui Aut NO; ch'io qui dico L^2 S; quel ch'io M^6; io qui R^1. 7 [**tanto ti priego ciò che 'l cor disia**] R^4; tu ssai che 'l cuore e ll'anima è in balia Vz; tanto ti priegho ciò è che io sia Aut NO M^6 R^1; tanto ti pregrerrò ciò che disia L^2 S. 8 [**mi dia**] R^4; e 'n Vz; in Aut NO L^2 S M^6 R^1.

46 3 [**portarne**] Aut NO L^2 S M^6 R^4; paterna Vz; portare R^1 (cf. *KnT* I, 2240: "ne veyne glorie") 5 **cierto** M^6 R^4; cercho Aut NO L^2 S R^1. 8 **me** dea Aut NO L^2 S M^6 R^1 R^4.

47. "Il modo truova tu, ch'i' non mi curo; [2244–7
o chi sie vinto o ch'i' sie vincitore
m'è poco caro, se non son sicuro
di possedere il disio del mio core;
però, idea, quel che tt'è men duro
piglia, e ssì fa ched io ne sia singniore;
fallo, i' te ne priego, o Citerea,
e cciò non mi negare, superna idea.

47. "You should find the manner, since I do not concern myself [about it]. Whether I be vanquished or I be victor is of little value to me, if I am not certain to possess the desire of my heart. Therefore, o goddess, take [the way] that is less difficult for you, and do so that I might be its master. Do this – I beg you of it, o Cytherea – and do not deny this to me, heavenly goddess.

48. "Gli tenpi tuoi saranno senpre orati [2251–3
da me, siccome dengni fermamente,
e di mortine ispesso incoronati;
e ongni tuo altare farò luciente
di fuoco, e sagrifici fien donati,
qu'al'alta dea si de'ciertamente;
e senpre il nome tuo per eccellenza
più c'altro idio arò i· riverenza.

48. "Your temples will be forever worshipped by me – as they are decidedly so worthy – and often crowned with myrtle. I will make your every altar bright with fire, and sacrifices will be offered: something that is certainly owed to the high goddess. And, because of its pre-eminence, I will always hold your name in greater reverence than that of any other god.

fol. 35^r 49. "E se t'è grave ciò ch'io ti dimando, [2254–6
de, fa che nel teantro qualche spada
prima mi fenda e, al mio cor forando,
costringhi che llo spirito fuor ne vada
con ongni vita, il canpo insanguinando;
ché cotal morte troppo più m'agrada [2257–8
che non sarebbe sanza lei la vita,
veggiendola non mia e ssì d' Arcita."

49. "And if what I ask of you is burdensome, well, at the start have some sword in the amphitheater slash me and, piercing [me] to my heart, compel my spirit to leave

***48.1** *orati*: a unique variant in *Vz*, this could be the source of Chaucer's "worshipe" (*KnT* I, 2251).
48.6 *de'* (= dee): 3rd person singular present.

47 1 **mi** M^6; ne Aut NO L^2 S R^1 R^4. 4 **core** L^2 S M^6 R^1 R^4; amore Aut NO. 8 **superna** o somma Aut L^2 S M^6 R^1 R^4; somma NO.
48 1 **orati** honorati Aut NO L^2 S R^1; ornati M^6 R^4. 6 **alta** M^6; tal Aut NO L^2 S R^1 R^4. **de'** deon Aut NO L^2 S R^1; denno R^4; *om* M^6.
49 2 **de** far Aut NO L^2 S M^6 R^1 R^4. **qualche** la Aut NO L^2 S M^6 R^1 R^4. 3 **me fenda** L^2 S R^4; prendi Aut NO; rendi M^6 R^1. **al** L^2 S M^6 il Aut NO R^1 R^4. 7 **sarebbe** farebbe Aut NO L^2 S M^6 R^1 R^4. 8 **e** L^2 S R^4; ma Aut NO M^6 R^1.

along with every trace of life, bloodying the battlefield. Because such a death would be more welcome to me than would be a life without her, seeing her not mine, but Arcita's."

50. Come d'Arcita a Marte l'orazione, + [1918–66
cierto così a Venere piatosa [1936–7
se n'andò sopra'l monte Cicherone
quella di Palamone, dove si posa
da Cieterea il tenpio e lla stagione
fra gli altissimi pini alquanto onbrosa;
alle quale apressandosi, [Vaghezza]
la prima fu che vidde in quell'alteza.

50. Just as Arcita's Prayer [went] to Mars, so indeed Palamone's went atop Mount Cichaeron to merciful Venus, where Cytheraea's temple stands and her domain, somewhat shaded amidst very tall pines. As she [the prayer] approached them, Desire was the first whom she saw in that exalted place.

[(51–2) *Passing through the delightful garden, the Prayer saw fountains, birds, rabbits, deer, and other animals.* (53) *She heard all sorts of musical instruments and singing, and she sensed the presence of flying spirits.* (54) *She saw Cupid and his daughter, Will, making arrows. Idleness and Memory also helped them with their work.*]

55. E poi vidde [in] quel passo Leggiadria + [1925–35
con Adorneza e Istabilitate,
e lla ismarrita in tutta Cortesia;
e vidde l'Arti c'ànno podestate
di fare altrui a forza far follia,
nel loro aspetto molto isfigurate
della 'magine nostra; e Van Diletto + [1932
con Gientilezza [vide] star soletto.

55. Then she saw in that path Loveliness with Array and Steadfastness, and Courtesy completely at a loss. She saw the Arts, which have the power to force others to commit folly – much distorted in their appearance from our own likeness. And she saw Vain Delight standing along with Gentility.

***50.2** The *alpha-kappa* variant *cierto* (indeed) could be the source of Chaucer's "soothly" (*KnT* I, 1936).

***50.3** *Cicherone* (cf. "Citheroun" *KnT* I, 1936): If Chaucer's MS contained this variant for Cithaeron, he would have known the proper form of the name from Statius and Ovid.

55.2 Chaucer translates this stanza closely in *PF*, but neither *Istabilitate* (steadfastness) nor *Affabilitate* (friendliness, the reading in *Aut*) is the source of his "Lust" (*PF* 219).

55.3 The translation depends on Havely's excellent rendering of the line.

50 2 **cierto** L[2] S M[6] R[1] R[4]; cerchò Aut NO. 5 **stagione** L[2]; magione Aut NO S M[6] R[1] R[4]. 6 **gli** L[2] S R[4]; *om* Aut NO M[6] R. 7 [**Vaghezza**] Aut NO L[2] S M[6] R[1] R[4]; Graveza Vz (cf. *KnT* I, 1925: "Desyr").

55 1 **E** M[6]; *om* Aut NO L[2]; poi S R[1] R[4]. [**in**] Aut NO L[2] S M[6] R[1] R[4]; *om* Vz. **passo** L[2] S M[6] R[1] R[4] + 29 MSS; passando Aut NO. 2 **Istabilitate** S M[2] N; Stabili- R[4] P[1] R[2]; Affabilitate Aut NO L[2] M[6] R[1]. *8 [**vide**] *Ed.* (cf. 56.1) vidde Aut NO L[2] S M[6] R[1] R[4]; vidi Vz.

56. Poi apresso a ssé vide Belleza
sanz'ornamento alcun, sé riguardando;
e vidde gir co· llei Piacievoleza,
e ll'una e ll'altra seco commendando;
po' vidde star co· llor la [Giovinezza]
destrera, adorna, molto festegiando;
e d'altra parte vidde il forlle Ardire, [1925
Lusinghe e Ruffian' insieme gire.

56. Then she saw Beauty nearby, without any adornment, gazing at herself; and she saw Agreeableness going around with her, each complimenting the other. She then saw Youth standing with them; [she was] sprightly, well-dressed, greatly celebrating. At a distance she saw Foolhardiness, Flattery and Procurement going around together.

57. A mezo il loco su alte colonne
di rame vidde un tenpio, il qual dintorno
danzando giovinetti vide e donne,
qual d'esse bella e qual d'abito adorno,
iscinte, iscalze, in capelli e in ghonne,
e in ciò sol disponevano il giorno;
po' sopra 'l tenpio vidde olitar' e
posarsi molte colonb' e rugghiare.

57. In the midst of the place upon high columns of copper she saw a temple. She saw young men and women dancing around it. Some of these women were beautiful and some wore beautiful clothing: barefoot, with hair and gowns undone. And in this alone they passed the day. Then above the temple she saw many doves fly and perch and coo.

[(58) *At the temple she saw Madonna Peace, Patience, Promises, Arts.* (59) *Inside the temple she encountered Sighs, burning Desires, Martyrdoms, and Jealousy.* (60) *Priapo held the place of honor there. Garlands and flowers adorned the temple.*]

56.6 destrera (*destra* Aut) is an example of the characteristic Latinisms in *Vz*.

56.7 *folle Ardire* (lit. insane effrontery). Note Chaucer's translation, "Foolhardynesse" (*KnT* I, 1925; *PF* 227).

57.7–8 *olitar'* is an uncommon form of *volitare* that Chaucer might not have understood. A unique variant in the next line, which substitutes the verb "perch" (*posarsi*) for the noun "sparrows" (*passere*), is an excellent source of the reading in the *Parliament of Fowls*: "And on the temple, of dowves white and fayre / Saw I syttnge many an hundred peyre" (237–8).

56 1 **vide** vide passar Aut NO L^2 S M^6 R^1 R^4. 5 **star** L^2 M^6 R^4; starsi Aut NO S R^1. **[Giovinezza]** Aut NO L^2 S M^6 R^1 R^4; Gientileza Vz. (cf. *KnT* I, 1926; *PF* 226: "Youthe") "Gientileza" is probably a copyist's error based on a remembrance of the name at 7.55.8. 6 **destrera** L^2 S R^4; *add* et Aut NO M^6 R^1. 7 **forlle** folle L^2 R^1; foll M^6; folla R^4*; illeg*: S.

57 1 **A** E 'n Aut NO L^2 S M^6 R^1 R^4. **su** in su Aut NO L^2 S M^6 R^4; in R^1. 2 **il** L^2 S M^6 R^4; al Aut NO R^1. 4 **d'esse** da sé Aut NO L^2 S M^6 R^1; d'essa R^4. 6 **disponevano** dispendevano Aut NO L^2 S; si spendano M^6; spendeano R^1; dispondano R^4. 7 **olitar' e** Vz S; volitare Aut NO M^6 R^4; volicare R^1; alitare L^2. (Since "olitare" also is in the authoritative S, it is treated as a variant of form "volitare.") 8 **posarsi** passere Aut NO L^2 S M^6 R^4. **colonb' e** et colombi Aut NO L^2 S R^4; colombi M^6.

fol. 35v 61. Quivi molt'archi a' cori di Diana
[vidde] apiccati e rotti, intra· qual' era
quel di Calistro, fatta Tramontana, [2056–9
Orsa; le pone v'eran della fiera
Atalanta ch' a correr fu sovrana,
e ancor l'almi di quell' altra altera
che partori il bel Paternopeo
nipote al chanidonolli Oneo.

61. She saw many bows of Diana's followers hung up and broken there; among them was that of Calistro[45] (who was made the North Star) the Bear. The apples of proud Atalanta, who was a champion at running, were there and also the weapons of that other arrogant woman who gave birth to handsome Paternopeo,[46] grandson of Oneo of Canidonoli.[47]

[(62) *Stories of famous lovers were painted on the walls, including the story of Hercules.* (63–6) *She learned that Venus was in the interior of the temple, lying nude on a couch. Venus, surrounded by her attendants, granted the Prayer's petition.*]

67. Da Palamon le voci adunque udite, [2438–41
subito gì la dea dove chiamata
era, per che allora fur sentite
diverse cose alla casa [namata]

61.3 F. N. Robinson (pp. 677–8) suggests that Chaucer's "Calistopee" (*KnT* I, 2056) may be a combination of Callisto and Calliope. Bennett (1976) calls it a nonce-form combining Callisto and Parte[r]nopeo in line 7 of the same octave. The name Calistopee may also have been constructed for the sake of rhyme (with "chastitee," *KnT* I, 2055). Note that *Vz* provides a precedent for altering words for the sake of rhyme at 7.37.1, 3: *bellatriti . . . infelliti*

61.3–4 *Tramontana, Orsa*: *tramontana* (from Lat. *trans* and *montem*) would normally be translated as "northern." In the late 14th century, the term also referred to the North Star (or lodestar), as Boccaccio indicates in his gloss to Tes. 7.50, where he relates the story of Callisto and her son Arcas and their transformations into bears and eventually into the constellations Ursa Minor and Ursa Major. (While Boccaccio's gloss to the *Teseida* does not specify that it was Callisto who was transformed into Ursa Minor, he does make this point in the *De gen. deor.* v. 49). In the tail of Ursa Minor, he notes, is to be found that star that we call the North Star (*quella stella che noi chiamiamo Tramontana* Limentani, p. 468.) In the gloss to 12.86.7 he repeats this identification of "tramontana" as the name of the lode star in the tail of Ursa Minor. In adapting *Teseida.* 61.3–4, Chaucer describes "Calistopee" as being changed first into a bear and then into the lodestar (*KnT* I, 2058–9), rather than into the constellation that includes the lodestar. If Chaucer's MS lacked Boccaccio's glosses, this could have led him to misconstrue the line. Instead of understanding her to be the one "who was made the northern Bear," he must have understood the description to mean the one "who was made the North Star, the Bear."

61.4 pone = pome This variant and the following are typical of the scribe's northern Italian dialect and spelling forms.

61.6 almi = armi

*61 2 [**vidde**] viddi Vz. 3 **Calistro** Chalistro M[6]; Calisto Aut L[2] S R[4]; Chalisto NO. 7 **Paternopeo** Parthenopeo Aut NO L[2] S R[4]; Parchenopeo M[6]. 8 **chanidonolli** al chalidonio Aut NO M[6]; alchuni L[2] S R[4]. **Oneo** M[6]; Oeneo Aut; Hoeneo NO; bomdineo [?] L[2] S; domolieneo R[4].

45 *Callisto.*

46 *Parthenopaeus.*

47 *Oeneus of Calydon.*

e sì nne nacque in ciel novella lite
intra Venere e Marte; ma trovata
da llor fu via e maestrevol arte
di far contenti i prieghi d'ongni parte.

67. Therefore, when she had heard [these] words from Palamone, the goddess went at once to the place where she was summoned. As a result unusual things were then heard in the famed house, and so a new dispute between Venus and Mars was born in the heavens. But a way was found by them and a masterful skill to satisfy the prayers of each faction.

[(68–9) *Palamone remained praying in the temple. The Athenians equally loved the two lovers.* (70) *Emilia, being more devout than the two lovers, prayed to Diana, the goddess who is more powerful in favor of her devotees than the other gods.*]

fol. 36^{r} 71. E lle servente sue tutte chiamate, + [2275, 2277–9, 2273–94
con corni pien di forte ragunare
le [fé] davanti a ssé e disse: "Andate,
e fate i tenpi di Diana mondare,
e [le veste e'] licori m'aparecchiate
e l'altre cose da sagrificare."
Elle n'andaron ed ella, in conpangnia
di molte savie donne, le seguia.

71. And when all her serving women were called, she had them all assemble before her with horns full of [something] strong and she said: "Go and cleanse the temples of Diana and get the garments and the liquors ready for me, and the other things necessary for sacrifice." They went away and she, in company with many wise women, followed them.

72. Fu mondo il tenpio e di be' drappi ornato, [2281, 2283, 2289
al quale ella pervenne, e quivi presto
tutto trovò ch'ella avie comandato;
e poi al loco [a] poche manifesto,
di [fontano] licori [il] dilicato

72.1 *Fu mondo*: Boccaccio's description of a temple that had been cleansed (fu mondo il tempio) becomes, in Chaucer, a description of a temple full of the smell of burning incense ("Smokynge the temple" *KnT* I, 2281). The easiest explanation is that, instead of *fu mondo*, Chaucer's MS had the erroneous reading *fumando*. Of the 56 MSS that contain the line, four copies (L^{4} A M T Pr) have the variant *fumando*, but these MSS are from the *beta* family. Another possibility is that Chaucer may have made the easy mistake of reading an *a* for an *o*. If so, this would be an excellent example of the *lectio facilior* that introduces error into a text. Finally, J. A. W. Bennett (1976, p. 83) argues that, even if Chaucer's MS read *fu mondo*, the smoke-filled temples elsewhere in the *Teseida* (7.42; 7.75.4–6; 11.85) inspired him to substitute incense for cleanliness.

67 4 **alla** M^{6}; en la Aut NO; e la L^{2} S R^{4}. *[**namata**] *Ed*; nomate Vz; sagrata L^{2} S M^{6} L^{1} R^{4}; sacrata Aut NO. 7 **e** con Aut NO M^{6}; di L^{2} S R^{4}.

71 2 **di forte** M^{6} R^{1} Bg; d'offerte Aut NO L^{2} S R^{4} (cf. *KnT* I, 2279: "of meeth") 3 [**fé**] Aut NO; fer Vz. 5 [**le veste e'**] Aut NO L^{2} S M^{6} R^{4}; li dengni Vz (cf. *KnT* I, 2277: "the clothes"). 8 **savie** L^{2} S R^{4}; honesta Aut NO M^{6}.

72 4 **al** L^{2} S R^{4}; in Aut NO; il M^{6}. [**a**] NO L^{2} S M^{6} R^{4}; ad Aut; *om* Vz. 5 [**fontano** . . . **il**] Aut NO M^{6}; nobili . . . e Vz; lontano . . . il L^{2} S R^{4} (cf. *KnT* I, 2283: "of a welle")

corpo lavossi, e po', fornito questo,
di bianchissima porpore vestissi,
e' biondi crini dagli veli iscoprissi.

72. The temple to which she came was cleansed and adorned with fine hangings. There she quickly found all that she had ordered. And then, in a place known to few, she washed her delicate body in the waters of a fountain. Then, once this had been accomplished, she dressed herself in the palest purple and she covered her blond hair with veils.

[(73) *Emilia honored the image of the goddess.*]

74. E coronò di quercia cireale, [2290–2
fatta venire a ssé piatosamente,
tutto il tenpio e 'l suo capo altrettale;
e fatto il grasso po' minutamente
spezare a servi, co· misura iguale
sopra l'altare, molto riverente
duo [rocchi] fecie di simil grandeza,
né ebbe l'un che ll'altro più dureza.

74. And she crowned the whole temple and her head as well with cereal oak, which she had piously ordered brought to her. And then once her servants had sliced the fat into small pieces and spread them uniformly upon the altar, she very devoutly made two pyres of similar size, so that one would last no longer than the other.

75. E po' con fiamma quivi acciese il foco, + [2295–6;
il qual di vino e di latte innaffiato 2293–4
per tre fiate tenperato un poco;
e po' lo 'ncienso prese e, seminato
sopra di quello, riempieva il loco
di fummo assai soave inn ongni lato;
e po' si fé più tortole recare,
e fecie il sangue lor nel fuoco andare.

75. And then with flames she lit the fire there, which, three times sprinkled with wine and milk, [was] dampened a bit. Then she took the incense and, once it was scattered over it [the fire], every part of the place filled with especially sweet fumes. Then in addition she had turtle doves brought and let their blood go on the fire.

76. E molti belli angnielletti bidienti,
alette al modo antico svenate,
si fé recare avanti alle suo gienti;

74 2 **a sé** assai Aut NO L^2 S M^6 R^4. 4 **e** poi Aut NO L^2 S M^6 R^4. **po'** pin Aut NO L^2 S M^6 R^4. *7 [**rocchi**] M^6; recchi Vz; rochi NO; roghi Aut; L^2 S R^4. (The word is spelled correctly in book 11: "rocco.") **grandeza** L^2 S R^4; grossezza Aut NO M^6. 8 **dureza** L^2 S R^4; d'altezza Aut NO M^6.

75 1 **E po' con fiamma quivi** Quindi con pia man v' Aut NO L^2 S M^6 R^4. 2 **il qual** et quel Aut NO L^2 S M^6 R^4. 8 **e fecie il . . . nel . . . andare** e 'l . . . sopra 'l . . . sprizzare Aut NO L^2 S M^6 R^4.

e tratti loro i chuori e lle churate,
ancor gli caldi spiriti battenti,
sopra gli acciesi fuochi l'à posate;
e cominciò piatosa nell'aspetto
a dir come apresso qui fie detto:

76. And she had many fine teething lambs, chosen according to ancient custom [and] bled, brought before her people. Once their hearts and viscera were taken out, with their spirits still beating warm, she placed them upon the lighted fires. And, with a devout expression, she began to speak, as is recounted below.

77. "O dea a chui la terra, [il cielo,] e 'l mare + [2297–9;
e' rengni di Pluton son manifesti 2297–2330
qualor ti piacie di que' [seguitare],
prendi gli mie [holocausti] modesti
in quella forma ched io gli fo fare;
ben so che dengnia di maggior che questi,
ma qui innanzi lo più non sapere
suplica, dea, lo mie buon volere."

77. "O goddess to whom the earth, the heaven and the sea, and the kingdoms of Pluto are shown – whichever of them [where] it pleases you to remain – take my modest offerings, in the form in which I have them carried out. Well do I know that you are worthy of greater than these, but henceforth, o goddess, let my good will substitute for my lack of knowledge."

[(78) *Emilia wept, then bowed and arose.*]

fol. 36^{v} 79. E cominciò con cotal vocie a dire:
"O casta dea de' boschi liveratricie [2304
la qual ti fai a vergini servire, [2300–8
e ssè delle tue ire vengiatricie, [2065–8
sì ccome Atteon poté sentire,
allora ch' e' più giovan e felicie,
della tua ira ma non del tuo nerbo
percosso, lasso!, si mutò in [cierbo],

77.8 suplica: The context requires a form of *supplire* (to supply; to substitute for), and Aut uses the appropriate subjunctive form: *suplisca*. But three-fourths of the MSS, including the *alpha-kappa* group, read *suplica*. This seems to be from *supplicare* (to beg, pray, implore), which does not make sense here. In this case, we use *suplica*, but the word is understood and translated as a variant form of *suplisca*.

76 1 **belli** belle L2 S R[4]; bianche Aut NO M[6]. 8 **a** R[4] chosì ad Aut NO L[2] S M[6]. **qui** *om* Aut NO L[2] S M[6] R[4].

77 1 [**il cielo**] Aut NO M[6]; tutta Vz; *om* L[2] S R[4] (cf. *KnT* I, 2298: " hevene") . *3 [**seguitare**] L[2] S R[4] + 5 MSS; seguitate Vz; visitare Aut NO M[6]. 4 [**holocausti**] Aut NO L[2] S M[6] R[4]; colli alti e Vz. **fo** so Aut NO L[2] S M[6] R[4]. 6 **che** sè Aut L[2] S M[6] R[4]; che sè NO. 7 **qui** L[2] S R[4]; *add* al Aut NO M[6].

79 1 **cotal** L[2] S R[4]; rotta Aut NO M[6]. 2 **liveratricie** lustratrice Aut NO L[2] S M[6] R[4]. 3 **servire** M[6]; seguire Aut NO L[2] S R[4]. 6 **giovan' e** giovin' che Aut NO L[2] S M[6] R[4]. 8 [**cierbo**] *Ed*; verbo Vz; M[6]; cervo Aut NO L[2]; verno S R[4]. (The spelling "cierbo" is characteristic of the scribe's usage.)

79. And she began to speak in such a voice: "O chaste goddess, savior of the woodlands, who make yourself of service to virgins and are vengeful in your anger, as Actaeon came to realize when, as a younger and luckier man, he was struck by your wrath instead of your bowstring [and] was changed, alas!, into a stag.

80. "odi le voci mie, se ne son dengnia,
e quelle per la tua gran dengnitade [2313
[triforme] priego che ttu le sostengnia;
e sed e' non ti fia difacultate,
a llor donar perfezion t'ingiengnia,
se mai ti puose il casto amor piatate
per vergine nessuna che pregasse
over per grazia ch'a tte dimandasse.

80. "hear my words, if I be worthy, and, for the sake of your great three-form dignity, I pray that you favor them. Unless these [words] be a hardship for you, use your skill to bring them to completion, if chaste love ever instilled pity in you for any virgin who prayed or asked for any favor from you.

81. "I' sono ancora delle tue ischiere [2307–10
vergine, assai più atto alla faretra
e a' boschi ciercare che a piaciere
per amore a marito; e [se] s'aretra
la tua memoria, bene ancor sapere
de' quanto fosse più duro che pietra
nostro valore contra Venere isciolta;
più che ragion segue sua voglia stolta.

81. "I am still part of your virgin company, much more adept at the quiver and at scouring the woods than at pleasing a husband with love. And if you would turn back your memory, you will indeed recall how our courage was harder than stone against dissolute Venus: rather than her reason, she follows her foolish appetites.

[(82–3) *She prayed that Diana would bring peace between the two young men. If the fates have decreed that she must marry, she begged Diana to help her to do what is proper.*]

84. "Coloro i qua' per me ne' ferri aguti
doman non sani s'avilupperanno,
caramente ti priego che gli aiuti;
i pianti miei, i qua' d'ongni lor danno
merito fie d'amore a llo· renduti,

81.2 *atto alla faretra* : adept at the quiver, i.e. skilled in archery

80 2 **dengnitade** M^6 L^8 Pr^2 T; deitate Aut NO; deitade L^2 S R^1. 3 [**triforme**] Aut NO; riferma Vz; t'informo L^2 S M^6 R^4 (cf. *KnT* I, 2313: "thre formes"). 6 **puose** punse Aut NO L^2 S M^6 R^4. **amor** L^2 S R^4; chor Aut NO M^6. 8 **per** NO L^2 S M^6 R^4; che Aut.

*81 4 [**se**] Aut NO L^2 S M^6 R^4; sa Vz. 7 **valore** voler Aut NO L^2 S M^6 R^4. 8 **più** chui più Aut L^2 S M^6 R^4; chi più NO. **sua** *om* Aut NO L^2 S M^6 R^4.

ti priego che ssi facci il loro affanno [2320–1
volgiere 'n dolcie pacie o altra cosa
ché lla lor fama sie più groliosa.

84. "As for those irrational men who will be setting upon each other with sharp weapons on my account tomorrow: I sincerely beg you that you help them. For my tears shed on their behalf for each of their wounds that occurs for the sake of love: I beg you that their misfortune be turned into sweet peace or some other thing, so that their fame will be more glorious.

85. "E sse gl'iddii avesson pur disposto [2323–5;
con etterna parola che cciò sia 2349–52
da llor seguito acciò c'ànno proposto,
fa che avengnia nelle braccia mia
colui a chui col vero più m'acosto
e cche con più fermeza mi disia,
chéd i' non so in me stesso nomare,
tanto ciascun piacievole mi pare."

85. "And if the gods have already decided by unchanging decree that what has been proposed may be accomplished, make it happen that that man will come into my arms whom I would truly prefer to receive and who desires me with greater steadfastness. For I myself do not know the one to choose, given that each one seems agreeable to me."

[(86–7) *She prayed that Diana would not let the one who lost her come to harm. She begged to be told who would win her, so that she might prepare herself.*]

88. Ardieno i fuochi mentre che pregava
dando soavi odori nel tenpio adorno,
ne' quali Emilia tuttora mirava,
quasi per quegli sanz'alcun sogiorno
veder dovesse ciò che disiava,
quando Diana il cor le [apparve] intorno
infarritratto disse: "Giovinetta, + [2348–57
tosto vedrai ciò che per te s'aspetta;

88. The fires burned while she prayed, spreading their sweet odors through the ornate temple. Emilia continued to gaze on them, as if by means of them she might, without any hesitation, see what she desired. Then Diana, surrounded by her armed attendants, appeared to her and said: "Young woman, soon you will see what awaits you.

84.8 *sie*: understood as a future tense

84 2 **sani** L^2 S savi Aut NO M^6 R^4. 4 **i pianti** M^6 R^4; e' pianti Aut NO L^2 S. 5 **merito fie d'amore a llo·** per merito d'amor sarien Aut NO L^2 S M^6 R^4. 6 **che ssi** cessi et Aut NO L^2 S M^6 R^4. 7 **o** *add* in Aut NO L^2 S M^6 R^4.

85 1 **avesson pur** forse ànno già Aut NO L^2 S R^4; me ànno M^6. 2 **ciò** e' Aut NO M^6; di L^2 S R^4. 4 **avengnia** e' vengha Aut NO; devengnia L^2 S M^6 R^4. 5 **vero** M^6; voler Aut NO L^2 S R^4.

88 1 **che** Emilia Aut NO L^2 S M^6 R^4. 6 **quando** L^2 R^4; *add* di Aut NO S M^6. [**apparve**] R^4 Aut NO; piacque Vz; parve L^2 S M^6. 7 **disse** et disser Aut NO L^2 S M^6 R^4.

fol. 37r 89. "già e nel cielo tra gl'idii confermato
che ttu sia sposa dell'un di costoro,
e Diana n'è lieta, ma cielato
poco ti fia qual d'eb'esser di loro,
se ben da te [nel] tenpio fie mirato
ciò che averrà non fuor di questo coro;
però atenta inver l'altare rimira
e vedrai ciò che 'l tuo cuor disia."

89. The gods in the heavens have already determined that you will be the spouse of one of them – and Diana is already content with this – but which one of them it must be will be hidden from you for a while. What will occur outside of this company may rather be observed by you within the temple. Therefore gaze intently at the altar and you will see what your heart desires."

90. E questo detto, sonar le saette [2358
della [faretra] di Diana bella,
e l'archo apers' e mossesi, né stette
più nulla lì di quella mai; isnella
ciascuna gì a' boschi onde venette.
Fremiro i cani, e il corno di quella
si sentì mormorare, onde i sengni
Emilia prese che' prieghi eran dengni.

90. Once she said this, the arrows in fair Diana's quiver resounded, and her bow was drawn and it moved. Nor did any of that [company] remain there any longer; each one swiftly returned to the wood whence she had come. The dogs trembled and her horn was heard to resonate. Emilia understood all of this as signs that her prayers were worthy.

91. La giovinetta le lagrime ispinse [2331–8
degli occhi belli, e dimorando atenta
più ver lo fuoco le luci sospinse;
né stette quasi che ll'una fu spenta,
po'per sé si racciese, e l'altra tinse
e tal divenne qual ora diventa
[quella] del zolfo, e lle punte menando,
e qua gie forte mormorando.

91. The young woman brushed the tears from her lovely eyes and, becoming more focused, she directed her lights to the fire[s]. Nor did she remain there [long] before one was just about extinguished and then re-lit itself. The other changed

91.3 *le luci*: the lights, i.e. her eyes

89 1 **confermato** è fermato Aut NO L² S M⁶ R⁴. 4 **fia** NO L² M⁶ R⁴; sia Aut S. 5 **[nel]** Aut NO L² S M⁶ R⁴; il Vz.

*90 2 **[faretra]** Aut L² S R⁴; ferita Vz; feretra NO; ferretra M⁶. 3 **apers' e** per sé Aut L² S M⁶ R⁴; prese NO. 4 **mai** L² R⁴; ma Aut NO S M⁶.

91 4 **quasi** guari Aut NO L² S M⁶ R⁴. 7 **[quella]** Aut NO S M⁶ R⁴; quelle L²; quale Vz. 8 **e qua gie** in qua in là Aut NO; in qua e in là L² S; in qua e là M⁶ R⁴.

color and now became transformed into that of sulfur. Its tongues flickering, it leaped here, roaring loudly.

92. E parien sangue gli acciesi tizoni, [2339–40
da' capi spenti tutti gien giemendo
lagrime tali, che spengneno i carboni;
e lle qua' cose Emilia veggiendo,
gli atti non prese né le condizioni
debitamente del fuoco, c'ardendo
si spense prima e poscia si racciese,
ma sol di ciò quel che le parve intese.

92. And it seemed as if there was blood on the burning firebrands. They wept from all their extinguished ends, shedding tears such that they extinguished the coals. Seeing these things, Emilia did not properly understand what was happening in the fire or why, when burning, it should first go out and then re-light itself – but rather [she understood] only those things that seemed to make sense to her.

93. E così nella camera dubiosa [2365
si ritornò com' ella n'era uscita,
ben che diciesse aver veduta cosa
che lle mostrava suo futura vita.
Ella passò quella notte angosciosa
infin che ongni stella fu fuggita,
po' si levò e rifeciesi bella
più che non fu mai mattutina istella.

93. And so she returned to her room just as full of doubts as she had been when she left, even though she might say that she had seen something that showed her future life. She spent that night in misery until every star had fled, then she arose and she made herself up to be more beautiful than the morning star ever was.

[(94) *When the moon was fading and the light began to show in the east (*95) *each of the lovers called his men to the temple in order to devise battle strategies. The companies then left the temples and went to meet Teseo.*]

96. Il gran Teseo, dagli alti sonni tolto, + [2523–5; 2492–2527
ancor le ricche camere tenea
del suo palagio, alla chu' corte molto,
molto gran populo cittadini vedea;
i qual vi s'era per veder racolto
che modi per costor vi si tenea
di ciò che ssi dovea il giorno fare
sol per Emilia bella conquistare.

92 2 **tutti gien** tututti Aut NO; tutti L^2 S M^6 R^4. 4 **e** *om* Aut NO L^2 S R^4; per M^6. 8 **parve** L^2 S R^4; piacque Aut NO M^6.

96 3 **alla** L^2 S M^6 R^4; en la Aut NO. 4 **molto gran** di Aut NO L^2 S M^6 R^4. **cittadini** *add* vi si Aut NO L^2 S M^6 R^4. 6 **costor** li due Aut NO L^2 S M^6 R^4. 7 **si dovea** e' doveano Aut NO L^2 S M^6 R^4. 8 **sol** M^6 R^4; *om* Aut NO L^2 S. **Emilia** L^2 S M^6 R^4; *add* la Aut NO.

96. Teseo the great, awakened from his splendid dreams, still remained in the rich rooms of his palace. In its courtyard he saw many, many citizens [of his] great nation. He had brought them there in order to see procedures that were to be followed there concerning those [two] men: what had to be done that day only in order to make a conquest of fair Emilia.

97. Quivi destrieri grandissimi vediesi [2506–7
con selle ricche d'ariento e d'oro,
e sfumanti di lor furor rodiensi,
tenuti da chi guardia avie di loro;
ringhiare e anitrire tutti sentiensi,
qual per amore, qual per odio tra lloro;
e ll'uno in qua e l'altro i· llà andava
di tali a piè, ed alcun cavalcava.

97. Steeds were to be seen there, their saddles rich with silver and gold. In their fury, they foamed and chomped while they were being restrained by those who kept watch over them. All were heard to neigh and snort – some out of the love, some out of the hatred between them. And they went here and there, [led] by some men on foot, and the occasional one was prancing.

98. Vedevasi venire i gran baroni,
co· robe istrane e di vari adornati,
e 'ntra tutti eran varie quistioni; [2514–5
qui [tre e] quattro e [là] sei adunati
tra llor mostrando diverse ragioni
di quel che credie degl'innamorati
che rimanesse il dì vettorioso;
facieano un mormorare tuommoltuoso.

98. The great barons were to be seen coming, with unusual robes adorned with various things. There were various discussions among everyone: here three and four, and there six gathered together offering each other various reasons about which of the lovers they believed would prevail that day as victor. They created a tumultuous discord.

fol. 37^{v} 99. L'aula grande d'alti cavalieri [2204–5
tutta piena e di diversa giente,
quivi aveva giullari e minestrieri
di diversi atti copiosamente,
di girfalchi, falconi e isparvieri,

97.3 Cf. "on the golden brydel / Gnawinge . . ." (*KnT* I, 2506–7). One could emend *di lor furor* ("in their fury") to the Aut reading, *li lor fren* ("their bridles"). Because "bridle" is implied in the context, however, the text was not emended.

97 3 **di . . . furor** li . . . fren Aut NO L^2 S M^6 R^4. 5 **tutti** spesso Aut NO L^2 S R^4; spessi M^6.
98 2 **co·** di Aut NO L^2 S M^6 R^4. **vari adornati** L^2 S R^4; varie addobbati Aut NO M^6. 4 **[tre e . . . là]** L^2 S R^4; tre là . . . gli M^6; tre là . . . lì Aut NO; tra gli . . . gli Vz (cf. *KnT* I, 2514: "thre ther"). 6 **che** *om* Aut NO L^2 S M^6; *var* R^4.

bracchi, levrieri, mastin veramente
su per le stanghe e in terra giaciere,
asai [alcun] gientil' e [belli] a vedere.

99. The majestic court was full of great knights and various people. Troubadours were there and minstrels [performing] a great number of feats; gyrfalcons, falcons, and sparrow-hawks, bloodhounds, greyhounds, [and] mastiffs as well, upon perches or lying on the floor – each one quite noble and beautiful to look at.

100. Tra queste gienti manifesto molto [2528–31
uscì Teseo co· real vestimento,
ov'è con somma reverenza acolto;
e con atto e onesto portamento
tutti gli vidde assai co· llieto volto;
e domandando s'ancora i dugiento
eran venuti, a chu' fu risposto
di "No, singniore, ma e' veranno tosto."

100. Notably conspicuous among these people, Teseo came out in royal attire, where he was received with the greatest honor. With his proper and honest bearing all saw his joyful appearance as he asked whether the two hundred had yet arrived. The answer was given: "No, my lord, but they will soon arrive."

[(101–2) *The two Thebans arrived at that moment and were greeted by a great shout. When Teseo arrived, everybody proceeded to the temple of Mars to offer sacrifices.* (103–5) *Teseo knighted the two young men. After they rejoined their companions, each man felt that his desire had cooled somewhat, as though he had misgivings.*]

106. E ciaschedun per sé divenne tale, + [1638–41
qual ne' foresti boschi il cacciatore,
a' rotti balzi acostatos', i· quale
il lion, muso per lungo romore,
aspetta e ferma in sé l'animo 'guale,
e nella faccia giela per tremore,
premendo i teli per forza tremanti,
e gli suo passi trieman tutti quanti.

***100.1** While *Aut* describes Theseus as magnificent (*magnifico*) in the presence of all the people, a unique variant in *Vz* describes him as being conspicuous (*manifesto*) before them. This could be the source of the statement that Theseus "was at a window set" (*KnT* I, 2528) so that all could admire him.

106.3 *a' rotti balzi* (lit., the broken cliffs): a gap in the cliffs; cf. Chaucer's "gappe" (*KnT* I, 1639).

99 2 **tutta** *add* era Aut NO L^2 S M^6 R^4. 5 **di** L^2 S R^4; *om* Aut NO M^6. **girfalchi** L^2 S R^4; *add* astor Aut NO M^6. 6 **levrieri** *add* et Aut NO L^2 S M^6 R^4. 7 **terra** L^2 S R^4; *add* ad Aut NO M^6. *8 **[alcun]** *Ed*; alcul Vz; a· chuor Aut NO L^2 S R^4; quelle M^6. **e** *om* Aut NO L^2 S M^6 R^4.
* **[belli]** belle Vz

100 1 **manifesto** magnifico Aut NO L^2 S M^6 R^4. 8 **di** *om* Aut NO L^2 S M^6 R^4. **singniore** L^2 S R^4; *add* mio Aut NO M^6.

106 2 **foresti** getuli Aut NO R^4; geti M^6; centuli L^2 S. 7 **per** M^6; con Aut NO L^2 S R^4. **tremanti** L^2 S M^6 R^4; sudanti Aut NO.

106. And each one, for his part, became like the hunter in a wooded forest: nearing a gap in the cliffs once the lion has been roused by a great deal of noise, he waits and steadies his courage. His face is cold with shivering, while he squeezes his weapons with trembling strength and all his footsteps shudder.

[(107) *Not knowing what is coming, the hunter wishes he had not set his trap. His fear sometimes lessens, sometimes increases.*]

108. Poch'era fuori della terra nel lito + [1885–1901
il teantro ritondo, che girava
un miglio, che non n'era meno un dito,
del quale un muro di marmo levava
inverso il cielo: sì alto e pulito
lavoro che qua su l'occhio straccava
a rimirarlo; e avi due entrate
con forti [porte] assa' ben lavorate.

108. The circular amphitheater was on the seashore a bit outside the city. It was a mile around, not one finger less. Its marble wall rose up toward the sky – a work so grand and gleaming that it strained the eye to look up at it. It had two entrances with fortified, rather well-adorned gates.

fol. 38r 109. Delle qua', l'una verso il sol nasciente
sopra colonne grandi era voltata,
l'altra mirava verso l'occidente,
come la prima apunto lavorata;
per [queste] entraro là dentro la giente:
d'altronde no, ché non v'era altr'[entrata];
nel mezo aveva quasi un tondo a sesta,
di spazio grande a ongni somma festa,

109. One of these, on great columns, was turned toward the rising sun; the other, constructed just like the first, faced the west. The people went inside through these and not from elsewhere, since there was no other entrance. In the middle it had a circle almost as [perfect as] one made by a compass – a space large enough for every great celebration.

***108.1** While the other MSS situate the amphitheater in a place (*sito*) outside Athens, a unique variant in *Vz* specifies that it was built on the seashore (*nel lito*). Chaucer locates the amphitheater in the grove where Palamon and Arcite met (*KnT* I, 1862). Since "dyken" and "dychen" were often used interchangeably, the dyke required to protect an amphitheater on the seashore could have inspired Chaucer's comment that the theater in the grove was "dyched al withoute" (*KnT* I, 1888).

108 1 **nel lito** sito Aut NO L² R⁴; usato M⁶; si sia S. 5 **e** L² S R⁴; con Aut NO; e si M⁶. 6 **qua su** quasi Aut NO L² S M⁶ R⁴. *8 **[porte]** Aut NO S M⁶ R⁴; porti Vz L².

*109 5 **[queste]** Aut NO; questo Vz; questa L² S R⁴; quest' M⁶. 6 **v'era altr'** v'aveva Aut NO; v'era L² S M⁶ R⁴. ***[entrata]** entata Vz. 7 **quasi un tondo** un pian ritondo Aut NO S M⁶; un piano ritto L² R⁴.

110. nel quale scale in cierchio si movieno,
e cierca 'n più di cinqueciento giri
insino al sommo del muro salieno
con gradi larghi di petrina miri
sopra de' quali la giente sedieno
a rimirare gli arenanti siri
e altri che ffaciessono alcun gioco,
sanza inpedir l'u· ll'altro in nessun loco. [1891–2

110. Tiers enclosed this in a circle, and nearly five hundred or more circuits rose up to the top of the wall, with ample steps of marvelous stone. The people sat upon these to watch the fighting noblemen and others engaged in various game[s], without one person in any way obstructing another.

[(111–12) *Teseo has had guards placed at the amphitheater, to prevent any violence.*]

113. Vennorv' i cittadini e tutte quante [2566–79
le belle donne, realmente hornate,
e qual per l'uno e qual per l'altro amante
prieghi porgieno, e, così adunate,
dopo tutte co· llieto senbiante
Ipolita vi venne, in veritate
più c'altra bella, Emilia co· llei,
a rimirar non men vaga di lei.

113. The citizens came and all of the beautiful women royally adorned. Some women offered prayers for one lover, and some for the other. When they had thus assembled, Ipolita, with a joyful expression, arrived there after the rest of them. In truth, she was more beautiful than any other woman; with her [was] Emilia – no less graceful to gaze upon than she.

114. Venuti adunque gli duo conpangnioni
armati di tutt'armi, inn esso entraro;
e ciaschedun co' suoi dichurioni
l'un dopo l'altro assa' ben si mostraro,
seguendo gli già detti lor pennoni,
come ne' tenpi dissi ch'ordinaro;
e dalla parte donde Euro soffia, [2581–3
entrò Arcita e tutta sua paroffia.

114.2 *in esso:* into the amphitheater

110 1 **nel** dal Aut NO L^2 S M^6 R^4. 2 **cierca 'n** cre· che 'n Aut NO; cre? con L^2; re con S; assai con R^4; e che a M^6. 3 **sommo** alto Aut NO L^2 S M^6 R^4. 4 **di** R^4; per Aut NO L^2 S M^6. 6 **arenanti siri** arenarii diri Aut; arenati disiri S R^4 L^2; attenati diri M^6; attenari diri NO. 7 **e** o Aut NO L^2 S R^4; se M^6.

113 8 **di** L^2; che Aut NO S M^6 R^4.

114 1 **conpangnioni** campioni Aut NO L^2 S M^6 R^4. 7 **parte** L^3 L^4 L^8 L^6 MA^1; porta Aut NO L^2 S M^6 R^4. 8 **e** con Aut NO L^2 S M^6 R^4.

114. Then when the two companions arrived, dressed in all their armor, they went into it. Each one made a good show of himself along with his captains, one after the other, following their already mentioned banners that, as I said, they had arranged in the temples. Arcita and all his party entered from that direction where Euro blows.

[(115) *Like a famished lion ready to attack, Arcita entered the amphitheater.* (116–18) *Arcita and his men gathered in their assigned place.*]

fol. 38^{v} 119. Qual per lo boscho il cinghial rovinoso,
po' ch' à di dietro a ssé sentito i cani,
le setole levate e ispumoso,
or qua or là pe' viottoli strani
rughiando va fuggiendo furioso,
[rami] ronpendo e schiantando selvani,
cotal entrò mirabilmente armato
Palamon quivi da ciascun mirato.

119. Like a destructive wild boar in the woods that, when it hears the dogs behind it, goes madly roaring here and there, its bristles raised and frothy, fleeing along unfamiliar paths, breaking branches and crashing through the woodlands: so Palamone, wonderfully armed, entered there admired by everyone.

[(120–1) *Palamone's men then entered and all gathered with him in the place assigned to them. Everyone awaited Teseo's command to sound the trumpet.* (122–5.2, 4–8;127–9) *Arcita saw Emilia and addressed a prayer to her that she would receive his love. Palamone made a similar speech to Emilia. The sound of the trumpet roused him.* (130–2) *Teseo announced the rules of combat: those who were taken would have to abandon their arms, anyone who left the field could not return, and the one who won the contest would also win the lady.* (133–4.5,7–8; 135–45) *Teseo ordered the second trumpet blast. Arcita spoke to his men, encouraging them to fight courageously and well. Palamone did the same. Inspired by these speeches, the troops greatly looked forward to the coming battle.*]

114.7 *e dalla parte donde Euro soffia* (from that direction where Euro blows). The line could be emended because *porta* (gate), the reading in Aut NO and the alpha-kappa MSS, seems to be reflected in Chaucer's "and westward, thurgh the gates" (*KnT* I, 2581). However, Robert Pratt ("Chaucer's Use of the *Teseida*," n.1) raised an interesting question about the line when he wondered whether Chaucer's MS might have read *porte* "gates"). This suggests the following hypothesis: Chaucer's copy contained the reading "parte"; once Chaucer translated "*dalla parte donde Euro soffia*" correctly as "westward," *parte* suggested *porte*, which he added to the line as "gates."

119 3 **le** M^{6}; con le Aut NO L^{2} S R^{4}. **ispumoso** L^{2} S M^{6} R^{4}; isquamoso Aut NO. *6 [**rami**] Aut NO L^{2} S M^{6} R^{4}; rapin Vz.

Book 8

[*Introductory sonnet*]

[(1–17) *After the third call was sounded, the two groups of combatants rushed together like swift floods. Palamone and Arcita charged each other. Other combatants fought on foot, and a few men were killed.* (18–25.3,5–8) *Various heroes met in combat.* (26) *Roaring like a tiger in search of her cubs, Diomede*[48] *fought fiercely when he saw that Ulisse was captured.* (27–8) *Various noblemen battled and were wounded.* (29–30) *Diomede was wounded and removed.* (31–7) *After violent struggles and the death of a few combatants, Minos was captured.* (38–43, 45) *Evandro and Siccheo*[49] *were so badly bruised in the fighting that their own men removed them.* (46–50) *Pelleo*[50] *was stunned by a blow and carried outside the amphitheater on his horse; when he came to his senses, he was enraged because, by the rules of combat, he could not return.* (51–5.1a,2–8; 56–7.1,3–8) *Because Ameto had wounded so many, Arcita attacked and a fierce battle ensued between their men.* (58–65) *Ida the Pisean tried to capture Arcita. After a struggle, he was captured by Arcita's men instead.* (66–77) *In response to this, Ameto attacked Arcita's standard bearer who was, however, guarded by Ligurgo.*[51] *Many others were wounded as the battle continued.* (78–85) *Arcita, exhausted, rested briefly. He glanced at Emilia, which was enough to restore him. Having recovered his strength, he terrified his opponents and fought marvelously. Palamone, on the other side, did the same.* (86–8) *When the dust had cleared, the field could be seen to be sprinkled with blood. Many of the men were bloodstained, as were all the weapons. The numbers on both sides were diminishing.* (89–93) *Teseo watched the battle from the sidelines, along with the defeated, disarmed combatants from each group. Ipolita wished that she could fight.* (94–110) *While watching the combat, Emilia was fearful that the souls of the men who died in the battle would haunt her. She lamented that love had made her suffer although she herself did not burn with desire. She did not know to which of the two men she would belong nor, since each was equally handsome, which one she ought to choose. While she pondered these things, she viewed the continuing carnage and heard the crowd shouting for one or another of the two sides.* (111–19) *When the combatants were becoming exhausted, Mars appeared to Arcita disguised in the form of Teseo and berated him, calling him a coward. Arcita became furious and fought all the more bravely. The battle continued to rage fiercely.* (120–3) *The stallion of Coronisi*[52] *bit Palamone's arm. Palamone fell and Arcita disarmed him. Palamone was enraged and was in despair because he had lost both the battle and Emilia.*]

fol. 46r 124. [Essa] acciò riguardava assa' dolente, + [2680–3
e sappiendo qua' patti eran tra lloro,
e già d'Arcita credé veramente
essere, l'animo suo sanza dimoro
nullo a llui divenne fervente
dell'amor d'esso e, già preso riparo,
per lui vettoria, piatosa credea,
né più di Palamone già le n' calea.

[48] Diomedes
[49] Evander and *Sichaeus*
[50] Peleus
[51] Lycurgus
[52] *Chromis*

124. She was watching this quite sorrowfully. Knowing about the agreements that had been [reached] between them, and [since] she believed that by now she truly was Arcita's, her feelings at once turned ardent with love for him. Having already taken shelter, she fervently hoped for his victory. Already she was no longer concerned about Palamone.

125. Così le fecie: il subito vedere
di chu' esser dovea mosse 'l cangiare!
Ciascun si guardi adunque di cadere
e del non presto potersi levare,
se non gli è forse caro di sapere
[chi] gli è amico e cchi nimico pare:
colui che 'n dubio [davanti] er' amato
or' è con cierto core abandonato.

125. This is how it happened to her: the sudden sight of the man for whom she was intended brought about the change! Hence a man should be careful of falling and not being able to get up quickly, unless perhaps it is not important that he know who is his friend or who seems to be his enemy. A man who was once loved with indecision is now abandoned with a confident heart.

126. Or loda seco Emilia la belleza
d'Arcita e tutt' i' nobil portamento;
or le parie più somma la grandeza
di lui e troppo maggior l'ardimento;
or crede i· llui aver più gientileza
e più cortese il riputa l'un ciento:
là ove prima le parieno uguali,
or le parie· tutti dusguali.

126. Now Emilia praises Arcita's fine appearance and all his aristocratic manners. Now his greatness seemed most excellent to her and his daring even greater still. Now she believes that he has greater breeding and she esteems him [to be] a hundred times more courtly. While at first they seemed the same to her, now they seem entirely different.

***124.6** Emilia's "taking shelter" (preso riparo) makes her more opportunistic in this variant line; *Aut* presents her as feeling the effects of love. The more cynical presentation in *Vz* is a better source of Chaucer's rather cynical description of Emilia in *KnT* I, 2680–3.

*124. 1 **[Essa]** L^2 R^4; Esse Vz; Et S; Emilya M^6. 3 **e** L^2 S M^6 R^4; *om* Aut NO. **veramente** L^2 S M^6 R^4; fermamente Aut NO. 5 **nullo a lui** a lui voltò et Aut NO; a lui volò et L^2 S M^6 R^4. 6 **preso riparo** per suo ristoro Aut NO L^2 S M^6 R^4. 7 **credea** R^4; chiedea Aut NO L^2 S M^6. 8 **n'** *om* Aut NO L^2 S M^6 R^4.

125 2 **dovea mosse 'l** esser credea pensier Aut NO; dovea di subito L^2; dovea subito S; esser dovea subito R^4; dovea e si M^6. *6 **[chi] gli** Aut NO L^2 S M^6 R^4; che gli Vz. **e** L^2 S M^6; o Aut NO R^4. **nimico** L^2 S M^6 R^4; amicho Aut NO. *7 **[davanti]** Aut NO M^6; davinti Vz; avanti L^2 S R^4.

126 3 **grandeza** prodezza Aut NO; bellezza L^2 R^4; destrezza S M^6. *5 **i** di L^2 S M^6 R^4; *om* Aut NO. 6 **e** L^2 S M^6 R^4; hor Aut NO. 8 **tutti** L^2 R^4; del tutto Aut NO; tututti S M^6.

[(127–8) *Now convinced that the gods had rewarded her with the better man, Emilia considered herself to be Arcita's spouse; fearful lest harm might come to him, she wished the conflict were over.* (129–31) *Although Palamone had been taken, he tried in vain to encourage his men to hold the field. Arcita and his men captured their remaining opponents. Aroused and delighted in his victory, Arcita paraded around the field with his much diminished troops.*]

Book 9

fol. 46^{r-v} Incomincia il libro nono del *Teseo*: in prima come [2684
Venere venne mandata con infernale furia a spaventare il cavallo /
d'Arcita; gli 'l fé cadere adosso.

Here begins the ninth book of the *Teseo*: first, how Venus was sent with [an] infernal fury to frighten Arcita's horse; she caused it to fall backwards on him.

[*Introductory sonnet*. 9.1–8, 12–14]

[(1–3) *Venus and Mars had seen the outcome of the battle. Venus told Mars that, with Arcita's victory, he had answered Arcita's prayer. Now it rested with her to fulfill her promise to Palamone, that he would win possession of Emilia. Mars agreed that she could do as she wished.* (4) *Venus had already traveled to the underworld and had arranged with Pluto that Crinis,*[53] *a foul fury, would do her bidding.* (5–6) *The fury, with serpent tresses, was hideous to behold. Following Venus' plan, she appeared in the amphitheater. Her arrival terrified everyone there; the amphitheater trembled.*]

7. Costei, nel chiaro di rasicurata, + [2686–91
non mutò forma né cangiò senbiante;
ma giù nel canpo tosto se n'andava,
là dove Arcita correva festante;
orribile com'era fu parata

* **Rubric** While Boccaccio's autograph contains 203 rubrics, MS *Vz* contains just four. Two of these rubrics bridge divisions in the work: rubric at end of the prologue and introducing the general sonnet to the poem; rubric at the end of bk. 8 and introducing the sonnet to bk. 9. The other two are narrative rubrics that introduce details in the plot: rubric to 9.1 (Venus sends an infernal fury to frighten Arcita's horse); rubric to 11.91 (Arcita's epitaph). The rubric to 9.1 could have supplied Chaucer's reference to a single infernal fury – "a furie infernal" (*KnT* I, 2684). The phrase does not have an exact source in the poem, where Venus is described as journeying to Dis and meeting several furies, none of whom is called infernal (9.4). One could argue, of course, that Chaucer recognized the source of the passage – Dante's three infernal furies ("tre furie infernal" *Inferno* 9.38) – from which Boccaccio fashioned his reference to the one infernal fury. One could as well point out that "infernal" needs no source when describing a fury. The most direct source, however, is the rubric to 9.1, which describes Venus as dealing with a single "infernale furia." That MS *Vz* contains only two narrative rubrics and that one of these is the single rubric that Chaucer uses as a source in *The Knight's Tale* is, it seems to us, an additional argument in favor of the authority of MS *Vz*.

Rubric: *lac* L^2 S R^4. ***Teseo*** *Theseyda* Aut NO. **in** et Aut NO. **venne** *om* Aut NO. **con** Erinis Aut NO.

[53] *Erinys*.

al corrente destrier tutta davante,
il qual per ispavento su levossi
e indietro cader tutto lasciossi.

7. Once she had been cheered by the light of day, she changed neither her appearance nor her expression. Instead she went right down onto the field where Arcita was riding in triumph. Horrible as she was, she placed herself directly in front of the galloping steed, which reared up in fear, lost all control and fell backwards.

8. Sotto a· qual cadde il contento Arcita,
e 'l forte arcione gli premette il petto
e sì gliel ruppe, che una ferita
tutto tenea il corpo al giovinetto,
che ffu in forse allora della vita
abandonar del gran dolor costretto,
per molti, che a llui corsono allora,
atato fu sanz'alcuna dimora.

8. Happy Arcita fell under it, and the hard saddlebow crushed his chest and pierced it. It seemed as if the whole body of the young man was a single wound, that he might be forced to lose his life because of his enormous suffering. He was assisted by many people who ran to him at once.

[(9) *They disengaged him with difficulty from the crushing saddle.* (10–13) *Seeing this, Emilia turned a deathly pale and lamented to herself about her short-lived happiness. Arcita's armor was removed and his face was washed, but he was unable to speak.* (14) *Agaminone*[54] *held the field for Arcita, ordering that all the conquered be treated courteously.* (15–21) *Once he was proclaimed victor, Egeo and the women rushed to aid Arcita, who was suffering and in great pain. Emilia silently cursed that love that had brought Arcita to this condition. Arcita's men were so overcome by sadness, that it seemed as if they had lost the battle. Palamone grieved for Arcita's fate and for his own.* (22–8) *Teseo called the victors together in the amphitheater and ordered that it be emptied of non combatants. He called his physicians to care for Arcita. Arcita was told that he had won both the battle and Emilia·. Arcita begged that he be allowed to die in Emilia's arms. Emilia told him that she could not bear to see his pain and that she would always love him. Her words gave him comfort.* (29–43, 45–6) *Teseo had a triumphal cart brought. Arcita sat in the cart along with Emilia, who was comforting him. The rest of the retinue arranged itself in the appropriate order and all proceeded from the amphitheater to the temple of Mars, where the arms were deposited. The triumphal march continued through the countryside, while the conquered kings kept their heads lowered as if in mourning.*]

7 6 **tutta** tosto Aut NO; forte L^2 S M^6 R^4. 7 **su** L^2 S M^6 R^4; in piè Aut NO.
8 1 **a·** il Aut NO L^2 S M^6 R^4. **il** M^6 R^4; il già Aut NO; già il L^2 S. 4 **tenea** pareva Aut NO L^2 S M^6 R^4. **al** M^6 R^4; e 'l Aut NO L^2 S.

[54] *Agamemnon.*

fol. 48[v] 48. In cotal guisa, con [alto] romore + [2694–9
d'infiniti stormenti e di gridare
che' popoli facien qui per honore
del grande Arcita e del suo operare,
giunsono al gran palazo del singnore,
e a llor piacque quivi dismontare;
e di fuor fatto ristar la più giente,
gir nella real sala pianamente.

48. In this manner, with the loud noise of a great number of instruments and the clamor that the people made in order to pay honor to Arcita's greatness and his deeds, they reached the lord's grand palace and they were glad to dismount there. Having most of the people wait outside, they went slowly into the royal hall.

49. Sopr'un gran letto, fatto quivi allora,
posato fu il faticato Arcita;
allato a cchui Ipolita dimora,
bella vie più che giemma margherita,
e di conforto sovente [il] rincora
con ornata parola e con ardita;
e simile fa Emilia sua sorella,
con altre molte, ciaschedun bella.

49. The exhausted Arcita was placed on a great bed, which had been set up there. Ipolita, even more beautiful than a pearl, stayed at his side and she continually offered encouragement to comfort him, with gracious and stirring words. Her sister Emilia did the same, as did many other lovely women.

[(50) *Palamone stood sorrowful and hopeless before Arcita.* (51–60) *Teseo told the vanquished that they must accept their fate and resign themselves to the will of the gods. He set them all free, except Palamone, who, he said, was to remain the prisoner of Emilia.* (61–2) *Palamone's men returned to their lodgings, changed their clothing, and sent for doctors to heal their wounds. Those who could do so returned to court, made peace with their former opponents, and celebrated Arcita's victory.* (63–4) *Palamone presented himself to Emilia as her prisoner and asked, in his misery, that she would condemn him to death.* (65–75) *Emilia told Palamone that, in other circumstances, she could have loved him, but that she can expect to love only one man. She encouraged him to find love in some other Greek city. She gave him his liberty, a ring, and a belt to wear during feasts, plus a horse and several weapons, telling him that he should remain the subject of Mars instead of Cupid.* (76–80) *Palamone thanked Emilia for her gifts, but insisted that he could love only her. Palamone changed his battle-stained clothing and returned to the palace, where all rejoiced to see him.* (81–3) *Arcita asked Teseo for Emilia's hand. Teseo granted his wish and the two were wed.*]

48 *1 **[alto]** Aut NO S M[6]; altro Vz; molto R[4]. 3 **qui** lì Aut NO S M[6] R[4].

Book 10

[*Introductory sonnet to book 10*]

[(1–9) *In order not to mar the festivities, the Greeks prepared a pyre in the amphitheater for the bodies of those slain in the combat. The bodies were burned at night and the ashes of the dead were deposited in the temple of Mars.* (10–15) *All the Greeks were healed of their wounds except Arcita, whose grave internal injuries resulted from the horse's fall. Arcita's wounds were judged as incurable and Teseo was counseled to make him comfortable during his last days.* (16–31) *When Arcita's condition worsened, he called Teseo. Arcita said that, although his marriage was unconsummated, he felt privileged because of his victory and he hoped that Palamone would someday be loved by Emilia.* (32–5) *Teseo tried to encourage Arcita by telling him that he would be cured and that Emilia loved him.* (36–47) *Arcita then had Palamone summoned. He lamented his coming death and asked Palamone to perform the proper funeral rites for him and to love and care for Emilia after his death.* (48–9, 51.1–5,7–8) *Palamone made light of Arcita's words, telling him that he would have children and a long life. Arcita replied, asking Palamone to carry out these requests.* (52–7) *Ipolita and Emilia came, trying to encourage Arcita. After gazing at Emilia, he sighed, saying that love could not stay in his heart but was unwilling to leave. Arcita said that Love and the soul of the dying person sometimes grieve together because death will soon expel them both. He expressed the hope that, when he died, Emilia would receive his homeless soul; then he wept aloud.* (58–9) *Arcita's words affected the ladies; Emilia lamented, saying that she could not live without him.* (60–3) *Arcita replied that Palamone was worthy to be wed – perhaps even more worthy than he – and that he hoped Emilia would marry him.* (64) *He said that he felt the coldness of death, and he told her that she had been fated to be Palamone's.*]

fol. 53ᵛ 65. “Ma non pertanto l'anima dolente [2768–9
che sse ne va per lo tuo amore piangiendo,
ti racomando, e priegoti c· a mente
ti sia tuttora; mentre ch'io vivendo,
qui starà sotto del bel ciel luciente;
a tte contenta la verrò; caendo,
i' me ne vo; non so se ttu verrai
là dov' i' sia, ch' i' ti riveggia mai.

65. “But nevertheless I commend to you the suffering soul that goes on its way weeping on account of its love for you, and I beg you always to keep it in your thoughts. As long as I am living it will remain here under the fine, shining heavens; I shall view it as something pleasing to you. I am fading away, I am leaving. I do not know whether you will come to where I shall be, so that I might ever see you again.

*49. 5 **[il]** Aut NO S R⁴; in Vz; 'l M⁶.

65.6 verrò caendo = vedrò calando; the scribe has altered the ending of “calando” in order to produce an end rhyme with “piangendo” and “vivendo” in lines 2 and 4. These variants indicate the degree to which the text in *Vz* has been transformed. It should be noted that Chaucer used only the first four lines of the octave.

65 4 **ch'io** che Aut NO S M⁶ R⁴. 5 **starà** starai Aut NO S M⁶; stai R⁴. 6 **la verrò** S M⁶ + *alpha*; l'aure Aut NO R⁴. **caendo** traendo Aut NO S M⁶ R⁴. 7 **i'** ch'i Aut NO S M⁶ R⁴.

66. "Gli utimi baci solamente aspetto [2781
da tte, o caro isposa, i qua' mi dei
ti priego molto; questo sol diletto
in vita omai atento, ond'io girei
isconsolato con sommo dispetto
s'i' non avessi, e ma' nonn oserei
gli occhi levare tra' morti innamorati,
ma senpre gli terre' fra llor bassati."

66. "I am only awaiting your last kisses, o dear spouse, which I sincerely beg that you give me. This is the only joy that I ever expect in this life. For I would leave disconsolate, with the greatest resentment, if I should not have [them] and I would not dare to raise my eyes in the company of dead lovers, but would always keep them downcast among them."

[(67–84) *Emilia responded, saying that she, not he, was suffering from the gods' wrath. Citerea took Acate, her betrothed, from her and was now taking Arcita. She wished she had never been born and said that now she understood the signs that Diana had given her. She wanted to die of grief, she said, but if she lived, she would remain a virgin and devotee of Diana. If Palamone wanted to marry, he would have to find another woman. After kissing Arcita, she would kiss no other man. Then she leaned over Arcita's bed and fainted; when she revived, she kissed him, telling him that he loved her more than she loved herself.* (85) *He replied that, now that she has kissed him, Jove could take his life whenever it pleases him. (86–8) The attendant lords and ladies lamented long and loudly. Afterward, they all tried to comfort Emilia and Arcita with gentle words.* (89–91) *Nine days later, Arcita expressed a desire to sacrifice to Mercury on the next day.* (92–3) *The day was cloudy; the altar had been prepared for the sacrifice, and Arcita spoke a prayer.* (94–9) *Arcita prayed to Mercury as the god who takes souls from their bodies and decides on their dwelling place after death. He begged Mercury to carry away his soul gently. He explained that he had not offended the gods. He pointed out that his taking up arms against Palamone was an evil, but that he was paying for it with his life. He finally begged Mercury to find a place for his soul in Elisium.* (100–1) *Palamone, in anguish, expressed his fear of what awaited Arcita in the afterlife.*]

fol. 55v 102. "O lass' a me! che ll'età giovinetta [2771–4
lascio sì tosto, alla quale sperava
ancor mostrar dov'è vertù perfetta:
tale speranza l'aldire mi mostrava.
Omè, che troppo la morte s'afretta,
e più che 'n nensun altro in me è plava;
e bene isforza, in ver me la sua ira
mostra quant'ella puote, e mi martira."

102.4, 6 aldire = ardire; plava = prava. Both readings are hypercorrections typically due to interventions by late fourteenth-century and early fifteenth-century northern Italian scribes and editors.

66 6 **on** non gli Aut NO S M6 R4.
102 1 **a** S M6; *om* Aut NO; *lac* R4. 2 **al** en Aut NO L2; nel S M6; *lac* R4. 3 **dov'è** di me Aut NO S M6; *lac* R4. 4 **mostrava** prestava Aut NO S M6; *lac* R4. 6 **nensun** alcun Aut NO S M6; *lac* R4. 7 **in me si** e bene Aut NO S M6; *lac* R4.

102. "Alas! that I am so soon departing that youthful stage of life where I still hoped to exhibit my talents fully realized; hope for such a thing taught me courage. Alas! since death is too hasty and is more perverse to me than to any other. So it strikes, exerts as much of its wrath as it can against me, and torments me."

[(103) *Arcita's strength has deserted him; because he could no longer struggle, he had to die.*]

104. "O bella Emilia, del mio cor disio, [2775–6
o bella Emilia, da me sola amata,
o dolcie Emilia, cuor del corpo mio,
ora sarai da me abandonata!
Oimè lasso! Non so quale idio
in ciò mi noccia con voglia turbata;
per te sola m'è noia il morire,
per te non sarò mai sanza languire."

104. "O lovely Emilia, desire of my heart – O lovely Emilia, my only love – O sweet Emilia, heart of my body: you are now to be abandoned by me! Ah me, alas! I do not know which god is injuring me with his deranged ill-will. Death troubles me for your sake alone. On your account I shall never be without misery."

[(105–10) *Arcita said that even if he received a place of honor in the afterlife, he would not be happy without Emilia. He would always be full of grief without her. He lamented all his friends, whom he would be leaving. He regretted that life would continue without him.* (111) *He spoke no more, but only looked at Emilia as he felt the approach of death.*]

fol. 56r 112. La quale in ciascun menbro era venuta + [2798–2809; 2798–2806
da' piedi in su venendo inverso il petto,
e ancor nelle braccia era perduta
la vital forza; sol nello 'ntelletto [2803–5
e nel cuore era ancor sostenuta
la poca vita; ma già sì ristretto
gli era il tristo cuor del mortal gielo,
c'agli occhi fé subitamente velo.

112. It had come into each of his limbs, traveling from his feet up toward his chest; the vital force in his arms was lost. Only in his mind and in his heart did a little bit of life still remain, but his sad heart was already so compressed by the deathly chill that it suddenly drew a veil over his eyes.

113. Ma po' ch'egli ebbe perduto il vedere
con seco cominciò a mormorare,

112.3 podere = potere. This is another example of the northern Italian accent of the MS.

104 7 **il** S; *add* mio Aut NO M6 R4

ongnior mancando più del suo podere;
né troppo fecie in ciò lungo durare,
ma 'l mormorio trasmutò in vere
parole, con assai basso parlare,
"A Dio, Emilia!", e più oltre non disse, [2808–9
ché ll'anima convenne si partisse.

113. But when he had lost his sight he began to murmur to himself, while his strength was failing more each moment. Nor did he long remain in this condition; instead, he changed his mumbling into clear words, saying in a very low voice: "Good-bye, Emilia!" He spoke no further, since his soul had to depart.

Book 11

[(1–3) *As Arcita's soul ascended toward the eighth sphere, he turned back to look at the earth and at his body. He laughed at the laments of the Greeks and then went to the place allotted to him by Mercury.* (4–5) *The Greeks wept when they realized that they had heard Arcita's last words. Emilia asked Arcita where he was going and said she wished to follow him.*]

fol. 56v 6. Ma poi che vide lui taciente e muto
e l'alma sua aver mutato ospizio [2809–10
da llui no· stato ma' più conosciuto,
con Palamone e piangiendo il tristo ufizio
feciere gli occhi travolti al transuto
chiusero – e per soperchio benifizio –
e il naso e lla bocca; poi ciascuno
si tirò indietro con sospetto alcuno.

6. But then she saw that he was silent and mute and that his soul had changed its residence to one that he had never before known. Therefore she and Palamone, weeping, performed the sad duty and closed his eyes, which had rolled back when he passed away, and – in an act of most excellent compassion – his nose and his mouth. Then each one drew back with some misgiving.

7. Non fer tal pianto di Prian le nuore, [2831–3
la moglie e lle figliuole, allor che morto
fu lor rechato il conperato Ettorre,
lor ben, lor duca e lor sommo diporto,
qual l'Ipolita fé per dolore
ch'ella sentì, e cierto non à torto;
Emilia co· llei e altre molte
antiche donne lì co· lloro racolte.

6 4 **e** *om* Aut NO S M⁶ R⁴. 6 **e per soperchio** M⁶; per suppremo Aut NO R⁴; supperno S. 8 **sospetto** aspecto Aut NO S M⁶ R⁴.

7 5 **per** S; *add* lo Aut NO S R⁴; quivi per M⁶. 7 **Emilia** M⁶; et Emilia Aut NO S R⁴. 8 **antiche** NO S M⁶ R⁴; atttiche Aut. **racolte** R⁴; accolte Aut NO S M⁶.

7. The daughters-in-law, the wife and the daughters of Priam made no greater lamentation when the ransomed corpse of Hector – their beloved, their lord, and their greatest delight – was brought back to them than did Ipolita because of the pain she felt (and she certainly was not wrong to do so). Emilia [was] with her, and also many other aged women who had gathered there with them.

8. Piangiendo [i] re offesi di piatate [2827–30
e da dolor, e piangie Palamone;
piangiea· gli altri d'ongni qualitate,
e d'età vecchio o giovane o garzone;
e come Atenne davante occupate
erano in festa, ora in [desollazione],
e tutte si vedeva lagrimose
e d'alti guai oscure e tenebrose.

8. Overwhelmed with compassion and distress, the kings were weeping and Palamone wept. All the others of every rank wept – the aged, the young, the youth. Just as [those in] Athens were before taken up in feasting, now they were in distress; all were to be seen tearful and sobbing loudly, melancholy and gloomy.

9. Niun potea racconsolar Teseo, [2837
sì avie posto i· llui perfetto amore,
il simile avea di Pelleo
e del buon Periton e di Nestore
e d'altri assai, e [ancor] d'Egieo;
il qual la bianca barba per dolore
tutta bangniata avea per Arcita,
allor passato della trista vita.

9. No one was able to console Teseo, since he had such great affection for him. The same was true of Pelleo, of good Periton,[55] of Nestor and of many others. It was also true of Egeo. He had completely drenched his white beard [with tears] on account of his grief for Arcita, who had just passed on from this sad life.

10. Ma come savio e huom che conosciea + [2839–42
i mondan casi e le cose avenute,
siccome que' c' assai veduto avea,
il dolor dentro istrinse con virtute,
per dare asempro a chiunque il vedea
di confortasi delle cose sute;

8.5 davante = davanti
9.2 avie =avea

8 1 [**i**] Aut NO; il Vz. 4 **e** M[6]; o Aut NO S R[4]. **giovane o** S M[6]; giovane Aut NO R[4]. 6 [**desollazione**] *Ed*; sollazione Vz; desolatione R[4]; consolatione S; consolazione M[6]. (Emendation based on scribe's spelling in *Vz*.) 7 **e tutte** tututte Aut NO; tutte R[4]; o tutte M[6]; così ora S.

9 4 **Periton** M[6] R[1] Perithoo Aut; Peritoo NO R[4]; Peritone S. 5 [**ancor**] *Ed*; aricor Vz; ancora S M[6] R[4]; anchora Aut NO.

[55] *Perithous*.

e po' s'[asisse] Palamone allato,
il qual faciea pianto ismisurato;

10. But since [Teseo] was wise and a man who understood worldly affairs and how things occur – such as the many things that he had seen – he nobly stifled his grief, in order to set an example for anyone who might look to him to see [how] to sustain oneself in such circumstances. Then he seated himself next to Palamone, who was sobbing uncontrollably.

11. e ingiengniossi con parole alquanto,
con quel silenzio ch'e' poté avere,
di volere tenperare il tristo pianto,
[ricordando] le cose antiche e vere;
le morte e' mutamenti e' duoli e 'l canto
l'un dopo l'altro spesso ongniun vedere;
ma mentre che parlav', ongnun piangiea
poco intendendo ciò che 'l diciea.

11. And he exerted himself greatly with words during the silence that he was able to command, since he wished to alleviate their sad cry by calling to mind deeds ancient and true. Deaths, change, pains, song – we often experience them one after the other. But while he was speaking, each of them was weeping, paying little attention to what he said.

[(12) *They did not heed his arguments and spent the day and night in bitter lamentation.*]

13. Quinci Teseo con sollecita cura + [2853–81;
co· sé cierca per solenne honore 2853–64
fare ad Arcita nella sepoltura;
né a cciò trasse angoscia né dolore,
ma [pensò] che nel bosco, [ov'e' rancura
aver] sovente solea d'amore,
farie conporre il rocco dentro a· [quale]
l'ufizio si conpuose funerale

13. Then Teseo searches within himself with particular care about how to do solemn honor to Arcita at his burial. He was impelled to this neither by grief nor by

10.5 asempro = esemplo: a northernism like "groria"

13–67 In describing the preparation of Arcite's funeral pyre, his cremation, and the celebration of the funeral games in his honor (*KnT* I, 2853–2962), Chaucer made use of two sources: these 55 stanzas from book 11 of the *Teseida* and their own source, book 6 of the *Thebaid*. See Wise, *Influence of Statius upon Chaucer*, pp. 107 ff for analysis and comparison of the accounts in the *Thebaid* and in *The Knight's Tale*.

*10 7 [**asisse**] *Ed.* afisse Vz S; asise Aut.

*11 4 [**ricordando**] Aut S M^6 R^4; ricordande Vz; richordando NO. 6 **ongniun** S M^6; ongn'uon Aut NO R^4.

13 4 **a** da Aut NO S R^4; *lac* M^6. **ciò** *add* il Aut NO S R^4; *lac* M^6. 5 [**pensò**] Aut NO S R^4; perso Vz; lac: M^6 5–6 [**ov' e' rancura aver**] S R^4 Aut NO; avie natura avie Vz; *om*: M^6. *7 [quale] S R^4; guale Vz; *om* M^6. 8 **conpuose** compiesse Aut NO S R^4; *lac* M^6.

pain. Instead, he decided that the woods where [Arcita] often used to suffer the pangs of love would be where he would arrange for the erection of the pyre where the funeral rites would be conducted.

fol. 57r 14. E comandò ch'una selva che stava [2865–9
a quel bosco vicina, vecchia molto,
fosse tagliata e cciò che bisongnava
per lo solenne rocco fosse acolto
dentro al boschetto, nel qual comandava
un' area si faciesse di tal colto:
monsonsi allora gli ministri tosto,
per far ciò che Teseo loro avie inposto.

14. He ordered that a very old wood in that forest nearby be cut down and that whatever was needed for the stately pyre be gathered together in the grove, where he commanded that a space be prepared for such a ritual. His servants quickly set about fulfilling what Teseo had commanded them.

15. E' fecie poi un [ferretro] venire [2870–3, 2875
reale a ssé davanti, e tosto fello
d'un drappo ad oro bellissimo fornire;
e similmente ancor fecie di quello
il morto Arcita tutto rivestire;
e poi il fecie a giacier porre in ello,
incoronato di fronde d'alloro,
co· ricco nastro rilegante d'oro.

15. He then ordered that a royal bier be brought to him. He had it draped at once in the finest cloth of gold and had Arcita's body clothed with this, too. Then he had him laid out crowned in laurel leaves, wrapping him with an ornate golden band.

16. E po' che ffu d'ongni parte luciente [2879–81
il nuovo giorno, egli il fecie portare
nella gran corte, ove tutta la giente
come volea il potea riguardare;
né crede alcuno che ssì fosse dolente
di Tebe allora il popolo a mirare,
quando gli sette e sette d'Anfione
figli fuor morte alla trista stagione.

16. And now that the new day shone everywhere, he had him brought into the great court [yard] where everyone who wished could see him. Nor can one believe that the Theban people could be seen as grief-stricken [as this] even when the seven and seven children of Anfione[56] died in that sad season.

[(17) *Weeping was heard throughout Athens.*]

15 1 [**ferretro**] *Ed*; ferretto Vz; feretro S R4; *om* M6. The emendation is based on the spelling of the word in *Vz*. The same misspelling occurs at 11.38.2.

[56] Amphion.

18. L'alta fatica e grande s'aparecchia, [2913
ciò è voler l'antico suol mostrare
[l'alto] Febo della selva vecchia;
la qual Teseo comandò tagliare
s'andasse, acciò ch'una pirra apparecchia
alla state di Chelte possan fare,
o se ssi puote, ancor la vuol maggiore,
in quanto fu più d'Arcita il valore.

18. The great and noble task is undertaken – that is, the goal of revealing the ancient soil of the old woodland to noble Phoebus. Teseo ordered it to be cut down so that a pyre might be prepared, which they could build like that made for Chelte.[57] He wishes, if possible, that it be even more magnificent since Arcita's valor was greater.

19. Essa toccava co· lle cime il cielo, [2915–17
e' braccia sparte e lle suo chiome liete
aveva molto, e di quell'alto velo
alla terra facieno; né più quiete
onbre avea Achaia; né giama' telo
l'avea offesa, o altro ferro sete
n'avea avuto; ma la lunga etade
. . .

19.1–7 Its treetops touched the sky and it had wide open branches and bright foliage in abundance, which covered the earth with a lofty veil. A more tranquil shade Archaia never had, nor had the ax ever harmed it or any other weapon thirsted after it; but its long age . . .

20. La qual non si credie che solamente [2925
gli uomini avesse li per 'tà passati,
ma si credie che lle ninphe sovente
e' faun' e llor greggie premutati
fosson da llei, che continovamente
di sterpi nuovamente pocreati
si ristorava, inn etterno durando,
e degli antichi suoi pochi mancando.

18.6 Chelte (Ofelte *Aut*: Opheltes) About 40% of the MSS (18 of 48) have variants on this name: Felte, Febo, Vesta, Plebo. The name appears elsewhere in MS *Vz* as Aphelte (6.14.2). Following his usual custom of omitting the classical allusions from the *Teseida*, Chaucer does not include any form of the name in *The Knight's Tale*.

19.8 The MS leaves a space to indicate a missing line: *d'essa tenean per degna deitate* (made men consider it to be like a divinity). Because Chaucer does not use the line, it is not supplied in this edition. The other *alpha-kappa* MSS (S, M^6, R^4) have the line, but it is also missing from *Ph*, a MS with which *Vz* uniquely shares some readings.

*18 3 **[l'alto]** R^4; l'alalto Vz; ad l'alto Aut NO S M^6. 4 **comandò** *add* ad Aut NO S M^6 R^4.
19. 8 *omitted line*: d'essa tenean per dengnia deitate Aut NO S M^6 R^4.

[57] *Opheltes*.

20. It was believed that not only had men passed by there through the ages, but it was also believed that nymphs and fauns and their flocks had often been transformed by it. Meanwhile it constantly restored itself with new-grown brush, and it continued on forever, with the loss of only a few of its ancient [trees].

21. Al miserabil loco soprastava
tagliamento continouo, del quale
ongni covil si vidde che vi stava;
e fuggì quindi ciascuno animale, [2929–30
e ongni ucciello i suo nidi lasciando,
temendo omai più non sentito male;
e alla lucie in quel giamai no stata
in poca d'ora si dà larga entrata.

21. Ceaseless hewing threatened the miserable place. Every den was exposed there; each animal therefore fled and the birds all abandoned their nests. They were terrified by an evil that they had never before felt. In less than an hour a wide entrance is given to the light, which had never before been there.

22. Quivi tagliati caddero gli alti faggi + [2921–3
e i morbidi tigli i qua' tagliati
sogliono ispaventar i fieri coraggi
nelle battaglie, molto adoperati;
né si difesor dagli nuovi oltraggi
gli 'scoli e i caomi ma tagliati
furono ancora, e 'l durante arcipresso
ad ongni bruna e il cierro con esso,

22. Cut down there, the high beech trees fell. So did the smooth lindens that most often served, when cut down, to make brave hearts fearful in battle. Nor did the durmast oaks and the chaomian[58] oaks defend themselves from these fresh outrages; instead they too were cut down, along with the cypress that withstands each winter and also the turkey oak.

22–3 Boccaccio describes the trees in complex, allusive stanzas; eventual scribal corruptions and variants have made the readings even more difficult to understand. While listing the trees, Chaucer opted not to use the complex references.

22.6, 8; 23.2 These lines list four species of oak felled for the funeral pyre of Arcita: the duramast oak, the chaonian oak, the turkey oak, and the holly oak. All three trees occur in variant spellings in *Vz*: *iscoli*, *caomi*, *cierro*, and *ilecci* (Aut: *exculi*, *caonii*, *cerro*, *ylici*). The correct forms of the first two were available to Chaucer in Ovid ("*aesculus*": *Metamorphoses* 10.91) and in Statius ("*Chaonium . . . nemus*": *Thebaid* 6.99). The third oak in the list is Boccaccio's own addition, while the correct form of the fourth was available to Chaucer in Ovid and Statius. Chaucer conflates the list into a generic reference: "okes" and "ook"(*KnT* I, 2866, 2921). See P. Boitani, "Chaucer and Lists of Trees," *Reading Medieval Studies* (U. of Reading) 2 (1976): 38–9 nn2–4, 40.

22.6 isculi = esculi This and the following readings are variants that are characteristic of the northern spelling of *Vz*.

21. 6 **omai il** mai Aut NO S M[6] R[4]
22 2 **tagliati** NO S M[6] R[4]; ferrati Aut. 6**'scoli** S M[6]; esculi Aut NO R[4]. **caomi** caonii Aut NO R[4]; corni S; cornioli M[6].

[58] *chaonian*.

23. e gli orni pien di pecie, nutrimento
d'ongni gran fiamma, e gl' ilecci soprani,
e 'l tasso, gli cu' sughi nocimento
soglion donare, e' frassini che' vani
e sanguiletti sol conbattimento
col [cedro], che per mani mai lontani
non sentito tra lloro né sgombrò sito
per sua vecchieza dove fosse unito.

23. And the ash trees full of resin (the nourishment of every great blaze), and the towering holly oaks, and the yew whose juices often bring harm, and the mountain ashes which, useless and bloody, are accustomed to combat, along with the cedar which, even into the far off past, was the one among them that was not dispossessed by human hands from the place to which it was united.

fol. 57^{v} 24. Tagliato fuvi l'audacie abete,
e il pin similmente, che odore
dà dale [tagliature], con sapete;
e il [fragil] corrilo, il bicolore
mirto, e con questi l'anno sanza sette,
del mare amico; e, d'ongni vincitore
primier, la palma fu tagliata ancora,
e l'olmo che di viti s'inamora.

24. The dauntless fir tree was cut down there and likewise the pine, which gives off a fragrance from its gashes, as you know, and the fragile hazel tree, the two-toned myrtle, and also among them the thirst-less alder, friend of the ocean. And even the palm tree, the first [prize] for every winner, was cut down, and the elm tree that cherishes the vines.

25. Donde la terra isconsolato pianto [2925–7
ne diede; e quindi ciascun altro idio
de' luoghi amati si partì intanto,
dolente girto e contra suo disio,
e l'albito dell'onbre par'ci è tanto
quel luogo amava, e ciascun semidio;

23.2 ilecci = ilici

23.5 sanguiletti = sanguilenti, a variant of *sanguinolenti;* sol = soglion (cf. 23. 4)

24.3 con = com

24.5 anno: (alno *Aut*) The variant spelling occurs in 14 of 53 MSS. If Chaucer did not understand the variant, he could have produced "alder" (*KnT* I, 2921) from the list of trees in Statius (*Thebaid* 6, 104).

25.4 girto = certo

25.5 albito = albitro

23 5 **e sanguiletti sol** sangui ber soglion de· Aut NO S M[6] R[4]. *6 [**cedro**] Aut NO R[4]; credo Vz; ciedo M[6]; *illeg* S. **mani** anni Aut NO S M[6] R[4]. 7 **tra lloro** tarlo Aut NO R[4]; si chalore M[6]; caldo S.

24 3 [**tagliature**] Aut; tagliatura Vz. 4 **e** NO *om* Aut S R[4]M[6]. 4 *[**fragil**] Aut NO R[4]; fragir Vz; frangibile S; frassini M[6]. **corilo** *add* et Aut NO S M[6]; *add* o R[4]. 7 **primier** premio Aut NO S R[4]; per premio M[6].

25 5 **par' ci è** Pan che Aut NO R[4]; pin che S; più che M[6]. 7**parenti** M[6] R[4]; partenti Aut NO L[2]; podere S.

e llor parenti ancor piangie la selva,
che forse lì ma più non si riserba.

25. For this reason the earth gave forth a disconsolate lament. So every other god thus abandoned their beloved haunts (grieving, of course, and against their will) and also the judge of shades – it seems that there is much [in] that place [that] he loved – and each demigod, too. Their families, too, wept for the woodland, which might not be able to reestablish itself there.

26. Adunque fu degli alberi tagliati [2913–17
un rocco fatto mirabilmente;
poco più furo i monti acomuati
sopra Tesaglia della folle giente,
inverso il cielo mattamente levati,
che fosse qui que· rocco eminente;
il qual dagli menistri fu tessuto
velociemente con ordine veduto.

26. In the end, a pyre was wonderfully made from the hewn trees. Only just a bit higher above Thessaly were the mountains heaped by that demented race – raised up insanely toward the heavens – than was this towering pyre. With observable order it was quickly woven together by the servants.

27. E' ffu di sotto di strame selvaggio + [2933–8; 2918
agrestamente fatto e di tronconi
d'alberi grossi, e ffu il suo spazio maggio;
po' fu di fronde di molte ragioni
tessuto, e fatto con troppo più saggio
avedimento, e di più condizioni
di grillande e di fiori fu poturato;
e questo suolo assai fu elevato.

27. It was ruggedly constructed of rough straw and great tree trunks at the base, which took up the greatest space. Next many kinds of boughs were woven into it. This was accomplished with much more careful precision. It was adorned with many types of garlands and flowers. This level was raised up exceedingly high.

28. Sopra di queste innarabil riccheze [2919–64
e quelle d'oriente con odori
mirabil fero delle lor belleze
il terzo suol conposto sopra fiori;
quivi lo 'ncienso, dove mai vecchieza

25.8 riserba = riserva.

26.3 acomuati = accumulati

27.7 poturato = pitturato

***28.1** While *Aut* describes Arabian riches (*l'arabe ricchezze*), a unique variant in *Vz* says that the riches are indescribable (*innarabil*). This indescribability might have inspired the lines (*KnT* I, 2919–64) that J. A. W. Bennett called "[p]erhaps the longest *occupatio* in English" (1,146).

26 8 **velociemente** S; *add* et Aut NO M[6] R[4]. **veduto** dovuto Aut NO S M[6] R[4].

non conobbe, ne fu dato agli ardore,
e il cienamo il qual più c'altro durante,
e 'l lengnio aloe che di sopra stante.

28. Above these, indescribable riches and those [riches] from the Orient together with fragrances made the third level, built on flowers, marvellous with their beauty. There, some of the incense that never knows old age was given over to the flames, with the cinnamon that lasts longer than any other and the aloe wood resting above.

29. Po' fu la somità di quella pira
d'un drappo inn ostro tirio con oro [2836
tutto coperto, a veder cosa mira
sì per lo valore e ssì per lo lavoro;
e, questo fatto, indietro ongnun si tira
e con tacito aspetto fa dimoro,
quegli atendendo che dovea venire
col morto corpo a tal cosa finire.

29. The summit of that pyre was a cloth of Tyrian purple all covered with gold: as marvelous a thing to see for its worth as for its craftsmanship. Once this was done, everyone stepped back and waited with silent expressions, watching for those who had to come with the corpse in order to bring that service to an end.

30. Già ongni parte era piena di pianto, + [2881–8
e già l'aula regia mughiava,
tale che di lontano bene altrettanto
nelle valli Ecco trista risonava;
e Palamone di locubre manto
coperto, nella corte si mostrava
co· rabuffata barba e tristo crine
e polveroso e aspro sanza fine.

30. Already every quarter was full of tears and already the royal court was howling in such a way that from a distance off in the valleys, sad Echo replied back just as loudly. Palamone appeared at court wrapped in a mourning cloak, with a ragged beard and pitiful hair that was dusty and totally unkempt.

31. E sopra il corpo misero d'Arcita,
non men dolente Emilia piangiea,
tutta nel viso palida e smarrita,
e circustanti più piangier faciea,
né dal corpo potea esser partita,
con tutto che Teseo gliele diciea;
anzi parea che suo sommo diporto
fosse mirare il suo Arcita morto.

28 1 **innarabil** l'arabe Aut NO S M^6 R^4. 5 **dove mai** il qual giamai Aut NO S M^6 R^4. 6 **ne** M^6; vi Aut NO S R^4. 7 **cienamo il qual** cennamo Aut NO S M^6 R^4. 8 **che** *om* Aut NO S M^6 R^4.

29 3 **tutto** S M^6; tinto Aut NO R^4.

31. And over Arcita's pitiful body, Emilia wept no less mournfully, her face all pale and bewildered, and this caused those standing around to weep all the more. Nor could she be made to part from the body, despite everything that Teseo said to her. In fact it seemed that her greatest solace was in gazing upon her dead Arcita.

[(32–4) *When the Argives arrived in the hall, a mournful wailing arose from the crowd. Egeo tried to comfort Palamone, who kept silent and wept because he had treated his friend as an enemy.*]

fol. 58^r 35. Quivi cavalli grandissimi, guardati [2889–93, 2895
per lui, furon coverti nobilmente,
e su vi fur, delle sue armi armati,
sopra ciascuno un nobile sergiente;
quivi l'esivie de' suo primi nati
furono apparecchiate parimente,
quivi [faretre] e archi con saette,
e più suo veste nobile e dilette.

35. The very large horses reserved for him there were nobly draped. On top of each and bearing his arms was a noble squire. His ancestors' spoils were also exhibited there. Quivers and bows with arrows were there and also his noble and splendid robes.

[(36) *In order to give full honors to Arcita, Teseo had him dressed in royal regalia.*]

37. E gli più nobili a chui gli vasi cari, [2901, 2907–8
di meli, di sangue e di latte novello
pien, si portava co· lamenti amari
sopra le braccia, prociedendo quello;
né si studiavan gli lor passi guari,
anzi soave, co· ll'aspetto bello
canbiato, andava l'uno a l'altro presso,
come l'ordine dato era conciesso.

37. And the finest of his precious vases, full of honey, blood, and new milk, were carried on their shoulders with bitter laments, preceding him. Nor did they quicken their pace very much. Instead, with their striking demeanor changed, they went calmly forward, one close upon the other, as allowed by the directive they were given.

***35.1** While the other MSS describe the horses in Arcita's funeral procession as being very tall (*altissimi*), a unique variant in *Vz* describes them as being very great in size (*grandissimi*). This could have been the basis of Chaucer's description of "steeds that weren grete" (*KnT* I, 2892).

35 1 **grandissimi** altissimi Aut NO S M^6 R^4. 4 **nobile sergiente** giovane sergente Aut R^4; giovane servente NO; nobile servente S; guerrier possente M^6. * 7 [**faretre**] NO S; caretre Vz; ferretre M^6; pharetre Aut R^4. The word is spelled correctly at 7.81.2. 8 **dilette** S; electe Aut NO M^6 R^4.

37 1 **E** S; *om* Aut NO M^6 R^4. **a chui** S M^6 R^4 achivi Aut NO L^2. 8 **era** avea Aut NO R^4; aviean S M^6.

38. Sopra le spalle, [de' Greci i] maggiori [2899–2900
il [ferretro] levarsi lagrimando,
e con esso d'Attene usciron fuori,
con alto pianto la giente gridando,
gl'iniqui iddii e gli loro errori
con alte boci spesso bestemiando;
infino al loco per la pira eletto
portaro i dugi il miserabil letto.

38. The bier was lifted upon the shoulders of the noblest of the Greeks as they wept. They went out of Athens with it, [while] the people loudly bewailed the unjust gods and their blunders, blaspheming repeatedly with loud voices. The leaders finally brought the pitiful bed to the place chosen for the pyre.

[(39) *They rested the bier on it and the people drew near to examine it.*]

40. Là venne Palamone, al quale Egieo [2905–6, 2909–12
dolente andava dal suo destro lato,
e dal sinistro gli venne Teseo,
po' gli altri greci tutto faserato;
Emilia poi apresso si vedeo,
con più debole senso sconsolato
a conpagnia, e essa in mano il foco
[funeral] recare al doloroso loco.

40. Palamone appeared there. The sorrowful Egieo[59] moved along at his right side and Teseo appeared at his left, then the other Greeks all grouped around. Emilia was then seen – with a more fragile countenance, inconsolable, in a company [of women]. She [had] a funeral flame in her hand to bring to the sorrowful place.

[(41–8) *Emilia described her sorrow for Arcita and blamed the gods for their lack of pity. She followed the accustomed ritual and lit the pyre. Then she fainted. Palamone had cut his hair and beard, which he cast upon the fire along with arms and jewels.* (49–50) *The fire became more intense. The jewelry, precious metals, and garments burned, along with all the contents of the pyre.*]

fol. 58ᵛ 51. E lle [cratere] de' vini spremanti [2949–50
e dello scuro sangue, e grazioso
candido latte, tutti fuminanti
sentieno ancora il foco poderoso;

40.4 faserato = fasciato.

38 1 [**de' Greci i**] Aut NO S R⁴ M⁶; gli regi Vz L⁶ M¹ R⁵ (cf. *KnT* I, 2899: "of the Grekes"). 2 [**ferretro**] *Ed*; ferretto Vz; feretro S R⁴; farite M⁶. (See 11.15.1.)

40 6 **senso** R⁴; sexo Aut NO S; sesto M⁶. 8 [**funeral**] S; feron Vz; feral Aut NO R⁴; final M⁶. (cf. *KnT* I, 2912: "funeral servyse") **recare** rechava Aut NO R⁴; tenea S M⁶.

[59] Aegeus.

e' maggior Gregi intorno tutti quanti
istavan e Palamon per lo noioso
rocco degli occhi torti, e simigliante
stavano le donne ad Emilia davante.

51. And the vases – with the sparkling wine and the dark blood and the appealing white milk all steaming – continued to feel the mighty flame. All the Greek noblemen stood around, as did Palamone, with their eyes turned away on account of the unpleasant pyre. The ladies likewise stood in front of Emilia.

[(52) *Egeo formed seven mounted squadrons of knights, each wearing a required funeral garment. A Greek elder led each squadron.*]

53. E a sinistra man correndo giro, + [2952–5
tre volte il rocco tutto intorniaro;
e la polvere alzò; il salir diro
delle fiamme pregava e risonaro
le lancie co· lle lancie; si feriro
per lo sovente intorniato amaro,
che quivi si facieno intorno intorno,
sopra 'l pi' pisti e sanz' alcun sogiorno.

53. And on the left they ran in a circle three times all around the pyre while the dust rose up. The cruel ascent of the flames sent up a prayer and lances clashed with lances. They were damaged on account of the frequent, bitter circling that was done there – round and round on beaten hooves and without any rest.

fol. 59r 54. Dieron quell'arme orribile fragore
quattro fiate, e altrettanto pianto
le donne diero co· misero dolore
e co· lle palme ripercosse alquanto;
po', dietro ciascheduno al suo rettore,
come l'ordine usato dava intanto,
sul destro braccio si voltavan tutti,
con nuovo gran dolore e aspri lutti.

54. Four times those weapons made a terrible clamor, while the women did the same, wailing in their wretched grief and sometimes striking their palms. Next, with each man behind his leader when the usual order was then given, all turned to the right with renewed deep grief and bitter mourning.

55.2 coirtura = covirtura

51 1 [**cratere**] Aut NO S R4] mitere Vz; chettere M6. (cf. *KnT* I, 2949: "coppes") **spremanti** spumanti Aut NO S M6 R4. 3 **fuminanti** fumanti Aut NO S M6 R4. 6 **e** ad Aut NO S M6 R4. 7 **torti** torli Aut NO S M6 R4. **e** e'l Aut NO M6; il S, R4.

53 1 **correndo** S M6; con tondo Aut NO R4. 4 **pregava** pieghava Aut NO R4; piangea S M6. 5 **colle** S M6; che alle Aut NO R4. 8 **pisti** presti Aut NO S M6 R4.

54 8 **gran dolore e aspri** giro et con dolore et Aut NO S M6 R4.

55. E cciò che essi sopra l'arme avieno [2948
forse portata lì per coirtura,
tutti quanti insieme si traieno,
quelle gittando nella calda arsura;
e i cavalli allora discoprieno
di lor coverte e di lor armadura;
e così il quarto giro fu fornito
per quella giente, come avete udito.

55. And whatever they had on over their armor, worn perhaps as a covering, they took off all at once, casting them into the hot blaze. Then they stripped their horses of their trappings and of their armor. And in this manner the fourth circuit was accomplished by these people, as you have heard.

[(56) *Each cast various battle armaments and accoutrements into the fire.* (57–8) *All was reduced to ashes by nightfall. The next day Egeo gathered the ashes into an urn, which he brought to the temple of Mars.* (59–68) *Various funeral games were ordered. Egeo awarded gifts to the competitors.* (69.1–3) *On the spot where the pyre had been, Palamone ordered built . . .* (70–90) *All the adventures of Arcita were represented in the temple, from Teseo's return from the Amazon kingdom, through his siege of Thebes and capture of Palamone and Arcita, to the contest in the amphitheater and the funeral pyre for Arcita. Palamone had a marble column set up in the temple, on which was set a golden urn. The urn had an inscription* (91) *that identified itself as containing the ashes of Arcita and warned of the effects of excessive love.*]

55 5 **allora** ancora Aut NO S M[6] R[4].

Book 12

[*Introductory sonnet*.12.1–13, 15]

[(1–2) *Emilia's continued mourning left her pale and thin.*]

fol. 61r 3. Già poi che furon più giorni passati [2967–9
dopo lo sventurato avenimento
co· lu' essendo gli greci adunati,
parve di gieneral consentimento
che tristi pianti omai fossor lasciati,
e il voler d'Arcita a conpimento
fosse [mandato], acciò che ll'amata
Emilia fosse a Palamon sposata.

3. Many days had already passed since the unfortunate event. When the Greeks assembled with [Teseo], the general consensus seemed that sad tears now ought to be left behind and that Arcita's wish should be carried out, so that his beloved Emilia could be wed to Palamone.

3 1 **Già** Ma Aut NO M[6] R[4]; Da S. * 7 [**mandato**] Aut NO S M[6] R[4]; mandata Vz.

4. Per che tosto chiamato Palamone, [2975–82, 2985–6
co· molti di que' re aconpangniato,
non sappiend' esso però la cagione,
di ner vestito e così tribolato
com'era, lu' seguì quella stagione;
e esso con quant'era se n'è entrato
dove co· molte donne si sedea
Emilia la quale ancor piangiea.

4. [Teseo] thus summoned Palamone, who came accompanied by many of the kings but without knowing the reason why. Dressed in black and as dejected as he was, he followed [them into] that place. And he, accompanied by as many as there were [with him], entered where Emilia, who was still weeping, was seated with several women.

5. E quivi poi c'ongni uomo taciente
si fu posto a sedere, Teseo istette
per lungo stato sanza dir niente;
ma già esso veggiendo tutti erette
l'orecchie pure a llui umilemente,
dentro tenendo le lagrime strette
c'agli occhi per piatà volle venire,
così parlando incominciò a dire:

5. When every man had silently taken his place there, Teseo stood for a long time without saying a thing. But once he saw that all had also raised their ears humbly towards him, and firmly holding back those tears that pity would have wanted to come to his eyes, he began to speak, saying what follows:

6. "Così come alcun che mai non visse [2843–6
non morì mai, così si può vedere
c'alcun non visse mai che non morisse;
e noi che or viviamo, quando piaciere
sarà di quel che 'l mondo ciercuiscie,
perciò morremo: adunque sostenere
il piacier degl'iddii lieti dobiamo,
poi c'ad esso resistere non possiamo.

6. "Just as there never lived a person who did not die, so it can be seen that no one has ever lived who may not die. As for us who are living now: when it pleases the one who sets limits on the world, we shall then die. We must therefore cheerfully bear with the pleasure of the gods, since we cannot defy it.

***4.1** *Vz* substitutes *tosto* (soon) for *Theseo* in *Aut*. It is clear from the context, that Theseus has sent for Palamone, so Chaucer's line (*KnT* I, 2975) naming Theseus will not require an emendation in this edition of *Vz*. The variant *tosto* could be source of Chaucer's "anon" in line 2975, however.

4 1 **tosto** Theseo Aut NO S M[6] R[4]. 5 **seguì** M[6]; *add* in Aut NO S R[4].
5 1 **taciente** R[4]; tacitamente Aut NO S M[6]. 3 **stato** spatio Aut NO S M[6] R[4]. 4 **esso** *om* Aut NO S M[6] R[4]. **tutti** di tututti Aut NO L[2]; di tutti R[4]; a ciascheduno S; ongni M[6].
6 5 **ciercuiscie** circunscrisse Aut NO S R[4]; in cotal guisse M[6].

7. “Le quercie, c'ànno sì lungo nutrimento [3017, 3019–25
e tanta vita quanto noi vedemo,
ànno pure alcun tenpo finimento;
le dure pietre ancor, che noi calchemo,
per accidenti vari mancamento
ancora avere, aperto lo sapemo;
e fiumi pieni esser seccati
veggiamo e alti monti esserne [nati].

7. “The oaks, which take their nourishment for so long and have such a life as we see – they, too, have a certain time limit; the hard stones, also, upon which we tread will still wear out through various circumstances, as we quite clearly know; and we see the spacious rivers dry up and the great mountains spring up from them.

8. “Degli uomini non cal dir, che assai [3027–30
è manifesto a quel che lla natura
l'acitta e à ttirati senpre mai
de' due termini all'uno: o a oscura
vecchieza piena d'infiniti guai,
e questo può da· [morte] più sicura
e terminata; overo a [morte, essendo]
giovani ancora, e più lieti vivendo.

8. “As regards men, there's no point in saying that it is well known that nature moves them and has always drawn them to one of two ends: either to dismal old age full of endless troubles – and this can give a death more certain and final – or to death while still young and living more joyfully.

9. “E cierto i' credo c'allora vivendo [3047–9
la morte sia quando di viver giova
il mondo; e 'l dove l'uon che à valendo
né de' curare; dovunque e' si truova,
fama il serva il suo debito erendo;
e 'l corpo che riman, null'altra prova
su in u· lloco che inn altro morto,
né ll'alma né più pena né men diporto.

9. “And indeed then I think that, for someone living, death should occur while he lives enjoying the world. And [as for] the place where, the man who has [any] worth ought not to worry. Wherever he might find himself, fame, as it moves about, will preserve its debt to him. As for the body left behind, it does not feel anything whether it be dead in one place or in another. The soul has no more pain, no less pleasure.

***7.7** While *Aut* describes ancient (*perenni*) rivers, *Vz* describes the rivers as *pieni*, that is, spacious, deep, full up. This variant is an excellent source of Chaucer's reference to the “brode ryver” (*KnT* I, 3024).

***7.8** Continuing the discussion, *Aut* describes other, new (*altri nuovi*) rivers that spring up from dry riverbeds. A unique variant in *Vz* changes the subject, describing high mounts (*alti monti*) that replace the dry rivers. The variant in *Vz* could be the source of Chaucer's “grete tounes” (*KnT* I, 3025).

7 7 **pieni** M[6] Bg A MT VzQ; perenni Aut NO R[4] + 30 MSS; alcuni S; per tempi P[2]. 8 **alti monti** altri nuovi Aut NO S M[6] R[4] + 41 MSS; altri monti Ph. * [**nati**] Aut NO S M[6] R[4]; ttati Vz.

fol. 61^{v} 10. "Del mondo dico ancora il simigliante, [3031–4
ché, ccome che alcuno anieghi in mare,
alcun si truova in sul suo letto istante,
alcun per lo suo sangue rivesciare
nelle battaglie, o in qualunque di quante
[maniere] non può morir, pure arivare
ad Acheronte a ciascun conviene
morir come si vuole o male o bene.

10. "As for the world, I still say the same thing: that is, just as someone drowns in the sea, someone else might find himself lying in bed; someone may have his blood spilled in battle or might die in any number of other ways. Yet to reach Acheron it is necessary for everyone to die as has been destined – whether badly or well.

11. "E però fare della neciessitate [3001–2; 3041–5
virtù, quanto bisongnia, è sapienza,
e il contrario è chiara vanitate,
e più in [quel] che n'à sperienza
che quel che mai no· ll'à ancora provate;
e cierto questa mia vera sentenzia
può luogo aver tra noi in qua dolenti
vivian di cose senpre contingienti;

11. "Therefore it is wise to make a virtue of necessity, as much as is required. The opposite is pure folly, and this is more so in someone who has experience of [life] than in someone who has never yet experienced it. Indeed this true axiom of mine can pertain to us who are miserably subsisting here on eternal uncertainties.

12. "anzi più tosto neciessario in tutto: [3047–9, 3055–60
cioè d'alcun la morte il cu' valore
fu tanto e tale, che grazioso frutto
di fama s'à lasciato dietro al fiore;
il che se ben pensiamo, ora al postutto
lasciar dovremo il misero dolore,
e intendere a vita valorosa
che ci aquistasse fama graziosa.

12. "Yet rather, one thing above all is essential: that is, the death of one whose valor was such that the blessed fruit of [his] fame has remained after the flower. If we consider this carefully, we must in the end now abandon wretched sadness and concern ourselves with a noble life that would gain a favorable reputation for us."

8 1 **cal** S; cal di Aut NO R^4; cal e'l M^6. 3 **acitta** tira Aut NO S M^6 R^4. 6 **può** poi Aut NO S R^4; pur M^6. [**morte**] Aut NO S M^6 R^4; monte Vz. 7 [**morte essendo**] Aut NO S M^6 R^4; Marte ofendo Vz.

9 1 **vivendo** migliore Aut NO S M^6 R^4. 3 **mondo** S M^6; modo Aut NO R^4. **valendo** valore Aut NO S M^6 R^4. 4 **né** nol Aut NO S M^6 R^4. **curare** *add* che Aut NO S M^6 R^4. 5 **erendo** honore Aut NO S M^6 R^4. 7 **su** fa Aut NO S M^6 R^4. 8 **alma né** alma n' a Aut NO S M^6 R^4**. pena né** M^6 pena et Aut NO S R^4.

10 3 **truova** muoia Aut NO S M^6 R^4. 5 **qualunque** qual vuoi Aut NO R^4; qual vuol M^6; qualuno S. 6 [**maniere**] Aut NO R^4 M^6; ma niente Vz; ma com.. S. **non** hom Aut NO S R^4; nom M^6.

11 4 [**quel**] Aut NO S; quegli Vz; quello M^6; *var*: R^4. 5 **che quel** R^4; che 'n quel Aut NO; che ad quel S; e quel M^6. 7 **in qua** i qua' Aut NO S M^6 R^4.

12 5 **ora** *om* Aut NO S M^6 R^4. 8 **graziosa** M^6; gloriosa Aut NO S R^4.

[(13) *He said that, while a certain amount of lamentation is correct, an excess can be harmful.* (14–15) *Arcita was certainly a brave hero who had all the appropriate honors at his death. Public mourning for Arcita was especially important, since it was necessary that the Athenians set a good example for all to see.* (16–18) *Arcita had been mourned enough, however; it was time to begin to be happy. It was time, he said, to honor Arcita's last wish, that Emilia be given to Palamone.*]

fol. 62r 19. "Però disposte queste nere veste [3068, 3070–2
e il pianto lasciato e il dolore,
comincieraˑ le liete e care feste;
e prima che ssi parta alcun singniore,
de' duo già detti nozze manifeste
cielebreren con debito splendore.
Disponetevi adunque i' ve ne priego,
e quel ch'i' voglio facciate sanza niego."

19. "Therefore once these black garments have been put aside and the weeping is finished and also the sadness, the happy and delightful festivities will begin. And before any of the lords should depart, they will participate in a public celebration of the wedding of these two with all the splendor that is due. Therefore prepare yourselves, I beg you, and carry out my will without any objection.

[(20–7.1–6,8; 28) *Palamone demurred, saying he could not in conscience marry Emilia since this would negate his love for Arcita. Arcita's dying wish, he argued, was made out of courtesy; to follow it would be villainous.* (29–32) *Teseo said that this was not true. He told Palamone that he wanted him to marry Emilia, and that he knew this was Palamone's own wish.* (33–7) *Palamone prayed to Jove, Diana, and Cytheraea – and also to the soul of Arcita – to ask their pardon if he obeyed Teseo.* (38) *Teseo instructed Emilia that she, too, should follow his wish.* (39–42) *Emilia replied that she would obey Teseo's command. But she feared that, since Diana had already killed Acate and Arcita, she would kill Palamone too.* (43) *Teseo told Emilia that she, and not the men, would have died if Diana had been offended.* (44–6) *All the barons returned to their dwellings; the next day they ceased their mourning, as did Teseo and the men along with Ipolita and the ladies* (47–50) *When the day for the wedding of Emilia and Palamone had arrived, the Greek kings accompanied Teseo and Palamone to the temple of Venus, where the ceremony would take place.* (51) *Ipolita and the other ladies went with Emilia to the temple.* (52–66) *The author invokes the aid of the Muses to help him describe the beauty of Emilia. Each part of Emilia's body is described and praised. (67–9) When Emilia arrived at the temple, the gods were invoked and the marriage ceremony was performed.* (70–4) *When they returned to the palace, the elaborate nuptial celebrations took place, attended by all.* (75–9.7) *Palamone passed an amorous night with Emilia in the bridal chamber and the next day he sent many gifts to the temple of Venus. The Greek kings joked with him about the bridal night.*]

19 1 **disposte** M6; diposte Aut NO S R4. 8 **e** M6; ad Aut NO R4; e a S.

fol. 64r 80. Durò la festa degli alti baroni + [2735–9
più giorni poi continovamente;
dove si dieron grandissimi doni
a ciascheduna maniera di giente;
ricchi vi furon ministieri e buffoni,
e qualunque altri prese parimente;
ma dopo il dì quindecimo si puose
fine alle feste liete e graziose.

80. The feasting of the great barons lasted several days – and continually at that. Most magnificent gifts were given to all manner of people there. Richly [rewarded] were the minstrels and jesters there, and everyone else equally received other [gifts]. But after the fifteenth day the joyous and elegant festivities came to an end.

[(81–2) *Two months had passed since the Greek kings had come to Athens. Before returning home, they took their leave of Egeo, Teseo, and Palamone. Palamone thanked them, but kept Arcita in his thoughts.*]

83. Partirsi adunque [i] re, e ciascun prese
quanto poté il camin suo più corto,
per tosto ritornare in suo paese;
e Palamone in gioia e in diporto
co· lla suo donna nobile e cortese
sì ssi rimase e con sommo conforto,
quel possedendo che più gli piaciea
e a cchui tutto il suo ben volea.

Finito I· Libro chiamato *Teseo*. Deo grazias. Amen

83. So after the kings had left, each one took the shortest route he could in order to return quickly to his own country. Palamone thus joyfully and delightedly stayed behind with his noble and courtly lady in the greatest of ease. He had her who most pleased him and to whom he gave all his love.

The book called *Teseo* is concluded. Thanks be to God. Amen.

80 6 **altri** altro Aut NO S M6 R4.
83 1 [**i**] Aut NO S M6 R4; il Vz. 6 **sì** lì Aut NO R4; et S; *om* M6.

II

Thebaid

(translated by William E. Coleman)[1]

[**Book 1**.1–6: *Brotherly strife (fraternas acies) and alternate sovereignty (alterna regna), which had tragic consequences for Thebes, are to be the themes of the poem. The poet explains that these themes had their source in the peculiar origins of the city.*][2]

1.7–14

[I would have to go] far in the past to tell the tale of that apprehensive farmer who cast upon the unhallowed ground the seed of a war not yet known;[3] and then if I were to continue with the tale (10) of Amphion who, with his song, induced the Tyrian mountain rocks to form the walls of Thebes,[4] which was the cause of the disastrous wrath of Bacchus against the city of his birth;[5] then cruel Juno's deed;[6] [and the story of] the [child] against whom wretched Athamas aimed his bow and why the mother of Palaemon did not shudder when she leaped into the immense Ionian Sea with her son.[7]

[7.15–170: *When Oedipus is imprisoned, he curses his sons, Polynices and Eteocles, and avenges himself by calling on Tesiphone, one of the Furies, to incite rivalry between the two. The two agree that each will rule Thebes in alternate years,*

1 I would like to acknowledge the help of my colleague Prof. Jacob Stern (Graduate Center, CUNY), who reviewed and corrected the following translation.

2 The following summary was based on that in A. D. Melville's translation: *Thebaid* (Oxford and New York: Oxford UP, 1992). For a more detailed synopsis of the poem, with maps and a list of principal characters, see Melville, pp. xlviii–lv, 2–3.

3 In order to create citizens for Thebes, Athena advised Cadmus, the founder of the city, to seed the earth with the teeth of a dragon consecrated to Mars. When fully armed soldiers sprang up, Cadmus was apprehensive that they posed a danger and so he threw a stone into their midst, setting off a battle among them. The five survivors were the first to inhabit the new city, and their martial values shaped the history of Thebes (Lactantii Placidi. *In Statii THEBAIDA Commentum*, I, ed. Robert Dale Sweeney [Stuttgart and Leipzig: Teubner, 1997], 1.7–8).

4 Famous for his skill in playing the lyre, Amphion constructed the walls of Thebes by moving the stones of Tyre with the sound of his music (LP 1.9–10).

5 Bacchus punished his Theban cousin Penteus, the king of Thebes, for opposing his cult. Falling into a delirium during the rites of Bacchus, Agave, the mother of Penteus, slew her son, thinking she had killed a wild beast (LP 1.10).

6 Jupiter seduced Cadmus's daughter Semele and from their union Bacchus was born. Then Juno tricked Semele into requesting her lover to appear to her in all his glory. When Jupiter did so, Semele was killed by exposure to his lightning bolts (LP 1.12).

7 Ino (or Leucothea) was the wife of Athamas and sister of Semele. She raised Bacchus with her own children, Learcus and Palaemon. Angry at Ino's protection of Bacchus, Juno drove Athamas mad. When he killed Learcus with an arrow, thinking him to be a deer, Ino tried to escape him by leaping into the sea with Palaemon, but the two drowned. The gods took pity on them, transforming them into deities. Ino became Mater Matuta, goddess of the morning, and Palaemon became Portunus, guardian of seaports (LP 1.12–14).

II

Statius, *Thebaid*

(from Publius Papinius Statius, *Thebais*, eds Alfred Klotz and Thomas C. Klinnert (Munich and Leipzig: K. G. Saur, 2001 [reprint of the 2nd ed. Leipzig: Teubner, 1973] , bk 1:7–14, 171–85; bk 4: 455–68, 494–9; bk 6:35–6, 54–65, 98–106, 110–3, 495–506; bk 7:34–61, 178–80; bk 9:606–36; bk 11:530–6, 539–40; bk 12:519–22, 702–5)

Book 1

.7 longa retro series, trepidum si Martis operti [1546 +[8]
agricolam infandis condentem proelia sulcis
expediam penitusque sequar, quo carmine muris
.10 iusserit Amphion Tyrios accedere montes,
unde graves irae cognata in moenia Baccho,
quod saevae Iunonis opus, cui sumpserit arcus
infelix Athamas, cur non expaverit ingens
.14 Ionium socio casura Palaemone mater.

[8] Bracketed numbers identify lines in *The Knight's Tale* whose source is the *Thebaid*. The + symbol indicates that the source continues elsewhere in the text. Consult Appendix, tables 1 and 3, to identify these additional lines.

while the other will go into exile. Eteocles wins the draw for the first year. After Polynices angrily departs into exile, the people begin to murmur.]

1.171–85

One [of them], who was inclined to hurt others with his poisonous, base speech and never to bow his head willingly before rulers, said, "Is this the plight that the cruel fates have decided to impose upon the people of Ogyges[9] – that we are constantly changing masters who terrify us and must profess hesitating loyalty to one regime and then the other? (175) They alternate their handling of the people's destinies, and in their hands our fate is uncertain. Will I always be assigned to serve one exile and then another? Is this what you had in mind for those who share this place, O great father of the gods and of the earth? (180) Or is the ancient curse [still] imposed upon Thebes, whereby Cadmus was commanded in vain to scour the Carpathian Sea in search of the pleasant burden of the Sidonian bull[10] [and] as a refugee he found a kingdom in the midst of the Hyantean fields[11] and transmitted (185) the curse of fraternal strife to his most distant descendants among those who were conceived in the furrows of the pregnant earth?"[12]

[1.186–720: *At an assembly of the gods, Jupiter announces his intention to destroy Thebes. When Juno protests, Jupiter sends Mercury to the underworld in order to bring Laius, father of Oedipus, back to the world above. Meanwhile, Polynices and Tydeus, a prince of Calydon, both arrive at the palace of king Adrastus in Argos. They meet and begin a fight, which is stopped by the king. Adrastus recognizes the two as the princes whom an oracle had foretold would marry his daughters. At a festival in honor of Apollo, Adrastus recounts the tale of Python and Coroebus.*]

[**Book 2**.1–743: *Transported from the underworld by Mercury, Laius appears to Eteocles in a dream and goads him to hatred of his brother. In Argos, Adrastus arranges the marriages of his two daughters; Argia is to wed Polynices, while Deipyle will marry Tydeus. During the ceremony Argia wears the fatal necklace of Harmonia, whose history is related and which is viewed as an evil omen. Tydeus is sent to Thebes to represent Polynices and to claim his right to rule. Eteocles fiercely rejects his claim and Tydeus flees the palace. Eteocles sends fifty assassins to slay Tydeus. Tydeus kills all of them except Maeon, whom he orders back to Thebes in order to report the news.*]

[**Book 3**.1–721: *Maeon reports the death of the Theban force to Eteocles and then commits suicide. The Thebans go to the place of the battle in order to seek their dead. Jupiter orders Mars to incite the Argives to war, while Venus pleads with*

9 The Thebans, since Ogyges was the first king of Thebes (LP 1.173–4).

10 In Sidon, the great city of Tyre, Jupiter took the form of a bull and approached Europa. Charmed by the bull, she mounted him, whereupon Jupiter dashed into the sea and swam away with his pleasant burden. Europa's father, King Agenor of Tyre, commanded Cadmus and his other children to search for their sister and not to return home without her. In vain Cadmus sought Europa throughout the Carpathian Sea, that part of the Aegean near the islands of Carpathus, Rhodes, and Crete (LP 1.181–93).

11 In Boeotia, where Cadmus founded Thebes (LP 1.181–3).

12 By creating the first citizens of Thebes from dragon's teeth sown in the earth (see n. 1, above), Cadmus doomed their descendants to the curse of fraternal strife (fraternas acies), a theme that is announced in the first line of the *Thebaid*.

atque aliquis, cui mens humili laesisse veneno
summa nec inpositos umquam cervice volenti
ferre duces, "hancne Ogygiis," ait, "aspera rebus
fata tulere vicem, totiens mutare timendos
alternoque iugo dubitantia subdere colla?
partiti versant populorum fata manuque
fortunam facere levem. semperne vicissim
exulibus servire dabor? tibi, summe deorum
terrarumque sator, sociis hanc addere mentem
sedit? an inde vetus Thebis extenditur omen,
ex quo Sidonii nequiquam blanda iuvenci
pondera Carpathio iussus sale quaerere Cadmus
exul Hyanteos invenit regna per agros,
fraternasque acies fetae telluris hiatu
augurium seros dimisit ad usque nepotes?"

Mars on behalf of the Thebans. Tydeus returns to Argos and relates the story of Eteocles' attempt on his life. Adrastus consults two seers. Their vision of swans destroyed by seven eagles predicts the deaths of the Argive leaders. While the Argives excitedly prepare for war, the seers remain silent until Capaneus forces one of them, Amphiaraus, to reveal the vision. When Capaneus hears the tale of impending disaster, he ridicules it. Polynices' wife Argia urges her father, king Adrastus, to make war on the Thebans.]

[**Book 4**.1–454: *Three years later, seven companies of Argives march off to war. The seven leaders are Adrastus, Polynices, Tydeus, Amphiaraus, Capaneus, Hippomedon, and young Parthenopaeus. Atalanta, the mother of Parthenopaeus, tries to dissuade him from fighting; when she fails, she entrusts her son to Adrastus's care. While the Thebans are preparing for war, Eteocles consults with the blind seer Tiresias, who has fires built for his ritual.*]

4.455–68

They then roll tree trunks there, and the sorrowful priest orders that fires be built: three for Hecate[13] and three for the virgin daughters of unholy Acheron.[14] As for the stack of pinewood for you, O ruler of Avernus,[15] deep though it is driven into the earth, it towers high into the air. Next to this and less imposing is an altar erected in honor (460) of Ceres of the underworld.[16] The tearful cypress entwines the front [of the pyres] and all their sides. And now the cattle, their lofty heads marked by the sword and sprinkled with pure meal, fall under the blow. Then the maiden Manto[17] collects the blood in the bowls and pours a libation. (465) After having completely encircled the pyres three times, she, [following] the custom of her honored father, places there the half-dead entrails and the still quivering viscera; nor does she delay in applying the devouring torches to the black branches.

[4.469–93: *While Tiresias is summoning the spirits of the underworld, Eteocles is terrified of the prophecy to come and tries to end the ritual.*]

4.494–9

Like a hunter who awaits a lion dislodged by an incessant uproar from the crags of the Gaetulian[18] forest where it had its den (496) he steels his courage and clutches the sweat-soaked lances in his grasp. His face is rigid with terror and his steps falter. [He does not know] what is coming and [what] its size [might be], but he recognizes the terrible meaning that its howling signified and measures its roaring with blind apprehension.

13 Since Hecate was associated with Diana, Luna, and Persephone, she was often represented with three heads, which explains the three fires lit in her honor (LP 4.456–60). She presided over spells and incantations.

14 Acheron was the stagnant river of the underworld. According to Lactantius Placidus (4.456–60), Acheron as father and Night as mother were parents of three furies: Allecto, Megaera, and Tisiphone.

15 Hades (Pluto), the god of the underworld (LP 4.457).

16 Persephone (LP 4.459–60).

17 The daughter of Tiresias, she was, like her father, a seer (LP 4.463).

18 belonging to the Gaetulians, in northwest Africa.

Book 4

.455 trunca dehinc nemora advolvunt, maestusque sacerdos [2293–4
tris Hecatae totidemque satis Acheronte nefasto
virginibus iubet esse focos; tibi, rector Averni,
quamquam infossus humo superat tamen agger in auras
pineus; hunc iuxta cumulo minor ara profundae
.460 erigitur Cereri; frontes atque omne cupressus
intexit plorata latus. iamque ardua ferro
signati capita et frugum libamine puro
in vulnus cecidere greges; tunc innuba Manto
exceptum pateris praelibat sanguen, et omnes
.465 ter circum acta pyras sancti de more parentis
semineces fibras et adhuc spirantia reddit
viscera, nec rapidas cunctatur frondibus atris
.468 subiectare faces. . . .

.494 qualis Gaetulae stabulantem ad confraga silvae [1638–48
venator longo motum clamore leonem
expectat firmans animum et sudantia nisu
tela premens; gelat ora pavor gressusque tremiscunt,
quis veniat quantusque, sed horrida signa frementis
.499 accipit et caeca metitur murmura cura.

[4.500–850: *The ancient kings and queens of Thebes appear from the underworld, accompanied by grieving spirits of the legendary Argive rulers. Tiresias predicts a Theban victory, but when he seeks information from the spirit of king Laius, he receives an unclear and mysterious response. When the Argives approach Thebes, Bacchus attempts to delay the army by ordering the river gods to cause a drought. In Nemea, however, the Argives discover a supply of water with the help of Hypsipyle.*]

[**Book 5**.1–753: *Adrastus asks Hypsipyle to relate her story. When the Lemnian women massacred their husbands, she rescued her father, king Thoas, and was eventually chosen queen of Lemnos. When the Argonauts sailed to Lemnos, the women first resisted them but then, under the influence of Venus, finally welcomed them. Jason seduced and married Hypsipyle; she bore twins, who would now be twenty years old. Pirates captured Hypsipyle and carried her off into slavery. She now serves Lycurgus, the king of Nemea, as caretaker to his infant son Opheltes. While Hypsipyle is telling her story to the Argives, Opheltes, whom she had left unattended, is killed by a huge serpent that is sacred to Jupiter. Hypsipyle is alarmed at the child's cries, rushes back to find the infant, and discovers his body. The Argives attack the snake and Capaneus kills it. When Hypsipyle is lamenting over the body of Opheltes, king Lycurgus attempts to kill her, but is restrained by the Argives. The twin sons of Hypsipyle arrive at the palace of Lycurgus and are reunited with their mother. Amphiaraus calms king Lycurgus and orders that funeral rituals be celebrated for Opheltes.*

[**Book 6**.1–34: *King Lycurgus mourns his dead son*]

6.35–6

. . . and [the grieving mother, queen Eurydice] aches to throw herself upon the mangled remains of her son and, as often as she does so, she is dragged from them and led away.

[6.37–53: *A magnificent funeral pyre is constructed.*]

6. 54–65

In the meantime the mound (55) destined for the flames and the infant's bier are entwined with sad branches and young cypress shoots. At the base is [a layer of] fresh-grown grass. Above this is a space more elaborately contrived with grassy garlands, and the pile is decorated with flowers that soon will perish. Then a third level in the heap is piled with the products of Arabia: (60) the riches of the East, lumps of aged incense, and cinnamon preserved since the time of an ancient war.[19] The highest levels resound with gold. At the summit a soft Tyrian[20] purple [covering] is raised up, sparkling everywhere with polished jewels; (64) in its center, within [a frame of] acanthus leaves, is woven [the image of] Linus[21] and the dogs that caused his death.

[19] While most MSS refer to Belo, a legendary king of Egypt or an eastern monarch, a variant reading refers to warfare (bello). Lactantius Placidus had the second reading, since his gloss refers to "veteris belli praedam" [the plunder of ancient war] (6.60–1).

[20] Tyre was famed in the ancient world for its purple dyes.

[21] The son of Apollo and Psamathe, he was exposed by his mother and mangled by dogs. His story is told in *Thebaid* 1.557ff (LP 6.64–6).

Book 6 [2853–2962

.35 . . . lacerasque super prorumpere nati [2129–52 +
relliquias ardet totiensque avolsa refertur

.54 tristibus interea ramis teneraque cupresso
damnatus flammae torus et puerile feretrum
texitur: ima virent agresti stramina cultu; [2933–8
proxima gramineis operosior area sertis,
et picturatus morituris floribus agger;
tertius adsurgens Arabum strue tollitur ordo
Eoas conplexus opes incanaque glebis
tura et ab antiquo durantia cinnama [bello].[22]
summa crepant auro, Tyrioque attollitur ostro
molle supercilium teretes hoc undique gemmae
inradiant, medio Linus intertextus acantho
letiferique canes: . . .

[22] Ed: Belo.

[6.66–97: *The Argives cut down an ancient wood in order to create a second funeral pyre.*]

6.98–106

The lofty beech tree falls and the grove of Chaonian[23] [oaks] and the cypress that is unharmed by the wintry cold. (100) The spruce trees, food for funeral fires, are knocked down and ash trees and the trunks of the holm-oak, and the yew with its poisonous sap and the mountain-ash tree that will drink the accursed blood of war,[24] and also the oak that cannot be rooted out of its site. Then the bold fir is split and the pine tree that smells pleasant when wounded; the alder, which is a friend of the sea,[25] (105) bows its untrimmed tops down to the ground, as does the elm, which is hospitable to vines.

[6.107–9: *The spirits and demigods who inhabited the wood flee their destroyed home.*]

6.110–13

Aged Pales and Silvanus, master of the shady forest,[26] and a crowd of demigods weep when they abandon these beloved places of leisure. As they depart, the forest groans along with them and the Nymphs cannot loosen these trees from their embraces.

[6.114–494: *Seven companies of Argives, each led by one of the seven Argive princes, circle the funeral pyre. A memorial temple is erected within nine days of the funeral. At the funeral games, Polynices, driving the famous horse Arion, is expected to win, but Apollo, who favors Amphiaraus, sends a fiend to frighten the animal.*]

6.495–506

A monstrous figure with snakes for hair, a face most ferocious in appearance – whether [Apollo] brought it forth from Erebus[27] or whether, with his skill, he created it for the present moment's [task] – it certainly was endowed with numberless terrors, this abomination that he raises up to the world above. The guardian of dark Lethe[28] would not have been able to look at it without fear (500) nor even the Eumenides[29] themselves without profound horror. It would have thrown the horses of the sun and the team of Mars into confusion during their

[23] In the *Metamorphosis* (10.90) Ovid includes the Chaonian oak in a list of trees (LP 6.98–106). It was named for the Chaones, a tribe from Epirus in northern Greece.

[24] Ash wood is used in making spears (LP 6.64–66).

[25] Because it does not absorb water, alder wood is often used in the construction of ships.

[26] The two were rustic deities worshipped by the Italic tribes. Pales was god of shepherds and cattle. Lactantius Placidus describes Silvanus as the lord of forest glades (6.111). He was associated with trees, both wild and cultivated.

[27] the god of darkness; by extension, the lower world.

[28] the river of forgetfulness in the infernal regions, from which the shades drank in order to forget their past.

[29] the Furies.

.98 . . . cadit ardua fagus, [2921–3
Chaonium que nemus brumaeque inlaesa cupressus,
.100 procumbunt piceae, flammis alimenta supremis,
ornique iliceaeque trabes metuendaque suco
taxus et infandos belli potura cruores
fraxinus atque situ non expugnabile robur.
hinc audax abies et odoro vulnere pinus
scinditur, adclinant intonsa cacumina terrae
.106 alnus amica fretis nec inhospita vitibus ulmus.

.110 . . . lincunt flentes dilecta locorum [2925–7
otia cana Pales Silvanusque arbiter umbrae
semideumque pecus, migrantibus adgemit illis
.113 silva, nec amplexae dimittunt robora Nymphae.

.495 anguicomam monstri effigiem, saevissima visu [2684
ora, movet sive ille Erebo seu finxit in astus
temporis, innumera certe formidine cultum
tollit in astra nefas. non illud ianitor atrae
inpavidus Lethes, non ipsae horrore sine alto
.500 Eumenides visisse queant, turbasset euntes
Solis equos Martisque iugum. nam flavus Arion
ut vidit, saliere iubae, atque erectus in armos
stat sociumque iugi comitesque utrimque laboris
secum alte suspendit equos. ruit ilicet exul
Aonius nexusque diu per terga volutus
.506 exuit; . . .

journey. So the moment golden Arion[30] saw it, his mane bristles and he halts, his shoulders raised up. He keeps his yoke-mate[31] in check and also the horses on either side that share his labor. (505) The Aonian exile[32] is immediately flung down and, being tossed on his back, drops the reins.

[6.507–946: *When Polynices falls, Amphiaraus wins the race. Parthenopaeus is leading in the footrace, but Idas passes him by cheating. When Adrastus orders that the race be started over, Parthenopaeus wins. Hippomedon wins the discus contest and Capaneus defeats Alcidamas in boxing. Tydeus beats Agylleus in wrestling. Adrastus shoots an arrow at a distant target; once it hits its mark, it returns to his quiver. This feat is interpreted as an omen that, of the seven princes, Adrastus alone will return to Argos after the war.*]

[**Book** 7.1–33: *In an effort to spur the Argives to battle, Jupiter sends Mercury to Mars, to instruct him that he should immediately begin the war.*]

7.34–61

He had spoken and the [god of] Cyllene[33] was approaching the fields of Thrace; (35) but while he was gliding down from the northern pole, the eternal tempest of the region and the mass of storm clouds stretched across the sky and the first blasts of the north wind tossed him in every direction. His golden cloak resounds with much hail, nor does his Arcadian sun-hat protect him very well. (40) Here he sees sterile forests – the shrines of Mars – and he shudders as he sees opposite him on Mount Haemus[34] where the gloomy house of Mars is ringed by a thousand furies. Its walls are constructed of iron, one steps on thresholds fitted with iron, its roofs rest upon iron-clad columns. (45) The ray of Phoebus is damaged [when it reflects] against it, and the light itself fears that place, and its stern glare saddens the stars. The guard is worthy of the place: insane Passion springs up at the doors and blind Impiety and Angers glowing red and bloodless Dread. (50) Deceit stands by with a hidden sword and Discord [is] holding a double-edged blade. The palace rumbles with countless Menaces. In the midst stands Virtue most sorrowful and joyful Rage, while armed Death with its bloodied face is seated. The only blood upon the altars is that of war and [the only] fire is that taken from burning cities. (55) Spread around are the spoils of [many] lands, and captive nations adorn the pediments of the temple. There were fragments of doors chiseled in iron and warships also and empty chariots and faces smashed by chariot wheels: one could almost even [hear] their groans. Such was it that every violence and every sort of wound [was there]. (60) [The god] himself was to be seen everywhere, but never with a yielding look.

[7.62–178a: *When Mars deludes the Argives into thinking that the Theban army is approaching, they rush to prepare themselves for battle. Meanwhile, in an effort to spare his native city, Bacchus appeals to Jupiter.*]

30 the famous horse of Adrastus that Polynices drove in the race.
31 i.e. the horse with which he shares the yoke.
32 Polynices was exiled because he drew the losing lot against his brother Eteocles; Aonia is a part of Boeotia.
33 Mercury.
34 in Thrace.

Book 7

.34 dixerat, et Tracum Cyllenius arva subibat; [1967–2050
atque illum Arctoae labentem cardine portae
tempestas aeterna plagae praetentaque caelo
agmina Nimborum primique Aquilonis hiatus
in diversa ferunt: crepat aurea grandine multa
palla, nec Arcadii bene protegit umbra galeri.
hic steriles delubra notat Mavortia silvas –
horrescitque tuens –, ubi mille furoribus illi
cingitur averso domus inmansueta sub Haemo.
ferrea compago laterum, ferro apta teruntur
limina, ferratis incumbunt tecta columnis.
laeditur adversum Phoebi iubar, ipsaque sedem [1987
lux timet, et durus contristat sidera fulgor.
digna loco statio: primus salit Impetus amens [1985
e foribus caecumque Nefas Iraeque rubentes [1995–2028
exanguesque Metus, occultisque ensibus adstant.
Insidiae geminumque tenens Discordia ferrum.
innumeris strepit aula Minis, tristissima Virtus
stat medio, laetusque Furor voltuque cruento
Mors armata sedet; Bellorum solus in aris
sanguis et incensis qui raptus ab urbibus ignis.
terrarum exuviae circum et fastigia templi [2027–30
captae insignibant gentes, caelataque ferro
fragmina portarum gellatricesque carinae, [2017
et vacui currus protritaque curribus ora, [2022–3
paene etiam gemitus; adeo vis omnis et omne
vulnus. ubique ipsum, sed non usquam ore remisso
.61 cernere erat: . . .

7.178b–80

"The sacred rituals of my ruined race and anything from a bad pregnancy that my mother surrendered to the tombs – where would you order these to go? To the forests of Lycurgus[35] in Thrace?"

[7.181–823: *In Thebes, Eteocles learns of the Argives' imminent arrival. Phorbas provides Antigone with a long and detailed description of the assembled Theban allies. Eteocles harangues his troops, striving to work them into a battle fever. The Argives camp within view of Thebes. Jocasta brings her daughters to the Argive camp and urges her son Polynices to come with her to Thebes in an effort to make peace with his brother Eteocles. Tydeus persuades Polynices not to go. Two tigers sacred to Bacchus are driven mad by the Fury and kill the charioteer of Amphiaraus. When Aconteus kills these sacred beasts, Jocasta is horrified and returns to Thebes. The battle begins; it is marked by extraordinary feats of courage and great carnage. Apollo, in disguise, fights along with Amphiaraus in the prince's chariot. Revealing himself, he warns Amphiaraus that he is soon to die. The earth quakes, a great fissure opens, and Amphiaraus drives his chariot into the chasm.*]

[**Book 8**: 1–766: *The arrival of Amphiaraus the seer dismays the inhabitants of the lower world and infuriates Pluto, who views him as an intruder. Pluto orders Tesiphone to inflict terrible punishment on the Argives, but Amphiaraus mollifies him. Amphiaraus's disappearance terrifies the Argives, who believe it to mean that their gods have abandoned them. Pursued by the Thebans, they retreat in disorder. When they regroup, the Argives choose Melamphus to succeed Amphiaraus as seer. He sets up an altar and prays to Earth, asking her not to harm the Argives. The Thebans and Argives join in battle, each side accomplishing great deeds and terrible slaughter. In the city, Ismene and Antigone discuss their trials and fears. On the battlefield, Tydeus almost kills Eteocles, but the Fury preserves the king for his later fight to the death with Polynices. Driven mad by Tisiphone, the dying Tydeus gnaws the head of Melanippus, the Theban who had mortally wounded him.*]

[**Book 9**: 1–605: *Appalled at the atrocity committed by Tydeus, the Thebans advance against the Argives. Eteocles tries to retain the body of Tydeus, but Tisiphone distracts him and the Thebans recover it. Hippomedon drives the Thebans to the river Ismenus, where further fighting and slaughter follow. Hippomedon slays Crenaeus, the son of Ismene. When Ismene locates her son's body, she reproaches the river, her father. When the river attempts to drown Hippomedon, Juno convinces Jupiter to spare him. When the river retreats, Hippomedon crawls to the bank, where he dies of his wounds. In the meantime, Atalanta, the mother of Parthenopaeus, prays to Diana to spare her son.*]

9.606–36

. . . Then [Atalanta][36] stood at the threshold of the goddess and she speaks the following prayer, but to no avail: "Great Virgin of the forests whose ungentle standards and ferocious warfare I serve, disdainful of my sex (610) in a manner not

[35] Lycurgus: the king of Nemea and supporter of the Argives; the funeral ritual and games for his son Opheltes are described in book 6.

[36] As a devotee of Diana, Atalanta had vowed chastity but then married Meleagrus and gave birth to Pathenopaeus.

178 . . . quo sacra tamen ritusque peremptae [2129–52 +
gentis et, in tumulos si quid male feta reliquit
mater, abire iubes? Thracen silavasque Lycurgi?

Book 9

606 . . . tunc limina divae [2297–330
adstitit et tali nequiquam voce precatur:
"virgo potens nemorum, cuius non mollia signa
militiamque trucem sexum indignata frequento
more nihil Graio – nec te gens aspera ritu
Colchis Amazoniaeve magis coluere catervae – :
si mihi non umquam thiasi ludusve protervae

at all Greek – and the barbarous race of Colchis[37] or the Amazon troop does not serve you any better in their ritual: if I have never joined the Bacchic dance or the amusement of shameless nights and, [if] though defiled by a detested union, I nevertheless did not handle the smooth Bacchic staff or the soft spun skeins,[38] (615) but even after marriage I stayed in the harsh wilds, still a hunter and in my heart unmarried; [and if] I did not try to hide my guilt in secret caves, but rather, having confessed, I showed my child and placed him trembling at your feet; [and if] he [was] not a weakling (620) but he crawled right to my bows [and] as a boy he cried for weapons with his tears and his first whimper: [if all this is true,] I pray for him – what do these terrifying nights and these dreams portend? – for him who now with bold longing has gone off to battle, trusting excessively – alas! – in you. Grant that I might see him (625) victorious in the war or, if I ask for too much, grant that I might at least see him![39] Let him toil and bear your arms here. Strike down those dreadful omens of evil. O Delian [goddess][40] of the woods, why do the hostile Maenads[41] and the Theban gods rule in our forests? Ah! me. Why so deeply – and may I be a failed diviner of the future – (630) why do I inwardly recognize the oak as an omen of such importance? But if sleep sends true predictions to my poor [mind], then by your mother's labors,[42] O kind Dictynna,[43] and your brother's[44] glory pierce this unhappy womb [of mine] with all your arrows. Let him be the first to hear of his poor mother's destruction!" (635) She spoke and saw that the stone [statue] of frosty Diana had dampened with falling tears.

[9.637–907: *While traveling to Thebes in response to Atalanta's prayer, Diana meets Apollo, who tells his sister that Parthenopaeus is fated to die. Despite this Diana tries to help Parthenopaeus by substituting her arrows for his, as a result of which he kills many Thebans. In disguise during the battle, Diana attempts to convince him to leave the field. When Mars, at Venus's urging, orders Diana away from the battle, Parthenopaeus is wounded and dies.*]

[**Book 10**. 1–939: *The Argives have lost four of their leaders. That night, the Thebans surround their camp. In response to the prayers of the Argive women, Juno sends Iris to the dwelling place of Sleep with the order that he prevent the Thebans from awaking. Thirty Argive warriors slay the sleeping Thebans. With Diana's help, the squires of Tydeus and Parthenopaeus discover their lords' bodies, but while they are bringing them to the Argive camp they are killed by a Theban patrol. The Argives assault Thebes and breach its walls. When Tiresias predicts the death of Creon's son, Menoeceus, Creon attempts to conceal the prophecy. Inspired by Valor to sacrifice his life for Thebes, Menoeceus ignores his father's pleas and kills himself. His mother laments for her dead son. While climbing the battlements of Thebes, Capaneus taunts Jupiter, who strikes him down with a lightning bolt.*]

[37] The Colchins burned human sacrifices (LP 9.610–11).

[38] That is, even though she was a wife, she had not resigned herself to domestic roles and to the Bacchic rituals, which were conducted by married women.

[39] Some MSS contain an added line after 625: "si non victorem, da tantum cernere victum!" [If not a victor, grant at least that I might behold him vanquished!]. The source of the line source is Lactantius Placidus's gloss to 624–5.

[40] Born on the island of Delos, Diana was called the Delian goddess.

[41] priestesses of Bacchus (LP 9.627–8).

[42] in giving birth (LP 9.632). The reference is to Diana's mother, Leto.

[43] one of Diana's names (LP 9.632).

[44] Apollo's.

noctis et, inviso quamvis temerata cubili,
non tamen aut teretes thyrsos aut mollia gessi
pensa, sed in tetricis et post conubia lustris,
sic quoque venatrix animumque innupta remansi.
nec mihi secretis culpam occultare sub antris
cura, sed ostendi prolem posuique trementem
ante tuos confessa pedes; nec degener ille
sanguinis inque meos reptavit protinus arcus,
tela puer lacrimis et prima voce proposcit:
hunc mihi – quid trepidae noctes somnusque minantur? –
hunc, precor, audaci qui nunc ad proelia voto
heu nimium tibi fisus abit, da visere belli
victorem, vel, si ampla peto, da visere tantum!
hic sudet tuaque arma ferat. preme dira malorum
signa; quid in nostris, nemoralis Delia, silvis
Maenades hostiles Thebanaque numina regnant?
ei mihi! cur penitus – simque augur cassa futuri! –,
cur penitus magnoque interpretor omine quercum?
quod si vera sopor miserae praesagia mittit,
per te maternos, mitis Distynna, labores
fraternumque decus, cunctis hunc fige sagittis
infelicem uterum; miserae sine funera matris
audiat ille prior!" dixit, fletuque soluto [2327
aspicit et niveae saxum maduisse Dianae.

[**Book 11**.1–529: *Seeing the manner of Capaneus's death, the Argives retreat. Tisiphone plots the fratricidal deaths of the two sons of Oedipus. She will drive Eteocles mad with rage and she enlists another fury, Megaera, to enflame Polynices. Polynices determines to engage Eteocles in mortal combat. Tisiphone prevents Eteocles' prayer of thanksgiving from reaching Jupiter. As Polynices approaches Thebes, Creon impels Eteocles to face his brother. While Jocasta beseeches Eteocles not to fight, Antigone, standing on the city walls, makes the same appeal to her brother Polynices below. He hesitates, but Eteocles, goaded by the Fury, insists on the fraternal combat. Adrastus tries in vain to convince the brothers not to fight.*]

11.530–36

As when Rage has hurled lightning-swift boars headlong into close contest and has raised the bristles high on their backs, their eyes quiver with fire and their crescent-shaped mouths with their curved tusks ring loud, [and] turning pale, a hunter gazes upon the combat from a nearby height and orders his hounds to be silent: (535) in such a manner did these eager men clash. They have not as yet dealt any mortal wounds, but the bleeding has begun and the villainy has been accomplished.

[11.537–38: *The watching Furies grieve that human rage can exceed their own.*]

11.539–40

Each one, in a rage, lusts for and seeks out his brother's life-blood, but does not know that his own is flowing.

[11.541–761: *When Eteocles and Polynices have killed each other, their parents and sisters come to lament over them. Oedipus intends to kill himself, but Antigone prevents him. Jocasta halfheartedly stabs herself, but Ismene binds the wound. Creon becomes ruler of Thebes. He commits sacrilege by refusing burial to the dead Argives. He banishes Oedipus from Thebes, restricting him to nearby mount Cithaeron.*]

[**Book 12**.1–518: *The Thebans bury their dead with full funeral honors. Creon has a grand pyre erected for Menoeceus and laments for his dead son. He sternly repeats his injunction against the burning and burial of the dead Argives. Argive widows have begun a journey to Thebes in order to bury their dead. Ornytus warns them of Creon's decree. All but Argia decide to travel to Athens in order to petition Theseus on behalf of their dead husbands. Entering the battlefield, Argia meets Antigone, who has determined to perform the funeral rituals for Polynices. They identify his body and carry it to the river Ismenus, wash it, and seek a pyre with embers, so that they can stoke a fire for Polynices. The pyre, which was for Eteocles, rebuffs the corpse of Polynices, bursting into two distinct flames. Theban guards seize the women and lead them to Creon. With Juno's help, the Argive women reach Athens where they are welcomed and housed in the temple of Clemency while they await the return of Theseus.*]

Book 11

.530 fulmineos veluti praeceps cum comminus egit [1660
ira sues strictisque erexit tergora saetis:
igne tremunt oculi, lunataque dentibus uncis
ora sonant; spectat pugnas de rupe propinqua
venator pallens canibusque silentia suadet;
sic avidi incurrunt; necdum letalia miscent
.536 volnera, sed coeptus sanguis, facinusque peractum est.

.539 fratris uterque furens cupit adfectatque cruorem
et nescit manare suum . . .

12.519–22[45]

And now after his harsh battle with the Scythian race,[46] the joyful applause and the shouting of the people, raised up to the stars, and the trumpet happy with the end of warfare announce the return home of Theseus in his laurelled chariot.

[12.523–701: *Evadne speaks for the Argive women, describing Creon's behavior and asking for Theseus's help. Having organized an army of Athenians and allies of Athens, Theseus marches on Thebes. The exhausted and dispirited Thebans offer little resistance.*]

12.702–5

No one is glorious with quivers [and] sword, no one is worthy to behold on his horse. Confidence in the palisade gives way. The [city] walls stand open on every side; the gates beg for protection. The former enemy holds [them]; the battlements are gone.

[12.706–819: *Theseus battles Creon and kills him. After the battle, the Athenians offer to make peace and are welcomed into Thebes. The Argive women perform the proper funeral rituals for their dead. An epilogue concludes the poem.*]

[45] Chaucer translates these lines in *Anelida and Arcite*, 22–8: "When Theseus, with werres longe and grete,/ The aspre folk of Cithe had overcome,/ With laurer corouned, in his char gold-bete,/ Hom to his contre-houses is he come;/ For which the peple, blissful al and somme,/ So cryëden that to the sterres hit wente,/ And him to honouren dide al her entente."

[46] The Amazons, who lived in Scythia.

Book 12

.519 iamque domos patrias Scythicae post aspera gentis [motto to *KnT*
proelia laurigero subeuntem Thesea curru
laetifici plausus missusque ad sidera vulgi
.522 clamor et emeritis hilaris tuba nuntiat armis.

.702 . . . non pharetris quisquam, non ense decorus,
non spectandus equo; cessat fiducia valli,
murorum patet omne latus, munimina portae [1331
.705 exposcunt: prior hostis habet; fastigia desunt:

III

Consolation of Philosophy

(Boethius, *Consolation of Philosophy*, trans. W. V. Cooper, The Temple Classics, ed. Israel Gollancz [London: J. M. Dent, 1902], 1 met. 5; 2. met. 8; 3 met. 9; 4. met. 6; selections from: 2 pr. 5; 3 pr. 2; 3 pr. 10; 3 met. 12; 4 pr. 6)

1. meter 5

"Founder of the star-studded universe,[1] resting on your eternal throne, you turn the swiftly rolling sky, and bind the stars to keep your law: so that [at your word] the moon now shines brightly with full face, ever turned to her brother's light,[2] and so she dims the lesser lights; or now pale, with darkened crescent, and nearer to the sun,[3] she loses her light. Cool rises the evening star[4] at night's first drawing near: the same is the morning star[5] who casts off the harness that she bore before, and, paling, meets the rising sun.[6] When winter's cold strips the trees, you set a shorter span to day. And when summer comes to warm, you change the short divisions of the night. Your power orders the seasons of the year, so that the western breeze[7] of spring brings back the leaves which winter's north wind[8] tears away; so that the dog-star's[9] heat scorches the ears of corn whose seed Arcturus[10] watched. Nothing breaks that ancient law: nothing leaves undone the work appointed to its place. Thus you rule all things within a fixed limit: the lives of men alone you scorn to restrain, as a guardian, within proper bounds.

1 Note Chaucer's metaphor for the design of the universe: "the wheel that bereth the sterres" (*Boece* 1–2).

2 In classical myth, the moon (under the control of Phoebe/Artemis/Diana) and the sun (under the control of her twin brother, Phoebus/Apollo) were considered to be sister and brother.

3 lit: Phoebus. In meter 5, Boethius merely names the celestial deities. In translating, Chaucer typically includes the name plus a description of its function ("the eve sterre, Hesperus" (11–2); "Zephirus, the debonere wynd" (22); "the wynd that hyghte Boreas" (23–4); "the sterre that highte Arcturus" (26–7); "the sterre Syrius" (28).

4 lit: Hesperus.

5 lit: Lucifer (the light bearer); refers to the planet Venus, when it appears as the morning star. Boethius preserves the classical names for the morning star (Lucifer) and the evening star (Hesperus); this distinction reflects the ancient belief that they were different bodies. His text, however, specifies the more "modern" understanding that they are the same heavenly body.

6 lit: Phoebus.

7 lit: Zephyrus.

8 lit: Borea.

9 lit: Sirius.

10 The brightest star in the constellation Bootes, its rising and setting portended foul weather.

III

Anicius Manlius Severinus Boethius, *De consolatione philosophiae*

(from *Patrologia Latina*, vol. 63 [1847], cols 634–40, 689–96, 718–20, 723–8, 758–69, 782–6, 813–23 with minor editing of punctuation, spelling, and capitalization. The single emendation, in brackets, is based on the text in *Corpus Scriptorum Ecclesiasticorum Latinorum* [CSEL] [vol. 67, Vienna, 1935])[11]

1. meter 5

O stelliferi conditor orbis,
qui perpetuo nixus solio
rapido caelum turbine versas
legemque pati sidera cogis,
ut nunc pleno lucida cornu, [6]
totis fratris obvia flammis
condat stellas luna minores;
nunc obscuro pallida cornu,
Phoebo propior lumina perdat.
Et qui primae tempore noctis [11]
agit algentes Hesperos ortus
solitas iterum mutet habenas,
Phoebi pallens Lucifer ortu.
Tu frondifluae frigore brumae
stringis lucem breviore mora: [16]
tu, cum fervida venerit aestas
agiles noctis dividis horas.
Tua vis varium temperat annum,
ut quas Boreae spiritus aufert,
revehat mitis Zephyrus frondes, [22]
quaeque Arcturus semina vidit,
Sirius altas urat segetes.
Nihil antiqua lege solutum
linquit propriae stationis opus.
Omnia certo fine gubernans, [31]
hominum solos respuis actus
merito, rector, cohibere modo.

[11] In the titles, the line numbering corresponds to that in Chaucer's *Boece*. The text of the *De consolatione* contains two types of line numbering. In the meters, the line numbers in the left margin are from the CSEL edition, while the line numbers in the right margin (in brackets) are from the *Boece*. This dual lineation is not possible in the prose sections, because the prose of the *Boece*, which is based on Boethius's original material and a French translation of Boethius, also includes glosses derived from Nicholas Trevet's commentary on the *Consolation*. The prose selections thus contain only the line numbers from the CSEL edition of the *De consolatione*, which are in boldface.

For why does fickle Fortune deal out such changing lots? The hurtful penalty is due to crime, but falls upon the sinless head: depraved men rest at ease on thrones aloft, and by their unjust lot can spurn beneath their hurtful heel the necks of virtuous men. Beneath obscuring shadows lies bright virtue hid: the just man bears the unjust's infamy. The [wicked][12] do not suffer for disavowed oaths, nor do they suffer for deceit glossed over with their lies. But when their will is to put forth their strength with triumph, they subdue the mightiest kings whom people without number fear. O you who weave the bonds of things, look down upon this pitiable earth! Mankind is no base part[13] of this great work and we are tossed on Fortune's wave. Restrain, our Guardian, the engulfing surge, and as you rule the unbounded heaven, with a like bond make true and firm these lands."

2. prose 5.90–5

18 "Or are you made happy by a long line of attendants? Surely if they are vicious, they are but a burden to the house, and full of injury to their master himself; while if they are honest, how can the honesty of others be counted among your possessions?"

2. prose 5.171–3

33 "Yet many a time do riches harm their possessors, since every man who is base, and for that reason more greedy of what is another's, thinks that he alone is worthy to possess whatever gold and precious stones exist."

2. meter 8

"That the universe with constancy makes changes all without discord, that the earth's elements, though contrary, abide in treaty bound, that Phœbus[14] in his golden car brings forth the rosy day so that Phoebe[15] rules the night that Hesperus[16] brought, so that the greedy sea confines its floods within bounds, so that it not be permissible [for it] to stretch its broad boundaries upon the earth by means of waves

[12] Chaucer supplies the plural noun "schrewes" (45).

[13] See Chaucer's expansion of the phrase: "We men, that ben noght a foul partie, but a fair partie of so greet a werk . . ." (52–3). This diffuseness in Chaucer's translation may be due to his using three sources for the *Boece*: Boethius's Latin, a French translation of Boethius, and the Latin commentary of Nicholas Trevet. These varied sources may also explain his habit (discussed below in the notes to 3 meter 9ff) of using double cognates to translate a single Latin word.

[14] In the *Boece*, Chaucer identifies the name: "Phebus, the sonne" (4).

[15] the name of Diana in her role of goddess of the moon; Chaucer omits the name, preferring "the moone" (6).

[16] the evening star.

Nam cur tantas lubrica versat
Fortuna vices? premit insontes
debita sceleri noxia poena.
At perversi resident celso
mores solio, sanctaque calcant
iniusta vice colla nocentes.
Latet obscuris condita virtus
clara tenebris, iustusque tulit
crimen iniqui.
Nil periuria, nil nocet ipsis
fraus, mendaci compta colore.
Sed cum libuit viribus uti,
quos innumeri metuunt populi,
summos gaudent subdere reges.
O iam miseras respice terras,
quisquis rerum foedera nectis!
Operis tanti pars non vilis
homines, quatimur fortunae salo.
Rapidos, rector, comprime fluctus
et, quo caelum regis immemsum,
firma stabiles foedere terras.

2. prose 5.90–5

18 An vero te longus ordo famulorum facit esse felicem? Qui si vitiosi moribus sint, perniciosa domus sarcina et ipsi domino vehementer inimica; sin vero probi, quonam modo in tuis opibus aliena probitas numerabitur?

2. prose 5.171–3

33 Atqui divitiae possidentibus persaepe nocuerunt, cum pessimus quisque eoque alieni magis avidus, quicquid auri usquam gemmarumque est, se solum, qui habeat dignissimum putat.

2. meter 8

Quod mundus stabili fide
concordes variat vices,
quod pugnantia semina
foedus perpetuum tenent,
quod Phoebus roseum diem
curru provehit aureo,
ut quas duxerit Hesperos
Phoebe noctibus imperet,
ut fluctus avidum mare
certo fine coherceat,
ne terris liceat vagis
latos tendere terminos,
hanc rerum seriem ligat
terras ac pelagus regens,

– all this harmony of things is bound by Love, which rules both earth and sea, and has its empire in the heavens too. If this [Love] should slacken its hold, all mutual love would change to war; and these would strive to undo the scheme which now their glorious movements carry out with trust and with accord. This [Love] also keeps peoples bound together, joined by a holy bond. This binds the sacred [tie] of wedlock with pure affections; this also speaks its bidding to all trustworthy friends. O happy would the race of mortals be, if that Love by which the universe is ruled, would rule your hearts!"

3. prose 2.25–8

"Some men believe that the highest good is to lack nothing, and so they are at pains to possess abundant riches. . . ."

3. prose 2.83–8

"But to return to the aims of men: even if their memory appears to be dull, their nature nevertheless seeks the highest good. It is as though a drunken man were seeking his home, but could not remember the way there."

3. meter 9[17]

"You who rule the universe with everlasting law, founder[18] of earth and heaven alike, who have bidden time to go forth from out Eternity, forever firm[19] yourself, yet giving movement unto all. No causes were outside you which could thence impel you to create this mass of changing matter, but within you there exists the very idea of perfect good, which resents nothing. You make all things follow that high pattern. You who are perfect beauty bear in your mind a world of beauty, making all in a like image, and bidding the perfect whole to complete[20] its perfect functions. All the first principles of nature[21] you bind together by [perfect orders as of] numbers, so that they may be balanced [each with its opposite]: cold with

[17] "In twenty-eight lines of astonishing poetic concentration and power, Boethius explores the central theological and cosmological ideas of Plato's *Timaeus* and fits them to his own conception of a personal God and to the whole process of his poetic vision." (Richard Green, trans., *Boethius, The Consolation of Philosophy*, Library of Liberal Arts [Indianapolis: Bobbs-Merrill, 1962], p. xxi.) The poem, probably the finest in the *De consolatione*, introduces Philosophy's prayer for divine help in demonstrating that supreme goodness and perfect happiness are in God and are God. During the Middle Ages, the poem elicited much study, citation, and commentary.

[18] Lit. sower; Chaucer's rendering of "sator" as "soowere and creatour" (1) reflects his habit of translating a word with two cognates. See other examples below.

[19] Chaucer translates "stabilis" with the double cognates, "stedefast and stable" (5–6).

[20] Chaucer renders "absoluere" as "have frely and absolut" (17).

[21] Lit: elements.

et caelo imperitans amor. [16]
Hic si frena remiserit,
quicquid nunc amat invicem
bellum continuo geret,
et quam nunc socia fide
pulchris motibus incitant [21]
certent soluere machinam.
Hic sancto populos quoque
iunctos foedere continent;
hic et coniugii sacrum
castis nectit amoribus; [23]
hic fidis etiam sua
dictat iura sodalibus.
O felix hominum genus,
si vestros animos amor
quo caelum regitur, regat! [26]

3. prose 2.25–8

5 Quorum quidem alii summum bonum esse nihilo indigere credentes, ut divitiis affluant elaborant. . . .

3. prose 2.83–8

13 Sed ad hominum studia revertor: quorum animus, et si caligante memoria, tamen bonum summum repetit, sed velut ebrius, domum quo tramite revertatur ignorat

3. meter 9

O qui perpetua mundum ratione gubernas,
terrarum caelique sator, qui tempus ab aevo
ire iubes, stabilisque manens das cuncta moveri;
quem non externae pepulerunt fingere causae
materiae fluitantis opus, verum insita summi [8]
forma boni, livore carens; tu cuncta superno
ducis ab exemplo, pulchrum pulcherrimus ipse
mundum mente gerens, similique [in] imagine formans
perfectasque iubens perfectum absoluere partes.
Tu numeris elementa ligas, ut frigora flammis, [18]
arida conveniant liquidis, ne purior ignis
evolet aut mersas deducant pondera terras.
Tu triplicis mediam naturae cuncta moventem
connectens animam per consona membra resolvis;
quae cum secta duos motum glomeravit in orbes, [27]
in semet reditura meat mentemque profundam
circuit, et simili convertit imagine caelum.
Tu causis animas paribus vitasque minores
provehis et levibus sublimes curribus aptans
in caelum terramque seris: quas lege benigna [35]

heat, and dry with moist together; thus fire, which is the purer [element], may not fly upward [too swiftly], nor may the weight of the solid earth drag it down. You make the threefold soul as an intermediate[22] which gives movement to all things, for you spread it abroad among the members of the universe, now working in accord. Thus is the soul divided as it takes its course, making two circles. Thereafter it returns unto itself and passes around the mind deep within; and in like manner it gives motion to the heavens to turn their course. You it is who carries forward with like inspiration these souls and lower lives. And fitting these sublime [souls] into weak vessels,[23] you send them abroad throughout the heavens and earth, and by your kindly law you turn them again to yourself and bring them to seek, by fire, to rise to you again.

"Grant then, O Father, that this mind of ours may rise to your throne of majesty. Grant that it may reach that fount of good. Grant, once the light has been provided, that it may fix the clear sights of its heart on you. Cast off[24] the clouds and burdens of this earthly world and shine forth upon us in your own true splendor. For you are the glory and the peaceful rest for gentle folk. To see you clearly is [our] goal. [You are] our beginning, our progress, our guide, our way, our very end."

3. prose 10. 25–30

5 "For nature does not start from degenerate or imperfect specimens, but starting from the perfect and ideal, it degenerates to these lower and weaker forms."

3. meter 12.52–5

47 "Who shall set a law to lovers? Love is a greater law unto itself."

4. prose 6.42–7

7 "The engendering of all things, the whole development of changeable natures, and every motion and progress in the world draw their causes, their order, and their forms from the unchanging mind of God. **8** This [divine mind], which is set in the fortress[25] of its own simplicity, establishes the manifold way in which events are carried out."

4. prose 6.146–65

18 "That course of Fate moves the heavens and the stars, moderates the first principles in their turns, and alters their forms by balanced interchangings. The same course renews all things that are born and wither away by similar advances of offspring[26] and seed. **19** This order also limits the actions and fortunes of men by an

22 "triplicis . . . animan": see Chaucer's "the mene soule of treble kynde moevynge alle thingis" (25–6).

23 Lit. carts, which Chaucer translates as "waynes or cartes" (34).

24 Chaucer translates "dissice" with dual cognates: "skatere thou and tobreke (43–4)."

25 A fine example of Chaucer's habit of "double translation" is his rendering of "in . . . arce composita": "iset and put in the tour (*that is to seyn, in the height*)" (48–9). The two cognates for "composita" are balanced by a translation of "arce" that is accompanied by Nicholas Trevet's gloss on the word.

26 Chaucer translates "fetuum" as "sexes," adding the gloss by Trevet: "*that is to seyn, male and female*" (152–3).

ad te conversas reduci facis igne reverti.
Da, Pater, augustam menti conscendere sedem,
da fontem lustrare boni, da luce reperta
in te conspicuos animi defigere visus.
Dissice terrenae nebulas et pondera molis, [43]
atque tuo splendore mica: tu namque serenum,
tu requies tranquilla piis; te cernere finis,
principium, vector, dux, semita, terminus idem.

3. Prose 10. 25–30

5 Neque enim ab deminutis, inconsummatisque natura rerum cepit exordium, sed ab integris, absolutisque procedens, in haec extrema atque effeta dilabitur.

3. Meter 12.52–5

47 Quis legem det amantibus?
Maior lex amor est sibi.

4. Prose 6.42–7

7 Omnium generatio rerum, cunctusque mutabilium naturarum progressus, et quicquid aliquo movetur modo, causas, ordinem, formas ex divinae mentis stabilitate sortitur.
8 Haec in suae simplicitatis arce composita, multiplicem rebus gerendis modum statuit.

4. Prose 6.146–65

18 Ea series caelum ac sidera movet, elementa in se invicem temperat, et alterna commutatione transformat. Eadem nascentia occidentiaque omnia per similes fetuum, seminumque renovat progressus. **19** Haec actus etiam, fortunasque hominum indissolubili causarum connexione constringit: quae cum ab immobilis Providentiae proficiscatur exordiis, ipsas quoque immutabiles esse necesse est. **20** Ita enim res optime reguntur, si manens in divina mente simplicitas, indeclinabilem causarum ordinem promat; hic vero ordo res mutabiles et alioqui temere fluituras propria incommutabilitate coherceat.

unbreakable bond of causes: and these causes must be unchangeable, as they proceed from the beginnings of an unchanging Providence. **20** Thus are things governed for the best if the simplicity which rests in the divine intelligence puts forth an unchangeable order of causes. This order restrains, by its own unchangeableness, changeable things, which might otherwise run hither and thither at random."

4. prose 6.214–24

29 "And who else is the preserver of the good and banisher of the evil, who but God, the guardian and healer of minds? **30** He [it is] who looks forth from the high watch-tower of his Providence, he is aware of what suits each man, and he provides him with what he knows will suit him. **31** Hence then comes[27] that conspicuous cause of wonder in the order of Fate, when [God] in his wisdom does that which amazes the ignorant."

4. meter 6

"If you would diligently behold with unsullied mind the laws[28] of the God of thunder[29] upon high, look to the highest point of heaven above. There, by a fair compact of things, the stars keep their ancient peace. The sun is hurried on by its whirl of fire, but does not impede the moon's[30] cool orb. The Bear[31] turns its rushing course around the highest pole of the universe. Never washed in the deep western [sea], and, though it sees the other constellations[32] sink, it never seeks to quench[33] its flames in the ocean stream. In just divisions of time does the evening star[34] foretell the coming of the late shadows, and Lucifer[35] brings back again the clear light of day. Thus does the interchanging bond of love bring round their never-failing courses; thus warlike strife is forever an exile from the starry realms. This unity rules the elements by fair limits, so that, striving by turns, moist things yield to dry, and cold things by faith unite with hot. The floating fire rises up on high, and the heavy matter of the earth subsides under [its own] weight. From these same causes, in warm spring the flowering season breathes its scents; the hot summer dries the grain;[36] autumn comes again with its burden of fruits;[37] falling rain bedews the winter. This disposition nourishes and brings forth everything on earth that has the breath of life; this is the same thing [that] seizes, hides, and carries away, overwhelming in the final death all that has arisen. Meanwhile the Creator

27 Note Chaucer's double translation of "fit": "comyth and . . . is don" (221).

28 Note Chaucer's double translation of "iura" as "the ryghtes or the lawes" (2).

29 lit. "of the thunderer"; the *Boece* adds Nicholas Trevet's gloss, "*that is to seyn, of God*" (3).

30 lit. "Phoebe's."

31 In order to specify that he is referring to the lodestar and not to the constellation of Ursa Minor, where it is to be found, Chaucer translates "Ursa" as "the sterre yclepid the Bere" (8). For a discussion of Chaucer's understanding of the distinction between the lodestar and its constellation, see notes to *Teseo* 7.61.3–4.

32 The word "sidera" could be translated as either stars or constellations; Chaucer understands it as "sterres" (14) in the *Boece* and elsewhere; see Introduction, n. 126.

33 lit: to dye (tingere); see Chaucer's "to deeyen his flaumbes in the see" (13).

34 lit: Vesper (i.e. Hesperus); see "Hesperus the steere" (*Bo* 15).

35 the "Light-bearer": one of the names of Venus, in her guise of morning star; see "Lucyfer the steere" (*Bo* 17). See above, 1 meter 5 n. 5.

36 "Cererem": either the grain or Ceres, the goddess of grain.

37 lit: of apples (Chaucer's translation, *Bo* 32–3).

4. Prose 6.214–24

29 Quis autem alius vel servator bonorum vel malorum depulsor quam rector ac medicator mentium Deus? **30** Qui, cum ex alta providentiae specula respexit, quid unicuique conveniat agnoscit et quod convenire novit accommodat. **31** Hinc iam fit illud fatalis ordinis insigne miraculum, cum ab sciente geritur quod stupeant ignorantes.

4. meter 6

Si vis celsi iura tonantis
pura sollers cernere mente,
aspice summi culmina cœli;
illic iusto fœdere rerum
veterem seruant sidera pacem. [6]
Non sol rutilo concitus igne
gelidum Phoebes impedit axem
nec quae summo vertice mundi
flectit rapidos Ursa meatus,
numquam occiduo lota profundo, [12]
cetera cernens sidera mergi,
cupit Oceano tingere flammas;
semper vicibus temporis æquis
Vesper seras nuntiat umbras,
revehitque diem Lucifer almum. [17]
Sic aeternos reficit cursus
alternus amor, sic astrigeris
bellum discors exulat oris.
Hæc concordia temperat æquis
elementa modis, ut pugnantia [23]
vicibus cedant humida siccis,
iungantque fidem frigora flammis,
pendulus ignis surgat in altum,
terraeque graves pondere sidant.
Iisdem causis vere tepenti [29]
spirat florifer annus odores,
æstas Cererem fervida siccat,
remeat pomis gravis autumnus,
hiemem defluus inrigat imber.
Hæc temperies alit ac profert [34]
quicquid vitam spirat in orbe:
eadem rapiens condit, et aufert
obitu mergens orta supremo.

sits on high, and rules all and guides [all] things, king and Lord, fount and source, Law [itself] and wise judge of justice, and what he stirs into motion, he draws back and halts. If he were not to recall them to their straight paths and set them again upon the circles of their courses, those things that stable order now holds together would be separated from their source and so would perish. This is the [bond of] love that is common to all things, and they seek [thus] to be held by the goal of the [common] good. In no other manner can they endure if they do not return again, restored by love, to the cause[38] which has given [them their] being."

[38] See Trevet's gloss: "*that is to seyn, to God*" (*Bo* 59–60).

Sedet interea conditor altus
rerumque regens flectit habenas, [40]
rex et dominus, fons et origo,
lex et sapiens arbiter æqui,
et quæ motu concitat ire,
sistit retrahens ac vaga firmat;
nam nisi rectos revocans itus [47]
flexos iterum cogat in orbes,
quæ nunc stabilis continet ordo,
dissaepta suo fonte fatiscant.
Hic est cunctis communis amor,
repetuntque boni fine teneri. [55]
Quia non aliter durare queunt
nisi converso rursus amore
refluant causæ quæ dedit esse.

The Miller's Tale[1]

PETER G. BEIDLER

Many medieval stories have features in common with Chaucer's *Miller's Tale* about two young suitors to the young wife of a rich old carpenter. All but one of these stories, however, are either too late or too distant in narrative structure from *The Miller's Tale* to have influenced it. That one is the anonymous fourteenth-century Middle Dutch tale known as *Heile van Beersele.*[2] While we cannot be sure that this one was Chaucer's actual source – that is, that he actually had this precise version of the story in his hands before he wrote the tale of John, Alisoun, Nicholas, and Absolon – I consider it the closest we have to Chaucer's source. To use a terminology that is gaining sway, I consider it to be a "hard analogue with near-source status."[3] Because *Heile van Beersele* would

[1] I am pleased to acknowledge here two men without whose generous help I could not have produced this chapter. First, Professor Henk Aertsen, of the Vrije Universiteit in Amsterdam, transcribed and translated the manuscript of *Heile van Beersele*. Second, Professor Geert Claassens, of the Katholieke Universiteit of Leuven, acted as general consultant to me. He was particularly helpful in verifying the lexical similarities between certain words and phrases in *The Miller's Tale* with cognate words and phrases in Middle Dutch, in verifying certain manuscript readings, and in dating the manuscript. Howell Chickering, of Amherst College, read through a draft of this paper and urged wise caution in my discussion of Chaucer's possible knowledge of Middle Dutch. I am fully responsible, of course, for the conclusions I suggest from what is at best slippery evidence. My translations of individual lines or phrases in this introduction are sometimes at slight variance with Aertsen's translations given below in the text proper.

[2] The unique MS in the Royal Library of Belgium in Brussels gives as the title to the story the couplet *Dits van Heilen van Beersele/ Die de .iii. jaghede te spele* [This is about Heile of Beersele who made a fool of those three men]. It is almost always referred to by the short title *Heile van Beersele*, with *Heile of Beersele* as its English equivalent, and I see no reason not to follow that sensible practice here.

[3] For a full definition, with examples, of the terms "source," "hard analogue," and "soft analogue," see Peter G. Beidler, "Just Say Yes, Chaucer Knew the *Decameron*," in *The Decameron and the Canterbury Tales*, ed. Leonard Michael Koff and Brenda Deen Schildgen (Madison, NJ: Fairleigh Dickinson University Press, 2000), pp. 41–2. In that terminology, a "source" is a work that, because of external evidence, narrative similarities, and verbal parallels, scholars can be sure Chaucer knew. A "hard analogue" is one that would have been available to Chaucer and that has certain striking parallels with his work, but not extended or exact verbal parallels. A "soft analogue" is one that, because of its remoteness in time or its different narrative strategies, Chaucer almost surely did not know. The term "hard analogue with near-source status" suggests that a work is old enough that Chaucer could have known it and that it gives close parallels in plot or characterization, even if there are few extended verbal parallels.

have been available to Chaucer and bears striking resemblances to his work, and because all other known analogues are either later than or distant from *The Miller's Tale*, I present in this chapter an edition and translation of only this one tale.[4] I discuss, however, and give citations for the various other more distant analogues that have been identified.[5]

The work of previous scholars

The existence of the Middle Dutch story of Heile was first pointed out in 1912 by Barnouw, who noted that in *Heile van Beersele* two different elements have been blended into one story: "(1) the jest of the man who let himself be scared by the prediction of a second flood, and (2) the story of the smith who, expecting to kiss his sweetheart's mouth, was made to kiss his rival's posteriors, on which he avenged himself with a red-hot iron from his smithy."[6] Barnouw, however, immediately dismissed the possibility that the Middle Dutch analogue was Chaucer's source. Rather, he said, Chaucer's source must have been a French fabliau, even though no French analogue to *The Miller's Tale* had yet been located. Indeed, Barnouw posited two lost French versions, one that had the role of one of the woman's suitors played by her husband, and a second story, without the husband, that had at one time been translated into the Middle Dutch story of *Heile van Beersele*. Curiously, without any textual or documentary evidence whatever, Barnouw stated that "our supposed French fabliau cannot have been an improved redaction of the Middle Dutch poem, but must have been based on the latter's French original."[7]

Despite his confused reasoning and lack of textual evidence, Barnouw's assertion that the Middle Dutch story was not Chaucer's source has not until now been seriously challenged. In his chapter on *The Miller's Tale* in Bryan and Dempster, the noted folklorist Stith Thompson joined Barnouw in asserting that "no direct literary source has ever been discovered for *The Miller's Tale*."[8] Although he knew about the Middle Dutch tale and even broke tradition for the 1941 *Sources and Analogues* by presenting it, not with the usual brief sidebar summary, but with a complete translation, he continued to echo Barnouw's

4 Erik Hertog, formerly of the Katholieke Universiteit of Leuven, has told me privately that he reached a similar conclusion about the special status of *Heile van Beersele* as the analogue most likely to be the source of *The Miller's Tale*. For Hertog's discussion of *Heile van Beersele*, see his monograph *Chaucer's Fabliaux as Analogues* (Leuven, 1991), pp. 105–30.

5 I am not interested here in two other "sources" for *The Miller's Tale* that Helen Cooper has identified, *The Knight's Tale* and the medieval city of Oxford. See her *Oxford Guides to Chaucer: The Canterbury Tales*, 2nd edn (Oxford, 1996). I do not deny, of course, that in some ways *The Miller's Tale* was shaped as a response to the preceding tale of rivals for the love of a beautiful young woman, nor do I deny that the setting for *The Miller's Tale* was influenced by the layout of Oxford itself. My concern here is with fictional tales that could have supplied Chaucer with the essentials of his narrative plot and with the various character types. I do not, of course, deny that other medieval tales could have suggested to Chaucer other minor elements that he adapted to *The Miller's Tale*.

6 A. J. Barnouw, "Chaucer's 'Milleres Tale,'" *Modern Language Review* 7 (1912): 145. The whole article is only four pages long (pp. 145–8).

7 Barnouw, p. 147.

8 Thompson's chapter appears on pp. 106–23. The quotation is taken from the brief introductory note on p. 106.

view that Chaucer's source was a "lost French fabliau," even though there was still no evidence whatsoever that such a work ever existed in France or elsewhere before, during, or after the fourteenth century.[9] For Thompson, the Middle Dutch analogue was interesting primarily because it was evidence for a French version:

> The argument for a lost French fabliau as Chaucer's immediate source is strengthened by the presence of a fourteenth-century fabliau in Flemish. This may be an adaptation of a contemporary French poem. Chaucer's version differs from it in many particulars. He places the seducer in the household, provides enough tubs for all three members, and forgets that the duped lover should appropriately be a smith.[10]

Thompson also misled scholars in another way. Working from his own central interest as a folklorist rather than as a Chaucerian, he focused scholarly attention on what he called the "three principal motifs" in *The Miller's Tale*. He was interested less in identifying the closest or most likely extant analogue to Chaucer's fabliau than in tracing those motifs in other literatures worldwide. In doing so he identified them in terms associated with his own *Motif-Index of Folk-Literature*: the flood (his number K 1522), the misdirected kiss (K 1225), and the branding (K 1577). All three motifs, of course, are present in *Heile van Beersele*, but because of the work of Barnouw and Thompson, many scholars have been isolating these elements from one another rather than looking for narratives in which they appear together, as in *Heile van Beersele*.

The ten analogues in the order Thompson gives them are (1) a fifteenth-century German tale by Hanz Folz, (2) a sixteenth-century English ballad, (3) a

9 Barnouw's and Thompson's notion of a lost French source has been remarkably persistent and influential in criticism of *The Miller's Tale*. Germaine Dempster in *Dramatic Irony in Chaucer* (Stanford, 1932) reports that "the lost source" for *The Miller's Tale* "was probably a French fabliau" (pp. 35–6). In Douglas Gray's Explanatory Notes to *The Miller's Tale* in *The Riverside Chaucer* (Boston, 1987) we read: "Chaucer may have found [the three principal motifs in the tale] combined in a single source, perhaps a French fabliau" (p. 842). Similarly, we read in Cooper's *Oxford Guides to Chaucer* that "Chaucer is generally assumed to have found the story in a French fabliau, now lost. The only direct trace of it in the text may be in the remark on John's finding no bread to sell in his fall (3821–2), apparently a translation of a French colloquialism" (p. 96). This last speculation, based apparently on the *Riverside* note (see p. 848), is slender evidence indeed for a lost French source. If the expression that John does not stop to sell bread or ale on his rapid descent from the roof-beam is indeed a French colloquialism, Chaucer's fluency in French suggests that he need not have learned it in a French source for *The Miller's Tale*. It is to her credit that Cooper points out that the Middle Dutch story of Heile is the only one of the various analogues "that could predate *The Miller's Tale*" and "serves to indicate the lines along which he modelled his own version" (p. 96).

10 Thompson, p. 106. Thompson's judgment that Chaucer "forgets" that the second lover should "appropriately be a smith" has not held up in recent criticism, which finds strong justification for Chaucer's making the second lover the parish clerk Absolon and for his creation of the blacksmith Gerveys to provide Absolon with the hot coulter. I am grateful to Geert Claassens for pointing out that both Barnouw and, following him, Thompson, and virtually all who talk about *Heile van Beersele*, inappropriately refer to it as the work of a "Flemish poet" or as having been written in "Flemish." Because the MS of *Heile van Beersele* is of Brabantine origin and because the story of Heile takes place in Antwerp, in the duchy of Brabant, it is inaccurate to refer to the story or its language as "Flemish." Accordingly, I have used the more general term "Middle Dutch" when referring to the MS and its language, and have reserved "Flemish" for the geographical location of Flanders, which was further to the west and closer to England.

sixteenth-century Italian tale by Morlini, (4) a late-fifteenth-century Italian tale by Masuccio, (5) a seventeenth-century English tale by Brewer, (6) the fourteenth-century Middle Dutch tale of Heile, (7) a sixteenth-century German tale by Schumann, (8) a nineteenth-century German popular tale, (9) a sixteenth-century German rendering of a Latin poem, and (10) a sixteenth-century German story by Hans Sachs. Of the ten analogues that Thompson singled out for specific mention in Bryan and Dempster, all but the Middle Dutch *Heile van Beersele* date from the fifteenth century or later and so could not have been known to Chaucer, at least in their surviving forms. Thompson dated the Middle Dutch manuscript as "second half of the fourteenth century,"[11] but he refused to grant it any special status for Chaucerians.

Thompson presented in Bryan and Dempster three full texts in addition to the Heile story. The first, Masuccio's Italian novella (Thompson's number 4), is dated 1476, nearly a century after Chaucer wrote *The Miller's Tale*. This story of Viola is broadly similar to Chaucer's tale, but it has both a husband and three visiting lovers rather than two, has no predicted flood, has no tubs at all, and has the third lover, the smith, be the favored lover of Viola and hero of the story.

The second, Schumann's German tale of a rich merchant (Thompson's number 7), is dated even later (1559). In it a merchant hears in church that fire and flood will ravage the earth at the Last Judgment. To protect himself, the merchant builds an iron-reinforced ship and suspends it by a large hawser outside his home, then climbs up a plank to sleep in it each night. His wife, sleeping alone in the house and feeling "night-hunger," takes up with both a young priest (not the one who preaches about the Last Judgment) and a smith. One night while the priest is with her the smith knocks on her window and asks for a kiss. The priest goes to the window and exposes his hindquarters for the smith to kiss. The smith then runs for a hot iron and brands the priest's backside when he bares it a second time. When the merchant hears the cry "water," he cuts the hawser suspending his ship, which crashes to the ground, and he is carried, half-dead, into his house.

The third, Hans Sach's German anecdote (Thompson's number 8) is also late (1537) and very distant from *The Miller's Tale*. In this sixty-line yarn, a smith is married to a lovely wife. To get rid of the husband so that he can have his way with the wife, the village priest predicts in church that a great rain is coming. The smith secretly suspends a kneading tub for himself in the rafters, but he makes no provision for his wife, who takes advantage of her husband's unexplained absence by accepting the priest into her bed. Later, when the smith's apprentice knocks at her chamber door and begs for a kiss, the priest puts his buttocks out the window. There is no explanation for why he selects the window when the apprentice is already in the house. Details in the rest of the story are somewhat similar to those in *The Miller's Tale*.

Thompson was aware that these three analogues were not likely sources of

[11] Thompson, p. 112. In the note he says vaguely that "the appearance of the manuscript indicates a date about 1400, more probably before than after." I shall have more to say about the date of the Middle Dutch MS at the end of this introduction.

The Miller's Tale, but he printed them because "they give us valuable suggestions touching the lost source" of *The Miller's Tale*.[12] Though he was convinced that the real source was French, it did not seem to bother him that not a single one of the ten analogues he cites is French. That fact that might have suggested to him either that this particular comic tale never appeared in France or that the plot of *The Miller's Tale* would have been something of an anomaly in the usual collections of French fabliaux.[13] Moreover, five of the analogues Thompson cites are in German, a language that Chaucer probably did not know, two are in English, two in Italian, and one in Middle Dutch. In part because of their dates and in part because of their narrative elements, I believe that except for the Middle Dutch tale, all of the stories that Thompson cites are more likely to have been influenced by *The Miller's Tale* than *The Miller's Tale* is to have been influenced by them.

In their chapter on *The Miller's Tale* in their collection of editions and translations of medieval fabliaux,[14] Benson and Andersson, curiously, give us no analogues that Chaucer was likely to have known and used. In addition to the versions by Masuccio, Schumann, and Sachs that Thompson had selected, they present eight more versions, two in Latin, two in English, and one each in Italian, French, German, and Swiss. The editors mention the Middle Dutch tale of Heile, but do not include it because it is printed and translated in Bryan and Dempster and because, like Thompson, they were interested not in identifying the closest analogue or most likely source for *The Miller's Tale* but in presenting works that "illustrate the general nature of . . . the fabliau."[15] How far Benson and Andersson stray from true analogues to *The Miller's Tale* is suggested by their inclusion of *Bérenger of the Long Arse*, a thirteenth-century French fabliau, which they admit that Chaucer "probably did not" know.[16] The central character is the son of a usurer who, to settle a debt owed him by a nobleman, has his lazy son made a knight and marries her to the nobleman's daughter. After some years of a disappointing marriage, the daughter, to prove her husband's worthlessness, disguises herself as a knight and challenges her foolish husband to a fight. In the end the cowardly husband agrees to kiss the challenger's arse rather than fight him. When the husband asks the strange knight what his name is, his wife answers, "Bérenger of the Long Arse." The story has no similarity with *The Miller's Tale* except possibly the fact that in it a

12 Bryan and Dempster, p. 107.

13 Sandra Pierson Prior, in "Parodying Typology and the Mystery Plays in the Miller's Tale," *Journal of Medieval and Renaissance Studies* 16 (1986), says for example that "the dominant role given to Nicholas is somewhat of a departure from the more common fabliau practice, which usually gives the wife the major responsibility in the tricky deceit of her husband" (p. 57 n3). More work needs to be done on the differences between Chaucer's practice in *The Miller's Tale* and "common fabliau practice." For example, three of the key physical properties of *The Miller's Tale* – a window as site for romancing, hanging tubs, and a hot poker used for revenge – do not appear in any of the Old French fabliaux that I have examined, whereas all appear in *Heile van Beersele*. My study, which includes a revision of my terminology for the terms "source" and "analogue," is now in press at *Studies in the Age of Chaucer*.

14 Larry D. Benson and Theodore M. Andersson, *The Literary Context of Chaucer's Fabliaux: Texts and Translations* (Indianapolis, IN, 1971), pp. 3–77.

15 Benson and Andersson, p. x.

16 Benson and Andersson, p. 11.

woman also bares her bottom for the kiss of a man she despises. Benson and Andersson also include Heinrich Wittenweiler's fifteenth-century "Ring," a long meandering tale having one unimportant scene in which a woman presents her buttocks at a window for a kiss. The kiss is never delivered, however, and the events surrounding that non-event have no connection with *The Miller's Tale*.

Benson and Andersson present in their chapter on the analogues of *The Miller's Tale* Apuleius's Latin "Tale of a Poor Fellow's Cuckoldry," from the second century BCE. This tale is about a clever wife who, caught with her lover when her husband comes home unexpectedly, hides her lover in a tub and then pretends that she has sold the tub to him at a generous price. This tale, unlike *The Miller's Tale*, has only two men, not three, the tub is on the floor, not suspended from the roof-beams, there is no predicted flood, no window scene, no buttocks kissing, no farting, no revenge with a hot poker, no broken arm. The climax of the tale is not the scorching of the buttocks or the punishment of the men – these plot elements do not appear at all – but rather the visitor's sex act with the wife as she leans forward over the tub to give her husband, now crouched in the tub, directions about how to clean it. The differences are far more impressive than the similarities. Besides, if Chaucer did know the story of the clever wife who hides her lover in a tub, then tells her husband that she has sold him the tub, he would have known it not in Apuleius's ancient Latin but in Boccaccio's fourteenth-century Italian. That tale becomes the second tale of the seventh day of the *Decameron*. Boccaccio elaborates on the plot in some interesting ways, but he does not change the basic outline of it that he learned from Apuleius.

The question of whether Chaucer knew Boccaccio's *Decameron* has been much debated, but many modern scholars are coming to believe that he did know it.[17] Although there is no one tale in the *Decameron* that can be said to serve as a source for *The Miller's Tale*, some half dozen of Boccaccio's hundred tales (*Decameron* III, 4 and 8; VII, 2, 4 and 6; and VIII, 7)[18] demonstrate elements that could have influenced Chaucer as he wrote *The Miller's Tale*. Still, although each of these tales has at least one element that can be said to be at least vaguely reminiscent of some elements we also find in *The Miller's Tale*, and although these tales are old enough that Chaucer could have known them in the versions that have come down to us, none of the parallels themselves provide convincing evidence of Chaucer's indebtedness to them.

Several other scholars have found suggestive hints that may indicate the sources of Chaucerian allusions or side-borrowings, or modern retellings of *The*

[17] See Helen Cooper's chapter on "The Frame" in vol.1 of *Sources and Analogues of the Canterbury Tales*, ed. Robert M. Correale and Mary Hamel (Cambridge: D. S. Brewer, 2002), esp. pp. 7–13, the various essays included in the Koff and Schildgen volume, and N. S. Thompson's *Chaucer, Boccaccio and the Debate of Love: A Comparative Study of the Decameron and the Canterbury Tales* (Oxford, 1996).

[18] See "Just Say Yes, Chaucer Knew the *Decameron*" (pp. 25–46) in Koff and Schildgen, where I discuss the essay by Donald McGrady, "Chaucer and the *Decameron* Reconsidered," *Chaucer Review* 12 (1977): 1–26. McGrady finds evidence that Chaucer drew from several of the tales in the *Decameron* when he wrote *The Miller's Tale*.

Miller's Tale, but they do not immediately concern us here. Among these are Harder,[19] Pearcy,[20] Bratcher and von Kreisler,[21] Poteet,[22] Vaughan,[23] and, more recently, Biggs and Howes.[24]

Chaucer, Flanders, and Middle Dutch

Having set aside the other analogues, I return to the Middle Dutch *Heile van Beersele*. In what follows I argue not, as Barnouw and others have done, that the Middle Dutch tale is collateral proof that Chaucer's real source was a French fabliau now lost, but that it was itself, if not assuredly the direct source of Chaucer's *Miller's Tale*, then the strongest candidate for that honor – what I have called a hard analogue with near-source status. Part of my argument lies in Chaucer's known personal connections with Flanders (what is now Belgium, though boundaries have shifted down through the years). The town of Bruges in western Flanders is, after all, less than a hundred miles from Dover, and Chaucer can be assumed to have made diplomatic or business-oriented trips there. It seems plausible, then, that he could have encountered some version of the story of Heile on one of his journeys. But even if he did not encounter it in Flanders, Flemish businessmen were known to travel to London with some frequency, and Chaucer could have heard the story from one of them, and even borrowed or purchased a written copy very similar to the one I print below.

Also relevant are Chaucer's own personal and family connections with the Low Countries. When Chaucer's patron John of Gaunt (that is, Ghent, a city just inland from Bruges), married Katherine Swynford, he married into a family from Hainault, a province on the southwestern border of Belgium bordering on France. When Chaucer himself married Phillipa Roet, he married the daughter of Paon de Roet, a knight of Hainault. In doing so he became a member of what

19 Kelsey B. Harder, "Chaucer's Use of the Mystery Plays in the *Miller's Tale*," *Modern Language Quarterly* 17 (1956): "Although we cannot dismiss the possibility that Chaucer based the tale on some literary source which has been lost, the connections with the mystery plays in this particular instance are too numerous and pervasive to be discounted" (p. 198).

20 Roy J. Pearcy, in "A Minor Analogue to the Branding in 'The Miller's Tale,'" *Notes and Queries* 214 (1969), reports that in one of Gautier le Leu's tales a foolish knight accidentally brands the backside of a sleeping guest, thinking it a wineskin. He hastens to admit that the parallel with the branding of Nicholas "is clearly not close" (p. 333).

21 James T. Bratcher and Nicolai von Kreisler, in "The Popularity of the *Miller's Tale*," *Southern Folklore Quarterly* 35 (1971) write that "In the United States alone, in this century, at least three analogues of the tale have circulated either orally or in printed form" (p. 325). One is an oral tale in Spanish collected in New Mexico, one an oral tale in English collected in Arkansas, and one a 1950s novel about a woman named Julie, from Joplin, Missouri.

22 Daniel P. Poteet II, in "Avoiding Women in Times of Affliction: An Analogue for the *'Miller's Tale'* A 3589–91," *Notes and Queries* 217 (1972): 89–90, finds a parallel between Nicholas's insistence that John not sleep with his wife the night of the "flood" and a similar suggestion in *Mirk's Festial.*

23 M. F. Vaughan, in "Chaucer's Imaginative One-Day Flood," *Philological Quarterly* 60 (1981), locates in popular tradition "a possible apocalyptic source" (p. 119) for the idea that the flood, unlike the biblical one, will come and disappear rapidly.

24 Frederick M. Biggs and Laura L. Howes, in "Theophany in the Miller's Tale," *Medium Ævum* 66 (1996), find what they call a "biblical source" (p. 268) in Exod. 33.23 for Nicholas's putting his arse out the window.

Garbáty calls "the Hainault Mafia."[25] I would not want to make too much of evidence that is, after all, circumstantial, but it seems entirely possible that Chaucer had visited the nearby Low Countries and that he was somewhat familiar with its language. Certainly it would have been very much to the advantage of any Englishman involved in finance, customs work, diplomacy, or commerce to know Middle Dutch. In addition to those incentives, Chaucer had a wife and patron with Flemish connections.

There are more direct indicators that Chaucer understood enough Middle Dutch that he could have made sense of a manuscript of *Heile van Beersele*. We find, for one thing, growing evidence that he was familiar with other narratives and plays in Middle Dutch.[26] Furthermore, we have not far to seek for evidence that Middle Dutch was in many ways similar to Middle English.

The Heile story is about an engaging young woman who makes separate arrangements with three men to come to her house for sexual services. In line 41 we read, "Terde was hare gebuer, .i. smet."[27] It would not have been so difficult for Chaucer to understand that the line meant, "Third was her neighbor, a smith." Here are some other examples of lines in the Heile story (with my modern English renderings) that Chaucer would have had little trouble understanding, even if he was not fully fluent in Middle Dutch:

27	Te comene daer si ware	To come where she was
53	Dus laghen si in hare jolijt	Thus lay they in their revelry (jolity)
56	Ende seide, "Heile, laet mi inne."	And said, "Heile, let me in."
57	"Ic ben hier."	"I am here."
59	Sprac Willem, "wie es daer?"	Said Willem, "who is there?"
67	Heile seide, "daer boven hangt .i. bac"	Heile said, "there above hangs a trough"
83	Beide met watre ende met viere	Both with water and with fire
87	Grote ende clene, jonge ende oude	Great and small, young and old
134	Ende staect int vier ende maket heet	And stuck it in the fire and made it hot
141	"Ochtic sta hier al den nacht"	"Or else stay here all night"
149	"Water, water, ic ben doet!"	"Water, water, I am dead!"
157	"Dwater es comen sekerlike"	"The water has come surely."

[25] Thomas J. Garbáty discusses Chaucer's many connections to Hainault in "Chaucer, the Customs, and the Hainault Connection," *Studies in the Age of Chaucer*, Proceedings no. 2 (1987): 95–102. Garbáty also cites evidence, admittedly slender, that some of Chaucer's own near ancestors came from the town of Malines, just north of medieval Hainault in the Duchy of Brabant. See also his humorous follow-up note in the *Chaucer Newsletter* 14 (no. 1, 1992): 2, 7.

[26] See Peter G. Beidler and Terese Decker, "*Lippijn*: A Middle Dutch Source for the *Merchant's Tale*?" in *Chaucer Review* 23 (1989): 236–50, and Peter G. Beidler, "The *Reeve's Tale* and Its Flemish Analogue," *Chaucer Review* 26 (1992): 283–92. The full text and translation of a Middle Dutch analogue to *The Reeve's Tale* appears in volume I of this edition of *Sources and Analogues*, pp. 56–67. Chaucer's knowledge of Middle Dutch is also apparent elsewhere. In *The Manciple's Tale*, for example, we read, "The Flemyng seith, and lerne it if thee leste,/ That litel janglyng causeth muchel reste" (IX, 349–50). That expression has been traced to a specific Flemish proverb, "Luttle onderwinds maakt grote rust" ["Little jangling makes great peace (rest)"]. See Donald Baker's note to these lines in *A Variorum Edition of The Works of Geoffrey Chaucer, Volume II: The Canterbury Tales* Part 10 *The Manciple's Tale* (Norman, OK, 1984), p. 126.

[27] All quotations from *Heile van Beersele* are cited by line number from my edition below.

Because so many of the words in the two languages are cognate, and because the phrasing and the grammatical structure of the two languages are often similar, it is entirely possible that Chaucer, given his interest and proficiency in various European languages and literatures, and used to dealing with Flemish merchants in London, perhaps with Flemish financiers in Bruges, and perhaps with members of his own family and the family of his patron, would have been able to make his way in reading the language of the Heile story.

I have noted (with the generous assistance of Geert Claassens) the Middle Dutch origins of a number of the unusual words in *The Miller's Tale*. These do not, of course, prove a definite connection between Chaucer's tale and *Heile van Beersele*, but they do suggest that Chaucer might well have known enough Middle Dutch to draw some of his words from that register. I cite the words in the order in which they appear in *The Miller's Tale*, with the line references all to *The Riverside Chaucer*. The asterisk (*) indicates that the word appears in *The Miller's Tale* but nowhere else in Chaucer:

lendes, * 3237 (also 3304): "A barmclooth . . ./ Upon hir lendes." The Middle Dutch (MD) noun "lende" (plural "lendes") refers to the side of the body, the thighs or groin (loins), but can in some contexts be a euphemism for a person's private parts.

tapes, * 3241: "The tapes of hir white voluper." The MD noun "tappe" means ribbon.

popelot, * 3253: "So gay a popelote." The MD noun "poppe" means doll.

crul, 3314: "Crul was his heer." The MD noun "crul" means curly. Used elsewhere in Chaucer only of the Squire in I 81.

strouted, * 3315: "strouted as a fanne large and brode." The MD verb "strooyen" means to spread out, with the preterite form being "stroyeden."

shode, 3316: "Ful streight and evene lay his joly shode." The MD noun "scheide" means parted hair. Used elsewhere in Chaucer only in *The Knight's Tale* in I 2007.

brewhous, * 3334: "nas brewhous ne taverne." The MD noun "brouhuus" means brewery.

tappestere, 3336: "Ther any gaylard tappestere was." The MD nouns "tapster" and "tapsteregge" mean barmaid, female bartender. Used elsewhere in Chaucer only of the Friar in I 142.

squaymous, * 3337–8: "somdeel squaymous/ Of fartyng." The MD adjective "scamel" means ashamed or sensitive.

shot, * 3358 (also 3695): "dressed hym up by a shot-wyndowe." The MD noun "schot" means a wooden board with which a door or window is closed. The verb "shot," of course, is used elsewhere in Chaucer.

capyng, * 3444: "Nicholas sat evere capyng upright." The MD verb "capen" means to stare or gaze, with overtones of the modern English "gape."

kiked, * 3445: "As he had kiked on the newe moone." The MD verb "kiken" means to look up, stare.

haspe, * 3470: "And by the haspe he haaf it of atones." The MD noun "haspe" means clamp, bolt, or shackle, in all instances referring to ways to close a door.

trogh, 3620 (also 3548, 3627): "He . . . geteth hym a knedyng trogh." The MD noun "troch/trog" means tub, especially one used for dough or for feeding domestic animals. Used elsewhere by Chaucer only in *The Reeve's Tale* in I 4043.

tubbe, * 3621 (also 3627): "And after that a tubbe." The MD noun "tubbe" means tub.

shaar, * 3763: "He sharpeth shaar." The MD noun "schare" refers to a cutting tool, specifically the part of a plow that cuts and turns over the earth.

kultour, * 3763 (also 3776, 3785, 3812): "He sharpeth shaar and kultour bisily." The

MD noun "couter" means a cutting tool, specifically that knife-like part of the plow that cuts the earth in front of the plow to make it easier for the plowshare to turn the earth over neatly.

I have not made a full study of the possible Middle Dutch origins of all of the words and phrases[28] in *The Miller's Tale*. Rather, I have selected above words that Chaucer used rarely. Thirteen of these words he uses only in *The Miller's Tale*; the rest he uses in only one other place. I do not mean to overstate a case that is, finally, uncertain. For some of these words we can also find cognates in other medieval languages besides Middle Dutch – Anglo-Norman, Old French, German, and Anglo-Saxon. And, to be sure, it may be mere coincidence that, in a tale for which the nearest analogue is a Middle Dutch narrative, Chaucer could have drawn from Middle Dutch so many words that he never or rarely used elsewhere. All I want to do here is establish the possibility that Chaucer knew enough Middle Dutch that he could have read *Heile van Beersele* with at least some comprehension.

Parallel elements

In claiming that *Heile van Beersele* was the most likely source for *The Miller's Tale* I am persuaded primarily by the many parallels between the plots, characters, and language in the two tales. I recognize, of course, that the two tales are different in many and important ways. For example, the Middle Dutch tale is only 190 lines long in the Germanic four-stress verse, while the English is 668 decasyllabic lines. In the Middle Dutch tale Heile is an unmarried prostitute, while Alisoun is a wife. In the Middle Dutch tale the first man is a presumably unmarried miller, while John is Alisoun's husband and a carpenter. In the Middle Dutch tale the first man hears the prediction of the flood that night, while John hears it a day or two earlier. In the Middle Dutch tale the tub is already suspended from the beam, while in Chaucer it is one of three gathered and hung there that day for a specific purpose. In the Middle Dutch tale the second man is a priest, while Nicholas is a student. In the Middle Dutch tale the third man is a smith who goes home to prepare a hot iron, while Absolon is a parish clerk who borrows the hot iron from a local smith. In the Middle Dutch tale the priest presents his buttocks out the window twice, while Alisoun presents her buttocks the first time, then lets Nicholas present his. And so on. The differences are many, most of them logically enough explained as adjustments that Chaucer made to suit his own narrative purposes as he transformed the brief and darkly misogynist Middle Dutch story about the evils of associating with prostitutes into a humorous send-up of unrealistic romances like *The Knight's Tale* and a light-hearted portrayal of foolish husbands, proud students, and corrupt clerics.

[28] Chaucer also used several phrases in *The Miller's Tale* that could easily have derived from Middle Dutch expressions. For example, Chaucer's "I nam nat lief" (3510) would have been rendered "Mi es niet lief" in MD, and would have meant "I do not like." Similarly, Chaucer's "ne roghte nat a bene" (3772) would have been rendered "ne roekte niet ene bone" in MD, and would have meant the same – "cared not a bean" or "couldn't care less."

Even while admitting – indeed, celebrating – these differences, I note that the broad similarities in plot and character are persuasive evidence of connection. In both tales a pretty young woman has three men wanting her. The first man is suspended in a tub while she makes love with the second. A third man shows up and wants to make love to her. She tries to send him away, but he insists on at least a kiss. Instead of kissing the woman's mouth, however, he kisses the buttocks presented to him out the window. The third man then, realizing that he has been tricked, runs angrily to fetch a hot iron, returns, and begs for a second kiss. When the second man presents his buttocks, the spurned lover strikes and burns him. The scorched lover's shouts for water cause the first man, above in the tub, to think that the great flood that he has been led to expect has indeed come. He cuts the rope suspending his tub and expects to float to safety, but there is no water beneath him and he falls to the floor. The stories end with statements reminding readers that the men who associate with pretty young women will be punished.

My claim is obviously not that the two tales are identical, but that Chaucer may well have learned the broad outlines of the tale from the earlier Middle Dutch story of Heile. That claim is strengthened by eighteen specific parallels that, taken together, urge the likelihood of direct influence. In some of them (numbers 5, 6, 8, 9, 10 and12–17) we find verbal parallels:

1. Excuses for telling a salacious tale. Both authors give excuses for telling an indecorous tale. The author of *Heile van Beersele* starts his tale by reporting that he tells it because a friend had made him promise to do so: "Vertellen sal, dore ene bede/ Die .i. goet geselle ane mi dede,/ Dies mi niet en woude verlaten" (11–13, "at the request that one good fellow made me, who would not leave me alone"). Chaucer gives a slightly different excuse: "for I moot reherce/ Hir tales alle, be they bettre or werse,/ Or elles falsen som of my mateere" (3173–5). Despite the differences, both authors feel the need to foreground the telling of a salacious tale with an explanation designed to head off blame for telling it.

2. Specific town. The author of *Heile van Beersele* gives the story a specific location in the town of Antwerp. Chaucer locates his story in Oxford. The towns are different, of course, but both authors felt the need to anchor their improbable narratives to a specific contemporary location.

3. Specific time indicators. In the story of Heile, the miller, the priest, and the smith make appointments at specific times in the night with Heile. Willem is to come in the early evening ("rechts in den avont" [38]), the priest when the evening bell is rung ("die slaepclocke hadde vernomen" [40]), and Hughe the smith when the night bell is rung ("die diefclocke geluut ware" [43]). The men come at the appointed times: Willem at dusk ("quam tuschen dach ende nacht" [47]), the priest in the evening ("dat was slaepcloc tijt" [54]), and the impatient smith perhaps just a bit early for his appointment because he thinks he has been waiting too long ("gemert boven sinen wille" [95]). Chaucer also specifies the times that the lovers come to perform their various activities. Although Alisoun makes no appointments with either Nicholas or Absolon, she, John, and Nicholas all climb into their tubs "whan it drow to nyght" (3633). Nicholas and Alisoun climb down their ladders just "Aboute corfew-tyme, or litel moore"

(3645) and then sport in bed "Til that the belle of laudes gan to rynge" (3655). Absolon knocks at Alisoun's window "at cokkes crowe" (3675). For Chaucer, of course, some of the actual times are later because he wants it to be light enough shortly after John comes crashing down that the neighbors can come in to look up into the roof, where John's tub had been suspended, and "laughen at his fantasye" (3840). Still, the specified times are generally parallel in the two tales.

4. Paying for sex. The prostitute Heile receives money for her sexual favors. Alisoun is a wife rather than a whore, but her suitor Absolon treats her as if she were a whore by sending her barter-gifts of wine and ale and cakes. He even offers money: "And, for she was of town, he profred meede;/ For som folk wol ben wonnen for richesse" (3380–1). Later, to get her to open her window for a second kiss he offers her his mother's gold ring: "Ful fyn it is, and therto wel ygrave" (3796). He has no such ring, but in offering it he treats the object of his unholy desires as if she were a prostitute like Heile.

5. Tubs hanging from "balkes." Heile tells Willem, her first lover, to hide in a tub hanging from a beam, "Ane die haenbalke es hi gebonden/ Met enen vasten zele wel" (70–1, "To the crossbeam it is securely bound with a strong rope"). Chaucer, too, specifies that the tubs hang by ropes from the beams, and uses the term "balkes": "hangynge in the balkes" (3626).

6. Drowning all the world. In proclaiming the coming great flood, the Middle Dutch priest predicts "Dat al die werelt verdrinken soude," (85, "That all the world shall be drowned"). Nicholas, similarly, predicts that "This world . . ./ Shal al be dreynt . . ./ Thus shal mankynde drenche" (3519–21). Note the verbal similarities "al"-"al," "werelt"-"world," "soude"-"shal," and "verdrinken"-"dreynt."

7. Knocking and clapping. Hughe the smith raps quietly when he comes to visit Heile: "Vore die dore clopte hi stille" (96, "On the door he knocked softly"). Absolon, similarly, makes his plan to "pryvely knokken at his wyndowe" (3676), and again "knokketh therwithal/ Upon the wyndowe, right as he dide er" (3788–9). And, of course, after Absolon's kiss, Alisoun "clapte the window to" (3740).

8. "Who is there?" Hearing the knocking, Willem asks Heile who is there: "Wie es daer?" (59), a line repeated in line 97 when Heile asks who is knocking. The question is asked again by Alisoun when Absolon knocks at her window: "Who is ther . . .?" (3790).

9. Enthusiastic arse-kissing. Hughe kisses the priest's arse with great enthusiasm: "custe spapen ers al dare/ Met soe heten sinne" (118–19, "kissed the priest's arse right there with such burning desire"). Absolon kisses Alisoun's arse with similar enthusiasm: "with his mouth he kiste hir naked ers/ Ful savourly" (3734–5). Note the verbal similarities "custe"-"kiste," and "ers"-"ers." It is interesting that Chaucer's reference to Absolon's "hoote love" growing cold just after the kiss (3754) may reflect the "heten sinne" of his counterpart's kiss.

10. Revengeful resolve. Both authors take us into the affronted lovers' thoughts, and both lovers think revenge. Hughe thinks, "hier com ic weder" (130, "I'll come back here"). Absolon thinks, "I shal thee quyte" (3746). And it

is interesting that Absolon's desire for vengeance – "Of this despit awroken for to be" (3752) – may well be an echo of the word "gewroken" used at the end of *Heile van Beersele*, where we are told that Hughe "hadde . . . hem wel gewroken" (185, "had avenged himself well"). In both tales the word for vengeance is used specifically with respect to the third lover's avenging the humiliation of the arse-kiss trick.

11. Nearby blacksmith shop. Both plots require that a blacksmith shop be near enough that the spurned visitor can go get a hot iron and return before it cools. Hughe the blacksmith's shop is close to Heile's dwelling: "Hine woende van daer niet verre" (132, "He lived from there not far"). Absolon's friend Gerveys lives just "over the strete" (3760).

12. All sweetness and love. Hughe says, "Heile, lieve minne/ Ic moet nu endelike inne,/ Ochtic moet cussen u mondekijn" (137–9, "Heile, dear love, I must now come in at last, or else I must kiss your little mouth"). Absolon says, "my sweete leef . . . if thou me kisse" (3792, 3797). Note the verbal similarities "cussen"-"kisse," and "lieve minne"-"my . . . leef." Chaucer expands the possessive-case Middle Dutch "lieve minne" into various other possessive-case epithets that Absolon uses with Alisoun: "my sweete cynamome" (3699), "lemman myn" (3700), and "my deerelyng" (3793).

13. Water! When the priest feels the hot iron, he cries out, repeating the word "water" twice: "Water, water, ic ben doet!" (149, "Water, water, I am dead!"). Nicholas, with obvious verbal similarity, cries out, "Help! Water! Water! Help . . .!" (3815). There may be an echo of "ic ben doet" in "wende for to dye" (3813) two lines earlier than the "Water! Water!" line in Chaucer.

14. It's come! Willem, above in the tub, thinks, "nu eest waerheide/ Van dat die pape te nacht seide./ Dwater es comen sekerlike" (155–7, "Now is happening what the priest said tonight. The water has come surely"). John, similarly, thinks, "Allas, now comth Nowelis flood!" (3818). Note the verbal similarities "nu"-"now," "comen"-"comth."

15. Severed rope. Willem takes his knife "Ende sneet ontwee den repe" (162, "And cut in two the rope"). John takes his axe and "smoot the corde atwo" (3820). Note the verbal similarities "sneet"-"smoot" and "ontwee"-"atwo."

16. And down comes all. With the rope severed, "quam Willem met allen/ Ter erden neder ghevallen" (168–9, "Willem came with everything falling down to the ground"). Similarly, "And doun gooth al . . ./ Upon the floor" (3821–3). Note the verbal similarities "allen"-"al."

17. A broken arm. The fall to the floor breaks Willem's arm: "hi doe brac ontwee/ sinen arm" (170–1, "he then broke in two his arm"). Like Willem, old John "brosten hadde his arm" (3829). Note the verbal similarities "brac"-"brosten" and "arm"-"arm."

18. The men are punished. For the Middle Dutch author all three men are punished, Willem with broken bones, the priest with a burned arse, and the smith with a misapplied kiss. Heile is not punished. For Chaucer, as well, John is punished with a broken bone, Nicholas with a burned arse, and Absolon with a misapplied kiss. Like Heile, Alisoun gets off without punishment.

I am aware, of course, that some of what I call verbal similarities may, taken individually, be no more than chance lexical parallels. Still, taken together with

the narrative parallels, the various lexical parallels between the two stories suggest the strong possibility of direct influence. There are other parallels, as well. The Middle Dutch "diefclocke" in line 43 ("thief-bell," the bell that signaled to town-dwellers that anyone found in the streets after it had rung may well be a thief) finds an echo in line 3791 of *The Miller's Tale*, where Alisoun wonders whether the late-arriving Absolon is "a theef." It is interesting that Willem is specifically said to "sit" in his trough (see line 87), just as John is (see lines 3637, 3641, 3819), rather than to lie or huddle or crouch or squat in it. There might be an echo of the Middle Dutch "mese" (121, titmouse) in the Middle English "if she hadde been a mous" (3346). And while we hear no verbal echo of the Middle Dutch "die cavele op end neder" (129, "vertical mouth" or "up and down mouth") in the Middle English "nether ye" (3852), it is interesting that both writers slyly compare "unmentionable" parts of a woman's body with mentionable parts of her face. Surely these accumulated parallels call into serious question the influential assumption, started so many years ago by Barnouw, that the true source of *The Miller's Tale* must have been in French. The sorts of parallels I have noted above suggest that the linguistic origins of the tale of the shenanigans of Alisoun and her lovers could be a Middle Dutch narrative. I can think of no good reason, then, not to assume a connection between *Heile van Beersele* and *The Miller's Tale*.

Which way the connection?

I have been saying that *Heile van Beersele*, or some near version of it, is directly connected with *The Miller's Tale*. We cannot ignore the possibility that Chaucer's narrative came first and influenced the Middle Dutch one, since we cannot identify the precise dates of either of them. That possibility has been suggested, directly or indirectly, more than once. Ross argues that Chaucer himself was the originator of the story,[29] as do Biggs and Howes.[30] I give here my

29 Thomas W. Ross, in his critical commentary to the tale in *A Variorum Edition of The Works of Geoffrey Chaucer, Volume II: The Canterbury Tales: The Miller's Tale* Part 3 (Norman, OK, 1983), wisely questions the existence of a lost French source, but, eager to give Chaucer credit for originality, he largely ignores the Middle Dutch story. "In the absence of evidence of a direct source," he tells us, "we must conclude that to Chaucer belongs the laurel for this masterpiece of narrative" (p. 6). My view is that accepting *Heile van Beersele* as the most likely source, far from denying Chaucer his full share of originality, helps scholars to measure the considerable extent of that originality.

30 In their 1996 *Medium Ævum* article, Biggs and Howes state that "The lack of motivation for the speech [that is, the priest's prediction of the end of the world in *Heile van Beersele*] . . . suggests that the author of *Heile* was influenced by Chaucer's version, rather than that the two stories descended from a common source" (p. 171). In a paper at the Medieval Congress in Kalamazoo, MI, in 1997, Frederick Biggs argued, on the basis his analysis of the characters, plots, and themes in *Heile van Beersele* and *The Miller's Tale*, that Chaucer originated the narrative and that his is the direct source of the simpler and less logical Middle Dutch one. In an expansion of that paper, just published as we go to press, "The Miller's Tale and Heile van Beersele," *Review of English Studies*, n.s. 56 (2005): 497–523, Biggs argues at length for the priority of Chaucer's version. He believes that *Heile van Beersele* is a poor retelling of the plot that Chaucer's created. Much of his evidence depends on his view of the unexplained and unlikely tub hanging from the beams in Heile's bedroom. I quite agree that Chaucer does a far better job of explaining how and why the tubs are there, but I think that Chaucer improved on the plot that he found in some version of the Heile story rather than that the author of the Heile story badly remembered or artistically botched his rendition of Chaucer's tale.

reasons for thinking that Chaucer's wonderfully complex tale is derived from the shorter, simpler, and more narrowly anecdotal Middle Dutch tale.

1. Date. Most scholars now think that Chaucer wrote *The Miller's Tale* in the 1390s, perhaps not long before his death, or in any case not earlier than the 1380s. We can be even less precise about the date of *Heile van Beersele*, though most who have studied the matter date it as Thompson did, in the second half of the fourteenth century. Geert Claassens, who in private correspondence supplied much of the information in this and the following paragraph, has made his own analysis of the date of the Thorpe MS: "It is indeed a beautiful manuscript, very neatly and regularly written. There are no illustrations, but there are lovely 'droleriën' connected to cadels (ornamented letters at the top of a page). There are funny faces, not really connected to the stories or structure of the book, but indicative of the care that the scribe took in producing it. It would appear that the initial purchaser of the manuscript would have paid a generous sum for it. I have checked for paleographical indications which might improve or narrow down the dating of the manuscript. There are surely no indications to date it into the fifteenth century – it's clear-cut fourteenth century – and some indications to place it around 1350. I think that a dating of around 1350–75 is rather safe. There are no indications that would justify a dating before 1350, but the use of the so-called 'tongue-e' at the end of the line, in combination with the sporadic use of small letters in the capital column, make a dating in the third quarter of the fourteenth century plausible. Until further evidence turns up, I would accept such a dating."

The Thorpe MS in the Royal Library of Brussels is difficult to date precisely in part because it is made up of two miscellanies that were bound together as a book in the early seventeenth century, with some of the quires put in the wrong place. The miscellany that contains the story of Heile is actually the more recent of the two. It is made up primarily of a Middle Dutch translation of the *Romance of the Rose*,[31] with five much shorter texts added at the end, almost as fillers. That these five are added at the end of a longer work suggests at least the possibility that those five texts were older than the manuscript itself, were circulated separately, and were merely transcribed into it – tacked on? – from earlier copies the scribe or workshop had at hand. If so, the Heile story may well be older than the miscellany manuscript itself, and thus may predate 1350. Certainly the beauty of the copy in the Thorpe MS and the lack of revisions or crossouts indicates that it is a professional copy of an existing text, not a text in the process of being created, and that suggests, as well, at least one pre-Thorpe copy that Chaucer could also have known.

Three of these shorter texts added after the end of the *Romance of the Rose* are "boerden" or short comic tales, and one of those three is *Heile van Beersele*. The other two are retellings of earlier stories about husbands, wives, and sexual relations. One, about a fisherman who pretends to cut off his penis to encourage

[31] It is tempting to imagine that Chaucer might have wanted to consult this Dutch version of the *Romance of the Rose*, and in doing so came across the *Heile van Beersele* attached to it, but that is mere speculation – at least until someone examines it to see if the Dutch *Romance* version might have influenced Chaucer's own version.

his wife to take a greater interest in having intercourse with him, is a reworking of a French fabliau. Another, about a woman who tries to accept a new lover in her bed while her husband sleeps next to her in the same bed, is a reworking of a tale familiar in German literature and in *Decameron* VII, 8. That both "boerden" are Middle Dutch reworkings of earlier story lines suggests at least the possibility that the third comic tale, *Heile van Beersele*, is one also. If so, then the actual composition of the story of Heile's adventures might well predate the version that appears in the Thorpe MS. And if that is so, then of course Chaucer might have seen an earlier copy or version of the story.

Though much of the thinking that goes into the dating of the Heile story is speculation, what we can say of that dating suggests that the Middle Dutch tale was probably written before the English one.

2. Authorship. We know that Chaucer wrote *The Miller's Tale*, and that he almost certainly traveled to the Low Countries, had contact with Flemish merchants, and knew some Middle Dutch. We know nothing of the author of *Heile van Beersele*, have no idea whether he knew Middle English or ever traveled to England. We know without any doubt that Chaucer had a deep interest in continental literature, that he had narrative sources for virtually all of his stories, and that he changed them in many ways to suit a fictional teller or to adapt them to his own narrative purposes. We know nothing whatever of the working habits of the original author of *Heile van Beersele*. It is more logical, then, to imagine Chaucer learning from a Middle Dutch story than to imagine an unnamed Middle Dutch writer traveling to England, acquiring a copy of a late manuscript of one of Chaucer's least-circulated tales, learning enough English to read it, and returning with it to Flanders to rewrite it as the inferior and less logical *Heile van Beersele*.

3. Language. Every medievalist knows the controversy about whether the Middle English *Everyman* preceded or followed the Middle Dutch *Elkerlijc*. Scholars from both nations wanted to claim original authorship for their countryman, but *Elkerlijc* finally emerged as the older one and the direct source of the English translation of it. The controversy about whether *The Miller's Tale* preceded or followed *Heile van Beersele* is less easy to settle on purely linguistic grounds, since we are dealing with two different versions of the sermon-kiss-burn-fall story, not with line-for-line translations from one to the other. Still, the fact that we find in *The Miller's Tale* a number of words that Chaucer uses nowhere else but that could derive from a Middle Dutch lexicon suggests that Chaucer may have been working from a Middle Dutch original when he wrote *The Miller's Tale*. It makes less sense to think that Chaucer came up with those words of possible Middle Dutch origin on his own, and that a Middle Dutch author then located a copy of the English tale and reworked it into Dutch, delighted to find that Chaucer's English had such a "Dutchy" orientation.

4. Literary quality. Both *Heile van Beersele* and *The Miller's Tale* are fast-paced and funny, but no one would claim that the Middle Dutch story is better literature than the English one. Not only is the English one longer and with a much more fully developed and logical plot line, but Chaucer's characters are brilliantly complex. To give only one example, in *Heile van Beersele* we have no explanation for the priest's preaching to Heile a sermon predicting the

end of the world after he has sex with her. In *The Miller's Tale*, on the other hand, we know precisely why Nicholas predicts that a second Flood is coming – because he wants to get rid of the foolish John so that he can bed Alisoun. It is possible that the Middle Dutch author read Nicholas's wonderfully logical and funny and in-character prediction and reduced it in his own tale to something illogical, unfunny, and out-of-character, but it is far easier to imagine that Chaucer saw the problems with what he found in his source and, as he did with so many other tales, improved on it. The evolution of stories is, after all, generally from simple to more complex, not from complex to simple. Incidentally, I do not mean to denigrate the Middle Dutch writer. Far from it. *Heile van Beersele* is a brilliant anecdote and there is no reason not to think that Chaucer admired it. I also think that the original author of *Heile van Beersele* was far more to be admired if he wrote the Heile story from scratch than if he knew Chaucer's more sophisticated version and, in the retelling of it, botched it. Both tellers are much to be admired, the Middle Dutch author for creating such a funny anecdote about a prostitute, the English author for retelling it as one of the most memorably funny marriage stories in all of British literature.

The evidence, then, indicates that *Heile van Beersele* and *The Miller's Tale* are connected, and the weight of probability is that the Middle Dutch tale, or a version very much like it, was a direct source of the English one. It is at least as old as Chaucer's, is in a language of which Chaucer knew at least the rudiments, from a country that he visited and with whose merchants he had frequent dealings. Far more than any of the other extant analogues, which are too distant in time, character, or plot to be considered sources, this one stands out as having a special relationship with Chaucer's story. We can with confidence take *Heile van Beersele* as the basis for comparison with *The Miller's Tale*. Scholars wanting to see what is most distinctively original about Chaucer's tale of Alisoun and her men must look carefully to the story of Heile and hers.

I

Heile of Beersele

(trans. Henk Aertsen)

This is about Heile of Beersele
Who made a fool of those three men.
You have often heard
Tell wonderful adventures
About all kinds of strange things
With accompaniment of the fiddle and singing
And sometimes with playing on the harp;
But such a strange story as in
Antwerp happened once,
Such a one all the people have
Not heard, I think,
As the one, in the Dutch language,
That I shall tell at a request
That one good fellow made me,
Who would not leave me alone.
In Antwerp in the Cow Gate Street[1]
Lived, as I understand,
A very frivolous woman
Named Heile of Beersele,[2]
Who often offered herself for sale
To good fellows whom she favored
And to whom she showed her skill.
Once it happened, as I heard tell,
That to her came three fellows
In one day, as I understand,
One after the other,
Who all asked her for favors,
That she would let them
Come to where she was;

[1] We believe "Coperstraten" to be a simplification or corruption of "Koepoortstraat," which is still the name of a street in the old center of Antwerp – literally "cow port street" or "cow gate street." We assume that in medieval Antwerp this street would have had an actual gate to permit cows daily egress to grazing lands outside the city proper. According to Kruyskamp, "the name of this street is still pronounced as *Koeperstraat* in the local Antwerp dialect" (p. 127).

[2] The name "Heile" was a fairly common name. It may be relevant that the noun "heile" in Middle Dutch means "blissful situation," "blessing," or "merriment." As for "Beersele," Kruyskamp (p. 109) identifies it with the modern town of Beersel just south of Brussels, but there are a number of problems with Kruyskamp's view. For one thing, it is then problematic why and how both Heile and Hughe are now living in Antwerp, more than thirty miles to the north. It may be that Beersele was a medieval village very near Antwerp, or even a section or quarter in Antwerp, and that the place name became submerged as the city grew around it.

I

Heile van Beersele[3]

(from Brussels, Royal Library MS II.1171, "Thorpe Manuscript," 1350–75, fols 330rb–331va)

Dits van Heilen van Beersele fol. 330rb
Die de .iii. jaghede te spele.
Ghi hebt gehoert te menegher ure
Vertrecken scone avonture
Van messeliken dinghen,
Beide vedelen ende singhen
Ende somtijt spelen metter herpen;
Maer alsoe vremde alse t'Antwerpen
Hier voermaels ene ghesciede,
Sone hebbe alle die liede
Niet gehoert, wanic wale,
Alsoe ic u in Dietscher tale
Vertellen sal, dore ene bede
Die .i. goet geselle ane mi dede,
Dies mi niet en woude verlaten.
  T'Antwerpen in der Coperstraten
Woende, alse ic mi versinne,
Ene harde goede ghesellinne
Ende hiet van Bersele Heile,
Die hare dicke maecte veile
Goeden gesellen dien sijs onste,
Ende dien si toende hare conste.
  Eens gevielt, hoerdic vertellen,
Dat ane hare quamen .iii. gesellen
Op enen dach, alsic versta,
Deen vore ende dander na,
Ende die hare alle om vrienscap baden fol. 330va
Dat si hen wilde ghestaden
Te comene daer si ware;

[3] This transcription is newly made from the "Thorpe MS," in the Koninklijke Bibliotheek (Royal Library) in Brussels, though comparisons have been made with the edition in C. Kruyskamp, *De middelnederlandse boerden* (The Hague: Martinus Nijhoff, 1957), pp. 109–14. I have made several small changes to make this edition more accessible to modern readers. For example, I have put the first couplet in italics to separate the title graphically from the tale itself, as well as the word "benedicamus" in line 180 to indicate that the word is Latin. I have added paragraph divisions to indicate natural narrative and conversational units. I have silently expanded abbreviations and used capital letters according to modern usage. I have switched the "v"/"u" and the "j"/"i" in certain places to aid modern readers. Thus, "auonture" becomes "avonture," (line 2, "adventure") and "iolijt" becomes "jolijt" (line 53, "jolity" or "revelry"). I have added all punctuation, including quotation marks, to reflect modern practice. Certain other forms have occasionally been silently changed to help readers of the Middle Dutch text to understand the meaning. For example, in line 14 "Tantwerpen" has been changed to "T'Antwerpen."

They wanted to speak to her
In secret and not otherwise.
As soon as Heile of Beersel realized
That such a wonderful thing had come her way,
She thought in her heart
That she would satisfy them all fully,
As long as she was in control.[4]
The first was, to be sure,
A miller called Willem Hoeft.
She told him to come as soon as it
Was early evening.
The second was a priest whom she told to come
As soon as he heard the evening bell.[5]
The third was her neighbor, a smith,
Whom she told to come as soon as
The night bell was rung.[6]
Thus, they all three took leave of her,
Full of good hope and in high spirits,
And each eagerly awaited his appointed hour.
When it came to the time between day and night,
Willem, who had been waiting, came.
Heile received him gladly
And was with him secretly;
They played the game of love,
For she knew that trade well.
Thus they lay in their revelry,
Until it was time for the evening bell.
Then came the eager priest
And said, "Heile, let me in;
I am here, you well know who."
"Ah, Heile, may God bless you,"
Willem said, "who is there?"
"Willem, I don't know, but
It seems to me it is the priest.
He would say a prayer over my head
And cure me from what ails me."
"Ah, dear Heile, whereto
Can I flee, then, hastily,
So that the priest cannot see me?"
Heile said, "up there hangs a trough
Which I have found convenient here
On many previous occasions;
To the crossbeam it is securely tied
With a strong rope.

[4] Literally, "her thumb did not fail her." In "The Flemish Analogue to Chaucer's *Miller's Tale*: Three Notes," *Notes and Queries* 138, [NS 40] (December 1993): 446–8, David Johnson gives several possible proverbial explanations for the thumb (*dume*) reference.

[5] The *slaepclocke* (lit. "sleep-bell") was rung to mark the transition from day to night and to tell the people it was time to go to bed.

[6] The *diefclocke* (lit. "thief-bell") indicated that anyone found in the streets after it was rung would be considered a thief.

Si wilden spreken jegen hare
Heimeleke ende anders niet.
    Alse Heile van Bersele siet
Dat hare soe scone gevel,
Peinset si in hare herte wel,
Si souds hem allen saden gerume,
Haer en faelgierde hare dume.
    Dat ierste was, des geloeft,
Een moeldre hiet Willem Hoeft.
Dien hiet si comen ter selver stont
Rechts in den avont.
Dander was .i. pape; dien hiet si comen
Alse hi die slaepclocke hadde vernomen.
Terde was hare gebuer, .i. smet;
Dien hiet si comen al ongelet
Alse die diefclocke geluut ware.
    Dus scieden si alle .iii. van hare
Van goeden troeste ende blide,
Ende elke wachte wel sijn getide.
    Alst quam tuschen dach ende nacht,
Quam Willem, diet hadde gewacht.
Heile ontfingkene blidelike
Ende was met hem heimelike.
Oec speelden si der minnen spel,
Want si conste dat ambacht wel.
Dus laghen si in hare jolijt,
Tote dat was slaepcloc tijt.
    Doe quam die pape met fieren sinne
Ende seide, "Heile, laet mi inne.
Ic ben hier, ghi wet wel wie."
    "Ay, Heile, dat u lieve ghescie,"
Sprac Willem, "wie es daer?"
    "Willem, in weets niet, maer
Het dunct mi die pape wesen.
Hi soude mi over thoeft lesen
Ende beteren mi dat mi deert."
    "Ay, lieve Heile, werweert
Maghic haestelike dan vlien, fol. 330vb
Dat mi die pape nine mach sien?"
    Heile seide, "daer boven hangt .i. bac,
Dies ic hier voermaels ghemac
Hadde te menegen stonden;
Ane die haenbalke es hi gebonden
Met enen vasten zele wel.

There you will be better off than anywhere else."
Then Willem told her to let the priest in
And fled into the trough.
Heile brought the priest in a pleasant mood,
And when they the sex-act[7]
Had done three times,
The priest began to quote
Many a word from the Gospels.
He also added
That the time was about to come
When God would destroy the world,
Both with water and with fire;
And that it was to happen soon,
That all the world would be drowned,
The great and the small, young and old.
This Willem heard where he was sitting
High above in that trough,
And thought it might well be true
Since priests read and explain it,
And the Gospel bears witness to it.
Meanwhile then came Hughe
Of Beersele, the smith,
Who thought he had remained outside too long
And had been waiting against his will.
On the door he knocked softly.
Heile spoke: "Who is there?"
"Ah, Heile, it is I, for sure."
Then Heile spoke: "You may not come in."
"Ah, Heile, my very dear love,
Will you then break your promise?
I must at any rate speak to you at last."
"You will not," Heile spoke, "at this moment,
For I am not very well;
You may not come in now."
"Ah, dear Heile, I beg you,
If I may at this moment,
That you will let me kiss your mouth."
Then Heile said to the priest,
"Ah, sir, let this young man kiss
Your behind, he will think no doubt
That it is I and no one else;
You never saw such a good joke."[8]
The priest got up in a hurry
And put his bottom mouth
At once before a little window,
And Hughe thought that it was Heile

[7] The Middle Dutch "wiekewake" is a hapax legomenon – that is to say, it appears only in this one context. That context, however, and the profession of Heile, make it clear enough that it refers to coitus or another sex act.

[8] For a discussion of this line, see Johnson, pp. 448–9.

Daer sidi bat dan ighering el."
Doe hiet Willem den pape in doen
Ende es in den bac gevloen.
Heile dede den pape te ghemake
Ende alsi die wiekewake
Driewerf hadden gheslaghen,
Ghinc die pape liggen ghewaghen
Uter ewangelien menech woert.
Oec soe seidi dit bat voert,
Dat die tijt noch soude comen
Dat God die werelt soude doemen,
Beide met watre ende met viere;
Ende dat soude wesen sciere,
Dat al die werelt verdrinken soude,
Grote ende clene, jonge ende oude.
Dit hoerde Willem daer hi sat
Boven hoge in ghenen bac,
Ende peinsde het mochte wel waer wesen
Sidermeer dat papen lesen,
Ende dewangelie gheeft getughe.
Hieren binnen soe quam Hughe
Van Bersele, die smet,
Die te langhe waende hebben gelet
Ende gemert boven sinen wille.
Vore die dore clopte hi stille.
Heile sprac: "Wie es daer?"
"Ay, Heile, dat benic vore waer."
Doe sprac Heile: "Ghine moget niet inne."
"Ay, Heile, wel lieve minne,
Seldi u gelof dan breken?
Ic moet u emmer endelike spreken."
"Ghine selt," sprac Heile, "teser stont,
Want in ben niet wel ghesont;
Ghine moget niet in comen nu." fol. 331ra
"Ay, lieve Heile, soe biddic u
Ochtic mach teser stont
Dat ghi mi cussen laet uwen mont."
Doe seide Heile toten pape,
"Ay, here, laet cussen desen knape
U achterste inde, hi sal wanen wel
Dat ict ben ende niemen el;
Sone saeghdi boerde nie soe goet."
Die pape stont op metter spoet
Ende sette die cavele sijn
Tehans vore een vensterkijn,
Ende Huge waende dat Heile ware

And kissed the priest's arse right there
With such burning desire
That his nose shot inside,
So that the smith, without doubt,
Very much imagined himself captured
Like a titmouse in the trap.[9]
He was beside himself with rage,
For he was not so foolish
As not to have felt and smelled
That he had kissed an arse,
For the mouth he thought was horizontal
And the bottom mouth vertical.
"Christ knows," he thought, "I'll come back here!"
He ran home as if he were mad;
He did not live far from there.
A big iron he took at once
And stuck it into the fire and made it hot,
So that it was red-hot, quite to his liking,
And ran with it to Heile's door
And called out, "Heile, dear love,
I must now come in at last,
Or else I must kiss your little mouth;
One of the two it must always be,
Or else I shall stand here all night.
The power of your love forces me to this."
The priest, who knew what to do,
Put once again his hindmost hole
Where he had put it before,
And the smith promptly stuck
The red-hot iron into his arse.
Then he loudly sang this verse,
"Water, water, I am dead!"
This he cried out in great fear
For a very long while;
The word died in his mouth.
Then Willem became much concerned,
Who lay hidden there above.
He thought, "now is happening
What the priest said tonight,
The water has surely come,
Now all the earth will be drowned;
But if I can float away,
This trough will keep me alive all right."
He grabbed his knife
And cut in two the rope
That the trough hung by.
Then Willem said this thing:

9 Middle Dutch *mese* means "titmouse" (a small bird) and not "mouse," which was Middle Dutch *muys*. There was apparently a bird trap of some sort that the titmouse reached its beak into for food, but was then trapped. Kruyskamp sees in *cloven* ("trap") a pun on the word for "groove" or "cleft" (p. 112).

Ende custe spapen ers al dare
Met soe heten sinne,
Dat sine nese vloech daer inne,
Soe dat die smet, sonder waen,
Harde wel waende sijn gevaen
Gelijc der mese inder cloven.
    Van torne wart hi al verscoven,
Want hine was niet soe verdoert,
Hine heeft ghevoelt ende gegoert
Dat hi gecust heeft .i. ers,
Want die mont dochte hem staen dwers
Ende die cavele op ende neder.
    "Wetkerst," peinst hi, "hier com ic weder!"
Hi liep thuus alse die was erre;
Hine woende van daer niet verre.
Een groet yser nam hi gereet
Ende staect int vier ende maket heet,
Soe dat gloyde wel ter cure,
Ende lieper mede vore Heilen dure
Ende riep, "Heile, lieve minne,
Ic moet nu endelike inne,
Ochtic moet cussen u mondekijn;
Deen vanden tween moet emmer sijn,
Ochtic sta hier al den nacht,
Hier toe dwingt mi uwer minnen cracht."
    Die pape die sijns niet vergat,
Hine sette weder sijn achterste gat
Daer hijt te voren hadde gheset, fol. 331rb
Ende die smet stac onghelet
Tgheloyende yser in den ers.
    Doe sanc hi lude dit vers:
"Water, water, ic ben doet!"
Dit riep hi met anxte groet
Ene harde lange stont;
Dat woerd verstarf hem in den mont.
    Doe wert Willem in groter sorghen,
Die daer boven lach geborghen.
Hi peinsde, "nu eest waerheide
Van dat die pape te nachte seide,
Dwater es comen sekerlike,
Nu sal verdrinken al erterike;
Maer eest dat ic henen drive,
Die bac houd mi wel te live."
Sijn mes hi gegrepe
Ende sneet ontwee den repe
Daer die bac mede hing.
    Doe seide Willem dese ding:

"Now if God and good fortune grant it,
Willem Hoeft will be sailing."
And thus Willem came with everything
Falling down to the ground,
Which caused him great pain,
For he then broke in two
His arm and his thigh.
The priest dashed into a corner
And thought that it was the devil.
Into a foul pit he fell there,
As people had me know,
He came home all shitty
And his arse all burned,
Put to scorn and shamed.
It would have been better if he had stayed at home
And had sung his *Benedicamus*.
This is how Heile's guests fared.
The smith also had a miserable time,
But he endured it much better,
Since he had raked[10] the priest's bottom;
With that he had avenged himself well.
With your leave this is said:
He who has dealings with whores,
Sorrow, injury, shame and pain
Will come to him—this is no joke;
That became very clear to Heile's guests.

[10] The MD word "cloyde" is difficult to translate precisely. The literal "clawed" is too harsh, but "scratched" and "stroked" seem to understate the scorching that actually takes place.

"Nu wouds God ende goed geval,
Ochte Willem Hoeft iet zeilen sal."
  Aldus quam Willem met allen
Ter erden neder ghevallen,
Dat hem dede harde wee,
Want hi doe brac ontwee
Sinen arm ende sinen die scinkel.
  Die pape scoet in een winkel
Ende waende dat die duvel ware;
In enen vulen putte viel hi dare,
Alsoe alsmen mi doet weten
Quam hi thuus al besceten
Ende sinen ers al verbrant,
Te sceerne gedreven ende ghescant.
Hi hadde bat gebleven thuus
Ende ghesongen sinen *benedicamus*.
  Aldus voeren Heilen gaste.
Die smet hadde oec onraste,
Maer hi verdroeght vele te bat,
Dies die pape cloyde sijn gat;
Daer met hadde hi hem wel gewroken. fol. 331va
  Met orlove es dit gesproken:
Wie met hoeren omme gheet,
Toren, scade, scande ende leet
Es hem nakende sonder spel;
Dat scene Heilen gasten wel.

The Man of Law's Prologue and Tale*

ROBERT M. CORREALE

The Man of Law's contribution to the storytelling contest in *The Canterbury Tales* consists of three parts commonly referred to as the *Introduction*, *Prologue* and *Tale.* Their relationships to each other and to the *Tales* as a whole are in many respects uncertain, resulting in a number of still unsolved problems, including the Man of Law's puzzling announcement that he will "speke in prose," (II, 96) just before giving his brief homily on poverty (II, 99–121) and telling his tale in verse.[1] The relationship between his *Prologue* and *Tale* has always been problematic. Many scholars have found little or no reason for any connection between them.[2] It had long been known, however, that the Lawyer's remarks on poverty in the *Prologue* and some of the passages in his *Tale* are derived from Pope Innocent III's *De Miseria Condicionis Humane*, which Chaucer claimed to have translated under the title "Of the Wreched Engendrynge of Mankynde" in the *Legend of Good Women* (*Prologue* G 414–15). In his study

* I am grateful to Professors Robert E. Lewis and Peter Nicholson for their helpful advice during the preparation of this chapter, and to Professors Joan Williamson (Emerita, LIU) and Jill Mann (Cambridge) for reading my translation of Trevet and offering several valuable suggestions for improving it.

1 For discussions of these problems, see Patricia Eberle's notes, with bibliographic references, in *The Riverside Chaucer*, pp. 854–63. All references to Chaucer's text are from this edition. See also Helen Cooper, *The Canterbury Tales*, 2nd edn (Oxford, 1996), pp. 123–7, and A. S. G. Edwards, "Critical Approaches to the *Man of Law's Tale*," in *Chaucer's Religious Tales*, ed. C. David Benson and Elizabeth Robertson (Cambridge, 1990), pp. 85–94.

2 Manly and Rickert found the Prologue "unnecessary," as lines 97–8 "sufficiently introduce the tale." *The Text of the Canterbury Tales*, 8 vols (Chicago, 1940), vol. 2, p. 448. F. N. Robinson, *The Works of Geoffrey Chaucer*, 2nd edn (Boston, 1957), termed the connection "rather far-fetched, and looks like an afterthought" (p. 691). Alfred David, "The Man of Law vs. Chaucer: A Case in Poetics," *PMLA* 82 (1967): 221, finds a connection in the use of the rhyme royal stanza, but in *The Strumpet Muse* (Bloomington, IN, and London, 1976), admits the connection "seems strained" (p. 127).

of the *De Miseria*, Robert E. Lewis defended Chaucer's claim and proved that he was working on this lost translation during the same period (1390–5) when he was writing the Man of Law's sequence.[3] But Lewis's study of the *De Miseria* was even more important for its argument in support of a connection between the *Prologue* and *Tale* based on Chaucer's use of the Pope's treatise as a source in both. For the Lawyer's comments on poverty, Chaucer used a condensed version of a passage at the beginning of the *De Miseria* (I.14.1–14), in which Innocent condemns the evils of poverty and the poor.[4] But in place of the denunciation of riches which concludes the Pope's remarks, Chaucer substitutes an apostrophe in praise of riches and wealthy merchants (II, 122–33). As Lewis argued, this design in the *Prologue* serves a dual purpose: it functions to highlight the Lawyer's concern for wealth and material success already mentioned in his portrait in the *The General Prologue*, and it provides a transition to the tale by linking merchants, the "fadres of tidynges" (129) and the merchant from whom the Lawyer learned his tale (132–3), to the merchants who figure prominently in its opening stanzas. Moreover, when composing *The Man of Law's Tale* (*MLT*) Chaucer also drew on five additional passages from the *De Miseria*, and these, according to Lewis, also serve to give it greater "moral seriousness" (II, 771–7, 925–31) and increased emphasis on "wo after gladnesse" (II, 421–7), one of its central themes.[5]

[3] Robert E. Lewis, ed., *De Miseria Condicionis Humane*, The Chaucer Library (Athens, GA, 1978), pp. 30–1.

[4] This passage and other lines from Innocent also appear in the Latin and French originals of *The Tale of Melibee*, and Juliette Dor believes certain divergences between Innocent's language and that of the *Prologue* are better explained by Chaucer's borrowing not from the *De Miseria* directly but from his own translation of them in the *Melibee*. See "L'enigme du Prologue du Conte de l'Homme de loi: Chaucer et l'auto-plagiat," in *The Medieval Translator, Traduire au Moyen Age*, vol. 5, ed. Roger Ellis and René Tixier (Brepols, 1996), pp. 376–89. If accepted, her argument would establish a link between *Melibee* and Chaucer's lost translation of the *De Miseria*, both of which have been proposed as candidates for the prose tale that Chaucer may have originally intended to assign to the Lawyer. The *Melibee* was put forward by J. S. P. Tatlock, *The Development and Chronology of Chaucer's Works* (London, 1907; rpt. 1963), pp. 188–97, and accepted by Carleton Brown as part of a larger argument that Fragment II originally began the *CT*; see "The Man of Law's Headlink and the Prologue of the *Canterbury Tales*," *Studies in Philology* 34 (1937): 8–35. Charles Owen claimed the *Melibee* was intended to begin the entire collection. See *Pilgrimage and Storytelling in the Canterbury Tales* (Norman, OK, 1977), pp. 25–31.

[5] Robert E. Lewis, "Chaucer's Artistic Use of Pope Innocent III's *De Miseria Humane Conditionis* in The Man of Law's Prologue and Tale," *PMLA* 81 (1966): 485–92. This study, notes Edwards (p. 88), was also influential in shifting the focus away from efforts to identify an historical figure behind the Man of Law – and from a real quarrel between Chaucer and Gower based on the Lawyer's references (II, 78–85) to stories of incest in Gower's *Confessio Amantis* (see John H. Fisher, *John Gower: Moral Philosopher and Friend of Chaucer* [New York University Press, 1964], pp. 289–92) – to a consideration of what the *Prologue* tells us about the Lawyer in relation to his *Tale.* It also produced a number of readings in which the Lawyer's materialism in the *Prologue,* contrasted with his rhetorical excesses and sentimental piety in the *Tale,* is seen as evidence of Chaucer's attempt to satirize him by pointing up his inadequacies as a storyteller. Derek Pearsall regards the *Tale* as a "puzzling performance," but would rather read it "as an independent poem," than try to rescue it by "ironizing" its narrator (*The Canterbury Tales* [London, 1985], pp. 258–9). Four of the passages from *De Miseria* are accompanied by Latin glosses which were written "either by Chaucer himself or by a scribe copying from his manuscript" (see Lewis's edition cited above, pp. 32–9, and his earlier "Glosses to the *Man of Law's Tale* from Pope Innocent's *De Miseria Humane Conditionis*," *Studies in Philology* 64 [1967]: 1–16).

For an opposing view, see Charles A. Owen, Jr., "The Alternative Reading of *The Canterbury Tales*: Chaucer's Text and the Early Manuscripts," *PMLA* 97 (1982): 240–1. Graham D. Caie, "Innocent III's 'De Miseria' as a Gloss on 'The Man of Law's Prologue' and 'Tale,'" *Neuphilologische Mitteilungen*

The main source of *The Man of Law's Tale*, as also of John Gower's "Tale of Constance" in *Confessio Amantis* (*CA* II, 587–1598), is the life of the saintly Constance of Rome found in *Les Cronicles*, an Anglo-Norman compilation of universal history from the Creation to the early fourteenth century (c. 1334) by the Oxford Dominican historian and scholar Nicholas Trevet.[6] The chronicle is dedicated to Princess Mary of Woodstock (1278–1332), sixth daughter of Edward I, who was a nun at Amesbury.[7] Trevet's life of Constance, the longest single story in the entire chronicle, belongs to a number of tales known as the Constance-saga, part of a much larger group of popular folktales and romances in many languages centered on the figure of the Calumniated Queen.[8] Originating in the East under Byzantine influence,[9] stories in the Constance cycle recount the life of "an innocent maiden who is banished by or flees from an unnatural [incestuous] father. She reaches a foreign land and marries its ruler. In her husband's absence she is falsely accused of giving birth to monstrous offspring and is banished with her child or children. Ultimately she is reunited to her husband, and in some versions, to her father as well."[10]

Trevet's story appears in the final section of his book, "les gestes des Apostles, Emperours, et Rois" ("the deeds of popes, emperors and kings"). He claims as his source "old Saxon chronicles" ("les aunciens croniqes des Sessouns"), but the story does not appear in any known Anglo-Saxon chronicle and his source, if he used a single source, remains unknown. It is clear that Trevet's narrative diverges from other versions of the Calumniated Queen tale in several important ways, but there is some difference of opinion as to whether these changes are original with him or are derived from another source. His most important change, the one that makes his tale unique among all previous stories in the Constance cycle, occurs in the opening episode of the plot. Instead of beginning her adventures in flight from her incestuous father, Constance

100 (1999): 175–85, discusses how the glosses reveal the disparity between Innocent's and the Man of Law's views of poverty and worldly possessions.

6 The discovery was made by the Swedish scholar P. O. Bäckström in *Svenska Folkböcker, Sagor, Legender, och Äfventyr,* 2 vols (Stockholm, 1845), I, 221–8. I adopt Ruth Dean's name for the chronicle and her spelling of Trevet's name. Dean describes the contents and purpose of the chronicle in "Nicholas Trevet, Historian," *Medieval Learning and Literature: Essays Presented to R. W. Hunt*, ed. J. J. G. Alexander and M. T. Gibson (Oxford, 1976), pp. 339–46; and M. Dominica Legge, *Anglo-Norman Literature and its Background* (Oxford, 1963), pp. 298–302.

7 Four manuscripts (Arundel, Magdalen, Rawlinson, Paris) contain in slightly different wording the dedication to Mary: "Ci commencement les cronicles qe frere Nichol Trivet escrit a ma dame Marie, la fille le roi d'Engleterre Edward le fitz Henri."

8 The classic study is Margaret Schlauch's *Chaucer's Constance and Accused Queens* (New York, 1927). See also Elizabeth Archibald, "The Flight from Incest: Two Late Classical Precursors of the Constance Theme," *Chaucer Review* 20 (1986): 259–72. Nancy B. Black studies the popularity of the genre in *Medieval Narratives of Accused Queens* (Gainesville, FL, 2003), using current literary, artistic and historical methods, and focusing chiefly on several non-Chaucerian texts. She discusses Trevet's, Chaucer's and Gower's versions as independent stories, and suggests that Chaucer "may have been influenced by several Continental stories of the empress of Rome, "in which spiritual development of the heroine is a central theme" (p. 137).

9 A. H. Krappe, "The Offa-Constance Legend," *Anglia* 61 (1937): 361, and Schlauch, "The Man of Law's Tale," in Bryan and Dempster, pp. 160–1. In an earlier study, A. B. Gough incorrectly asserted that the primitive form of the story was a pre-historic Anglian folk-tale. See *The Constance Saga, Palaestra* XXIII (Berlin, 1902), p. 13.

10 Lillian Hornstein, in *A Manual of the Writings in Middle English, 1050–1500*, ed. J. Burke Severs, vol.1 (New Haven, CT, 1967), p. 120.

leaves home in obedience to her father's demand that she marry a Saracen prince who has agreed to convert to Christianity if she will become his wife.

Lillian Hornstein suggested that Trevet invented this "conversion story," using as his model a tale relating the marriage of a Tartar khan to an Armenian princess, a tale which appears in numerous European and British chronicles and is also found in the Middle English romance *The King of Tars* (*KT*). Hornstein listed several ways in which Trevet's version agrees more closely with this story in *KT* than with any other analogues, including such details as greater emphasis on the heroine's Christian piety, her marriage as a means of fostering peace and friendship between Christians and Saracens, and the Saracen's promise to give the Christians freedom of trade, worship, and control of Jerusalem and other holy places. Acquaintance with *KT* would also help to explain two other elements in Trevet's story. In *KT,* the heroine's departure from home to enter a forced marriage with a heathen Sultan causes her great sorrow and arouses much pity. The same kind of mourning occurs in Trevet's version, presumably as an unexplained survival from *KT*, for the Sultan's decision to become a Christian would seem to eliminate the main reason for Constance's sorrow. From *KT*, in which the heroine pretends to adopt the Sultan's religion, Trevet may also have taken the motif of the hypocrisy of the Sultaness, who cloaks her scheme to murder her son and the Christians under the pretense of becoming a Christian herself.[11]

Margaret Schlauch also believed that Trevet invented the conversion story as part of a larger plan to create an original work of fiction by transforming a popular romantic tale into a morally edifying story for a royal nun. For this purpose, she argued, he drew on several sources, including two stories of persecuted queens that he surely could have known, the *Vita Offae Primi*, the first part of the *Vitae duorum Offarum*, written in England c. 1250 and once believed to have been the work of Matthew Paris, and the French romance *La belle Hélène de Constantinople*. After fleeing from their incestuous fathers, the heroines in both works find refuge in England, marry the English king (Offa in the Latin, Henry in the French), and are falsely accused in exchanged letters carried by drunken messengers. The *Vita* is set in Northern England, where Trevet locates the king's mother's castle (Knaresburgh), and the heroine's husband goes to aid the King of Northumbria in a war against the Scots, as does Trevet's King Alla.[12] From *La belle Hélène*, Schlauch suggested, he may have found the main plot of his story and the idea of beginning it in the Eastern empire during the reign of the historical Emperor Tiberius Constantius of Constantinople (578–2), whose son Mauritius (Maurice) of Cappadocia ruled after him (582–603/04). The influence of *La belle Hélène* has been rendered somewhat doubtful by its recent editor Claude Roussel, who dates it mid-

[11] "Trivet's Constance and the King of Tars," *Modern Language Notes* 55 (1940): 354–7, and Hornstein, *A Manual of the Writings in Middle English*, pp. 130–1, 289–90. See also Judith Perryman, *The King of Tars*, edited from Auchinleck MS, Advocates 19.2.1 (Heidelberg, 1980), pp. 53–4.

[12] "The Man of Law's Tale," in Bryan and Dempster, pp. 156–7; the Latin text, with marginal English summaries, is printed in *Originals and Analogues of Some of Chaucer's Canterbury Tales*, ed. F. J. Furnivall, E. Brock and W. A. Clouston, Chaucer Society 2nd series, nos 7, 10, 15, 20, 22 (London, 1872), pp. 71–84.

fourteenth century, but it is possible Trevet may have known an earlier oral version or a lost written one.[13] In a later study, Schlauch argued that Trevet's decision to use Maurice and Constance as leading characters in his story may have resulted from his acquaintance with a pious Latin tale in which the Byzantine emperor Maurice and his wife Constance are portrayed as exemplary Christian rulers whose lives "harmonized with the saga of pathos and suffering [Trevet] was about to unfold."[14] Moreover, having eliminated the incestuous father, he further modified the plot by duplicating in the first part of his story the persecution of the heroine by a resentful mother-in-law who is found both in the second part of *La belle Hélène* and in other analogues, a change suggested by a story in Archbishop William of Tyre's *A History of Deeds Done Beyond the Sea* in which the marriage of a Christian princess to a Saracen is impeded by a wicked mother-in-law.[15]

Two other scholars, however, have rejected the argument that Trevet invented the conversion story at the beginning of his tale. Commenting on Trevet's pseudo-historical account in which Constance becomes the mother of Maurice by the Anglo-Saxon King Aella (Alla), instead of the wife of Maurice, as she was in history, Alexander Krappe concluded that he was following an older, lost original model in Latin or Norman French, "carried to Europe by the first crusaders," which was presumably a "compilation like those of Wace and Jeffrey Gaimar, professing to satisfy the curiosity of the Normans about the past history of the British Isles."[16] More recently, Phillip Wynn, who denies "any proof of Trevet's originality," has identified a version of the conversion story in the *Annales Eutychii*, a chronicle written in Arabic c. 937 by the Greek Orthodox patriarch of Alexandria. According to Wynn, both Eutychius and Trevet tell the same story of a pagan king (the historical Sassanid Chosroes II in Eutychius), who writes to the Roman (Byzantine) emperor asking to marry his daughter. In both stories the emperor agrees only on condition that the king convert to Christianity. In both, the pagan monarch agrees to this condition (though Chosroes II remained a Zoroastrian) despite the opposition of his court, and the emperor sends his daughter in the company of a great retinue. Maurice also plays a leading role in both stories, as father-Emperor in Eutychius and as the grandson and successor to the Emperor Tiberius in Trevet. Other parallels include mention of the heroine's beauty and wisdom, a treaty ensuring peace between the two rulers and their realms as part of the marriage agreement, some skepticism on the part of Chosroes and his courtiers concerning the divinity of

[13] Claude Roussel, ed., *La belle Hélène de Constantinople: chanson de geste du XIVe siècle* (Geneva: Droz, 1995), "nous considérerons … que *La belle Hélène* a dû être composée vers le milieu du XIVe siècle" (p. 95). See also Barbara N. Sargent-Baur, who argues that *Le Roman de la Manekine*, written "before the early 1330s" by Philippe de Remi, is closer to Trevet's tale. Despite the lack of evidence that Trevet ever saw this work and the numerous differences between the two plots, she proposes that Trevet was not telling a story different from Philippe's but "telling the same story differently" while "exploiting and adapting other materials" (p. 99). See "*Peregrinatio:* Joïe, Constance, and their Tale(s)," in *Philologies Old and New*, The Edward C. Armstrong Monographs on Medieval Literature, no. 12, ed. Joan T. Grimbert and Carol Chase (Princeton, 2001), pp. 93–108.

[14] Margaret Schlauch, "Historical Precursors of Chaucer's Constance," *Philological Quarterly* 29 (1950): 403.

[15] Schlauch, "Historical Precursors," pp. 407–12.

[16] Alexander Krappe, "The Offa-Constance Legend," *Anglia* 61 (1937): 368–9.

Christ, and the heroine's very tearful departure from her father. Taken together, all these similarities, Wynn argues, prove that Eutychius's story represents "the earliest extant version of the conversion story later found in Trevet," and that the form of the story of Chosroes as Trevet knew it was transmitted to the West, as Krappe and others pointed out, by the crusaders.[17]

Whatever its origin, the conversion story is not Trevet's only addition that serves to give his version of the Constance legend a distinctively religious and specifically Christian tone. As Schlauch pointed out, he also added two miracles (Hermengild's restoration of the blind Briton's sight and the destruction of Constance's accuser by a divine hand), gave the names of sixth century saints and rulers to some of his fictional characters, and introduced other minor incidents. Some of these additions may have been drawn from the kinds of hagiographical works Schlauch mentions, such as Bede's *De ratione temporum*,[18] but some could also have been imported from, or been suggested by, other parts of Trevet's own history. *Les Cronicles* is filled with stories and legends of martyrs, saints and miracles. Perhaps with his royal patroness in mind, Trevet added a miracle of the Virgin Mary to his account of the reign of Pope Pelagius, who is also mentioned in the Constance story.[19] Alexander Rutherford lists some thirty other miracles scattered throughout the pages of the chronicle, including an account of a blind man's regaining his sight.[20]

Several of the characters in the Constance story, as Schlauch also noticed, are given the names of historical figures who in one way or another promoted the Christian faith. The constable's wife is named after St Hermengild, a Spanish prince whose conversion to Catholicism by his wife parallels King Alla's conversion by his wife Constance. This saint's martyrdom by his Arian father is mentioned by Trevet as having occurred during the reign of the Emperor Tiberius ("Tyberie") immediately before the story of Constance.[21] Trevet also framed his story by two events relating to the conversion of the English. At the beginning of his account of the reign of Tiberius, just prior to his mention of St Hermengild (fol. 62va), he tells the famous story of how Pope Gregory the Great, then an archdeacon at Rome, conceived the idea of sending Christian missionaries to England when he saw the young subjects of King Aelle (Alla) of Northumberland in the Roman slave market. Then, during the reign of the

17 Phillip Wynn, "The Conversion Story in Nicholas Trevet's 'Tale of Constance,'" *Viator* 13 (1982): 260, 267–70, 272–4.

18 Bryan and Dempster, pp. 158–9.

19 Known as "The Jew of Bourges," this miracle is an example of one of the oldest miracles of the Virgin and contains several elements found in *The Prioress's Tale*. "En le temps cist emperour Justin et le pape Pelagie, avint en la cite de Bruges qe un enfaunt Judeu, par ses compaignons Cristiens [q'estoient] de lui bien amez, fu amene en l'eglise Nostre Dame pur resceivre le corps Dieux, pur quele chose son pere Judeu le fist gettre en un fourn ardant de flaume. Mes par Cristiens fu estret sanz blemure, et afferma qe la femme q'estoit en l'eglise depeinte tenaunt son enfaunt enchasa de son mantel la flaume del fourneys, qe ne lui poeit noser. Lors lui Cristiens pristrent le pere Judeu et lui mistrent mesme la fourn, et meyntenaunt come une herece estoit ars et a cendres." Cited from Paris, Bibl. Nationale, MS français, 9687, fol. 61rb. All citations from *Les Cronicles* are from this manuscript. A longer Middle English version of the miracle is printed below among the analogues of *The Prioress's Tale*, see pp. 593–4 and 600–4.

20 Alexander Rutherford, "The Anglo-Norman Chronicle of Nicholas Trevet: Text, with Historical, Philological and Literary Study," unpublished dissertation (University of London, 1932), p. 42.

21 Bryan and Dempster, p. 158. In the Paris manuscript of *Les Cronicles* the story appears on fol. 62va.

Emperor Maurice, which follows immediately after his story of Constance (fols 70b–va), Trevet recounts how Gregory sent St Augustine to convert England, and this, as Macaulay surmised, "may have had something to do with the story that Maurice was partly of English origin."[22] Another example of how *Les Cronicles* may have contributed to the story of Constance can be seen in the language Trevet uses to describe his heroine. It was Geoffrey of Monmouth, Schlauch reminds us, who created the legend that St Helena, the mother of Constantine, was English. Geoffrey of course was one of Trevet's sources in *Les Cronicles*, and when writing his account of the life of St Helena, Trevet translated almost word for word Geoffrey's description of her virtue, beauty and accomplishments (my emphasis).

> Ceste Seint Heleine estoit femme de ***grant vertue***, et passoit ***en beauté*** totes les puceles de Brutaigne . . . et n'estoit trové une autre issint ***endoctriné*** en instrumenz ***de musiqe et les sept artz qe l'en apele liberals***, qar son piere Koel ***n'avoit autre enfant*** qi poet aprés son roialme governer, et pur ceo s'afforsa qe ele fust issint ***endoctriné*** qe ele put regnir aprés lui. (fol. 49a)[23]

> [This Saint Helen was a woman of great virtue, and she surpassed in beauty all the young maidens of Britain…and there was found no other maiden so skilled in musical instruments and the seven liberal arts, for her father King Cole had no other child who could afterwards govern his kingdom and therefore determined that she be so educated that she would be able to rule after him.]

Later, when writing the story of Constance, Trevet gave the name Helena to Constance's cousin, the wife of senator Arsenius; however, it is evident that his vision of Constance was shaped by what he knew of the earlier legendary St Helena, for as the italicized words in both passages reveal, he used much of the same language from his earlier portrait of St Helena to describe Constance's education, sanctity, and great beauty.

> Cist Tyberie . . . engendra (fol. 63a) de sa femme Ytalie une fille apelé Constance. Et pur ceo ***qe nul autre enfaunt avoit***, pur ceo a grant diligence la fist enseigner la foi Cristiene, et ***endoctriner*** par mestres sachauntz en ***les sept sciences***, qe sount logiciene, naturele, morale, astronomie, geometrie, ***musiqe***, perspective, qe sont philosophies seculers apelez, et la fist ***endoctriner*** en

[22] G. C. Macaulay, ed., *The Complete Works of John Gower*, 4 vols (1899–1902; rpt. Grosse Pointe, MI, 1968), II, 484. Cited by Schlauch in Bryan and Dempster, p. 158. All citations from Gower are from Macaulay's edition. V. A. Kolve, in *Chaucer and the Imagery of Narrative: The First Five Canterbury Tales* (Stanford University Press, 1984), argues that Chaucer (like Trevet and Gower) was attracted to the story of Constance as history not only because it dealt with the conversion of the English, but because it "constituted part of an even larger true history, the spreading of the faith, the Christianization of Europe" (p. 299).

[23] For Trevet's use of Geoffrey of Monmouth, see Dean, "Nicholas Trevet, Historian," p. 340. Trevet's description is based on either the variant version of the *Historia Regum Britanniae*, ed. Jacob Hammer, The Mediaeval Academy of America (Cambridge, MA, 1951), Book 6, p. 90, lines 119–23 ("Helenam nomine, pulchram valde ac formosam, artibusque liberalibus edoctam: sed et in musicis instrumentis non reperiebatur talis, nec erat regi Coel filius, qui regni solio potiretur. Unde ita patri cara exstiterat, ut artibus omnibus imbui eam faceret, quo facilius et sapientius regnum post illum regere nosset"), or similar wording in the later poem, *Historia Regum Britannie*, ed. and trans. Neil Wright (Cambridge: D. S. Brewer, 1991), Book 4, p. 102, lines 306–11. Cf. the Vulgate version, *The Historia Regum Britanniae of Geoffrey of Monmouth*, ed. Acton Griscom (New York and London, 1929), p. 338.

> diverses langages. . . . Constance estoit de totes gentz, riches et povres sanz comparison de lui ou de nule de la terre plus grantment preisé de bounté et ***de seinteté*** et de ***merveillouse beauté***. Et lui fu avis qe si sa loaunge et sa gloire fu ja anientie pur le grant pris de Constance. (fol. 66a)
>
> [this Tiberius . . . begot on his wife Italy a daughter named Constance. And because he had no other child, with great diligence he had her taught the Christian faith and instructed by learned masters in the seven sciences, which are logic, physics, morals, astronomy, geometry, music, and optics, called the secular sciences, and had her instructed in various languages. . . . Constance, by all people rich and poor, was, without comparison to her [Domild] or any other lady in the land, more highly praised for goodness and holiness and marvelous beauty. And it seemed to her [Domild] that her praise and glory were already brought to nothing because of the great esteem for Constance.]

Clearly, then, whatever other sources Trevet used in fashioning his story of Constance, he was influenced to a larger extent than Schlauch or others have realized by people and events recorded elsewhere in his own chronicle.

Besides being the source of Chaucer's *Tale*, Trevet's chronicle is also of course the immediate source of Gower's "Tale of Constance" in *Confessio Amantis* (*CA*, II, 587–1598). Like their common source, both English poems open with the conversion story – in Chaucer's tale the "Sowdan of Surrye" (*MLT*, II, 177) has agreed to convert to Christianity if "he shal han Custance in mariage" (*MLT*, II, 241) – and both poets follow the same story line in the French.[24] Similarities in plot and language prove that both Chaucer and Gower used Trevet independently,[25] and though there has been some difference of opinion about which one of the English poems preceded the other, the consensus is that Gower wrote first and Chaucer borrowed from him. Tatlock noted that the Lawyer's condemnation of "unkynde abhomynacions" (*MLProl*, II, 78–85) is likely an allusion to the stories of incest such as those of Canacee and Apollonius of Tyre that Gower told in the *Confessio Amantis*. He also argued for Gower's priority because in two places near the end of his *Tale*, Chaucer refers to both Gower's and Trevet's versions when he disagrees with what "Som men wolde seyn" about the child Maurice being sent to invite King Alla to a feast (*MLT*, II, 1109), and to invite the Emperor to dinner (*MLT*, II, 1086).[26] Schlauch believed Gower wrote first because his "rather mediocre narrative shows no sign of demonstrable influence by Chaucer's more original and

[24] As Schlauch (*Chaucer's Constance and Accused Queens*, pp. 132–3) and others have noted, a trace of the incest motif in other stories of calumniated queens like *Emaré* and *La Manekine* may be detected in the versions of Trevet, Chaucer and Gower where Constance "shows her reticence and aversion to telling anything about herself" or about her father when she arrives in Northumberland and later in Rome.

[25] Emil Lücke,"Das Leben der Constanze bei Trivet, Gower und Chaucer," *Anglia* 14 (1892): 77–122, 147–85.

[26] Tatlock, *Development and Chronology*, pp. 172–5, 183–6. Peter Nicholson has correctly observed that the Man of Law has distorted Trevet's and Gower's versions in these two places: in the first scene Constance only "urges her son to stand where Alla will be sure to see him," and in the second, Maurice is no longer a child. He thinks the allusions are "Chaucer's joking but friendly way of acknowledging … his indebtedness to Gower for the tale." See "Chaucer Borrows from Gower: The Sources of the *Man of Law's Tale*," in R. F. Yeager, ed., *Chaucer and Gower: Difference, Mutuality, Exchange*, ELS (English Literary Studies), Monograph Series, no. 51 (Victoria, British Columbia: 1991), pp. 93–4.

moving tale"; however, she found that Tatlock's evidence provided only "slight indications" for Gower's priority.[27]

Schlauch's views were accepted by Edward Block in his study of Chaucer's sources.[28] Block focused primarily on Chaucer's debt to Trevet, providing a detailed analysis of the various kinds of changes he made in reshaping Trevet's tale into what Block considered a work of "greater originality, imaginative power, and conscious artistry" than had been previously realized (p. 572). Even though there are only about 200 lines of *The Man of Law's Tale*, a little less than twenty percent of the whole, in which he follows Trevet closely (p. 574), Chaucer follows the main outline of Trevet's plot, retaining all the main episodes while adding the council scenes of the Sultan and his mother (*MLT*, 204–31, 326–43), the formal hearing before King Alla on the murder of Hermengyld (*MLT*, 606–89), and the scene with Custance and her infant Maurice before her second exile (*MLT*, 825–75). In Part III of his *Tale*, Chaucer changes the sequence of events in his source. After Constance is exiled from Northumberland, Trevet relates her wanderings at sea, her arrival in the heathen orient, and her escape from the attempted rape by Telous. Then he shifts his attention to Alla, who returns victorious from the wars in Scotland, discovers his mother's treachery and kills her. Trevet then narrates the rescue of Constance by her father's Roman fleet sailing home from its sack of Surrye in reprisal for the massacre at the Sultan's pre-nuptial marriage feast. By contrast, Chaucer first narrates Alla's homecoming and his execution of Donegild. Then he returns to Custance at sea and describes her escape from the wicked steward and her rescue by the Romans in that order. To keep his main focus on Custance, Chaucer also omits or condenses many non-essential incidents and details, deletes several of Trevet's characters, reduces the roles of others, and suppresses the names of all but Custance, her husband King Alla, Hermengyld, Donegild (Trevet's Domilde), and Maurice (p. 578). His numerous additions – including biblical allusions, prayers to God, Christ and Mary, moralizing comments and rhetorical apostrophes – increase the pathos and religious intensity of the *Tale* and give it a heightened moral tone.[29] Some of these additions "stress the Christian piety of Alla, the constable and Maurice" (p. 588), but most

27 Bryan and Dempster, pp. 155–6. For a survey of all the arguments, see Schlauch, *Chaucer's Constance and Accused Queens*, pp. 132–4; Edmund Brock, "Preface to Trevet's Life of Constance," in *Originals and Analogues*, pp. iii–xii; Walter W. Skeat, *The Complete Works of Geoffrey Chaucer*, 6 vols (Oxford, 1894), III, 409, 413–17; V, 145–65; Macaulay, *Complete Works*, II, 483–4. Helen Cooper describes the relationship between the two English tales as "unsettled," but admits that the "balance of probabilities is that Chaucer knew Gower's version" (*The Canterbury Tales*, p. 128).

28 Edward A. Block, "Originality, Controlling Purpose, and Craftsmanship in Chaucer's *Man of Law's Tale*," *PMLA* 68 (1953): 572–616, 600–1 n. 78.

29 For the sources of these additions, several of which are indicated by glosses in the manuscripts, see Eberle's notes in *The Riverside Chaucer*, pp. 857 and ff. See also John A. Yunck, "Religious Elements in Chaucer's *Man of Law's Tale*," *English Literary History* 27 (1960): 249–61; Robert T. Farrell, "Chaucer's Use of the Theme of the Help of God in The Man of Law's Tale," *Neuphilologische Mitteilungen* 71 (1970): 239–43; Roger Ellis, *Patterns of Religious Narrative in The Canterbury Tales* (Totowa, NJ: Barnes and Noble, 1986), pp. 119–68, and R. M. Correale, "Chaucer's Constance and The Sorrowing Mary: The Man of Law's Tale, 841–54," *Marian Library Studies* (University of Dayton) n.s. 26 (1998–2000): 287–94. In *Imagery of Narrative* (pp. 297–358) Kolve employs the medieval iconographical tradition to explore the tale's central images of the rudderless ship and the sea as polysemous symbols of the Christian's spiritual journey through life.

of them are centered on Custance, especially in places like the judgment hall scene (*MLT*, II, 610–18, 621–61) for the purpose of portraying her as a more passive, holier woman than she is in Trevet (p. 587) and at the same time a more human figure by "describing her emotions, behavior, and appearance during crucial incidents in her life" (pp. 612–13). As a result of these changes and additions, it is difficult to define precisely the genre of Chaucer's tale, combining as it does elements of folktale, romance and saint's life.[30]

According to Block, Gower contributed only forty words in nine different passages to Chaucer's *Tale.*[31] Block thus gave most readers the impression, in Peter Nicholson's words, that "Gower's influence on Chaucer, while demonstrable, was almost entirely negligible."[32] To correct this impression, Nicholson offered a detailed comparison of all three stories that developed a quite different picture of how Chaucer used both Trevet and Gower as his sources, turning from one text to the other in the manuscripts that lay before him. It was Gower's shorter, more focused version, he contended, that Chaucer followed as he omitted a mass of unnecessary details from Trevet's plot. The real significance of the verbal parallels in passages cited by Block is that they provided a memorable image or picture that Chaucer adopted in his various descriptions of such elements as the slaughter of the Sultan and the Christians by the Sultan's mother at the pre-nuptial feast, of Constance's rudderless ship, of the blind man's simple appeal to Hermengyld to restore his sight, of the false knight's creeping to the bed where Constance and Hermengyld were asleep in order to murder Hermengyld.[33] More importantly, it was Gower's depiction of Constance as a helpless, innocent, suffering woman in several other scenes – as when she is exiled from Northumberland with her infant son, when she is attacked by the renegade steward, and when she is reunited with her husband and father in Rome – that inspired Chaucer's vision of her.[34] For these reasons, Nicholson argued, not only was Chaucer's debt to Gower greater than Block (and others) were willing to acknowledge, but that Gower provided Chaucer's "most important model," that "it was Gower's tale rather than Trevet's which Chaucer chose to retell," and, however "pallid or threadbare" it may seem to modern readers

[30] There has been much debate about the genre of *MLT*, which has been variously defined as "hagiographical romance," "pious exemplum" and "sentimental tale." See Paul Clogan, "The Narrative Style of *The Man of Law's Tale*," *Medievalia et Humanistica* n.s. 8 (1977): 8–35; Michael R. Paull, "The Influence of the Saint's Legend Genre in the *Man of Law's Tale*," *Chaucer Review* 5 (1971): 179–94; Pearsall, *The Canterbury Tales*, p. 260; and the summary of other opinions in Edwards, "Critical Approaches," p. 87. Kolve (note 22 above) regards it mainly as history.

[31] Block (pp. 600–2, 609–11) compares Chaucer's lines *MLT* 430 and Gower's *CA* 689; *MLT* 439 and *CA* 709; *MLT* 535 and *CA* 749–51; *MLT* 561–2 and *CA* 766; *MLT* 599 and *CA* 828; *MLT* 683 and *CA* 907; *MLT* 721 and *CA* 932; *MLT* 799 and *CA* 1031; *MLT* 825 and *CA* 1055–7. To these Eberle (p. 857) adds "the most important parallel between Chaucer's and Gower's versions, the pathetic scene with Custance and her child as she leaves Northumberland," *MLT* 834–68 and *CA* 1054–83.

[32] Peter Nicholson, "*The Man of Law's Tale*: What Chaucer Really Owed to Gower," *Chaucer Review* 26 (1991): 153–74.

[33] Nicholson, *ibid.*, pp. 157–8, 161, 170–1. Robert F. Yeager describes the "richness and complexity" of Gower's imagery "at once similar to Chaucer's and yet uniquely his" own, in "John Gower's Images: 'The Tale of Constance' and 'The Man of Law's Tale,' " in *Speaking Images: Essays in Honor of V. A. Kolve*, ed. R. F. Yeager and Charlotte Morse (Asheville, NC: Pegasus Press, 2001), pp. 525–57. See especially pp. 527–8, 540–2 for some images mentioned by Block.

[34] Nicholson, "*The Man of Law's Tale*," pp. 164, 167–70.

familiar with Chaucer's "imaginatively much richer" story, Gower's version is the more appropriate starting point when assessing Chaucer's achievement.[35]

In addition to works already mentioned, such as *La belle Hélène*, *La Manekine*, *The King of Tars*, there are numerous other analogues to *The Man of Law's Tale*, including a group of stories called the "Eustace-Constance-Florence-Griselda Legends."[36] Of these, the closest to Chaucer's is the Middle English *Emaré*, a tail-rhyme romance surviving in only one fifteenth-century manuscript, Cotton Caligula A. 2, which may have been composed as early as 1400.[37] Emaré, who like Custance is the only child of an emperor, rejects her father's incestuous advances and is set adrift in a boat "Wythowte anker or ore" (275). Thereafter the story line is similar to that found in Chaucer. She lands in Wales, marries the king over the objections of his mother, who accuses her of being a "fende" (446), and soon conceives. When her husband goes to war to aid the king of France against the Saracens, she gives birth to a son, but is again exiled at sea in a rudderless boat by her mother-in-law's use of faked letters carried by a drunken messenger. She and her infant son find refuge in Rome, where she is finally reunited with her husband and then her father. D. Thomas Hanks, Jr., lists several resemblances in words and phrases between *Emaré* and *The Man of Law's Tale* that are not found in Trevet or Gower. To cite one example, the reference in the faked letter that the "the qwene had born a devyll,/ Durste no mon come her hende" (536–7) contains references to the monstrous child and people's avoidance of the infant in similar language and in the same order as found in Chaucer: "The lettre spak the queene delivered was/ Of so horrible a feendly creature/ That in the castel noon so hardy was/ That any while dorste ther endure" (*MLT*, 750–3).[38] However, despite these resemblances the Saracens do not directly affect the fate of the heroine, Emaré is not portrayed as a Christian saint like Chaucer's Custance, nor is she protected during her trials by God or the Virgin Mary, but by a magic robe made of gold cloth. A more distant analogue, with a much different story line, but which may have contributed details to Chaucer's *Tale*, appears in the *Decameron* 5.2. Both long-suffering Christian heroines have similar names – Gostanza and Custance – and when washed ashore in strange lands both speak a similar language: Gostanza in "latino" (probably Italian) and Custance in "A maner Latyn corrupt" (*MLT*, 519), whereas Trevet's Constance, fluent in many languages, speaks in Saxon.[39]

35 Nicholson, *Ibid.*, p. 171. In a less detailed, more impressionistic, comparison of the two versions, Masayoshi Itô in *John Gower, The Medieval Poet* (Tokyo, 1976), concludes that Chaucer's achievement consists in writing a tale that has more complex characters, includes a tactful use of humor, and is "paradoxically more religious and philosophical than Gower's," thereby arousing "more universal interest" (p. 36).

36 See Hornstein, *A Manual of the Writings in Middle English*, pp. 121–32, 278–91, and Schlauch, *Chaucer's Constance and Accused Queens*, pp. 69–114.

37 *Emaré* in *Six Middle English Romances*, ed. and introduction by Maldwyn Mills (London: Dent, 1973), pp. xiii–xv, 46–74. All citations are from this edition. Mills refers to Chaucer's tale as *Emare*'s "more pious first cousin" (p. xiii, n2). A more extended summary and comparison to Chaucer's and Gower's versions are provided in Neil D. Isaacs, "Constance in Fourteenth-century England," *Neuphilologische Mitteilungen* 59 (1958): 260–77.

38 D. Thomas Hanks, Jr., "*Emaré:* An Influence on The *Man of Law's Tale*," *Chaucer Review* 18 (1983): 182–5.

39 See Thomas McNeal, "Chaucer and The Decameron," *Modern Language Notes* 53 (1938): 257–8; Cooper, *The Canterbury Tales*, p. 128; and Eberle's note to line 519 in *The Riverside Chaucer*.

Finally, three glosses at the beginning of the tale, drawn from astrological works, indicate the role of fate and the stars in dooming Custance's first marriage. The first gloss, from Bernardus Silvestris's *Megacosmos* (III.39–40, 43–4), appears next to lines 194–203, where the Man of Law compares the heavens to a book in which one might have read the Sultan's impending death because of his love for Custance. The second gloss, from Ptolemy's *Almagest* (Bk. 1, ch. 8), occurs at lines 295–301, where the narrator rails against the cruelty of the planets, especially Mars, who has "slayn" the approaching marriage between the Sultan and Custance. The third gloss, from the *Liber Electionum* of the Arab astrologer Zael Benbriz, appears next to lines 309–15, where Custance's father is denounced for failing to seek the advice of an astrologer ("philosophre") about Custance's horoscope prior to her ill-fated journey to the "Barbre nacioun" for the marriage.[40] As the glosses indicate, these astrological sources are somewhat misquoted and misinterpreted by the Man of Law to underscore the baleful influence of Fortune on Custance's early life, a theme that contrasts sharply with that of God's providential care of her in the rest of the tale.[41]

MANUSCRIPTS AND TEXTS

Les Cronicles survives in eleven Anglo-Norman manuscripts and an early fifteenth-century Middle English translation.[42] Two of the French copies contain

40 The glosses are printed in Manly and Rickert (III, 493), translated in *The Riverside Chaucer*, pp. 858–9, and appear with their source texts in Graham D. Caie, "'This was a thrifty tale for the nones': Chaucer's Man of Law," in *Chaucer in Perspective: Middle English Essays in Honour of Norman Blake*, ed. Geoffrey Lester (Sheffield, 1999). pp. 47–60.

41 Cooper (*The Canterbury Tales*, p. 128) observes that by adapting these references "to give much gloomier applications than their originals suggest," Chaucer raises "unsettling questions about the final thematic import of the Tale." However, J. D. North (*Chaucer's Universe* [Oxford, 1988], p. 497), claims that Chaucer is adhering to the medieval orthodox Christian position: "although the planets have some influence on inferior events, the human will is free" and in the final analysis "everything is controlled by the power of God." Caie ("'This was a thrifty tale for the nones'", p. 59) argues that Chaucer deliberately misconstrued his sources to show the Man of Law is too much concerned with "the things of this world and is spiritually lacking." Caie also comments on the "twists" and "misquotation" in these glosses in "The Significance of Marginal Glosses in the Earliest Manuscripts of *The Canterbury Tales*," in *Chaucer and Scriptural Tradition*, ed. David L. Jeffrey (Ottawa, 1984), pp. 85–8. For further commentary on astrology in the tale, see Skeat, V, 147–52; W. C. Curry, *Chaucer and the Mediaeval Sciences*, 2nd edn rev. (New York, 1960), pp. 164–94; Chauncey Wood, *Chaucer and the Country of the Stars* (Princeton, 1970), pp. 208–34; Dorothy B. Loomis, "Constance and the Stars," in *Chaucerian Problems and Perspectives: Essays Presented to Paul E. Beichner*, ed. E. Vasta and Z. P. Thundy (Notre Dame, IN, 1979), pp. 207–20; J. C. Eade, "'We ben to lewed or to slowe': Chaucer's Astronomy and Audience Participation," in *Studies in the Age of Chaucer* 4 (1982): 76–82; and North, *Chaucer's Universe*, pp. 484–98.

42 This list of manuscripts, with the same sigla but in different order, is taken from Ruth J. Dean, "Nicholas Trevet, Historian," pp. 351–2. For fuller descriptions of all the manuscripts and their textual histories, see Dean's articles, "The Manuscripts of Nicholas Trevet's Anglo-Norman *Cronicles*," *Medievalia et Humanistica*, 14 (1962): 95–105, and "An Essay in Anglo-Norman Palaeography," in *Studies in French Language and Medieval Literature Presented to Professor Mildred K. Pope* (Manchester, 1939), pp. 79–87. See also *Anglo-Norman Literature: A Guide to Texts and Manuscripts*, ed. Ruth J. Dean in collaboration with Maureen B. M. Boulton, Anglo-Norman Text Society (London, 1999), pp. 47–8. The ME translation survives in Cambridge, Mass., Harvard MS Eng 938, fols 9ra–91rb, XV^2. See C. U. Faye and W. H. Bond, *Supplement to the Census of Medieval and*

only small portions of the work copied in post-medieval times. The other nine, listed below, are all written in English hands, and all except Stockholm belong to the fourteenth century.

A	London, British Libr., Arundel 56, fols 2–77	c. 1375
M	Oxford, Magdalen Coll. 45 (138), fols 1–97v	c. 1335–40
F	Oxford, Bodleian, Fairfax 10 (S.C. 3890), fols 1ra–106ra	XIVm
T	Cambridge, Trinity Coll. 0.4.32, fols 1ra–101va	XIV m 1360
S	Stockholm, Kungliga Bibl., D.1311a (III), pp. 1–27	c. 1400
P	Paris, Bibl. Nationale, franç. 9687, fols 1va–114va	c. 1340–50
R	Oxford, Bodleian, Rawlinson B.178 (S.C. 11545), fols 1–66	c. 1335–50
L	Leyden, Universiteitsbibl. Voss. Gall. F.6, fols 1–93v	XIV 4/4
D	Oxford, Bodleian, Douce 119 (S.C. 21693), fols 1(=1a)–69v	XIV 1/4

The first five of these manuscripts, and the ME translation, end with Trevet's account of the disputed election in 1330 of Louis of Bavaria as Holy Roman Emperor. The others, with the exception of Douce which breaks off incomplete during the reign of Richard I (Lionheart), each have a lengthy continuation describing the struggles of Louis with the papacy and his condemnation on charges of heresy, and then conclude with the decision of Edward II of England to invade Scotland. The manuscripts of this second group also share differences in the presentation of material relating to early British history as well as other textual variants. On the basis of this evidence, and the examination of several test passages, Ruth Dean has shown that Trevet's book, as we have it, exists in two separate authorial redactions, one represented by manuscripts A M F T S (Family A) and the other by P R L D (Family B), and a text from either redaction might have been presented to Princess Mary before she died in 1332, though Trevet continued working on the chronicle until about 1334.[43] Dean also noticed the existence of subgroups AM, FT, and PR. The Stockholm manuscript belongs to the same subgroup as FT, but it has many unique readings and additions of words and phrases, suggesting either that the scribe's exemplar contained readings found nowhere else in the manuscript tradition, or that the scribe himself edited it quite freely.[44] Douce, which is textually closely related to PR, has several large gaps, including the omission of most of the story of Constance. Leyden, the other member of this family, appears to have been contaminated in a number of places by readings from the A-type manuscripts,

Renaissance Manuscripts in the United States and Canada (New York, 1962), p. 228. Two editions of this translation have been prepared as doctoral dissertations in American universities: by William V. Whitehead (Harvard, 1961), and Christine M. Rose (Tufts, 1985), the latter with the "Brut Continuation" from the same manuscript. Rose has given a more detailed description of the manuscript and has speculated that a Middle English version of *Les Cronicles* might have been known to Chaucer and Gower in the fourteenth century. See "The Provenance of the Trevet *Chronicle* (MS Eng 938)," *Harvard Library Bulletin*, n.s. 3 (1992–93): 38–55.

43 Dean, "Nicholas Trevet, Historian," pp. 346–8. My own collation of all the manuscripts for a new edition of the entire chronicle confirms Dean's findings.

44 An example of this "editing"occurs in the italicized words and phrases in the following sentences. "Donc qaunt Thelous par dures manaces la voloit afforcer *et* ele *luy* respount par *resouns sages et bels si dit* lenfaunt Moris qi ia estoit ii aunz entiers puis qil estoit exile dengleterre poeit avoir entendement et memoire de chose fait en sa presence. *Puit avenir grant peril ceste* fu sa colour soy defendre de pecche" (Stockholm MS, p. 167). See p. 317, lines 384–9 in the edition of the French text below.

although there is not much evidence of such conflation in the story of Constance.

The two French texts that students of Chaucer's and Gower's versions have traditionally consulted were printed by Edmund Brock for the Chaucer Society in 1872 and by Margaret Schlauch in Bryan and Dempster in 1941. Brock edited the story from Arundel, corrected at times by readings from Stockholm; he learned about the existence of four other manuscripts (M T R D) only after his edition was set in type.[45] Schlauch, who did not know about the existence of Leyden and did not examine Fairfax, attempted to find the copy closest to Trevet's original. She believed the A-texts generally preserved a greater number of Anglo-Norman dialect characteristics than the others, and she selected Magdalen as her base text because it has fewer obvious kinds of corruptions than Fairfax and Trinity, because it is older and more clearly Norman and has fewer glaring grammatical errors than Arundel and Stockholm. She included variants from the other copies "only when they improve on M."[46]

In the course of preparing the text of the entire chronicle for The Chaucer Library series, however, I have attempted to find the manuscript that comes closest to the one that Chaucer knew and used, and the method I have used to identify this manuscript is the same that Severs used to identify the Latin and French source manuscripts of *The Clerk's Tale*.[47] Each passage in which the readings of the Anglo-Norman texts diverge from the others has been compared with the corresponding passage in Chaucer's works where the influence of *Les Cronicles* has been, or might be, detected. According to this method the manuscript having the largest number of correspondences and requiring the fewest emendations will be the one that best represents Chaucer's manuscript. Because Chaucer gave free rein to his imagination while transforming Trevet's story into *The Man of Law's Tale*, following his source in only some 200 lines, when these lines are compared with the variants in the French texts only about two dozen passages provide any evidence that helps to identify Chaucer's source manuscript, and the weight of this evidence clearly favors the B-texts (P R L D) over the A-texts (A M F T S). Among the B-texts, Douce eliminates itself because it lacks most of the story of Constance. Leyden has the complete text, but in three of its sentences (pp. 307, lines 180–2; 309, line 222; 323, line 504 below) the scribe omits a word or phrase that appears in *The Man of Law's Tale* (lines 566, 597, 1004). Only Paris and Rawlinson, then, are the remaining contenders to represent Chaucer's manuscript and choosing between them is not easy. Paris is

[45] See *Originals and Analogues*, pp. iii–xii, 1–53. The Middle English version of Trevet's story is edited by W. A. Clouston in the same volume, pp. 221–50, along with some Asiatic and other European analogues, also edited by Clouston, pp. 365–414.

[46] Bryan and Dempster, pp. 163–4. Three of the sigla Schlauch uses for the manuscripts are different from those I have adopted: she uses Ar for A, G for T, and Fr for P. To avoid a great deal of confusion, anyone using her text should note that she was "not able to include variants from the text of F" (p. 162); but actually she used the sigil F, not Fr, when citing variants from the Paris manuscript. In the only edition of the entire chronicle to date, Rutherford used Rawlinson as his base text, which he regarded as typically normal Anglo-Norman, and included variants from Magdalen, Arundel, Trinity and Douce. See "The Anglo-Norman Chronicle of Nicholas Trevet," pp. 7–12.

[47] J. Burke Severs, *The Literary Relationships of Chaucer's "Clerkes Tale"* (Yale University Press, 1942; rpt. Hamden, CT, 1972), pp. 108, 191–2.

the earlier copy but both are closely related textually. The omission in Paris of a little phrase (*e sanz viron*) from Trevet's first exile scene may seem to give Rawlinson a slight edge, but the evidence is inconclusive because both manuscripts have the same phrase in the second exile scene. On the basis of the evidence in the Constance story alone, therefore, either Rawlinson or Paris could represent Chaucer's source manuscript.[48]

But Robert Pratt argued that Chaucer read more of the chronicle than just the life of Constance and used material from several other sections of it, especially his reference to Maurice's honoring the church in the conclusion of *The Man of Law's Tale* (1121–7), and also in several other works including *Anelida and Arcite*, *The Pardoner's Tale*, *The Wife of Bath's Tale* and *The Squire's Tale*. Chaucer may also have relied on Trevet for allusions to Caesar's triumph (*MLT*, 400, *MkT*, 2695–6), and the Demon-Yeoman's remark about Phitonissa and Samuel in *The Friar's Tale* (1511–12). When Trevet's language is compared with the corresponding passages in these poems, the comparisons provide evidence against all the surviving French texts except Paris, and in two passages that may have influenced the Pardoner's and Squire's allusions to the stories of Lot and Moses they give votes against Rawlinson, which lacks most of Trevet's redaction of Genesis and virtually all of Exodus.[49] The Paris manuscript therefore comes closest to representing Chaucer's copy, though it is not the manuscript Chaucer himself consulted. Paris has therefore been selected as the base text for The Chaucer Library edition, and is used for the edition of the Constance story printed here.

The manuscript that Gower consulted while writing "The Tale of Constance" was probably not much different from that which lay on Chaucer's desk as he wrote *The Man of Law's Tale*. All the available evidence indicates that both poets used a copy like one of the B-texts (P R L), and there is no evidence to prove that they did not in fact use the same manuscript.[50] Nicholson has even speculated that Gower may have been the "source" of Chaucer's copy. He based this hypothesis on the well known friendship of the two poets, on the fact that Gower was evidently the first to retell Trevet's story, and on his argument that, contrary to Pratt's surmise that Chaucer may have had access to Trevet's history through one of his noble patrons, *Les Cronicles* had apparently no wide circulation in court circles or among these patrons.[51] Nicholson cited the spellings of the names of the

[48] Correale, "Chaucer's Manuscript," pp. 240–54.

[49] See Robert A. Pratt, "Chaucer and *Les Cronicles* of Nicholas Trevet," in *Studies in Language, Literature, and Culture of the Middle Ages and Later*, ed. E. Bagby Atwood and Archibald A. Hill (Austin, TX, 1969), pp. 303–11, and Correale, "Chaucer's Manuscript," pp. 255–7. Nicholson is not persuaded by any of these "points of resemblance"; the only evidence he accepts of Chaucer's actual borrowing from another part of Trevet's history is his reference to Maurice honoring the church (*MLT* 1121–7), which "is important because it indicates that Chaucer had a manuscript of the entire *Chronicles*, not just an excerpt containing the tale of Constance" ("Chaucer Borrows From Gower," pp. 88–9).

[50] R. M. Correale, "Gower's Source Manuscript of Nicholas Trevet's *Les Cronicles*," in *John Gower: Recent Readings,* ed. R. F. Yeager, Medieval Institute Publications (Kalamazoo, MI, 1989), pp. 133–157.

[51] According to an inventory in 1397 two copies of *Les Cronicles* belonged to the library of Thomas of Woodstock, great-nephew of Princess Mary and brother of John of Gaunt, leading Pratt to conclude that it was "clearly a history well known to the family of Edward III" (p. 311). But Nicholson believes "there is no reason to connect Chaucer with either copy" ("Chaucer Borrows from Gower," p. 87), for

characters in both Chaucer's and Gower's versions, most of which are found only in A-texts, as further evidence that both poets worked from a similar manuscript.[52] That manuscript does not survive, but an edition of Trevet's story based on the Paris manuscript will give a clear picture of the kind of source text Chaucer and Gower handled while composing their versions of the Constance legend.

I. Schlauch did not print any extracts from Pope Innocent III's *De Miseria Condicionis Humane* in Bryan and Dempster. But because of its importance as a source for *The Man of Law's Prologue and Tale*, all six passages discussed at the beginning of this article are reprinted below from Lewis's edition of Innocent's treatise.

II. The text of Trevet's story of Constance presented here is an accurate transcription of the text found in the Paris manuscript, with the following exceptions: (a) abbreviations have been silently expanded in conformity with forms appearing in full elsewhere in the manuscript; (b) i/j and u/v have been distinguished according to accepted modern usage; (c) though attention has been paid to them, the scribe's practices regarding capitalization, punctuation, and sentence division have not been reproduced, instead modern English usage has been followed where required or where it seemed reasonable; (d) the editor is also responsible for paragraph divisions. Folio numbers of the base manuscript have been inserted into the text in parentheses.

In the critical apparatus, the lemma is given first, followed by any rejected readings from P, then all the variant readings in the order R L (D) A M F T S, as in the following examples:

> 49 **s'assentesit** sassentit L; sassentiseit A; se assent FT; sassenti S.

The reading **s'assentesit** of the base text is found in PRM; L has *sassentit*; A reads *sassentiseit*; FT have *se assent*; and S has *sassenti.*

> 144 **un clef** RLFT; en chef P; le une clef AM; un clefz S.

The reading *en chef* of the base text P has been rejected as erroneous; the emended reading **un clef** is found in RLFT; *le une clef* is the reading of AM; and S has *un clefz.*

Variant readings in D are listed beginning in line 493.

The apparatus includes all important differences in word choice and meaning. Minor differences in spelling are excluded as for example the masculine pronoun *li/lui* and *fu/f(e)ust/fuist* when they are variant spellings, as very frequently in LFTS, of the third person preterite. Also excluded are minor disagreements in number and gender of nouns and pronouns, dittography (except *Lumere* in line 238 in M) and minor inversions of words and phrases. The

as Jeanne Krochalis has pointed out, the books belonging to Thomas "came from the library of his wife's home at Pleshy, and many were probably inherited from her father, Humphrey de Bohun." See "The Books and Reading of Henry V and his Circle," *Chaucer Review* 23 (1988): 50–1. Paris is the most elaborately decorated manuscript and contains several illustrations, suggesting that it was produced for a particular library or some nobleman (Dean, "The Manuscripts," pp. 100–1, 103–4); it may have belonged at one time to Philip the Bold and his wife Margaret of Flanders, and later to Philip's brother, John, Duke of Berry (see Correale, "Chaucer's Manuscript," pp. 262–3).

52 Nicholson, "Chaucer Borrows from Gower," pp. 91–3; Correale, "Chaucer's Manuscript," pp. 250–1, and "Gower's Source Manuscript," pp. 148–50.

variant spellings of all proper names are given either in the critical apparatus or in a note to the text (*Hermegild*) The variants C*onstance*/*Constaunce* are not recorded, but *Custaunce*/*Custance* (Chaucer's spelling) are listed.

In the list of variants, the spelling given is that of the first textual witness following the variant. Thus, in line 506 **bons** beaux LAMFTS, the spelling **bons** (good) is that of the base manuscript P, but the other manuscripts with that reading (RD) have *bones*. *Beaux* (beautiful, fair) is the reading of L, but *bieus* is the spelling in AM, *bealx* is in FT, and *beals* in S.

In the apparatus, three abbreviations are used: *add* (added), *corr* (corrected), *om* (omitted). An asterisk is used to indicate a reading closer to Chaucer's English (175 ***devers la marine** de veer la marine AMFT; devers marine S.)

No modern translation of the Trevet's story has appeared since Brock's translation in 1872, and I have consulted it regularly in preparing my own translation, which aims to be more literal than literary.

III. The text of Gower's "Tale of Constance" is reproduced from G. C. Macaulay's edition (note 22 above), though in many places I have revised capitalization and punctuation to bring them more into line with modern practice. Macaulay's text is based on Bodleian Library MS Fairfax 3, the earliest copy of what Macaulay labeled the "third recension" of the poem. For Macaulay's description of his editorial practices see *Complete Works*, II.clviii–clix. Macaulay's edition reprints the Latin marginal glosses, summarizing the major incidents in the tale, that appear in Fairfax and most other early copies. These are omitted here, but vocabulary glosses have been added.

I

Of the Misery of the Human Condition

(trans. Robert Enzer Lewis)

I. The poor are indeed oppressed by starvation, tortured by need, hunger, thirst, cold, nakedness; they become worthless and waste away, are despised and confounded. O miserable condition of a beggar! If he begs, he is confounded with shame, and if he does not beg, he is consumed with want, and indeed is compelled by necessity to beg. He maintains that God is unjust because he does not dispense properly; he accuses his neighbor of being evil because he does not help fully; he is offended, he complains, he curses. Consider the opinion of the wise man on this subject: "It is better to die than to want." "The poor man shall be hateful even to his own neighbor." "All the days of the poor are evil." "The brethren of the poor man hate him, and even his friends have departed far from him."

II. Sudden woe always follows worldly joy, and what begins with gladness ends in sorrow. Worldly happiness is indeed sprinkled with many bitternesses. He knew this who said: "Laughter shall be mingled with sorrow, and mourning takes hold of the ends of joy." . . . Sound counsel: "In the day of good things be not unmindful of evils."

III. What is more unsightly than a drunkard, in whose mouth is a stench, in whose body a trembling; who utters foolish things, betrays secrets; whose reason is taken away, whose face is transformed? "For there is no secret where drunkenness reigneth."

IV. O extreme foulness of desire, which not only weakens, but debilitates the body; not only defiles the soul, but pollutes the person . . . sorrow and repentance always follow.

V. "From the morning until the evening the time shall be changed." . . . "They take the timbrel and the harp and rejoice at the sound of the organ."

VI. Who indeed has ever spent one whole delightful day in his own pleasure, whom the guilt of conscience or an attack of anger or the agitation of concupiscence has not disturbed in some part of the day? Whom the spite of envy or the burning of avarice or the swelling of pride has not vexed? Whom some loss or offense or passion has not upset?

I

Lotario Dei Segni, *De Miseria Condicionis Humane*

(from Lotario Dei Segni (Pope Innocent III), *De Miseria Condicionis Humane*, ed. and trans. Robert Enzer Lewis, The Chaucer Library [Athens, GA: University of Georgia Press, 1978], pp. 114–15, 128–31, 166–9, 170–1)

I. *MLTPro* 99–121, *De Miseria*. I. 14.1–14

Pauperes enim premuntur inedia, cruciantur erumpna, fame, siti, frigore, nuditate; vilescunt et contabescunt, spernuntur et confunduntur. O miserabilis condicio mendicantis! Et si petit, pudore confunditur, et si non petit, egestate consumitur, set ut mendicet necessitate compellitur. Deum causatur iniquum quod non recte dividat; proximum criminatur malignum quod non plene subveniat; indignatur, murmurat, inprecatur. Adverte super hoc sentenciam sapientis: "Melius est mori quam indigere." "Eciam proximo suo pauper odiosus erit." "Omnes dies pauperis mali." "Fratres hominis pauperis oderunt eum, insuper et amici procul recesserunt ab eo."

II. *MLT* 421–7, *De Miseria* I.21.1–5, 13–14

Semper mundane letitie tristicia repentina succedit, et quod incipit a gaudio desinit in merore. Mundana quippe felicitas multis amaritudinibus est respersa. Noverat hoc ille qui dixerat: "Risus dolore miscebitur, et extrema gaudii luctus occupat." . . . Salubre consilium: "In die bonorum ne immemor sis malorum."

III. *MLT* 771–7, *De Miseria* II. 19. 1–4

Quid turpius ebrioso, cui fetor est in ore, tremor in corpore; qui promit stulta, prodit occulta; cui mens alienatur, facies transformatur? "Nullum enim secretum ubi regnat ebrietas."

IV. *MLT* 925–31, *De Miseria* II. 21.5–8, 12–13

O extrema libidinis turpitudo, que non solum effeminat, set corpus enervat; non solum maculat animam, set fedat personam . . . semper secuntur dolor et penitencia.

V. *MLT* 1132–4, *De Miseria*. I .20.10–11, 12–13

"A mane usque ad vesperam mutabitur tempus." . . . "Tenent tympanum et cytharam et gaudent ad sonitum organi."

VI. *MLT* 1135–8, *De Miseria* I. 20. 1–7

Quis unquam vel unicam diem duxerit totam in sua delectacione iocundam, quem in aliqua parte diei reatus consciencie vel impetus ire vel motus concupiscencie non turbaverit? Quem livor invidie vel ardor avaricie vel tumor superbie non vexaverit? Quem aliqua iactura vel offensa vel passio non commoverit?

II

Nicholas Trevet, "Of the Noble Lady Constance"

(trans. R. M. Correale)

(1–9) In the time of this Emperor Tiberius [Constantine] as the old Saxon chronicles relate, there was a youth named Maurice, who was not more than eighteen years old when he was appointed by Tiberius to the empire, a very handsome youth, exceedingly strong for his age, and wise and keen of mind. This Maurice, according to the aforementioned history of the Saxons, was the son of Constance, the daughter of Tiberius, by a king of the Saxons – the aforesaid Alla, who was the second king of Northumbria – and was said to be of Cappadocia because for twelve years he was reared in the court of Senator Tarquinius of Rome, who was from Cappadocia.

(10–24) Then the story informs us that this Tiberius, when he governed the court and provinces of the empire under the Emperor Justin, as mentioned before, begot on his wife Italy a daughter named Constance. And because he had no other child, with great diligence he had her taught the Christian faith and instructed by learned masters in the seven sciences, which are logic, physics, morals, astronomy, geometry, music, and optics, called the secular sciences, and had her taught various languages. Then when she had begun her thirteenth year, there came to the court of her father Tiberius heathen merchants from the great Saracen land carrying much diverse and rich merchandise; Constance went down to see their riches and asked them about their land and their religion. And when she understood that they were heathens, she preached the Christian faith to them. And when they had assented to the Christian faith, she had them baptized and instructed perfectly in the faith of Jesus Christ.

(25–38) Then they returned to their country. And when they had acknowledged the faith before their Saracen neighbors and family, they were accused concerning their faith before the high Sultan. And after they were brought before him they were rebuked by their wise men for their faith, that they should believe in a crucified and mortal man. But after they had sufficiently defended the religion of Jesus Christ

1 **cist** cesti FT. **emperour** *om* S. **Tyberie** Thiberie AM; Teborie S. **Constantin** AMFTS; *om* PRL. **dient** devant L. 2 **aunciens** uns AMFTS. **des Sessouns** *om* AMFTS. **juvencele** tresvailaunt chevaler del pais de Capadoce AMFTS. 2–3 **Moriz qi n'estoit** Cist Moris fu eslu (esluz FT) par le avantdit Thiberie (de Tyberie S) destre emperour ou lui et lui dona femme Constaunce sa fille et la (le F, lui T) clama son heire Mes come dient lez aunciene cronikes de sessouns cist nestoit AMFTS. 3 **disoit** dissept AM. **quant** RLAMFTS; *om* P. **fu** estoit FT. **Tyberie** Thiberie A. 4 **graciouse** *add* juvencel AMFTS. 5 **Morice** Moriz L; *om* AMFTS. 6 ***Alla** Alle AMFTS (*so throughout*). **avauntdit** avantnome AMFTS. 7 **Northumbre** Northumberland S. **Capadoce** Capedoce F. 8 **norri** norre S. **Tarquinius** Tarquinnus AM. **de Rome** *om* FT. 10 **cist** cest L; cesti FT. **Tyberie** *add* Constantin AMFTS. 11 **dit** *add* al comencement del quarantime sisme (.xlvii. FTS) estoire AMFTS. 12 **Ytalie** Ytaile F. **apelé** *om* AMFTS. 13 **a** od S. 15 **logiciene** LAMS; *om* P; logicienez FT. 16 **perspective** RLAMFTS; perspeitive P. **philosophies** philosophres T. 17 **endoctriner** *add* par mestres sachanz L. 19 **Sarizine** paisine L. **trop** FT; *om* PLAM; trops R; multz S. 20 **lour richesses** lez richesses S. 21 **lour creaunce** la creance S. **entendi** LAMFTS; etendi PR. 23 **assentu** assenti S. **Cristiene** *om* LAMFT. **en** *om* S. 24 **foi** ley FT. 27 **devaunt** de L. **par** de FTS. 29 **puis** *om* FS. **defendu** defendi S. **loi** RA; *om* P; lei LMFT; foy S.

II

Nicholas Trevet, "De la noble femme Constance"[1]

(from *Les Cronicles*: Paris BN, MS français 9687, fols 62vb-69va)

(fol.62vb) En le temps cist emperour Tyberie [Constantin], come dient les aunciens croniqes des Sessouns, estoit un juvencele apelé Moriz, qi n'estoit mes de disoit anz [quant] il fu ordiné par Tyberie a l'empire, trop graciouse et mervaillousement vigerous de son age et de sen sages et agu. Cist Morice, solonc l'estoire de Sessons avantdite, estoit le fitz Constaunce, la fille Tyberie, de un roi de Sessons, Alla avauntdit, qi estoit le second roi de Northumbre, et fu dit de Capadoce, qar dusze anz estoit norri en la court le senatour Tarquinius de Rome, q'estoit de Capadoce.

Dount fait assavoir qe cist Tyberie, taunt come il governa la court et les provinces de l'empire souz l'emperour Justin, come avaunt est dit, engendra (fol.63a) de sa femme Ytalie une fille apelé Constance. Et pur ceo qe nul autre enfaunt avoit, pur ceo a grant diligence la fist enseigner la foi Cristiene, et endoctriner par mestres sachauntz en les sept sciences, qe sount [logiciene], naturele, morale, astronomie, geometrie, musiqe, [perspective], qe sont philosophies seculers apelez, et la fist endoctriner en diverses langages. Puis quant ele estoit entré le treszisme an de son age, viendrent a la court son pere Tyberie marchaunz paens hors de la grant Sarizine, aportauntz [trop] diverses et riches marchaundises, a queux descendi Constaunce pur aviser lour richesses, si lour demanda de lour terre et de lour creaunce. Et quant ele [entendi] q'il estoient paens, lour precha la foi Cristiene. Et puis q'il avoient assentu a la foi Cristiene les fist baptizer et enseigner parfitement en la foi Jhesu Crist.

Puis retournerent a lour terre. Et quant reconustrent la foi devaunt lour veisins et parentz Sarazins, estoient accusez a l'haut soudan de lour foi. Et aprés q'il estoient amenez devaunt lui, furent repris par les sages de lour ley, q'il devient crere en un homme crucifié et mortel. Mes puis q'il avoient suffisaument defendu la [loi] Jhesu Crist encontre les

[1] Trevet's story of Constance appears in his *estoire* on the Emperor Tiberius Constantine. The title I use is used as a marginal gloss at the beginning of the story in the Leyden MS, fol. 49v.

against the heathens, who no longer knew how to contradict it, they began to praise the maid Constance, who had converted them, for her very high and noble mind and wisdom, and great and wondrous beauty, and gentility and noble lineage; by these words the Sultan, greatly overcome with love for the maid, as he was a young man, sent again those same Christians she had already converted to the faith to Tiberius and his daughter, and with them a heathen emir with great array and wealth and gifts, asking for the maid in marriage, with great promise of peace and alliance between the lands of the Christians and Saracens.

(39–49) And after he had conferred about this request with Pope John III, who was mentioned before in the preceding chapter, and other important persons of Holy Church and the Roman senators, he replied to the emir and the messengers that if the Sultan would agree to deny his idols and his false beliefs and receive baptism and the religion of Jesus Christ, Tiberius by this agreement would assent to the alliance, but in no other form. And thereupon he sent his letters to the Sultan and greatly honored the messengers. And these men on their return, above all things praised the maiden to the Sultan, and also the nobility, the court, and the courteous rule of Tiberius. And before the Sultan and all his council, the emir vowed to become a Christian himself if the Sultan gave consent.

(50–62) Then after a few days the Sultan sent this same emir and official messengers from among the greatest men of the land, and in their safe conduct twelve Saracen children, sons of the leading Saracens, as hostages to Tiberius in the form of security for his daughter; and moreover he gave his full consent to the ordinance of the Christians, and also sent his sealed letters of good and entire peace between all Christians and Saracens, and free passage to travel freely for trade, and to visit the holy places of the Sepulchre, Mount Calvary, Bethlehem, Nazareth, the Valley of Jehoshaphat, and all other holy places within the boundaries of his control. And he surrendered the city of Jerusalem to the lordship of the Christians to live in, and gave liberty to the Christian bishops and their clergy to preach and to instruct the people of his land in the true faith, and to baptize, to build churches, and to destroy the temples of idols.

(63–72) And moreover to this effect he sent his letters by high-ranking persons to the pope and the clergy, to Tiberius and the maid Constance, and to all the senate with rich gifts and treasures. And through their negotiations they all agreed to this arrangement, and in time ordered the maiden to go from her father's house and from

30 **plus** *om* FTS. **contredire** attendre L. **comenserent** comencerunt A; come comencerent S. 31 **qi** LAMFTS; qil PR. **convertu** converti L; convertiz et pleinement enseigne S. **trop haut** tres haut LFT. **noble** trop noble F; tres noble T. 34 **ceux** ses L. 35 **ia** qil AM. **convertuz** convertiz L; converti AM; convertez FTS. **admirail** admirable S. 36 **a sa** sa LA. 37 **d'aliaunce** de liance F. **entre** contre AM. 38 **de** *om* S. 39 **avoit** LAMFTS; avant PR. **demaunde** demaunda S. 40 **le Tiercz** *om* AMFTS. **proschein** quarantisme sisme AM; .xlvii. FTS. 42 **as** as ses F; a ses T. **si** *om* S. **se** *om* L. 43 **maumetz** maumes leis L; maumes S. **ley** foy FTS. 44 **a ceste** en cest FTS. **se** *om* FTS. **a** R; et P; al LAMFTS. 44–5 **en . . . fourme** en autre manere L; autrement T. 45 **manda** comaunda S. 46 **cist** cesti F; ceux T; ils S. 48 **Tyberie** Thiberie M. **le . . . et devaunt** *om* A. 49 **s'assentesit** sassentit L; sassentiseit A; se assent FT; sassenti S. 50 **jours** temps L. **maunda** *om* FTS. **cist** cesti AMFT; cest S. **et** LAMFTS; set PR. 52 **hostages** en hostages A. 54 **a l'ordinaunce** de l'ordinance AMFTS. **asselez** ensealees L. 54–5 **de bone** *om* AM. 55 **Sarrasins** Cristiens FTS. **et fraunch** en franche FTS. 56 **fraunchement** *om* L. **de marchaunder** et marchandier LAMFT; *om* S. **pur** puis FTS. 57 **lieus del** *om* L. **Sepulture** sepultures L. 58 **Nazareth . . . Josephat** *om* L. **Josephat** Iosaphath R; Josaphat M; Josophath S. **seintz** lieux seintz S. 60 **a** *om* S. 61 **les gentz** la gent FT. **sa terre** la terre de S. 62 **de maunetz** et maumentz FT; des maumes S. 65 **grantz** S; *om* PRLAMFT. **pur** par FTS (*passim*). **comunes** conues FTS.

paens, qi ne savoient plus contredire, comenserent de preiser la pucele Constaunce, [qi] les avoit convertu, de trop haut et noble sen et sapience, et de grant et merveillous beauté et genterise et noblesce de sanc; par quels paroles lui soudan, trop suppris de l'amour de la pucele, com il estoit homme de jeu(fol.63b)ven age, maunda de novele meismes ceux Cristiens ia convertuz a la foi, et ovesqe eux un admirail paen ove grant aparail et richesces et presens a Tyberie et a sa fille, endemaundant la pucele en mariage, ove grant promesse de pees et d'aliaunce entre les parties de Cristiens et Sarazins.

Et puis qe Tyberie [avoit] counseillé sour ceste demaunde le pape Johan le Tiercz, de qi est avantdit en le proschein estoire, et les autres grantz de Seinte Eglise, et les Romeins del Senat, respoundi a l'admirail et as messagers, qe si lui soudan se voleit assenter de reneer ses maumetz et sa mescreauntz et resceivre baptesme et la ley Jhesu Crist, a ceste covenaunt Tyberius se assenteroit [a] alliaunce, mes ne pas en autre fourme. Et sur ceo manda ses lettres a lui soudan et grantment honura les messagers. Et cist, a lour retourner, sour totes riens preiserent la pucele a lui soudan, et la nobleie et la court et la genti seignurie Tyberie. Et lui admirail devant le soudan et devaunt tote son counsail se vowa a la foi Cristiene, si le soudan s'assentesit.

Puis aprés poi de jours, le soudan maunda mesme cist admirail [et] solempnes messagers des plus grant de sa terre, et, en lour condut, dusze enfauntz Sarazins, fitz a grant Sarazins, hostages a Tyberie en fourme de seurté pur sa fille. Et a ceo manda son assent, haut et bas, a l'ordinaunce des Cristiens; et a ceo envoia ses lettres asselez de bone et entiere pees entre touz Cristiens et touz Sarrasins, et fraunch pas (fol.63va) sage de aler fraunchement de marchaunder, et pur visiter les seintz lieus del Sepulture et del mount de Calvarie et de Bethleem et de Nazareth et del vaal de Josephat, et tous autres seintz deinz les marches de son pouer. Et la cité de Jerusalem abandona a la seignurie des Cristiens pur enhabiter, et fraunchises as evesqes Cristiens et a lour clergie de precher et enseigner les gentz de sa terre la droite foi, et de baptizer, et de eglises faire et les temples de maunetz destrure.

Et a ceo envoia ses lettres a l'apostoille et a la clergie, et a Tyberie et a la pucele Constance, et a tut le senat, ove riches dons et tresours par [grantz] persons. Et pur lour comunes sur ceste maundement

her acquaintances among foreign barbarians with great grief, tears, outcry, noise and lament from the whole city of Rome. On this voyage was sent a cardinal bishop and a cardinal priest with a large number of clergy, and a senator of Rome with noble knights in grand and rich apparel, and a large number of Christians, some of whom went there on pilgrimage and others to take possession of Jerusalem.

(73–84) It happened that the Sultan's mother, who was still living – Alas! it was the will of God – seeing that her religion was already on the point of being destroyed by Christians, who were in the Saracen land, plotted evil and treason. Then, after she made a secret alliance by covenant with seven hundred Saracens to commit themselves to live or die in the quarrel, she went to her son, when she heard the coming of the maiden and the Christians was very near – within a few days' journey from the land – and began to thank and praise God that he had intended to adopt the Christian faith; and she swore to him that for a long time she secretly had this same resolve. Then finally she begged her son, the Sultan, that he would grant her the first feast before the wedding, and thanking her, he consented. Then the maiden and the Christians were received by the Sultan and his mother with great honor and great splendor.

(85–99) And on the first day of her arrival the feast was provided in the palace of the Sultaness; and the banquet was so arranged that all the Christian and Saracen males should eat in the hall of the Sultan, and at the feast in the hall of the Sultaness there should be only women, except for the seven hundred hired Saracens, who were assigned to serve at both feasts. And when the feast was most joyful, these seven hundred hirelings, with another large multitude of their retainers, came armed upon those eating. And according to the order of the Sultaness, they killed all the Christian men and women, except only the maiden, and they killed the Sultan and the emir and the other converts to the Christian faith. And everywhere in the court they put to death whomever they found among the common Christian people. But when they first heard the commotion, three young Christian men escaped and came to Rome and reported to the Emperor the mischief and treason, and the death, as they supposed, of his daughter Constance. At this news the Emperor and all the clergy and the Senate were dismayed, and great grief was displayed throughout Rome.

(100–116) In this manner Constance remained alone, entirely destitute in the hands of her enemies. Then after she would not deny her faith, neither for any favorable promise of wealth or honor, nor for any threat of punishment or death, the

66 **s'acordereient** sacorderent LAMFTS. 68 **cel** *om* L; *add* temps FTS. 69 **envoié** *om* T. **et . . . Cardinal** *om* FT. 70 **un** RLMFTS; une PA. **noble** grande et noble FS. **ove grant** e grant AM; et ove grant FTS. 71 **grant nombre** ove grant nombre AM; grant noble nombre FT. **qe** y qi LS. 72 **pelrinage** pelrinages LF. 73 **sil** si ne AMS; sil ne FT. 75 **qe furent** qestoient FT; survenauntz S. **Sarasine** sa reaume L. 76 **cenz** *om* AM. 77 **vient** mist AMFTS. 78 **bien** *om* L. 79 **a poi de** apres de deux FTS. **mult** a molt FT. **mercier** *om* L. **q'il** qel AM. 80 **foi** ley LAMFTS. 82 **il** luy S. 83 **fu** feurent T. 85 **lour** sa FTS. 85–6 **la soudane** FT; le soudane PRLAMS. 86 **q'en** qe AMFS. **lui soudan** la soudane FT. 87 **mangassent** mangerent L. **en** *om* L. 88 **soudane** la soudane RL; le soudan AFT; le soudane M; la sodane sa miere S. **sauve** sauntz AMFTS. **lowés** lowis AFT. 90 **lowés** lowis AMFT. **autre** *om* L. 91 **retenaunce** RL; recenaunce P; reteinaunce AM; retenance FTS. **mangantz** mangeauncez A. 92 **occirent** tuerent AMFTS. 93 **convertuz** convertiez AMS. 94 **Cristiene** *om* AMS. **Et** RLAMFTS; *om* P. 95 **mistrent** RLAMFTS; mustrent P. **valletz** veils S. **eschaperent** eschapirent L; eschaperont M. 96 **counterent** counteront FT. 98 **entenderent** entendirent LAMS. 99 **senat** LAMFTS; sanat PR. **et** RLAMFTS; a P. **fu** RLAMS; *om* P; feust FT. **parmi** par demy S. 100 **degarré** desgarri T. **la main** les meyns AMFTS. **ses** des FT. 101 **bele** *om* LFT. **de richesse** ne richesse FT.

touz s'acordereient, et en temps maunderent la pucele hors de la meson son piere et hors de sa conoissaunce entre estranges barbaryns a grant deol et lermes et crie et noyse et plente de tote la cité de Rome. En cel voiage estoit envoié un evesqe Cardinal et un prestre Cardinal ove grant nombre de clergie, et [un] senatour de Rome ove noble chivalerie ove grant et riche apparail, et grant nombre de Cristiens qe y alerent, les uns pur pelrinage, les autres pur la seisine de Jerusalem.

Avient qe la mere le soudan qe uncore vivoit – Allas! sil fut la volenté Dieux – veaunt qe sa ley estoit ja en poynt d'estre destrute par Cristiens qe furent en Sarasine, s'en pensa de mal et de treson. Dount puis qe ele avoit privé alliaunce de covenaunt ov sept cenz Sarasins qe s'abandonerent de vivre et morer en la querele vient(fol.63vb)a son fitz quant ele oy la venue de la pucele et des Cristiens bien pres de la terre a poi de journeys, et comensa mult mercier et loer dieux q'il avoit le purpos de la foi Cristiene, et lui jura qe par grant temps avoit ele esté en mesme la volenté privément; dount finaument pria son fitz le soudan qe lui grantast la primere feste avaunt les esposailles, et il enmerciaunt lui octrai. Puis fu la pucele et les Cristiens resceuz del sodan et de sa mere a grant honour et a grant nobleie.

Et le primer jour de lour venue fu le feste purveu en la paleis [la] soudane; et estoit la mangerie ordeiné issint q'en les hales lui soudan mangassent touz les mals Cristiens et Sarazins, et q'en les hales et en la feste soudane fuissent soules femmes sauve lé sept cenz sarazins lowés qe furent ordinez pur service de l'une feste et de l'autre. Et ceux sept cenz lowés, quant la feste fut plus lee, vindrent armés ove une autre grant multitude de lour [retenaunce] sur les mangantz. Et solenc l'ordinance de la soudane occirent touz les Cristiens madles et femeles fors soul la pucele; et occirent le soudan et l'admiral et les autres convertuz a la foi Cristiene. [Et] par tote la court quant q'il troverent del comune people des Cristiens [mistrent] a la mort. Mes trois valletz Cristiens eschaperent quant primerement oirent l'affray, et viendrent a Rome, et counterent a l'emperour la mescheaunce et le traison et la mort sa fille Constance com il entenderent. A ceste novele estoit l'emperour et tote la clergie et le [senat] (fol.64a) affraez, [et] grant deol [fu] demené parmi Rome.

A ceste manere demora Constance soul, tote degarré en la main ses enemis. Puis, aprés qe ele ne voleit pur nule bele promesse de richesse ne de honur, ne pur nul manace de peine ne de mort, reneier sa foi, le

Sultaness – that member of the devil! – planned a new torture for her, which, though it came entirely from her cruel will, nevertheless the providence of God was not lacking therein, which never fails those in tribulation who have hope in him. Then the Sultaness caused a boat to be stored with food, bread called biscuit, peas, beans, sugar, honey and wine to sustain the life of the maiden for three years. And in the boat she had placed all the riches and treasure which Emperor Tiberius had sent with the maid Constance, his daughter; and she had Constance put into this boat without sail, oar, or any kind of human aid. And she had her taken by other ships to the high sea where no land was visible to them; and the sailors left her all alone and commended her to the four winds. But God was her mariner, for during the three whole years she was led on the great ocean, in all that time she never saw man or ship, but God alone comforted and counseled her by his words.

(117–128) Then in the eighth month of the fourth year, God, who steered the ship of the holy man Noah in the great Flood, sent a favorable wind and drove the boat to England, beneath a castle in the kingdom of Northumberland, near Humber; and the ship landed on the eve of the Nativity of Our Lord Jesus Christ. And when the sailors, who were near the shore in their ship, saw this marvel – namely a maiden of fair and noble form, but pale, in unusual attire, and furnished with great treasure – they went to the warden of the castle, who at that time was a Saxon named Olda (for the Britons had already lost control of the island, as is related above in the end of the story of the Emperor Justinian the Great) and told him of the marvel. And this Olda went down to the maid in her boat and asked about her condition.

(129–144) And she, as one who was skilled in various languages, as mentioned above, answered him in Saxon, which was Olda's language, and told him that as to her religion she was of the Christian faith; as to her lineage she was born of rich and noble family, and that because of her lineage she was given in marriage to a great prince, but because she displeased the great ones of the land she was in such manner exiled. And in her words she would reveal nothing about the Emperor Tiberius, her father, nor about the Sultan, for the story of the murder of the Sultan and the Christians was already known throughout all lands. And when Olda had heard her speak his language so competently and found such great treasure with her, he supposed she was the daughter of some king of the Saxons beyond the sea, as of Germany, or Saxony,

103 **la soudane** le sodane S. **enpensa** pensa FTS. **de une** de lui AM. 104 **vensit** vienesit A; venist FT. **n'i** ne LFTS. **failli** faille L. **point** unqes FT. 105 **faut** failli point S. **ount** sont L. 106 **estoffer** estorier AMFTS. **nef** nefs M. 107 **et de meel** se de meel M. 108 **cel** *om* L. **tote** *om* A. 110–11 **et *sanz viron** RL; *om* P; et sauntz neviroun AM; et sanz naviron FTS. 113 **comaunderent** comaunder A. **venz** nefze FTS. 114 **son** RLAMFTS; *om* P. **entiers** *om* FTS. **mené** mesme AM; *om* S. 115 **en tut** AMS; ove P; en RL; ou tout FT. **ne nef** nef S. **n'encontra** LAMFTS; ne nentra PR. 116 **l'avoit** AMFTS; avoit PRL. **confort** counforte AMS; confortez FT. **counseilé** AMFS; conseiler PRL; conseillez T. **sa** *om* FT. 117 **le oitime** LAMFTS; lei oitime PR. 117–18 **le seint homme** leint homme T; *om* S. 118 **Noé** Nee FT. 119 **Northumbreland** Northombre AM; Northumbre FTS. 120 **Hombre** Humbre AMFTS. **Nostre Seignur** *om* AMFTS. 121 **nef** nefs LAM. 122–3 **genti affeiture** gentz(?)affeiture L; de gentil feture S. 123 **estoffé** feossez FT; stoffe S. 124 **noun** a noun LAMT; son noun S. 125 **Olda** Elda AM(*so throughout*). **Brutons** Bretouns AMT; Britons FS. **de l'ysle** del iste FT. **avant** devant FT. 126 **l'estoire . . . Grant** quarantisme quint estoire AMFTS. 127 **cist** *om* AMFTS. **sa nef** la nef FT. **lui** la FT. 129 **ele** RLAMFTS; al P. 130 **q'estoit** qe fust L. 133 **ele** *om* L; qil FT. 134 **tiele** cele FT. **Et** Mes S. **riens** rieil L. 136 **l'aventure** lave(?)L. **Cristiens** Cristient M. 137 **conue** RLAMFTS; come P. 138 **lange** langage FT. **si** *om* T.

membre au diable, la soudane, se enpensa de une novel tourment, qe tut le vensit de cruele volunté, nepurquant la purveaunce Dieux n'i failli point, qi en tribulacion ja ne faut as ceux qe ount en lui esperance. Dount ele fist estoffer un nef de vitaile de pain q'est apelé bisquit, et de pois et de feves et de zucre et de meel et de vin pur sustenaunce de la vie de la pucele pur trois anz. Et en cel nef fist mettre tote la richesse et le tresour qe l'emperour Tyberie avoit mandé ove la pucele Constance, sa fille; et en cel nef fist la soudane mettre la pucele sanz sigle [et sanz viron] et sanz chescune manere de eide de homme. Et issint la fist mener par autres nefs tanqe a la haute mere ove nule terre lour aparut; et issint les mariners la lesserent soule et la comaunderent a qatre venz. Mes Dieux estoit [son] mariner, qar par trois anz entiers fu ele mené en le grant occean, [en tut] le temps unqes homme ne nef ne vist ne [n'encontra], mes Deux soul [l'avoit] confort et [counseilé] de sa parlaunce.

Puis [le oitime] mois del quart an, Dieux, qi governa le nef le seint homme Noé en le grant deluve, maunda un vent covenable et enchasa la nef en Engleterre desouz une chastel en le roialme de Northumbreland, pres Hombre, et ariva la nef la veille de la (fol.64b) Nativité Nostre Seignur Jhesu Crist. Et quant lé mariners q'estoient pres de la rivail en lour nef virent ceste merveil, c'est assavoir une pucele de bele et genti affeiture, mes descolouré, en strange atir et estoffé de grant tresour, alerent al gardein del chastel qe adonqe estoit un Sessoin q'avoit noun Olda – qar les Brutons avoient ja perdue la seignurie de l'ysle, come avant est counté en la fin de l'estoire l'emperour Justinian le Grant – et lui counterent la merveil. Et cist Olda descendi a la pucele en sa nef, et lui demaunda de son estre.

Et [ele] lui respoundi en Sessoneis, qe fu langage Olda, come cele q'estoit aprise en diverses langages, come avant est dit, et lui disoit qe quant a sa creance ele estoit de Cristiene foi; quant a linage qe ele estoit de riches et nobles gentz estret; et qe par son linage estoit ele doné en mariage a un grant prince, mes pur ceo qe ele desplut as grantz de la terre, pur ceo fu ele en tiele manere exilé. Et entre ses ditz riens ne voleit reconustre de Tyberie l'emperour, son piere, ne del soudan, qar l'aventure del murdre del soudan et de les Cristiens lui estoit ia [conue] par totes terres. Et puis qe Olda l'avoit oy si renablement parler sa lange, et trova ove lui si grant tresour, esperoit qe ele estoit fille de ascun roi des Sessouns outre mere, come d'Alemayne, oue de Sessoine,

or Sweden, or Denmark, and with great joy he received her courteously and honorably into his castle; and the treasure that he had found with her he shut within a chest with a double lock, and gave the maid one key to the chest and the other he kept for himself. And he ordered his wife to receive the maiden honorably in her chamber.

(145–151) Then, after a short time, when she was well refreshed with good food and comforted with baths and other conveniences, she recovered her beauty and her fair color. And although she was wondrously fair in body, nevertheless she excelled in the beauty of virtues, as one whom God had predestined for grace and virtue in temptation and joy. Then when Hermegild, Olda's wife, perceived her noble and virtuous way of life, she was so much taken by love for her that nothing could happen to her that she would not do according to her will.

(152–173) Then, when she had affirmed this promise to her several times, one day as Hermegild again repeated this promise to her, the holy maiden answered her: "and since there is nothing," she said, "that you will not do at my wish then you yourself will be such as I am." And Hermegild answered her: "to that," she said, "I can never attain, for on earth you are peerless in virtue." And Constance answered her, "You may come to it if you believe in that God, who is lord of all virtue." (For Hermegild and Olda and the other Saxons who had control over the land were still pagans.) And Hermegild listened humbly and devoutly to the teaching of the faith from the mouth of Constance, who taught her the power of God in the creation of the whole world, and the vengeance he took for sin in the great Flood, and afterwards by plunging the great cities into hell for sin, with men and beasts and whatever else was therein. Then she showed her the great love of God in his birth, and his meekness and virtue in his passion and death, and the power of the divinity of Jesus Christ in his resurrection and ascension, and all about the nature of only one God and three persons in the coming of the Holy Spirit. And when she had instructed her for many days concerning the faith and the sacraments and the commandments, then she taught her to love and desire the joy of heaven and to hate the pains of hell. Then Hermegild, after this instruction, devoutly begged to be baptized according to the form of Holy Church, but because her husband was a pagan she could not yet achieve her purpose.

(174–189) And so it happened as Olda and Hermegild and Constance went one day toward the sea and the fishermen fishing in the sea, they saw coming towards them a poor blind Christian Briton. He, who was unknown to them all, but taught by the Holy Spirit, began to cry out before all, "Hermegild, wife of Olda and disciple of

140 **joye** LAMFTS; ioyse PR. 141 **son** le AM. 142 **einz** deinz FTS. **souz** deinz S. **serrure** ferrure L. **bailla** *add* a T. 143 **un clef** RLFT; en chef P; le une clef AM; un clefz S. **soi** lui FT. 144 **damoisele** pucele AM. 145 **un** *om* T. **avigouré** aviboire L. 147 **sa bele** bel FTS. **de merveil** a marvaille LAMFT; et merveille S. 148 **cele** *om* L. 149 **vertue** a vertue FTS. **en** S; et PRLAM; a FT. **temptacion** temptacions S. **et joie** a joye S. 150 **sa noble** le noble S. 154 **ne est** est S. **dit** fist T. 155 **tiele** celle S. 156 **porrai** purra S. 157 **vertue** vertues FS. **Constance** Custaunce AM. **respount** respondist FTS. **poet** poiez LAMFTS. 158 **tote vertue** touz vertues S. 159 **Qar** *om* AM. **seignurie** fourme FTS. 160 **estoient** estoien L. 161 **escota** RLAMFTS; escoca P. 163 **de pecché** *om* AM. 164 **ove** et AM. 165 **en sa** et sa FTS. **deboneretė** boneirte AM. 166 **mort** RLAMFTS; morut P. 167 **en sa (1)** et sa L. **de un** en un FTS. 168 **persones** *add* en trinite A. **en la** et en la AL. **par** *om* TS. 169 **comaundementz** .x. comandementz Puis S. 170 **haier** *om* AMFTS. **d'enfern** *add* douter AM; *add* de eschuer S. 171 **aprés** apris F; aprist S. 172 **poeit** poiast S. 173 **purcevre** pursuir LFT; pursuer S. 174 **Olda** Elda A; Helda M. 175 ***devers la marine** de veer la marine AMFT; devers marine S. **pessoners** *repeated* P; pessours FT. 176 **encontraunt** et contront F; et contrent T. **Cist** cesti FT. 177 **a crier** crier LS; de crier AM.

ou de Suece, oue de Denemarche. Et a grant [joye], courteisement et honurablement, la resceut en son chastel; et le tresour q'il avoit ove lui trové ferma einz une huche souz double serrure, de quel il bailla la pucele [un clef] et devers soi retient (fol.64va) l'autre. Et comanda sa compaigne qe ele resceut la damoisele honurablement en sa chaumbre.

Puis, aprés un poi de temps, qe ele estoit bien avigouré de bones viaundes et conforté de bains et d'autres eesementz, ele reprist sa beauté et sa bele colour. Et tut fut ele bele de merveil de corps, nepurquant ele passa en beauté de vertues come cele qe Dieux avoit predestiné a grace et vertue [en] temptacion et joie. Dont quant Hermegild,[2] la femme Olda, apparceut sa noble vie et vertuouse taunt fu de s'amour suppris, qe riens ne lui poet avenir qe ele ne freit a sa volunté.

Lors, quant plusours foitz lui avoit ceste parole affermé, un jour come Hermegild lui reherca autrefoitz la parole, la seinte pucele lui respoundi: "Et pus qe riens ne est," dit ele, "qe vous ne frez a ma volenté, dount vous serretz meisme tiele come jeo sui." Et Hermegild lui respondi: "A ceo," dist ele, "ja ne porrai jeo attendre, qar vous estes en terre sanz piere en vertue." Et Constance lui respount: "A ceo poet vous venir, si crere vodrez en celui Dieux, qi est Seignour de tote vertue." (Qar Hermegild et Olda et les autres Sessons q'avoient donc la seignurie de la terre estoient encore paens.) Et Hermegild houmblement et devoutement [escota] la doctrine de la foi par la bouche Constaunce, qe lui aprist la puissaunce Dieux en la fesaunce de tut le mond, et sa vengaunce q'il prist de pecché par le grant deluvie, et aprés par les grantz citez q'il effoudri en enfern pur pecché ove hommes et bestes et quantqe leins estoit. Puis lui moustra le grant amour Dieux en sa nessaunce (fol.64vb) et sa debonereté et vertue en sa [mort] et en sa passion, et la vertue de la deité Jhesu Crist en sa Resurection et en sa Assension, et tote la nature de un soul Dieux et treis persones, en la venue del Seint Espirit. Et quant par plusours jours l'avoit de la foi apris et les sacrementz et les comaundementz, lui aprist amour et desir a la joie de ciel et haier les peines d'enfern. Dont Hermegild, aprés ceste aprise, devoutement pria d'estre baptizé solonc la fourme de Seinte Eglise; mes pur ceo qe son baron estoit paen, ele ne poeit encore purcevre son purpos.

Et avient qe auxi come Olda et Hermegild et Constance alerent un jour devers la marine et les pessoners pessauntz en la mere, et voient encontraunt un povre Cristien Bruton enveuglés. Cist, q'estoit de touz estrange mes apris del Seint Esperit, comensa a crier devaunt touz:

[2] The constable's wife's name appears in various forms in sixteen lines. **PRL** have *Hermegild*, except in line 224, where they have *Hermigild*, and in 182 where it is omitted in **L**. **AM** have *Hermi(y)ngild* in 149, 153, 155, 178, 222, 243, and *Hermigild* in 180, 182, 190. **A** has *Hermi(y)gi(y)ld(e)* in 159, 160, 171, 174, 183, 224, 234. **M** has *Hermingi(y)ld* in 159, 160, 174, 224, 234 and *Hermigi(y)ld* in 171, 183. **FS** have *Hermigild* everywhere. **T** has *Hermigild* in 149, 171 and *Hermegilde* in all others.

Constance, I pray you in the name of Jesus Christ, in whom you believe, to make the sign of the cross on my blind eyes." At that cry, Hermegild, greatly frightened, was dismayed, but Constance, perceiving the power of God in the blind man's cry, strengthened Hermegild and said to her: "Lady, do not hide the power God has given you." And Hermegild, before Olda and his retinue which followed him, in good and firm faith made the holy cross on the eyes of the blind man, and said to him in her Saxon language: "Blind man, in the name of Jesus, slain on the cross, have thy sight." And he was immediately given sight and saw well and clearly. When Olda had seen this, he wondered greatly where his wife had learned her admirable skill. And after he had asked her, she replied that if he would listen to her advice he should perform such a marvel and even greater ones.

(190–202) Then Hermegild and Constance did not cease to preach the faith of Jesus Christ to Olda and all his household, and they sheltered and cared for this poor Briton for the love of Jesus Christ. Then Olda very joyfully received teaching in the faith, and by common agreement they sent the Briton secretly into Wales, where most of the Britons had fled (as mentioned above in the end of the story of the Emperor Justinian the Great) to bring from there a British bishop who might baptize Olda and his wife and their household. And in the meantime Olda caused their idols, which they had worshipped, to be smashed and ordered them thrown into the latrine. Then this poor Briton, returning from Wales, brought with him Lucius, one of the bishops of Wales, who was from Bangor. This Lucius, after he had tested and proven that Olda, with his wife and household, were taught according to the true form of the Christian faith, praised God devoutly and baptized them in the number of four score and eleven.

(203–209) Then Olda, by great deliberation and private counsel with himself, went to his lord Alla, the aforesaid king of Northumberland, and in private conference told him about the maid Constance, as he who by great trust for honesty and good sense had the supreme command of the realm after the king. And when the king had listened to all his words in private consultation between the two of them, he was greatly desirous to see and speak with the maid. And because of this desire he promised Olda that he would come in secret to visit her.

(210–226) At this same time, a Saxon knight of Olda's household, one among the others already baptized, to whom Olda had entrusted the keeping of the castle until his return from the king, was by secret temptation smitten with love for the

178 **te pri** le pri M. 179 **Crist** *om* AM. **facet** facetz RFTS; face L; facis AM. 180 **estut** estoit AMS. **abaié** esbai FT. 180–2 **mes *Constaunce . . . *conforta Hermegild . . . dist** *om* L. 181 **Dieux** *add* estre estre S. **en** RAMFTS; et P. 182 **te** vous FT. 183 **devaunt** davant T. **sui** feust FT. 184 **enveuglé** veuglez S. 184–5 **sa langage** la lange L. 185 **Bisne** Bisene AM; Bisigne FT; Bisine S. **in** AMS; en PRLFT. **rode** RLAMFT; rede P; ye rode S. **thi** yi RA; 3i M. 186 **siht** sight LAT; sith M; sigh F; sigth S. **sil** cist L; *om* A; si M; cil S. **meintenaunte** RLAMTS; meintenaunce P; *om* F. **aluminé** illumine S. 187 **clerement** crerement L. 188 **sa bele** si bele LAMFT; celle belle S. 189 **merveil** merveillement FT; meistre et merveile S. 190 ***de precher** *om* AM. 191 **foi** RLFTS; fu P; fey AM. 191–2 **Et cil . . . Crist** *om* FTS. 191 **recetterent** receurent AM. 193 **en** a FTS. **Wales** Gales AMFTS (*so throughout*). 194 **plus** plusours S. **fuit** Puis FTS. 194–5 **de l'estoire . . . Grant** del quarauntisme quinte (.xlv. FTS) estoire AMFTS. 196 **et lour** ove lour FT; et sa S. 197 **maunetz** maumez L; Mahounet A; Mahouneth M; Mahouns FTS. **avoient** avoit FTS. 198 **Cist** cesti FT. **povre** *om* L. **retournant** retournoit S. 199 **q'estoit** *om* AMFTS. **de Bangor** a Bangor F; et Bangor T. **Cist** cesti T. 200 **q'il** *om* L; ceo qil AM. 201 **foi Cristiene** ley et fey AM; foi TS. **devoutement** RLAMFTS; devoitement P. 202 **baptiza** baptize F. 203 **lui** counta la pucele Constance *add and erased* S. 204 **Northumbre** Northumberlond S. 205 **leauté** beaute FT. 206 **sa** la FTS. 207 **fu** *om* F; estoit T. 208 **desir** *add* parfournir T. 209 **la** le FT; luy S. **vindroit** voudroit LF; vorroit T. 212 **par** en S.

"Hermegild, la femme Olda et la disciple Constance, te pri en le noun Jhesu Crist, en qi tu creiz, qe tu me facet le signe de la crois sur mes eux enveuglés." A ceste parole, Hermegild, trop affraié, estut abaié, mes Constaunce, entendant la vertue Dieux [en] la parole l'eveugle, conforta Hermegild, et lui dist: "Ne muscez pas, dame, la vertue qe Dieux te ad doné." Et Hermegild, devaunt Olda et sa meine qe lui sui, de bone foi et ferme fist sus les euz de lui enveuglé la seinte croiz et lui dit en sa langage Sessoine: "Bisne man [in] Jhesu name in [rode] yslawe, have thi siht." Et sil [meintenaunte] fu aluminé et regardoit bien (fol.65a) et clerement. Quant Olda avoit ceo veu, mult s'enmerveilla ou sa femme avoit aprise sa bele mestrie. Et aprés q'il avoit demandé, ele lui respoundi qe si il escotast son conseil, tiel merveil freit et plus grande.

Puis Hermegild et Constance ne cesserent de precher a Olda et a tut sa meiné la [foi] Jhesu Crist. Et cil povre Breton recetterent et sustindrent pur l'amur Jhesu Crist. Lors Olda trop joyousement receut la doctrine de la foi; et par comune assent maunderent privément le dit Brutoun en Wales, ou estoient le plus de Brutons fuit, come avant est dit en la fin de l'estoire l'emperour Justinian le Grant, pur amener de illeoqes un evesqe Bruton qe put Olda et sa femme et lour meiné baptizer. Et en le mene temps Olda fist debruser lour maunetz q'il avoient aouré, et les comaunda gettre en longaines. Puis cist povre Bruton, retournant de Wales, amena ovesqe lui Lucius, un des evesqes de Wales, q'estoit de Bangor. Cist Lucius, aprés q'il avoit assaé et esprové qe Olda ove sa femme et sa meiné estoient solom droite fourme de la foi Cristiene enformé, loa Deux [devoutement] et les baptiza al noumbre de quatre vinz et unze.

Puis Olda par grant avisement et privé conseil de lui mesmes, ala a son seignour Alla, le roi de Northumbre avantnomé, et en privé conseil lui conta de la pucele Constance, come sely qi par grant affiance de leauté et sen avoit sa soverein garde del roialme aprés le roi. Et quant le roi avoit touz ces ditz en privee conseil entre eux deux escotez, mult fu desirous de la pucele veer et parler. Et a cest desir (fol.65b) promist a Olda q'il privément la vindroit visiter.

Et en cel mesme temps un chivaler Sessoun de la mené Olda, entre les autres ja baptizé, a qi Olda avoit baillé la garde del chastel tanqe a sa venue del roi, estoit par privé temptacion suppris en l'amur

maid Constance. And because in Olda's absence all the keeping was left to him, by evil instigation and temptation of the devil he went to tempt the maid Constance to consent to carnal sin. And after she had reproved him one time and another, the third time she reviled him with great indignation, saying he was like a dog, who after the holy sacrament of his baptism, wanted to return to his filth. Then, fearing he would be accused for his misdeed before Olda at his return, he plotted evil. For at daybreak after the night when Olda was to enter the castle on his return from the king, and when Hermegild and Constance were asleep after long vigils and prayers, this knight, who was wholly caught in the devil's grip, cut the throat of Hermegild, Olda's wife, by the side of Constance, who was sound asleep in the same bed. And when he had performed the crime, he hid the bloody knife under the pillow of the maid Constance.

(227–252) Thereupon, after a short time, Olda entered the castle, and went in haste to his wife's chamber to tell her the news of the king's coming. And, Constance, who had been awakened by the noise, thinking the lady asleep, moved her hand to wake her. And when she felt that her body was all wet with blood, in great alarm she cried out, "My lady is dead!" At which cry, Olda and those present, greatly amazed at the word, as those who knew nothing of the crime – shouting "Light!" – found the throat of Hermegild hideously cut and her body all covered in her blood. And when all bewailed the cruelty, demanding the truth from Constance, this traitor, who had committed the crime, loudly blamed the death on the maiden; and on the pretext that he took the lady's death more to heart than the others, he leaped about in all directions like a man deranged until he had found the knife where he himself had hidden it, and showing the instrument of the crime before all, with a loud cry he accused the maiden of treason. But Olda, who could not believe such cruelty of the maiden, vigorously defended her. And this evil man took in his hands the book of the aforesaid Bishop Lucius, which was a book of the gospels that the holy women Hermegild and Constance had beside them every night for devotion; and on this book he swore, crying out that so help him God, the gospel and his baptism, which he had just recently received, Constance was the murderer of the lady. He had scarcely finished the accusation when a closed hand like a man's fist appeared before Olda and all who were present and struck such a blow on the nape of the felon's neck that both his eyes flew out of his head and his teeth out of his mouth, and the criminal fell, struck down to the ground. And at this a voice said in the hearing of all, "You were placing a stumbling block against

213–14 **pur . . . demoree** *om* AM. 213 **Olda** *om* S. 214 **emprise** aprise AMS; appriser FT. 216 **q'ele l'avoit** que ele avoit AM; qil avoit luy S. 217 **reveli en disaunt** reculi et disoit S. **si** sa S. 218 **sacrement** RLAMFTS; sacrementz P. **sa** son LAMFTS. **merderie** merdayle S. **cist** cil LFTS. 219 **fu** serroit S. 220 **purveut** purveint AM; purvoit FT; purveit S. 221 **l'en retournaunt** en soun retourner S. 222 ***et Constance** *om* L. **fortment** estoient forment AMFTS. 223 ***chivaler** *om* AMFTS. **pris** LAMFTS; pres PR. 224 **en costé** e ceste A; e coste M; a cost FT; a coste S. **fortement** fu forment LAMFTS. 225 **la** sa S. **musca** mussea FT. 226 **desouz . . . Constance** desouz sa *corr* la oriler Constance R; en Constaunt lorier AM; et Constance lorir FT; aderer loriler Constance S. **la pucele** *om* S. 227 **chastiel** *add* mitant S. **a la** en la FT. 230 **lui veiller** la veiler LAMS. **lui(2)***om* S. **moil** meil L; moilez FT. 231 **dit** *repeated* P. **criaunt** RLAMFS; creaunt P; criante T. 233 **Lumere** *repeated* AM. 234 **en son sanc** en saunc AMS; de sanc FT. 236 **cist** celi FT. **la (2)** RLAMFTS; *om* P. 237 **la mort** lamour de la dame S. 238 **sailli de** sailli a AM. 239 **le avoit** avoit S. **moustrant** demonstraunt S. 241 **tiele** cele AMFTS. **sil** cil AMFS. 242 **ses** *om* AMS. 244 **costé** costes FTS. 245 **criaunt** criauns R. **eidast** eydeit A. **qe** qil FT. **ja** *om* FTS. 246 **Constaunce** Custaunce A; *Custance M. **felonesse** felonie TS. **mourdrere** de mourdre FT; pur mourdrer S. 247 **parfini** fini A; parfine LFT. **enclose** close LAMFTS. **poyn** RLAMFT; poym P; poyne S.

la pucele Constance. Et pur ceo q'en l'abscence Olda tote la garde lui estoit demoree, par malveise emprise et temptacioun del diable ala susquere la pucele Constance de assent de pecché charnel. Et puis q'ele l'avoit repris une foiz et autre, la tierce foitz ov grant queor lui reveli en disaunt q'il estoit com chien, qe aprés si seinte [sacrement] de son baptesme voleit retourner a sa merderie. Puis cist, dotaunt q'il fu accusee de sa mesprise a son seignur Olda a son retourner, de mal se purveut. Qar en la journaunte de la nuyt a quel Olda devoit entrer le chastel l'en retournaunt del roi, puis qe Hermegild et Constance fortment endormies aprés longes veiles et oreisons, cist chivaler, qi tut estoit [pris] en la main al diable, trencha la gowle Hermigild, sa dame, en costé Constance, qi fortement endormie en mesme le lit. Et quant il avoit parfait la felonie, musca le cotel senglaunt desouz le oriler Constance la pucele.

A ceo aprés poi de temps, entra Olda le chastiel, et en hast vient a la chaumbre sa compaine pur counter novele de la venue le roi. Et Constance, qe ove la noise estoit aveillé, quidaunt la dame dormaunte, lui moveit la mein pur lui veiller. Et quant ele senti qe le corps lui estoit tut moil de sanc, a grant affrai (fol.65va) dit en [criaunt], "Ma dame est morte!" A quele parole Olda et qi estoient en presente, trop abaiez de la parole, com ceux qe rienz n'entendirent la felonie, acrianz, "Lumere!" troverent la gowle Hermegild hidousement trenché et le corps tut envolupé en son sanc. Et quant touz acrierent la crueuté, en demandant de Constance la verité, cist tretres q'avoit fait la felonie, hugement surmist [la] mort sur la pucele, et, par contenaunce qe la mort lui estoit plus pres a queor qe as autres, sailli de tote partz come homme aragé, tant'qil eust trové le cotel la ou il le avoit mesmes muscé; et devant touz moustrant le instrument de la felonie, a huge crie apela la pucele de treson. Mes Olda, qi ne poeit tiele crueuté penser de la pucele, bonement la defendi. Et sil malveis en hast prist entre ses mains le livere l'evesqe Lucius, avantnomé, q'estoit livre des Evangeils, quel les seint femmes Hermegild et Constaunce, chescune nuyt par devocion avoient en costé eles; et sur cel livre jura en criaunt si Dieux lui eidast et l'Evangeil et son baptisme, qe ja novelement avoit resceu, qe Constaunce[3] fu la felonesse mourdrere la dame. A peine avoit parfini la parole qe un main enclose come [poyn] de homme apparut devant Olda et quantq'estoient en presence, et feri tiel coup en le haterel le feloun, que ambedeux les eux lui envolerent de la teste et les dentz

3 Trevet's heroine's name is commonly spelled *Constance* or *Constaunce* in all the manuscripts (63 times in P); Chaucer's spelling, *Custance*, appears only in this line in M; *Custaunce* is the reading in A in this line and in AM (lines 157, 506, 545, 574).

the daughter of mother Church; this you have done and I have not remained silent."

(253–258) And because the arrival of the king was near, Olda would not render judgment on the treason until his coming, and put the felon into prison. Then within a few days the king sentenced him to death. Then because of the great love he had for the maiden and because of the miracles shown by God, King Alla had himself baptized by the aforesaid Bishop Lucius, and he married the maiden, who conceived a male child by the king.

(259–265) Then after half a year passed, news came to the king that the people of Albany, who are the Scots, had passed their boundaries and made war on the king's land. Then by common counsel the king assembled his army to repulse his enemies, and before his departure toward Scotland, he gave his wife, the Queen Constance, into the keeping of Olda, the constable of the castle, and to Lucius, bishop of Bangor, and charged them that when she was delivered of her child they should let him know the news quickly. And above all things he charged them that the queen be completely at her ease.

(266–279) At that time King Alla's mother was still alive, a fair lady and proud of heart who very mortally hated Queen Constance, for she was extremely angry that King Alla, for the love of a foreign woman whose lineage was unknown to him, had abandoned his former religion which all his ancestors had loyally and earnestly kept. Moreover, great envy had wounded her heart because Constance, by all people rich and poor, was, without comparison to her or any other lady in the land, more highly praised for goodness and holiness and marvelous beauty. And it seemed to her that her praise and glory were already brought to nothing because of the great esteem for Constance. And the songs which the maidens of the land composed and sung about Constance greatly increased her wrath. The mother's name was Domild. Then when God and nature willed, Constance gave birth to a male child, handsome and large, well-begotten and well-born; and at his baptism he was named Maurice. Then Olda and Lucius hastily sent the king gracious news of the queen, who was healthy and joyful, and of his child which she delivered.

(280–289) At that time, Domild, the king's mother, was at Knaresborough, between England and Scotland, thus as in a middle place. It happened that the messenger sent by Olda and Lucius went through Knaresborough to carry and tell the king's mother the good news, as he properly supposed. And when she heard the news, she feigned very great joy in the sight of the people and gave the messenger very large and rich gifts in a show of joy. But she intended more than she said, for that night she made the messenger so drunk with an evil drink which took hold of

250 **abatu . . . terre** abatu a la batu a la terre P. 251 **l'oy** loyaunce A. 252 **hoc** hec AS. **non tacui** *tacui AM. 253–4 **le roi . . . venue** *om* A. 253 **pur ceo(2)** *om* FT. 254 **et mist** Mes mist L. 256 **lui** se LMFTS; soy A. 257 **un** *om* AM. 260 **guerreient** guerrirent AMS. 262 **Escoz** Scoce S. **en** et L. 264 **savoir** a savoir T. 265 **ses** choses S. 266 **estoit** feu T. **bele** *om* A. 267 **grant** auant M. ***engain** dedeyne A; engin FT; envie S. 269 **leaument** *om* A. 270 **grant** *om* S. **estoit** AMFTS; *om* PRL. 271 **gentz** *om* T. **nule** *add* autre S. 272 **grantment** RLAMS; grantmement P; grandement FT. 273 **fu (1)** fui *corr* fu P. **si** *om* LAMFTS. **sa (1)** soun S. **anientie** R; anience P; anientee LFT; anentize A; anentie M; aneintee S. **de** RLAMFTS; des P. 274 **lui** la FT; *om* S. 275 **mere** mare M. **noun** a noun LAMFTS. **Downilde** Domulde AS; Deumylde M; Domild F; Domilde T. 276 **d'un** dune S. **bel** *add* enfaunt AMFT; bien bel S. 277 **nee** norre nee M. **nomé** appele FT. 278 **de(1). . .qe fu** que la roine feust FT. **qe . . . heité** qi fu seigne S. 279 **ele** *om* S. 280 **Downild** Downilde L; Domulde AS; Doumilde M; Domigild F; Domigilde T. **Knaresbourgh** Knaresburgh LFTS; Knaresbourgh A; Knaresbourth M (*same variants in line 282*). 281 **lieu** la AM. **maundé** maunda M. 282 **pur** et S. 283 **ele** come ele S. **feint** fit LFT; fesoit S. 284 **trop** tres F. 285 **cel nuyt** L; ele mit PR; cele nuyt AM; cele noet F; cele noyt T; cell nuyt S. 286 **boire** beyuere AM. **ses** les LAMFTS.

hors de la bouche, et le feloun chei abatu a la terre. Et a ceo dit un voiz en l'oy de (fol.65vb) touz: "Adversus filiam matris ecclesie ponebas scandalum; hoc fecisti et non tacui."

Et pur ceo qe la venue le roi fu pres, pur ceo ne voleit Olda jugement doner sur la treson jesqe a sa venue, et mist le feloun en prison. Puis deinz poi de jours par le roi fu le jugement doné de sa mort. Puis le roi, pur le grant amour q'il avoit a la pucele, et pur les miracles par Dieux moustrez, le roi Alla lui fist baptizer de l'evesqe Lucius avantnomé, et esposa la pucele qe conceut del roi un enfant madle.

Puis a un demy an passé, vient novele al roi qe les gentz de Albanie, qe sont les Escoz, furent passés lour boundes et guerreient les terres le roi. Dont par comune counseil le roi assembla son host de reboter ses enemis, et avant son departir vers Escoz, bailla la reyne Constance, sa femme, en la garde Olda, le conestable del chastiel, et a Lucius, evesqe de Bangor, si lour charga qe quant ele fut delivrés d'enfant, q'il lui fesoient hastiement savoir la novele. Et sour tote riens lour charga qe la reyne fust a totes ses eeses.

Unqorre a cel temps estoit la miere le roi Alla en vie, bele dame et fere de corage, et qe trop mortuement hey la reyne Constance; qar grant engain avoit qe le roi Alla avoit, pur l'amour une femme estrange et qui linage lui n'estoit pas conu, sa primer ley guerpi, quele touz ses auncestres avoient leaument et entierement gardez. D'autre part grant envie lui avoit le queor naufré, qe Constance [estoit] de totes gentz, riches et povres (fol.66a) sanz comparison de lui ou de nule de la terre plus [grantment] preisé de bounté et de seinteté et de merveillouse beauté. Et lui fu avis qe si sa loaunge et sa gloire fu ja [anientie] pur le grant pris [de] Constance. Et mult lui encrut sa ire les chaunsouns qe les puceles de la terre fesoient et chauntoient de lui. La mere avoit noun Downilde. Puis, quant Dieux et nature voleient, Constance fu delivrés d'un enfaunt madle, bel et grant et bien engendré et bien nee; et al baptesme fu nomé Moriz. Puis Olda et Lucius hastivement manderent novele graciouse al roi de la reyne, qe fu seigne et heité, et de son enfaunt dont ele estoit delivrés.

A cel temps estoit Downild,[4] la mere le roi, a Knaresbourgh entre Engleterre et Escoz, auxi com en lieu mene. Avient qe le messager maundé par Olda et Lucius ala par Knaresbourgh pur porter et nouncier a la mere le roi bone novele, com il quidoit par reson. Et ele, oye la novele, feint trop grant joye en agarde des gentz, et al messager dona trop grant dons et riches en moustrance de joie. Mes plus pensa qe ne dit, qar [cel nuyt] enyvri taunt le massager d'une maliciouse boire, qe lui purprist la cervele, et si fort lui lya ses senz, q'il jeust com

4 Chaucer's spelling *Donegild* does not appear in any manuscript. The closest spelling is *Domigild(e)* which is found in this line in FT.

his brain and bound his senses so strongly that he lay as if insensible, like a dead man. Then by the consent and advice of her clerk she opened the messenger's box and opened the letters sent to the king by Count Olda and Bishop Lucius, and counterfeited them under the same seals.

(290–304) And in the names of the said lords she wrote other letters bearing the news that Queen Constance, entrusted to their care after the king's departure, was changed in manner and condition as if into another creature, for she was an evil spirit in the form of a woman; and the wonders she wrought, which seemed to be miracles, were the acts of an evil spirit in her body: "whereto witnesses the child born of her, which does not resemble a human form, but a cursed form, hideous and woeful. And therefore, lord King, that shame might not come to your person and your royal honor, for show we caused another child to be baptized and named him Maurice; and the other devilish form we have shut up secretly in an iron cage until it please your lordship to send back word what is to be done, for your honor, with Constance and her hideous offspring. These marvels we write to your lordship with sorrow and tears, according as we were charged by your sovereign command to send you all the truth about your wife and her delivery; and the matter is unknown to the bearer of these [letters], who supposes he knows otherwise than is the case."

(305–317) Then in the morning the messenger arose, very sick and unhappy because of the mischief of the drink that had poisoned his brain; and after false embraces and false promises from Domild, he went his way, charged to return by the same road [he took] on his departure from the king. And when he came to the king, he related to him by word of mouth the truthful and joyful news. But the letters made him turn to grief and caused him to be disbelieved; for when he had looked at the letters, the king was instantly seized with great sorrow and deep thought and with great threats of punishment forbade the messenger to speak anything about his wife and child. And immediately he wrote back to Olda and Lucius, replying to the letters which he believed he had received by their sending and order, that although the news was astonishing to him, and, saving the grace of such trustworthy men writing [it], almost unbelievable, he commanded that without any contradiction they should have his wife and her monster kept safely until his return.

(318–335) Then with these letters the foolish messenger returned at an unlucky hour to Domild, and when he arrived there he complained bitterly about the king's expression and his dull-witted manner. But the traitress comforted him greatly with

287 **sanz** homme sanz S. **le seon** de soun ATS. 289 **les seals** ceux seals S. 290 **tele** tieles FT. **sentence** RLAMS; seintete P; sentences FT. 291 **en lour** a lour S. **puis** LAMFTS; pur PR. 292 **en condicion** condicion FT. 294 **sembloient** semblaient L; semblent A; sembleint M. **fesantz** fesances LMFS; faitz A. **del . . . espirit** des mauveis espiritz FS. 295 **ne** *om* F. 296 **a ta** ta FTS. 297 **a hontage** hontage L. **feismes** femmes(?)FT. 298 **baptizer** baptize AM. **privément** LAMFTS; prveement PR. 299 **nous** vous LS. **estut faire** estoit fere AM; estez a faire S. 301 **dolour** dolurs L. **ce** *om* LAMS. **fumes** LFTS; fumus PR; sumus A; sumes M. 302 **seignurel** *om* L. **a** de S. **toi** *om* FT. **tote** la S. 305 **a** RLAMFTS; *om* P. **se** sen L. **tut malade** RLAMFTS; *om* P. 307 **Downilde** Domylde A; Dounylde M; Domilde FTS. 308 **mesme** par mesme A. **il estoit** AFT; *om* PRL; estoit MS. 309 **lez lettres** A; lettre PRMFT; la lettre LS. **fist (1)** firent A. 310 **suppris** suspira L. 311 **defendi** descendi FTS. **a** ove FTS. **manaces** manace LFT; minasses S. 312 **a(2)** *om* AMFTS. 314 **maundement** comandement FT. **comandaunt** comaundement AM; comandoit FTS. **tut** LAMFTS; tu PR. 315 **leles** lele A; bele M. **escrivaunt** escrivantz LFTS. 316–17 **son retourner** sa venue L. 318 **ove** *om* S. **Downild** Downilde R; Domylde AM; Domilde FTS. 319 **estoit la** il estoit F; il y estoit T. **pleinoit** pleynout AM. **lourd** *om* A; lorud S. 320 **Mes** *om* L. **la tretresce . . . semblaunt** *moved to line 321 after* fait L. **le conforta** se conforta S. **de son** de sen R; dessouz S.

sanz sen et come homme mort. Puis par l'assent et le counseil le seon clerc overi la boiste le massager et oevri les lettres maundez al roi par le Counte Olda et l'evesqe Lucius, et les fausa desouz meismes les seals.

Et escript en lé nouns les ditz seignurs autres lettres tele [sentence] portaunt qe la reyne Constance bailé en lour garde [puis] le departir le roi fu en manere et en condicion (fol.66b) changé come en un autre creature, qar ele fu malveis espirit en fourme de femme; dount les merveilles qe ele fist, qe sembloient miracles, furent fesantz del mauveis espirit en son corps. "A quoi tesmoigne l'enfaunt de lui nee, qe ne resemble pas a fourme de homme, mes a une maudite fourme hidouse et dolerouse. Et pur ceo, sire roi, qe a ta persone ne vensit a hontage et a ton real honur, feismes en moustraunce un autre enfaunt baptizer et le nomams Moriz, et l'autre fourme demoniac avons [privément] fermé en un cage de fer tanq'il pleise a ta seignurie remaunder qe nous estut faire a toun honur de Constance et de sa hidouse engendrure. Cestes merveilles escrivons a ta seignurie ove dolour et lermes selonc ce qe nous [fumes] chargez par toun seignurel comandement a toi tote verité maunder de ta femme et de sa deliveraunce; et al portour de cestes la chose est desconue, qi autre quide savoir q'il ne seet."

Puis [a] matin se leva le massager [tut malade] et desheité pur la malice del boire qi lui avoit la cervele envenimé, et aprés faux embracementz et fauses promesses de Downilde, s'en ala son chemin, chargé de retourner, a son departir del roi, mesme le chemin. Et quant [il estoit] al roi venuz, de bouche lui counta veritable novele et joyouse. Mes [lez lettres] le fist tourner a dolour, et le fist noncreable, qar le roi, quant il avoit les lettres regardé, hastivement suppris de la grande dolour et parfound pensee, defendi al messager, a grant manaces de peine, qe riens de sa femme ne de l'enfaunt parlast. Et meintenant reescript a Olda et a Lucius en responaunt a les lettres q'il (fol.66va) entendi avoir resceu de lour maundement et comandaunt, qe [tut] lui fussent les noveles merveillouses, et, sauvé la grace de si leles gentz et escrivaunt, apoi noun creables, comaunda qe sanz nul contredit feissent sa femme sauvement garder et le moustre de lui tanqe a son retourner.

Puis ove cestes lettres retourna le fol messager a mal houre par Downild, et quant estoit la venuz, durement se pleinoit de la chiere le roi et de son lourd semblaunt. Mes la tretresce mult le conforta de son faux semblaunt, et cele nuyt

her false show, and made him drink as before. And after she had opened and looked at the king's letters, she understood that this order was by no means favorable to her. Then under the same seal of the king she wrote to Olda and Lucius in the king's name with such intention as to answer the first letters sent by them: that, because in a foreign country one may often hear more news than at home in the neighborhood, therefore, by reason that he had heard news that if his wife Constance remained in the land it would bring war and the destruction of the whole country by foreign nations. Thus he ordered Olda, on pain of forfeiting his life, his lands and whatever else he owned, and disinheritance of all his lineage, that within four days after reading the letters he should have a boat prepared and provisioned for five years with food and drink for Constance, and put into the boat the same treasure that was found in her former boat, and that she with her infant Maurice should be exiled from the country in this boat in the same manner as she entered the land, without sail and without oar, and without any other device. And he commanded Lucius, bishop of Bangor, the same thing on pain of perpetual imprisonment.

(336–350) Then when the said lords had received these letters, they expressed great grief and great sorrow. And because the holy lady perceived their manner to be quite changed and dejected, and because no message had come to her from the king, she suspected the death of her lord, and with great prayer begged them that no truth be hidden from her. Then the messenger told her that the king had given him such a harsh reception that he would hear no word concerning the lady or the child. Then the lords, with great sorrow and tears, showed her the king's letter. But Constance, filled with God, and ready for all his will and ordinances, said to them: "May the day never come that the land should be destroyed because of me and that because of me my dear friends should suffer death or harm. But since my exile pleases God and my lord the king, I must accept it in good will, in the hope that God will bring a harsh beginning to a good end, and he will be able to save me on the sea who on land and sea is almighty."

(351–359) Then on the fourth day she was exiled with Maurice, her dear son, who learned seamanship young. And there was so much sorrow and crying and weeping in the city and town, by rich and poor, old and young, when they heard the woeful news that no heart can comprehend it, for all the people mourned her; and though he was not at fault all people cursed King Alla. And after her boat was already brought by other ships upon the high seas, where neither England nor any other land was

321 **l'enyvri** yverie L. **l'avoit fait** *om* AM; avoit fait FTS. **les lettres** *repeated* PR. 322 **overt** overtez FS; overez T. **mandement** comandement FTS. 323 **le roi** *om* A. 324 **tiele** celle S. **par (1)** pur S. **qe** Et S. 325 **en** *om* L. 326 **ceo** ce que FTS. **q'il** LAMFTS; qele PR. 327 **avendroit** devindroit S. **a** en S. **guerre et** *om* FTS. 328 **comanda** manda FTS. 329 **et(2)** LAMFTS; *om* PR. 330 ***vitaille** viande FT. 331 **la nef** celle nief FT. 332 **viroun** enviroun AM; mariner FT; naviroun S. 333 **engin** RLAMFTS; egin P. **enfaunt** fiz S. 336 **les dites** ceux ditz L. **cestes** lez S. 337 **grant(2)** *om* L. **demenoient** fesoient FT; enavoient S. 339 **ne** *om* LTS. 341 **lui fist** se fist S. 342 **Puis** *add* que S. 344 **et(1)** se FT. **preste** RLAM; presce P; prist FTS. **a . . . volentez** de tote a sa volente FT. 345 **le jour** ceo jour AM. 346 **fust** feusse T. **et** ne T. **moi** *om* S. **eussent mort ou** eusez mort ou LAM; sount(?)mys en S. 347 **a mon** mon S. 348 **dure** par dure S. 349 **me** *om* L. **en(3)** *om* LFT. 350 **puissaunce** puissant FT. 351 **douce fuitz** enfaunt et tresdouce fitz S. 352 **marinage** marinages S. 353 **cité** citees T; la cite S. **ville** villes FT; en ville S. 354 **le poeit** nele pout AM; ne purroit FT; ne poit S. 355 **weymentoient** waimenterent LFTS; weymentent A; weymenteient M. **tut . . . coupe** toutes mistrent il coupe FT; tut nust il la coupe S. **touz** *add* luy S. 357 **en** *om* AMFTS.

l'enyvri come autrefoitz l'avoit fait. Et puis qe ele avoit les lettres le roi overt et regardé, aparceut qe cel mandement ne lui fust de riens favorable. Dount desoutz meisme le seal au roi escript a Olda et Lucius en la persone le roi en tiele sentence com par respouns faire a les primers lettres par eux maundés: qe, pur ceo q'en estrange pais peut homme sovent noveles oier plus qe a meson en veisenage, pur ceo par la reson [q'il] avoit noveles oi de Constance sa femme qe, si ele en la terre demorat, ceo avendroit a guerre et destruction de tote la terre par estrange nacions. Pur ceo comanda a Olda en forfeiture de vie et de ses terres et quant q'il avoit [et] desheritement de tut son linage, qe deinz qatre jours aprés les lettres luez feist aparailler un nef et vitaille pur cink anz de manger et de boire pur Constance, et en la nef mettre mesme le tresour qe fu en sa primere nef trové, et q'en mesme la manere en cel nef saunz sigle et saunz viroun ou saunz nule autre [engin] fust ov soun enfaunt Moriz de la terre exillé, come ele en la terre entra. Et mesme(fol.66vb) la chose comaunda a Lucius, evesqe de Bangor, sur peine de perpetuel prisonement.

Puis quant les dites seignours avoient cestes lettres resceu, grant doel et grant dolour demenoient. Et pur ceo qe la benoite dame apparceut lour semblaunt trop chaungé et mournes, et qe a lui nule mandement ne estoit del roi venuz, soucha la mort son seignour; et a grant priere lour requist qe nule verité lui feust celee. Lors lui dist lui messager qe lui roi lui fist si dure encontrer q'il ne voleit de la dame ne de l'enfaunt nule parole oier. Puis les seignours lui ount les lettres le roi moustree ove grant dolour et lermes. Mes Constance pleine de Dieux et [preste] a tote ses volentez et a ses ordinances, lour dist: "Ja ne viegne le jour qe pour moi la terre fust destrute, et qe pur moi mes chiers amis eussent mort ou moleste. Mes puis qe a Diex pleist et a mon seignur le roi moun exil, a bon gree le doi prendre en esperaunce qe dure comencement amenera Dieux a bone fin, et q'il me purra en la mere sauver qui en mere et en terre est de tute puissaunce."

Lors le quart jour fu ele exilé ove Moriz soun douce fuitz, qi jeuvenes aprist marinage. Et taunt de dolour et crie et plour fu en cité et ville, de riches et povres, veuz et jeuvens, quant oyrent la dolorouse novele, qe nul qeor le poeit comprendre, qar tote gentz la weymentoient, et tut n'ust il coupe, al roi Alla touz maudisoient. Et puis qe sa nef par autre navie estoit ja amené en la haute mere, ou ja en Engleterre ne autre terre (fol.67a) lour apparut, les mariners

visible to them, with great grief the sailors commended her to God, praying that she might return again to the land with joy.

(360–372) Then God guided her boat as far as the sea of Spain towards the eastern shore under a castle of a heathen emir. This emir had as his seneschal an apostate from the Christian faith named Telous. This Telous, when he saw the lady with her son brought from her ship before the emir, had great pity on her, and by him she was most graciously received. And after she had been refreshed with food and drink, she would not lodge anywhere else in the evening except in her boat, for they were heathens and she put more trust in floating on the uninhabitable sea under God's guidance than to dwell among the enemies of God. Then God, who never proves false to his friends during tribulation, gave her grace before the emir, for he ordered the aforesaid Telous, his seneschal, to take care of her so that no evil or ill-treatment should come to the lady from anyone.

(373–382) And Telous, very glad and joyous for the charge, went down alone in the dead of night carrying a large treasure of gold and silver and precious stones. And when he had admitted his fault to the lady, in that he who had been a Christian was a renegade traitor towards God for fear of death and the desire for worldly honor, he asked her that he might put himself with her into the hand of God, to return to his faith by the grace of God in some place among Christians. Then cast off from the land with the help of his close friends, they came to the high sea. And the Enemy, who everywhere strove to cause evil, moved the apostate knight by a grievous temptation to entice the lady to consent to sin.

(383–394) But God, to whom she had given her heart since childhood, would not allow her to assent to such evil. Then when this Telous would force her with harsh threats, she restrained his folly by reason, for the child Maurice, as it was already two full years since he was exiled from England, might have understanding and remembrance of a thing done in his presence then. This therefore was her pretext to protect herself from sin. And she asked Telous to look on all sides to see if he might spy any land, and when they might reach land she would fulfill his desire in a suitable place. And he, who was at this promise very much on the alert, standing in the front of the ship, looked on all sides to see if he could see land. And while he was most anxious, Constance, to safeguard her chastity, came secretly behind his back and pushed him into the sea.

358 **en priant** supriant L; en priauntz S. 359 **a joie** ove joie S. 361 **desouz** RLAMFTS; desourt(?)P. **Cist** cesti FT. 362 **Telous** Thelous AMS. 363 **Cist** cesti FT. **Telous** *om* AMFTS. 364 **fust** L; *om* PR; fut A; fu M; feust FT; fuist S. 365 **refete** RLAMS; refece P; refaite FT. 366 **par** *om* FT. 367 **meuth** moutz L; mout AM; mielz FT; meuz S. **avoit** *om* L. **espoiraunce** esperast L. 369 **herberger** RLAMFTS; horberger P. **fause** faut AFTS. 371 **Telous** Thelous AMS. **en** ent F. 373 **Telous** Thelous AMS. 375 **quant** LAMFTS; *om* PR. **cil** sil L. 377 **mettre** mestre S. 378 **ascun** en aucun T. **Dieu** AT; *om* PRLMFS. 379 **aloinez** allies FT. 380 **a** en S. **s'afforsca** sen force AM; se force F; se afforce T; enforce S. 381 **a** as L; par T; en S. 382 **d'enticer** de tempter S. **de pecché** a pecche F. 383 **ele** il F. **son** LAMFTS; sa PR. **de enfaunce** daffiaunce A. 384 **cist** cesti FT; *om* S. **Telouus** Telous RL; Theolous AM; Tholous FT; Thelous S. 385 **dures** *om* FT. 385–6 **refreint . . . qar** luy respount par resouns sages et bels si dit S. 385 **resoun** resons FT. 388 **adonqe Dount** puit avenir grant peril S. **ceste . . . colour** ele feina colour FT. 389 **Tylous** Telous LFT; Thelous AMS. **q'il . . . totes** qe savisa par touz S. **parz** parties FT. **s'il** si AM. 392 **l'avaunt** le vant AM; la haute FTS. **s'avisa** avisa LAMFTS. **s'il** si AMFT. 394 **rere** deriere T. **le** ele lui A.

a grantz dolours la comanderent a Dieux, en priant qe enquore poet ele a joie a la terre retourner.

Lors Dieux gya sa nef tanqe en la mere d'Espaine enver la terre de l'orient [desouz] un chastiel de un admirail de paens. Cist admirail avoit le seon seneschal un renee de la foi Christiene, Telous nomé. Cist Telous, quant il vist la dame de sa nef amenee ove son fitz devaunt l'admirail grant pité en avoit et par lui [fust] mult graciousement recewe. Et aprés qe ele estoit bien [refete] de manger et de boire, asoir ne voleit par aillours mes en sa nef herberger, qar il estoient paens, et ele meuth avoit sa espoiraunce en la gaste mer souz le governement Deux floter qe entre les enemis Dieux [herberger]. Lors Dieux, qi a ses amis ja ne fause en tribulacioun, dona a lui grace devaunt l'admirail, qar il comanda a lui avantdit Telous, son seneschal, q'il en eust cure, qe mal ne moleste par nulli avenist a la dame.

Et Telous de la garde trop lee et joiouse en la nuit parfounde descendi soul, portaunt graunt tresour de or et de argent et peres precious. Et [quant] avoit reconu a la dame son errour, qe cil q'avoit esté Christien fu tretres renez enver Dieux pur pour de mort et pur covetise de terrene honur, lui pria q'il se put ove lui mettre en la mein Dieux, pur retourner ascun liu a sa foi par la grace [Dieu] entre Cristiens. Puis, par eide de ses priveez aloinez de la terre viendrent a l'haute mere. Et l'enemi, qi par tut s'afforsca de mal faire, (fol.67b) moveit le chivaler renee a grevouse temptacion d'enticer la dame a consent de pecché.

Mes Dieux, a qi ele avoit doné [son] queor de enfaunce, ne la voleit soeffrer assentier a tiel mal. Dount qaunt cist Telouus, par dures manaces la voleit afforcer, ele refreint sa folie par resoun, qar l'enfaunt Moriz, qi ja estoit de dieux aunz entiers puis q'il estoit exiléx d'Engleterre, poeit avoir entendement et memoire de chose faite en sa presence adonqe. Dount ceste fu sa colour pour soi defendre de pecché. Et pria a Tylous q'il avisat de totes parz s'il peut nule terre veer, et qaunt a la terre puissent attendre en lieu covenable, parfreit son talent. Et cil, sur ceste promesse mult curiouse, esteaunt en l'avaunt partie de la nef de totes parz s'avisa s'il nul terre poeit veer. Et taunt come fu plus curious, Constance, pur sa chasteté sauver, priveement lui vient rere au dos et le trebucha en la mere.

(395–405) During this time King Alla, having already gained the victory in Scotland over his enemies the Picts, hastened into England with great desire and sorrow, for he was told by travelers that by his command his holy wife Constance was already banished from the land with her son Maurice. And as the king made his way through cities in England by day, there came toward him men and women, children and old people, and they reviled him with crying and insults, throwing mud and filth and large stones on him and his men, and women and naked children out of spite showed him their backsides; and so severe was the persecution that it was necessary for him and his army henceforth to conduct their journeys by night.

(406–416) Then, when in great fear for his life, he had come to the aforesaid castle, he had Olda and Lucius summoned, demanding in a great rage [to know] where his wife Constance was, whom they called an evil spirit in the form of a woman, and what had become of the fiendish monster, his child. And they, amazed at the words, said they knew nothing of such a thing, but that his wife was good and holy, and his child fair and gracious. And, like a madman, he asked them what reason moved them to send such treasonable letters as he could openly show them. Then, seeing the letters from one side and the other the king knew nothing of the letters he saw sealed with his own seal, no more than did they of the other side. Then they could not suspect treachery in any quarter but from the messenger.

(417–432) And the messenger said finally that he felt guilty of no treason; nonetheless he fully admitted to them his drunkenness in the court of Domild, the king's mother, and if there were treason there was the source. The king, by now wholly inflamed with wrath, began to travel by night until he came to where his mother was. And when he had entered where his mother was already asleep, he cried out to her in a terrifying voice, "Traitress!" and ordered her to show speedily the letters which she had treacherously counterfeited. And she, suddenly overcome with fear, and seeing the king like a man out of his mind, holding his naked sword over her, and fully aware she was guilty of such great treachery, begging for mercy, without more delay she confessed to all her crime. And the king with great fierceness told her she would have such mercy as her treason required. "For you had no pity on me, nor on my wife, nor my child, neither will I have any pity on you!" And with that he struck off her head and [cut] her body to pieces as she lay naked in her bed. Then Alla solemnly vowed before Lucius, bishop of Bangor, that he would never marry a wife until the mercy of God should send him news of Constance.

396 **Puteus** Picteis LA; Pycteis M; Putes FT. 398 **fitz** douce fitz S. 400 **en** on T. **encountrauntz** encontrarius A. 402 **et les** dles A. 403 **lour derere** LAMFTS; son PR. 404 **covient** covenoit LAMFTS. **et son** en son T; ove soun S. **ost** RAMF; ostoit P; host LTS. **desormés** *om* S. 406 **il estoit** il avoit S. 409 **monstre** Moris FT. **ceux** eux L. **abais** abaiez FT. 409–10 **la parole** cel parole T. 410 **rienz** *add* ne L. **tiel** celle FTS. 411 **sa engendrure** soun enfaunt nee S. 412 **moveit** meuoit S. **tresoneles** tressonables FT. 413 **lour** *om* S. **poeit** purroit FTS. 414 **riens** *om* FT. **q'il** quex il S. 415 **desouz** de AMFTS. **ceux** deux F. 417 **cist** il FT. ***messager** *om* AMFTS. **de senti** se senti LAMFTS. 418 **reconust . . . yveresce** reconoist qe sa yveresce F; reconoist qen yvery estoit T. **Downild** Downilde RL; Dommylde AM; Domilde FTS. 419 **treson** nulle treisone FT. 420 **tanq'il** tant come L. **ou** a *corr* ou S. 421 **endormie** endormis AM. **ove** en FT. **la** *om* F. 422 **qe ele** queles ele L; quex S. 423 **tretrousement** tresonousement FT; tresserousement S. 425 **bien sachaunt** elle sachante bien FT. **en** et FT; *om* S. 426 **reconoissoit** reconust T. **a** ai *corr* a P; od S. 427 **force** ferce R; ferte AMFTS. **tiele** nul AM. **mercy** *om* FTS. **averoit** en averoit L; nen avereyt A; ne en avereyt M; avoit F. **come** mes com AM. 428 **n'en avetz** nen aviez LAMFT; ne avoistez S. 429 **ne averai** nen averai L; averai FT; avera S. **a ceo** ove ce FT. 429–30 **a pieces** en pieces FT. 430 **jeut** iut A; tut M; geust FT. **vow** awove S. 431 **de Bangor** *om* S. 432 **envoiast** enveiat AM; envoieit FT.

Deinz cest temps le roi Alla, ja esploité de la victorie en Escoce de les Puteus, ses enemis, a grant desir et dolour se hasta en Engleterre, qar counté lui estoit par entrealanz qe sa benoite femme Constaunce ja estoit par son comaundement de sa terre ove son fitz Morice exilez. Et come lui roi erra son chemin par citez et viles de jour en Engleterre, lui vindrent encountrauntz hommes et femmes enfauntz et veillard, et le revilerent de crie et ledeng, gettauntz sur lui et les seons tay et ordure et grosses peres, et femmes et enfauntz devestutz par despit lui moustrerent [lour] derere; et taunt dure fu la (fol.67va) persecucion qe lui covient et son [ost] desormés de nuyt prendre lour journeis.

Puis, quant il estoit a l'avantdit chastel venuz a graunt pour de sa vie, fist apeler Olda et Lucius, a grant felonie demaundaunt ou fu sa femme Constance, q'il appellerent malveis espirit en fourme de femme, et ou fu devenuz le demoniac monstre soun enfaunt. Et ceux, abais de la parole, se disoient rienz savoir de tiel chose, mes qe sa femme estoit bone et seinte et sa engendrure bele et graciouse. Et cil come homme aragé lour demaunda quele reson lour moveit si tresoneles lettres a lui maunder, come apertement lour poeit moustrer. Puis, vewes les lettres d'une part et d'autre, ja le roi les lettres riens ne conoissoit q'il vist desouz son seal assealés, ne ceux de l'autre part ausint. Dont d'autre part ne savoient soucher la treson mes vers le massager.

Et cist messager finaument dit qe de nule treson de senti coupable; nepurquant bien lour reconust de sa yveresce en la court Downild, la mere le roi, et si treson fust, la fu la source. Et le roi, ja tut enflaumé de ire, comensa de nuiz errer tanq'il vient ou sa miere estoit. Et quant estoit entré sour sa mere ja endormie, ove hidouse voiz la escria "tretresce!" et lui comanda hastivement moustrer les lettres qe ele avoit tretrousement fausé. Et ele, sudeinement supprise de pour, et veaunt le roi com homme hors de sen, tenant l'espei nue outre lui, et bien sachaunt soi coupable de si grant treison, sanz plus de relees en priaunt mercy reconoissoit (fol.67vb) tote sa felonie. Et le roi a grant force lui dist qe tiele mercy averoit come sa tresoun demaunda. "Qar de moi, ne de ma femme, ne de mon enfaunt vous n'en avetz pité, ne jeo de vous ja pité ne averai." Et a ceo lui coupa la teste et les corps tut a pieces come ele jeut nue en son lit. Lors Alla sollempnement fist son vow devaunt Lucius, l'evesqe de Bangor, qe james femme n'esposeroit tanqe la misericorde Dieux lui envoiast noveles de Constance.

(433–445) Then Constance, the third year after she had drowned Telous in the sea, which was the fifth year of this exile, as she was floating on the sea, saw far off what appeared to her to be a wood. And as God, her very good and courteous guide, steered her boat nearer and nearer, she at last perceived that it was the masts of a large navy which lay in the harbor of a city by the sea. And when the sailors saw a boat floating so wondrously on the sea, they supposed it had been a ship abandoned by its crew during a storm. But when they came nearer, they found a woman and a five-year old child richly provisioned with treasure but very lacking in food. And after the sailors had questioned the lady, they brought her and her child into the city to a palace where a Roman senator, not unknown to the lady, was harbored.

(446–59) This senator was named Arsenius of Cappadocia, a very wise and worthy knight, very excellent in learning, and a much-loved and intimate adviser of the Emperor Tiberius Constantine, the father of Constance. When he saw Constance, Arsenius in no way recognized her, which the lady accepted with great joy. And she knew him well, for she had seen him often in the house of her father the Emperor. This Arsenius was the commander of all that navy. And after he had asked the lady several questions about her condition and her fortune, she had wisely answered them, without revealing anything about her lineage or the Emperor, [that] though her fortune was not entirely favorable as regards the world, it was completely favorable with respect to God; and because she was married to a rich lord who had begotten the child, [but] to whom she, by her fortune, was not pleasing in all respects, therefore she suffered such hardship.

(460–472) And after he had asked her name, and she had answered him that she was named Couste, for so the Saxons called her, then the lady asked him what was the meaning of that great fleet which he led. And he replied that this was the fleet of the Emperor Tiberius, sent by him to the Holy Land against the Saracens, who had treacherously murdered the Emperor's daughter Constance and a great number of Christians, and the Sultan and his allies who were friends of the Christians; and he told her that on all sides God had given them happy results over their enemies: for the Sultaness was burnt and more than eleven thousand Saracens slain, but not one Christian in his army was lost or wounded, and that he and his soldiers had found the bodies of all the Christians who were murdered by the Saracens except only the body of Constance, who, according to the Saracens' report, was drowned in the sea.

433 **q'ele** qil S. **nei** vew L. **Telous** Theolous A; Theelous M. 434 **flotaunte** RM; flocaunte P; flotante LT; floutaunt A; flotant FS. 435 **loins** lio *corr* loins P; loigne S. **apparut** apparceust L; apparer AMFTS. 436 **curteis** tres curteis T. **gya** governa et gya A. 437 **mastz de un** R; mast de un P; mast de une L; mastode une AM; mastez une F; mastes dune TS. 438 **mere** rivere FT. **un nef** la nef L. 439 **flotaunte** RM; flotaunce P; flotante LT; floutaunt A; flotant FS. 440 **voidé** veude AM. 441 **estoffés** estoppez FT. 442 **povres** *om* A. 446 **Cist** cesti FT. **senatour** *om* AMFTS. **Arsenius** Arcenius LFTS; Arcemius AM. 448 **Cist** cesti FT. 449 **Arsenius** *om* AMFTS. **riens** *add* ne T. 450 **qe la . . . conoissoit** *om* FTS. **ele** cele AM. 451 **Cist** cest F; cesti T. **Arsenius** Arcemius AM; Arcenius FTS. 452 **cele** tut cele LAMFTS. 453 **son estre** sa estre T. **ele** et ele PRLAMFTS. 454 **respoundu** respondi S. **qe** ou PR; et LAMFTS; qe *substituted to improve syntax and clarify the meaning of the sentence.* 455 **ne lui estoit** nestoit FT. **tote graciouse** trop gracious S. 456 **ele(1)** *om* FTS. 457 **sa** *om* L. 460 **avoit respondu** respondist S. 461 **Couste** Coste FT. 462 **il** *add* lui LAM; *add* la FT; *om* S. 462–3 **qe c'estoit** qestoit S. 464 ***mourdré** *om* FS; occis T. **la . . . l'emperour** sa fille AM. 467 **errous** oeverouse FT. 468 **tuez** estoient tuez T. **un** om L. **n'estoit** ne fuist S. 469 **avoient** avoit L. 470 **et son** en son A. 471 **le dit de** lez ditz dez S.

Puis ceste Constance, le tierce anz aprés q'ele avoit nei Telous en la mere, qe fu le quint an de ceste exil, com ele fu [flotaunte] sour la mere, regardoit de loins lui apparut com un bois. Et com son trebon et curteis gyour, Dieux, gya sa nef plus pres et plus a la fin apparceut qe ceo estoient [mastz de un] grant navie qe reposa en le porte de une cité sur la mere. Et quant les mariners virent un nef si merveilousement sur la mere [flotaunte] soucherent qe ceo eust esté une nef par tempeste voidé de ses mariners. Mes quant estoient venuz adés, troverent une femme et un enfaunt de cink anz richement estoffés de tresour mes trop povres de vitailles. Et aprés qe les mariners avoient la dame aresonez, amenerent lui et son enfaunt en la citee a un paleis, ou un senatour de Rome, non pas de la pucele desconu estoit recetté.

Cist senatour estoit apelé Arsenius de Capadoce, tres sages chivaler et pruz et mult excellent en lettrure, et de l'emperour Tyberie Constantin, le pere Constaunce, mult amee et secré. Cist Arsenius, (fol.68a) quant il vist Constance, de riens la conoissoit, qe la dame prist a grant joie. Et ele assetz le conoissoit, qar assez l'avoit veu en la mesoun l'emperour son pere. Cist Arsenius estoit dustre de cele navie. Et puis q'il avoit demaundé la dame plusours demaundes de son estre et de sa fortune, ele lui avoit sagement respoundu sanz rien descoverer de son linage ou de l'emperour, [qe] pur ceo qe sa fortune ne lui estoit selonc le secle tote graciouse, tote lui plust ele solonc Dieux; et pur ceo qe ele estoit marié a un riche seignur qi avoit engendree l'enfaunt, a qi par sa fortune ele n'estoit pas pleisaunte en touz pointz, pur ceo soeffri ele tiele penaunce.

Et puis q'il avoit son noun demaundé, et ele lui avoit respondu qe ele estoit Couste nomé, qar issit l'apelerent les Sessoneis, puis lui demanda la dame qoi amonta cele grant navie q'il amena. Et il respoundi qe c'estoit la navie l'emperour Tyberie, envoié par lui en la Terre Seinte encontre les Sarasins, q'avoient tretrousement mourdré la fille l'emperour Constaunce et grant nombre des Christiens, et le soudan et ses aliez, q'estoient amys as Christiens; et lui disoit qe de totes partz Dieux lour avoit doné errous esploite de leur enemis, qar la soudane fu arse, et de Sarazins estoient plus de unze mil tuez, mes unqes un Christien n'estoit perdu ne naufré en son ost, et qe touz les corps de Christiens avoient il et son ost trovez, qe par Sarazins estoient mourdrez fors soulement le corps Constaunce, qe selonc le dit de Sarazins (fol.68b) estoit né en la mere.

(473–483) Then the maiden asked him that she might pass in his protection to Rome. And Arsenius granted [it] to her with much joy, and took her, her son, and all her treasure into his keeping. And when they were come to Rome, he commended Couste to his Roman wife Helen, the daughter of Salustius, the brother of the Emperor Tiberius and Constance's uncle. This Helen, Constance's cousin, loved her cousin and her kinsman Maurice so tenderly that she had no other joy so great in her life. And perhaps her joy would have been increased if Constance had told her all the truth. Then Constance, with her son Maurice, lived twelve entire years in the company of Arsenius and Helen, a lady of all holiness and goodness. And Arsenius and Helen, who had no children, loved and nurtured Maurice as their son, and proclaimed him as their heir.

(484–494) In this same time, Alla the king of England, by advice of Lucius, bishop of Bangor, and Olda his constable, went with his men to make a pilgrimage to Rome, and to have absolution from the Pope for the murder of his mother. At the same time, he entrusted the keeping of his kingdom to his son Edwyn, who was the third king after him. And when Alla was seven days journey from Rome, he sent Olda ahead to make honorable provision before him. And when Olda was come to Rome, and had inquired where the king of England and his retinue might honorably lodge, he was answered that Arsenius, the senator of the city, was nobly endowed with several castles and good palaces. Then, at that news Olda went to Arsenius to request [lodging], and he kindly had shown him his castles and manors, which were already emptied without any delay.

(495–512) And after Olda had honorably chosen for the king, Arsenius returned from there to his palace. And when he had entered his wife's chamber where Constance was, he asked them if they wished to hear news, and told them that Alla, king of England, would come into the city within ten days and would be lodged in his castles, and for that reason he had sent his marshal, a great count and chamberlain. And when Constance heard the news, for secret and hidden joy, she fell down in a swoon; and after her spirits had returned to her, to their question of what ailed her, she excused herself by [citing] weakness of her mind which she acquired at sea. Then before the said ten days when King Alla was coming near to the city of Rome, Senator Arsenius, who was to receive him in his castles, went to meet him honorably with all the knighthood of Rome and the rich Roman citizens, and they received him courteously. And when the senator's wife Helen and Constance stood

473–4 **a Rome** Rome FT. 474 **Arsenius** Arcenius LFT; Arsemius AM. **a grant** od grant S. 475 **puis** quant FT. **estoient** estoit A. **recomaunda** recomande L. 476 **Couste** Custe AM; Coste FT. **Salustius** Salustieus FT. 479 **peut** puis F; puisse T. **eust escrue** est escrue L. 480 **eust** *om* AM. **tote** *om* L. 481 **Arsenie** Arcenie L; Arsemye AM; Arseni S (*Brock reads Arsenius*). 482 **bounté** verite AM. **Arsenius** Arcenius LFT; Arsemius AM. **Heleine** Heleinure D. **avoient** navoient AM. 483 **amur** lour amour S. **et noreture** LAMFTS; en noreture PRD. 484 **Alle** Alla L. 485 **conestable** seneschall et conestable AM. **faire** *om* FTS. **le pilrinage** soun pilrinage LAMFTS. 487 **roi** *om* L. **lui** *om* S. 488 **Alle** Alla L. 489 **contre lui** *om* AM. **enquis** conquis AM. 490 **et ses** ov sez S. **puissent** *add* estre L. **herberger** herbergetz D. **respoundu** responde S. 491 **Arsenius** Arcenius LS; Arsemius AMF. **la cité** Rome S. **bons** beaux LAMFTS. 492 **Arsenius** Arsemius AM; Arcenius S. 493 **moustrer** moustre S. **voidés** veudez AM. 494 **demoraunt** demourance A. 495 **pur le roi** *om* FT. **choisi** choise D. **Arsenius** Arsemius AM. 496 **sa chambre** la chambre LAMFTS. **entré** en D. **estoit (2)** *add* en PRD; *add* et L. 497 **oier** *add* nouueles M. **Alle** Alla L. 498 **en vile** a vile L; en la ville S. **en ses** e sez M; en ceux S. 501 **lui** *om* FTS. **demaunde** demaunda S. **devoit** deuot M. **acundut** excusa FT. **par** pur L. 502 **sa** *om* FTS. **deins** eynz AM. **ditz** *om* FTS. 503 **Alle** Alla L. **en** *om* S. **pres a** pres de S. **Arsenius** Arsemius AM. 504–05 **dein . . . *honurablement . . . Rome** *om* L. 505 **riches** *om* FT. 506 **la femme** le femme D. **Heleine** LAMFTS; Heliene PRD. **Constaunce** Custaunce AM. **esteurent** esteirent A.

Puis lui pria la pucele qe ele poet en son condut passer tanqe a Rome. Et Arsenius a grant joie lui graunta, et la prist en sa garde et son fitz et tut son tresour. Et puis q'il estoient a Rome venuz, recomaunda Couste a sa femme Romeine, Heleyne, la fille Salustius, le frere l'emperour Tyberie, et le uncle Constaunce. Ceste Heleyne, la nece Constaunce, taunt tendrement ama sa nece et Moriz soun cosin, qe autre si graunt joie en sa vie n'avoit. Et peut estre qe sa joie ly eust escrue, si Constaunce lui eust tote verité counté. Puis Constaunce[5] ov son fitz Moriz demora en la compaignie Arsenie et Heleine duzze anz entiers, dame de tut seinteté et bounté. Et Arsenius et Heleine, qe nul engendrure avoient, Moriz en amur [et] noreture come lour fitz, et lui clamerent lour eir.

En cel mesme temps Alle,[6] le roi de Engleterre, par le counseil Lucius, evesqe de Bangor, et Olda, son conestable, ala ove gentz pur faire le pilrinage a Rome et de avoir absolucion del pape de l'occision sa mere. En meisme le temps bailla la garde de son roialme a Edwyn, son fitz, q'estoit le tierce roi aprés lui. Et quant Alle estoit a sept journés de Rome, maunda Olda devant pour honurable purveaunce faire contre lui. Et quant Olda estoit a Rome venuz et avoit enquis ou le roi d'Engleterre et ses gentz puissent honurablement herberger, lui fu respoundu qe Arsenius, le senatur de la cité, estoit noblement dowé de plusours chasteus et bons paleis. Puis a ceste novele Olda ala a Arsenius dé (fol.68va) ceo prier, et il bonement lui fist moustrer ses chasteus et maners, q'estoient ja voidés saunz nul demoraunt.

Et puis qe Olda avoit pur le roi honurablement choisi, Arsenius s'en est retourné a son paleis. Et puis q'il estoit en sa chambre sa femme entré, oue estoit Constaunce, lour demanda si eles voleient noveles oier, et lour counta qe Alle, rois d'Engleterre, deinz les dis jours vendreit en vile et serroit herbergé en ses chastels, et a ceo avoit maundé un grant counte et chastelein son mareschal. Et quant Constaunce oi la novele, de privee et celé joie chei en paumeson; et puis qe ses espiriz lui estoient revenuz, a lour demaunde quele devoit, se acundut par feblesce de sa cervel, qe lui avint en la mere. Puis deins les ditz dis jours quant Alle le rois fu en venaunt pres a la cité de Rome, Arsenius le senatur, qi le devoit resceivre dein ses chastels, lui ala encountraunt honurablement ove tote la chivalerie de Rome et ove les riches citezeins Romeins, et lui resceut corteisement. Et come la femme le senatur [Heleine] et Constaunce esteurent sur un

[5] The final part of the story in the Douce manuscript (D) begins here.
[6] From here to the end of the story, the name of the king in the Paris text is **Alle** instead of **Alla.**

upon a balcony filled with steps that they might see the king of England and look at the procession of mounted knights, a knight who had seen the king on the road before his coming into the city and was assigned to point out the person of the king for the ladies, pointed him out to them as he rode under the platform and said, "Ladies, that is King Alla." And hearing his name mentioned the king looked upwards; and when Constance saw his face she fell down in a swoon beside Helen, who supposed it to be nothing but her weakness.

(513–532) At this time of the king's coming to Rome, Maurice began his eighteenth year. He was secretly instructed by his mother Constance that, when he might go to the feast with his lord the senator, he should neglect all other things and place himself before the king of England, when he should be seated at dinner, in order to serve him, and that he should stir nowhere out of the king's sight, and that he should strive to serve him well and courteously, for he greatly resembled his mother. Then when the king saw the youth standing before him, he was greatly taken aback by the resemblance and asked him whose son he was; and he answered that he was the son of the senator Arsenius, who sat on his right. And at the king's asking, the senator told him that he held him as his son because he had made him his heir. And he knew his mother well, but not his father, for his mother would never reveal that to him in twelve years' time. And the youth did not know him because he and his mother were sent into exile when he was only ten weeks old. At that, the king asked the youth his name, and he replied that his name was Maurice. Then the king became very thoughtful, on account of the name, the resemblance in the face, and the words of the senator, and he asked the senator, if he pleased, to show him the youth's mother. And he answered him that she was in his house. Upon [hearing] this, the king, greatly comforted, caused the dinner to be hurried.

(533–543) And when he was come down to the senator's palace, his wife appeared, coming towards him with the senator's wife. And after he had greeted the lady of the palace, the king, clearly recognizing her, went to kiss and embrace his wife. And he made such open expressions of love that the senator, and all who were there, were not a little amazed. And at that the king cried out loudly, "I have found my wife!" Then Olda and Lucius greeted the lady, and with great joy thanked God, who never fails those who have hope in him. On the morrow, the king went to receive his absolution for the death of his mother, and when he had told Pope Pelagius, before named, all the events, the Pope gave thanks to God.

(544–559) Then, after the king had dwelt forty days in Rome, one night Constance begged him to request the emperor, who lived twelve leagues from

507 **bretasce** bretarch S (*also line 510*). **puissent** purroient T. **le rois** lez rois D. 508 **chivauché** chivalrie AM. **un chivaler** une chivaler D. **avant** devaunt S. 509 **estoit** qi estoit LAMFTS. 509 **sa** la AM. 510 **ci** si AMS. 511 **nomé** nomer AMS; *om* FT. 512 **mes** qe FT. **sa** a sa L; *om* AMFTS. 514 **Cist** cesti FT. 516 **fust** estoit FT. 518 **servir** lui servir AM; le roi servir T. **il(2)** RLDAM; ele P; *om* FTS. 519 **resembla** resemblast T. 520 **et . . . estoit** *repeated* A. 521 **il respoundi** ly respoundi AMS; il lui respoundi FT. **Arsenie** Arseni D; a Arsemie AM. **seoit** site A. 522 **destre** *add* a la table FT. **sa** ce FT. **demande** demaunda DTS. **lui** qi lui FT. 525 **la mere** sa mere FTS. 526 **n'estoit** il estoit L; il nestoit S. 527 **respound** respont L; respondi AMS; le respondi F; lui respondi T. **lui** le roi LAMFTS. 529 **si lui** sil lui T. 530 **il** ele S. 532 **manger** maungerie S. 533 **descendu** descendi LFTS. 537 **i** LAMFT; *om* PRD; ia S. **en** *om* LAMFTS. 538 **haut** hast L. **J'ay trové** jeo ta trove L. 540 **en** *om* A. **esperaunce** affiaunce AM. 541 **a prendre** de prendre L. **son** une D. 545 **Constance** Custaunce AM.

bretasce ordiné de gré, qe eles puissent ver le rois d'Engleterre et aviser le chivauché, un chivaler, qi avoit veu le rois avant sa venue a la cité par chemin et estoit assigné pur les dames moustrer la persone le roi, lour moustra sa persone com il chivacha desus le bretache, et dist: "Veez ci, dames, lui rois Alle." Et le roi, oiaunt son noun nomé, regarda vers mount; et quant Constaunce vist son visage, chei enpres de Heleine (fol.68vb) paumé, qe ne quidoit autre mes sa feblesse.

A cest temps de la venue le rois a Rome comensa Moriz son dis et oitisme an. Cist estoit apris privément de sa mere Constaunce qe, quant il irreit a la feste ove son seignur le senatur, qe, totes autres choses lessez, se meist devant le rois d'Engleterre, quant il fust assis a manger pur lui servir, et qe de nule part se remuat hors del regard al roi, et qe il se afforsat bien et curtoisement servir, qar [il] durement resembla sa mere. Puis quant le rois regarda l'enfaunt esteaunt devaunt lui, trop fu suppris de la resemblance et lui demaunda qi fitz il estoit; et il respoundi q'il estoit fitz Arsenie le senatour, que li seoit a destre. Et a sa demande le senatur lui dist qe son fitz le tient il, pur ceo q'il l'avoit fait son heir. Et sa mere savoit il bien, mes noun pas son pere, qar unqe sa mere ceo ne lui voleit reconustre en le temps de duzze aunz. Et le juvencel ne savoit qar la mere et lui estoient mis en exil quant n'estoit forqe de dis semains. A ceo le rois demaunda del juvencele son noun, et il respound qe son non fu Morice. Dount lui devient en grant pensee et del noun et de la resemblaunce de visage et pur les ditz le senatur, et demanda del senatur si lui plust faire moustraunce de la dame la mere le juvencel. Et il lui respondi qe ele estoit en sa meson. Sur ceo le rois, trop confortee, fist haster le manger.

Et quant il estoit descendu al paleis le senatur, parust sa femme qe lui venoit encontre ove la femme le (fol.69a) senatour. Et le roi, aprés q'il avoit la dame del paleis salué, par certeine conoisaunce ala sa femme enbracer et beiser. Et taunt apeert monstraunces d'amur ly fesoit, qe le senatur et la dame et quantqe [i] estoient, n'estoient pas poi en merveillet. Et le roi a ceo tut en haut escrie: "J'ay trové ma femme!" Puis Olda et Lucius ount salué la dame et a grant joie ount Dieux mercié, qe jammes ne faut a ceals qe en lui ount esperaunce. Lendemain le rois ala a prendre son absolucion de la mort sa mere, et puis q'il avoit counté al pape Pelagie, avant nomé, totes les aventures, le pape rendi graces a Dieu.

Puis, aprés qaraunte jours qe le rois avoit demoré a Rome, un nuyt lui pria Constance q'il mandast a l'empere, qi demorra de Rome a duzze

Rome, that he would do him the honor to be pleased to dine with him at Rome. And because the request pleased the king, Constance charged her son Maurice with the message. And she told him if the emperor would not grant his petition, then he should entreat him for the love he had to the soul of his daughter Constance, for she knew well that then the emperor would not deny his request, as he did to no one who, for his daughter's soul, begged him for anything. And when Maurice was come before the emperor with his honorable company and had delivered his message on behalf of his father the king, the emperor greatly taken by surprise with love for the youth, weeping, said to his knights: "God, how wondrously this youth resembles my daughter Constance." And after he had given Maurice great gifts, but would not grant his petition, because, for the grief which he suffered for his daughter whom he thought dead, he would never afterwards eat at a joyful feast nor hear the minstrel's song. Then Maurice begged him according to the aforesaid form, and the emperor granted his request.

(560–577) It happened on her birthday, the vigil of the feast of St. John the Baptist, when the feast was to be held on the following day, that Constance said to the king that for his courtesy he should ride honorably to meet the emperor so as to receive him into the city, and so it was done. And when all the noble chivalry of Rome, with the citizens, came honorably into the company of the king, Constance prayed her lord to alight from his horse to meet the emperor, whom she already saw coming near, on foot. And before the whole company, Constance took her lord the king in her right hand and her son Maurice in her left, and went to greet her father in these words: "My lord and fair father Tiberius, I, your daughter Constance, thank God, who has granted me life even to this day, that I see you in health." And after he had heard and knew well his daughter, his heart was seized with such sudden joy that he had almost fallen from his horse, but King Alla and his son Maurice supported him. Then, as fitting, they made great joy. And Constance told her father all her adventures, and how she had already lived twelve years in the house of the senator Arsenius and Helen, who then for the first time recognized her cousin, her uncle's daughter.

(578–585) Then after another forty days, when King Alla wished to return to his own country, the Emperor Tiberius, with the consent of Pope Pelagius and the entire Senate of Rome, because of his old age, took Maurice as his companion emperor and named him his heir. And he was called Maurice of Cappadocia because of

546 **lues** relues D. ***vousist** vensist S. 547 **Moriz** Morice AMFT. 548 **message** messager AF. 549 **avoit** *om* T. 550 **sa** son A; la FT. 551 **ne fist** fist FT; le fist S. **qe** RLDAMFS; *om* P; qi T. **l'alme . . . fille** sa alme S. 552 **Moriz** Morice AMFT. 553 **son message** sa message S. 554 **cist** cel AM; cest FT. 555–6 **q'il . . . doné** il dona a Moris S. 556 **Morice** Moriz L. 557 **pur ceo qe** *om* S. **q'il avoit** qis avoit FT. 557–8 **q'il . . . mort** qi quida ele estre mort qi S. 557 **quidoit** quida LAMFT. 558 **voleit** veloit D. **de joie** *om* L. 559 **Moriz** Morice AMF; Moris TS. **lui(2)** tost lui S. 561 ***le feste** le maungerie S. **suaunt** ensuaunt AMFTS. **roi** *add* et lui pria S. 562 **q'il** *om* A. **chivachast** chivaucha FTS. 563 **fait** fest AM. **tote** *om* AMFTS. 565 **seignour** *add* le roy S. 566 **de pres** den prees S. ***a pee** S; *om* PRLDAMFT. 567 **la mein** sa mein TS. 567–8 **destre . . . meyn** RD; *om* P; destre et Morice son fitz en la LAMFTS. 568 **son pere saluer** a son pere L. 571 **out** ust S. **bien conu** vieu com A; bien com M. 573 **destrer** destre LF. **Alle** Allee S. **Moriz** Moris AM; Morice FT. **supportoient** suppotterent LAM; suppowerent FT; supponerent S. 574 **demenerent** demeneroun D. **Constaunce** Custaunce AM. **pere** *add* lemperour S. 575 **ses** LDAMFTS; ces PR. 576 **Arsenie** Arsemie M. **conusait** reconissoit L; reconuseyt AM; reconoit FT; reconusoit S. **la** RLAMFTS; le PD. 578 **autres** *om* FTS. 579 **voleit** *om* AMFTS. **retourner** returna AMFTS. **en son pais** vers Engleterre S. 581 **Moriz(1)** Morice AMFTS. **Morice (2)** Moriz L; Moris AMS.

lues, q'il vousist lui faire l'onur q'il lui plust ove lui manger a Rome. Et puis qe la priere plust au roi, Constaunce charga son fitz Moriz del message. Et lui dist si l'emperour ne lui grantast point sa priere, qe dunqe lui requeist pour l'amour q'il avoit a l'alme sa fille Constaunce, qar dunqe savoit ele bien qe l'emperour ne lui denieroit pas sa demande, come a nulli ne fist, [qe] pur l'alme sa fille riens ly priast. Puis, quant Moriz estoit devaunt l'emperour venuz ove compaignie honurable et avoit son message fait de part le roi son pere, l'emperour, trop surpris de l'amur le juvencel, dit a ses chivalers enploraunt: "Dieux! com cist juvencel mervoilousement resemble ma fille Constaunce." Et puis q'il avoit a Morice doné grantz douns, (fol.69b) mes ne lui voleit otreier sa prier, pur ceo qe pour le doil q'il avoit pris pur sa fille q'il quidoit mort, unques aprés ne voleit a feste de joie manger ne mynstraucie oier. Donc lui pria Moriz selonc la fourme avantdite, et l'emperour lui granta.

Avynt la veile Seint Johan le Baptistre, la feste de sa nativité, quant le feste se devoit faire le jour suaunt, Constaunce dist au roi qe a sa curteisie q'il chivachast honurablement encontre l'emperour pur lui resceivre en la cité, et ensi fut fait. Et quant tote la noble chivalrie de Rome ove les citeseins vindreint en la compaignie le rois honurablement, Constance pria son seignour de descendre de son destrer encontre l'emperour, qi ele ja vist venir de pres [a pee]. Et Constaunce devaunt tote la compaignie prist son seignur le roi en la mein [destre et Moriz son fitz en la meyn] senestre, et vient son pere saluer en cestes paroles: "Mon seignour et beau pere Tyberie, jeo, Constaunce, vostre fille, mercie Dieux qe encore a ceste jour m'ad graunté la vie, qe jeo vous vei en saunté." Et puis qe l'emperour out sa fille oi et bien conu, ja de si sudeine joie avoit le queor suppris qe apoi estoit de son destrer tresbuché, mes lui rois Alle et son fitz Moriz le supportoient. Dont a bon droit grant joie demenerent. Et Constaunce conta a son pere totes [ses] aventures et coment ele avoit ja douze anz demoré en la meson le senatur Arsenie et Heleine, qe ore primerement conusait sa nece, [la] fille son uncle.

Puis aprés autres qaraunte jour passez, quant le roi Alle s'en voleit retourner en son pais, l'emperour Tyberie, (fol.69va) par assent le pape Pelagie et de tut le Senat de Rome, pur sa veilesce, prist Moriz compaignon de l'emperour et lui clama son heir. Et estoit Morice

Arsenius, who was from Cappadocia, as mentioned above in the beginning of this story. This Maurice was called by the Romans in Latin: "Mauricius Christianisimus Imperator," that is to say, "Maurice the Christian Emperor."

(586–598) Then Alla, the king of England, the ninth month after he had come to England, rendered his soul to God, piously and devoutly. And almost half a year afterwards, Constance, who was [held] in great honor and love by all the land, returned to Rome because of the news she heard of her father's illness, and the thirteenth day after her arrival Tiberius died piously in the arms of his daughter and gave up his soul to God. And she, a year later, departed to God in the year of the Incarnation five hundred eighty-four, on St Clement's day, and was buried at Rome near her father in the church of St Peter. And Olda, who had brought Constance back to Rome, died devoutly at Tours, while returning to England, and was buried by Lucius, aforesaid bishop of Bangor, in the church of St. Martin. Then Lucius returned to his church of Bangor. The body of Alla was buried in the church of St Amphibel at Winchester, where he died.

582 **Capadoce (1)** Capadouce D. **par** pur AM; Puis S. **Arsenie** Arseni D; Arsemie AM; Arsenye S. **q'estoit** qest T. **Capadoce(2)** Capedoce F. 583 **Moriz** Moris LAMS; Morice FT. **fu** estoit FTS. 584 **Imperator** Emperator S. **ceo est** qest L. **Moriz** Morice DAMFT; Moris S. 586 **Alle** Ale D. 587 **et devoutement** *om* AM. 588 **aprés** pres S. 590 **aprés sa** de sa FTS. **seintement** *add* et devoutement FT. 591 **fille** *add* Constance S. 592 **trespassa** passa FT; trepassoit S. 595 **devers** vers AMT; envers FS. 597–8 **de Bangor . . . a(2)** *om* A. 597 **Alle** le roy Alle roy dengleterre S. 598 **a l'eglise** *om* D; en laglise S. **Amphibel** Alphyge F; Alphege T; Amphibe S. **morut** R (*corr from* enorut) LAMFTS; enorut PD.

de Capadoce nomé par Arsenie, q'estoit de Capadoce, come avant est dit al comencement de ceste estoire. Cist Moriz fu apellé dé Romeins en Latin, "Mauricius Christianisimus Imperator," ceo est a dire, "Moriz le Christiene Emperour."

Puis Alle, le roi d'Engleterre, le neofisme moiz aprés q'il estoit venuz en Engleterre, rendi l'alme a Dieu seintement et devoutement. Et apoi aprés un demi an Constaunce, qe en grant honur et amour estoit a tote la terre, retourna a Rome pur la novele qe ele oit de la maladie son pere, et le treszime jour aprés sa venue morut Tyberie seintement deinz les braz sa fille, et rendi l'alme a Dieux. Et ele aprés un an trespassa a Dieux, l'an de l'Incarnacion cink cenz oitantisme quart, le jour Seint Clement, et fu enterré a Rome pres de son pere en l'eglise Seint Pere. Et Olda, qe avoit Constaunce remené a Rome, en retournaunt devers Engleterre, morut devoutement a Tours, et par Lucius, evesqe de Bangor avantdit, fu enterré en l'eglise Seint Martin. Puis Lucius retourna a sa eglise de Bangor. Le corps Alle fu enterré a l'eglise Seint Amphibel a Wyncestre, ou il [morut].

III

John Gower, "Tale of Constance"

(from *Confessio Amantis*, ed. G. C. Macaulay, *The Complete Works of John Gower*, [1901; rpt. Grosse Pointe, MI, 1968], vol. 2, pp.146-73)

A worthi kniht in Cristes lawe*	religion
Of grete Rome, as is the sawe*,	saying
The sceptre hadde forto rihte*;	rule
Tiberie Constantin he hihte*,	was named
Whos wif was cleped* Ytalie.	called
Bot thei togedre of progenie	
No children hadde bot a maide,	
And sche the God so wel apaide*	pleased
That al the wide worldes fame	
Spak worschipe* of hire* goode name.	honorably/her
Constance, as the cronique seith,	
Sche hihte, and was so ful of feith	
That the greteste* of Barbarie*,	nobility/heathen nation
Of hem* whiche usen marchandie*,	them/engage in trading
Sche hath converted as thei come	
To hire upon a time in Rome,	
To schewen such thing as thei broghte,	
Whiche worthili of hem sche boghte.	
And over that in such a wise*	manner
Sche hath hem with hire wordes wise	
Of Cristes feith so full enformed*	instructed
That thei therto ben all conformed,	
So that baptesme thei receiven	
And alle here*false goddes weyven*.	their/abandon
Whan thei ben of the feith certein,	
Thei gon to Barbarie ayein,	
And ther the Souldan for hem sente	
And axeth* hem to what entente	asks
Thei have here ferste feith forsake.	
And thei, whiche hadden undertake	
The rihte feith to kepe and holde,	
The matiere of here tale tolde	
With al the hole circumstance*.	full detail
And whan the Souldan of Constance	
Upon the point that thei ansuerde	
The beaute and the grace herde,	
As he which thanne was to wedde,	
In alle haste his cause spedde*	advanced
To sende for the mariage.	
And furthermor with good corage*	intention
He seith, be so* he mai hire have,	provided
That Crist, which cam this world to save,	

He woll believe; and this recorded,
Thei ben on either side acorded.
And therupon to make an ende
The Souldan hise hostages sende
To Rome, of princes sones tuelve,
Wherof the fader in himselve
Was glad, and with the Pope avised*   having consulted with the Pope
Tuo Cardinals he hath assissed*   appointed
With othre lordes many mo*,   more
That with his doghter scholden go
To se the Souldan be converted.
Bot that which nevere was wel herted*,   benevolent
Envie, tho* began travaile*   then/to work
In destourbance of this spousaile
So prively* that non was war*.   secretly/aware
The moder which this Souldan bar
Was thanne alyve, and thoghte this
Unto hirself: "If it so is
Mi sone him wedde in this manere,
Than have I lost my joies hiere
For myn astat* schal so be lassed*."   status/diminished
Thenkende* thus sche hath compassed*   thinking/plotted
Be sleihte how that sche may beguile
Hire sone; and fell* withinne a while,   it befell
Betwen hem two* whan that thei were,   together by themselves
Sche feigneth wordes in his ere,
And in this wise gan to seie:
"Mi Sone, I am be* double weie   by
With al myn herte glad and blithe,
For that miself have ofte sithe*   times
Desired thou wolt, as men seith,
Receive and take a newe feith
Which schal be forthringe of thi lif;
And ek* so worschipful a wif,   also
The doughter of an emperour,
To wedde it schal be gret honour.
Forthi*, mi Sone, I you beseche*   therefore/implore
That I such grace mihte areche*   obtain
Whan that my doughter come schal,
That I mai thanne in special,
So as me thenkth* it is honeste*,   it seems to me/right
Be thilke which* the ferste feste   that one who
Schal make unto hire welcominge."
The Souldan granteth hire axinge*,   request
And sche therof was glad ynowh*,   very glad
For under that anon she drowh*   formed
With false wordes that sche spak
Covine* of deth behinde his bak.   Conspiracy
And therupon hire ordinance
She made so, that whan Constance
Was come forth with the Romeins,

Of clerkes* and of citezeins,   clergy
A riche feste sche hem made;
And most whan that thei weren glade,
With fals covine which sche hadde
Hire clos* envie tho sche spradde,   hidden
And alle tho* that hadden be   those
Or in apert or in prive*   Either publicly or privately
Of conseil to the mariage,
Sche slowh hem in a sodein rage
Endlong* the bord* as thei be set,   all along/ table
So that it myhte noght be let*;   prevented
Hire oghne* sone was noght quit*,   own/ spared
Bot deide upon the same plit*.   circumstance
Bot what the hihe God wol spare
It mai for no peril misfare*.   go wrong
This worthi maiden which was there
Stod thanne, as who seith, ded for feere,
To se the feste how that it stod,
Which al was torned into blod.
The dissh forthwith the coppe and al
Bebled* thei weren overal*.   all covered with blood
Sche sih* hem deie on every side;   saw
No wonder thogh* sche wepte and cride   if
Makende* many a wofull mone.   making
Whan al was slain bot sche al one,
This olde fend*, this Sarazine,   fiend
Let take anon this Constantine
With al the good* sche thider broghte,   goods
And hath ordeined, as sche thoghte,
A nakid* schip withoute stiere*   empty/rudder
In which the good and hire* in fiere*,   (Constance)/together
Vitailed full* for yeres fyve;   filled with food
Wher that the wynd it wolde dryve,
Sche putte upon the wawes* wilde.   waves

Bot he which alle thing mai schilde,
Thre yer, til that sche cam to londe,
Hire schip to stiere* hath take in honde   guide
And in Northumberlond aryveth*.   it arrives
And happeth* thanne that sche dryveth*   it happens/sails
Under a castel with the flod*,   by the tidal river
Which upon Humber banke stod
And was the kynges oghne also,
The which Allee was cleped tho,
A Saxon and a worthi knyht,
Bot he believeth noght ariht.
Of this castell was chastellein*   warden
Elda, the kinges chamberlein,
A knyhtly man after his lawe;
And whan he sih upon the wawe
The schip drivende* al one* so*,   sailing/alone/in that way
He bad anon men scholden go

To se* what it betokne mai*.   see/might portend
This was upon a somer dai,
The schip was loked* and sche founde.   searched
Elda withinne a litel stounde*   short time
It wiste*, and with his wif anon   knew
Toward this yonge ladi gon,
Wher that thei founden gret richesse;
Bot sche hire* wolde noght confesse   herself
Whan thei hire axen what sche was.
And natheles upon the cas*   as it happened
Out of the schip with gret worschipe
Thei toke hire into felaschipe,
As thei that weren of hir glade.
Bot sche no maner joie made,
Bot sorweth sore*of that sche fond*   sorely/because she found
No Cristendom in thilke lond;
Bot elles* sche hath al hire wille,   otherwise
And thus with hem sche duelleth stille*.   quietly
Dame Hermyngheld, which was the wif
Of Elda, lich her oghne lif
Constance loveth; and fell so,
Spekende* alday betwen hem two,   speaking
Thurgh grace of goddes pourveance*   providence
This maiden tawhte the creance*   faith
Unto this wif so parfitly,
Upon a dai that faste by*   very soon
In presence of hire housebonde,
Wher thei go walkende on the stronde*,   shore
A blind man, which cam there lad*,   led
Unto this wif, criende he bad*,   begged
With bothe hise hondes up and preide
To hire, and in this wise he seide:
"O Hermyngeld, which* Cristes feith,   who
Enformed as Constance seith,
Received hast, yif* me my sihte."   give
Upon his word hire herte afflihte*   trembled
Thenkende what was best to done,
Bot natheles sche herde his bone*   prayer
And seide, "In trust of Cristes lawe,
Which don was*on the crois and slawe*,   who was put/slain
Thou bysne* man, behold and se."   blind
With that to God upon his kne
Thonkende*, he tok* his sihte anon,   giving thanks/received
Wherof thei merveile everychon,
Bot Elda wondreth most of alle.
This open thing which is befalle
Concludeth* him be such a weie   persuades
That he the feith mot* nede obeie.   must
Now lest* what fell upon this thing.   listen
This Elda forth unto the king
A morwe tok his weie and rod*,   rode

And Hermyngeld at home abod*	remained
Forth* with Constance wel at ese.	continually
Elda, which thoghte his king to plese,	
As he that thanne unwedded was,	
Of Constance al the pleine cas	
Als goodliche as he cowthe* tolde.	knew how
The king was glad and seide he wolde	
Come thider upon such a wise*	such a way
That he him mihte of hire avise,*	observe
The time apointed forth withal.	
This Elda triste* in special	trusted
Upon a knyht, whom fro childhode	
He hadde updrawe* into manhode.	reared
To him he tolde al that he thoghte,	
Wherof that after him forthoghte*;	he repented
And natheles at thilke tide*	time
Unto his wif he bad him ride	
To make redi alle thing	
Ayein* the cominge of the king,	in anticipation of
And seith that he himself tofore*	beforehand
Thenkth* forto come, and bad therfore	intends
That he him kepe*, and told him whanne.	await
This knyht rod forth his weie thanne;	
And soth* was that of time passed	truth
He hadde in al his wit compassed	
How he Constance myhte winne.	
Bot he sih tho no sped* therinne,	success
Wherof his lust began t'abate*,	to decline
And that* was love is thanne hate;	what
Of hire honour he hadde Envie,	
So that upon his tricherie	
A lesinge* in his herte he caste*.	deceit /plotted
Til he cam home he hieth* faste,	hurries
And doth* his ladi t'understonde	causes
The message of hire housebonde.	
And therupon the longe dai	
Thei setten thinges in arrai*,	place
That al was as it scholde be	
Of every thing in his* degree;	its
And whan it cam into the nyht,	
This wif hire hath to bedde dyht*,	retired
Wher that this maiden with hire lay.	
This false knyht upon delay	
Hath taried til thei were aslepe,	
As he that wolde his time kepe*	await
His dedly werkes to fulfille;	
And to the bed he stalketh stille*	quietly
Wher that he wiste was the wif,	
And in his hond a rasour knif	
He bar, with which hire throte he cutte,	
And prively the knif he putte	

Under that other beddes side
Wher that Constance lai beside.
Elda cam hom the same nyht,
And stille with a prive* lyht,   dim
As he that wolde noght awake
His wif, he hath his weie take
Into the chambre, and ther liggende*   lying
He fond his dede wif bledende*,   bleeding
Wher that Constance faste by
Was falle aslepe; and sodeinly
He cride alowd, and sche awok,
And forth withal sche caste a lok
And sih this ladi blede there,
Wherof swounende ded* for fere*   fainting dead away/fear
Sche was, and stille as eny ston
She lay, and Elda therupon
Into the castell clepeth oute,
And up sterte* every man aboute,   jumped
Into the chambre and forth thei wente.
Bot he, which alle untrouthe mente,
This false knyht, among hem alle
Upon this thing which is befalle
Seith that Constance hath don this dede*;   deed
And to the bed with that he yede*   went
After the falshed of his speche,
And made* him there forto seche*,   pretended/search
And fond the knif wher he it leide,
And thanne he cride and thanne he seide,
"Lo, seth* the knif al blody hiere!   see
What nedeth more in this matiere
To axe?" And thus hire innocence
He sclaundreth* there in audience*   slanders/publicly
With false wordes whiche he feigneth.
Bot yit for al that evere he pleigneth*,   despite all his accusations
Elda no full credence tok.
And happeth that ther lay a bok,
Upon the which, whan he it sih,
This knyht hath swore and seid on hih*   loudly
That alle men it mihte wite*,   know
"Now be this bok which hier is write,
Constance is gultif*, wel I wot*."   guilty/know
With that the hond of hevene him smot
In tokne of that he was forswore*,   perjured
That he hath bothe hise yhen* lore*,   eyes/lost
Out of his hed the same stounde*   instant
Thei sterte*, and so thei weren founde.   burst out
A vois was herd whan that they felle,
Which seide, "O dampned man to helle,
Lo, thus hath God the sclaundre wroke*   avenged
That thou ayein Constance hast spoke;
Beknow the sothe* er that thou dye."   make known the truth

And he told out* his felonie,	confessed
And starf* forth with his tale anon.	died
Into the ground, wher alle gon,	
This dede lady was begrave*.	buried
Elda, which thoghte his honour save,	
Al that he mai* restreigneth sorwe.	as best he may
For the seconde day a morwe*	in the morning
The king cam, as thei were acorded,	
And whan it was to him recorded*	related
What God hath wroght upon this chaunce,	
He tok it into remembrance	
And thoghte more than he seide.	
For al his hole* herte he leide	whole
Upon Constance, and seide he scholde	
For love of hire, if that sche wolde,	
Baptesme take* and Cristes feith	be baptized
Believe, and over that* he seith	in addition
He wol hire wedde, and upon this	
Asseured ech til other is*.	each to the other is betrothed
And forto make schorte tales,	
Ther cam a bisschop out of Wales	
Fro Bangor, and Lucie* he hihte,	Lucius
Which thurgh the grace of God almihte	
The king with many an other mo	
Hath cristned, and betwen hem tuo	
He hath fulfild* the mariage.	performed
Bot for no lust* ne for no rage*	pleasure/sexual passion
Sche tolde hem nevere what sche was;	
And natheles upon the cas	
The king was glad, how so it stod,	
For wel he wiste and understod	
Sche was a noble creature.	
The hihe makere of nature	
Hire hath visited in a throwe*,	in a (short)while
That it was openliche knowe	
Sche was with childe be the king,	
Wherof above al other thing	
He thonketh God and was riht glad.	
And fell that time he was bestad*	engaged
Upon a were* and moste ride;	war
And whil he scholde there abide,	
He lefte at hom to kepe his wif	
Suche as he knew of holi lif,	
Elda, forth with the bisschop eke.	
And he with pouer* goth to seke	troops
Ayein the Scottes forto fonde*	wage
The werre which he tok on honde.	
The time set of kinde* is come:	by nature
This lady hath hire chambre nome*,	taken, gone to
And of a sone bore full,	
Wherof that sche was joiefull,	

Sche was delivered sauf and sone*.	safe and sound
The bisshop, as it was to done,	
Yaf* him baptesme and Moris calleth;	gave
And therupon, as it befalleth,	
With lettres writen of record*	as proof
Thei sende unto here liege lord,	
That kepers weren of the qweene.	
And he that scholde go betwene,	
The messager, to Knaresburgh,	
Which toun he scholde passe thurgh,	
Ridende cam the ferste day.	
The kinges moder there lay,	
Whos rihte name was Domilde,	
Which after* al the cause spilde*.	afterward/destroyed
For he which thonk deserve wolde,	
Unto this ladi goth and tolde	
Of his message al how it ferde.	
And sche with feigned joie it herde	
And yaf him yiftes* largely*;	gifts/generously
Bot in the nyht al prively	
Sche tok the lettres whiche he hadde,	
Fro point to point and overradde*,	read them over point by point
As sche that was thurghout untrewe,	
And let do wryten othre newe*	had other new ones written
In stede of hem, and thus thei spieke:	
"Oure liege lord, we thee beseke*	pray, entreat
That thou with ous* ne be noght wroth*,	us/angry
Though we such thing as is thee loth*	displeasing to you
Upon oure trowthe certefie.	
Thi wif, which is of faierie*,	supernatural creature
Of such a child delivered is	
Fro kinde* which stant all amis;	nature
Bot for* it scholde noght be seie*,	because/seen
We have it kept out of the weie	
For drede of pure* worldes schame,	very
A povere child and in the name	
Of thilke which is so misbore	
We toke, and therto we be swore	
That non bot only thou and we	
Schal knowen of this privete*.	secret
Moris it hatte*, and thus men wene*	is named/think
That it was boren of the qweene	
And of thin oghne bodi gete*.	begotten
Bot this thing mai noght be foryete*,	forgotten
That thou ne sende ous word anon	
What is thi wille therupon."	
This lettre, as thou hast herd devise*,	told
Was contrefet in such a wise	
That noman scholde it aperceive*,	perceive, realize
And sche, which thoghte to deceive,	
It leith wher sche that other tok.	

This messager, whan he awok,
And wiste nothing how it was,
Aros and rod the grete pas*   swiftly
And tok this lettre to the king.
And whan he sih this wonder thing,
He makth the messager no chiere*,   welcome
Bot natheles in wys manere
He wrot ayein, and yaf hem charge
That thei ne soffre* noght at large   allow
His wif to go, bot kepe hire stille
Til thei have herd mor of his wille.
This messager was yifteles*,   giftless
Bot with this lettre natheles,
Or be him lief or be him loth*,   whether he like it or not
In alle haste ayein he goth
Be Knaresburgh, and as he wente
Unto the moder, his entente
Of that he fond toward the king
He tolde; and sche upon this thing,
Seith that he scholde abide al nyht
And made him feste and chiere ariht,
Feignende as thogh sche cowthe* him thonk*.   owed/thanks
Bot he with strong wyn which he dronk
Forth with the travail of the day
Was drunke, aslepe and while he lay,
Sche hath hise lettres overseie*   examined
And formed in an other weie.
   Ther was a newe lettre write,
Which seith: "I do you forto wite*   I command you to know
That thurgh the conseil of you tuo
I stonde in point to ben undo,
As he which is a king deposed.
For every man it hath supposed,
How that my wif Constance is faie*;   bewitched
And if that I, thei sein, delaie
To put hire out of compaignie,
The worschipe of my regalie*   throne (rule)
Is lore*; and over this thei telle   lost
Hire child schal noght among hem duelle,
To cleymen* eny heritage.   claim
So can I se non avantage,
Bot al is lost, if sche abide.
Forthi to loke on every side
Toward the meschief as it is,
I charge you and bidde* this,   demand
That ye the same schip vitaile,
In which that sche tok arivaile*,   arrived
Therinne and putteth bothe tuo,
Hireself forthwith hire child also,
And so forth broght unto the depe
Betaketh* hire the see* to kepe.   Commit/sea

Of foure daies time I sette,
That ye this thing no longer lette*, — delay
So that your lif be noght forsfet." — forfeit
And thus this lettre contrefet
The messager, which was unwar,
Upon the kingeshalve* bar*, — king's behalf/bore
And where he scholde it hath betake*. — taken
Bot whan that thei have hiede* take, — heed
And rad* that writen is withinne, — read
So gret a sorwe thei beginne*, — begin to have
As* thei here oghne moder sihen* — As if/ had seen
Brent in a fyr before here yhen;
Ther was wepinge and ther was wo,
Bot finaly the thing is do.
   Upon the see thei have hire broght,
Bot sche the cause wiste noght,
And thus upon the flod thei wone*, — dwell
This ladi with hire yonge sone.
And thanne hire handes to the hevene
Sche strawhte*, and with a milde stevene* — reached/voice
Knelende upon hire bare kne
Sche seide, "O hihe mageste,
Which sest* the point of every trowthe, — sees
Tak of thi wofull womman rowthe* — pity
And of this child that I schal kepe."
And with that word sche gan to wepe,
Swounende as ded, and ther sche lay.
 Bot he which alle thinges may* — may do
Conforteth hire, and ate laste
Sche loketh and hire yhen caste
Upon hire child and seide this:
"Of me no maner charge* it is — not important
What sorwe I soffre, bot of thee
Me thenkth it is a gret pite,
For if I sterve* thou schalt deie. — die
So mot I nedes be that weie
For moderhed and for tendresse
With al myn hole besinesse* — full attention
Ordeigne me for thilke office*, — duty
As sche which schal be thi norrice*." — nurse
Thus was sche strengthed forto stonde;
And tho sche tok hire child in honde
And yaf it sowke, and evere among* — at times
Sche wepte, and otherwhile* song — sometimes
To rocke with hire child aslepe.
And thus hire oghne child to kepe
Sche hath under the goddes cure*. — care
   And so fell upon aventure*, — by chance
Whan thilke yer hath mad his ende,
Hire schip, so as it moste wende
Thurgh strengthe of wynd which God hath yive*, — given

Estward was into Spaigne drive
Riht faste under a castell wall
Wher that an hethen amirall* — emir
Was lord, and he a stieward hadde,
Oon Theloüs, which al was badde,
A fals knyht and a renegat*. — apostate
He goth to loke in what astat
The schip was come, and there he fond
Forth with a child upon hire hond
This lady, wher sche was al one.
He tok good hiede of the persone,
And sih sche was a worthi wiht*, — person
And thoghte he wolde upon the nyht
Demene* hire at his oghne wille, — deal with (i.e.sexually)
And let hire be therinne stille,
That mo men sih sche noght that dai.
At goddes wille and thus sche lai,
Unknowe what hire schal betide.
And fell so that be nyhtes tide
This knyht withoute felaschipe
Hath take a bot* and cam to schipe, — boat
And thoghte of hire his lust to take,
And swor if sche him daunger make* — resists his desire
That certeinly sche scholde deie.
Sche sih ther was non other weie,
And seide he scholde hire wel conforte,
That he ferst loke* out ate porte* — should look/ portside
That noman were nyh the stede* — near the place
Which myhte knowe what thei dede,
And thanne he mai do what he wolde.
He was riht glad that sche so tolde,
And to the porte anon he ferde.
Sche preide God and he hire herde,
And sodeinliche he was out throwe
And dreynt*, and tho began to blowe — drowned
A wynd menable* fro the lond, — favorable
And thus the myhti Goddes hond
Hire hath conveied and defended.
    And whan thre yer be full despended*, — passed
Hire schip was drive upon a dai,
Wher that a gret navye lay
Of schipes, al the world* at ones*. — entirely/at one time
And as God wolde for the nones* — this time
Hire schip goth in among hem alle,
And stinte* noght, er it be falle — stopped
And hath the vessell undergete*, — come under
Which maister* was of al the flete, — chief
Bot there it resteth and abod.
This grete schip on anker rod;
The lord cam forth and whan he sih
That other ligge* abord* so nyh, — other(ship)lay alongside

He wondreth what it myhte be,
And bad men to gon in and se.
This ladi tho was crope* aside, had crept
As sche that wolde hireselven hide,
For sche ne wiste what thei were.
Thei soghte aboute and founde hir there
And broghten up hire child and hire;
And therupon this lord to spire* inquire
Began, fro whenne that sche cam,
And what sche was. Quod* sche,"I am said
A womman wofully bestad*. afflicted
I hadde a lord, and thus he bad* ordered
That I forth with my litel sone
Upon the wawes scholden wone,
Bot why the cause* was, I not*. reason/do not know
Bot he which alle thinges wot
Yit hath, I thonke him, of his miht
Mi child and me so kept upriht
That we be save bothe tuo."
This lord hire axeth overmo
How sche believeth, and sche seith,
"I lieve* and triste in Cristes feith, believe
Which deide upon the rode tree*." rood tree, cross
"What is thi name?" tho quod he.
"Mi name is Couste," sche him seide,
Bot forthermor for noght he preide
Of hire astat to knowe plein,
Sche wolde him nothing elles sein
Bot of hir name, which sche feigneth*; dissembles
Alle othre thinges sche restreigneth,
That a word more sche ne tolde.
This lord thanne axeth if sche wolde
With him abide in compaignie,
And seide he cam fro Barbarie
To Romeward, and hom he wente.
Tho sche supposeth what it mente,
And seith sche wolde with him wende
And duelle unto hire lyves ende,
Be so it be to his plesance*. Provided that he agreed
And thus upon here aqueintance
He tolde hire pleinly as it stod,
Of Rome how that the gentil blod
In Barbarie was betraied,
And therupon he hath assaied* undertaken
Be werre, and taken such vengance
That non of al thilke alliance,
Be whom the tresoun was compassed,
Is from the swerd alyve passed;
Bot of Constance hou it was,
That cowthe he knowe be no cas,
Wher sche becam*, so as he seide. What became of her

Hire ere unto his word sche leide,
Bot forther made sche no chiere*. — outward acknowledgement
And natheles in this matiere
It happeth thilke time so,
This lord, with whom sche scholde go,
Of Rome was the senatour,
And of hir fader th'emperour
His brother doughter hath to wyve,
Which hath hir fader ek alyve,
And was Salustes cleped tho;
This wif Heleine hihte also,
To whom Constance was cousine.
Thus to the sike a medicine
Hath God ordeined of his grace,
That forthwith in the same place
This senatour his trowthe plihte* — pledged
For evere, whil he live mihte,
To kepe in worschipe and in welthe,
Be so that God wol yive hire helthe,
This ladi, which fortune him sende.
And thus be schipe forth sailende
Hire and hir child to Rome he broghte,
And to his wif tho he besoghte
To take hire into compaignie.
And sche, which cowthe of courtesie
Al that a good wif scholde konne*, — know
Was inly glad that sche hath wonne
The felaschip of so good on*. — person
Til tuelve yeres were agon,
This Emperoures dowhter Custe
Forth with the dowhter of Saluste
Was kept, bot noman redily
Knew what sche was, and noght forthi* — nevertheless
Thei thoghten wel sche hadde be
In hire astat of hih degre,
And every lif* hire loveth wel. — person
Now herke how thilke unstable whel,
Which evere torneth, wente aboute*. — turned again
The king Allee, whil he was oute*, — away(at war)
As thou tofore hast herd this cas,
Deceived thurgh his moder was.
Bot whan that he cam hom ayein,
He axeth of his chamberlein
And of the bisschop ek also,
Wher thei the qweene hadden do*. — had put
And thei answerde, there he bad,
And have him thilke lettre rad,
Which he hem sende for warant,
And tolde him pleinli as it stant,
And sein, it thoghte hem* gret pite — it seemed to them
To se so worthi on as sche,

With such a child as ther was bore,
So sodeinly to be forlore*.   lost
He axeth hem what child that were;
And thei him seiden, that naghere*,   nowhere
In al the world thogh men it soghte,
Was nevere womman that forth broghte
A fairer child than it was on.
And thanne he axede hem anon
Whi thei ne hadden write so.
Thei tolden so thei hadden do.
He seide, "Nay." Thei seiden, "Yis."
The lettre schewed rad it is,
Which thei forsoken* everidel*.   denied/ completely
Tho was it understonde wel
That ther is tresoun in the thing.
The messager tofore the king
Was broght and sodeinliche opposed*;   questioned
And he, which nothing hath supposed
Bot alle wel, began to seie
That he nagher upon the weie
Abod, bot only in a stede*;   one place
And cause why that he so dede
Was, as he wente to and fro,
At Knaresburgh be nyhtes tuo
The kinges moder made him duelle.
And whan the king it herde telle,
Withinne his herte he wiste als faste*   immediately
The treson which his moder caste*.   had perpetrated
And thoghte he wolde noght abide,
Bot forth riht in the same tide
He tok his hors and rod anon.
With him ther riden manion*,   many a one
To Knaresburgh and forth thei wente,
And lich the fyr which tunder* hente*,   tinder/catches
In such a rage, as seith the bok,
His moder sodeinliche he tok
And seide unto hir in this wise:
"O beste of helle, in what juise*   by what punishment
Hast thou deserved forto deie,
That hast so falsly put aweie
With tresoun of thi bacbitinge
The treweste at my knowlechinge
Of wyves and the most honeste?
Bot I wol make this beheste*,   vow
I schal be venged* er I go."   avenged
And let a fyr do make* tho,   fire be made
And bad men forto caste hire inne.
Bot ferst sche tolde out al the sinne,
And dede hem alle forto wite*   let them all know
How sche the lettres hadde write,
Fro point to point as it was wroght*.   done

And tho sche was to dethe broght
And brent tofore hire sones yhe;
Wherof these othre, whiche it sihe
And herden how the cause stod,
Sein* that the juggement is good,   say
Of that hir sone hire hath so served.
For sche it hadde wel deserved
Thurgh tresoun of hire false tunge,
Which thurgh the lond was after sunge,
Constance and every wiht compleigneth.   And everybody mourns for Constance
Bot he, whom alle wo distreigneth*,   torments
This sorghfull king, was so bestad*   troubled
That he schal nevermor be glad,
He seith, eftsone* forto wedde,   again
Til that he wiste how that sche spedde*,   fared
Which hadde ben his ferste wif.
And thus his yonge unlusti* lif   listless
He dryveth forth so as he mai.
  Til it befell upon a dai,
Whan he hise werres hadde achieved,
And thoghte he wolde be relieved*   restored
Of soule hele upon the feith*   to health of soul by means of the faith
Which he hath take, thanne he seith
That he to Rome in pelrinage*   pilgrimage
Wol go, wher Pope was Pelage*,   Pelagius
To take his absolucioun.
And upon this condicioun
He made Edwyn his lieutenant,
Which heir to him was apparant,
That he the lond in his absence
Schal reule; and thus be providence
Of alle thinges wel begon
He tok his leve and forth is gon.
Elda, which tho was with him there,
Er thei fulliche at Rome were,
Was sent tofore to pourveie*;   make provision
And he his guide upon the weie,
In help to ben his herbergour*,   attendant sent ahead to find lodging
Hath axed who was senatour,
That he his name myhte kenne*.   know
Of Capadoce, he seide, Arcenne
He hihte, and was a worthi kniht.
To him goth Elda tho forth riht
And tolde him of his lord tidinge*,   news
And preide that for his comynge
He wolde assigne him herbergage*;   lodging
And he so dede of good corage.
  Whan al is do that was to done,

The king himself cam after sone.
This senatour, whan that he com
To Couste and to his wif at hom,
Hath told how such a king Allee
Of gret array to the citee
Was come; and Couste upon his tale
With herte clos* and colour pale constricted
Aswoune fell, and he merveileth
So sodeinly what thing hire eyleth,
And cawhte hire up, and whan sche wok,
Sche syketh* with a pitous lok sighs
And feigneth seknesse of the see;
Bot it was for the king Allee,
For joie which fell in hire thoght
That God him hath to toune broght.
This king hath spoke with the Pope
And told al that he cowthe agrope*, discover
What grieveth in his conscience;
And thanne he thoghte in reverence
Of his astat, er that he wente,
To make a feste, and thus he sente
Unto the senatour to come
Upon the morwe and othre some,
To sitte with him at the mete*. at dinner
This tale hath Couste noght foryete,
Bot to Moris hire sone tolde,
That he upon the morwe scholde
In al that evere he cowthe and mihte
Be present in the kinges sihte,
So that the king him ofte sihe*. might see
Moris tofore the kinges yhe
Upon the morwe, wher he sat,
Fulofte stod, and upon that
The king his chiere* upon him caste, look
And in his face him thoghte als faste
He sih his oghne wif Constance;
For nature as in resemblance
Of face hem liketh so to clothe,
That thei were of a suite* bothe. suit
The king was moeved in his thoght
Of that he seth, and knoweth it noght;
This child he loveth kindely*, naturally
And yit he wot no cause why.
Bot wel he sih and understod
That he toward Arcenne stod,
And axeth him anon riht there,
If that this child his sone were.
He seide, "Yee, so I him calle,
And wolde it were so befalle,
Bot it is al in other wise."

And tho began he to devise

How he the childes moder fond
Upon the see from every lond
Withinne a schip was stiereles*, | which was rudderless
And how this ladi helpeles
Forth with hir child he hath forthdrawe*. | fostered
The king hath understonde his sawe,
The childes name and axeth tho,
And what the moder hihte also
That he him wolde telle he preide.
"Moris this child is hote*," he seide, | named
"His moder hatte Couste, and this
I not what maner name it is."
But Allee wiste wel ynowh,
Wherof somdiel* smylende he lowh*; | somewhat/laughed
For Couste in Saxoun is to sein
Constance upon the word Romein.
Bot who that cowthe specefie
What tho fell in his fantasie*, | imagination
And how his wit aboute renneth
Upon the love in which he brenneth,
It were a wonder forto hiere.
For he was nouther ther ne hiere,
Bot clene out of himself aweie
That he not what to thenke or seie,
So fain* he wolde* it were sche. | eagerly/ wished
Wherof his hertes privete* | secret place
Began the werre of yee and nay,
The which in such balance lay
That contenance* for a throwe | composure
He loste, til he mihte knowe
The sothe; bot in his memoire
The man which lith in purgatoire
Desireth noght the hevene more,
That he ne longeth al so sore
To wite what him schal betide.
And whan the bordes* were aside | tables
And every man was rise aboute,
The king hath weyved* al the route*, | dismissed/ company
And with the senatour al one
He spak and preide him of a bone*, | favor
To se this Couste, wher sche duelleth
At hom with him, so as he telleth.
The senatour was wel appaied*; | pleased
This thing no lengere is delaied.
To se this Couste goth the king;
And sche was warned of the thing,
And with Heleine forth sche cam
Ayein* the king, and he tho nam* | toward/took
Good hiede, and whan he sih his wif,
Anon with al his hertes lif
He cawhte hire in his arm and kiste.

Was nevere wiht that sih ne wiste
A man that more joie made,
Wherof thei weren alle glade
Whiche herde tellen of this chance.
  This king tho with his wif Constance,
Which hadde a gret part of his wille*, desire
In Rome for a time stille
Abod and made him wel at ese.
Bot so yit cowthe he nevere plese* he never knew how to please
His wif that sche him wolde sein
Of hire astat the trowthe plein,
Of what contre that sche was bore,
Ne what sche was, and yit therfore
With al his wit he hath don sieke.
Thus as they lihe abedde and spieke,
Sche preide him and conseileth bothe
That for the worschipe of hem bothe,
So as hire thoghte it were honeste,
He wolde an honourable feste
Make, er he wente, in the cite,
Wher th'emperour himself schal be.
He graunteth al that sche him preide.
Bot as men in that time seide,
This emperour fro thilke day
That ferst his dowhter wente away
He was thanne after nevere glad;
Bot what that eny man him bad
Of grace* for his dowhter sake, favor
That grace wolde he noght forsake*. deny
And thus ful gret almesse* he dede, almsgiving
Wherof sche hadde many a bede*. many prayers
  This emperour out of the toun
Withinne a ten mile environ*, all around
Where as it thoghte him for the beste,
Hath sondry places forto reste;
And as fortune wolde tho,
He was duellende at on of tho.
The king Allee forth with th'assent
Of Couste his wif hath thider sent
Moris his sone, as he was taght,
To th'emperour, and he goth straght
And in his fader half* besoghte, behalf
As he which his lordschipe soghte,
That of his hihe worthinesse
He wolde do so gret meknesse* humility
His oghne toun to come and se,
And yive a time in the cite,
So that his fader mihte him gete
That he wolde ones with him ete.
This lord hath granted his requeste,
And whan the dai was of the feste,

In worschipe of here emperour
The king and ek the senatour
Forth with here wyves bothe tuo,
With many a lord and lady mo,
On horse riden him ayein,
Till it befell, upon a plein
Thei sihen wher he was comende.
With that Constance anon preiende
Spak to hir lord that he abyde,
So that sche mai tofore ryde,
To ben upon his bienvenue* welcoming
The ferste which schal him salue*. greet
And thus after hire lordes graunt,
Upon a mule whyt amblaunt* ambling
Forth with a fewe rod this qweene.
Thei wondren what sche wolde mene,
And riden after softe pas*; slowly
Bot whan this ladi come was
To th'emperour, in his presence
Sche seide alowd in audience,
"Mi lord, mi fader, wel you be*! may you be well
And of this time that I se
Youre honour and your goode hele,
Which is the helpe of my querele*, complaint
I thonke unto the goddes myht."
For joie his herte was affliht* excited
Of that sche tolde in remembrance;
And whanne he wiste it was Constance,
Was nevere fader half so blithe.
Wepende he keste* hire ofte sithe, kissed
So was his herte al overcome;
For thogh his moder were come
Fro deth to lyve out of the grave,
He mihte nomor wonder have
Than he hath whan that he hire sih.
With that hire oghne lord cam nyh
And is to th'emperour obeied*; makes obeisance
Bot whan the fortune is bewreied*, revealed
How that Constance is come aboute,
So hard an herte was non oute,
That he for pite tho ne wepte.
   Arcennus, which hire fond and kepte,
Was thanne glad of that is falle,
So that with joie among hem alle
Thei riden in at Rome gate.
This Emperour thoghte al to late* all too long
Til that the Pope were come,
And of the lordes sende some
To preie him that he wolde haste;
And he cam forth in alle haste,
And whan that he the tale herde,

How wonderly this chance ferde,
He thonketh God of his miracle,
To whos miht mai be non obstacle.
The king a noble feste hem made,
And thus thei weren alle glade.
A parlement*, er that thei wente, — council
Thei setten unto this entente,
To puten Rome in full espeir* — hope
That Moris was apparant heir
And scholde abide with hem stille,
For such was al the londes wille.
Whan every thing was fulli spoke,
Of sorwe and queint* was al the smoke, — quenched
Tho tok his leve Allee the king,
And with full many a riche thing,
Which th'emperour him hadde yive,
He goth a glad lif forto live;
For he Constance hath in his hond,
Which was the confort of his lond.
For whan that he cam hom ayein,
Ther is no tunge it mihte sein
What joie was that ilke* stounde — same
Of that he hath his qweene founde,
Which ferst was sent of Goddes sonde*, — by God's decree
Whan sche was drive upon the stronde,
Be whom the misbelieve of sinne
Was left*, and Cristes feith cam inne — forsaken
To hem that whilom* were blinde. — formerly
Bot he which hindreth every kinde
And for no gold mai be forboght*, — bought off
The deth, comende er he be soght,
Tok with this king such aqueintance
That he with al his retenance* — retinue
Ne mihte noght defende his lif;
And thus he parteth from his wif,
Which thanne made sorwe ynowh.
And therupon hire herte drowh
To leven Engelond for evere
And go wher that sche hadde levere*, — rather (be)
To Rome, whenne* that sche cam. — whence
And thus of al the lond sche nam
Hir leve, and goth to Rome ayein.
And after that* the bokes sein, — according as
She was noght there bot a throwe,
Whan deth of kinde hath overthrowe
Hir worthi fader, which men seide
That he betwen hire armes deide.
And afterward the yer suiende* — following
The God hath mad of hire an ende,
And fro this worldes faierie* — deceits, fantasies
Hath take hire into compaignie.

Moris hir sone was corouned,
Which so ferforth* was abandouned*   completely/ devoted
To Cristes feith, that men him calle
Moris the Cristeneste* of alle.   most Christian

The Wife of Bath's Prologue

RALPH HANNA AND TRAUGOTT LAWLER

The Wife of Bath's Prologue is surely among the most original and vital of Chaucer's poems, and yet it is also the one most deeply involved in literary tradition. That tradition, even at its most serious (as with Jerome), was always

allied with satire, and it certainly had its comic manifestations, most notably in the *Roman de la Rose*. But nothing in the tradition approaches the rich comedy of the Wife of Bath. Part of that comedy lies in the witty use Chaucer made of texts, and we present here both passages he surely used (from Jerome, Theophrastus, Walter Map, Jean de Meun, and a few lesser authors), and some that may or may not be sources but at least illustrate the tradition and cast some light on many of his lines (Matheolus and Eustache Deschamps).

The tradition of identifying the sources of *The Wife of Bath's Prologue* is virtually contemporary with Chaucer. The Ellesmere manuscript, whose "aura of authority" is especially evident in the Wife's prologue, gives forty-one quotations of sources in its margins; the Egerton manuscript gives fifty-five, almost all from the bible, though many are illustrative parallels (or implied attacks on the wife) rather than sources.[1] We have tried to honor the Ellesmere glossator in what we print. More than half of his glosses are to lines 1–183 and are taken from Jerome's *Adversus Jovinianum*; most are biblical verses, but they are cited because Jerome cites them. The glossator was quite thorough: every passage of Jerome we print below is cited, at least in part, in the Ellesmere glosses.

We begin, then, with the three major authors in the Wife's fifth husband Jankyn's "book of wikked wyves":

> He hadde a book that gladly, nyght and day,
> For his desport he wolde rede alway;
> He cleped it Valerie and Theofraste,
> At which book he lough alwey ful faste.
> And eek ther was somtyme a clerk at Rome,
> A cardinal, that highte Seint Jerome,
> That made a book agayn Jovinian . . . (*WB Prol*, III, 669–75)[2]

We print three texts by these three authors in the order in which the Wife names them, which Jankyn's title suggests is the order in which he has them in his book: first Walter Map's *Dissuasio Valerii ad Ruffinum* (c. 1175); then the

[1] All are printed in John M. Manly and Edith Rickert, eds, *The Text of the Canterbury Tales*, 3.1 (Chicago, 1940), pp. 496–502. The Ellesmere glosses are also printed *ad loc.* in Paul G. Ruggiers, ed., *The Canterbury Tales: A Facsimile and Transcription of the Hengwrt Manuscript, with Variants from the Ellesmere Manuscript* (Norman, OK, and Folkestone, UK, 1979), and are clearly readable in *The Ellesmere Manuscript of Chaucer's Canterbury Tales: A Working Facsimile*, with Introduction by Ralph Hanna (Cambridge, 1989). The phrase "aura of authority" is Charles A. Owen, Jr.'s, from his seminal essay "The Alternative Reading of *The Canterbury Tales*: Chaucer's Text and the Early Manuscripts," *PMLA* 97 (1982): 237–50; he discusses glossing on pp. 238–44; the quoted phrase is on 241. See also Daniel S. Silvia, Jr., "Glosses to the *Canterbury Tales* from St Jerome's *Epistola Adversus Jovinianum*," *Studies in Philology* 62 (1965): 28–39, and the illuminating analysis of all the glosses in both Ellesmere and Egerton in Susan Schibanoff, "The New Reader and Female Textuality in Two Early Commentaries on Chaucer," *Studies in the Age of Chaucer* 10 (1988): 71–108.

[2] The phrase "book of wikked wyves" is at III, 685. Jerome was not a cardinal. The belief, stemming apparently from his secretaryship to Pope Damasus in Rome from 382 to 385, was widespread, and enshrined in Italian art of Chaucer's time. He perhaps knew the sentence in the *Golden Legend* that "at the age of twenty-nine Jerome was ordained a cardinal priest in the church of Rome" (Jacobus de Voragine, *The Golden Legend: Readings on the Saints*, trans. William Granger Ryan [Princeton, 1993], 2.212); see also PL 22: 202; J. N. D. Kelly, *Jerome: His Life, Writings, and Controversies* (London, 1975), p. 83; Maria Letizia Casanova, "Iconographia," in the entry "Girolamo" in *Bibliotheca sanctorum* 6 (Rome, 1965), cols 1132–7; and F. Lanzoni, "La Leggenda di S. Girolamo," *Miscellanea Geronimiana* (Rome, 1920), pp. 32–5.

"Liber de Nuptiis," the so-called "Liber Aureolus" or "Golden Book" of the Greek writer Theophrastus (c. 370–288 BCE), which we have only because Jerome quoted it in full in *Adversus Jovinianum* (if he didn't make it up); then *Adversus Jovinianum* (393) itself. These are the major sources simply because they constitute the standard contents of medieval anti-matrimonial collections, the books that presumably gave Chaucer the idea for Jankyn's book. He drew on the standard set of selections from *Adversus Jovinianum* that appeared in those collections for various of the Wife's (and Jankyn's) dicta, though he went to the full text for the Wife's opening discussion of the relative value of marriage and virginity (9–162), in which she says the kind of thing Jerome says Jovinian said. He drew on Theophrastus's diatribe against marriage and women for the charges the Wife puts in the mouth of her old husbands (235–378). He drew on Map's *Epistola Valerii* just for two of the stories Jankyn likes to read from his book (747–64) and one sly remark (491–2), though the very idea of Jankyn may have been prompted by Map, who throughout implies that the chief readership of anti-matrimonial literature is married men who regret having married. Unless that prompting was at secondhand, through the figure of the Jealous Husband in the *Roman de la Rose*, who himself quotes Map.[3]

That text, Jean de Meun's continuation of the *Roman de la Rose* (c. 1275), though neither mentioned by Chaucer nor quoted by the Ellesmere glossator, was Chaucer's final major source, and we next print a series of passages from it. Many of those are utterances by Jean's "La Vieille," the Old Woman or Duenna who is quite evidently the major model for the Wife (though the Wife lacks her bitterness and cynicism);[4] others are by the Friend, who lists the tortures suffered by the Jealous Husband, and quotes him. We do not print Ovid (though "Ovides Art" is one of the texts in Jankyn's book), since there is no clear evidence that Chaucer made direct use of him, as Jean de Meun certainly did: the bawd Dipsas of *Amores* 1.8 is surely the model for Jean's Duenna and so an ultimate ancestor of the Wife of Bath; and the instructions to women in *Ars*

3 For a full treatment of medieval Latin anti-feminist collections and Chaucer's use of them, see *Jankyn's Book of Wikked Wyves*, vol. 1: *The Primary Texts*, edited by the present authors using materials collected by Karl Young and Robert A. Pratt (Athens, GA, 1997; hereafter cited as *JBWW1*). Since our purpose there was to present not Chaucer's sources but books of wicked wives, we printed from *Adversus Jovinianum* only the selections (1.28, 29, and 41–9) that occur typically in such books, though we acknowledged that Chaucer certainly consulted Jerome's full text; see pp. 97, 113. Thus Chaucer imagines and presents the Wife as knowing Jerome from her husband's book, but he himself in fact called on the full text as he wrote her prologue; of the fourteen passages we print below, only four (those cited from *JBWW1*) occur in the standard selections. We discuss the Jealous Husband of the *Roman* on p. 63. We don't see any strong evidence that Chaucer consulted the commentaries (which we will present in our second volume). Jill Mann has written trenchantly on how Chaucer transmuted his anti-feminist sources; see her *Geoffrey Chaucer* (Hemel Hempstead, UK, 1991), pp. 48–55, 70–86.

4 In his brilliant essay, "Some Implications of Nature's Femininity in Medieval Poetry," in *Approaches to Nature in the Middle Ages,* ed. Lawrence D. Roberts (Binghamton, NY, 1982), pp. 47–62, Winthrop Wetherbee argues persuasively that Jean's character Nature is as much an influence on Chaucer's conception of the Wife as La Vieille. "Like Nature in her long plea for procreation the Wyf displays a prodigious intellectual and imaginative energy in affirming her sexual role, but there is also, as in Nature's long speech, an element of uncertainty; for both figures sexual assertiveness is balanced by deep feelings of betrayal and resentment" (60). There are no obvious passages from Nature's long confession to Genius in the *Roman* for us to print, but we refer our readers to this profound and important essay.

amatoria 3 and *Amores* 3.4 play a role as well.[5] And in accordance with the principles of this volume we print nothing from the Bible, though the wisdom books – Proverbs is in Jankyn's book – are a major source and so are Paul's Epistles (though everything Chaucer uses from them is in *Adversus Jovinianum*). Paul's notion of the marital debt (I Cor. 7.3, cited in *Adversus Jovinianum* 1.7) and Ecclus. 25.30, on when the wife has the *maistrie*, are at the heart of Chaucer's conception.[6] We do give the text of four brief sources of particular passages, all cited or quoted in the Ellesmere margins: several anecdotes by Valerius Maximus, used at lines 460–3 and 641–9,[7] some sayings of Ptolemy's (180–3, 323–7), some astrological material from "Almansor" and "Hermes" relevant at 609–20 and 697–705, and the fable of the man and the lion (692).

All those are undoubted sources. Our final selections, from "Matheolus" and Eustache Deschamps, have a more uncertain status. In Bryan and Dempster, Bartlett J.Whiting printed seven pages of passages from Deschamps's *Miroir de Mariage*, all of them cited by Lowes in his long-unquestioned article of 1911.[8] In that article Lowes granted that all the passages he treated came ultimately from Jerome and Theophrastus, but again and again he argued that Chaucer showed verbal debts to Deschamps. In 1971 Zacharias P. Thundy, in the course of presenting his claim that Matheolus (whose name we know only from the title of his poem, *Lamentationes Matheoli* [c. 1290], and internal references in it) was a major source for the Wife's Prologue, argued also that the *Miroir de Mariage* was unknown until its publication in 1406, and that the apparent likenesses to it in Chaucer came about because both he and Deschamps made use of Matheolus.[9] But Thundy's article has not commanded general assent, for in it he undermines his own argument about Matheolus by claiming far more than the evidence he represents warrants; and little attention has been paid to what he says about Deschamps. We ourselves have publicly dismissed Thundy's argument

5 See Richard L. Hoffmann, *Ovid and the Canterbury Tales* (Philadelphia, PA, 1966), pp. 129–44, and Michael A. Calabrese, *Chaucer's Ovidian Arts of Love* (Gainesville, FL, 1994), pp. 81–111. Charles Muscatine, "The Wife of Bath and Gautier's *La Veuve*," in *Romance Studies in Memory of Edward Billings Ham*, ed. Urban T. Holmes (Hayward, CA, 1967), pp. 109–14, points out the many similarities between the Wife and Gautier's La Veuve; he argues that (since there are "too few verbal resemblances") "*La Veuve* was one of the poems that Chaucer did not read but heard" (p. 114). And Lee Patterson, " 'For the Wyves Love of Bathe': Feminine Rhetoric and Poetic Resolution in the *Roman de la Rose* and the Canterbury Tales," *Speculum* 58 (1983): 656–95, shows the relevance of the thirteenth-century Latin poem *De vetula*, translated into French as *La vieille* by Jean Lefèvre in 1370. Patterson is expanding on William Matthews, "The Wife of Bath and All Her Sect," *Viator* 5 (1974): 413–43.

6 As noted (though with erroneous page numbers) in the *Riverside Chaucer*, G. R. Owst, *Literature and Pulpit in Medieval England* (Oxford, 1961), pp. 385–6, suggests that the picture of a woman as "garrulous and vagrant" in Proverbs 7.10–12 is the ultimate source of both Noah's wife in the mysteries and the Wife of Bath.

7 We doubt that Chaucer subscribed to the curiously common medieval supposition that the Valerius of the *Epistola Valerii* was Valerius Maximus, since anyone who reads it with any attention, as Chaucer certainly did, must see that it is by a Christian author.

8 John Livingston Lowes, "Chaucer and the *Miroir de Mariage*," *Modern Philology* 8 (1910–11): 165–86, 305–34.

9 Zacharias P. Thundy, "Matheolus, Chaucer, and the Wife of Bath," in *Chaucerian Problems and Perspectives: Essays Presented to Paul E. Beichner, C.S.C.*, ed. Edward Vasta and Zacharias P. Thundy (Notre Dame, 1979), pp. 24–58. Jehan Le Fèvre made a French translation of Matheolus in 1371–72, which Chaucer might have known instead of, or in addition to, the Latin; but since whether he did or not is unclear, we cite the Latin only.

for treating Matheolus as a major source as "uncompelling, for the most part lacking exact verbal resemblance to Chaucer's text and concentrated in commonplaces."[10]

We have, however, since made our own independent study of Matheolus's poem, and have revised our position somewhat. There is after all some verbal resemblance – in "quoniam," for instance, and "shrewed Lamech," and "I sitte at hoom" – and a number of motifs and ideas not paralleled in the major sources. So while we remain unconvinced by the details of Thundy's presentation, we have come to think his thesis in the main right, and we print here both unique passages and a few places that are indeed commonplaces and yet contain some wording that suggests Chaucer's. We also think he may be right about Deschamps. Lowes too has overstated his case; most of the verbal resemblances he calls attention to seem very slight.[11] Still they have a certain weight, not to mention a certain Chaucerian quality, and since Deschamps clearly knew Chaucer's work we think it at least possible that Chaucer may have seen his through some private means, so that the "publication" of the *Miroir* in 1406 is not an insuperable obstacle. It is at least an analogue, and we agree with James Wimsatt's modest conclusion that "there are parallels that show Chaucer's marriage discussions could have been inspired in part by it,"[12] and so we print the passages Whiting printed, though we have shortened several of them.

[10] *JBWW1*, p. 5n.

[11] As they seemed to James I. Wimsatt: "the particular echoes of Deschamps that Lowes alleges are not impressive," *Chaucer and his French Contemporaries: Natural Music in the Fourteenth Century* (Toronto, 1991), p. 270. For earlier doubts, see Thundy, p. 51.

[12] Wimsatt, p. 271. Wimsatt devotes an entire judicious chapter to the question of Deschamps's relation to Chaucer, and is generally skeptical about influence without ruling it out. Pratt, building on remarks of Skeat, argued ("A Note on Chaucer and the *Policraticus* of John of Salisbury," *Modern Language Notes* 65 (1950): 243–6) that the three instances listed in lines 765–71 have "parallels" in *Policraticus*: that 766–8 is an adaptation of Petronius's story of The Widow of Ephesus, told by John at 8.11, and 769–70 of the story of Jael and Sisara, retold from Judges 4.17–22 by John at 8.20; and that 771 might have been prompted by John's mentioning poison a few sentences after giving the story of Judith beheading Holofernes (8.20). But the last argument is trivial; further (as Pratt knows) neither Holofernes nor Sisara was the husband of the woman who killed him; and the widow of Ephesus not only did not kill her husband (as Pratt acknowledges), she also did not lie with her lover in the bedroom, as Chaucer implies, but by the tomb. Thus (revising our silent agreement with Pratt in *JBWW1*, p. 83 n. 144), we are disinclined to count the *Policraticus* (though 8.11 brings together a good many anti-feminist materials, including Jerome and Theophrastus) among the sources of the *Wife of Bath's Prologue.*

I

Walter Map, ***Valerius to Ruffinus on why he should not get married***

Pacuvius, in tears, said to his neighbor Arrius, "Friend, I have an unlucky tree in my yard, from which my first wife hanged herself, and then my second, and now my third, too." Arrius said to him, "You amaze me. Do you always cry at happy endings?" And again, "Good gods, how many expenses that tree has suspended for you." And third, "Friend, give me some cuttings from that tree that I may plant." Friend, I am afraid lest you should need to beg cuttings from that tree at a time when they cannot be found.

Sulpicius felt where his shoe pinched him and divorced his wife who was noble and chaste. Friend, look out, lest the shoe which you will not be able to get off pinch you.

Livia killed her husband whom she hated too much, Lucilia hers whom she loved too much. The one mixed aconite on purpose; the other, deceived, offered madness to drink instead of the cup of love. Friend, these two are opposites, they wanted completely different things; but neither missed the proper end of female deceit, namely evil. Women advance by various and different paths; on whatever twisted roads they may wander, on however many perverse ways they may stray, there is a single outcome, a single goal of all their ways, a single head and common destination of all their divergences – malice. Take the experience of these two as an example of the fact that a woman will put everything at risk, both what she loves and what she hates, and is skilled in bringing harm when she wants to, which is always; and often she does harm when she is trying to help, and so it turns out that she brings harm even when she does not want to.

II

Theophrastus, ***Marriage***

Theophrastus's book about marriage, in which he asks whether a wise man should marry, is said to be worth its weight in gold. And after specifying that, yes, occasionally a wise man might venture on marriage – if the woman is beautiful, virtuous, and from a good family, and he himself healthy and rich – he immediately concludes: but all these things rarely coexist in a marriage. Therefore a wise man should not marry.

I

Walter Map, *Dissuasio Valerii ad Rufinum*

(from *Jankyn's Book of Wikked Wyves, 1: The Primary Texts (JBWW1)*, ed. and trans. Ralph Hanna and Traugott Lawler, The Chaucer Library [Athens and London: University of Georgia Press, 1997], pp. 121–47)

Pacuvius flens ait Arrio vicino suo, "Amice, arborem habeo in orto meo infelicem, de qua se prima uxor mea suspendit, et postmodum secunda, et jam nunc tercia." Cui Arrius, "Miror te in tantis successibus lacrimas invenisse." Et iterum, "Dii boni, quot dispendia tibi arbor illa suspendit." Et tercio, "Amice, dede michi de arbore illa surculos quos seram." Amice, metuo ne et te oporteat arboris illius surculos mendicare cum inveniri non poterunt.

Sensit Sulpicius ubi ipsum calceus suus premebat, qui ab uxore nobili et casta divertit. Amice, cave ne te premat calceus qui avelli non possit. (lines 198–208, p. 137)

Livia virum suum interfecit quem nimis odit; Lucilia suum quem nimis amavit. Illa sponte miscuit achoniton; hec decepta furorem propinavit pro amoris poculo. Amice, contrariis contenderunt votis iste; neutra tamen defraudata est fine fraudis feminee proprio, id est malo. Variis et diversis incedunt semitis femine; quibuscumque amfractibus errent, quantiscumque devient inviis, unicus est exitus, unica omnium viarum suarum meta, unicum capud et conventus omnium diversitatum suarum, malicia. Exemplo harum experimentum cape, quod audax est ad omnia quecumque amat vel odit femina, et artificiosa nocere cum vult, quod semper est; et frequenter, cum juvare parat, obest, unde fit ut noceat, et nolens. (lines 238–50, pp. 139–41)

II

Theophrastus, *Liber de Nuptiis*

(from *Jankyn's Book of Wikked Wyves, 1: The Primary Texts (JBWW1)*, ed. and trans. Ralph Hanna and Traugott Lawler, The Chaucer Library [Athens and London: University of Georgia Press, 1997], pp. 149–55)

Fertur aureolus Theophrasti liber de nuptiis, in quo querit an vir sapiens ducat uxorem. Et cum definisset, si pulchra esset, si bene morata, si honestis parentibus, si ipse sanus ac dives, sic sapientem inire aliquando matrimonium, statim intulit: hec autem raro in nuptiis universa concordant. Non est igitur uxor ducenda sapienti.

For first, marriage impedes the pursuit of philosophy, nor may any man serve both books and a wife. There are many things which are necessary for married women's practices: expensive clothes, gold, gems, shopping sprees, maids, all kinds of furniture, litters, a gilt two-wheeled chariot. Then, all night long, the nagging complaints: "That woman looks so much prettier when she goes out; this one is honored by everyone; when women get together, they despise me as a wretch. Why were you staring at the woman next door? What were you talking about with the maid? What did you bring home from the market?" We cannot even have a friend or a companion.[1] She suspects that if we love someone else we must hate her. If there is a really learned teacher in another city, we can neither leave our wife behind nor travel there with that baggage.

It is hard to support a poor one, a torment to put up with a rich one. Add to that that there is no picking out a wife, but we have to take whatever comes along. If she has a temper, if she is foolish, malformed, proud, smelly, whatever vice it is, we learn of it only after the wedding. A horse, a donkey, a bull, a dog, and the most worthless slaves, even clothes and kettles, a wooden stool, a goblet, and an earthen pitcher are all tested first and then bought or not. Only a wife is not shown, lest she should displease before she is wed.

Her face must always be noticed and her beauty praised, lest, if you look at another woman, she'll think that she displeases you. You have to call her "lady," celebrate her birthday, toast her health, and wish for her to outlive you. You have to show deference to her nurse and her maid, the servant from her father's house, and her foster-child, and her handsome attendant and her curly-haired "assistant," and her eunuch, gelded to prolong her pleasure and to make it safe: behind these titles there is an adulterer hiding. You have to love everybody she loves, whether you want to or not.[2]

If you put her in charge of the whole household, you become one of the servants. If you keep some matters for your own judgment, she will think you don't trust her, and turn to hatred and bickering, and, if you do not change your mind immediately, she will get the poison ready. If you let into the house old women and goldsmiths and soothsayers and peddlers of gems and of silk clothing, it is a threat to her chastity; if you keep them out, she takes offense because you suspect her. But in truth what does even diligent watchfulness avail, since an immodest wife cannot be guarded, and a modest one should not be? Necessity is a faithless watchkeeper over chastity; and only a woman who could have sinned if she wanted to can truly be called modest. A beautiful wife will be quickly surrounded by lovers, an ugly one will have difficulty restraining her desires. What many love is hard to keep; to have what no one else wants is irksome. Still it is less painful to have an ugly wife than to keep a beauty. Nothing is safe that the whole population is longing and sighing for. One man tempts by his shape, another by his brains, another by his jokes, yet another by his generosity. What is attacked from all sides will fall, one way or another.

People take wives to manage their household, to care for them when they are sick, and to avoid loneliness. But a faithful servant will manage things much better, one obedient to his master's authority and complying with his way of running

[1] Chaucer misunderstands this line, taking it as one more complaint from the wife; see III, 243–5. Perhaps, though, his Latin text had "possum" for "possumus." Deschamps seems to misunderstand it in a different way, also taking it as part of the wife's complaint, but translating "amicum" as "mari"; see 1607.

[2] The translation printed here of Theophrastus is revised slightly from our version in *JBWW1*.

Primum enim impediri studia philosophie, nec posse quemquam libris et uxori pariter inservire. Multa esse que matronarum usibus necessaria sunt: preciose vestes, aurum, gemme, sumptus, ancille, suppellex varia, lectice, et esseda deaurata. Dein per totas noctes garrule conquestiones: "Illa ornatior procedit in publicum; hec honoratur ab omnibus; ego in conventu feminarum misella despicior. Cur aspitiebas vicinam? Quid cum ancillula loquebaris? De foro veniens quid attulisti?" Non amicum habere possumus, non sodalem. Alterius amorem suum odium suspicatur. Si doctissimus preceptor in qualibet urbium fuerit, nec uxorem relinquere nec cum sarcina ire possumus.

Pauperem alere difficile est, divitem ferre tormentum. Adde quod nulla est uxoris electio, sed qualiscumque obvenerit habenda. Si iracunda, si fatua, si deformis, si superba, si fetida, quodcumque vitii est, post nuptias discimus. Equus, asinus, bos, canis, et vilissima mancipia, vestes quoque et lebetes, sedile ligneum, calix, et urceolus fictilis probantur prius et sic emuntur. Sola uxor non ostenditur, ne ante displiceat quam ducatur.

Attendenda est semper eius facies et pulchritudo laudanda, ne si alteram aspexeris, se estimet displicere. Vocanda domina, celebrandus natalis eius, jurandum per salutem illius, ut sit superstes optandum. Honoranda nutrix eius et gerula, servus paternus et alumpnus et formosus assecla et procurator calamistratus et in longam securamque libidinem exectus spado, sub quibus nominibus adulteri delitescunt. Quoscumque illa dilexerit ingratis amandi.

Si totam ei domum regendam commisseris, serviendum est. Si aliquid tuo arbitrio reservaveris, fidem sibi haberi non putabit et in odium vertetur ac jurgia et nisi cito consulueris, parabit venena. Anus et aurifices et ariolos et institores gemmarum sericarumque vestium si intromiseris, periculum pudicitie est; si prohibueris, suspitionis injuria. Verum quid prodest etiam diligens custodia, cum uxor impudica servari non possit, pudica non debeat? Infida enim custos est castitatis necessitas; et illa vere pudica dicenda est cui licuit peccare, si voluit. Pulchra cito adamatur, feda facile concupiscit. Difficile custoditur quod plures amant; molestum est possidere quod nemo habere dignetur. Minore tamen miseria deformis habetur quam formosa servatur. Nichil tutum est in quo tocius populi vota suspirant. Alius forma, alius ingenio, alius facetiis, alius liberalitate sollicitat. Aliquo modo expugnatur quod undique incessitur.

Quod si propter dispensationem domus et languoris solatia et fugam solitudinis ducuntur uxores, multo melius servus fidelis dispensat, obediens auctoritati domini et dispensationi eius obtemperans, quam uxor, que in eo se

things, than a wife, who thinks herself the mistress in this alone, that she should do the opposite of her husband's will, that is, what she likes, not what she is told. As for waiting on us when we are sick, friends and household slaves we have bound to us by our kindness to them can do that better than a woman who will weep and blame us, and sell us floods of tears in hope of the inheritance and, by making a great show of her own anxiety, drive her poor sick husband to despair.

III

Jerome, *Against Jovinian*

He (i.e., Jovinian) hurries to Abraham, Isaac, and Jacob, the first of whom had three wives, the second one, the third four: Leah, Rachel, Bilhah, and Zilpah (cf. Gen. 29, 30); and he points out that Abraham was blessed with a son as a reward for his faith.

As if to say, "It's good to eat wheat bread, and the finest wheat flour." And yet I grant that a man who is overcome with hunger should eat barley rather than cow manure. Doesn't barley have its own kind of purity if the alternative is dung?

Here my adversary goes wild in his utter exultation, and says this, as if battering the wall of virginity with his heftiest ram: "See," he says, "the Apostle confesses that he has no precept from the Lord about virgins; and he who has laid down the law for husbands and wives won't dare command what God has not taught him to." And rightly so. For what is taught is commanded; what is commanded must be done; if what must be done is not done, there is punishment. There is no point in commanding what is a matter of free will for the one to whom the command is made. If the Lord had commanded virginity, he would seem to have condemned marriage, and to have taken away the seed-bed of man from which virginity comes. If he had cut off the root, how would he look for fruit? If he hadn't first laid the foundation, how was he to build the building and put the roof on to cover everything from above? Enough digging will undo a mountain, men penetrate the very bowels of the earth to find gold – and when out of the tiniest particles, first by the blast of the furnace and then by the deft hand of the goldsmith, the bracelet takes shape, the man called blessed is not the one who sifted the gold from the mud but the one who wears the gold in all its beauty. So don't be surprised if between the titillations of the flesh and the allurements of sin we aren't forced to be angels, only encouraged. For counsel asks us to offer obedience freely, whereas command requires us to obey like servants.

estimat dominam, si adversum viri faciat voluntatem, id est quod placet, non quod jubetur. Assidere autem egrotanti magis possunt amici et vernule beneficiis obligati quam illa que nobis imputet lacrimas suas et hereditatis spe vendat illuviem et sollicitudinem jactans, languentis animum desperatione conturbet. (lines 1–60, pp. 151–5)

III

Jerome, *Adversus Jovinianum*

(from J.-P. Migne, ed., *Patrologia latina* XXIII [Paris, 1845], cols 216–61, or from *JBWW1*, pp. 175–91, as specified[1])

Currit ad Abraham, Isaac, et Jacob, e quibus prior trigamus, secundus monogamus, tertius quatuor uxorum est: Liae, Rachel, Balae, et Zelphae; et asserit Abraham ob fidei meritum benedictionem in generatione filii accepisse. (1.5, Migne col. 216; cf. 1.19, Migne col. 237)

Velut si quis definiat, "Bonum est triticeo pane vesci, et edere purissimam similam." Tamen ne quis compulsus fame comedat stercus bubulum, concedo ei, ut vescatur et hordeo. Num idcirco frumentum non habebit puritatem suam, si fimo hordeum praeferatur? (1.7, Migne col. 219)

Hic adversarius tota exsultacione bacchatur: hoc velut fortissimo ariete virginitatis murum quatiens, "Ecce," inquit, "Apostolus profitetur de virginibus, Domini se non habere praeceptum; et qui cum auctoritate de maritis et uxoribus jusserat, non audet imperare quod Dominus non praecepit." Et recte. Quod enim praecipitur, imperatur; quod imperatur, necesse est fieri; quod necesse est fieri, nisi fiat, poenam habet. Frustra enim jubetur quod in arbitrio ejus ponitur cui jussum est. Si virginitatem Dominus imperasset, videbatur nuptias condemnare, et hominis auferre seminarium unde et ipsa virginitas nascitur. Si praecidisset radicem, quomodo fruges quaereret? Nisi ante fundamenta jecisset, qua ratione aedificium exstrueret et operturum cuncta desuper culmen imponeret? Multo labore fossorum subvertuntur montes, terrarum pene inferna penetrantur ut inveniatur aurum – cumque de granis minutissimis prius conflatione fornacis, deinde callida artificis manu fuerit monile compactum, non ille beatus vocatur qui de luto excrevit aurum, sed qui auri utitur pulchritudine. Noli igitur admirari si inter titillationes carnis et incentiva vitiorum angelorum vitam non exigimur, sed docemur. Quia ubi consilium datur, offerentis arbitrium est; ubi praeceptum, necessitas est servientis. (1.12, Migne col. 227; cf. 1.36, Migne col. 259)

[1] Some silent changes have been made to Migne's punctuation and capitalization.

It's plain why the Apostle says, "Now, concerning virgins I have no commandment of the Lord": precisely because the Lord had already said, "All men take not this word, but they to whom it is given" and "He that can [30] take, let him take it." The President of the Games offers the prize, invites us to the race, holds up in his hand the reward of virginity. He points to the pure fountain, and cries, "If any man thirst, let him come to me and drink," "He that can take, let him take it."

The man who has a wife is spoken of as a debtor, as uncircumcised, as the slave of his wife – and [35] like bad slaves he has a leash on him.

Just as he allows virgins to marry on account of the danger of fornication, and makes excusable what is not in itself desirable, so for the same reason of avoiding fornication he allows widows to marry again. For it is better to have one husband, though he be the second or the third, than many lovers; that is, it is more tolerable [40] to be a prostitute to one man than to many. At least the Samaritan woman in John's gospel who says she has a sixth husband is rebuked by the Lord because he is not her husband. For where there is a number of husbands, there ceases to be any husband, since a husband is properly one. One rib at the beginning was turned into one wife, "and they shall be two," God says, "in one flesh" – not three or four, [45] since they are no longer two if they are more than two. Lamech, a murderer, a man with blood on his hands, was the first to divide one flesh between two wives. The same punishment of the flood wiped out both fratricide and bigamy.

Since Paul has urged those who have wives to be like those who don't, it wouldn't be consistent for him to require a widow who has become a Christian to marry again, [50] and the reason there is no definite number of wives one can have is that if a man gets married after he is converted, even if it's his third or fourth wife, she is considered to be his first. . . . I don't condemn bigamists, trigamists, or, if I may say, octagamists. I will say further that I will welcome any whorechaser as long as he repents. What is equally allowed must be weighed on an equal scale. [55]

As for the command "Increase and multiply, and fill the earth," it was necessary first for matter to be planted and grow so that there would be something to be cut off later. And let's think about what "fill the earth" means. Marriage fills earth, virginity heaven.

[60] And who may be silent about what Solomon writes in a riddle? "The horseleech had three daughters who were much beloved, but they were never satisfied, and for her fourth daughter it is not enough to say, 'It is enough': hell and the love of a woman and the earth which is not satisfied with water; and the fire will not say, 'It is enough.'" If the horseleech is the devil, the very beloved daughters of the devil are those things that cannot be satisfied with the blood of those they kill – [65] hell and the love of a woman and parched earth and blazing fire. This is not said about a whore nor about an adulteress, but the love of women in general is reproached here, that love which can never be satisfied, which when you put it out catches fire again, and which after plenty is needy again, and which makes a man's mind feminine and does not allow it to think of anything else except the passion it feeds.

[70] There is a similar proverb right after that one: "Three things trouble the earth, and the fourth it cannot endure: if a slave rules, and if a fool is filled with

In propatulo est cur Apostolus dixerit, "De virginibus autem praeceptum Domini non habeo" (1 Cor. 7.25): profecto quia praemiserat Dominus, "Non omnes capiunt verbum, sed quibus datum est" (Matt. 19.11) et, "Qui potest capere, capiat" (Matt. 19.12). Proponit *agonothetes* praemium, invitat ad cursum, tenet in manu virginitatis bravium: ostendit purissimam fontem et clamitat: "Qui sitit, veniat, et bibat" (John 7.37), "Qui potest capere, capiat" (1.12, Migne col. 228).

Qui uxorem habet ut debitor dicitur, et esse in praeputio, et servus uxoris, et quod malorum servorum est alligatus. (1.12, Migne col. 229).

Quomodo enim virginibus ob fornicationis periculum concedit nuptias, et excusabile facit, quod per se non appetitur, ita ob eamdem fornicationem vitandam concedit viduis secunda matrimonia. Melius est enim licet alterum et tercium, unum virum nosse, quam plurimos: id est, tolerabilius est uni homini prostitutam esse quam multis. Siquidem et illa in Evangelio Joannis Samaritana, sextum se maritum habere dicens, arguitur a Domino quod non sit vir eius (John 4.17). Ubi enim numerus maritorum est, ibi vir, qui proprie unus est, esse desiit. Una costa a principio in unam uxorem versa est, "et erunt," inquit, "duo in carne una" (Gen. 2.24). Non tres, neque quatuor, alioquin jam non duo, si plures. Primus Lamech sanguinarius et homicida unam carnem in duas divisit uxores: fratricidium et digamiam, eadem cataclysmi poena delevit (Gen. 4.18–24). (1.14, Migne col. 233)

Nec enim consequens esset ut Apostolus post baptisma viro mortuo jubeat alteri nubere, cum habentibus quoque uxores praeceperit ut sic sint quasi non habentes (cf. I Cor. 7.29), et ob hanc causam non esse uxorum numerum definitum: quia post baptisma Christi, etiam si tertia et quarta uxor fuerit, quasi prima reputetur. . . . Non damno digamos, immo nec trigamos, et, si dici potest, octogamos: plus aliquid inferam, etiam scortatorem recipio poenitentem. Quicquid aequaliter licet, aequali lance pensandum est. (1.15, Migne col. 234)

Quod autem ait, "Crescite et multiplicamini, et replete terram" (Gen. 1.28), necesse fuit prius plantare silvam et crescere, ut esset quod postea posset excidi. Simulque consideranda vis verbi, "replete terram." Nuptiae terram replent, virginitas paradisum. (1.16, Migne col. 235)

Illud vero quis taceat quod sub enigmate scribitur? "Sanguisuge tres filie erant dilectione dilecte, sed iste non saturate erant, et quarte non sufficit dicere 'satis est': infernus et amor mulieris et terra que non saciatur aqua; et ignis non dicet 'satis est' " (cf. Prov. 30.15–16). Si sanguisuga diabolus est, diaboli filie sunt dilectione dilecte, que saciari interfectorum cruore non possunt: infernus, et amor mulieris et terra arens et ignis exestuans. Non hic de meretrice, non de adultera dicitur, sed amor mulieris generaliter acusatur, qui semper insaciabilis est, qui extinctus accenditur, et post copiam rursum inops est, animumque virilem effeminat, et excepta passione quam sustinet, aliud non sinit cogitare.

Simile quid et in sequenti parabola legimus: "Per tria movetur terra, quartum autem non potest ferre: si servus regnet, et stultus si saturetur panibus, et odiosa uxor si habeat virum bonum, et ancilla si eiciat dominam

bread, and if a hateful wife has a good husband, and if a bondwoman casts out her lady." Look, here too a wife is listed among the greatest of evils. But if you answer, "But it says 'a hateful wife,'" I will say to you what I said above: just to be in danger of that is serious enough. For every bridegroom is in a state of uncertainty about whether he is marrying a hateful or a lovable woman. If he has married a hateful woman, she cannot be endured; if a lovable one, her love is compared to hell and parched earth and fire.

And why, you will say, were genitals made? Why were we built by the wisest of creators so that we burn for each other and naturally want to couple? . . . I could indeed have pointed out that just as the posterior of the body, and the passage through which the belly's wastes are discharged, is hidden from the eyes, put as it were behind our back, so what is under the stomach, for discharging humors and liquids by which the body's veins are irrigated, was concealed by God. But since those same organs, that fabric of the genitals, our distinguishing part and that of women, and the chambers concealed within the vulva for receiving and nourishing fetuses, proclaim difference of sex, I will reply briefly. . . . What does the apostle mean by exhorting us to continence if it is against nature? What does our Lord himself mean when he teaches about the variety of eunuchs? The Apostle calls us to share his celibacy: shouldn't he constantly hear back, why do you have a penis, Paul? Why are you distinct from the female sex in your beard, your hair, in the clear otherness of your members? Why don't you have big breasts? Why aren't you wide below and slim above? Your voice is too unrefined, your speech too rough, your eyebrows too hairy. What good is it to have all those manly features if you won't touch a woman? . . . Our Lord and Savior, "who, being in the form of God," deigned to take "the form of a servant," "becoming obedient" to the Father "unto death, even to the death of the cross" – what need had he to be born with these members that he wasn't to use? He was even circumcised, as if to parade what sex he was. Why did he castrate John the Apostle and John the Baptist for the love of him, after he had made them born male? We believe in Christ; let us follow Christ's example.

And my opponent's objection that the Lord went to Cana in Galilee and took full part in the wedding festivities by turning water into wine doesn't bother me in the least. . . . It just strengthens my case, in fact, for by going to only one wedding he taught us we should marry only once. . . . For the church doesn't condemn marriage, just gives it a lowly place; doesn't throw it out, but makes use of it; for it knows, as I have said, that in a great household there are gold and silver vessels, yes, but wooden and clay ones too, and that some vessels are treasured, some scorned; and whoever has cleansed himself will be a treasured, needed vessel, ready for any good service.

I know that I have included far more in this catalogue of women than the conventions of examples allow, and that I may be justly blamed by a learned reader. But what else can I do, when women these days will push the authority of St. Paul at me, and recite the rules about multiple marriage by heart before their first husband is even buried?

Socrates had two wives, Xanthippe, and Myron the granddaughter of Aristides. They were always bickering with each other, and he was accustomed to laugh at them because they fought over him – the ugliest man, with ape's nostrils, a bald

suam" (cf. Prov. 30.21–3). Ecce, et hic inter malorum magnitudinem uxor ponitur. Quod si responderis, "sed uxor odiosa," dicam tibi quod et supra: at hoc periculum in memet fieri grave est. Qui enim ducit uxorem in ambiguo est, utrum odiosam an amabilem ducat. Si odiosam duxerit, ferri non potest; si amabilem, amor illius inferno et arenti terre et incendio comparatur. (*JBWW1*, pp. 189–91, lines 429–50; 1. 28, Migne col. 250)

Et cur, inquies, creata sunt genitalia, et sic a conditore sapientissimo fabricati sumus ut mutuum nostri patiamur ardorem, et gestiamus in naturalem copulam? . . . Poteram quidem dicere, quomodo posterior pars corporis et meatus per quem alvi stercora egeruntur relegatus est ab oculis, et quasi post tergum positus, ita et hic qui sub ventre est, ad digerendos humores et potus quibus venae corporis irrigantur, a Deo conditus est. Sed quoniam ipsa organa et genitalium fabrica, et nostra feminarumque discretio, et receptacula vulvae ad suscipiendos et coalendos fetus condita, sexus differentiam predicant, hoc breviter respondebo. . . . Quid sibi autem vult apostolus, ut ad continentiam cohortetur (e.g. I Cor. 7–8, Gal. 5.23), si contra naturam est? Quid ipse Dominus qui eunuchorum precipit varietates (Matt. 19.12)? Certe apostolus, qui ad suam nos provocat pudicitiam (I Cor. 7–8), debet constanter audire, cur portas veretrum, o Paule? Cur a sexu feminarum, barba, pilis, aliaque membrorum qualitate distingueris? Cur tuae non intumescunt papillae, non dilatantur renes, non pectus arctatur? Vox obsoletior est, sermo ferocior, et hirsutius supercilium. Frustra haec omnia virorum habes, si complexu non uteris feminarum. . . . Dominus noster atque Salvator, "qui cum in forma Dei esset . . . formam servi" dignatus est assumere, "factus obediens" Patri "usque ad mortem, [mortem autem] crucis" (Phil. 2.6–8), quid necesse erat, ut in his membris nasceretur, quibus usurus non erat? Qui certe ut sexum ostenderet, etiam circumcisus est. Cur Joannem apostolum et Baptistam sua dilectione castravit, quos viros nasci fecerat? Qui ergo in Christum credimus, Christi sectemur exempla. (1.36, Migne cols. 260–1)

Ex quo nequaquam nos illud poterit impedire, quod adversarius objicit, fuisse Dominum in Cana Galilaeae, et nuptiarum festa celebrasse quando aquas vertit in vinum. . . . Quamquam et hoc pro nobis. Qui enim semel venit ad nuptias, semel docuit esse nubendum. . . . Ecclesia enim matrimonia non damnat, sed subjicit; nec abjicit, sed dispensat, sciens, ut supra diximus, in domo magna non solum esse vasa aurea et argentea, sed et lignea et fictilia, et alia esse in honorem, alia in contumeliam; et quicumque se mundaverit, eum futurum esse vas honorabile et necessarium, in omne opus bonum praeparatum. (1.40, Migne cols. 269–70)

Sentio in katalogo feminarum multo me plura dixisse quam exemplorum patitur consuetudo et a lectore erudito juste posse reprehendi. Sed quid faciam, cum mihi mulieres nostri temporis apostoli ingerant auctoritatem; et necdum elato funere prioris viri, memoriter digamie precepta decantent? (*JBWW1*, p. 175, lines 231–6; 1.47, Migne col. 276)

Socrates Xantippen et Miro neptem Aristidis, duas habebat uxores. Que cum crebro inter se jurgarentur, et ille eas irridere esset solitus, quod propter se – fedissimum hominem simis naribus, recalva fronte, pilosis humeris, et

forehead, hairy shoulders, and bowlegs. In the end they turned their energy on him [120] and persecuted him for a long time, punishing him and putting him to flight. Once, when he had stood up to Xanthippe as she poured out endless abuse from an upper story, she poured dirty water on him, and he responded with nothing further than wiping his head and saying, "I knew it was coming. I knew it would rain after a thunder like that."

[125] We read of a certain noble man among the Romans who, when his friends criticized him because he had divorced a wife who was beautiful, chaste, and rich, put out his foot and said to them, "And this shoe which you see looks new and elegant to you, but no one except me knows where it pinches me." Herodotus writes that a woman takes off her modesty when she takes off her dress. And our comic author thinks it is a lucky man who has [130] never married.

What can I say about Pasiphaë, the Clytemnestras, and the Eriphyles? The first of them, who was filled to the brim with self-indulgence, just as expected, since she was the wife of a king, is said to have wanted to sleep with a bull; the second to have killed her husband for the sake of her lover; and the third to have betrayed Amphiaraus and preferred a golden necklace to her husband's safety.

IV

Jean de Meun, *The Romance of the Rose*

(Friend) Only a big fool would be stingy about a thing like that (i.e. what Jealousy withholds). It's the candle in the lantern: you could light up a thousand other candles with it and not find its flame any smaller.[1] Everybody who isn't a blockhead understands this comparison. (7379–84)

(Friend, quoting Theophrastus's *Golden Book*) If a man takes a poor wife, he is going to have to feed and clothe her and keep her in shoes; and if he thinks he can raise himself by marrying rich, he will find her so uppity and proud, so presumptuous and arrogant that it will be a big pain for him to put up with her. If she's pretty, they'll all come running, chase her, seek to honor her, punch and wrestle each other for her, strain and battle over her, strive to serve her, surround her, woo her, hover near her, covet her – and in the end they will have her, they press her so, for a tower besieged on all sides will hardly escape being taken.

If she's ugly, she will try to please them all. And how is somebody supposed to

[1] Cf. Ovid, *Ars amatoria* 3.93, "Quis vetet adposito lumen de lumine sumi?" [Who would keep anyone from taking a light from his light?] Cited and discussed in Richard L. Hoffmann, *Ovid and the Canterbury Tales* (Philadelphia, PA, 1966), pp. 129–30, and Michael A. Calabrese, *Chaucer's Ovidian Arts of Love* (Gainesville, FL, 1994), pp. 88–9.

repandis cruribus – disceptarent. Novissime verterunt in eum inpetum, et male multatum fugientemque diu persecute sunt. Quodam autem tempore cum infinita convitia ex superiori loco ingerenti Xantippe restitisset, aqua perfusus inmunda, nichil amplius respondit quam capite deterso, "Sciebam," inquit, "futurum, ut ista tonitrua imber sequeretur." (*JBWW1*, p. 177, lines 252–61; 1.48, Migne cols 278–9)

Legimus quemdam apud Romanos nobilem, cum eum amici arguerent quare uxorem formosam et castam et divitem repudiasset, protendisse pedem et dixisse eis, "Et hic soccus quem cernitis videtur vobis novus et elegans, sed nemo scit preter me ubi me premat." Scribit Erodotus quod mulier cum veste deponat et verecundiam. Et noster comicus fortunatum putat qui uxorem nunquam duxerit.

Quid referam Phasiphen, Clitemestras, et Eripilas? Quarum prima delitiis fluens, quippe ut regis uxor, tauri dicitur expetisse concubitus; alia occidisse virum ob amorem adulteri; tertia prodidisse Amphiaraum et saluti viri monile aureum pretulisse. (*JBWW1*, pp. 179–81, lines 290–302; 1.48, Migne cols 279–80)

IV

Jean de Meun, *Le Roman de la Rose*

(from *Le Roman de la Rose,* ed. Félix Lecoy, vols 1–3, [Paris, 1965–70])

7379 Mout est fols qui tel chose esperne;
c'est la chandele en la lanterne;
qui mil en i alumeroit,
ja meins de feu n'i troveroit.
7383 Chascuns set le similitude,
se mout n'a l'entendement rude.
…

8549 Et qui veust povre fame prendre,
a norrir la l'esteut entendre,
et a vestir et a chaucier;
et s'il tant se cuide essaucier
qu'il la prengne riche forment,
au soffrir la ra grant torment,
tant la trove orgueilleuse et fiere
et seurquidee et bobanciere.
S'el rest bele, tuit i aqueurent,
tuit la porsivent, tuit l'anneurent,
tuit i hurtent, tuit i travaillent,
tuit i luitent, tuit i bataillent,
tuit a li servir s'estudient,
tuit li vont entor, tuit la prient,

guard either a thing that everybody is fighting over, or one who wants all who see her? (8549–70)

(The friend has just argued, after Theophrastus, that when you buy a horse you examine it carefully with no cover on it.) But you get a wife without an examination: win or lose, pleasure or grief, she'll never show herself for fear of putting you off before she's married. Once she sees the thing is done, then and only then she shows her malice, then it appears if she has any faults in her, then she makes you feel her true character, and what a fool she's made of you, when repentance is useless. (8642–52)

(The Jealous Husband is speaking) They go up and down the streets to see and be seen, and to make their beaux want to sleep with them. That's why they dress up for dances and for church, for nobody would do that if she didn't think that she'd be looked at, and think that was the quickest way to please those she could seduce.[2] (8999–9008)

(The Jealous Husband) Even at night, when you're lying in bed naked right next to me, you won't let me touch you; for when I want to put my arms around you and kiss you and give you pleasure, and I'm all hot, you sulk like a little devil, and won't turn towards me no matter what I do. (9058–66)

(The Jealous Husband) This Hercules according to Solinus was seven feet tall – no

[2] Cf. Ovid, *Ars amatoria* 1.99 (On women at the games) "Spectatum veniunt; veniunt spectentur ut ipsae:/ Ille locus casti damna pudoris habet" [They go to see and to be seen; that's a good place to lose your chastity]. Cited and discussed in Hoffmann, 1966, p. 140 and Calabrese, 1994, pp. 93–4.

tuit i musent, tuit la covoitent,
si l'ont en la fin, tant esploitent,
car tour de toutes parz assise
enviz eschape d'estre prise.

S'el rest lede, el veust a touz plere.
Et conment porroit nus ce fere
qu'il gart chose que tuit guerroient
ou qui veust touz ceuz qui la voient?
…

Mes l'en prent fame sanz espreuve,
ne ja n'i sera descoverte,
ne por gaaigne ne por perte,
ne por solaz ne por mesese,
por ce, sanz plus, qu'el ne desplese
devant qu'ele soit espousee.
Et quant el voit la chose outree,
lors primes moutre sa malice,
lors pert s'el a sus soi nul vice,
lors fet au fol ses meurs sentir,
quant riens n'i vaut le repentir.
…

… et vont traçant par mi les rues
por voair, por estre veües,
por fere aus compaignons desir
de volair avec eus gesir.
Por ce portent eus les cointises
aus queroles at aus iglises
car ja nule ce ne feïst
s'el ne cuidast qu'an la veïst
et que par ce plus tost pleüst
a ceus que decevoir peüst.
…

Neïs la nuit, quant vos gisiez
en mon lit lez moi toute nue,
n'i poez vos estre tenue;
car quant je vos veill embracier
por vos besier et soulacier,
et sui plus forment eschaufez,
vos rechiniez conme maufez
ne vers moi, por riens que je face,
ne volez torner vostre face.
…

Cist Herculés avoit, selonc
l'aucteur Solin, .VII. piez de lonc,
n'onc ne pot a quantité graindre
nus homz, si com il dit, attaindre.

man, he says, was ever taller. Hercules had many adventures: he vanquished twelve horrible monsters; and when he had won the twelfth adventure, he could not get through a thirteenth,[3] the one with his girlfriend Deianira, who used the poisoned shirt to make his skin all on fire with the poison and tear it apart. His heart had already been made crazy with love for Iole. Thus Hercules who had so many good qualities was beaten by a woman. And thus Samson, who wouldn't have feared ten men any more than ten apples if he'd had his hair, was deceived by Dalila. (9157–76)

(Friend) Thus handsome young gentlemen in the know all should work hard to keep their girlfriends without harping on their shortcomings. Women don't like being corrected . . . And so she hates whoever corrects her. (9929–33, 9950)

(The Duenna) I tell you, if when I was your age I were as smart about the games lovers play as I am now – for I was a great beauty then, but now I have to moan and complain when I look at my ruined face and see how relentlessly it's wrinkled, and remember how my beauty used to make the young men dance . . . (12731–9)

(The Duenna) I was pretty, and young and silly and foolish; I never was at the school of love where they taught the theory of it – but I know everything from doing it. The experiments I've been conducting all my life have made me smart about it. Now I know about it down to its last encounter, and it just isn't right that I should fail to pass on to you the useful things I know from having tested it out so fully. It's a kindness to give young people advice. (12771–81)

[3] See *Dissuasio Valerii*, *JBWW1* p. 141, lines 261–2. We discuss Jean de Meun's Appropriations of Valerius in *JBWW1*, pp. 63–4.

Cist Herculés ot mout d'encontres,
il vainqui .xii. horribles montres;
et quant ot vaincu le dozieme,
onc ne pot chevir du trezieme,
9165 ce fu de Deïanira,
s'amie, qui li descira
sa char de venin toute esprise
par la venimeuse chemise.
Si ravoit il por Yolé
9170 son queur ja d'amors affolé.
Ainsinc fu par fame dontez
Herculés, qui tant ot bontez.
Ausinc Sanson, qui pas .X. homes
ne redoutast ne quel .X. pomes
s'il eüst ses cheveux eüz,
9176 fu par Dallida deceüz.

…

9929 Ainsinc a garder leur amies,
sanz reprendre de leur folies,
doivent tuit estre diligent
li biauz vallet, li preuz, le gent.
9933 Fames n'ont cure de chasti …
…

9950 Si het quiconques la chastoie.
…

12731 Sachiez, se je fusse ausinc sage,
quant j'estoie de vostre aage,
des geus d'amors con je suis ores
– car de trop grant biauté fui lores,
12735 mes or m'esteut pleindre et gemir,
quant mon vis esfacié remir
et voi que froncir le covient,
quant de ma biauté me sovient
qui ces vallez fesoit triper …
…

12771 Bele iere, et jenne et nice et fole,
n'onc ne fui d'Amors a escole
ou l'en leüst la theorique,
mes je sai tout par la practique.
12775 Experimenz m'en ont fet sage,
que j'ai hantez tout mon aage;
or en sai jusqu'a la bataille,
si n'est pas droiz que je vos faille
des biens aprendre que je sai,
12780 puis que tant esprovez les ai.
Bien fet que jennes genz conseille.

(The Duenna) Oh Lord, it (i.e. my past) pleases me still when I look back on it; I take great delight in the thought and my members shiver when I bring back the good times and the gay life my heart still yearns for; my whole body is young again when I think of it and remember it; it does me all the good in the world to recall all that, for at least I've had my fun, even if they took advantage of me. A young woman isn't wasting her time when she leads a gay life, especially if she's looking to cover expenses. (12902–18)

(The Duenna instructs the Lover in the games of love) Dear son, never try generosity; have your heart in several places: never put it in just one place; don't give it, don't lend it, but sell it good and dear and always to the highest bidder; and make sure that the buyer doesn't get a bargain. (13007–14)

(The Duenna) A mouse has very poor protection and takes a big risk when he goes out foraging if he has only one hole to run to. (13120–2)

(The Duenna) Any woman who does that (loves one man only) is a fool. She should have several boyfriends and strive if she can to please them so much that she makes them all very uneasy. (13239–42)

(The Duenna) And let her keep her chamber of Venus clean, like a good girl. (13305–6)

(The Duenna) And once a woman gets drunk she loses all her inhibitions; she says whatever comes into her head, and is at the mercy of any man when she has put herself in such a parlous state.[4] (13422–6)

4 Cf. Ovid, *Ars amatoria* 3.765–6: "Turpe jacens mulier multo madefacta Lyaeo:/ Dignast concubitus quoslibet illa pati." [A woman lying drunk with too much wine is a shameful thing: whoever lies down with her, and whatever he does, she deserves it.] Cited and discussed in Hoffmann, 1966, p. 135, and Calabrese, 1994, pp. 92–3.

. . .

Par Dieu, si me plest il oncores
quant je m'i sui bien porpensee;
mout me delite en ma pensee
et me resbaudissent li menbre
quant de mon bon tens me remembre
et de la jolivete vie
dom mes queurs a si grant envie;
tout me rejovenist le cors
quant g'i pens et quant jou recors;
touz les biens du monde me fet
quant me souvient de tout le fet,
qu'au mains ai je ma joie eüe,
conbien qu'il m'aient deceüe.
Jenne dame n'est pas oiseuse
quant el maine vie joieuse,
meesmement cele qui pense
d'aquerre a fere sa despense.
. . .

Biau filz, ja larges ne saiez;
en pluseurs leus le queur aiez,
en un seul leu ja non metez
ne nou donez ne ne pretez,
mes vendez le bien chierement
et torjorz par enchierement;
et gardez que nus qui l'achat
n'i puisse fere bon achat.
. . .

Mout a soriz povre secours
et fet en grant perill sa druige
qui n'a q'un pertuis a refuige.
. . .

Fole est fame qui si l'a mis,
ainz doit avoir pluseurs amis
et fere, s'el peut, que tant plese
que touz les mete a grant mesese.
. . .

Et conme bone baisselete,
Tiegne la chambre Venus nete.
. . .

Et puis que fame est anivree,
il n'a point en li de deffanse
et jangle tout quan qu'ele panse,
et est a touz habandonee
quant a tel meschief s'est donee.

(The Duenna) A woman who is wise will pluck love's fruit while she's in the flower of her age. (13453–4)

(The Duenna) Let her go often to the principal church and make appearances at weddings, processions, games, feasts, dances, for in such places the god of love holds school and celebrates high mass for his pupils – and so does the goddess. (13492–8)

(The Duenna) In the same way a woman ought to spread her nets everywhere to catch all the men, for she can't know from whom she might have grace. (13559–62)

(The Duenna, on what a woman should say when she submits) I believe you have enchanted me. (13661)

(The Duenna) A woman is a fool if she doesn't pluck her lover down to the last feather; for the better she can pluck him the better she will keep him, and the dearer she sells herself the dearer she'll be held; for what one gets for nothing, one usually discounts, as if it were worth no more than a piece of bark.[5] If he loses it, he doesn't care – nothing like the way he'd care if he'd paid a lot for it. (13667–78)

(The Duenna, on receiving a lover) Then the lady has to sigh and seem angry and attack him and badger him, and say that he would never have been so late unless there was a reason, and that he is keeping another woman in his house, whoever she is, and having more fun with her. (13793–800)

5 Dean Spruill Fansler, *Chaucer and the Roman de la Rose* (New York, 1914), pp. 74–7, shows that this figure of speech, what he calls "picturesque negation", and E. Koeppel, "Chauceriana," *Anglia* 14 (1892): 262 (quoted by Fansler) calls "gemeinschaftliche Ausdrücke der Geringschätzung" (common expressions of contempt), i.e., expressing contempt for something by comparing it to a commonplace object of no value, is a feature of Chaucer's style probably derived from Jean de Meun. Fansler lists sixty-five examples in Chaucer and forty-six in Jean de Meun's portion of the *Roman*.

...

13453 Le fruiz d'amors, se fame est sage,
cueille an la fleur de son aage.
...

13492 Sovant aille a la mestre iglise
et face visitacions
a noces, a processions,
a geus, a festes, a queroles,
car en tex leus tient ses escoles
e chante a ses deciples messe
li dex d'Amors et la deesse.
...

13559 Ausinc doit fame par tout tendre
ses raiz por touz les homes prendre,
car por ce qu'el ne peut savoir
des quex el puist la grace avoir . . .
...

13661 Si croi qu'ous m'avez anchantee.
...

13667 Fole es qui son ami ne plume
jusqu'a la darreniere plume;
car qui mieuz plumer le savra
c'iert cele qui meilleur l'avra
et qui plus iert chiere tenue,
quant plus chier se sera vendue;
car ce que l'an a por noiant
trop le va l'en plus vistoiant;
l'an nou prise pas une escorse;
se l'an le pert, l'en n'i fet force,
au mains si grant ne si notee
con qui l'avroit chier achatee.
...

13793 Puis doit la dame sopirer
et sai par samblant aïrer,
et l'assaille et li queure seure
et die que si grant demeure
n'a il mie fet sanz reson
et qu'il tenoit en sa meson
autre fame, quel qu'ele soit,
dom li solaz mieuz li plesoit.
...

(The Duenna) Nobody can put a guard on a woman if she doesn't guard herself. Even if it were Argus guarding her and watching her with his hundred eyes . . . his guard would be worth nothing.[6] (14351–4, 14363)

(The Duenna) I gave it all (the gifts I'd had from earlier lovers) to a louse who did too shameful things to me, and yet he was the one who pleased me most. I called all the others my friends, but he's the only one I loved so much; but I have to say he valued me about as much as a pea, and he used to tell me so. He was bad, I've never seen a worse. He never stopped despising me; he called me a common whore, the louse – he didn't love me at all. A woman has very poor judgment, and I was a woman, head to toe. I've never loved a man who loved me, but if this rat had dislocated my shoulder or fractured my skull, I believe I'd have thanked him for it. He wouldn't have known how to batter me in a way that I wouldn't then let him back on top of me, for he knew very well how to make peace no matter how badly he'd treated me. He would never batter me so badly, or hit me or drag me across the floor or cut or bruise my face, that he wouldn't ask my forgiveness before he went out the door; he would never insult me so badly that he wouldn't signal for peace and then soothe me with his touches, and so we had peace and concord once more. That's how he had me on his leash, for he was a genius at making up, that cheat, that traitor, that robber. I couldn't live without him, I would have followed him anywhere. (14448–82)

(Genius) Anybody who tells his wife his secrets has made her the boss. No man who is born of woman, unless he's drunk or out of his mind, should tell a woman anything that shouldn't come out, if he doesn't want to hear it repeated by someone

6 Cf. Ovid, *Ars amatoria* 3.617–18: "Tot licet observent, adsit modo certa voluntas,/ Quot fuerant Argo lumina, verba dabis" [Though you be observed by as many people as Argus had eyes, as long as your will stays firm you will find the words to deceive them]. Cited and discussed in Hoffmann,1966, pp. 131–3. As Hoffmann points out, the number of eyes is specified as one hundred in *Metamorphoses* 1.625, 721.

14351 Nus ne peut metre en fame garde,
s'ele meïsmes ne se garde.
Se c'iert Argus qui la gardast
et de ses .C. euz l'esgardast,
...

14363 n'i vaudroit sa garde mes rien.
...

14448 ... tretout donoie a un ribaut,
qui trop de honte me fesoit,
mes c'iert cil qui plus me plesoit.
Les autres touz amis clamoie,
mes li tant seulement amoie;
mes sachiez qu'il ne me prisoit
un pois, et bien le me disoit.
Mauvés iert, onques ne vi pire,
onc ne me cessa de despire;
putain conmune me clamoit
li ribauz, qui point ne m'amoit.
Fame a trop povre jugement,
et je fui fame droitement.
Onc n'amoi home qui m'amast;
mes se cil ribauz m'antamast
l'espaule, ou ma teste eüst quasse,
sachiez que je l'en merciasse.
Il ne me seüst ja tant batre
que seur moi nou feïsse enbatre,
qu'il savoit trop bien sa pes fere,
ja tant ne m'eüst fet contrere.
Ja tant ne m'eüst maumenee
ne batue ne trahinee,
ne mon vis blecié ne nerci,
qu'ainceis ne me criast merci
que de la place se meüst;
ja tant dit honte ne m'eüst
que de pes ne m'amonetast
et que lors ne me rafetast:
si ravions pes et concorde.
Ainsinc m'avoit prise en sa corde,
car trop estoit fiers rafetierres
li faus, li traïstres, li lierres.
Sanz celi ne poïsse vivre,
celi vosisse tourjorz sivre.
...

16317 Et quiconques dit a sa fame
ses secrez, il an fet sa dame.
Nus hom qui soit de mere nez,
s'i n'est ivres ou forsenez,
ne doit a fame reveler

else. It would be better to flee the country than tell a woman what should be kept secret, no matter how loyal or sweet she is. If he's about to do something in secret and sees a woman coming, he'd better stop, for even at the risk of bodily harm she will tell it, I assure you, though she may bide her time; even if nobody asks her about it, she will tell it all, she doesn't need outside encouragement; she won't keep quiet about it for anything in the world. So what if he might yell at her or hurt her: she'll think she'll die if it doesn't jump out of her mouth. (16317–38)

(Nature) Certainly they (i.e., women) swear and lie more boldly than any man. (18106–7)

V

Valerius Maximus, *Memorable Doings and Sayings*

9. (Publicia and Licinia poisoned their husbands, and were quickly strangled by their own relatives) The severity of these men in exacting revenge was prompted by a great crime, while Ignatius Mecennus's was prompted by a much smaller cause: just because his wife drank wine he beat her with his staff and killed her – and no one accused him of murder or even blamed him, because everybody thought she had paid the price of violating sobriety in a most exemplary way. And of course it's true that any woman who likes her drop too much closes the door to virtue and opens the door to vice.

nule riens qui face a celer,
se d'autrui ne la veust oïr.
Mieuz vandroit du païs foïr
que dire a fame chose a tere,
tant soit leaus ne debonere.
Ne ja nul fet secré ne face,
s'il voit fame venir en place;
car s'il i a perill de cors,
el le dira, bien le recors,
conbien que longuement atande;
et se nus riens ne l'an demande,
le dira ele vraement
sanz estrange amonestement:
por nule riens ne s'an teroit.
A son avis morte seroit
s'il ne li saillet de la bouche,
s'il i a perill ou reprouche.
. . .

18106 Plus hardiemant que nus hom
certeinement jurent et mantent.

V

Valerius Maximus, *Facta et Dicta Memorabilia*

(from Valerius Maximus, *Facta et Dicta Memorabilia*, ed. John Briscoe [Stuttgart and Leipzig: Teubner, 1998], vol. 1 of 2, Book VI, chapter 3, "De Severitate", pp 393–4)[1]

Book VI, 3. 9. Magno scelere horum severitas ad exigendam vindictam concitata est, Egnati autem Mecenni[2] longe minore de causa, qui uxorem, quod vinum bibisset, fusti percussam interemit, idque factum non accusatore tantum, sed etiam reprehensore caruit, unoquoque existimante optimo illam exemplo violatae

[1] Robert A. Pratt, "Chaucer and the Hand that Fed Him," *Speculum* 41 (1966): 619–42, gives evidence (620–3) to suggest that Chaucer took the *exempla* in III, 460–2 and 642–9 not directly from Valerius Maximus but from the *Communiloquium* of the Franciscan John of Wales, a manual of material for preachers. Both passages are accompanied by glosses in Ellesmere and several other manuscripts citing the place in Valerius Maximus, but these citations too are probably drawn from John of Wales. Pratt also notes that John's statements are closer to the text of the epitome of Valerius Maximus made, probably in the fourth century, by Julius Paris than to the text of Valerius himself. This reads (Briscoe, *ed. cit.*, 2.727): "Egnatius Metenius uxorem suam, quod vinum bibisset, fuste percussit. C. Sulpicius uxorem dimisit, quod eam capite operto [*sic*] foris versatam cognoverat. . . . P. Sempronius Sophus coniugem suam repudii nota adfecit, quod se ignorante ludos spectatum ierat." It is not clear why Briscoe does not emend "operto" (covered) to "aperto" (as in his text of Valerius), since the whole point is that she is uncovered.

[2] Briscoe cites three manuscripts with the variant *Metelli*; John of Wales says, "Ait Valerius, libro vj, capitulo iij, quod Metellius uxorem eo quod vinum bibisset fuste percussam interemit" (quoted by Pratt, p. 621).

10. How rigid was the husbandly arrogance of Caius Sulpicius Gallus? He divorced his wife because he found out that she had gone outside with nothing on her head. He issued his opinion bluntly (though it had a certain logic): "The law requires you," he said, "to turn to my eyes alone for an appreciation of your beauty. Make yourself up for them, for them be lovely, entrust yourself to their unerring judgment. If anybody sees you but me, you've invited it, you've provoked it, surely – and gossip and scandal will surely follow."

12. (Section 11 mentions Quintus Antistius Vetus, who divorced his wife for talking with a freedwoman in public; section 12 concludes the chapter) In the same list belongs Publius Sempronius Sophus, who branded his wife with the stigma of divorce simply because she dared to watch the games without his knowing it. So that's the way it used to be for women; it must have kept their minds on the straight and narrow.

VI

Gerard of Cremona, Preface to Ptolemy's *Almagest*

18. If you don't learn from others' mistakes, others will learn from yours.
19. The hands of the intellect hold the reins of the soul.
20. A leader who keeps a firm rein on the people won't need a lot of soldiers.
21. Trustworthiness is a consoling friend; even if you don't manage it yourself, you will have found yourself exacting it.
22. The relief of being alone takes sorrow away, but a crowd is a fearsome thing that takes away one's peace of mind.
23. You raise yourself above others when you don't care whose hands the world seems to be in.

sobrietati poenas pependisse. Et sane quaecumque femina vini usum immoderate appetit, omnibus et virtutibus januam claudit et delictis aperit.
10. Horridum C. quoque Sulpici Gali maritale supercilium: nam uxorem dimisit quod eam capite aperto foris versatam cognoverat, abscisa sententia, sed tamen aliqua ratione munita: "Lex enim," inquit, "tibi meos tantum praefinit oculos quibus formam tuam adprobes. His decoris instrumenta compara, his esto speciosa, horum te certiori crede notitiae. Ulterior tui conspectus supervacua inritatione arcessitus in suspicione et crimine haereat necesse est."

12. Jungendus est his P. Sempronius Sophus, qui conjugem repudii nota adfecit, nihil aliud quam se ignorante ludos ausam spectare. Ergo, dum sic olim feminis occurritur, mens earum a delictis aberat.

VI

Gerard of Cremona, Preface to Ptolemy's *Almagest*

(from Gerard of Cremona, *Preface to Ptolemy's Almagest*, ed. Karl Young from British Library MS Burney 275, fol. 390r)[1]

18. Qui per alios non corrigitur, alii per ipsum [corrigentur][2].
19. Manus intellectuum animarum tenent habenas.
20. Vulgi habenas regere melius est quam multos habere milites.
21. Fiducia est socius consolans, quam licet non consequaris, eam tamen angariasti.

22. Securitas solitudinis dolorem removet, et pavor multitudinis consolacionem aufert.
23. Inter homines alcior existit qui non curat in cuius manu sit mundus.

[1] Karl Young, "Chaucer's Aphorisms from Ptolemy," *Studies in Philology* 34 (1937): 1–7. Ewald Flügel had earlier published Gerard's preface from an edition of the *Almagest* printed at Venice in 1515 ("Ueber einige Stellen aus dem Almagestum Cl. Ptolomei bei Chaucer und im Rosenroman," *Anglia* 18 [1896]: 133–40); Young's point was simply to give the text from a manuscript of the fourteenth century. Gerard took the preface to his translation of the *Almagest*, as he says, from an Arabic work, *The Choicest Maxims and Best Sayings*, by Abu al-Wafa al-Mubashshir ibn Fatik, compiled in 1048–49. See Dorothee Metlitzki, *The Matter of Araby in Medieval England* (New Haven, CT, and London, 1977), p. 112. Young prints the entire preface with its thirty-four sayings, of which the Wife cites sayings numbers 18 and 23; to provide a little context, we print the intervening sayings as well. Young considers but rejects the possibility that Chaucer knew the sayings not from Gerard but from Walter Burley's entry on Ptolemy in his *Vita omnium philosophorum et poetarum*; we agree with him that the assertion that the aphorisms are from the *Almagest* points to direct knowledge of Gerard's text.

[2] MS **non corrigentur**, an evident error which also appears in the 1515 print, but not in Burley. See Young, pp. 5–7.

VII

"Romulus," Fable 44: The Man and the Lion

Bravery and other virtues lie not in words but in deeds, and things ought to be proved by real actions, not by empty words. Here's a story about that. Once a man and a lion were arguing over which was stronger and braver. As they were looking for evidence to solve the argument, the man said, "Come with me to a tomb I know, and I'll show you a picture of a lion killed by a man." When they got there and he showed the lion the picture, the lion said, "Who painted this picture? If lions could paint, it would show a lion killing a man. But now you come with me, and I'll give you real evidence that the lion kills the man." They went to an amphitheater where many criminals had been sent into the arena, and the lion said, "We're not looking at a painting here, but something actually done." What this fable proves is that a lying painting is soon outdone by the truth – and truth will always shine out more clearly, even though fools despise it.

VII

"Romulus," Fabula XLIV: Homo et leo

(from *Aesop's Fables in the Latin Version of "Romulus,"* ed. Johannes Fredericus Nilant, *Fabulae antiquae ex Phaedro . . . accedunt Romuli fabulae Aesopiae* [Leiden, 1709], pp. 130–2)[1]

Profert subsequens fabula, quod audacia et ceterae virtutes non in verbis, sed in factis consistunt, quia omnia factis probanda sunt, non inanibus verbis.

Jam dudum homo et leo quandam inter se contentionem habuerunt, quis illorum esset superior et audacior. Cumque hujus altercationis testimonium quaererent, dixit ille homo: "Veni mecum ad unum tumulum, atque illic ostendam tibi pictam esse imaginem leonis occisi ab homine." Cumque ad tumulum illum ambo venissent, simul demonstravit leoni hanc imaginem occisi leonis ab homine. Cui leo inquit, "Quis hanc imaginem pinxit?" Ad haec leo ait, "At si leo pingere nosset, hominem a leone superatum pingeret." Cui leo iterum dixit, "At tu veni mecum, et demonstrabo tibi verum testimonium, ubi leo hominem suffocavit." Et veniunt ubi multi rei in amphitheatro inclusi erant, et dixit illi leo, "Hic colorum testimonia non sunt, sed opus factum veritate firmatur." Quapropter haec fabula probat mendacium colore compositum veritate superari; et veritas semper solet clarius clarescere, quamvis ab insipientibus despiciatur.

[1] This Latin prose version, known from its editor as the "Romulus Nilantii," is a medieval adaptation of the so-called "Romulus vulgaris," a work of the fourth century wrongly ascribed to Romulus, and widely circulated in the Middle Ages; see Léopold Hervieux, *Les fabulistes latins*, 2nd edn (Paris, 1883–89; rpt. New York, 1967), 1. 330. In that version, which Nilant prints in a footnote, the lion does not ask a question but simply states, "Hoc ab Homine pictum est." Chaucer may have known the more elaborate version by Marie de France (*Fables* 37), based on this, in which the lion asks, "Ki fist ceste semblance ici?/ Humme u lïuns – Itant me di!" [Who made this picture here? A man or a lion – tell me!"], but this plain version has the essential story. The Ellesmere gloss "Quis pinxit leonem?" is presumably the glossator's inexact memory of this Latin text. We have made some silent changes to Nilant's punctuation and capitalization.

VIII

"Almansor" (Al-Isrà'ìlì), *Judgments or Propositions*

2. The exaltation of any of the seven planets is said to be in the sign in which it experiences utter opposition from another planet, as the exaltation of the Sun in Aries, which is the fall of Saturn – for the sun is bright and Saturn dark. Or the exaltation of Jupiter in Cancer where Mars falls – and Jupiter desires justice and Mars signifies injustice. And likewise the exaltation of Mercury in Virgo, which is the fall of Venus: for Mercury signifies knowledge and philosophy but Venus signifies singing, sharp desires, and whatever brings pleasure to the body.

14. Anybody at whose birth malign planets are in the ascendant will have an ugly mark on their face.[1]

1 Almansor calls the good planets (Jupiter, Mercury, Venus, the Sun) "fortunae" and the malign planets ("Saturn, Mars, the Moon) "infortunae."

VIII

"Almansor" (Al-Israʾili), *Judicia seu Propositiones*

(from *Liber quadripartiti Ptholomaei, centiloquii ejusdem, centiloquium Hermetis centum quinquagenta propositiones Almansoris* . . . [Venice, 1493],[2] fol. 120v)

2. Cujusquam planetarum septem exaltatio in illo loco esse dicitur in quo substantialiter patitur ab alio contrarium, veluti Solis in Ariete qui Saturni casus est. Sol enim habet claritatem, Saturnus tenebrositatem, et ut Jovis in Cancro in quo Mars cadit, quorum alter cupit justitiam, alter vero significat injustitiam. Et sic Mercurii in Virgine qui casus est Veneris; alter namque significat scientiam et philosophiam, altera vero [cantus],[3] alacritates, et quicquid est saporiferum corpori.[4]

14. Cuicunque fuerint in ascendente infortune, turpem notam in facie patietur.[5]

2 An anthology of Latin translations of Arabic texts on astronomy and astrology, consisting of Ptolemy's *Quadripartitum* and fourteen shorter texts by various authors: besides Hermes and Almansor, Bethem, Zahel, and Messahala. The complete title of the tract by "Almansor" is as follows: "Almansoris iudicia seu propositiones: Incipiunt capitula stellarum oblata regi magno Saracenorum ab Almansore astrologo et a Platone Tyburtino translata," fol. 120v. For "Almansor," see George Sarton, *Introduction to the History of Science*, vol. 2 (Baltimore, 1931), p. 178; Sarton astutely suggests that "ab Almansore" (which means "the conqueror") should be "Almansori" and is part of the title of the king, whom he identifies (from the name Alchacham that appears in some prints) as al-Hakim al-Mansur, Fatimid caliph from 996 to 1020. This conjecture is confirmed by Fuat Sezgin in his *Geschichte des arabischen Schrifttums*, vol. 7 (Leiden, 1979), pp. 175–6. He has identified the original Arabic text in MS Oxford Bodleian Marsh 663, in which the author's name appears as (in Sezgin's words) "der jüdische Astrologe Al-Israʾili, über den wir zur Zeit nichts wissen," along with a dedication to the above-named caliph (whose reign Sezgin gives as 996–1021). For the translator Plato of Tivoli (12th century), see Sarton, pp. 177–9. The Latin text is edited, translated into French, and discussed by Jean-Claude Vadet, "Les aphorismes latins d'Almansor, essai d'interprétation," *Annales Islamologiques* 5 (1963): 31–130.

3 cantus: so Ellesmere, Vadet (see previous note); causat Venice 1493.

4 This passage is quoted in the margin of Ellesmere fol. 73b and identified as "In libro Mansor primo." First the statement "Utraque cadit ubi alia exaltatur" [Each falls as the other is brought high, fol. 73a] is put next to line 702, then this passage is quoted (with "etc." replacing "Solis . . . casus est" and the entire second sentence) next to line 705.

5 Quoted in the margin of Ellesmere fol. 72b next to line 609 (with reference to line 619) and identified as "Mansor amphorismorum 14." It is followed immediately by the quotation from Hermes below, which does refer to lines 609–14.

IX

"Hermes," *One Hundred Aphorisms*

6. Venus is the opposite of Mercury: he loves languages and learning, she loves pleasure.
25. When a girl is born and any one of the mansions of Venus is ascendant and Mars is in them, or if any of the mansions of Mars is ascendant and Venus is in them, she will be a lustful woman; and likewise if she has Capricorn in the ascendant.

X

Matheolus, *Lamentations*

For this reason Lamech deserves to be punished seven times over, whatever Jerome says. Why did that miserable man take two wives? Wasn't one woman enough to satisfy ten? Damn! because of Lamech, Lamech, cursed Lamech I've forfeited my clerical rights and my cassock. (175–80)

There is no rest for the husband, fifteen times a day and night passion is his lot; he is tortured continually. I swear, marital torment is a lot worse than the torment of hell. (341–4)

Look at me, I've gone deaf from arguing. (518)

IX

"Hermes," *Liber Aphorismorum Centum*

(from *Liber quadripartiti Ptholomaei* [Venice, 1493, see above], fol. 117r)

6. Opponitur Venus Mercurio. Hic quidem sermones et disciplinas, illa vero voluptates et delectationes amplectitur.
25. In nativitatibus mulierum, cum fuerit ascendens aliqua de domibus Veneris, Marte existente in eis, vel de domibus Martis, Venere existente in eis, erit mulier impudica; idem erit si in ascendente Capricornum habuerit.[1]

X

Matheolus, *Lamentationes*

(from Matheolus, *Lamentationes*, ed. A.-G. van Hamel, 2 vols [Paris, 1892], vol. 1)

Hac in septuplum Lamech ratione meretur
Puniri, quitquid per Jheronimum recitetur.
Cur miser iste duas uxores accipiebat?
Nonne decem mulier satis unica sufficiebat?
Heu! propter Lamech, Lamech, Lamech maledictum
Cleri perdidimus, sicut puto, jus et amictum.
...

341 Nulla viro requies, cum nocte dieque legatur
Passio quindecies illi; semper cruciatur.
Est, Mediuffidius! tormentum connubiale
344 Jam multo gravius quam tormentum stigiale.
...

518 Surdus factus pro litibus, en! sum.
...

[1] Identified in Ellesmere as follows: "he hermes in libro fiducie amphorismorum 25o" [Thus Hermes in the book of trusty aphorisms [literally, of aphorisms of trustworthiness], in the 25th aphorism]. The first statement in this aphorism is incorrectly treated in the notes in *Riverside Chaucer* as belonging to the quotation from Almansor. "Hermes" is the mythical Hermes Trismegistus. The book of 100 aphorisms attributed to him, also called *Centiloquium*, was translated from Arabic, or compiled from Arabic sources, by Stephen of Messina during the reign of Manfred, King of Sicily, to whom it is dedicated, i.e. between 1258 and 1266. It had a wide circulation; for a list of 81 manuscripts, see Paolo Lucentini and Vittoria Perrone Compagni, *I testi e i codici di Eremete nel Medioevo* (Florence, 2001), pp. 27–32.

Whatever I do or say to Petra, she twists my words back against me. (557–8)

Summer is gone for me, it's winter now, I have no staying power. (571–2)

My wife wants it, but I can't; she asks for her rights, I say no, I just can't pay. (577–8)

She brings up on her side the rule that if a shriveled purse can't pay because it's empty, corporal punishment is mandated by law as recompense for the injury. (582–4)

To start an argument she pretends that her husband has been caught with a mistress. (686–7)

Better to marry a serpent or a lion than a contentious wife. (692–3)

Though she cries on the outside because her husband is dead, she sings within because she's got herself another one. (862–3)

She hates the people her husband likes. You can look it up in Cato: "A woman hates the people her husband likes." (872–4)

While her husband lies on his bier and the wife is crying, she's also thinking ahead, thinking back, who to marry and how, once her three days are up. That's women's way. (953–5)

Indeed, as soon as her first husband is buried she's on the lookout for another, because she can't live alone. (976–7)

557 Quitquid ago vel dico Petre, mox verba retorquet
In caput ipsa meum.
...

571 Mea preterit estas,
Cui succedit hiems, est nulla morosa potestas.
...

577 Vult uxor, sed ego nequeo; petit hec sua jura;
Non solvendo nego factus;
...

582 Allegat enim Petra pro se
Jus, quod si nequeat inopis rugosa crumena
Solvere, pro noxa statuatur corpore pena.[1]
...

686 Ut moveat litem, nuper cum pelice captum
Sponsum fingit.
...

692 Junge serpentem potius tibi sive leonem
Quam contendentem sponsam. (692–93)[2]
...

862 Nam licet exterius ploret moriente marito,
Concinit interius alio consorte petito.
...

872 Quos diligit ipse maritus
Odit eos penitus. Super hiis vult Cato requiri.
Hic inquit: "Mulier quos conjunx diligit odit."[3]
...

953 Dum jacet in feretro conjunx, uxor lacrimando
Cogitat ante, retro, cui nubere, quomodo, quando
Post spatium tridui poterit; mos est mulierum.
...

976 Immo, viro primo tumulato querit habere
Femina mox alium, quia nescit sola manere.
...

1 See also lines 2075–7: (When the man is old and the woman young) "Debita conjugii petit illa, libidine plena,/ Sed quid ei solvat penitus vacuata crumena/ Non habet" [She wants the conjugal debt, but his empty purse doesn't have anything to pay her with].

2 Ecclus. 15.16. See also lines 3738–9: "tutior est homini comitiva leonis/ Quam fedus sponse rixose conditionis" [A man is safer with a lion than with a wife who likes to argue].

3 *Disticha Catonis* 1.8.

Women's envy is too much: every single one of them thinks her neighbor is better dressed than she is. She blames her husband for that, she says, "Damn you, I don't even dare go outside," and then come the phony tears. "What's bothering my pretty miss?," he says. "I sit at home naked! Can't you see that every one of our neighbors is dressed so as to outclass me? Here I am, so much higher class than they are, and yet they put me to shame." And so either he has to buy his wife clothes or put up with a thousand arguments a day. (1107–16)

They (nuns) pretend they want to see their mothers and fathers, that their brothers and relatives are lying sick: in order to satiate their *quoniams* and their *quippes* they wander all over the country – yes, yes, they get out of their cloister as often as they can! (1235–9)[4]

(An old woman instructs a young woman on the delights of the flesh) My daughter, didn't God make man and woman so instrumented as to do the act of joy? (1390–1)

She's such a liar that if you haven't done anything she can blame you for she just makes it up. She also often denies what you've actually seen her doing: she weeps, she swears, she lies to cover her guilt; she's never at a loss for an excuse; as often as she can she convicts her husband of the very thing she's guilty of. She knows the old tricks, and she knows the new tricks. (1605–10)

You couldn't keep her with a castle wall. (1886)

[4] This passage is misinterpreted by Thundy, who quotes the French "Pour faire charnelement congnoistre/ Leur *quoniam* et leur *quippe*," translating "To know carnally their *quoniam* (female genitals) and their *quippe* (male genitals)." Rather it means "to give their *quoniams* and their *quippes* some carnal knowledge." The two Latin words are synonyms (both mean "because"; they can be used in tandem for emphasis, as in line 3038, quoted below), and they both refer to the same thing here. Christine Hilary, in her note to WBP III, 608 in the *Riverside Chaucer,* claims, unaccountably, that the passage says that "men and women rush . . . 'To make carnally acquainted their *quoniam* (female genitals) and *quippe* (male genitals).' " But the subject of the sentence in both Latin and French is women (nuns), not men at all, and Latin *suis* and French *leur* can only mean "their," that is, "the women's." Thus both these Latin conjunctions are applied to female genitals, as they are again at lines 1368–9, "Ut vetulam facias risus vultu dare leto,/ Per 'quoniam' capias vel eam per 'quippe' teneto" [Do you want to make an old woman laugh? Grab her by the *quoniam*, hold her by the *quippe*]. Facetious grammatical play is common in the poem; the origin of this little joke may be line 1209, "Os vulve Salomon vocat insatiabile quippe,/ Fundo vulva caret" If you put the comma before "quippe," this means "Solomon calls the mouth of the womb insatiable (Prov. 30.15–16), for the vulva has no bottom." But you can put it after, as van Hamel does, and read "Solomon calls the mouth of the womb an insatiable *quippe* . . ." That is, to Matheolus's way of thinking, a woman, always in heat and never at a loss for words, can always find a reason for sex. Indeed, her *quoniam* is her *raison d'être*.

1107 Est livor nimius mulierum; cuique videtur
Quod sua nobilius semper vicina paretur.
Damnat ob hoc sponsum, cui dicit: "Vir maledicte
1110 Ausa foras non sum profisci." Postea ficte
Plorat. "Pulcra soror mea," dicit vir, "quid habetis?"
"In lare nuda moror; vicinam quanque videtis
Nostram nobiliter ornatam; grandior esse
Deberem, breviter, ego sum minor." Inde necesse
Est, aut ut vestes uxori comparet ille,
1116 Aut quod quottidie patiatur jurgia mille.
…

1235 Patres et matres se fingunt velle videre,
Infirmos fratres consanguineosque jacere,
Ut sacient "quoniam" cum "quippe" suis spaciantur
Per totam patriam, sic, sic quam sepe vagantur
1239 Extra claustra.
…

1390 Filia, nonne virum fecit Deus et mulierem
Instrumentatos, facerent ut leticie rem?
…

1605 Est mendax adeo quod, si non inveniatur
Presens, hoc ideo factum scelus inficiatur.
Visaque sepe negat, flet, jurat, ut inde reatum
Mendax ipsa tegat; quid dicat, in ore paratum
Mox habet; hec scelere proprio quam sepe virumque
1610 Convincit, vere Vetus atque Novum scit utrumque.
…

1886 Ut serves illam, nil proficiet tibi vallum.
…

A peasant woman will singe all of a cat's fur so that it won't be stolen for that fur. Oh, how I would like those long-trailing dresses burnt, and those torques and those horn-hats – telltale signs of lechery that (along with the women's seductive ways) tempt wife-stealers to try to win such women away from their husbands. (1939–44)

Nature didn't make you to be the partner of just one honey, but equipped you for any of them, if you're up to it. Solomon is proof enough of that, and some holy patriarchs besides had several wives – men then had much more vigor than we do now. (2289–93)

Let me say – it's on the tip of my tongue – it may be too bold – Christ, you didn't have the nerve to get married. (2393–5)

Where on earth did we get the rule that a woman you're about to marry can't be tested like a cow or a horse? Since you (Christ) know very well that our law warns us that the more there is at stake the more carefully we have to guard against being deceived. (2425–8)

(Christ is speaking to the dreamer in reply) Look, I don't want sinners to die, I'm their redeemer, I fought for them. When you've paid a lot for something you don't just throw it away, and so I've decided to make several purgatories for them to purify themselves in – treatment makes sick people better – and the best one is marriage. You've already experienced punishment, I needn't reopen it; rather I'd say that even those who have been toasted on a flaming gridiron don't suffer as much pain as those who are imprisoned in marriage. There is no greater martyrdom than day-to-day pain like yours, refined in the furnace of marriage. You are truly a martyr, and so if you take your suffering well have no doubt that after you die you're coming straight to me: nothing will stand in your way, no punishment will intervene, and why? because you will have already been purified under your wife. (3024–38)

(Christ is still speaking) It's necessary and right for cities and towns to be replenished with babies. If male hadn't joined with female, there would be no religious orders now, no Peter to be keeper of the keys; and so would the clergy please stop contradicting me on this? (3515–18)

1939 Cunctam murilegi comburit rustica pellem,
Ne pro pelle legi possit. Nam sic ego vellem
Caudatas vestes, torques cum cornibus uri,
Luxurie testes, per quas occasio furi,
Instructo Venere, datur, ut tales mulieres
1944 Sponsis substrahere nitantur.
…

2289 Ut fieres socius non te natura creavit
Ysse solius, sed propter quanque paravit
Te, si sufficeres. Salomon satis ista probavit.
Sic etiam quidam sancti patres habuerunt
2293 Plures, qui multo plus quam nos tunc valuerunt.[5]
…

2393 Dicam, michi cum sit in ore,
Nescio si temere, non ausus, Christe, fuisti
Uxorem capere.
…

2425 Unde locus, quod non uxor ducenda probatur,
Sicut bos et equus; cum, sicut scis, caveatur,
In nostro jure, quod, ubi magis est metuendum,
Circumspectius est, ne decipiatur, agendum.
…

3024 O! peccatorum quia mortem nolo, redemptor
Et pugil ipsorum, cum res non debeat emptor
Emptas tam care pessundare, janque parare
Idcirco volui sibi purgatoria plura,
3028 Ut se purgarent; egros sanat data cura;
Inter que majus est conjugium. Quia nosti
Penas, non resero; tamen hoc dico, quia tosti
Ferro flammifico, tot penas non patiuntur
3032 Quod patiuntur ei qui conjugio capiuntur.
Non est martirium majus quam continuata
Pena velut tua, conjugii fornace probata.
Es vere martir; ergo, bene si patiaris,
3036 Non dubites quin me post mortis bella sequaris,
Obice sublato, nulla pena mediante,
Quippe sub uxore quoniam purgatus es ante.
…

3515 Expedit atque decet urbes et castra repleri
Filiolis. Nisi se junxisset mas mulieri,
Nil modo religio, nil Petrus claviger esset;
Ergo clerus in his michi contradicere cesset!

5 See also lines 153–4, where Matheolus is defending bigamy: "Quidam sancti patres habuerunt/ Plures, felices qui non minus inde fuerunt" [Some holy patriarchs had several wives, and they were no less happy for it].

XI

Eustache Deschamps, *The Mirror of Marriage*

(Répertoire de Science, i.e., Wisdom, writing to Franc Vouloir, Free Will, a young man considering getting married) (1539) A man who takes a wife will get her just as he takes her for she'll be covered up before. But afterwards her true ways will be on display, and she will make them felt up close by him, and he will suffer them like a martyr; then she will make all her vices appear. (1550) It seems to me that a man who buys something that he can't return and doesn't examine it first is a fool. If you want to buy livestock, whether to keep or to sell off one by one, whether it's oxen, cows, sheep, or pigs, you'll look up and down the body – the stomach, the tail, the head, the teeth if it is a young animal – and you'll put them to the test. (1560) With horses too, I know, when they're trying to sell them to you they'll trot them out for show, you'll see them warm and cool, and under the saddle, as is only right, to make sure they're not broken down, and feel their joints to make sure they're not lame, and mount them and prick their sides with your spurs. (1570) But that's not how it goes for noblemen or any men who take wives, for they hide their faults from sight, and men take them without knowing what they will later show, as I'll get to in full detail. When the measly pleasure of the bed has gone on for a few nights, then the great torments will start because you won't be able to bring her full pleasure (1580) without exhausting your body, and then you'll want to rest. God knows that you

XI

Eustache Deschamps, *Le Miroir de Mariage*

(from, *Le Miroir de Mariage,* ed. Gaston Raynaud, *Oeuvres Complètes de Eustache Deschamps*, 11 vols [Paris: Firmin Didot, 1878–1903], vol. 9, 1894, pp. 53–131)

Qui prandra femme, cilz l'ara
Toute tele qu'il la prandra,
...

Car par devant se couverra;
Mes ses meurs après ouverra,
Et de près les fera sentir
A tel qui en sera martir;
Lors fera aparoir ses vices.
Si me semble que cilz est nices
Qui, sanz cerchier ce qu'il veult prandre,
L'achate et ne le puet reprandre.
Se tu veulz achater bestail
Pour garder ou vendre a detail,
Soit buefs, vaiches, brebiz ou pors,
Tu le verras au long du corps,
Ou ventre, en la queue, en la teste
Et es dens, s'il est juene beste,
Et les metteras a l'essay;
Et des chevaulx encore sçay,
Quant ilz vendront en ton encontre,
Ilz troteront dessus la monstre,
Tu les verras et chaux et frois,
Et soubz la selle, c'est bien drois,
Qu'ilz ne soient rouz ou cassez;
Et qu'ilz ne soient mespassez,
Leur tasteras parmi les jointes;
Sus monteras, et donrras pointes
Es costez de tes esperons.
Mais autrement va des barons
Et des aultres qui prannent femmes,
Car sanz vir queuvrent leur diffames,
Et les prannent sanz ce sçavoir
Qu'elles font depuis apparoir,
Comme plus a plain sera dit.
Quant le povre deduit du lit
Est passé par aucunes nuis,
Lors te saudront les grans ennuis,
Car tu ne pourras achever
Son delit sanz ton corps grever,
Qui adonc reposer vouldras;
Mais Dieux scet que tu ne pourras

won't be able to pay the debt of pleasure that she asks of you. Then she will want to have buckles and brooches and you won't be rich enough to keep up her standard of living. She'll see her neighbors (1590) her aunts, her cousins wearing new clothes, and the complaints will start, and the weeping, and your wife will say, "Mother of God! look at the attention so-and-so gets, look at her clothes and her jewelry, and look at me: they all despise me and call me "poor sad her." But I know what's going on. (1600) I see you looking at her when she comes out, our neighbor I mean, I get it. You don't care about me. You've got something going with our maid; when you came back from shopping the other day, what did you bring her? Oh, it was a hard day when you married me! You're no husband, no companion. If you were good to me and not in love with somebody else (1610) you wouldn't come home as late as you do!"

(1625) If you marry somebody because she's pretty she'll never bring you peace because every man who comes along will want her, and it will be a hard thing for you to keep what every man wants (1630) and pursues and covets, you have a hundred eyes against you, and lecherous desire is always after beauty, which is contrary to chastity.

(1736) If you marry an ugly woman no man will envy you – but what deadlier life is there than to have something that nobody else wants, and so have it all alone?

Rendre le deu qu'elle demande
Quant au delit. Or yert engrande
D'avoir fremillez et affiches
Et tu ne seras pas si riches
Que tu puisses continuer
Son estat et renouveler;
Et elle verra ses voisines,
Ses parentes et ses cousines,
Qui nouvelles robes aront;
Adonc plains et plours te saudront
Et complaintes de par ta fame,
Qui te dira: "Par Nostre Dame,
Celle est en publique hounourée,
Bien vestue et bien acesmée,
Et entre toutes suy despite
Et povre, maleureuse ditte!
Mais je voy bien a quoy il tient:
Vous regardez, quant elle vient,
No voisine, bien m'en perçoy,
Car vous n'avez cure de moy;
Vous jouez a no chamberiere;
Quant du marchié venis arriere,
L'autre jour, que li apportas?
Las! de dure heure m'espousas!
Je n'ay mari ne compaignon.
Certes se vous me fussez bon,
Et vous n'amissiez autre part,
Vous ne venissiez pas si tart
Comme vous faictes a l'ostel!"
…

Se tu la prens, qu'elle soit belle,
Tu n'aras jamais paix a elle,
Car chascuns la couvoitera,
Et dure chose a toy sera
De garder ce que un chascun voite
Et qu'il poursuit et qu'il couvoite,
Car tu as contre toy cent oeulx,
Et li desirs luxurieux
Est toutes fois contre beauté,
Qui est contraire au chasteté.
…

S'il est qui preingne femme laide,
Nulz homs n'ara sur elle envie;
Et ou sera plus mortel vie
Qu'a cellui qui possidera
Ce que nulz avoir ne vourra,
Que il possidera touz seulx?
…

(1753) A pretty wife is hard to tame, an ugly one too embarrassing. If you take a rich wife, you can bet on constant reproaches.[1] If she's poor, it will be windy weather all the time, and the torture of putting up with her. (1760) If you want to end your life in peace, you've got to adore her face whatever mood she's in. Whether she's pretty, ugly, or malformed, pretend that she's loved by you . And you don't have to just praise her beauty, you also have to keep yourself from looking at anybody else. You've got to call her "My Lady," and swear by Our Lady that she surpasses every other woman in goodness. (1770) You have to celebrate her birthday (and her beloved nurse's too); and her grandfather, her brother, her uncle, her father – you've got to honor them all, love them, be nice to them to your fingertips, and entertain their entire retinue and come up with whatever they need.

(1877) They always want to be the boss, and if you let them deck their hair with gold thread or dress up in silk and other rare fabrics, what will you be doing? You'll be nourishing the vice of immodesty, which will destroy their chastity.

(When her husband dies) (1971) She won't even listen to talk about a funeral service or chanting, all she'll accept is a low mass; and as they carry the corpse to the grave, she'll be looking them over, trying to pick out who to have next.

(Your mother-in-law will say) (3208) "If your wife stagnates in the house keeping the embers from going out, she'll lose all her value. Your name will sink, it won't be

[1] Literally, "It's earnest-money and a snare to have reproaches often." See *OED*, s.v. God's-penny.

Belle femme est envix domptée,
Et la laide est trop ahontée.
Se tu prans femme qui soit riche,
C'est le denier Dieu et la briche
D'avoir des reprouches souvent;
S'elle est povre, ce n'est que vent
Et tourment d'elle soustenir.
S'en paix veulz ta vie finir,
Quelque chiere que femme face,
Il te fault encliner sa face.
Soit belle, laide ou difformée,
Fain qu'elle soit de toy amée:
Il couvient sa beauté louer,
Et te tien d'autre regarder;
Il fault qu'apelée soit dame,
Et que tu jures Nostre Dame
Qu'elle passe tout en bonté.
Le jour de sa nativité
Te doit estre concelebrable,
Et le sa nourice amiable,
Son aieul, son frere et son oncle
Et son pere doiz tu a l'ongle
Honourer, amer, conjouir,
Leurs mesgnies et gens jouir
Et livrer tout ce qu'il lui fault.
. . .

Tousjours veulent estre maistresses,
Et se tu consens que leurs tresses
A fil d'or soient galonnées
Et qu'elles soient ordonnées
De soye et de fins autres draps,
Que feras tu? Tu nourriras
La vice d'impudicité,
Qui destruira leur chasteté.
. . .

Du service, obseque et les lays
Oir vouldra parler jamais,
Excepté d'une courte messe;
Et regardera, en la presse
A porter le deffunct en terre,
Quel mari elle pourra querre
Et avoir après cesti cy.
. . .

"Se ta femme crout en maison
Et garde le feu et les cendres,
Elle en vault pis, tes noms est mendres;
D'oneur ne sçara tant ne quant,
S'iert comme une chievre vacant

honored at all, and she'll be like a loose nanny goat who can't do anything but chew on grass, or like a cat in the hearth that burns its hair and singes it."

(3600) When she gets home she has to deceive her husband, who has been waiting a long time for her and, God! how angry he is over the delay! And right away she starts to cry and get all worked up: "Oh my! I have so much to do, I haven't sat down all day! Why was I ever born? I've bought everything I needed (3610) I was out of all kinds of things. I haven't drunk or eaten a thing all day, and if I say so myself I've bought more flax, hemp, seed, and the yarn I get yelled at for, and a distaff, and more needles, spindles, reels, and sieves for twenty Parisian sous than any other wife in Paris or anywhere else could have bought for forty. (3620) You only make a fool of yourself, nagging me as you do; you go try to get what I got! You'd get a lot less for that price; you're decked out like a real prelate, sure! I wouldn't have a shoelace, or a piece of bread all year if I weren't out buying morning and evening! You don't get involved at all. (3630) But when a wife does well her husband will torment her and never treat her well. I can tell it by your face! Ask your chambermaid if I've been where I shouldn't! It's been a pain to buy all this stuff, and now I wish I hadn't bothered." Then she dumps it all out in the house in front of her husband (3640) who is pretty well disarmed by hearing this defense, and in his heart he is sorry that he has done wrong by blaming her so.

Then to throw off all blame she leaps up and flees to her room and goes to bed crying to fool her husband more.

Qui ne scet que brouter et paistre,
Ou comme un chat qui est en l'aistre,
Qui brulle son poil et qui l'art."

Il fault que son mari deçoive
. . .

Au revenir, qui longuement
L'a attendue; et Dieux! comment
Il se cource de la demeure!
Et elle se commence en l'eure
A plourer at a esmouvoir;
"Lasse! j'en doy bien tant avoir,
Qui ne finay huy a journée
D'aler! De maleure fuy née!
J'ay achaté ce qu'il me fault
Et dont j'avoye grant default;
Je ne bu huy ne ne mangay,
Et si m'ose vanter que j'ay
De lin, de chanvre et de semence,
Et de filé dont on me tance,
D'aguilles, cannoulle et fuseaux,
De desvoudoirs, de bureteaux
Plus pour .xx. soulz de parisis,
Que n'aroit femme de Paris
Ne d'ailleurs pour .xl. solz.
Je croy que vous devenez fols
Qui ainsis m'alez riotant:
Or en alez querir autant!
Et je croy que vous y faurrez
Pour le pris: vous estes fourrez
Et vestus comme un droiz prelas!
Il ne me faulroit pas un las
Ne ceans un morsiau de pain
Que je n'achate soir et main.
Mesler ne vous voulez de rien.
Mais puis que femme fera bien,
Son mari la tourmentera
Ne jamès bien ne lui fera;
Bien l'apperçoy a vostre chiere.
Demandez a vo chamberiere
Se j'ay en mauvais lieu esté:
J'ay tout ce mesniage acheté
A grant paine: je m'en repent."
Puis le desvelope et l'espent
Par l'ostel devant son mary,
Qui est a la moité guari,
Quant il oit ainsy sa deffense,
Et bien en son cuer se pourpense
Que mal fait quant ainsi la blame.
Lors pour elle jetter de blame,

Her maid goes in to keep her company, and returns (3650) grieving and long-faced. The husband asks her what his wife is doing, and the clever maid answers, "My lady is unhappy that she ever married such a husband."

(If the husband complains that she cruises too much, his wife accuses him back) (3920) "You have begged our chambermaid for love two or three times. You've been several times also to see Helot and Eudeline, Isabel, Margot, and Catherine, and you've slept with whores. That's why you're always on me, for a thief won't trust a thief, the bad don't trust the good and so think that everybody is a thief. (3930) There's nobody worse than you anywhere on earth, I know it; all we ever do is argue. I've put up with your sinning for too long; how can you call me a slut? I'm better than you, and more faithful to you than you are to me, I swear it. Oh! You doubt me? Do I come from a place (3940) where they grow fools? There are no whores in my family; go check up on the women of your family! " Then she pretends to be enraged, and cries so horribly and weeps from such depth that she seems to have gone crazy. "Oh, me!," she goes, "He won't even let me go to church! (3950) I can't have Robin or Walter or any man as my friend!" Thus she lies to him, thus she manipulates him, thus she deceives and confuses him – as many women do.

Fuit en sa chambre d'un escueil
Et se couche la larme a l'ueil,
Pur plus son mary assoter.
Et adonc la va convoier
Sa chamberiere, et s'en retourne;
Dolente est et fait chiere mourne;
Et ly maris la tient de plait,
Demendans que sa femme fait.
Et la chamberiere engigneuse
Respond: "Ma dame est maleureuse,
Quant onques tel homme espousa."
...

"Vous avez nostre chamberiere
Requis d'amour .ii. fois ou trois;
Vous estes alez pluseurs fois
Veoir Helot et Eudeline,
Ysabel, Margot, Kateline
Et couché aux femmes communes.
De la me viennent les rancunes,
Car lerres le larron mescroit,
Ne ly mauvès le bon ne croit,
Ains cuide que chascuns soit lerres;
On ne verroit en nulles terres
Plus mescreant de vous sanz failles;
Tousjours avons plaiz et batailles.
J'ay long temps souffert vo pechié:
Comment m'avez vous reprouchié
Que j'estoie trop villotiere?
Meilleur vous suy et plus entiere
Que vous ne m'estes, par ma foy!
Lasse! vous doubtez vous de moy?
Je ne suy pas du lieu venue
Que pour fole soye tenue;
En mon linaige n'a putain:
Prenez les vostres par la main
Et celles de vostre linaige."
Et lors fait semblant qu'elle enrraige,
Et crie si horriblement,
Et ploure si parfondement
Qu'il samble qu'elle soit dervée:
"Hé lasse!" fait elle, "il me vée
Neis que je voise au moustier!
Si n'ay je Robin ne Gautier
Ne homme, dont je soie acointe!"
Ainsis ly ment, ainsis l'apointe,
Ainsis le deçoit et confont,
Ainsis pluseurs femmes le font.

The Wife of Bath's Tale

JOHN WITHRINGTON AND P. J. C. FIELD

The Wife of Bath's Tale makes use of two folklore motifs: in one a "Loathly Lady" is transformed into a beautiful woman, while the other involves answering the question "What is it that women most desire?"[1] G. H. Maynadier's study remains the most comprehensive discussion of the origins of the Loathly Lady motif in the context of Chaucer's tale, and it was he who first proposed that the theme of sovereignty found in early Irish analogues made its way into British folklore, although whether by a Scandinavian or Welsh route, he was not sure.[2] Sigmund Eisner reinforced the theory of an Irish origin, introduced to England via first Wales and then France, but argued that the concept of sovereignty over territory, present in the Irish tales, was transformed into the concept of sovereignty over a husband in the English analogues.[3] However, the dramatic nature of the Loathly Lady and her transformations has understandably proven attractive for story-tellers from different places and in different ages, so much so that examples have been found as far apart as the Orient and Texas.[4] In *The Taming*

[1] See Stith Thompson, *Motif-Index of Folk-Literature: A Classification of Narrative Elements in Folktales, Ballads, Myths, Fables, Medieval Romances, Exempla, Fabliaux, Jest Books, and Local Legends* (Bloomington and London, 1966), motifs D 732 and H 1388.1 respectively.

[2] G. H. Maynadier, *The Wife of Bath's Tale: Its Sources and Analogues* (London, 1901).

[3] Sigmund Eisner, *A Tale of Wonder: A Source Study of the Wife of Bath's Tale* (Wexford, 1957). J. K. Bollard ("Sovereignty and the Loathly Lady in English, Welsh and Irish," *Leeds Studies in English* 17 [1986]: 196–9) argued, however, that tales of the transformation of a Loathly Lady were unlikely to have come to England from France, and that English analogues tend to include the motif of the riddle. See also Michael Aguirre, "The Riddle of Sovereignty," *Modern Language Review* 88 (1993): 273–82.

[4] Ananda K. Coomaraswamy, "On the Loathly Bride," *Speculum* 20 (1945): 391–404; Ann Carpenter, "The Loathly Lady in Texas Lore," *Journal of the American Studies Association of Texas* 5 (1974): 48–53. Juan Manuel's *El Conde Lucanor*, written in 1335, would also seem to draw upon some of the themes found in *The Wife of Bath's Tale* (See Jesús L. Serrano Reyes, *Didactismo y Moralismo en*

of the Shrew Petruchio vows to woo Katherina "Be she as foul as was Florentius' love," which implies that by Shakespeare's time the episode in Gower's *Confessio Amantis* was well known. Indeed, the enduring popularity of these themes, not least through dissemination of *The Wife of Bath's Tale* itself, is manifest through versions continuing to the present day. For example the seventeenth-century ballad *A New Sonnet of a Knight and a Fair Virgin* is clearly based upon Chaucer's tale, while in more recent times the Loathly Lady motif is represented by the inclusion of the character Dame Ragnell in Thomas Berger's novel *Arthur Rex* (1978) and the retelling of the story for a children's audience in *Sir Gawain and the Loathly Lady* (1985), written by Selina Hastings and illustrated by Juan Wijngaard.[5] As a result, the selections in this chapter comprise only the closest analogues to Chaucer's text. In particular, the ballads *King Henry* and *The Knight and the Shepherd's Daughter* have been omitted on the grounds that, while both may reflect various aspects of *The Wife of Bath's Tale*, they are not analogues in the strictest sense of the word.[6] Thus, *King Henry* features a monstrous hag with a monstrous appetite, who is transformed into a fair lady when the eponymous King accedes to her request to lie next to her, but the ballad differs from Chaucer's version of events in that a riddle is not imposed, the hag actually visits the hero as opposed to the hero coming across her in the course of a quest, and the male protagonist is seemingly not offered the "fair or foul" choice in the marriage bed.[7] *The Knight and the Shepherd's Daughter* was first suggested by Maynadier as a possible analogue for the rape scene in *The Wife of Bath's Tale*, but the similarities are fewer than in a

Geoffrey Chaucer y Don Juan Manuel: Un estudio comparatizo textual [Córboda, 1996], pp. 101–6; we are grateful to Professor Serrano Reyes for drawing our attention to this text).

5 The ballad *A New Sonnet of a Knight and a Fair Virgin* was published in the collection *A crowne garland of goulden roses*, ed. Richard Johnson (London, 1612). (See *A Short-Title Catalogue of Books Printed in England, Scotland, Wales, & Ireland, and of English Books Printed Abroad, 1475–1640*, ed. A. W. Pollard and G. R. Redgrave, rev. W. A. Jackson, F. S. Ferguson and Katharine F. Pantzer, 2 vols [London, 1976–86], item 14672.) The indebtedness of the ballad to *The Canterbury Tales* was remarked upon by Thomas Warton in a letter to Thomas Percy dated 20 October 1762: "It is the old Story of Q. Guenever desiring to know *What* women love most." (*The Correspondence of Thomas Percy and Thomas Warton*, ed. M. G. Robinson and Leah Dennis [Baton Rouge, LA, 1951], p. 52.) Percy included *The Marriage of Sir Gawain* in his *Reliques of Ancient English Poetry* of 1765, but not the "Sonnet."

6 See *English and Scottish Popular Ballads*, ed. F. J. Child, 5 vols (Boston, 1882–98; rpt. New York, 1965). *King Henry* is ballad number 32. The text of *The Knight and the Shepherd's Daughter* may be found in Child, number 110. Percy included the text in his *Reliques*, concluding that the ballad was Elizabethan in origin.

7 Maynadier, p. 111. Laura Sumner ("The Weddynge of Sir Gawen and Dame Ragnell," *Smith College Studies in Modern Languages* 5 [1924], p. xvii) suggested that the day/night choice was reflected in line 2 of stanza 19 of *King Henry*, when the King asks "how lang'll this last wi me?" Margaret Schlauch ("The Marital Dilemma in the *Wife of Bath's Tale*," *PMLA* 61 [1946]: 417) agrees that "this hero too . . . was first asked to choose between nocturnal and diurnal beauty on a part-time basis." The argument however is weak. In Chaucer's version and the three main analogues, the Loathly Lady's assurance that she will remain beautiful follows immediately upon the hero yielding to her the choice in the fair/foul dilemma. The question asked by King Henry actually follows not upon a tense question and answer session, but a good night's sleep (stanza 18). There is no indication that he has been forced to choose between fair and foul, and the prize of the fair lady may simply be a reward for passing a test which requires enduring foulness as opposed to answering a seemingly impossible question.

number of other marginal texts suggested since Maynadier's time.[8] Only three analogues can be said truly to follow Chaucer's *Wife of Bath's Tale* closely. They are Gower's "Tale of Florent," from his *Confessio Amantis*, the anonymous poem known as *The Weddyng of Syr Gawen and Dame Ragnell*, and the anonymous ballad *The Marriage of Sir Gawain*. Of the three, only the "Tale of Florent" can be dated with any certainty.[9] The *Confessio Amantis* was composed in its first version by 1390, revised between June 1390 and June 1391, and revised again about the time of Henry IV's accession in 1399. The latter recension represents what is believed to be Gower's final version of the *Confessio*, and it survives in eleven manuscripts, one of which, Oxford, Bodleian Library MS Fairfax 3, is the source of the other ten. The Fairfax manuscript therefore provides the most authoritative text of the *Confessio*, and of "The Tale of Florent" in particular. Given that *The Wife of Bath's Tale* is generally thought to have been written in the early to mid 1390s it is possible that the two texts were actually contemporaneous: both, in fact, make striking use of the owl's supposed reluctance to be seen in daytime as a metaphor for the heroes' reluctance to be seen abroad with their Loathly Ladies.[10] However, not enough is known about Chaucer and Gower for it to be worthwhile speculating as to which of the two texts was written first, let alone whether they were indebted to each other or had a common source.

The Weddyng of Syr Gawen and Dame Ragnell exists uniquely in Oxford, Bodleian Library, MS Rawlinson C.86. The text is the work of one hand throughout and the manuscript itself, which is likely to have been preserved in or near London, has been dated to "around or even a little after 1500."[11] The dialect of the poem is likely to have been Midlands in origin, and it has been suggested that the scribe who copied the text came from the south Staffordshire region.[12] Unfortunately the text as we have it suffers from corruptions that make it impossible to say with certainty how accurately it reflects the poet's original

[8] Those suggested include the *Life of St Cuthbert*, *Sir Degare* and French *pastourelles*. See George R. Coffman, "Another Analogue for the Violation of the Maiden in the *Wife of Bath's Tale*," *Modern Language Notes* 59 (1944): 271–4; Laura Hibbard Loomis, "Chaucer and the Breton Lays of the Auchinleck MS," *Studies in Philology* 38 (1941): 14–33; Helen Cooper, *The Canterbury Tales*, Oxford Guides to Chaucer (Oxford, 1989; rev. 1996), p. 159.

[9] See John H. Fisher, R. Wayne Hamm, Peter G. Beidler and Robert F. Yeager, "John Gower," in *A Manual of the Writings in Middle English*, ed. J. Burke Severs and Albert E. Hartung, vol. 7 (New Haven, CT, 1986), pp. 2195–7, 2202–10. The *Confessio Amantis* exists in three recensions, surviving in a total of forty-nine manuscripts.

[10] See lines 1079–82 of *The Wife of Bath's Tale* and lines 1727–31 of the "Tale of Florent." *The Weddyng of Syr Gawen and Dame Ragnell* also refers to an owl in lines 310–16, but seemingly as a metaphor for ugliness. However, this figure of speech may simply be proverbial in origin rather than evidence of common ancestry. See *Proverbs and Proverbial Phrases from English Writings Mainly Before 1500*, ed. Bartlett Jere Whiting and Helen Wescott Whiting (Cambridge, MA., 1968), G 382.

[11] J. J. Griffiths, "A Re-examination of Oxford, Bodleian Library, MS Rawlinson C.86," *Archiv für das Studium der neueren Sprachen und Literaturen* 219 (1982): 387. See also Julia Boffey, *Manuscripts of English Courtly Love Lyrics in the Later Middle Ages,* Manuscript Studies I (Cambridge, 1985), pp. 125–6, and Julia Boffey and Carole Meale, "Selecting the Text: Rawlinson C.86 and Some Other Books for London Readers," *Regionalism in Late Medieval Manuscripts and Texts: Essays Celebrating the Publication of "A Linguistic Atlas of Late Medieval English,"* ed. Felicity Riddy (Cambridge, 1991), pp. 43–69.

[12] Lucia Glanville, "A New Edition of the Middle English Romance *The Weddynge of Syr Gawen and Dame Ragnell*," unpub. B.Litt. thesis (University of Oxford, 1958), pp. 11–22.

work. In several places tail lines have an extra stress (e.g. 36, 227, 242), occasionally lines are overlong (e.g. 167–8), and as Lucia Glanville notes, the opening couplets themselves are "overweighted with extra syllables."[13] On a number of occasions the structure collapses completely (84–96, 137–48, 176–206, 231–9, 270–3, 338–41, 414–18, 440–8, 515–20). Many of these breakdowns seem to have been prompted by the omission of a line or two, but elsewhere additions to the text seem responsible for the damage: for example, lines 231–9 are probably the result of an attempt to "improve" upon the original description of Ragnell's ugliness. Lines 199–203 and 408–13 are obviously indebted to *The Wife of Bath's Tale* itself.[14] The identity of the author of *The Weddyng of Syr Gawen and Dame Ragnell* is not known, but one suggestion has been that the poet was Sir Thomas Malory.[15] A contrary view suggests that the poem is by an anonymous author who plays ironically upon allusions to Malory's *Le Morte Darthur*, an interpretation which would date composition of the text to approximately the last quarter of the fifteenth century.[16] *The Marriage of Sir Gawain* is preserved uniquely in London, British Library, MS Add. 27879, the so-called "Percy Folio." The Folio is thought to date from about 1650, and the dialect of the single scribe responsible for transcribing the texts seems to be from Lancashire.[17] The manuscript as a whole was famously rescued by Thomas Percy, who found it being used by the maids to light fires at the house of his friend, Humphrey Pitt. Folios 2–27 of the manuscript itself have survived only as half leaves, presumably as a result of the pages being torn in two in order to provide kindling. It is unfortunate that *The Marriage of Sir Gawain* should have been written in this particular part of the manuscript, or we would have had a more complete version of the ballad. Assigning a date for the composition of the *Marriage* is impossible, although in his enthusiastic belief that these collected ballads represented the descendants of a Golden Age of minstrelsy, Percy declared to Thomas Warton that Chaucer had been indebted to *The Marriage of Sir Gawain* for *The Wife of Bath's Tale*.[18] However, the fact that one of the other Arthurian ballads in the Percy Folio, *King Arthur's Death*, has been dated to a time after 1584 should act as a cautionary note for those who would regress the written ballad to an oral archetype contemporaneous with or even predating *The Canterbury Tales*.[19]

[13] Glanville, pp. 39–40.

[14] Cf. *WOBT* 925–8.

[15] P. J. C. Field, "Malory and *The Wedding of Sir Gawain and Dame Ragnell*," *Archiv für das Studium der neueren Sprachen und Literaturen* 219 (1982): 374–81.

[16] Stephen H. A. Shepherd, "No poet has his travesty alone: *The Weddynge of Sir Gawen and Dame Ragnell*," in *Romance Reading on the Book: Essays on Medieval Narrative presented to Maldwyn Mills*, ed. Jennifer Fellows, Rosalind Field, Gillian Rogers, and Judith Weiss (Cardiff, 1996), pp. 112–28.

[17] The manuscript was edited and published by John W. Hales and Frederick J. Furnivall as *Bishop Percy's Folio Manuscript* (London, 1867–68; rpt. Detroit, MI, 1968). It has been dated and described by G. Guddat-Figge, *Catalogue of Manuscripts Containing Middle English Romances* (Munich, 1972), pp. 151–9.

[18] Letter to Thomas Warton dated 28 May 1761, preserved as London, British Library, MS Add. 42560. See Robinson and Dennis, pp. 2–3.

[19] For the dating of *King Arthur's Death*, see Robert H. Wilson, "Malory and the Ballad *King Arthur's Death*," *Medievalia et Humanistica* 6 (Cambridge, 1975): 139–49. For a discussion of other Percy Folio ballads indebted to texts printed in the sixteenth or early seventeenth century, see Joseph

Of *The Wife of Bath's Tale* it has been observed that "Perhaps no other Canterbury tale has been more universally admired with less agreement about what is really admirable in it."[20] For what is undoubtedly one of the most popular and analysed of *The Canterbury Tales*, the fact remains that after centuries of scholarship only three analogues for this particular tale have been identified. Of these, only Gower's version is contemporary with that of Chaucer, and while the remaining two analogues evidently have much in common, not least their Arthurian setting, it is impossible to say whether one was based upon the other, or both derive from a common source.

For this chapter we have gone back to Oxford, Bodleian Library, MS Fairfax 3 as the base text for "The Tale of Florent" on the grounds explained above. The manuscript fortunately is written in a very good late fourteenth-century hand, which has been carefully edited and corrected by the main scribe. The revisions are so detailed as to suggest that Gower himself must have supervised them.[21] *The Weddyng of Syr Gawen and Dame Ragnell* appears in the Rawlinson MS as an uninterrupted series of lines, with no visual indication of the six-line tail-rhyme structure which underpins it. The text published here attempts to recreate stanzaic breaks as they accord with this scheme, but a complete reconstruction of the original has not been attempted, because of the corruption of the text.[22] In the case of *The Marriage of Sir Gawain* the published text is taken from the Percy Folio, with stanzaic breaks marking divisions laid down in the manuscript. Owing to the state of the Percy Folio, a number of readings have been taken from the earlier edition by Hales and Furnivall.[23]

Donatelli, "The Percy Folio Manuscript: A Seventeenth-Century Context for Medieval Poetry," *English Manuscript Studies, 1100–1700, Vol IV*, ed. Peter Beal and Jeremy Griffiths (Oxford, 1993), pp. 122–4.

20 Robert J. Meyer, "Chaucer's Tandem Romances: A Generic Approach to the *Wife of Bath's Tale* as Palinode," *Chaucer Review* 18 (1984): 222. For a comprehensive review of scholarship concerning Chaucer's Tale, see *Chaucer's "Wife of Bath's Prologue" and "Tale." An Annotated Bibliography 1900 to 1995*, ed. Peter G. Beidler and Elizabeth M. Biebel (Toronto, 1998).

21 Gower, *Confessio Amantis*, ed. Russell A. Peck (New York, 1968), p. vi.

22 For previous critical editions which have addressed these issues see John Withrington, *The Wedding of Sir Gawain and Dame Ragnell*, Lancaster Modern Spelling Texts 2 (Lancaster, 1991), and Stephen H. A. Shepherd, *Middle English Romances* (New York, 1995), pp. 243–67.

23 The damage inflicted upon the manuscript is not restricted to the the tearing in half of the opening pages by Humphrey Pitt's maids. In his enthusiasm to preserve the manuscript as a whole Percy records on fol. 1v that he sent it to "an ignorant Bookbinder, who pared the margin," and on fol. 124v he admits to having torn out several pages of the manuscript to send to the printers. Subsequent repairs made by F. J. Furnivall and others to help preserve the Folio for posterity have also obscured a number of readings now accessible only through the Hales and Furnivall edition. (See the Introduction by F. J. Furnivall in Hales and Furnivall, vol. I, sections 3 and 9.)

I

The Tale of Florent

(from Oxford, Bodleian Library, MS Fairfax 3 [c. 1399], fols 16a–18c)

Here the Confessor gives an example in commendation of obedience against those disobedient in love. In it he says that, when a certain very beautiful daughter of the King of Sicily in the flower of her youth was transformed into a most loathsome old hag by the spells of her stepmother, Florentius, nephew of the then Emperor Claudius, a knight exceptionally strenuous in arms and devoted to the laws of love, marvellously changed her back into her former beauty by his obedience in love.[1]

(fol.16a)	Mi sone, and I thee rede* this,	counsel
	What so befalle of other weie,	
	That thou to loves heste* obeie	command
	Als ferr as thou it myht suffise:	
	For ofte* sithe in such a wise	often
	Obedience in love availeth,	
	Wher al a mannes strengthe faileth;	
	Wherof, if that the list to wite*	if you want to know about it
	In a cronique as it is write,	
	A gret ensample* thou myht fynde,	example
	Which now is come to my mynde. /	
(fol.16b)	Ther was whilom* be daies olde*	once; in olden times
	A worthi knyght, and as men tolde	
	He was neveou* to th'emperour	nephew
	And of his court a courteour:	
	Wifles* he was, Florent he hihte,*	wifeless; was called
	He was a man that mochel myhte,	
	Of armes he was desirous,	
	Chivalerous and amorous,	
	And for the fame of worldes speche,	
	Strange aventures forto seche,*	seek out
	He rod the marches al aboute.	
	And fell a time, as he was oute,	
	Fortune, which may every thred	
	Tobreke* and knette* of mannes sped,*	break; tie up; success
	Schop,* as this knyht rod in a pas,*	contrived; pass/narrow place
	That he be strengthe take was,	
	And to a castell thei him ladde,	
	Wher that he fewe frendes hadde;	
	For so it fell that ilke stounde*	at that same time
	That he hath with a dedly wounde	
	Feihtende his oghne hondes* slain	with his own hands

[1] This is a translation of the Latin marginal rubric that stands at the head of the tale in the Fairfax manuscript.

Branchus, which to the capitain
Was sone and heir, wherof ben wrothe
The fader and the moder bothe.
That knyht Branchus was of his hond*   in his actions
The worthieste of al his lond,
And fain thei wolden do vengance
Upon Florent, bot remembrance
That thei toke of his worthinesse
Of knyhthod and of gentilesse,
And how he stod of cousinage
To th'emperour, made hem assuage,
And dorsten noght slen* him for fere;   they dared not slay
In gret desputeisoun thei were
Among hemself, what was the beste.
Ther was a lady, the slyheste
Of alle that men knewe tho,*   then
So old sche myhte unethes go,*   hardly walk
And was grantdame unto the dede;*   dead man
And sche with that began to rede,*   advise
And seide how sche wol bringe him inne,*   trap him
That sche schal him to dethe winne,
Al only of his oghne grant*   entirely by his own permission
Thurgh strengthe of verray covenant
Withoute blame of eny wiht.*   man
Anon sche sende for this kniht, /
(fol.16c) And of hire sone* sche alleide*   grandson; adduced
The deth, and thus to him sche seide:
"Florent, how so thou be to wyte*   to blame
Of Branchus deth, men schal respite
As now to take vengement,
Be so thou stonde in juggement
Upon certein condicioun,
That thou unto a questioun
Which I schal axe* schalt ansuere,   ask
And over this thou schalt ek* swere,   also
That if thou of the sothe* faile,   truth
Ther schal non other thing availe
That thou ne schalt thi deth receive.
And for men schal thee noght deceive,
That thou therof myght ben avised,*   given proper advice
Thou schalt have day and tyme assised*   set
And leve saufly* forto wende,*   safely; go
Be so* that at thi daies ende   provided
Thou come ayein with thin avys.
This knyht, which worthi was and wys,
This lady preith that he may wite,*   know
And have it under seales write,
What questioun it scholde be
For which he schal in that degree
Stonde of his lif in jeupartie.

With that sche feigneth compaignie,*   friendship
And seith: "Florent, on love it hongeth,
Al that to myn axinge longeth:
What alle wommen most desire
This wole I axe, and in th'empire
Wher as thou hast most knowlechinge
Tak conseil upon this axinge."
Florent this thing hath undertake,
The day was set, the time take,
Under his seal he wrot his oth,
In such a wise and forth he goth
Hom to his emes* court ayein,   uncle's
To whom his aventure plein
He tolde, of that* him is befalle.   what
And upon that thei weren alle
The wiseste of the lond asent,
Bot natheles of on* assent*   one; sent for
Thei myhte noght acorde plat,*   plainly
On seide this, an othre that.
After the disposicioun
Of naturel complexioun /
(fol.16d) To som womman it is plesance,
That to an othre is grevance;
Bot such a thing in special,
Which to hem alle in general
Is most plesant, and most desired
Above alle othre and most conspired,*   agreed upon
Such o* thing conne thei noght finde   one
Be constellacion ne kinde;
And thus Florent withoute cure
Mot* stonde upon his aventure,   must
And is al schape* unto the lere,*   prepared; loss
As in defalte of his answere.
This knyght hath levere forto dye
Than breke his trowthe and forto lye
In place ther as he was swore,
And schapth him gon ayein therfore.
Whan time cam he tok his leve,
That lengere wolde he noght beleve,*   remain
And preith his em* he be noght wroth,   uncle
For that is a point of his oth,
He seith, that no man schal him wreke*   avenge
Thogh afterward men hiere speke
That he par aventure* deie.   by chance
And thus he wente forth his weie
Alone as knyht aventurous,
And in his thoght was curious
To wite what was best to do;
And as he rod al one so,
And cam nyh ther he wolde be,
In a forest under a tre

He syh wher sat a creature,
A lothly wommannysch figure,
That forto speke of fleisch and bon
So foul yit syh* he nevere non. — saw
This knyght behield hir redely,
And as he wolde have passed by,
Sche cleped* him and bad abide; — called
And he his horse heved* aside — head
Tho* torneth, and to hire he rod — then
And there he hoveth and abod,
To wite what sche wolde mene.
And sche began him to bemene,* — explain
And seide: "Florent, be thi name,
Thou hast on honde such a game,
That bot* thou be the betre avised, — unless
Thi deth is schapen and devised, /
(fol.17a) That al the world ne mai the* save, — thee
Bot if* that thou my conseil have." — unless
Florent, whan he this tale herde,
Unto this olde wyht* answerde — creature
And of hir conseil he hir preide.
And sche ayein to him thus seide:
"Florent, if I for the so schape,
That thou thurgh me thi deth ascape
And take worschipe of thi dede,
What schal I have to my mede?"* — reward
"What thing," quod he, "that thou wold axe."
"I bidde* nevere a betre taxe," — ask for
Quod sche, "bot ferst, er thou be sped,* — gone
Thou schalt me leve such a wedd,* — pledge
That I wol have thi trowthe in honde
That thou schalt be myn housebonde."
"Nay," seith Florent, "that may noght be."
"Ryd thanne forth thi wey," quod sche,
"And if thou go withoute red,* — counsel
Thou schalt be sekerliche* ded." — truly
Florent behihte* hire good ynowh — promised
Of lond, of rent, of park, of plowh,
Bot al that compteth* sche at noght. — accounts
Tho fell this knyht in mochel thoght,
Now goth he forth, now comth ayein,
He wot noght what is best to sein,
And thoghte, as he rod to and fro,
That chese he mot* on of the tuo: — must
Or* forto take hire to his wif, — either
Or elles forto lese* his lif. — lose
And thanne he caste his avantage,
That sche was of so gret an age,
That sche mai live bot a while
And thoghte put hire in an ile,* — isle
Wher that noman hire scholde knowe,

Til sche with deth were overthrowe.
And thus this yonge lusti knyht
Unto this olde lothly wiht* — creature
Tho seide: "If that non other chance
Mai make my deliverance,
Bot only thilke same speche
Which, as thou seist, thou schalt me teche,
Have hier myn hond, I schal thee wedde,"
And thus his trowthe* he leith* to wedde.* — honour; gives; pledge
With that sche frounceth* up the browe; — wrinkles
"This covenant I wol allowe." /
(fol.17b) Sche seith, "If eny other thing
Bot that thou hast of my techyng
Fro deth thi body mai respite,
I woll thee of thi trowthe* acquite,* — promise; release
And elles be non other weie.
Now herkne me what I schal seie:
Whan thou art come into the place,
Wher now thei maken gret manace
And upon this comynge abyde,
Thei wole anon the same tide* — time
Oppose thee of thin answere.
I wot thou wolt no thing forbere
Of that thou wenest* be thi beste, — think
And if thou myht so finde reste,
Wel is, for thanne is ther nomore.
And elles this schal be my lore,
That thou schalte seie, upon this molde* — earth
That alle wommen lievest wolde* — most desire
Be soverein of mannes love:
For what womman is so above,
Sche hath, as who seith, al hire will,
And elles may sche noght fulfille
What thing hir were lievest have.
With this answere thou schalt save
Thiself, and other wise noght.
And whan thou hast thin ende wroght,
Com hier ayein, thou schalt me finde,
And let nothing out of thi minde."
He goth him forth with hevy chiere,
As he that not* in what manere — knows not
He mai this worldes joie atteigne:
For if he deie, he hath a peine,
And if he live, he mot him binde
To such on* which of alle kinde — a one
Of wommen is th'unsemlieste:
Thus wot he noght what is the beste
Bot be him lief* or be him loth,* — pleasant; unpleasant

230 **th'unsemlieste**: MS þunsemylieste

Unto the castell forth he goth
His full answere forto yive,
Or forto deie, or forto live.
Forth with his conseil cam the lord,
The thinges stoden of record,
He sende up for the lady sone,
And forth sche cam, that olde mone.* shrew
In presence of the remenant
The strengthe of al the covenant /
(fol.17c) Tho was reherced openly,
And to Florent sche bad forthi
That he schal tellen his avis.* opinion
As he that woot what is the pris,
Florent seith al that evere he couthe,
Bot such word cam ther non to mowthe,
That he for yifte or for beheste* promise
Mihte eny wise his deth areste.
And thus he tarieth longe and late,
Til that this lady bad algate* nevertheless
That he schal for the dom* final judgement
Yif his answere in special
Of that sche hadde him ferst opposed:* put to
And thanne he hath trewly supposed
That he him may of nothing yelpe,* boast
Bot if so be tho wordes helpe,
Whiche as the womman hath him tawht;
Whereof he hath an hope cawht
That he schal ben excused so,
And tolde out plein* his wille tho. plainly
And whan that this matrone herde
The manere how this knyht ansuerde,
Sche seide: "Ha treson! wo thee be,
That hast thus told the privite
Which alle wommen most desire!
I wolde that thou were afire!"
Bot natheles in such a plit
Florent of his answere is quit;
And tho began his sorwe newe,
For he mot gon, or ben untrewe,
To hire which his trowthe* hadde. promise
Bot he, which alle schame dradde,
Goth forth in stede of his penance,
And takth the fortune of his chance,
As he that was with trowthe affaited.* oppressed/put down
This olde wyht* him hath awaited creature
In place wher as he hire lefte:
Florent his wofull heved uplefte
And syh* this vecke* wher sche sat, saw; hag
Which was the lothlieste what* thing
That evere man caste on his yhe:* eye
Hire nase bass,* hire browes hyhe, low

Hire yhen smale and depe set,
Hire chekes ben with teres wet,
And rivelen* as an emty skyn — wrinkled
Hangende doun unto the chin, /
(fol.17d) Hire lippes schrunken ben for age,
Ther was no grace in the visage,
Hir front* was nargh,* hir lockes hore,* — face; narrow; grey
Sche loketh forth as doth a more,* — Moor
Hire necke is schort, hir schuldres courbe,* — bent
That myghte a mannes lust destourbe,
Hire body gret and nothing smal,
And schortly to descrive hire al,
Sche hath no lith* withoute a lak; — limb
Bot lich unto the wollesak
Sche proferth hire* unto this knyght, — offers herself
And bad him, as he hath behyt,* — promised
So as sche hath ben his warant
That he hire holde covenant,
And be the bridel sche him seseth,
Bot godd wot how that sche him pleseth
Of suche wordes as sche spekth:
Him thenkth welnyh his herte brekth
For sorwe that he may noghe fle,
Bot if he wolde untrewe be.
Loke, how a sek* man for his hele* — sick; health
Takth baldemoine* with canele,* — gentian; cinnamon
And with the mirre* takth the sucre, — myrrh
Ryght upon such a maner lucre
Stant Florent, as in this diete:
He drinkth the bitre with the swete,
He medleth sorwe with likynge,
And liveth, as who seith, deyinge;
His youthe schal be cast aweie
Upon such on which as the weie
Is old and lothly overal.
Bot nede he mot* that nede schal: — must
He wolde algate* his trowthe holde, — always
As every knyht thereto is holde,
What happ so evere him is befalle;
Thogh sche be the fouleste of alle,
Yet to th'onour of wommanhiede
Him thoghte he scholde taken hiede;
So that for pure gentilesse,
As he hire couthe best adresce,* — manage/cope with
In ragges, as sche was totore,* — tattered
He set hire on his hors tofore
And forth he takth his weie softe;
No wonder thogh he siketh* ofte, — sighs
Bot as an oule* fleth by nyhte — owl
Out of alle othre briddes syhte, /
(fol.18a) Right so this knyght on daies brode

In clos him hield, and schop his rode
On nyhtes time, til the tyde
That he cam there he wolde abide;
And prively withoute noise
He bringth this foule grete coise*   rump
To his castell in such a wise
That noman myhte hire schappe avise,
Til sche into the chambre cam:
Wher he his prive conseil nam*   took
Of suche men as he most troste,*   trusted
And tolde hem that he nedes moste
This beste* wedde to his wif,   beast
For elles hadde he lost his lif.
The prive wommen were asent,*   sent for
That scholden ben of his assent:
Hire ragges thei anon* of drawe,*   quickly; take off
And, as it was that time lawe,
She hadde bath, sche hadde reste,
And was arraied to the beste.
Bot with no craft of combes brode
Thei myhte hire hore lockes schode,*   divide
And sche ne wolde noght be schore*   shorn
For no conseil, and thei therfore,
With such atyr as tho was used,
Ordeinen that it was excused,
And hid so craftelich aboute,
That noman myhte sen hem oute.
Bot when sche was fulliche arraied
And hire atyr was al assaied,
Tho was sche foulere on to se,*   fouler to look on
Bot yit it may non other be:
Thei were wedded in the nyht –
So wo begon was nevere knyht
As he was thanne of mariage.
And sche began to pleie and rage,
As who seith, I am wel ynowh;
Bot he therof nothing ne lowh,*   laughed
For sche tok thanne chiere on honde*   then began to be merry
And clepeth him hire housebonde,
And seith, "My lorde, go we to bedde,
For I to that entente wedde,
That thou schalt be my worldes blisse:"
And profreth him with that to kisse,
As sche a lusti lady were.
His body myhte wel be there, /
(fol.18b) Bot as of thoght and of memoire
His herte was in purgatoire.
Bot yit for strengthe of matrimoine
He myhte make non essoine,*   excuse
That he ne mot algates plie*   can in any way avoid submitting
To gon to bedde of compaignie;

And whan thei were abedde naked,
Withoute slep he was awaked,
He torneth on that other side,
For that he wolde hise yhen* hyde   eyes
Fro lokynge on that foule wyht
The chambre was al full of lyht,
The courtins were of cendal thinne,*   thin rich silk
This newe bryd which lay withinne,
Thogh it be noght with his acord,
In armes sche beclipte* hire lord,   embraced
And preide, as he was torned fro,
He wolde him torne ayeinward tho;
"For now," sche seith, "we ben bothe on."*   one
And he lay stille as eny ston,
Bot ever in on sche spak and preide,
And bad him thenke on that he seide,
Whan that he tok hire be the hond.
He herde and understod the bond,
How he was set to his penance,
And as it were a man in trance
He torneth him al sodeinly,
And syh a lady lay him by
Of eyhtetiene wynter age,
Which was the fairest of visage
That evere in al this world he syh:
And as he wolde have take hire nyh,
Sche put hire hand and be his leve
Besoghte him that he wolde leve,*   stop
And seith that forto wynne or lese
He mot on of tuo thinges chese:
Wher he wold have hire such on nyht,
Or elles upon daies lyht,
For he schal noght have bothe tuo.
And he began to sorwe tho
In many a wise, and caste his thoght,
Bot for al that yit cowthe he noght
Devise himself which was the beste.
And she, that wolde his hertes reste,
Preith that he scholde chese algate,
Til ate laste longe and late /
(fol.18c) He seide: "O ye, my lyves hele,
Sey what you list in my querele,
I not* what ansuere I schal yive;*   know not; give
Bot evere whil that I may live,
I wol that ye be my maistresse,
For I can noghte miselve gesse
Which is the beste unto my chois.
Thus grante I yow myn hole vois,

400 **foule**: MS fole

Ches for ous bothen, I you preie;
And what as evere that ye seie,
Riht as ye wole, so wol I."
"Mi lord," sche seide, "grant merci,
For of this word that ye now sein,
That ye have mad me soverein,
Mi destine* is overpassed, destiny
That nevere hierafter schal be lassed* made less
Mi beaute, which that I now have,
Til I be take into my grave;
Bot nyght and day as I am now
I schal alwey be such to yow.
The kinges dowter of Cizile
I am, and fell bot siththe awhile,* it befell only a while ago
As I was with my fader late,
That my stepmoder for an hate,
Which toward me sche hath begonne,
Forschop* me, til I hadde wonne transformed
The love and sovereinete
Of what knyht that in his degre
Alle othre passeth of good name;
And, as men sein, ye ben the same,
The dede proeveth it is so:
Thus am I youres evermo."
Tho was plesance and joye ynowh,
Echon with other pleide and lowh;* laughed
Their live longe and wel thei ferde,
And clerkes that this chance herde
Thei writen it in evidence,
To teche how that obedience
Mai wel fortune a man to love
And sette him in his lust above,
As it befell unto this knyht.

[Ends]

II

[*The Weddyng of Syr Gawen and Dame Ragnell*]

(from Oxford, Bodleian Library, MS Rawlinson C.86 [c. 1500], fols 128v–140r)

Lythe* and lystenyth the lif of a lord riche, — harken *(fol.128v)*
The while that he lyvid was none hym liche,
    Nether in bowre ne in halle.
In the tyme of Arthoure thys adventure betyd,
And of the greatt adventure that he hymself dyd,
    That Kyng curteys & royall.

Of alle kynges Arture beryth the flowyr,
And of alle knyghthod he bare away the honour
    Where so ever he wentt.
In his contrey was nothyng butt chyvalry,
And knyghtes were belovid [by] that doughty,
    For cowardes were evermore shent.* — shamed

Nowe, wyll ye lyst a whyle to my talkyng,
I shall you tell of Arthoure the Kyng,
    How ones hym befell.
On huntyng he was in Ingleswod,
With alle his bold knyghtes good:
    Nowe herken to my spell!* — tale

The Kyng was sett att his trestyll-tree,* — hunting station/hideout
With his bowe to sle* the wylde venere,* — kill; game
    And hys lordes were sett hym besyde;
As the Kyng stode, then was he ware
Where a greatt hartt was and a fayre,
    And forth fast dyd he glyde.* — go/move

The hartt was in a braken ferne,* — thicket of fern
And hard the houndes, and stode full derne:
    Alle that sawe the Kyng.
"Hold you styll, every man,
And I woll goo myself, yf I can,
    With craft of stalkyng."/

The Kyng in hys hand toke a bowe, — *(fol.129r)*
And wodmanly he stowpyd lowe,
    To stalk unto that dere;

11 **by** omitted in MS

23 "Where a large, fair hart was." 26 "And heard the hounds, and stood completely quietly/secretly." The hart freezes on hearing the hounds, hoping to avoid detection.

When that he cam the dere full nere,
The dere lept forthe into a brere,* briar patch
And ever the Kyng went nere and nere.

So Kyng Arthure went awhyle
After the dere (I trowe* half a myle), believe
And no man with hym went;
And att the last to the dere he lett flye,
And smote hym sore and sewerly,
Suche grace God hym sent.

Doun the dere tumblyd [so deron],
And fell into a greatt brake of feron;* thicket of fern
The Kyng folowyd full fast.
Anon the Kyng bothe ferce* and fell* fierce; bold
Was with the dere, and dyd hym [serve well],
And after the grasse* he taste.* fat; tested

As the Kyng was with the dere alone,
Streyght ther cam to hym a quaynt grome,
Armyd well and sure;
A knyght full strong and of greatt myght,
And grymly wordes to the Kyng he sayd:
"Well i-mett, Kyng Arthour!

Thou hast me done wrong many a yere,
And wofully I shall quytte* the* here: repay; you
I hold thy lyfe-days nyghe done!
Thou hast gevyn my landes in certayn
Wyth greatt wrong unto Syr Gawen.
Whate sayest thou, kyng alone?"

"Syr Knyght, whate is thy name with honour?"
"Syr King," he sayd, "Gromer Somer Joure,
I tell the nowe with ryght.* truly
"A, Syr Gromer Somer, bethynk the well,
To sle me here honour getyst thou no dell:*/ none at all
Bethynk* the, thou artt a knyght. remember *(fol.129v)*

Yf thou sle me nowe in thys case,
Alle knyghtes woll refuse the in every place,
That shame shall never the froo.*

34 **nere**: nygh, then amended
43 **so deron**: soderon
47 **serve well**: servell

40–1 "Finally he loosed an arrow at the deer, which struck the deer surely and sorely." 43 Possibly "so derne," i.e. hidden/out of view, or misreading several times removed for "suddenly." 47 Possibly derived from OF "surveiller," i.e. to examine, but the sense is that Arthur finishes off the deer, delivering the coup de grace after the initial shot. 48 Having dispatched the deer, Arthur assesses the quality of his kill: the thicker the fat, the better. 50 "Immediately there came to him a strange man." 69 "[And the] shame will always be with you."

Lett be thy wyll* and folowe wytt,*   passion; reason
And* that is amys I shall amend itt,   if
    And thou wolt, or that I goo."

"Nay," sayd Syr Gromer Somer, "by Hevyn Kyng!
So shalt thou nott skape* withoute lesyng,*   escape; deceit
    I have the nowe att avayll;
Yf I shold lett the thus goo with mokery,
Anoder tyme thou wolt me defye:
    Of that I shall nott fayll."

"Now," sayd the Kyng, "So God me save,
Save my lyfe, and whate thou wolt crave,
    I shall now graunt itt the.
Shame thou shalt have to sle me in venere,*   hunting
Thou armyd and I clothyd butt in grene, perde!"

"Alle thys shall nott help the, sekyrly,*   certainly
For I woll nother lond ne gold, truly;
Butt yf* thou grant me att a certayn day   unless
Suche as I shall sett,* and in thys same araye."*   stipulate; garb

"Yes," sayd the Kyng, "lo, here my hand!"
"Ye,* butt abyde, Kyng, and here me a stound.*   yea/yes; a while
Fyrst thow shalt swere upon my sword broun*   bright
To shewe me att thy comyng whate wemen love best, in feld and town;
And thou shalt mete me here, withouten send,*   unaccompanied
Evyn att this day xii monethes end;
And thou shalt swere upon my swerd good,
That of thy knyghtes shall none com with the, by the Rood,*   Cross
Nowther [fremde]* ne freynd.   stranger

And yf thou bryng nott answere withoute fayll,
Thyne hed thou shalt lose for thy travayll:*/   effort/pains
Thys shall nowe be thyne oth.   *(fol.129r*)*
Whate sayst thou, Kyng? Lett se! Have done!"
"Syr, I graunt* to thys, now lett me gone;*   agree; go
    Though itt be to me full loth.*   repellent

I ensure* the, as I am true Kyng,   assure/promise
To com agayn att thys xii monethes [endyng],
    And bryng the thyne answere."
"Now go thy way, Kyng Arthure,
Thy lyfe is in my hand, I am full sure,
    Of thy sorowe thow artt nott ware.

96 **fremde**: frende
104 **endyng**: end

83 "While you are armed, and I am just clothed in green!" 99 The MS has been ascribed two folios with the number "129." The latter of the two folios has had an asterisk added as a prefix in the MS in order to distinguish it from its predecessor.

Abyde, Kyng Arthure, a lytell whyle!
Loke nott today thou me begyle,
  And kepe alle thyng in close.* secret
For and I wyst, by Mary mylde,
Thou woldyst betray me in the feld,
  Thy lyf fyrst sholdyst thou lose."

"Nay," sayd Kyng Arthure, "that may nott be,
Untrewe knyght shalt thou never fynde me:
  To dye yett were me lever!
Farwell, Syr Knyght, and evyll mett,
I woll com, and* I be on lyve att the day sett, if
  Though I shold scape never."

The Kyng his bugle gan* blowe, did
That hard every knyght and itt gan knowe,* recognise
  Unto hym can* they rake.* did; hurry
Ther they fond the Kyng and the dere,
With sembland sad and hevy chere,
  That had no lust to layk.

"Go we home nowe to Carlyll,
Thys hyntyng lykys me nott well,"
So sayd Kyng Arthure.
Alle the lordes knewe by his countenaunce/
That the Kyng had mett with sume dysturbaunce. *(fol.129v*)*

Unto Carlyll then the Kyng cam,
Butt of his hevynesse knewe no man,
  Hys hartt was wonder* hevy; wondrously
In thys hevynesse he dyd abyde
That many of his knyghtes mervaylyd that tyde.

Tyll, att the last, Syr Gawen
To the Kyng he sayd than,
"Syr, me marvaylyth ryght sore
Whate thyng that thou sorowyst fore."
Then answeryd the Kyng as tyght,* at once
"I shall the tell, gentyll Gawen knyght.
In the forest as I was this daye,
Ther I mett with a knight in his araye,
And serteyn wordes to me he gan sayn,* say
And chargyd* me I shold hym nott bewrayne;* commanded; betray

His councell* must I kepe therfore, secret
Or els I am forswore."* perjured
"Nay, drede you nott, lord, by Mary flower!

112–14 "For by gracious Mary, if I thought that you would betray me in the field of battle, I would make sure first that you lost your life." 117 "I would sooner die!" 126 "That had no inclination for further sport."

I am nott that man that wold you dishonour,
Nother by evyn ne by moron."

"Forsoth, I was on huntyng in Ingleswod –
Thowe knowest well I slewe an hartt, by the Rode,
Alle mysylf alon –
Ther mett I with a knyght armyd sure.* — fully
His name he told me was Syr Gromer Somer Joure;
Therfor I make my mone.* — lament

Ther that knyght fast dyd me threte,
And wold have slayn me with greatt heatt,
Butt I spak fayre agayn.
Wepyns with me ther had I none.
Alas! my worshypp* therfor is nowe gone." — honour/renown
"What therof?" sayd Gawen.

"Whatt nedys more? I shall nott lye,
He wold have slayn me ther withoute mercy,/
And that me was fulle loth! — *(fol.130r)*
He made me to swere that att the xii monethes end,
That I shold mete hym ther in the same kynde,* — manner/state of dress
To that I plyght* my trowith.* — gave; word

And also I shold tell hym att the same day,
Whate wemen desyren moste, in good faye;* — faith
My lyf els shold I le[s]e.
This oth I made unto that knyght,
And that I shold never tell itt to no wight,* — person
Of thys I myght nott chese.* — choose

And also I shold com in none oder araye,
Butt evyn as I was the same daye;
And yf I faylyd of myne answere,
I wott* I shal be slayn ryght there. — know
Blame me nott though I be a wofull man,
Alle thys is my drede and fere."

"Ye, Syr, make* good chere; — be of
Lett make your hors redy
To ryde into straunge* contrey; — unfamiliar
And ever wheras ye mete owther man or woman, in faye,
Ask of theym whate thay therto saye.
And I shall also ryde anoder waye,
And enquere of every man and woman, and gett whatt I may
Of every man and woman's answere,
And in a boke I shall theym wryte."

172 **lese**: leve

151 "Neither by evening nor morning," i.e. never; 158–60 "There, that knight quickly threatened me, and would have killed me in his fury, except that I spoke courteously to him."

"I graunt"*, sayd the Kyng as tyte. agree
"Ytt is well advysed, Gawen the good,
Evyn by the Holy Rood."
Sone were the[y] bothe redy,
Gawen and the Kyng, wytterly.* certainly
The Kyng rode on way, and Gawen anoder,
And ever enquyred of man, woman and other
Whate wemen desyred moste dere.

Somme sayd they lovyd to be well arayd,* dressed
Somme sayd they lovyd to be fayre prayed;*/ wooed
Somme sayd they lovyd a lusty man *(fol.130v)*
That in theyr armys can clypp* them and kysse them than; embrace
Somme sayd one,* somme sayd other; one (thing)
And so had Gawen getyn many an answer.
By that* Gawen had geten whate he maye the time
And come agayn by a certeyn daye,

Syr Gawen had goten answerys so many
That he had made a boke greatt, wytterly;
To the courte he cam agayn.
By that was the Kyng comyn with hys boke,
And eyther on other's pamplett* dyd loke. book
"Thys may nott fay[l]!" sayd Gawen.

"By God," sayd the Kyng, "I drede me sore,
I cast* me to seke* a lytell more intend; search
In Yngleswod Forest.
I have butt a moneth to* my day sett, until
I may hapen on somme good tydynges to hytt –
Thys thynkyth me nowe best."

"Do as ye lyst," then Gawen sayd,
"Whatsoever ye do, I hold me payd,* satisfied
Hytt is good to be spyrryng!* enquiring
Doute you nott, lord, ye shall well spede:
Sume of your sawes shall help att nede,
Els itt were yll lykyng."

Kyng Arthoure rode forth on the other* day, next
Into Yngleswod as hys gate* laye, way
And ther he mett with a lady;
She was as ungoodly* a creature ugly
As ever man sawe, withoute* mesure. beyond
Kyng Arthure mervaylyd securly.* certainly

194 **they**: the
212 **fayl**: ffayd

213 "By God," said the King, "I am deeply afraid." 222–4 "Do not doubt, lord, that you will succeed. Some of the responses you have gathered will help, otherwise it would be unwelcome news!"

Her face was red, her nose snotyd withall,
Her mowith* wyde, her teth yalowe over all, [mouth]
With bleryd eyen gretter than a ball,
Her mowith was nott to lak;/
Her teth hyng over he[r] lyppes, [*(fol.131r)*]
Her chekys [w]yde as wemens' hyppes,
A lute* she bare upon her bak. [hump?]
Her nek long and therto greatt,* [thick]
Her here cloteryd on an hepe,

In the sholders she was a yard brode,
Hangyng pappys to be an hors lode;
And lyke a barell she was made;
And to reherse the fowlnesse of that lady,
Ther is no tung may tell, securly,
Of lothlynesse inowghe she had.

She satt on a palfray was gay begon,
With gold besett and many a precious stone,
Ther was an unsemely*syght; [inappropriate]
So fowll a creature withoute mesure,
To ryde so gayly, I you ensure,* [assure/guarantee]
Ytt was no reason ne ryght.

She rode to Arthoure, and thus she sayd:
"God spede, Syr Kyng! I am well payd
That I have with the mett;
Speke with me, I rede,* or* thou goo, [advise; before]
For thy lyfe is in my hand, I warn the soo,
That shalt thou fynde, and I itt nott lett."

"Why, whatt wold ye, lady, nowe with me?"
"Syr, I wold fayn nowe speke with the,
And tell the tydynges good;
For alle the answerys that thou canst yelpe,* [boast]
None of theym alle shall the helpe,
That shalt thou knowe, by the Rood!

Thou wenyst* I knowe nott thy councell;* [believest; secret]
Butt I warn the, I knowe itt every deall:* [part]
Yf I help the nott, thou art butt dead!
Graunt me, Syr Kyng, butt one thyng,/
And for thy lyfe, I make warrauntyng,* [guarantee *(fol.131v)*]
Or elles* thou shalt lose thy hed." [else]

235 **her**: he
236 **wyde**: syde
266 **Yf I help the nott**: Butt I warn the yf I help the nott

234 "Her mouth was not lacking," i.e. not small. 239 "Her hair was piled in a heap on her head." 241 "Her pendulous breasts were big enough to be a load for a horse." 246 "She rode a gayly bedecked palfrey." 257 "You shall find this out, if I do not prevent it."

"Whate mean you, lady? Tell me tyght,* — immediately
For of thy wordes I have great dispyte:* — contempt
To* you I have no nede. — for

Whate is your desyre, fayre lady?
Lett me wete* shortly,* — know; briefly
Whate is your meanyng;
And why my lyfe is in your hand.
Tell me, and I shall you warraunt
Alle your oun askyng."

"Forsoth," sayd the lady, "I am no qued;* — evil person/deceiver
Thou must graunt me a knyght to wed:
His name is Syr Gawen.
And suche covenaunt* I woll make the: — agreement
Butt thorowe myne answere thy lyf savyd be,
Elles lett my desyre be in vayne;

And yf myne answere save thy lyf,
Graunt me to be Gawens wyf.
Advyse* the nowe, Syr Kyng, — consider
For itt must be so, or thou artt butt dead!
Chose nowe, for thou mayste sone lose thyne hed:
Tell me nowe in hying."* — haste

"Mary!" sayd the Kyng, "I maye nott graunt the
To make warraunt Syr Gawen to wed the;
Alle lyeth in hym alon.
Butt and itt be so, I woll do my labour
In savyng of my lyfe to make itt secour;
To Gawen woll I make my mone."

"Well," sayd she, "nowe go home agayn,
And fayre wordes speke to Syr Gawen,
For thy lyf I may save;
Thoughe I be foull, yett am I gaye,* — vigorous/lively
Thourgh me thy lyf save he maye,
Or sewer thy deth to have."

"Alas!" he sayd, "nowe woo is me,
That I shold cause Gawen to wed the,/
For he wol be loth* to saye naye. — reluctant *(fol.132r)*
So foull a lady as ye ar nowe one
Sawe I never in my lyfe on ground gone;
I nott* whate I do may." — know not

"No force,* Syr Kyng, though I be foull, — matter
Choyse for a make* hath an owll. — mate
Thou getest of me no more.
When thou comyst agayn to thyne answer,
Ryght in this place I shall mete the here,
Or elles I wott* thou artt lore.* — know; lost

"Now farewell," sayd the Kyng, "lady [fowll]."
"Ye, Syr," she sayd, "ther is a byrd men call an owll,
And yett a lady I am."
"Whate is your name? I pray you tell me."
"Syr Kyng, I hight* Dame Ragnell, truly, — am called
That never yett begylyd man."

"Dame Ragnell, nowe have good daye."
"Syr Kyng, God spede the on thy way,
Ryght here I shall the mete."
Thus they departyd fayre and well,
The Kyng full sone com to Carlyll,
And his hartt hevy and greatt.* — sad

The fyrst man he mett was Syr Gawen,
That unto the Kyng thus gan sayn,
"Syr, howe have ye sped?"* — fared
"Forsoth," sayd the Kyng, "never so yll!"* — badly
Alas, I am in poynt* myself to spyll,* — on the point of; kill
For nedely I most be ded!"

"Nay," sayd Gawen, "that may nott be,
I had lever myself be dead, so mott I the;
Thys is ill* tydand."* — bad; news
"Gawen, I mett today with the fowlyst lady
That ever I sawe, sertenly;

She sayd to me my lyfe she wold save,
Butt fyrst she wold the to husbond have;
Wherfor I am wo-begon,
Thus in my hartt I make my mone."/

"Ys this all?" then sayd Gawen. — *(fol.132v)*
"I shall wed her, and wed her agayn,
Thowgh she were a fend;* — fiend
Thowgh she were as foull as Belsabub,
Her shall I wed, by the Rood,
Or elles were nott I your frende.

For ye ar my Kyng with honour,
And have worshypt* me in many a stowre;* — honoured; battle
Therfor shall I nott lett.* — shrink/hold back
To save your lyfe, lorde, itt were my parte,* — duty
Or were I false and a greatt coward,
And my worshypp is the bett."

315 **fowll** omitted from line 315, and instead concludes the previous line.
334 "So may I thrive, I would rather be dead myself."

"Iwys,* Gawen, I mett her in Inglyswod, — indeed
She told me her name, by the Rode,
That itt was Dame Ragnell;
She told me butt* I had of her answere, — that unless
Elles alle my laboure is never the nere,
Thus she gan me tell.

And butt yf her answere help me well,
Elles lett her have her desyre no dele,
This was her covenaunt;
And yf her answere help me, and none other,* — no other (answer)
Then wold she have you: here is all togeder;
That made she warraunt."

"As for this," sayd Gawen, "[it] shall not lett.* — hinder
I woll wed her att whate tyme ye woll sett,
I pray you make no care;
For and she were the moste fowlyst wyght* — creature
That ever men myght se with syght,
For your love I woll nott spare."

"Garamercy,* Gawen," then sayd Kyng Arthor, — many thanks
"Of alle knyghtes thou berest the flowre,
That ever yett I fond;
My worshypp and my lyf thou savyst for ever,
Therfore my love shall nott frome the dyssevyr/* — part
As* I am Kyng in lond." — while *(fol.133r)*

Then within v or vi days,
The Kyng must nedys goo his ways
To bere his answere.
The Kyng and Syr Gawen rode oute of toun,
No man with them, butt they alone,
Neder ferre ne nere.

When the Kyng was within the forest,
"Syr Gawen, farewell, I must go west;
Thou shalt no furder goo."
"My lord, God spede you on your jorney,
I wold* I shold nowe ryde your way, — would (prefer that)
For to departe I am ryght wo."

The Kyng had rydden butt a while,
Lytell more then the space of a myle,
Or* he mett Dame Ragnell. — before
"A, Syr Kyng, ye arre nowe welcum here;
I wott* ye ryde to bere your answere: — believe
That woll avayll you no dele!"

366 **it** omitted in MS.

383 "from either far away or nearby." 395 "That will help you not in the slightest!"

"Nowe," sayd the Kyng, "sithe* itt woll none other be, since
Tell me your answere nowe, and my lyf save me:
Gawen shall you wed.
So he hath promysed me my lyf to save,
And your desyre nowe shall ye have,
Both in bowre* and in bed. chamber

Therfor tell me nowe alle in hast,
Whate woll help now att last –
Have done! I may nott tary."
"Syr," quod* Dame Ragnell, "nowe shalt thou knowe said
Whate wemen desyren moste, of high and lowe,
From this I woll nott varaye.

Sum[m]e men sayn we desyre to be fayre,
Also we desyre to have repayre* resort
Of diverse straunge men;
Also we love to have lust in bed,/
And often we desyre to wed, *(fol.133v)*
Thus ye men nott ken.* know

Yett we desyre anoder maner thyng,
To be holden* nott old, butt fresshe and yong, considered
With flatryng and glosyng and quaynt gyn,
So ye men may us wemen ever wyn
Of whate ye woll crave.

Ye goo full nyse, I woll nott lye,
Butt there is one thyng is alle oure fantasye,
And that nowe shall ye knowe:
We desyren of men above alle maner thyng
To have the sovereynte, withoute lesyng,* lying
Of alle, both hygh and lowe.

For where we have sovereynte alle is ourys,
Though a knyght be nevere so ferys,* fierce
And ever the mastry* wynne; mastery/superiority
Of the moste manlyest is oure desyre,
To have the sovereynte of such a syre,
Suche is oure crafte* and gynne.* cunning; intention

Therfore wend, Syr Kyng, on thy way,
And tell that knyght, as I the saye,
That itt is as we desyren moste;

408 **Summe**: sumne

416 "With flattery, smooth talking and clever trickery."
419 "You (men) are really quite clever at this, I won't deny it." Alternatively misreading for "Ye goo full nyghe", i.e. 'You get close to the truth'. 424 "Over everybody, of both high and low estate."

He wol be wroth and unsought,* — implacable/irreconcilable
And curse her fast that itt the taught,
For his laboure is lost.

Go forth, Syr Kyng, and hold promyse,
For thy lyfe is sure nowe in alle wyse,* — respects
That dare I wele undertake."

The Kyng rode forth a greatt shake,* — speed
As fast as he myght gate,* — go
Thorowe myre, more, and fenne
Whereas the place was sygnyd* and sett* then./ — appointed; agreed
Evyn ther with Syr Gromer he mett, — *(fol.134r)*
And stern wordes to the Kyng he spak with that;
"Com of,* Syr Kyng, nowe lett se — along
Of thyne answere, whate itt shal be,
For I am redy grathyd."* — prepared

The Kyng pullyd oute bokes twayne;* — two
"Syr, ther is myne answer, I dare sayn,
For somme woll help att nede."
Syr Gromer lokyd on theym everychon;* — every one
"Nay, nay, Syr Kyng, thou artt butt a dead man –
Therfor nowe shalt thou blede!"

"Abyde, Syr Gromer," sayd Kyng Arthoure,
"I have one answere shall make ale sure."
"Let se," then sayd Syr Gromer,
"Or els, so God me help, as I the say,
Thy deth thou shalt have with large* paye,* — great; pleasure
I tell the nowe ensure."* — assuredly

"Now," sayd the Kyng, "I se as I gesse,
In the is butt a lytell gentilnesse,
By God that ay* is helpand.* — always; helping (us all)
Here is oure answere and that is alle,
That wemen desyren moste speciall,
Both of fre and bond.

I saye no more, butt above al thyng
Wemen desyre sovereynte, for that is theyr lykyng,
And that is ther moste desyre;
To have the rewll of the manlyest men,
And then ar they well, thus they me dyd ken,* — teach
To rule the, Gromer syre."

466 "Both those who are free, and those who are servants," i.e. everybody. 467 originally concluded by repeating "of fre and bond" from the previous line. This was then deleted and "above al thyng" inserted; 469 originally started "And is that," the second word being deleted by the scribe on realising the mistake.

"And she that told the nowe, Syr Arthoure,
I pray to God I maye se her bren* on a fyr, burn
For that was my suster, Dame Ragnell;/
That old stott! God geve he[r] shame, *(fol.134v)*
Elles had I made the full tame;
Nowe have I lost moche travayll.* effort/hard work

Go where thou wolt, Kyng Arthoure,
For of me thou maiste be ever sure;
Alas! that I ever se this day;
Nowe, well I wott,* myne enime thou wolt be, know
And att suche a pryk* shall I never gett the – advantage
My song may be well-awaye!"

"No," sayd the Kyng, "that make I warraunt,
Some harnys* I woll have to make me defendaunt, armour
That make I God avowe;
In suche a plyght shallt thou never me fynde,
And yf thou do, lett me bete* and bynde,* (be) beaten; bound
As is for* thy best [prowe]."* to; advantage

"Nowe have good day," sayd Syr Gromer,
"Fare wele," sayd Syr Arthoure, "so mott I the,
I am glad I have so sped."
Kyng Arthoure turnyd hys hors into the playn,
And sone he mett with Dame Ragnell agayn,
In the same place and stede.* location

"Syr Kyng, I am glad ye have sped well,
I told howe itt wold be, every dell;
Nowe hold* that ye have hyght.* keep to; promised
Syn I have savyd your lyf, and none other,
Gawen must me wed, Syr Arthoure,
That* is a full gentill knyght." who

"No, lady; that* I you hight I shall nott fayll, what
So ye wol be rulyd by my councell,
Your will then shall ye have."
"Nay, Syr Kyng, nowe woll I nott soo,
Openly I wol be weddyd or I parte the froo,/
Elles shame woll [I] have! *(fol.135r)*

476 **her**: he
490 **prowe**: prouf
508 **I**: ye

476 "Stott" or "scott" are equally valid readings. While both words can mean a cow or a horse, and while there was a long-standing English tradition of using the word "scott", i.e. someone of Scottish origin, as a term of abuse in its own right, there is evidence that the word "stott" meant a slut. (See "The Marriage", line 111, where Gromer's counterpart calls the hag a "hore".) 484 "I have good reason to lament." 485–7 "I guarantee that next time I shall be wearing armour to protect myself, I swear to God."

Ryde before, and I woll com after,
Unto thy courte, Syr Kyng Arthoure;
Of no man I woll shame.
Bethynk* you how I have savyd your lyf. remember
Therfor with me nowe shall ye nott stryfe,* contest/argue
For and* ye do, ye be to blame!" if

The Kyng of* her had greatt shame, because of
Butt forthe she rood,* though he were grevyd,* rode; unhappy
Tyll they cam to Karlyle forth they mevyd.
Into the courte she rode hym by,
For no man wold she spare, securly –
Itt likyd the Kyng full yll!

Alle the contraye had wonder greatt
Fro whens she com, that foule unswete,
They sawe never of so fowlle a thyng;
Into the hall she went, in certen:
"Arthoure, Kyng, lett fetche me Syr Gaweyn,
Before* the knyghtes, alle in hying,* in front of; haste

That I may nowe be made sekyr;
In welle and wo trowith-plyght us togeder
Before alle thy chyvalry.* knights (here present)
This is your graunt. Lett se! Have done!
Fett* forth Syr Gawen, my love, anon,* bring; immediately
For lenger taryeng kepe nott I!"

Then cam forth Syr Gawen the knyght;
"Syr, I am redy of that I you hyght,
Alle forwardes* to fulfyll." agreements
"God have mercy," sayd Dame Ragnell then,
"For thy sake I wold I were a fayre woman,/
For thou art of so good wyll." *(fol.135v)*

Ther Syr Gawen to her his trowth plyght,
In well and in woo, as he was a true knyght;
Then was Dame Ragnell fayn.* pleased
"Alas!" then sayd Dame Gaynour;
So sayd alle the ladyes in her bower,* chamber
And wept for Syr Gawen.

"Alas!" then sayd both Kyng and knyght,
That ever he shold wed such a wyght,
She was so fowll and horyble.
She had two teth on every* syde, either
As borys' tuskes, I woll nott hyde,
Of length a large handfull.

528 "For better or worse, betroth us together." 532 "I cannot wait any longer!"
549 "Just like boar's tusks, I won't deny it."

The one tusk went up, and the other doun;
A mowth full wyde, and fowll i-grown,
With grey herys* many on;* hairs; (many a) one
Her lyppes laye lumpryd* on her chyn; lumped
Nek forsoth on her was none i-seen, –
She was a lothly on!

She wold nott be weddyd in no maner,
Butt* there were made a krye* in alle the shyre, unless; proclamation
Both in town and in borowe.
Alle the ladyes nowe of the lond,
She lett kry to com to hand,
To kepe that brydalle thorowe.* complete

So itt befyll after on a daye,
That maryed shold be that fowll [maye]* maid
Unto Syr Gawen.
The daye was comyn the daye shold be,
Therof the ladyes had greatt pitey;
"Alas!" then gan* they sayn.* did; say

The Queen prayd Dame Ragnell sekerly/
To be maryed in the mornyng erly, *(fol. 136r)*
"As pryvaly* as we may." secretly/discreetly
"Nay," she sayd, "by Hevyn Kyng,
That woll I never for no thyng,
For ought* that ye can saye; anything

I wol be weddyd alle openly,
For with the Kyng suche covenaunt made I;
I putt you oute of dowte.
I woll nott to church tyll high masse tyme,
And in the open halle I woll dyne,
In myddys* of alle the rowte."* the midst; company

"I am greed,"* sayd Dame Gaynour, agreed
"Butt me wold thynk more honour,
And your worshypp moste . . ."
"Ye, as for that, lady, God you save,
This daye my worshypp woll I have,
I tell you withoute boste."

She made her* redy to church to fare,* herself; go
And alle the states* that there ware, people of every rank
Syrs, withoute lesyng.
She was arayd in the richest maner,
More fressher than Dame Gaynour:

564 **maye**: is inserted after fowll
569 **"dayes"** deleted after "prayd" and "Dame" inserted.

582–3 "But I was thinking it would be more honourable and better for you if . . ."

Her arayment was worth iii thousand mark
Of good red* nobles, styff* and stark,*   gold; strong; sturdy
    So rychely she was begon.*   adorned
For alle her rayment she bare the bell
Of fowlenesse that ever I hard tell,
    So fowll a sowe sawe never man!

For to make a shortt conclusion./
When she was weddyd, they hyed* theym home,   hurried *(fol.136v)*
    To mete* alle they went.   dinner
This fowll lady bygan the high dese,*   dais
She was full foull and nott curteys,
    So sayd they alle verament.*   truly

When the servyce cam her before,
She ete as moche as vi that ther wore,
    That mervaylyd many a man;
Her nayles were long ynches iii^{e},
Therwith she breke* her mete* ungoodly,*   broke; food; unseemly
    Therfore, she ete alone.

She ette iii^{e} capons and also curlues iii^{e},
And greatt bake metes she ete up, perde,*   to be sure
    Al[l] men therof had mervayll;
Ther was no mete cam her before
Butt she ete itt up, lesse and more,
    That praty fowll damesell!

    All men then that ever her sawe,
Bad the devill her bonys gnawe,
    Both knyght and squyre.
So she ete tyll mete was done,
Tyll they drewe clothes* and had wasshen,   cloths
    As is the gyse* and maner.*   custom; practice

Many men wold speke of diverse service,
I trowe ye may wete inowghe ther was,
    Both of tame and wylde;
In King Arthour's courte ther was no wontt,
That myght be gotten with mannys hond,
    Noder in forest ne in feld.

Ther were mynstralles of diverse contrey . . . /

[A leaf of the manuscript is missing at this point. The wedding festivities would have been described, and the retiring to bed of the newly married couple.]

592 **thousand**: m^{1}
612 **All men**: Almen

595–6 "Notwithstanding her finery she was the ugliest woman I heard tell of."
604 "When it was her turned to be served food."

"A, Syr Gawen, syn* I have you wed, *(fol. 137r)* since
Shewe me your cortesy in bed –
    With ryght itt may nott be denyed!

Iwyse,* Syr Gawen," that lady sayd, certainly
"And I were fayre ye wold do anoder brayd,
    Butt of wedlock ye take no hed.
Yett for Arthours sake, kysse me att the leste,
I pray you do this att my request:
    Lett se howe ye can spede!"* get on

Syr Gawen sayd, "I woll do more
Then for to kysse, and God before!"
    He turnyd hym her untill.
He sawe her the fayrest creature
That ever he sawe, withoute mesure.* any doubt
    She sayd, "Whatt is your wyll?"

"A, Ihesu!" [he] sayd, "whate ar ye?"
"Syr, I am your wyf, securly;
    Why ar ye so unkynde?"* unnaturally unkind
"A, lady, I am to blame;
I cry* you mercy,* my fayre madame – beg (of); my apologies
    Itt was nott in my mynde.

A, lady! Ye are fayre in my syght,
And today ye were the foulyst wyght
    That ever I sawe with myne [ie].* eye
Wele* is me, my lady, I have you thus"; happy
And brasyd* her in his armys, and gan her kysse, embraced
    And made greatt joye, sycurly.

"Syr," she sayd, "thus shall ye me have.
Chese of the one – so God me save,
    My beawty woll nott hold;* keep
Wheder ye woll have me fayre on* nyght[es] by
And as foull on days to alle men sightes,/

Or els to have me fayre on days, *(fol.137v)*
And on nyghtes on the fowlyst wyse.
    The one ye must nedes have;
Chese the one or the oder.
Chese on, Syr Knyght! Which you is lever,
    Your worshypp for to save?"

644 **he**: she
652 **ie**: ien
659 **nyghtes**: nyght

633 "If I were beautiful you would be behaving differently." 640 "He turned himself towards her." 649 "It was not my intention." 665–6 "Make your choice, Sir Knight! Which of the two (options) will you prefer, in order to save your honour?"

"Alas!" sayd Gawen, "the choyse is hard;
To chese the best itt is froward;*   difficult
Wheder* choyse that I chese,*   whichever; make
To have you fayre on nyghtes and no more,
That wold greve my hartt ryght sore,
And my worshypp shold I [lese].

And yf I desyre on days to have you fayre,
Then on nyghtes I shold have a symple* repayre.*   poor; reward
Now fayn wold I chose the best!
I ne wott in this world whatt I shall saye!
Butt do as ye lyst* nowe, my lady gaye,   prefer
The choyse I putt in your fyst.

Evyn* as ye woll,* I putt itt in your hand,   just; wish
Lose* me when ye lyst, for I am bond;*   release; bound
I putt the choyse in you;
Both body and goodes, hartt, and every dele,*   part
Ys alle your oun, for to by and sell –
That make I God avowe!"

"Garamercy,* corteys* knyght," sayd the lady,   thank you; courteous
"Of alle erthly knyghtes blyssyd mott* thou be,   may
For now am I worshyppyd;
Thou shall have me fayre both day and nyght,
And ever whyle I lyve as fayre and bryght;
Therfore be nott grevyd.*   dismayed/upset

For I was shapen by nygramancy,*   necromancy
With* my stepdame, God have on her mercy,   by
And by enchauntement,
And shold have bene oderwyse, understond,
Evyn tyll the best of Englond/
Had wedyd me, verament.*   truly *(fol.138r)*

And also he shold geve me the sovereynte
Of alle his body and goodes, sycurly,
Thus was I disformyd;*   deformed
And thou, Syr Knyght, curteys Gawen,
Has gevyn me the sovereynte serteyn,
That woll nott wroth the, erly ne late.

Kysse me, Syr Knyght, evyn now here,
I pray the, be glad, and make good chere,
For well is me begon!"

672 **lese**: lose

694–5 "And, understand, would have remained this way until the best knight in England . . ." 702 "And I will never anger you, at any time." 705 "For all has turned out well for me!"

Ther they made joye oute of mynde,
So was itt reason and cours of kynde,
They two theymself alone.

She thankyd God and Mary mylde
She was recovered of [that] she was defoylyd,* defiled
So dyd Syr Gawen;
He made myrth alle in her boure,
And thankyd of alle oure Savyoure,
I tell you, in certeyn.

With joye & myrth they wakyd* tyll daye, stayed awake
And than wold ryse that fayre [maye],
"Ye shall nott," Syr Gawen sayd,
"We woll lye & slepe tyll pryme,
And then lett the Kyng call us to dyne."
"I am greed,"* then sayd the mayd. agreed

Thus itt passyd forth tyll mid-daye.
"[Syrs]," quod the Kyng, "lett us go and asaye* find out
Yf Syr Gawen be on lyve.
I am full ferd* of* Syr Gawen, afraid; for
Nowe, lest the fende have hym slayn,
Nowe wold I fayn preve.* find out

Go we nowe," sayd Arthoure the Kyng.
"We woll go se theyr uprysyng,/
Howe well that he hath sped." *(fol.138v)*
They cam to the chambre, alle in certeyn:
"Aryse!" sayd the Kyng to Syr Gawen,
"Why slepyst thou so long in bed?"

"Mary," quod Gawen, "Syr Kyng, sicurly,
I wold be glad, and ye wold lett me be,
For I am full well att eas;
Abyde, ye shall se the dore undone,
I trowe that ye woll say I am well goon,
I am full loth to ryse!"

Syr Gawen rose, and in his hand he toke
His fayr lady, and to the dore he shoke,* went
And opynyd the dore full fayre;* elegantly
She stod in her smok all by [that syre],
Her [her] was to her knees as red as gold wyre,
"Lo! this is my repayre.* reward

710 **that**: that that
716 **maye**: mayd
722 **Syrs**: Syr
743 **her**: hed

707 "As was reasonable and quite natural."
737 "I think that you will agree that I have been fortunate." 742 "the fyre" deleted and "that fyre" succeeds. Most editions read this as "that syre," but either reading is possible.

Lo!" sayd Gawen Arthoure untill,*   unto
"Syr, this is my wyfe, Dame Ragnell,
That savyd onys* your lyfe."   once
He told the Kyng and the Queen hem beforn*   in front of them
Howe sodenly from her shap she dyd torne,*   transform
"My lord, nowe be youre leve."

And whate was the cause* she forshapen* was,   reason; changed
Syr Gawen told the Kyng both more and lesse.
"I thank God," sayd the Queen,
"I wenyd,* Syr Gawen, she wold the have myscaryed;*   thought; harmed
Therfore in my hartt I was sore agrevyd;
Butt the contrary is here seen."

Ther was game, revell* and playe,   revelry
And every man to other gan saye:
"She is a fayre wyght!
Than the Kyng them alle gan tell
How did [help] hym att nede Dame Ragnell,
"Or my dethe had bene dyght."*   the result

Ther the Kyng told the Queen, by the Rood,
Howe he was bestad* in Ingleswod/   beset
With* Syr Gromer Somer Joure;   by *(fol.139r)*
And whate othe the knyght made hym swere,
"Or elles he had slayn me ryght there,
Withoute mercy or mesure."

This same lady, Dame Ragnell,
From my deth she dyd help me ryght well,
Alle for the love of Gawen."
Then Gawen told the Kyng alle togeder
Howe forshapen she was with* her stepmoder,   by
Tyll* a knyght had holpen her agayn;   until

Ther she told the Kyng fayre and well
Howe Gawen gave her the sovereynte every dell,
And whate choyse she gave to hym;
"God thank hym of* his curtesye,   for
He savid me from chaunce* and vilony,*   misfortune; shame
That was full foull and grym.

Therfore, curteys knyght and hend* Gawen,   gracious
Shall I never wrath* the, serteyn,   anger
That promyse nowe here I make –
Whilles that I lyve I shal be obaysaunt,*   obedient
To God above I shall itt warraunt,*   swear
And never with you to debate."*   quarrel

761 **help**: held

"Garamercy, lady," then sayd Gawen,
"With you I hold me full well content,
And that I trust to fynde."
He sayd, "My love shall she have,
Therafter nede she never more crave,
For she hath bene to me so kynde."

The Queen sayd, and the ladyes alle,
"She is the fayrest nowe in this halle,
I swere by Seynt John!
My love, lady, ye shall have ever,
For that ye savid my lord Arthoure,
As I am a gentilwoman."

Syr Gawen gatt* on her Gyngolyn,/ begat
That was a good knyght of strength and kynn, *(fol.139v)*
And of the Table Round.
Att every greatt fest that lady shold be,
Of fayrenesse she bare away the bewtye,
Wher* she yed* on the ground. wherever; went

Gawen lovyd that lady Dame Ragnell,
In alle his lyfe he lovyd none so well,
I tell you withoute lesyng;* lie
As a coward he lay by her both day and nyght,
Never wold he haunt justyng aryght;
Theratt mervayled [Arthoure the Kyng].

She prayd the Kyng, for his gentilnes,
"To be good lord to Syr Gromer, iwysse,
Of that to you he hath offendyd."
"Yes, lady, that shall I nowe* for your sake, now do
For I wott well he may nott amendes make,
He dyd to me full unhend!"

Nowe for to make you a short conclusyon,
I cast* me for to make an end full sone intend
Of this gentyll lady.
She lyvyd with Syr Gawen butt yerys v.
That grevyd* Gawen alle his lyfe, distressed
I tell you, securly.

In her lyfe she grevyd hym never,
Therfor was never woman to hym lever,* more dear
Thus leves my talkyng;
She was the fayrest lady of ale Englond
When she was on lyve, I understand,
So sayd Arthoure the Kyng.

810 **MS** reads "Ther att mervayled Kyng Arthoure."

808–9 "He would lie by her, day and night, in a slothful way, not even attending to jousting." 816 "He treated me disgracefully!"

Thus endyth the adventure of Kyng Arthoure,
That oft in his days was grevyd sore,
And of the weddyng of Gawen.
Gawen was weddyd oft in his days,
Butt so well he never lovyd woman always,/
As I have hard men sayn. *(fol.140r)*

This adventure befell in Ingleswod,
As good Kyng Arthoure on huntyng yod,
Thus have I hard men tell.
Nowe God as thou were in Bethleme born,
Suffer never her* soules be forlorne* their; lost
In the brynnyng fyre of hell!

And Jhesu, as thou were borne of a virgyn,
Help hym oute of sorowe that this tale dyd devyne,* recount
And that nowe in alle hast.
For he is besett with gaylours many,
That kepen hym full sewerly,
With wyles* wrong and wraste.* wiles; powerful

Nowe God as thou art veray Kyng [royall],
Help hym oute of daunger that made this tale,
For therin he hath bene long;
And of* greatt pety help thy servaunt, out of
For body and soull I yeld into thyne hand,
For paynes he hath strong.

Here endyth "The Weddyng of
Syr Gawen and Dame Ragnell
For helpyng of Kyng Arthoure"

847 **royall**: ryoall

III

The Marriage of Sir Gawaine

(from London, British Library, MS Additional 27879 [c. 1650], pp. 46–52)

(p.46) Kinge Arthur lives in merry Carleile,
    & seemely is to see,
& there he hath with him [Queene] Genever,
    That bride* soe bright of blee.* — lady; fair of face

And there he hath with him Queene Geneve[r],
    That bride soe bright in bower,
& all his barons about him stoode
    That were both stiffe* & stowre.* — bold; strong

The King kept a royall Christmasse
    Of mirth & great honor,
[& when] . . . /

[Half a page is missing at this point. The missing text probably included Arthur's encounter with the bold baron at Tarn Wadling, the ultimatum whether to fight or pay a ransom, and the terms by which Arthur has to return to the baron.]

(p.47) "And bring me word what thing it is
    That a woman most desire.
This shalbe thy ransome, Arthur," he sayes,
    "for I'le have noe other hier."

King Arthur then held up his hand,
    According thene as was the law;
He tooke his leave of the baron there,
    & homeward can he draw.* — did he go

And when he came to merry Carlile,
    To his chamber he is gone,
& ther came to him his cozen* Sir Gawaine — kinsman
    As he did make his mone.* — complaint

And there came to him his cozen Sir Gawaine
    That was a curteous knight,
"Why sigh you soe sore, unckle Arthur," he said,
    "Or who hath done thee unright?"* — wrong

1 **Kinge Arthur**: MS Kinge Arthur in. final word is struck through
3 **Queene**: MS Qqueene
5 **Genever**: final letter presumed
11 **& when**: adopted from the Hales & Furnivall edition; hereafter H&F

"O peace, O peace, thou gentle Gawaine,
That faire may thee beffall,
For if thou knew my sighing soe deepe,
Thou wold not mervaile att all;

"For when I came to Tearne Wadling,
A bold barron there I fand,* found
With a great club upon his backe,
Standing stiffe & strong;

"And he asked me wether I wold fight,
Or from him I shold begone,
O[r] else I must him a ransome pay
& soe depart him from.

"To fight with him I saw noe cause,
Methought it was not meet,* appropriate
For he was stiffe & strong withall,
His strokes were* nothing sweete; would have been

"Therfor this is my ransome, Gawaine,
I ought to him to pay:
I must come againe,* as I am sworne, return
Upon the New Yeer's day.

["And I must bring him word what thing it is . . ."] /

[Half a page is missing at this point. The missing text probably included the decision by Arthur and Gawaine to search separately for answers to the riddle, and events building up to the deadline imposed by the baron.]

(p.48) Then King Arthur drest him* for to ryde got ready
In one soe rich array
Toward the fore-said Tearne Wadling,
That he might keepe his day.

And as he rode over a more,
He see a lady where shee sate
Betwixt an oke & a greene hollen:* holly bush/tree
She was cladd in red scarlett.

Then there as shold have stood her mouth
Then there was sett her eye,
The other was in her forhead fast
The way that she might see.

38 **Or else**: o else

29 "that good fortune will come your way"; 33 The line may have concluded originally rhyming with the words "me fang," i.e. "takes me prisoner," with "strang," i.e. "strong" concluding line 36. See also lines 85–7; 48 Text partly reconstructed from H&F; 50 in particularly splendid clothes; 57–9 "Where her mouth should have been was set an eye, while the other was in her forehead."

Her nose was crooked & turnd outward,
Her mouth stood foule a-wry;
A worse formed lady than she was
Never man saw with his eye!

To halch* upon him, King Arthur,   greet
This lady was full faine,*   inclined
But King Arthur had forgott his lesson,*   manners/courtesy
What he shold say againe.*   in return

"What knight art thou," the lady sayd,
"That will not speak to me?"
Of me be thou nothing dismayd
Tho' I be ugly to see;

"For I have halched you curteouslye,
& you will not me againe;
Yett I may happen, Sir Knight," shee said,
"To ease thee of thy paine."

"Give* thou ease* me, lady" he said,   if; assist
"Or helpe me any thing,*   in any way
Thou shalt have gentle Gawaine, my cozen,
& marry him with a ring."

"Why, if I help thee not, thou noble King Arthur,
Of thy owne heart's desiringe,
[Of gentle Gawaine . . . "] /

[Half a page is missing at this point. The missing text probably included Arthur agreeing to the hag's terms in order to save his life.]

(p.49) And when he came to the Tearne Wadling,
The baron there cold* he [finde],   did
With a great weapon on his backe,
Standing stiffe & stronge.

And then he tooke King Arthur's letters in his hand
& away he cold them fling,
& then he puld out a good browne* sword,   bright
& cryd* himselfe a king.   proclaimed

And he sayd, "I have thee & thy land, Arthur,
To doe as it pleaseth me,
For this is not thy ransome sure:
Therfore yeeld thee to me."

61 **outward**: The text seems originally to have read "toward," and a subsequent hand, probably Percy, corrected to the present reading.
85 **finde**: frinde

83 Text partly reconstructed from H&F. 94 "This is not according to the terms of our agreement."

And then bespoke him noble Arthur,
    & bad him hold his hand,
"& give me leave to speake my mind
    In defence of all my land."

He said "As I came over a more,
    I see a lady where shee sate
Betweene an oke & a green hollen;
    Shee was clad in red scarlett;

"And she says 'A woman will have her will,
    & this is all her cheef desire':
Doe me right, as thou art a baron of skill,
    This is thy ransome & all thy hyer."

He sayes, "An early vengeance light* on her!   befall
    She walkes on yonder more;
It was my sister that told thee this;
    & she is a misshappen hore!

"But heer I'le make mine avow to God
    To doe her an evill turne,
For an* ever I may thate fowle theefe get[t],   if
    In a fyer I will her burne!" /

[Half a page is missing at this point. The missing text probably included Arthur's return to Carlisle, and an account of his adventures and need to return with his knights to Tarn Wadling.]

[T]he 2nd Part

(p.50) Sir Lancelott & Sir Steven bold
    They rode with them that day,
And the formost of the company
    There rode the steward Kay.

Soe did Sir Banier & Sir Bore,
    Sir Garrett with them soe gay,
Soe did Sir Tristeram that gentle knight,
    To the forrest fresh & gay.

And when he came to the greene fforrest,
    Underneath a greene holly tree
Their sate that lady in red scarlet
    That unseemly was to see.

106 skill: sckill

106 "Do right by me, as you are a reasonable fellow." 114 Text partly reconstructed from H&F. The subsequent reference to "The 2nd Part" of the text is in the scribal hand, with the opening letter taken from H&F.

Sir Kay beheld this Lady's face
    & looked uppon her swire,*   neck
"Whosoever kisses this lady," he sayes,
    "Of his kisse he stands in feare!"

Sir Kay beheld the lady againe,
    & looked upon her snout,
"Whosoever kisses this lady," he saies,
    "Of his kisse he stands in doubt!"

"Peace, cozen Kay," then said Sir Gawaine,
    "Amend thee of thy life;*   change your ways
For there is a knight amongst us all
    That must marry her to his wife."

"What! Wedd her to wiffe?" then said Sir Kay,
    "In the divell's name anon!
Gett me a wiffe where e're I may,
    For I had rather be s[l]aine!"

Then some tooke up their hawkes in hast,
    & some tooke up their hounds,
& some sware they wold not marry her
    For citties nor for townes.

And then be-spake him noble King Arthur,
    & sware there "By this day,
"For a litle foule sight & misliking . . . " /

[Half a page is missing at this point. The missing text probably included Gawain's formal and public agreement to marry the hag, the return to Carlisle and the wedding ceremony and celebrations, and the subsequent retiring to bed of the married couple.]

(p.51) Then shee said "Choose thee, gentle Gawaine,
    Truth as I doe say,
Wether thou will have me in this liknesse
    In the night or else in the day."

And then bespake him gentle Gawaine,
    With* one soe mild of moode,   to
'Sayes, "Well I know what I wold say –
God grant it may be good!"*   the right thing to say

"To have thee fowle in the night
    When I with thee shold play;
Yet I had rather, if I might,
    Have thee fowle in the day."

143 **slaine**: shaine
147 **For citties nor for townes**: For citty nor for towne

"What! When lords goe with ther [f]eires,"* shee said, companions
"Both to the ale & wine?
Alas! Then I must hyde myselfe,
I must not goe withinne."* accompany you

And then bespake him gentle Gawaine,
'Said "Lady, that's but a skill;
And because thou art my owne lady,
Thou shalt have all thy will."

Then she said, "Blesed be thou gentle Gawain[e],
This day that I thee see;
For as thou see me att this time,
From henc[e]forth I wil be:

"My father was an old knight,
& yett it chanced soe
That he marryed a younge lady
That brought me to this woe.

"Shee witched me, being a faire young lad[y],
To the greene forrest to dwell;
& there I must walke in woman's liknesse,
Most like a feend of hell.

"She witched my brother to [a carlish] . . . /

[Half a page is missing at this point. The missing text probably included a complete explanation from Gawain's wife of the magic inflicted upon both her and her brother. Gawain then introduces her to the court.]

(p.52) "That looked soe foule, & that was wont
On the wild more to goe."

Come kisse her, brother Kay," then said Sir Gawaine,
"& amend the* of thy liffe; thee
I sweare this is the same lady
That I marryed to my wiffe!"

Sir Kay kissed that lady bright,* fair
Standing upon his ffeete;

163 **feires**: seires
174 **henceforth**: hencforth

168 "Lady, this was simply one line of reasoning that I was putting forward." 171 Text partly reconstructed from H&F. 179 Text partly reconstructed from H&F. 183 Again, with the incomplete state of the MS it is impossible to know what originally was written: "carlish" is the most plausible reading of this particular word, and the succeeding word could have begun with the letter "b." Hales and Furnivall recorded the enigmatic transcription "a Carlist B . . .," while Percy himself in the margin of the MS glossed the penultimate word as "churlish." "Carlish baron" is one possible reading. Percy's own imaginative reconstruction of the ballad, which he published in his *Reliques of Ancient English Poetry* in 1765, at this point has "She witched my brother to a carlish boore."

He swore, as he was trew knight,
The spice was never soe sweete.

"Well, cozen Gawaine," sayes Sir Kay,
"Thy chance is fallen arright;
For thou hast gotten one of the fairest maids
I ever saw with my sight."

"It is my fortune," said Sir Gawaine;
"For my unckle Arthur's sake
I am glad as grasse wold be of raine,
Great joy that I may take."

Sir Gawaine tooke the lady by the one arme,
Sir Kay tooke her by the tother,
They led her straight to King Arthur
As they were brother & brother.

King Arthur welcomed them there all,
& soe did Lady Genever, his Queene,
With all the knights of the Round Table
Most seemly to be seene.

King Arthur beheld that lady faire
That was soe faire & bright;
He thanked Christ in trinity
For Sir Gawaine, that gentle knight.

Soe did the knights, both more & lesse,
Rejoyced all that day
For the good chance that hapened was
To Sir Gawaine & his lady gay.

217 Taken from H&F. Cropping of the MS prevents unambiguous confirmation of this reading, but the reading from H&F is consistent with the text that survives.

The Summoner's Prologue and Tale

CHRISTINE RICHARDSON-HAY

The *Prologue* to *The Summoner's Tale* begins another round in the quarrel between the Summoner and the Friar, whose own tale about a summoner carried off to hell has just very effectively discredited not only this particular Canterbury summoner, but summoners in general. In the preamble to his tale, the Summoner is quick to draw an association between the devil and friars, suggesting thereby their rightful place in hell. His anecdote about a friar who is ravished to hell in a vision is blatantly provocative. Seeing no other friars there, the friar asks the angel who is acting as his guide if any friars ever come into hell. For an answer, the angel leads him to Satan, from whose "ers" swarm, as bees from a hive, "Twenty thousand freres on a route" (III, 1695).[1]

Visions of hell are, of course, common in medieval literature and Satan is often depicted as occupying the lowest place there (Dante, *Inferno*, 34.28ff). Chaucer's version of this motif in the Summoner's *Prologue* is distinguished by the image of Satan's "ers" and its location as a place of punishment for the miscreant and sinful, although this kind of story and this way of representing Satan did occur in the Middle Ages, "usually in vulgar jests or curses."[2] Without reference to friars, Chaucer uses the same motif in *The Romaunt of the Rose* to indicate how the sinful Wikked Tonge will be punished: "For thou shalt for this synne dwelle/ Right in the devels ers of helle" (7575–6).[3]

Similar portrayals of Satan appear in the art of the period. Francisco Traini's

[1] All quotations from Chaucer are from *The Riverside Chaucer*. For the imagery of the swarming bees, see *Troilus and Criseyde*, 2.193; 4.1356; *Roman de la Rose*, 8721–2. The abundance of friars in hell is also described in the poem "Against Friars." See Poem 140 in *The Oxford Book of Medieval English Verse*, ed. Celia and Kenneth Sisam (Oxford, 1970), p. 368, lines 93–6.

[2] F. N. Robinson, ed., *The Works of Geoffrey Chaucer*, 2nd edn (Boston: Houghton Mifflin, 1957), p. 706.

[3] D. S. Fansler regards the phrase "the devels ers of helle" as proverbial. See *Chaucer and the Roman de la Rose* (New York, 1914; rpt. Gloucester, MA: Peter Smith, 1965), pp. 164–5.

The Last Judgement, a fresco in the Camposanto of Pisa, which may have been seen by Chaucer during his travels in Italy in 1373, presents a powerful illustration of Satan's defecation of man the sinner.[4] Both Giotto's *Last Judgment* (c. 1306) at Padua and the *Last Judgment* of Giusto di Menabuoi in the parish church of Viboldone near Milan also depict a large Satan consuming and excreting sinners.[5] Moreover, the entrance to hell in medieval painting and drama was often a gaping mouth, and several other medieval Italian paintings depict a Satan who, "eating and defecating sinners, bears on his lower abdomen the features of a second face, of which his anus is the mouth."[6] Medieval manuscript illustration, in which sinners or those allied with the devil were sometimes depicted revering the buttocks of Satan or another devil, presumably would have complemented and enhanced this imagery.[7] It is obvious that the image of Satan in the Summoner's *Prologue* belongs to what J. F. Plummer calls "a deep and vigorous medieval tradition of scatological eschatology" (p. 7).

No literary source has ever been found for the Summoner's anecdote,[8] but it is generally regarded as a parody of a story about the Virgin Mary's care and protection of members of religious orders, which had apparently by Chaucer's day gained general currency.[9] The earliest example is attributed to the thirteenth-century Cistercian monk Caesarius of Heisterbach, in his *Dialogus Miraculorum* (VII, 59). In this version, a Cistercian monk who is carried up to heaven is unable to find any members of his own order, despite a large presence of the other orders. He weeps and expresses his disappointment to the Virgin, who opens her cloak to reveal a multitude of his brothers, declaring: "Those of the Cistercian Order are so dear to me and so beloved that I cherish them in my bosom."[10] This theme was quickly taken over by the mendicant orders, in particular the Dominicans, who adapted it to illustrate the life of St Dominic. In one

4 Robert A. Pratt reproduces this image in *The Tales of Canterbury* (Boston: Houghton Mifflin, 1974), p. 296. See also Theodore Spencer, "Chaucer's Hell: A Study in Medieval Convention," *Speculum* 2 (1927): 196–7.

5 See Spencer, *Ibid.*, p. 196, and Pratt, *Ibid.*, p. 295.

6 J. F. Plummer, ed., *The Summoner's Tale*, A Variorum Edition of the Works of Geoffrey Chaucer, Vol. II: The Canterbury Tales, Part VII (Norman, OK, and London: University of Oklahoma Press, 1995), p. 6. See also R. Hughes, *Heaven and Hell in Western Art* (New York: Stein and Day, 1968), p. 32 and R. Cavendish, *Visions of Heaven and Hell* (London: Orbis, 1977), p. 15.

7 See L. M. C. Randall, *Images in the Margins of Gothic Manuscripts* (Berkeley and Los Angeles: University of California Press, 1966), pp. 192–4 and Karl P. Wentersdorf, "The Symbolic Significance of *Figurae Scatologicae* in Gothic Manuscripts," in *Word, Spectacle and Picture*, ed. Clifford Davidson (Kalamazoo, MI: Medieval Institute Publications, 1984), pp. 1–19. Wentersdorf (p. 11) cites two references of the common insult "to kiss the devil's arse" from the Wakefield (Towneley) play of Abel (lines 266, 287), underscoring it with the practice of the *osculum infame* as revealed by witchcraft and heresy trials of the Middle Ages (and later). Both Beryl Rowland (*Blind Beasts: Chaucer's Animal World* [Kent, OH: Kent State University Press, 1971], p. 71) and R. E. Jungman (" 'Covent' in the *Summoner's Tale*," *Mississippi Folklore Register* 14 [1980]: 20–3) refer to accusations by the enemies of the friars of their connection to witchcraft.

8 John V. Fleming suggests "an echo of a tradition" in the Lollard exegesis of Isaiah 9:15: " '*Rome* is the verye Nest of Antichrist. And out of that Nest cometh all his Disciples. Of whom Prelates, Prestes, and Monkes are The Bodye, and these pylde Fryers are the Tayle which covereth his most fylthye Part.' " See "The Summoner's Prologue: An Iconographic Adjustment," *Chaucer Review* 2 (1967): 95 n. 2.

9 First noted by J. S. P. Tatlock, "Notes on Chaucer: The Canterbury Tales," *Modern Language Notes* 29 (1914): 143.

10 *The Dialogue on Miracles*, trans. H. Von E. Scott and C. C. Swinton Bland (London, 1929), I, 546; quoted by Fleming, pp. 95–6.

version, the saint weeps when he is unable to find any members of his order in heaven. Christ himself intervenes to give Dominic the reassurance he seeks, saying, "I have entrusted your Order to my Mother," and beneath Mary's cloak, Dominic "saw a huge multitude of the Brothers of his Order, embraced by the safe-keeping of an unparalleled protection, and in the arms of an incomparable love."[11]

Inevitably, this theme was popular with the Carmelites, who had always regarded themselves as Mary's Men and their Order as *totus marianus*. In their iconography the Virgin is often dressed in the Carmelite habit, which she spreads over a group of friars kneeling before her.[12] In addition, this theme has parallels in the Marian painting tradition of the *Maria Misericordia* (the Virgin of Mercy), where the Virgin Mary is depicted protecting her devotees by shielding them in heaven under her cloak. This image of the Virgin of Mercy was, appropriately, often the device on the confraternal seals used to authenticate what were known as letters of fraternity (cf. III, 2128). These were issued by friars to laypeople who, as part of their penance for their sins, would donate or make a bequest of money to the friars in their wills.[13] That Caesarius's story was known by critics of the mendicant orders is evident from a reference in *Pierce the Ploughman's Crede* (c. 1394). In this Wyclifite attack on the friars, the motif of the Virgin's protection accords with the cynicism of the Summoner, Pierce having been told that if he donates money to the Franciscans, "seynt Fraunces his-self schall folden the in his cope,/ And presente the to the trynitie and praie for thy synnes" (126–7).[14]

The Summoner's Tale is an unabashed and scurrilous example of Chaucer's fabliau art. Its central incident (2121–64), the "satiric legacy," is based on a theme as ancient as the biblical story of Jacob and Esau and one which is widespread in both popular and literary traditions.[15] In stories of this kind, a sick or dying person manages, usually without difficulty, to convince greedy and hypocritical attendants (relatives, visitors, or self-serving clerics) of the value and desirability of a worthless object, which would then, as the person's death approached, be promised or bequeathed to them. The humor of these stories lay in the deception the dying person practised upon his heirs and in their reaction to the bequest, which, if disagreeable, could be totally objectionable. In

[11] *Acta Sanctorum* (Paris edn) August, vol. 1, p. 580 (my translation). This version is quoted by Fleming (p. 97), who notes that a variant of this story "was widely circulated" in the *Vitae Fratrum*, a sourcebook of exempla used by the Dominicans. A number of other Dominican versions are listed by André Duval, "La Dévotion mariale dans l'Ordre des Frères Prècheurs," in *Maria, Études sur la Sainte Vierge* (Paris, 1952), II, 739n.

[12] Cécile Edmond, *L'Iconographie Carmélitaine dans les anciens Pays-Bas méridianaux* (Brussels, 1961), vol. 1, p. 107.

[13] See Fleming, "An Iconographic Adjustment," pp. 100–1. R. W. Hanning agrees that the Summoner's *Prologue* can be read as a parody of the *Maria Misericordia*. See "Roasting a Friar, Mis-Taking a Wife and Other Acts of Textual Harassment in Chaucer's *Canterbury Tales*," *Studies in the Age of Chaucer* 7 (1985): 14.

[14] Ed. W. W. Skeat, EETS OS 30 (London: Trübner, 1873).

[15] *The Literary Context of Chaucer's Fabliaux*, ed. Theodore M. Andersson and Larry D. Benson (Indianapolis, IN, and New York, 1971), pp. 339–40. For examples from the ballad tradition, see F. J. Child, *English and Popular Ballads* (Cambridge, 1882–98), vol. 1, pp. 143–4. Note also R. J. Pearcy, "Structural Models for the Fabliaux and the Summoner's Tale Analogues," *Fabula* 15 (1974): 103–13.

Chaucer's tale, the sick but angry and frustrated Thomas convinces the unctuous and ever persistent Friar John to "grope" his nether parts in expectation of a generous reward. Rather than any prize, however, the "wind" of the wheedling Friar's sermonizing is aptly paid in kind with a magnificent fart. Not allowing the friar to lose even this, the tale ends with an ingenious solution which actually allows him to gain his rightful share of the fart.

The Summoner's Tale has no definite source. The closest known analogue is the French fabliau, *Li Dis de le vescie à Prestre* ("The Tale of the Priest's Bladder"), written in the early fourteenth century by Jacques de Basieux.[16] It tells of a wealthy and clever priest living near Antwerp who becomes terminally ill and, wishing to make a good end, bequeathes all his possessions, even the sheets on his bed, to his friends and colleagues, naming each one and having his plan officially notarized. When two Jacobin (Dominican) friars arrive at his house, they refuse to believe nothing remains and try to persuade him to bequeath some of his wealth to their convent, even if it means revoking some of the gifts he has already made. Angered, but retaining his self-control, the priest decides to avenge himself by promising them a jewel of inestimable value which he says he still has in his possession. Having asked them to come back the next day with their prior, the friars, in high expectation, return as requested with others from their convent, although not the prior. With these friars, the mayor and town councillors in attendance, the wily priest makes his bequest which, he carefully stipulates, the friars cannot have until he has died. He says he has never given this object into the keeping of anyone else and loves it like his life. In response to the friars' eager request to know what it is, he bequeathes them his bladder, telling them good humoredly that when cleaned it is better than leather and will serve them well to hold their pepper. Humiliated and rebuked before all the townsfolk, the friars return home.

Li Dis was probably based on one of the common jests of the time told at the expense of the mendicant friars. There is some similarity between it and *The Summoner's Tale*, but "few exact resemblances"[17] and some important differences. Unlike the priest's bladder, Thomas's gift is not a legacy, but the proposed donation (immediately enacted) of a man who still lives (2129–30). Nor is there any correspondence between the priest's delighted announcement about the jewel he still owns and Thomas's trick to get the friar to physically "grope" him for his reward. Then, unlike the conclusion of the French tale in which the friars return home chastened, Friar John, in search of a meal, goes to the house of the lord of the village. Complaining of the insult he has received, his grievance then provides the opportunity for initiating the final and similarly debased episode of the squire's solution. W. M. Hart suggested that had Chaucer known this fabliau while composing *The Summoner's Tale*, he would surely have developed further the ironic possibilities, both in speech and situation, offered by the character of the priest, just as he had developed similar material in *The Friar's Tale*. Granting some thematic similarities, the two tales are clearly

[16] Text and translation of the tale are included at the end of the chapter.

[17] Benson and Andersson, p. 340.

distinct narratives which represent the separate workings of two different imaginations.[18]

Two other stories have been mentioned as possible analogues to *The Summoner's Tale*. One is an anecdote about a bequest made by Jean de Meun to the Jacobin friars in Paris. Having received their guarantee that he would be buried in their church, Jean is supposed to have bequeathed them a heavy chest which he orders not to be opened until after his death, when it is discovered to be filled with lead. The other is a tale from *Til Eulenspiegel*, "How Howleglas Deceived his Ghostly Father," in which a greedy priest convinces the sick Howleglas that he should donate the money he has acquired by a sinful life to the priest. He promises in return to sing Masses for him after his death. Howleglas agrees and asks him to come back the next day, preparing in the meantime an earthenware pot by filling it halfway with turds and placing a little money on the top to conceal them. On the following day when the priest pulls his hand covered with excrement from the pot, he condemns Howleglas's deception as a trick against God and religion. Howleglas merely comments blithely that it is the priest's own greed that is the real evil here. Cursing him, the priest departs and does not return when Howleglas calls after him to remind him of the money he has left behind.[19] Despite the theme of the "satiric legacy," there are no verbal parallels or close similarities in terms of character, plot or literary intention between these tales and *The Summoner's Tale*.[20]

Apart from the literary analogues to *The Summoner's Tale*, what is also central to the tale's main frame of reference is the controversy that arose during the early Middle Ages over the evolution and growth of the friars and their mendicant orders. Early on, the friars had been called "pseudoapostoli," either in the sense of figures like the Pharisees who merely feigned to be Apostles, or as eschatological figures, the so-called "new apostles" of the last age of the world – a reference to the apocalyptic theories of Joachim, Abbot of Fiore (1132–1202), which were widely propagated in the mid thirteenth century. The Franciscans in particular represented themselves as the new apostles at the end of time, using the text of 2 Timothy 3:1 to support their claim ("Know also this, that in the last days, shall come dangerous times"). Out of this there grew a general tradition of antifraternalism, so that by the second half of the fourteenth century, antifraternal criticism had become an established commonplace, ranging in genre from learned polemical treatises and sermons, to poems, popular songs, and satire.

Chaucer makes free and independent use of it in *The Summoner's Tale*, incorporating it into his narrative with an almost seamless quality. He clothes the character, the speech and action of the Friar with those features which had

18 "The Summoner's Tale," in Bryan and Dempster, pp. 276–7. Hart finds a dozen "resemblances or similarities, in thought if not in phrasing" (p. 277 and note 2).

19 Benson and Andersson mention the anecdote about Jean de Meun (pp. 339–40) and provide an English translation of the tale of Howleglas (pp. 360–1).

20 Pearcy (p. 105) remarks how these similarities "have been allowed to conceal some fundamental differences between the tales. Analysis of deep structure will demonstrate that both *Li Dis de le vescie à prestre* and 'How Howleglas Deceived his Ghostly Father' are essentially as close to other tales not belonging to the satiric legacy type as they are to the *Summoner's Tale*."

become a part of the rhetorical stock-in-trade of the antifraternalists' polemic, even the biblical verses they cited. For example, alluding directly to Matthew 4:19 ("And he saith unto them, Follow me, and I will make you fishers of men" [cf. Luke 5:10]), the Friar boasts "I walke and fisshe Cristen mennes soules/ To yelden Jhesu Crist his propre rente" (1820–1). This was a traditional reference that had been used as far back as 1247 by Matthew Paris, one of the friars' first critics (cf. *The Romaunt of the Rose*, 7490–1). He termed them "no longer fishers of men, but fishers for coins" (*Chronica Majora*, IV, 635; cf. Rutebeuf, *Des Jacobins*, 33–6).[21]

A major issue that evoked hostility against the friars was the right of mendicants to hear confessions (III, 1815–18; 2093)[22] and preach (III, 1711–34; 1788–92; 1818; 2281–2). The secular clergy regarded the friars as interfering in matters which were rightly the province of the parish priest, but more importantly the friars' actions also deprived the clergy of their accustomed dues. These are activities which Friar John carries out energetically (cf. I, 215–24; *The Romaunt of the Rose*, 6364–70), motivated (in accordance with the antifraternalists), less by a concern for the souls of his audience or their penance and absolution, than his own material interests ("Whan folk in chirche had yeve him what hem leste," 1735 cf. 1754–6). Not only, it was said, did a friar steal a person's material goods, but he lost that person's soul and condemned him to damnation as well. Certainly, any assurance the audience of Friar John has about their own spiritual safety is a delusion. Although the Friar's companion wrote down the names of all the people who gave him something, "Ascaunces that he wolde for hem preye" (1745), he has only to be out of sight to have already erased their names. Chaucer concludes that the Friar served his congregation "with nyfles and with fables" (1760).

In contradiction to such claims, the friars themselves professed their ability (the result of their religious knowledge and insight) to probe and illustrate with more spiritual consequence the literal surface of the Bible. The friars' justification for this "spiritual" interpretation of scripture was 2 Corinthians 3:6 ("the letter killeth, but the spirit quickeneth"), and after a successful day's preaching, Friar John himself makes allusion to this ("Glosynge is a glorious thyng, certeyn,/ For lettre sleeth, so as we clerkes seyn" [1793–4 cf. 1918–23; *Piers Plowman*, B. XIII. 73–4]). Letters of fraternity ("letters of bretherhed") were another advantage offered by the friars to their congregation. In *The Summoner's Tale*, Thomas is one of these favoured brothers (2126–8) and, in keeping with antifraternal cynicism which pointed to benefaction rather than religious virtue

[21] These references are noted by N. Havely, "Chaucer, Boccaccio and the Friars," in *Chaucer and the Italian Trecento*, ed. P. Boitani (Cambridge, 1983), p. 251. The lord's pronouncement to the Friar "Ye been the salt of the erthe and the savour" (2196), a reference to Matt. 5:13 (cf. Luke 14:34–5) and a description by Christ of his disciples, is a similar use of antifraternal terminology (cf. Richard de Bury, *Philobiblon*, chapter 6, ed. E. C. Thomas, *The Love of Books: The Philobiblon of Richard de Bury* (London, 1888; rpt. New York: Cooper Square Publishers, 1966), p. 38.

[22] In "Anticlerical Satire as Theological Essay: Chaucer's Summoner's Tale," *Thalia: Studies in Literary Humor* 6 (1983): 15, J. V. Fleming notes how Thomas's reply to the Friar, who has called on him to make a confession (2094–8), would seem to derive from a "spurious" passage which survives in Fragment C of *The Romaunt of the Rose* (6390–400). See also Ronald Sutherland, ed., *The Romaunt of the Rose and Le Roman de la Rose* (Oxford: B. Blackwell, 1967), p. xxxiii.

as the factor which decided the granting of these, Thomas has donated generously to the friars over the years (1949–53). Acting as a critic within the tale itself, Thomas is not actually convinced by the special favour of this brotherhood (2094–8), although it was to this piece of paper rather than to their own effort that people often looked for spiritual assurance.

Always fundamental to the overall criticism of the friars was St Francis's founding of the friars' orders and their way of life upon begging and the principle of "evangelical poverty." Having been inspired by Luke 10:1–12 (Christ's instructions to the apostles before sending them out to preach the Gospel),[23] St Francis decreed a life of austerity, discipline and self-control ("And having food and raiment let us be therewith content," 1 Tim. 6:8).[24] Thus St Francis and his early followers claimed to own nothing, dressed as well as poor men could, slept wherever was available and ate whatever was provided for them. The possession of money was forbidden and the friars were admonished for even touching it. It is this apostolic life that Friar John repeatedly claims he and his brothers have restored. Following the example of Jesus, the friars "Been wedded to poverte and continence,/ To charite, humblesse, and abstinence,/ . . . To wepynge, misericorde, and clennesse." (1907–8, 1910, cf. 1873; 1876; 1881–4; 1935–7).

Inevitably, the friars' contraventions of their strict life-style led to accusations of their wealth, a situation complemented by their apparent greed and avarice. It is without any sense of scruple that Faus-Semblant boasts, "We always pretend to be poor, but no matter how we complain, we are the ones, let me tell you, who have everything without having anything" (*Roman de la Rose*, 11675).[25] In particular, the friars' claims of humility and poverty were sorely tried by the reputed splendour of their clothing, their diet and by their extensive libraries and the size and grandeur of their convents ("alas! a threefold care of superfluities, viz., of the stomach, of dress, and of houses").[26]

In *The Summoner's Tale*, Chaucer thrusts at the friars with a double-edged sword as he brings together references both to the size of the new convent the Friar is proposing (1718; 1974–80), and the extent of the present convent's library (2099–2108). And, while the Friar, who is well equipped (1736–7; 1740 cf. Mark 6:8), goes busily "hous by hous" (1765), his decision to stop at Thomas's house is only decided by the superiority of its hospitality ("an hous ther he was wont to be/ Refresshed moore than in an hundred placis," 1766–7). In doing this, the Friar is also flouting one of the most fundamental of St Francis's precepts ("And in the same house remain, eating and drinking such things as they give: for the labourer is worthy of his hire. Go not from house to house," Luke 10:7, cf. Matthew 10:9–11; 1 Tim. 5:18). Slyly, Chaucer allows this Friar who so blatantly seeks anything he can get from everyone he visits (1738–9; 1746–53) to openly quote this verse back to Thomas: "The hye God

23 Cf. Matt. 10:5–15; Mark 6:7–13; Luke 9:3–5.

24 See *François d'Assise Écrits*, ed. Théophile Desbonnets, *et al.* (Paris: Les Éditions du Cerf, 1981), pp. 182–4, and "The Rule of Saint Francis of Assisi," *Readings in Medieval History*, ed. P. J. Geary (Ontario, Canada: Broadview Press Ltd., 1989), pp. 486–93.

25 C. Dahlberg, trans., *The Romance of the Rose* (Princeton: Princeton University Press, 1971), p. 204.

26 Richard de Bury, *Philobiblon*, chapter 6, p. 40.

. . . / Seith that the werkman worthy is his hyre" (1972–3). It is almost farcical therefore, coming as it also does after his ordering of a large meal (1836–42), that Friar John announces with so much self-congratulation and a reference to 1 Cor. 6:13: "My spirit hath his fostryng in the Bible./ The body is ay so redy and penyble/ To wake, that my stomak is destroyed." (1845–7). Describing himself as a man "of litel sustenaunce" (1844), who is satisfied merely with "hoomly suffisaunce" (1843), ironical allusions to Matthew 4:4 and 1 Tim. 6:8 (cf. Job 23:12), the Friar goes on to compare himself to Moses, Elijah and Aaron (1885ff), his hypocrisy even extending to a couple of brief attacks on gluttony (1916, 1927).[27] Plainly it is in the historical environment of the tale, that is, the basic principles and activity of the fraternal movement, that some of the fundamental sources of *The Summoner's Tale* are to be found. This is Chaucer's response to a contemporary social attitude.

No literary source has been found for the concluding incident of Jankyn's solution to the problem of "ars-metrike" (2222).[28] Yet it is possible that Chaucer, who compares Jankyn's knowledge to the great classical scientists, Euclid or Ptolemy (2289), may have been indebted to medieval scientific theory regarding the action or movement of "soun" and "savour" as found in Albertus Magnus's *Liber de sensu et sensato.*[29] Albertus's theory illustrates how a number of people are able to see, hear and smell the same thing simultaneously ("hoc modo idem simul multi vident et audiunt et odorant"). Chaucer probably had access to Albertus's theory through its reproduction in the *Parva naturalia*, which he also appears to have used for the *Nun's Priest's Tale*.

At the same time, it is in this final section of the tale that the association the friars make between themselves and the first Apostles takes on a special significance. In imitation of the twelve apostles and Christ, the friars had established their orders in houses of thirteen ("For thrittene is a covent, as I gesse," 2259) and it becomes the Friar's problem to divide the fart he has been granted equally between himself and the other members of his convent (2131–4). The solution the lord's squire proposes, that would re-enact the gift of the fart by sitting Friar John at the hub of a cartwheel, "his nose upright under the nave" (2266) and each of the twelve other friars at the end of one of the wheel's twelve spokes

27 While discussing the pomp and gluttony of monks with Thomas, Friar John compares them at line 1929 to Jovinian, the fourth-century heretical monk who provoked St Jerome's *Epistola adversus Jovinianum.* It appears that this work may be the source for the biblical *exempla* of Lazarus and Dives, Elijah, Aaron and the expulsion of man from Paradise which occur in the tale. See F. Tupper, "Chaucer's Bed's Head," *Modern Language Notes* 30 (1915): 8–9, and E. Koeppel, "Chauceriana," *Anglia* 13 (1891): 174–86.

28 R. F. Green notes how the division of the fart has "a very precise literary (or rather quasi-literary) parallel . . . in a courtly collection of riddles and verbal games preserved in a manuscript from northern France of 1470 (Chantilly, Musée Condé MS 654)" in "A Possible Source for Chaucer's Summoner's Tale," *English Language Notes* 24 (1987): 25. One of the riddles actually asks how a fart can be divided into twelve parts, the answer (in translation) reading: "Make the fart in the middle of a wheel, with twelve people, each with his nose in the twelve holes, so that each shall thus get his share." Green is aware that this riddle may in fact have *The Summoner's Tale* as its source. He also suggests that a much earlier version of this type of riddle may have inspired the question in *The Summoner's Tale*.

29 Robert A. Pratt, "Albertus Magnus and the Problem of Sound and Odor in the Summoner's Tale," *Philological Quarterly* 57 (1978): 267–8.

(2243–85), has been discovered to be an ingenious reversal of the descent of the Holy Spirit at Pentecost.[30]

The scriptural basis of this is Acts 2:1–13 which described Pentecost as the time when, according to the promise of Christ, the Holy Spirit would appear to the Apostles, gathered together in one place. It was this event that established Christ's Church on earth, as the Apostles, filled with the Holy Spirit's "gift of tongues," then went forth to spread Christ's word throughout the world.[31] Medieval iconographic representations of the descent of the Holy Spirit upon the Apostles either depict the Apostles in a circular grouping like a wheel, or use a wheel-image for its illustration.[32] Rays for example often emanate from a centre point, such as a dove, to each of the apostles.[33] The suggested division of the fart into twelve through the spokes of a wagon wheel in *The Summoner's Tale* is "a highly sophisticated and formally perfect thrust at the inversion of the Holy Spirit among the corrupt friars."[34]

Equally, it is with pointed reference to the "fruits" of the Pentecostal Feast (Numbers 28:26–31; Leviticus 23:15–22), a feast of thanksgiving at the end of the grain harvest (fifty days after Passover), and commonly associated with the "primitiae" or "first fruits" of the harvest, that the squire predicts that it is Friar John who will receive "the firste fruyt" (2277) of Thomas's benefaction.[35] Offerings were made to the Lord throughout the feast, which were to be of "sweet savour" (Leviticus 23:18; Numbers 28:24), a blatant antithesis to the "savour" of the fart (2226, cf. 2196) in *The Summoner's Tale*. The Holy Spirit, who traditionally appeared and entered like a "mighty wind" (Acts 2:2), becomes in *The Summoner's Tale* a windy blast from the anus of an angry man,

30 The pioneering studies of this argument are by B. S. Levy, "Biblical Parody in the *Summoner's Tale*," *Tennessee Studies in Literature* 11 (1966): 45–60; A. Levitan, "The Parody of Pentecost in Chaucer's Summoner's Tale," *University of Toronto Quarterly* 40 (1971): 236–46, and Penn R. Szittya, "The Friar as False Apostle: Antifraternal Exegesis and the *Summoner's Tale*," *Studies in Philology* 71 (1974): 23. See also V. A. Kolve, "Chaucer's Wheel of False Religion: Theology and Obscenity in the *Summoner's Tale*," in *The Centre and its Compass: Studies in Medieval Literature in Honor of Professor John Leyerle*, ed. Robert A. Taylor, et al. (Kalamazoo, MI: Medieval Institute Publications, 1993), pp. 265–96.

31 Friar John's long-windedness, his "glosyng," his hypocritical preaching for gain and pretentious affectation are therefore a part of this Pentecostal parody. These actions demonstrate his misuse of his gift of tongues.

32 For the association between friars and wheels (e.g. Dante's *Paradiso*, cantos 10–12), see Levitan, pp. 241–4, and Szittya, p. 29.

33 Levitan provides illustrations which date from the early twelfth century to the late fourteenth, pp. 242–5. K. P. Wentersdorf suggests that "the notion of the cartwheel came to Chaucer from the medieval concept of the twelve winds of heaven, sometimes depicted iconographically as a cartwheel, with each wind depicted as a face blowing along one of the spokes towards the hub." See "The Motif of Exorcism in the Summoner's Tale," *Studies in Short Fiction* 17 (1980): 254. He refers to a wheel-shaped wind-circle in a twelfth-century English manuscript of Bede's *De natura rerum* which is reproduced by Donald Howard, *The Idea of the Canterbury Tales* (Berkeley: University of California Press, 1976), p. 204, fig. 11.

34 Levitan, p. 244.

35 Fleming comments how the humour of the Pentecostal parody "requires the correlation of the image with that of the Maria Misericordia in the tale's prologue. The number of the Apostles at Pentecost was twelve (Acts I. 26), but 'thrittene is a covent, as I gesse,' with Fr John, its most 'worthy' member, at its centre. Likewise in the Gothic iconography of Pentecost there is also a thirteenth and most worthy member around whom the twelve apostles are reverently gathered. The thirteenth 'apostle' is the Virgin Mary, the vessel of mercy . . . Thus the tale ends as it began, with a jarring iconographic burlesque." See "Anticlerical Satire as Theological Essay," pp. 18–19.

contradicting all he should represent. There may even be a significance in the designation of Thomas's benefaction as a "yifte" (2146). The Holy Spirit was traditionally regarded as "donum Dei" ("the gift of God," Acts 2:38).[36]

In contrast to much of the rest of the tale, the three *exempla* which Friar John uses in his preaching to Thomas to demonstrate the sinfulness and danger of anger (2005–10) have a recognised source. Chaucer specifically attributes the first *exemplum* to Seneca (2018), but all three, which concern Piso, Cyrus and Cambyses can be found in Seneca's treatise *De Ira* (1.18.3–6; 3.14.1–6; 3.21.1–3). It seems inevitable in a tale that has anger as one of its major themes that Chaucer should turn to a treatise so wholly concerned with examining the morality of this sin. Yet, despite Chaucer's reference to Seneca, his source may not have actually been the *De Ira*, but a medieval compilation by the thirteenth century Franciscan theologian John of Wales. He taught at Oxford and Paris and was the author of a number of works which, drawing upon various classical and medieval writings, were used as manuals for preachers, or handbooks for general moral edification. The longest and most popular of these was the *Communiloquium sive summa collationum*. Robert A. Pratt has argued that similarities in narrative detail and the order in which the three *exempla* appear in *The Summoner's Tale* and the *Communiloquium* reveal that "Chaucer's retelling of each anecdote is closer to John of Wales' redaction than to the original story as told by Seneca."[37] In the *exemplum* about Piso, for example, Pratt points out how Seneca mentions Piso by name, whereas he is nameless in both John of Wales and Chaucer. Seneca's Piso orders the soldier who has returned without his comrade to be immediately executed, whereas in John of Wales another soldier, and in Chaucer another knight, leads him off to a place of execution. Then, while the centurion in *De Ira* leads the condemned man back to Piso, the centurion in John of Wales and in Chaucer leads both the condemned man and his returned comrade back to the judge. Furthermore, as the men are condemned, they are numbered (i.e. "Dixitque primo . . . Secundo dixit . . . Tertio dixit") in both the *Communiloquium* and Chaucer's tale, a specification Seneca does not make. Finally, John of Wales has combined the two stories of Cambyses and Cyrus, separated by seven chapters in the *De Ira*.[38] It has therefore been decided to print John of Wales' versions of these *exempla* instead of Seneca's.

[36] See Szittya, p. 27. He further recognizes the Friar's earlier association of himself with Moses and Elijah (1885–93) as another anticipation of "the pseudo-Pentecost of the final scene" (p. 26). Elijah was recognized as a "Pentecostal figure" (i.e. 1 Kings 19:11–12), as was Moses, who received the Law at Sinai on the fiftieth day after Passover, the time of the Pentecostal Feast. Cf. I. Lancashire, "Moses, Elijah and the Back Parts of God: Satiric Scatology in Chaucer's *Summoner's Tale*," *Mosaic* 14 (1981): 17–30 (especially, 18ff).

[37] Robert A. Pratt, "Chaucer and the Hand that Fed Him," *Speculum* 41 (1966): 627.

[38] Pratt, "Chaucer and the Hand that Fed Him," pp. 627–8. The further difference asserted by Pratt (p. 628) that it is a personified Anger who condemns the three men in *De Ira* and not Piso (as in John of Wales and Chaucer) is erroneous. Pratt appears to have mistaken Seneca's exclamatory comment on anger ("O quam sollers est iracundia ad fingendas causas furoris," *De Ira,* 1.18.6) as a personification of Anger which then becomes the subject of *De Ira*'s following use of "inquit" (i.e. "Te," inquit, "duci iubeo, quia damnatus es"). The subject of Seneca's "inquit" is, in fact, Piso.

I

John of Wales, *Communiloquium sive summa collationum*, I.iv.4

(reprinted from text cited by R. A. Pratt in *Speculum* 41 [1966]: 628; my translation)

Unde narrat Seneca . . . de quodam iudice tyrannico, qui ex ira damnavit tres innocentes milites, unum quia redierat de via sine suo socio, imponens ei quod illum interfecisset, precepitque alteri militi ut eum duceret ad locum supplicii. Qui cum esset eductus venit commilito socius sanus, quem videns centurio cui fuerat preceptum alium occidere, reduxit ambos ad iudicem. Quos cum vidit tyrannus iratus est. Dixitque primo: Te iubeo interfici, quia damnatus. Secundo dixit: Et te similiter, quia causa damnationis commilitoni fuisti. Tertio dixit: Et te iubeo occidi, quia iussus occidere, imperatori non paruisti. Unde Seneca ibi: O quam sollers est iracundia ad fingendas causas furoris: tres hi puniti sunt ob unius innocentiam. Excogitavit iste quemadmodum tria faceret crimina cum nullum inveniret.

[Whereby Seneca tells . . . about a certain tyrannical judge who, because of his anger condemned three innocent soldiers, one, because he had returned from his journey without his companion, accusing him that he had killed him. He ordered a second soldier to take him to a place of execution. When he had been taken there, the fellow-soldier, his companion arrived there, safe and well. Seeing him, the centurion who had been ordered to kill the other soldier, led both back to the judge. When the tyrant saw them he became angry. And to the first, he said: I order you to be killed, because you were condemned. To the second, he said: And you similarly, because you were the cause of your fellow-soldier's condemnation. To the third he said: And I order you to be killed, because having been ordered to kill, you did not obey your commander. Whence Seneca says here: O how clever is anger in devising reasons for its mad fury: these three were punished because of the innocence of one of them. It contrived that three crimes be committed because it had discovered none.]

II

John of Wales, *Communiloquium sive summa collationum*, I.iii.11

(reprinted from text cited by R. A. Pratt in *Speculum* 41 [1966]: 630; my translation)

Similiter [Seneca] narrat de rege cambise quem cum nimis deditum vino unus ex carissimis monebat ut parcius biberet, turpem esse dicens in rege ebrietatem quem oculi omnium auresque sequerentur. Respondit ille, ut scias oculos post vinum esse in officio et manus approbabo. Deinde bibit liberalius quam ante et iubet filium illius stare ex opposito et intendens arcum cor adolescentis transfixit, et respiciens patrem interrogavit si satis certam haberet manum. At ille negavit apollinem potuisse se certius dimittere. O cruentum regem! O dignum ira dei! Similiter narrat ibidem de tyto[39] qui cum versus babiloniam festinaret ad bellum nec posset transire amnem gisen et esset ibi unus equus regius submersus, ira commotus iuravit seipsum amnem divisurum ut etiam non transiri sed calcari a feminis posset, quem postea divisit in .ccclx. rivulos.

[Similarly Seneca tells of King Cambyses who, since he was too much addicted to wine, one of his dearest friends warned that he should drink more sparingly, saying that drunkenness in a king, whom the eyes and ears of everyone follow, is a shameful thing. The former answered, "In order that you may know that (even) after drinking wine, my eyes and hands perform their duty, I will prove it to you." Then he drinks more liberally than previously, and orders the son of his friend to stand before him, and drawing his bow, he pierced the heart of the youth. And looking again at the father, he asked if his hand was steady enough. And he said that Apollo could not have shot more surely. O cruel king! O [king] worthy of God's anger! Likewise, in the same place, Seneca tells of Cyrus who, when hastening to war against the Babylonians, was unable to cross the river Gyndes. And when one of the horses of the king was drowned there, he, roused by anger, swore that he would divide the whole river so that women could not only cross it, but could trample it under foot. After that, he divided the river into three hundred and sixty streams.]

The likelihood of Chaucer's use of the *Communiloquium* is strengthened by his inclusion of a verse from the Book of Proverbs (22:24–5) immediately following the retelling of these tales: "Ne be no felawe to an irous man,/ Ne with no wood man walke by the weye,/ Lest thee repente" (2086–8). The same verse is quoted by John of Wales in the *Communiloquium* (I.viii.2): "[E]st tamen societas malorum vitanda, quia dicitur Prover.xxij: Noli esse amicus homini iracundo neque ambules cum homine furioso ne discas semitas eius." ["The company of evil people must be avoided, because it is said in Proverbs 22: Do not be a friend to an angry man, nor walk with an angry man lest you should take his pathway"].[40] The evidence of Chaucer's use of the *Communiloquium* becomes even more convincing with his

[39] Pratt implies that "tyto" is a variant reading for "Syro" which also occurs in some editions (see "Chaucer and the Hand that Fed Him," p. 630 n. 31). Its translation here as "Cyrus" derives directly from Seneca (*De Ira*, 3.21.1). Chaucer also uses "Cirus" at III, 2079.

[40] See Pratt, "Chaucer and the Hand that Fed Him," p. 631 (my translation).

subsequent statement: "For whoso wolde us fro this world bireve,/ So God me save, Thomas, by youre leve,/ He wolde bireve out of this world the sonne." (2111–13). Again the same sentiments, with Cicero as authority (*De Amicitia*, 13.47), are expressed in the *Communiloquium* (II.vii.3).[41]

[41] In the lines following the *exemplum* of King Cambyses, Chaucer uses the phrase "Syngeth *Placebo*" (2075). J. V. Fleming points to the influence of the *Roman de Fauvel* in Chaucer's use of it in "Anticlerical Satire as Theological Essay," p. 15.

III

The Tale of the Priest's Bladder

(from *The Literary Context of Chaucer's Fabliaux*, ed. Larry D. Benson and Theodore M. Andersson [Indianapolis, IN, and New York, 1971], pp. 345–59)[42]

Instead of a fabliau, I shall tell you
A true story, as I have heard tell,
Of a priest who dwelt
[4] Near Antwerp. What he had acquired
In the way of possessions was very great,
For he was filled with good sense.
He had not spent everything;
[8] He had taken care to save,
And thus he was a rich and prosperous man.
Of beef cattle and cows, [sheep] and grain
He had so much that one could not count them.
[12] But Death, who spares neither [king],
Duke nor count, had summoned him with his messenger
To the inevitable departure.
He became dropsical;
[16] [It was known by everyone]
That he had [no] promise of a long life.
This priest, who had a deep desire
To die well and justly,
[20] Sent right away
For his dean and all his friends,
And put his possessions into their hands
To give out and divide up
[24] When they should see that his soul
[Will have to] leave his body.
Not jewels, cushions, pots, nor benches,
Mattresses, linens, not even a tablecloth,
[28] Sheep, mutton, beef, not even his cape –
Nothing remained to him that he did not give away.
And he named each person
To whom he wished his things to be given.

42 The translation of Benson and Andersson is based on the text of *Li Dis de le vescie à prestre* in *Recueil Général des Fabliaux XIIIe et XIVe Siècles* III, ed. A. de Montaiglon and G. Raynaud (1878; rpt. New York: Burt Franklin, 1964), pp. 106–17. Any alteration of their translation is signified by the use of brackets. Benson and Andersson's line numbering has also been changed to match that of the French (*NRCF*) text.

III

Li Dis de le vescie à prestre

(from *Nouveau Recueil Complet des Fabliaux* (*NRCF*) X, ed. W. Noomen [Van Gorcum, Assen, 1998], pp. 295–303)

En lieu de fable vos dirai
Un voirs, ensi k'oï dire ai,
D'un prestre ki estoit manans
Deleis Anwiers. Li revenans[43]
Estoit mult biaus de son avoir,
Car plains estoit de grant savoir,
Si n'avoit pas tot despendut.
A amassier avoit tendut,
S'estoit riches hons et moblés:
Buez et vaches, brebis et bleiz[44]
Avoit tant c'on n'en savoit conte.
Mais li mors, qui roi, duc ne conte[45]
N'espargne, l'ot par son message
Somont al naturel passage:
Eutropikes ert devenus,
De nul home n'estoit conus[46]
Ki li promesist longe vie.
Li prestes, qui out grant envie
De bien morir et justement,
Manda tost et isnelement
Son doiien et toz ses amis:
Son avoir entre lor mains mist
Por donner et por departir,
Cant ilh verront que departir
De son cors estovera l'ame.[47]
Jowel, cossin, pot ne escame,
Cuete, tuelle, neiz une nape,
Brebis, moutons, buef, ne sa chape
Ne li remaint que tot ne donne;
Et nome chasconne persone
A cui ilh wet c'on doinst ses chozes.

[43] Noomen changes "remanans," found in the manuscript and subsequent editions of the text, to "revenans." The meaning of "revenans" ("revenue") is more appropriate, but he also argues (p. 380) that the occurrence of the more obscure "remanans" could actually have been a scribal alteration of "revanans."

[44] Benson and Andersson do not translate "brebis" [sheep].

[45] Benson and Andersson do not translate "roi" [king].

[46] Noomen cites the manuscript reading "tenus" as "leçon qui donne des difficultés d'interpretation." He instead adopts "conus" which makes better sense and which may, because of palaeographic propinquity, be the original reading corrupted by a later scribe unfamiliar with "l'ancienne langue" (p. 380).

[47] Benson and Andersson translate "estovera" as "was striving to."

He had public, not private,
Letters written and notarized
On this-more I can't tell you.
In short, whatever he had
He gave away as best he knew how.
Since he had no hope
Of any relief from his illness,
For his disease was severe.
At this time two Jacobin friars
Had set out from Antwerp to preach;
They greatly desired to profit themselves
By putting back on the right path any who strayed.
They came directly forth on their way
Until they arrived at the priest's house.
They expected to be invited in there
For eating, for pleasure, and for a feast,
For they had been there before.
But they neither [ate nor drank],
For they have found the priest ill.
Nevertheless, they ask him
About his state and about his condition;
They feel his hands, his face,
His feet, and they look at his legs
And carefully examine his whole body.
Thus it was clear to them indeed
That he could not be cured of his malady,
And that surely he must die of it;
It had been allowed to develop for such a long time
That it is not easy to cure.
"[But] said the one to the other [it is clear]
"[That from now on we should take care that]
From the possessions he has amassed
He should leave our house twenty pounds
As a bequest for repairing our books;

Descovertes – et non pas clozes –[48]
Lettres saeler et escrire
En fist, que ne le vos puis dire
Plus briement quant que il avoit.
Il dona tot quant qu'il savoit,
Con chil qui n'avoit esperance
D'avoir de son mal aligance,
Car sa maladie ert amere.
Atant se sont d'Anwier dui frere
De saint Jake issu por prechier,
Qui mult se wellent estachier[49]
Cant aucun desviiet ravoient.[50]
Cele part tot droit ont lor voie,
Si sunt chil le prestre venus:
Iestre quidarent retenus
Al mangier a joie et a feste,
Si c'autrefois esté i furent.[51]
Mais ne mangierent ne ne burent,[52]
Car malade ont trové le prestre.
Nonporquant li ont de son estre
Demandé et de son afaire;
Ses mains manient, son viaire,
Ses piés, ses jambes regarderent
Et tot son cors mult bien tansterent;
Si lor sembla bien par droiture
C'awoir ne poist de son mal cure,
K'i ne l'en coviengne morir:
Trop lonc tans l'a laisié norrir,
Si n'est pas legiers a curer.
"Mais des or nos covient curer,[53]
Dist l'uns a l'autre, c'est passé[54]
Ke de l'avoir k'a amassé
Doinst a nostre maison vint livres
A lé por refaire nos livres:

[48] The priest had his will drawn up in the form of a *letter patente* which allowed its contents to be made public. The contents of a *letter close* by contrast remained confidential. See Noomen, p. 380.

[49] Noomen (p. 380) interprets this line etymologically as the friars' conceit or vain pride in their religious activity rather than a specific desire to enrich themselves, i.e. "*estachier* signifiant 'ériger.'"

[50] Montaiglon and Raynaud (p. 358) note that reading the line *Cant aucuns desviiet ravoie* would correct the defective rhyme.

[51] Montaiglon and Raynaud (p. 358) point out that a line is missing here in their manuscript and accordingly (like Benson and Andersson) they number this absent line as line 48. Noomen notes that, although line 47 stands alone in the pattern of the tale's rhyme scheme ("Bien que le vers soit orphelin," p. 381), the passage is nonetheless coherent, and an irregularity possibly due to the author himself. In order that the line numbering of text and translation continue to coincide, the absent line in Benson and Andersson's translation has been omitted.

[52] Benson and Andersson use the future tense, "they will neither eat nor drink."

[53] Benson and Andersson's translation of this line reads, "Although we should care for him." "Mais des or" does not, however, mean "although" and the object of "curer" is the clause dependent on the subjunctive verb "doinst" in line 64.

[54] The phrase "c'est passé" is an aside meaning "it is clear; it is settled." See the *NRCF* glossary and Hart's gloss in Bryan and Dempster (p. 279 n. 2). Benson and Andersson translate this phrase, "it is too late for that."

If we could manage that
It would be pleasing to our prior
[68] And our brothers would rejoice."
"You speak the truth, by God our Father,
Friar Louis. [Now it will appear which (of us friars)
Will speak to him most eloquently]
[72] And reveal our need to him."
To the priest, who was in grave danger
From his illness, they said straightway,
"Sir, your illness afflicts you severely,
[76] And you seem to us gravely ill.
You must think of your soul;
Give something from your possessions for God."
Said the priest, "I cannot think
[80] That I have held back anything – not a [cloak or tunic]
Nor even the sheets against which I rub myself.
I have given all for God."
"But," say the friars, "how have you
[84] Ordered your business?
The Scriptures warn us
That one must be careful to whom one makes gifts
And be sure that they are given to the person
[88] To whom one wishes to give alms."
The priest answered agreeably,
"To my poor relations I have given
Sheep, and cows, and calves,
[92] And to the poor of this town
I have also given, by Saint Giles,
Some grain that is worth more than ten pounds,
So that I might be delivered
[96] From any wrongs that I have done them,
Since I have made my living among them;
And I have given to orphan girls
And to orphaned lads and to nuns
[100] And to people with small means,
And I have also left, for their daily bread,
One hundred sous to the Franciscan friars."
"These alms are very fine,
[104] But to the friars of our house
Have you [done justice]?"
This the two friars said to the priest.
"No indeed." "How could this be?
[108] In our house there are so many good men,
And we are such close neighbors to you
And we live so soberly

Se nos le poons ensi faire,
A no prius devera plaire
Et si en seront liet no frere.
– Vos dites voir, par Dieu no pere,
Frere Lowis, or i parra
Liqueis miez a lui parlera[55]
Et mostrera nostre besongne!"
Al prestre, qui out grant esoingne
De maladie, ont dit sans faille:
"Sire, chis maus mult vos travaille,
Vos nos sambleis mult agreveis.
De vostre ame penser deveis:
Doneis por Dieu de vostre avoir!"
Dist li prestes: "Ne puis savoir
K'aie caché sorcot ne cote,[56]
Neis les linchués a coi me frote,
Ke tout n'aie por Deu doné.
– Coment aveis vos ordené,
Dient li frere, vo besongne?
Li Escriture nos temongne
C'on doit garder a cui on done,
S'emploiiet est a la persone
A cui on wet aumone faire."
Li prestes respont sans contraire:
"J'ai a mes povres parentiaus
Doné brebis, vaces et viaus;
Et as povres de cele vilhe
Ai doné ausi, par saint Gilhe,
De bleis qui vaut plus de dis livres,
Por ce ke je soie delivres
De ce k'ai envers iaus mespris,
Car entor iaus mon vivre ai pris.
Si ai doné as orfenines,
A orfenins et a beguines,
Et a gens de povre puisance;
Et si ai laisiet por pitance
Cent souz as freres des Cordeles.
– Ces amuenes se sunt mult beles!
Et as freres de no maison
Aveis vos fait nule raison?"[57]
Ce dient li doi frere al prestre.
"Naie voir! – Ce conment puet estre?
En maison a tant de preudomes,
Et a vos prochain voisien somes,
Et si vivons mult sobrement:

55 Benson and Andersson translate lines 70–1, "Now I shall prepare my best snares, and I shall speak to him." Neither of the verbs "parra" nor "parlera" has, however, a first-person ending.

56 The phrase "sorcot ne cote" means "cloak or tunic." Benson and Andersson's "not a coat" omits one of the garments. (See Noomen's note, p. 381.)

57 Benson and Andersson translate "Fait nule raison" as "had no thought for."

That you will not die justly
[112] If you do not leave us something of yours."
The priest, completely astonished,
Answered, "By the eyes of my head,
I have nothing to give, neither grain nor beast,
[116] Gold nor silver, cup nor bowl."
Each of the friars reproaches him
And shows him by examples
That he could retract one of his gifts
[120] And call it back to give to them,
"[We would be willing] to take great pains
That your soul should be set right,
For in this place has been set forth –
[124] Many times and well – our teaching;
And the alms are especially good
Which are given to our house.
We do not wear fine shirts,
[128] And we live [off charity].
God knows, [we don't say it
For the value of your money]"
The priest hears this and is enraged by it,
[132] And he thinks that he will be avenged for it
If he can, and that he will trick them;
They are going to suffer for pressing him so closely.
Then he answers the friars,
[136] "I have decided that I should give you
A jewel that I have always loved very much
And love still. By Saint Peter,
I have nothing nearly so valuable.
[140] I would not take a thousand marks of silver for it,
And, if I were in good health,
I would not let another have it
For two hundred marks.
[144] God directed you here;
Bring your prior to me,
And I shall tell you about it
Before my life fails me."
[148] The friars, without sadness or wrath,
Answer, "God bless you for this!
When do you want us to return
And bring our prior?"
[152] "Tomorrow, if it pleases God I am here,

Vos ne moreis pas justement
Se del vostre ne nos laiiés."
Li prestes trestous esmaiés
Respont: "Par les oelz de ma teste!
A doner n'ai ne bleif ne beste,
Or ne argent, chanap ne cope."
Chascons des freres li rencope,
Et li mostre par exemplaire
K'ilh puet bien un des dons retraire
Et rapeler por iaus doner:
"Nos nos vorimes mult pener[58]
Ke vostre ame fust adrechie,
Car chaiens a esté drechie
Soventesfois bien nostre escuele;
Et li amuene si est biele
Ki est a nostre maison mise:
Nos ne vestons nulle chemise,
Et si vivomes en pitance.[59]
Se sache Dieus, por la valhance
De vostre argent nel disons mie!"[60]
Li prestre l'ot, si s'en gramie
Et pense qu'il s'en vengera,
S'ilh puet, et qu'il les trufera:
Mar le vont or si pres tenant!
As freres respont maintenant:
"Appenseis sui: doner vos welh
Un jowel ke mult amer suel
Et aime encore. Par saint Piere,
Je n'ai chose gaires plus chiere:
Milh mars d'argent n'en prenderoie,
Et se je bien haitiés estoie,
Je n'en voroie miés avoir
Deus cens marchies d'autre avoir.[61]
Diez vos a chaiiens asseneis:
Vostre prieus me ramineis,
Si vos en ferai conissanche
Ains que de vie aie faillance."
Li frere sans duel et sans ire
Ont respondut: "Dieus le vos mire!
Cant voleis vos que revenons
Et nostre prieuz ramenrons?
– Demain. Je sui ou Diew plaisir:

[58] "Vorimes" is a conditional verb. Benson and Andersson translate it using the past tense, "we have been willing."

[59] "Pitance" is food given as alms. Hence, "we live off charity," rather than Benson and Andersson's "on poor food."

[60] Characteristically, the friars are saying, "we do not boast about our holy life in order to persuade you to leave us a legacy." Benson and Andersson translate lines 129–30, "as to the value/ Of your money, we say nothing."

[61] "Marchie" is more specifically a "piece of land yielding an income of a mark" (see Noomen's note, p. 381; and Tobler-Lommatzsch s.v. marchiee, col. 1140).

You shall take your bequest,
[Before I am in too bad a way."]
Straightway the friars were
[156] On their way; to Antwerp they came
And called together their chapter.
Each told what befell,
But they had no concern for making a long tale,
[160] But shouted out in the assembly,
"Bring forth a good feast!
We have gained two hundred pounds
From a priest whom we know,
[164] Ill in a small village."
Friar Nicholas and Friar Giles,
Friar William and Friar Ansel,
Came to hear this news,
[168] Which very greatly pleased them.
They ordered huge fishes,
Old wine and new, custards and pastries.
This great feast was quickly brought forth;
[172] Each thinks himself well at ease;
They do not drink cheap wine;
With drinking and eating they are well entertained,
And they kiss their cups for the priest
[176] Who promised them the jewel.
When they had poured in their heads
This good wine, they made a great festival:
They rang their bells resoundingly
[180] As if for the relics of a saint.
There was not a neighbor who did not bless himself
[And those who see it, marvel]
They came racing to the preachers
[184] To see the great marvel.
None of the friars could keep
From acting in a disorderly way,
For each of them had befuddled his head
[188] With good wine and with their food.
By their bizarre looks
And their postures and their manners
They seemed indeed to be out of their minds;
[192] All who saw it wondered at it.
Then Friar Louis draws himself up
To ask exactly how
They could best
[196] Obtain their bequest from the priest.
"Tomorrow, before Mass is sung,
It will be well to be on our way."

Vo premesse deveis saisir
Ains que je trop aggreveis soie."[62]
Atant ont acuelli lor voie
Li frere; a Anwier sont venu,
Si ont lor chapitre tenu.
Chascons s'aventure raconte;
Mais chil n'ont cure de lonc conte,
Ains ont dit haut en audience:
"Faites venir bone pitance:
Deus cens livres gaangniet avons
A un prestre ke nos savons
Malade chi a une vilhe."
Frere Nichole et frere Gilhe,
Frere Guilhiame et frere Ansiaus
Vinrent oïr ces mos nouviauz,
Ki mult forment lor abelissent.
De ces grans poisons mander fisent,
Viez vin, novel, fions et pasteis.
Chil grans mangier fu mult hasteis.
Chascuns de lui bien aisier pense;
Ne burent pas vin de despense!
De boire et de mangier bien s'aisent:
Por le prestre le hanap baisent
Ki le jowel lor ot promis.
Cant en lor testes orent mis
De ce bon vin, grant feste fisent.
Lor cloches sovent en bondissent,
Ausi con ilh awist corsaint;
N'i a voisin qui ne se saint,
Et se merveillent qu'il avoient:[63]
Qui miez miés as Preschors s'avoient
Por la grant merveilhe esgarder.
Nus d'iaus ne se savoit garder
De mener vie deshoneste,
Car chascons a ferré la teste
De bon vin et de lor pitance;
A lor diverse contenance,
Et al maintieng et a lor estre
Semblerent bien hors de sens estre:
Chascons ki les voit s'en merveilhe.
Et frere Lowis s'aparailhe
De demander confaitement
Il poroient plus sagement
Al prestre querre lor promesse.
"Demain, anchois c'on chante messe,
Se fera bon mettre a la voie,

[62] In Benson and Andersson this line is translated, "Although I shall be greatly troubled." The sick man, however, pretends to want to give his legacy before his sickness makes him too ill to do so. The *NRCF* glossary offers "décliner" as a gloss for "agrever" in this line.

[63] Benson and Andersson translate line 182, "And wonder whom the feast honored."

Each says, "As Jesus may save me,
[200] Before Death seizes him,
[However the thing turns out]
We must have knowledge of our gift,
We will have a great alms-gift there,
[204] But one must take great trouble for it.
Friar Louis, whom do you want
To take with you? Tell us now!"
"Friar William, the hermit,
[208] Will go there, and Friar Nicholas,
For they [will know] how to speak well,
And also Friar Robert will come,
For there is no wiser convert here,
[212] And he will carry our breviary.
We need not bother with our prior."
Thus the business is settled.
The next day they were on their way
[216] Straight to the priest's house.
They did not worry about being early,
But, before the day had ended,
They wished they had stayed
[220] In their house at Antwerp.
Straightway they greeted
The priest, and saluted him in God's name;
Then they asked if he felt any change,
[224] Any easing of his illness.
The priest very politely
Said, "You are indeed welcome;
I have not forgotten
[228] The gift that I promised you,
For indeed I am still so inclined;
Have the town councillors come
And the mayor, so that in the future
[232] There will be no trouble for you.
In their presence I shall gladly
Do this for you,
And I shall name this thing to you
[236] And I shall tell you where it is."
While the priest was yet speaking,
Friar Robert so busied himself
That he brought the mayor
[240] And all the councillors as well.
The four friars, as I have heard,
Nobly greeted them.
The priest, who was very clever,
[244] Then straightway spoke out
And said to them exactly thus,

Dist chascons, se Jhesu m'avoie,
Anchois ke li mors le sorprengne;
Si, conment ke la chose prengne,[64]
De no don aions conissance.
Nos i arons mainte pitance,
Si s'en doit on mult bien pener!
Frere Lowis, les queis miner
I voreis vos? Or le nos dite!
– Frere Guilhiames, li ermites,
En venra et frere Nicoles:
Bien saront dire la parole;[65]
Et si venra frere Robiers:
Çaiens n'a si sage convers,
Si portera no breviaire.
De no prieus n'avons ke faire."
Ensi ont le plait otriiet.
L'endemain se sont avoiiet
Tot droit vers la maison le prestre.
Ja n'i cuidierent a tans estre,
Mais ans ke li jors fu passeis
Amassent ilh mieus estre asseis
A Anwiers dedens lor maison!
Atant ont le prestre a raison
Mis et de Deu l'ont salué;
Puis demandent s'il a mué
Son mal en nul aligement.
Li prestes mult tres sagement
Lor dist: "Bien soiiés vos venu!
Je n'ai mie desconeü
Le don ke promis vos avoie:
Encors en sui je bien en voie.
Faites les eschevins venir
Et le maieur, si k'awenir
Ne vos en puist nule grevance;
Devant iaus la reconissance
Mult volentiers vos en ferai
Et la choze vos nomerai,
Et vos dirai u ele ert prise."
Entrués ke li prestes devise,
Frere Robers a tant pené
K'ilh a le maieur aminé
Et toz les eschevins ensemble.
Li quatre frere, ce me samble,
Les ont hautement benvigniés.
Li prestes, qui fu ensigniés,
Si a parlé promierement
Et lor a dit sifaitement:

64 The *NRCF* glosses this phrase: "quel que soit le tour que prend l'affaire" (s.v. prendre, p. 428). Benson and Andersson translate, "Of how one gets the thing."

65 "Saront" is future tense. Benson and Andersson translate it as present tense, "they know."

"My lords, you are my friends;
By God, now listen to me:
[248] Friar Louis and Friar Simon
Came to me yesterday to give a sermon
[Because they thought me to be in health],
But God in His providence had planted
[252] In me a disease so severe
That it is clear I will never recover from it.
They came and looked at me,
And then they asked me
[256] If I had thought of my soul
And I said to them, by our Lady,
That I had given away everything.
They asked if I had provided
[260] Any gift for their house,
And I said no; as God may save me,
I had not thought of it,
And now they had come too late.
[264] I had nothing more to give.
'No?' they said, too far astray
[I see you]: you will die in a state of sin
If you persist in this intent
[268] And do not give us something of your goods.'
And I, by the holy Our Father,
Did not wish to die in a state of sin.
I therefore considered this for so long
[272] That I thought of a thing
That I have locked in my possession,
That I greatly love and hold very dear,
But I grant it to them in such a manner
[276] That they will not have it as long as I live,
For [I will never give] it
Into anyone's keeping save my own.
Know you that I deeply love it
[280] And will love it all my life;
Without covetousness or envy
I give it to them in your presence,
And let no one raise any dispute about it."
[284] The [five] friars say to the priest,

"Sangnor, vos estes mi ami:
Por Dieu, or entendeis a mi!
Frere Lowis, frere Symons
Vinrent ier chi faire sermons,
K'ilh me cuidoient en santé;[66]
Mais Dieus par sa grasce a planté
En moi maladie si grieve
C'aparant est ke mais n'en lieve.
Il me virent et esgarderent,
Et aprés si me demanderent
Se j'avoie pensé de m'ame;
Et je lor dis, par Nostre Dame,
Ke j'avoie trestot donet.
Ilh demanderent s'ordiné
A lor maison riens nee avoie,
Et je dis non: se Dieus m'avoie,
Il ne m'en estoit sovenu;
Or estoient trop tart venu,
Je n'avoie mais que doner.
'Non, dissent ilh, trop mal mener
Vos voi:[67] mavaisement moreis
S'en cestui propoz demoreis,
Se vos ne nos doneis del vostre.'
Et je, par sainte Patenostre,
Ne welh pas morir malement;
Si ai pensé si longement
K'apenseis me sui d'une coze
Ke j'ai en mon porpris encloze,
Ke j'aime mult et ting mult chiere.
Mais je lor doin en tel maniere
K'ilh ne l'aront tant con vivrai,
Car onkes ne le delivrai[68]
En autrui garde k'en la moie;
Sachiés que durement l'amoie
Et amerai toute ma vie.
Sans convoitise et sans envie
Lor done chi en vo presence.
– Et que nos n'i amenés tenche,[69]
Dient al prestre li cinc frere,[70]

66 Benson and Andersson translate this line, "That they might bring me back to health."

67 Benson and Andersson translate "Vos voi" as "You are going."

68 "Delivrai" is future tense. Benson and Andersson translate it as past tense, "I have given."

69 The attribution of this line to the priest is changed by Noomen (p. 382) to the friars. Wishing to have absolute certainty concerning their rights to the legacy (cf. lines 114–20), the friars invite the priest to specify their bequest in front of witnesses. Hence Noomen translates lines 283–5: "Et pour que vous ne nous attiriez pas de contestation à propos de ce don (disent les cinq frères au prêtre), dites en quoi il consiste" (p. 382).

70 The number five ("cinc"), also found in the Montaiglon and Raynaud text (".v."), is changed in Benson and Andersson to four ("IIII") because only four friars have been mentioned and named in lines 205–10; 241. Line 213 also explicitly discounts the presence of the friars' Prior. This discrepancy is noted by Hart in Bryan and Dempster (p. 283 n. 4; p. 285 n. 2), where the number ".v." is nevertheless retained.

"Good father, tell us what this thing is!"
  "Indeed, I will; it is my bladder.
If you see that it is well cleaned,
[288] It will be better than leather
And last you much longer.
You can put your pepper in it."
  "Have you brought us here
[292] To fool us, false stubborn priest?
You intended to shame us,
But you will never profit from this, by St. Obert,
Though you now consider us fools."
[296] "But you considered me a beast
When you wanted me to take back
The gifts that I had given.
Indeed, you made my blood boil
[300] When you wanted me to recall them.
Indeed, I told you that I had
Neither pot nor pail nor anything to give;
But you wanted to convince me
[304] That the alms would be better bestowed on you
Than in any place I would have given them,
Because you are the best of all."
  The Jacobins hang their heads,
[308] And then turned themselves back
Toward their house with sorry faces;
And all those who lived around there
Nearly fainted from laughing
[312] At the trick of the bladder
Which the priest had so praised
To the Jacobins, who drank on it,
And feasted, and received for it
[316] Rations of wine and fish.
  Jacques de Baisieux, in truth,
Translated this from Flemish into French
[319] Because he so enjoyed the trick.

Dite quel choze c'est, biaz pere!
– Volentiers voir, c'est me vesie:
Se la voiiés, bien netoiie
Mieus que de corduan varra
Et plus longement vos durra,
Se poreis ens metre vo poivre.
– Nos aveis vos ci por dechoivre
Mandeis, foz prestres entesté?
Avoir nos cuidiés ahonteis,
Mais nen aveis, par saint Obert,
Bien nos teneis or por bobert!
– Mais vos por beste me teneis,
Cant les dons que je ai doneis
Me voleis faire retolhir.
Bien me faites le sanc bolir,
Ki voleis que je le rapiele!
Bien vos dis que pot ne paele,
Ne riens nee a doner n'avoie;
Or me voleis metre en tel voie
K'en vos soit mieus l'amouene asise
K'en liew u je l'ewise mise,
Por ce que de tos melhor estes."
Li Jacobin baisent les testes,
Si se sont retorné arriere
Vers lor maison a triste chiere.
Et tot chil qui la demorerent
De ris en aise se pamerent
Por la trufe de la vesie,
Que li prestes ot tant prisie
As Jacobins, qui bien en burent
Et mangierent et en rechurent
De vin et de poissons pitance.
Jakes de Baisiu, sans dotance,
L'a de tieus en romanç rimee
Por la trufe qu'il a amee.

The Merchant's Tale

N. S. THOMPSON

The Merchant's Tale is a well-known type in medieval narrative,[1] but an exact source is difficult to pinpoint. Nineteenth-century research uncovered several ancient Oriental tales illustrating the wiles of women that show some similarity,[2] but the husband is sighted and the wife's trickery performed on the

[1] According to the head note in the *Riverside Chaucer* (p. 884), it contains three parts: January's deliberations on marriage (1245–1688), January's wedding to the understanding between May and Damian (1689–2020), and then the deception story (2021–2418). All citations from Chaucer are from this edition.

[2] See W. A. Clouston, "The Enchanted Tree: Asiatic Versions and Analogues of Chaucer's *Merchant's*

ground with the husband in the tree (as in *Decameron* VII, 9). Transmission of such tales, many in framed collections typified by the *Thousand and One Nights*, would have occurred in contact with the Muslim world in and around the Mediterranean from Mozarabic Spain to the Levant. Later Latin versions suggest that the story of a blind husband cuckolded by his wife in a pear tree had become current across Europe by the fifteenth century, most probably translated for a clerical or goliardic audience from the vernacular.[3] In this type, a classical god sees what is going on and decides to restore the husband's sight, while another god (or goddess) gives the wife a prompt reply to get her out of her predicament. The wife's excuse is that she understood such an act would restore her husband's sight. These analogues, printed in earlier collections of Chaucer's sources and analogues,[4] are too distant in time and geography for the aims of this edition, but the type is conveniently found in a fifteenth-century French translation put into English by William Caxton, in an appendix to his collection of Aesopian fables: *The book of the subtyl historyes and fables of Esope* (1484).[5] Closer to a tradition Chaucer was most likely acquainted with is the Italian novella, and it is most probably from this type that the versions in Latin verse derive.[6] A version exists in the late twelfth-early thirteenth century manuscript of "il libro di novelle e di be' parlare gentile" ("the book of speaking well and courteously"),[7] in the Codice Panciatichiano-Palatino 32 (Florence, Biblioteca Nazionale). Here God and St Peter look down on the event, but the act of giving a witty reply to the wife is tempered by an antifeminist strain (the *moralitas* ending), as in the Oriental tales. On a more concrete level, some suggestive fragments for January's character appear in two works by Boccaccio, the *Comedia delle ninfe fiorentine* (1341–2) and the *Decameron* II, 10 (1350). Boccaccio's own version of the pear tree story in *Decameron* VII, 9 exhibits the same sophisticated development of its source,[8] and provides a model for how

Tale," in *Originals and Analogues of Some of Chaucer's Canterbury Tales*, ed. F. J. Furnivall, E. Brock and W. A. Clouston, Chaucer Society, Second Series, 7, 10, 15, 20, 22 (London, 1872–87), pp. 341–64; and A. C. Lee, *The Decameron: Its Sources and Analogues* (London: Nutt), 1909, pp. 234–5. For the later ones that have come to light, see Vittore Branca, ed., *Giovanni Boccaccio: Decameron* (Torino: Einaudi, 1980), p. 861, note to VII, 9.

3 One such is in verse, *Adolphi Fabulae*, 1315 ("Fable of Adolphus") found in a Vienna manuscript but, as Dempster points out, "Nothing suggests that he [Chaucer] read Adolphus" (p. 341). A second is a prose version, "De cæco et eius uxore ac rivali," from Steinhöwel's *Aesop*, 1476 or 1477, which adds the agency of the gods (Mercury and Venus). "De cæco" was later translated into French by Julian Macho or Julien des Augustins under the title, *Les Subtilles Fables de Esope translatéez de latin en françois par Reverend Docteur en Theologie Frere Julien des Augustins de Lyon, auecques les Fables d'Avien, et Alfonce etc.* (Lyons, 1480). The French is printed in Bryan and Dempster, pp. 355–6.

4 See Bryan and Dempster, pp. 352–5, and *Originals and Analogues*, pp.177–85.

5 Caxton's version, which is presented as one of his twelve "fables of Alfonce," is a close translation of the French version by Julian Macho cited above, and follows the French in substituting Venus for Mercury (as in the Latin) as the deity who restores the husband's sight. The British Library copy is available on line at http://wwwlib.umi.com/eebo/image/11597.

6 An excellent introduction to the tradition is given in *Novelle italiane: Il Duecento, Il Trecento*, ed. Lucia Battaglia Ricci (Milan: Garzanti, 1982), pp. vii–xlvi.

7 See Sebastiano Lo Nigro, "Per il testo del'Novellino,' " *Giornale Storico della Letteratura Italiana*, CXLI (1964): 51–102. This wording of the title has to be taken with a good deal of irony considering the content of some narratives, including the one under discussion.

8 This is one of the few novelle in the *Decameron* with an identifiable source, namely the *Comoedia Lydiae*, once attributed to Matthew of Vendôme, which Boccaccio copied into his miscellany Codice Laurenziano XXXIII. With some slight divergences, Boccaccio follows the outline of this Latin poem,

Chaucer could have created his own sophisticated narratives from the much cruder analogue versions, not only in the *Merchant's Tale* but also in the tales of the Miller, Reeve and the Shipman. In artistry, all these tales are far superior to the French fabliaux and early Italian novelle, which contain no localized setting and depict anonymous (often two-dimensional) characters in a crude tit-for-tat plot. Some comments follow on the materials printed here and, in the light of them, further suggestions are made as to how Chaucer may have constructed and elaborated his tale.

Advice on marriage

Chaucer's portrait of January begins with a long discussion of the pros and cons of marriage (IV, 1263–1579), beginning with what could be the narrator's voice, or perhaps January's (in free indirect discourse),[9] followed later by the views of his two brothers, Placebo and Justinus. Placebo argues on January's side for a young wife, while Justinus is against a marriage between an old man and a young woman. The passage has its inspiration, if not its direct source, in *Le Miroir de Mariage* by Eustache Deschamps (c.1340–c.1404).[10] *Le Miroir* is a long poem on marriage (12,103 lines) in which several allegorical personifications offer conflicting advice to "Franc Vouloir" (Free Will), who is of marriageable age, on the question of whether or not he should marry. His "False Friends" – "Desir," "Folie," "Servitute" and "Faintise" (Desire, Folly, Servitude and Deceit) – argue for marriage, while "Répertoire de Science" (Repository of Learning), a bookish and clerical figure, argues against it. In style and tone, Deschamps's poem often follows discussions on marriage in the *Roman de la Rose*, especially in Repository of Learning's letter (XIV–LXXV),[11] but where it possesses the *Roman*'s breadth of learning and debate it is short on the latter's wit and *double entendre*. Although *Le Miroir* contains much practical discussion on such matters as the difficulties of marrying a beautiful woman (XVIII) or the effects of having children (XXIII), it also retains some of the same complex ironies found in the *Roman* – for example, Genius's antifeminist speech to Nature (*Roman*, 16323ff) on the subject of women and marriage – especially when Deschamps has the collective False Friends speak for marriage and Repository of Learning, an equally prejudiced figure, speak against it.

Lines 1296–1306 of *The Merchant's Tale* on the preferability of a good servant to a wife have long been known to come from the section of St Jerome's *Epistola adversus Jovinianum* c. 393 ("Letter against Jovinian"). This letter, in which Jerome defends the superiority of virginity to wedlock (among other

but his style and treatment are as far removed from the source as Chaucer's so-called "fabliaux" are from theirs. The same tale is also found in the *Adolphi Fabulae: De cœco et eius uxore* and Caxton's *Fables of Aesop*, 1480 (see notes 3 and 4 above). All three texts, with part of the *Comoedia Lydiae*, along with a study of "Asiatic Versions," are printed by Clouston in *Originals and Analogues*, pp. 341–64.

9 See *Riverside Chaucer*, p. 885, note to IV, 1267–1392.

10 Deschamps also wrote a good many courtly lyrics, including the well-known *balade* in praise of Chaucer ("O Socratès plains de philosophie"). See Derek Brewer, ed., *Chaucer: The Critical Heritage* (London: Routledge and Kegan Paul, 1978), p. 40.

11 See the speech of "Ami" in the *Roman*, 8455–9492.

subjects), contains a lengthy quotation from an otherwise lost book known as the *Liber de Nuptiis* ("The Book on Marriage") whose author, according to Jerome, is Theophrastus (c. 372–288), a Greek philosopher and follower of Aristotle. Chaucer names Theophrastus directly in *The Merchant's Tale* (IV, 1295), and also, together with Jerome, in *The Wife of Bath's Prologue* as one of the authors included in Jankyn's "book of wikked wyves" (III, 685): "He cleped it Valerie and Theofraste,/ At which book he lough alwey ful faste./ And eek ther was somtyme a clerk at Rome,/ A cardinal, that highte Seint Jerome,/ That made a book agayn Jovinian" (III, 671–5). Jerome's letter was extremely popular as a source of quotation, especially the passage attributed to Theophrastus.

January gives a list of virtuous wives from the Old Testament who offered good counsel (IV, 1362–74). These wives are mentioned in the *Miroir*, but also in Albertano of Brescia's, *Liber consolationis et consilii*, the ultimate source of Chaucer's *Melibee* by way of the French translation, the *Livre de Mellibee* by Renaud de Louens, which also contains a good deal of discussion on women and marriage. Because the topic was a popular one, with arguments about marriage so diffuse as to be the common currency of many writers, other works such as Jehan Le Fèvre's, *Les Lamentations de Matheolus* (a translation of the Latin *Matheolus*) and the *Roman de la Rose,* which is cited specifically in *The Merchant's Tale* (IV, 2032) with reference to January's garden, cannot be discounted as general influences on Chaucer's tale. January's affectionate love language (IV, 2138–48) echoes verses from the biblical Song of Solomon (Canticle of Canticles),[12] the same verses that also appear in *adversus Jovinianum* (I, 30–1), but in a different context. In the nuptial blessing of May during the marriage ceremony in the tale (1701–8), she is enjoined to follow the biblical examples of "Sarra and Rebekke/ In wysdom and in trouthe of mariage" (1705–6). There is a clear reference here to the Collect prayer that follows the blessing of the bride in the Marriage Service of the *Sarum Manual*, where these virtuous women are mentioned (along with Rachel). *The Merchant's Tale* also abounds in references to several other authors, such as Seneca, Cato, Martianus Capella, and Ovid, and the amount of exemplary reference and mock high apostrophe mark it as distinctly Chaucerian and similar in this regard to *The Nun's Priest's Tale.*

Description of an aged husband and young wife

The figure of an aged husband appears in *The Miller's Tale*, *The Reeve's Prologue and Tale* (see lines I, 3867–98 on old men), and in the *Wife of Bath's Prologue* in the descriptions of her first three husbands. In *The Merchant's Tale*, Chaucer has combined the basic deception of a blind man in a pear tree with a complex portrait of a *senex amans*, who also happens to be a Lombard merchant, therefore a merchant *per eccellenza*. Italian merchants were well known and successful enough in London to merit the opprobrium of Gower in his *Miroir de l'Omme* (25429–32): "Mais gaigne qui voldra gaigner,/ L'en porra trop esmerveiller/ En nostre terre a mon avis/ Des Lumbardz . . ." ("But no

[12] Song Sol. 2:10–12; 4:1, 7–12.

matter who wants to gain, it is to be marvelled, it seems to me, at the Lombards in our country . . .") who, Gower goes on to say, treat the country as their own.[13] To make January into an Italian merchant who becomes blind represents a highly significant change in Chaucer's treatment of the *senex amans*, for it adds a rich layer of symbolism to the critical analysis of marital imbalance between an old man and a young wife begun in *The Miller's Tale*.

But it is to Boccaccio's *Comedia delle ninfe fiorentine* (known also as *Ameto* from the title given it in the Renaissance), that Chaucer probably owes a greater debt. The *Comedia* is an allegory in which the rough young shepherd Ameto comes across seven nymphs in a forest and hears them relate their personal histories of love out of wedlock. It contains an animated portrait of an aged husband and his difficulties in paying the marriage debt to an eager young wife.

Boccaccio's use of a ribald gardening metaphor for the sexual act is worth noting as a possible suggestion for the development of January's garden into his place of sexual obsession. More importantly, Boccaccio's mention of an elaborate wedding ceremony, moving house, the physical descriptions of the husband's harsh bristles, his pressure on the nymph Agapes's white neck, similar to January's bristles rubbing May's tender face, and the slack skin about the husband's neck[14] suggest that the *Comedia,* if not a direct source, may have exerted a strong influence on some of the elements in *The Merchant's Tale*, especially on the elaboration of January's beard, that is fashionably shaven, yet so pointedly sharp. Boccaccio, like Chaucer, also presents the lovemaking of the aged husband from the young woman's point of view, a crucial perspective not found in any of the other narrative analogues, from which follow certain descriptive details, comment on the husband's performance, and the young woman's sleeping late after a wakeful night. The level of domestic intimacy given to January and May is one that offers a rare anticipation of the modern novel.

It is also tempting to see something of *Decameron* II, 10 in the portrait of January. The description of an aged husband who cannot satisfy his young wife is less explicit than the metaphorically rich depiction by Agapes in the *Comedia delle ninfe fiorentine*, but the story in the *Decameron* contains three elements of interest to readers of *The Merchant's Tale*: an old man's wilful search for an unsuitably young wife, his use of "vernaccia" and restorative potions, and his language of love. The rich old judge, Riccardo di Chinzica, makes a great effort looking about to find a beautiful young wife, and only succeeds when a young wife (like Agapes) is offered by her parents. The marriage is celebrated with great festivity. Whereas Riccardo finds it necessary to fortify himself after his amatory efforts, January takes the precaution of doing so before the enterprise, but his use of preparations and "vernage" (IV, 1807; Boccaccio's "vernaccia") for his "corage" is highly reminiscent of Riccardo's post-coital *remedia amoris*. It must be said that Chaucer makes January a more enthusiastic lover than Riccardo, but (like Agapes and Bartolomea) May can not applaud his "pleying"

13 G. C. Macaulay, ed., *The Complete Works of John Gower*, 4 vols (1899–1902; rpt. Grosse Pointe, MI, 1968), I, 281.

14 Chaucer mentions this twice, at lines 1849 and 1853.

at all (IV, 1847–54). Riccardo's inappropriate efforts at the sweet language of love also suggest an antecedent for January (2138–49), albeit the latter's language contains firm echoes of the *Song of Solomon,* perhaps suggested ironically by January's enclosed garden. Finally, Chaucer uses the correct term "palays" (IV, 2415) for the kind of city dwelling January inhabits, namely what Boccaccio calls a "palazzo."

The pear tree story

The appearance of the pear tree story in Europe is most likely owing to an Oriental source that became translated culturally, as well as linguistically, into the type of short exemplary narrative widely popular with both preachers and the lay audience. The earliest Western version of the story is found in a collection of *novelle* mentioned above: "il libro di novelle e di be' parlare gentile" ("the book of speaking well and courteously") found in the codex Panciatichiano-Palatino 32 in Florence. Some of its material was edited in the Renaissance under the title *Le ciento novelle antike*,[15] and in the nineteenth century the collection became known as *Il novellino*.[16] The Florence manuscript title is important because it foregrounds the importance of wit and elegance in the collection, despite the sometimes ribald material, as in the pear tree *novella*. The thrust of this tale is not the cuckolding of the husband, but the reply that gets the lady out of trouble, which is then used as an instrument for the antifeminist comment ending the tale. Nearer to Chaucer's own time, two versions seem to have been available. The most likely would have been something like the *Novellino* version, where God and St Peter take a hand in matters and where the wife's response to excuse herself for being caught *in flagrante* is seen as crucial for vilifying woman, rather than the action itself. The second would be a Latin fable, where classical gods intervene in the action. However, as the Caxton translation of the Aesopian fable shows, there is little in such a fable to whet the appetite of a writer like Chaucer, whereas the *Novellino* version offers the wonderfully laconic repartee of God and St Peter and such detail as the husband clasping the tree so that no one may ascend after his wife, a detail Chaucer also includes.[17] Generally, Chaucer's work has the feel of popular tradition, rather than the academic (where he used or translated a Latin source there is usually a mediating text in French), but like Boccaccio he then raises popular narrative to a high level of literary art. It is interesting that both authors use the stylistic ploy of seeming to portray a serious courtly love triangle, with the young lovers as potentially "refined" protagonists, only for the narrative to collapse into low farce.

Having said this, it is nevertheless difficult to argue from direct parallels that any of the narrative material printed below is a source, yet if one is to take direct

[15] See Carlo Gualteruzzi, ed., *Le ciento novelle antike* (Bologna: Girolamo Benedetti, 1525).

[16] See the edition of Lorenzo Sonzogno, Milan 1836.

[17] See IV, 2341–3 where May actually tells January to take the pear tree in his arms because she knows that he does not trust her. Interestingly, the illustration in Caxton's *Aesop* (folio cxxxij) shows the husband clasping the tree, while the lovers are in it, a detail that possibly comes from a knowledge of *The Merchant's Tale*.

verbal parallel alone to be the "rule" for determining a source, then the literary historian risks losing much of the rich flow of ideas from one author to another that otherwise comes under the heading of "influence." Thus, although Boccaccio's version of the pear tree story contains few close parallels to *The Merchant's Tale*, I suggest it could have provided Chaucer with a model for how to create a more richly elaborated narrative than any other similar story that had previously appeared. Clearly, Boccaccio has taken the tasks enjoined on Lidia from his original (in the *Comoedia Lydiae*) as the greater part of his narrative; the pear tree episode is part of Lidia's bravado in proving to her lover Pirro that she can fool her husband before his very eyes.[18] Significantly, Boccaccio's treatment is realistic, with no intervention from any deity or deities, and Nicostrato's age (compounded by his hunting) is the main source of Lidia's physical dissatisfaction. But such elements as style, character, register and general literary sophistication, while they recall *Decameron* II, 10, also point to the way Chaucer elaborates his tale. If one conjectures a basic narrative such as the Caxton version –

An attractive wife invites her lover to climb the pear tree in her garden, then takes her blind husband there and also climbs the tree. The husband hears the noise made by the two lovers and protests. The god(s) restore his sight, but the wife claims she was told by Venus (or some other figure) that the remedy was to make love to a young man in a tree, which the husband accepts.

– and then one recalls the *Novellino* version and *Decameron* novelle, it is possible to see exactly how Chaucer has proceeded in creating his version in *The Merchant's Tale* by using and combining the following five elements:

(1) The creation of January as a "named" Lombard merchant with a long amorous history, who seeks to minimize further transgression by acquiring a lawful (and youthful) sex partner. His inner life is depicted in a lengthy deliberation on marriage, aided by the reflections of Placebo and Justinus (most probably from Deschamps, with extra material from St Jerome and Albertano of Brescia). January's subsequent loss of sight becomes a crucial reflection of his moral and spiritual blindness.

(2) January is further developed, possibly with material from Boccaccio, as a *senex amans*, a rich materialist who cherishes his young wife as a physical treasure, almost as if she were a casket opened and closed by a key; but also, more especially, as a "garden of Venus," she becomes his "paradys terrestre" (IV, 1332). January's values are revealed in a parodic inversion of the love expressed in the Song of Songs for the *hortus conclusus*.

(3) God and St Peter and/or Jupiter and Venus become Pluto and Proserpine, who exercise a great sway on events: when Pluto decides to restore January's sight, it is Proserpine who says she will retaliate by giving May a prompt response (IV, 2316–17), in keeping with the "bel parlare" tradition.

[18] An Oriental version that depicts the cuckolding in the tree as a similar boast on the part of the wife can be found in a "Turkish Version," printed in *Originals and Analogues*, pp. 351–2. See also Carol Falvo Heffernan, "Three Unnoticed Links between Matthew of Vendôme's *Comedia Lidie* and *Chaucer's Merchant's Tale*," *Notes & Queries*, n.s. 50.2 (2003): 158–62.

(4) Sympathy is initially created for May as the victim of a selfish and lustful *senex*, and is further developed as she and Damian appear to act the roles of courtly lovers who are thwarted by January. Despite the narrator's apostrophe to treacherous servants (IV, 1783–94), Damian is presented as a "gentil squier" (1907ff), very much in the mould of Pirro. But May's disposal of a love letter in the "pryvee" (1954) detracts from her being "fulfilled of pitee" (1995) for him, and Damian's unadorned "throng" (2353) has little of finesse about it. Chaucer here draws a very fine line between the expectations of courtly refinements in two lovers and the actual realistic – even grotesque – detail that follows, which is strongly reminiscent of the way Boccaccio presents his love triangle in *Decameron* VII, 9, blending the refined and the grotesque before descending into popular ribaldry.

(5) While keeping the wife's altruistic excuse that she is with a man in a tree in order to bring back the husband's sight, Chaucer has May say that she was only "struggling" with Damian in order to have January's sight restored, which elicits January's stern counterclaim that she was doing much more than that (IV, 2371–83). Although January finally concedes he was seeing things, and agrees with May that persons who regain their sight after a period of blindness can not trust their eyes, the quibble adds a realistic touch to an otherwise ludicrous proposition.

In sum, Chaucer's great artistic coup in the *Merchant's Tale* is to meld January's sexual possession of May with his possession of a private and secret pleasure garden to create a rich layer of poetic symbolism that undergirds the continuing indictment of the mercantile worlds of *The Wife of Bath's Prologue* and *The Shipman's Tale* (among other *Tales*) where "al is for to selle" (III, 414). Naturally, he could simply have set up his own mirror in the market place to gain his picture of this world, but the material collected here shows how some literary seeds could have been planted from elsewhere.

I

Eustache Deschamps, *The Mirror of Marriage*

(trans. P. Rand and N. S. Thompson)

[The author ('acteur') speaks.]

33–5 If the true friend is aware of it when you act badly, he will make sure to tell you in order to protect you . . .

42–6 But, upon my soul, the false friend blandishes, flatters and deceives, and trims with the wind, and will approve your foolishness to please you . . .

[Free Will reports what his 'False Friends' have told him, especially that he should marry while he is still young, 87–105.]

106–16 Besides, he who burns in the flames of lust lives foolishly and against Holy Writ: therefore, it is better to marry than to burn. For Saint Paul tells us in the *Epistles*[1] he wrote for us that marriage is a very good path to take, as long as it be taken in order to reproduce: in doing so one avoids many a sin that might besmirch one . . .

217–28 Marriage is a very sweet union, it is two bodies united, who are joined together in one flesh by the law, and keep on loving one another near and far. A man should hold sway outside the home, while a woman should govern inside. She is so gentle of speech, she serves her husband, kissing and embracing him and, when he is troubled, she works to calm his temper. If he is suffering, she looks after him and watches over him tenderly . . .

[1] I Cor. 7:9.

I

Eustache Deschamps, *Le Miroir de Mariage*

(from *Œuvres complètes de Eustache Deschamps*, ed. G. Raynaud, Société des anciens textes français [Paris: 1894], vol. IX, pp. 4–5, 6–7, 10–11, 12–13, 15, 17, 19, 27–8, 55–6, 98–9, 293–6)

[The author ('acteur') speaks.]

33 Le vray amy, se tu faiz mal,
Lui saichant, par especial
Le te dira pour toy garder.
. . .
42 Mais le faulx ami, par ma teste,
Blandist, flatte et va decepvent,
Et se tourne avecques le vent
Et consentira ta folie
Pour toy plaire . . .

[Franc Vouloir reports what his False Friends have told him, especially that he should marry while he is young, 87–105.]

106 . . . cilz vit folement
Et contre la Saincte Escripture,
Quant il art ou feu de luxure.[2]
Dont mieulx vault marier qu'ardoir,
Car saint Pol le nous fait sçavoir
Es epistres qu'il nous envoye,
Mariage est moult bonne voye
Qui la prant en entencion
De faire generacion:
On en laist maint autre pechié
De quoy on puet estre entechié.
. . .
217 C'est tresdoulce conjunction,
Ce sont deux corps en union,
En une char par la loy joins,
Qui s'entraiment et près et loins.
Homs doit par dehors ordonner,
Femme doit dedenz gouverner:
Elle est si doulce en sa parole,
Son mari sert, baise et acole,
Et fait, quant il est a martire,
Qu'elle le puisse getter d'ire.
S'il a griefté, celle le garde,
Et piteusement le resgarde . . .

[2] I Cor. 7:9.

231–4 She runs his house and his livestock too. She is vigilant, wise and skilful, and sees to it that nothing is wasted . . .

239–44 She knows how to save money so as to be able to spend it when necessary, unlike an unfamiliar household [of servants] who would empty coffers and barns alike, and think only of pilfering, and of passing the time in idleness.

252–6 Tobit lost his eyesight[3] but his wife helped him and was humble, gentle and kind, and set herself to the task of looking after him until God restored his vision . . .

275–7 This same Sarah of whom we are speaking was so faithful that she is named in blessings and at weddings[4] . . .

280–3 There was once a king who loved many women and he vowed that he would never take a wife . . .

290–4 Many of his bastards put themselves forward as his heir and destroyed the kingdom; and when some of the king's neighbours saw this, they destroyed them and reigned, dividing the kingdom up amongst themselves . . .

369–74 Thus it is wise to have lawful descendants and to take as a wife a kindly woman of good, respectable parents, so that for want of heirs one's land is not given or left to rogues or knaves . . .

418–30 See to it therefore that your brightness does not fail and is not extinguished, and that through marriage the everlasting light that is beautiful in the eyes of the world and pleasing to God springs forth from you, and that your wife might be a help to you in your old age, just as the aged Anne was to the great Tobit. And do not damn yourself by falling in this benighted time into carnal sin, for your future life would thereby be shortened and in the end your soul would be damned . . .

3 Tobit 2:12–23, Apocrypha.

4 See reference to Sarah and the virtuous women in the *Sarum Manual* Collect prayer, p. 500 below.

. . .
231 Elle gouverne son hostel
Et son bestail d'autre costel;
Elle est guettant, saige et apperte,
Et voit que rien ne voist a perte;
. . .
239 Espargnier scet et avoir soing
Pour le despendre a un besoing:
Ce ne fait pas mesgnie estrange,
Qui vuide l'escrin et la grange
Et ne pense fors de rober,
244 De po faire et de temps passer . . .
. . .
252 Thobie perdit sa lueur,
Mais sa femme lui fut aidable,
Treshumble, doulce et charitable,
Et a lui garder entendi
256 Tant que Dieux clarté lui rendi;
. . .
275 Celle Saire que nous disons
Fut si loyal qu'es benissons
Est nommée et es espousailles.
. . .
280 . . . Il fut uns roys
Qui diverses femmes ama
Et son propos en ce ferma
Que il n'aroit jamais espouse . . .
. . .
290 Maint bastart se vouldrent faire hoir
Qui le royaume destruisirent;
Et quant aucuns voisins ce virent,
Les destruisirent et regnerent,
294 Entr'eulx le regne diviserent . . .
. . .
369 Si fait bon avoir droicte ligne
Et espouser femme benigne
D'onnestes parens et de bons
Tant qu'a merdailles n'a garsons
Par deffault d'oirs ne soit donnée
374 Terre d'autruy n'abandonnée.
. . .
418 Or garde donc par quel maniere
Ta clarté n'estaingne ne faille,
Et que par mariage saille
De toy lumiere pardurable,
Belle au monde, a Dieu agreable,
Et que ta femme en tes vieulx jours
Soit a ta vieillesse secours,
425 Ainsi comme fut la vieille Anne
Au grant Thobie. Et ne te dampne
De suir en ce temps obscur

[Free Will speaks to Desire, Folly, Servitude and Deceit.]

493–504 And I am truly in need of advice. And it seems to me that I saw, when I was a child at school, a saying of Solomon's which said quite clearly: "if you do anything, do it wisely, with an eye always on the end." And elsewhere he said in Latin, from which the French has it, that one should never do anything without advice, for the man who acts on advice meets with success in his undertakings . . .

722–31 But I want to have a wife who is kind, humble, unaffected, not talkative, hard-working, not haughty, young and pure of hand and mouth, wise and graceful, and who is between at least fifteen or sixteen and twenty years old, who is rich and of a good family, who has a healthy body and who is beautiful, and as gentle as a dove, obedient to me in all things . . .

746–73 And, if I give her children, let her love, tend and nurture them like a mother and sweet nurse, and let her save money in order to feed them and to help them achieve a good situation in life. If I can find a woman like this I shall love her more than any other mortal soul, I shall end my days joyfully, I shall have neither troubles nor disturbances, I shall be merry and happy, I shall always be in great comfort and at a safe remove from those dangers that come from foolish harlots. No-one will have joy like mine. I shall live according to the law. She will be the refuge of my youth and the support of my old age, sustaining me when I am frail. And when it is time for me to pay nature's tribute, she will take care of my soul, which she will pray for. My friends will not do this. And my children who remain after me will remember me, their father. Thus my light will remain untarnished after me here. And I believe that this is the best way . . .

Pechié de char, car ou futur
En seroit ta vie abregiée,
Et en la fin t'ame dampnée . . .
. . .

[Franc Vouloir speaks to Desir, Folie, Servitute and Faintise.]

. . . S'ay bien mestier d'avoir advis.
Et si me samble que je vis,
Comme je fu enfant d'escole,
De Salemon une parole,
Qui disoit assez plainement:
<Se tu faiz rien, fay saigement,
Et resgarde en tous temps la fin.>
Et ailleurs disoit en latin,
De quoi le françois veult retraire,
Qu'om ne doit nulle chose faire
Sanz conseil, car qui de lui euvre,
A bonne fin vient de son euvre . . .
. . .

[After summarising arguments against marriage (lines 665-720), Franc Vouloir speaks in its favour.]

Mais avoir vueil femme benigne,
Humble, simple, po enparlée,
Bien besongnant, pou eslevée,
Juene et chaste de bouche et mains,
Saige et gente, et qui ait du mains
De .xv., .xvi. ou a vint ans,
Qui soit riche et de bons parans,
Qui ait bon corps et qui soit belle,
Et doulce comme columbelle,
Obeissant a moy en tout . . .
. . .

Et se je des enfans lui fais,
Qu'elle les aimt, garde et nourrice,
Comme mere et douce nourrice,
Et espargne pour les nourrir
Et pour eulx a estat venir.
Se j'en puis trover une tele,
Plus l'ameray que riens mortele,
En joie fineray mon temps,
Je n'aray noise ne contemps,
Je seray gaiz et envoisés,
Je seray tousjours bien aisés
Et hors de ces aultres perils
De foles femmes qui sont vils;
Nulz n'avra tel joie com moy:
Je viveray selon la loy.
S'iert le retret de ma jonesse,
S'iert le baston de ma vieillesse,
Soustenent ma fragilité,

[Free Will writes to his 'vray ami' (true friend) Repository of Learning for his opinion on what the False Friends have said, and receives a long letter in return that details women's vices and the woes of marriage with help from many authorities.]

1617 And even if the husband is wise . . .

1622–30 He cannot avoid conflict with his wife, once he has taken her, nor the burden she represents. If you take as a wife a beautiful woman you will know no peace, for everyone will desire her, and it will be extremely difficult for you to preserve for yourself what everyone pursues, seeks and desires . . .

2922–9 Juvenal takes issue with husbands and maintains that no woman remains chaste if she is pursued and pressed, for it is in her nature to be pliable and to offer succour to all men, and that this yielding to men is the least of the sins that stain the heart of woman[5] . . .

2943–53 Furthermore, Herodotus says that in order to procure her own pleasure, a woman is not in the least ashamed to lift up her dress, wherever she may be, so that someone may have his way with her. And if she is caught in the act, providing she manages to cover herself again quickly, she is so artful with her tongue that she will always outargue her accuser . . .

5 See *Le Roman de la Rose*, lines 9145–6.

Et quant je seray exité
A paier le treu de nature,
Celle ara de m'ame la cure
Et prira pour l'ame de my:
Ce ne feront pas mi amy;
Et mes enfens qui demourront
Moy leur pere ramenbreront:
Ainsi demourra ma lumiere
Glorieuse ça en arriere,
Et croy que ce sera le mieulx . . .
. . .

[Franc Vouloir writes to his 'vray ami' (true friend) 'Répertoire de Science' for his opinion on what the false friends have said and receives a long letter in return that details women's vices and the woes of marriage, with help from many authorities.]

Et encor soit ly maris saiges . . .

Ne puet il eschuer la guerre
De sa femme, puis qu'il l'a prise,
Ne la sarcine de l'emprise.
Se tu la prens, qu'elle soit belle,
Tu n'aras jamais paix a elle,
Car chascuns la couvoitera,
Et dure chose a toy sera
De garder ce que un chascun voite
Et qu'il poursuit et qu'il couvoite
. . .
Juvenaulx les mariez tance
Et content qu'il n'est femme chaste,
S'on la poursuit et s'on la haste;
Que la nature est enclinable
D'estre a tout homme secourable,
Et que c'est ly mendres pechiez
Dont cuer de femme est entechiez[6]
Que de livrer bersault aux hommes.
. . .
Erodotes encor raconte
Que la femme n'a point de honte,
Pour son grant delit achever,
De sa robe prandre et lever
En quelque lieu, en quelque place,
Tant que aucuns sa volunté face;
Et s'elle y estoit prinse apperte,
Mais qu'elle soit tost recouverte,
Tant se scet de sa langue aidier

6 Taken from *Le Roman de la Rose*, lines 9145–6: "Que c'est li mendres des pechiés/ Dont cuer de fame est entechiez."

[The False Friends counter Repository of Learning's antifeminist arguments with examples of virtuous women.]

9063–7 Moreover, to tell the truth, I find that in their sufferings women have been a hundred thousand times more constant and pious than men . . .

9097–9100 For I would dare to bet that for every example one could find in literature of a woman who has acted badly, I could find a thousand good ones . . .

9107–16 What did Judith do for her city, whose blood she spared, when, only lightly armed, she cut off Holofernes's head? And then the fair maid, alone with her maidservant, carried it to the city of Bethulia, as the Bible tells me; at daybreak it was hung on the walls and her people were saved.

9124–5 And is not Esther[7] worthy of great reward for her humility?

9135–52 She did so much by her prayers that she saved her people, who were marked for death. In the end Haman was proved wrong, so that on the gallows that he had raised to hang Mordecai, against God and against reason, he was hanged in front of his house. Mordecai ruled in his place, and comported himself wisely; he was second after Ahasuerus. Thus Esther, the holy mother, saved and protected her people, who would [otherwise] have been destroyed and slain because of Haman and false envy. Is it not then a beautiful way to live: to have a beautiful and good lady, and to find such a wife?

[The poem eventually breaks off during a long discussion between Free Will and Folly on events of the Hundred Years War, including the battles of Crécy and Poitiers.]

7 See Book of Esther.

Qu'elle ara droit par son plaidier
Encontre cellui qui l'accuse.

[The False Friends counter Répertoire de Science's antifeminist arguments with examples of virtuous women.]

Et encores, pour le voir dire,
Trueve femmes en leur martire
Avoir esté cent mille tans
Plus devotes et plus constans
Assez que les hommes ne furent . . .
. . .
Car j'oseray gaigier et mettre
Que pour une qu'om treuve en lettre
Qui a mal fait, j'en trouveray
Mille bonnes . . .
. . .
Que fist Judith pour sa cité
Dont elle a le sang respité,
Quant elle a petit de harnès
Couppa le chief Holofernès?
Et adonc l'apporta la belle,
Seulement lui et son ancelle,
En Bethulie la cité,
Ce m'a la Bible recité;
Au main fut pandu sur les murs:
Si demoura ses peuples surs.
. . .
Ne rest digne de grant desserte
Hester pour son humilité . . .
. . .
Et tant fist par son orison
Qu'elle impetra la garison
De son peuple qui estoit mort.
Amam en ot au derrain tort,
Qu'au traistre qu'il ot fait lever
Pour Mardocheon encroer
Contre Dieu et contre raison,
Fut pandus devant sa maison.
Mardocheus pour lui regna,
Qui saigement se gouverna;
Secons fut après Assuere.
Ainsis Hester, la saincte mere,
Son peuple sauva et guari,
Qui estoit dampné et peri
Par Aman et par fausse envie.
N'est ce pas donques belle vie
Que d'avoir belle et bonne dame
Et de trover une tel femme?

II

St Jerome, *Letter against Jovinian*

(trans. W. H. Fremantle, *The Principal Works of St Jerome* [New York: Christian Literature Co., 1893], p. 385)

Men marry, indeed, so as to get a manager for the house, to solace weariness, to banish solitude; but a faithful slave is a far better manager, more submissive to the master, more observant of his ways, than a wife who thinks she proves herself mistress if she acts in opposition to her husband, that is, if she does what pleases her, not what she is commanded. But friends, and servants who are under the obligation of benefits received, are better able to wait upon us in sickness than a wife who makes us responsible for her tears (she will sell you enough to make a deluge, for the hope of a legacy), boasts of her anxiety, but drives her sick husband to the distraction of despair.

III

Albertano of Brescia, *The Book of Consolation and Advice*

(trans. C. W. Marx, in *Women Defamed and Women Defended: An Anthology of Medieval Texts*, ed. Alcuin Blamires [Oxford, 1992], pp. 240–1)

Chapter V: In Praise of Women.
When you have heard these arguments for the justification of women, you may hear and understand five other reasons why it can be shown that women are good and especially kind partners in marriage, and that their counsel should be listened to and, if it is good, followed. First, because it is commonly said, "counsel from women is either excessively valuable or quite worthless." I understand "excessively valuable" as "most highly valued," because there is nothing superfluous about it, just as is said about the friends of God, "Your friends, O God, are esteemed beyond measure." [Psalm 138:17] And certainly, although there are villainous women whose counsel is worthless, nevertheless, the best counsel is found in many. For Jacob through the good counsel of his mother Rebecca obtained the blessing of his father Isaac and dominion over his brothers. In the same way Judith, through her good counsel, freed the city in which she dwelt from the hands of Holofernes, who wanted to destroy it in a siege. Also, Abigail through her own good counsel freed her husband Nabal from the anger of King David who wanted to kill him. In a similar way, Esther raised up the Jews through her good counsel along with Mordecai during the reign of King Ahasuerus. And so, many examples can be found of the innumerable good women and their counsel.

II

St. Jerome, *Epistola adversus Jovinianum*, I. 47

(from *Patrologia Latina*, ed. J.-P. Migne [Paris, 1845], vol. 23, cols 277–8)

Quod si propter dispensationem domus et languoris solatia, et fugam solitudinis, ducuntur uxores: multo melius servus fidelis dispensat, obediens auctoritati domini, et dispositioni ejus obtemperans, quam uxor, quae in eo se existimat dominam, si adversum viri faciat voluntatem, id est, quod placet, non quod jubetur. Assidere autem aegrotanti magis possunt amici, et vernulae beneficiis obligati, quam illa quae nobis imputat lacrymas suas haereditatis spe vendit illuviem, et sollicitudinem jactans, languentis animum desperatione conturbat.

III

Albertano of Brescia, *Liber consolationis et consilii*

(ed. Thor Sundby, Chaucer Society, 2nd series, 8 [London: 1873], pp. 16–17)[1]

Caput V: De Laude Mulierum

Hijs ad excusationem mulierum auditis, audias et intelligas quinque alias rationes, quibus probari potest, mulieres esse bonas et maxime benignas conjuges, earumque consilium esse audiendum et, si bonum est, servandum. Primo, quia vulgo dici consuevit: Consilium feminile aut nimis carum aut nimis vile. *Nimis carum*, intelligo: id est *carissimum*, ut non notetur per hoc superfluitas, sicut de amicis Dei dicitur: "*Nimis* honorati sunt amici tui, Deus." [Psalm 138:17] Et certe, licet enim multae mulieres pessimæ sint, quarum consilium est vile, tamen in multis invenitur optimum consilium. Jacob enim per bonum consilium matris suae Rebeccæ adeptus est patris sui Ysaac benedictionem et super fratribus suis dominatum. Similiter et Judith per bonum suum consilium liberavit civitatem, in qua morabatur, de manibus Holofernis, qui illam obsidendo destruere volebat. Similiter et Abigail per suum bonum consilium virum suum Nabal ab ira David regis liberavit, qui eum interficere volebat. Simili modo et Hester Judæos per suum bonum consilium simul cum Mardochæo, in regno Assueri regis, sublimavit. Et ita de infinitis bonis mulieribus earumque consiliis infinita possent repiriri exempla.

[1] For the French text, see *Sources and Analogues of the Canterbury Tales*, ed. Robert M. Correale and Mary Hamel (Cambridge: D. S. Brewer, 2002), vol. 1. 321ff. The passage itself is found on pp. 340–1.

[cf. *The Tale of Melibee* IV, 1098–1102 (*Riverside*, p. 221):
Loo, Jacob by good conseil of his mooder Rebekka wan the benysoun of Ysaak his fader and the lordshipe over alle his bretheren./ Judith by hire good conseil delivered the citee of Bethulie, in which she dwelled, out of the handes of Olofernus, that hadde it biseged and wolde have al destroyed it./ Abygail delivered Nabal hir housbonde fro David the kyng, that wolde have slayn hym, and apaysed the ire of the kyng by hir wit and by hir good conseillyng./ Hester by hir good conseil enhaunced greetly the peple of God in the regne of Assuerus the kyng./ And the same bountee in good conseillyng of many a good womman may men telle.]

IV

Collect after the Marriage Blessing, *The Sarum Manual*

(trans. F. E. Warren, *The Sarum Missal in English*, Part II [London, 1913], pp. 155–6)

O God, by whom woman is joined to man, and the union, instituted in the beginning, is gifted with that blessing, which alone has not been taken away either through the punishment of original sin, or through the sentence of the deluge, look graciously, we beseech thee, on this thy handmaiden, who now to be joined in wedlock, seeketh to be guarded by thy protection. May the yoke of love and peace be upon her; may she be a faithful and chaste wife in Christ, and abide a follower of holy matrons. May she be amiable to her husband as Rachel, wise as Rebecca, long-lived and faithful as Sara. Let not the father of lies get any advantage over her through her doings; bound to thy faith and thy commandments may she remain united to one man; may she flee all unlawful unions; may she fortify her weakness with the strength of discipline. May she be bashful and grave, reverential and modest, well-instructed in heavenly doctrine. May she be fruitful in child-bearing, innocent and of good report, attaining to a desired old age, seeing her children's children unto the third and fourth generation; and may she attain the rest of the blessed, and to the kingdom of heaven.

IV

Collect after the Marriage Blessing, *The Sarum Manual*

(from A. Jefferies Collins, ed., *Manuale ad vsum percelebris ecclesie sarisburiensis*, Henry Bradshaw Society XCI [London, 1960], p. 54)

Ordo ad faciendum sponsalia: (excerpt)

Deus, per quem mulier iungitur viro et societas principaliter ordinata ea benedictione donatur: que sola nec per originalis peccati penam/ nec per diluuii est ablata sententiam *.respice*. Respice propitius super hanc famulam tuam que maritali iungenda consortio: tua que se expetit protectione muniri. Sit in ea iugum dilectionis et pacis: fidelis et casta nubat in christo: imitatrixque sanctarum permaneat feminarum. Sit amabilis vt rachel viro: sapiens vt rebecca: longeua et fidelis vt sara. Nichil in ea ex actibus suis ille auctor preuaricationis vsurpet: nexa fidei mandatisque permaneat vni thoro iuncta/ contactus illicitos fugiat/ muniatque infirmitatem suam robore discipline. Sit verecundia grauis/ pudore venerabilis/ doctrinis celestibus erudita. Sit fecunda in sobole/ sit probata et innocens: et ad optatam perueniat senectutem: et videat filios filiorum suorum vsque in tertiam et quartam progeniem: et ad beatorum requiem atque ad celestia regna perueniat.

V

Comedy of the Florentine Nymphs

(trans. N.S. Thompson)

XXXII *(Agapes speaks)*:
(1–24) Now, nymphs, it is hard for me to believe that it is less honourable to remain silent about one's parents than it is to speak openly. One is not worthy of note, while the other is worthy of infamy, not for herself, but for her family, I would say, had I not been born of them. Thus are their forebears known, and they have grown up in vice, not knowing themselves how to love, one having gouged the poor people with a sharp nail, the other having bled them dry with a flattering tongue. But I, not following their evil ways, well known because of them, no longer care if this is so: therefore, as you have done, so will I [i.e. tell her story].

In Achaea, the beautiful part of Greece, rises a mountain at the foot of which runs a small stream. In summer it barely has a ripple, but during storms it is full. Here rough satyrs lived in the early days of habitation, along with the nymphs who lived there. From such rough types came my father's forebears who, given that Amphion had moved hard stones with the sound of his clear lyre for building Thebes, so they with their own hands ordered them into the shape of high walls. But because fortune, who blindly deals out the world's goods, gave these unworthy people many riches, they abandoned their first crafts which, although more humble, would have served them better as more useful, and gave themselves up to following the clever practices of Mercury [i.e. became merchants]. O they were much more suited to the hoes of Saturn [god of agriculture]! The notoriety of their pleasures, which was to fall as soon as it rose, fills the world. From plebeians mixed with nobility, barely knowing themselves, and through their accumulated wealth having begun to hope like Phlegreus and his followers [the Giants], they search the sky with a brazen thought. And the hidden vendetta, already begun in anger against their deceit, is veiled from the eyes that must shortly close in eternal sleep.

(25–56) Well, why should I talk at length divining my wrongs? My father is of those who, crossing the little stream by an ancient bridge, came to the lands inhabited by my mother; he found her relatives, more rich than noble, were working beyond the reasonable nature of Amanthus, creating coin from coin [i.e. as bankers]; on a gold ground, they bore a silver horned Phebea in a vermilion sash [arms of the

V

Giovanni Boccaccio, *La comedia delle ninfe fiorentine*[1]

(ed. Antonio Enzo Quaglio, *Tutte le opere di Giovanni Boccaccio*, ed. Vittore Branca, vol. 2 [Milan: Mondadori, 1964], pp. 772–6)

[XXXII] – Appena mi si lascia credere, o ninfe, che non fosse così onesto il tacere come sia il parlare de' miei parenti, de' quali l'uno non degno di fama e l'altra d'infamia degna, non per lei ma per li suoi, riputerei, se io non ne fossi nata; tali i loro antecessori si conoscono, e essi, ne' vizii cresciuti e male saputisi fare amare, però che l'uno con tagliente unghione ha laniato il misero popolo, l'altro con lusinghevole lingua leccando l'ha munto di sangue. Ma io, non seguente le loro malizie, notissima per quelli, non curo se più mi fo nota: e però, come voi avete fatto, e io farò. In Acaia, bellissima parte di Grecia, surge un monte appiè del quale corre un picciolo fiume, ne' tempi estivi poverissimo d'onde e abondante di quelle negli acquazzosi, sopra il quale agresti satiri furono ne' primi tempi d'abitare costumati con le ninfe quelli luoghi colenti. Tra quelli così rozzi nacquero i primi del padre mio, li quali, sì come Anfione col suono della chiara cetera le dure pietre mosse a chiudere Tebe, così essi con le propie mani già molte ne costrinsero stare in ordine d'alte mura. E come che la fortuna, ciecamente trattante i beni mondani, indegni gli traesse a molte copie, lasciate le prime arti, le quali, avvegna che più umili, sanza fallo più utili sarebbono loro riuscite, si dierono a seguitare di Mercurio l'astuzie: oh quanto più degni a' ligoni di Saturno! La fama delle loro delizie, così subita ancora casura come salio, riempie il mondo; e essi, di plebei mescolati tra' nobili, male conoscenti di se medesimo, per gli accumulati beni entrati nella speranza di Flagrareo e de' seguaci, con tempesto pensiero cercano il cielo; e l'occulta vendetta, con giusta ira già mossa a' falli loro, si cela agli occhi che si debbono in poco tempo chiudere di morte etterna.

Deh, perché mi distendo io più a vaticinare i danni miei? Il padre mio è di questi, il quale, passate le poche onde per antico ponte, pervenne a' luoghi abitati dalla mia madre; i parenti della quale, più ricchi che nobili, trovò che intendevano, oltre alla naturale ragione d'Amatuta, a fare partorire i metalli a' metalli medesimi, e tutti d'oro coperti, portavano in vermiglia cintura la inargentata Febea con le sue corna. Non curo questi dello abominevole

[1] Boccaccio's first frame tale, the *Comedia* is an allegory in which the nymphs represent a theological or cardinal virtue (Lia=Faith; Agapes=Charity; Adiona=Temperance; Emilia=Justice; Fiammetta= Hope; Acrimonia= Fortitude; Mopsa=Prudence) and temper the lovers they acquire (who represent a defect or vice) with a beneficial influence. Collectively, the narratives add up to an education in Christian love for Ameto, who is transformed by his love for the nymph Lia, and achieves salvation through faith. Because several nymphs are associated by heraldic devices with certain Florentine families, it has been suggested that there is a realistic centre to these portraits (see Quaglio's note, p. 947), especially in the case of Agapes, whose heraldic device suggests her membership in the Strozzi family. The barbed comments against usury and following "di Mercurio l'astuzie" (the craft of Mercury, i.e. they were merchants) place her narrative firmly in a mercantile context, even if the exact identification of individuals is more problematic. The classicizing frame is perhaps also of interest because of Chaucer's reference to Amphion and the creation of Thebes (see IV, 1715–17).

Strozzi family]. Not caring for the abominable trade, but desirous of money, of which they enjoyed a huge quantity, he was joined to my mother by the laws of Juno, and took her to his property, where I, born from them, was raised with a pious education. My childhood passed simply. I was not troubled by many studies nor noted by the gods. But, when I was older and grown in beauty, with my whole heart I desired to marry. I hoped the gods had promised me to a worthy young man, someone in build and age like me, who was beautiful. But my idea was one thing and the heavens disposed something else. Although I possessed a beauty I had long cultivated, an old man was given me, whereby I sorrowed, no matter how rich he was. But I dared not let the sorrow escape my lips. Coming from patronage circles and "helping" towards the above mentioned civil questions [i.e. his money secured the marriage], having perhaps seen more ages than the renewing stag, he was reduced by time into misshapen form. The few white hairs on his head bear clear witness to this; and his cheeks, with rough folds, and his wrinkled forehead and huge hairy beard, as sharp as the quill of a porcupine, bear it even more. Moreover, and it pleases me even less, he has eyes more red than white, hidden under knitted brows, covered with long hairs, and they water continuously. His lips hang down like those of a long-eared donkey, without any colour, pallid, giving the impression they are badly shaped, worn and yellow, rather than reddish, with broken teeth, many of which are missing; and his thin neck hides neither bone nor vein, but rather, it trembles very often with the head, shaking the faded parts. And the weak arms and the withered chest and calloused hands and the dried up body, with all that follows, respond in even worse measure. And going everywhere bent over, he keeps his eyes on the ground, as if thinking that it will soon receive him; and it should have received him, given that he has been deprived of his reason for many years.

(57–83) Fate delivered me to him, who accepted me happily into his properties; where I still stay with him sometimes in the silent night; and with him, no matter how long Phoebus is from the earth, no night is short. As we lie in the soft bed, he takes me in his arms and weighs unpleasantly on my pure white neck. And after not so much as kissing me many times with his stinking mouth as slobbering over mine, he touches my pretty breasts with his trembling hands, and then goes over every part of my unfortunate body and, with ill-sounding whispers in my ears, he offers flattery; and, ice cold himself, he thinks he will inflame me with such attentions: where I would sooner light his soul than his miserable body. O nymphs, have compassion on my troubles! After he has wasted most of the night with these trifles, he struggles in vain to cultivate the gardens of Venus; and seeking with an old ploughshare to break the ground that desires gracious seed, he works in vain: so that, worn out by age, his sharp part bending over like the curved willow, it refuses to perform the necessary office in the firm pasture. Beaten, he rests for a while, and then labours a second and third time, and many others he tries again with all his will; and with many procedures he tries to put into effect that which is impossible for him to perform; and in this fashion he has me pass away the night with unpleasant horse-play and indecent acts, sleepless and exasperated. With his head empty of any sap, content with little sleep, he keeps me awake in disgust with yet more talk. He tells me of his youth and how on his own he could satisfy many women, or he tells me of his lovers and the things he did for them; and sometimes he tells me of the heavenly gods and condemns their deceptions with vituperative censure and other things beyond the limits of the holy law [of marriage]; and if any evil came of this transgression, he relates it. And then when I think he is ready for sleep, he begins to say at the top of his voice:

mestiere di coloro, ma cupido di denari, de' quali quelli abondavano gran quantità, mediante di quelli con giunonica legge la mia madre si giunse e quella seco trasse alle sue case, là dove io, nata di loro, con pietoso studio fui nutricata; e la mia età puerile passò semplice, né mi furono a cura alcuni studii né nota deità nulla. Ma, già multiplicata negli anni e in bellezza, con tutto l'animo desiderava le nozze mie, le quali sperava che gl'iddii avessero promesse a degno giovane, per aspetto e per età simile a me, che era bella; ma il mio pensiero era ad una cosa e i cieli ne dispuosero un'altra. Però che a possedere le bellezze da me lungo tempo studiate fu dato un vecchio, avvegna che copioso, onde io mi dolsi; ma non osò passare i denti il mio dolore. Elli da' patrocinanti le quistioni civili sopra nominate [aiutato], avente forse veduti più secoli che il rinnovante cervio, dagli anni in poca forma era tirato. E la testa con pochi capelli e bianchi ne danno certissimo indizio; e le sue guance, per crespezza ruvide, e la fronte rugosa e la barba grossa e prolissa, né più né meno pugnente che le penne d'uno istrice, più certa me ne rendono assai. Egli ha ancora, che più mi spiace, gli occhi più rossi che bianchi, nascosi sotto grottose ciglia, folte di lunghi peli; e continuo son lagrimosi. Le labbra sue sono come quelle dell'orecchiuto asino pendule e sanza alcuno colore, palide, danti luogo alla vista de' male composti e logori e gialli, anzi più tosto rugginosi, e fracidi denti, de' quali il numero in molte parti si vede scemo; e il sottile collo né osso né vena nasconde, anzi, tremante spesso con tutto il capo, muove le vizze parti. E così le braccia deboli e il secco petto e le callose mani e il già voto corpo, con quanto poi seguita, alle parti predette rispondono con proporzione più dannabile. E nel suo andare continuamente curvo, la terra rimira, la quale credo contempli lui tosto dovere ricevere; e ora l'avesse ella già ricevuto, però che sua ragione gli ha di molti anni levata.

A costui mi concessero i fati, il quale lieto mi raccolse nelle sue case; dove io ancora dimorante alcuna volta con lui, nella tacita notte, delle quali mai niuna con esso, quanto che Febo si lontani alla terra, vi sento corta, istanti nel morbido letto, me raccoglie nelle sue braccia e di non piacevole peso prieme il candido collo. E poi che egli ha molte volte con la fetida bocca non baciata ma scombavata la mia, con le tremanti mani tasta i vaghi pomi, e quindi le muove a ciascuna parte del mio male arrivato corpo, e con mormorii ne' miei orecchi sonevoli male, mi porge lusinghe, e freddissimo si crede me di sé accendere con cotali atti: là dove io più tosto di lui accendo l'animo che 'l misero corpo. O ninfe, abbiate ora compassione alle mie noie! Poi che egli ha gran parte della notte tirata con queste ciance, gli orti di Venere invano si fatica di cultivare; e cercante con vecchio bomere fendere la terra di quelli disiderante i graziosi semi, lavora indarno: però che quello, dalla antichità roso, come la lenta salice la sua aguta parte volgendo in cerchio, nel sodo maggese il debito uficio recusa d'adoperare. Onde elli, vinto, alquanto si posa, e quindi alla seconda fatica e alla terza appresso e poi a molte invano risurge con l'animo; e con diversi atti s'ingegna di recare ad effetto ciò che per lui non è possibile di compiersi; e per questo modo la notte tutta di spiacevoli ruzzamenti e di sconvenevoli atti, sanza sonno, accidiosa mi fa trapassare. Egli, col capo voto d'umidità, contento di poco sonno, con nuovi ragionamenti, sanza dormire, invita mi tiene. Egli mi racconta i tempi della sua giovanezza e come egli a molte femine solo saria bastato, o dice i suoi amori e le cose fatte per quelli; e tale volta mette mano alle storie de' celestiali iddii e danna con vituperevole riprensione i furti loro e di qualunque altro passante i termini della santa legge; e se per questo trapassamento mai n'avenne alcuno

(84–96) "O young woman, happy among others, how gracious were the gods to you when they gave you to me rather than to a younger man! There is no mother hovering over your pleasures, you are in my house alone and my woman; you need not suspect that the love of another woman would draw me away; I have given you all the clothes and everything else pleasing to you. You are my only comfort and joy; there is no moment more pleasant in my life than when you are in my arms and your lips are against mine. If you had happened to go to a younger man, few of these things would be yours; young men have their minds on a thousand loves; the ones they frequent most are the ones they love least. They leave their wives cold and alone and fearful in the cold bed for the most part of the night and crazily go off seeking other women; but I will never leave you. Why should there be anyone more dear to me than you? The gods forbid that I would ever change you for another."

(97–111) But after listening so long, led by the evil breath from his mouth into extreme suffering, I demand silence and tell him to sleep, but to no avail. And if I want to go anywhere else, he makes such an effort and seizes me in his thin arms and either keeps me there or, light on his feet, follows me wherever I might go. And just as day is almost near, I manage to separate him from me and have him sleep a little: this happens with him snoring loudly and stopping me from sleeping; so that almost desperate I pray to the gods that day come so that I might leave his side and go and lie somewhere else. These actions, although my aged husband still goes through them, with me still being without satisfaction, have brought me almost to the point of desperation. But through the useful advice given to me I propose to serve Venus, and to her divinity, more merciful than any other, I thought to air my sufferings and seek from her some remedy by which to bear them with less hardship. And after the advice, I followed through to the effect. I came to these temples hereabouts from my region and, offering my devotion as required, I began to pray before the holy altars in this way . . .

male, egli il racconta. E poi con più intero parlare, quando io credo ch'egli voglia dormire, ricomincia e dice:

<O giovane donna, tra l'altre molto felice, quanto ti furono graziosi gl'iddii che più tosto a me che a uno più giovane ti concessono! A me non madre soprastante a' tuoi piaceri, tu sola se' della mia casa e di me donna; di me non puoi dubitare che amore d'altra donna mi ti tolga; da me i vestiri e tutte quelle cose che a grado ti sono, a te sono concedute. Tu se' sola bene e riposo di me; niuna volta m'è graziosa la vita, se non mentre tu nelle mie braccia dimori e la tua bocca s'accosta alla mia. Se tu fossi pervenuta alle mani d'uno più giovane, poche di queste cose ti sarieno concedute; i giovani hanno gli animi divisi in mille amori; quella che è meno amata da loro è colei di cui essi hanno maggiore copia. Elli lasciano la maggiore parte delle notti le loro spose sole e paurose nel freddo letto e vanno cercando follemente le altrui; ma io mai da te non mi diparto. E perché me ne sarebbe alcuna più cara di te? Cessino l'iddii che io mai per alcuna altra ti cambi>.

Ma io, dopo molto ascoltare, quasi dal pessimo fiato della sua bocca condotta ad estremo supplicio, gl'impongo silenzio e dico che dorma; ma poco mi vale. E s'io in altra parte mi voglio voltare, egli, sforzantesi e con le deboli braccia strignentemi, o mi ritiene o, lieve di carne, si volge con meco dovunque io mi volgo. E appena, già al giorno, vicini posso fare che da me diviso si dorma alquanto: la qual cosa s'avviene pur ch'e' faccia, ronfando forte il mio sonno impedisce; onde io, quasi disperata, agl'iddii cerco il giorno acciò che, da lato a lui levandomi, altrove mi possa posare. Questi atti, avvegna che ancora il mio vecchio li servi, essendo io sanza alcuna consolazione, quasi a disperazione m'aveano recata. Ma per utile consiglio a me dato proposi di servire Venere, e alla sua deità più che altra pietosa pensai dolermi de' miei affanni e di cercare ad essa alcuno rimedio per lo quale con meno fatica li sostenessi; e come fu l'avviso, così seguitai con l'effetto. Io venni dalle mie parti a questi templi vicini, e in quelli, divota secondo il bisogno, dinanzi a' santi altari così cominciai a pregare . . .

[Agapes prays to Venus and, not knowing whether she is waking or dreaming, is transported by dove-drawn chariot to 'Mount Cythera' where Venus presents her with Apiros (the 'cold one'), her lover.]

VI

Giovanni Boccaccio, *Decameron* II, 10

(trans. N. S. Thompson)

Paganino of Monaco steals the wife of Messer Ricciardo di Chinzica who, when he finds her whereabouts, goes and befriends Paganino and asks for her return; Paganino offers to do so, if she is agreeable; but she does not want to return and, when Messer Riccardo dies, she becomes Paganino's wife.

(1–4) Each one of the honourable company commended the queen's story (II, 9) very highly for its beauty and, most of all, Dioneo, who was the last speaker left. When he had finished his remarks, he began:
(5–16) Fair ladies, one aspect of the queen's tale has made me change my mind about the one I was to tell, so I will change it for another, and that aspect, although it turned out well for him in the end, was the idiocy of Bernabò and any men like him who believe that while they travel the world taking pleasure with one woman here and another one there, the women left at home sit with their hands on their laps, as if we who are born, grow up and live with them did not know what it is they desire. In telling this next tale, I will show you the foolishness of such people, at the same time showing the even greater folly of those who, thinking themselves more powerful than nature, believe they can perform the impossible with fantastic arguments and try to make other people be like them, no matter how much it stretches the bounds of nature.

(17–31) There was once a judge in Pisa blessed with more fancy than bodily strength, whose name was Messer Riccardo di Chinzica, who thought he could perhaps satisfy a wife using the same methods he did for his studies and, being very rich, *he made every effort to find a woman for his wife who was both young and beautiful* whereas, if he had been able to advise himself as well as he did others, he should have looked for neither one nor the other. But the thing came about because Messer Lotto Gualandi gave him as wife one of his daughters, whose name was Bartolomea, one of the most beautiful and charming young ladies of Pisa, where there are few women who do not look like a skinny lizard. *The judge took her to his house with great festivity but, after a huge and magnificent ceremony*, on the first night he only managed to touch her once to consummate the marriage, and then he almost had to throw in the towel; *in the morning, seeing as he was thin, wrinkled and weary, he had to treat himself with vernaccia,*[1] *delicate restorative sweetmeats, and other preparations in order to return to the land of the living.*

(32–45) So this Man of the Bench, now a better judge of his forces that he was before, quickly began to teach his wife a calendar that was excellent for children

[1] A name that today applies to many different local wines.

VI

Giovanni Boccaccio, *Decameron* II, 10

(from *Giovanni Boccaccio, Decameron*, ed. Vittore Branca, 2nd edn, [Torino: Einaudi, 1980], pp. 303–14)[2]

Paganino da Monaco ruba la moglie a messer Ricciardo di Chinzica; il quale, sappiendo dove ella è, va, e diventa amico di Paganino; raddomandagliele, e egli, dove ella voglia, gliele concede; ella non vuol con lui tornare e, morto messer Ricciardo, moglie di Paganin diviene.

Ciascuno della onesta brigata sommamente commendò per bella la novella della loro reina contata, e massimamente Dioneo, al qual solo per la presente giornata restava il novellare. Il quale, dopo molte commendazioni di quella fatte, disse:

– Belle donne, una parte della novella della reina m'ha fatto mutar consiglio di dirne una, che all'animo m'era, a doverne un'altra dire: e questa è la bestialità di Bernabò, come che bene ne gli avvenisse, e di tutti gli altri che quello si danno a credere che esso di creder mostrava: cioè che essi, andando per lo mondo e con questa e con quella ora una volta ora un'altra sollazzandosi, s'immaginan che le donne a casa rimase si tengan le mani a cintola, quasi noi non conosciamo, che tra esse nasciamo e cresciamo e stiamo, di che elle sien vaghe. La qual dicendo, a un'ora vi mostrerò chente sia la sciocchezza di questi cotali, e quanto ancora sia maggior quella di coloro li quali, sé piú che la natura possenti estimando, si credon quello con dimostrazioni favolose potere che essi non possono, e sforzansi d'altrui recare a quello che essi sono, non patendolo la natura di chi è tirato.

Fu adunque in Pisa un giudice, piú che di corporal forza dotato d'ingegno, il cui nome fu messer Riccardo di Chinzica; il quale, forse credendosi con quelle medesime opere sodisfare alla moglie che egli faceva agli studii, essendo molto ricco, *con non piccola sollecitudine cercò d'avere e bella e giovane donna per moglie*, dove e l'uno e l'altro, se cosí avesse saputo consigliar sé come altrui faceva, doveva fuggire. E quello gli venne fatto, per ciò che messer Lotto Gualandi per moglie gli diede una sua figliuola il cui nome era Bartolomea, una delle piú belle e delle piú vaghe giovani di Pisa, come che poche ve n'abbiano che lucertole verminare non paiano. *La quale il giudice menata con grandissima festa a casa sua, e fatte le nozze belle e magnifiche*, pur per la prima notte incappò una volta per consumare il matrimonio a toccarla e di poco fallò che egli quella una non fece tavola; *il quale poi la mattina, sí come colui che era magro e secco e di poco spirito, convenne che con vernaccia e con confetti ristorativi e con altri argomenti nel mondo si ritornasse.*

Or questo messer lo giudice, migliore stimatore delle sue forze che stato non era avanti, incominciò a insegnare a costei un calendaro buono da

2 Line numbering and all italics in Italian and English translation are mine.

learning to read,[3] or perhaps it was one made in Ravenna.[4] As a result, according to what he showed her, there was not a day that was not a holy day, sometimes many together, out of respect for which, for various reasons, he said that a man and a woman should refrain from conjugal relations adding, on top of this, days of fasting, Ember days, vigils for the Apostles and a thousand other saints, and Fridays, Saturdays, the Lord's Day itself, as well as Lent and certain phases of the moon and many other instances, thinking that perhaps a civic holiday should be taken from being in bed with a woman in the way he sometimes took a day off from summing up his cases. And this fashion continued for a long time, causing grave melancholy in the young lady, as he touched her perhaps once a month and barely that, *at the same time watching her very closely so that there was no opportunity for anyone else to teach her the days on which to work as he had taught her the days for rest.*

(46–61) Then it chanced to be very hot and Messer Riccardo wanted to take a short break on a very beautiful property of his near Monte Nero [south of Livorno], taking his beautiful wife with him, and stay there several days to enjoy the cool air. In order to give her some recreation while they were there, he organized two boats for a day of fishing, taking one boat himself with the fishermen, his wife in the second with other ladies to watch. So absorbed was he that, without being aware of it, they went several miles out to sea. And while they were giving their attention to the spectacle, a small galley captained by Paganino da Monaco, a well-known corsair of those days, seeing the boats suddenly steered towards them, and overtook them. As they could not escape quickly enough, Paganino was able to close in on the one containing the women and, with Riccardo watching from the shore, seeing only the beautiful lady in it and not paying attention to anything else, he placed her in his galley and went away There is no need to wonder how sorrowful the judge felt on seeing this, *given that he was so jealous as to suspect the very air about him.* He complained about the evil of corsairs in Pisa and elsewhere to no avail, without knowing who had taken his wife or where he had taken her.

(62–70) But all was well with Paganino seeing such a beauty and, having no wife, he thought to keep her and, as she was in a flood of tears, began to comfort her with sweet words. But when night came, the calendar having dropped out of his belt, and every high day and holiday gone from his mind, he began to comfort her more with actions than with the words that seemed to be of little use by day. Indeed, he consoled her in such a way that, well before they reached Monaco, both the judge and his laws had passed from her mind and she began to live a more enjoyable life with Paganino who, carrying her off to Monaco, maintained her there honourably as his wife, as well as the gentle consolation he gave her both night and day.

(71–82) Some time later, when news of his wife's whereabouts came to the ears of Messer Riccardo, thinking that he alone knew what to do, he set about going after her with a burning desire, ready to pay any amount of money to release her. Putting to sea, he crossed to Monaco where they caught sight of each other. In the evening she told Paganino and informed him of Riccardo's intentions. The following morning, seeing Paganino, Messer Riccardo went up to him and in less than no time formed a bond of friendship and intimacy, while Paganino pretended to know him and waited to see what he would do. When the time seemed right, in his best and most pleasing manner, Messer Riccardo revealed the reason why he had come, entreating him to take whatever he pleased in return for his wife.

3 i.e., one with many holidays.

4 The city was noted for its great number of churches, and thus many holidays for their patron saints.

fanciulli che stanno a leggere e forse già stato fatto a Ravenna. Per ciò che, secondo che egli le mostrava, niun dí era che non solamente una festa ma molte non ne fossero, a reverenza delle quali per diverse cagioni mostrava l'uomo e la donna doversi abstenere da cosí fatti congiugnimenti, sopra questi aggiugnendo digiuni e quatro tempora e vigilie d'apostoli e di mille altri santi e venerdí e sabati e la domenica del Signore e la quaresima tutta, e certi punti della luna e altre eccezion molte, avvisandosi forse che cosí feria far si convenisse con le donne nel letto, come egli faceva talvolta piatendo alle civili. E questa maniera, non senza grave malinconia della donna, a cui forse una volta ne toccava il mese e appena, lungamente tenne, *sempre guardandola bene, non forse alcuno altro le 'nsegnasse conoscere li dí da lavorare, come egli l'aveva insegnate le feste.*

Avvenne che, essendo il caldo grande, a messer Riccardo venne disidero d'andarsi a diportare a un suo luogo molto bello vicino a Monte Nero, e quivi per prendere aere dimorarsi alcun giorno, e con seco menò la sua bella donna. E quivi standosi, per darle alcuna consolazione fece un giorno pescare, e sopra due barchette, egli in su una co' pescatori e ella in su un'altra con altre donne, andarono a vedere; e tirandogli il diletto parecchi miglia quasi senza accorgersene n'andarono infra mare. E mentre che essi piú attenti stavano a riguardare, subito una galeotta di Paganin da Mare, allora molto famoso corsale, sopravenne e, vedute le barche, si dirizzò a loro; le quali non poteron sí tosto fuggire, che Paganin non giugnesse quella ove eran le donne: nella quale veggendo la bella donna, senza altro volerne, quella, veggente messer Riccardo che già era in terra, sopra la sua galeotta posta andò via. La qual cosa veggendo messer lo giudice, *il quale era sí geloso che temeva dell'aere stesso, se esso fu dolente non è da dimandare.* Egli senza pro, e in Pisa e altrove, si dolfe della malvagità de' corsari, senza sapere chi la moglie tolta gli avesse o dove portatala.

A Paganino, veggendola cosí bella, parve star bene; e non avendo moglie, si pensò di sempre tenersi costei, e lei che forte piagnea cominciò dolcemente a confortare. E venuta la notte, essendo a lui il calendaro caduto da cintola e ogni festa o feria uscita di mente, la cominciò a confortar co' fatti, parendogli che poco fossero il dí giovate le parole; e per sí fatta maniera la racconsolò, che, prima che a Monaco giugnessero, e il giudice e le sue leggi le furono uscite di mente, e cominciò a viver piú lietamente del mondo con Paganino; il quale, a Monaco menatala, oltre alle consolazioni che di dí e di notte le dava, onoratamente come sua moglie la tenea.

Poi a certo tempo pervenuto agli orecchi di messer Riccardo dove la sua donna fosse, con ardentissimo disidero, avvisandosi niuno interamente saper far ciò che a ciò bisognava, esso stesso dispose d'andar per lei, disposto a spendere per lo riscatto di lei ogni quantità di denari: e, messosi in mare, se n'andò a Monaco e quivi la vide e ella lui, la quale poi la sera a Paganino il disse e lui della sua intenzione informò. La seguente mattina messer Riccardo, veggendo Paganino, con lui s'accontò e fece in poca d'ora una gran dimestichezza e amistà, infignendosi Paganino di conoscerlo e aspettando a che riuscir volesse; per che, quando tempo parve a messer Riccardo, come meglio seppe e il piú piacevolmente la cagione per la quale venuto era gli discoperse, pregandolo che quello che gli piacesse prendesse e la donna gli rendesse.

(83–93) With a broad smile on his face, Paganino replied, "Messer, you are most welcome and, keeping it brief, I will tell you this: it is true I have a young lady in my house, but I do not know if she is your wife or the wife of another, because I do not know you nor anything about her, except that she has been living with me for some time. If, as you say, you are her husband, I will take you to her, because you seem a likeable and courteous man to me, and I am sure she will easily recognize you. If she says that it is indeed as you say it is, and she wishes to leave with you, for the sake of your likeableness, you can give whatever it pleases you to give me to release her; but if this is not the case, it would be dishonest to take her away, because I am a young man and can look after a young woman as well as any other [young man], especially one who is the best looking I have ever seen."
(94–7) Then Messer Riccardo said, "She certainly is my wife, and if you take me to her, you will soon see her throw herself immediately around my neck; I ask no more than you have indicated."

(98) "All right," said Paganino, "Let us go."
(99–106) So they went to Paganino's house and when they were in one of his rooms, Paganino called for her. She came from her chamber neatly arrayed and dressed and entered the room where Messer Riccardo was with Paganino, but she addressed Messer Riccardo no differently than she would have done any other stranger he brought into the house. Seeing which, the judge, who expected to have been given a warm welcome, was greatly amazed and said to himself, "Perhaps the melancholy and long sorrow I have had since I lost her have so disfigured me that she does not recognize me."
(167–12) So he said, "Dear lady, it cost me a great deal to take you fishing. I have never felt a pain like the one since I lost you, and yet you do not seem to recognize me, so cold is your attitude. Can you not see that I am your Messer Riccardo, come here to pay whatever is asked by this gentleman, in whose house we are, in order to take you away and have you back again, and he in his goodness, given that I wish it, will give you back."
(113–15) Turning to him with just the touch of a smile, the lady said, "Are you speaking to me, sir? Are you sure you have not mistaken me, because as far as I am concerned I do not remember ever having seen you before."
(116–17) Messer Riccardo said, "What are you saying? Look at me closely. If you decide to have a clear memory, you will see that I am your Riccardo di Chinzica."
(118–20) The lady said, "Messer, you must forgive me, perhaps it is not an honest thing for me, as you imagine, to look closely at you, but nevertheless I have looked at you enough to know that I have never seen you before."
(121–6) Messer Riccardo thought that she was saying this out of fear of Paganino, not wanting to admit in his presence that she knew him. So, after a while, he asked Paganino if he would kindly allow him to speak to her in private. Paganino said he was very happy, so long as he did not attempt to kiss her against her wishes, and he asked the lady to go into her chamber with him and hear what he had to say and reply as she wished.
(127–31) When they were sitting down alone in the room together, Messer Riccardo began to say: "*Well, heart of my heart, my sweet soul, my hope, now do you recognize your Riccardo that loves you more than himself*? How can this be? Am I so disfigured? *Well, light of my life, look at me a little.*"

(132–55) The lady, who had begun to laugh, did not let him utter another word, but said, "Please understand that I am not so scatterbrained as not to know that you are

Al quale Paganino con lieto viso rispose: <Messer, voi siate il ben venuto, e rispondendo in brieve vi dico cosí: egli è vero che io ho una giovane in casa, la quale non so se vostra moglie o d'altrui si sia, per ciò che voi io non conosco né lei altressí se non in tanto quanto ella è meco alcun tempo dimorata. Se voi siete suo marito, come voi dite, io, per ciò che piacevol gentile uom mi parete, vi menerò da lei, e son certo che ella vi conoscerà bene. Se essa dice che cosí sia come voi dite e vogliasene con voi venire, per amor della vostra piacevolezza quello che voi medesimo vorrete per riscatto di lei mi darete; ove cosí non fosse, voi fareste villania a volerlami torre, per ciò che io son giovane uomo e posso cosí come un altro tenere una femina, e spezialmente lei che è la piú piacevole che io vidi mai>.

Disse allora messer Riccardo: <Per certo ella è mia moglie, e se tu mi meni dove ella sia, tu il vederai tosto: ella mi si gitterà incontanente al collo; e per ciò non domando che altramente sia se non come tu medesimo hai divisato>.

<Adunque> disse Paganino <andiamo>.

Andatisene adunque nella casa di Paganino e stando in una sua sala, Paganino la fece chiamare; e ella vestita e acconcia uscí d'una camera e quivi venne dove messer Riccardo con Paganino era, né altramente fece motto a messer Riccardo che fatto s'avrebbe a un altro forestiere che con Paganino in casa sua venuto fosse. Il che vedendo il giudice, che aspettava di dovere essere con grandissima festa ricevuto da lei, si maravigliò forte e seco stesso cominciò a dire: <Forse che la malinconia e il lungo dolore che io ho avuto poscia che io la perdei m'ha sí trasfigurato, che ella non mi riconosce>.

Per che egli disse: <Donna, caro mi costa il menarti a pescare, per ciò che simil dolore non si sentí mai a quello che io ho poscia portato che io ti perdei, e tu non par che mi riconoschi, sí salvaticamente motto mi fai. Non vedi tu che io sono il tuo messer Riccardo, venuto qui per pagare ciò che volesse questo gentile uomo in casa cui noi siamo, per riaverti e per menartene? e egli, la sua mercé, per ciò che io voglio mi ti rende>.

La donna rivolta a lui, un cotal pocolin sorridendo, disse: <Messere, dite voi a me? Guardate che voi non m'abbiate colta in iscambio, ché, quanto è io, non mi ricordo che io vi vedessi giammai>.

Disse messer Riccardo: <Guarda ciò che tu di', guatami bene: se tu ti vorrai ben ricordare, tu vedrai bene che io sono il tuo Riccardo di Chinzica>.

La donna disse: <Messere, voi mi perdonerete: forse non è egli cosí onesta cosa a me, come voi v'immaginate, il molto guardarvi, ma io v'ho nondimeno tanto guardato, che io conosco che io mai piú non vi vidi>.

Imaginossi messer Riccardo che ella questo facesse per tema di Paganino, di non volere in sua presenza confessar di conoscerlo: per che dopo alquanto chiese di grazia a Paganino che in camera solo con essolei le potesse parlare. Paganin disse che gli piacea, sí veramente che egli non la dovesse contra suo piacere basciare; e alla donna commandò che con lui in camera andasse e udisse ciò che egli volesse dire e come le piacesse gli rispondesse.

Andatisene adunque in camera la donna e messer Riccardo soli, come a sedere si furon posti, incominciò messer Riccardo a dire: <*Deh, cuore del corpo mio, anima mia dolce, speranza mia, or non riconosci tu Riccardo tuo che t'ama piú che se medesimo?* come può questo esser? son io cosí trasfigurato? *deh, occhio mio bello, guatami pure un poco*>.

La donna incominciò a ridere e senza lasciarlo dir piú disse: <Ben sapete che io non sono sí smimorata, che io non conosca che voi siete messer

Riccardo di Chinzica, my husband; but, while I was with you, you showed yourself so poor at "knowing" [Biblical sense] me that if you were wise or are, as you like to be held, you should have had enough understanding to see that I was young, ripe for picking and full of energy, and therefore have realized what a young woman needs besides clothes and food, even if for shame she does not say: and you know how much you provided of that. If the study of law pleased you more than a wife, you should not have taken one; indeed, you did not seem to me to be a judge, but rather a proclaimer of festivals and holidays and fasts and vigils, you knew them all so well. And I will also say this, that if you had given as many days of rest to the workers on your estates as you gave to the one charged with cultivating my little plot, you would not have reaped a single ear of corn. I know I have come across this man, as God – the pious guardian of my youth – has willed, and with whom I now share this room, where we have no knowledge of holidays, I mean those days of rest which you, devoted more to God than the service of women, used to celebrate so much; nor has a Saturday or a Friday, a vigil or an Ember day or Lent, that lasts so long, ever entered through that door; but rather we work all the time and make hay there. When Matins sounded last night, I know how it went from beginning to end. So I intend to stay with him and work while I am young and reserve days of rest and pilgrimage and fasting for when I am old, and with good speed you can go back as you can and have your days of rest as much as you like."

(156–67) Messer Riccardo felt an unbearable pain on hearing these words and, as soon as he saw her stop speaking, he said, "Oh, *my sweet soul*, what do you think you are saying? Have you no regard for the honour of your family nor your own? Would you rather stay here in mortal sin as this man's strumpet, than as my wife in Pisa? As soon as he is bored with you, he will throw you out with great shame, whereas I will hold you dear for ever, and even if I did not wish it you will always be the lady of my house. Must you abandon your honour and me, *who love you more than my own life*, because of this dishonest and disorderly appetite? *My dear hope*, let us have no more of this, come away with me: I will make an effort from here on in, since I know your desire; so *my good sweet lady,* change your mind and come with me, seeing as I have not felt well since you were taken away from me."

(168–87) To which the lady replied, "I no longer care that anyone is jealous about my honour, now that it barely matters. How I wish my parents had cared when they gave me to you! If they did not care about my honour then, I do not intend to care about theirs now. And as to living in mortal sin, I certainly intend his pestle to go into my mortar. Please do not be solicitous about me any longer. And I will say this to you, that here I feel I am Paganino's wife, while at Pisa I felt I was your strumpet, thinking how many quarters of the moon and geometric calculations had to be made before our two planets came together, whereas here Paganino holds me in his arms all night and squeezes and bites me, and how he treats me God alone can tell you. And you say that you will make an effort? How? By playing quits or being thrashed into it? I can see what a great horseman you have become since I last saw you! Now be off, and put an effort into living, as you seem so drawn and weary as to barely belong to the world. And one more thing: if he should ever leave me, which he does not seem disposed to do, as long as I wish to stay, I would never come back to you, who – if anyone squeezed you – would not even make one bowl of broth, as I know to my great cost and with interest to pay on top of it! No, I would look elsewhere for my living. To repeat: there are no days of rest nor

Riccardo di Chinzica mio marito; ma voi, mentre che io fui con voi, mostraste assai male di conoscer me, per ciò che se voi eravate savio o sete, come volete esser tenuto, dovavate bene avere tanto conoscimento, che voi dovavate vedere che io era giovane e fresca e gagliarda, e per conseguente cognoscere quello che alle giovani donne, oltre al vestire e al mangiare, benché elle per vergogna nol dicano, si richiede: il che come voi il faciavate, voi il vi sapete. E se egli v'era piú a grado lo studio delle leggi che la moglie, voi non dovavate pigliarla; benché a me non parve mai che voi giudice foste, anzi mi paravate un banditor di sagre e di feste, sí ben le sapavate, e le digiune e le vigilie. E dicovi che se voi aveste tante feste fatte fare a' lavoratori che le vostre possession lavorano, quante faciavate fare a colui che il mio piccol campicello aveva a lavorare, voi non avreste mai ricolto granel di grano. Sommi abbattuta a costui, che ha voluto Idio sí come pietoso raguardatore della mia giovanezza, col quale io mi sto in questa camera, nella quale non si sa che cosa festa sia, dico di quelle feste che voi, piú divoto a Dio che a' servigi delle donne, cotante celebravate; né mai dentro a quello uscio entrò né sabato né venerdí né vigilia né quatro tempora né quaresima, ch'è cosí lunga, anzi di dí e di notte ci si lavora e battecisi la lana; e poi che questa notte sonò mattutino, so bene come il fatto andò da una volta in sú. E però con lui intendo di starmi e di lavorare mentre sarò giovane, e le feste e le perdonanze e' digiuni serbarmi a far quando sarò vecchia; e voi con la buona ventura sí ve n'andate il piú tosto che voi potete, e senza me fate feste quante vi piace>.

Messer Riccardo, udendo queste parole, sosteneva dolore incomportabile, e disse, poi che lei tacer vide: <Deh, *anima mia dolce*, che parole son quelle che tu di'? or non hai tu riguardo all'onore de' parenti tuoi e al tuo? vuoi tu innanzi star qui per bagascia di costui e in peccato mortale, che a Pisa mia moglie? Costui, quando tu gli sarai rincresciuta, con gran vitupero di te medesima ti caccerà via: io t'avrò sempre cara e sempre, ancora che io non volessi, sarai donna della casa mia. Dei tu per questo appetito disordinato e disonesto lasciar l'onor tuo e me, *che t'amo piú che la vita mia?* Deh, *speranza mia cara*, non dir piú cosí, voglitene venir con meco: io da quinci innanzi, poscia che io conosco il tuo disidero, mi sforzerò; e però, *ben mio dolce*, muta consiglio e vientene meco, ché mai ben non sentii poscia che tu tolta mi fosti>.

A cui la donna rispose: <Del mio onore non intendo io che persona, ora che non si può, sia piú di me tenera: fosserne stati i parenti miei quando mi diedero a voi! Li quali se non furono allora del mio, io non intendo d'essere al presente del loro; e se io ora sto in peccato mortaio, io starò quando che sia in imbeccato pestello: non ne siate piú tenero di me. E dicovi cosí, che qui mi pare esser moglie di Paganino e a Pisa mi pareva esser vostra bagascia, pensando che per punti di luna e per isquadri di geometria si convenieno tra voi e me congiugnere i pianeti, dove qui Paganino tutta la notte mi tiene in braccio e strignemi e mordemi, e come egli mi conci Dio vel dica per me. Anche dite voi che vi sforzerete: e di che? di farla in tre pace e rizzare a mazzata? Io so che voi siete divenuto un pro' cavaliere poscia che io non vi vidi! Andate, e sforzatevi di vivere, ché mi pare anzi che no che voi ci stiate a pigione, sí tisicuzzo e tristanzuol mi parete. E ancor vi dico piú: che quando costui mi lascerà, che non mi pare a ciò disposto dove io voglia stare, io non intendo per ciò di mai tornare a voi, di cui, tutto premendovi, non si farebbe uno scodellino di salsa, per ciò che con mio grandissimo danno e interesse vi stetti una volta: per che in altra parte cercherei mia civanza. Di che da capo vi

vigils where I intend to remain, therefore leave as soon as you can, with God's blessing, before I cry out that you are trying to force me against my will."

(188–94) Seeing that he was being taken apart, and only then realizing his stupidity in taking a young woman for a wife when he was impotent, he went out of the room in pain and sadness and had many words with Paganino, but they did not do a scrap of good. In the end, having accomplished nothing, he left the lady and returned to Pisa, where he lost his mind through sorrow, so that when he walked through the city, he could only reply to those who greeted him or asked him anything "No holiday for the old hole" and after a short time he died.

(195–9) When Paganino heard this, knowing how much the lady loved him, he made her his lawful wife and, without ever thinking of days of rest or vigils or Lent, they worked as long as their legs would let them and gave themselves a good time. For which, my dear ladies, it seems to me that Sir Bernabò's disputation with Ambruogiulo put the cart before the horse.[5]

[5] Refers to the preceding novella, II, 9.

dico che qui non ha festa né vigilia, laonde io intendo di starmi; e per ciò, come piú tosto potete, v'andate con Dio, se non che io griderò che voi mi vogliate sforzare>.

Messer Riccardo, veggendosi a mal partito e pure allora conoscendo la sua follia d'aver moglie giovane tolta essendo spossato, dolente e tristo s'uscí della camera e disse parole assai a Paganino le quali non montavano un frullo. E ultimamente, senza alcuna cosa aver fatta, lasciata la donna, a Pisa si ritornò; e in tanta mattezza per dolor cadde, che andando per Pisa, a chiunque il salutava o d'alcuna cosa il domandava, niuna altra cosa rispondeva, se non: <Il mal furo non vuol festa>; e dopo non molto tempo si morí.

Il che Paganin sentendo e conoscendo l'amore che la donna gli portava, per sua legittima moglie la sposò, e senza mai guardar festa o vigilia o far quaresima, quanto le gambe ne gli poteron portare lavorarono e buon tempo si diedono. Per la qual cosa, donne mie care, mi pare che ser Bernabò disputando con Ambruogiuolo cavalcasse la capra inverso il chino. –

VII

Il Novellino

(trans. N. S. Thompson)

Once upon a time there was a rich man, and he had a very beautiful lady for his wife; and this man loved her very dearly, but was very jealous. Then it happened that, as it pleases God, this man suffered an illness in his eyes and became blind, so that he could not see the light. It also came about that this man would never leave his wife; he kept her by his side everywhere and would not let her leave him, for fear that she might deceive him.

It also happened that a man of the neighbourhood fell in love with this lady, and could not see how he could speak with her because her husband was always with her; and this man was dying for love of her and told her so by his looks; and the lady, seeing him so much in love with her, took pity on him and said by her looks, "You see how I am, he never leaves me!" So the good man knew neither what to say or do, and it seemed by his appearances that he would die, finding no way to be with the lady, and the lady, seeing the gentlemanly way the man acted, took pity (again), and decided to give herself to him. She made a tube out of a long cane and put it to the ear of this courteous man and spoke to him in this manner, so that her husband would not hear, and said to the courteous man, "I feel pity for you, and so I have decided to give myself to you. Go into our garden and climb into a pear tree that has lots of pears and wait for me up there, and I will come up to you."

The good man went immediately to the garden and climbed the pear tree and waited for the lady. At this time the lady entered and wanted to give herself to the good man, but her husband was always with her, and she said, "I have a taste for those pears that are up in that tree, they are so good." Her husband said, "Call for somebody to pick them." And the lady said, "I will pick them myself, otherwise there's no fun in it." Then she went up towards the pear tree and her husband went with her to the foot of the tree, and the lady climbed up, while the husband embraced the trunk so that no one could climb up behind her. Now the lady was in the pear tree with the friend who was waiting for her and they enjoyed great pleasure together, so that the pear tree was bending this way and that with the pears falling to earth all over the husband. The husband called out, "What are you doing up there, woman. Why don't you come down? You're making the pears fall." And the lady answered him, "I only want the pears of a certain branch, I don't want any others."

Now I want you to know that the Lord God and St Peter were watching all this, and St Peter said to the Lord God, "Do you see the trick this lady is playing on her husband? Well, make the husband see the light, so that he can see what his wife is doing." And the Lord God said, "I tell you, St Peter, that as soon as he regains his sight, the lady will find a reason, an excuse, yet I'll make him see

VII

Il Novellino

(from Guido Biagi, ed., *Le Novelle Antiche dei Codici Panciatichiano-Palatino 138 e Laurenziano-Gaddiano 193* [Florence: Sansoni, 1880], CLV, pp. 199–201)[1]

A uno tenpo era uno riccho homo, ed avea una molto bella donna per molglie; et questo homo le volea tutto il suo bene, ed erane molto geloso. Or avenne, chome piacque a Dio, che questo homo li venne uno male nelgli occhi, donde aciechò; sicchè non vedea lume. Ora avenía che questo homo no' si partía da la molglie; tuttavía la tenea sì che no' la lasciava partire da ssè, per tema ch'ella no lli facesse fallo.

Ora avenne, che uno homo della contrada invaghío di questa donna, et non vedea chome le potesse favelare, però che 'l marito era tuttavía cho' lei: et questo homo moría di lei per senbianti ch'elli faciea a la donna; et la donna, vedendolo chosìe inamorato di lei, sìe ne le' (n)crebe, et disse per senbianti: Tue vedi chome io posso, chè questi non si parte mai da me! Sì che il buono homo non sapea che si fare nè che si dire, et parea che volese morire per senbianti: altro modo no' sapea trovare chome s'avenisse cholla donna; et la donna, vedendo i modi di questo gentile homo chome faciea, sì ne le '(n)crebe, et pensò di volere servire chostui. Ora fecie fare uno chanone di canna lungho, et puoselo a l'orecchie di questo gentile homo, et favelolli in questo modo, però che non volea che 'l marito l'odisse: et disse a questo gentile homo: Di te m'incresce, e però oe pensato di servirti: vattine nel giardino nostro, et sali in su 'n uno pero che v'àe molte belle pere, et aspettami là suso, ed io veròe là sùe a te.

Il buono homo inchontanente n'andò nel giardino, et salíe in sul pero, ed aspettava la donna. Ora venne il tenpo che la donna era nel giardino, e volea andare a servire il buono homo, et il marito era tuttavía co' lei, et la donna disse: E' m'è venuto volglia di quelle pere che sono in sùe quello pero, che sono cosíe belle. E' marito disse: Chiama chi ti ne cholgha. Et la donna disse: Io me ne cholglierò pure io, ch'altrimenti no' mi ne gioverebe. Alotta si mosse la donna per andare in sul pero, et il marito si mosse e venne co' lei infino a piè del pero, et la donna andoe in sùe il pero; et il marito abraccia il pedale del pero, perchè non v'andasse persona dietro le'. Or avenne che la donna fue sùe pero cho' l'amico che lla aspettava, e istavano in grande solazzo, e il pero si menava tutto, sì che le pere chadevano in terra a dosso al marito. Onde disse il marito: Che fai tue, donna, che no 'ne vieni? tue fai cadere tante pere. Et la donna li rispuose: Io volea delle pere d'uno ramo: non ne potea avere altrimenti.

Ora volglio che sapiate che Domenedio et San Piero, vedendo questo fatto, disse San Piero a Domenedio: No' vedi tue la beffa che quella donna fae al marito? Dè! fae che 'l marito vegha lume, sicchè elli vegha cioe che la molglie fae. Et Domenedio disse: Io ti dicho, San Piero, che sì tosto chome elli vedrà lume, la donna averà trovata la chagione, cioè la schusa, e però volglio che

[1] The manuscript previously numbered 138 is now number 32 in the Biblioteca Nazionale, Florence.

the light and you'll see what she says." The husband regained his sight and looked upwards and saw what the lady was doing. He then said to her, "What are you doing with this man? You do no honour to yourself nor to me, it's not how a faithful woman behaves." And the lady replied immediately and said, "If I had not done this with him, you would never have seen the light." Hearing this, the husband was then content. And so you see how faithful married women and young girls are, and how they quickly find an excuse.

VIII

Giovanni Boccaccio, *Decameron* VII, 9

(trans. N. S. Thompson)

Lydia, the wife of Nicostratos, loves Pyrrhus who, in order to believe her, sets her three tasks, which she accomplishes. In addition, she makes love to him in front of Nicostratos and has him believe that what he has seen was not true.

(1–4) Neifile's novella [VII, 8] was so well received that the ladies could neither refrain from laughing, nor from discussing it, no matter how many times the king [Dioneo], having asked Panfilo to start his tale, demanded silence. When they were finally quiet, Panfilo began:
(5–12) Dear ladies, I believe that there is nothing, no matter how serious or risky, that would not be attempted by someone fervently in love; although this has been shown in many of our *novelle*, I nevertheless believe that the one I am about to tell will prove the point even more, when you hear of a woman on whom fortune shone more favourably than the light of reason. I would therefore not advise any woman to risk following in the footsteps of this one of whom I am about to speak, because fortune is not always so well disposed, nor are all the world's men so easily fooled.

(13–24) In Argos, the very ancient Greek city, famed more for its kings of old than its size, there lived a nobleman by the name of Nicostratos to whom, when he was already nearing old age, fortune gave a wife no less bold than beautiful, whose name was Lydia. Given that he was noble and rich, this man possessed many servants, dogs and birds, as hunting was his great delight; among these servants was a charming young man, well dressed, handsome and capable of carrying out any service, whose name was Pyrrhus, whom Nicostratos loved and trusted above all others. Lydia fell so strongly in love with this young man that day and night her thoughts dwelled on him, but whether Pyrrhus did not notice or desire this love, he showed no concern about it, which caused the lady deep pain in her spirit.

vega lume, et vedrai quello ch'ella dirae. Ora vidde lume et guatò in sùe, et vidde quello che la donna faciea. Alora disse a la donna: Che fate voi co' cotesto homo? non è onore ned a voi ed a me, et non è lealtà di donna. Et la donna rispuose incontanente di subito, et disse: S'io non avessi fatto chosíe con chostui, tue non n'averesti mai veduto lume. Alotta udendo il marito chosíe dire, istette contento. Et chosíe vedete chome le donne et le femine sono leali, et chome trovano tosto la schusa.

VIII

Giovanni Boccaccio, *Decameron* VII, 9

(from *Giovanni Boccaccio, Decameron*, ed. Vittore Branca [Torino: Einaudi, 1980], pp. 861–75)[1]

Lidia moglie di Nicostrato ama Pirro: il quale, acciò che credere il possa, le chiede tre cose le quali ella gli fa tutte; e oltre a questo in presenza di Nicostrato si sollazza con lui e a Nicostrato fa credere che non sia vero quello che ha veduto.

Tanto era piaciuta la novella di Neifile, che né di ridere né di ragionar di quella si potevano le donne tenere, quantunque il re piú volte silenzio loro avesse imposto, avendo comandato a Panfilo che la sua dicesse: ma pur poi che tacquero, cosí Panfilo incominciò:

– Io non credo, reverende donne, che niuna cosa sia, quantunque sia grave e dubbiosa, che a far non ardisca chi ferventemente ama; la qual cosa, quantunque in assai novelle sia stato dimostrato, nondimeno io il mi credo molto piú con una che dirvi intendo mostrare, dove udirete d'una donna alla quale nelle sue opere fu troppo piú favorevole la fortuna che la ragione avveduta. E per ciò non consiglierei io alcuna che dietro alle pedate di colei, di cui dire intendo, s'arrischiasse d'andare, per ciò che non sempre è la fortuna disposta, né sono al mondo tutti gli uomini abbagliati igualmente.

In Argo, antichissima città d'Acaia, per li suoi passati re molto piú famosa che grande, fu già uno nobile uomo il quale appellato fu Nicostrato, a cui già vicino alla vecchiezza la fortuna concedette per moglie una gran donna non meno ardita che bella, detta per nome Lidia. Teneva costui, sí come nobile uomo e ricco, molta famiglia e cani e uccegli, e grandissimo diletto prendea nelle cacce; e aveva tra gli altri suoi famigliari un giovinetto leggiadro e addorno e bello della persona e destro a qualunque cosa avesse voluta fare, chiamato Pirro, il quale Nicostrato oltre a ogn'altro amava e piú di lui si fidava. Di costui Lidia s'innamorò forte, tanto che né dí né notte che in altra parte che con lui aver poteva il pensiere: del quale amore o che Pirro non s'avvedesse o non volesse niente mostrava se ne curasse; di che la donna intollerabile noia portava all'animo.

[1] All line numbering is my own.

(25–44) Ready to do anything to make him know her feelings, she called to her one of her maids named Lusca, whom she greatly trusted, and said: “Lusca, the benefits you have received from me should make you faithful and obedient: so take care that what I now tell you will be heard by no person other than the one whom I will mention. As you can see, Lusca, I am a young woman full of life, rich, and in possession of everything anyone could wish for, and have nothing to complain of except for one thing and, that is, that when considered against mine my husband’s age is too great, with the result that in that thing in which young women take most delight I have little satisfaction. And yet, given that my desires are the same as anyone else’s, for some time I have considered the fact that, given fortune has been so unkind in giving me a husband who is old, I do not wish to be an enemy to myself in being unable to find a pathway to my pleasure and well being. And having reasoned in this way, as in other things, I have taken the decision, seeing that he is more worthy than anyone else, that our servant Pyrrhus should satisfy them with his embraces. I have placed so great a love in him that I can only feel well when I see him or think about him: and if I do not soon find myself in his arms I feel sure that I will die. Therefore, if you care about my life, when you go to him please make my love known to him in whatever way you think best, and beg him on my behalf that he kindly come to see me, when you go to fetch him.”

(45–54) The servant said she would do so willingly. As soon as the occasion presented itself, she took Pyrrhus to one side and to the best of her ability conveyed her mistress’s desire. Upon hearing this, Pyrrhus was greatly amazed, having suspected nothing before, and had the idea that the woman had been made to say these things to test him, so he immediately replied in a brusque manner: “Lusca, I cannot believe what you have said comes from my mistress, watch what you say, therefore, and if they do come from her, I do not believe she would tell you her heart; but if she did, my master gives me greater honour than I can merit, so that as long as I hold my life dear, I could do him no such disservice; therefore take care that you no longer say such things to me.”

(55–8) Unabashed by his severe words, Lusca said: “Pyrrhus, I will speak the words my mistress commanded me to speak about this and on any other matter whenever she pleases, whether it agree with you or annoy you. What a beast you are!”

(59–66) Upset by Pyrrhus’s words, she returned to her mistress who, upon hearing what he had to say, wished she were dead. Some days later, she again spoke to the servant and said: “Lusca, as you know, an oak is not felled by one stroke; it seems that, unhappily for me, he wishes to appear loyal, so you should try again and, choosing an opportune moment, reveal all of my ardour and see to it in everything there will be a result; if nothing comes of it, however, I should die and he would feel it was a trick and where we seek his love, we will find only hate.”

(67–94) The servant consoled her mistress and, seeking Pyrrhus out, finding him cheerful and well disposed, she said: “Pyrrhus, some days ago I revealed the burning love that your mistress and mine feels for you; again I want to remind you that if you show her the hard face that you did the other day, you can live in the surety she will not live long. Therefore, I beg you to consider conceding to her wishes; but if you persist in your obstinacy, then I can only take you for a fool, when I had previously thought you wise. Think what glory it will bring you to be loved by such a beautiful well-born woman who loves you above all else! Beside this, how thankful you will be to fortune thinking that she has offered you such a

E disposta del tutto di fargliele sentire, chiamò a sé una sua cameriera nomata Lusca, della quale ella si confidava molto, e sí le disse: < Lusca, li benifici li quali tu hai da me ricevuti ti debbono fare obediente e fedele: e per ciò guarda che quello che io al presente ti dirò niuna persona senta già mai se non colui al quale da me ti fia imposto. Come tu vedi, Lusca, io son giovane e fresca donna e piena e copiosa di tutte quelle cose che alcuna può disiderare, e brievemente fuor che d'una non mi posso ramaricare: e questa è che gli anni del mio marito son troppi se co' miei si misurano, per la qual cosa di quello che le giovani donne prendono piú piacere io vivo poco contenta. E pur come l'altre disiderandolo, è buona pezza che io diliberai meco di non volere, se la fortuna m'è stata poco amica in darmi cosí vecchio marito, essere io nimica di me medesima in non saper trovar modo a' miei diletti e alla mia salute. E per avergli cosí compiuti in questo come nell'altre cose, ho per partito preso di volere, sí come di ciò piú degno che alcun altro, che il nostro Pirro co' suoi abbracciamenti gli supplisca, e ho tanto amore in lui posto, che io non sento mai bene se non tanto quanto io il veggio o di lui penso: e se io senza indugio non mi ritruovo seco per certo io me ne credo morire. E per ciò, se la mia vita t'è cara, per quel modo che miglior ti parrà, il mio amore gli significherai e sí 'l pregherrai da mia parte che gli piaccia di venire a me quando tu per lui andrai>.

La cameriera disse che volentieri; e come prima tempo e luogo le parve, tratto Pirro da parte, quanto seppe il meglio l'ambasciata gli fece della sua donna. La qual cosa udendo Pirro si maravigliò forte, sí come colui che mai d'alcuna cosa avveduto non se n'era, e dubitò non la donna ciò facesse dirgli per tentarlo; per che subito e ruvidamente rispose: < Lusca, io non posso credere che queste parole vengano della mia donna, e per ciò guarda quel che tu parli; e se pure da lei venissero, non credo che con l'animo dir te le faccia; e se pur con l'animo dir le facesse, il mio signore mi fa piú onore che che io non vaglio, io non farei a lui sí fatto altraggio per la vita mia; e però guarda che tu più di sí fatte cose non mi ragioni>.

La Lusca non sbigottita per lo suo rigido parlare gli disse: <Pirro, e di queste e d'ogn'altra cosa che la mia donna m'imporrà ti parlerò io quante volte ella il mi comanderà, o piacere o noia che egli ti debbia essere: ma tu se' una bestia!>

E turbatetta con le parole di Pirro se ne tornò alla donna, la quale udendole disiderò morire; e dopo alcun giorno riparlò alla cameriera e disse: <Lusca, tu sai che per lo primo colpo non cade la quercia; per che a me pare che tu da capo ritorni a colui che in mio progiudicio nuovamente vuol divenir leale, e prendendo tempo convenevole gli mostra interamente il mio ardore e in tutto t'integna di far che la cosa abbia effetto; però che, se così s'intralasciasse, io ne morrei e egli si crederebbe essere stato beffato; e, dove il suo amor cerchiamo, ne seguirebbe odio>.

La cameriera confortò la donna, e cercato di Pirro il trovò lieto e ben disposto e sì gli disse: <Pirro, io ti mostrai pochi dí sono in quanto fuoco la tua donna e mia stea per l'amor che ella ti porta, e ora da capo te ne rifò certo, che, dove tu in su la durezza che l'altrieri dimostrasti dimori, vivi sicuro che ella viverà poco. Per che io ti priego che ti piaccia di consolarla del suo disiderio; e dove tu pure in su la tua obstinazione stessi duro, là dove io per molto savio t'aveva, io t'avrò per uno scioccone. Che gloria ti può egli essere che una cosí fatta donna, cosí bella, cosí gentile te sopra ogn'altra cosa ami! Appresso questo, quanto ti puo' tu conoscere alla fortuna obligato, pensando

thing suited to the desires of your youth and, moreover, a ready refuge for your needs. What young men of your age do you know who would be better off than you in pleasure, if you were wise? What other young man could you find who could possibly be as you would be in arms, in chivalry, in clothes and money, if you gave her your love? Open your heart to what I say and think again, remember that fortune only smiles and opens her arms once and whoever does not know how to receive her and subsequently finds himself poor and needy only has himself and not her to blame. And beyond this, there is no need for any loyalty between servant and master such as there is between friends and so it should be; indeed, as far as they can, servants should act in return according to the manner they have been treated. If you had a beautiful wife or mother or daughter or sister that Nicostratos desired, do you think he would be thinking of loyalty in the same way that you are showing with regard to his wife? You are foolish if you think so! Of this you can be sure, if flattery and prayers were not enough, then whatever you thought, force would prevail. Let us therefore treat them and their things as they treat us and our things. Use the blessing of fortune: do not cast it away, go to her and receive her willingly, as certainly, if you do not, without further ado the death of the young woman will follow without a doubt, and you will then repent many times, so that you will also wish you were dead."

(95–106) Pyrrhus, who had several times thought again about what Lusca had said, had already decided that, if she returned, he would give a different reply and do everything to please the lady, if he could verify that he were not being put to the test. He thus replied: "Lusca, I know all that you say to be true, but I also know that my master is very wise and shrewd, and taking all the facts in hand I greatly fear that, under his guidance and will, she is doing this to test me. Therefore if she will do three things I ask to be done to give me some guarantee, certainly there is nothing that I would not quickly do at her command. These three things are firstly, that in the presence of Nicostratos she kill his best sparrow hawk, next that she send me a lock of his beard, and thirdly, one of his good teeth."

(107–12) These things seemed difficult to Lusca and even more so to her mistress; but Love, that great comforter and grand master of advice, made her decide to do them and she sent word via her servant saying that she would fully do what he asked and very soon; moreover, given that he thought Nicostratos so wise, she said that she would take her pleasure with Pyrrhus in Nicostatos's presence and have him believe it had not taken place.

(113–20) Pyrrhus waited for what the noble lady might accomplish. Several days later, after Nicostratos had given a large dinner to certain noblemen according to his custom, and the tables had been taken away, wearing a richly embroidered green velvet gown, the lady left her room and came to where the men were. Seeing Pyrrhus and the others, she went to the perch beside Nicostratos where his dearly loved hawk stood and, untying it as if she wanted to lift it up, she took it by the jesses and dashed it against the wall, killing it.

(121–32) When Nicostratos cried out at her "Woman, what have you done?", she would not reply but turned to the noblemen with whom he had dined and said, "Sirs, I could hardly avenge myself against a king who insulted me if I had no courage to take my revenge on a hawk. You should know that this bird has long deprived me of all the time that ought to be spent by men in pleasing women: as soon as dawn comes Nicostratos rises, mounts his horse with his hawk in his hand and is away to

che ella t'abbia parata dinanzi cosí fatta cosa e a' disideri della tua giovanezza atta e ancora un cosí fatto rifugio a' tuoi bisogni! Qual tuo pari conosci tu che per via di diletto meglio stea che starai tu, se tu sarai savio? quale altro troverrai tu che in arme, in cavalli, in robe e in denari possa star come tu starai, volendo il tuo amor concedere a costei? Apri adunque l'animo alle mie parole e in te ritorna: ricordati che una volta senza più suole avvenire che la fortuna si fa altrui incontro col viso lieto e col grembo aperto; la quale chi allora non sa ricevere, poi trovandosi povero e mendico, di sé e non di lei s'ha a ramaricare. E oltre a questo non si vuol quella lealtà tra servidori usare e signori, che tra gli amici e par si conviene; anzi gli deono cosí i servidori trattare, in quel che possono, come essi da loro trattati sono. Speri tu, se tu avessi o bella moglie o madre o figliuola o sorella che a Nicostrato piacesse, che egli andasse la lealtà ritrovando che tu servar vuoi a lui della sua donna? Sciocco se' se tu 'l credi: abbi di certo, se le lusinghe e' prieghi non bastassono, che che ne dovesse a te parere, e' vi si adoperrebbe la forza. Trattiamo adunque loro e le lor cose come essi noi e le nostre trattano. Usa il benificio della fortuna: non la cacciare, falleti incontro e lei vegnente ricevi, ché per certo, se tu nol fai, lasciamo stare la morte la qual senza fallo alla tua donna ne seguirà, ma tu ancora te ne penterai tante volte, che tu ne vorrai morire>.

Pirro, il qual piú fiate sopra le parole che la Lusca dette gli avea avea ripensato, per partito avea preso che, se ella a lui ritornasse, di fare altra risposta e del tutto recarsi a compiacere alla donna, dove certificar si potesse che tentato non fosse; e per ciò rispuose: < Vedi, Lusca, tutte le cose che tu mi di' io le conosco vere: ma io conosco d'altra parte il mio signore molto savio e molto avveduto, e ponendomi tutti i suoi fatti in mano, io temo forte che Lidia con consiglio e voler di lui questo non faccia per dovermi tentare; e per ciò, dove tre cose che io domanderò voglia fare a chiarezza di me, per certo niuna cosa mi comanderà poi che io prestamente non faccia. E quelle tre cose che io voglia son queste: primieramente che in presenzia di Nicostrato ella uccida il suo buono sparviere, appresso che ella mi mandi una ciochetta della barba di Nicostrato, e ultimamente un dente di quegli di lui medesimo, de' migliori>.

Queste cose parvono alla Lusca gravi e alla donna gravissime: ma pure Amore, che è buono confortatore e gran maestro di consigli, le fece diliberar di farlo, e per la sua cameriera gli mandò dicendo che quello che egli aveva addimandato pienamente farebbe, e tosto; e oltre a ciò, per ciò che egli cosí savio reputava Nicostrato, disse che in presenzia di lui con Pirro si sollazzerebbe e a Nicostrato farebbe credere che ciò non fosse vero.

Pirro adunque cominciò a aspettare quello che far dovesse la gentil donna: la quale, avendo ivi a pochi dí Nicostrato dato un gran desinare, sí come usava spesse volte di fare a certi gentili uomini e essendo già levate le tavole, vestita d'uno sciamito verde e ornato e uscita della sua camera, in quella sala venne dove costoro erano; e veggente Pirro e ciascuno altro, se n'andò alla stanga sopra la quale lo sparviere era cotanto da Nicostrato tenuto caro, e scioltolo quasi in mano sel volesse levare e presolo per li geti al muro il percosse e ucciselo.

E gridando verso lei Nicostrato: <Oimè, donna, che hai tu fatto?> niente a lui rispose, ma rivolta a' gentili uomini che con lui avevan mangiato disse: <Signori, mal prenderei vendetta d'un re che mi facesse dispetto se d'uno sparviere non avessi ardir di pigliarla. Voi dovete sapere che questo uccello tutto il tempo da dovere esser prestato dagli uomini al piacer delle donne lungamente m'ha tolto; per ciò che, sì come l'aurora suole apparire,

the open fields to see it fly, while I remain alone and dissatisfied in bed; for this reason I have often wished to do what I have now done, with no other reason for delay than simply waiting to do it in the presence of men who would be righteous judges of my case, as I believe you to be."

(133–8) Hearing this, believing her emotions towards Nicostratos to be no different than her words, all the noble men laughed and turning to Nicostratos, who was enraged, said: "How well the lady has done to avenge her ill treatment with the hawk's death!" When the lady returned to her room, they soothed Nicostratos's discomposure into laughter with various witty comments on the matter.

(139–40) Having witnessed all this, Pyrrhus said to himself, "The lady has made a high start in her love towards me. May God grant that she persist!"

(141–51) Several days after Lydia killed the hawk, she was in her room with Nicostratos, caressing him and teasing him, when he caught her by the hair and gave her the idea to put into effect Pyrrhus's second request: she soon had Nicostratos by a small lock of his beard and, laughing, pulled so hard that it came away from his chin. When Nicostratos complained, she said: "Now what's the matter? Pulling such a face because I took six whiskers from your beard! You should have felt what I did when you pulled my hair just now!" As they continued talking pleasurably, the lady carefully kept the whiskers she had taken from him and sent them to her beloved the very same day.

(152–63) But the third request gave the lady much more thought; even so, seeing that she was highly imaginative and Love gave her extra inspiration, she managed to think of a way in which she could bring it about. Two fathers had given their sons to Nicostratos so that, since they were of noble birth, they might learn courtly manners under his roof; one carved for him at the table, and the other poured out his drink. Lydia called them both to her and gave them to understand that there was a problem with their breath, instructing them that when they served Nicostratos they should incline their heads away as far as possible, nor say a word of this to anyone. Believing her, the young men began to behave as she said, so that the lady was able to ask Nicostratos: "Have you noticed what those young men do when they serve you?"

(164–5) Nicostratos replied: "Indeed I have! In fact, I wanted to ask them why they did it myself."

(166–71) To which the lady responded: "There is no need, I can tell you myself, and have kept quiet about it for a while so as not to upset you, but now that I see others are beginning to notice, there is no point in hiding the fact. This manner of theirs is caused by nothing other than the fact that your breath smells horribly foul, and I don't know the reason, only that it used not to; and this is a very ugly thing since you have to deal with the gentry, so I shall have to find a way to cure it."

(172–3) So Nicostratos said: "What could it be? Do I have a rotten tooth or two?"

(174–80) Lydia replied: "Perhaps so." Leading him to a window, she made him open his mouth and after looking at it on both sides, she said: "Oh, Nicostratos, how can you have suffered so? You have a tooth on this side that, it seems to me, is not only carious, but totally rotten and certainly, if it remains in your mouth, it will

così Nicostrato s'è levato e salito a cavallo col suo sparviere in mano n'è andato alle pianure aperte a vederlo volare; e io, qual voi mi vedete, sola e malcontenta nel letto mi son rimasa; per la qual cosa ho piú volte avuta voglia di far ciò che io ho ora fatto, né altra cagione m'ha di ciò ritenuta se non l'aspettar di farlo in presenzia d'uomini che giusti giudici sieno alla mia querela, sí come io credo che voi sarete>.

I gentili uomini che l'udivano, credendo non altramenti esser fatta la sua affezione a Nicostrato che sonasser le parole, ridendo ciascuno e verso Nicostrato rivolti, che turbato era, cominciarono a dire: <Deh, come la donna ha ben fatto a vendicar la sua ingiuria con la morte dello sparviere!> e con diversi motti sopra cosí fatta materia, essendosi già la donna in camera ritornata, in riso rivolsero il cruccio di Nicostrato.

Pirro, veduto questo, seco medesimo disse: <Alti principii ha dati la donna a' miei felici amori: faccia Idio che ella perseveri!>

Ucciso adunque da Lidia lo sparviere, non trapassar molti giorni che, essendo ella nella sua camera insieme con Nicostrato, faccendogli carezze con lui incominciò a cianciare, e egli per sollazzo alquanto tiratala per li capelli le diè cagione di mandare a effetto la seconda cosa a lei domandata da Pirro: e prestamente lui per un picciolo lucignoletto preso della sua barba e ridendo, sí forte il tirò, che tutto dal mento gliele divelse. Di che ramaricandosi Nicostrato, ella disse: <Or che avesti, che fai cotal viso per ciò che io t'ho tratti forse sei peli della barba? Tu non sentivi quel ch'io, quando tu mi tiravi testeso i capelli!> E cosí d'una parola in un'altra continuando il lor sollazzo, la donna cautamente guardò la ciocca della barba che tratta gli avea e il dí medesimo la mandò al suo caro amante.

Della terza cosa entrò la donna in piú pensiero; ma pur, sí come quella che era d'alto ingegno e amor la faceva vie piú, s'ebbe pensato che modo tener dovesse a darle compimento. E avendo Nicostrato due fanciulli datigli da' padri loro acciò che in casa sua, però che gentili uomini erano, apparassono alcun costume, de' quali quando Nicostrato mangiava l'uno gli tagliava innanzi e l'altro gli dava bere, fattigli chiamare ammenduni fece lor vedere che la bocca putiva loro e ammaestrogli che, quando a Nicostrato servissono, tirassono il capo indietro il piú che potessono né questo mai dicessono a persona. I giovinetti, credendole, cominciarono a tener quella maniera che la donna aveva lor mostrata; per che ella una volta domandò Nicostrato: <Se'ti tu accorto di ciò che questi fanciulli fanno quando ti servono?>

Disse Nicostrato: <Mai sí, anzi gli ho io voluti domandare perché il facciano>.

A cui la donna disse: <Non fare, ché io il ti so dire io, e holti buona pezza taciuto per non fartene noia: ma ora che io m'accorgo che altri comincia a avvedersene, non è piú da celarloti. Questo non t'avien per altro se non che la bocca ti pute fieramente, e non so qual si sia la cagione per ciò che ciò non soleva essere; e questa è bruttissima cosa avendo tu a usare co' gentili uomini, e per ciò si vorrebe veder modo da curarla>.

Disse allora Nicostrato: <Che potrebbe ciò essere? avrei io in bocca dente niuno guasto?>

A cui Lidia disse: <Forse che sí>; e menatolo a una finestra, gli fece aprire la bocca, e poscia che ella ebbe d'una parte e d'altra riguardato disse: <O Nicostrato, e come il puoi tu tanto aver patito? Tu n'hai uno da questa parte il quale, per quello che mi paia, non solamente è magagnato ma egli è

infect those next to it. I advise you, therefore, to have it out before it gets much worse."

(181–2) Thereon Nicostratos said, "Given that this seems to be the case, you have my consent, and send without delay for a surgeon who can extract it."
(183–9) But the lady replied: "It is not pleasing to God that a surgeon should take care of this; it seems to me that it is in such shape that I could do it very well myself. And besides, these surgeons are so cruel when they work that my heart could not suffer in any way to see or hear you in the hands of anyone else; I will do it all myself, so that if it pains you too much at least I can leave off, which a surgeon would not do."

(190–202) Having called for the instruments from a servant and sent everyone out of the room, she kept only Lusca by her side. Locking themselves in, they laid Nicostratos down on a table, one holding him firmly, the other performing the extraction by brute force, putting the pincers in his mouth and taking the tooth out, no matter how much he cried out in pain; this tooth they kept and, taking another that Lydia had which was dreadfully decayed, they showed it to Nicostratos who was half dead with pain, saying: "Look what you had in your mouth all this time!" Believing this to be the case, however the great pain he had suffered and however much he remonstrated, now that it was out, Nicostratos seemed to think he felt better. Comforted by one thing and another, the pain alleviated, he went out of the room. Taking the tooth, the lady immediately sent it to her beloved who was now certain of her affection and prepared himself for the delights to follow.

(203–12) Every hour seeming like a thousand before she could be with him, but wishing to accomplish this discreetely, yet maintain the promise she had made, the lady pretended to be ill. Visited by Nicostratos, it being near meal time one day, and seeing no one with him but Pyrrhus, she asked them to accompany her to the garden to alleviate her discomfort. With Nicostratos at one side and Pyrrhus the other, they took her to the garden and set her down on a little lawn at the foot of a pear tree. After they had sat there for a while, the lady – who had already told Pyrrhus what she was about to do – said: "Pyrrhus, I should greatly like to have one of those pears. Would you climb up there and throw some down?"

(213–19) Pyrrhus soon climbed up and began to throw down some pears and while he was doing so burst out: "Oh, sir, what are you doing? And you, my lady, how is it you are not ashamed to allow it in my presence? Do you think I am blind? You were even gravely ill just now, how is it you are so quickly recovered that you can do such things? You surely have many beautiful rooms if you wish to do so! Why don't you go and do them there? It would be more seemly than in my presence!"

(220) Turning to her husband, the lady said: "What is Pyrrhus talking about? Is he raving mad?"
(221–2) Then Pyrrhus said: "I am not mad, my lady. Do you think I can't see?"

(223–4) Greatly amazed, Nicostratos said: "Pyrrhus, I really think you must be dreaming."
(225–7) Pyrrhus replied: "My lord, I'm not dreaming at all, nor are you. Indeed, you are shaking so well, that if it were this pear tree there would be no fruit left on it!"

tutto fracido, e fermamente, se tu il terrai guari in bocca, egli guasterà quegli che son dallato: per che io ti consiglierei che tu il ne cacciassi fuori prima che l'opera andasse piú innanzi>.

Disse allora Nicostrato: <Da poi che egli ti pare, e egli mi piace: mandisi senza piú indugio per uno maestro il qual mel tragga>.

Al quale la donna disse: <Non piaccia a Dio che qui per questo venga maestro: e' mi pare che egli stea in maniera che senza alcun maestro io medesima tel trarrò ottimamente. E d'altra parte questi maestri son sí crudeli a far questi servigi, che il cuore nol mi patirebbe per niuna maniera di vederti o di sentirti tralle mani a niuno; e per ciò del tutto io voglio fare io medesima, ché almeno, se egli ti dorrà troppo, ti lascerò io incontanente: quello che il maestro non farebbe>.

Fattisi adunque venire i ferri da tal servigio e mandato fuori della camera ogni persona, solamente seco la Lusca ritenne; e dentro serratesi, fecero distender Nicostrato sopra un desco, e messegli le tanaglie in bocca e preso uno de' denti suoi, quantunque egli forte per dolor gridasse, tenuto fermamente dall'una, fu dall'altra per viva forza un dente tirato fuori; e quel serbatosi e presone un altro il quale sconciamente magagnato Lidia aveva in mano, a lui doloroso e quasi mezzo morto il mostrarono, dicendo: <Vedi quello che tu hai tenuto in bocca già è cotanto>. Egli credendoselo, quantunque gravissima pena sostenuta avesse e molto se ne ramaricasse, pur, poi che fuor n'era, gli parve esser guerito: e con una cosa e con altra riconfortato, essendo la pena alleviata, s'uscí della camera. La donna, preso il dente, tantosto al suo amante il mandò: il quale già certo del suo amore sé a ogni suo piacere offerse apparecchiato.

La donna, disiderosa di farlo piú sicuro e parendole ancora ogni ora mille che con lui fosse, volendo quello che proferto gli avea attenergli, fatto sembiante d'essere inferma e essendo un dí appresso mangiare da Nicostrato visitata, non veggendo con lui altro che Pirro, il pregò per alleggiamento della sua noia che aiutar la dovessero a andare infino nel giardino. Per che Nicostrato dall'un de' lati e Pirro dall'altro presala, nel giardin la portarono e in un pratello a piè d'un bel pero la posarono: dove stati alquanto sedendosi, disse la donna, che già avea fatto informar Pirro di ciò che avesse a fare: <Pirro, io ho gran disidero d'avere di quelle pere, e però e montavi suso e gittane giú alquante>.

Pirro, prestamente salitovi, cominciò a gittar giú delle pere: e mentre le gittava cominciò a dire: <Eh, messere, che è ciò che voi fate? e voi, madonna, come non vi vergognate di sofferirlo in mia presenza? credete voi che io sia cieco? Voi eravate pur testé cosí forte malata: come siete voi sí tosto guerita, che voi facciate tai cose? le quali se pur far volete, voi avete tante belle camere: perché non in alcuna di quelle a far queste cose ve n'andate? e sarà più onesto che farlo in mia presenza!>

La donna rivolta al marito disse: <Che dice Pirro? farnetica egli?>

Disse allora Pirro: <Non farnetico no, madonna: non credete voi che io veggia?>

Nicostrato si maravigliava forte, e disse: <Pirro, veramente io credo che tu sogni>.

Al quale Pirro rispose: <Signor mio, non sogno né mica, né voi anche non sognate, anzi vi dimenate ben sí, che se cosí si dimenasse questo pero, egli non ce ne rimarrebbe sú niuna>.

(228–31) Then the lady said: "What can this be? Could it be true that what he says appears to him to be true? If – God preserve me – I was as healthy as I was, I would climb up there to see the marvels he claims he can see."

(232–4) From the pear tree Pyrrhus continued to broadcast his wonders, to which Nicostratos responded: "Get down!" When he came down, Nicostratos asked him: "What do you say you can see?"
(235–7) Pyrrhus said: "I believe you take me for a fool or a dreamer: if I must be plain, I saw you lying on top of your lady; then as I came down I saw you rise and place yourself where you are sitting now."
(238–9) "Certainly," said Nicostratos, "You were foolish in this because we have not, since you were up in that tree, been in any other place than you see us now."
(240–1) To which Pyrrhus replied, "Why are we even discussing this? Indeed I did see you, and if I saw you, then it was only on your property."
(242–7) With each passing moment Nicostratos was more amazed, so that he said: "Well, I'm going to see if this pear tree is bewitched and if it is true that whoever is up there can see amazing things!" and he climbed up. As soon as he was up, the lady began to take her pleasure with Pyrrhus; seeing this, Nicostratos began to cry out: "O evil woman, what are you doing? And you, Pyrrhus, in whom I had most trust?" And speaking thus be began to climb down from the pear tree.
(248–50) The lady and Pyrrhus said: "We are sitting here". Seeing him descend they went back to their seats as they were when he left them. When Nicostratos was down and saw them exactly as he had left them, he began to curse them.
(251–63) To which Pyrrhus replied: "Nicostratos, now I truly confess that, as you said earlier, I saw falsely when I was up in the pear tree. And I know it by no other way than this, that I see and know that you have seen falsely what I saw when I was in the pear tree; and nothing else should convince you that I am speaking the truth but the consideration that your lady, who is the most honest and more wise than any other, could ever wish to do you such an outrage and be led to do it beneath your very eyes; for myself I should like to say that I would sooner see myself hanged and quartered before I even thought about it, never mind actually doing it in your presence. Certainly the blame for this illusion must come from the pear tree; no one in the world could have dissuaded me that you were not in a carnal act with your lady, had I not heard you say that you saw me performing that which I certainly know I would not think of doing, let alone act out."

(264–9) Next the lady, who was quite disturbed, rose to her feet and said: "Well, perdition take you, if you think me so stupid that if I wished to behave as dishonestly as you say that I should do so before your very eyes. You can be sure that, whatever desire ever came over me, I should never come here, but think I would be able to find one of our rooms covertly and in such a manner that I should be surprised were you ever to hear about it."
(270–3) It seemed to Nicostratos that both were telling the truth that they would never have conducted themselves in such a fashion before him, so he left off his blame for their actions and began to speak of the strange fact and miraculous change of sight that occurred to whoever climbed the pear tree.

Disse la donna allora: <Che può questo essere? potrebbe egli esser vero che gli paresse vero ciò ch'e' dice? Se Dio mi salvi, se io fossi sana come io fui già, che io vi sarrei suso per vedere che maraviglie sieno queste che costui dice che vede>.

Pirro di 'n sul pero pur diceva e continuava queste novelle; al quale Nicostrato disse: < Scendi giú>, e elgi scese; a cui egli disse: <Che di' tu che vedi?>

Disse Pirro: <Io credo che voi m'abbiate per ismemorato o per trasognato: vedeva voi addosso alla donna vostra, poi pur dir mel conviene; e poi discendendo, io vi vidi levare e porvi costí dove voi siete a sedere>.

<Fermamente> disse Nicostrato <eri tu in questo smemorato, ché noi non ci siamo, poi che in sul pero salisti, punto mossi se non come tu vedi>.

Al quale Pirro disse: <Perché ne facciam noi quistione? Io vi pur vidi; e se io vi vidi, io vi vidi in sul vostro>.

Nicostrato piú ognora si maravigliava, tanto che egli disse: <Ben vo' vedere se questo pero è incantato e che chi v'è sú vegga le maraviglie!> e montovvi sú; sopra il quale come egli fu, la donna insieme con Pirro s'incominciarono a sollazzare; il che Nicostrato veggendo cominciò a gridare: <Ahi rea femina, che è quel che tu fai? e tu, Pirro, di cui io piú mi fidava?> e cosí dicendo cominciò a scender del pero.

La donna e Pirro dicevan: <Noi ci seggiamo>; e lui veggendo discendere a seder si tornarono in quella guisa che lasciati gli avea. Come Nicostrato fu giú e vide costoro dove lasciati gli avea, cosí lor cominciò a dir villania.

Al quale Pirro disse:<Nicostrato, ora veramente confesso io che, come voi diciavate davanti, che io falsamente vedessi mentre fui sopra il pero; né a altro il conosco se non a questo, che io veggio e so che voi falsamente avete veduto. E che io dica il vero, niun'altra cosa vel mostri se non[2] l'aver riguardo e pensare a che ora la vostra donna, la quale è onestissima e piú savia che altra, volendo di tal cosa farvi oltraggio, si recherebbe a farlo davanti agli occhi vostri; di me non vo' dire, che mi lascerei prima squartare che io il pur pensassi, non che io il venissi a fare in vostra presenzia. Per che di certo la magagna di questo trasvedere dee procedere del pero; per ciò che tutto il mondo non m'avrebbe fatto discredere che voi qui non foste con la vostra donna carnalmente giaciuto, se io non udissi dire a voi che egli vi fosse paruto che io facessi quello che io so certissimamente che io non pensai, non che io facessi mai>.

La donna appresso, che quasi tutta turbata s'era levata in piè, cominciò a dire: <Sia con la mala ventura, se tu m'hai per sí poco sentita, che, se io volessi attendere a queste tristezze che tu di' che vedevi, io le venissi a fare dinanzi agli occhi tuoi. Sii certo di questo, che, qualora volontà me ne venisse, io non verrei qui, anzi mi crederei sapere essere in una delle nostre camere e in maniera che gran cosa mi parrebbe che tu il risapessi già mai>.

Nicostrato, al quale vero parea ciò che dicea l'uno e l'altro, che essi quivi dinanzi a lui mai a tale atto non si dovessero esser condotti, lasciate stare le parole e le riprensioni di tal maniera, cominciò a ragionare della novità del fatto e del miracolo della vista che cosí si cambiava a chi sú vi montava.

[2] In line 254, the words "E che io . . . mostri se non" are a correction taken from *Giovanni Boccaccio, Decameron, edizione critica secondo l'autografo hamiltoniano*, a cura di Vittore Branca (Firenze: L'Accademia della Crusca, 1976), p. 494.

(274–82) But the lady, who looked upset by the opinion that Nicostratos showed he had of her, said: "Truly this pear tree will never produce any other shameful vision about me or any other woman, if I have my way; therefore, Pyrrhus, run and get an axe and shortly you will avenge both of us by cutting it down, though it would be as well to apply it to the head of Nicostratos who, without any consideration whatsoever, lets the eyes of his reason be so quickly blinded. For whatever your eyes were telling you, you should not have allowed your mind to believe or even think of it."

(283–7) Pyrrhus soon went for the axe and chopped down the pear tree, seeing which the lady said to Nicostratos: "Now that I see the enemy of my virtue fallen, my anger has gone." Nicostratos begged for her pardon and she graciously gave it, cautioning him never to presume anything again about her, who loved him more than herself, once and forever more.

(288–90) And so the unfortunate dupe of a husband went back with her and her lover to the mansion where later, in a more leisurely fashion, Pyrrhus and Lydia took pleasure and delight in each other many times. And may God grant the same to us.

Ma la donna, che della opinione che Nicostrato mostrava d'avere avuta di lei si mostrava turbata, disse: <Veramente questo pero non ne farà mai piú niuna, né a me né a altra donna, di queste vergogne, se io potrò; e per ciò, Pirro, corri e va e reca una scure e a un'ora te e me vendica tagliandolo, come che molto meglio sarebbe a dar con essa in capo a Nicostrato, il quale senza considerazione alcuna cosí tosto si lasciò abbagliar gli occhi dello 'ntelletto: ché, quantunque a quegli che tu hai in testa paresse ciò che tu di', per niuna cosa dovevi nel giudicio della tua mente comprendere o consentir che ciò fosse>.

Pirro prestissimo andò per la scure e tagliò il pero: il quale come la donna vide caduto, disse verso Nicostrato: <Poscia che io veggio abbattuto il nemico della mia onestà, la mia ira è ita via>; e a Nicostrato, che di ciò la pregava, benignamente perdonò, imponendogli che piú non gli avvenisse di presummere, di colei che piú che sé l'amava, una cosí fatta cosa già mai.

Cosí il misero marito schernito con lei insieme e col suo amante nel palagio se ne tornarono, nel quale poi molte volte Pirro di Lidia e ella di lui con piú agio presero piacere e diletto. Dio ce ne dea a noi.

IX

William Caxton, "The xii fable of a blynd man and of his wyf"

(from *The book of the subtyl hystoryes and Fables of Esope*, in *Originals and Analogues of Some of Chaucer's Canterbury Tales*, ed. F. J. Furnivall, E. Brock and W. A. Clouston, London: Chaucer Society, Second series, Part II, no. 11 [1875], pp. 181–2)

There was somtyme a blynd man whiche had a fayre wyf/ of the whiche he was moche Ialous/ He kepte her so that she myght not goo no wher/ For euer he had her by the hand/ And after that she was enamoured of a gentil felawe/ they coude not fynde the maner ne no place for to fulfylle theyr wyll/ but notwithstandyng the woman whiche was subtyle and Ingenyous counceylled to her frende that he shold come in to her hows/ and that he shold entre in to the gardyn and that there he shold clymme vpon a pere tree/ And he did as she told hym/ and when they had made theyr enterpryse/ the woman came ageyne in to the hows/ and sayd to her husbond/ My frend I praye yow that ye wylle go in to our gardyn for to disporte vs a lytel whyle there/ of the whiche prayer the blynd man was wel content/ and sayd to his wyf/ wel my good frend I will wel/ lete vs go thyder/ And as they were vnder the pere tree/ she sayd to her husband/ My frende I praye the to lete me goo vpon the pere tre/ And I shalle gader for vs bothe some fayre peres/ Wel my frend sayd the blynd man/ I wylle wel & gra*u*nt therto/ And when she was vpon the tree/ the yong man begann to shake the pere tree at one syde/ and the yonge woman atthe other syde/ And as the blynd man herd thus hard shake the pere tree/ and the noyse whiche they made/ he sayde to them/ Ha a euylle woman/ how be it that I see hit not/ Neuertheles I fele and vnderstande hit well/ But I praye to the goddes/ that they vouchesauf to sende me my syght ageyne/ And as soone as he had made his prayer Iupiter rendryd to hym his syght ageyn ¶ And whanne he sawe that pagent vpon the pere tree/ he sayd to his wyf Ha vnhappy woman/ I shalle neuer haue no Ioye with the/ And by cause that the yonge woman was ready in speche and malycious/ she ansuerd forthwith to her husbond/ My frend thow arte wel beholden and bounden to me/ For by cause [of me] and for the loue the goddes haue [to me they have] restored to the thy syght/ wherof I thanke alle the goddes and goddesses/ whiche haue enhaunced and herd my prayer/ For I desyryng moche that thow myght see me/ cessed neuer day ne nyght to pray them/ that they wold rendre to the thy syghte/ wherfore the goddesse Venus vysybly shewed her self to me/ and sayd/ that yf I wold doo somme playsyr to the sayd yonge man/ she shold restore to the thy syght/ And thus I am cause of it And thenne the good man sayd to her/ My ryght dere wyf & goode frende/ I remercye and thanke yow gretely/ For ryght ye haue and I grete wronge.

The Physician's Tale

KENNETH BLEETH

The story of the maiden Virginia, her father Virginius, and the corrupt judge Appius that forms the basis of *The Physician's Tale* began life as a piece of Roman historiography – perhaps invented to illustrate the abuse of power by the decemviri – and found its definitive form in Book 3 of Livy's history of Rome.[1] The Physician names Livy as the story's author in the opening line of his tale. As commentators long have recognized, however, this attribution merely translates a line – "Si con dit Titus Livius"– from the *Roman de la Rose*, and thus signals Chaucer's dependence on the condensed retelling of Livy's anecdote in Jean de Meun's portion of the *Roman*. Of the ninety lines that make up the narrative portion of the tale, twenty or so are close imitations of the *Roman,* where it appears as part of Reason's discourse on the superiority of love to justice.[2] But verbal echoes are not the only evidence for Chaucer's indebtedness to Jean de Meun. Other parallels – the names of the principal characters (Livy's Appius Claudius and Marcus Claudius are called simply Appius and Claudius respectively in both the *Roman* and in Chaucer); the omission of elements central to Livy's version of the story such as the references to Icilius, Virginia's

[1] See Joerg O. Fichte, "Incident – History – Exemplum – Novella: The Transformation of History in Chaucer's *Physician's Tale*," *Florilegium* 5 (1983): 191–6, and R. M. Ogilvy, *A Commentary on Livy, Books 1–5* (Oxford, 1965), pp. 476–9. Ogilvy notes that "the story of Verginia is entirely devoid of historical foundation" (p. 477).

[2] Compare VI, 1 and *Roman* 5594; VI, 168–9 and *Roman* 5612–14; VI, 184–5 and *Roman* 5605–6; VI, 188–9 and *Roman* 5608–9; VI, 205–6 and *Roman* 5630–1; VI, 225 and *Roman* 5635; VI, 255–7 and *Roman* 5637–9; VI, 258–62 and *Roman* 5640–6; VI, 275–6 and *Roman* 5657–8. Less certain parallels are VI, 135–8 and *Roman* 5596–8; VI, 210 and *Roman* 5632–3.

betrothed, and the fully developed historical context; and Virginia's death by beheading in the *Roman* and Chaucer instead of by stabbing as in Livy – all identify the French poem as the primary source of Chaucer's tale.[3]

In his chapter on *The Physician's Tale* in Bryan and Dempster, Edgar Shannon noted details in Chaucer's treatment of the story not present in Jean de Meun that seemed to him to echo Livy's narrative – for example, the reference to Virginius's wife (VI, 5, 118–19; cf. *uxor* [Livy 44, p. 541]); Virginia as an only child (VI, 6; cf. *unica filia* [Livy 45, p. 543]); Virginia's "excellent beautee" (VI, 7, 39; cf. *virginem . . . forma excellentem* [Livy 44, p. 541]); Virginia's journey to "the toun/ Toward a temple" (VI, 118–19; cf. *Virgini venienti in forum – ibi namque in tabernaculis litterarum ludi erant* [Livy 44, p. 541]); the epithet "strong of freendes," used of both Virginius and Virginia (VI, 4, 135; cf. Livy 44, p. 541; 46, p. 543; 47, p. 545); and Virginius's absence when Claudius makes his initial charge (VI, 171–3; cf. Livy 44, p. 541; 45, 46, p. 543). From this evidence, Shannon concluded that Chaucer used Livy to supplement the barebones account of the story in the *Roman*.[4] But the similarities of diction adduced by Shannon are inexact, and parallels of situation (e.g. Virginius's absence from the court when Claudius first makes his charge) can be explained as logical developments from Jean de Meun's narrative. The case for Chaucer's direct knowledge of the Latin historian is not compelling, and most scholars who have investigated the question would agree with Thomas Lounsbury, who in 1892 declared that "the tale of Virginia . . . is evidence . . . that the poet knew nothing of Livy."[5]

3 Chaucer's poem nowhere reflects the influence of two other fourteenth-century versions of the story – Gower's treatment in the *Confessio amantis* (7:5131–306) and chapter 56 of Boccaccio's *De mulieribus claris*. For an argument that Chaucer could have known the *Confessio amantis* (at least by hearsay) when he wrote *The Physician's Tale*, see William H. Brown, Jr., "Chaucer, Livy, and Bersuire: The Roman Materials of *The Physician's Tale*," *On Language: Rhetorica, Phonologica, Syntactica. A Festschrift for Robert P. Stockwell from his Friends and Colleagues*, ed. Caroline Duncan-Rose and Theo Venneman (London and New York, 1988), p. 48 n. 6.

4 Bryan and Dempster, pp. 401–7.

5 Thomas R. Lounsbury, *Studies in Chaucer* (New York, 1892), vol. 2, p. 281. Others who question Chaucer's use of Livy include W. W. Skeat, ed., *The Complete Works of Geoffrey Chaucer, Edited from Numerous Manuscripts* (London, 1894–7), vol. 3, p. 435; vol. 5, p. 260; vol. 6, ci; John Koch, "Chaucers Belesenheit in den römischen Klassikern," *Englische Studien* 57 (1923): 58–9; Bruce Harbert, "Chaucer and the Latin Classics," in *Geoffrey Chaucer*, ed. D. S. Brewer (London, 1974), pp. 142–3; C. David Benson, *The Riverside Chaucer*, p. 902; Derek Pearsall, *The Life of Geoffrey Chaucer: A Critical Biography* (Oxford and Cambridge, MA, 1992), pp. 33, 81, 241; Helen Cooper, *The Canterbury Tales*, 2nd edn (Oxford, 1996), p. 250. For an opposing view, see George R. Coffman, "Chaucer's Library and Literary Heritage for the *Canterbury Tales*," *Studies in Philology* 38 (1941): 580. Brown, "Chaucer, Livy, and Bersuire," pp. 42–8, also detects Livy's influence in Chaucer's use of reiteration and his emphasis on chastity, but suggests that Chaucer could have read Livy in Pierre Bersuire's translation (c. 1355). Although one may agree in principle that Chaucer would have been more likely to "choose contemporary French over Golden Latin," a comparison of Bersuire's translation with Livy's Latin reveals no details not in the original that provide positive evidence for Chaucer's knowledge of the vernacular version. The same conclusion applies to Simon of Hesdin's translation into French of Valerius Maximus's *Memorabilia* (c. 1376), which includes much material from Livy (for Simon as a possible source for Chaucer, see John P. McCall, *Chaucer Among the Gods: The Poetics of Classical Myth* [University Park, PA, and London, 1979], p. 178 n. 35), and to an anonymous fourteenth-century Italian translation of Livy: Claudio Dalmazzo, ed., *La prima deca di Tito Livio, volgarizzamento del buon secolo publicato dal manoscritto Torinese, riveduto sul latino e corretto co'frammenti del codice Adriani del 1326 col testo Riccardiano del 1352 e con altre varielezioni*, 2 vols (Torino, 1845–6). The Appius and Virginia story is in vol. 1, pp. 305–28.

The Physician's Tale contains a number of passages that have no equivalents either in Livy or in Jean's version: Nature's speech (VI, 9–29); the description of Virginia's beauty and her "maidenly virtues" (VI, 30–71; 105–17); the addresses to parents and guardians (VI, 72–102); the dialogue of Virginius and Virginia (VI, 213–53); and the closing *moralitas* (VI, 277–86). The last two of these passages appear to be original with Chaucer.[6] The sources that have been suggested for the other set-pieces demonstrate with particular clarity the truth of C. S. Lewis's observation that medieval authors "hardly ever attempt to write anything unless someone has written it before."[7] When texts are layered with citations and paraphrases of earlier authorities, it frequently proves impossible to isolate a specific source for an oft-cited anecdote or piece of doctrine. Moreover, the desire to pin down the precise point of origin for topoi with widespread currency misrepresents both the rich intertextuality of medieval writing and the manner in which Chaucer's extensive but unsystematic reading made its way into his poems.

Nature's monologue, for example, has been quarried for allusions to Ovid, Cicero, Juvenal, the *Ovidius moralizatus*, and, in particular, Jean de Meun, whose Nature, like Chaucer's, identifies herself as God's "vicaire" (*Roman de la Rose* 16782, 19507), and who describes the goddess in hyperbolic language reminiscent of Nature's account of Virginia's beauty in Chaucer.[8] But Jean inherited the trope of Nature as *vicaria Dei* from Alanus de Insulis's *De planctu naturae*, which has itself been proposed as a source for Chaucer's lines.[9] In making his case for the *De eruditione filiorum nobilium* of Vincent of Beauvais as a model for the account of Virginia's "maidenly virtues," Karl Young cites a passage in which Vincent condemns the use of cosmetics that he believes to be closer to the essential significance of the description of Nature's "painting" of Virginia's figure (VI, 32–6) than the lines in the *Roman*.[10] And Carolyn Collette, quoting part of a Wycliffite treatise, suggests that Nature's language of painting and counterfeiting is best understood in relation to the late medieval discourse on the power of images.[11] Although each of these glosses adds something to our comprehension of Nature's speech, they do so not by identifying material that

[6] The parallels between the dialogue of Virginius and Virginia and the treatments of Abraham's sacrifice of Isaac in the English mystery cycles cited by Anne Lancashire in "Chaucer and the Sacrifice of Isaac," *Chaucer Review* 9 (1975): 320–3, fall short of proving Lancashire's contention that the latter tradition "lies behind" Chaucer's handling of his scene. Cooper (*Canterbury Tales*, p. 14) notes the possible relevance to *The Physician's Tale* of the material on the damnation of unjust judges in John Bromyard's *Summa praedicantium*, which appears in Bromyard's text just after a version of the cock and the fox story that Chaucer may have used in composing *The Nun's Priest's Tale*.

[7] C. S. Lewis, *Studies in Medieval and Renaissance Literature* (Cambridge, 1966), p. 37.

[8] See the notes to lines 9–29 and 31–9 in *The Physician's Tale. A Variorum Edition of the Works of Geoffrey Chaucer*, vol. 2, part 17, ed. Helen Storm Corsa (Norman, OK, 1987); for Juvenal, see William Kupersmith, "Chaucer's Physician's Tale and the Tenth Satire of Juvenal," *English Language Notes* 34 (1986): 20–3.

[9] Barbara Bartholomew, *Fortuna and Natura: A Reading of Three Chaucer Narratives* (The Hague, 1966), pp. 52–3; Geraldine Sesak Branca, "Experience versus Authority: Chaucer's Physician and Fourteenth-Century Science," unpublished dissertation (University of Illinois, Champaign-Urbana, 1971), pp. 91–2.

[10] Karl Young, "The Maidenly Virtues of Chaucer's Virginia," *Speculum* 16 (1941): 345–6.

[11] Carolyn P. Collette, "'Peyntyng with Greet Cost': Virginia as Image in the *Physician's Tale*," *Chaucer Yearbook* 2 (1995): 49–62.

Chaucer was directly imitating or even (except in the case of Ovid and the *Roman*) that he had necessarily read. Rather, they direct our attention to what Michael Riffaterre calls the "vast terra incognita of other texts," written but also remembered, that link themselves to any given text, and that a medieval audience would have brought to bear on its experience of a literary work.[12]

The scholarship on the portrait of Virginia and the addresses to parents and guardians leads us to a book that Chaucer almost certainly knew, and demonstrates as well why Chaucer probably had read only a small fraction of the works that a complete list of the "sources" identified by modern commentators would imply that he was acquainted with. In 1915, Frederick Tupper (styling himself a "source-hunter . . . keen in his quest") argued for Chaucer's indebtedness to St Ambrose's *De virginibus*, offering as evidence seven passages that in his view exemplified the poet's "generous use" of the treatise.[13] Shannon was sufficiently persuaded by the similarities between Chaucer's Virginia and Ambrose's type of the consecrated virgin to include five of Tupper's excerpts in his chapter on *The Physician's Tale.*[14] In the article referred to above (published in the same year as Bryan and Dempster's volume), Young acknowledges that Tupper was on the right path, but offers *De eruditione* – "a treatise less remote and considerably more comprehensive and relevant than Ambrose's tract" – as a more likely source of Chaucer's inspiration.[15] Like the rest of Vincent's treatise, the sections cited by Young – those concerned with the education of girls – are for the most part a collection of classical, medieval, and, especially, patristic utterances, which may themselves have been drawn from florilegia. In these chapters, Jerome (particularly the letters and the *Ad Jovinianum*) and Ambrose are quoted most frequently; Vincent's citations encompass most of the material traced by Tupper to *De virginibus*, and include two of Tupper's passages *verbatim*.

Young's suggestion that Chaucer had access to a compilation that included a wide range of patristic doctrine was taken to the next stage by Martha S. Waller, who in 1976 suggested that a single source – a fourteenth-century Castilian translation of and commentary on Giles of Rome's *De regimine principium* by Juan García de Castrojeriz – may lie behind the portrait of Virginia and the depiction of the manner in which she chooses death rather than dishonor.[16] According to Waller, Castrojeriz's work "account[s] for nearly every phrase of the Physician's Tale not suggested by the *Roman de la Rose*," and allows us to imagine Chaucer consulting one author who brings together most of the commonplaces on virginity in a single volume rather than gathering materials from half a dozen separate authorities.[17]

[12] Michael Riffaterre, "The Mind's Eye: Memory and Textuality," *The New Medievalism*, ed. Marina S. Brownlee, Kevin Brownlee, and Stephen G. Nichols (Baltimore and London, 1991), p. 33.

[13] Frederick Tupper, "Chaucer's Bed's Head," *Modern Language Notes* 30 (1915): 5–7.

[14] Bryan and Dempster, pp. 407–8.

[15] Young, "Maidenly Virtues," p. 340.

[16] Martha S. Waller, "The Physician's Tale: Geoffrey Chaucer and Fray Juan García de Castrojeriz," *Speculum* 51 (1976): 292–306.

[17] Waller, p. 296.

It is precisely the plausibility of Waller's hypothesis about Chaucer's working methods that constitutes the strength of Glending Olson's response to her article, in which he demonstrates that Castrojeriz relied heavily on John of Wales's thirteenth-century preacher's manual, the *Communiloquium*, a work that, on the basis of independent evidence, we know Chaucer was familiar with.[18] The similarities between the Spanish commentary and *The Physician's Tale*, Olson maintains, prove not that Chaucer had read Castrojeriz, but rather that both authors had made use of the *Communiloquium*. Although the verbal parallels between the *Communiloquium* and *The Physician's Tale* are less striking than those Pratt found for *The Wife of Bath's Prologue and Tale*, *The Summoner's Tale*, and *The Pardoner's Tale*, almost everything in lines 39–104 of Chaucer's poem has some point of correspondence with the chapters on the education of children and the proper behavior for women in parts 2 and 3 of John of Wales's compendium.[19] The *Communiloquium*, moreover, contains many of the biblical and patristic citations (notably from Jerome, but also from Ambrose's treatises on virginity) included by Vincent in *De eruditione*. Although the presence of this material in John of Wales weakens Young's case for Chaucer's direct knowledge of *De eruditione*, I print excepts from the latter to demonstrate the degree of overlap that exists in medieval writings on virginity, and the consequent obstacles to tracing Chaucer's use of a given topos to a particular authority.[20] Chaucer didn't require a specific source for his account of Virginia's virtues and his admonitions to parents and guardians, but if he had wanted to find assembled in one place most of the traditional discourses on virginity and the education of children, he would have needed to go no further than an anthology of *sententiae*, extracts, and illustrative anecdotes like those in the *Communiloquium*.

18 Glending Olson, "Juan García de Castrojeriz and John of Wales: A Note on Chaucer's Reading," *Speculum* 64 (1989): 106–10. On Chaucer's knowledge of the *Communiloquium*, see Robert A. Pratt, "Chaucer and the Hand that Fed Him," *Speculum* 41 (1966): 619–42, and Pearsall, *Geoffrey Chaucer*, pp. 243–4. A preliminary list of institutions and individuals who owned copies of John of Wales's works up to the mid-sixteenth century includes 31 entries for the *Communiloquium* in English locations; see Jenny Swanson, *John of Wales: A Study of the Works and Ideas of a Thirteenth-Century Friar* (Cambridge, 1989), pp. 262–71. On the use of John of Wales by Castrojeriz, see Ana Maria Huélama San José, "El *Communiloquium* de Juan de Gales en las Letras Castellanas," *Actas del VI Congreso Internacional de la Asociación Hispánica de Literatura Medieval*, ed. José Manuel Lucía Megías (Alcalá, 1997), vol. 2, pp. 825–8.

19 Some of the material in the *Communiloquium* that seems to be recalled in *The Physician's Tale* appears in close proximity to passages that Chaucer incontrovertibly made use of elsewhere in the *Tales*; for example, the retelling of the anecdote from Valerius Maximus that, as Pratt has shown (pp. 620–1), lies behind lines 460–7 of *The Wife of Bath's Prologue*, occurs in the context of John's comments on sobriety as a preserver of women's chastity (see below, p. 559). As Olson points out, all observations about Chaucer's use of the *Communiloquium* must be provisional in the absence of a detailed study of the manuscripts (p. 107 n. 2).

20 Compared to the relatively large number of manuscripts of the *Communiloquium* for which we have medieval English records (see note 18, above), a survey of manuscripts of Vincent's minor works lists only two pre-fifteenth-century manuscripts of *De eruditione* in English libraries; see R. J. Schneider and J. B. Voorbij, "A Hand-list of Manuscripts of the Minor Treatises of Vincent of Beauvais," *Vincent of Beauvais Newsletter* 12 (1987): 3–11.

I

Titus Livius, *From the Founding of Rome*, III, 44–48, 58

(trans. B. O. Foster [Cambridge, MA, and London: Harvard University Press, 1922])

44. This outrage was followed by another, committed in Rome, which was inspired by lust and was no less shocking in its consequences than that which had led, through the rape and the death of Lucretia, to the expulsion of the Tarquinii from the City and from their throne; thus not only did the same end befall the decemvirs as had befallen the kings, but the same cause deprived them of their power. Appius Claudius was seized with the desire to debauch a certain maiden belonging to the plebs. The girl's father, Lucius Verginius, a centurion of rank, was serving on Algidus, a man of exemplary life at home and in the army. His wife had been brought up in the same principles, and his children were being trained in them. He had betrothed his daughter to the former tribune Lucius Icilius, an active man of proven courage in the cause of the plebeians. She was a grown girl, remarkably beautiful, and Appius, crazed with love, attempted to seduce her with money and promises. But finding that her modesty was proof against everything, he resolved on a course of cruel and tyrannical violence. He commissioned Marcus Claudius, his client, to claim the girl as his slave, and not to yield to those who demanded her liberation, thinking that the absence of the maiden's father afforded an opportunity for the wrong. As Verginia was entering the Forum – for there, in booths, were the elementary schools – the minister of the decemvir's lust laid his hands upon her, and calling her the daughter of his bond-woman and herself a slave, commanded her to follow him, and threatened to drag her off by force if she hung back. Terror made the maiden speechless, but the cries of her nurse imploring help of the Quirites quickly brought a crowd about them. The names of Verginius her father and of her betrothed Icilius were known and popular. Their acquaintance were led to support the girl out of regard for them; the crowd was influenced by the shamelessness of the attempt. She was already safe from violence, when the claimant protested that there was no occasion for the people to become excited; he was proceeding lawfully, not by force. He then summoned the girl to court. She was advised by her supporters to follow him, and they went before the tribunal of Appius. The plaintiff acted out a comedy familiar to the judge, since it was he and no other who had invented the plot: The girl had been born, said Marcus, in his house, and had thence been stealthily conveyed to the home of Verginius and palmed off upon him as his own; he had good evidence for what he said, and would prove it even though Verginius himself were judge, who was more wronged than he was; meanwhile it was right that the hand-maid should follow her master. The friends of the girl said that Verginius was absent on the service of the state; he would be at hand in two days' time if he were given notice of the matter; it was unjust that a man should be involved in litigation about his children when away from home; they therefore requested Appius to leave the case open until the father arrived, and in accordance with the law he had himself proposed, grant the custody of the girl to the defendants, nor suffer a grown maiden's honour to be jeopardized before her freedom should be adjudicated.

I

Titus Livius, *Ab urbe condita*, III, 44–48, 58

(from *Livy*, Books III and IV, ed. and trans. B. O. Foster [Cambridge, MA, and London: Harvard University Press, 1922], vol. 2, pp. 142–60; 196, 199)

44. Sequitur aliud in urbe nefas ab libidine ortum, haud minus foedo eventu quam quod per stuprum caedemque Lucretiae urbe regnoque Tarquinios expulerat, ut non finis solum idem decemviris qui regibus sed causa etiam eadem imperii amittendi esset. Ap. Claudium virginis plebeiae stuprandae libido cepit. Pater virginis, L. Verginius, honestum ordinem in Algido ducebat, vir exempli recti domi militiaeque. Perinde uxor instituta fuerat liberique instituebantur. Desponderat filiam L. Icilio tribunicio, viro acri et pro causa plebis expertae virtutis. Hanc virginem adultam forma excellentem Appius amore amens pretio ac spe perlicere adortus, postquam omnia pudore saepta animadvertit, ad crudelem superbamque vim animum convertit. M. Claudio clienti negotium dedit ut virginem in servitutem adsereret neque cederet secundum libertatem postulantibus vindicias, quod pater puellae abesset locum iniuriae esse ratus. Virgini venienti in forum – ibi namque in tabernaculis litterarum ludi erant – minister decemviri libidinis manum iniecit, serva sua natam servamque appellans, sequique se iubebat: cunctantem vi abstracturum. Pavida puella stupente ad clamorem nutricis fidem Quiritium implorantis fit concursus. Vergini patris sponsique Icili populare nomen celebrabatur. Notos gratia eorum, turbam indignitas rei virgini conciliat. Iam a vi tuta erat, cum adsertor nihil opus esse multitudine concitata ait; se iure grassari, non vi. Vocat puellam in ius. Auctoribus qui aderant ut sequeretur, ad tribunal Appi perventum est. Notam iudici fabulam petitor, quippe apud ipsum auctorem argumenti, peragit: puellam domi suae natam furtoque inde in domum Vergini translatam suppositam ei esse; id se indicio compertum adferre probaturumque vel ipso Verginio iudice, ad quem maior pars iniuriae eius pertineat; interim dominum sequi ancillam aequum esse. Advocati puellae, cum Verginium rei publicae causa dixissent abesse, biduo adfuturum si nuntiatum ei sit, iniquum esse absentem de liberis dimicare, postulant ut rem integram in patris adventum differat, lege ab ipso lata vindicias det secundum libertatem, neu patiatur virginem adultam famae prius quam libertatis periculum adire.

45. Appius prefaced his decision by saying that it was evident how much he favoured liberty from that very law which the friends of Verginius made the pretext for their claim; but the law would afford liberty a sure protection only if it varied neither with causes nor with persons; for in the case of others who were claimed as free, the demand was legal, since any one might bring an action: in the case of one who was under the authority of a father there was no one else to whom the master ought to yield the custody; accordingly he decreed that the father should be summoned, and that meanwhile the claimant should not relinquish his right, but should take the girl in charge and guarantee that she should be produced at the coming of him who was called her father.

Against the injustice of the decree, though many murmured their disapproval, there was not a single man who dared to stand out; when Publius Numitorius, the girl's great-uncle, and her lover Icilius, arrived on the scene. When a path had been opened for them through the throng, since the crowd believed that the intervention of Icilius would be particularly effectual in resisting Appius, the lictor cried that the case had been decided, and as Icilius began to protest, attempted to thrust him aside. Even a placid nature would have been incensed by so violent an insult. "You must use iron to rid yourself of me, Appius," he cried, "that you may carry through in silence what you desire should be concealed. This maiden I am going to wed; and I intend that my bride shall be chaste. So call together all your colleagues' lictors too; bid them make ready rods and axes: the promised wife of Icilius shall not pass the night outside her father's house. No! If you have taken from the Roman plebs the assistance of the tribunes and the right of appeal, two citadels for the defence of liberty, it has not therefore been granted to your lust to lord it over our children and our wives as well! Vent your rage upon our backs and our necks: let our chastity at least be safe. If that shall be assailed, I will call on the Quirites here present to protect my bride, Verginius will invoke the help of the soldiers in behalf of his only daughter, and all of us will implore the protection of gods and men; nor shall you ever repeat that decree of yours without shedding our blood. I ask you, Appius, to consider earnestly whither you are going. Let Verginius decide what to do about his daughter, when he comes; but of one thing he may rest assured: if he yields to this man's claim, he will have to seek a husband for her. As for me, in defense of the freedom of my bride I will sooner die than prove disloyal."

46. The crowd was deeply moved and a conflict appeared to be imminent. The lictors had surrounded Icilius, but had nevertheless gone no further than to threaten him, since Appius declared that it was not a question of Verginia's defense by Icilius, but of a turbulent fellow, who even now breathed the spirit of the tribunate, seeking an opportunity to stir up strife. He would furnish him no excuse for it that day; but that he might know now that the concession had not been made to his own wantonness but to the absent Verginius, to the name of father, and to liberty, he would not pronounce judgment that day nor deliver a decision; he would request Marcus Claudius to waive his right and suffer the girl to remain at large until the morrow; but unless the father should appear the next day, he gave notice to Icilius and to those like Icilius that the proposer of his law would not fail to support it, nor the decemvir be wanting in firmness; and in any case he should not call together his colleagues' lictors to repress the instigators of sedition, but rest content with his own.

The time for accomplishing the wrong having been postponed, the girl's supporters went apart by themselves, and decided that first of all the brother of Icilius and the son of Numitorius, active young men, should proceed straight to the City gate and make all possible haste to the camp, to summon Verginius; for the

45. Appius decreto praefatur, quam libertati faverit eam ipsam legem declarare quam Vergini amici postulationi suae praetendant; ceterum ita in ea firmum libertati fore praesidium si nec causis nec personis variet; in aliis enim qui adserantur in libertatem quia quivis lege agere possit, id iuris esse: in ea quae in patris manu sit neminem esse alium cui dominus possessione cedat. Placere itaque patrem arcessiri, interea iuris sui iacturam adsertorem non facere quin ducat puellam sistendamque in adventum eius qui pater dicatur promittat.

Adversus iniuriam decreti cum multi magis fremerent quam quisquam unus recusare auderet, P. Numitorius, puellae avus, et sponsus Icilius interveniunt; dataque inter turbam via, cum multitudo Icili maxime interventu resisti posse Appio crederet, lictor decresse ait vociferantemque Icilium submovet. Placidum quoque ingenium tam atrox iniuria accendisset. "Ferro hinc tibi submovendus sum, Appi" inquit, "ut tacitum feras quod celari vis. Virginem ego hanc sum ducturus nuptamque pudicam habiturus. Proinde omnes collegarum quoque lictores convoca; expediri virgas et secures iube; non manebit extra domum patris sponsa Icili. Non, si tribunicium auxilium et provocationem plebi Romanae, duas arces libertatis tuendae, ademistis, ideo in liberos quoque nostros coniugesque regnum vestrae libidini datum est. Saevite in tergum et in cervices nostras: pudicitia saltem in tuto sit. Huic si vis adferetur, ego praesentium Quiritium pro sponsa, Verginius militum pro unica filia, omnes deorum hominumque implorabimus fidem, neque tu istud unquam decretum sine caede nostra referes. Postulo, Appi, etiam atque etiam consideres quo progrediare. Verginius viderit de filia ubi venerit quid agat; hoc tantum sciat, sibi si huius vindiciis cesserit condicionem filiae quaerendam esse. Me vindicantem sponsam in libertatem vita citius deseret quam fides."

46. Concitata multitudo erat certamenque instare videbatur. Lictores Icilium circumsteterant; nec ultra minas tamen processum est, cum Appius non Verginiam defendi ab Icilio, sed inquietum hominem et tribunatum etiam nunc spirantem locum seditionis quaerere diceret. Non praebiturum se illi eo die materiam; sed ut iam sciret non id petulantiae suae sed Verginio absenti et patrio nomini et libertati datum, ius eo die se non dicturum neque decretum interpositurum: a M. Claudio petiturum, ut decederet iure suo vindicarique puellam in posterum diem pateretur; quod nisi pater postero die adfuisset, denuntiare se Icilio similibusque Icili, neque legi suae latorem neque decemviro constantiam defore. Nec se utique collegarum lictores convocaturum ad coercendos seditionis auctores: contentum se suis lictoribus fore.

Cum dilatum tempus iniuriae esset secessissentque advocati puellae, placuit omnium primum fratrem Icili filiumque Numitori, impigros iuvenes, pergere inde recta ad portam, et quantum adcelerari posset Verginium acciri e castris: in eo verti puellae salutem, si postero die vindex iniuriae ad tempus praesto esset. Iussi pergunt citatisque equis nuntium ad patrem perferunt. Cum instaret adsertor puellae ut vindicaret sponsoresque daret, atque id ipsum agi diceret Icilius, sedulo tempus

maiden's safety turned on her protector's being at hand in time. They set out the moment they got their orders, and galloping their horses, carried the message through to the father. When the claimant of the girl pressed Icilius to furnish the sureties required of her guarantor, and Icilius said that it was precisely that which he was considering (though he was doing his best to consume time, that the messengers who had been dispatched to the camp might get a start on the way), the people began on every side to raise their hands, and every man of them to indicate his readiness to go bail for Icilius. And Icilius said, with tears in his eyes, "I am grateful to you; tomorrow I will use your services; of sureties I now have enough." So Verginia was surrendered, on the security of her kinsmen. Appius waited a little while, that he might not appear to have sat for this case only, and when nobody applied to him – for all other matters were forgotten in men's concern over this, – he went to his house and wrote to his colleagues in camp that they should grant no furlough to Verginius, and should even detain him in custody. His base design was too late, as it deserved to be; Verginius had already got his leave and had set out in the fore-part of the night, nor was it until early the next morning that the letters for detaining him were delivered, to no purpose.

47. But in the City, as the citizens at break of day were standing in the Forum, agog with expectation, Verginius, dressed in sordid clothes and leading his daughter, who was also meanly clad and was attended by a number of matrons, came down into the market-place with a vast throng of supporters. He then began to go about and canvass people, and not merely to ask their aid as a favour, but to claim it as his due, saying that he stood daily in the battle-line in defence of their children and their wives; that there was no man of whom more strenuous and courageous deeds in war could be related – to what end, if despite the safety of the City those outrages which were dreaded as the worst that could follow a city's capture must be suffered by their children? Pleading thus, as if in a kind of public appeal, he went about amongst the people. Similar appeals were thrown out by Icilius; but the women who attended them were more moving, as they wept in silence, than any words. In the face of all these things Appius hardened his heart – so violent was the madness, as it may more truly be called than love, that had overthrown his reason – and mounted the tribunal. The plaintiff was actually uttering a few words of complaint, on the score of having been balked of his rights the day before through partiality, when, before he could finish his demand, or Verginius be given an opportunity to answer, Appius interrupted him. The discourse with which he led up to his decree may perhaps be truthfully represented in some one of the old accounts, but since I can nowhere discover one that is plausible, in view of the enormity of the decision, it seems my duty to set forth the naked fact, upon which all agree, that he adjudged Verginia to him who claimed her as his slave. At first everybody was rooted to the spot in amazement at so outrageous a proceeding, and for a little while after the silence was unbroken. Then, when Marcus Claudius was making his way through the group of matrons to lay hold upon the girl, and had been greeted by the women with wails and lamentations, Verginius shook his fist at Appius and cried, "It was to Icilius, Appius, not to you that I betrothed my daughter; and it was for wedlock, not dishonour, that I brought her up. Would you have men imitate the beasts of the field and the forest in promiscuous gratification of their lust? Whether these people propose to tolerate such conduct I do not know: I cannot believe that those who have arms will endure it."

The claimant of the maiden was being forced back by the ring of women and supporters who surrounded her, when silence was commanded by a herald;

terens dum praeciperent iter nuntii missi in castra, manus tollere undique multitudo et se quisque paratum ad spondendum Icilio ostendere. Atque ille lacrimabundus "Gratum est" inquit; "crastina die vestra opera utar; sponsorum nunc satis est." Ita vindicatur Verginia spondentibus propinquis. Appius paulisper moratus ne eius rei causa sedisse videretur, postquam omissis rebus aliis prae cura unius nemo adibat, domum se recepit collegisque in castra scribit, ne Verginio commeatum dent atque etiam in custodia habeant. Improbum consilium serum, ut debuit, fuit, et iam commeatu sumpto profectus Verginius prima vigilia erat, cum postero die mane de retinendo eo nequiquam litterae redduntur.

47. At in urbe prima luce cum civitas in foro exspectatione erecta staret, Verginius sordidatus filiam secum obsoleta veste comitantibus aliquot matronis cum ingenti advocatione in forum deducit. Circumire ibi et prensare homines coepit et non orare solum precariam opem, sed pro debita petere: se pro liberis eorum ac coniugibus cottidie in acie stare, nec alium virum esse cuius strenue ac fortiter facta in bello plura memorari possent; quid prodesse si, incolumi urbe, quae capta ultima timeantur liberis suis sint patienda? Haec prope contionabundus circumibat homines. Similia his ab Icilio iactabantur. Comitatus muliebris plus tacito fletu quam ulla vox movebat. Adversus quae omnia obstinato animo Appius – tanta vis amentiae verius quam amoris mentem turbaverat – in tribunal escendit, et ultro querente pauca petitore quod ius sibi pridie per ambitionem dictum non esset, priusquam aut ille postulatum perageret aut Verginio respondendi daretur locus, Appius interfatur. Quem decreto sermonem praetenderit, forsan aliquem verum auctores antiqui tradiderint: quia nusquam ullum in tanta foeditate decreti veri similem invenio, id quod constat nudum videtur proponendum, decresse vindicias secundum servitutem. Primo stupor omnes admiratione rei tam atrocis defixit; silentium inde aliquamdiu tenuit. Dein cum M. Claudius circumstantibus matronis iret ad prehendendam virginem, lamentabilisque eum mulierum comploratio excepisset, Verginius intentans in Appium manus, "Icilio" inquit, "Appi, non tibi filiam despondi et ad nuptias, non ad stuprum educavi. Placet pecudum ferarumque ritu promisce in concubitus ruere? Passurine haec isti sint, nescio: non spero esse passuros illos, qui arma habent."

Cum repelleretur adsertor virginis a globo mulierum circumstantiumque advocatorum, silentium factum per praeconem.

48. and the decemvir, crazed with lust, declared that he knew, not only from the abusive words uttered by Icilius the day before and the violence of Verginius, which he could prove by the testimony of the Roman People, but also from definite information, that all through the night meetings had been held in the City to promote sedition. Accordingly, having been aware of the approaching struggle, he had come down into the Forum with armed men, not that he might do violence to any peaceable citizen, but to coerce, conformably to the dignity of his office, those who would disturb the nation's peace. "You will therefore," he cried, "best be quiet! Go, lictor, remove the mob and open a way for the master to seize his slave!" When he had wrathfully thundered out these words, the crowd parted spontaneously and left the girl standing there, a prey to villainy. Then Verginius, seeing no help anywhere, said, "I ask you, Appius, first to pardon a father's grief if I have somewhat harshly inveighed against you; and then to suffer me to question the nurse here, in the maiden's presence, what all this means, that if I have been falsely called a father, I may go away with a less troubled spirit." Permission being granted, he led his daughter and the nurse apart, to the booths near the shrine of Cloacina, now known as the "New Booths," and there, snatching a knife from a butcher, he exclaimed, "Thus, my daughter, in the only way I can, do I assert your freedom!" He then stabbed her to the heart, and, looking back to the tribunal, cried, "Tis you, Appius, and your life I devote to destruction with this blood!" The shout which broke forth at the dreadful deed roused Appius, and he ordered Verginius to be seized. But Verginius made a passage for himself with his knife wherever he came, and was also protected by a crowd of men who attached themselves to him, and so reached the City gate. Icilius and Numitorius lifted up the lifeless body and showed it to the people, bewailing the crime of Appius, the girl's unhappy beauty, and the necessity that had constrained her father. After them came the matrons crying aloud, "Was it on these terms that children were brought into the world? Were these the rewards of chastity?" – with such other complaints as are prompted at a time like this by a woman's anguish, and are so much the more pitiful as their lack of self-control makes them the more give way to grief. The men, and especially Icilius, spoke only of the tribunician power; of the right of appeal to the people which had been taken from them; and of their resentment at the nation's wrongs.

Chapters 56–58 are Livy's account of the trial Appius and his co-conspirators; Appius is sent to jail and a day is set for the continuance of his trial.

58. . . . And so Appius, cut off from hope, did not wait for the appointed day to come, but killed himself . . . Marcus Claudius also, the claimant of Verginia, was cited and condemned, but at the instance of Verginius himself, the extreme penalty was remitted; and being allowed to depart, he went into exile at Tibur.

48. Decemivir alienatus ad libidinem animo negat ex hesterno tantum convicio Icili violentiaque Vergini, cuius testem populum Romanum habeat, sed certis quoque indiciis compertum se habere nocte tota coetus in urbe factos esse ad movendam seditionem. Itaque se haud inscium eius dimicationis cum armatis descendisse, non ut quemquam quietum violaret, sed ut turbantes civitatis otium pro maiestate imperii coerceret. "Proinde quiesse erit melius. I," inquit, "lictor, submove turbam et da viam domino ad prehendendum mancipium." Cum haec intonuisset plenus irae, multitudo ipsa se sua sponte dimovit desertaque praeda iniuriae puella stabat. Tum Verginius ubi nihil usquam auxilii vidit, "Quaeso" inquit, "Appi, primum ignosce patrio dolori, si quo inclementius in te sum invectus; deinde sinas hic coram virgine nutricem percontari quid hoc rei sit, ut si falso pater dictus sum aequiore hinc animo discedam." Data venia seducit filiam ac nutricem prope Cloacinae ad tabernas quibus nunc novis est nomen atque ibi ab lanio cultro arrepto, " Hoc te uno quo possum" ait "modo, filia, in libertatem vindico." Pectus deinde puellae transfigit respectansque ad tribunal "Te" inquit, "Appi, tuumque caput sanguine hoc consecro." Clamore ad tam atrox facinus orto excitus Appius comprehendi Verginium iubet. Ille ferro quacumque ibat viam facere, donec multitudine etiam prosequentium tuente ad portam perrexit. Icilius Numitoriusque exsangue corpus sublatum ostentant populo; scelus Appi, puellae infelicem formam, necessitatem patris deplorant. Sequentes clamitant matronae: eamne liberorum procreandorum condicionem, ea pudicitiae praemia esse? – cetera quae in tali re muliebris dolor, quo est maestior imbecillo animo, eo miserabilia magis querentibus subicit. Virorum et maxime Icili vox tota tribuniciae potestatis ac provocationis ad populum ereptae publicarumque indignationum erat.

Chapters 56–58 are Livy's account of the trial of Appius and his co-conspirators; Appius is sent to jail and a day is set for the continuance of his trial.

58. . . . Itaque spe incisa, priusquam prodicta dies adesset, Appius mortem sibi conscivit. . . . Et M. Claudius, adsertor Verginiae, die dicta damnatus, ipso remittente Verginio ultimam poenam dismissus Tibur exsulatum abiit.

II

Guillaume de Lorris and Jean de Meun, *The Romance of the Rose*, lines 5589–5658

(trans. Frances Horgan [Oxford, 1994], pp. 86–7)

Reason speaks to the Lover about corrupt judges.

Did Appius not deserve to be hanged when, according to Titus Livy (5595), who is well able to give an account of those events, he caused his servant to bring a false case supported by false witnesses against the maiden Virginia, daughter of Virginius, because he was unable to intimidate the maiden, who wanted nothing to do with him or his lustful desires? The wretch said in court: (5600) "Lord judge, give judgement in my favour, for the maiden is mine. I shall prove against any man alive that she is my slave, for wherever she was brought up, (5605) she was taken from my house at birth, by my faith, and given to Virginius. I therefore call upon you, Lord Appius, to deliver my slave to me, (5610) for it is right that she should serve me and not the man who brought her up. If Virginius denies this, I am ready to prove it all, and I can find good witnesses."

Thus spoke the evil traitor, (5615) who was the servant of the false judge, and the case proceeded in such a way that before Virginius could speak (5620) (and he was quite ready to reply and confound his enemies),

Appius gave a hasty judgement to the effect that the maiden should be given to the servant without delay. (5625)

II

Guillaume de Lorris and Jean de Meun, *Le Roman de la Rose*, lines 5589–5658

(from *Le Roman de la Rose*, ed. Ernest Langlois, II [Paris: Champion, 1920], 263–6)

Reason speaks to the Lover about corrupt judges.

Ne fist bien Appius a pendre
Qui fist a son sergent emprendre
Par faus tesmoinz fausse querele
Contre Virgine la pucele,
Qui fu fille Virginius,
Si con dit Titus Livius,
Qui bien set le cas raconter?
Pour ce qu'il ne poait donter
La pucele, qui n'avait cure
Ne de lui ne de sa luxure,
Li ribauz dist en audience:
"Sire juiges, donez sentence
Pour mei, car la pucele est meie;
Pour ma serve la prouveraie
Contre touz ceus qui sont en vie,
Car, ou qu'ele ait esté nourrie,
De mon ostel me fu emblee
Des lors, par [foi],[21] qu'ele fu nee,
E bailliee a Virginius:
Si vous requier, sire Appius,
Que vous me delivrez ma serve,
Car il est dreiz qu'ele me serve,
Non pas celui qui l'a nourrie;
E se Virginius le nie,
Tout ce sui je prez de prouver,
Car bons tesmoinz en puis trouver."
Ainsinc palait li maus traïstres,
Qui dou faus juige estait menistres,
E con li plaiz ainsinc alast,
Ainz que Virginius palast,
Qui touz estait prez de respondre,
Pour ses aversaires confondre,
Juija par hastive sentence
Appius que, senz atendance,
Fust la pucele au serf rendue.
E quant la chose a entendue
Li beaus preudon devant nomez,

[21] **foi** *MS* po (foi *supplied from other MSS; see Langlois, p. 264*).

And when that fine and worthy man whom I have mentioned, that excellent and renowned knight Virginius heard it, realizing that he could not defend his daughter against Appius (5630) but would be forced to give her up and deliver her body to shame, he found a terrible way of exchanging shame for injury. For if Titus Livy does not lie, (5635) in love rather than in hate he instantly cut off the head of his beautiful daughter Virginia and then presented it to the judge before all, in open court. (5640) According to the story, the judge at once commanded that he be seized and led away to be killed or hanged, but he was neither killed nor hanged, for the people defended him, (5645) since all were moved to pity as soon as the facts were known. Appius was imprisoned for this injustice, and hastily killed himself (5650) before the day of his trial, while Claudius, the plaintiff, would have been sentenced to die like a thief had Virginius in his pity not spared him (5655) and implored the people to send him into exile. All the witnesses to Claudius' case were condemned to death.'

Bons chevaliers, bien renomez,
C'est a saveir Virginius,
Qui bien veit que vers Appius
Ne peut pas sa fille defendre,
Ainz li couvient par force rendre
E son cors livrer a hontage,
Si change honte pour domage
Par merveilleus apensement,
Se Titus Livius ne ment;
Car il, par amour, senz haïne,
A sa bele fille Virgine
Tantost a la teste copee
E puis au juige presentee,
Devant touz, en plein consistoire;
E li juiges, selonc l'estoire,
Le comanda tantost a prendre,
Pour lui mener ocierre ou pendre.
Mais ne l'ocist ne ne pendi,
Car li peuples le defendi,
Qui fu touz de pitié meüz
Si tost con li faiz fu seüz.
Puis fu pour cete mesprison
Appius mis en la prison,
E s'ocist la hastivement
Ainz le jour de son juigement;
E Claudius li chalengierres
Juigiez iert a mort come lierres
Se ne l'en eüst respitié
Virginius par sa pitié,
Qui tant vost le peuple preier
Qu'en essil le fist enveier;
E tuit cil condanné moururent
Qui tesmoing de sa cause furent.

III

Vincent of Beauvais, *On the Education of Noble Children*

(trans. Joann Silverberg and Kenneth Bleeth)[22]

(1) Virginia's maidenly virtues (VI, 43–54):

Again, Ambrose has given us in the Blessed Virgin a model of complete integrity and maturity in maidenly habits and bearing, saying in Book 2 of *On Virginity*: "Let Mary's virginity be reinscribed in you in image, and from her let shine forth in you, as in a mirror, the beauty of chastity and the model of virtue; she was a virgin in body and mind, humble of heart, dignified in her words, prudent in spirit, very reserved in her speech. There was nothing fierce in her eyes, nothing insolent in her words, nothing immodest in her deeds. There was no affectation in her bearing, no lack of restraint in her step, no immodesty in her voice, so that the beauty of her body became a likeness of her mind and the very shape of uprightness."

(2) Virginia's "mesure . . . of beryng and array" (VI, 47):

Excessive adornment consists of rare and expensive garments, carefully arranged hair, painting of the face and suchlike, concerning which John says in his *Dialogue to Basilius*, Book 6: "A face and eyes made beautiful through painting, cheeks stained with rouge, elaborate hairdos, dyed hair, expensive clothing, shining gems, fragrant unguents, and whatever else is involved in womanly adornment are just so much weight to burden the spirit unless it is all enclosed in a very vigorous purity." Let their clothing be decorous, displaying neither licentiousness nor wantonness nor pride.

(3) Virginia's modesty and decorum in speech (VI, 48–54):

But silence especially becomes virgins, according to Ambrose in Book 3 of *On Virginity*: . . . "The social round," he says, "wears down a girl's shyness: she tries to appear sophisticated, and then boldness breaks out, laughter creeps in, modesty slips away. And so I would rather see virgins to talk too little than talk too much." Let her be modest in speech, then: quiet, not a chatterer; a peacemaker, not a wrangler.

(4) Virginia's zeal in avoiding idleness (VI, 56–7):

As John Chrysostom says (*On Matthew*, Book 2): "a woman sitting around with nothing to do behind closed doors falls easily into carnal sin, especially since this

[22] In the English translations of *De eruditione* and John of Wales's *Communiloquium*, biblical citations follow the form of the Douai-Rheims Version, adjusted to fit authorial context and with modernization of pronouns and the third person singular of verbs. We are indebted to Traugott Lawler for his helpful suggestions regarding the translation of *De eruditione* and the text and translation of the *Communiloquium*.

III

Vincent of Beauvais, *De eruditione filiorum nobilium*

(from Arpad Steiner, ed. [Cambridge, MA: Mediaeval Academy of America, 1938], pp. 172–4, 176–7, 179–81, 187–9, 192–4, 203)[23]

(1) Virginia's maidenly virtues (VI, 43–54):

Porro de universa morum ac gestuum puellarium honestate et maturitate ponit exemplum idem Ambrosius in Beata Virgine, dicens in II libro *De virginitate*: "Sit vobis . . . in ymagine descripta virginitas Marie, e qua velut speculo refulgeat species castitatis et forma virtutis . . . virgo erat . . . corpore . . . et mente . . . corde humilis, verbis gravis, animo prudens, loquendi [parcior][24] . . . Nichil torvum in oculis, nichil procax in verbis, nichil in actu inverecundum. Non gestus fractior, non incessus solucior, non vox petulancior, ut ipsa species corporis simulacrum fieret mentis et figura probitatis."[25] (Steiner, pp. 193–4)

(2) Virginia's "mesure . . . of beryng and array" (VI, 47):

Ornatus autem superfluus consistit in vestium exquisicione et crinium conposicione et faciei depictione et huiusmodi, de quibus dicit Johannes in *Dyalogo ad Basilium*, libro vi: "Pulcritudo vultus et oculi depicti, infecte maxille et capitis ornatus et tinctura crinium ac vestes preciose, gemmarumque splendor et pigmentorum odor et alia que pertinent ad mundum muliebrem gravia sunt ad perturbandum animum, nisi multo castitatis vigore concluserit."[26] . . . Sit ergo habitus ordinatus, nichil habens lascivum vel impudicum vel etiam superbum. (Steiner, pp. 181, 203)

(3) Virginia's modesty and decorum in speech (VI, 48–54):

Sed et taciturnitas virgines decet precipue juxta illud Ambrosii in libro III *De virginitate*: . . . "Teritur," inquit, "officiis pudor, audacia emicat, risus subrepit, modestia solvitur dum urbanitas affectatur. . . . Itaque sermonem virgini malim deesse quam superesse."[27] . . . Sit et in verbo modesta, scilicet non garula sed taciturna, non litigiosa sed pacifica. (Steiner, pp. 192, 194, 203)

(4) Virginia's zeal in avoiding idleness (VI, 56–7):

Ut enim dicit Johannes Crisostomus *Super Matheum*, libro II: "Mulier in quiete

[23] The numbers of Jerome's letters in the excerpts from *De eruditione* and John of Wales's *Communiloquium* have been silently adjusted to those in *Patrologia Latina* (*PL*), vol. 22.

[24] **parcior** *MS* pericior

[25] *De virginibus* 2.2.6–7 (*PL* 16:220).

[26] St John Chrysostom, *De sacerdotio* 6.2 (*PG* 48:679).

[27] *De virginibus* 3.3.9 (*PL* 16:234).

vice is easily bred of idleness and leisure." Concerning work, he [i.e. Jerome] also says in his letter *To the Maiden Demetrias*: "Every idle person, as we have read, is in a state of desire. Therefore you must not stop working just because God's bounty has left you needing nothing: rather for that very reason you must labor along with everyone else, so that being always occupied you may think only of what pertains to the service of the Lord."

(5) Virginia's abstention from wine (VI, 58–60):

And so Jerome says the same thing about the pleasure of food and drink, in the same place as above: "Eating meat and drinking wine and filling the belly is the seedbed of lust." And he also writes in his letter *To a Mother and Daughter* that it is difficult to stay chaste at a banquet. Hence Ovid says, too, in Book 2 of *On the Remedies [of Love]*, that "wines prepare minds for lechery." Solomon says the same thing in Proverbs 20, "a lecherous thing is wine." Conversely, Terence says in *The Eunuch* that "without food and wine, love grows cold."

(6) Virginia's avoidance of unseemly social gatherings (VI, 61–71):

Keep watch, I say, over the bodies of those in the state of girlhood, which tends towards lechery; don't let them gad about everywhere to dances or shows or banquets, but keep them safe at home, for if they gad about they will desire, or be desired. Jerome, in his letter *To a Mother and Daughter*: "You will be in the company of married men and women, you will see other people's kisses. In the midst of this, one of the guests or others present, since he won't look at other men's wives, will keep looking at you who have no chaperone, communicate to you with nods and convey with glances what he fears to say in words. Amidst such great enticements to pleasure, lust overcomes even iron wills and in virgins creates all the more hunger, since one considers sweeter what one doesn't know."

(7) The responsibility of governesses for safeguarding their charges (VI, 72–92):

Therefore Jerome writes in his letter *To Laeta on the Education of a Daughter*, "Give her," he says, "a companion in holiness whose conversation and bearing and dress may be an education in virtue. Never let her go out in public without you. Let her take delight not in a companion carefully groomed and shapely, who pours out sweet songs in liquid notes, but in someone stern, pale, and gloomy looking." He also writes the same thing in his letter *To the Maiden Demetrias*, speaking as follows: "You should choose as your companions serious women, particularly virgins and widows, whose ways are sober, whose talk is reserved and whose modesty is unstained, because the character and aims of mistresses are usually judged by the characters of their maids and companions."

sedens inclusa facile in peccatum carnis labitur, maxime quia vicium hoc ex vacacione et ocio facile nascitur."[28] . . . De operacione quoque dicit [i.e. Jerome] idem *Ad Demetriadem virginem*: "In desideriis, ut legimus, est omnis ociosus.[29] Nec ideo tibi ab opere cessandum est, quia Deo propicio nulla re indiges, sed ideo cum omnibus laborandum est, ut per occasionem operis nichil aliud cogites nisi quod ad Domini pertinet servitutem."[30] (Steiner, pp. 176–7)

(5) Virginia's abstention from wine (VI, 58–60):

Itaque de voluptate cibi et potus dicit idem Jeronimus, ubi supra: "Esus carnium et potus vini atque saturitas ventris seminarium est libidinis."[31] Idem quoque scribit in epistola *Ad matrem et filiam* inter epulas difficile servari pudiciciam.[32] Hinc et Ovidius in libro *De remediis* ii: "Vina parant animos Veneri."[33] Idem quoque dicit Salomon in *[Liber] Proverbiorum* xx: "luxuriosa res est vinum." Econtra vero dicit Therencius in *Eunucho*: "Sine Cerere et Bacho friget Venus."[34] (Steiner, pp. 179–80)

(6) Virginia's avoidance of unseemly social gatherings (VI, 61–71):

Serva, inquam, corpus illarum in etate puellari que prona est lascivie, scilicet ut non passim ad choreas vel spectacula vel convivia evagentur, sed in domo custodiantur, ne vagantes concupiscant vel concupiscantur . . . Jeronimus . . . in epistola *Ad matrem et filiam* . . .: "Inter viros et matronas erit tibi convivium, aliena oscula spectabis . . . Inter hec aliquis convivancium vel assistencium, quoniam alienas uxores non videbit, te que custodem non habes sepius respectabit, loquetur nutibus et quicquid metuit dicere, significabit aspectibus. Inter has et tantas illecebras voluptatum eciam ferreas mentes libido domat, que majorem in virginibus patitur famem, dum dulcius putat esse quod nescit. . . ."[35] (Steiner, pp. 172–3, 188–9)

(7) The responsibility of governesses for safeguarding their charges (VI, 72–92):

Ideo scribit Jeronimus [*Ad Laetam*][36] de institucione filie. "Trade," inquit, "ei comitem sanctitatis . . . cuius [et][37] sermo et incessus et habitus doctrina virtutum sit . . . Nunquam absque te in publicum procedat . . . Placeat ei comes nequaquam compta atque formosa, que liquido gutture carmen dulce moduletur, sed gravis, pallens . . . subtristis."[38] Idem quoque describit *Ad Demetriadem virginem*, hoc modo dicens: "Graves femine, maximeque virgines ac vidue tibi comites eligantur

28 *Incerti auctoris opus imperfectum in Matthaeum* 40.28 (*PG* 56:850).
29 Proverbs 13:4 (LXX).
30 *Epistolae* 130 (15) (*PL* 22:1119).
31 *Adversus Jovinianum* 2.7 (*PL* 23:310).
32 *Epistolae* 117 (6) (*PL* 22:957).
33 Ovid, *Remedia amoris*, line 805.
34 Terence, *Eunuchus* IV.v. 6.
35 *Epistolae* 117 (6–7) (*PL* 22:957).
36 **Ad Laetam** *MS* alethe
37 **et** *MS* est
38 *Epistolae* 107 (13, 9) (*PL* 22:877, 875).

(8) The responsibility of fathers and mothers for the rearing and discipline of their children (VI, 93–100):

Therefore as far as is in him a father must be on guard against all these things for the daughter of his flesh – and so Ecclesiasticus goes on to say, "keep a sure watch over a shameless daughter," that is, one who tends toward dissoluteness since youth is hot, "lest at any time she make you become a laughingstock to your enemies, and a byword in the city, and a reproach among the people, and she make you ashamed before all the multitude." Therefore Scripture rightly exhorts parents scrupulously to guard their virgin daughters and bring them up with discipline, lest they relax the reins to their lust and pleasure or at any time provide an occasion for disgrace either to themselves or their parents.

(9) This mayde upon a day wente in the toun
Toward a temple, with hire mooder deere,
As is of yonge maydens the manere. (VI, 118–20)

Because of all this, Jerome says in his letter *To Laeta on the Education of a Daughter*: "Never let her go out in public without you, or visit the basilicas of the martyrs or churches without her mother, or let any curly-haired youth smile at her."

quarum conversacio sit probata, sermo moderatus, verecundia sancta. . . . Mores siquidem et studia dominarum plerumque judicantur ex moribus ancillarum et comitum."[39] (Steiner, pp. 187–8)

(8) The responsibility of fathers and mothers for the rearing and discipline of their children (VI, 93–100):

Hec igitur omnia debet pater carnalis filie sue, quantum in ipso est precavere. Unde adhuc ibidem subjungitur: "Super filiam luxuriosam," id est ad luxuriam propter etatis fervorem pronam, "confirma custodiam, ne quando faciat te in opprobrium venire a detractione in civitate et objeccione plebis et confundat te in multitudine populi."[40] . . . Ideoque recte Scriptura parentes solicite filiam virginem custodire monet ac cum disciplina nutrire, ne lascivie vel voluptati frena relaxet vel aliqua occasione sibi atque parentibus causam infamie prestet. (Steiner, p. 174)

(9) This mayde upon a day wente in the toun
Toward a temple, with hire mooder deere,
As is of yonge maydens the manere. (VI, 118–20)

Propter hec omnia dicit Jeronimus [*Ad Laetam*][41] de institucione filie: . . . "Nunquam absque te in publicam procedat, basilicas quoque martyrum et ecclesias sine matre non adeat, nec ullus ei juvenis [cincinnatus][42] arrideat."[43] (Steiner, p. 176)

[39] *Epistolae* 130 (18) (*PL* 22:1121–2).
[40] Ecclesiasticus 42:11.
[41] **Ad Laetam** *MS* ad adletham
[42] **cincinnatus** *MS* circumnatus
[43] *Epistolae* 107 (9) (*PL* 22:875).

IV

John of Wales, *Communiloquium*

(trans. Joann Silverberg and Kenneth Bleeth)

2.2.1 *That fathers should raise their sons and daughters subject to well-ordered instruction.*
And first fathers and mothers should be exhorted to educate their sons in a disciplined fashion. *Ethics* 8: "A father is responsible for his son's existence, nurture, and training." Ecclesiasticus 7:25: "Do you have sons? instruct them." Therefore a father's strictness in rebuking his sons is to be praised, as long as it is not excessive. Conversely, parents' negligence in rebuking and censuring their sons is much to be criticized, and the sins of the sons are in some way to be imputed to them, and God's punishment sometimes visited on them for their negligence. Such was the case with Eli: because he was remiss in rebuking his insolent sons, he was justly punished by God (I Kings 3:13); whence Gregory in his *Dialogues* (4.17) tells of a fifteen-year-old boy who had become accustomed to blaspheming God, and who was therefore struck dead by God in the bosom of his father. And rightly so, as much to punish the father for not censuring him as to punish the son, and so that he would not grow in greater evils as he grew in age. As if [a son] were to say to his father: "Because you did not chastise me but allowed me to devote myself to sin, I am right to take my revenge on you." Whence also parents should not set a bad example for their children.

3.1.2 *On the instruction of women with regard to sobriety.*
Women should be silent, not talkative, nor should they be idle nor be gadabouts nor inquisitive. Moreover, women should especially be admonished to be sober and moderate in consuming intoxicating drinks. They should most diligently practice sobriety, which is the preserver of chastity. "Without food and wine, love grows cold," says the comic poet, and Jerome repeats this in Epistle 54. And in aiming at such sobriety, that is, at being perfect, sober, and chaste, women ought to be shaped from their infancy and youth by the example of the nurse of St. Augustine's mother. *[John here repeats Augustine's account, in* Confessions *9.8, of how his mother Monica gave up drinking after she was rebuked by a serving-girl.]*

3.1.3 *How women ought to conduct themselves in regard to chastity.*
Valerius Maximus provides many examples of chaste women who were careful and diligent in protecting their modesty and chastity, who preferred to give up their lives rather than their chastity and modesty. Likewise he tells of a certain man who killed his own daughter because Apius Claudius, relying on the power of his high position, sought to debauch her; he preferred to be the murderer of a chaste daughter than the father of a defiled one.

IV

John of Wales, *Communiloquium*

(from *Communiloquium* [Venice: Georgius Arravabenis, 1496])

2.2.1 *Quod patres nutriant filios [et filias]*[44] *suos sub ordinata disciplina.*
Et primo sunt admonendi patres [et matres][45] ad erudiendum filios disciplinabiliter . . . *Etica* viii: "pater filio est causa essendi, causa nutrimenti, et causa discipline."[46] Ecclesiasticus vii [25]: "Filii tibi sunt? erudi illos." [fol. 71v] . . . Severitas ergo paterna commendanda est in correptione filiorum dummodo non habeat excessum . . . Econverso negligentia parentum in castigando filios et corripiendo multum vituperanda et illorum peccata eis imputanda aliquo modo et pena eis aliquando a Deo inflicta pro eorum negligentia. Sicut fuit de Heli quia negligens fuit in corripiendo filios insolentes a Deo merito est punitus (i. Regum. iii [13]); unde narrat Gregorius, *Dialogorum* (iv.[xviii]) de puero quinquenni qui consueverat Deum blasfemare quod fuit percussus a Deo in sinu patris et mortuus.[47] Et hoc juste, tam in penam patris quia non corripuit eum quam in penam pueri, et ne cresceret in malis majoribus crescente etate. . . . Quasi scilicet diceret patri: "Quia non castigasti me sed me permisisti vacare peccatis, merito de te vindictam capio." Unde et parentes ne relinquerent malum [exemplum][48] filiis. [fol. 73r]

3.1.2 *De instructione mulierum quo ad sobrietatem.*
Mulieres . . . sint tacite non loquentes . . . et non sint ociose vel vage vel curiose. . . . Specialiter autem sunt mulieres admonendi quod sint sobrie et moderate in alimentis inebriativis . . . Magna . . . diligentia debent mulieres studere sobrietati que conservativa est pudicitie. "Sine enim Cerere et Baco frigere Venus," ait comicus,[49] et recitat Hieronymus Epistola liv[50] . . . Et ad hanc sobrietatem, ut scilicet mulieres sint perfecte, sobrie, et caste, debent [fol. 89r]/ a juventute et infantia informari exemplo nutricis matris Beati Augustini. *[John here repeats Augustine's account, in* Confessions *9.8, of how his mother Monica gave up drinking after she was rebuked by a serving-girl.]* [fol. 89v]

3.1.3 *Quales debent esse mulieres quo ad castitatem.* [fol. 89v]
[Valerius Maximus] ponit multa exempla de pudicis mulieribus que sollicite fuerunt et diligentes in custodienda pudicitia et castitate, que maluerunt vitam amittere quam castitatem et pudicitiam . . . Similiter narrat de quodam qui filiam suam occidit eo quod Apius Claudius potestatis viribus fretus stuprum eius expeteret, malens esse pudice filie interemptor quam corrupte pater. [fol. 90r]

44 **et filias** Strasburg: Jordanus de Quedlinburg, 1489; *om.* Venice 1496.
45 **et matres** Strasburg 1489; *om.* Venice 1496.
46 Aristotle, *Ethics* 8.12.
47 *PL* 77:349.
48 **exemplum** Strasburg 1489; exemplam, Venice 1496.
49 Terence, *Eunuchus* IV.v.6.
50 *Epistolae* 54 (9) (*PL* 22:554).

3.1.4 *How women should conduct themselves with regard to stillness and silence.*
Women who are thus chaste should be admonished to be still and silent as well; lest they be an occasion for others to sin and lest they themselves lapse into sin, they should not be unrestrained, excitable, talkative or idle.

3.1.5 *That women should be modest in their adornments.*
Women should be cautioned that they should be clothed in ornaments fitting even for nuns. I Peter 3:3: "Let your adorning not be the outward plaiting of the hair, or the wearing of gold, or the putting on of apparel." Whence Jerome in Epistle 38 has much to say concerning those who adorn themselves immodestly: "Women who paint their faces with rouge and tint their eyes are a temptation to the eyes of Christians."

3.2.2 *Concerning the molding of children*
And just as they should be molded in infancy, so in the next stage that is called childhood, especially from sins that need to be guarded against. For at that age arise lusts and desires. Whence Ecclesiasticus 7:26: "do you have daughters? have a care of their body, and show not your countenance gay towards them," thus permitting them to be wanton. And Jerome treats this subject fully in his letter concerning the rearing of a daughter, where he says: "Let her learn to hear and speak nothing but what pertains to the fear of the Lord. She should not understand foul words nor know any worldly songs. Her still tender tongue should be steeped in the sweetness of the psalms, and she should stay far away from the wantonness of boys. Her maids and attendants should avoid worldly associations." He continues: "If you take prudent care to prevent your daughter from being bitten by a viper, why do you not show the same concern to keep her from being struck by the hammer of anger, from walking out with Dinah, from playing about or inspiring songs?" After she is sufficiently grown up, she should go to the temple with her parents and not be found among crowds.

3.6.3 *About the molding of virgins, the loss of virginity, and the punishment of those who violate it.*
The Apostle describes what a virgin should be like in I Corinthians 7:34, where he says "the unmarried woman and the virgin thinks on the things of the Lord, that she may be holy both in body and in spirit." A virgin should therefore be unstained in holiness both within and without. Likewise a virgin should be sober in frugality and abstinence, as Jerome says in the letter referred to above: "If experience gives my advice weight, I would begin by urging that, as the bride of Christ, she avoid wine as she would poison. For wine is the first weapon that devils use against the young." He continues: "Wine and youth are the twin fuels of pleasure's fire. Why do we add oil to the flame? Why do we add fresh fuel to a body that is already on fire? Your diet should be spare and your belly never full. Fast daily, and when you do eat, avoid satiety." A virgin should also be docile and obedient in humility, following the example of the Blessed Virgin, the Mother of God, in whom virginity has been proclaimed sacred. A virgin should also practice virtuous silence and be shy out of modesty. Jerome states in his letter *To Demetrias*: "A virgin's speech should be prudent, modest, and infrequent, valued not so much for eloquence as for decency. Everyone admires you for your modesty when you are silent, and for your prudence when you speak." And on the same matter: "No disparagement should issue from a virgin's mouth"; and later, "frivolous talk should be avoided." A virgin should be quiet and seek the society of honest companions; she should not wander about at

3.1.4 *Quales debent esse mulieres quo ad quietem et taciturnitatem.*
Mulieres sic caste sunt admonende ut sint quiete et tacite . . . ne sint aliis occasio ad peccandum et ne ipse labantur in peccatum, non debent esse vage, inquiete, garule nec ociose. [fol. 91r]

3.1.5 *Quod mulieres sint in ornamentis temperate.*
Sunt etiam admonende ut sint ornamentis competentibus et religiosis indute. I Petri iii [3]: "Quarum non sit extrinsecus capillatura aut circumdatio auri aut vestimentorum cultus" . . . Unde de impudice se ornantibus multum loquitur Hieronymus, Epistola xxxviii: "Ille oculos Christianos scandalizant . . . que purpurisso et quibusdam fucis ora oculosque depingunt."[51] [fol. 91v]

3.2.2 *De informatione puerorum.*
Et sicut sunt informandi in infantia, sic in sequenti gradu etatis que dicitur pueritia, maxime a peccatis cavendis. In ipsa enim etate insurgunt libidines et concupiscentie [fol. 93r] . . . Unde Ecclesiasticus vii [26]: "Filie tibi sunt? Serva corpus illarum, et ne ostendas hilarem faciem tuam ad eas," scilicet permittendo illas lascivire. Et de hoc sufficienter Hieronymus epistola . . . de institutione filie, ubi ait, "Nihil aliud discat audire vel loqui nisi quod pertinet ad timorem Domini. Turpia non intelligat, cantica mundana ignoret, adhuc tenera lingua psalmis dulcibus imbuatur; procul sit lascivia puerorum. Puelle et pedisece a secularibus consortiis arceantur."[52] Sequitur: "Si sollicita et prudens es ne filia percutiatur a vipera, cur non eadem cura provides ne feriatur a maleo ire, ne egrediatur cum [Dyna],[53] nec ludat nec trahat cantus?"[54] Postquam grandiuscula est pergat ad templum cum parentibus nec inter turbas inveniatur. [fol. 93v]

3.6.3 *De informatione virginum et defectu virginitatis et de pena violantium eam.* [fol. 104v]
Qualis autem debet esse virgo Apostolus describit, I Corinthios vii [34], ubi ait: "Mulier innupta et virgo cogitat que Domini sunt, ut sit sancta et corpore et spiritu." Debet igitur esse virgo sanctitate interiori et exteriori immaculata. . . . Item virgo debet esse frugalitate et abstinentia sobria, unde Hieronymus dicta epistola: "Si experto creditur, hoc primum moneo: ut sponsa Christi vinum fugiat pro veneno. Hec adversus adolescentiam prima arma sunt [fol.105r]/ demonum." Sequitur: "Vinum et adolescentia duplex incendium voluptatis. Quid oleum flamme adicimus? Quid ardenti corpusculo fomenta ignium ministramus? . . . Moderatus cibus et nunquam venter expletus. Sint tibi quottidiana jejunia et refectio saturitatem fugiens."[55] Item debet esse virgo humilitate subjecta et timida; exemplo Beate Virginis matris Dei, in qua dedicatur sacra virginitas . . . Item debet esse tacita silentio virtuoso et pudore verecunda. Ait Hieronymus *Ad Demetriadem* epistola . . .: "Sit sermo virginis prudens, modestus et rarus, nec tam eloquentia preciosus quam

[51] *Epistolae* 38 (3) (*PL* 22:464).
[52] *Epistolae* 107 (4) (*PL* 22:871).
[53] **dyna** Strasburg 1489 (see Genesis 34:1); Diana, Venice 1496.
[54] *Epistolae* 107 (7) (*PL* 22:873).
[55] *Epistolae* 22 (8, 17) (*PL* 22:399, 404).

random in the squares and streets. Whence Jerome in the aforementioned letter: "Go out in public only infrequently. You will never lack a reason for going out if you always go out when there is need."

pudore. Mirantur omnes te tacente tuam verecundiam, te loquente prudentiam." Et ibidem: "Nunquam detractio ex virginis ore procedat." Et post: "Sermo ociosus vitandus est."[56] . . . Item debet esse quieta et honesta societate comitata, non vaga discurrens per plateas et vicos . . . Unde Hieronymus dicta epistola: "Rarus sit egressus in publicum. Nunquam causa deerit procedendi, si semper, cum necesse fuerit, fueris processura."[57] [fol. 105v]

[56] Pelagius, *Ad Demetriadem* 19 (*S. Hieronymi opera supposititia*; *PL* 30:33, 34).
[57] *Epistolae* 22 (17) (*PL* 22:404).

The Shipman's Tale

JOHN SCATTERGOOD

The Shipman's Tale is a fabliau, a short comic story of financial and sexual deception firmly located in a bourgeois setting. Neither the prosperous merchant of St Denis, nor his attractive spendthrift wife are given names, and since the unscrupulous and lecherous monk is called Daun John, which was practically a generic name for a cleric, it has seemed to many scholars that Chaucer was trying to write something archetypal in the fabliau genre.[1] Yet, paradoxically, the physical world of the tale – the layout of the merchant's house and garden at St Denis, the details of his business trips to Bruges and Paris, the ways in which loans are raised and repaid at a mercantile and personal level – is precisely articulated and suggests that Chaucer took a lot of trouble to be exact and accurate, to give a contemporaneous authenticity to his story.[2] There is a paradox too in relation to the place of the tale in the Canterbury sequence: after *The Man of Law's Tale*, ostensibly to prevent the Parson from preaching Lollardy to the pilgrims, the Shipman offers to tell a tale (II, 1178–90), but most editors choose to place the tale as the first of Fragment VII. And again, there is some doubt as to whether the tale was originally intended for the Shipman: the ostensible identification of the teller with a woman, because of the pronouns "we," "us," and

I am much indebted to my colleague Corinna Salvadori Lonergan for her generous and discerning help, both with the intricacies of scholarship on Boccaccio and Sercambi, and with the equal difficulties of seeking to render Boccaccio's nuanced language into English. I am also immensely grateful to Peter Nicholson for his constructive comments on a number of points in relation to this chapter.

1 D. S. Brewer in his chapter on the fabliaux in *Companion to Chaucer Studies*, ed. Beryl Rowland (Toronto, New York, London: Oxford University Press, 1968), p. 259, says it is "closer to the pure fabliau type" than Chaucer's other comic stories. For other interesting explorations of the question of the tale's generic relations see Peter Nicholson, "The 'Shipman's Tale' and the Fabliaux," *English Literary History* 45 (1978): 583–96, and Joerg Fichte, "Chaucer's *Shipman's Tale* within the Context of the French Fabliaux Tradition," in *Chaucer's Frame Tales: The Physical and the Metaphysical*, ed. Joerg O. Fichte (Tübingen: Narr, 1987; Cambridge: D. S. Brewer, 1987), pp. 51–66.

2 See my article "The Originality of *The Shipman's Tale*," *Chaucer Review* 11 (1976–7): 210–31 (rpt. in *Reading the Past: Essays on Medieval and Renaissance Literature* [Dublin: Four Courts Press, 1996], pp. 146–64). On the intricacies of mercantile borrowing in the tale see Kenneth S. Cahn, "Chaucer's Merchants and the Foreign Exchange: An Introduction to Medieval Finance," *Studies in the Age of Chaucer* 2 (1980): 81–119.

"oure" in lines VII, 10–19 which are spoken by a woman, has inevitably led to speculation that the tale might have been intended at one stage for the Wife of Bath.[3] Chaucer had evidently done a lot of work on this tale but had not quite finished with it. The seemingly typical tale raises a great many problems, and the question of its sources is not the least of them.

In 1941, basing his conclusions on extensive folkloric research done in 1930 into the type-story known as "the lover's gift regained," John Webster Spargo concluded, in perhaps an overly reductive way, that the closest analogues to *The Shipman's Tale* were Boccaccio's *Decameron* 8.1, and Sercambi's *Novella* XXXII, but that neither was Chaucer's source: "In the absence of an authentic source, the likeliest thing that can be said is that, if we had one, it would probably be an Old French fabliau very similar to *The Shipman's Tale*, of which the atmosphere is all French."[4] This is a view that is regularly restated, most recently, with great clarity, by John Hines. He points to the French setting, the swearing by French saints, St Martin, St Denis, and possibly St Ivo of Chartres (148, 152, 227), and the use of the French phrase "Quy la?" [Who is there?] at 214. He might also have added the reference to the traitorous "Genylon of Fraunce" at 194. He does add the interesting observation that the setting of the tale in north-eastern France locates it in "the true home of the fabliau."[5] But though *The Shipman's Tale* is set in France and Flanders it does not follow that its source has to have had a similar location: the French fabliau *Le Meunier et les II Clercs* is convincingly transposed by Chaucer in *The Reeve's Tale* to Cambridge and its environs. And it would surely not have been beyond his capacities to give this tale a setting appropriate to a ship's captain who sailed frequently to France (I, 397, 408–9) or to the Wife of Bath, a clothmaker whose skill surpassed that of her counterparts in Ypres and Ghent, two of the principal Flemish cloth towns (I, 448). The argument for a French source cannot be based on the setting of *The Shipman's Tale*: when Chaucer used a source he sometimes altered the location of the story, and there are reasons for thinking he may have done so here.

Spargo is emphatically dismissive of the possibility that any of the *novelle* of Boccaccio or Sercambi could be Chaucer's source. He persuades himself that Chaucer did not use these stories because their plots are more complicated than that of *The Shipman's Tale* and because Chaucer, in his view, had a "tendency in general" to keep to plots as he found them.[6] This is, at best, debatable and other scholars, not surprisingly, have taken a different view. Robert Pratt in 1940 held that the claims of Sercambi's *Novella* XXXII as Chaucer's possible

[3] On this question see Philip Appleman, "The 'Shipman's Tale,' and the Wife of Bath," *Notes and Queries* 201 (1956): 372–3; Robert L. Chapman, "The Shipman's Tale was Meant for the Shipman," *Modern Language Notes* 71 (1956): 4–5; Robert A. Pratt, "The Development of the Wife of Bath" in *Studies in Medieval Literature in Honor of Professor Albert Croll Baugh*, ed. MacEdward Leach (Philadelphia: University of Pennysylvania Press, 1961), pp. 45–79; Murray Copeland, "*The Shipman's Tale*: Chaucer and Boccaccio," *Medium Aevum* 35 (1966): 11–28 especially pp. 25–6.

[4] See J. W. Spargo, *Chaucer's Shipman's Tale: The Lover's Gift Regained*, Folklore Fellows Communications 91 (Helsinki, 1930), summarized in Bryan and Dempster, pp. 439–46. The quotation is from p. 439.

[5] See John Hines, *The Fabliau in English* (London and New York: Longman, 1993), p. 72.

[6] For this argument see *Chaucer's Shipman's Tale: The Lover's Gift Regained*, pp. 11–13.

source were "too hastily discarded," and compared, in tabular fashion, various similarities between that novella, *Decameron* 8.1, and *The Shipman's Tale*.[7] In 1971 Richard Guerin reviewed the material and came to much the same conclusions, but added the interesting possibility that Chaucer may have used *Decameron* 8.2, another "lover's gift regained" story, as well. When the parish priest of Varlungo approaches Monna Belcolore at her house, knowing that her husband is away, she says: "O sere, voi siate il ben venuto: che andate voi zaconato per questo caldo?" [Oh sir, you are welcome. But what are you doing gadding about in this heat?].[8] Guerin points to similar lines in *The Shipman's Tale* as Daun John counsels the merchant before his trip to Bruges:

> I prey yow, cosyn, wisely that ye ryde.
> Governeth yow also of youre diete
> Atemprely, and namely in this hete. (VII, 260–2)

This detail, and the fact that the lover in *Decameron* 8.2 is a cleric and not a soldier as in the other two analogues persuade him that "while definite proof is lacking it seems not unreasonable to assume that Chaucer may have known all three analogues."[9] But there is another piece of evidence he might have adduced. In *Decameron* 8.2 Monna Belcolore, in return for her favours, asks for the money as a loan (*prestate*), not as a gift, and says she needs it for clothes in order to keep up social appearances:

> ". . . e se voi mi prestate cinque lire, che so che l'avete, io ricoglierò dall'usuraio la gonnella mia del perso e lo scaggiale dai dì delle feste che io recai a marito, ché vedete che non ci posso andare a santo né in niun buon luogo, perché io non l'ho; e io sempre mai poscia farò ciò che voi vorrete."
>
> [". . . and if you would lend me five lire, which I know you have, I shall redeem my dark purple gown and the fancy belt I wear on feast days which I had in my dowry, for you see I cannot go to church or to any fine place because I do not have them, and afterwards I shall always do what you want."]

This is strikingly similar to the bargain negotiated in *The Shipman's Tale*. The merchant's wife tells Daun John that she owes money for clothes she has bought, to maintain her husband's honour, and asks for him to "lene" her this sum, though "lene" can mean "give" as well as "lend,"[10] one of the many puns in this tale:

> But by that ilke Lord that for us bledde,
> For his honour, myself for to arraye,
> A Sonday next I moste nedes paye
> An hundred frankes, or ellis I am lorn.
> Yet were me levere that I were unborn
> Than me were doon a sclaundre or vileynye;

7 See Robert A. Pratt, "Chaucer's Shipman's Tale and Sercambi," *Modern Language Notes* 55 (1940): 142–5.

8 See *Tutte Le Opere di Giovanni Boccaccio*, ed. Vittore Branca, 10 vols (Verona: Arnaldo Mondadori, 1964–2000), IV.674–80 for this story. It is possible here that *zaconato* might mean "out of breath."

9 See Richard Guerin, "*The Shipman's Tale*: The Italian Analogues," *English Studies* 52 (1971): 412–19.

10 See *A Chaucer Glossary*, compiled by Norman Davis, Douglas Gray, Patricia Ingram and Anne Wallace-Hadrill (Oxford: Clarendon Press, 1979), s.v. le(e)n(e), *v*. The editors think the word means "lend" as it is used here, but the ambiguity is interesting.

And if myn housbonde eek it myghte espye,
I nere but lost; and therfore I yow preye,
Lene me this somme, or ellis moot I deye. (VII, 178–86)

For this she will be at his service "right as yow list devise" (192). Because there are features of *Decameron* 8.2 and *The Shipman's Tale* which cannot be paralleled elsewhere, this story of Boccaccio's has to be regarded as a possible source for Chaucer, though it contains much that was not used and, indeed, much that is incompatible.

Peter Nicholson, in fact, in a detailed study of "the lover's gift regained" type of story, sees distinct differences between *Decameron* 8.1 and 8.2. The second story has a "more traditional form" where the "gift" is an object, here a "cloak," but 8.1 is original in that the nexus of exchange is money: "The new type of bargain . . . depends on the substitution of money, the prerogative of the bourgeoisie, for the miscellaneous object of barter, for the woman must not be able to recognize the gift as the property of her husband though she must be compelled by the formal conventions of contracts to give it up in the end. The introduction of the loan is clearly the most significant innovation." As his argument proceeds a disjunction appears in the history of this type of story which effectively separates the urban and the pastoral worlds and the literary from the folkloric: "The use of money itself might have come from another tale but it is in fact only with the *Decameron* that commerce and sex become so closely allied. No earlier literary tale suggests the sort of bargaining that occurs here, nor does the Aarne-Thompson type index provide any popular story with this motif that might have served as a model." And it might be recalled at this point that the narrator of *Decameron* 8.2 calls it a story of peasant lechery (*uno amorazzo contadino*), and that the tale is full of rural details. Nicholson continues arguing that the essential originality of *Decameron* 8.1 could have derived from 8.2 "in which the priest's cloak is a deposit" instead of the money Monna Belcolore originally asks for, and that this story provides "the earliest suggestion for the use of money within the traditional tale."[11] Though Nicholson himself does not go so far as to say this, one reasonable implication of his findings is that Chaucer could have derived much of what he used as a source for *The Shipman's Tale* from *Decameron* 8.1 including the bourgeois mercantile setting, though, if he had access to this story it is not easy to argue that he could not have had access to *Decameron* 8.2 also.

All of which leaves the vexed question of Sercambi's *Novelle*. Story XXXII is set in the same bourgeois mercantile world as *Decameron* 8.1 and *The Shipman's Tale*, but in Perugia, the principal city of Umbria, instead of Milan or Paris and Bruges. In the same way, the husband is a merchant who sometimes lends money, and the lover is somebody who is prepared to raise a loan, albeit in an unscrupulous way. Spargo said that "Sercambi's Novella XXXII has precisely the relationship to *Decameron* 8.1 that one would expect if the conventional view is accepted that Sercambi's entire collection is an imitation of

[11] See Peter Nicholson, "The Medieval Tale of the Lover's Gift Regained," *Fabula: Journal of Folklore Studies* 21 (1980): 200–22.

Boccaccio's."[12] But, as the researches of Pratt and Guerin have shown, there are important details in *The Shipman's Tale* which do not appear in Boccaccio but which are to be found in Sercambi: the assignation and the payment of the money is negotiated for the following Sunday (307); on the day following the conversation between the wife and the lover the husband departs from the city (299), the wife and the lover spend the following night together (313–19); when the "loan" is returned the husband expresses surprise that the wife has not told him of the fact (388–99). But a relationship between Sercambi's *Novelle* and *The Shipman's Tale* is made problematic by the likely date of the Italian collection, which Giovanni Sinicropi dates as no earlier than 1400, too late, therefore for it to be a possible source for Chaucer's story.[13] However, two eighteenth-century documents – one a marginal note by Bernardino Baroni in a book on Lucchese authors and the other a letter by his nephew Luigi to Gaetano Poggiali dated 17 July 1793 – hint at the possibility of an earlier version of the *Novelle*. Luigi refers to a manuscript of Sercambi which was entitled "Novelliero di Ser Giovanni Sercambi, lucchese": it was written, he says, in 1374 and contained 100 stories. Bernardino likewise mentions a Sercambi manuscript, in the possession of the family, containing a hundred stories told by men and women fleeing the plague in Lucca on a journey through Tuscany. The only known surviving copy of the *Novelle* (now in the Biblioteca Trivulziana in Milan) contains 155 stories, and the journey described takes the travellers on a circuitous route throughout most of northern Italy, well outside the bounds of Tuscany. Yet Sinicropi and others have largely discredited the evidence of the Baroni family, and believe that there was no other version of the *Novelle*: what the Baroni were describing, not very accurately, was the Trivulziano MS. It is unlikely, with the evidence we have at present, that the matter can be settled one way or the other. After a detailed and judicious review of the question Peter Nicholson writes: "At the end of the eighteenth century the Baroni family of Lucca owned a manuscript of Sercambi's work which might have been different from the one we now have. Unless and until that manuscript or a copy of it is found, we can tell very little about what it contained."[14] It is worth pointing out also that, even if we do accept the possibility that there was a version of Sercambi's collection which contained a hundred stories, there is no certainty that it included *Novella* XXXII, since it would have been only two thirds as long as the surviving collection.

So, though the possibility that Sercambi's *Novella* XXXII was one of Chaucer's sources for *The Shipman's Tale* cannot be definitively dismissed, the evidence that it might be is unreliable. The case with *Decameron* 8.1 and 8.2, however, is very different. If Sercambi is excluded from consideration, these

[12] See Spargo in Bryan and Dempster, p. 439. I number the *novella* according to Sinicropi's edition (see next note).

[13] See Giovanni Sercambi, *Novelle*, ed. Giovanni Sinicropi, 2 vols, Scrittori d'Italia, nos. 250–1 (Bari: Laterza, 1972). His discussion of the "lost" version, in the course of which he prints the two documents from the Baroni family, is on pp. 801–10. For earlier arguments against the existence of the "Novelliere" see Luciano Rossi, "Per il testo del Novelliere di Giovanni Sercambi," *Cultura Neolatina* 28 (1968): 16–63, 89–104. Sinicropi has updated his account of the arguments in his second edition of Sercambi, *Novelle, Nuovo testo critico con studio introduttivo e note* (Florence: Le Lettere, 1995), pp. 32–47.

[14] See Peter Nicholson, "The Two Versions of Sercambi's *Novelle*," *Italica* 53 (1976): 201–13.

stories are the closest analogues to *The Shipman's Tale* and may even be its sources. If they are, it may be that Chaucer did not simply derive plot features from Boccaccio but something in terms of ambience. If Chaucer's decision to locate his story in a bourgeois mercantile world derives from *Decameron* 8.1, it suggests that those interested in sources and analogues have to broaden their fields of vision and take into account literary emphases which have not been traditionally part of their agenda.

I

Giovanni Boccaccio, *Decameron* 8.1

(trans. John Scattergood)

Now, there was once in Milan a German mercenary soldier, whose name was Gulfardo, a brave man and very loyal to those with whom he took service, an uncommon characteristic amongst Germans. And because he was most reliable in paying back any money that he borrowed, many merchants could be found who, at a low rate of interest, would lend him any amount of money. While he was living in Milan, this man fixed his affection on a beautiful woman called Madonna Ambruogia, wife of a very wealthy merchant whose name was Guasparruolo Cagastraccio, who was his good acquaintance and friend. He loved her most discreetly, without the husband or anyone else noticing, and one day he sent word to her asking her courteously if she might be pleased to grant him her love, and that for his part he was ready to be at her service in whatever she might command. The lady, after much inconsequential talk,[15] came to the conclusion that she was ready to be at his service in whatever Gulfardo wished on the following two conditions: the first was that he must never reveal the affair to anybody; the second was that, since for some business of her own she had need of two hundred gold florins, she wished that he would, because he was a rich man, give them to her, and immediately forever she would be at his service.

Listening to her avarice, Gulfardo became offended at the baseness of someone he believed to be an honourable lady, and his passionate love turned almost to hate. He decided he should trick her, and sent back word that he would very willingly do that and whatever other things, within his power, that she wanted which would please her. For this purpose she was to go ahead and send him word when she wished him to go to her, and he would bring the money with him, and nobody, moreover, would hear anything of it except a colleague of his, whom he trusted much, and who was always party to whatever he did. The lady, or rather the worthless woman,[16] was pleased at hearing this, and sent him word that her husband Guasparruolo had to go on business, in a few days time, as far as Genoa, and then she would let him know and send for him.

15 *Novelle* usually means "gossip," "tittle-tattle," "chit-chat." The implication is that Madonna Ambruogia is talking around the proposal so as to negotiate a position.

16 Boccaccio uses the social difference between *donna* and *femina* to reinforce the moral point.

I

Giovanni Boccaccio, *Il Decamerone* 8.1

(from *Tutte Le Opere di Giovanni Boccaccio*, ed. Vittore Branca, 10 vols [Verona: Arnaldo Mondadori, 1964–2000], IV.670–3, 5–18)

Fu adunque già in Melano un tedesco al soldo, il cui nome fu Gulfardo, pro' della persona e assai leale a coloro ne' cui servigi si mettea, il che rade volte suole de' tedeschi avvenire. E per ciò che egli era nelle prestanze de' denari che fatte gli erano lealissimo renditore, assai mercatanti avrebbe trovati che per piccolo utile ogni quantità di denari gli avrebber prestata. Pose costui, in Melan dimorando, l'amor suo in una donna assai bella chiamata madonna Ambruogia, moglie d'un ricco mercatante che aveva nome Guasparruol Cagastraccio, il quale era assai suo conoscente e amico: e amandola assai discretamente, senza avvedersene il marito né altri, le mandò un giorno a parlare, pregandola che le dovesse piacere d'essergli del suo amor cortese e che egli era dalla sua parte presto a dover far ciò che ella gli comandasse. La donna dopo molte novelle, venne a questa conclusione, che ella era presta di far ciò che Gulfardo volesse dove due cose ne dovesser seguire: l'una, che questo non dovesse mai per lui esser manifestato a alcuna persona; l' altra, che, con ciò fosse cosa che ella avesse per alcuna sua cosa bisogno di fiorini dugento d'oro, voleva che egli, che ricco uomo era, gliele donasse, e appresso sempre sarebbe al suo servigio.

Gulfardo, udendo la 'ngordigia di costei, isdegnato per la viltà di lei la quale egli credeva che fosse una valente donna, quasi in odio transmutò il fervente amore e pensò di doverla beffare: e mandolle dicendo che molto volontieri e quello e ogni altra cosa, che egli potesse, che le piacesse; e per ciò mandassegli pure a dire quando ella volesse che egli andasse a lei, ché egli gliele porterebbe, né che mai di questa cosa alcun sentirebbe, se non un suo compagno di cui egli si fidava molto e che sempre in sua compagnia andava in ciò che faceva. La donna, anzi cattiva femina, udendo questo fu contenta, e mandogli dicendo che Guasparruolo suo marito doveva ivi a pochi dì per sue bisogne andare insino a Genova, e allora ella gliele farebbe assapere e manderebbe per lui.

At a convenient moment, Gulfardo went to Guasparruolo and said: "I am doing some business of my own, for which I need two hundred gold florins, which I want you to lend me at the rate of interest which you charged me on other occasions." Guasparruolo said that he would gladly do so, and straightaway counted out the money.

A few days later Guasparruolo went to Genoa, as the lady had said, so the lady sent to Gulfardo that he should come to her and bring the two hundred gold florins. Gulfardo, taking his colleague with him, went to the lady's house. Finding her waiting for him, the first thing he did was to put into her hands those two hundred gold florins, in the sight of his companion, and said these very words to her: "Lady, take this money and give it to your husband when he returns."

The lady took it and did not perceive why Gulfardo had spoken as he did, but believed he did that so that his companion would not be aware that he was giving it to her as a payment,[17] so she said: "I shall willingly, but I want to see how much there is." Having spread it out on a table, and having found that there were two hundred florins, she put it away very pleased with herself. And she turned to Gulfardo and, having led him to her bedroom, she gratified him with her body, not only on that night but on many others before her husband returned from Genoa.

When Guasparruolo had returned from Genoa, straightaway Gulfardo, having ascertained[18] that his wife would be with him, went to him and said to him in her presence: "Guasparruolo, the money, those two hundred gold florins that you lent me the other day, they were of no use to me because I could not complete the business for which I took them, and so I brought them back here immediately to your wife and gave them to her, and so cancel my debt."[19]

Guasparruolo turned to his wife and asked her if she had received it. She, who could see the evidence, could not deny it but said: "Yes, I did receive it, but until now I did not remember to tell you of it."

Then Guasparruolo said: "Gulfardo, I am satisfied. Go with God for I shall properly adjust your account."

Gulfardo went away, leaving the scorned lady to hand over to her husband the dishonourable payment for her worthless conduct, and thus the shrewd lover, without payment, took his pleasure of his avaricious mistress.

[17] *prezzo* properly means "price," such as one might pay for an item purchased. It is pointedly preferred to a word such as *pagamento* or *ricompensa*.

[18] *appostato* has the sense of " having spied things out" or even "having lain in wait."

[19] *ragione* is used here and a few lines later in the technical sense of "financial terms," as in the Modern Italian *ragione di scambio*, "terms of trade."

Gulfardo, quando tempo gli parve, se n'andò a Guasparruolo e sì gli disse: "Io son per fare un mio fatto per lo quale mi bisognan fiorini dugento d' oro, li quali io voglio che tu mi presti con quello utile che tu mi suogli prestar degli altri." Guasparruolo disse che volentieri e di presente gli annoverò i denari.

Ivi a pochi giorni Guasparruolo andò a Genova, come la donna aveva detto; per la qual cosa la donna mandò a Gulfardo che a lei dovesse venire e recare li dugento fiorin d'oro. Gulfardo, preso il compagno suo, se n'andò a casa della donna; e trovatala che l'aspettava, la prima cosa che fece, le mise in mano questi dugento fiorin d'oro, veggente il suo compagno, e sì le disse: "Madonna, tenete questi denari e daretegli a vostro marito quando sarà tornato."

La donna gli prese e non s'avide perché Gulfardo dicesse così, ma si credette che egli il facesse acciò che il compagno suo non s'accorgesse che egli a lei per via di prezzo gli desse; per che ella disse: "Io il farò volentieri ma io voglio veder quanti sono"; e versatigli sopra una tavola e trovatigli esser dugento, seco forte contenta gli ripose. E tornò a Gulfardo e, lui nella sua camera menato, non solamente quella notte ma molte altre, avanti che il marito tornasse da Genova, della sua persona gli sodisfece.

Tornato Guasparuolo da Genova, di presente Gulfardo, avendo appostato che insieme con la moglie era, se n'andò a lui e in presenza di lei disse: "Guasparruolo, i denari, cioè li dugento fiorin d'oro che l'altrier mi prestasti, non m'ebber luogo, per ciò che io non potei fornir la bisogna per la quale gli presi: e per ciò io gli recai qui di presente alla donna tua e sì gliele diedi, e per ciò dannerai la mia ragione."

Guasparruolo, volto alla moglie, la domandò se avuti gli avea; ella, che quivi vedeva il testimonio, nol seppe negare ma disse: "Mai sì che io gli ebbi, né m'era ancor ricordata di dirloti."

Disse allora Guasparruolo: "Gulfardo, io son contento: andatevi pur con Dio, ché io acconcerò bene la vostra ragione."

Gulfardo partitosi, e la donna rimasa scornata diede al marito il disonesto prezzo della sua cattività: e così il sagace amante senza costo godé della sua avara donna.

II

Giovanni Boccaccio, *Decameron* 8.2

(trans. John Scattergood)

I tell you then, once in Varlungo,[20] a village very close to here [i.e. Florence], as each of you ladies knows or may have heard, there was a priest, capable and vigorous in the service of women, who, though he did not know how to read very well, yet with many good and holy aphorisms entertained his parishioners on Sundays at the foot of the elm-tree.[21] And, when the men had gone elsewhere, he was better than any priest who had been there before at visiting their wives, bringing for them, into their houses, feast-day stuff, and holy water, and sometimes some small candle-ends, and giving them his blessing.

Now it happened that, among the womenfolk of the parish who had pleased him most, he fancied one above all the others: she was called Monna Belcolore, the wife of a labourer who called himself Bentivegna del Mazzo. The truth is that she really was a pretty and fresh country lass, brown-skinned, and very sturdy, and was better at grinding[22] than anybody else. And beyond that, she knew how to play the tambourine,[23] and sing "The water runs in the mill-race,"[24] and lead the round dance and the skipping dance, when the occasion presented itself, better than any of her neighbours, with a fine and dainty handkerchief in her hand. Because of these things, my lord the priest lusted after her so deeply that he was led to distraction, and all day sauntered about so as to be able to catch sight of her. And when on Sunday morning he was aware of her in church, he would intone the *kyrie* or the *sanctus*, exerting himself greatly to show himself to be a great singer, though he seemed to bray like an ass, but when he did not see her there he would pass over them discreetly. Yet he managed to behave so that Bentivegna del Mazzo did not notice it, nor any neighbouring woman that he had. And in order the better to be intimate with Monna Belcolore the priest gave her gifts from time to time: sometimes he brought her a small bunch of fresh garlic, of which he had the best in the neighbourhood in his kitchen garden, which he tended with his own hands, and sometimes a little basket of broad beans, and at times a bunch of spring onions or shallots. And when he saw the opportunity he would gaze at her in a surly manner, to rebuke her in an affectionate way, and she would respond in a huff, making a pretence of not noticing. She kept her distance in a really reserved manner, because of which my lord the priest could make no headway.

Now, one day about noon when the priest was wandering here and there about the district, it happened that he encountered Bentivegna del Mazzo, with a donkey laden with things in front of him, and greeted him and asked him where he was going.

[20] This is Valdarno, then a few miles from Florence, but now incorporated into the suburbs of the city.

[21] In country villages, elm trees were often situated close to the church, and groups often gathered in their shade. Compare *Decameron,* 8.6. 41.

[22] The word *macinare* is used here and throughout the story in a double sense: to grind herbs or spices in a mortar, and to copulate.

[23] A *cembalo* here is probably a tambourine with bells. See the last sentence of the story.

[24] A song, evidently popular at the time and sexually suggestive.

II

Giovanni Boccaccio, *Il Decamerone* 8.2

(from *Tutte Le Opere di Giovanni Boccaccio*, ed. Vittore Branca, 10 vols [Verona: Arnaldo Mondadori, 1976], IV.674,6 – 680,47)

Dico adunque che a Varlungo, villa assai vicina di qui, come ciascuna di voi o sa o puote avere udito, fu un valente prete e gagliardo della persona ne' servigi delle donne, il quale, come che legger non sapesse troppo, pur con molte buone e sante parolozze la domenica a piè dell'olmo ricreava i suoi popolani; e meglio le lor donne, quando essi in alcuna parte andavano, che altro prete che prima vi fosse stato, visitava, portando loro della festa e dell'acqua benedetta e alcun moccolo di candela talvolta infino a casa, dando loro la sua benedizione.

Ora avvenne che, tra l'altre sue popolane che prima gli eran piaciute, una sopra tutte ne gli piacque, che aveva nome monna Belcolore, moglie d'un lavoratore che si facea chiamare Bentivegna del Mazzo; la qual nel vero era pure una piacevole e fresca foresozza, brunazza e ben tarchiata e atta a meglio saper macinar che alcuna altra; e oltre a ciò era quella che meglio sapeva sonare il cembalo e cantare *L' acqua corre la borrana* e menar la ridda e il ballonchio, quando bisogno faceva, che vicina che ella avesse, con bel moccichino e gente in mano. Per le quali cose messer lo prete ne 'nvaghì sì forte, che egli ne menava smanie e tutto il dì andava aiato per poterla vedere; e quando la domenica mattina la sentiva in chiesa, diceva un *Kyrie* e un *Sanctus* sforzandosi ben di mostrarsi un gran maestro di canto, che pareva uno asino che ragghiasse, dove, quando non la vi vedea, si passava assai leggiermente; ma pur sapeva sì fare, che Bentivegna del Mazzo non se ne avvedeva, né ancora vicina che egli avesse. E per poter più avere la dimestichezza di monna Belcolore, a otta a otta la presentava: e quando le mandava un mazzuol d'agli freschi, ch' egli aveva i piú belli della contrada in un suo orto che egli lavorava a sue mani, e quando un canestruccio di baccelli e talora un mazzuolo di cipolle malige o di scalogni; e, quando si vedeva tempo, guatatala un poco in cagnesco, per amorevolezza la rimorchiava, e ella cotal salvatichetta, faccendo vista di non avvedersene, andava pure oltre in contegno; per che messer lo prete non ne poteva venire a capo.

Ora avvenne un dì che, andando il prete di fitto meriggio per la contrada or qua or là zazeato, scontrò Bentivegna del Mazzo con uno asino pien di cose innanzi, e fattogli motto il domandò dove egli andava.

To which Bentivegna replied: “Truly, sir, in good faith, I am going as far as the city for something I need to do. And I am carrying these things to master Bonaccorri da Ginestreto (35) to get him to help me, because the judge of penal causes has cited me before the court by means of his attorney to answer a peremptory summons.”[25]

The delighted priest said: “Well done, my son! Now go with my blessing and return soon. And if you happen to see Lapuccio or Naldino, do not let it slip your mind to tell them to send me those thongs for my flails.” (40)

Bentivegna said that it would be done; and the priest thought that, while he was making his way to Florence, now would be the time to go to Belcolore and try his luck, and he made his way on foot without stopping until he was at her house. When he entered he said: “May God bring you good! Is anybody at home?”

Belcolore, who had gone to the attic, heard him and said: “O sir, you are (45) welcome. What are you doing gadding about in this heat?”

The priest replied: “As I hope for God’s blessing, I have come to keep you company for a short time, because I met your man going to the city.”

Belcolore came down, took a seat, and began to pick over the sprouts’ seed that her husband had threshed a little earlier. The priest began by saying: (50) “Well, Belcolore, are you always going to make me die in this way?”

Belcolore began to laugh and said: “Oh, am I doing something to you?”

The priest said: “You do nothing to me, but you do not allow me to do to you what I wish and which God commands.”

Belcolore said: “Alas! Go away with you, without delay. But do priests do these sorts of things?” (55)

The priest replied: “Indeed, and we do this better than other men. And why not? And I shall tell you further, we do a much better job of work. And do you know why? Because we grind only when we have plenty.[26] But, truly, it would be more to your advantage[27] if you kept quiet and let me get on with it.”

Belcolore said: “Of what possible advantage could this be to me? You (60) are all meaner than the Devil.”[28]

Then the priest said: “I do not know about that. Just ask. Would you like a pair of shoes or a silk headband, or a length of fine carded wool? Or what would you like?”

Belcolore said: “Generous, indeed, of you, sir. I have all those in plenty. But if you wish me well, why not do me a service, and I would do as you wished?” (65)

Then the priest said: “Say what you want, and I will do it gladly.”

Belcolore then said: “It is necessary for me to go to Florence on Saturday to take in the wool I have spun and to get my spinning-wheel repaired, and if you would lend me five lire, which I know that you have, I shall redeem from the pawnbroker my dark purple gown (70) and the fancy belt I wear on feast days which I had in my dowry, for you see I cannot go to church[29] or to any fine place because I do not have them, and afterwards I shall always do what you want.”

[25] The unsophisticated Bentivegna garbles the difficult words in this passage: *vicenda* for “accenda,” *parentorio* for “perentorio,” *pericolatore* for “procuratore,” *dificio* for “maleficio.” The implication is that he is very much out of his depth with the law.

[26] Again with a sexual pun on *macinare.*

[27] *uopo* properly means “need,” “necessity.”

[28] Boccaccio uses the word *fistolo*, meaning literally “ulcer,” but in Tuscan usage a slang word meaning “evil spirit” or “devil.”

[29] The phrase Belcolore uses is *a santo*, perhaps for “a luogo santo” meaning “to the holy place,” that is “to church.”

A cui Bentivegna rispose: "Gnaffé, sere, in buona verità io vo infino a città per alcuna mia vicenda: e porto queste cose a ser Bonaccorri da Ginestreto, ché m'aiuti di non so che m'ha fatto richiedere per una comparigione del parentorio per lo pericolator suo il giudice del dificio."

Il prete lieto disse: "Ben fai, figliuole; or va con la mia benedizione e torna tosto; e se ti venisse veduto Lapuccio o Naldino, non t'esca di mente di dir loro che mi rechino quelle combine per li coreggiati miei."

Bentivegna disse che sarebbe fatto; e venendosene verso Firenze, si pensò il prete che ora era tempo d'andare alla Belcolore e di provar sua ventura; e messasi la via tra' piedi non ristette sì fu a casa di lei; e entrato dentro disse: "Dio ci mandi bene: chi è di qua?"

La Belcolore, che era andata in balco, udendol disse: "O sere, voi siate il ben venuto: che andate voi zaconato per questo caldo?"

Il prete rispose: "Se Dio mi dea bene, che io mi veniva a star con teco un pezzo, per ciò che io trovai l'uom tuo che andava a città."

La Belcolore, scesa giù, si pose a sedere e cominciò a nettare sementa di cavolini che il marito avea poco innanzi trebbiati. Il prete le cominciò a dire: "Bene, Belcolore, de'mi tu far sempre mai morire a questo modo?"

La Belcolore cominciò a ridere e a dire: "O che ve fo io?"

Disse il prete: "Non mi fai nulla ma tu non mi lasci fare a te quel che io vorrei e che Idio comandò."

Disse la Belcolore: "Deh! andante andate: o fanno i preti così fatte cose?"

Il prete rispose: "Sì facciam noi meglio che gli altri uomini: o perché no? E dicoti più, che noi facciamo vie miglior lavorio; e sai perché? perché noi maciniamo a raccolta: ma in verità bene a tuo uopo, se tu stai cheta e lascimi fare."

Disse la Belcolore: "O che bene a mio uopo potrebbe esser questo? ché siete tutti quanti più scarsi che 'l fistolo."

Allora il prete disse: "Io non so, chiedi pur tu: o vuogli un paio di scarpette o vuogli un frenello o vuogli una bella fetta di stame o ciò che tu vuogli."

Disse la Belcolore: "Frate, bene sta! Io me n'ho di coteste cose; ma se voi mi volete cotanto bene, ché non mi fate voi un servigio, e io farò ciò che voi vorrete?"

Allora disse il prete: "Di ciò che tu vuogli, e io il farò volentieri."

La Belcolore allora disse: "Egli mi conviene andar sabato a Firenze a render lana che ho filata e a far racconciare il filatoio mio: e se voi mi prestate cinque lire, che so che l'avete, io ricoglierò dall'usuraio la gonnella mia del perso e lo scaggiale dai dì delle feste che io recai a marito, ché vedete che non ci posso andare a santo né in niun buon luogo, perché io non l'ho; e io sempre mai poscia farò ciò che voi vorrete."

The priest replied: “May God give me a good year, but I do not have the money with me. But believe me before Saturday comes, I shall see to it that you have it very willingly.”

“Indeed,” said Belcolore, “you all make such great promises, but afterwards you keep none of them. Do you think you can do with me what you did with Biliuzza, whom you dazzled with your words? By my faith in God, you are not going to do that; and she went to the bad for what you caused. If you do not have it with you, go and fetch it.”

“For pity’s sake,” said the priest, “do not make me go all the way back to my house, for you can see that my luck is high just now because there is nobody about, and perhaps when I return there will be somebody or other to get in our way. And I do not know when I might do as well as now.”

And she said: “So be it! If you want to go, go. If not drop it.”

Seeing that she was not disposed to do what would please him without a guarantee though he wanted to proceed with no guarantee, the priest said: “Look, you will not trust me to bring you the money. So that you may trust me I shall leave a pledge, this blue woollen cloak of mine.”

Belcolore turned up her nose and said: “Yes, and this cloak, what is it worth?”

The priest said: “What do you mean? What is it worth? I want you to know that this is Flanders cloth from Douai, from as far away as ‘Trouai’, and there are pieces of this among our people which they have got from ‘Quadrouai’.[30] And it is not a fortnight since that I bought it from Lotto, the second-hand dealer, for seven good lire, and then I got it cheap for five soldi less than its value, according to what Buglietto tells me who you know is very expert on these blue woollen fabrics.”

“Oh, is it?”, said Belcolore, “May God help me, I would never have believed it. But give it to me first.”

My lord the priest, who had his weapon at the ready,[31] took off his cloak and gave it to her, and she, after she had put it away safely, said: “Sir, let us go to the shed here where nobody ever goes.” And so they went.

And there, the priest, giving her the sweetest wet kisses in the world and making her feel as if she was in heaven,[32] solaced himself with her for a long time. Then he departed in his cassock, as if he had come from officiating at a wedding, and went back to the church.

There, thinking that however many candles’ ends he might receive in a year by way of offerings would not make up half the value of the five lire, he perceived he had done badly and regretted having left his cloak, and began to think what he might do to repossess it without cost. And because he was pretty cunning, he devised an all too good plan as to what he should do to get it back, and this fell into place. The next day, which was a feast day, he sent a neighbour’s young boy to the house of Monna Belcolore, and asked her as a favour that she might please lend him her stone mortar, because Binguccio dal Poggio and Nuto Buglietti were to dine with him later, and he wanted to make a sauce for them. Belcolore sent it to him.

[30] The priest seeks to impress here by citing a faraway place and by arithmetical progression. *Douai* is indeed in Flanders and was a cloth-making town. But he uses a pun on *due* (two) and Douai, and invents two other towns based on *tre* (three) and *quattro* (four).

[31] The phrase *aveva carica la balestra* means literally “had loaded his crossbow” and here indicates his sexual arousal.

[32] The phrase Boccaccio uses is *faccendola parente di messer Domenedio*, which means literally “making her kinswoman to the Lord God Almighty,” an expression indicating sexual rapture.

Rispose il prete: “Se Dio mi dea il buono anno, io non gli ho allato: ma credimi che prima che sabato sia, io farò che tu gli avrai molto volontieri.”

“Si,” disse la Belcolore “tutti siete così gran promettitori, e poscia non attenete altrui nulla: credete voi fare a me come voi faceste alla Biliuzza, che se n'andò col ceteratoio? Alla fé di Dio non farete, ché ella n'è divenuta femina di mondo pur per ciò: se voi non gli avete, e voi andate per essi.”

“Deh !” disse il prete “non mi fare ora andare infino a casa, ché vedi che ho così ritta la ventura testé che non c'è persona, e forse quand'io ci tornassi ci sarebbe chi che sia che c'impaccerebbe: e io non so quando e' mi si venga così ben fatto come ora.”

E ella disse: “Bene sta: se voi volete andar, sì andate; se non, sì ve ne durate.”

Il prete, veggendo che ella non era acconcia a far cosa che gli piacesse se non a *salvum me fac,* e egli volea fare *sine costodia,* disse: “Ecco, tu non mi credi che io te gli rechi; acciò che tu mi creda io ti lascerò pegno questo mio tabarro di sbiavato.”

La Belcolore levò alto il viso e disse: “Sì, cotesto tabarro, o che vale egli?”

Disse il prete: “Come, che vale? Io voglio che tu sappi ch'egli è di duagio infino in treagio, e hacci di quegli nel popolo nostro che il tengon di quattragio; e non ha ancora quindici dì che mi costò da Lotto rigattiere delle lire ben sette, e ebbine buon mercato de' soldi ben cinque, per quel che mi dica Buglietto, che sai che si cognosce così bene di questi panni sbiavati.”

“O sie?” disse la Belcolore “se Dio m'aiuti, io non l'avrei mai creduto: ma datemelo in prima.”

Messer lo prete, che aveva carica la balestra, trattosi il tabarro gliele diede; e ella, poi che riposto l'ebbe, disse: “Sere, andiancene qua nella capanna, ché non vi vien mai persona”; e così fecero.

E quivi il prete, dandole i più dolci basciozzi del mondo e faccendola parente di messer Domenedio, con lei una gran pezza si sollazzò: poscia partitosi in gonnella, che pareva che venisse da servire a nozze, se ne tornò al santo.

Quivi, pensando che quanti moccoli ricoglieva in tutto l'anno d'offerta non valeva la metà di cinque lire, gli parve aver mal fatto e pentessi d'avere lasciato il tabarro e cominciò a pensare in che modo riaver lo potesse senza costo. E per ciò che alquanto era maliziosetto, s'avisò troppo bene come dovesse fare a riaverlo, e vennegli fatto: per ciò che il dì seguente, essendo festa, egli mandò un fanciullo d'un suo vicino in casa questa monna Belcolore, e mandolla pregando che le piacesse di prestargli il mortaio suo della pietra, per ciò che desinava la mattina con lui Binguccio dal Poggio e Nuto Buglietti, sì che egli voleva far della salsa. La Belcolore gliele mandò.

And when it approached dinnertime the priest watched to see when Bentivegna dal Mazzo and Belcolore sat down to eat, and called his clerk and said to him: "Take this mortar and carry it back to Belcolore, and say 'My master thanks you very much, and can he have back the cloak that the young boy left as a pledge?' " The clerk went to Belcolore's house with this mortar and found her together with Bentivegna at table eating. Then he set down the mortar and delivered the priest's message.

Belcolore, hearing him ask for the cloak, wanted to reply, but Bentivegna looking very cross, said "So then, you are taking a pledge from the priest? I have a mind to give you a good hard smack in the face. Give it back to him immediately, a plague on you. And look to it that whatever he wants, I tell you, even if it is that donkey of ours, and more, he is not to be refused."

Belcolore, grumbling, got up, went to the chest at the foot of the bed, took the cloak out, and gave it to the clerk, and said: "Say this to your master from me: 'Belcolore says that she prays to God that you will not again grind more sauce in her mortar.[33] She has been less than honourably treated.' "

The clerk went back with the cloak and took the message to his master, to which the priest, laughing, replied: "Tell her, when you see her, that if she does not lend me the mortar I shall not lend her the pestle. It cuts both ways."

Bentivegna believed that his wife had spoken these words because he had scolded her, and took no notice. But Belcolore fell out with the priest and refused to talk to him until the grape-harvest. After that, because the priest had threatened to have her sent to be chewed by the great Lucifer, and because of the great fear she had of it, and what with the fermented grape juice he sent her and the roast chestnuts, she made her peace with him and they caroused and revelled more times together subsequently. And instead of the five lire the priest had new skin put on her tambourine and added a little bell to it, and she was satisfied.[34]

[33] *Mortaio* is here used, as often, in a sexual sense, as is *pestello* later. Both continue the puns on *macinare*.

[34] For an interesting essay on the problematics of translating Boccaccio see G. H. McWilliam, "On Translating the 'Decameron,' " in *Essays in Honour of John Humphreys Whitfield, presented to him on his retirement from the Serena Chair of Italian at the University of Birmingham*, ed. H. C. Davis, D. G. Rees, J. M. Hatwell and G. W. Slowey (London: St. George's Press for the Department of Italian, University of Birmingham, 1975), pp. 71–83. He has some pertinent comments on the difficulties of rendering the Florentine demotic of 8.2.

E come fu in su l'ora del desinare, el prete appostò quando Bentivegna del Mazzo e la Belcolore manicassero; e chiamato il cherico suo gli disse: "Togli quel mortaio e riportalo alla Belcolore, e dì: 'Dice il sere che gran mercé, e che voi gli rimandiate il tabarro che il fanciullo vi lasciò per ricordanza.'" Il cherico andò a casa della Belcolore con questo mortaio e trovolla insieme con Bentivegna a desco che desinavano; quivi posto giù il mortaio fece l'ambasciata del prete.

La Belcolore udendosi richiedere il tabarro volle rispondere; ma Bentivegna con un mal viso disse: "Dunque toi tu ricordanza al sere? Fo boto a Cristo che mi vien voglia di darti un gran sergozzone: va rendigliel tosto, che canciola te nasca! e guarda che di cosa che voglia mai, io dico s'e' volesse l'asino nostro, non ch'altro, non gli sia detto di no."

La Belcolore brontolando si levò, e andatasene al soppediano ne trasse il tabarro e diello al cherico e disse: "Dirai così al sere da mia parte: 'La Belcolore dice che fa prego a Dio che voi non pesterete mai più salsa in suo mortaio: non l'avete voi sì bello onor fatto di questa.'"

Il cherico se n'andò col tabarro e fece l'ambasciata al sere; a cui il prete ridendo disse: "Dira'le, quando tu la vedrai, che s'ella non ci presterà il mortaio, io non presterò a lei il pestello; vada l'un per l'altro."

Bentivegna si credeva che la moglie quelle parole dicesse perché egli l'aveva garrito, e non se ne curò; ma la Belcolore venne in iscrezio col sere e tennegli favella insino a vendemmia. Poscia, avendola minacciata il prete di farnela andare in bocca del lucifero maggiore, per bella paura entro, col mosto e con le castagne calde si rappatumò con lui, e più volte insieme fecer poi gozzoviglia. E in iscambio delle cinque lire le fece il prete rincartare il cembal suo e appiccovvi un sonagliuzzo, e ella fu contenta.

The Prioress's Prologue and Tale

LAUREL BROUGHTON

Chaucer's Prioress tells a miracle of the Virgin, one of the most popular forms of narrative in the Middle Ages. These tales tend to be simple, focused exempla, designed to reinforce specific aspects of Marian devotion. In creating *The Prioress's Tale* Chaucer has drawn on a number of cultural and literary influences to produce a complex and multi-layered narrative that transcends its genre.[1] Because of these many layers, *The Prioress's Prologue* and *Tale* present numerous challenges for those wishing to pursue its sources and analogues. Each makes direct and indirect reference to the Sarum Missal, Sarum Breviary, and Primer, as demonstrated by Madeleva, Hamilton, Wenk, Maltman and Collette. Although *The Prioress's Tale* is a miracle of the Virgin, no clear source can be identified for the version the Prioress tells. Instead, Carleton Brown, writing in 1941, identified thirty-two analogues of the story, which he divides into three groups labelled A, B and C,[2] and Chaucer's *Tale* seems to combine elements from all three groups. Since Brown's study, other scholars have identified additional analogues, bringing the number to thirty-eight, and these, along with other saints' legends and "The Ballad of the Jew's Daughter" augment our understanding of *The Prioress's Tale.*

THE PRIORESS'S PROLOGUE

The Prioress's Sequence begins with a prologue in which the Prioress invokes the Virgin's assistance in the telling of her tale. Brown did not discuss the *Prologue*, but its possible sources, though too numerous and fragmentary to print here, nevertheless deserve examination. The *Prologue* richly reflects medieval Marian devotion and bears a strong relationship to liturgical sources as well as to the *Prologue* to *The Second Nun's Tale* and Canto XXXIII of Dante's *Paradiso*.

Chaucer heads *The Prioress's Prologue* with *Domine Dominus Noster*, the first words of Psalm 8 in the Sarum Breviary, and the first seven lines of the *Prologue* paraphrase the opening verses (2–3, Vulgate) of this psalm, beginning with "O Lord, oure Lord, thy name how merveilous/ Is in this large world ysprad" (VII, 453–4) (Domine, Dominus noster,/ Quam admirabile est nomen

I wish to thank the Dean's Fund of the College of Arts and Sciences and the Graduate College of the University of Vermont, whose generous grants made possible much of the research that appears in this chapter. Also, my deep appreciation goes to Carolyn Collette for her careful reading of this chapter and to Jeanne Krochalis, Mary Hamel, Priscilla Throop and Anne Clark for their invaluable help with translations from the Latin.

[1] See Beverly Boyd's excellent summary in *A Variorum Edition of the Works of Geoffrey Chaucer, Volume II, The Canterbury Tales, The Prioress's Tale, Part Twenty* (Norman: University of Oklahoma Press, 1987), pp. 4–26.

[2] Carleton F. Brown, "The Prioress's Tale," in Bryan and Dempster, pp. 447–85.

tuum in universa terra!). Chaucer's Prioress would certainly have been well-acquainted with this psalm, for it was recited in the canonical hours of the Divine Office in the breviary, especially in the commemorative Office of the Virgin, liturgical services that secular clerics in major orders and men and women in religious orders in the fourteenth century were obligated to pray daily.[3] This psalm was also said in the Little Office of the Virgin, a shorter liturgical service modeled on the Divine Office, which was a popular daily devotion observed by clergy and lay people in the Middle Ages, and by the fourteenth century had become an added obligation on all clergy and religious who were bound to the recitation of the Divine Office.[4] Sister Madeleva, believing that the Little Office was Chaucer's source for the *Prologue*, cited additional parallels between several prayers in it and the Prioress's words, including her reference to Mary as "O bussh unbrent, brennynge in Moyses sighte" (VII, 468), echoing "Rubum, quem viderat Moyses incombustum," an antiphon said at Lauds after Advent.[5] Verses 2–3 of Psalm 8 were also used in reverse order as the introit to the mass on the feast of the Holy Innocents (December 28).[6] Both Madeleva and Hamilton used the modern Roman Breviary to identify these parallels, but Psalm 8:2–3 was also used in the English Sarum rite and appears frequently throughout the liturgical year in the Sarum Missal and Breviary.[7] The probability that Chaucer's audience would have recognized echoes of Psalm 8 and these other prayers is enhanced by the fact that the Little Office also formed the first part of the Middle English *Prymer,* which first appeared in the fourteenth century and was used as a schoolbook for children like the Prioress's "litel clergeon" (VII, 517, 541) and as a layperson's prayerbook.[8] While all this

3 See Pierre Salmon, *The Breviary through the Centuries*, trans. Sister David Mary (Collegeville, MN: Liturgical Press, 1962), pp. 15–16. (Authorized English version of *L'office divin: Histoire de la formation du bréviaire*, Lex Orandi 27 [Paris, 1959]). John Harper, in *The Forms and Orders of Western Liturgy from the Tenth to the Eighteenth Century* (Oxford, 1991) notes that Psalm 8 was prayed regularly in the secular "use" at Sunday Matins and in the monastic "use" at Tuesday Prime (p. 243).

4 See Edmund Bishop, "On the Origin of the Prymer," in *The Prymer*, ed. Henry Littlehales, EETS OS 109 (London, 1895, 1897), Part 2, p. xxxv. See also Beverly Boyd, *Chaucer and the Liturgy* (Philadelphia, 1967), p. 66. Harper calls attention to the distinction between the Commemorative Office that "displaced the Office of the day once a week, most often on Saturday," and the Little Office which "was said in addition to the main Office of the day," sometimes recited aloud in choir and other times said individually either in or out of choir (pp. 133–4).

5 Sister M. Madeleva, *Chaucer's Nuns and Other Essays* (New York: Appleton, 1925; rpt. Port Washington, NY: Kennikat, 1965), pp. 30–5. The essay also appears in *A Lost Language and Other Essays on Chaucer* (New York, 1951). She cites parallels between lines 460–6 and the antiphon at Matins, "Vouchsafe that I may praise thee, O sacred Virgin; give me strength against my enemies"; and between lines 473–9 and the first responsory prayer at Matins, "O holy and immaculate virginity, I know not with what praises to extol thee," and the absolution at Matins, "By the prayers and merits of the blessed Mary ever Virgin and of all the Saints, may the Lord bring us to the kingdom of heaven." These parallels and their Latin originals are printed by Boyd, *Variorum*, pp. 4–5.

6 Marie Padgett Hamilton, "Echoes of Childermas in the Tale of the Prioress," *Modern Language Review* 34 (1939): 2–3. She cites Robinson's note in *The Poetical Works of Chaucer* (Cambridge, MA, 1933), p. 841, crediting Joseph Dwight for bringing this information about Psalm 8 to his attention.

7 In the Sarum Use, the Little Office was incorporated into the regular Office (Bishop, pp. xxxvi–xxxvii). Psalm 8 was recited at Matins of the Virgin for Advent in the Commemorative Office, and at Sunday and Monday Matins in the Little Office. See *Breviarium ad usum insignis ecclesiae Sarum*, ed. Francis Procter and Christopher Wordsworth (Cambridge, 1879–86; rpt. Farnborough, Hampshire, 1970), 1.34, 2.286.

8 Bishop, p. xxxvii. See also William Maskell, *Monumenta Ritualia Ecclesiae Anglicanae*, vol. 3 (Oxford, 1882).

suggests the familiarity of Psalm 8 to Chaucer's audience, it is not possible to determine whether Chaucer's source was the Little Office or the Divine Office because, as Boyd points out, there was no uniform breviary of the Divine Office, and because that Office "commemorates the feasts of the Virgin Mary, for which there was a common heritage of liturgical materials"; moreover, such an identification isn't necessary because Chaucer has interwoven and layered various liturgical allusions, some found in more than one source, to create the rich fabric of *The Prioress's Sequence*.[9]

Carolyn Collette, while arguing for similarities between *The Prioress's Prologue* and that of the Second Nun, also identifies vernacular primers and the daily recital of Offices of the Virgin as expressions of late medieval English lay piety, thereby underscoring the fact that these texts were familiar to Chaucer and his audience.[10] She also further analyzes Chaucer's method of interweaving and layering liturgical allusions in the *The Prioress's Prologue*, pointing out additional echoes and references to prayers in the Little Office, including Psalm 19:7 at Matins; *O gloriosa domina* and *O gloriosa dei genetrix* at Lauds; *Rubum quem* at Sext; Psalm 131 (Vulgate 130), recited during Compline; and the anthem at Sext in addition to bidding prayers at Vespers, Compline and Matins.[11]

Collette is not the first to explore the parallels between *The Prioress's Prologue* and the Second Nun's *Invocatio ad Mariam;* scholars from Skeat onward have noted the resemblance between them. In her exclamation about Mary's unique relationship to Christ – "O mooder Mayde, O mayde Mooder free" (VII, 467) – the Prioress echoes the paradox in the first line of the prayer Dante assigns to St Bernard in *Paradiso*, Canto XXXIII : "Vergine madre, figlia del tuo figlo" ["Virgin mother, daughter of thy son"].[12] Beverly Boyd, in her discussion of the complex interrelationship between Dante's invocation and *The Prioress's Prologue*, cites Pratt's discussion of the *Prologue* as an example of how Chaucer reworked some material from his own earlier work instead of going to another source.[13] By placing Dante's words in lines 16–21 from the same Canto XXXIII, side by side with the words of the Prioress and the Second Nun (shown below in italics), Pratt indicates clearly the relationship between them and argues that in the *Prioress's Prologue* Chaucer borrowed from his own, presumably earlier, *Prologue* to the *Second Nun's Tale* of St Cecilia. rather than from Dante.[14]

[9] Boyd, *Variorum*, pp. 5–6.

[10] Carolyn P. Collette, "Chaucer's Discourse of Mariology: Gaining the Right to Speak," *Art and Context in Late Medieval English Narrative*, ed. Robert R. Edwards (Cambridge: D. S. Brewer, 1994), p. 128.

[11] Collette, *Ibid.*, pp. 127–47. For the prayers mentioned above see Littlehales, *The Prymer*, 105 (Part 1), pp. 3, 12, 13, 24, 32. See also the discussion of *The Second Nun's Prologue* by Sherry L. Reames in *Sources and Analogues of the Canterbury Tales*, ed. R. M. Correale and Mary Hamel (Cambridge: D. S. Brewer, 2002), vol. 1, pp. 491–3.

[12] John D. Sinclair, *Dante's Paradiso* (New York: Oxford University Press, 1939; rpt. 1972), p. 479.

[13] See Boyd, *Variorum*, pp. 6–8.

[14] Robert A. Pratt, "Chaucer Borrowing from Himself," *Modern Language Notes* 7 (1946): 259–61. While it is possible that all three passages may have derived from a common source, that source has not yet been identified. Charles Singleton, in his edition of the *Divine Comedy, Paradiso*, vol. 2, Commentary, Canto XXXIII (Princeton University Press, 1975), p. 560, notes the relationship to *The Second Nun's Prologue* but cites no source for this prayer to the Virgin that Dante assigns to St Bernard in *Paradiso*, Canto XXXIII, lines 1–39.

Dante, Canto XXXIII (16–21)	*Second Nun's Prologue* (VIII, 50–6)	*Prioress's Prologue* (VII, 474–80)
La tua benignità non pur soccorre a chi domanda, ma ***molte*** ***fiate*** liberamente al dimandar precorre. In te misericordia, in te pietate, in ***te magnificenza***, in te s'aduna quantunque in creatura è di bontate	Assembled is in thee ***magnificence***/ With mercy, goodnesse, and with swich pitee/ That thou, that art the sonne of excellence/ Nat oonly helpest hem that preyen thee,/ But ***often tyme of thy*** ***benygnytee***/ Ful frely, ***er that men thyn*** ***help biseche***,/ ***Thou goost biforn*** and art hir lyves leche.	Lady, thy bountee, thy ***magnificence***/ Thy vertu and thy grete humylitee/ Ther may no tonge expresse in no science;/ For somtyme, Lady, er men praye to thee,/ ***Thou goost biforn of thy*** ***benyngnytee,***/ And getest us the lyght, of thy preyere,/ To gyden us unto thy Sone so deere.

THE PRIORESS'S TALE

Carleton Brown, in both his earlier *Study of the Miracle of Our Lady*, and in his chapter in Bryan and Dempster, focuses on identifying the closest analogues to *The Prioress's Tale* and establishing the relationships between the analogues. In doing so, he neglects to discuss the tale in the larger context of miracles of the Virgin. The remainder of this introduction will summarize Brown's work, discuss liturgical sources, other saints' lives, and ballads that may have contributed to creation of *The Prioress's Tale*; explore the larger context of miracles of the Virgin; and present analogues identified since Brown's time.

Brown's work

In his 1910 *Study*, Brown identified twenty-six miracles of the Virgin which he considered to be close analogues of *The Prioress's Tale*. In his 1941 reworking of the subject, he revises the number to thirty-two. He includes tales that contain protagonists killed by Jews for singing praises to the Virgin and divides these into three groups identified as A (13 tales), B (10 tales) and C (9 tales plus Chaucer's). The story as it appears in Group A he outlines as follows.[15]

Group A:

1. A boy sings *Gaude Maria* in a Jewish neighborhood, provoking the anger of the residents.
2. A Jew, or group of Jews, kills and buries the child.
3. The boy's mother searches for him and hears his voice as she goes by the Jew's house.
4. The boy is exhumed, alive and unharmed.
5. In most versions, the Jews convert as a result of the miracle. In some versions, however, they are punished.

[15] Carleton F. Brown, *A Study of the Miracle of Our Lady Told by Chaucer's Prioress* (London: The Chaucer Society, 1910), pp. 1–50; and Bryan and Dempster, pp. 447–50.

The next group changes the form of the narrative by introducing important modifications:

Group B:

1. The boy is a chorister, singing regularly in church.
2. The mother disappears from the tale.
3. The murderer hears the boy singing as he did before he was killed.
4. The Jews confess the crime and are converted before Christians learn of it.

The versions in the third group are not influenced by Group B, but diverge from those in Group A in the following ways:

Group C:

1. *Gaude Maria* is replaced by the antiphon *Alma redemptoris mater* in seven versions. *Gaude Maria* appears in one version, *Ave regina* in one, and *Sancta Maria* in one.
2. The boy's body is thrown into a cloaca or jakes.
3. The story ends with the boy's funeral, during which he continues to sing.

Attempting to define the genealogy of the legend, Brown posits that Group A constitutes the trunk from which Groups B and C branch off.[16] He notes two strains in Group A, one related to A4, attributed to Caesarius of Heisterbach (an attribution now refuted),[17] the other related to A3, Gautier of Coincy's version, and postulates undiscovered sources for each of these strains, which he calls Ur-Caesarius and Ur-Gautier respectively. He also acknowledges that "a confusion of elements from different groups" exists in some analogues. In A10, for example, the victim is not a young scholar or choirboy, but a mature clerk whose mother oddly enough appears on the scene and whose body, like the bodies of the dead boys in the Group C tradition, is thrown into a privy ("jakes").[18] Margaret H. Statler explores the "confusion" Brown mentions, showing that similarities between *The Prioress's Tale*, C1 and Ur-Caesarius include a description of the child's continual singing as he passed from school through Jewry, the conspiracy of the Jews to murder the child, and the recording of the mother's plea to the Jews and their denial of any knowledge of the child. Similarities between Chaucer's *Tale*, C9, C10, and Ur-Gautier include the child's account of Mary's appearance to him, condemnation of the Jews in strong terms even using the proverb "Mordre wol out," and closer correspondence

16 Brown, *Study*, p. 57.

17 Alfons Hilka, *Die Beiden ersten Bücher der Libri VIII Miraculorum*, vol. 3 of *Die Wundergeschichten des Caesarius von Heisterbach*, Publikationen der Gesellschaft für rheinische Geschichtskunde, no. 43 (Bonn: Peter Hanstein, 1937), pp. 201–2, attributes A4 to someone else, maybe another brother at Heisterbach. See also Evelyn Faye Wilson, ed., *The Stella Maris of John of Garland*, Medieval Academy of America Publication no. 45 (Cambridge, MA, 1946), pp. 55–9, who traces sources of Caesarius and Pseudo-Caesarius to Cistercian collections of Mary miracles.

18 Bryan and Dempster, p. 451.

between the ages of Gautier's "clerconcel" and Chaucer's "clergeon" than in any other version of the legend.[19]

Within Group C, Brown identifies a subgroup which he designates the "magical objects" group.[20] In these four versions, including Chaucer's *Tale*, the Virgin places an object in the child's mouth that enables him to continue singing.

C5	Vernon Manuscript	lily
C6	*The Prioress's Tale*	greyn
C9	Alphonsus a Spina	gem
C10	Trinity Cambridge O.9.38	pebble

After exploring the relationship of *The Prioress's Tale* to the three other versions within this subgroup and to C1, Brown concludes that none of the known analogues could have been Chaucer's direct source and theorizes that an intermediate text served as a source for *The Prioress's Tale*, C9 and C10.

Liturgical sources

Brown pays little attention to the liturgical sources of the *The Prioress's Tale*; however, like the *Prologue*, it is also rich in liturgical allusions. As Marie Hamilton has shown, the Prioress's paraphrases of, and references to, several biblical texts are found in the Sarum Missal propers of the mass for the feast of Holy Innocents (December 28) known as Childermas, which Chaucer undoubtedly had in mind when writing the *Tale*. The first two verses of Psalm 8 are used in the Introit of this mass (Cf. *PrT*, VII, 607–8), singers of the "song al newe" who follow the "Whyte Lamb celestial" (VII, 579–85) are mentioned in the reading from the Apocalypse (Revelation) 14:1–5, and the reference to Rachel weeping for her children (VII, 627) recalls both the gospel reading (Matt. 2:13) and the Communion prayer of Childermas. Finding a relationship between Childermas and the Feast of St Nicholas, she postulates from this evidence that Chaucer's source for *The Prioress's Tale* was a Childermas sermon he heard preached by a "boy bishop," perhaps at Lincoln Cathedral.[21] J. C. Wenk also recognizes the allusions to the Feast of Holy Innocents

19 Margaret H. Statler, "The Analogues of Chaucer's 'Prioress' Tale': The Relation of Group C to Group A," *PMLA* 65 (1950): 899–909 (correspondences listed above discussed on pp. 902–3 and 907–8 respectively).

20 Bryan and Dempster, pp. 457–60. Other tales in Group C form a "liturgical" subgroup in which the miracle centers on the child's introduction of the hymn *Salve sancta parens* into the funeral mass.

21 Marie P. Hamilton, "Echoes of Childermas in the Tale of the Prioress," *Modern Language Review* 34 (1939): 1–8 (rpt. *Chaucer: Modern Essays in Criticism*, ed. Edward Wagenknecht [New York, 1959], pp. 88–97). Boyd agrees that Chaucer was thinking of Childermas when he wrote *PrT*, but not that he got the idea from a sermon at a Childermas celebration. The strongest modern case for its origins in Childermas, she thinks, is John C. Hirsh's argument ("Reopening the *Prioress's Tale*," *Chaucer Review* 10 [1975]: 32) that the boy's death is parallel with Christ's in the mass and both define the theme of salvation in the tale (see *Variorum*, pp. 5–6). Hamilton points out Chaucer's connection to Lincoln Cathedral through his wife Philippa and his sister-in-law, Katherine Swynford. See also Sumner Ferris, "Chaucer at Lincoln: 'The Prioress's Tale' as Political Poem," *Chaucer Review* 15 (1981): 295–321, who argues on the basis of conjectural evidence that Chaucer composed *The Prioress's Tale* for Richard II's visit to Lincoln on March 26, 1387.

(December 28) in the *Tale*, and points out a connection between it and the feast of St Thomas of Canterbury (Thomas Becket) on December 29 through the commemorative prayer which immediately followed the Magnificat at Vespers on Holy Innocents, which recalls the martyrdom of Thomas by the swords of the wicked while praising God in Canterbury cathedral just as the little "clergeon" was slain while singing Mary's praises.[22]

By noting this memorial collect, Wenk anticipates the work of Sister Nicholas Maltman, who identifies liturgical references to the feast of St Thomas of Canterbury in *The Prioress's Tale.* She points out that the responsory *Jacet granum* was sung after the third lesson at Matins of this feast, and the prosa *Clangat pastor*, which also makes reference to the "granum," was sung at the altar of St Thomas during a commemorative procession at second Vespers of Holy Innocents. She therefore contends that these inspired Chaucer's use of the "greyn" (VII, 662) as the magical object that sustains the clergeon's singing, and whose precise meaning has troubled scholars ever since.[23]

The clergeon's song itself constitutes another reference to the liturgy. The boy sings *Alma redemptoris mater*, an antiphon probably dating from the late eleventh century, which praises the Virgin and commemorates the Incarnation.[24] Chaucer was certainly imitating his source when he chose to highlight this antiphon since it is the one that, as noted above by Brown, appears in the Group C analogues that are closest to his tale. There is no evidence to support Hamilton's assumption that this antiphon was sung in the Middle Ages, as in modern times, during Advent or after Christmas as in the Feast of the Holy Innocents.[25] But Chaucer would probably have known it from its place in the Sarum Breviary, where it was the designated or optional antiphon at Vespers during the summer months, and between the Octave of Trinity Sunday and the beginning of Advent.[26] Davidson has also studied the musical setting for *Alma redemptoris*, reconstructing from the Sarum Use antiphonal books what she believes to be the version performed in England during Chaucer's time, which differs in both pitch and rhythm from the version found in the modern *Liber usualis*, and would therefore been difficult for Chaucer's clergeon to learn.[27] She attests to the popularity of the antiphon, and argues for the suitability of the *Alma redemptoris* because it emphasizes Mary's maternal nature, which resonates with images in the rest of the tale, thus seconding Boyd's assertion

[22] J. C. Wenk, "On the Sources of *The Prioress's Tale*," *Mediaeval Studies* 17 (1955): 214–19, prayer on 217.

[23] Sr. Nicholas Maltman, O.P., "The Divine Granary or the End of the Prioress's 'Greyn,'" *Chaucer Review* 17 (1982): 163–70. For discussions of the many interpretations of "greyn," see the note to line 662 in *The Riverside Chaucer*, p. 916, and Boyd's long note in *Variorum*, pp. 160–1.

[24] Hilda Graef, *Mary: A History of Doctrine and Devotion* (London: Sheed and Ward, 1985, combined edition), pp. 229–30. See also Harper, *Forms and Orders*, pp. 130ff.

[25] Hamilton, "Echoes of Childermas," p. 5 n. 4. Harper (p. 132) indicates that in the the post-Tridentine Roman Breviary *Alma redemptoris* is the prescribed antiphon from first Vespers of Advent through second Vespers of the Purification (February 2).

[26] Audrey Davidson, "*Alma Redemptoris Mater*: The Little Clergeon's Song," in *Substance and Manner: Studies in Music and the Other Arts* (Saint Paul, MN: Hiawatha Press, 1977), pp. 21–9.

[27] Davidson, pp. 23, 29.

that the liturgical allusions in *The Prioress's Tale* stem from the canonical hours.[28]

Other saints' lives

At the end of her tale the Prioress invokes the name of little Hugh of Lincoln: "O yonge Hugh of Lyncoln, slayn also/ With cursed Jewes" (VII, 684–5), a reference that has been investigated by scholars as another possible source for her tale. This child, who was believed to have been martyred by Jews in 1255, became the subject of a saint's cult centered at Lincoln Cathedral, where Chaucer's wife Philippa had close ties.[29] Gavin Langmuir examined in great detail the circumstances surrounding Hugh's death and identified two traditions engendered by it: a popular one described in three contemporary chronicles, an Anglo-Norman ballad, and Hugh's shrine at Lincoln, and a literary tradition preserved in the ballad of "Sir Hugh" or "The Jew's Daughter," collected by Francis Child in some twenty-one different versions in the nineteenth century.[30] The first tradition, based on thirteenth-century historical reports relating that the eight-year old Hugh's body was found in a well near the house of a Jew where Jews had gathered for a wedding, led to the popular belief that he had been murdered in some sort of ritual sacrifice. The story contributed to a belief that Jews crucified Christian children, for which there was no evidence, but which "most fully developed in England [spread] to the continent, where it brought death and suffering to Jews down to the twentieth century."[31] The second tradition, exemplified by the ballad known as "The Jew's Daughter," little resembles either the story of ritual murder or that of the singing boy in Chaucer's tale. It tells of how a Jew's daughter entices a young boy, Sir Hugh, into her house to retrieve a ball he has kicked through the window. She stabs him and throws his body into a well in the house where his mother later finds him because the body speaks. Thomas Percy included a version of the ballad in his *Reliques* and associated it with *The Prioress's Tale*, even though it is clearly quite different from it and makes no reference to Lincoln.[32] In his 1910 study, Brown supposed that C

28 Davidson, pp. 25–9. See also Boyd's note in *Variorum*, p. 15, and p. 16 for Davidson's reconstructed musical version of the *Alma*.

29 Hamilton, p. 7. For a complete discussion of the history of Little Hugh of Lincoln, see Gavin I. Langmuir, "The Knight's Tale of Young Hugh of Lincoln," *Speculum* 47 (1972): 459–82. Boyd lists the historical record in *Variorum*, pp. 166–7, note to lines 1874–5.

30 Langmuir (p. 460 n. 3) cites as sources for the first tradition the following chronicles: Matthew Paris, *Chron. Maj*. v, pp. 516–19, 546, 552; *Ann. Mon*., I, pp. 340–6, 348 (Burton Annals); and II, pp. 346–8 (Waverly Annals). He locates the Anglo-Norman ballad in Francisque Michel, *Hughes de Lincoln* (Paris, 1834), pp. 1–16. In addition to these sources, an account of Hugh of Lincoln appears in *Castleford's Chronicle* XI.xviii, EETS OS 306 (Oxford, 1996), pp. 1000–4.

31 Langmuir, pp. 461–2. The Anglo-Norman ballad, summarized by Boyd, contains more details. "Hugh is tortured and crucified, his heart then eaten by his tormentors; three times they try to dispose of the body – in the earth, in a privy, and in a well – and three times the body reappears. These details indicate just how virulent and hysterical anti-Semitism in England could be and how the miraculous element could be commensurately magnified." Boyd, *Variorum*, p. 18. Langmuir discusses this ballad on pp. 466–9.

32 See Langmuir, p. 460 nn. 8–9, citing Francis James Child, *The English and Scottish Popular Ballads*, 5 vols in 3 (New York, 1956), III, 233–54; IV, 497; V, 241; and Thomas Percy, *Reliques of Ancient English Poetry*, 2nd edn (London: Dodsley, 1767), I, 35–8.

versions of "The Child Slain by Jews" might have been influenced by the stories of the Hugh's death, but later retracted this view, noting that C1 dates from before Hugh's death "by nearly half a century," though the tragic ending in Group C may well reflect "earlier stories of Jewish atrocities which were circulating in England."[33]

In addition to the Hugh of Lincoln story, commentators have identified other saints' legends that bear some resemblance to the tale. Gerould notes similarities between *The Prioress's Tale* and a legend of St Mauritius in which the saint tells a poor widow who has lost her son that she will hear the voice of the dead boy singing with the monks in the choir when she attends divine service.[34] Sherman Hawkins finds an interesting analogue in the story of the death of St Kenelm, recounted by Chanticleer in *The Nun's Priest's Tale* (VII, 3110–20), interesting for it shows yet another example of Chaucer's intertextual mingling in *The Canterbury Tales*. As Hawkins points out, St Kenelm's story has several similarities to that of the little clergeon, including Kenelm's age of seven years, his martyrdom while he sings, and the miraculous recovery of his body.[35]

Another influence on the tale is suggested by the Prioress's association of the clergeon's readiness to learn "Cristes mooder deere,/ To worshipe ay" (VII, 510–11) with the precocious holiness of St Nicholas, who "so yong to Crist dide reverence" (515). Hamilton has observed that the feast of St Nicholas (December 6) was closely associated with Childermas, and, as Boyd points out, Chaucer was surely familiar with well-known play of *St Nicholas and the Schoolboys*, which tells of a child's being dismembered at an inn and then being resurrected by the instigation of the Saint.[36]

Miracles of the Virgin

While exploring the liturgical and historical connections in *The Prioress's Tale* can shed light on the possible sources of Chaucer's inspiration, as well as reveal its rich and multi-layered poetic fabric, the *Tale* is best understood in the context of its genre. The Prioress tells a miracle of the Virgin, a form of popular literature pervading medieval culture in Chaucer's time. Many of these legends originated out of the desire to promote feasts and teach various forms of Marian devotion.[37] Boyd correctly notes that the miracle Chaucer chooses to tell was deeply embedded in the popular culture of fourteenth-century England.[38]

[33] Bryan and Dempster, p. 455; *Study*, pp. 87–95.

[34] Gordon H. Gerould, "An Early Analogue of Chaucer's *Prioress's Tale*," *Modern Language Notes* 24 (1909): 132–3. Versions of this story also appear in *The Golden Legend* and the *Miracula* of Gregory of Tours.

[35] Sherman Hawkins, "Chaucer's Prioress and the Sacrifice of Praise," *Journal of English and Germanic Philology* 63 (1964): 622–4.

[36] See Hamilton, pp. 5–6, on the relationship between St Nicholas and Childermas, and Boyd (*Variorum*, p. 14), on the play of St Nicholas, which is printed in *Chief Pre-Shakespearean Drama*, ed. Joseph Q. Adams (Boston, 1924), pp. 59–62.

[37] Graef, pp. 229ff, discusses the origins of miracles of the Virgin. See also Marina Warner, *Alone of All her Sex* (New York, 1983). R. W. Southern, "The English Origins of 'Miracles of the Virgin,'" *Medieval and Renaissance Studies* 4 (1958): 176–216, argues that the earliest collections of miracles of the Virgin were made in England.

[38] Boyd, *Variorum*, p. 8.

Although no direct source for this tale has yet been identified, a number of analogues exist, appearing in both Latin and vernacular languages. These analogues fall into two thematic categories: lily miracles and legends in which Mary, a representative of the new dispensation, opposes Jews, who represent the old dispensation. Statler suggests the influence of an additional topos common to Mary legends, that of the dying child.[39]

The Prioress's Tale belongs to the group of Mary legends called the lily miracles, which contain two major components: a protagonist who recites "Ave Maria" or some other Marian text or hymn which commemorates the Incarnation; and a miraculous manifestation in the person's mouth. In the prototypical lily miracle, the protagonist prays "Ave Maria" devoutly throughout his life. He dies, is buried and shortly thereafter, a flower appears at his grave site. When his body is exhumed, members of his community find the flower to be rooted in the dead man's mouth. This prototypical miracle gives rise to several elaborations and variations. Some versions of the miracle vary the prayer, or the flower, or even both, as does *The Prioress's Tale.* Even in the variant versions, however, the didactic purpose behind the lily miracle remains clear: to celebrate, even actively participate in, the Incarnation. The protagonist re-enacts the Incarnational moment by repeating the angel Gabriel's salutation to the Virgin and is rewarded with a miraculous manifestation in the mouth, usually a lily, which is not only a symbol of the Virgin, but a symbol of the physical presence of Christ.[40] The versions most closely related to *The Prioress's Tale* retain this didactic purpose.

As the largest single subgroup of miracles of the Virgin, lily miracles appear in numerous Middle English collections including:

South English Legendary (c. 1300)
Tanner MS 407 (late fifteenth century)
British Library Additional MS 39996 (early fifteenth century)
Vernon MS (1370–1400)
Caxton's *Golden Legend* (1483)
Alphabet of Tales (fifteenth century)
Speculum Sacerdotale (3 examples) (c. 1425)
Wynken de Worde's *Myracles of Our Blessed Lady* (1496)

Among the oldest miracles of the Virgin are legends in which Mary successfully opposes a Jew or a community of Jews, resulting in their punishment or conversion. The best-known representative of this genre, "The Jewish Boy," sometimes called "The Jew of Bourges," tells of a Jewish boy who takes communion with his Christian friends on Easter Sunday. When his father discovers this, he throws the child into a hot oven. The child's mother alarms the community which flocks to rescue the boy. When they open the oven, they find the boy unharmed, because, as he tells them, the Virgin protected him. The father is

[39] Statler, p. 898, n. 7.

[40] For a more detailed discussion of the Incarnational aspects of the lily miracles, see Laurel Broughton, "Ave Maria: The Incarnational Aesthetic and Mary Miracle Collections," *Studia Mystica* 20 (1999): 1–14.

thrown into the same oven and the rest of the Jewish community converts to Christianity. This tale contains many of the elements found in *The Prioress's Tale* including the attempt to murder the child for his act of faith, the protection of the Virgin and the punishment of the murderer.

While the optimal outcome of Mary's confrontations with the Jewish community in these legends is their conversion, the Jews in many of them suffer violent punishments. "Toledo," another widespread legend in this subgroup tells of Mary's voice heard during Mass on the Feast of the Assumption (August 15) accusing the Jews of continuing to torture her Son. When a search of the city reveals a group of Jews torturing and crucifying a wax image of Christ, they are condemned to death. Other tales in which Jews are punished include "The Jew of Toulouse," "Mary Image Insulted," and "Relentless Jew Killed by Lightning."

Miracles of the old vs. new dispensation type appear in the following Middle English collections:

South English Legendary (c. 1300)
Vernon MS (1370–1400)
Mirk's *Festial* (1415)
British Library Additional MS 39996 (early fifteenth century)
Gilte Legende (1438)
Brotherton Collection MS 501 (c. 1456)
Alphabet of Tales (fifteenth century)
Caxton's *Golden Legend* (1483)

Many Mary legends concern the death of children and occasionally their subsequent resuscitation, although these miracles don't sort themselves as clearly into a subgroup with similar plots or outcomes, as do the lily miracles or the old vs. new dispensation miracles. Statler points specifically to "Son restored to life."[41] In this tale, after a woman prays to Mary for a child, she bears a son who dies at an early age. The woman beseeches the Virgin to restore her son to life and the child awakes as if from a sleep. This legend is not as widespread as "The Child Slain by Jews," but it does appear in Latin and French versions as well as in the Middle English collection noted by Statler.[42]

The closest group of analogues to *The Prioress's Tale* combines elements from both the lily miracles and the old/new dispensation legends. One legend of this type, often called "The Child Slain by Jews," first appears in the early twelfth century.[43] In this tale the protagonist sings a hymn in praise of the Virgin. The hymn – usually *Gaude Maria*, occasionally *Alma redemptoris* or another hymn, in keeping with the lily miracle pattern described above – always commemorates the Incarnation. The child's singing arouses the anger of a Jew, or community of Jews, who kills the singer. However, the protagonist continues to sing after death and in many versions is restored to life.

[41] British Library Additional MS 39996, see Statler, p. 898 n. 7.

[42] Latin versions of this tale can be found in British Library Additional MS 18346 and John of Garland's *Stella Maris*. French versions appear in Jean Mielot, *Miracles de Nostre Dame* (Douce 374) and Bibliothèque Nationale MS 12593.

[43] See Brown, *Study*, p. 55.

New analogues

Since the publication of Brown's revised study in Bryan and Dempster, several analogues to *The Prioress's Tale* have come to light. Rather than place these within Brown's A, B, and C groups, which would entail renumbering several of the miracles, I have put them into a new category, designated "New Analogues" (**NA**). These are as follows:

NA1. Alfonso X, Cantiga no. 6. In 1996, Fernadez-Corugedo identified this cantiga as an analogue to *The Prioress's Tale.*[44] Following Mettmann, he dates the cantigas, written in Galician-Portuguese, between 1257 and 1283. This version clearly follows the pattern of analogues in Brown's Group A.[45] The young boy sings *Gaude Maria* to obtain alms for his widowed mother. A Jew takes offense and splits his head with an ax, burying him in the wine cellar. When the boy fails to return home, his anguished mother searches for him and prays to the Virgin to return him to her dead or alive. She then hears the boy singing *Gaude Maria.* The gathered crowd rescues the child from the grave and the Jew is burned to death.

NA2. Sidney Sussex MS 95.2.85. Although Brown provided a text for this version in his 1910 study, he rejected it as an analogue because the protagonist is a monk rather than a schoolboy.[46] For Brown this version represented a "willful perversion" of the tale; the importance of such "distortions" he quickly dismissed as "mere sporadic and abortive variants. They exerted no influence . . . in the development of the story, and consequently introduced no confusion into the type."[47] However, he included in his 1941 assessment an exemplum from Bromyard's *Summa praedicantium* (A10) in which the protagonist is a mature clerk. I therefore add Sidney Sussex 95.2.85 to this list of "new" analogues. This tale provides an interesting twist on the standard plot, for in it the monk who sings *Gaude Maria* requests an electuary (honey based drink) from a Jewish apothecary. After he is murdered, he is suspended in a "fovea" or pit, a word occasionally used as a euphemism for sewer or jakes.[48] Chaucer also uses "pit," which the Prioress redefines as "wardrobe":

> This cursed Jew hym hente, and heeld hym faste,
> And kitte his throte, and in a pit hym caste.
> I seye that in a wardrobe they hym threwe
> Where as thise Jewes purgen hire entraille. (VII, 570–3)

[44] Santiago Gonzalez Fernandez-Corugedo, "A Marian Miracle in England and Spain: Alfonso X's 'Cantigas de Santa Maria' no. 6 and Chaucer's 'The Prioress's Tale,' " in *Medieval Studies: Proceedings of the IIIrd International Conference of the Spanish Society for Medieval English Language and Literature*, ed. Luis A. Lazaro Lafuente, Jose Simon, and Ricardo J. Sola Buil (Madrid: Universidad de Alcala de Henares, 1996), pp. 151–75.

[45] Fernandez-Corugedo, p. 156–8.

[46] "In this version we are startled to find that the victim of the Jews is not a boy of tender years, but a monk. On this account I decided not to admit this version into my company of analogues." Brown, *Study,* p. 51.

[47] Brown, *Study*, p. 53.

[48] R. E. Latham, *Revised Medieval Latin Word-List from British and Irish Sources, with Supplement* (London: The British Academy, 1965; rpt. with supplement 1980).

Brown identifies the cloaca as a hallmark of Group C. Like the connections Statler points out between certain A and C versions, the pit in NA2 forms a bridge between Groups B and C. Brown himself called the Sidney Sussex version "a conglomerate, in which are recognizable elements which properly belong respectively to the A, B, and C Groups."[49] Perhaps he was reluctant to include this version in his list of analogues because it blurs the neat distinctions he tries to maintain between his three groups.

NA3. Balliol Oxford 228, fol. 290r. R. A. B. Mynors notes this version, which resembles analogues in Group C, was not printed by Brown in either his 1910 study or in his 1941 revision. It dates from the fourteenth or fifteenth century and is written in an English book hand, but there is no further information regarding the provenance of the manuscript, whose grammar suggests a corrupt source or an inept scribe.[50] This version of the miracle resembles other Group C type legends that focus on the miraculous introduction of the hymn *Salve sancta parens* into the funeral service, rather than the magical objects subgroup.[51] Although the manuscript containing NA3 may have been compiled during Chaucer's lifetime, given the tale's focus on the liturgical aspect of the story rather than on the magical object, if Chaucer knew it, it probably did not influence his telling of this legend.

Trinity College, Dublin, MS 167, Chapters 107 and 254. This manuscript contains two previously unidentified analogues to *The Prioress's Tale.* It dates from the late fourteenth to the early fifteenth century, possibly from Chaucer's lifetime but most likely too late to have been known to him. Ker places it at Fountains Abbey in the fifteenth century.[52] It is the second largest extant collection of miracles of the Virgin, containing approximately 475 legends, superseded only by the number in Sidney Sussex MS 95.

NA4. Trinity College, Dublin, 167, Chapter 107, fol. 36v, col. 1. This version bears a strong resemblance to C7 (Sidney Sussex MS 95) and therefore belongs in Brown's Group C because it includes both the cloaca and the funeral scene. In this version the young scholar sings *Gaude Maria* as he returns home from school every day. When he does not come home as usual, his parents and schoolmates search for him. On the third day they hear his voice singing and find his body, which they carry to the church of the Virgin. The cantor begins the mass for the dead but the murdered child begins to sing *Salve sancta parens*, the Mass of the Virgin. The third time this happens they continue *Salve sancta parens* to completion.

While in places the language of NA4 parallels that of C7, it is not a word-for-word copy. In many places Trinity Dublin 167 uses more simple and direct diction. The most significant variation in plot occurs at the end. In C7 the

[49] Brown, *Study*, p. 80.

[50] *Catalogue of the Manuscripts of Balliol College Oxford*, compiled by R. A. B. Mynors (Oxford, 1963), p. 234.

[51] See note 20 above.

[52] N. R. Ker, *Medieval Libraries of Great Britain* (London: Offices of the Royal Historical Society, 1964), p. 88; and Marvin L. Colker, *Trinity College Library Dublin: Descriptive Catalogue of the Mediaeval and Renaissance Latin Manuscripts* (Brookfield, VT: published for Trinity College Library, Dublin, by Scolar Press, 1991), pp. 284–304.

community buries the child's body, whereas NA4 ends with the singing of *Salve sancta parens*. The NA4 version could have been the source for C7, but probably not the reverse, given the number of embellishments found in the Sidney Sussex version. A more likely scenario is that they derived from the same source.

Given the dates of the manuscript, however, NA4 most likely could not have served as Chaucer's source for it lacks two of the distinguishing features of *The Prioress's Tale*: the antiphon *Alma redemptoris mater*, and what Brown calls "the magical object." Although this version of "The Child Slain by Jews" may tell us nothing new about *The Prioress's Tale*, it stands as yet another witness to the popularity of this particular legend, especially in England.

NA5. Trinity College, Dublin, MS 167, Chapter 254, fol. 69v, col. 2. Like NA4, this legend is closely related to the Sidney Sussex MS 95 version found in NA2, but while the plots are similar, the wording is not. NA2 is again much more elaborate in language and in embroidering the story line. However, major elements of the plot remain the same, including the "electuaria," the disposal of the body in a pit, the apothecary's repentance after hearing the body still singing, and the retrieval and placement of the body before the altar of the Virgin. NA2 also emphasizes the monk's taunting of the Jewish neighborhood, describes the electuary as necessary and the monk's ignorance of the Jew's evil intent, and most significantly, his revival through the intervention of the Virgin and the telling of his miraculous tale.These embellishments don't appear in the NA5 version. However, NA5 contains an elaboration, albeit enigmatic, of its own, as it ends with a short list of miracles "they" (the recently converted Jews?) found most pleasing to remember.

NA6. Trinity College, Dublin, MS 277. This manuscript contains a two-line summary of the "Child Slain by Jews" in support of singing *Alma redemptoris mater*. The Trinity College Dublin Library catalogue dates this manuscript to mid-fifteenth-century England, suggesting a connection with York, but giving no specific information on provenance.[53] Although short, this summary significantly assumes that its reader will be familiar with the story of the murdered scholar.

The closest analogue

Of all the known analogues to *The Prioress's Tale*, the version found in the Vernon MS "The Child Slain by Jews," (C5) remains the closest. Brown discounted the importance of this version, however, considering it to be a fluke among the "magical objects" subgroup of Group C, not only because the lily in the poem would be of doubtful value as an aid to singing, but also because this incident was transferred bodily from the a different Latin version. Moreover, he claims it could not be the immediate source of *The Prioress's Tale* because it lacks verbal similarities to Chaucer's work and "it is doubtful whether the Vernon manuscript was written early enough for Chaucer to have known it."[54]

[53] See *Trinity College Dublin Catalogue*, pp. 531–2.
[54] Bryan and Dempster, pp. 458, 461.

He argued instead that C1 is the only known analogue that could be considered Chaucer's direct source because it "not only supplies the main features of Chaucer's story but agrees closely in a number of the details." Among these agreements, he lists Chaucer's (1) mentioning of the clergeon singing his anthem through Jewry, (2) his dramatizing the resentment of the Jews at the song, (3) his reference to the Jews taking counsel together to kill the child, (4) his stress on the anxiety of the boy's mother, (5) his statement that the mother got news of the boy, and (6) his description of the mother's appeal to the Jews. At the same time, Brown points out a similar number of disagreements in details between Chaucer and C1 that are found in one or both of the versions C9 and C10. He is led therefore to posit the existence of an unknown, intermediate version which was the direct source of Chaucer's poem and these later Latin versions.[55]

Boyd, however, takes a different view: after analyzing all the analogues, she concludes that the lily miracle in C5 is the "closest analogue known," though not the direct source.[56] Brown's desire for a "realistic" magical object has perhaps blinded him to the contribution that the tale of "The Child Slain by Jews" makes to our understanding of *The Prioress's Tale.* In fact, his grounds for dismissal are the very reasons why we should consider, and even value, the Vernon miracle's relationship to lily miracles and to *The Prioress's Tale.* For if, as suggested above, the tale mixes elements of lily miracles with those of the old/new dispensation group, then the lily may indeed be the most appropriate object to appear in the child's throat, because it reveals the Incarnational piety that characterizes the lily genre, and helps us to find the answer to the riddle of the "greyn" by suggesting that we look for this magical object's Incarnational significance.

55 Bryan and Dempster, pp. 461–4.

56 Boyd, *Variorum*, p. 12; she discusses all the analogues known to Brown on pp. 11–14.

I

"A Lily Grows from the Mouth of a Clerk Buried outside the Churchyard"

(from British Library Additional MS 39996, fol. 80a, ed. Ruth Wilson Tryon, "Miracles of Our Lady in Middle English Verse," *PMLA* 38 [1923]: 365–7)

Anoþer miracle ʒe may here	
As hit was in alle manere	
A clerke served oure lady ay	
And for hir love wolde psalmes say	
So at þe laste fel a caas	
Uppon a felde he swolten* was	killed
Schrifte ne housel* hade he noght	confession nor communion
But oure lady was in his þoght	
Er þe soule passed away	
He saide Ave Maria aye	
When þat he was fonde dede	
Þai saide hit was þe beste rede*	course of action
Þere make a pitte and laye hym ynne	
He was not schryven* of his synne	confessed
When þai hade so saide	
Þe pitt was made þe clerk in laide	
Þai prayed to God Almyghty	
On his soule to have mercy	
And þen by þe þridde day	
Fel a grace ful verray	
Of his mouþe sprange a floure	
Whyte as lilie of coloure	
Þe spyre foure fote longe	
Þe leves a partie rede* amonge	partly red
Uppon þe leves proprely	
Was writen þus Ave Marie[1]	
As a man come on þe felde	
Upon þe biriynge* he behelde	grave
Þere as þe floure sprongen wes	
Þe . . . newe baren of gresse	
He ʒede to þe kirke þerone	
And tolde [hit to] þe persone*	parson
Þe persone þen and oþer mo	
lered* and lewed* also	learned/ ignorant
Wenten þider for to se	
Wheþer [hit] myght [so]þe be	
Þai seghen* verray in her sight	saw
Þe floure of oure lady myght	

1 26 **þus** MS is blurred here. Tryon doesn't explain brackets (lines 32, 36) or ellipsis (line 30).

To þe[2] bisshop þai ʒede to telle
A þe grace as hit bifelle
Þai prayed of leve to have
To take þe body of þe grave
Þe bisshop wiþ gode chere
ʒaf hem his powere*   permission, spiritual authority
Þai ʒede aʒayn hastily
And toke up þe body
And bare hit into holy place
And biried hit as worþi was
Wiþ ful grete solempnitie
For he was holy in alle degre

II

"How a Jew putte his sone in a brennyngge ovene"

(from Vernon MS, Oxford, Bodleian Library, MS Eng. poet. a. 1. Ed. Carl Horstmann, *Minor Poems of the Vernon Manuscript*, vol. 1, EETS OS 98 [London, 1892], pp. 149–54)

Lord, Makere of alle þing,
Almihti God in Maieste,
Þat ever was wiþ-oute biginning
And art and evermore schal be:
Graunte us boþe miht and space
So to serve þe to pay*,   please
þat we mowe þorw þi grace
Wone wiþ þe for evere and ay!
Of þe Miracles of ure ladi
We ouhten wel to haven in Muynde,
Þat writen beþ in soþ stori,
How helplich heo* is evere to Monkynde*.   she, mankind
Sum-tyme fel* in on Cite –   happened
Herkneþ wel, and ʒe may here –
As Jewes weren I-wont to be
Among þe cristen and wone I-fere*:   together
Þe Cristene woneden* in On halve   lived
Of þat Cite, as I þe hete*,   tell
And alle þe Jewes bi hem-selve
Were stihlet* to wone* in a strete.   compelled/ to live
Þe Cristene children in a Crofte*   field
I-mad hem hedden a wel feir plas.
Þer-Inne a Jewes child ful ofte
Wiþ hem to pleyen I-wont he was.

2 Tryon's edition misprints "be" for "þe."

Þe childes ffader nom non hede*,   took no heed
Ne to his child he sette non eiȝe,
Þerfore þe child boþe come and eode*   went
As ofte as evere hem luste* to pleye.   pleased
So ofte to pleyen hem fel i-fere
Þe Jewes son on heore pleyes coude*,   knew their games
Þat riht as on of hem he were;
Wiþ loue þerfore þei him alouwede.
At an Aster tyme* bi-tidde,   Easter time
Whon cristen made solempnite –
A Menskful* Munstre* was mad amidde,   beautiful/ church
As semed best, in þat Citéé:
Þerto þe cristene peple can drawe,
To here boþe Mateyns and eke Masse,
As falleþ by þe Cristene lawe
Boþe to more and eke to lasse;
Everi mon in his array,
Boþe housbonde and wyf also,
As falleþ wel for asterday
And al as cristene men schul do.
Þe children foleweden heore fadres in-fere,
As þei weore evere I-wont to do.
Þe Jewes child wiþ wel good chere
Wiþ hem wel fayn* was for to go.   eager
Wiþ-Inne þe chirche whon he was Riht,
Him þouhte he nas neuer er so glad
As he was of þat semeli* siht,   beautiful
Such on bi-fore never seȝe he had:
Boþe laumpes and tapers, brenninde briht,
And Auters curiousliche de-peynte*   skillfully decorated with color
Images ful deinteousliche* i-diht*,   elegantly/ made
And guld* of moni a good corseynt*.   gilt/ saint's shrine (body)
A comeli qween in O Chayer
fful semeli sat, al greiþed* in golde,   dressed
A blisful* Babe on Arm heo beer,   blessed
fful kyngly Corouned, as he scholde.
Of þat ladi þe child tok hede,
And of þat blisful Babe also,
Hou folk bi-foren heore bedes* bede*,   prayers/ prayed
As cristen Men beþ wont to do
Þe Jewes child evere tok such ȝeme*   heed
To alle sihtes þat he þer seiȝ,
Him þhouȝte hem alle so swete to seme
ffor Joye him þouȝte I-Ravessched neih.
Whon heiȝ-Masse of þat day was do,
Þe Prest bad alle men knelen a-doun:
Wiþ Confiteor, as falleþ þer-to,
He ȝiveþ hem Absolucioun;
He biddeþ hem More and lasse also,
To vengen heor saviour busken hem boun*.   made ready to take Communion

Þe Jewes child tok tente* þer-to,   attention
Among the cristene he dude* him doun.   knelt
Among þe pres þauh he were poselet*,   confused
He spared no-þing for no drede
Among þe cristene til he were hoselet*;   he should have taken Communion
Of such a child me tok non hede.
To ende whon alle þing was brouht
And everi cristene drouh him hom,
Þe Jeuh þorw toune his child haþ souht,
And saih wher he from chirche com.
He asked his sone wher he hedde ben,
Whil he hedde souht him al þat day.
Al riht as he hedde i-don and seon,
Þe child him rikenet* al þe a-Ray   told
His ffader þerfore wox wood-wroþ*,   angry to the point of madness
And seid anon: "þou getest þi mede!"
And to his hovene al hot he goþ,
Þat glemede as glowyng as a glede*.   live coal
In to þe hovene þe child he caste:
To askes* he þouȝte þe child to brenne;   ashes
And wiþ þe Mouþ-ston he stekeþ him faste,
And þouhte þat never couþ scholde him kenne*   acquaintance should find him out
Þerof whon his moder herde,
In a stude* þer as heo stood,   place
As ffrayed* in ffrenesye* heo ferde*,   frightened/ frenzy/ acted
ffor wo heo wente as waxen wood,
Ever hotyng out*, heo tar hire her*,   crying out,/ tore her hair
In everi stret of þat Citee,
Nou In, Nou out, so everiwher;
Men wondret on hire and hedde pite.
Boþe Meir and Bailifs of þe toun,
Whon þei herden of þat cri,
Þei aresten hire bi Resoun,
A[nd] maden chalange enchesun whi*   reason why
Heo criede so in þat Cite
And putte þe Peple in such affray,
To serwen in such solempnite,
and nomeliche on heore Aster-day.
As sone as heo mihte sece of wepe,
Þis was þe seyinge of hire sawe*:   story
"Sires, ȝe han þis Citéé to kepe,
As lordus han to lede þe lawe:
Allas, Allas, I am i-schent,
And help of ow me mot bi-hoven,
I prey ow of Just Juggement,
Mi cause I schal bi-fore ȝou proven:
Mi hosebonde haþ my child ibrent,
I-stopped him in a glouwyng hoven;
Goth seoþ, sires, bi on assent,

And I schal ȝive ow gold to gloven*."   gold to gloves (reward)
Boþe Meir and Baylifs wiþ folk i-fere
To þe Jewes hovene ben gon.
As sone as þei þider come were,
Þe Meir Comaundet: "doþ doun þe ston."
Þer everi Mon wel mihte i-seo
Þe hovene-Roof, þat was so round,
Hou hit was Blasyng al of bleo*   brilliance (Boyd: livid)
As glouwyng glos*, from Roof to grount   glass
Þe child sat þere boþe hol and sound,
Ne nouht I-harmet, hond ny her,
A-Midde þe gledes of þe ground,
As he seete in Cool Erber*.   grassy area
Þe childes Moder, whon heo þat seih,
Hire þouhte heo nas never er so glad;
In to þe hovene heo sturte* him neih,   jumped
Þus sone wiþ hire him out heo had.
And al þe peple þere present
Wondred on þat selly* siht,   blessed
And heried* god wiþ good entent,   praised
ffor Miracle is more þen Monnes miht.
Hou he haþ non harmes hent
Among þe brondes þat brenneþ so briht,
Þei asken of him bi on assent.
Þe child onswered a-non-riht:
"Of alle þe Murþes þat I have had
In al my lyf ȝit hider-to
Ne was I nevere of gleo so glad
As aftur I was In þe hovene I-do!
Boþe Brondes and Gledes, trustily,
Þat weren bi-neþen under my fote,
As feire floures, feiþfully,
As special spices me þhouȝte hem swote*;   sweet
Þe Blisful Qwen, þat Maiden Milde,
Þat sitteþ in Chirche in hih Chayer
Wiþ þat comely kyng, hire childe,
Þat Blisful Babe, on Barm heo ber,
ffrom alle þe schydes* þei cunne me schilde   firewood
ffrom gledes and brondes þat brende so cler,
ffrom all þe flaumes þat flowen so wilde,
Þat never non mihte neihȝe me ner*."   come near me
Boþe Men and wymmen, al þat þer wore,
Þei herieden God hertily,
Boþe luytel* and muche, lasse and more,   little
Of þis Miracle, witerly*.   without doubt
Þe Jewesse þorw hir sones sawe
Was convertet to crist a-non;
Þe Child tok hym to cristes lawe,
And alle þe Jewes everichon.
Þe Meir sat on þe* Jeuh him-selve,   sat in judgment upon
Fforte* beo Juge of his trespas;   for to

To siggen* þe soþe i-sworen were twelve,   to say
To ȝiven heore verdyt in þat caas.
    Þei counseiled i-vere* vppon þat caas,   together
And comen aȝeyn bi on assent;
Þe wordes of þat verdyt was:
"In þat same hovene he schulde be brent."
    Þus is endet þis stori
Of þe Miracle
I-writen a-bove.
God graunt us Joy
In hevene an hih,
Ihesu, for þi Moder love.   Amen.

III

Alfonso El Sabio, Songs of Holy Mary: Song 6 "How Holy Mary revived a little boy killed by a Jew for singing *Gaude Virgo Maria*"

(Alfonso El Sabio, *Songs of Holy Mary*, trans. Kathleen Kulp-Hill [Tempe: Arizona Center for Medieval and Renaissance Studies, 2000], pp. 11–12)

(1–11) She who is descended from the lineage of good King David is mindful, trust my word, of him who suffers evil for her sake.

Concerning this, the Sacred Writings, which neither lie nor err, tell us a great miracle performed in England by the Holy Virgin Mary, with whom the Jews have great quarrel because Jesus Christ, who reproves them, was born of her.

(12–16) There was in England a poor woman whose lawful husband had died. She had a son from him, who gave her great consolation. Therefore, she offered him to Holy Mary.

(17–21) The boy was wonderfully gifted and handsome and very quick at learning all he heard. Furthermore, he sang so well, sweetly and pleasantly, that he excelled everyone in his land and beyond.

III

(NA1) **Alfonso X, El Sabio, Cantiga 6: "Esta é como Santa Maria ressucitou ao menỹo que o judeu matara porque cantava *Gaude Virgo Maria*"** [1]

(from *Cantigas de Santa Maria*, ed. Walter Mettmann, vol. 1 [Madrid: Clasicos Castalia, 1986], pp. 72–5)

A que do bon rey Davi
de seu linnage decende,
nenbra-lle, creed' a mi,
de quen por ela mal prende.

Porend' a Sant' Escritura, | que non mente nen erra,
nos conta un gran miragre | que fez en Engraterra
a Virgen Santa Maria, | con que judeus an gran guerra
porque naceu Jesu-Cristo | dela, que os reprende.
A que do bon rei Davi . . .

Avia en Engraterra | hũa moller menguada,
a que morreu o marido, | con que era casada;
mas ficou-lle del un fillo, | con que foi mui confortada,
e log' a Santa Maria | o offereu porende.
A que do bon rei Davi . . .

O menỹ' a maravilla | er' apost' e fremoso,
e d' aprender quant' oya | era muit' engẽoso;
e demais tan ben cantava, | tan manss' e tan saboroso,
que vencia quantos eran | en ssa terr' e alende.
A que do bon rei Davi . . .

[1] I have followed Mettmann's line numbering, which includes the title as part of the text.

(22–6) The song the boy sang best, and which most pleased whoever heard it, was the song which says *Gaude Virgo Maria* and then berates the Jew, who takes great exception to it.

(27–31) The boy sang this song so well that anyone who heard it at once seized upon him and disputed with the others to take the child with him, saying: "I shall give you supper or a nice tidbit."

(32–6) Because of this, the boy said: "Mother, in all frankness, I advise you that from now on you cease to beg, for Holy Mary gives you all that you wish through me. Let her provide, for she is very generous."

(37-41) Then, on a feast day when many Jews and Christians were gathered together and were playing dice, the boy sang. All were very pleased, except a Jew, who hated him for it.

(42–6) The Jew heeded well what the boy was singing, and when the people went away, he took him to his house. He struck him such a blow with an ax that he split open his head down to his teeth, just as one splits wood.

(47–51) After the boy was dead, the Jew quickly buried him in the wine cellar where he kept his casks. He caused the boy's mother to spend a very bad night, poor woman, for she went about seeking her son hither and yon.

(52–6) The unfortunate woman, weeping piteously, asked all she saw if they had seen him. A man told her: "I saw him when a Jew who sells used clothing took him away with him."

(57–61) When the people heard this, they ran to the place. The mother of the boy was wailing and crying: "Tell me what you are doing, my son. Can you not hear me that you do not come to your mother, who fears that you are dead?"

E o cantar que o moço | mais aposto dizia,
e de que sse mais pagava | quen quer que o oya,
era un cantar en que diz: "Gaude Virgo Maria";
e pois diz mal do judeu, que sobr' aquesto contende.
A que do bon rei Davi . . .

Este cantar o menỹo | atan ben o cantava,
que qualquer que o oya | tan toste o fillava
e por leva-lo consigo | conos outros barallava,
dizend': "Eu dar-ll-ei que jante, | e demais que merende."
A que do bon rei Davi . . .

Sobr' esto diss' o menỹo: | "Madre, fe que devedes,
de oge mais vos consello | que o pedir leixedes,
pois vos dá Santa Maria | por mi quanto vos queredes,
e leixad' ela despenda, | pois que tan ben despende."
A que do bon rei Davi . . .

Depois, un dia de festa, | en que foron juntados
muitos judeus crischãos | e que jogavan dados,
enton cantou o menỹo; | e foron en mui pagados
todos, senon en judeu que lle quis gran male des ende.
A que do bon rei Davi . . .

No que o moço cantava | o judeu meteu mentes,
e levó-o a ssa casa, | pois se foron as gentes;
e deu-lle tal dũa acha, | que ben atro enos dentes
o fendeu bẽes assi, ben como quen lenna fende.
A que do bon rei Davi . . .

Poi-lo menỹo fo morto, | o judeu muit' agỹa
soterró-o na adega, | u sas cubas tĩya;
mas deu mui maa noite | a sa madre, a mesqỹa,
que o andava buscando | e dalend' e daquende.
A que do bon rei Davi . . .

A coitada por seu fillo | ya muito chorando
e a quantos ela viia, | a todos preguntando
se o viran; o un ome | lle diss'; "Eu o vi ben quando
un judeu o levou sigo, | que os panos revende."
A que do bon rei Davi . . .

As gentes, quand' est' oiron, | foron alá correndo,
e a madre do menỹo | braadand' e dizendo:
"Di-mi que fazes, meu fillo, | ou que estás atendendo,
que non vees a ta madre, | que ja sa mort' entende."
A que do bon rei Davi . . .

(62–6) Then she said, “Holy Mary, My Lady, you who are haven for the unfortunate, give me my son dead or alive, however it may be. If not, you will do me great wrong, and I shall say that he who trusts in your benevolence is much mistaken.”

(67–71) Then the boy, from the grave in which the Jew had buried him, began to sing “Gaude Maria” in a loud, clear voice. Never had he sung so well for the pleasure of the glorious one who defends her faithful.

(72–6) Then all the people who were assembled there went running to the house whence issued the voice. They took the boy, alive and well, from the place the Jew had put him. They all said: “What a fragrance surrounds him!”

(77–81) The mother then asked her son what he had felt, and he told her how the Jew had struck him, and he had gotten very sleepy and afterward went fast asleep until Holy Mary said to him: “Arise from there,

(82–6) “for you have slept a long time. You have become a sleepyhead and have forgotten the song of mine you used to sing. But arise and sing it at once, better than you have ever sung, so that no one can find fault with it.”

(87–91) When the boy said that, all who were there went at once to the Jews and killed them all. The one who had struck the boy they burned in the fire, saying: “He who commits such a deed reaps such a reward.”

Pois diss': "Ai, Santa Maria, | Sennor, tu que es porto
u ar[r]iban os coytados, | dá-me meu fillo morto
ou viv' ou qual quer que seja; | se non, farás-me gran torto,
e direi que mui mal erra | queno teu ben atende."
A que do bon rei Davi . . .

O menỹ' enton da fossa, | en que o soterrara
o judeu, começou logo | en voz alta e clara
a cantar "Gaude Maria," | que nunca tan ben cantara,
por prazer da Gloriosa, | que seus servos defende.
A que do bon rei Davi . . .

Enton tod' aquela gente | que y juntada era
foron correnď' aa casa | ond' essa voz vẽera,
e sacaron o menỹo | du o judeu o posera
viv' e são, e dizian | todos: "Que ben recende!"
A que do bon rei Davi . . .

A madr' enton a seu fillo | preguntou que sentira;
e ele lle contou como | o judeu o ferira,
e que ouvera tal sono | que sempre depois dormira,
ata que Santa Maria | lle disse: "Leva-t' ende;
A que do bon rei Davi . . .

Ca muito per ás dormido, | dormidor te feziste,
e o cantar que dizias | meu ja escaeciste;
mas leva-t' e di-o logo | mellor que nunca dissiste,
assi que achar non possa | null' om' y que emende."
A que do bon rei Davi . . .

Quand' esto diss' o menỹo, | quantos s'y acertaron
aos judeus foron logo | e todo-los mataron;
e aquel que o ferira | eno fogo o queimaron,
dizendo : "Quen faz tal feito, | desta guisa o rende."
A que do bon rei Davi . . .

IV

"Concerning a monk, slain by a Jew for singing *Gaude Maria* but raised from death by Christ's blessed mother"

There was in a certain monastery a monk devoted to the blessed Virgin Mary. In her honor on every night he was accustomed to sing the responsory *Gaude Maria* in a sonorous voice. And because the cell of the foresaid monk bordered on the city, a certain Jew living nearby was accustomed to hear him singing it. Therefore, being astonished that the monk so devoutly sang the said responsory, he inquired of his neighbor what was meant by "Erubescat judeus infelix" (Let the unhappy Jew blush). He was answered that every night that monk did not cease to abuse the Jews. Thus, vehemently angered within himself by that phrase, he thought to himself how he would kill the monk or cause him some bodily harm. At last, at a certain late hour the monk, ignorant of the intended malice, entered the Jew's apothecary in order to procure necessary electuaries*. And when, by the Jew's command, he went further in (to the shop) for the sake of examining better goods, the Jew, thinking the time opportune for carrying out his villainy, attacked the monk, and threw him, slaughtered, in a certain pit, and covered him with stones and other household filth. Then the next night he heard the monk singing the same responsory in his customary manner. Therefore coming to the pit and finding his dead body, he marvelled greatly. And when he had heard this many times, fearing lest he be discovered, he went to the abbot of the place, begging indulgence for what he had done against him, promising he would do whatever he ordered him. The abbot, truly ignorant of what he had done, humbly pardoned him. Then the Jew, having received forgiveness, indicated to the abbot, in sequence, the manner of the deed. Then, with the villainy of the Jew discovered, they raised the body of the dead monk from the pit, and placed it before the altar of blessed Mary. And when there was weeping and great confusion in church for the sudden death of such a great brother, the man revived and rising he stood on his own feet and told everyone how the mother of Christ had obtained his life from her son. And thus, the Jew seeing what she had done, believing, hastened to be baptized. But also many other unbelievers, because of this miracle, accepted the catholic faith and baptism with other sacraments of the church, to the praise and glory of the name of Christ, who wants all people to be saved and to come to the acknowledgement of his name.

* **electuaries:** : medicinal mixtures made with a honey or syrup base

IV

(NA2) "**De quodam monacho cantante Responsorium *Gaude Maria* a judeo jugulato set per Beatam Christi matrem a morte suscitato**"

(from Sidney Sussex College Cambridge MS 95.2.85, fols 87v–88)

Erat in quodam monasterio monachus beate virgini marie devotus. In cuius honore qualibet nocte responsorium *Gaude Maria* solebat voce sonora cantare. Et quia cella predicti monachi contigua erat civitati quidam judeus habitacione vicinus hoc ipsum cantantem audire consuevit. Admirans itaque quod monachus tam devote predictum responsorium cantaret sciscitabatur a proximo suo quid esset dictu Erubescat judeus infelix. Responsum est ei quod qualibet nocte monachus ille judeis maledicere non cessabat. Unde occasione illius clausuli vehementer stomachatus intra se meditabatur. Qualiter predictum monachum interficeret, vel aliquam corporis ei molestiam. Quodam tandem sero monachus concepte malicie ignarus judei apothecam intravit. ut electuaria necessaria compararet. Et dum profundius meliora scrutandi gracia ductu judei descendisset. judeus malicie complende tempus oportunum existimans irruit in monachum trucidatum que in quandam foveam projecit. et lapidibus ac aliis domus sordibus occuluit. Nocte igitur sequente monachum ipsum audivit. more solito idem responsorium cantantem. Veniens itaque ad foveam invento eius corpore defuncto mirabatur valde. Et cum hoc multociens audisset, timens ne deprehenderetur, venit ad abbatem loci petens ab eo indulgenciam de hoc quod fecerat contra eum promittens se facturum quidquid illi preciperet. Abbas vero quod fecerat ignorans humiliter condonavit ei. Tunc judeus percepta venia indicavit abbati per ordinem modum facti. Tunc inventa judei nequicia monachi corpus defuncti de puteo sublevantes ante altare Beate Marie posuerunt. Cumque fletus et confusio magna fieret in ecclesia pro tanti fratris morte subita, revixit homo et surgens stetit super pedes suos, et narravit omnibus quomodo Mater Christi vitam a filio sibi impetraverat. Videns itaque judeus quod factum fuerat ad baptismum credens convolavit. Sed et multi alii infideles huius miraculi occasione fidem catholicam et baptismum cum aliis ecclesie sacramentis susceperunt. ad laudem et gloriam nominis christi qui vult omnes homines salvos fieri et ad agnicionem sui nominis venire.

V

"About a certain boy accustomed to sing *Alma Redemptoris Mater*"

It happened that a certain boy on his walk to school and on his way home out of habit would sing the antiphon *Alma redemptoris mater*. The Jews of that city, hearing that he sang so joyously about the most sweet mother Mary, were indignant. Day and night, they lay in wait for the boy, [to see] if by any means they could or would dare to kill him. They set an ambush for him on a certain day when on his way from school to lunch he would return by their doors. Just as he was accustomed, he sang with a clear voice. Thus those malignant Jews, seeing no one in the street, by fraud and deception called the boy into their house and immediately killed him and discarded his body in the privy. His mother, however, waiting for him through the day and night, sought her son and greatly suffered. And coming to the school the next day she asked the master if he knew where her son was. He responded, "I did not see him after he went to lunch yesterday with his friends." But the woman, groaning, with his friends sought her son through the whole town. When he was not found, she turned down through the Jewish quarter toward her house. The mother heard, along with other Christians, her son singing *Alma redemptoris mater*, just as he was accustomed. And following the boy's voice, when they came to the house of the Jew who killed him, they asked him whether he would restore the boy whom they heard singing. But he, not hearing that voice, said, "Go and search for him." Moreover, those Christians with the voice as a guide, coming to the privy where the boy was lying, drew him from the privy and carried him to the church. When, however, the cantor began the mass for the dead, *Requiem eternam*, the boy with clear voice began *Salve sancte parens*. But the cantor began *Requiem eternam* a second time; the boy's voice hindered it, beginning *Salve sancte parens*. Hearing this, they celebrated the service of the glorious Virgin Mary while he rested in peace helped by the sweetest Mary.

VI

"A boy singing *Gaude Maria* is killed for whom *Salve sancta parens* is sung from heaven"

A certain schoolboy, still a child, well educated in chant, had a sweet and melodious voice. Every day at vespers when he returned home from school, he sang in a high voice the responsory of holy Virgin Mary, namely *Gaude Maria*, in honor of blessed Mary, God's mother. The boy's singing voice exhilarated all. But the perfidious Jews, incited by envy, attempting to suppress the praises of blessed Mary, one day apprehended and suddenly killed the boy as he passed singing by their door at vespers. In reproach to the blessed Virgin they suspended his body in a privy. The

V

(NA3) "**De quodam puero qui solebat psallere *Alma Redemptoris Mater***"

(from Balliol College MS 228, fol. 290r, col. 1)

Factum est ut quidam puer ex consuetudine versus scolas et ingressu versus domum antiphone scilicet *Alma redemptoris mater* decantaret. Judei civitatis audientes quia de dulcissima matre maria adeo gratanter cantaret indignati sunt; die nocteque insidiantes puero si quo modo possent et audissent ipsum occidere; et ponentes ei insideas quadam die cum de scolis ad prandium rediret per hostia sua sicut solebat clara voce cecinit. At illi maligni judei neminem videntes in vico per fraudes et decepciones vocaverunt puerum in domum suam et statim occiderunt eum et in cloacam corpus eius posuerunt. Expectans autem mater eius per diem et noctem filium suum quesivit et multum condoluit et veniens ad scolas in crastino quesivit a magistro si sciret ubi filius suus esset, qui respondit postquam ad prandium suum heri cum sociis suis ivit non vidi illum. At illa ingemiscens cum amicis suis per totam villam filium quesivit quo non invento cum declinavit per Judaismum versus domum suam audivit mater cum ceteris christianis filium suum cantantem *Alma redemptoris mater* sicut solebat et vocem pueri sequentes cum pervenerunt ad domum judei qui eum occidit interrogaverunt eum ut puerum quem cantantem audierunt redderet At ille vocem non audiens dixit Ite et querite illum. Illi autem christiani ad cloacam voce duce venientes ubi iacebat puer extraxerunt eum a cloaca et ad ecclesiam deferentes. Cum autem missam defunctorum *Requiem eternam* [cantor] inciperet. Audita est vox pueri clara voce incipiens *Salve sancta parens* At cantor incipiens bis *Requiem* [*eternam*] vox pueri obvians ei incipiens *Salve sancta parens*. Hoc ipsi audientes servicium gloriose virginis marie celebrantes ipso in pace quiescente adiuvante dulcissima maria.

20 **cantor** canter MS
21 **eternam** eterrnam MS

VI

(NA4) "***Gaude Maria* reponsorium puer cantans occiditur pro quo *Salve sancta parens* celitus decantatur**"

(from Trinity College Dublin MS 167, chapter 107, fol. 36v, col. 1)

Scolaris quidam adhuc parvulus in cantu satis edoctus vocem habens dulcem et canoram singulis diebus quando de scolis ad vesperum reverteretur domum Responsorium de sancta maria virgine scilicet *Gaude Maria* in honore beate marie dei genitricis ex celsa voce decantavit ita quod vox pueri cantantis omnes exhilaravit. Sed perfidi judei laudes beate marie supprimere conantes invidia stimulante puerum cantantem quadam die ad vesperum et per ostium eorum transeuntem apprehenderunt et subito interfecerunt: ac in [opprobrium]

boy, not having returned home in his customary manner, was sought among relatives and friends by his parents and schoolmates for two days and was not discovered. However, on the third day, at vespers they heard the voice of someone singing the same responsory which the boy used to sing and it seemed that the boy himself was singing in his customary way. Moreover, this voice did not cease to sing outside the Jews' house where the boy was hanging, until Christians, rushing in through the Jews' closed door, reached the body. Now the body was carried with great honor to the church of the blessed Virgin. On the next day, with all the students of the city gathered then at church so that they might be present at the mass to be celebrated reverently for him, the cantor began *Requiem eternam* as is the custom for the dead. Suddenly a clear voice, as if from the boy himself, was heard from the coffin, beginning the office of the holy Virgin, *Salve sancta parens.* Soon the stupefied cantor fell silent and the boyish voice heard earlier was silent. Again the cantor began *Requiem*; that most sweet voice solemnly resounded in all ears, *Salve sancte parens.* Similarly, a third time. Then, by God's inspiration and persuaded by the advice of the scholars, the cantors proceeded with the whole office of the blessed Virgin and mass.

VIIa

"A monk singing the reponsory *Gaude Maria*, killed by a Jew"

A certain monk used to sing the responsorium *Gaude Maria* each night. And because he uttered the verse "Let the unhappy Jew blush," a certain Jew who lived near the monastery was most violently angry with him. When he asked what "Let the unhappy Jew blush" meant, the answer was that each night the monk would not cease to revile the Jews. However, on a certain night the monk entered the Jew's apothecary shop and when he had gone far within for the sake of certain electuaries, the Jew, having flung him in a certain pit, stoned him to death with large stones. However, hearing him singing again the same responsory of God's mother and coming to the pit, the Jew was amazed to find the dead body. And when he heard this many times he came to the abbot begging his pardon for what he had done against him. When he promised he would do whatever the abbot would command, he received forgiveness because the abbot did not know what he had done. Then, the villainy of the Jew having been discovered, the monks put the body of the dead man before the altar of blessed Mary. And when the weeping and confusion in the church was great, the mother of God obtained from her Son the resuscitation of the monk. Henceforth many infidels were converted to the catholic faith and received baptism with other sacraments of the church. The miracles of the blessed Virgin they considered most pleasing to remember were about the young Cistercian monk who was carried off, and about the choirs of the blessed Virgin shown to him, and about the apple thrown back and forth between virgins, and that the blessed Virgin told St Margaret that she would put it in its place.[1]

[1] The miracles listed in this enigmatic passage still need to be identified.

beate virginis eius corpus in cloaca suspenderunt. Puer vero more solito [non] domum non regressus inter cognatos et notos a parentibus et conscolaribus biduo quesitus est nec inventus Tercia autem die ad vesperum audita enim ab eis vox cantantis idem responsorium quod puer cantare consueverat et videbatur ipse puer more solito decantans. Et hec vox extra in domo judeorum ubi puer suspendebatur non destitit cantare: donec christiani per judeorum ostium preclusum irruentes ad corpus pervenerunt. Quod quidem corpus cum ingenti honore ad ecclesiam beate virginis allatum est. Convenientibus igitur in crastino omnibus scolaribus urbis ad ecclesiam ut pro eo misse celebrande reverenter interessent: incepit cantor *Requiem eternam* ut mos est pro defunctis. Statim que audita in loculo est veluti ab ipso puero vox clara: inchoans officium de sancta virgine. *Salve sancta parens.* Mox que cantor stupefactus subticuit et vox puerilis prius audita siluit Iterum cantore incipiente. Requiem personuit in auribus omnium vox illa [dulcissima] et sollempniter. *Salve sancta parens.* Similiter et tercio. Cantores igitur inspirante deo et persuadente discipulorum consilio: totum officium de beata virgine et missam prosecuti sunt.

7 **opprobrium** oppribrium MS
8 **non** *expunged in MS*
21 **dulcissima** ducissima MS

VIIa

(NA5) "**Monachus cantans responsorium *Gaude Maria***"

(from Trinity College Dublin MS 167, capitulum 254, fol. 69v, col. 2)

Monachus quidam cantabat responsorium *Gaude Maria* qualibet nocte. Et/(fol.70r) quia dicebat in versu erubescat judeus infelix: quidam judeus qui prope monasterium morabatur erat iratus vehementissime contra eum. Ipso enim querente quid esset dictu. Erubescat judeus infelix responsum fuit ei quod qualibet nocte monachus ille judeis maledicere non cessaret. Quadam autem nocte monachus judei apothecam introivit et dum propter electuria quedam profundius descendisset judeus projectum illum in quamdam foveam magnis lapidibus trucidavit. Iterum autem judeus audiens ipsum cantare idem responsorium matris dei et veniens ad foveam invento eius corpore defuncto mirabatur. Et cum hoc multociens audisset venit ad abbatem petens ab eo indulgenciam de hoc quod fecerat contra eum. Cumque promisisset se facturum quidquid abbas preciperet veniam optinuit quia abbas hoc quod fecerat ignorabat. Tunc inventa judei nequicia monachi corpus defuncti ante altare beate Marie posuerunt. Cumque in ecclesia fletus et confusio magna esset mater dei resuscitationem monachi a filio impetravit. Et postmodum multi infideles conversi fuerunt ad fidem catholicam et baptismum cum aliis sacramentis ecclesie susceperunt et miracula beate viriginis gratissima habuerunt memorandum de monacho adolescente cisterciensis ordinis rapto et de choreis beate virginis sibi ostensis et de pomo inter virgines hinc inde iactato et quod beata virgo dixit sancte margarete ut ipsum reponeret loco suo.

VIIb

[*Alma Redemptoris Mater*]

Moreover, a boy killed by Jews sang this after death, *Alma redemptoris mater* . . .

VIII

[Boy killed for singing *Alma Redemptoris Mater*]

(1–7) There was across the sea, in the land of the Albigensians in a town called Carcassone, a rich man, a burgess or a knight I know not, supporting a certain poor old woman who, as long as she could freely use her feet to walk, was accustomed to come to his table and be refreshed. Later, indeed, she was not able to approach the table of the rich man herself, from too great a weakness of body and age; she arranged to have the provisions designated for her to be carried from the house of that rich man by her own small son.
(8–16) Indeed, the boy was a clerk who had a clear voice. In going, moreover, and returning he always used to sing this antiphon in the hearing of all: *Alma redemptoris mater*, etc., and when he would finish it, he would start again. The course and direction of the route was such that from the small house of his mother to the house of the rich man it was necessary to go through the quarter where Jews were living. When every day he passed by the Jews singing the antiphon, they disputed with each other, saying, "That boy who frequently travels through us so often repeats that song in reproach of us and derision of our people," and they blasphemed that revered and sweet name of the one who brought forth salvation for the world.
(17–23) The impiety of the Jews grew. The boy, truly ignorant of their evil thoughts, did not cease from his accustomed daily singing. The impious ones were considering, therefore, in what way they could kill the boy. Having formed a plan,

3 Literally, "to use the paces of her feet" ("quamdiu gressibus pedum uti").

VIIb

(NA6) [*Alma Redemptoris Mater*]

(from Trinity College, Dublin, MS 277, p. 118)

Hanc autem puer a judeis occisus post mortem decantabat *Alma redemptoris mater que per via celi porta manes et stella maris et cetera.*

TEXTS FROM CARLETON BROWN'S GROUP C[1]

VIII

(C1) [Boy killed for singing *Alma Redemptoris Mater*]

(from Corpus Christi College, Oxford, MS 32, Art. 19 [thirteenth century])

(fol.92) Fuit in transmarinis homo dives, burgensis an miles fuerit nescio, in terra Albigeorum in villa que dicitur Carcassum, habens vetulam quandam pauperem qui quamdiu gressibus pedum libere uti potuit ad mensam ipsius venire et refici consuevit. Postquam vero ex nimia corporis et etatis inbecillitate ad mensam divitis accedere per se non potuit, per proprium filium suum parvulum fecit sibi constitutam annonam de domo eiusdem divitis deferri.

Puer vero clericus erat habens vocem claram. In eundo autem et redeundo semper in omnium audiencia cantabat hanc antiphonam: *Alma redemptoris mater* etc. et cum finisset eam reincipiebat. Ratio vero et dispositio ita se habebat itineris ut a domuncula matris sue ad domum divitis per vicum ubi judei manebant transire necesse esset. Qui dum singulis diebus per judeos transiret antiphonam cantando, litigabant judei ad invicem dicentes, "Garcio iste qui frequenter transit per nos in obprobrium nostrum et derisum generis nostri tociens replicat canticum illud," et blasphemabant reverendum illud et suave nomen illius qui sal[u]tem edidit mundo.

Crescebat impietas judeorum. Puer vero malignarum cogitationum ignarus cotidie a solito cantu non cessabat. Cogitabant ergo impii quomodo puerum

[1] I have reprinted here the texts of Carleton Brown's Group C (with the exception of C6: *The Prioress's Tale*), which he identifies as the closest analogues to *The Prioress's Tale*, and his explanatory notes. A. G. Rigg, in his translation of C10, notes several possible misreadings in Brown's transcription. (See *The Canterbury Tales: Nine Tales and the General Prologue,* ed. V. A. Kolve and Glending Olson [New York and London: Norton, 1989], p. 418n.) Because of this, I have collated Brown's transcriptions against the originals (with the exception of C5, reprinted from EETS OS 98, and C9), and noted possible alternative readings where appropriate. The only other changes to these texts as they appear in Bryan and Dempster are the conversions u/v and i/j, and the expansion of & to et.

they designated two who would seize the boy as he passed by. He was seized and thus led into an interior chamber, and when the Jews had gathered around him, they began, with very great cruelty to attack him. Cutting the belly of the innocent boy in the shape of a cross, they drew out his innards and, together with the body, they threw them into the privy.

(24–30) Although these things had thus happened, the grace of God was not absent in such a cruel deed, for when the boy was dragged inside, when he was cut, when he was flung away, either he himself or the angel who had been appointed to him by the Lord did not stop singing. But during all that the impious ones impiously did to him, the same voice, the same song was heard by Christians who were passing through that place, although not one of them was aware that the boy was being treated in this manner. The Jews, indeed, did not hear the voice from within.

(31–41) When, however, at the appointed hour the boy did not return to his mother, she began to be concerned for her son. However, thinking by chance that he was sent somewhere by the man from whom she received her daily ration, she held out until morning. When the boy did not return the following day, the mother, impatient of delay, began to walk, leaning on a walking stick. Grief moreover, and sadness for her son were restoring to her the strength which age had consumed. She was going, therefore, seeking her son, and she was told that on the previous day at that hour he had entered into the house of that Jew. Coming, therefore, to the door, she pounded, shouting "Return to me my son whom I hear singing within." Indeed, as soon as she approached that area she heard a voice which she knew to be her son's. But those who were inside, thinking they could lie hidden, said she was delirious and, shamefully pushing her back, they affirmed they knew absolutely nothing about the son whom she was seeking.

(42–6) Indeed, the distressed woman went to the mayor of the town. That man, having sent subordinates, commanded that this was to be investigated. They, entering the house, immediately heard the voice of the boy, but also many Christians rushing up heard the voice, and searching they found the place and they drew the body out. And in a marvelous way, all Christians who were present heard the melody and song; indeed the Jews alone heard nothing from that place.

(47–50) Therefore, with great honor and exultation of the clergy as well as the people, the body of the innocent was carried to the church and reverently buried. Nor did that marvelous voice cease to the praise and glory of the glorious Virgin Mary until the body was buried.

47 Literally, "dancing in the street" ("tripudio").

interficerent. Initoque consilio constituerunt duos qui puerum pertranseuntem raperent. Raptus itaque ductus est in interius cubiculum, congregatisque circa eum judeis nimia crudelitate ceperunt grassari in eum. Nam ventrem innocentis pueri scindentes in modum crucis, interiora eius extraxerunt et ea simul cum corpore in cloacam projecerunt.

Cum hec ita fierent, in tam crudeli facto gracia dei non defuit, nam cum intrinsecus puer traheretur, cum secaretur, cum proiceretur, a cantu tamen non destitit, vel ipse vel angelus cui a domino jussum est. Sed inter omnia que circa eum impie impii operati sunt eadem vox, idem cantus audiebatur a christianis (fol.92v) qui per locum illum transibant, licet nullus eorum adverteret quod hoc modo puer tractaretur. Judei vero vocem penitus non audiebant.

Cum autem ad horam constitutam puer non rediret ad matrem, cepit esse sollicita pro filio. Tamen estimans forte quod aliquorsum ab eo mitteretur a quo annonam cotidianam suscipiebat, sustinuit usque mane. Puero vero non revertente sequenti die, mater impaciens more baculo innixa cepit ire. Dolor autem et tristicia filii reparabant ei vires quas etas consumpserat. Ibat igitur filium querens, dictumque est ei quia heri hora illa intravit in domum illius judei. Veniens igitur ad ostium, pulsavit clamans, "Reddite mihi filium meum quem intrinsecus audio cantantem." Statim enim ex quo accessit ad partem illam audivit notam sibi filii sui vocem. Hii vero qui intrinsecus erant, putantes se posse latere, delirare eam dicebant, et turpiter eam repellentes, affirmabant se omnino de filio quem querebat nihil scire.

Illa vero angustiata majorem ville adiit. Ille missis ministris jussit inquiri quid hoc esset. Qui intrantes domum statim vocem audierunt pueri, sed et multi christianorum concurrentes audierunt vocem, requirentesque invenerunt locum, corpus extraxerunt. Miroque modo omnes christiani qui aderant audierunt melodiam et cantum, soli vero judei nichil inde audierunt.

Cum magno igitur honore et tripudio tam cleri quam populi ad ecclesiam corpus innocentis est delatum et venerabiliter sepultum. Nec cessavit vox illa admirabilis donec corpus sepeliretur ad laudem et gloriam gloriose virginis Marie.

IX

(C2) *Alma Redemptoris Mater*

(from British Library Additional MS 46919, fol. 205v [formerly Phillipps MS 8336], early fourteenth century)[1]

Holy moder, þat bere cryst	
Buggere* of monkunde,	redeemer
Þou art ʒat* of hevene blisse	gate
Þat prest wey ʒyfst* and bunde*.	quick, handily
Þou sterre of se rer* op þe volk	rise
Þat rysing haveht in munde.	
In þe þou bere þyn holy vader,	
Þat mayden were after and raþer*,	before
Whar-of* so wondreth kunde*.	at which / nature
Of gabrieles mouþe/	
þou vonge* þylke 'Aue';	received
Lesne ous of sunne nouþe*,	Release us of sin now
so woe bisecheth þe. AMEN.	

Hic nota de filio vidue qui semper eundo ad scolas et redeundo de scolis consueuit istam antiphonam decantare; propter quod a iudeis per quos transitum fecit "puer marie" dicebatur; quem ipsi tandem occiderunt et in cloacam projecerunt, qui tamen a cantu non cessauit; etc.

[Here note about the son of a widow who always going to school, and returning from school, was accustomed to sing this antiphon; on this account he was called "boy of Mary" by the Jews by whom he passed. At last they killed him and threw him into a privy, but he ceased not from singing.]

1 As Brown points out (Bryan and Dempster, p. 468), notes in this manuscript attribute this Middle English translation and sixteen other hymns to Fr. William Herebert, a Franciscan who died in 1333 and was buried in the friars' convent at Hereford.

X

[Boy sings *Ave regina* after his head is cut off]

(1–9) There was a certain Christian boy living in a city where there were many Jews. He always sang the antiphon, namely *Ave regina* in front of the Jews and their houses. Wherefore the Jews much envied him and finally by deceit and small gifts drew him into their house and in the most interior room they cut off his head. After this, truly, the boy's mother came, seeking her son, always hearing the son's voice singing *Ave regina* but she was not able to find him. Thereupon, indeed, she went to the magistrates of the city, telling them how the Jews held her son in prison and entreated that they might come with her and liberate her son.

(10–15) Those coming all heard the voice and entering and searching found the boy dead and carried him to church for burying. When they had to sing a mass for him, they did not know whether they ought to sing the mass for the dead, that is *Requiem eternam*, or of holy Mary, that is *Salve*. And while they were considering these things, the dead boy rose and began with loud voice *Salve sancta parens*, etc.

XI

[Boy killed for singing *Sancta Maria*]

Also a certain boy daily returning from school by the door of a certain Jew was accustomed to sing *Sancta maria* etc. about the blessed Virgin. Seizing him, a Jew threw him into a privy near Toledo and how he began *Salve sancta parens* when the priest had begun the requiem, and how after *Agnus dei* he came to life again.

X

(C3) **[Boy sings *Ave regina* after his head is cut off]**

(from British Library Additional MS 11579, fol. 5v [early fourteenth century])

Erat quidam puer christianus manens in civitate una ubi multi Judei erant. Qui semper Antiphonam. scilicet *Ave regina* cantabat coram judeis et domibus eorum. Quare judei multum invidebant ei et tandem per fraudem et munuscula trahebant eum in domibus eorum in ultimo t[h]alamo et amputaverunt capud eius. post hec vero veniens mater pueri querens filium suum semper audiendo vocem filii cantantem *Ave regina* set non potuit invenire eum. Deinde vero ivit ad magistros civitatis narrando eis quomodo judei tenuerunt filium suum in carcere et petiit ut venirent secum et liberarent filium suum.

Qui venientes omnes vocem audierunt et intrantes et querentes invenerunt puerum mortuum. et detulerunt eum ad ecclesiam ad sepeliendum. et cum deberent cantare missam pro eo ignorabant utrum deberent cantare missam pro mortuis. scilicet *Requiem eternam* vel de sancta Maria. scilicet *Salve*. Et dum hec cogitabant, surrexit mortuus et incepit magna voce *Salve sancta parens* etc.

XI

(C4) **[Boy killed for singing *Sancta Maria*]**

(from British Library Royal MS 12.E.I, art. 19, fol. 170 [early fourteenth century])

Item quidam puer cotidie revertens de scolis cotidie per ostium cuiusdam judei solebat cantare *Sancta maria* etc de beata virgine. quem judeus apprehendens projecit in cloacham apud tholetum et qualiter incepit *Salve sancta parens*. quando sacerdos inceperat requiem et qualiter post *Agnus dei* revixit.

XII

(C5) **"Hou þe Jewes, in Despit of Ure Lady, þrewe a Chyld in a Gonge"**

(from Vernon MS, Bodleian Library, MS Eng. poet. a. 1 [late fourteenth century]. Ed. Carl Horstmann, *Minor Poems of the Vernon MS*, EETS OS 98 [1892], pp. 141–5)

Text	Gloss
(fol.124a) Wose* loueþ wel ure ladi,	Whoever
Heo wol quiten his wille wel whi*,	(*meaning uncertain*)
Oþur in his lyf or at his ende:	
Þe ladi is so freo* and hende*.	generous/ gracious
Hit fel [so] sum-tyme in Parys,	
As witnesseþ in holy writ Storys.	
In þe Cite bi-fel þis cas:	
A pore child was of porchas*,	property
Þat wiþ þe Beggeri* þat he con wynne	proceeds of begging
He fond sumdel what of his kinne*,	he supported some of his family
His ffader, his Moder, and eke him-self;	
He begged in Cite bi everi half*.	everywhere
Þe child non oþur Craftus couþe	
But winne his lyflode wiþ his Mouþe.	
Þe Childes vois was swete and cler,	
Men lusted* his song wiþ riht good cher;	listened to
Wiþ his song þat was ful swete	
He gat Mete from strete to strete.	
Men herked his song ful likyngly:	
Hit was an Antimne of ure lady,	
He song þat Antimne everi-wher,	
I-Called *Alma redemptoris mater*,	
Þat is forþrihtly to mene:	
"Godus Moder, Mylde and Clene,	
Heuene ȝate* and Sterre of se,	gate
Save þi peple from synne and we*."	woe
Þat song was holden deynteous*,	excellent
Þe child song hit from hous to hous.	
ffor he song hit so lykynglye*,	pleasingly, attractively
Þe Jewes hedde alle to hym Envye*.	malice
Til hit fel on a seters-day*	Saturday
Þe Childes wey þorw þe Jewerie lay:	
Þe Jewes hedden þat song in hayn*,	hatred
Þerfore þei schope* þe child be slayn.	brought about
So lykingly þe Child song þer,	
So lustily song he never er.	
On of þe Jewes Malicious	
Tilled* þe child in to his hous;	enticed
His Malice þere he gan to kuyþe*:	made known
He Cutte þe childes þrote alswiþe*.	immediately
Þe child ne spared nout for þat wrong,	

But neuer-þe-latere* song forþ his song; nevertheless
Whon he hedde endet, he eft bi-gon,
His syngyng couþe stoppe no mon.
Þer-of þe Jeuh was sore anuyet*. annoyed, troubled
Leste his Malice mihte ben aspyet,
Þe Jeuh bi-þouhte him of a gynne*: plan, scheme
In to a gonge-put* fer wiþ-Inne privy pit
Þe child adoun þer-Inne he þrong*. thrust, threw
Þe child song evere þe same song;
So lustily þe child con* crie, did
Þat song he never er so hyȝe:
Men mihte him here fer and neer,
Þe Childes vois was so heiȝ and cleer.
Þe Childes moder was wont to a-byde
Every day til þe Non-tyde,
Þen was he wont to bringe heom* mete, them
Such as he mihte wiþ his song gete.
Bote þat day was þe tyme a-past.
Þerfore his Moder was sore a-gast;
Wiþ syk and serwe in eueri strete
Heo souhte wher heo mihte wiþ him mete.
Bote whon heo com in to þe Jewery,
Heo herde his vois so clere of cry.
Aftur þat vois his Modur dreuh:
Wher he was Inne, þerbi heo kneuh.
Þen of hire child heo asked a siht.
Þe Jew wiþ-nayted* him anon-riht, denied
And seide þer nas non such child þrinne*. therein
Þe childes Moder ȝit nolde not blinne*, cease
But ever þe Moder criede in on*. continually
Þe Jeuh seide evere þer nas such non.
Þen seide þe wommon: "Þou seist wrong,
He is her-Inne, I knowe his song."
Þe Jeuh bi-gon to stare and swere
And seide þer com non such child þere.
But never-þe-latere men mihte here
Þe child song evere so loude and clere,
And ever þe lengor, herre* and herre, higher
Men mihte him here boþe fer and nerre.
Þe Modur coude non oþur won:
To Meir and Baylyfs heo is gon,
Heo pleyneþ þe Jeuh haþ don hire wrong
To stelen hire sone so for his song;
Heo preyeþ to don hire lawe and riht*, justice
Hire sone don come* bi-fore heore siht; make her son come
Heo preyeþ þe Meir par Charite
Of him to have freo lyvere*. legal delivery
Þenne heo telleþ þe Meir a-Mong* meanwhile
Hou heo lyveþ bi hire sone song.
Þe Meir þen haþ of hire pite,
And sumneþ þe folk of þat Cite.

He telleþ hem of þat wommons sawe*, story
And seiþ he mot don hire þe lawe,
And hoteþ* hem wiþ hym to wende, commands
To Bringe þis wommons cause to ende.
Whon þei cum þider, for al heore noyse
Anon þei herde þe childes voyse,
Riht as an Angeles vois hit were,
Þei herde him never synge so clere.
Þer þe Meir makeþ entre,
And of þe child he askeþ lyvere.
Þe Jeuh may nouȝt þe Meir refuse,
Ne of þe child hym wel excuse,
But nede he moste knouleche his wrong,
A-teynt* bi þe childes songe. proven guilty
Þe Meir let serchen hym, so longe,
Til he was founden in þe gonge,
fful depe I-drouned in fulþe of fen*. dung
Þe Meir het drawe þe child up þen, that the child be drawn up
Wiþ ffen and ffulþe riht foule bi-whorven*, bespattered
And eke þe childes þrote I-corven.
Anon-riht, er þei passede forþere,
Þe Jeuh was Jugget for þat Morþere.
And er þe peple passede in-sonder,
Þe Bisschop was comen to seo þat wonder.
In presence of Bisschop and alle I-fere* together
Þe child song evere I-liche* clere. alike, equally
Þe Bisschop serchede wiþ his hond:
Wiþinne be childes þrote he fond
A Lilie flour, so briht and cler,
So feir a Lylie nas nevere seȝen er,
Wiþ guldene lettres everiwher:
Alma redemptoris mater.
Anon þat lilie out was taken,
Þe childes song bi-gon to slaken,
Þat swete song was herd no more;
But as a ded cors* þe child lay þore. corpse, there
Þe Bisschop wiþ gret solempnete
Bad bere þe cors þorw al þe Cite:
And hym-self wiþ processioun
Com wiþ þe Cors þorw al þe toun,
Wiþ prestes and clerkes þat couþen syngen,
And alle þe Belles he het hem ryngen,
Wiþ torches Brennynge and cloþus riche,
Wiþ worschipe þei ladden þat holi liche*. body
In to þe Munstre whon þei kem,
Bi-gonne þe Masse of Requiem,
As for þe dede Men is wont.
But þus sone þei weren i-stunt*: stopped, halted
Þe Cors a-Ros in heore presens,
Bi-gon þen *Salve sancta parens.*
Men mihte wel witen þe soþe þer-bi:

Þe child hedde i-servet ur swete ladi,
Þat worschipede* him so on erþe her — honored
And brouhte his soule to blisse al cler.
    Þerfore i rede* þat everi mon — advise
Serve þat ladi wel as he con,
And love hire in his beste wyse:
Heo wol wel quite him his servise.
Now, Marie, for þi Muchele miht
Help us to hevene þat is so briht!

XIII

"A boy singing *Gaude Maria* is killed by Jews"

(1–9) A certain other student, still a small boy, well-educated in chant, having a sweet and melodious voice, almost every day at vespers when he returned home from school, was accustomed to sing in a high voice the responsory of the blessed Virgin, namely, *Gaude Maria virgo*, in honor of Saint Mary, God's mother. Therefore the voice of the boy singing cheered all kindly people by whom he passed. But incited by envy, the perfidious Jews who lived in those parts, undertaking to suppress the praises of the glorious Virgin, apprehended and suddenly killed that boy passing by their door on a certain day at vespers time. Moreover, in reproach of the blessed Virgin, they hid his body by throwing it in a privy.

(10–17) The boy, indeed, having not returned home in his accustomed manner, was sought among friends and acquaintances by parents and fellow students for two days but not discovered. However, on the third day at vespers time they heard a voice of one singing the same responsory which the living boy was accustomed to sing, and it seemed the same boy's voice singing according to his habit. And from the house of the Jews where the boy was hanging, this voice ceased not to sound until Christians, forcing in the Jews' closed door, came to the body. Indeed, with great joy, the body was carried honorably to the church of the blessed Virgin and placed together with its bier in front of the great altar.

(18–31) The next day, indeed, with all the students of the same city gathered at the church with the people so that they might be present at the mass to be celebrated reverently for him and they might pray devoutly for his soul, and offer their own gifts to God, the cantor began the office *Requiem eternam* as is the custom to sing for the dead. And behold suddenly a clear voice resonating with sweet melody was heard from the coffin, just as if from that boy, beginning the office of the blessed Virgin, *Salve sancte parens*. Soon the stupefied cantor fell silent and the boyish voice heard before likewise was silent. Noticing this, the cantor again intoned *Requiem eternam*; in everyone's ears that mellifluous voice, suppressing the voice of the cantor, solemnly began again: *Salve sancte parens*. And this was done a third time. Therefore, marvelling greatly, the priests, with God inspiring and the people urging, continued the whole office of the blessed Virgin with the mass. When the mass was finished, they entrusted the body to earth, glorifying and praising God and his mother Mary to whom, with her Son, be honor forever. Amen.

XIII

(C7) **"De puero cantante responsorium *Gaude Maria* a Judeis occiso pro quo salve" sancta parens celitus decantari auditur**

(from Sidney Sussex College Cambridge MS 95, Lib. II, cap. 84 [1409])

Alter quidam scolaris adhuc puerulus in cantu satis edoctus vocem habens dulcem et canorem singulis fere diebus cum de scolis ad vesperum reverteretur domum Responsorium de beata virgine, scilicet *Gaude Maria virgo*, in honorem sancte Marie dei genitricis excelsa voce cantare consuevit, itaque omnes benivolos per quos transivit vox pueri cantantis exhillaravit. Sed perfidi judei qui in illis partibus habitabant laudes gloriose virginis supprimere conantes invidia stimulante puerum illum quadam die ad vesperum per hostium eorum transeuntem apprehenderunt et subito interfecerunt, ac in opprobrium beate virginis corpus eius in cloacam proicientes occuluerunt.

Puer vero more solito domum non regressus inter cognatos et notos a parentibus et conscolaribus biduo quesitus est nec inventus. Tercia autem die ad vesperum audita est ab eis vox cantantis idem responsorium quod puer vivens cantare consueverat, et videbatur idem puer more suo decantans. Et hec vox de domo judeorum ubi puer suspendebatur non destitit resonare donec christiani per judeorum ostium preclusum irruentes ad corpus devenirent. Quod quidem corpus cum ingenti gaudio honorifice ad ecclesiam beate virginis allatum coram majus altare cum feretro deponitur.

In crastino vero scolaribus omnibus eiusdem urbis ad ecclesiam cum populo convenientibus ut misse pro eo celebrande reverenter interessent et pro eius anima devocius orarent, ac munera sua deo offerrent, incepit cantor officium *Requiem eternam* sicud mos est pro defunctis canere. Et ecce subito vox clara resonans audita est de loculo veluti ab ipso puero dulci modulamine officium inchoans de beata virgine, *Salva sancta parens*. Mox cantor stupefactus subticuit et vox puerilis prius audita similiter siluit. Quod attendens cantor *Requiem eternam* iterum personuit, auribus omnium vox illa dulcissona vocem cantoris comprimens solenniter reincepit: *Salve sancta parens*. Et hoc factum est tercio. Vehementer igitur admirantes clerici inspirante deo et persuadente populo totum officium de beata virgine cum missa prosecuti sunt. ffinita missa corpus terre tradiderunt glorificantes et laudantes deum eiusque genitricem Mariam cui cum filio sit honor in secula seculorum. Amen.

XIV

"About the boy killed by Jews who ceased not to sing the antiphon *Alma redemptoris* until the Office of the Funeral was completed"

(1–14) In the land of the Albigensians was a certain powerful and noble rich man who was accustomed to feed a certain old woman from his table, as long as she was able to come. When however, because of weakness, she was unable to come by herself, the rich man made sufficient provision to be carried to her from his house by her small son. Indeed, the boy was a clerk and, as was fitting for his age, a clear voice rang out from his throat. Moreover, in coming and going, he was accustomed to sing the antiphon *Alma redemptoris mater* in the hearing of all. And when he had finished it he used to begin it again, and thus when he went or when he returned, the sacred melody did not cease to come from the boy's mouth. Indeed, the direction of the route was such that from his mother's little house to the rich man's house he was bound to pass through the quarter of the Jews. Praising the blessed Virgin every day with clear voice, he walked among the Jews; indignant, inflamed, with great complaint they spoke to each other, saying: "This boy who frequently passes by us daily repeats that song in derision and reproach of our people." And they began to blaspheme the name of the Virgin Mary.
(15–20) The impiety of the Jews increased from day to day so that they were very assiduously thinking that they should kill the boy. And they said: "What shall we do?" And with a plan devised, they appointed two who might seize the passing boy. And they did that. And so he was seized and led into an interior room and, with the Jews congregated around him raging with excessive cruelty, they cut the stomach of the innocent through the middle and extracting his innards, they threw them, together with his body, into a privy.
(21–7) When these things were done, divine grace did not fail. For when the boy was dragged inside, cut and foully thrown into the privy, either he himself or perchance his angel ceased not from singing just as had been ordained by the Lord. But always the same voice, the same song was heard by Christians who were passing through that place, although none of them perceived that the boy had been treated in this way by those perfidious Jews. But although the Christians, just as it is said, clearly experienced the voice of the singer, the Jews did not experience the voice and song at all.
(28–37) When, however, the boy did not return as usual at the appropriate hour, the mother began to be anxious for her son. She held out however until morning. On the next day, leaning on a walking stick, she began to go around seeking her son. The strength, in fact, which age had consumed, grief and sadness for her son restored. When, however, she searched very assiduously all around, she was told that the boy had entered into the house of a Jew at such an hour. Thus coming to the door where she had heard her son had entered, the mother pounded, saying: "Return

XIV

(C8) **"De puero a Judeis interfecto qui antiphonam *Alma Redemptoris* cantare non cessavit donec Funeris Officium conpleretur"**

(from Sidney Sussex College Cambridge MS 95, Lib. II, cap. 87, fols 88r–89 [1409])

In terra Albegeorum erat quidam dives potens et nobilis qui quandam vetulam quamdiu ire poterat de mensa sua reficere consueverat. Postquam autem per se pre debilitate venire nequiverat, per filium eius quem habebat parvulum fecit sibi dives de domo sua annonam sufficientem deferri. Puer vero clericus erat et sicud illi etati convenit vox clara ab eius gutture resonabat. In eundo autem et redeundo antiphonam *Alma redemptoris mater* in omnium audiencia decantare consueverat. Et cum finisset eam iterum incipiebat, sicque quando ibat vel quando redibat ista sacra melodia de ore pueri non cessabat. Disposicio vero itineris ita se habebat, ut a matris sue domuncula ad domum divitis per vicum judeorum transire deberet. Qui cum diebus singulis sic beatam virginem clare voce laudans per judeos incederet grandi murmure [stomochati] accensi adinvicem loquebantur dicentes: "Puer iste qui frequenter transit per nos cotidie replicat illud canticum in generis nostri derisum et obprobrium." Et ceperunt nomen Marie virginis blasphemare.

Crescebat de die in diem judeorum impietas et ut puerum interficerent attencius cogitabant. Et dicebant: "Quid faciemus?" Initoque consilio statuerunt duos qui puerum raperent transeuntem. Quod et fecerunt. Raptus itaque ductus est in interius cubiculum et congregatis circa eum judeis nimia crudelitate debacantes ventrem innocentis [scinderunt] per medium et interiora eius extrahentes simul cum corpore in cloacam projecerunt.

Cumque hec fierent, divina gracia non defuit. Nam cum intrinsecus puer traheretur, secaretur, et in cloacam turpiter proiceretur, a cantu non destitit vel ipse vel forte angelus eius sicud a domino fuerit ordinatum. Sed semper eadem vox idem cantus a christianis qui per locum illum transibant audiebatur, licet nullus eorum adverteret quod puer hoc modo ab ipsis perfidis judeis tractaretur. Sed licet christiani sicud dictum est vocem cantantis evidenter sunt experti, judei tamen vocem et cantum sunt penitus inexperti.

Cum autem puer ad horam constitutam ex more non rediret, cepit pro filio mater sollicitari. Sustinuit tamen usque mane. In crastino vero baculo innixa cepit [circuire] filium suum querens. Vires enim quas etas consumpserat, dolor et tristicia filii reparabant. Cum autem attencius circum circa quereret, dictum est ei quia in domum talis judei puer illa hora intravit. Veniens itaque mater ad ostium ubi filium eius audierat intrasse, pulsavit dicens: "Reddite mihi filium meum quem intrinsecus audio more solito decantantem." Ex quo

12 **stomochati** stomachati (Brown)
19 **scinderunt** sciderunt MS (and Brown)
30 **circuire** circumire (Brown)
44 **occecata** obcecata MS (and Brown)

to me my son whom I hear singing inside in his usual way." For from the time when she approached this area, she perceived a voice known to be her son's. But the Jews who were inside were saying she was delirious, and claiming that they knew nothing about her son, they drove her shamefully from the door.
(38–43) Going back, she told this news to the rich man. Servants sent by him, entering the house of the Jew, heard at once the voice of the boy. And also many Christians likewise, rushing together to that sight, assembled and diligently searched. They found the place and, grieving, they extracted the body of the boy from the privy. Indeed, in an astonishing manner, all the Christians heard the melody and song, but only because of their faithlessness the Jews did not hear.

(44–7) Therefore, with great honor and joy, the body of the innocent was carried to the church and in that same place was reverently buried. And the wondrous voice did not cease until the priest and people completed the service of the funeral and in praise of Christ's mother returned to their own homes.

(48–52) And so that this antiphon might be made manifest to those present who don't know it, it seems fitting to insert it: "Kind mother of the redeemer who are the open door of heaven and star of the sea, help the fallen to rise (you) who care for the people; you who, while nature marvelled, gave birth to your own holy father, Virgin before and after taking that Ave from Gabriel's lips, have mercy on us sinners."

XV

Alfonsus a Spina, "The Expulsion of the Jews from England"

(trans. Priscilla Throop)

(1–14) There was a third expulsion of the Jews from England. A two-fold cause is given for this expulsion, the first of which I read in certain miracle stories as follows. In Lincoln, a city of the King of England, occurred a certain miracle which God wished to reveal through prayers of the blessed Virgin. A certain poor widow woman had a son named Alphonse. She handed him over to be taught the alphabet, and after he knew how to read, she entrusted him for training in the rudiments of grammar and music. (8) Although he made progress in grammar, he was very gifted in music. And since this woman was poor, she entrusted him to a certain religious man of her family, so that he might at least provide for him from his sustenance. And so it was done that daily, after his lessons, he received a meal with the monk. The boy was ten years old. His usual habit was to go first to church everyday, then to his lectures, and at meal time, as was said, to the house of the monk. At night he returned to his mother's house.

enim ad partem illam accessit, filii sui vocem notam intellexit. Sed judei qui intrinsecus erant eam delirare dicebant, nil se scire de suo filio asserentes turpiter ab ostio repellebant.

Recedens ipsa nunciavit hoc diviti. A quo missi ministri domum judei intrantes statim vocem pueri audierunt. Sed et multi christianorum similiter concurrentes ad istud spectaculum convenerunt et diligenter requirentes locum invenerunt, sicque corpus pueri de cloacha merentes extraxerunt. Miro quidem modo omnes christiani melodiam et cantum audierunt, sed sola judeorum [ocecata] perfidia non audivit.

Cum magno igitur honore et gaudio corpus innocentis ad ecclesiam defertur, et ibidem venerabiliter sepelitur. Nec cessavit vox ista admirabilis donec clerus et populus obsequium funeris explerent, et in laude matris christi ad propria remearent.

Et ut hec antiphona nescientibus manifestetur presentibus illam interserere congruum videtur: Alma redemptoris mater que pervia celi porta manens et stella maris succurre cadenti surgere qui curat populo tu que genuisti natura mirante tuum sanctum genitorem virgo prius ac posterius Gabrielis ab ore sumens illud ave peccatorum miserere.

XV

(C9) **Alphonsus a Spina, "De expulsione Judeorum de regno Anglorum"**

(from *Fortalicium fidei contra Judeos, Saracenos, aliosque Christiane fidei inimicos* [1458–60][1]

Tercia judeorum expulsio fuit a regno anglie cuius expulsionis causa duplex assignatur quarum primam legi in quibusdam miraculis sub ordine qui sequitur. In li[n]conia civitate regis anglie, Accidit quoddam miraculum quod deus voluit ostendere precibus beate virginis. Unde mulier quedam vidua et paupercula filium quendam nomine Alfonsum habebat, quem tradidit ad docendum primas litteras et postquam scivit legere tradidit imbuendum rudimentis gra[m]maticalibus et in musica; qui licet in gra[m]maticalibus processerit, in musicis tamen gratissimus erat. Et quia predicta mulier paupercula erat recommendavit illum cuidam religioso sui generis, ut de victu saltem ipsi provideret: et ita factum est, quia cottidie post lectiones suas recipiebat suam refectionem cum predicto religioso. Erat autem predictus puer etatis annorum x., cuius erat consuetudo ordinata ut primo cottidie iret ad ecclesiam deinde ad scolas et hora refectionis, ut dictum est, ad domum religiosi. Nocte vero ad matris domicilium se convertebat.

1 Alphonsus a Spina was a convert from Judaism. When he wrote the *Fortalicium* he was Doctor of Theology in the Franciscan College at Salamanca, and later bishop of Thermopylae in Greece. Brown reprints the text from the Basel edition, c. 1475. See Bryan and Dempster, p. 477.

(15–43) Since he often heard that famous antiphon *Alma redemptoris* sung in church, he conceived such a great devotion for the blessed Virgin and he so imprinted on his mind the antiphon that wherever he went, both night and day, through the streets and roads, as boys are wont, he sang that antiphon very sweetly in a high voice. When he went to or returned from his mother's house, his path was through a certain Jewish quarter. Frequently hearing that song of the Virgin from the youth's mouth, one of them asked a learned Christian the meaning of that chant, since it was so sweet. (23) And when he learned that it was an antiphon which was sung by believers in church to the praise of the blessed Virgin Mary, mother of the redeemer, Jesus Christ, the true messiah, he conceived a resentment and devised a crime. He held a meeting with his accomplices, whose hearts the devil possessed, how they might deliver to death and kill the child. They saw an opportune time when the child would pass (29) through their quarter singing the said antiphon in a high voice. Suddenly, as if by roaring lions, he was seized and shut up in a certain house, while they plotted the means of his death. And they determined that his tongue, with which he praised the blessed Virgin, should be pulled out from the opposite side of his head. Secondly, that also his heart, with which he thought about the chant, should be ripped out, and finally that his body be thrown in a very deep and very unclean place and one full of stench: that place was their adjoining latrine; so that not a single trace of him could be found. And so it was done. (36) But the blessed Virgin, who is the mother of mercy and pity, does not commit to oblivion any service whatsoever done for her. As soon as that most devoted singer of hers had been thrown into that fetid place, she was there present to him and put in his mouth a certain precious stone in place of his tongue, and he immediately began to sing, just as before, the antiphon, indeed better and louder than before. Neither did he cease any time day or night from that song, and the little boy stayed in such a way in that place for four days.

(44–55) When indeed his mother saw that he did not come home as usual, she went with a quick gait to the house of the monk and then to the lecture halls, and was not able to find him. The anxious woman was running about everywhere through the city to find her son, if possible, and (48) by God's will, at the end of four days, the woman passed through the quarter in which her son had been killed and thrown into the latrine. And behold: the voice of her son, singing very sweetly the chant of the Virgin, which she had heard from him very often, resounded in her ears. Having heard it, the woman began to shout, and many people gathered around, and with them a judge of the city. They entered that house in which the voice was heard, and at last the youth was found in the place described, and pulled out. He never ceased from that very sweet chant, although he was dead.

(56–78) He was dressed in different (i.e. clean) clothes by the men who had come there, and the bishop of the town was notified. He came immediately to the sight, and ordered that he be placed with honor on a certain bed, and so he was led in a solemn procession, with great honor, to the cathedral church (59) of the city; yet he always continued his song. When they were gathered together in the church, the bishop celebrated divine service and delivered a solemn sermon and ordered all the listeners to pour out devout prayers, so that by the prayers of the blessed Virgin,

Cum autem sepe in ecclesia illam preclaram antiphonam *Alma redemptoris* audiret cantare, tantam devocionem concepit in virgine beata et sic menti impressit predictam antiphonam quod [quocumque] iret de die et de nocte per vicos et plateas more puerorum supradictam antiphonam alta voce dulcissime cantabat. transitus autem eius erat, cum iret ad domum matris vel rediret ab eadem, per vicum quendam judeorum; qui audientes frequenter predictam virginis cantacionem ab ore juvenis [quidam] illorum habuit querere a quodam docto christiano, quis esset sensus illius cantacionis cum eius cantus tam dulcis esset. Et ut cognovit quod illa erat antiphona quedam que ad laudem et honorem virginis beate marie matris redemptoris ihesu christi veri messie decantabatur a fidelibus in ecclesia, concepit dolorem et peperit iniquitatem: quod consilium habuit cum suis complicibus quorum corda dyabolus possidebat, quomodo predictum infantem morti traderent et occiderent. hora ergo oportuna observata cum parvulus predictus alta voce cantando predictam antiphonam transiret per eorum vicum, subito sicut a rugientibus leonibus rapitur et reclusus in domo quadam de modo mortis eius tractaverunt. Et diffinitum est inter eos quod eius lingua cum qua beatam virginem laudabat extraheretur per oppositam capitis partem; secundo quod extraheretur etiam eius cor cum quo cogitabat predictam cantacionem; et ultimo quod corpus eius proiceretur in loco profundissimo et immundissimo fetoribusque pleno qui locus erat eorum continua latrina, ut nullatenus signum eius inveniri posset: et factum est sic. Set virgo beata, que mater est misericordie et pietatis nec oblivioni tradit servicium quodcunque sibi factum, statim sic ille devotissimus suus cantor in predicto loco fetito fuit projectus, Affuit presens eidem et posuit in eius ore lapidem quendam preciosum, qui locum lingue suppleret, et statim cepit cantare sicut prius predictam antiphonam ymmo melius et alcius quam primo: nec aliquando cessabat de die nec de nocte a predicto cantu, et tali modo stetit in predicto loco parvulus ille iiii. diebus.

Cum vero mater eius videret quod sicut consueverat ad domum eius non veniret, celeri gressu ad domum supradicti religiosi pervenit ac deinde ad scolas, nec poterat invenire. Discurrebat undique per civitatem anxia mulier si posset alicubi invenire filium suum, et disponente deo in fine iiii. dierum predictorum mulier illa transivit per vicum illum in quo filius suus fuerat occisus et in latrinam projectus; et ecce vox filii sui cantantis dulcissime cantacionem illam virginis, quam sepissime ab eo audierat, insonuit in auribus eius. Quo audito clamoribus magnis predicta mulier clamare cepit, et congregate sunt multe gentes et cum eis judex civitatis, intraverunt que domum illam in qua vox illa audiebatur, et finaliter inventus est juvenis in loco predicto et extractus; nec unquam cessabat a cantu illo dulcissimo licet mortuus foret.

Indutusque aliis vestimentis per dominos qui ibidem venerant, notificatum est episcopo civitatis, qui illico veniens ad spectaculum precepit quod poneretur honorifice in quodam lecto; et sic deductus est cum solenni processione et magno honore ad ecclesiam cathedralem predicte civitatis: semper tamen continuabat canticum suum. convenientibus ergo in unum ad predictam ecclesiam dictus episcopus celebravit et fecit solempnem sermonem precepitque omnibus audientibus, quod devotas funderent

17 **quocumque** quincunque (Brown)
21 **quidam** quidem (Brown)

God would deign to reveal this secret. When the sermon was over, it pleased the Most High and His most blessed mother, that (65) the treachery and cruelty of the very impious Jews was detected: at that very hour the little boy arose and stood on his feet in the bed in which he was lying, and pulled from his mouth the one very precious stone. With a happy, joyful face he told all the people how it had happened to him, just as was said, and how the blessed Virgin had come to him and placed the stone in his mouth so that he would not cease, although dead, from her praise, so that the glory of her Son would be revealed for the salvation of believers and for the perdition (71) of the hateful and unbelievers. After this he called the bishop to himself and gave him the kiss of peace and likewise his mother. He informed those in the holy assembly of the whole populace that he is ascending into heaven in the company of the glorious Virgin. He handed the precious stone to the bishop so he could put it on the altar with other relics. This done, he signed himself with the sign of the holy cross and, readying himself on the bed, entrusted his soul to the Savior. He was honorably buried in a marble tomb which, as people say (77) for a long time put forth precious stones until a certain pernicious heresy arose in the same place.

(79–87) And the king of the realm, when he learned of the Jews' unspeakable and horrible crime, and because of many other things the Jews did to the outrage and affront of Jesus Christ our Savior and of his most blessed mother, which he discovered by an inquiry to seek out the truth of the matter, after deliberate and timely consideration, ordered that, on an assigned day, all the Jews found in the kingdom would be killed. (84) Those who thought better of it [i.e. converted to Christianity] were [not killed like the others but only] despoiled of all their goods, and baptised and expelled from the entire kingdom of England. From that time no Jew ever lived, nor lives, nor dared to appear there, since he would be killed immediately, if he were recognized.

orationes ut precibus beate virginis deus dignaretur revelare hoc secretum. Finito vero sermone placuit altissimo et sue beatissime matri quod fuit detecta impiissimorum judeorum prodicio et crudelitas, quia eadem hora surrexit parvulus ille et stetit pedes in lecto in quo jacebat et extraxit ab ore suo unum preciosissimum lapidem. Dixitque omni populo leta et hylari facie qualiter sibi acciderat, sicut dictum est, et quomodo virgo beata ad eum venerat et posuerat dictum lapidem in ore eius ut non cessaret [licet][2] mortuus ab eius laude, et ut ostenderetur gloria filii sui in salutem credencium et perdicionem odiencium et incredulorum. Post hec autem vocavit ad se episcopum et dedit sibi pacem similiter et matri, et sancta expedicione ab omni populo certificavit eos, quod ascendit ad celos in societate virginis gloriose, et tradidit predictum lapidem preciosum episcopo, ut poneret cum aliis reliquiis in altari. Quo facto, signaculo sancte crucis se insignivit et coaptans se lecto animam tradidit salvatori. qui honorifice sepultus fuit quodam in sepulcro marmoreo, quod multo tempore preciosos lapides, ut fertur, emanavit quousque quedam pestifera heresis ibidem orta fuit.

Rex vero predicti regni, cum cognovit tam nephandum et horridum judeorum crimen et propter multa alia que invenit veridica inquisicione que predicti judei operabantur in contumeliam et injuriam jhesu christi salvatoris nostri et sue beatissime matris, ex deliberato et maturo consilio assignata die precepit, quod occiderentur omnes judei quotquot possent inveniri in predicto regno suo. Et illi qui melius deliberaverunt fuerunt totaliter expoliati ab omnibus bonis et signati[3] ac expulsi a toto regno anglie. Et ab illo tempore nunquam amplius ibi habitavit, nec habitat, nec ausus est apparere aliquis judeus, quia statim occideretur si cognosceretur.

2 Brown's emendation to supply a missing word.

3 This sentence is open to a number of possible readings because *signati* can mean *signed, inscribed, put on a list, marked in some way*. It also means *baptised, confirmed, signed with the sign of the cross*.

XVI

"The Story of the *Alma Redemptoris Mater*"

(trans. A. G. Rigg in *Geoffrey Chaucer, The Canterbury Tales: Nine Tales and the General Prologue*, ed. V. A. Kolve and Glending Olson [New York: Norton,1989], pp. 418–23)

(1–7) The Mother of Grace never forgets those who remember her, and so the memory of her should be continually brought to mind; praise should be lavished upon her, and we should preach her mighty works as often as possible. Although the treasure-chest of all goodness has no need of our good offices, nevertheless it is beneficial and salutary for us to heap praises on her goodness. I have, therefore, decided to take care to entrust the following chapter to writing, so that the story may come to the notice of future generations, and so that those who hear it may be inspired all the more deeply and firmly to remember the Virgin.

(8–21) There was once a certain boy born and bred in the city of Toledo; by the diligence of his mother he was sent to be instructed at school; he learned to dot his "i"s and to make the forms of letters; he learned the alphabet, and how to marry letter to letters and figure to figures properly. When he had learned how to join letters, he gladly passed on to music, in order that the understanding of the voice might be open to him as well as knowledge acquired by words. Every day he dutifully made his reading, according to what the authority of his teacher required of him. Each day, when he had fulfilled his educational duty, the hour of mealtime followed, and this little boy then used to go to the house of a canon of Mother Church; by the help of this canon the boy relieved his hunger and cheated the demands of that most importunate of debt-collectors, his stomach. He went there in hope of satisfying his hunger with the rich man's crumbs; every day he was given a measure of the crumbs which fell from the table of his masters and of the fragments left over by those who had eaten. He carefully collected everything that was given him, not in a shepherd's bag but in a little pocket at his breast; for his own use he kept the smallest and most worthless scraps, setting aside the bigger and better portions for his mother. O Lord, you who look into and know our hearts – you know what lies within man!

The following notes are based on Rigg's comments and annotations. All biblical quotations are from the Vulgate. Rigg (p. 418) notes that MS Trinity College, Cambridge, O.9.38 was compiled c. 1450, mainly from much earlier materials, though several stylistic features of this story resemble those of another Latin narrative in the [manuscript], both of which may have been "retouched" by the scribe who added his own rhetorical embellishments for literary effect, including frequent, though not always apt, biblical quotation. "There is, however, no a priori reason for saying that Chaucer could not have known the story in a version very close to this." **29–30** Brown "notes the presence of a rhyme on which this conceit is based in another MS, but in fact a later hand has added it in this text also; the rhyme puns on *amor*, *clamor vox*, *votum*, etc." **34** Hos. 10:11 the biblical passage does not clarify the meaning of this line. **53–4,** "their rejoicing was as that of him who eats the poor in secret," cf. Hab. 3:14; **105** "second Joseph out of the pit," cf. Gen. 37:28; **111** "a door of circumstance," cf. Ps. 140:3; **129** their tears "were on their cheeks," Lam. 1:2; cf. Joel 2:23; **143–4** "the amazement of Nature" an exact rendering of "natura mirante, from the antiphon *Alma redemptoris mater*. **169** for the image of the two walls meeting at the cornerstone, see Eph. 2:11–22 and Ps. 117:22, the antiphon for the Magnificat on December 22. For a similar interpretation of the union of circumcised and uncircumcised by St Gregory, see *The Christ of Cynewulf*, ed. A. S. Cook (1900; rpt. Hamden: Archon Books, 1964), p.75.

XVI

(C10) "De cantu *Alma Redemptoris Mater*"

(from Trinity College Cambridge MS O.9.38, late fifteenth to early sixteenth century)

(fol.37) Cum mater gracie sui memorum immemor nequaquam existat jugiter ipsius est memoria memoranda, laus ipsi tribuenda propensius et profusius sunt ipsius magnalia predicanda, licet bonorum operum non egeat tocius archa bonitatis tamen utile et salubre est ipsius bonitatem laudibus cumulare. Provide sequens capitulum commendandum duximus attramento ut ad noticiam perveniat posterorum et qui audierint ad memoriam virginis sanccius et interius accendantur.

Puer quidam in urbe toletana natus et nutritus matris sue diligencia mediante scolarum subditus discipline, iota et apices non preteriens nectere, didicit elementa et literas literis figuram figuris fideliter maritare. Cognito conjugio literarum feliciter ad musicam pertransivit ut tam vocis quam [verbi] eidem pateret intellectus diebus singulis soluit debitum leccionis secundum quod eidem prescripsit auctoritas magistralis. Diete debito persoluto hora prandii succedente domum cuiusdam canonici matricis ecclesie puer pauperculus adire consuevit. Cuius suffragio relevabat famem et ventris molestissimi exactoris exaccionem deludebat. Cupiebat saturari de micis divitis et dabatur ei cotidie ad mensuram de micis que cadebant de mensa dominorum et de fragmentis que superfuerunt hiis qui manducaverant. Puer quod ei dabatur non in pera pastorali set in sacculo pectorali provide recollegit quod minus fuit et peius in usus convertens proprios, majus et melius sue reservans genetrici. O cordium cognitor et inspector tu nosti quod esset in homine.

10 **verbi** verbis MS

Notes to text. A. G. Rigg, in *The Canterbury Tales*, ed. V. A. Kolve and Glending Olson (New York: Norton, 1989), p. 418 n. 1, indicates the following corrections and emendations that he thinks should be made to the text as presented by Brown: I have incorporated Rigg's corrections and emendations into the text. Rigg corrects Brown (in boldface) as follows: **25 precanere** read precavere; **48 animis** *delete*; **96 cunque** *read* scilicet; **115 quanto** *read* quanta; **124 suo** *read* sue; **151 monumentum** *read* monimentum. These corrections agree with the manuscript. At line 48 Brown most likely read the expunged "ac" as an abbreviation. Rigg suggests the following emendations: **10 figura** *read* figuram; **34 doctam** *read* docta; **115 que** *read* qui; **141 excitato** *read* excitatus. In each of these instances Brown has correctly transcribed the manuscript.

Brown's own notes are as follows: **31 perorare:** the following words are scribbled in a fifteenth-century hand on the last page of Trinity Coll., Camb., MS 1055: "Non vox sed voturn [MS vocurn], non musica cordula sed cor,/ Non clamor sed amor cantat in aure dei." **34 effraim:** Cf. Hos. 10:11; **39 diffitetur:** difficetur MS; **56 resecatur** rececatur MS; **57 resecato** rececato MS; **91 indicantes** indicantis *corr to* indicantes; **115 devote** de devote MS, *scribal repetition*; **136 reseratur** resaratur MS; **141 non** *added in same hand*; **143 nam que** naq naq3 MS; **153 tocius** tociens *deleted*, tocius *added*; **164 siciens** sciciens MS; **169 circumcisione** circursicione MS; **170 parietes** paritea *corr* parietes; **172 Sic** Sic sic MS.

(22–32) One day the boy was assigned as his daily schoolwork that sweet and delightful antiphon in praise of the Virgin Mother, whose opening line is *Alma redemptoris mater*. The boy was anxious not to suffer the terrifying taunts of his schoolmaster, (25) and so he carefully learned the antiphon by heart, and meditated on it, both because it was difficult to learn and because it is a delightful song to sing. In my opinion, however, he learned and sang the antiphon so often not so much because of the sweetness of the song as because of the memory and love of the Virgin Mother. For more worthy than the string of the harp is the heart of the player who prays out of love. The judge who judges the hearts of men is more affected by the love from the heart than by the loudness of the harp, more by the prayer than by the voice which makes the prayer: when one learns to pray in faith one also learns to speak with beauty. Why is this? Because the voice never sounds pleasant unless the spirit leads the voice and prayer in the singing.

(33–50) One day, when the hour of breakfast had arrived, the boy, who had earned rest by his hard work, was released from school; he practiced with effect what he had learned from usage, like the calf of Ephraim who was taught to love treading. He proceeded in the direction of the house of the canon by whose mercy he used to relieve his own misfortune. By chance he happened to go into the courtyards of Jewry where that stiffnecked race lived, that detestable family – the race which objects to the fruitfulness of the Virgin Mary and denies that the Son of God was made incarnate in a virgin's womb. A great number of the sons of the synagogue had gathered together in a house there, strengthening by their number that brotherhood of iniquity, that oppressive branch of sin. The boy arrived close by the house, singing the antiphon (43) we have mentioned above, the *Alma redemptoris mater*. His intention was to pass through the area, but he did not get through unharmed. Among the Jews was a certain young Hebrew boy who had been taught a little Latin and understood the Latin idiom. They heard the song, and wondered what it was; Satan came among them, and one of them asked the Hebrew who knew Latin what the Christian boy was singing. The Hebrew replied that the boy was singing an antiphon composed in praise of the Virgin Mary; its delightful sweetness was intended to inspire the minds of the listeners to the memory of Mary. At the mention of the name of the Virgin, the Jew cried out; Satan put it into his heart to betray and kill the innocent boy.

(51–62) He therefore treacherously asked his colleague to bring the boy in: if he couldn't do what was required simply by asking, he was to offer the boy a bribe. So the innocent boy was summoned and brought in, introduced – or, rather, traduced. They took firm hold of him; "their rejoicing was as that of him who eats the poor in secret." Without delay they made themselves ready for the murder, and prepared to condemn the innocent boy to death. The lamb was seized by the wolves; one of them set a knife to his throat, (55) and his tongue was cruelly cut out; his stomach was opened and his heart and liver taken out. They imagined that they were offering a double sacrifice, firstly by cutting the throat from which emerged the voice of praise, and secondly by tearing out the heart which incessantly meditated on the memory of the Virgin. They thought they were obeying God, but in fact they were making a sacrifice not to God but to the devils of hell. It is usual for malice to cease after death, but although they had killed the boy, their malice did not come to an end: they threw his corpse into a place of the coarsest filth, where nature purges itself in secret.

(63–6) Immediately the blessed mother of the Redeemer arrived by his side; her gracious mercy was present; she appeared to place a white pebble (which looked very like a stone) on and within the mouth of the dead boy. When the pebble had

Assignabatur puero quadam die pro dieta illa dilectabilis et suavis Antiphona in laudem matris virginis confecta cuius est caput et principium *Alma redemptoris mater.* Puer contumelias et terrores magistri cupiens precavere Antiphonam memoratam assidue ruminabat, tum quia sciendum est difficilis, tum quia delectabilis ad canendum. Amplius ipsum credo ob memoriam et amorem matris virginis Antiphonam decantasse memoratam, quam ob cantus dulcedinem tociens id fecisse; minus enim prodest corda cythare quam cor cytharedi supplicantis ex affectu. Plus amor cordis quam cordis clamor, plus votum quam vox, judicem interpellat hominum corda judicantem quia cum didicit orare fideliter novit feliciter perorare. Quare? quia nunquam sonat vox amene nisi vocis et voti animus sit precentor.

Cum hora prandii a scolis (fol.37v) quadam die puerum absoluisset et labore quietem subrogasset, puer, ut vitula effraim trituram docta diligere quod ab usu didicit hoc exercuit cum effectu, domum adit canonici de cuius misericordia suam miseriam depellebat. Contigit ipsum forte ingredi plateas Judaismi, ubi gens dure cervicis et domus exasperans habitabat, que Marie virginis fecunditati contradicens dei filium incarnatum in virginis utero diffitetur. ffilii synagoge quam plurimi in domo quadam fuerant congregati et ibi colligacio iniquitatis et deprimens peccati fasciculus ex ipsorum multitudine amplius fuerat roboratus. Ad hanc domum puer venit dictam decantans Antiphonam *Alma redemptoris mater,* transire cupiens, set illesus non transivit. Affuit inter eos quidam adolescens de pueris hebreorum in lingua latina parumper eruditus quia latinum intelligens ydeoma. Audiunt cantilenam et mirantur et quia fuit sathan inter eos ecce unus ex illis inquirit ab hebreo qui literas novit latinorum, quid puer concineret christianus. Respondit hebreus puerum Antiphonam in laudem matris virginis confectam decantare ut ipsius melliflua suavitas ad marie memoriam accenderet auditores. Audito virginis nomine judeus exclamavit et ecce sathanas misit in cor eius ut puerum traderet et interficeret innocentem.

Rogat ergo collegam fraudulenter ut puerum introducat et si prece non possit saltem precio faciat quod deposcit. Innocens vocatur et introducitur, trahitur ymmo magis traditur. Nam tenetur et facta est exultacio eorum sicut eius qui devorat pauperem in abscondito. Sine mora se preparant occisioni ut condempnent innocentem. Agnum lupi rapiunt. Apponit unus cultrum gutturi, lingua crudeliter resecatur, reseratur venter et cor extrahitur cum pulmone. Duplex se credunt offerre sacrificium, gutture resecato quo vox laudis est egressa, extracto corde quod virginis memoriam non desiit meditari: arbitrantur obsequium se prestare deo set ymmo ymmolabant demoniis et non deo. Livor post fata solet quiescere, set extincto puero livor non quievit, quia corpus extinctum in locum proicitur extreme vilitatis ubi natura se purgat per secessum.

Affuit continuo *Alma redemptoris mater* quia affuit ipsius misericordia graciosa ut extincto videbatur lapillum album set saxo simillimum ori ipsius apponens et imponens: (fol.38) lapillo imposito cor et guttur mortui reserant,

been put in place, the boy's heart and throat opened up; his voice and power of speech returned, and he began to sing the *Alma redemptoris mater.*

(67–89) In the meantime the boy's mother was anxious at his delay: he was her only son. She was alarmed at his unusually long delay, and suddenly began to be afraid and frightened at his daylong absence. For a mother does not easily forget the child of her womb and the joy that a man is born into the world. Thus, scarcely in control of herself she set aside her domestic task, and went out into the courtyards and walked through the streets of the town; everywhere she looked at the passersby, and carefully scrutinized everyone she met. But nowhere did she see the face of her son. She walked on and on, into the Jewish quarter, scarcely able to support herself for her grief: her soul slept for weariness when she pictured as dead the child whom she had loved in life. She was now close to the house where the progeny of vipers had committed the crime. Suddenly the anxious mother (77) heard her son singing the *Alma redemptoris mater*: that is, she heard his voice, but she saw no one. She stopped in amazement, but just as a sheep recognizes its lamb by its bleat alone, so this mother recognized her own son by the uniqueness of his singing voice: she was in labour close to death when she bore him, and so now she was in labour again, shouting and not sparing her voice. She could not put a guard on her mouth; however hoarse her throat became through her shouting, she incessantly cried out at the doors of her bloody enemies, "Give me back my son! Give me back my son!" As she repeated the words again and again, her grief was opened up. Time and again, as she stood outside the house she begged the Jews for her son, but the cruel and treacherous Jews would not give her any satisfaction; on stumbling feet she went to the house of the canon, and told him the whole sequence of events. In great grief and sorrow for the boy, the canon came to the house and demanded back the body from the murderers, but the perfidious Jews still refused to satisfy his demand in any way. Nevertheless he also heard and recognized the voice of the innocent child sweetly singing the *Alma redemptoris mater.*

(90–104) Together they ran to the Archbishop of the city of Toledo and told him the sequence of events. He gathered a huge company of armed men and quickly went to investigate. He entered the guilty and treacherous house, breaking down the doors in his way, and roughly ordered the killer to produce the remains of the murdered innocent as quickly as possible – for he was sure that the boy was dead, in view of the great secrecy with which the malicious Jews had hidden him. All of them had conspired in the murder, but the main culprit in the murder, fearing the majesty of the Archbishop, confessed the truth of all his wickedness – how, out of envy at the mother of the Redeemer, he had extinguished the life of an innocent child, just because he had sung such a sweet song in honour of the Virgin Mother. After his confession of the crime, or rather his conviction – he put himself under the judgment of the Archbishop, and asked him for his mercy rather than his condemnation. (100) He led the Archbishop by the hand, for all was darkness and gloom where the boy lay dead in the depths. The singing voice was their leader and guide, and at last they arrived where the dead boy miraculously continued to sing the *Alma redemptoris mater* without ceasing – for when the dead boy's voice had finished the end of the antiphon, it would begin the same song over again throughout the whole day.

(105–112) The boy was lifted out, like a second Joseph out of the pit; with speed and rejoicing he was taken to the church. The song to the Virgin did not leave his lips; continually he sang the *Alma redemptoris mater.* The people were summoned, and the clergy were present in complete devotion. The Archbishop began to celebrate the divine office in honour of the blessed Virgin. The moment came when

redit vox cum organo et decantat puer mortuus *Alma redemptoris mater.*

Interim angit mora pueri mentem sue genitricis. Erat enim unicus filius matris sue. Miratur quod moram faciat longiorem et de mora diuturna subito timet et stupescit. Non enim de facili obliviscitur mater infantem uteri sui propter gaudium quia natus est homo in mundum. Effecta ergo fere sui impaciens opus manuum pretermittit, plateas ingreditur et vicos circuit civitatis circumspicit undique venientes oculo subtili obvios intuetur. Set nusquam filii sui faciem deprehendit: ultro graditur et ultra progreditur et ingreditur judaismum, vix se sustinens pre dolore quia dormitavit anima eius pre tedio cum ipsum quem dilexerat viventem mortuum estimabat. ffit iam vicina domui qua facinus exercuit progenies viperarum audit mater anxia filium suum decantantem *Alma redemptoris mater.* Audiebat quidem vocem set neminem videbat. Idcirco stabat stupefacta set tamen velut ovis solo balatu agnum, sic et ipsa filium proprium proprietate vocis et organi recognoscit, laborabat mater sustinens puerum periendo. Idcirco laborat clamans ori proprio non parcendo non potuit ori suo custodiam; set licet clamando rauce facte fuissent fauces sue tamen clamat indesinenter ad hostia hostium cruentorum: "Reddite filium meum! Reddite filium meum!" Verbi geminacio dolorem animi detegebat. Extra domum filium suum repetit a judeis, set cum non satisfaceret crudelitas perfidorum in offenso pede adit domum canonici pretaxati, eidem ex ordine referens universa. Accedit canonicus plangens puerum et deplorans. Ab interfectoribus repetit interfectum, set eorum perfidia ipsius voto nullatenus satisfecit. Audit tamen et ipse vocem cognitam innocentis decantantis suaviter *Alma redemptoris mater.*

Currunt ergo pariter ad Archiepiscopum urbis tolletane eidem rei seriem indicantes. Qui cum innumera manu armatorum currens ad spectaculum, locum perfidie conscium est ingressus, hostia confringit obstancia et severius precipit peremptori ut innocentis perempti eximie cicius ostendantur. Credidit enim extinctum quem tanta malicia secrecius occultabat. Universi in puerum necem consencerunt, set pueri precipuus interfector formidans Archiepiscopi majestatem tocius nequicie veritatem confitetur quomodo scilicet (fol.38v) ob invidiam conceptam contra Redemptoris matrem puerum innoxium suffocavit, eo quod in matris virginis memoriam tam suavem concinnit cantilenam. Confessus ymmo magis convictus ex scelere Archipresulis judicio se subjecit, misericordiam amplius expetens quam censuram, Archipresul ad manum trahitur. Erant enim ibi tenebre et caligo ubi puer mortuus jacuit in profundo. Tandem voce duce et ductrice ad locum ipsum pervenitur ubi miraculose sine intermissione concinebat puer mortuus *Alma redemptoris mater.* Cum enim vox extincti antiphone finem explicasset idem canticum tota die incepit iterato.

Extrahitur ergo puer tanquam alter Joseph de cisterna, et tam festive quam festine ad ecclesiam deportatur, nec recedit ab eius ore preconium virginale quia assidue concinit *Alma redemptoris mater.* Convocato populo, clero cum devocione maxima assistente, incipit Archipresul in honore beate virginis divina celebrare. Venit hora qua silencium assistentibus imperatur

the congregation was ordered to be silent; the preacher began to speak, bringing a message of salvation through the gospel. At this moment the boy also became quiet, and placed "a door of circumstance" on his lips, so that the words of the gospel would not be misheard or misunderstood because of the sound of his voice.

(113–26) The congregation listened with faith and devotion to the reading, and when the message of salvation was over, once again the boy miraculously began to sing the antiphon. How great then was the pious devotion of the clergy's prayers! How great was the effusion of tears among the congregation in its place, when the dead boy began again what he had just stopped, going through in his song what he had just passed over in silence! The health-giving Host was offered devoutly on the altar and the memory of the Lord's Passion worshipped, and all this time the boy's voice continued to sing of the purity of Mary. When the mysteries of our Redemption had been performed, the Archbishop turned to the congregation and delivered a sermon in praise of the innocence of the Virgin – though while he reverently called to memory the mother, of course he did not neglect to honour Christ as well. At the end of the sermon he wept and encouraged the clergy and people altogether to beseech the Virgin's Son with the aroma of devotion and the sweet scent of pious prayer, and to pray by the merits of his mother and the prayers of the precious Virgin that Christ should deign to restore the boy to life, and breathe the breath of life into the dead corpse.

(127–44) The clergy and the people poured out their souls within themselves, giving out their hearts like water in the sight of the Lord, letting their tears flow in a willing shower in the evening, a shower of tears, for their tears "were on their cheeks." They prayed in supplication; in faith they beseeched; they were not beset by a cloud of mistrust about the efficacy of their prayer, for it went straight up to the court of the Trinity: their faith swiftly penetrated to heaven, and their blessed trust was faithfully and joyfully repaid. (134) In reply to their public and private prayers, the Virgin Mother (as I imagine) looked into the face of Christ and beseeched Him in what I picture as a familiar fashion; and immediately the boy's cut throat was allowed to breathe again, his previously torn flesh was restored fully, and his tongue, which sang divine praise, was given back to him; his heart and liver which had been removed were put back again, or were created anew by divine aid. His soul was summoned back again into its vessel and vehicle, and the boy became whole again; the immortal spirit was again married to the dead flesh. He who was dead came to life again and returned; the boy awoke, aroused, as it were, from a deep sleep. Even now he did not cease his praise of Mary, and his sweet voice continued to sing the *Alma redemptoris mater*. Truly blessed are you, Mother of the Redeemer, for coming to the help of the dead boy who lacked the power to rise again: she who, to the amazement of Nature, gave birth to her own father, again astonished Nature by pouring back the vital spirit into the dead child through the intercession of her prayer.

(146–52) At the sight of this amazing miracle, the congregation of the faithful rejoiced, and at the sight they dissolved into tears: they still wondered if it was an illusion. When they looked at the revived boy's face, they discovered the pebble which Mary had placed in his mouth; they removed it, and immediately he stopped his singing of the antiphon. He lost the impelling power of speech which before had not allowed him to be silent. The pebble was placed as a sign in the cathedral church, to act as a monument of the event and as evidence of the miracle, to be kept there for ever.

cum aperitur vox predicantis bonum annunciantis salutem per evangelium. Silet puer ori suo apponens ostium circumstancie ne vox ipsius verba evangelica minus intelligi faciat vel audiri.

Auditur evangelium a circumstantibus tam fideliter quam devote. Ipsoque perlecto salubriter mirabiliter reincepit puer cantilenam *Alma redemptoris mater*. O quanta in clero devota votorum devocio! quanta in populo qui stabat in gradu suo lacrimarum effusio cum extinctus repeciit quod nuper omisit! Iterans vocis organo quod prius silencio pretermisit. Cum reverencia tractatur hostia salutaris in altari recolitur memoria dominice passionis organo innocencie marie preconium concinente. Expletis redempcionis nostre misteriis Archipresul se ad populum convertens sermonem texit in laudem pudicicie virginalis nec christi preconium reticet vel occultat dum marie matris eius memoriam venerabiliter representat. In fine sermonis clerum et populum cum lacrimis exhortatur ut cum devocionis aromate cum pie oracionis thure unanimiter natum de virgine deprecentur quatinus meritis matris sue et prece virginis preciose dignetur puerum reddere redivivum et eidem mortuo, vite spiraculum inspirare.

Plebs et clerus effundunt in se animas suas effundunt sicut aquam cor suum in conspectu domini (fol.39) fundentes pluviam voluntariam ac ymbrem serotinum lacrimarum quia lacrime sue in maxillis suis. Orant suppliciter et supplicant confidenter, nec est eis opposita nubes diffidencie ne transiret oracio quia ascendit usque ad consistorium trinitatis. ffides enim eorum celos penetravit celeriter et eorum felix confidencia tam fiducialiter quam feliciter impetravit.

Oracione facta publica seu privata, matre virgine ut arbitror respiciente in faciem christi filii sui et ipsum ut credo familiariter deprecante, subito guttur pueri precisus reseratur, pellis prius dissuta integre restauratur, lingua redditur divina canenti preconia, cor cum pulmone aut prius ablatum restituitur aut concessum divinitus de novo procreatur. Anima ad vas suum et sui vehiculum revocatur et homo [fit] integer carni mortue iterum se maritat spiritus immortalis. Revixit qui mortuus fuerat et recedit, puer quasi de gravi sompno excitatus; set tamen marie preconium non pretermittit set organo mellifluo concinit *Alma redemptoris mater*. O vere alma redemptoris mater que sic succurrit egenti surgere defuncto puero, nam que genitorem natura mirante suum genuit, vitalem spiritum natura mirante mortuo sic infudit sue precis remedio mediante.

Exultat turba fidelium visa miraculi novitate et de visione resol[u]untur in lacrimas universi putantes tamen fantasma esse. Intuentur faciem redivivi, lapillum per mariam impositum in ore reperiunt, inventum extrahunt et redivivus continuo antiphonam pretermittit *Alma redemptoris mater*. Amisit organum qui prius silencium non admisit. Lapis ille in signum repositus est in ecclesia cathedrali in monimentum rei et miraculi testimonium perpetuo reservandus.

138 **fit** fiat MS

(153–61) The Archbishop now asked the boy to tell him the whole sequence and order of the affair, and he answered the pontiff to his satisfaction, giving him a full and true account of the whole series of events – the crime of the Jews, his own martyrdom and the assistance of the Virgin Mary. He attributed everything to the Mother of God: whatever had happened to him was done by the Mother of Grace, who had thus aided his wretchedness from the abundance of her mercy. As he told his story, he pointed with his finger at the murderer, but this boy, who had been raised from death, prayed humbly but insistently that his murderer should not be condemned to die for the crime. At last the boy rose, and gave thanks fully to his saviour, the Virgin and, now made whole in every particular, lived long after in the city of Toledo.

(162–75) The Jew was more sure of his punishment than hopeful for mercy, but after seeing the miracle he confessed himself guilty and worthy of execution; nevertheless, he asked first to be bathed by the saving water of baptism. The Archbishop was more eager for the saving of a soul than for the punishment of the crime; he baptized the Jew and entrusted him to the church; having marked him with the sign of our faith, he remitted the penalty and pardoned the crime. Afterward the Jew, who had before been the most impious persecutor of the name of the Virgin, became her most pious devotee. There was also an infidel who (167) witnessed the miracle and who became a member of the Christian faith. Thus, in the faith of Christ, the two walls of the cornerstone, from both circumcised and uncircumcised, were joined together. The second man, now a believer instead of an infidel, was prosperous and very rich: he built a church in honour of the Virgin Mother, where her memory is memorably celebrated. Thus the kindly Mother of the Redeemer helps everyone with success; by her deserts may she commend to God those of us who are mindful of her, and help them by her good actions. AMEN

Inquirit ergo pontifex a puero tocius rei seriem et tenorem, et ipse pro voto pontifici satisfaciens, rei processum excessum judeorum sui martirium et virginis marie suffragium veraciter enarravit. Totumque dei genetrici ascribebat quicquid circa ipsum actum est per matrem gracie, que de sue habundancia misericordie ipsius miserie sic subvenit. Inter alia suo digito demonstravit occisorem, et vere resuscitatus a mortuis pro suo peremptore ne mortis reus morti traderetur instanter et humiliter supplicavit. Surgens tandem puer grates uberimas sue reddidit salvatrici, totusque factus incolumis vixit diucius in urbe tolletana.

Judeus plus venia desperans quam vindicta viso miraculo se reum mortis confitetur set tamen perfundi se postulat lavacro salutari. Pontifex (fol.39v) salutem anime eius siciens non criminis ulcionem judeum baptizatum consignat ecclesie et caractare fidei nostre insignito remittit penam pariter et offensam. Qui postmodum effectus est Marie piissimus venerator qui prius fuerat sui nominis impiissimus persecutor. Gentilis eciam quidam ad hoc venit spectaculum set dum huiusmodi fieret spectator miraculi fidei se subdidit christiane. Ut sic in fide christi lapidis angularis ex circumcisione et prepucio duo parietes jungerentur. Ipse quoque fidus de perfidio, dives opum et habundans diviciis in honorem matris virginis ecclesiam fabricavit, ubi virginis memoria memoriter celebratur. Sic alma redemptoris mater utrique subvenit cum effectu, que sui memores deo commendet meritis et iuvet beneficiis.

AMEN.

Sir Thopas

JOANNE A. CHARBONNEAU

FIT ONE

FIT TWO

FIT THREE

APPENDIX

Chaucer's tale of *Sir Thopas*, the most imitative and derivative of all the *Canterbury Tales*, has no known single source or analogue, but instead borrows extensively from romances and ballads with echoes from these popular works in virtually every line. Unlike most of the other tales in the Canterbury collection, *Sir Thopas* is not really a tale at all, but is instead a hodgepodge of common rhetorical devices and popular plot motifs. Filled with conventional diction, paralyzingly bad meter and stereotypical catalogues, the poem must be seen as a parody or satire – a position most scholars have maintained, following the lead

of Richard Hurd, who in 1911 claimed *Thopas* was "Don Quixote in little."[1] Most also agree that part of the Chaucerian joke is his passing off this potpourri, this deliberately interrupted narrative, as a coherent tale. Major disagreements, however, revolve around questions of who or what is being lampooned. In 1922 Lilian Winstanley argued that the whole poem was "intended as a satire against Philip van Artevelde."[2] Later, John Manly observed that Chaucer's contemporaries were accustomed to poke fun at the "efforts of the Flemish *bourgeoisie* to ape the manners of the English and French aristocracy"and would have "recognized unhesitatingly the object of satire was the ridiculous pretentiousness of these Flemings."[3] Although F. N. Robinson doubted the association between Thopas and Philip, he nevertheless endorsed the Flemish theory as "very probable."[4] But other scholars have found little internal evidence to support the Flemish theory and have begun to reconsider its legitimacy. If the poem is meant to satririze or parody any particular Fleming or group of Flemings, their identities are certainly obscure.[5] Chaucer's only concrete satiric suggestion is in placing the birth of Thopas in Flanders.

Thomas Tyrwhitt, on the other hand, voiced what has since become a modern critical commonplace when he stated that *Sir Thopas* was intended to ridicule the "palpable-gross fictions" [i.e. Middle English metrical romances] of their time, especially "the meanness of their language and versification."[6] Because they are derivative in nature and most often translated from French or Anglo-Norman originals, the Middle English metrical romances have often been viewed as inferior, debased, and popular in the pejorative sense – the works of hacks[7] – especially when set beside such highly sophisticated romances as *Sir Gawain and the Green Knight* and Chaucer's own *Troilus and Criseyde.* Recently, however, critics have begun to rehabilitate these much-maligned popular texts,[8] a task made

1 *Letters on Chivalry and Romance*, ed. Edith J. Morley (London, 1911), pp. 147, 172ff. Hurd is also quoted in Caroline Spurgeon, *Five Hundred Years of Chaucer Criticism and Allusion, 1357–1900* (Cambridge, 1925), vol. 1, p. 422.

2 Lilian Winstanley, ed., *The Prioress's Tale and The Tale of Sir Thopas* (Cambridge, 1922), p. lxviii.

3 John Matthews Manly, "*Sir Thopas*: A Satire," *Essays and Studies* 13 (1928): 60.

4 F. N. Robinson, ed., *The Complete Works of Geoffrey Chaucer*, 2nd edn (Boston, 1957), p. 737.

5 John Burrow has identified another poem describing the "unheroic doings of Flemish townsfolk," but the parallels betweeen it and Chaucer's tale could be found in virtually any other Middle English verse romance. See "Chaucer's *Sir Thopas* and *La Prise de Nuevile*," *Yearbook of English Studies* 14 (1984): 44–55. Walter Scheps sums up the critique of the Flemish theory by noting that Thopas's birth in Flanders is the only piece of "flimsy evidence" that earlier scholars had to support it. See "Sir Thopas: The Bourgeois Knight, the Minstrel and the Critics," *Tennessee Studies in Literature* 11 (1966): 42 n. 27.

6 Thomas Tyrwhitt, *The Poetical Works of Geoffrey Chaucer* (London, 1843), p. lxvi.

7 A. C. Gibbs, in *Middle English Romances* (London, 1966), p. 37, says of *Emaré* that it illustrates "the depths of ineptitude to which an English medieval romance could sink."

8 Earlier and still useful studies of Middle English romance are Laura Hibbard Loomis, *Medieval Romance in England: A Study of the Sources and Analogues of the Non-Cyclic Metrical Romances* (New York, 1954), and Dieter Mehl, *The Middle English Romances of the Thirteenth and Fourteenth Centuries* (London, 1969). This reassessment has been aided recently by new critical editions such as the readily accessible TEAMS editions (also available on line). See also Joanne A. Rice's *Middle English Romance: An Annotated Bibliography, 1955–1985* (New York, 1987), and the following collections of essays: *Studies in Medieval English Romances: Some New Approaches*, ed. Derek Brewer (Cambridge, 1988); *Companion to Middle English Romance*, ed. Henk Aertsen and Alasdair A. MacDonald (Amsterdam, 1990); *Romance in Medieval England*, ed. Maldwyn Mills, Jennifer Fellows and Carol M. Meale (Cambridge, 1991); *Romance Reading on the Book: Essays on Medieval Narrative*

much more difficult in the case of *Sir Thopas* because many readers have tended to agree with the Host's condemnation of its "drasty rymyng," and by extension, to view such romances as *nat worth a toord* (VII, 930). The Host, of course, does not necessarily represent Chaucer's own estimation of these poems, and many modern scholars have questioned the traditional view that Chaucer rejected the native English romance tradition, especially in light of his own appropriation of the diction, formulaic conventions, and even compositional methods of the romances in serious contexts within his own work, especially in the *Troilus*. John Burrow, for example, has argued that *Sir Thopas* should not be viewed simply as a parody of popular English minstrelsy, but as a "cartoon" that illuminates "many of the weaknesses and some of the strengths of the hacks" as well as of the poet himself.[9] Alan Gaylord has taken this approach one step further, suggesting that the subject of parody in *Sir Thopas* is not Middle English romances at all, "but the fancies and temptations of [Chaucer's] own practice."[10] Other critics have cautioned against applying modern aesthetics, which denigrates formulaic language, to Chaucer's attitudes towards the poetic practices of his own time.[11] Yet, despite these studies, most modern scholars, following Tyrwhitt, have believed that Chaucer's poem *is meant* to be a parody or satire of the extravagances or general faults of the romances. That said, there is some question as to whether in *Sir Thopas* Chaucer is poking fun at *all* varieties of Middle English romances or only at specific types. For many reasons from meter to the physical layout on the page, tail-rhyme romances seem to be the main butt of Chaucer's satire.

First, tail-rhyme romances typically are composed in stanzas of twelve lines divided into four groups of three, each group containing, as a rule, a couplet with four accents to the line, and a concluding "tail" line with three accents.[12]

Presented to Maldwyn Mills, ed. Jennifer Fellows, Rosalind Field, Gillian Rogers, and Judith Weiss (Cardiff, 1996); *Tradition and Transformation in Medieval Romance*, ed. Rosalind Field (Cambridge, UK, 1999); *The Spirit of Medieval English Popular Romance*, ed. Ad Putter and Jane Gilbert (Harlow, England, 2000); and *The Matter of Identity in Medieval Romance*, ed. Phillipa Hardman (Cambridge, 2002).

9 John A. Burrow, *Ricardian Poetry* (New Haven, CT, 1971), p. 14.

10 Alan Gaylord, "The Moment of *Sir Thopas*: Towards a New Look at Chaucer's Language," *Chaucer Review* 16 (1982): 320.

11 Nancy M. Bradbury, "Chaucerian Minstrelsy: *Sir Thopas*, *Troilus and Criseyde* and English Metrical Romance," in *Tradition and Transformation in Medieval Romance*, pp. 115–24, has also noted elements of Chaucer's own poetics in the tale and questioned the assumptions of post-modern critics that formulaic language is *per se* inartistic. Jane Gilbert, "A Theoretical Introduction," in *The Spirit of Medieval English Popular Romance*, p. 29, reiterates the importance of "reworking conventional aesthetic criteria" especially when dealing with so-called popular romances. In "Genre and Authority: The Eighteenth-Century Creation of Chaucerian Burlesque," *Huntington Library Quarterly* 48 (1985): 345–62, Joseph A. Dane discusses how such eighteenth-century figures as Hurd, Warton, Warburton, Percy, and Tyrwhitt grappled with Chaucerian tales in terms of an emerging critical vocabulary including parody, burlesque, and travesty. He argues that Chaucer could not have written *Sir Thopas* as a parody or burlesque if the "generic categories which these words tend to create did not exist." Other scholars have found clear distinctions between parody, satire and burlesque in their studies concerning the sensibility, critical idiom and the role of formulae in the romances and Chaucer's own poetry. See Susan Wittig, *Stylistic and Narrative Structures in the Middle English Romances* (Austin, TX, 1978), and Jesse M. Gellrich, *Discourse and Dominion in the Fourteenth Century: Oral Contexts of Writing in Philosophy, Politics, and Poetry* (Princeton, 1995).

12 A. Mcl.Trounce, "The English Tail-Rhyme Romances," *Medium Ævum* 1 (1932): 87–108, 162–82; *Medium Ævum* 2 (1933): 34–57, 189–98; *Medium Ævum* 3 (1934): 30–50.

Sir Thopas, however, has no twelve-line stanzas, but rather four stanzas of ten lines, one stanza of seven lines, and the remaining twenty-six stanzas of six lines each – a pattern obviously intended to represent a telescoping of the usual tail-rhyme stanza form and purposely manipulated "to produce bathos."[13] That Chaucer intended to draw attention to his poem as a tail-rhyme romance and also to parody the form is suggested by the physical layout of the poem in four of the landmark manuscripts of *The Canterbury Tales* – Hengwrt, Ellesmere, Cambridge University College Dd.4.24, and Cambridge University College Gg.4.27. In these manuscripts the poem appears in an eye-catching layout consisting of rhyming lines joined together with brackets, the tail-rhyme line appearing as a second column, and the bob-lines forming almost a third column. This design – whether the scribes' idea, or more likely Chaucer's own – seems to have been based on a well-known tradition, as one would expect of a successful parody of a genre.[14] In addition to mimicking, and perhaps parodying, the form of the English tail-rhyme romances, Chaucer also parodies their vocabulary, rhetoric and syntax, as the following extracts fully demonstrate.

Chaucer's familiarity with and knowledge of Middle English romances are patently evident and explicit. Towards the end of *Sir Thopas*, Chaucer refers specifically to six titles of "romances of prys,/ of Horn Child and of Ypotys,/ of Beves and Sir Gy,/ of Sir Lybeux, and Pleyndamour . . ." (VII, 897–900), and in his very last stanza he alludes to a seventh romance "Sire Percyvell (VII, 916). *Ypotys* stands out as the anomaly in this list, and it is likely that Chaucer included the didactic poem among the known popular chivalric romances as a joke, as name recognition of a serious and moral poem (which *Thopas* is not). It is also possible, given the inclusion of *Horn Childe*, that Chaucer is drawing attention to another "child" hero, the wise, young boy Ypotys, who stands in contrast to Thopas as hero. The other work from this list that is problematic is *Pleyndamour*, the only text that is unknown today. Although it may be lost, this work may never have existed at all since the name *Pleyndamour* is similar to many other names of heroes and heroines ending in *-amour* found scattered throughout the pages of Middle English romance. The titular heroes of *Sir Eglamour of Artois* and *Sir Triamour* are examples, as are Triamour in both *Guy of Warwick* and in *Sir Launfal*, Lady Doceamour in *Bevis of Hamton*, Dame

13 Walter Scheps, "Sir Thopas: The Bourgeois Knight, the Minstrel and the Critics," p. 41 n. 8.

14 Rhiannon Purdie in a forthcoming book *Anglicizing Romance* provides manuscript evidence to counter the position taken by Judith Tschann, "The Layout of *Sir Thopas* in the Ellesmere, Hengwrt, Cambridge Dd.4.24, and Cambridge Gg.4.27 Manuscripts," *Chaucer Review* 20 (1985): 1–13, who argues that, although the layout of *Sir Thopas* in the four Chaucer manuscripts is "extravagant, a bit puzzling, and very conspicuous," Chaucer was not parodying the physical layout of Middle English tail-rhyme romances. Instead, Purdie clearly indicates that graphic tail-rhyme is used for *Beues of Hampton* (cited in *Sir Thopas*) in the late-fourteenth-century MS Egerton 2862 (fols 45r–49v), and the early-fifteenth-century Caius College MS 175. *Sir Isumbras,* also in this Caius College MS, is laid out the same way there, in the mid-fifteenth-century Advocates MS 19.3.1, and the faded mid-fourteenth-century scrap, Gray's Inn MS 20, which predates Chaucer's work by some decades. Robert Thornton, the enthusiastic fifteenth-century preserver of romances, used graphic tail-rhyme for his British Library Additional MS 31042 copies of the *Sege of Melayne* and *Duke Roland and Sir Otuel of Spain*, as well as for the sixteen-line stanzas of *Sir Degrevant* in Lincoln MS 91. "Even the arrangement of the absurd little bob-lines in *Sir Thopas* – set in a third column to the right of the tail-lines – has a precedent in the layout of those rhymed-alliterative poems such as the *Pistill of Susan*."

d'Amore in *Lybeaus Desconus*, and Lady Lufamour in *Sir Perceval of Galles*. Whether Chaucer invented the name *Pleyndamour* or took it from a now-lost source, he was obviously using it to burlesque the names of romance characters.[15]

Of the romances specifically named by Chaucer, half (*Guy of Warwick*, *Bevis of Hamton*, *Horn Childe*) exist in the famous Auchinleck manuscript, which includes a total of sixteen Middle English romances. Among them, *Amis and Amiloun* is of particular interest in terms of a character named Child Amourant (Emerald), which may have influenced Chaucer's naming of his hero as both a child and jewel (topaz). The Auchinleck *Guy* has a giant named Amourant, possibly the source of Thopas's giant adversary, renamed Olifaunt. The fact that Chaucer alludes to the *Horn* poem, which survives only in this manuscript, with *Guy* (the poem with the largest number of verbal parallels to *Thopas*) and *Bevis* (with its six-line, tail-rhyme stanza whose opening provides the closest and longest example of direct borrowing) leads to the conclusion that Chaucer had seen and read this famous manuscript, which was copied by scribes in London 1330–40, near the time of Chaucer's birth. Although there is no direct evidence for this claim and only circumstantial evidence that the Auchinleck manuscript remained in London during the fourteenth century, this manuscript does account for parallels to *Thopas* that exist in no other extant collection.[16] In addition to *Amis and Amiloun*, *Bevis*, *Guy*, and the unique extant text of *Horn Childe*, this miscellany also includes *Sir Degaré*, *Kyng Alisaunder*, *Otuel*, *Richard Coeur de Lion*, and the unique copy of *Reinbrun* – all probable sources or analogues of Chaucer's tale of Thopas.

Of the remaining romances that Chaucer actually names in his text, both *Ypotys* and the only extant copy of *Lybeaus Desconus* are found in the fifteenth-century MS Cotton Caligula A.2, which also has versions of *Thomas of Erceldoune*, *Sir Launfal*, *Octavian*, and *Sir Eglamour of Artois* – all possible sources of Chaucer's *Thopas* if the assumption is made that they existed in an earlier exemplar. Found also in Cotton Caligula A.2 are the *Trentals* of St Gregory (a pope) and a life of St Jerome (considered a cardinal)[17] tantalizing

[15] Although Chaucer could have invented *Pleyndamour* based on these other names, Malory makes reference to a knight named Playn de Amours in *Le Morte Darthur* (Book IX), who is one of the three brothers met by the hero La Cote Mal Taillé, whose adventures parallel those of Lybeaus Desconus, the very hero mentioned by Chaucer in the same line as *Pleyndamour* in the text of *Sir Thopas* (VII, 900). Where Malory found it is unknown; it does not appear in any extant manuscript of the French prose *Tristan*, the most likely source for this part of Malory's story. But as Robinson points out, it "appears to have been in actual use in the fifteenth century," and is the name of "one of the scribes of Cambridge MS Ff.1.6: 'Nomen scriptoris Nicholaus plenus amoris' (perhaps a Latinization of Pleyndamour or Fullalove, though it may be a mere rime-tag)," p. 740, note to line 897.

[16] Dates are referred to by Derek Pearsall and I. C. Cunningham, from their introduction to *The Auchinleck Manuscript, National Library of Scotland Advocates' MS 19.2.1*, facsimile edition (London, 1979), p. vii. Helen Cooper mentions texts in the Auchinleck manuscript that provide "a number of parallels to *Sir Thopas* that are found nowhere else," but then softens that claim by saying "it is not impossible that Chaucer knew it," *The Canterbury Tales*, p. 301.

[17] According to Loomis (Bryan and Dempster, pp. 488–9 n. 5), "in medieval art Jerome was represented with a cardinal's hat from the end of the thirteenth century (cf. K. Kuenstle, *Ikonographie der Heiligen* [Freiburg-in-Breisgau, 1926], p. 299). Two illuminations in a splendid Bible executed in England in the latter part of the fourteenth century, probably for Richard II, show Jerome with the cardinal's hat (cf. Brit. Mus., Roy. I E IX, fols 230, 234 [reproduced by Eric Millar, *English Illuminations of the XIVth Century* (Paris, 1928), plates 74, 77])."

possibilities for *romances that been roiales,/ Of popes and of cardinales* in *Sir Thopas* (VII, 848–9). The hero Perceval, also mentioned in *Sir Thopas*, is found in a Middle English romance, extant only in the Thornton MS, which also contains another version of *Thomas of Erceldoune*. Chaucer then seems to have had access to or familiarity with at least the manuscript collections or prototypes of Auchinleck, Cotton Caligula A.2, and Thornton.

Of all the works most likely known to Chaucer, the extremely popular *Guy of Warwick* is clearly a major source for *Sir Thopas*. This is apparent in terms of narrative motifs and descriptions as well as phraseology and even specific rhyme schemes. Caroline Strong[18] has provided forty verbal parallels between the two texts. If the resemblances seem coincidental given the conventionality of romance vocabulary, the clinching piece of evidence is that *Guy* contains close parallels to two of the Host's nasty comments about the pilgrim-Chaucer's tale about Thopas in the prologue to the *Tale of Melibee*. In fact, the expression *not worth a tord* is found evidently only in three literary texts.[19] From *Guy of Warwick*, Chaucer also could have borrowed a giant, references to Termagaunt, the carbuncle in the arming scene, the binding effect of love, the specifics of Thopas's physical description (white skin, red *rode*, yellow hair, and the word *syklatoun*), specific references to riding (bestriding and pricking, especially), and most dramatically many specific rhyme schemes, the most notable being the four rhyming words *contree*, *see*, *free*, *contree* in the same order in the second stanza of both poems.

Guy of Warwick, however, does not account for all of the material found in *Sir Thopas*. Most noticeably absent is the elf queen or fairy mistress motif, which Chaucer could have borrowed from *Sir Launfal* or *Thomas of Erceldoune*; a lady of supernatural qualities is also found in *Lybeaus Desconus* and a fairy king and Other World kingdom in *Sir Orfeo*. Both *Lybeaus Desconus* and *Sir Launfal* are the works of Thomas Chestre, a contemporary of Chaucer's, so these works were no doubt accessible to Chaucer and his fellow Londoners. Chaucer may also have drawn from *Roman de la Rose* and probably had heard or read other romances and listened to many popular ballads. Although manuscripts of the Robin Hood ballads are later in date, oral versions are likely to have been circulating during Chaucer's time. Certainly the hero's interest in wrestling and archery and the band of *myrie men* (VII, 839) suggest familiarity with the popular ballads. *Gamelyn*, which survives in some manuscripts of the *Canterbury Tales* as a spurious *Cook's Tale*, has the hero wrestling for a ram and joining a group of archer-outlaws, following the Robin Hood model. That poem is also distinguished by its repeated formula, *Liþeth, and lestneþ and holdeþ ȝour tonge*.[20]

[18] Caroline Strong, "Sir Thopas and Sir Guy, II," *Modern Language Notes* 23 (1908): 102–6.

[19] The host says, "Now swich a rym the devel I biteche!" (VII, 924), which is paralleled to "þe deuel biteche ich ȝou ichon" (*Guy*, line 5834) as well as the Host's "Thy drasty rymyng is nat worth a toord!" (VII, 930), paralleled with "Þou nart nouȝt worþ a tord!" (*Guy*, line 3704). The *OED* gives only these two references for the uncommon (in literary works at any rate) expression *not worth a tord*; however, the expression is also found in *Otuel and Roland* when a Saracen is accused of saying "that oure god vas nouȝt worth a tord" (line 1322).

[20] Helen Cooper, *The Canterbury Tales*, p. 302.

Topaz as name and gem: The name Topas, although never associated with a male in Middle English romances,[21] is nonetheless a name for females in several of these works. In *Richard Coeur de Lion*, for example, Topas is listed as one of the children of Henry I and a sister to Richard: *þe þrydde hys sustyr Topyas.*[22] This is purely fictitious since historically there is no known sister of Richard's by that name. The name occurs as well in both *Floris and Blanchefleur* as the name of the heroine's mother and in *Il Filocolo*, Boccaccio's work, which Chaucer seemed to know well.[23] Chaucer, then, appears to have appropriated a feminine name for his knightly hero. Skeat neatly sums up the joke by simply stating that Topas was an excellent choice of a name for Chaucer's mock-hero who is "such a gem of a knight."[24] Determining what, if anything, the topaz as a gem signified for Chaucer and his contemporaries is of utmost importance before assigning probable significance or interpretation of the name for Chaucer's hero. This matter is still being debated by scholars, many of whom until fairly recently, following the lead of Woodburn O. Ross,[25] took for granted that the topaz was the symbol of chastity or a protection against sensuality and unchastity.[26] In 1976, John Conley tried to sort out the various contexts in which the topaz appeared: lapidarial, biblical, exegetical, heraldic, and chivalric.[27] Challenging Ross's hypothesis, Conley concluded that the reputation of the topaz was as the most precious and brightest of gems, not primarily as the gem of chastity after all.[28] He brings in evidence from Chaucer himself who uses the emerald (not the topaz) as the gem of chastity in the *Prioress's Tale* (VII, 609). E. S. Kooper[29] brings to light another property of the topaz, hitherto overlooked, but more significant to this tale than the property of chastity, and that is its property as a hollow mirror, which inverts images. In his chart listing the distribution in over twenty-one lapidaries of the three most common properties associated with the topaz, he discovered its inverting property was mentioned with even

21 The name is attached to a male, however, in an anti-Lollard poem dating from 1401: "The Reply of Friar Daw Topias with Jack Upland's Rejoinder," in *Political Poems and Songs Relating to English History*, ed. Thomas Wright, Rolls Series no. 14, vol. 2 (London, 1861), pp. 39–114. W. H. Schofield, *Chivalry in English Literature* (Cambridge, 1912), notes that Watriquet de Couvin praised his patron Gauchier de Châtillon, the Constable of France, who died in 1329 with the non-satiric words: "C'estoit la jemme et la topasse/ Des haus hommes, touz les passoit/ D'onneur faire" (p. 278).

22 *Richard Coeur de Lion* in *Der mittelenglische Versroman über Richard Löwenherz*, ed. Karl Brunner (Vienna, 1913), p. 90, line 204.

23 The line from *Il Filocolo* is "una nobilissima giovane romana, nata della gente Giulia, e Giulia Topazia nominata" from *Opere volgari di Giovanni Boccaccio* (Florence, 1829), vol. 7, I. i, pp. 13–14.

24 W. W. Skeat, ed., *The Complete Works of Geoffrey Chaucer,* 6 vols (Oxford, 1900), V. 183.

25 "Possible Significance of the Name *Thopas*," *Modern Language Notes* 45 (1930): 172–4.

26 F. N. Robinson in the Explanatory Notes to his 1957 edition says that the name may imply the "further symbolism of purity, inasmuch as the topaz was worn by young girls as a charm against luxury" (p. 737); Charles W. Dunn also says "the name suggests the gem of chastity" (*A Chaucer Reader* [New York, 1952], p. 50); E. Talbot Donaldson notes that the hero's chastity is "perhaps symbolized in his name, Topaze, the stone of chastity" (*Chaucer's Poetry: An Anthology for the Modern Reader* [New York, 1958], p. 935). Robert A. Pratt notes "the topaz was a symbol of chastity" (*The Canterbury Tales* [New York, 1974], p. 161). Editors from 1933 until 1974, then, have ignored the warnings of Skeat, who said that Thopas was merely "an excellent title for such a gem of a knight" (V. 183), to which A. C. Baugh added that apart from that symbolism, no other "need be supposed" (*Chaucer's Major Poetry* [New York, 1963], p. 347).

27 John Conley, "The Peculiar Name Thopas," *Studies in Philology* 73 (1976): 42–61.

28 Conley, *ibid.*, especially pp. 52–61.

29 "Inverted Images in Chaucer's *Tale of Sir Thopas*," *Studia Neophilologica* 56 (1984): 147–54.

more frequency than chastity. Obviously this property would have particular satiric reverberations for Chaucer and his audience in this tale of all others that mirrors and inverts many of the conventions of chivalry and metrical romance.

For the purposes of this chapter, *Sir Thopas* is divided into the three fits suggested by the manuscript tradition,[30] and the various episodes or motifs within each fit are then numbered. (All the quoted extracts are numbered sequentially throughout the chapter, and these numbers also appear after the bibliographic information in the alphabetized list of editions in the Appendix.) From the organization of his tale into fits, it is apparent that Chaucer included parallels and similar ordering devices for each of the three fits: each has a minstrel opening, a typical romance catalogue, a stereotypical description, and suggestions of action to come. The halving of each fit seems intentional: Chaucer begins with 18 stanzas, then moves to 9, and ends with 4½ – progressive halvings. If this design is as deliberate as it seems, then, as John Burrow has noted, the ratio is that of the diapason, the numerical expression of the principle that was thought to govern the order of the universe.[31] Lee Patterson sees the "disparity between this grandiose conception of cosmic harmony and the thematically ill-shaped and diminutive *Sir Thopas* [as] part of the joke."[32] From this perspective, the tale is deliberately incomplete, one that Chaucer never intended to finish. "The layout also serves as a comment of the form, as the intellectual or narrative content of the columns dwindles towards nothing as one moves across the page."[33] From the appearance of the poem on the page to the ever-shortening divisions of the poem, Chaucer reinforces the joke that the tale ends before its action really begins.

For contemporary audiences, Chaucer's placing of his diminutive hero's residence in the non-exotic, too real world of Flanders[34] instead of in a fairyland or exotic, distant faraway country would have been a source of humor. As if

[30] Hengwrt, Ellesmere, Cambridge Dd.4.24 and Cambridge Gg.4.27 (as well as eleven other manuscripts) all agree on marking a fit division at line 891. The paraph mark of Gg was missed by John Burrow, as it was not visible in the facsimile, so that his count of fourteen manuscripts (see "*Sir Thopas*: An Agony in Three Fits," *Review of English Studies* NS 22 [1971]: 54–8; rpt. in Burrow, *Essays On Medieval Literature* [New York, 1984]), is one short of the fifteen that Tschann mentions. Burrow also lists twelve manuscripts (including Ellesmere and Hengwrt) which indicate a new fit at line 833, thus dividing the poem into three, rather than two fits. See also Phillipa Hardman, "Fitt Divisions in Middle English Romances: A Consideration of the Evidence," *Yearbook of English Studies* 22 (1992): 63–80.

[31] John Burrow, "*Sir Thopas*, An Agony," pp. 54–8. E. A. Jones, in '"Loo, Lordes Myne, Heere is a Fit!' The Structure of Chaucer's *Sir Thopas*," *Review of English Studies* NS 51 (2000): 248–52, takes Burrow's argument one step further by emphasizing Chaucer's familiarity with Neoplatonic arithmetical traditions and his possible use of the perfect number 28 and other significant ratios in terms of medieval cosmology and divine creation. Jones sees the poem divided into two sections, one of 176 lines, followed by the interjection or interruption of "*Loo, lordes myne, heere is a fit*" (VII, 888), followed by lines totalling 28 (a Perfect number). See also Derek Brewer, "Arithmetic and the Mentality of Chaucer," in *Literature in Fourteenth-Century England*, ed. Piero Boitani and Anna Torti (Tübingen, 1983), pp. 155–64.

[32] Lee Patterson, "'What Man Artow?' Authorial Self-Definition in *The Tale of Sir Thopas* and *The Tale of Melibee*," *Studies in the Age of Chaucer* 11 (1989): 124.

[33] Helen Cooper, *The Canterbury Tales*, p. 300.

[34] Winstanley, *The Prioress's Tale* and *The Tale of Sir Thopas*, notes that the father of Philip van Artevelde (a possible prototype for Thopas) "devoted himself in a quite special way to the interests of Poperinghe" (p. lxxi). W. W. Lawrence suggests that this town might have been chosen for its comic-sounding name and associations with commonplace things. See "Satire in Sir Thopas," *PMLA* 50 (1935): 81–91.

Flanders were not satiric enough, according to Gibbs and Manly, the men of Poperinghe, the town where Thopas was born, had a traditional reputation for stupidity.[35] To make matters worse, Chaucer rhymes *fer contree* with *al biyonde the see*; in the same stanza he repeats *contree* to rhyme with *free* – a striking parallel to the second stanza of *Guy of Warwick*. Even the most impoverished rhyme schemes in Middle English verse romances are not usually this blatantly bad. From *Guy*, Chaucer also borrowed the rather unusual rhyme *entent* with *verrayment* as well as the juxtaposition of *al of a knyght* with *his name was*. From *Sir Eglamour*, a close analogue to Chaucer's own words in *Thopas*, Chaucer may have borrowed both the division of his poem into fits as well as the phraseology *I was born in Artas;/ Syr Prymsamour my fadyr was,/ The lord of þat countre*. Thopas is described as a *doghty swayn* but the conventional collocation of *doghty* with *dede* is lacking.[36] Instead Chaucer undercuts his hero's courage by rhyming *swayn* with Thopas's white face of *payndemayn* – perhaps to suggest that his bravery is mere appearance or that his white face denotes fear, not courage. By casting doubt on the aristocratic and chivalric nature of Thopas's birth, by undercutting the hero in a few lines instead of establishing his noble lineage, Chaucer calls Thopas's fitness for knighthood into question.

FIT ONE

I. Minstrel Opening and Introduction of Hero

Many narratives in Middle English – whether intended to be heard or read, whether primarily learned or not, whether secular or religious – begin with the traditional call to listen carefully and not disrupt the story about to be told.[37] The command *lesteneð* or *herkeneð* within the first stanzas is so common that Chaucer's opening *Listeth, lordes, in good entent,/ And I wol telle verrayment* fits this quite ordinary and normal pattern. For Chaucer, however, the verb is unique in his corpus of work; the most common word he uses in other works is

[35] A. C. Gibbs, *Middle English Romance*, p. 118. Manly ("Sir Thopas: A Satire," pp. 52–70) infers from the *Cronycke van Nederlent* that the men of Poperinghe were seen by contemporaries as stupid. He also draws attention to the fact that the actual lord of Poperinghe was the Abbot of St Bertin.

[36] This phrase *doghty in dede* was a stock descriptor. See *Amis*, lines 178, 442, 466; *Guy of Warwick*, stanza 10, line 6; *Isumbras*, line 9, *Lybeaus Desconus*, line 6; *Octavian B*, line 18, *Otuel and Roland*, lines 617, 749, and 826; *Sir Degrevant*, line 12; *Sir Perceval of Gales*, ed. J. Campion and F. Holthausen (Heidelberg, 1913), line 18n, p. 76.

[37] Albert C. Baugh has written extensively on the role of conventional language and improvisation in Middle English romance in a series of articles: "Convention and Individuality in the Middle English Romance," in *Medieval Literature and Folklore Studies: Essays in Honor of Francis Lee Utley*, ed. Jerome Mandel and Bruce A. Rosenberg (New Brunswick, NJ, 1970), pp. 123–46; "Improvisation in the Middle English Romance," *Proceedings of the American Philosophical Society* 103 (1959): 418–54; and "The Middle English Romance: Some Questions of Creation, Presentation, and Preservation," *Speculum* 42 (1967): 1–31. See also D. S. Brewer, "The Relationship of Chaucer to the English and European Traditions," in *Chaucer and Chaucerians*, ed. D. S. Brewer (London, 1966), pp. 3–15; P. M. Kean, *Chaucer and the Making of English Poetry* (London, 1972), pp. 5–23; and William A. Quinn and Audley S. Hall, *Jongleur: A Modified Theory of Oral Improvisation and its Effects on the Performance and Transmission of Middle English Romance* (Washington, DC, 1982).

hark or *hearken*.[38] In terms of oral address to the audience and minstrel opening, *Sir Thopas* seems to have drawn heavily upon the Guy story, including some rhyme schemes, although the diction is commonplace in oral poetry. Both *Sir Degaré* and *Sir Eglamour of Artois* echo certain rhymes as well as the standard references to listening and tournaments. After calls to attention, most poets usually establish the identity and lineage of their heroes, emphasizing feats of arms or other chivalric accomplishments. Chaucer instead unexpectedly places the otherwise conventional-sounding words *of myrthe and of solas* at the very point in the text when readers expect the naming of the hero and his lineage. The opening two stanzas are thus a wonderful mixture of stock phrases and stereotypical patterns found elsewhere, primarily in verse romances such as *Guy of Warwick* and *Bevis of Hamton*.

1. *Amis and Amiloun*

1	For goddes loue in trinyte	
	Al þat ben* hend* herkeniþ* to me,	are/ courteous, gentle/ listen
	I pray ȝow*, par amoure,*	you/ as a favor
	What sum-tyme fel* *beȝond þe see*	befell
5	[Of] two barons of grete bounte	
	(from Sutherland MS; these lines are missing in Auchinleck)	
	. . .	
1886	Wiþ tong* *as y** ȝou *tel* may, –	tongue/ I
	It was midwinter tide*,	time
	. . .	
173	Alle þe lond spac* of hem* þo*,	spoke/ them/ then
	Boþe in tour* & toun;	castle
175	In to what stede* þat þai went,	whatever place
	To iustes* oþer to *turnament*,	jousts
	Sir Amis & sir Amiloun,	

2. *Athelston*

7	*Lystnes, lordyngys* þat ben hende,	
	. . .	
64	Þorwȝ* þe myȝt off *Goddys gras*	Through

3. *Bevis of Hamton*

7	*Ich wile* ȝow *tellen* al to gadre* –	together
	Of þat *kniȝt* and of *is* fadre*,	his

4. *Earl of Toulouse*

475	Thus dwellyd the Erle in þat place	
	Wyth game*, *myrthe*, and grete *solase*,	amusement

[38] See Larry Benson, *A Glossarial Concordance to the Riverside Chaucer* (New York, 1993).

5. *Guy of Warwick*

1635		A kniȝt icham* of *fer cuntre*;	I am
		…	
2449		*Lordinges, listeneþ* to me now!	
		…	
4793		Of Gyes felawes* *y wille* ȝou *telle*	companions
		…	
7292		For soþe y ȝou telle may,	
stanza 1	1	God graunt hem heuen blis to mede*	as reward
		Þat herken to mi romaunce rede*	read aloud
		Al of a gentil *kniȝt*:	
		Þe best bodi* he was at nede*	person (knight)/ in danger
	5	Þat euer miȝt bistriden stede*,	horse
		& freest* founde in fiȝt*.	most noble/ battle
		Þe word of him ful wide it ran,	
		Ouer al þis warld þe priis* he wan	prize
		As man most of miȝt.	
	10	Balder bern* was non in bi*:	Bolder warrior/ in town
		His name was hoten* *sir* Gij	called
		Of Warwike, wise & wiȝt*.	valiant
stanza 2	1	Wiȝt he was, for soþe to say,	
		& holden for priis* in eueri play*	most excellent/ tournament
		As kniȝt of gret bounde*.	valor
		Out of þis lond he went his way	
	5	Þurch* mani diuers cuntray,	Through
		Þat was *biȝond þe see*.	
		Seþþen* he com into Inglond,	Afterwards
		& Aþelston þe king he fond,	
		Þat was boþe hende & *fre*.	
	10	For his loue, ich vnder-stond,	
		He slouȝ* a dragoun in Norþhumberlond,	slew
		Ful fer in þe norþ cuntre.	
stanza 44	1	Now herken, & ȝe may here	
		In gest*, ȝif* ȝe wil *listen* & lere*,	story/ if/ learn
		…	
stanza 238	5	Þe king seyd, '*lordinges* alle,	
		Mine men ȝe ben, *verrament**.	truly
		…	
	9	Ich biseche ȝou wiþ gode *entent*,	
		…	
1675		At ich* plas & *turnament*	each
		Gij hadde þe priis *verrament.*	

6. *Horn Childe*

1	Mi leue* frende dere,	dear
	Herken & ȝe may here,	
	& ȝe wil vnder stonde;	
	…	
7	*Y wil* ȝou *telle* of kinges tvo,	
	Hende haþeolf* was on of þo*,	Hathealf/ one of those
	Þat weld* al inglelond;	ruled

7. *Ipomadon A*

16	Thereffore in þe world where euer he went,	
	In Iustys or in *tur[na]mente,*	
	Euer more the pryce he wan.	

8. *Ipomydon B*

1	Mekely, *lordyngis* gentyll and *fre*,	
	Lystene a while and herken to me:	
	I shall you *telle of a* kynge,	
	A *dowghty** man, with owte lesynge*;	strong, valiant/ lying
	…	
11	Of Poyle-lond* *lord was he*,	Poland(?)
	Gold and syluer he had plente,	
	…	
15	*Hys name was* kynge Ermones.	

9. *Life of St. Alexius*

1	*Lesteneþ* alle, and herkeneþ me,	
	ȝonge and olde, bonde* & fre*,	slave/ freeman
	And ich ȝow *telle* sone,	
	How a ȝong* man, *gent* and *fre*,	young
5	By-gan þis worldis wele* to fle:	wealth, fortune
	Y-born he was in Rome.	

10. *Lybeaus Desconus*

4	Þat harkeneþ of a conquerour,	
	Wys of wytte and whyȝt* werrour	valiant
	And *douȝty* man yn dede.	
	Hys name was called Geynleyn,	
	…	
434	Harkeneþ, *lordynges* fre,	

11. *Octavian B*

1	Mekyll and littill*, olde and ȝynge*,	All (great and small)/ young
	Herkyns all to my talkynge*,	words

Of whaym I will ȝow kythe*; — tell
. . .
17 And leuede* in joye and grete honoure, — lived
And *doghety* was of dede*. — actions
In *tornament* nor in no fyghte
20 In þe werlde þer ne was a bettir *knyghte*
. . .
22 Octouyane *was his name* thrugheowte;

12. ***Otuel and Roland***

1 Herkenyth, *lord*ynges, & ȝeuyth *lyst** — listen
. . .
35 thorowe the *grace of god* almyȝt.
. . .
340 hys douȝter*, so *fayre and gent*, — daughter

13. ***Sir Degaré***

1 Kniȝtus þat [werey* sometime in lande]† — made war
Ferli* fele* wolde fonde, — wonders/ many
And sechen* auentures bi niȝt and dai, — seek
Hou ȝhe* miȝte here* strengthe asai*; — they/ their/ try, prove
5 So dede* a *knyȝt, Sire* Degarree: — did
Ich wille ȝou *telle* wat man was he.
. . .
11 Þer nas no man, *verraiment*,
Þat miȝte in werre ne in *tornament*,
Ne in iustes for noþing,
Him out of his sadel bring,

† (supplied by the Cambridge MS)

14. ***Sir Degrevant***

9 *I will* ȝow *telle of a knyghte*:

15. ***Sir Eglamour of Artois***

7 *I will* ȝow *telle of a knyghte*
Þat was bothe hardy and wyght,
. . .
126 He hath serued vs many a day,
Full trewly *in* hys *entent* –
In iustyng and in *turnament*
. . .
934 Sche sayde, 'I was *born* in Artas;
Syr Prymsamour my *fadyr was*,
The *lord of þat countre*.

(lines 126–8 and 934–6 from MS Cotton Caligula A.2)

16. *Sir Isumbras*

7 *I wyll you tell of a knyghte*
That *dowghty* was in eche a fyghte,
In towne and eke* in felde; — also
His name was called *sir* Ysumbras:
Swilke* a *knyghte*, als he was, — Such
Now lyffes* nane in lede*. — lives/ on earth

17. *Sir Perceval of Galles*

1 Lef*, *lythes* to me, — Friend
Two wordes or thre,
Off one þat was faire and *fre*
And fell* in his fighte. — fierce

18. *Thomas of Erceldoune*

255 Than ladyes come, bothe *faire & gent*,

19. *Torrent of Portyngale*

10 *I Schall* yow *tell*, ore I hense pase,
Off a knyght, þat *Dowghtty wase*,
In Rome ase clarkys ffynde.
. . .
337 *Lorddes*, and* ye wol* *lythe*, — if/ will
. . .
1089 *Lordys*, and ye *liston* wold*, — would

20. *Ypotys*

1 He þat wyll of wysdome lere,
Herkeneth now, & ȝe may *here*
Of a tale of holy wryte* – — scripture
Seynt Jon þe euangelist wytnesseth hyt:
How hyt befell yn grete Rome,

II. Description of Hero

Verse romances often paid attention to the attributes, both physical and moral, of both the hero and heroine; however, physical description was most extensive in terms of female bodies while character traits – most importantly courage, nobility, and strength of arms – were usually noted for the male heroes.[39] Phrases such as *hardy & wyght* are common for men, but missing from *Thopas*. That Chaucer's hero looks more like a child or woman (not the

[39] W. C. Curry, *The Middle English Ideal of Personal Beauty* (Baltimore, 1916) is still a good source of the language used to describe physical attributes.

expected knightly or aristocratic hero) is exacerbated by Chaucer's use of the descriptors *whit was his face* and *rede as rose* (VII, 725, 726) and later *sydes smale* (VII, 836) – attributes common for women and children, but rare for men.[40] The diminution of the hero is further enhanced when one realizes that Chaucer most likely borrowed certain characteristics – girdle, shoes, and even beard – from a dwarf in *Lybeaus Desconus*.[41] Certain critics believe that Chaucer intended Sir Thopas to be deliberately effeminate or even, as George Williams has claimed, homosexual.[42] Manly offers a different interpretation by drawing attention instead to details suggestive of trade: "The comparison of his face with fine bread, his complexion with a dye for cloth, his beard with a coloring for pies and meats and confectionery; the shoes of cordewain leather, the brown Bruges hose – all suggest the tradesman, as does the silk robe that cost 'many a jane' (ha'penny)."[43] Certainly the expensive, often exotic clothing from India and from Tars, the *sendall* and the *syklatoun*, are worn by many romance heroes to denote high status and stature; however, Thopas's robe of *syklatoun* is juxtaposed to his Bruges hose and further devalued by the crass reference to how much it cost.[44] Another interpretation of the description of Thopas centers on the possibility that Chaucer intended his audience to see parallels to puppets, a clever allusion to Chaucer as author who pulls all the strings.[45] In this regard, Thopas's diminutive stature and unreal exploits fit into a paradigm that is not nonsensical or simply silly, but rather indicative of the clever manipulations of Chaucer, the master poet.

40 Loomis suggests that punning "on the word *flour* probably led Chaucer to his own variant, *whit as payndemayn*, a word found in the romances only in *Thopas* and in *Degrevant*, vs. 1291, *þay profird hym payndemayne*; also vs. 1409, *Paynedemayn . . . Scho fett*." See Bryan and Dempster, p. 504 n. 2.

41 Only in *Lybeaus Desconus* are the three items found together: the yellow beard, the girdle and shoes; however, the collocation of the beard and girdle with the rhyme *wax/fax* is found in *Reinbrun*, stanza 34, lines 10–12 and in *Bevis*, lines 2243–4. *Sir Degaré*, lines 783–90, mentions only the yellow beard and shoes of the dwarf, but not the girdle. Further clinching evidence for *Lybeaus Desconus* as the model for *Thopas* in the descriptors for the hero is the inclusion of *whyt face*, a good *nose*, and *rose her rode was red* – all in one stanza, lines 880–91.

42 George Williams, *A New View of Chaucer* (Durham, NC, 1965), pp. 147–9. He tries to prove that the poem is ripe with "phallic, or autoerotic, or homosexual innuendos" (p. 147), but his views have been seen as too extreme and sometimes misguided. See especially Richard L. Greene, "The Hunt Is Up, Sir Thopas: Irony, Pun, and Ritual," *Notes and Queries* NS 13 (1966): 169–71, and Chauncy Wood, "Chaucer and 'Sir Thopas': Irony and Concupiscence," *Texas Studies in Literature and Language* 14 (1972/73): 389–403.

43 John Matthews Manly, *The Canterbury Tales* (New York, 1928), p. 630.

44 Loomis credits Kölbing (*English Studies* 11 [1888]: 499) with noting "that the French *Ipomadon*, vs. 1625, has *solleres de cordewan*; but found no other parallel except from sources later than *Thopas*. *Of Brugges* parodies the *of India* and *of Tars* of the romances. *Syklatoun* is a comparatively rare word found in the romances only in *Guy* A, vs. 2835 . . . and in *Richard*, vs. 5268, both poems in the Auchinleck MS, and in *Florence of Rome* (ed. Vietor), vs. 177, a story not apparently known to Chaucer" (Bryan and Dempster, p. 504 n. 4).

45 Ann S. Haskell, "Sir Thopas: The Puppet's Puppet," *Chaucer Review* 9 (1975): 253–61, argues that there is a distinct possibility that Chaucer intends the audience to see associations with literal puppets since romances seemed to form a part of medieval puppet repertoires and a puppet-hero would be an "effective commentary on the lifelessness of an obsolescent literary type" (p. 253).

21. *Athelston*

70 Al-so *whyt*, so lylye-flour,
Red, as rose, off here* colour, — her
As *bryȝt*, as blosme on brere*. — briar
. . .
582 From hym þey token þe *rede scarlet*,
Boþe *hosyn* and *schoon*, þat weren hym met*, — suitable
þat fel al for a knyȝt.

22. *Bevis of Hamton*

2243 *His berd was* ȝelw*, to is* brest wax*, — yellow/ his/ grew
And *to his gerdel* heng is fax*. — hair

23. *Guy of Warwick*[46]

65 Hir skynne *was white* of brighte coloure;
. . .
68 Browes bente* and *nose* well sittyng; — arched brows
. . .

706 Þerl* dubbed sir Gij þe fre, — The earl
& wiþ him tventi god gomis*, — men
. . .
709 Of cloth of Tars & riche cendel* — silk
Was he[r] dobbeing* euerich a del*; — adornment/ part
Þe panis* al of fow* & griis*, — lining/ fur/ grey fur
Þe mantels* weren of michel priis, — cloaks
. . .
2835 Gode cloþes of *sikelatoun* & Alisaundrinis,
Peloure* of Matre, & pu[r]per* & biis*, — Fur/ purple/ fine linen
To ȝour wille as ȝe may se;
. . .
5688 Oysel sche hete* wiþ þe *rode so rede*. — was called, named
. . .
6107 *His here**, þat was ȝalu and briȝt, — hair

24. *Ipomadon A*

361 He was large of lyme* and lythe* — limb/ body
. . .
367 His dobelett was of *red* welvet,
Off bryght golde botuns* ibete* — buttons/ decorated
. . .

[46] Only lines 65 and 68 are taken from Cambridge Caius College MS 107 since the parallel lines in the Auchinleck MS are lost. The excerpts show that *Guy* has references to white skin, rosy cheeks, good nose, yellow hair, *sikelatoun*, and the cost of clothing although in scattered references throughout the poem, not concentrated in one stanza as they are in *Lybeaus*.

370	His mantell was of *skarlett* fyne,	
	Furryd wyth good armyne*,	ermine
	Ther myght no better been;	
	The bordoure* all of red sendell,	border
	That araye became hym wele	
375	To wete* wythouten wene*.	to be sure/ doubt
	A noble countenavnce he hade;	
	…	
379	Also bryght his coloure shone	
	All hym lovyd that lokyd hym one*,	on
	Bothe lord and lady shene.	
	…	
2456	Lyghttly was he clade to ryde	
	In a mantell panyd wyth pryde	
	And semys* sette grette plente.	seams
	…	
2462	*Hose* he had of clothe *of* Ynde*,	blue cloth
	Suche shull no man now fynde,	
	To seke all crystyante*.	christendom
	Spurrys of gold he had vpon;	
	Was neuer kyng better weryd* none	dressed
	Ne no man in no degre.	

25. ***King Horn***

9	He hadde a sone þat het horn,	
	Fairer ne miste* non beo born.	might
	…	
13	Fairer nis* non þane he was,	is not
	He was briȝt so* þe glas,	as
	He *was whit* so þe flur,	
	Rose red was his colur.	

26. ***Lybeaus Desconus***

109	Þat mayde was clepede* Elene,	named
	Gentyll, bryȝt and schene:	
	…	
115	Sche was clodeþ* in tars,	clothed
	Rowme* and nodyng skars*,	full/ close-fitting
	Pelured wyth blaunner*;	white fur
	Her sadell and her brydell yn fere*	together
	Full of dyamandys were:	
120	Melk* was her destrere*.	Milk-white/ war horse
	Þe dwerke* was clodeþ yn ynde,	dwarf
	Be-fore and ek be-hynde:	
	Stout* he was and pert*.	Haughty/ smart
	…	
126	Hys surcote was ouert*.	open
	Hys berd was yelow as ony wax,	

To hys gerdell henge þe plex*:† braid of hair
J* dar well say yn certe. I
130 Hys *schon wer* wy*th* gold y-dyȝt
And kopeþ* as a knyȝt, slashed
Þat semede no pouert.
…
880 *As* þe *rose* her *rode* was *red*;
Þe her* schon on hyr heed hair
As gold wyre* schyneþ bryȝt. thread
Ayder* browe as selken þrede each
…
885 Hyr *nose* was strath* and ryȝt. straight
Her eyen* gray as glas, eyes
Melk *whyt was* he[r] *face*:
So seyde þat* her sygh* wyth syȝt*. that one/ saw/ sight

† Lambeth MS, line 137, reads: "To his girdyll hange his fax."

27. ***Otuel and Roland***

1573 with helm and breny* bryȝt, coat of mail
with pencelys* of *sykelatoun*, streamers

28. ***Reinbrun***

stanza 34 10 *His berde was* to is brest y-wax,
To his gerder heng is fax:

29. ***Seven Sages of Rome***[47]

51 The iij mayster* was a lyght* man third master (sage)/ slight
With louesum* lere* as *whytte as* swanne, handsome/ skin
Hys here was crypse* and noo thyng rous*, curly/ shaggy, unkempt
His name was callyd Lentyllous.
…
97 An other master come anon,
The ffayrest of them euerychon,
Jesse *was his name* jhoote*, called
100 Withowt weme* from hede to fote. blemish
His here was yelow as the *safferon,*
He loked lustely* as a ffawcon*. vigorous/ falcon

30. ***Sir Degaré***

780 Þer com a dwerw into þe halle.
Four fet of lengthe was in him;

[47] Lines 51–4 come from a fifteenth-century manuscript (British Library MS Egerton 1995), and lines 97–101 are from a sixteenth-century manuscript (Oxford Balliol College MS 354), both printed in *The Seven Sages of Rome*, ed. Karl Brunner, EETS OS 191 (Oxford, 1933), pp. 2, 4. The Auchinleck MS is missing the first 122 lines of the poem, which may have contained a source for *saffroun hair*.

His visage was stout* and grim*; strong/ fierce
Boþe *his berd* and his fax
Was crisp an *ʒhalew* as wax;
Grete sscholdres and quarré*; square
Riʒt stoutliche loked he;
Mochele* were hise fet and honde large
Ase þe meste* man of þe londe; greatest
He was iclothed wel ariʒt,
His sschon icouped as a kniʒt;

31. ***Sir Launfal***

241 *Hare* faces were whyt* as snow on downe*; their/ hillside
Har *rode was red*, here eyn were browne
. . .
259 Launfal hem grauntede curteyslyche,
And wente with hem myldelyche*; meekly
  Þey wheryn *whyt as* floure.
. . .
277 He fond yn þe pauyloun
Þe Kynges douʒter of Olyroun,
  Dame Tryamoure þat hyʒte;
280 Here *fadyr was* kyng of fayrye* the other-world
. . .
283 In þe pauyloun he fond a bed of prys
. . .
286 Þerinne lay þat lady *gent*
Þat aftere Sir Launfal hedde ysent,
  Þat lefsom lemede* bryʒt. beautiful one
. . .
292 Sche was as wh*yt as* lylye yn May
Or snow þat sneweþ* yn wynterys day: snows
. . .
295 Þe *rede rose*, whan sche ys newe,
Aʒens* here rode* nes nauʒt* of hewe*, Compared with/ complexion/ there is not/ color

III. Hero's Activities

The nature of Chaucer's humor is evident in the unaristocratic, perhaps even effeminate, nature of Thopas's activities and his accoutrements as well as the disjointed, abrupt switches of topic from stanza five to stanza eight of the poem. At first, Thopas seems engaged in a variety of activities to demonstrate his versatility and skills: he hunts deer;[48] he rides with a goshawk; he is an archer and a wrestler; however, these activities are undercut in several ways. First, his *grey goshauk* is unusual in romance texts as a companion for a knight, who is more often accompanied by a falcon. In these romances, the goshawk is associated

[48] *Guy of Warwick*, lines 6341–2, provides the unusual *wilde dere* rhyming with *riuer*. See below, p. 670.

primarily with women: a *gentil goshawk* is sent by a lady to her love in *Horn Childe* (line 338), and a lady goes with *goshauke and with gentyll fawcon* in *Squire of Low Degree* (line 775). Another possibility is the connection between a yeoman and a goshawk, another diminution in the stature of the hero of this tale.[49] Even more damning is Thopas's interest in archery and wrestling, which were not considered knightly sports or arenas for knightly prowess. They suggest instead the yeomen heroes of balladry.[50]

After these dubious attributes of the hero, Chaucer abruptly switches in stanza six to Thopas's effect on women. *Ful many a mayde, bright in bour,/ They moorne for hym paramour* (VII, 742–3) is most likely an allusion to the many ladies in *Guy of Warwick* who are *bright in bower*, a common alliterative phrase. Like Guy, Thopas resists them, but in the unusual phrasing without analogues in the romances: *But he was chaast and no lechour,/ And sweete as is the brembul flour/ That bereth the rede hepe* (VII, 745–7). Here, the hero is reduced even further by being compared to a dog rose.

The next stanza begins with the sort of filler lines that give tail-rhyme romances a bad reputation: *And so bifel upon a day,/ For sothe, as I yow telle may* (VII, 748–9)[51] followed by Thopas riding out on his grey steed with a *launcegay* and long sword. The lancegay, a short lance, was not the usual weapon for combat and was often used in parades, not in serious battle, although examples in the *OED* do not bear out the idea that this is a frivolous weapon.

Then he *priketh* (variations of the word appear eight times in eighty-four lines) through a forest with *many a wilde best,/ Ye, bothe bukke and hare;/ And as he priketh north and est,/ I telle it yow, hym hadde almest/ Bitid a sory care* (VII, 755–59). For most of these stanzas, *Guy of Warwick* provides the richest sources of materials for Chaucer's humor as the following extracts demonstrate, even in terms of the rhymes *fair forest* with *wilde best* and the unusual *wilde dere* rhyme with *riuer*.[52] Although mounting, riding, and

[49] Manly, *Canterbury Tales*, line 1928n, p. 631, quoted Dame Berners, *Boke of Hawkyng*: "Ther is a Goshawke and that hawke is for a yeman." Rachel Hands, however, brings evidence from a correspondence between Sir John Paston and a relative concerning a goshawk. See *Notes and Queries* 216 (1971): 85–8, and Robin Oggins, "Falconry and Medieval Social Status," *Mediaevalia* 12 (1989): 43–55.

[50] Gamelyn wrestles for the prize of a ram, and yeomen wrestle in some of the ballads. See *Gest of Robyn Hode* (in *English and Scottish Popular Ballads Edited from the Collection of Francis James Child*, ed. Helen Child Sargent and George Lyman Kittredge [Boston, 1904], no. 117, stanza 135, p. 263). For Chaucer's consistently negative depiction of yeomen, see T. A. Shippey, "*The Tale of Gamelyn*: Class Warfare and the Embarrassments of Genre," in *The Spirit of Medieval English Popular Romance*, pp. 78–96.

[51] The catch phrase "and so it happened one day" is a poor transition, but found in many ballad refrains as well as in other romances. See *Guy of Warwick*, the opening lines of stanzas 5, 8 and 11; *Otuel and Roland*, line 701, and a variant in *Sir Cawline*, a ballad with a 5-headed giant (*English and Scottish Popular Ballads*, no. 61, stanza 41, p. 117). Asservations of truth-telling are also commonplace with numerous romance and ballads echoes; for the expression *Ffor soþe as I yow say*, see "Robin Hood and Monk" (*English and Scottish Popular Ballads*, no. 119, stanzas 48, 60, 63, 66, and 78, pp. 282–6.)

[52] There is some question whether Chaucer intended humor in juxtaposing the wild beasts with the buck and hare, which do not strike modern readers as particularly wild, ferocious, or savage. S. I. Tucker, "*Sir Thopas* and the Wild Beasts," *Review of English Studies* NS 10 (1959): 54–6, notes that *wild* meaning *undomesticated* was a perfectly acceptable usage in Chaucer's time and that hunters thought these animals "no ignoble quarry"; however, the deer and hare, because of their timidity, may be seen as anticlimactic. Beryl Rowland, in "Chaucer's 'Bukke and Hare' (Thop, VII, 756)," *English Language Notes* 2 (1964): 6–8), sees sexual innuendo in these lines; however, Richard L. Greene in

bestriding are common in the romances, few heroes rival Thopas in their *pricking*.[53]

32. ***Athelston***

69 In þe world *was non here pere*: — equal, peer

33. **General Prologue to *Canterbury Tales***

545 The MILLERE was a stout carl for the nones;
Ful byg he was of brawn, and eek of bones.
That proved wel, for over al ther he cam,
At *wrastlynge* he wolde have alwey the *ram*.

34. ***Gamelyn***

171 Ther was þer bysiden cryed* a *wrastlyng*, — announced
And þerfor þer was sette vp *a ram* and a ryng;
And Gamelyn was in good wil to wende þerto,
For to preuen his might what he cowþe* do. — could, knew how
…
279 Tho þat* wardeynes* were of þat *wrastlyng* — Those who/ officials
Come and broughte Gamelyn þe *ram* and þe ryng,
And seyden, "Haue, Gamelyn þe ryng and þe *ram*
For þe best wrasteler þat euer here cam."

35. ***Guy of Warwick***

stanza 256 10 He was so michel & so strong,
& þer-to so wonderliche long:
In þe world *was non his pere*.

36. ***Octavian A***

895 At *wrestelyng* & at þe stoncastynge
He wan þe prys wythout lesynge,
Þer nas* noþer old ne ȝynge — was not
So mochell of strengh,

37. ***Reinbrun***

stanza 107 10 For þow ert of gret power:
In al þis world *þer nis þe per*
þat man finde miȝte.

"The Hunt Is Up, Sir Thopas: Irony, Pun, Ritual" dismisses these claims by arguing that these animals are labeled appropriately as *wild* and that the only source of satire can be found in the fact that bucks, male deer of at least five years of age, belonged to the beast of chase and the hare was a beast of venery.

[53] Caroline Strong, "Sir Thopas and Sir Guy, II," p. 103, notes that over "forty times in *Guy* a knight comes pricking," but it must be remembered that *Guy* is one of the longest Middle English romances.

...
stanza 113 7 For he is man of gret power:
In al þis world *þer nis is per*,
Ne of so meche mounde*. strength

Hunting and hawking by a river or in a forest:

38. *Guy of Warwick*

171 Of wodes & *riuer* & oþer game:
...
175 Michel he couþe of *hauk* & hounde,
Of estriche faucouns of gret mounde.
...
2797 To pleyn hem þai went bi *riuer*
þat of *wilde* foule ful were;
To her wille an *hunting* hij* gos, they
2800 To chace þe hert* & þe ros*. hart/ deer
...
6340 In þe cite were mani & mo.
In þat on half* orn* *þe riuer*, one half/ ran
In þat oþer half forest wiþ *wilde dere*.
...
6719 Þai comen into *a fair forest,*
Þer þai fond a bore, *a wilde best*.

39. *Ipomydon B*

61 Bothe of howndis & *haukis* game;
Aftir he taught hym all & same
In se*, in feld and eke in *ryuere,* sea
In wodde to chase the *wild dere*
65 And in the feld to *ryde* a *stede**, horse, steed
That all men had joy of his dede.

40. *King Edward and the Shepherd*[54]

422 Þer is no *hert* ne *bucke* so wode* wild, mad

[54] See *King Edward and the Shepherd* in *Middle English Metrical Romances*, ed. W. H. French and C. B. Hale (New York, 1930). This poem is in the fifteenth-century Cambridge University Library MS Ff.5.48, but was composed probably "at about the end of the fourteenth century"; from "references to the Black Prince (928, 972) and Warenne, the very date of the fictitious adventure can be set as not long after 1340" (p. 949). This poem also includes a sling shot and stones cast, conventional diction such as *be Goddis grace* (line 259), *qwyte as any swan* (line 365), *Vndir a forest fayre* (line 254), mention of hart and buck (line 422), and *But his sidis shulde blede* (line 234) suggestive of *His sydes were al blood* in *Sir Thopas (*VII, 777). Chaucer's familiarity with the common language of balladry and popular, oral poetry and songs is clear through such echoes.

41. ***Sir Degrevant***

41	Oþer gammnes he louede* mare:	loved
	Grewhundes for *buk* and bare,	
	For herte, hynde*, and for *hare*,	female deer
	By dayes and by nyghte;	
	. . .	
49	He walde be vp or* daye	before
	To *hunt* and to *ryvaye**;	hunt or hawk along the river bank

42. ***Sir Orfeo***

304	Sexti leuedis* on hors ride,	sixty ladies
	. . .	
307	& ich* a *faucoun on hond* bere,	each
	And *riden on haukin* bi *o riuere**.	by a river

43. ***Sir Perceval of Galles***

209	Thus he welke* in þe lande,	walked
	With hys darte *in his hande*;	
	. . .	
213	He wolde schote with his spere	
	Bestes and oþer gere*,	game
215	As many als he myghte bere;	
	He was a gude knaue!	
	Smalle birdes wolde he slo,	
	Hertys, hyndeȝ also;	

Ladies, often bright in bower, who desire the hero:

44. ***Guy of Warwick***

stanza 11	6	Of leuedis *briȝt in bour*.	
		Þerl seyd to sir Gij hende & fre,	
		'Tel me þe soþe, par charite,	
		Y pray þe *par amoure**:	if you please
stanza 15	7	Miche* semly* folk was gadred þare	many/ fair, comely
		Of erls, barouns lasse* & mare,	less
		& leuedis *briȝt in bour*.	
		. . .	
237		Þat day Gij dede his miȝt	
		To serue þritti* maidens *briȝt*;	thirty
		Al an-amourd* on him þai were,	enamored
240		& loued Gij for his feir chere.	
		Þer of no ȝaf* he riȝt nouȝt,	gave
		Al anoþer* it was his þouȝt:	another entirely
		On Felice þat was so briȝt,	
		Gij hir loued wiþ al his miȝt;	

45. *Ipomadon A*

698	The lady was full woo.	
	She thynkys to haue Ipomadon,	
	…	
908	No thynge sche *slepyd* all the nyght,	
	But ofte tymes turnyd and sadely* syte*;	heavily/ sighed

46. *Lybeaus Desconus*

1413	For sche was *bryȝt* and schene.	
	Alas he ne hadde y-be *chast!*[55]	

Hero ambling, bestriding, leaping, pricking, going forth on his horse:

47. *Amis and Amiloun*

973	Amorwe* sir Amis made him ȝare*	On the next day/ ready
	…	
976	For noþing nold* he spare*,	would not/ stop
	He *priked** þe stede þat him bare	rode
	Boþe niȝt & day.	
	So long he *priked* wiþ-outen abod*	delay
980	Þe stede þat he on rode	
	In a fer cuntray	
	Was ouercomen & fel doun ded;	
	…	
1191	For no-þing wold he spare.	
	He priked his stede niȝt & day,	
	As a gentil kniȝt, stout & gay*,	finely dressed

48. *Bevis of Hamton*

1942	A gode *stede* ȝhe* let forþ drawe	she
	And sadeled hit & wel adiȝt*,	dressed, made ready
	And Beues, þat hendi kniȝt,	
	Into þe sadel a lippte*,	leapt
	Þat no stirop* he ne drippte*.	stirrup/ touched

49. *Guy of Warwick*

1601	Þan *he* lepe *opon his stede,*	
	…	
3864	On hors he lepe wiþ-outen stirop,	
	…	
stanza 259 1	Sir Gij lepe *on his stede* fot hot*,	quickly
	…	
4723	Opon a mule sche *warþ** anon,	climbed

[55] This is the only place where the lady *bright* is juxtaposed with the chastity of the hero.

. . .
6986 Nim* þi stede, & *worþ* þeron. Take

50. *Ipomydon B*

1488 Ipomydon sterte vp that tyde*, time
Anone *he worthyd vppon his stede*,
They *rode* to gedyr with good spede;

51. *Sir Degaré*

421 And lep *vpon hiis* palefrai,
And doht him forȝ* in his wai; set out
. . .
723 Forȝ *he rod* in his wai
Mani a pas and mani iurnai;
725 So longe he passede into *west*
Þat he com into þeld* *fforest* the old
Þer he was biȝeten* som while. stayed
Þerinne *he rideȝ* mani a mile;
Mani a dai he ride gan;

52. *Sir Launfal*

217 Pouerly* þe knyȝt to hors gan sprynge; miserably, wretchedly
For to dryue away lokynge*, to avoid notice
He rood toward þe west.

53. *Torrent of Portyngale*

627 On he dyd* hys harnes a-geyne donned
And worthe on hys sted, serteyne,
And thetherward he sowght.
. . .
864 Thus *he worthe on a stede.*
In* hys wey Cryst hyme sped, On

IV. Catalogues of Herbs and Birds

Lists or catalogues of various items from birds and flowers to spices were part of medieval poetic conventions, perhaps suggested by the rhetorical device of *amplificatio*. However, many writers took such lists to excess so that they became a mere listing of names or specific items extended for many, many lines with no apparent context or *raison d'être*. In this regard, *Squire of Low Degree* is one of the worst offenders of all the metrical romances.[56] Mead points out that

[56] William J. Farrell, "Chaucer's Use of the Catalogue," *Texas Studies in Literature and Language* 5 (1963): 70, argues that Chaucer is satirizing the "padding techniques of his less able contemporaries" and that these unnecessary digressions kill whatever spark of interest the story might have kindled.

in terms of bird lists, "Chaucer needed only to parody himself."[57] *Sir Thopas* for all its shortness of length contains excesses in terms of lists (the hero's physical attributes, his pastimes, spices, birds, foods, the arming of hero, and the names of heroes). The exotic spices – licorice, cetewale or zedoary, clove and nutmeg – none of which grows in Flanders, are comically substituted for the expected tree lists. J. A. Burrow notes that the passage "belongs to a tradition of descriptions of paradisal woods and gardens best represented by the *Roman de la rose*"[58] with which it also shares the odd term *clove-gelofre* and the unusual rhyme *gylofre/cofre*. In a self-referential move, Chaucer may be alluding to his own lovers, Absolon with his *love-longynge*, and hende Nicolas *as sweete as is the roote/ Of lycorys or any cetewale*.[59] In other romances, birds are associated with love-longing; however, in *Squire of Low Degree*, the birds comfort the hero instead of sending him into anguish. Interestingly, this text also has a swallow *whippynge to and fro*, perhaps suggesting Thopas's frenetic movements in the next few lines.

In this second list of birds – sparrowhawk, parrot, thrush and wooddove – the parrot is the anomaly among the other birds.[60] The thrush or dove has been associated with lovers,[61] but in St Gregory's *Dialogues*, the devil in the likeness of a *merula* (merle) tempted St Benedict to commit a sin of impurity, most likely a sin of the flesh.[62] This could be an irony used by Chaucer for his chaste knight.

Bird and Herbs

54. *Annot and Johon*

21	He is _papeiai_* in pyn þat beteþ me my bale*;	parrot/ "who cures my pain for me when I am in torment"
	to trewe tortle* in a tour y telle þe mi tale;	turtledove
	he is _þrustle_* þryuen in þro* þat _singeþ_ in sale*,	thrush/ virtuous in strife/ hall
	þe wilde laueroc* ant wolc* ant _þe wodewale_*;	lark/ hawk/ singing bird

57 William E. Mead, *Squyr of Lowe Degre* (Boston, 1904), p. lxiv. The *sperhauk*, *douve*, *popinjay*, and *throstel* are all mentioned in *Parliament of Fowls*, lines 338–64. The Prologue to the *Legend of Good Women*, F 139–40, includes *somme songen clere/ Layes of love, that joye it was to here*, and *Troilus*, II. 920–2, includes a nightingale that *Ful loude song ayein the moone shene,/ Peraunter in his briddes wise a lay/ Of love, that made hire herte fressh and gay*.

58 *The Riverside Chaucer*, p. 919, note to lines 760–65. All four spices grow in Love's garden in the *Roman de la Rose* so that the association of love to these exotic spices is directly relevant to *Thopas*.

59 See *The Miller's Tale*, I, 3349 and 3206–7.

60 The harsh sounds of a parrot are at odds with the melodies of other birds, but not all of the birds cited here are songbirds. See lines 19–20 of Thomas Hoccleve's *Praise of His Lady*: "Hir comly body shape as a foot-bal;/ And shee syngith ful lyk a pape-Iay – " in *Secular Lyrics of the XIVth and XVth Centuries*, ed. Rossell Hope Robbins (Oxford, 1952), p. 223.

61 Ovid, *Ars amatoria*, II. 269, recommends them as appropriate gifts to one's lover, and the turtledove has a long history of associations with lovers.

62 This allusion is noted by Mortimer J. Donovan, "*Sir Thopas*, 772–4," *Neuphilologische Mitteilungen* 57 (1956): 237–46, who states that to fourteenth-century readers, "*thrustel* denoted the song-thrush, or throstle, also called *mavis* (<L. *maviscus*) and was loosely identified with the *merle* (L. *merula*) or blackbird, which, in fact, belongs to the same family" (p. 238). Importantly, according to Donovan, Bishop Waerferth's translation of St Gregory's *Dialogues* reads *þrostle* as the translation of *merula* (p. 240). Gregory's story of St Benedict's temptation by a devil in the form of a thrush is also found in Robert Mannyng of Brunne's *Handlyng Synne*, ed. Idelle Sullens, Medieval & Renaissance Texts and Studies (Binghamton, NY, 1983), pp. 188–9, lines 7475–98.

55. *Guy of Warwick*

4502 Þe weder was hot in somers tide.
In May it was also ich wene*, — think, suppose
When floures sprede & *springeþ* grene:

56. *Land of Cockaygne*

73 Þe rote is gingeuir* and galingale*, — ginger/ spice
Þe siouns* beþ* al *sedwale**, — shoots/ are/ zedoary
Trie maces* beþ þe flure, — choice maces (spices)
Þe rind*, canel* of swet odur, — bark/ cinnamon
Þe frute, *gilofre** of gode smakke*. — clove/ flavor
Of cucubes* þer nis no lakke; — cubebs (spicy seeds)
Þer beþ rosis of rede ble*, — color
And lilie likful* for to se; — delightful
...
96 Þ*rostil*, þruisse, and niȝtingale,
Chalandre* and *wodwale**, — larks/ golden orioles
And oþer briddes wiþout tale*, — count
Þat stinteþ neuer by har miȝt
Miri* to sing dai and niȝt. — merrily, happily

57. *Otuel and Roland*

187 "the brydde that syttyth on the bowe
...
641 And whenne the fowlys songon on the rys*, — branch
...
675 whenne foules synge *on the spray**, — branch

58. *Squire of Low Degree*

43 On euery braunche sate *byrdes* thre,
Syngynge with great melody,
The lauorocke and the nightyngale,
The ruddocke*, the *woodwale*, — robin
The pee* and the *popiniaye*, — magpie
The thrustele saynge both nyght and daye,
The marlyn*, and the wrenne also, — merlin hawk
The swalowe whippynge to and fro,
The *iaye** iangled* them amonge, — jay/ chattered
The larke began that mery songe,
The sparowe spredde her *on her spraye,*
The mauys* songe with notes full gaye, — mavis
The nuthake* with her notes newe, — nuthatch
The sterlynge* set her notes full trewe, — starling
The goldefynche made full mery chere,
Whan she was bente vpon a brere,
And many other foules mo,
The osyll*, and the thrusshe also; — blackbird

And they sange wyth notes *clere*,
In confortynge that squyere.

59. *Thomas of Erceldoune*

29 I herde *þe jaye, & þe throstyll cokke*,
The Mawys menyde* hir of hir songe, — sang plaintively
Þe wodewale beryde als a belle*, — sang clearly(?)
. . .
121 *Downe þane lyghte** þat lady bryghte, — alighted
Vndir-nethe þat grenewode *spraye*;
And, als the storye tellis full ryghte,
Seuene sythis* by hir he laye. — times
. . .
177 Scho *lede* hym in-till a faire herbere*, — enclosed garden
Whare frwte* was g[ro]wan[d gret plentee;] — fruit
Pere and appill, both ryppe þay were,
The date, and als the damasee*; — Damson plum
Þe fygge, and als so þe wyneberye*; — grape
The nyghtgales byggande* on þair neste; — building
Þe *papeioyes* faste abowte gane flye;
And throstylls sange wolde* hafe no reste. — (who) would

V. Hero's Love-longing

It would be difficult to find a medieval metrical romance without some love element. Indeed, the combination of love and chivalric adventure, so typical of romance, is not absent in this tale.[63] Thus, Chaucer would have many places to look for sources of parody and excess. Even the love-longing brought on by bird song has precedents in both *Guy of Warwick* and *Thomas of Erceldoune* when the hero, after hearing the birds singing, lay *in longynge* (extract no. 65) and then dreams of a fairy mistress. From this poem as well as *Sir Launfal*, Chaucer seems to have borrowed not only the fairy mistress and forest setting, but specific phrasing and rhymes. The *dappill graye* horse and saddle of *roelle bone* come directly from *Thomas* (extract no. 123) as well as the *throstyll cokke* and *papeioyes* of earlier lines (extract no. 59). From *Launfal* Chaucer takes the private nature of love and a form of the word *privily* (extract no. 79). Part of the humor of *Thopas* may derive from the fact that the hero only dreams about this lover and never actually sees her or meets her, unlike other narratives in which the fairy mistress is an active force and integral part of the story. The expression *hardy fiers corage* can be found in *The Knight's Tale* (I, 1945), but Chaucer usually favors *ful devout corage*. Again, *Guy of Warwick* offers an immediate

[63] In "Chivalry and Courtly Love," *Peritia* 2 (1983): 149–69, M. H. Keen explores the role of love as a spur to virtue and self-achievement in chivalric contexts, a phenomenon that Chaucer mocks in this tale.

source for many of the hero's activities; however, other romance heroes also provide fodder for Chaucer: Amis, Ipomadon, Torrent and Perceval all sleep or rest, sometimes with their horses, although none brings fodder with him.

Pricking of horse that brings on weariness:

60. ***Guy of Warwick***

stanza 97 4 Þai *priked þe stedes* þat þai on sete,
& smiten* togider wiþ dentes grete*, — strike/ hard blows
& ferd* *as* þai *wer wode**, — behaved/ enraged
. . .
stanza 181 10 & *priked* riȝt *as he wer wode*
. . .
stanza 251 4 Sir Gij opon þat stede wond* — hoisted himself
Wiþ a gode glaiue* in hond, — lance
& *priked* him forþ his way,
&, when he com to *þe plas*
Þer þe batayl loked* was, — decreed, ordered
Gij *liȝt* wiþ-outen delay,

61. ***Ipomadon A***

Ipomadon was wonder sore* — sad
As he gan *thorow the foreste fare*,
He lyght vnder a tre
There flovris were *spryngand*, swete of smell;
For-*wery* on slepe he fell
On his cosyns knee.

Bird song and love-longing:

62. ***Guy of Warwick***

4519 So michel he herd þo foules sing,
Þat him þouȝt he was in gret *longing*.

63. ***Ipomadon A***

2444 Into a *foreste feyre* and grene
Ther foulys *song* al bedene* — together (in harmony)
On bowes bothe lesse and more.
The frithe* was full of swete flouris – — woodland
Who lyst* to love paramowres — wished
Grette lykyng had byn there.
Ipomadon forgettys nouȝte
To haue his *leman* in his thoughte,
That made hym sigh full sore.

64. *Lybeaus Desconus*

Þys somerys day ys long,
Mery ys þe fowles *song*
A[nd] notes of þe nyȝtyngales.
Þat tyme Lybeauus com ryde
Be a ryuer syde
And saw a greet cyte

65. *Thomas of Erceldoune*

That alle þe wode a-bowte me ronge.
Allonne *in longynge* thus als j *laye*,
Vndyre-nethe a semely tree,
(Saw I wher a lady gay
Came ridand* ouer a louely le*.)†   [riding/ lea]

† Final 2 lines from MS Cambridge University Library Ff.5.48

Lying down and the subsequent dream of the elf queen after complaints about the binding power of love:

66. *Amis and Amiloun*

In to a wilde *forest* he cam
Bitven þe day & þe niȝt.
So strong slepe ȝede* him on,   [led]
To win al þis warldes won*,   [reward]
No ferþer he no miȝt.
  Þe kniȝt, þat was so hende & fre,
Wel fair he *layd him* vnder a tre
& fel in slepe þat tide.

67. *Guy of Warwick*

stanza 5
Ac, swete Felice,' he seyd þan,
'Y no schal neuer spouse* wiman   [marry]
Whiles þou art oliue*.'   [alive]
…

stanza 6
Þan answerd þat swete wiȝt*,   [woman]
& seyd oȝain* to him ful riȝt*:   [in reply/ directly]
  'Bi him þat schope* mankinne*,   [made/ mankind]
Icham desired day & niȝt
Of erl, baroun, & mani a kniȝt.
  For noþing wil þai blinne*.   [cease]
Ac Gij,' sche seyd, 'hende & fre,
Al mi loue is layd on þe:
  Our loue schal neuer tvinne*,   [end]
& bot ich haue þe to *make**   [mate, husband]
Oþer lord nil* y non *take*,   [will not]
  For al þis warld to winne.'

. . .
437 Loue me doþ* to grounde falle, — makes
Þat y ne may stond stef* wiþ alle. — straight
. . .
477 Allas, Felice, þat ich stounde,
Þi *loue* me haþ so *ybounde!*
. . .
stanza 11 10 Hastow ment* euer in þi liue — intended
Spouse ani wiman to wiue
  Þat falleþ to þine anour*?' — Who comes within your high rank

stanza 12 4 Bi nouȝt þat y tel can
Y nil neuer spouse wiman
  Saue on* is fre & hende.' — Except one (who)
. . .
stanza 24 6 Þi *loue* me haþ so *y-bounde**, — imprisoned
. . .
486 Allas! to grounde icham ybrouȝt!
. . .
499 Þerl for him sori was,
Þer liked non in that plas:

68. ***Ipomadon A***

7182 That *love* full sore hyr *bovndyn* hathe.

69. ***Ipomydon B***

1457 Ipomydon come by a *foreste*,
A while he thoght there to rest,
He was forwakyd* & all *werye*; — worn out by lack of sleep
To hys men he sayd on hye:
"*Slepe* I muste, with oute fayle,
For I am *wery* for travayle!"

70. ***Seven Sages of Rome***

3235 "Lord," said þe maister, "þis es no ly*. — lie
In þe kingdom of Hungery
Wond* a nobil knyght whylom*, — lived/ once
A rightwis man and whise of dome*. — judgement
He dremyd þus opon *a nyght*,
Þat he lufed a lady bryght,
Bot he ne wist* in what *contre* — did not know
Þat þe lady myght *funden* be.
Him thoght he knew hir wele bi kinde*, — nature
And wele he hopid he sold* hir finde. — should
Þat same time dremyd þat ladi bright,
And thoght þat sho sold luf a knight;
Bot sho wist noght of what land,

Ne in whate stede* he was dweland,   place
Ne his name knew sho nathing;

71. ***Sir Launfal***

220 Þe weþer was hot þe vndern-tyde*;   morning
He *lyȝte adoun* and gan abyde
  Vnder *a fayr forest*;
And for hete of þe wedere,
Hys mantell he felde* togydere,   folded
225 And sette hym *doun* to reste;
…
229 As he sat, yn sorow and sore*,   distress
He sawe come out of holtes hore*   grey woods
  Gentyll maydenes two;
…
301 Sche seyde, "Launfal, my *lemman** swete,   lover, darling
Al my ioye for þe y lete*,   abandon, renounce
  Swetyng paramour:
Þer nys no man yn Cristenté
305 Þat y loue so moche as þe,
  Kyng neyþer emperoure!"
Launfal beheld þat swete wyȝth* –   lady
…
315 Be nauȝt aschamed of me.
Yf þou wylt truly to me *take*,
And alle wemen for me *forsake*,
  Ryche i wyll make þe.

72. ***Sir Perceval of Galles***

1205 Now fonde he no sekirnes*,   security
Bot vnder þe walle þer he was,
A faire *place* he hym chese*,   selected
  And down there he lighte.
He laide hym doun in þat tyde;
1210 *His stede* stode hym besyde:
The fole* was fayne* for to byde* –   foal/ glad/ rest
  Was *wery* for þe fyght.

Riding out in search of elf queen:

73. ***Otuel and Roland***

172 A-ȝeynes a knyȝt to *prike* a stede,
…
415 smyten her horsys and let hem *go*,
…
434 A-none a-ȝeyn to hors they sprong:

752 He smot hys hors and let hym *gone*,
. . .
759 Smyten here hors and *gonne* to ryde
. . .
839 Rowlond vp stert & nouȝt ne lay,
And *in-to the sadyl* that was so gay,
Smertelyche* gan he sprynge. — briskly
. . .
1370 he lep to hors and nouȝt abode,

74. *Thomas of Erceldoune*

95 I ryde aftyre this wylde fee,
My raches* rynnys* at my devyse*.' — hounds/ running/ command
'If þou be parelde* moste of prysee, — spoken of, heralded
And here rydis thus in thy folye,
Of lufe, lady, als þou erte wysse*, — instructed
Þou gyffe me leue to lye the bye!'

was ther noon/ That to him durste ride or goon,/ Neither wyf ne childe:

75. *Guy of Warwick*

45 *In* all Englond *ne was ther none*
That durste in wrath ayenste hym goon.
(Caius MS only)
. . .
133 Þer nas kni[ȝ]t in Inglonde
Þat wiþ wretþe* *durst him* atstonde*. — anger/ stand up to him
. . .
139 *Þe[r] nas* man in al þis londe
Þat durst him do schame no schonde*, — disgrace
. . .
stanza 148 7 In þis warld is man non
Þat oȝaines him *durst gon*,
Herl*, baroun, no kniȝt, — Earl
. . .
1677 *Was þer non* in al þat lond,
Þat his dent miȝt astond*. — withstand
. . .
2827 Þritti mile men may *riden & gon*,
Ne schal men finde man *non*;

76. *Ipomydon B*

77 He ys a myghty man for the nonys
And wele ishape with grete bonys.
In all *that contre was there none*,
To hym myght cast þe tre* ne stone. — tree

77. ***Otuel and Roland***

518 ne schulle we fynde in no londe
None that schall vs withstonde, –
neythyr kyng *ne* kny3t.

pryve woon:

78. ***Guy of Warwick***

4518 *In priue* stede stode Gij þere;

79. ***Sir Launfal***

352 Hy seyde to hym, "Syr gantyl Kny3t,
And þou wylt speke with me any wy3t,* any time
To a derne* stede þou gon: secret
Well *priuyly* i woll come to þe –

VI. Fight with the Giant

The introduction of a giant into the idyllic setting is a little unusual, although not the presence of a giant as a worthy opponent testing the mettle of the hero in metrical romances.[64] Giants occur in many Middle English romances, including *Lybeaus Desconus*, *Guy of Warwick*, *Bevis of Hamton*, *Sir Eglamour*, *Sir Launfal*, *Sir Degaré*, *Sir Perceval*, and *Torrent of Portyngale.* No romance, however, has a giant named Olifant or one with multiple heads; usually size alone emphasized the worthiness of the bigger-than-life opponent to the hero.[65] *Guy of Warwick*, *Bevis*, *Lybeaus*, *Sir Eglamour*, and *Torrent of Portyngale* all have horse-killing giants; however, only *Guy of Warwick* and *Lybeaus* contain the collocation of a horse-killing giant, the presence of the lady, and the expression *grace of God. Lybeaus* further is probably responsible for the *geaunt/ Termagaunt* rhyme although *Guy* also rhymes *Termagaunt*, but with *Amoraunt*, the name of the giant. *Guy* might have suggested postponed combat, but Thopas's reason for delay because of lack of armor recalls *Lybeaus*. Both romances emphasize the diminutive nature of the hero in contrast to the giant,

[64] For a strikingly different interpretation of the giant in Lacanian terms, see Jeffrey Jerome Cohen, "The Giant of Self Figuration: Diminishing Masculinity in Chaucer's 'Tale of *Sir Thopas*,'" in *Of Giants: Sex, Monsters, and the Middle Ages*, Medieval Cultures 17 (Minneapolis, MN, 1999), pp. 96–118. For Cohen, the giant represents monstrous masculinity, sexual aggession and anarchic violence – tendencies that the chivalric hero must conquer within himself.

[65] In Icelandic and Irish stories, many-headed giants appear (see Thompson, *Motif-Index*, F531.1.2.2), and there is a five-headed giant in the ballad of Sir Cawline (*English and Scottish Popular Ballads*, no. 61, stanza 30, p. 116). The name *Oliphant* or *elephant* may in itself be humorous, but Winstanley (p. lxxvii) reminds us that the horn of Roland was called *Olifaunt* and "as such it was symbolic of French chivalry and the army which opposed Philip van Artevelde was almost entirely composed of the French noblesse . . ." Athough this suggestion may seem far-fetched, nonetheless, the name *Oliphant* surely brings to mind – now as it must also have in Chaucer's time – the tragic hero Roland and his fighting against all odds.

and Guy is even called *child* and Lybeaus *ȝyng and lyte*. Chaucer may also have had in mind the David and Goliath stories; in *Cursor Mundi*, David is called *childe David*.[66] The hero in *Torrent of Portyngale*, who also throws stones at a giant, may have suggested the appearance of the *fel staf-slynge* in *Thopas* (VII, 829); however in all these stories, as well as ballads with woodland heroes with sling shots, it is the protagonist who throws stones, not the giant – presumably to keep a safe distance from the formidable foe.

The humor of the lines concluding the escape of Thopas: *And al it was thurgh Goddes gras,/ And thurgh his fair berynge* (VII, 831–2) may be suggested by the equally anticlimatic line in *Sir Eglamour*: *Thorowe Goddis helpe and his knefe* (line 331). But even there, the knife is more useful than good looks.

80. *Guy of Warwick*

stanza 62	1	Þan dede he com forþ* a Sarrazine,	he made come forth
		…	
	7	He is so michel & vnrede*,	huge and monstrous
		Of his siȝt a man may drede,	
		Wiþ tong as y þe telle.	
		…	
stanza 63	1	For he is so michel of bodi y-piȝt*,	well-built
		Oȝains him tvelue men haue no miȝt,	
		Ben þai neuer so strong;	
		For he is four fot, sikerly*,	surely
		More þan ani man stont* him bi*:	(who) stands /beside him
		So wonderliche* he is long*.	extremely/ tall
		…	
stanza 121	1	'Hold þi pes*,' seyd Amoraunt,	Be silent
		'For, *bi* mi lord sir *Teruagaunt*,	
		…	
stanza 126	5	Þi liif þou schalt astite* forgon,	immediately
		Þi bodi schal atvinne*,	(be cut) in two
		& þine heued, *bi Teruagaunt*,	
		Mi leman schal haue to presaunt*,	as a gift
		Þat comly is of kinne*.	noble birth
		…	
stanza 263	1	& Gij hent* his swerd an hond,	seized
		& heteliche* smot to Colbrond:	fiercely
		As a *child* he stode him vnder.	

81. *Lybeaus Desconus*

1243	For a lady of prys,	
	Wyth rode reed as rose on ryse,	
	þys countre ys yn dowte*;	danger
	A *geaunt* hatte Mauugys,	

66 Laura Hibbard Loomis, "Sir Thopas and David and Goliath," *Modern Language Notes* 51 (1936): 311.

Nowher hys per þer nys,
Her haþ be-leyde* abowte.   beseiged
He ys blak as ony pych*,   pitch
1250 Nower þer ys non swych
Of dede sterne* and stoute;   fierce
. . .
1300 And þat fyle* *geaunt*   horrible
þat leuede* yn *Termagaunt*,   believed
Þat day to deye yn fyȝt.

82. ***Sir Eglamour of Artois***

301 When he come ware* *þe geant* was,   where
'Gude sir,' he sayd, 'þou latt me passe,
If þat it be thi will.'
'Nay, traytour! þou arte tane*!   taken
305 My chefe herte hase þou [sclayne: Cotton MS]
þat sall þe lyk full ill!'

To þe knyght þe geaunt gun gaa*;   did go
An iryn clube he gan hym taa*,   take

83. ***Torrent of Portyngale***

1260 The Gyaunt shipped in a while
And sett hym oute in an yle,
That was grow both grene and gay.
Sir Torrent com *prekand* on a stede,
Richely armed in his wede;
. . .
1287 The Giaunt said: 'So must I the*,   thrive, prosper
Sir, thou art welcom to me,
Thy deth is not to layn*!'   not to be concealed

Queene of Fairye with her music:

84. ***Lybeaus Desconus***

1426 Sche made hym melodye
Of all manere menstracy
Þat man myȝte descryue*.   describe
. . .
1432 Wyth fantasme* and *fayrye**   illusion/ magic
Þus sche blerede hys yȝe*,   deceived him
Þat euell mot sche þryue*.   that she may prosper ill

85. ***Thomas of Erceldoune***

256 With curtassye to hir knelande.
Harpe & fethill bothe þay fande*,   try

	Getterne*, and als so þe sawtrye*;	guitar/ psaltery
	Lutte* and rybybe* bothe gangande*,	lute/ violin/ playing (going)
	And all manere of mynstralsye.	

The child seyde, 'Also moote I thee'

86. *Sir Eglamour of Artois*

229	The knyght *sayd, 'So mot I the**,	So may I prosper
	At my iournaye wolde I bee!'	
	He buskede* and mad hym ȝare*.	hastened/ ready
	'Bot a lyttill here by weste*	by the west
	A geant hase a *forest* –	

Postponing the fight (stanza 17)

87. *Cursor Mundi*

7519	Gas* and fettis* me nou in hi*,	go/ fetch/ in haste
	Min aun* *armur* to *child* daui*."	own/ David

88. *Guy of Warwick*

stanza 64 7	When he seye Amoraunt so grim*	monstrous
	(Þer durst no man fiȝt wiþ him:	
	So grille* he was on grounde),	fierce
	Þan asked he respite til* a day,	for
	To finde anoþer ȝif he may	
	Oȝaines him durst* founde*.	dared/ fight

89. *Otuel and Roland*

231	A*morwe* er it were day-lyȝt	
	and er the sonne schon bryȝt	
	…	
1200	"*To-morwe y wyl* thyder come,	

Giant attacks, and Thopas escapes:

90. *Cursor Mundi*

7485	I trou* treuly in godes miht,	believe
	Þat i sal* vndertake þe fight,	shall
	Agayn Goly þat es sua* grim,	so
	Wid *goddes grace sle sal* i him;	
	…	
7531	He tok fiue *stanis* þar war round,	
	And putt þaim in his scrip* þat stound*,	bag/ time
	And said, "dos* away þis ger*,	put away/ armour

	For certis i can na* armis ber,	no
	…	
	Þan said golias, “þu art bot dede.”	
	Dauid said, “þat take i godd to rede*.”	advise
	Said goli, “wil þu fight wid me?”	
	“I rede bi-time* þat þu heþen* fle.”	soon/ heathen
	“Fle þat wenis* haue þe werre,	(you) who thinks
	For ar i fle i sal come nerre.”	
	wid þis a *ston* he laid in *slinge,*	
	Sua stalworthli* he lett it suinge*,	strongly/ swing
	Þat in his front* þe ston he fest*,	forehead/ fastened
	Þat both his eyen* vte* þai brest*.	eyes/ out/ burst
	…	
7593	Dauid went ham* wid gret honour,	home
	All thankid *godd* þair creatour,	

91. ***Guy of Warwick***

stanza 100 1	Sir Amoraunt was agreued in hert,	
	& smote to Gij a dint ful smert	
	…	
stanza 101 1	Þe sadel bowe he clef* atvo,	split
	Þe stedes nek he dede also,	
	Wiþ his grimli* brond*.	deadly/ sword
	…	
stanza 110 1	Tel me,’ he seyd, ‘wennes* þou be;	whence
	For þou art strong, so mot y the,	
	& of michel miȝt.’	
	…	
stanza 117 1	Amoraunt was ful egre* of mode,	enraged
	& smot to Gij as* he wer wode*	as if/ mad
	…	
7	Of his scholder þe swerd glod* doun,	struck
	Þat boþe plates* & hauberioun*	plate armor/ coat of mail
	He carf* atvo, y pliȝt*,	cut/ I swear
	Al to þe naked hide*, y-wis,	skin
	& nouȝt of flesche atamed* is	pierced
	Þurch grace of god almiȝt.	
	…	
stanza 118 10	& when Gij seye* þat fair *grace**,	saw/ miracle
	Þat noþing wounded he was,	
	Iesu he þanked on heye.	
	…	
stanza 269 9	*þurch grace of godes* sond*	God’s grace
	Ded he feld* þe glotoun* þare.	slew/ villain

92. ***Lybeaus Desconus***

1258	Yf *God* me *grace* sende,
	Er þys day come to ende

Wyth fyȝt Y schall hym spylle*. kill
. . .
1264 Þey* Y be ȝyng and lyte, Though
To hym ȝyt wyll Y smyte,
Do God all hys wylle!'
Þey ryden forþ all þre
Toward þat fayre cyte,
Me[n] clepeþ hyt Ylle d'Ore.
1270 Mauugeys þey gonne y-se
Vp-on þe bregge of tre*, bridge of wood
Bold as wylde bore.
. . .
1279 He cryde to hym yn despyte*, hatred
'Say, þou felaw yn whyt,
Tell me what art þou!
Torne hom agayn all-so tyt*, quickly
For þy owene profyt,
Yef þow louede þy prow*.' advantage
1285 Lybeauus seyde anoon ryȝt*, immediately
'Artour made me knyȝt,
To hym J made avow
Þat Y ne schulde neuer turne bak;
þer-fore, þou deuell yn blak,
1290 Make þe redy now!'

Syr Lybeauus and Maugys
On stedes prowde of prys
To-gedere ryde full ryȝt.
Boþe lardes and ladyes
. . .
1315 Maugys was queynte* and quede* cunning/ evil
And smot of þe stedes heed
þat all fell out þe brayne;
Þe stede fell doune deed,
Lybeauus noþyng ne sede
1320 Bot start hym vp agayn*. up toward him
. . .
1387 Þe geaunt þys gan se,
J-*slawe* þat he schulde be,
And flauȝ* wyth myȝt and mayn. hastened
. . .
1396 He wente *yn-to þe toun;*
Wyth fayr processioun
Þat folk *com* hym *agayn*.

93. *Sir Eglamour of Artois*

313 He *sayd*, 'Traytour, whate dose þou here
In my foreste to stele my dere?
Here sall þou habyde*!' abide
Sir Eglamour his swerde owt drowthe*, drew

Thorowe Goddis helpe *and his* knefe*   sword
Thus hase *þe geant* loste his lyfe –

94. ***Sir Perceval of Galles***

The geant stode in his holde*,   castle
That had those londis in wolde*:   possession
Saw Perceuell, þat was bolde,
  One his lande dryfe*;   galloped over
He calde one his portere:
"How-gate* may this fare?   By what means
I se a bolde man ȝare*   rapidly
  On my lande ryfe*.   come
. . .
Hym were better hafe bene at Rome,
  So euer mote i thryfe!"
. . .
Than said Perceuell the fre,
"*Thurgh grace of God* so *sall i* the,
And siche geanteȝ as ȝe –
  Sle thaym in the felde!"

Siche metyng* was seldom sene;   strife
The dales* dynned* thaym bytwene   valleys/ resounded
For dynttis þat þay gaffe bydene*   each other
  When þay so mett.

95. ***Torrent of Portyngale***

Tho sir Torent went nere Cate, . . .
  He thought, he wold hym haue *slayn.*
The theff couth* no better wonne*,   was able/ to abide
In to the see rennyth he sone,
  As faste as he myght ffare.
Sir Torrent gaderid cobled *stonys*,
Good and handsom ffor the nonys,
  That good and round ware;
Meny of them to hym he *caste*,
He threw *stonys* on hym so faste,
  That he was sad and sare.
To the ground he did hym fell,
Men myght here the fend yell
  Halfe a myle and mare.

FIT TWO

VII. Minstrel Opening

Chaucer begins fit two with a minstrel-like call to attention common to metrical romances and his own first fit. Here the first two lines are nearly identical with those of *Bevis of Hamton*, including the verb *roune*; however, the description of Thopas's *sydes smale* (VII, 836) seems reminiscent of the lady in *Sir Launfal* with her *myddyll small*.

96. ***Bevis of Hamton***

1 *Lordinges, herkneþ to me tale*!
Is *merier þan þe niȝtingale*,
Þat y schel* singe; shall
Of a kniȝt *ich wile ȝow roune**, tell
Beues a hiȝte of Hamtoune,
Wiþ outen lesing.
. . .
1829 And rod ouer *dale & doun,*
Til he com to a gret toun;

97. ***Otuel and Roland***

715 Lordynges, wyl ȝe now here?
here names, *y wylle* that *ȝow* wyte*, know
As in frensche it ys y-wrete*. written
Now lesteneth to lere!

98. ***Richard Coeur de Lion***

6723 Now *herkenes* of *my* tale soþ,
Þowȝ* j swere ȝow none oþ*! Though/ oath

99. ***Sir Launfal***

942 Þat lofsom lemede lyȝt.

Þe lady was clad yn purpere palle*, rich cloth
With gentyll body and *myddyll small*,
Þat semely was of syȝt.

VIII. Game and Glee

Yet again, Chaucer interrupts any ongoing action; this time it is stopping for *game and glee* (VII, 840) before Thopas must fight the *geaunt with hevedes*

three (VII, 842) (a humorous rhyme).[67] Chaucer thus undercuts the momentum of the hero and the reader's interest in his future exploits by these kinds of stalling devices. Instead of providing suspense and building excitement, these plot impediments leave readers wondering whether Thopas will ever meet his giant and engage in the expected ritualistic combat of chivalric heroes.

100. ***Cursor Mundi***

7443 Þai broght wid þaim Goli, þat etin*, — giant
. . .
7447 Be-tuix his eyen, thre fote brad,
Ful laith* it was his visage made. — handsome
Of bodi grett, in graynys* lang, — legs
vnsterly* semid he to be strang; — stern, fierce
Sex elne* and mare he was on hiht*, — ells/ tall
He was all armid forto fight.
Of his mete* was mesur nan, — meal
He wild ete seuen schep his an*. — seven of his own sheep
Þan said he,"quar es nu saul king*? — where is now King Saul

101. ***Guy of Warwick***

stanza 14 4 Now for fourteniȝt it schal be
Þe bridal* hold wiþ *gamen & gle* — wedding
At Warwike in þat tyde.'
. . .
stanza 16 10 Þer was mirþe & melody,
And al maner *menstracie*
As ȝe may forþeward here.
. . .
stanza 17 1 Þer was trumpes* & tabour*, — horn players/ drummers
Fiþel*, croude*, & harpour*, — fiddlers/ croude players/ harpers
Her craftes* for to kiþe*, — Their skills/ show
Organisters* & gode stiuours*, — Organists/ bagpipers
Minstrels of mouþe*, & mani dysour*, — Story-tellers/ jesters
To glade þo bernes bliþe*. — To make those people happy

102. ***Ipomadon A***

184 Ipomadon servyd in the hall,
And herde the knyghttys wordys all
Of that damysell.
So grette good of her he spake,
Hym thoughte [hys] hertte asvunder brake
Wyth syghynge and vnsyle*. — unhappiness

[67] Winstanley (p. lxxiv) suggests that the three-headed giant might represent the armies of Charles VI, the Count of Flanders, and the Duke of Burgundy that opposed Philip van Artevelde; however, this kind of allegorical reading is not suggested by Thopas's adventures.

103. ***Kyng Alisaunder***

1034	Now gynniþ* þe *geste** of nobles	begins/ story
	At þeo feste was trumpyng	
	Pipyng and eke taboryng	
	Sytolyng* and ek harpyng	playing on citoles (kind of guitar)
	Knyf pleyng and ek syngyng	
	Carolyng and turmentyng*	participating in tournaments
1040	Wrastlyng and ek flymyng*.	fencing (?)

104. ***Octavian A***

67	Ther myȝth *men* here *menstralcye*,	
	Trompys, taborus & cornettys crye,	
	Roowte*, gyterne, lute & sawtrye,	fiddle (stringed instrument)
70	Fydelys & oþyr mo;	
	In Parys greet melodye	
	They maden þo.	

105. ***Otuel and Roland***

628	with moche melodye:
	he held fest ryche and *ryall,*
	for-sothe in the kyngys halle,
	with myrthe and *mynstrel*sye.

106. ***Richard Coeur de Lion***

4643	Trumpes blewen, tabours dasshen*	striking of drums
	…	
4649	Off ryche *wyn* þer was plente,	
	Pyment* and ryche clarre*.	spiced wine/ claret

107. ***Squire of Low Degree***

1069	There was myrth and melody	
	With harpe, getron, and sautry,	
	With rote, ribible*, and clokarde*,	rebec (kind of lute)/ bells
	With pypes, organs, and bumbarde*,	bassoon
	*Wy*th other *mynstrelles* them amonge,	
	With sytolphe* and with sautry songe,	citoles
1075	With fydle, recorde*, and dowcemere*,	recorder/ dulcimer
	With trompette and with claryon clere,	
	With dulcet pipes of many cordes;	

108. ***Thomas of Erceldoune***

260	And all manere of *mynstrals*ye.
	…
268	*Reuelle* amanges þame was full ryfe.

	Knyghtis dawnesede* by three and three,	daunced
	There was revelle, *gamene,* and playe;	

IX. Catalogues of Wine, Spices

This catalogue, the second in *Sir Thopas* (VII, 851–6), is unusual for its references to sweetness, suggestive of a child's sweet tooth: the *mazelyn*, *the roial spicerye*, *gyngebreed*, and *lycorys*. Descriptions of feasts are common in Middle English romances, but few (with the notable exception of *Kyng Alisaunder*) dwell on the spices alone as this one does.

109. *Annot and Johon*

33	such *licoris* mai leche* from Lyne to Lone*;	physician/ rivers in Devonshire and Lancashire
	such *sucre* mon secheþ þat saneþ* men sone*;	heals/ quickly
	…	
38	ase quibibe* ant *comyn* cud is in crone*,	cubeb/ cummin known by its top
	cud comyn in court, canel in cofre*,	in a chest
	wiþ *gyngyure* ant sedewale ant þe gylofre.	

110. *Kyng Alisaunder*

5514	Forþ Alisaundre gan wende	
	Til he com to þeo trowes* ende	woods
	Note mugge* and þeo sedewale	nutmeg
	On heom smulliþ* and þe wodewale	smells
	Þeo canel and þe *licoris*	
	And *swete* sauour ymeynt* ywis	mingled together
	Þeo gilofre quybibe and mace	
	Gynger comyn ȝauen odour of grace	
	And vndur sonne* of alle spices	in the world
	Þey hadden sauour wiþ delices	

111. *Richard Coeur de Lion*

4247	Þey soden* fflesch*, rost and brede,	boiled meat/ roasted meat
	And to þe soper faste þey ȝede.	
	Plente þer was of bred and *wyn*,	
	Pyment, clarry, good and *ffyn**;	in plenty
	Off cranes, swannes, and venysoun,	
	Partryhches, plouers*, and heroun,	plovers
	Off larkes, and smale volatyle*.	birds

112. *Sir Launfal*

341	Þe cloþ was spred, þe bord* was sette,	table
	Þey wente to hare sopere.	

343 Mete and drynk þey hadde *afyn*,
Pyement, claré, and Reynysch *wyn*,

113. ***Squire of Low Degree***

316 And serued the Kynge ryght royally
With deynty meates that were dere*, precious
With partryche, pecoke, and plouere,
With byrdes in bread ybake,
The tele*, the ducke, and the drake, teal (wild duck)

X. Arming of the Hero

As in other instances, the description of arming the hero provided opportunities for excess, although battle gear was an essential component of any fighting knight.[68] For a poem in which the protagonist never does get to fight, the four-stanza, 31-line description of Thopas's arming (VIII, 857–87) may be seen as a clear example of Chaucerian excess. Whether, as Manly suggested the whole passage is "absurd from beginning to end" is open to question.[69] For example, the *aketoun*, which Manly claims was "specifically the defensive armour of the common foot soldier"[70] was worn by many romance heroes, including the heroes in *Bevis*, *Guy*, *Lybeaus*, *Richard Coeur de Lion*, *Seege of Melayne*, *Roman de Gaydon*, and *Otuel and Roland*.[71] Likewise, the harbergeoun and hauberk were familiar during Chaucer's time. The one satiric touch that virtually everyone agrees upon is the reference concerning *cote-armour/ As whit as is a lilye flour* (VII, 866–7). The coat-armor should have displayed Sir Thopas's armorial bearings, and thus should not have been blank.[72] The descriptor *whit as is a lilye flour* usually applies to women, as it does in two lines in *Sir Launfal*: *Þey wheryn whyt as floure* and *Sche was as whyt as lylye yn May* (extract no. 31). Thopas's shield does not depict the usual lion or eagle, but rather a *bores heed*. The great war-horse or destrier is instead a *dappull gray* which goes at an amble (VII, 884–5), not the pace one would expect. In the early Middle Ages, the color in descending order of prestige for war-horses is white, piebald, skewbald, any color with white feet and face, but "war-horses of almost every colour are mentioned in the poems, including spotted, chestnut, bay, innumerable shades of grey (including iron grey, dappled, or otherwise), sorrel, and roan."[73]

68 See Derek Brewer, "The Arming of the Warrior in European Literature and Chaucer," in *Chaucerian Problems and Perspectives: Essays Presented to Paul E. Beichner*, ed. Edward Vasta and Zacharias P. Thundy (Notre Dame, IN, 1979), pp. 221–43.

69 Manly, "*Sir Thopas*: A Satire," p. 70.

70 Manly, *Ibid.*

71 Irving Linn, "The Arming of Sir Thopas," *Modern Language Notes* 51 (1936): 300–11, especially 303–5.

72 Linn, p. 306. However, Stephen J. Herben, Jr., points out that white, although not an heraldic color, was the usual representation of argent; further, references to white arms are found elsewhere, with no absurdity or satire intended. See "Arms and Armor in Chaucer," *Speculum* 12 (1937): 480–1. See also extracts no. 117 from *Ipomadon A* and no. 119 from *Octavian*.

73 Léon Gautier, *Chivalry*, ed. Jacques Levron, trans. D. C. Dunning (New York, 1959), p. 333.

Chaucer follows *Guy* and *Lybeaus* in terms of phrasing and specific combinations of words not found elsewhere. Guy wears a hauberk from Jerusalem, a *charbocle* for decoration, a *flour* on his helm while Lybeaus in MS Cotton Caligula A.2 wears a *sherte*, white *gypell*, *sheeld* of gold with boars' heads and a *spear head scharp yground*. Thopas's *jambeux* of *quyrboilly*, his ivory sword *shethe* and his *helm of latoun* have no exact parallels in romance literature and are most likely Chaucer's own additions to the accoutrements of his knight.[74] It is peculiar that Chaucer would pay attention to the ivory sheath without mentioning the more important sword, which often has a proper name in romance and epics. That Thopas is lacking a sword and spurs is telling.[75] His spear (VII, 881) is made of *fyn ciprees*, a wood not known for its strength and sometimes associated with cemeteries and death. Shafts were preferably made of ash (the strongest and toughest wood); other woods of choice were applewood, hornbeam, pine, laurel and sycamore.[76]

In VII, 872, Thopas swears on ale and bread. Many critics have pointed out that knights usually swear by saints, God, Mary, or aristocratic objects such as peacocks, swans or herons.[77] In Middle English romance, knights swear *bi Crist and Seint Iohan* (*Havelok*, line 2563), *Goddes book* (*Gamelyn*, line 91), *Seynt Rycher* (*Gamelyn*, lines 137 and 619); *by Cristes ore* (*Gamelyn*, line 231), *Goddes berd* (*Gamelyn*, line 295); *Seynt Anne* (*Athelston*, line 669), and *God Almiȝti* (*Degaré*, line 415). None swears by ale and bread. *Kyng Alisaunder*, however, provides a possible source of the rhyming of dead and bread (*Areches he hutte; now he is ded,/ N'ul he no more ete bred*, lines 247–8) as well as of another unusual rhyming of *mawe* with *slawe*: (*Jn litel while was mony y slaw,/ And y smyte þoruȝ wombe and mawe*, lines 1253–4).

74 Manly ("*Sir Thopas*: A Satire," p. 70) argued that the arms of Thopas represented comic absurdities and deliberate mistakes, but Herben ("Arms and Armor in Chaucer," p. 481) argues that it is a "fairly realistic description of the successive stages of arming" and thus the satire "must reside in the over-elaboration of detail and in the emphasis upon the obvious." See also Claude Blair, *European Armour, circa 1066 to circa 1700* (London, 1958), and *Complete Encyclopaedia of Arms & Weapons*, ed. Leonid Tarassuk and Claude Blair (London, 1982).

75 In investiture ceremonies, the sword and spurs were the culminating acts for a knight. In degrading an unworthy knight the symbolic action consisted in depriving him of sword and spurs, as was set forth in *The Booke of Honor and Armes* printed in 1590: "In the raigne of King Edward IV, it appeared a knight was degraded in this sort. First after the publication of his offense, his guilt spurs were beaten from his heels, then his sword taken from him and broken" (Linn, p. 310).

76 Gautier, *Chivalry*, p. 321.

77 Baugh, *Chaucer's Major Poetry*, note to line 2062, p. 350. W. W. Skeat suggested that the oath was a "ridiculous imitation of the vows made by the swan, the heron, the pheasant, or the peacock, on solemn occasions" (*Works,* V. 196). Cf. *Voeux de Paon* (Vows of the Peacock) of Jacques de Longuyon as well as the poem *The Vows of the Heron*, which recounts the taking of oaths at the court of Edward III. For further references on the custom, see Eleanor Hammond, *English Verse between Chaucer and Surrey* (Durham, NC, 1927), pp. 414–15. Beatrice White, in "Two Chaucer Notes. 1. Proper Names in the *Canterbury Tales*; 2. A 'Minced Oath' in *Sir Thopas*," *Neuphilologische Mitteilungen* 64 (1963): 170–5, sees the "mealy-mouthed" hero substituting a minced or idle oath for a blasphemous oath on the eucharistic wine and bread; she further thinks this is ironic in light of the violent Flemish youths in the *Pardoner's Tale*, who use "grete and dampnable" oaths, something our hero from Flanders might be expected to do as well.

114. _**Bevis of Hamton**_

	King Ermin þo anon riʒte	
	Dobbede Beues vn-to kniʒte	
	And ʒaf him a _scheld_ gode & sur*	reliable
	. . .	
979	Beues dede on is _actoun_*,	quilted jacket
	Hit was worþ mani a toun;	
	An _hauberk_ him brouʒte þat mai*,	maiden
	So seiden alle þat hit isai*:	saw
	Hit was wel iwrouʒt* & faire,	made
	Non egge tol* miʒte it nouʒt paire*.	sword, blade?/ damage
	After þat ʒhe* ʒaf him a _stede_,	she
	Þat swiþe* gode was at nede*,	very/ in time of need

115. _**Cursor Mundi**_

7521	_Helm_ and _habiryun_ on him þai did*,	put, placed
	And gird him wid a suord emid;	

116. _**Guy of Warwick**_

stanza 91	Gij was ful wele in armes diʒt	
	Wiþ _helme_, & _plate_, & brini* briʒt,	coat of mail
	Þe best þat euer ware.	
	Þe _hauberk_ he hadde was _renis_*,[78]	from region of the Rhine
	Þat was king Clarels, y-wis,	
	In Ierusalem when he was þare.	
	. . .	
2328	Wiþ white hauberkes & wiþ scheldes.	
	. . .	
3849	He oxed* his armes hastiliche,	asked for
	And men es him brouʒt sikerliche.	
	Hosen of iren* he haþ on drawe,	leg guards of iron
	Non better nar* bi þo dawe*.	are not/ day
	In a strong _hauberk_ he gan him schrede*,	cut
	Who so it wered, þe ded no þurt him drede.	
	An _helme_ he haþ on him don:	
	Better no wered neuer kniʒt non;	
	The sercle of gold þer-on was wrouʒt,	
	For half a cite no worþ it bouʒt*:	the worth of half a city would not buy it
	. . .	
3861	Seþþe he gert him wiþ a brond	
	Þat was y-made in eluene lond*.	fairy-land
	His scheld about his nek he tok,	
	On hors he lepe wiþ-outen stirop,	
	On hond he nam a _spere_ kerueinde*,	sharp-pointed

[78] The word _renis_ occurs in the Auchinleck MS, miswritten for _ieuis_ (Jewish). See H. S. Ficke, "'_Iewes Werk_,'" _Philological Quarterly_ 7 (1928): 82–5, on the reputation of Jews as expert armourers, and in the metal-working industries, especially in Toledo, which had a large Jewish community.

		Out of þe cite he was rideinde.	
		…	
3873		Wel y-armed on his *stede*,	
		A launce he bar gode at nede.	
		…	
4129		Gij anon asked* *his stede* þo,	asked for
		His spere, & his swerd also:	
		In his hond a gode swerd he bar;	
		…	
stanza 92	4	As bri3t as ani siluer it was:	
		Þe halle schon þerof as sonne* of glas*,	sun/ glass
		For soþe wiþouten fayle.	
		His *helme* was of so michel mi3t,	
		Was neuer man ouer-comen in fi3t	
		Þat hadde it on his ventayle*.	face plate
		…	
stanza 93	1	A gode swerd he hadde, wiþ-outen faile*,	without doubt
		Þat was Ectors in Troye batayle,	
		In gest as so men fint*.	find
		…	
	7	Hose & gambisoun* so gode kni3t schold,	jacket
		A targe* listed* wiþ *gold*	shield/ bordered
		About his swere* he hint*.	neck/ carried
		…	
stanza 249		& Gij was armed swiþe wel	
	5	In a *gode hauberk* of stiel	
		Wrou3t of þe best lawe*.	Made in the best way
		An *helme* he hadde of michel mi3t	
		With a ce[r]cle of *gold*, þat schon bri3t,	
		Wiþ precious stones on rawe*.	in a row
	10	In þe frunt stode a *char-bukel** ston:	carbuncle
		As *bri3t* as ani sonne it schon	
		Þat glemes vnder schawe*.	in the dark
		…	
stanza 250	1	On þat *helme* stode a *flour*:	
		Wrou3t it was of diuers colour;	
		…	
stanza 250	5	Gloues, & gambisoun, & hosen of mayle	
		As gode kni3t haue scholde.	
		Girt* he was wiþ a gode brond	armed
		Wele kerueand, bi-forn his hond	
		A targe listed wiþ *gold*,	

117. ***Ipomadon A***

2390	Abowte his neke a white *scheld*,	
	A *white* spere in his hand he helde,	
	The pensell white I wene.	

118. ***Lybeaus Desconus***

217	To army* þer knyȝtes wer fayn*:	arm/ glad
	Þe ferste was Syr Gaweyn,	
	Þat oþer, Syr Perceuale,	
220	Þe þyrþe, Syr Eweyn,	
	Þe ferþde was Syr Agrafrayn:	
	So seyþ the Frenȝsch tale.	
	Þey caste on hym *a scherte* of selk*,	silk
	A gypell* as *whyte* as melk,	short tunic
225	Jn þat semely sale,	
	And syȝt* an *hawberk* bryȝt	then
	Þat rychely was a-dyȝt	
	Wyth mayles* þykke and smale.	iron rings
	Gaweyn, hys owene syre,	
230	Heng abowte hys swyre	
	A *scheld wyth* a gryffoun;	
	And Launcelet hym broȝt a *sper*,	
	Jn werre wyth hym well to were*,	defend
	And also a fell fachoun*;	sharp sword
235	And Syr Oweyn hym broȝt a *stede*	
	…	
238	And an *helm* of ryche atyre	
	Þat was stele and noon yre*	iron
	Perceuale sette on hys croun*.	head
	…	
1174	Hys fomen wer well boun	
	To perce hys *acketoun*,	
	Gypell, mayl and *plate*.	
	…	
1567	*Hys scheld was of gold* fyn,	
	Þre *bores heddes* þer-*jnne*	
	As blak as brond y-brent*;	piece of burning wood
	…	
1573	And of þe same paynture*	style of painting
	Was lyngell* and trappure*,	horse's harness strap/ horse cloth
1575	J-*wroȝt* well fayre and gent*.	tastefully
	Hys schaft* was strong wyth-all,	lance
	…	
1603	Þo he tok a schaft rounde	
	Wyth cornall* *scharp y-grounde*	lance head
	And ryde be ryȝt* resoun.	(proper) correct

119. ***Octavian A***

1677	Þe kyng of Ierusalem gan lede	
	Þe ferst batayle;	
	Melk *whyte armes*, yn ryme I rede,	
1680	Was hare parayle*.	equipment

120. *Otuel and Roland*[79]

282 On hym an *haketoun* thay gonne done
Ouer hys *hauberk* that bryȝt *schon*,
That ryche was of mayle.
And it made y-wys
That was whylom denys* prentys* — Diones (fabled British blacksmith)/ apprentice
Off a trewe entayle*. — order of succession
Estre of langares*, that was lel*, — Estout de Legres (French baron)/ loyal
brouȝt hym an *helm* off steel
fful strong to a-ssayle*. — assault

The *helm* was grene as glas.
Tha[t] whylome auȝt* galyas*, — owned/ Goliath
And sythe kyng barbatyan*. — King Brachant
hym gert in that plas
with dorundale* that good was, — Roland's sword
That he by-fore wanne.
Duk reyner hym brouȝt a *schyld,*
A fayrer myȝt haue be non in feld,
And that wel many a man telle can,
with a lyon there-Inne raumpande*. — leaping (rampant)
That whylome aught* a geante, — owned
That was a douȝty man.

Tho olyuer hym brouȝt *a spere*,
As good as any man myȝt bere
In feld to batayle,
kyng, knyȝt, or any ryder
Myȝt it ful wel were
hys enymye to assayle.
The duk terry sette a-none
The spores that of gold schone,
ffor-sothe with-oute fayle.

121. *Sir Eglamour of Artois*

235 Wyth *syprese* trees growand lang;

122. *Squire of Low Degree*

211 *In* the myddes of your *sheld* ther shal be set
A ladyes *head*, with many a frete*; — ornament

[79] Although the Fillingham manuscript is fifteenth-century, O'Sullivan argues that the extant text is most likely copied from a version in existence before the middle of the fourteenth century and that a pre-Chaucerian date of composition (no later than the first quarter of the fourteenth century) is suggested. (An earlier version is found in the Auchinleck MS.) See M. I. O'Sullivan, *Firumbras and Otuel and Roland*, EETS OS 198 (Oxford, 1935), pp. xx and lxvii. This arming of Roland is also similar to the arming of Otuel, lines 357–86, and of Clarel, lines 1217–46, in the same text. According to Linn, all these descriptions (roughly the same length as that in *Thopas*) provide correspondences with Chaucer's text in mentioning the aketoun, hauberk, shield, helmet and saddle and "present closer resemblances than any other English romances now known" ("The Arming of Sir Thopas," p. 310).

123. ***Thomas of Erceldoune***

41	Hir palfraye* was a dappill graye,	saddle horse
	. . .	
46	Swylke one ne saghe j neuer none;	
	Als dose þe sonne on someres daye,	
	Þat faire lady hir selfe scho *schone.*	
	Hir selle it was of *roelle bone**,	ivory
50	ffull semely was þat syghte to see!	
	. . .	
62	Hir cropoure was of Orpharë*;	made by a goldsmith
	And als clere golde hir *brydill it schone*,	
	. . .	
68	Hire lire* was *white* as any swan.	calf of leg

(MS Cambridge Ff.5.48)

Swearing oath, line 872

124. ***Athelston***

169	Þanne *swoor* þe kyng be cros and roode*:	Christ's cross
	'Meete ne drynk schal do me goode,	
	Tyl þat he be dede,	

125. ***Avowis of Alexander***

5151	"Lordingis," said auld* Cassamus,	old
	"Be* all our Goddis and be Marcus,	by
	I rede* we to the pacok* do	advise/ peacock
	The vsage that coustumit* is thair-to.	customary
5155	In this countre the vsage is	
	That ilk man avow* sall his auyse*;	swear/ vow
	. . .	
5207	"This mete for douchty ordaned is,	
	That worthy ar ladeis for to kis.	
	Heirto suld* men avow heyly*,	should/ loudly
5210	And syne* fulfill douchtelly,	then
	Of armes and of amouris* samin*;	armours/ together
	And I sall first begin the gammin!"	
	. . .	
5287	That I sall licht in middes the feild	
	With *helme, haubrek, spere and sheild*,	
	. . .	
5290	Thare sall I duell with thame* and fecht*,	them/ fight
	Outher leif or dee* quhether* God will send,	either life or death/ whatever

126. ***Lybeaus Desconus***

406	But o þyng greuyþ me sore:	
	Þat he haþ do me swore	
	Vp-on hys fawchoun bryȝt	

Þat Y ne schall neuer-more,
410 Tyll Y come Artour be-fore,
Soiourne* day ne nyȝt. — delay, stay

127. *Seven Sages of Rome*†

505 He *swore* anon, *by* saynt Vyncent,
"I schal nevere hete* *brede*, — eat
Here* the thyfe traytour *by dede*." — Ere, before
. . .
1630 Quod the emperour to the emperesse,
"By hym that made matyns* and messe*, — Matins/ mass
I nyll* to morwen ete no *brede* — will not
Er the thef traytour *be ded*."

† These lines are from MS Cambridge University Library Dd.I.17, ed. Thomas Wright for Percy Society 16, *Early English Poetry, Ballads, and Popular Literature of the Middle Ages* (London, 1846; rpt. New York, 1965).

128. *Sir Degrevant*

1753 Þan þe Erle wexe* wode*, — grew/ angry
And *swore* by bane and by blode:
'Þar sall na mete do me gud
  Or* I se þe dy!' — before

129. *Sir Eglamour of Artois*

567   This fend will felly* fyghte.' — fiercely
Sir Eglamour said, 'By þe rode,
I sall assaye hym þofe* he be wode, — though
  And sla* hym thorow Goddis myghte!' — kill

130. *Sir Perceval of Galles*

381 He sware by grete Goddeȝ myȝte,
"I schall holde* þat i hafe highte*; — keep/ promised
"Bot-if þe Kyng make me knyghte,
  To-morne i sall hym sloo!"
. . .
Hade i bene in the stede* — that place
930 Þer* he was done to þe *dede*, — Where
I solde neuer hafe etyn *brede*
  Are* i hade sene hym bren*." — Before/ burn

131. *Sir Triamour*

97 Then was the quene wonder wrothe,
And swere mony a grete othe,
. . .
103 Y trowe y schalle never ete *bred*
Tylle thou be broght to the *dedd*,

"Bityde what bityde":

132. ***Bevis of Hamton***

351 *Be-tyde*, what so euer *be-tyde*,
...
663 Certes,' said Beues, 'tyde, what wyll be-tyde
(Chetham MS 8009)

133. ***Sir Degaré***

741 To his knaue he seide, "Tide wat tide,

134. ***Sir Orfeo***

339 Parfay!' quaþ he, 'Tide wat bitide,

135. ***Squire of Low Degree***

276 *Betyde* of you *what* so *betyde*;

XI. Announcement of End of Fit

It is entirely possible that announcing the end of the fit derives from *Sir Eglamour* since that romance breaks from the tail-rhyme pattern to add: *Make we mery, so haue we blysse!/ For þys ys þe fyrst fytte iwys* repeated in virtually identical lines for the second and third fits as well. The phrase *here [is] a fit* is also found in *Thomas of Erceldoune* and some later ballads.[80]

136. ***Sir Degrevant***

after line 368 Her endyth þe first *fit*
Howe say ye? will ye *any more of hit.*[81]

137. **Sir Eglamour***

343 Make we mery, so haue we blysse!
For þys ys þe fyrst *fytte*, iwys,
...

* These lines are from MS Cotton Caligula A.2, and are so numbered in Richardson's edition.

80 See especially the ballad of Adam Bell (*English and Scottish Popular Ballads*, no. 116, stanza 51, p. 248, and stanza 97, p. 251).

81 These two lines written in different hands are inserted after line 368 in Cambridge University Library MS Ff.1.6, of *Sir Degrevant*, and thus may be the insertion of a scribe familiar with *Sir Thopas* rather than lines that Chaucer may have adapted. This manuscript contains Chaucerian texts, but not *The Canterbury Tales*. See Eleanor Hammond, *Chaucer: A Bibliographical Manual* (New York, 1933), pp. 343–6.

634 This ys þe secund *fytte* of þis:
Makes mery, so haue y blys!
. . .
904 Makes mery, for yt ys beste,
For þis ys þe laste geste
(variant: the thrydd fytt of owre geste)

FIT THREE

XII. Minstrel Opening

Unlike most minstrel openings, this one is almost abusive in telling the company to be quiet so that the poet can continue. To ask the audience to *Holde* their *tongue* (in *Gamelyn*) or *sitte stille* is as rude as these overt directions to the audience usually get. Chaucer then continues with the traditional appeal to listen: *herkneth to my spelle* (VII, 893) and falls back into the minstrel story-telling mode. Chaucer adds to the humor by describing the inactive knight Thopas as the one who *bereth the flour/ Of roial chivalry!* (VII, 901–2). The addition of *roial* is totally superfluous for even the best knights.

138. *Amis and Amiloun*

1189 *Now*, hende, *herkeneþ*, & y schal say
Hou þat sir Amiloun went his way;

139. *Bevis of Hamton*

1484 For to hiȝe* wiþ our *spelle*: hasten

140. *Gamelyn*

169 Liþeth, and *lestneþ* and *holdeþ ȝour* tonge,
And ȝe schul heere talkyng of Gamelyn þe yonge.

141. *Guy of Warwick*

3997 *Listeneþ* now & sitteþ stille:
. . .
4790 More ȝe schul here ȝif ȝe wille
. . .
4794 So y finde in mi *spelle*,
. . .
4819 Now wende we oȝain to our *spelle*,
Þat ȝe me herd er þan telle

142. ***Ipomadon A***

701 Thus turnythe she tow and fro.
Att the laste, of *love drewry** — illicit love
Dystrwes* defawte* of *chevallrye*: — cures (destroys?)/ loss
'Alas why [ys] [it] so?

143. ***Kyng Alisaunder***

29 *Now* pais* *holdiþ* and leteþ cheste* — peace/ wrangling
And ȝe schole here anoble ieste
Of Alisaundre þeo riche kyng
…
39 ȝef ȝe wolen sitte stille
Ful feole* *Y wol ȝow telle* — many things
…
1233 Listeniþ now sire and dame
Now bygynniþ aneowe game

144. ***Seven Sages of Rome***

1 Lordynges þat here likes to dwell,
Leues ȝowre speche and *heres þis spell.*
I sal ȝow tel, if I haue tome*, — leisure
Of þe Seuen Sages of Rome.
5 Whilom lifed* a nobil man; — lived
His name was Dyoclician.

he bereth the flour/ Of roial chivalry!

145. ***Guy of Warwick***

1560 Þe *flour of* kniȝtes is sleyn þis day.
…
stanza 67 12 'In warld þai *bere the flour.*'

146. ***Lybeaus Desconus***

1529 And *flowr of chyualrye*

147. ***Octavian A***

27 *Of chyualrye he hadde þe flour,*
That any man wyste;
Here of a nobyll conquerour
30 Ye mowyth* lyste. — may

148. ***Torrent of Portyngale***

2494 Of all the Justis*, that there ware, — jousts
Torent the *floure* a way *bare*

XIII. Catalogue of Heroes

It is not uncommon to find lists of heroes in romance literature, often as a way of establishing the stature and reputation of the hero or as a way of showing how many heroic works the author knew. Either way, it seems like consummate showmanship with little real meaning.

149. **Cursor Mundi**

[Me]n ȝernis* iestis for to here, — yearn, desire
And *romance* rede on maner ser,
Of alexander þe conquerour,
Of Iuli cesar þe emperour
[Of grece & Tr]oye þe strong strijf,
[Þere many thosand lesis] hir lijf,
[O brut* þ]at berne bolde of hand — Brutus
[First Conqu]erour of meri ingland;
[Of] king arthour, þat was so riche,
[W]as non in his time funden suiche;
Of ferlijs* þat his knigh[t]es fell, — marvels
[Of] auntris did i. here of tell,
[Of] wawain*, kay, and other stabil, — Gawain
[For] to were þe runde tabil.
Hou king charlis* and rouland* faght – — Charlemagne/ Roland
Wid sarazins ne wald þai neuer be saght*; – — reconciled
O tristrem, and ysoude þe suete,
Hu þai wid luffe first gan mete;
Of king ionet and ysumbras,
Of ydoyne, and of amadas*; — Amadace
Storijs of diuers thinges,
Of princes, prelates, and of kinges,

(Supplied by Cotton Vespasian MS A.3)

150. ***Laud Troy Book***

Many speken of men that *romaunces* rede
That were sumtyme doughti in dede,
…
Off Bevis, Gy, and of Gauwayn,
Off kyng Richard, & of Owayn,
Off Tristram, and of Percyuale,
Off Rouland Ris, and Aglauale,
Off Archeroun, and of Octouian,
Off Charles, & of Cassibaldan,
Off Hauelok, *Horne,* & of Wade; –

151. *Otuel and Roland*

ther was Rowland, and Olyuer,
and syr Otuel, and Oger, –
In hert ys nouȝt to huyde, –
Esteryche of langares, and syr turpyn,
Archel, Etus, & syr Geryn,
Nemes, and syr Reyner.

152. *Richard Coeur de Lion*

Ffele* *romaunses* men maken newe, Many
Off goode knyȝtes, stronge and trewe;
Off here dedys men rede *romaunce*,
Boþe in Engeland and in Ffraunce:
Off Rowelond, and off Olyuer,
And off euery Doseper*; champion
Off Alisaundre, and Charlemayn;
Off kyng Arthour, and off Gawayn,
How þey were knyghtes goode and curteys;
Off Turpyn, and of Oger Daneys;
Off Troye men rede in ryme,
What werre þer was in olde tyme;
Off Ector, and off Achylles,
What folk þey slowe in þat pres*. throng (crowd)
. . .
J wole rede *romaunce* non
Off Pertenope, ne of Ypomadon,
Off Alisaunder, ne of Charlemayn,
Off Arthour, ne off Sere Gawayn,
Nor off Sere Launcelet-de-Lake,
Off Beffs, ne Gy, ne Sere Vrrake,
Ne off Ury, ne of Octauyan,
Ne off Hector, the stronge man,
Off Jason, ne off Hercules,
Ne off Eneas, ne off Achylles.
I wene neuere, par ma fay,
Þat in þe tyme off here day,
Dede ony off hem so douȝty dede
Off strong batayle and gret wyȝthede,
As dede Kyng Rychard, saun fayle,
At Jaffe in þat batayle

153. *Sir Launfal*

Sere Perseuall and Sere Gawayn,
Syr Gyheryes and Syr Agrafrayn
  And Launcelet du Lake;
Syr Kay and Syr Ewayn,
Þat well couþe fyȝte yn playn*, in full (battle)
  Bateles for to take*; engage in

Kyng Banbooȝt and Kyng Bos –
Of ham þer was a greet los*: fame
Men sawe þo nowhere here make*; – equal
Syre Galafre and Syr Launfale,
Whereof a noble tale
Among vs schall awake.

154. *Speculum Vitae*

I warne ȝow ferst at þe begynnyng,
I wil make no veyn* spekyng vain
Of dedes of armes ne of amours,
Os* don mynstreles and oþer gestours, as
Þat make spekyng in many a place
Of Octouian and Isanbrace
And of many oþer gestes,
And namely whan þei come to festes,
Ne *of Beus* of Hamptoun,
Þat was a [MS *of*] knyht of gret renoun,
Ne *of sir Gy* of Warewyk,
Al þow it mowe som men like,
I thenke my spekeng schal not be;
For I holde þat nowht bot vanyte.
…

53 Þere fore gode men þat be now here,
Lysten to me and ȝe may here,
Whow* ȝe schal reule ȝowre lyf How

155. *Squire of Low Degree*

77 Or els so bolde in eche fyght,
As was Syr Lybius that gentell knyght,
Or els so bolde in chyualry
As Syr Gawayne, or Syr Guy;
Or els so doughty of my hande
As was the gyaunte Syr Colbrande.

XIV. Riding Out

The last section of *Sir Thopas* describes not a heroic battle against the giant, but rather Thopas setting out on his horse for an adventure that never happens. These lines are packed with *non sequiturs* and abrupt shifts. The words *goode steede al he bistrood* (VII, 903) are stereotypical and found in many romances as the following extracts demonstrate; however, the next action verb, the gliding, is unusual, puzzling, and possibly humorous, given the comparison to a

spark: *And forth upon his wey he glood/ As sparcle out of the bronde.*[82] The action is slowed even further, almost stalling altogether, with the description of Thopas's crest: *Upon his creest he bar a tour,/ And therinne stiked a lilie flour* (VII, 906–7). Towers were not uncommon on crests, but sticking a lily on it is.[83] This could be an allusion to the *fleur-de-lis* associated with French royalty or to Guy of Warwick, who bore a flower on his crest.[84] Chaucer abruptly switches from a description of the crest to a description of the hero as the *knyght auntrous*, a common designator found in many of the Middle English romances, including *Lybeaus*, *Richard*, *Sir Degaré*, *Sir Degrevant*, and *Sir Eglamour*, but nothing in the text supports this description. Like Gawain, Generides, and the hero of *Squire of Low Degree*, Thopas finds himself in an inhospitable environment, alone without shelter for the night. Sleeping in the woods alone with his horse eating *herbes fyne and goode* (VII, 914) while he drinks from the well, like Sir Perceval, is ironic. The last adjectival phrase, *worly under wede*, is unusual for Chaucer, who might have found it in *Guy* or *Amis and Amiloun*; however, these kinds of alliterative phrases were ubiquitous.[85] The poem ends abruptly and anticlimactically with *Til on a day* – a suggestion of important things to come; the rest of the line is easily anticipated with the cliché *it so bifel.*

his goode steede al he bistrood/ And forth upon his wey he glood/ As sparcle out of the bronde

156. *Bevis of Hamton*

1827 A* restede him þer a lite tide, — He
His gode stede he gan *be-stride*
And rod ouer dale & doun,

157. *Guy of Warwick*

5463 Wiþ scharp spors* þai smiten her stede, — spurs
& sprongen forþ so spark* on glede*. — spark/ live coal

6411 *His gode stede he bi-strod,*
And of-tok hem wiþ-outen abod.
…

82 The furious and swift actions of a knight have been compared to sparks from a fire or flint. See Whiting S 561–9. This furious pace, however, is belied by the verb *glood.* Ann Haskell points to this puzzling verb instead of the expected galloping as further indication of Thopas as puppet. See "Sir Thopas: The Puppet's Puppet," pp. 255–6.

83 John Burrow (*Riverside Chaucer*, n. 906, p. 922) notes that helmets "often bore distinctive crests (though *creest* here refers not to the crest itself but to the top of the helmet to which it is fixed; see MED s.v. *creste* 3 [a]). The heraldic crest may or may not carry the same device as the shield. In this case it does not." See J. Woodward, *A Treatise on Heraldry* (Edinburgh, 1896), vol. 2, pp. 235–6, and *Fairbairn's Book of Crests*, ed. A. C. Fox-Davies (Edinburgh, 1892), plates 156–7 for towers on crests.

84 See Blair, *European Armour*, figure 86.

85 John Burrow, "'Worly under wede' in *Sir Thopas*," *Chaucer Review* 3 (1969): 170–3; rpt. in *Essays on Medieval Literature* (New York, 1984), finds this expression in *Emaré*, *Amis and Amiloun*, *Golagros and Gawain*, *William of Palerne*, and five times in *Awntyrs of Arthure*.

Stanza 1 4 Þe best bodi he was at nede
Þat euer miȝt *bistriden stede*,
…
488 Y brenne so *spark* on glede.

158. *Laud Troy Book*

28 That euere *by-strod* any *stede*,

159. *Lybeaus Desconus*

622 Lybeaus was redy boun
And lepte out of þe arsoun* saddle
As sperk þoȝ *out of glede*
…
769 *Hys stede he be-*gan *stryde*,

160. *Otuel and Roland*

445 And fouȝten as they were wode,
…
492 the fyr out sprang as *spark of* flynt,
…
1432 the fyr sprange oute as *sparcle of* glede, –
…
1515 that feer flye out as *sparkyl of* flynt,
…
1831 that fyre flye out as *sparke of* flynt.

161. *Reinbrun*

Stanza 76 7 Amorwe Reinbroun aros erly,
And armede him ful hastely,
For to winne pris.
10 A *gode stede he bestrod,*
& forþ a wente wiþ-oute abod* delay
To þe forest, ywis.

162. *Sir Degaré*

495 *His gode stede he gan bistride*;

163. *Sir Isumbras*

457 When he was horsede on a *stede*,
He sprange forthe, *als sparke one glede*,
With grymly* growndyn* gare*. fiercely/ honed/ spear

164. ***Torrent of Portyngale***

502 Tho *he be-strod* a noble *sted,*

knight auntrous

165. ***Confessio Amantis*, Book I**

1522 And thus he wente forth his weie
Alone as a *knyht aventurous,*

166. ***Lybeaus Desconus***

1117 Jn-to þe wode þey rode
And Lybeauus þer-out aboþe
As *aunterous kny3t* yn pryde.
. . .
1831 Þat on rod yn-to þe halle
And þer he gan to kalle*, call
'Syr kny3t aunterous!

167. ***Richard Coeur de Lion***

271 As a *knyght auentorous.*
His atyre was orgulous*: prideful
All togyder coleblacke
. . .
275 *Upon his creste* a rauen stode,
. . .
285 He bare a shafte that was grete and stronge,
It was fourtene fote long;
. . .
502 Tyde me lyff, or tyde me deth,
I shal mete hym 3yff j may!'
The *aunterous*, wiþ gret deray*, outcry
. . .
507 Hys schuldre wiþ hys schafft he brak,
. . .
511 The *aunterous* þo turnyd agayn,
And houyd* stylle* for to seyn waited/ quietly
Who durste iouste wiþ hym more.

168. ***Sir Degaré***

1006 Iich am an *aunterous kni3t,*
For to seche werre and fi3t."

169. ***Sir Degrevant***

421 Scho lokide on þat cheualerouse
And said, '*Knyghte aunterus,*

…
1385 'Welcome,' scho said, '*Sir Aunterous,*
Me thynke þou art meruelous;

170. *Sir Eglamour of Artois*

469 He sayde, 'My name ys *Antorus*;
…
1229 He was *aunterous* in þe feld:
…
1249 He sayd, 'No, Mari! I am *aunterus in stowre** — ready to fight in battle
For a lady, as whyte as flowre,
  To wynne here ȝyf I may.'

(Cotton MS)

171. *Squire of Low Degree*

175 And ryde through many a peryllous place
As a *venterous* man, to seke your grace,

nolde slepen in noon hous

172. *Generides*

3918 And furth* with all the Sowdon had aspyed — thereafter
Wythynne the logge* wher *lay* Generides, — lodge
In his harnes *slepyng* still opece*. — quietly

173. *Lybeaus Desconus*

241 Þe knyȝt to hors gan spryng
And rod to Artour þe kyng
And seyde, 'My lord hende:
ȝef me þy blessynge,
245 Anoon* wyth-oute dwellynge: — At once
My wyll ys for-to wende.'

174. *Sir Gawain and the Green Knight*

729 Ner slayn wyth þe slete he *sleped in* his yrnes* — armor
Mo nyȝtez þen innoghe in naked rokkez*, — More nights than enough on bare rocks

175. *Squire of Low Degree*

177 Ouer *hylles and dales* and hye mountaines,
In wethers wete, both hayle and raynes,
And yf ye may no harbroughe* se*, — lodging/ see
Than must ye lodge vnder a tre,
Among the beastes wyld and tame,

And euer you wyll gette* your name; enhance
183 *And in your armure must ye lye*,
Eeuery nyght than by and by,

***baiteth* his horse:**

176. ***Torrent of Portyngale***

Down light this gentill knyght,
To Rest hym a litull wight,
  And vnbrydelid his stede
And let hym *bayte** on the ground, feed
And aventid hym* in that stound*, recovered his breath/ time
  There of he had gret nede.

drinking from the well:

177. ***Sir Perceval of Galles***

His righte name was *Percyuell*,
He was ffosterde in the felle*, wilds
He dranke water of þe welle:
  And ȝitt was he wyghte*. powerful, valiant

worthly under wede

178. ***Amis and Amiloun***

466 He is douhtiest in dede
& *worþliest in* eueri *wede*[86]
& chosen for priis & flour.

179. ***Duk Moraud***[87]

36 I am dowty in dede!
I am *worly in wede*!
I am semly on stede!

180. ***Guy of Warwick***

stanza 10 9 Þat *worþly were in wede.*

[86] See note to line 30 in Kölbing's edition *Amis and Amiloun* (Heilbronn, 1884) for the nearly identical lines 138, 443, and 453.

[87] This fourteenth-century fragment has been edited by J. Q. Adams, *Chief Pre-Shakespearean Dramas* (Cambridge, 1924), pp. 207–11. The word *worly* appears twice, in lines 37 and 79; the variant *worlych* also appears twice, in lines 55 and 160 although the expression *worly under wede* appears just once (line 37) juxtaposed to the *dowty in dede*. John Burrow draws attention to this reference and concludes that the word belongs to the "general stock of well-worn native poetic words and forms" (see "'Worly under wede' in *Sir Thopas*," p. 173).

181. ***Laud Troy Book***

27 But of the *worthi*est wyght *in wede*
That euere *by-strod* any *stede,*
Spekes no man, ne in romaunce redes
Off his batayle ne of his dedis.

182. ***Octavian B***

21 No *worthier vndir wede.*

183. ***Otuel and Roland***

941 Tho Roulond, *worthy on wede,*

Last half line: Til on a day –

184. ***Amis and Amiloun***

1885 So it bifel þat selue *day*, –

185. ***Sir Perceval of Galles***

2141 So it byfelle app*on a day*,
Now þe sothe als i sall say,
Mi lorde went hym to play*. take his pleasure

APPENDIX

Editions of Middle English Texts

Amis and Amiloun, ed. MacEdward Leach, EETS OS 203 (London, 1937; rpt. 1960). See extracts nos 1, 47, 66, 138, 178, 184.

Annot and Johon, in *The Harley Lyrics: The Middle English Lyrics of MS Harley 2253*, ed. G. L. Brook (Manchester, 1964), pp. 31–2. See extracts nos 54, 109.

Athelston, ed. Julius Zupitza in *Englische Studien* 13 (1889): 331–414; and *Englische Studien* 14 (1890): 321–44 [from Cambridge College Caius MS 175]. See extracts nos 2, 21, 32, 124.

Avowis of Alexander, in *The Buik of Alexander*, ed. R. L. G. Ritchie (Edinburgh, 1921–29), vol. 3, pp. 248–351. See extract no. 125.

Bevis of Hamton, in *The Romance of Sir Beues of Hamtoun*, ed. Eugen Kölbing, EETS ES 46, 48, 65 (London, 1885, 1886, 1894; rpt. one volume, 1975). See extracts nos 3, 22, 48, 96, 114, 132, 139, 156.

Confessio amantis, in *The English Works of John Gower*, ed. G. C. Macaulay, EETS ES 81 (Oxford, 1957), vol. 1. See extract no.165.

Cursor Mundi, ed. Richard Morris, EETS OS 57, 59, 62, 66, 68, 99, 101 (London, 1874–93) [from MS Göttingen Theol.107]. See extracts nos 87, 90, 100, 115, 149.

Duk Moraud, in *Chief Pre-Shakespearean Dramas*, ed. J. Q. Adams (Cambridge, 1924), pp. 207–11. See extract no. 179.

Earl of Toulouse, in *Middle English Metrical Romances*, ed. Walter H. French and Charles B. Hale (New York, 1930), pp. 383–419. See extract no. 4.

Gamelyn, in *Middle English Metrical Romances*, ed. Walter H. French and Charles B. Hale (New York, 1930), pp. 209–35. See extracts nos 34, 140.

Generydes, ed. W. Aldis Wright, EETS OS 55, 70 (London, 1873, 1878; rpt. one volume, 1973). See extract no. 172.

Guy of Warwick, ed. Julius Zupitza, EETS ES 42, 49, 59 (London, 1883–91; rpt. one volume, 1966) [from MSS Auchinleck and Caius 107]. See extracts nos 5, 23, 35, 38, 44, 49, 55, 60, 62, 67, 75, 78, 80, 88, 91, 101, 116, 141, 145, 157, 180.

Horn Childe, in *King Horn: A Middle English Romance*, ed. Joseph Hall (Oxford, 1901), pp. 179–92. See extract no. 6.

Ipomadon A (stanzaic version), ed. Rhiannon Purdie, EETS OS 316 (Oxford, 2001) [from MS Chetham 8009]. See extracts nos 7, 24, 45, 61, 63, 68, 102, 117, 142.

Ipomydon B or *The Lyfe of Ipomydon* (couplet version), *Ipomedon in drei englischen Bearbeitungen*, ed. E. Kölbing (Breslau, 1889), pp. 257–319; 454–61 [from MS Harley 2252]. See extracts nos 8, 39, 50, 69, 76.

King Edward and the Shepherd, in *Middle English Metrical Romances*, ed. Walter H. French and Charles B. Hale (New York, 1930), pp. 949–85. See extract no. 40.

King Horn: A Middle English Romance, ed. Joseph Hall (Oxford, 1901), pp. 1–177. See extract no. 25.

Kyng Alisaunder, ed. G. V. Smithers, EETS OS 227 (London, 1952; rpt. 1961) [from Laud MS Misc. 622, including Lincoln's Inn MS 150]. See extracts nos 103, 110, 143.

Land of Cokaygne, in *Altenglische Sprachproben*, ed. Eduard Mätzner (Berlin, 1867–1900), vol. 1, p. 150. See extract no. 56.

Laud Troy Book: A Romance of about 1400 A.D., ed. J. Ernst Wülfing, EETS OS 121, 122 (London, 1902–03; rpt. one volume, 1988) [from MS Laud Misc. 595]. See extracts nos 150, 158, 181.

Life of St Alexius, in *Adam Davy's 5 Dreams About Edward II, The Life of St Alexius, Solomon's Book of Wisdom, St Jeremie's 15 Tokens Before Doomsday, The Lamentacion of Souls*, ed. F. J. Furnivall, EETS OS 69 (London, 1878), pp. 17–79. See extract no. 9.

Lybeaus Desconus, ed. M. Mills, EETS OS 261 (London, 1969) [from MS Cotton Caligula A.2]. See extracts nos 10, 26, 46, 64, 81, 84, 92, 118, 126, 146, 159, 166, 173.

Octavian A (southern version, six-line stanzas), in *Octovian Imperator*, ed. Frances McSparran, Middle English Texts 11 (Heidelberg, 1979) [from MS Cotton Caligula A.2]. See extracts nos 36, 104, 119, 147.

Octavian B (northern version, twelve-line stanzas), in *Octavian*, ed. Frances McSparran, EETS OS 289 (London, 1986). [from MS Lincoln 91]. See extracts nos11 and 182.

Otuel and Roland, in *Firumbras and Otuel and Roland*, ed. Mary Isabelle O'Sullivan, EETS OS 198 (London, 1935; rpt. 1971), pp. 59–153. See extracts nos 12, 27, 57, 73, 77, 89, 97, 105, 120, 151, 160, 183.

Reinbrun, in *Guy of Warwick*, ed. Julius Zupitza, EETS ES 42, 49, 59 (London, 1883–91; rpt. one volume, 1966), pp. 631–74. See extracts nos 28, 37, 161.

Richard Coeur de Lion, in *Der mittelenglische Versroman über Richard Löwenherz*, ed. Karl Brunner (Vienna, 1913) [from MS Caius Cambridge 175]. See extracts nos 98, 106, 111, 152, 167.

Seven Sages of Rome, ed. Killis Campbell (Boston, 1907; rpt. 1975) [from MS Cotton

Galba E.9]. See extracts nos 29, 70, 127, 144 (for 29 and 127, see above footnotes on pp. 666 and 700 respectively).

Sir Degaré, in *Middle English Metrical Romances*, ed. Walter H. French and Charles B. Hale (New York, 1930), pp. 287–320. See extracts nos 13, 30, 51, 133, 162, 168.

Sir Degrevant, in *The Romance of Sir Degrevant: A Parallel-Text Edition*, ed. L. F. Casson, EETS OS 221 (London, 1949) [from MSS Lincoln A.5.2 and 91 and Cambridge University Library Ff.1.6] . See extracts nos 14, 41, 128, 136, 169.

Sir Eglamour of Artois, ed. Frances E. Richardson, EETS OS 256 (London, 1965) [MS Lincoln 91, with lines supplied from Cotton Caligula A.2 as noted]. See extracts nos15, 82, 86, 93, 121, 129, 137, 170.

Sir Gawain and the Green Knight, ed. J. R. R. Tolkien and E. V. Gordon, 2nd edn, revised by Norman Davis (Oxford, 1967). See extract no. 174.

Sir Isumbras, in *Sir Ysumbras*, ed. G. Schleich, Palaestra 15 (Berlin, 1901) and in *Six Middle English Romances*, ed. M. Mills, Everyman Library 90 (London, 1973). See extracts no. 16 (lines 7–9, Mills; 10–12, Schleich) and no. 163 (Schleich).

Sir Launfal, in *Middle English Metrical Romances*, ed. Walter H. French and Charles B. Hale (New York, 1930), pp. 345–80. See extracts nos 31, 52, 71, 79, 99, 112, 153.

Sir Orfeo, ed. A. J. Bliss (Oxford, 1966). See extracts nos 42, 134.

Sir Perceval of Galles, in *Middle English Metrical Romances*, ed. Walter H. French and Charles B. Hale (New York, 1930), pp. 531–603. See extracts nos 17, 43, 72, 94, 130, 177, 185.

Sir Triamour, The Romance of Syr Tryamoure, in *Early English Poetry, Ballads, and Popular Literature of the Middle Ages*, ed. James O. Halliwell, Percy Society 16 (London, 1846, pp.1–63; rpt. 1965). See extract no. 31.

Speculum Vitae, ed. J. Ullmann in *Englische Studien* 7 (1884): 468–72 [first 370 lines only]. See extract no. 154.

Squire of Low Degree, in *Middle English Metrical Romances*, ed. Walter H. French and Charles B. Hale (New York, 1930), pp. 721–55. See extracts nos 58, 107, 113, 122, 135, 155, 171, 175.

Thomas of Erceldoune, in *The Romance and Prophecies of Thomas of Erceldoune, Printed from Five Manuscripts*, ed. James A. H. Murray, EETS OS 61 (London, 1875; rpt. 1987). See extracts nos 18, 59, 65, 74, 85, 108, 123.

Torrent of Portyngale, ed. E. Adam, EETS ES 51 (London, 1887; rpt. 1973). See extracts nos 19, 53, 83, 95, 148, 164, 176.

Ypotys, in *Altenglische Legenden*, ed. Carl Horstmann (Heilbronn, 1881), pp. 511–26. See extract no. 20.

The Canon's Yeoman's Tale

CAROLYN P. COLLETTE AND VINCENT DIMARCO

The Canon's Yeoman's Tale is extraordinary among *The Canterbury Tales* in having neither any known major sources nor analogues that suggest the early existence of a primary source.[1] This anomaly has encouraged various suppositions about the autobiographical nature of the tale, resulting in a body of mid-twentieth-century criticism focusing on Chaucer's putative suspicion of alchemy or the equally factitious hypothesis that Chaucer was himself the dupe of an alchemical trickster; this latter is an ancient Chaucerian tradition given authority by Tyrwhitt, who had written that the poet's "sudden resentment had determined Chaucer to interrupt the regular course of his work, in order to insert a Satire against the Alchemists."[2] This theory was advanced by such influential twentieth-century scholars as John Matthews Manly, who adduced a wealth of historical documentation of alchemical activity in Chaucer's milieu to hint at his likely acquaintance with the alchemist William Shuchirch, and to conclude with this disingenuous suggestion:

> Is it too wild a speculation to wonder whether Chaucer himself had been a victim? Is there no hint of bitterness in his satire? Certain lines in the *Canon's Yeoman's Tale* – what manuscripts and editors call Part II – suggest very strongly that that tale was originally composed, not for inclusion in the Canterbury series, but to be read or recited to an audience which included some canons of the church. I refer of course to lines 992ff . . . I do not dare to suggest that the tale was read at Windsor, but I will say that if it had been read there, the canons there would have been very apt to think of Brother William Shuchirch . . .[3]

And, indeed, the vast majority of critical studies of the tale assume Chaucer's thoroughly critical, satirical stance.

But the speculation that Chaucer was the victim of an alchemical sting, or that he was the dupe of some adept practicing in the world of late fourteenth-century London – an idea, it seems, nurtured by modern ambivalence toward the alchemical enterprise – rivals another well-documented historical tradition, articulated consistently in the fifteenth, sixteenth, and seventeenth centuries, that Chaucer possessed a deep and extensive knowledge of the terms and techniques of alchemy because he was himself an adept. Francis Thynne, correcting

The authors gratefully acknowledge the kind assistance in the preparation of this chapter of Professors Donald Cheney, Alex Page, and Harlan Sturm of the University of Massachusetts (Amherst), as well as Robert Correale, Mary Hamel, and Jill Mann.

1 Chaucer's authorship of the tale, while generally accepted, is still a matter of critical discussion. Norman F. Blake's recent edition of *The Canterbury Tales* (*The Canterbury Tales by Geoffrey Chaucer, Edited from the Hengwrt Manuscript*, York Medieval Texts, 2nd series [London, 1980]), calls attention to the fact that the tale is not included in the early Hengwrt manuscript. Peter Brown, in "Is the 'Canon's Yeoman's Tale' Apocryphal?" *English Studies* 6 (1983): 481–90, offers a reasoned response to the implications of Blake's argument, at the same time acknowledging the inconsistencies of tone and style between the first and second parts of the tale, and in its second part between the story of the deception and the last fifty-four lines. Albert E. Hartung makes a similar point in "'Pars Secunda' and the Development of the *Canon's Yeoman's Tale*," *Chaucer Review* 12 (1977): 111–28. On the inclusion of the tale in the manuscripts of *The Canterbury Tales* see E. T. Donaldson, "The Manuscripts of Chaucer's Works and their Use," in *Geoffrey Chaucer: Writers and Their Background*, ed. Derek Brewer (London, 1974), pp. 85–108.

2 *The Poetical Works of Geoffrey Chaucer with an Essay on His Language and Versification*, ed. Thomas Tyrwhitt (London, 1843), p. lxviii.

3 John Matthews Manly, *Some New Light on Chaucer* (New York, 1926), pp. 246–7.

errors in alchemical terms in Thomas Speght's 1598 edition of Chaucer, asserted Chaucer's expertise in the field.[4] Thynne included Chaucer among the great alchemists of the Middle Ages in his 1573 poem on the subject which spoke of "the learned Raymund Lyully/ the inglishe frier olde Bacone, & the good britishe Riplye,/ with Arnolde of the new towne, & the wise & princely legate [sic]/ the famous grave Sir Geffray chaucer come to light but of late/ the morall Gower . . . / Then Noorton of whome Bristowe may bragge."[5]

In the early modern period it was often thought that Chaucer's alchemical knowledge derived from Gower's instruction of his fellow poet in the art.[6] In 1652, Elias Ashmole declared in reference to *The Canon's Yeoman's Tale:* "Now as Concerning Chaucer (the Author of this Tale) he is ranked amongst the *Hermetick Philosophers,* and his *Master* in this *Science was Sir John Gower*, whose familiar and neere acquaintance began at the *Inner Temple* . . ."[7] Thus it is not surprising that another correlative Renaissance tradition linked Chaucer's skill as a poet with the importance of poetry in conveying the secrets of hermetic arts. As Robert Schuler points out, the English alchemical tradition in the early Renaissance was conveyed largely in poetical works into which Chaucer's work, like Gower's, fit seamlessly:

> It is not generally recognized, first of all, that there was a strong tradition of medieval and Renaissance alchemical poetry into which the *Canon's Yeoman's Tale* was easily assimilated, and of which it seemed a natural part. The fifteenth century in particular produced dozens of alchemical poems, including two masterpieces, George Ripley's *The Compound of Alchymie* or *Twelve Gates* (1471) in over 2500 lines of rhyme-royal stanzas, and the 3102-line *Ordinal* by Norton (1477). Both exist in many manuscripts (twenty-four and thirty-two respectively), including some from the sixteenth century which contain alchemical material associated with Chaucer. It is important to remember, in fact, that poetic texts actually constituted the main vernacular alchemical tradition from the fifteenth through the sixteenth century.[8]

Michela Pereira demonstrates the importance of such secular lines of transmission in late medieval and early modern alchemical knowledge, suggesting the secular and learned, as opposed to the academic and ecclesiastically-controlled,

[4] *Francis Thynne's Animadversions upon Speght's First (1598) Edition of Chaucer's Works*, ed. G. H. Kingsley, EETS OS 9 (London, 1865), pp. 9, 32–3, 36, 38.

[5] *Animadversions*, p. 135. He also points to Chaucer's apparent discrimination between the philosophy of alchemy and the tricksters who fed off ignorance and hope, by observing that both Chaucer and Norton "plenteously vnfolde" the tricks of false alchemists in their work.

[6] George G. Fox in *The Medieval Sciences in the Works of John Gower* (Princeton, 1931), pp. 156ff argues that Gower is mistakenly credited with the greater knowledge.

[7] *Theatrum Chemicum Britannicum, Containing Severall Poeticall Pieces of our Famous English Philosophers, who have written the Hermetique Mysteries in their owne Ancient Language Faithfully Collected into one Volume with Annotations thereon by Elias Ashmole, Esq.* (London, 1652). Reprinted with introduction by Allen G. Debus, Sources of Science Series, 39 (New York, 1967), p. 470. On Chaucer and alchemy in the sixteenth century, see also Stanton J. Linden, *Darke Hieroglyphicks: Alchemy in English Literature from Chaucer to the Restoration* (Lexington, KY, 1996), and Gareth W. Dunleavy, "The Chaucer Ascription in Trinity College, Dublin, MS D.2.8," *Ambix* 12 (1965): 2–31; for the opposite Renaissance tradition, that Chaucer was critical of alchemy, see Caroline Spurgeon, *Five Hundred Years of Chaucer Criticism and Allusion 1357–1900*, 3 vols (New York, 1960), I, 90–125.

[8] Robert M. Schuler, "The Renaissance Chaucer as Alchemist," *Viator* 53 (1984): 306.

nature of alchemical knowledge in this period: "Except for the recipes, whose link with oral transmission implies a somewhat different range of problems, the existence of vernacular alchemical texts from the first half of the fourteenth century seems therefore to have been fostered by the nonacademic status of cultivated alchemists and by their experimental frame of mind."[9]

In spite of these assertions from this Renaissance tradition, the depth of Chaucer's knowledge of alchemy and the nature of his interest remain important but unknown factors in understanding the origins of *The Canon's Yeoman's Tale*. The most useful approach to determining the materials on which Chaucer drew to create the tale is to place Chaucer and his story of alchemy within a living intellectual tradition, and to show how many texts his own work echoes, and how fully he incorporated the subjects and protean discourse of alchemy in his tale. While we may never know for certain Chaucer's full attitude toward alchemy, we can safely conclude that he was hardly alone among his generation of writers in his interest in the subject.

Late medieval discussions of alchemy reveal a variety of opinions. Jean de Meun had treated alchemy at some length in the *Roman de la Rose,* incorporating into the fabric of his poem the conventional alchemical discourse of how art strives with nature.[10] Gower, apparently embracing the philosophy of alchemy, articulated fundamental alchemical principles concerning the unity of all matter in the *Confessio Amantis*. Lydgate translated the pseudo-Aristotle's *Letter of Alexander* in the *Secreta Secretorum*, a text that affirms the mystery of alchemy in terms that echo the ending of *The Canon's Yeoman's Tale*. Philippe de Mézières used a metaphor of alchemy and medicine to structure the social criticism of *Le Songe du Vieil Pelerin.*[11] By contrast, Petrarch wrote against alchemy in *De remediis utriusque fortunae*; and in her *Avisioun,* Christine de Pizan roundly condemned alchemy as a corrupt folly that led to loss of money and time, even though (because?) her own father was an adept. Whatever their particular positions on the merits or faults of the alchemical enterprise, all these writers demonstrate a degree of knowledge of both the theory and the practice of alchemy in their own time; by referring to and citing alchemy – if only to excoriate it – they imply its topical currency in their intellectual circles.[12] The bifurcation of their attitudes is instructive, because it suggests that the combination of criticism and acceptance that characterizes Chaucer's story of alchemy – criticism in terms of the three tricks, acceptance in terms of the last fifty-four

[9] "Alchemy and the Use of Vernacular Languages in the Late Middle Ages," *Speculum* 74 (1999): 356.

[10] *Romance of the Rose*, lines 16005–248. This is a passage which Chaucer also seems to have drawn on in part for his description of Virginia in *The Physician's Tale*, lines 7–29.

[11] For the passages from *Piers Plowman*, Gower, Lydgate, Christine de Pizan and Petrarch, see below. For the full text of Christine's discussion of alchemy, see folios 43v to 45r of *Lavision-Christine*, ed. Sister Mary Louis Towner (Washington, D.C., 1932), pp. 137ff. For *Le Songe du Vieil Pelerin*, see the edition by G. W. Coopland, 2 vols (Cambridge, 1969), and Carolyn Collette, "Reading Chaucer through Philippe de Mézières: Alchemy, the Individual and the Good Society," *Courtly Literature and Clerical Culture,* ed. Christoph Huber and Henrike Lähnemann (Tübingen: Attempto Verlag, 2002), pp. 177–94.

[12] On the intellectual climate in which alchemy flourished and a general history of medieval alchemy, see Lynn Thorndike, *A History of Magic and Experimental Science,* 8 vols (New York, 1923–58), especially vol. 3.

lines – reflects a cultural ambivalence in late-medieval Europe regarding the radical claims and the potential value of alchemy.[13]

Although we can place Chaucer's tale of alchemy within this contemporary literary context, it is also likely that his awareness of alchemy was as much a product of experience as of learned authority. One need not postulate an autobiographical origin of the tale to realize that its action and details may reflect Chaucer's awareness of fourteenth-century London practice. As Dorothea Waley Singer and others have shown, the historical record of alchemical activity in fourteenth-century England reveals that alchemical experimentation was not at all an unusual phenomenon, and was one of more than passing interest to the English crown. To Manly's evidence of the intersection of Chaucer's world and that of the adepts we can add the historical documents that Singer includes in Appendix II of her *Catalogue of Latin and Vernacular Alchemical Manuscripts*.[14] Although Singer's choice of documents claims to be no more than a representative selection, it provides a sense of the texture and details of alchemical activity, while at the same time depicting the crown's continuing interest in such processes. A document from 1329, for example, requests that Johannes le Rous and Magister Willelmus de Dalby, who were reputed to have made silver metal by means of alchemy, be brought to the king, with the implements of their art: "cum instrumentis et aliis rebus quibuscumque dictam artem contingentibus secum inventis" (Singer, III, 778). Their arrest, we may assume, had as much to do with gaining access to their knowledge as with controlling their activities.

An even more intriguing document is a petition brought by one Thomas de Euerwyke, an alchemist who was able "ouerrir par la sience de Alconemie et faire argent en plate," which he accomplished "en presence de bones gentz de Londres, et l'argent assaie par les orfeures de meisme la Citee et troue bon."[15] [to work by the science of Alchemy to create silver plate . . . in the presence of the good people of London, and the silver assayed by the goldsmiths of the same city was found to be genuine] Euerwyke was subsequently approached by a certain Thomas Crop, who invited him to bring his alchemical instruments into his home, and "qant le dit Thomas Crop feuest aparceu de la sience, voillant auoir le dit Thomas de Euerwyke en daunger, par collusion entre lui et autres de la Citee enprisona le dit Thomas de Euerwyke en la meson le dit Thomas Corp [*sic*] en Londres." [When the said Thomas Crop was acquainted with the science, wishing to place the said Thomas de Euerwyke in his control, with

[13] Part of this world of common knowledge included the distinction between spritually focused alchemists who worked with metals, reading and writing alchemical texts allegorically, and another group variously called "Puffers" or "Geber's Cooks," who carried out their operations on all kinds of organic substances, and read the alchemical texts literally. On this distinction see John Reidy, "The Unity of the 'The Canon's Yeoman's Tale,' " *PMLA* 80 (1965): 31–7.

[14] Dorothea Waley Singer, *Catalogue of Latin and Vernacular Alchemical Manuscripts in Great Britain and Ireland Dating from before the XVI Century*, 3 vols (Brussels, 1928–31), III, Appendix II, pp. 777ff.

[15] Singer, III, 778–9. The Crown's interest in alchemy is an entirely separate subject; judging from the documents Singer has gathered, it was lively and continuous. She also includes a 1350 document regarding an alchemist named John de Walden, who received "de Thesauro Domini Regis per manus Philippi de Weston quingenta scuta auri et viginti libras argenti ad comodum Regis inde faciendum per artem Alkemie" (p. 780); he was imprisoned for more than seven years in the Tower, so we must assume that his alchemy did not work.

others of the city he imprisoned the said Thomas de Euerwyke in his home in London.] He proceeded to charge Euerwyke with a debt which led to his being imprisoned in Newgate, "et lui detient son elixir et ses autres instrumenz et autres biens et chateux a la mountance de xl li; dont le dit Thomas de Euerwyke prie pur Dieu qe il pleise ordeiner pur sa deliuirrance, et faire venir le dit Thomas Corp oue le elixer et les instrumenz auant diz, issint q'il puisse deuant eux ouerrir et prouer sa sience ou autres queux il plerra au Roi assigner, et qe les faux obligacions puissont estre dampnetz" [and he (Crop) kept his elixir and his other instruments and other goods and chattels to the value of forty pounds; for which the said Thomas de Euerwyke asks that, please God, he be delivered and that the said Thomas Crop be made to come with the elixir and the instruments, before mentioned, that he may before them work and prove his science, or before others whom it may please the King to assign, and that the false obligations be invalidated] (Singer, III, 778–9).

Equally interesting is a document from the year 1374 which accuses one Willelmus de Brumleye, *capellanus,* of counterfeiting:

> Memorandum quod die mercurii proxima post festum Sancti Andree, coram domino Rege apud Westmonasterium venit quidam Willelmus de Brumleye capellanus nuper commorans cum Priore de Hermodes Worth per consilium domini Regis cum quatuor peciis auri controfacti super ipsum captis . . . et expresse cognovit quod ipse fecit pecias predictas cum arte Alconomie de auro et argento et aliis medicinis, videlicet sal armoniak, vitriol, et solermonik; et quod fuit in faciendo per quinque septimanas; et quod ipse venit cum peciis predictis apud Turrim London' ad Gautron, custodem monete domini Regis, et optulit ei pecias predictas ad vendendum si sibi videbatur quod alicuius essent valoris, et quod ipse antea vendidit prefato Gautron, quandam peciam huiusmodi metalli pro xviii solidis, set cuius ponderis erat ignorat. Et dicit quod ipse fecit metallum predictum per doctrinam Willelmi Shitchirch [sic], canonici Capelle domini Regis de Wyndesore . . . (Singer, III, 781)
>
> [Recorded that on the Wednesday next after the feast of St. Andrew, to the King's court at Westminster came a certain William de Brumley, chaplain, lately dwelling with the Prior of Harmandsworth, arrested by order of the King's Council, with four counterfeit pieces of gold upon him. He expressly acknowledged that he had, by the art of alchemy, made these pieces from gold and silver and other medicines, to wit *sal armoniak, vitriol* and *solermonik.* The process had occupied him five weeks, and he had taken the pieces to Gautron, the keeper of the King's mint at the Tower, and offered to sell them to him if they appeared to him of any value. William had before sold to Gautron a piece of this sort of metal for eighteen shillings, but of what weight it was he did not know. He said that he made the metal according to the teaching of William Shuchirch, canon of the king's chapel of Windsor . . .][16]

Documents such as these open a window on the place of alchemy in Chaucer's world, to reveal the generic and realistic nature of much of what

[16] Translation that of H. G. Richardson (p. 39) in "Year Books and Plea Rolls as Sources of Historical Information," *Transactions of the Royal Historical Society*, fourth series, vol. 5 (London, 1922), pp. 28–70.

might be termed the background action in the tale. The domestic nature of experiments in the art, the sharing of the secret recipes, the prominence of ecclesiasts among those connected to alchemy[17] all function as essential albeit background elements in the logical progress of Chaucer's tale. Furthermore, such details in the historical record indisputably ground the various incidental details of setting and effect in *The Canon's Yeoman's Tale* in contemporary fourteenth-century reality.

Records of the Guild of Goldsmiths from the late fourteenth century also corroborate the verisimilitude of incidental elements of Chaucer's tale of alchemy. After the duplicitous canon in Chaucer's tale has played his trick, he proposes that he and the priest "gon/ With thise thre teynes, whiche that we han wroght,/ To som goldsmyth and wite if they been oght."[18] (VIII, 1331–3). At the goldsmith's the "teynes three" were "putte . . . in assay/ To fir and hamer; myghte no man seye nay,/ But that they weren as hem oghte be" (VIII, 1337–40). The records of the Goldsmiths' Guild reveal a world of metal-working concerned with trickery, hidden workshops and madness, all elements of Chaucer's depiction of alchemy. The company's first charter fixes the site and function of goldsmiths' shops, expressly forbidding them to inhabit the "obscure turnings and by-lanes and streets" which constitute the world of Chaucer's alchemists; by warning against those who enter into the apparently common practices of counterfeiting and debasing precious metals, the charter implies the existence of a lively trade in such dishonest practices:

> . . . that of late, not only the merchants and strangers brought counterfeit sterling into the nation, and many also of the trade of goldsmiths kept shops in obscure turnings and by-lanes and streets, – but did buy vessels of gold and silver secretly and without enquiry, and immediately melting them down, did make the metal into plate, and sell it to merchants trading beyond the sea . . . and so they made false work of gold and silver . . . These deceptions as well as others charged against the cutlers, – who are said to have covered tin so subtly and with such slight, that the same could not be discovered from fine silver . . .[19]

The records of the Goldsmiths' Guild, together with the crown documents regarding the apprehension of counterfeiters and false alchemists, suggest the intersection of these two worlds, both apparently known to Chaucer, who places his alchemists and their attempts to manufacture false gold in precisely those locations that the guild suspects and tries to control, i.e., in "hernes and lanes blynde," where "thise robbours and thise theves by kynde/ Holden hir pryvee fereful residence" (VIII, 658–60). Similarly, guild documents from 16 Richard II cite the perilous nature of the goldsmiths' work in terms that evoke the Yeoman's description of the hazards of alchemy: "They state that Edward, the king's late grandfather, at the suit of the goldsmiths of the city of London,

[17] On the dominance of Friars and other ecclesiasts in the field see Thorndike, vol. 3, 213ff.

[18] All citations of *The Canon's Yeoman's Tale* are from *The Riverside Chaucer,* ed. Larry D. Benson (Boston, 1987).

[19] William Herbert, ed., *The History of the Twelve Great Livery Companies of London*, 2 vols (London, 1836), II, 129; his translation.

'suggesting to him, how that many persons of that trade, by fire and the smoke of quicksilver, had lost their sight; and that others of them, by the working in that trade, became so crazed and infirm, that they were disabled to subsist, but of relief from others. . . .' " (*Twelve Great Livery Companies*, II, p. 156).

Such documents suggest that *The Canon's Yeoman's Tale* need not have been generated out of anger or humiliation to have been a combination of authority and experience, the details of which were based both on Chaucer's London life and on his reading.

It is impossible to infer from *The Canon's Yeoman's Tale* the full range of alchemical texts Chaucer read, in large part because his presentation of alchemy is both general and eclectic.[20] Contextualizing the tale within the corpus of alchemical literature presumably available to him shows that he uses the discourses and the common alchemical themes to be found in a wide variety of texts.[21] In the years since Bryan and Dempster's volume of sources and analogues appeared, a number of scholars have demonstrated several specific echoes of particular alchemical authors and texts in Chaucer's tale. Following the earlier lead of S. Foster Damon,[22] Pauline Aiken argued for Chaucer's acquaintance with alchemy on the basis of his reading in Vincent of Beauvais' *Speculum Naturale*, especially the eighth book. She asserted that Chaucer's terminology in the tale followed Beauvais' so closely that his text was Chaucer's source of Part I of the tale.[23] Joseph E. Grennen concluded that Chaucer's knowledge of alchemical literature was extensive if not deep,[24] and that Chaucer depended on his audience's knowledge of alchemical literature for his verbal echoes and puns. Edgar H. Duncan ventured a conservative opinion that Chaucer did indeed know the *Rosarium* attributed to Arnaldus de Villa Nova, as well as the *De Secreta* attributed to the same author. He argued at length and in some detail for Chaucer's apparent extensive indebtedness to Geber's *Sum of Perfection,* finding "the lists of alchemical substances, apparatus, processes, etc. thrown out by the yeoman more nearly paralleled in Geber's *Sum* than in any other treatise."[25]

The various conclusions reached by these scholars who have tried to identify Chaucer's sources demonstrate that the nature of the corpus of alchemical literature – its conventional technical language, its self-reflexivity, and its comparative stability over time – makes it difficult to identify with a high degree of certainty any particular sources of the various elements of the tale. We can, however, identify some conventional topoi and themes that Chaucer did and

20 While Chaucer is unusual among alchemical writers in specifying the amounts of material used in Pars II of *The Canon's Yeoman's Tale*, he is also unusually sketchy in his description of processes and materials in Pars I.

21 On this subject Thorndike is invaluable in laying out the various conventions of alchemy and its labyrinthine, metaphorical discourses.

22 "Chaucer and Alchemy," *PMLA* 39 (1924): 782–8. Damon argued that Chaucer had "evidently been a serious student of alchemy," p. 788.

23 Pauline Aiken, "Vincent of Beauvais and Chaucer's Knowledge of Alchemy," *Studies in Philology* 41 (1944): 371–89.

24 Joseph E. Grennen, "The Canon's Yeoman's Alchemical 'Mass,' " *Studies in Philology* 62 (1965): 547.

25 "The Literature of Alchemy and Chaucer's *Canon's Yeoman's Tale*: Framework, Theme, and Characters," *Speculum* 43 (1968): 642.

didn't use. As Aiken did, we can note that Chaucer's text does not include allegorical and mystical passages that appear in so many late medieval alchemical texts.[26] We observe, moreover, that Chaucer's materials (VIII, 805–15) include a series of corrupt ingredients, bodily wastes, and bodily fluids that not all alchemists used, but which appear in a strain of alchemical texts which includes the work of John of Rupiscessa, translated into English by the fifteenth century as *The Book of Quinte Essence*; it provides multiple recipes for making the elixir, *quinte essence*, out of corrupt waste materials.[27]

The Canon's Yeoman's Tale is unusual in pre-fifteenth-century alchemical literature because it conjoins an exposé of deception and a declaration of faith in the *work*. Norton's fifteenth-century *The Ordinal of Alchemy* also includes such a combination, beginning with an affirmation of "holye Alchymye" as "A wonderful science, secrete philosophie,/ A singuler grace & gyfte of almyghtie,/ which neuir was fownde bi labour of man."[28] Within a hundred and fifty lines, however, the author warns of "The fals man" who "walkith fro towne to towne,/ For the moste parte with a thredbare gowne,/ Euyr serching with diligent a-wayte/ To wyn his pray with som fals disceyte" (*Ordinal*, 323–6). Norton, however, cites Chaucer (line 1162) as an alchemical authority, so his combination of affirmation and skepticism may in fact derive from Chaucer's own combination of explication of alchemical trickery and affirmation of alchemical truth.

An even more apposite example, because it shows no knowledge of Chaucer's text, is the *De chemico miraculo* attributed to Bernard of Treves,[29] which records its author's history of failure over the course of decades in various alchemical investigations with a number of reputed adepts, then concludes in an

26 While he uses the common terms for processes, equipment, and materials, Chaucer does not explain any process in detail, either using a shorthand addressed to a knowledgeable audience like his sixteenth-century readers, or playing with the language's obscurity and unstable referents. He is unusual, too, in that his story of the alchemical deception indicates specific amounts of materials to be used. Unlike most earlier alchemical treatises, *CYT* specifies materials in terms of ounces: see VIII, 756–76, 1102–4, 1112, 1163, 1308. This fact and the fact that he refers to the process of alchemy as *multiplication*, a term that does not appear in English as a synomym for alchemy until early in the fifteenth century (in a document from the reign of Henry IV), suggest that he wrote the tale with an ear to current usage and an eye to "modern" practices.

27 *The Book of Quinte Essence or the Fifth Being*, ed. Frederick J. Furnivall, EETS OS 16 (London, 1866). See the first part of the *Book* on methods of preparation which feature horse dung. It is arguable that the Yeoman's description of these materials marks his canon as one of the puffers, not a true alchemist.

28 *Thomas Norton's The Ordinal of Alchemy*, ed. John Reidy, EETS OS 272 (London, 1975), p. 10, lines 182–5.

29 Bernard was a contemporary of Thomas of Bologna, father of Christine de Pizan and a noted alchemist and physician at the court of Charles V; after a scandal regarding a medication Thomas was said to have furnished the King, he wrote to Bernard, a recognized adept, regarding both the science of medicine and alchemy. Bernard's response, an extended corrective to various of Thomas's alchemical theories, is neatly summarized by Lynn Thorndike, *History of Magic and Experimental Science*, vol. 3, pp. 624–6. *De chemico miraculo,* which in an aside Thorndike likened to *The Canon's Yeoman's Tale*, is treated on pp. 621–4. The treatise purports to be written in the middle of the fifteenth century and relates the reminiscences of a practitioner supposedly in his eighties; but Thorndike notes that the text's references to "Raymundus" suggest a later date, since "it was doubtful if the Lullian alchemical collection was yet in circulation during the life of the genuine Bernard of Treves."

assertion of the efficacy of "this precious science and worthye arte"[30] – even to the extent of communicating (albeit under the veil of an impenetrable allegory) alchemy's most valuable secrets.[31] The author speaks of "seducers and sophisticall fellowes" encountered during his frustrating years of alchemical research, but limits this reference to those alchemists who attract would-be adepts to their misguided experiments, rather than, it seems, attracting out-and-out confidence men.[32] Like the Canon's Yeoman (VIII, 734–6, 782–3, 832–3, etc.), the writer emphasizes the extent to which studying with these false masters has impoverished him: 800 crowns lost while working through the principles laid down by Rasis, another 2000 testing the theories of Geber, 300 more on other so-called authorities, and on and on, year after year. Also, again reminiscent of the Canon's Yeoman, the author's health has been seriously impaired by his obsessive pursuit of the Philosophers' Stone: experiments with distillations of vitriol, conducted under the tutelage of a "certayn other learned devyne, a notarye of Berges," produced vapors "whereof caused me to fall into a moste vehement quartern fever, which held me 14 months."[33]

Moreover, in this treatise, as in Chaucer's tale, the exposé of fruitless experimentation is presented with such copious lists of substances and processes as to leave the impression that the narrator remains entranced by his subject, even as he satirizes it. The author's descriptions of manifold failures – trying to produce the Philosophers' Stone from salt; dissolving "the best silver, copper, and other metalle" in "strong water," combining the products after a year, hoping in vain for crystals to form; undertaking bizarre operations with a "famous monk and learned clarke," one Galfridus Leporis, on 2000 hard-boiled hens' eggs (the yolks and whites prepared for thirty separate distillations, the shells calcinated "into a wonderfull whitness")[34] occasion various explanations of what must have gone wrong, as in Chaucer's *Tale* (922–50), yet encourage further experimentation, rather than convince the researcher to give up.

30 We quote *De chemico miraculo* from the English translation in Bodley MS Ashmole 1487, fol. 182r; in this translation, the treatise begins with a dedication of "Lord Bernard earle of the marsches of Treuiers in Germanye" to "the noble Doctor Thomas of Bononye, gouernour of france (and philosopher most learned), the 12 of May 1453," as if it were Bernard's Response to Thomas, a different text.

31 This "parable," as the writer terms it, occupies much of the last three folios (194–7).

32 The writer of *De chemico miraculo* (fol. 182r) denies as a "grosse and follishe opynion" of the common people the familiar charge (*CYT,* VIII, 742–7) that alchemists who have lost their money delight in making others poor and unhappy: "they wold [rather] haue lefte a fame of them selues after their deathe, then infamye and dispraise."

33 Fol. 184v. Elsewhere he notes that along with the loss of a considerable fortune, "I had almoste eryed my selfe to deathe" (fol. 184r).

34 These operations are summarized on fols 184–6.

ANALOGUES

I

John Gower, *Confessio Amantis*

(from John Gower, *Confessio Amantis*, ed. G. C. Macaulay, EETS ES 81 [rpt. 1969], pp. 367–8, 371, 369, Book 4, lines 2457–83; 2580–99; 2531–40)

Among those of Chaucer's contemporaries who wrote about alchemy, John Gower stands as the most interesting and the most important in respect to analogues to Chaucer's work. In book four of the *Confessio Amantis,* Gower discusses alchemy in generic philosophical terms. At several points within this broad-ranging treatment, however, he touches on points Chaucer also includes in his much more narrowly-focused tale. One such place is Gower's description of the spirits of alchemy and the planetary correlations with specific metals, echoing *The Canon's Yeoman's Tale,* lines 819–35.

And also with gret diligence	
Thei founden* thilke experience,*	discovered; knowledge from observation
Which cleped is Alconomie,	
Wherof the Selver multeplie	
Thei made and ek the gold also.	
And forto telle hou it is so,	
Of bodies sevene in special	
With foure spiritz joynt withal	
Stant* the substance* of this matiere.	stands; essence
The bodies whiche I speke of hiere	
Of the Planetes ben begonne:	
The gold is titled* to the Sonne,	dedicated
The mone of Selver hath his part,	
And Iren that stant* upon Mart,	depends
The Led after Satorne groweth,	
And Jupiter the Bras bestoweth,	
The Coper set is to Venus,	
And to his part Mercurius	
Hath the quikselver, as it falleth,*	happens
The which, after the bok it calleth,*	according as the book calls it
Is ferst of thilke fowre named	
Of Spiritz, whiche ben proclamed;	
And the spirit which is secounde	
In Sal Armoniak* is founde:	ammonium chloride
The thridde spirit Sulphur is;	
The ferthe suiende*after this	following
Arcennicum* be name is hote.*	Arsenic; is called

The "spirits" (volatile substances) and "bodies" (non-volatile substances) are traditional alchemical lore, associated with the planetary identifications of the

various metals described at length by "Geber" (Abu Musa Jabir ibn Hayyaan) in his *Sum of Perfection*.[35] Avicenna classed quicksilver as a spirit only, and his opinion was reproduced by Vincent of Beauvais (*Speculum Naturale* 8.62) though elsewhere, as noted by Aiken, Vincent seems to suggest otherwise.[36] Chaucer and Gower clearly identify Mercury as both spirit and body. Moreover, both poets then go on to complain of the difficulties and expense in preparing the Elixir, yet each remains hopeful of the outcome (see *CYT*, VIII, 862–72):

Bot now it stant al otherwise;
Thei speken faste* of thilke Ston,   eagerly
Bot hou to make it, nou wot non
After the sothe experience.
And natheles gret diligence
Thei setten upon thilke dede,
And spille* more than thei spede;*   waste; succeed
For allewey thei finde a lette,*   impediment
Which bringeth in poverte and dette
To hem that riche were afore:
The lost is had, the lucre* is lore,*   money; lost
To gete a pound thei spenden fyve;
I not hou such a craft schal thryve
In the manere as it is used:
It were betre be refused
Than forto worchen upon weene*   operate in uncertainty
In thing which stant noght as thei weene.*   think
Bot noght forthi, who that it knewe,
The science of himself* is trewe   knowledge itself
Upon the forme* as it was founded. . . .   in the manner

Finally, both Chaucer (VIII, 799–801) and Gower agree against many of the prevailing authorities in allowing for the use of herbs in the preparation of the elixir.[37]

These olde Philosophres wyse
Be weie of kinde* in sondri wise   in the natural course
Thre Stones maden thurgh clergie.*   learning
The ferste, if I schal specefie,
Was *lapis vegetabilis,*
Of which the propre vertu is
To mannes hele* forto serve,   health
As forto kepe and to preserve
The bodi fro siknesses alle,
Til deth of kinde upon him falle.

[35] *The Works of Geber, Englished by Richard Russell, 1678*, ed. E. J. Holmyard (London and New York, 1928), Part 3, chapters 8–13.
[36] Aiken, *Studies in Philology* 41(1944): 379.
[37] Edgar H. Duncan, "The Yeoman's Canon's 'Silver Citrinacioun,'" *Modern Philology* 37 (1940): 260.

Here Gower appears to rely on the theories of Roger Bacon who, in his notes on the *Secreta Secretorum*,[38] pronounced on the virtues of a vegetable preparation, and in the *Opus Majus*[39] saw the elixir/Philosopher's Stone/medicine as that which would not only procure an advantage for the state in the removal of impurities from base metals and the multiplication of gold, but would "be able to remove the corruptions of the human body to such an extent that it would prolong life for many ages" (see Appendix below, p. 746).

II

William Langland, *Piers Plowman*, Passus XI

(from *Piers Plowman: The A Version*, ed. George Kane (London: Athlone Press, 1960), pp. 412–13, lines 155–64)

William Langland appears to have been less enthusiastic than either Gower or Chaucer, and much more wary of alchemical promises, and of alchemists. The A Text of *Piers Plowman*, written at least a decade before Chaucer set to work on *The Canterbury Tales*, presents Dame Study's criticism of vain and dangerous subjects in a passage that describes alchemy as a deceitful science that holds back its devotees from prosperity, is injurious to the mind, and is associated with the devil, whether haste is part of the process, or not:

Astronomye is hard þing & euil for to knowe;	
Geometrie & geomesie* is gynful* of speche;	geomancy; deceitful
þat þinkeþ werche wiþ þo þre þriueþ wel late,*	He who intends to work with these three will never succeed.
For sorcerie is þe souerayn* bok þat to þat science longiþ.*	chief; belongs
ʒet arn þere febicchis of Forellis* of many manis wittes,	alchemical tricks of contrivances (?)
Experimentis of alkenemye of albertis* makyng,	Albert the Great's
Nigromancie* & per[i]mansie* þe pouke to reisen;	necromancy; and pyromancy
ʒif þou þenke do wel deile þerewith neuere.	
Alle þise sciences, sikir,* I myself	surely
Foundit hem formest* folk to desceyue.	principally

[38] *Opera Hactenus Inedita Rogeri Baconi*, ed. R. Steele, vol. 5 (Oxford, 1920), p. 117.
[39] *The Opus Majus of Roger Bacon*, trans. Robert Belle Burke, vol. 2 (Philadelphia, 1928), p. 627.

III

Lydgate, The Secund pistil that kyng Alysaundre sent to his maistir Aristotiles

(from *Lydgate and Burgh's Secrees of Old Philisoffres*, ed. Robert Steele, EETS ES 66 [London, 1894], pp.18–19, lines 554–6, 570–2, 582–8)

Writing self-consciously in the shadow of Chaucer's genius, John Lydgate also engaged the subject of alchemy in his translation of *The Secund pistill that kyng Alysaundre sent to his maistir Aristotiles,* a text that touches on some of the same alchemical themes Chaucer developed. Lydgate devotes an extended section of his translation to the poverty that alchemy can generate (cf. *CYT*, VIII, 677–83, 740–5, 865–82, *passim*). The secret at the heart of alchemy is so well hidden that most practicioners find themselves ruined:

But the fals Erryng hath fonnyd* many Oon; — fooled
And brought hem afftir in ful greet Rerage,* — arrears
By expensys and Outragious Costage.
...
It is no Crafft poore men tassaye,* — to try
It Causith Coffres and Chestys to be bare,
Marryth wyttes, and braynes doth Affraye;
Yit be wryting this book doth declare,
And be Resouns lyst nat for to spare,
With goldeyn Resouns in taast moost lykerous,
Thyng per ignotum prevyd per ignocius.* — the unknown thing is explained by the more unknown

Lydgate ends this section with an echo of Chaucer's own concluding "This is *ignotum per ignocius*" (VIII, 1457).

In disavowing his own ability or interest in alchemy – "I was nevir noon expert Ioweler,/ In suych materys to putte my Sylff in prees/ With philisoffres myn Eyen wer nat Cleer" (554–6) – Lydgate echoes the correlation of clear eyesight and alchemy that Gower implies in his description of the effect of the animal stone. Chaucer's tale, too, is replete with references to sight and blindness,[40] a common trope for understanding in his culture, and a crucial element of the alchemical process, because sight was an important means of validating what appeared in alchemical experiments.[41]

[40] On the subject of alchemy and vision see Carolyn P. Collette, *Species, Phantasms and Images: Vision and Medieval Psychology in the Canterbury Tales* (Ann Arbor, MI, 2001), pp. 128ff.

[41] Chaucer's deployment of a pervasive sight/blindness theme in the tale, as well as Gower's and Lydgate's inclusion of the subject, attests to a well-established tradition of the importance of the alchemist's senses in the success of the art. The author of *The New Pearl of Great Price,* trans. A. E. Waite (London: V. Stuart, 1963), discussing the connection between learning and doing, theory and praxis, assumes the central role of the human senses, particularly sight, in the art: "Hence it is all but impossible, as we may learn from Geber in his *Sum of Perfection,* for a blind man, or one whose sense

IV

Thomas Norton, *The Ordinal of Alchemy*

(*Thomas Norton's Ordinal of Alchemy*, ed. John Reidy, EETS OS 272 [London, 1975], pp. 14, 26–7, 38, lines 323–36, 757–78, 1151–66)

Thomas Norton's *The Ordinal of Alchemy* accepts and builds on Chaucer's tale as an alchemical text. Norton's reliance on Chaucer and his reproduction of many of Chaucer's themes show that Chaucer's tale was accepted into the world of alchemical literature not as a criticism of alchemy, but as a combination of affirmation of the enterprise and exposé of the "puffers" and charlatans who misunderstood and distorted the art. Norton refers to Chaucer in a section in which he addresses one "Tonsile," an unidentified character whom Reidy surmises to have been one of Norton's unsuccessful alchemical contemporaries:

Another stone, Tonsile, ye most haue with-alle,
Or els ye fawte your chyef Materialle.
which is a stone glorious, faire, and bright,
In handlyng a stone, & a stone in syght;
A stone glitiryng with perspicuyte,* — transparency
Beyng of wondirful diaphanyte;* — transparency
The price of a vnce* conveniently — ounce
Is xx. *shillings*, or welnere therbye.
Hire name is Magnesia, few peple hir know;
She is fownd in hye placis as wel as in lowe.
Plato knew hir propertie, & callid hir bi hir name,
And chawcer rehersith how titanos is þe same,
In þe Canon his tale, saynge: whate is thuse
But Quod Ignotum per magis ignocius?
That is to say, whate may this be
But vnknow bi more vnknow named is she?

of touch is defective, or for a man without hands, to be successful in our Magistery. The experience of sight is essential, more especially at the end of the decoction; when all superfluous matter has been removed, the artist will behold an awful and amazing splendour, the occultation of Sol in Luna, the marriage of East and West, the union of heaven and earth, and the conjunction, as the ancients tell us, of the spiritual with the corporeal . . . The study of books cannot be dispensed with, but the study of books alone is not sufficient. There must be a profound natural faculty for interpreting the significance of those symbols and analogies of the philosophers, which in one place have one meaning and in another a different. For, as Morien tells us, all books on Alchemy are figuratively written" (pp. 133–6). Geber had written, "if any *Man* have not his *Organs compleat*, he cannot by himself come to the *Compleatment* of this *Work*; no more than if he were *Blind* or wanted his *Limbs* . . . Therefore, we say, he that hath not a *Natural Ingenuity*, and *Soul*, searching and subtily scrutinizing *Natural Principles*, the *Fundamentals of Nature*, and *Artifices* which can follow *Nature*, in the properties of her *Action*, cannot find the true *Radix* of this most precious *Science*." See *The Works of Geber*, ed. E. J. Holmyard (London, 1928), pp. 26–7.

Norton also devotes a section of his work to the expense and the other costs of alchemy. In this he repeats a theme found in many serious alchemical texts, as well as in Chaucer's tale, as he warns that *multiplying* is not for poor men. Norton uses the term *multiply* to refer, as does Chaucer, to the entire process of alchemy, not just to the preparation of the elixir or *medicine* of the stone. Warning that those who want to pursue the science of alchemy must be able to distinguish false practitioners from true, he draws the following picture of false alchemists, a picture that combines the habits and appearance of Chaucer's Canon and his Yeoman in the First Part of the tale with the trickery of the false canon of the Second Part:

The fals man walkith fro towne to towne,
For the moste parte with a thredbare gowne,
Euyr serching with diligent a-wayte* — watch
To wyn* his pray* with som fals disceyte. — gain; desired object
Of swering and lesyng* such wil not cese, — lying
To say how thei can siluer plate encrese;
And euyr thei rayle* with periurye, — assert vehemently
Sayng how thei can multiplye
Gold and siluer, and in suche wise
with promyse thei please the covetyse,
And causith his mynde to be on hym sett;
Then falshode and couetyse be fully mett,
But afterwarde, within a litille while,
The multiplier doth hym begyle.

Norton, moreover, makes a special point about the need for patience, as does Chaucer in the Yeoman's description (VIII, 932–54) of how his master deals with alchemical failure:

The litill boke wrete of þe philosophers fest,
Seythe: omnis festinacio ex parte diaboli est.* — all haste is of the devil's party
Wherfore þat man shalle sonest spede
which with grete leysere wisely wille procede.
Vppon assay ye shalle trewly knowe
That who most hastith he trewly shalbe slow,
For he with hast shall bryng his werke arere* — in arrears
Somtyme a monyth, & somtyme an hole yere;
And in þis arte it shal euyre be so,
That hasty mane shal neuir fayle of woo.
Also of haste ye may trewly be sure,
That she leuythe no thinge clene & pure.
The devill hathe none so subtile wyle
As with hastynes yow to begyle;
Therfore ofte tymes he wille assawte
youre mynde with hast to make defawte.* — mistake
He shall fynde grace in towne & londe
whiche can hastynes alle tymys withstonde;

I say alle tymes, for in oone puncte of tyme
Haste may destroye alle youre engyne;
Therfore alle haste eschewe & feere
As if that she a deville were.[42]

V

Ramón Llull, *Libre de Meravelles*

(from Ramón Llull, *Libre de Meravelles*, ed. Mn. Salvador Galmés [Barcelona: Editorial Barcino, 1932], vol. 2, pp. 82–3; trans. Anthony Bonner, *Selected Works of Ramon Llull* [Princeton and Guildford, Surrey: Princeton University Press, 1985], vol. 2, pp. 778–9)[43]

While the preceding texts show that Chaucer participated in a tradition of English alchemical writing, a closer look at specific parts of his tale in the context of particular analogues and probable or possible sources indicates his indebtedness to the wider tradition of alchemical literature. As Willa Babcock Folch-Pi first pointed out,[44] a fairly close analogue to the first of Chaucer's alchemist's deceptions of the gullible and cupidinous priest exists in the *Fèlix Libre de Meravelles (Fèlix or Book of Wonders)*, composed c. 1288 by the Catalan philosopher, mystic, Christian apologist, and missionary Ramón Llull (c. 1232–1316). Llull's work received medieval translations into Spanish, Italian, and French, the latter preserved in a fifteenth-century MS belonging to Louis de Bruges, a counselor of the dukes of Burgundy (1422–92).

Llull, who never set foot in England, and whose genuine works explicitly deny the possibility of the alchemical transmutation of metals, became associated soon after his death with a number of alchemical treatises. He was widely believed to have learned from Arnaldus de Villa Nova the art of transforming base metals into gold, and to have gone to England to make gold for Edward III (who gained the throne a full decade after Llull's death!), on the condition that the monies derived would be used to finance a crusade; but once Llull realized

[42] This conventional topos appears across the spectrum of late medieval alchemical writing. Geber's *Sum of Perfection* says, "Yet you must not think all this can be effected by *Preparation* at once, in a very short *Time*, as a few *Days* and *Hours*; but in respect of other *Modern Physicians*, and also in respect of the *Operation* of *Nature*, the *Verity* of the *Work* is sooner terminated this way. Whence the *Philosopher* saith, *It is a Medicine requiring a long space of time*. Wherefore I tell you, you must patiently sustain *Labour*, because the work will be long; and indeed *Festination* is from the *Devil's* part: Therefore let him that hath not *Patience* desist from the *Work*, for credulity will hinder him making overmuch haste. And every *Natural Action* hath its determinate *Measure* and *Time*, in which it is terminated, viz. in a greater or lesser space. For this *Work Three Things* are necessary, namely *Patience, Length of Time* and *Aptness* of *Instruments*; of which we speak to the *Artificer*, in the *Sum of the Perfection of our Magistery* . . ." (p. 17).

[43] Cf. the text from the edition of Jerónimo Rosselló quoted by Willa Babcock Folch-Pi in "Ramón Llull's 'Fèlix' and Chaucer's 'Canon's Yeoman's Tale,' " *Notes and Queries* 212 (1967): 10–11.

[44] Folch-Pi, pp. 10–11.

Edward's interest was not sincere, he supposedly left England without revealing his secret. As Bonner suggests,[45] the legend was probably fueled by the fact that the first alchemical text that came to be ascribed to Llull, the *Testamentum* (1332), was apparently written by a Catalan alchemist living in London.[46]

In Book VI, Chapter 36 of the *Libre de Meravelles* are presented Llull's arguments for the impossibility of transmutation, which the "philosopher," speaking for the author, notes must entail substantial and accidental transmutation, i.e. of both form and matter along with their accidents; "and such a task . . . can not be done artificially, for nature needs all her powers to do it." All elements, the argument continues, have been seeking their own perfection since the Creation; such perfection consists in each element being "by itself, simple, and without corruption." But since God has mixed the qualities of the elements, i.e. heat, moisture, cold and dryness, it is impossible for one element to exist without another. Moreover, "no metal wants to change its being into that of another being, since if it changed its being into that of another being, it would no longer be that being it prefers to be." To answer the question, then, of why one could be so fond of the art of alchemy, since it is not a true art, the philosopher relates the following exemplum.

> En .I^{a}. terra se sdevench que .I. hom pençà com pogués ajustar molt gran tresaur, e vendech tot quant havia, E en .I^{a}. terra molt luny ell anà a .I. rey, e dix que ell era alquimista. Aquell rey hac molt gran plaser de sa venguda, e féu-li donar hostal e tot ço que mester havia. Aquell hom hac mès aur molt en .III. bústies, en les quals havia decocció de erbes, e era aquella decocció en semblant de latovari. Denant lo rey mès aquell hom .I^{a}. de aquelles bústies en la caulera hon fonia moltes dobles que el rey li havia donades, per tal que les muntiplicàs. L'aur qui era en la bústie pessave .M. dobles, e el rey n'avia meses .II.M. en la caldera; e a la fi pesà la missa del aur .III.M. dobles. Per .III. vegades féu açò lo hom, e el rey cuydà's que fos alquimista segons veritat. A la fi: que lo hom fugí ab gran còpia de aur que el rey li havia comanat per tal que.l muntiplicàs; car cuydave's que lo coffit qui ere en les bústies, hagués virtut per la qual l'aur muntiplicàs en la fornal.
>
> [In a certain land it happened that a man devised a scheme for amassing great wealth. He sold all his belongings and went to the king of a far-away land, saying he was an alchemist. This king was very pleased at his arrival, and ordered that he be given lodging and whatever else he needed. This man had put a large amount of gold in three containers, in which there was a brew of herbs made to look like an electuary. In front of the king he placed one of these containers in a caldron in which he was melting the many pistoles the king had given him so he would multiply them. The gold in the container weighed one thousand pistoles, and the king had put two thousand in the cauldron, with the result that in the end the mass of gold weighed three thousand pistoles. The man did this three times, and the king thought he was a true

[45] *Selected Works of Ramon Llull (1232–1316)*, ed. and trans. Anthony Bonner (Princeton, 1985), vol. 1, p. 73.

[46] See J. Batista Roca, "Catàlech de les obres lulianes d'Oxford," *Boletin de la Real Academia de Buenas Letras de Barcelona* 8 (1915–16): 205–6; and P. Bohigas, "El repertori de manuscrits catalans. Missió a Anglaterra," *Estudis Universitaris Catalans* 12 (1927): 419–27.

alchemist. In the end the man ran off with a large amount of the gold the king had given him to multiply, for the king thought the mixture in the containers had the power to multiply gold when heated.]

VI

Don Juan Manuel, *El Conde Lucanor*

(from Juan Manuel, *El Conde Lucanor: A Collection of Mediaeval Spanish Stories*, ed. and trans. John England [Warminster: Aris & Phillips, 1987], no. 20, pp. 128–9, 130–1)

Llull's story of alchemical deception, almost certainly derived from some oriental or Arabic original, itself finds analogues in the *Libro del cavallero Zifar* (early fourteenth century) and the hugely influential *El Conde Lucanor* of Don Juan Manuel. In the former, the alchemist conspires with a spice vendor to sell to the king a secret powder the alchemist has made from ground-up coins. Added to the base metal in the heated furnace, the powder turns to a molten mass of silver. Naturally the greedy king is eager to pay the alchemist to secure more powder, supposedly available only in the alchemist's homeland; but it is clear he will never return.[47] As Juan Manuel relates it in *El Conde Lucanor*, the filings of 100 doubloons are turned into pellets to which he gives the name *tabardíe*; they are melted in the king's presence to produce gold, and the king pays dearly in his hope to obtain more. J. L. Serrano Reyes[48] has proposed, in arguments not all of equal worth, Chaucer's direct knowledge of Juan Manuel's work, which was composed some thirty-three years before the poet's trip to Spain in 1367. One might well expect coincidental similarities of diction and phrasing in analogous treatments of corresponding alchemical deception; nevertherless, a number of the verbal parallels Serrano Reyes adduces merit notice:

> Et aquel golfín tomó çient doblas et limólas, et de aquellas limaduras fizo, con otras cosas que puso con ellas, çient pellas, et cada una de aquellas pellas pesava una dobla, et demás las otras cosas que él mezcló con las limaduras de las doblas
>
> [So the confidence-trickster took a hundred doubloons, and filed them down, and with the filings and other things which he added to them, he made one hundred balls, each the weight of one doubloon plus the other things he mixed with the filings from the doubloons. (See *CYT*, VIII, 1159–68)]

47 *The Book of the Knight Zifar: A Translation of El Libro del Cavallero Zifar*, trans. Charles L. Nelson (Lexington, KY, 1983), pp. 268–73.

48 Jesús L. Serrano Reyes, *Didactismo y Moralismo en Geoffrey Chaucer y Don Juan Manuel: Un Estudio Comparativo Textual* (Córdoba: Universidad de Córdoba, 1996). The passages cited above from England's edition are found in Reyes' book on pp. 342, 323, 295, respectively.

> Et desque el rey vio que de cosa que costaba dos o tres dineros, salía una dobla, fue muy alegre et tóvose por el más bien andante del mundo . . .
>
> [The king was delighted to see something which cost two or three pence turn into a doubloon, and considered himself the most fortunate man in the world . . . (See *CYT*, VIII, 1240–2)]
>
> Et desque el golfín lo tovo en su poder, fuesse su ca(r)rera et nunca tornó al rey. Et assí fincó el rey engañado por su mal recabdo.
>
> [When the confidence-trickster had the money in his possession, he went his way and never returned to the king; and in this way the king was deceived by his own foolishness. (See *CYT*, VIII, 1381–5)]

Also noteworthy is the stylistic habit shared by both texts of phrases introduced by *et/and* followed by a verb and *et/and* followed by a subject.[49]

VII

Desiderius Erasmus, *Colloquies*

(from *The Colloquies of Erasmus*, trans. Craig R. Thompson [Chicago and London: University of Chicago Press, 1965], pp. 252–3)

A story in a form rather closely resembling Chaucer's tale is found in the *Colloquies* of Desiderus Erasmus (1466 or 1467–1536), as was brought to scholarly attention almost a century ago by H. de Vocht, but anticipated, we find, as early as 1624 by John Wilson in his comedy, *The Cheats*.[50] Erasmus (who in his 1526 defense of his work, entitled *The Usefulness of the Colloquies*, referred to alchemy as "by no means the slightest of human afflictions . . . a disorder so intoxicating, once it strikes a man, that it beguiles even the learned and prudent") treats the fraudulent practices of its devotees in two colloquies. In "Alchemy" (first printed 1524), he describes how an alchemist gains the confidence of a rich and esteemed gentleman through what appears to be his dedication to the science, his scrupulousness and patience, his self-criticism, and religious devotion. Specific laboratory procedures are not described. But in "Beggar Talk" an alchemist describes to one of his old friends his success as a charlatan after leaving the ranks of professional paupers. Misoponus ("hater of work") tells how he warns prospective dupes not to trust practitioners of the art too readily, since so many are cheats; how he expects his clients to be convinced

[49] See Serrano Reyes, pp. 108, 295, 323; see also pp. 310–12 for comparative tables and, on the repetitive style of both versions, *XX*, pp. 300–8.

[50] H. de Vocht, "Chaucer and Erasmus," *Englische Studien* 41 (1910): 385–92, and see Wilson's *The Cheats*, as quoted in Caroline F. E. Spurgeon, *Five Hundred Years of Chaucer Criticism and Allusion 1357–1900* (New York, 1960), vol. 1, p. 240: "Did not *Apulejus* take the Rise of his *Golde Asse*, from *Lucan's Lucius?* and *Erasmus*, his *Alcumnistica*, from *Chaucer's Canon's Yeomans Tale*? and *Ben Jonson* his more happy *Alchymist* from both?"

by their own eyes; and how he bids them perform the entire operation by themselves while he looks on from a distance, etc. He then relates the secret:

> The whole trick turns on one coal prepared for this purpose. I hollow it out and insert molten silver, the amount I predict must be yielded. After the powder is spread over this, I make ready the pot so it's surrounded by live coals not only below and on the sides but also above. I convince them this is part of the art. Among the coals placed on top I lay the one containing silver or gold. Melted by the heat, this flows down on the other stuff, say tin or bronze, which liquefies. When refining takes place, what was mixed with it is discovered. . . . When he's done everything according to my directions, I just step up before the alchemic vessel is moved and look around to make sure nothing's been accidentally omitted. I remark that one or two coals seem to be missing on top. Without being noticed I lay mine on. I pretend I've taken it from the pile of other coals, but it's been so placed there beforehand that it's not recognizable and it fools him. I pick it up.

Erasmus, who spent considerable time in England before writing the *Colloquies* (including time in Oxford, 1498–9, and later on the faculty at Cambridge, soon after the accession of Henry VIII), nowhere directly mentions Chaucer or his works, but a letter of his written in 1519, and referring to his friend John Colet in the time before 1493, has been taken to refer to Colet's reading of Chaucer and Gower. The supposed reference is somewhat vague, but suggests the possibility that Erasmus might have known of *The Canon's Yeoman's Tale* indirectly, from one of the English humanists.[51]

This particular deception was apparently of some wide currency; in a learned exposé of eighteenth-century alchemical tricks, the renowned scientist Etienne François Geoffroy l'aîné (1672–1731) begins his report to the Académie Royale des Sciences with notice of the deception which turns on the preparation of charcoal filled with gold or silver powder (oxide?), sealed with wax or sawdust, or charcoal suffused with a solution containing those precious metals, which, as in Chaucer's Tale, yields its treasure when subjected to heat.[52]

51 Spurgeon, *Five Hundred Years of Chaucer Criticism*, vol. 1, p. 73, quotes from the letter as follows: "Habet gens Britannica, qui hoc praestiteru*n*t apud suos, quod Dantes ac Petrarcha apud Italos. Et horum euoluendis scriptis linguam expoliuit [he, Colet] iam tum se praeparans ad praeconium sermonis Euangelici."

52 M. Geoffroy l'aîné, "Des Supercheries concernant la Pierre Philosophale," *Mémoires de l'Académie Royale des Sciences*, in *Histoire de l'Académie Royale des Sciences, 1722* (Paris, 1778), pp. 374–5: "D'autres fois ils font un trou dans un charbon où ils coulent de la poudre d'or ou d'argent qu'ils renferment avec de la cire, ou bien ils imbibent des charbons des dissolutions de ces méteaux, & ils les font mettre en poudre pour projetter sur les matieres qu'ils doivent transmuer."

VIII

Giovanni Sercambi, *Novelle*

(from *Novelle of Sercambi*, ed. Giovanni Sinicropi [Florence: Casa Editrice le Lettre Novella, 1995], XXII, De Falsari[o], vol. 1, pp. 256–7, paragraphs 17–18; pp. 258–9, paragraph 22)

The Canon's second deception of the gullible priest (VIII, 1265–82), in which an ounce of silver is introduced through a hollow tube stopped with wax, which is used to stir the coals, finds an analogue in Novella XXII, "De Falsari," of the *Novelle* of Giovanni Sercambi, which Spargo in Bryan and Dempster printed from the sole extant manuscript, Milan, Trivulzian Library MS 193 (fifteenth century). R. A. Pratt and Karl Young[53] accepted the legend of a version of the work written in 1374 but no longer extant; Chaucer, they speculated, could have heard of Sercambi's early version on his 1378 trip to Milan, whose rulers "were collectors of books and patrons of literature" (p. 32). But the only form of the work we possess indicates through internal evidence a date of composition no earlier than the mid-1380s. Moreover, Luciano Rossi has argued convincingly that the hypothetical lost shorter form of the work in fact never existed, and that the *Novelle* was not composed until 1400 or later.[54]

A proven thief, Giuda d'Ascoli, operating in Siena under the alias Zaccagna, surreptitously buries a large quantity of an earth named "ocra," laced with "orpimento" (i.e. arsenic trisulfide, yellow arsenic; cf. *CYT*, VIII, 759, 774, 823) on the property of Pitullo; he tells him this will serve as the gold to be multiplied alchemically. Pitullo is of course interested and wishes to proceed.

> . . . il tesoro trovon[n]o; e fu questa vena piú di x corbelli e quella ne portonno a casa di Pitullo. Zaccagna menò Pitullo a Siena e compronno cruzuoli da fondere oro e tornoro in villa. E quine edificò uno fornello e, preso uno paio di bilance, pesò once vi di quella vena e quella misse in uno cruzuolo faccendo gran fuoco. Zaccagna, avendo in bocca granella d'oro piú di oncia una, soffiando con uno cannone innel cruzuolo lo mettea e la polvere n'uscía fuori. Faccendo fuoco e soffiando, verga, disse Zaccagna a Pitullo: "Porta quest'oro a Siena e vendelo, e non lo dare per meno di fiorini viii, però ch'è buon oro; e cerca orafi e battilori." E di vero l'oro valea piú di viii fiorine bene uno mezzo. Pitullo ch'avea veduto mettere la vena innel cruzuolo e non s'era acorto dell'oro messo per Zaccagna: "Di certo la vena trovata vale molti fiorini; forsi tanti che miglior mercadante di Siena non ne farè' tanti." E questo era il suo parlare mentre che a Siena andava.

> [. . . they found the treasure; there was a lode of more than ten basketsful that they took to Pitullo's house. Zaccagna brought Pitullo to Siena and they

53 Bryan and Dempster, pp. 21–33.

54 See Helen Cooper, "Sources and Analogues of Chaucer's *Canterbury Tales*: Reviewing the Work," *Studies in the Age of Chaucer* 19 (1997): 183–210 (p. 185), rpt. as "The Frame" in *Sources and Analogues of The Canterbury Tales*, ed. Robert M. Correale and Mary Hamel, vol. I (Cambridge: D. S. Brewer, 2002), pp. 1–22.

bought crucibles to cast gold and returned to the villa. And there he built a furnace, and taking a set of balances he measured out six ounces of that lode and put it in a crucible at high flame. Zaccagna, holding in his mouth a grain of gold weighing over an ounce and blowing through a tube put it into the crucible and the powder came out of it. Building up the fire and blowing, eventually he smelted out that ounce of gold that Zaccagna had put into the crucible. And casting it in a stick, Zaccagna said to Pitullo: "Take this gold to Siena and sell it, and don't let it go for less than eight florins, for it's good gold; seek out goldsmiths and goldbeaters." And in truth the gold was worth a good half more than eight florins. Pitullo, who had seen the lode put into the crucible and was not aware of the gold put in by Zaccagna, replied: "Surely the lode we've found is worth many florins; perhaps so many that the best merchant of Siena wouldn't make so many." And this was what he said as he went off to Siena.]

Pitullo pays Zaccagna 1000 florins for a demonstration of the secret process:

E presa once vi di quella terra e messa a fuoco, Zaccagna tenea uno cannone in mano, Pitullo un altro. E mentre che 'l fuoco si facea, Zaccagna dicea: "Soffia cosí." E mentre ch'e' soffiava, misse innel cruzuolo oncia una a buon peso d'oro. Pitullo disse: "Io cosí farò." Zaccagna disse: "Or soffia." Pitullo soffia. Zaccagna disse: "Soffia forte." Pitullo soffiava. E questo fe' molte volte, tanto quell'oro fu strutto. Gittato in verga, disse Pitullo: "Ormai saprò fare."

[And taking six ounces of that earth and putting it into the fire, Zaccagna held one tube in his hand and Pitullo another. And while the fire was building up, Zaccagna said: "Blow like this." And while he was blowing, he put into the crucible a good ounce of gold. Pitullo said: "I'll do it like that." Zaccagna said: "Now blow." Pitullo blew. Zaccagna said: "Blow hard." Pitullo kept on blowing. And he did this many times, so much that the gold melted. Casting it into a stick, Pitullo said: "Now I'll know how to do it."]

But after numerous unsuccessful attempts by himself, Pitullo wises up. The authorities are summoned and Zaccagna is apprehended. He confesses under torture, and is burnt as a "falsario," i.e. a counterfeiter.

Interestingly, a close analogue of the false canon's second trick is also recorded by Étienne François Geoffroy, in which a hollowed-out rod, filled with some preparation of gold or silver, and stopped up with sawdust, is used to stir the coals.[55]

[55] Geoffroy, "Des Supercheries concernant la Pierre Philosophale," p. 375: "Ils se servent de baguettes ou de petits morceaux de bois creusés à leur extrémité, dont le trou est rempli de limaille d'or ou d'argent, & qui est rebouché avec la sciure fine du même bois. Ils remuent les matieres fondues avec la baguette qui, en se brûlant, laisse dans le creuset le métal fin qu'elle contenoit."

IX

Pseudo-Albertus Magnus, *Libellus de Alchimia*

(from *Libellus de Alchimia in B. Alberti Magni . . . Opera Omnia*, ed. A. and A. Borgnet, vol. 37 [Paris, 1898], p. 547; translation from *Libellus de Alchimia ascribed to Albertus Magnus*, trans. Sister Virginia Heines, S.C.N. [Berkeley and Los Angeles: University of California Press, 1958], p. 6)

A deception along the same lines as Chaucer's false canon's third trick (VIII, 1296ff), in which he secretly substitutes a *teyne* of silver for copper which has been cast into an ingot, is mentioned in the *Libellus de Alchimia* as a trick often forced upon those alchemists who, despite some measure of success, have exhausted the financial resources necessary to continue the processes (see above, p. 724):

> Unde pauperibus non valet ars ista, quia ad minus vult habere expensas duobus annis. Et si contingat in opere errare, vel prolongare, quod non perveniat ad egestatem, ut in pluribus sum expertus. Vidi alios qui sublimationes faciebant puras et bonas ad quinque sublimationes: et quum plures facere non valebant, sophisticabant, et Venerem dealbabant, addentes quintam vel sextam partem Lunae, et seipsos et alios decipiebant.
>
> [Hence this art is of no value to paupers, because one must have enough for expenses for at least two years. Thus, if one should happen to err in one's work or prolong it, one need not be reduced to penury, as I have seen occur many times. I have seen some who made pure and good sublimations as many as five times, but then were unable to make any more and became deceitful; they whitened Copper, adding five or six parts of Silver, and thus cheated both themselves and others.]

X

Arnaldus de Villa Nova, *De Lapide Philosophorum*

(from Arnaldus de Villa Nova, *De lapide Philosophorum* [*Opera*, Lyons, 1532], fol. 304r; cited by J. L. Lowes, *Modern Language Notes* 28 [1913]: 229, and J. Spargo in Bryan and Dempster, p. 698)

With the deceptions of the false canon unmasked, Chaucer's narrator declares the utter futility of the alchemical science (VIII, 1397–9, 1420–2), in appearing to draw the tale to a close with a warning well borne out by what we have seen in the preceding narrative: "Withdraweth the fir, lest it to faste brenne;/ Medleth namoore with that art, I mene,/ For if ye doon, youre thrift is goon ful clene" (VIII, 1423–5). Yet the appeal to authority immediately following ("And right

as swithe I wol yow tellen heere/ What philosophres seyn in this mateere" 1426–7) can hardly be said to reinforce this position, because the last fifty-four lines of the tale, which begin with a quotation of the alchemist Arnaldus de Villa Nova on the proper preparation of quicksilver by sulphur, assume the science's viability; this passage explains the difficulty in understanding its secrets as a reflection of God's desire to bestow alchemical knowledge only on those he wishes to enlighten, and exhorts those who would work against God's will to abandon their pursuit of the Philosophers' Stone. The tale then concludes with the hope that God will relieve the sufferings of "every trewe man" (VIII, 1472–81).

The Canon's Yeoman's allusion (VIII, 1428ff) to Arnaldus's *Rosarie*, i.e. *Rosarium philosophorum* ("Rose Garland of the Philosophers") is incorrect, for as J. L. Lowes pointed out, the lines are based closely on the following lines from Arnaldus's less well-known treatise, *De lapide Philosophorum* ("On the Philosophers' Stone"):

> Dixit discipulus quare dicunt philosophi quod mercurius non moritur nisi cum fratre interficiatur: magister dixit primus eorum qui dixit fuit hermes qui dixit quod draco nunquam moritur nisi cum fratre interficiatur: vult dicere quod mercurius nunquam moritur id est congelatur nisi cum fratre suo id est sole et luna.
>
> [The disciple said, Why do the philosophers say that mercury does not die unless slain with (his) brother? The master said, The first of those who spoke was Hermes who said the dragon never dies unless he is slain with his brother. (By this) he wishes to say that mercury never dies, that is, hardens, except with his brother, that is the sun and the moon.]

In this passage, Arnaldus does not refer to Hermes as the "philosophres fader" (VIII, 1434), though the (conventional) idea may be implied in Arnaldus's "primus eorum qui dixit fuit hermes."[56] It should further be noted that the passage from the *De lapide* quoted above does not identify the "brother" of Mercury, which is sulphur, thought to be derived from gold and silver (sol et luna). The identification, which may well have been common knowledge and for which Chaucer required no specific source, is made, however, in Arnaldus's *Rosarium*, the text to which Chaucer explicitly alludes.

Chaucer further draws on the *De lapide* in the immediately following lines

[56] Cf., however, a more explicit statement of the epithet in Albertus Magnus, *De Mineralibus* (ed. Borgnet, vol. 5, p. 81): "Scimus autem ex his quae in scientia *Peri geneseos* determinata sunt, quod inter habentia symbolum in materia et virtutibus et potentiis naturalibus, facilis est transmutatio ad invicem. Propter quod et multorum Philosophorum, quorum tamen pater est Hermes Trismegistus, qui Propheta Philosophorum vocatur, assertio est, circularem esse metallorum generationem, et ex se invicem, sicut et circularis est generatio elementorum." [We know, from what has been determined in the science of *Generation and Corruption* that among [things] having a common property in their material, powers, and potentuialities, the transmutation of any one into another is easy. And this is the reason for the assertion of many philosophers – whose father is Hermes Trismegistus, called the prophet of philosophers – that the production of metals is cyclical, from each other, just as the production of the elements is cyclical.] Translation from Albertus Magnus, *Book of Marvels*, trans. Dorothea Wyckoff (Oxford, 1967), p. 200.

(VIII, 1441–7), as was demonstrated by Karl Young and, independently, by Edgar Hill Duncan.[57]

> Ars igitur ista non est nisi de occultis philosophorum. Nulli igitur a[d] ha[n]c scientia[m] veniant nisi primo audiverunt logica[m] & postea ph[ilosoph]iam & sciant causas & naturas rerum atq[ue] elementorum. Aliter frustra fatigarent anima[m] suam & corpus suum. . . . Dixit discipulus que verba sunt[:] non intelligo. Et ille: nonne oportet q[uod] ego occulte[m] tibi hoc secretum secretorum sicut fecerunt ph[ilosoph]i: quod non est de hac scientia sicut de aliis dictum est. (*De Lapide,* fol. 303v)
>
> [Therefore that art is not unless concerning the secrets of the philosophers. None, therefore, may come to this science until they have first heard logic and afterward philosophy and know the causes and natures of things and elements. Otherwise they fatigue their minds and bodies in vain. . . . The disciple said: What your words are I do not understand. And he: Is it not necessary that I should hide from you this secret of secrets as the philosophers have done, because it has not been told of this science as it has been of others? (Duncan's translation)]

XI

Arnaldus de Villa Nova, *Rosarium*

(from Arnaldus de Villa Nova, *Rosarium*, in J. J. Manget, *Bibliotheca Chemica Curiosa* [Geneva, 1702], vol. 1, pp. 664–5; cited and translated by Edgar H. Duncan, *Modern Language Notes* 57 (1942): 31–3)

> Qui ergo argentum vivum cum Sole & Luna tingere novit, venit ad arcanum, quod dicitur Sulphur album, optimum ad argentum, quod cum rubeum efficitur, erit sulphur rubeum optimum ad aurum. Ab illis igitur corporibus extrahitur sulphur nimium album & rubeum, cum in ipsis sit purissima sulphuris substantia. . . . Pater enim ejus est Sol, Luna mater est; quia ex illis corporibus cum suo sulphure . . . nostra elicitur medicina.
>
> [Who therefore knows to tinct mercury with Sol and Luna comes to the arcane, which is called white Sulphur, best for silver, which when it is made red, will be red sulphur best for gold. From those bodies, therefore, the exceedingly white and red sulphur is extracted, since in them is the purest substance of sulphur. . . . For its father is Sol; Luna is its mother, for from those bodies with their sulphur . . . is our medicine extracted.]

[57] Karl Young, "The 'Secree of Secrees' of Chaucer's Canon's Yeoman," *Modern Language Notes* 58 (1943): 98–105; Duncan, "Arnold of the Newe Toun," *Modern Language Notes* 57 (1942): 31–3.

XII

Senior Zadith, *Tabula Chemica*

(from the Latin rendering of the *Kitab Mā' al-Wareqī*, ed. H. E. Stapleton and M. Hidāyat Husain, in M. Turāb 'ali, *Three Arabic Treatises on Alchemy by Muhammad bin Umail*, in *Memoirs of the Asiatic Society of Bengal* 12 [Calcutta, 1933], p. 180)

Tyrwhitt first noted that Chaucer's allusion to the "book Senior" (VIII, 1448–60) is that entitled *Senioris Zadith fil. Hamuelis Tabula Chemica*, which Ruska[58] identified as a Latin translation of an Arabic commentary on an allegorical alchemical poem entitled "Epistle of the Sun to the Crescent Moon."

> Dixit Salomon rex: recipe lapidem qui dicitur Thitarios; et est lapis rubeus, albus, citrinus, niger, habens multa nomina et diversos colores. . . . Dixit Sapiens: assigna mihi illum. Dixit: [et] est corpus magnesiae nobile, quod commendarunt omnes Philosophi. Dixit (Sapiens): quid est magnesia? Respondit: magnesia est aqua composita, congelata, quae repugnat igni. . . . Et dixit Plato: unumquodque est unum. . . .
>
> [King Solomon said: take the stone which is called Thitarios; it is a red stone, white, yellow, black, having many names and diverse colors. . . . The wise one said: Assign that one to me. He said: it is the noble substance magnesia, which all the philosophers commend. The wise one said: What is magnesia? He answered: Magnesia is water composed and congealed, which opposes fire. . . . And Plato said: every single thing is one. . . .]

Ruska noted the possibility that Chaucer's *Titanos* (VIII, 1454) for the nonsensical reading "Tithanos" in the text first printed by Zetzner (*Theatrum Chemicum,* 1622) shows he had access to a better MS (the Arabic at this point transcribing the Greek *titanus*, "chalk"? "gypsum"?).[59] "Solomon," who speaks this sentence in the Latin text, apparently represents the translator's substitution for the mysterious philosopher "Qalimus" in the Arabic text. Edgar Hill Duncan, in an unpublished paper, noted that a fourteenth-century manuscript of the work, Trinity College, Cambridge, MS 1122, annotates the word "senior" as "i. Plato" (i.e. Plato), thus partially explaining Chaucer's speaker of the lines.[60] And indeed, even in the printed edition above in which Solomon figures, the name of Plato occurs three times only a few lines below, as Skeat noticed.[61]

58 Julius Ruska, "Chaucer und das Buch Senior," *Anglia* 61 (1937): 136–7.

59 Cf. Thomas Norton's *The Ordinal of Alchemy*, lines 1159ff.

60 See John Reidy's note to VIII, 1448–71 in *The Riverside Chaucer*.

61 W. W. Skeat, *The Works of Geoffrey Chaucer,* vol. 5 (Oxford, 1894), p. 433 (note to VIII, 1450). Edgar H. Duncan, in "The Literature of Alchemy and Chaucer's Canon's Yeoman's Tale," *Speculum* 43 (1968): 654, has shown Chaucer's reliance on a later passage from this same work for the immediately subsequent lines, VIII, 1461–71: "Et hoc est secretum, super quo juraverunt, quod non indicarent in aliquo libro. Nec aliquis eorum declarabit hoc, & attribuerunt illud deo glorioso, ut inspiraret illud cui vellet, & prohibeat a quo vellet" (Stapleton and Husain, p. 183) [And this is the secret about which they have sworn that they would not reveal it in any book nor anyone of them declare it. And they have attributed it to the glorious God that he may inspire it to whom he wishes and prohibit [it] from whom he wishes] (trans. Duncan, p. 654, from the text as found in Vienna, Österreiches National Bibliothek, Cod. Vindob. 5477, fol. 34v).

Though Chaucer probably was dependent on the *book Senior* for the idea of the divinely sanctioned secrets of alchemy, the idea was a popular one among the adepts, as the following quotations indicate.

XIII

Anonymous, *L'Obratge dels Philosophes*

(from *L'Alchimie Médiévale: L'Obratge dels Philosophes, La Soma et les Manuscrits d'Oil*, ed. Suzanne Thiolier-Méjean [Paris: Université de Paris-Sorbonne, 1999], p.176)

Dels quals secrets a home carnal a un tot solet non deves revelar, quar maldich serias en la revelation del secret, car nengun homme non pot tolre ne hostar a qui Dieu lo vol revelar; a el s'apartent revelar et non a autre, car don de Dieu es sobeyran et non de home mortel, el qual Dieu fa tota gracia que ly ha plagut de revelar los secrets que el ha pausatz en las forsas de natura.

[You should not reveal these secrets to any living person, not to one, for you will be cursed by the revelation of the secret: no one can remove or take it away from one whom God wishes it revealed to; it is for God to reveal it and none other, because a gift of God is sovereign, but not the gift of a mortal to whom God has graciously revealed the secrets which he has placed in the forces of nature.]

XIV

Pseudo-Thomas Aquinas, *Aurora Consurgens*

(from *Aurora Consurgens: A Document Attributed to Thomas Aquinas on the Problem of Opposites in Alchemy*, ed. Marie-Louise von Franz; trans. R. F. C. Hull and A. S. B. Glover, Bollingen Series 77 [New York: Pantheon Books, 1966], pp. 122–3)

Et super hoc iuraverunt omnes philosophi, ne in aliquo loco scriptotenus ponerent lucide, sed attribuerunt glorioso Deo, ut revelaret cui vult et prohiberet a quo vult, quia in ipso est magnum sophisma et obscuritas sapientum.

[And of this have all the philosophers sworn, that they would nowhere set it forth clearly in writing, but they have left it to the glorious God, to reveal it to whom he will and withhold it from whom he will, for in him is great cunning and the secrecy of the wise].

APPENDIX

Texts and Documents Illustrating Differing Opinions about the Value and Utility of Alchemy in Chaucer's World

The ambivalence noted above in the attitudes expressed in *The Canon's Yeoman's Tale* toward alchemy and its ultimate value also appears in a variety of late medieval texts; we print here extracts from several of them in modern English translations.

XV

Decree of Pope John XXII

(from *The Decree of Pope John XXII against the crime of alchemy*, c. 1317; Latin and English texts cited in J. R. Partington, "Albertus Magnus on Alchemy," *Ambix* 1 [1937]: 15–16)

Poor themselves, the alchemists promise riches which are not forthcoming; wise also in their own conceit, they fall into the ditch which they themselves have digged. For there is no doubt that the professors of this art of alchemy make fun of each other because, conscious of their own ignorance, they are surprised at those who say anything of this kind about themselves; when the truth sought does not come to them they fix on a day [for their experiment] and exhaust their arts; then they dissimulate [their failure] so that finally, though there is no such thing in nature, they pretend to make genuine gold and silver by a sophistic transmutation; to such an extent does their damned and damnable temerity go that they stamp upon the base metal the characters of public money for believing eyes, and it is only in this way that they deceive the ignorant populace as to the alchemic fire of their furnace. Wishing to banish such practices for all time, we have determined by this formal edict that whoever shall make gold or silver of this kind or shall order it to be made, provided the attempt actually ensues, or whoever shall knowingly assist those actually engaged in such a process, or whoever knowingly shall make use of such gold or silver either by selling it or giving it in payment for debt, shall be compelled as a penalty to pay into the public treasury, to be used for the poor, as much by weight of genuine gold or silver as there may be of alchemical metal, provided it be proved lawfully that they have been guilty in any of the aforesaid ways; as for those who persist in making alchemical gold, or, as has been said, in using it knowingly, let them be branded with the mark of perpetual infamy. . . . And if the delinquents are clerics, besides the aforesaid penalties they shall be deprived of any benefices they shall hold and shall be declared incapable of holding any further benefices.[62]

62 Partington, p. 16, notes that Pope John XXII was himself represented as an alchemist, with works on the science (falsely) attributed to him. See also, Petrarch, *De alchimia*, in *De remediis utriusque*

XVI

Christine de Pizan, *Lavision-Christine*

(from Christine de Pizan, *Christine's Vision,* trans. Glenda K. McLeod, Garland Library of Medieval Literature [New York and London, 1993], pp. 82–3)

The speaker, Lombre, the shadow of Opinion, addresses the author regarding Alchemists:

> Here, however, is what deceives the workers in this science: they say and declare that since it is unsuitable for ignorant boors to discover so noble a secret, the authors wanted to hide it for the benefit of the clever so it might not be stolen or taken away by oafs. And the deception occurs here. For everyone so convinced believes he is among the cleverest and is deceived in his understanding as he studies these books, whose words yield their interpretation in such double meanings that the most clear-sighted see nothing at all. Then I establish myself within them, however, and make them believe that by joining the sublime metals in various ways (specifying how and to what end they should be mixed from various materials and fed into the fire) they will obtain the art of nature, and the mixture will be converted after a time to gold or silver. One person understands the manner of composition in one way, however, and another in another; and the workers keep it secret, not conferring together for fear their ideas and methods may tell another how to discover the road to success. Few if any work as the others do; hence as they put some solid material into water or powder or something else, they waste and lose time and foolishly spend much money for the vain hope that perchance comforts them in their error because of a meager showing or suggestion of some unusual congelation from the different mixtures and the fire. They think that through these things, which are completely frivolous and lead to madness and misery, they will arrive at the level to which they aspire. All day and night they tend the fire, contemplating a furnace. Ill fed and ill clothed, they feed on the wind and build castles in the air, thinking how comfortable they will be and how much money they will manage when they know how to make gold. And why do you think that from such alchemists frequently arise great charlatans, who deceive the lords and make them believe that if they had a little money, they undoubtedly would have already acquired a great secret? They would draw a huge profit from them, and so by a show of subtle truth in this science, they reveal a token of some apparently genuine substance, and in the end all comes to nothing just as you have seen in your own lifetime concerning several who had a considerable reputation and in whom many believed. . . .[63]

fortunae; text from the 1648 edition printed by J. W. Spargo, in Bryan and Dempster, pp. 692–3; translation in *Petrarch's Remedies for Fortune Fair and Foul*, ed. Conrad H. Rawski (Bloomington, IN, 1991), vol. 1, pp. 299–300.

63 At this point, Christine's interlocutor alludes to Bernard of Treves (see pp. 723, above): "such as the one in Germany named master Bernard – who made himself so famous by his position and who did so many things (he even sent letters to your father) that quite a few people believed in him, students went to him from everywhere, and in the end everything was found to be lies and baubles. . . ." The original text can be found in *Lavision-Christine*, ed. Sister Mary Louis Towner (Washington, D.C., 1932).

XVII

Petrus Antonius Bonus, *Pretiosa margarita novella*

(from *The New Pearl of Great Price,* ed. and trans. A. E. Waite [London: V. Stuart, 1963], pp. 11–19)[64]

BONUS: Do you not know that all who practice this art are very anxious to keep it a secret from the whole world?
LACINIUS: Alas! Is it, then, a profane pursuit?
BONUS: That is the opinion of the vulgar. But the art is sacred, and all its adepts are sanctified and pure. For "men either discover it because they are holy, or it makes them holy."
LACINIUS: That is not the opinion of the present age. People say that this art is unbecoming not only a godly but even an honest man.
BONUS: And do you also echo the ignorant babble of the vulgar?
LACINIUS: Would it were of the vulgar only! But I know that it is the opinion of all classes, both high and low, learned and ignorant.
BONUS: Can it be true? Surely they must be thinking of those sophistical impostors who are a disgrace to our science. Such men are not philosophers, but thieves and robbers: between us and them there is all the difference of day and night, good and evil, God and mammon. But, nevertheless, by their wicked and shameless practices, they have succeeded in making our blessed Art a byword among the vulgar. Yet it is essentially an art which can never become known to any but honest and god-fearing persons. Was not the inventor of this Art, the thrice-great Hermes, a person of signal sanctity? . . .
LACINIUS: Alas, that this glorious and heavenly magistery should be regarded by many as a mere fraud and imposture!
BONUS: No wonder, if overweening and ignorant persons such as carpenters, weavers, smiths, take upon themselves to set up laboratories, and to pretend to a knowledge of our Art. The universal prevalence of impostors naturally makes people think that our whole Art is a fraud from beginning to end.
LACINIUS: But is this knowledge not also sought by learned men, nobles, princes, and even by kings?
BONUS: Yes, but the motive which prompts them all is an illiberal love of gold. Their hearts are as hard as the flints which they wish to change into the precious metals, and they are as ignorant withal of the elementary facts of Nature as the poorest labourer. The consequence is that they fall an easy prey to impostors and itinerant charlatans, and spend their lives in foolishly experimenting with arsenic, sulphur, and all manner of solvents. Thus, instead of learning to prepare the Stone, they dissipate their money, and have empty pockets for their pains.

[64] Latin text, *Pretiosa margarita novella de thesauro, ac pretiosissimo philosophorum lapide* . . . (c. 1330), ed. J. W. Spargo in Bryan and Dempster, pp. 695–7.

XVIII

Roger Bacon, *Opus Majus*

(from *The Opus Majus of Roger Bacon*, trans. Robert Belle Burke [Philadelphia: University of Pennsylvania Press, 1928], vol. 2, pp. 626–7)

There have always been a few who during their life have known this secret of alchemy; and this science does not go beyond that. But experimental science by means of Aristotle's Secrets of Secrets knows how to produce gold not only of twenty-four degrees but of thirty and forty degrees and of as many degrees as we desire. For this reason Aristotle said to Alexander, "I wish to disclose the greatest secret"; and it really is the greatest secret, for not only would it procure an advantage for the state and for every one his desire because of the sufficiency of gold, but what is infinitely more, would prolong life. For that medicine which would remove all the impurities and corruptions of a baser metal, so that it should become silver and purest gold, is thought by scientists to be able to remove the corruptions of the human body to such an extent that it would prolong life for many ages.[65]

XIX

Jean de Meun, *Le Roman de la Rose*

(from *The Romance of the Rose*, trans. Frances Horgan [Oxford and New York, 1994], pp. 248–9, lines 16053–118)

It is worthy of note, nevertheless, that alchemy is a true art, and that anyone who worked at it seriously would discover great marvels. Whatever may be true of species, individuals at least, when subjected to the operations of the intellect, can be changed into so many different forms, and their complexions so altered by various transformations, that this change can rob them of their original species and put them into a different one. Have we not seen how those who are expert in glass-making can, through a simple process of purification, use ferns to produce both ash and glass? Yet glass is not fern, nor fern glass. And when we have thunder and lightning, we often see stones fall from the clouds, although they did not rise as stones. Experts may know what causes matter to be changed into different species. And thus species are transformed, or rather their individuals are alienated from them in substance and appearance, by Art in the case of glass and by Nature in the case of the stones.

[65] Latin text in *The Opus Majus of Roger Bacon*, ed. John Henry Bridges (Frankfurt am Main: Minerva, 1964), vol. 2, p. 215. Cf. Bacon's notes on the relevant portion of the *Secretum Secretorum*, in *Secretum Secretorum cum glossis et notulis*, ed. Robert Steele in *Opera hactenus inedita Rogeri Baconi*, fasc. 5 (Oxford, 1920), pp. 114–16.

The same could be done with metals, if one could manage to do it, by removing impurities from the impure metals and refining them into a pure state; they are of similar complexion and have great affinities with one another, for they are all of one substance, no matter how Nature may modify it. Books tell us that they were all born in different ways, in mines down in the earth, from sulphur and quicksilver. And so, if anyone had the skill to prepare spirits in such a way that they had the power to enter bodies but were unable to fly away once they had entered, provided they found the bodies to be well purified, and provided the sulphur, whether white or red, did not burn, a man with such knowledge might do what he liked with metals. The masters of alchemy produce pure gold from pure silver, using things that cost almost nothing to add weight and colour to them; with pure gold they make precious stones, bright and desirable, and they strip other metals of their forms, using potions that are white and penetrating and pure to transform them into pure silver. But such things will never be achieved by those who indulge in trickery: even if they labour all their lives, they will never catch up with Nature.[66]

66 French text in Guillaume de Lorris and Jean de Meun, *Le Roman de la Rose*, ed. Félix Lecoy, CFMA 95 (Paris: Honoré Champion, 1973), vol. 2, pp. 238–40. Chaucer drew on the description of the manufacture of glass from fern ashes in this passage (lines 16066–71) for his account of the magic ring in the *Squire's Tale* (V.253–7). See Correale and Hamel, *Sources and Analogues of the Canterbury Tales*, vol. I, p. 207.

The Manciple's Tale

EDWARD WHEATLEY

James A. Work asserted in 1941 that *The Manciple's Tale* had no one source but was cobbled together from Chaucer's memories of a common story and related materials;[1] no scholar since then has convincingly undermined that assertion. The story of Phoebus, his unfaithful wife, and a tattling bird that the god changes from white to black circulated in a number of different texts, one of which was a work to which Chaucer alludes frequently in his poetry, Ovid's *Metamorphoses*. However, the Latin story differs in several significant details from Chaucer's. Ovid gives Phebus's wife's name as Coronis, which Chaucer omits; Ovid's raven travels to find the absent Phebus whereas in Chaucer the wife's infidelity occurs while the crow is caged at home, where he waits for his master to return; and Ovid's Coronis pleads for the life of the child in her womb as Phebus threatens to kill her, but the nameless wife in Chaucer's tale is not described as pregnant. Chaucer also adds the crow's loss of his singing voice as punishment.

The *Ovide moralisé* (c. 1225) and Guillaume de Machaut's *Le livre du voir dit* (c. 1365) also include versions of this fable that resemble Chaucer's in tone and, to some extent, in the focus upon unwise speech, but both of these versions follow Ovid more closely than Chaucer's does. The story also appears in John

[1] Bryan and Dempster, pp. 699–700.

Gower's *Confessio Amantis*, where the emphasis on proverbial wisdom addressed to "Mi sone" strongly resembles the self-consciously labored, parodic concluding lines of Chaucer's tale. However, there is no conclusive evidence that Chaucer knew Gower's version, which is shorter than *The Manciple's Tale* and differs from it in a number of ways; in fact, Gower's tale may not predate Chaucer's at all. Another strong Middle English analogue for the tale is *The Seven Sages of Rome*, a translation of the French *Li Romans des sept sages*; the version printed here is from the Auchinleck Manuscript.

Since Work wrote, the critical history relating to Chaucer's sources has been divided between those who claim special connections between *The Manciple's Tale* and one or more of these five texts, and those who argue against Chaucer's direct use of any of them. In the first group, J. Burke Severs noted twenty-one similarities between Chaucer's poem and the two French texts.[2] On the other hand, Britton Harwood convincingly examined many of the points in which *The Manciple's Tale* differs from all of the texts named above.[3] In 1984, Donald C. Baker summarized the critical history on these issues as follows:

> If there is a source in any specific sense for Chaucer's poem, it has been lost. It is far more likely, as most now recognize, that *The Manciple's Tale* was in its imaginative conception an amalgam of the Phoebus stories with which Chaucer was familiar . . . an amalgam that probably originated not in Chaucer's returning to any of the stories but to his recalling those details from his reading and listening that suited his own purposes in telling the story.[4]

In this assessment, Baker anticipated the recent research of Carruthers[5] and other scholars who have reestablished the place of memory in medieval writing and rhetorical practice.

Work detected in *The Manciple's Tale* allusions to such texts as the *Integumenta Ovidii*, Boethius's *Consolation of Philosophy*, and Jean de Meun's *Roman de la Rose*. However, inasmuch as Chaucer probably generated the narrative of Phoebus and the crow from his memory of one or more texts, it is equally probable that he would not have needed to consult source texts in order to remember the brief citations of proverbial wisdom and etiological detail that punctuate *The Manciple's Tale*. The explanatory notes to the tale in *The Riverside Chaucer* identify the most important of these proverbs and allusions, and James Work reproduces similar passages from earlier texts in Bryan and Dempster (pp. 719–22).

2 "Is the *Manciple's Tale* a Success?" *Journal of English and Germanic Philology* 51 (1952): 1–16.

3 "Language and the Real: Chaucer's Manciple," *Chaucer Review* 6 (1972): 268–79.

4 *A Variorum Edition of the Works of Geoffrey Chaucer*, Volume II: *The Canterbury Tales, Part 10: The Manciple's Tale*, ed. Donald C. Baker (Norman, OK: University of Oklahoma Press, 1984), p. 9.

5 Mary Carruthers, *The Book of Memory: A Study of Memory in Medieval Culture* (Cambridge: Cambridge University Press, 1990).

I

Ovid, *Metamorphoses*

(trans. Frank Justus Miller)

. . . peacocks [were] but lately decked with the slain Argus' eyes at the same time that thy plumage, talking raven, though white before, had been suddenly changed to black. For he had once been a bird of silvery-white plumage, so that he rivalled the spotless doves, nor yielded to the geese which one day were to save the Capitol with their watchful cries, nor to the river-loving swan. But his tongue was his undoing. Through his tongue's fault the talking bird, which once was white, was now the opposite of white. (534–41)

In all Thessaly there was no fairer maid than Coronis of Larissa. She surely found favour in thy eyes, O Delphic god, so long as she was chaste – or undetected. But the bird of Phoebus discovered her unchastity, and was posting with all speed, hardhearted tell-tale, to his master to disclose the sin he had spied out. The gossiping crow followed him on flapping wings and asked the news. But when he heard the real object of the trip he said: "Tis no profitable journey you are taking, my friend. Scorn not the forewarning of my tongue. See what I used to be and what I am now, and then ask the reason for it. (542–50)

. . . My punishment ought to be a warning to all birds not to invite trouble by talking too much" (564–5).

In reply to all this the raven said: "On your own head, I pray, be the evil that warning portends; I scorn the idle presage," continued on his way to his master, and then told him that he had seen Coronis lying beside the youth of Thessaly. When that charge was heard the laurel glided from the lover's head; together countenance and colour changed, and the quill dropped from the hand of the god. And as his heart became hot with swelling anger he seized his accustomed arms, strung his bent bow from the horns, and transfixed with unerring shaft the bosom which had been so often pressed to his own.

I

Ovid, *Metamorphoses*, Book II

(from *Ovid, Metamorphoses*, ed. and trans. Frank Justus Miller, vol. 1 [Cambridge: Harvard University Press, 1977], pp. 96–104)

. . . tam nuper pictis caeso pavonibus Argo
quam tu nuper eras, cum candidus ante fuisses,
corve loquax, subito nigrantis versus in alas.
nam fuit haec quondam niveis argentea pennis
ales, ut aequaret totas sine labe columbas,
nec servaturis vigili Capitolia voce
cederet anseribus nec amanti flumina cygno.
lingua fuit damno: lingua faciente loquaci
qui color albus erat, nunc est contrarius albo •
Pulchrior in tota quam Larisaea Coronis
non fuit Haemonia: placuit tibi, Delphice, certe,
dum vel casta fuit vel inobservata, sed ales
sensit adulterium Phoebeius, utque latentem
detegeret culpam, non exorabilis index,
ad dominum tendebat iter. quem garrula motis
consequitur pennis, scitetur ut omnia, cornix
auditaque viae causa "non utile carpis"
inquit "iter: ne sperne meae praesagia linguae!
quid fuerim quid simque vide meritumque require . . .

[The crow tells of Athena's attempt to hide the motherless child Ericthonius in a box; she orders three sisters to keep it closed and guard it. One of the three, Aglauros, opens the box to find the boy with a snake stretched alongside him. When the crow tells Athena of Aglauros's disobedience, the goddess punishes him by dismissing him as her attendant. Lines 552–64]

. . . mea poena volucres
admonuisse potest, ne voce pericula quaerant.

[The crow tells of her past life as a beautiful princess who was pursued by the amorous Neptune while walking along the beach. She cried out for help, and Athena transformed her into a crow. Lines 566–95]

. . . Talia dicenti "tibi" ait "revocamina" corvus
"sint, precor, ista malo: nos vanum spernimus omen."
nec coeptum dimittit iter dominoque iacentem
cum iuvene Haemonio vidisse Coronida narrat.
laurea delapsa est audito crimine amantis,
et pariter vultusque deo plectrumque colorque
excidit, utque animus tumida fervebat ab ira,
arma adsueta capit flexumque a cornibus arcum
tendit et illa suo totiens cum pectore iuncta

The smitten maid groaned in agony, and, as the arrow was drawn out, her white limbs were drenched with her red blood. "'Twas right, O Phoebus," she said, "that I should suffer thus from you, but first I should have borne my child. But now two of us shall die in one." And while she spoke her life ebbed out with her streaming blood, and soon her body, its life all spent, lay cold in death.

The lover, alas! too late repents his cruel act; he hates himself because he listened to the tale and was so quick to break out in wrath; he hates the bird by which he has been compelled to know the offence that brought his grief; bow and hand he hates, and with that hand the hasty arrows too. He fondles the fallen girl, and too late tries to bring help and to conquer fate; but his healing arts are exercised in vain. (596–618)

But the raven, which had hoped only for reward from his truth-telling, he forbad to take its place among white birds. (631–2)

II

Ovid Moralised

(trans. †*George Reinecke*)

The raven . . . once had a white color, whiter than swan or snow on branch or white dove or white wild goose, – their white was not whiter or lovelier than the raven used to have. He was blackened by his ignorance; thus was his color changed from white to black by his folly, and his vile jangling tongue, which was hurtful and deceitful, caused him to become newly black. Now will I tell you how this happened. (2143) – In Thessaly there was a girl most agreeable and lovely; she had fresh delicate coloring. Coronis was the name of this lass,

indevitato traiecit pectora telo.
icta dedit gemitum tractoque a corpore ferro
candida puniceo perfudit membra cruore
et dixit: "potui poenas tibi, Phoebe, dedisse,
sed peperisse prius; duo nunc moriemur in una."
hactenus, et pariter vitam cum sanguine fudit;
corpus inane animae frigus letale secutum est.
Paenitet heu! sero poenae crudelis amantem,
seque, quod audierit, quod sic exarserit, odit;
odit avem, per quam crimen causamque dolendi
scire coactus erat, nec non arcumque manumque
odit cumque manu temeraria tela sagittas
conlapsamque fovet seraque ope vincere fata
nititur et medicas exerect inaniter artes.

[Apollo places Coronis on a funeral pyre but snatches his unborn son from her womb before he is burned. Lines 619–30]

sperantemque sibi non falsae praemia linguae
inter aves albas vetuit consistere corvum.

II

Ovide moralisé

(from *Ovide moralisé. Poème du commencement du quatorzième siècle*, ed. C. de Boer, Verhandelingen der Koninklijke Akademie van Wetenschappen te Amsterdam [Amsterdam: Johannes Müller, 1915], vol. 1, pp. 217–18, lines 2130–63, 2351–75; p. 224, lines 2449–54)

Li corbiaus, qui premierement
Avoit eü la coulour blanche
Plus que cignes – ne noif sor branche,
Ne blans coulons ne blance gante
N'ot coulour plus blanche et plus gante
Que li corbiaux soloit avoir –
Nercis fu par son non savoir,
Si fu muee sa coulour
De blanc en noir, par sa folour,
Et sa vilz langue jenglerresse,
Qui fu nuisable et tricheresse,
L'ot fet nercir nouvelement.
Or vous raconterai comment.
– En Thesale ot une pucele,
La plus plesant et la plus bele.
La colour avoit fresche et fine.
Coronis ot non la meschine,

born in the town of Larissa; she was of great nobility. Phoebus loved her for a long time, but the lovely one secretly loved another young squire. Phoebus then owned a bird which is called a raven. At that time none could find a finer one; its feathers were fine and delicate and whiter than new-fallen snow, though later blackened for his jangling. He saw the lechery of the adulterer and the girl. (2160) He goes to Phoebus to tell him the news concerning what he had seen. The crow caught up with him and asked where he was going.

(2351) Then he goes to Phoebus and recounts the villainy and great shame done to him by Coronis, and how she had broken her love bond, and was acquainted with a new adulterer, to whom she gave her affection; thus was she proved to be at fault and caught in present transgression. (2359) When Phoebus heard of the vile actions and the shame of his beloved, he was most sorrowful and downcast; his harp fell from his hands as did the bow which he held. He forgot all pleasures; the crown fell from his head. He was most saddened and miserable. He fell into a mood of great anger; in this anger and rage which had taken hold of his heart, he picked up his bow and arrows. He strings the bow and shoots the arrow. (2372) Nought was lacking when he drew; rather the arrow pierced to the heart of the lovely one whom he had so loved. This was a pity, and a sin!

Nee en Laurisse la cité,
Si fu de grant nobilité.
Phebus l'ama moult longuement,
Mes la bele celeement
Amoit un autre damoisiau.
Phebus ot lors un sien oisiau
Que l'en seult apeler corbiau.
Lors ne trouvast l'en nul plus biau.
La plume avoit bele et deugiee
Et plus blanche que noif negiee,
Puis nerci par sa jenglerie.
Cil aperçut la lecherie
De l'avoultire a la pucele.
A Phebus vait, pour la nouvele
Dire de ce qu'il ot veü
La cornille l'a conseü
Si li demande ou il aloit.

[The crow counsels the raven not to tell his master of the adulterous liaison. The crow then recounts the story of Vulcan, Pallas, "Euritonium," and Aglaros, as well as the tale of her earlier metamorphosis from maiden to bird in order to thwart the advances of Neptune.]

Lors vait a Phebus, si li conte
La vilonnie et la grant honte
Que Coronis li avoit faite,
Et comme elle a s'amor enfraite,
S'a nouvel avoutre acointié,
Cui elle a donné s'amistié,
Si l'en a reprise prouvee
Et en present forfait trouvee.
Quant Phebus oit la vilanie
Et la reprouche de s'amie,
Trop fu dolens, trop s'esbahi.
Sa harpe des mains li cheï
Et li arçons que il tenoit.
De nul geu ne li souvenoit.
La coronne li chut dou chief.
Trop fu a duel et a meschief.
Trop ot grant ire en son corage.
En cele ire et en cele rage,
Dont il avoit le cuer espris,
A son arc et ses fleches pris.
L'arc entoise et la fleche trait.
Ne failli mie a celui trait,
Ains a jusqu'au cuer entamee
La bele qu'il ot tant amee.
Ce fu damages et pechiez!

[The dying Coronis tells Phebus that although she deserves death because of her adultery, he should have allowed her to live because of the unborn child she is

(2449) The raven expected a reward for the news he had carried. But Phoebus gives him evil for it. Quite other than what he expected, he gave him black feathers and turned his whiteness into black. (2455)

III

Guillaume de Machaut, *The Book of the True Poem*

(trans. R. Barton Palmer)

How the White Crow's Feathers Turned Black

At one time the crow had feathers
Whiter than snow on the branch,
Whiter than the dove, the goose, or swan,
Whiter than the hawthorn flower.
In short, he was in no way ugly,
Being whiter than milk itself.
Phoebus loved him quite dearly
And took more enjoyment in him
Than in his little bow or harp,
Which he often plucked and played.
Now I'll tell you how it happened
His whiteness changed to black.
In Thessaly was a maiden
Becoming and pretty,
The woman most praised for gracefulness
Then living in all that country;
Born she was in the city of Larissea,
And so she wasn't foolish or uncultivated,
But rather sophisticated, bright, and wise,
Belonging to a noble lineage.
The maiden's name was Coronis.
Phoebus loved her with a pure affection
So firmly established in his heart

carrying. He tries unsuccessfully to revive her, then he consigns her body to the funeral pyre but rescues his son "Escupalius" from her womb.]

Li corbiaus atendoit merite
De la nouvele qu'il ot dite,
Et Phebus male la li rent:
Autre qu'il n'aloit esperent:
Noire plume li a donnee,
Et sa blanchour en noir tornee.

[The narrator "explicates" the tale by saying that the raven allegorically represents a servant in Phebus's household; he then retells the story briefly, substituting the servant for the bird.]

III

Guillaume de Machaut, *Le Livre dou Voir Dit*

(from *Le Livre dou Voir Dit* (The Book of the True Poem), ed. Daniel Leech-Wilkinson, trans. R. Barton Palmer [New York: Garland, 1998], pp. 537–55, lines 7792–7881, 7988–8131)

Comment li corbiaus blans fu muez en plume noire

Li corbiaus iadis plume blanche
Avoit • plus que la noif seur branche
Ne que coulon • gente • ne cisne •
Ne que la fleur de laube espine
Brief en li navoit riens de lait
Car il estoit plus blanc que lait
Phebus lamoit moult chierement
Et y prenoit esbatement
Plus quen son arson nen sa harpe
Dont il sesbat souvent et harpe
Or vous dirai comment ce avint
Que sa blancheur noire devint
En thessalle ot une pucelle
Qui estoit avenant et belle
Et de grace la plus loee
Qui fust en toute la contree
Nee en la cite de laurice
Fu • si nestoit rude ne nice
Eins estoit cointe aperte et sage
Et estraite de haut lignage
Coronis ot non la meschine
Phebus lamoit damour si fine
Si fermement et de tel cuer

He was at no time unmindful of her.
But she loved a young man
More than Phoebus did his white bird.
In short, she cared for nothing else so much.
And this came out clearly in the end.
For the crow spied the two together,
Locked in Nature's way, I think,
With each one taking pleasure in it,
Just as Nature teaches them to do.
When the crow spotted this adultery,
He began to curse them,
Swearing a great oath
That he'd go quickly to tell
Phoebus the terrible lechery
Of his beloved that he'd witnessed.
He struck the air with his wings
And, not saying another word, flew off
To report to Phoebus this news
Of the young man and the pretty girl,
How he had discovered them
Right there in the very deed.
The raven, who met up with him,
Took to flight at this encounter
And asked eagerly where that one intended flying,
For he was flying on in such haste.
The crow answered at once,
Relating from beginning to end
The adultery of Coronis,
And saying he was going to tell Phoebus
Because he didn't intend to conceal the shame
Done his lord by not telling him.

How the Raven Chastised and Corrected the Crow

After the raven heard him out,
She said: 'Crow, this much I'll tell you:
If you trust me, don't make the journey.
Stop and turn back.
Attend to what I say to you,
For in not a word will I lie.
Some things should be kept secret.
Do you think that Phoebus, your lord,
Won't be sorrowful and woebegone;
That he won't have a head full of pain
When you tell him the wickedness
Of Coronis, who is his beloved?
Do you think he'll be grateful
And raise you up to an even higher station?
Not at all! Truly, he'll hate you
And never wish you well.
Now the portrait that speaks has said

Quil ne loubliast a nul fuer
Mais elle amoit un damoisel
Plus que phebus son blanc oisel
Brief • riens tant namoit autre chose
Bien y parut a la parclose
Car li corbiaus les vit ensamble
Joins par nature ce me samble
Que chascuns prenoit son deduit
Si com nature les y duit
Quant li corbiaus vit lavoutire
Il les commensa a maudire
Et si iura grant sairement
Quil yroit dire isnellement
A phebus la grant lecherie
Quil a veu en son amie
De ses eles lair acola
Et sans plus dire sen vola
Pour dire a phebus la nouvelle
Dou damoisel et de la belle
Comment il les avoit trouve
Presentement en fait prouve
La corneille qui lencontra
Pris son vol en son encontre a
Moult enquist ou voler voloit
Qui si hastivement voloit
Li corbiaus tantost li respont
Et de chief en chief li espont
De coronis tout lavoutire
Et dit qua phebus le va dire
Car pas ne wet celer la honte
De son signeur quil ne li conte

Comment la corneille reprist et chastia le corbel

Quant li corneille lentendi
Elle dist corbiaus tant ten di
Se tu men crois tu niras pas
Arreste • et vole par compas
Et enten ce que ie diray
Car ia de mot nen mentiray
Tout voire ne sont pas bon a dire
Cuidez tu que phebus ton sire
Ne soit dolens et a meschief
Et quil nait bien mal en son chief
Quant tu li diras villonnie
De coronis qui est samie
Cuides tu quil ten sache gre
Et ten mette en plus haut degre
Nennil voir einsois te harra
Et iamais bien ne te vorra
Et limage qui parle a dit

Something notable here above:
That the one bringing bad tidings
Cannot come late to the door.
Things often go wrong when you speak the truth,
And you can easily understand
How a great misfortune can befall you.
I know very well what I'm saying
Because I used to be mistress
In the house of Pallas,
Where I was greatly honored.
Now I'm on the outs to my dishonor,
And all for speaking the truth.
Was this not a great injustice?
Listen and heed my warning;
Look to how I correct you
Because the man abandons his folly with dignity
Who corrects himself by another's example.
Now I'll tell you what happened to me,
And more than twenty years have since passed.
…

The crow refuses to heed this advice,
Saying that it will never rest
Until after having told the whole truth
About Coronis to Phoebus.
He flaps his wings, flies off.
He's hardly well schooled,
For often misfortune's the result
When a man speaks who should keep silent,
And he'll receive the wages
Reason pays out to blabbermouths,
Or at least to those who have dealings
With people of high station.
Beating the air with his wings,
The crow took off flying
Without path or highway;
He searched so much, wandered so far
He came right to Thessaly.
There Phoebus was in a palace
Crafted of gold, silver, and precious gems,
Well and richly carved.
The hall and all the places around it
Quite softly resounded

Ci dessus un notable dit
Que tart ne puet venir a porte
Qui maises nouvelles aporte
Souvent meschiet de dire voir
Et tu pues clerment savoir
Que grant mauls ten puet avenir
Je men say bien a quoy tenir
Car ie fui maistresse iadis
En la maison de palladis
Et y estoie a grant honnour
Or en suis hors a deshonnour
Et tout pour dire verite
Ne fu ce grant iniquite
Escoute et retien mon chastoy
Et voy comment ie te chastoy
Car noblement laist sa folie
Cils qui par autrui se chastie
Or te diray ce qui mavint
Il a ia des ans plus de vint

[The raven, who once held a place of honor in Pallas Athena's household, tells the crow of Vulcan's unrequited passion for the goddess. Vulcan "spills his seed" on the earth, which brings forth the monster Eresichton. Pallas locks him in a chest that is opened by Aglauros, who reveals the secret of the monster's existence. Expecting a reward, the raven hastens to tell Pallas what Aglauros has done, but the furious goddess banishes the bird and bestows her favor on the owl instead. Therefore, according to the raven, the crow should not bear bad news to his master.]

Li corbiaus dist que non fera
Et que iamais ne cessera
Tant qua phebus ait recite
De coronis la verite
Il fiert de lele et si sen vole
Na pas este a bonne escole
Car il avient souvent contraire
De parler quant on se doit taire
Si quil en ara tele paie
Comme raison aus gengleurs paie
Au mains a ceuls qui ont a faire
A gens qui sont de bon affaire
De ses eles lair acolant
Sen va li corbiaus en volant
Sans voie et sans chemin ferre
Tant a serchie tant a erre
Quil est venus droit a thessale
Phebus estoit en une sale
Dor dargent et de pierrerie
Bien et richement entaillie
Dou son qui de sa harpe yssoit
Moult doucement restentissoit

With the music of the harp.
In no chamber or tower
Could it not be heard.
The white crow began
To rejoice quite heartily upon hearing it;
He expected great treatment and a great reward,
But he didn't get this wish.
He's like the swan who sings
And celebrates on the brink of death.
For he's a great fool who determines
To say what might annoy
His lord when he's at ease.
And truly too much talk's unwelcome,
Nor ever, not day or night,
Is gossiping called for.
Spying the house of Phoebus,
The crow, hastening, whipped through the air
And flew quickly in that direction.
Phoebus saw and so asked him
To tell, explain
Why he'd come, because for quite long
He'd taken his pleasure elsewhere.
Right away the crow told him
The outrage, the ugly deed, and the shame
Of Coronis, the adultery too.
Even further he said: 'Good sir,
By all the sacraments one celebrates,
In this very misdeed I spied them.
I decided to tell you,
And this is why I've come.'
When Phoebus heard the news
From the crow, who said the beautiful woman
He loved with a pure and whole heart
Had abandoned him to take up with another man,
The crown fell from his head,
And the harp, which sounds softly,
Fell from his hands to his feet.
Had he been pierced by two swords
Through the body, he'd not have been
More grief-stricken than he was about his beloved,
Of whom it had been reported to him
That she'd played him false.
But it isn't necessary
That everything one says be the truth
– Nor is there truth in a quarter
Of what one says, so God preserve me!
Phoebus very mightily tormented himself,
Complained much, went quite mad;
So much ill he felt, so much misery
In his rage and anger.
By chance he spied that beautiful woman.

La sale et tous li lieus dentour
Nil ni avoit chambre ne tour
Dont on ne le peust oir
Li blans corbiaus a resioir
Se prist moult fort • quant il entent
Grant chiere et grant salaire attent
Mais il faurra a son entente
Il ressamble au cisne qui chante
Et resioist contre sa mort
Car cils est trop fols qui samort
A dire chose qui desplaise
A son signeur quant il est aise
Et vraiement trop parler nuit
Nonques ne de iour ne de nuit
Ne fu janglerie en saison
Quant li corbiaus vit la maison
De phebus lair fent et depart
Et tost sen vole celle part
Phebus le vit si li commande
Que raison li die et li rende
Dont il vient • car moult longuement
A pris hors son esbatement
Li corbiaus en leure li conte
Loutrage le lait et la honte
De coronis et lavoutire
Et encor li dist il biau sire
Par tous les sacremens quon fait
Je les vi en present meffait
A vous le di ie y sui tenus
Et pour ce suis ie ci venus
    Quant phebus oy la nouvelle
Dou corbel qui dist que la bele
Quil aimme de fin cuer entier
Le laist pour un autre acointier
De son chief chey sa coronne
Et sa harpe qui souef sonne
De ses mains chei a ses piez
Sil fust ferus de .ij. espiez
Parmi le corps il ne fust mie
Plus dolens quil est pour samie
De ce quon li a raporte
Que vers li a fait faussete
Mais ce nest pas neccessite
Que quan quon dit soit verite
Nen ce quon dit na pas le quart
De verite se diex me gart
Phebus trop forment se tourmente
Trop se complaint trop se demente
Trop a de mal et de dolour
En sa rage et en sa furour
Daventure la belle vit

Listen now to what he did.
He seized his bow, put an arrow on the string,
And so violently loosed it
He struck Coronis in the chest
Because he'd been cuckolded.
Coronis fell down in a heap.
Her heart failed, in her head
The vision grew dim, and from the wound
The blood ran down upon the ground.
Dying, she said: 'Alas, miserable one!
I see well I'll die soon,
And yet I've not deserved death
If I have not served you to your liking.
Friend, now you acted too hastily
Because you've killed two with one blow.
Listen, at least, to my complaint.
Pregnant with your child I am,
And this baby has done no wrong,
Sweet friend, the one you gave me.'
With this word she gave up her soul.
After Phoebus listened to that beauty
And saw she was now completely dead,
He was quite grievously distressed,
Very angry, quite filled with sorrow.
He cursed all birds that fly,
Especially the crow,
Whose body was fairest of all.
He cursed the bow and arrow,
The hand that had drawn it,
The hour, the season, and the day,
That ever he'd seen it dawn.
He had the corpse treated with balm,
With an ointment of great value,
And this was done so skillfully
She seemed still very much alive.
In the temple of the goddess Venus
He had her put with great pomp.
But he had her split and opened
Before all this was done and the child removed,
Who was afterward of great renown.
Aesculapius was his name,
And he knew more about surgery
Than any man then living,
For he made the dead come back to life,
So I find in my book.
The crow was awaiting a reward
For the tidings he'd brought.
This he desired greatly, was quite eager for.
Phoebus noticed him and looked him over,
Saying: 'In remembrance of this
Your white feathers will henceforth be black.

Or orez comme il se chevit
Larc prist • la flesche mist en coche
Et si roidement la descoche
Qua coronis la traite ou pis
Pour ce quil estoit acoupis
Coronis chiet toute estendue
Li cuers li faut et la veue
Li trouble en chief et de la plaie
Li sans iusqua la terre raie
En morant dist lasse dolente
Bien voy que la mors mest presente
Et se nay pas mort desservi
Sen gre ne vous ai bien servi
Amis • mais vous vous hastez trop
Qui .ij. en tuez a un cop
Au mains entendez ma complainte
Je sui de vous grosse et enseinte
Et li enfes na riens meffait
Dous amis que vous mavez fait
Apres ce mot lame rendi
Quant phebus la bele entendi
Et quil vit quelle est toute morte
Trop mortelment se desconforte
Trop fu courciez trop fu dolens
Il maudist tous oisiaus volans
Especiaument le corbel
Qui dessus tous avoit corps bel
Il maudist larc et la saiette
Et la main dont il lavoit traite
Leure • le temps • et la iournee
Quant onques la vit aiournee
Le corps fist aromatiser
Dongnement quon doit moult priser
Fait par maniere si soutive
Quelle samble encor toute vive
En temple venus la deesse
La fist mettre a moult grant richesse
Mais il la fist ouvrir et fendre
Avant toute ouevre et lenfant prendre
Qui fu puis de moult grant renon
Esculapius ot a non
Et si sceut plus de surgerie
Que nul homme qui fust en vie
Car il faisoit les mors revivre
Si com ie le truis en mon livre
Li corbiaus attendoit merite
De la nouvelle quil a ditte
Moult le desire moult li tarde
Phebus le vit et le regarde
Et dist en signe de memoire
Sera ta blanche plume noire

And all the crows who have white feathers
Will have them blacker than ink
Forever in perpetuity.
It will never be otherwise
Because of your malicious gossiping,
Which has stolen from me the love
Of the most beautiful woman in the world,
And it could be she's innocent
In this matter and that you've lied to me;
So I'm sorrowful, grief-stricken, and distraught.
You'll do nothing but jabber henceforth.
A mean eagle can squeeze the life out of you!
Be off! You're banished from my court.
Come again, and here you'll find shame.'
This is how the crow was rewarded.
And he flew off completely dismayed
And became a thief; that's it in a nutshell.
And this many men know quite well,
For in all the places he frequents,
He does nothing but jabber and make noise.

Et tuit li corbel qui lont blanche
Laront plus noire que nest anche
A tousiours perpetuelment
Ne sera iamais autrement
Pour ta mauvaise ianglerie
Qui ma tollu ma druerie
De la plus bele de ce monde
Et puet estre quelle estoit monde
De ce fait • et que menti mas
Dont dolens sui tristes et mas
Jamais ne feras que iangler
Maus aigles te puist estrangler
Va ten de ma court yes banis
Se plus y viens tu yes honnis
Einsi fu li corbiaus paiez
Si sen vola tous esmaiez
Et devint lerres cest la somme
Et si li scevent bien maint homme
Quen tous les leus ou il repaire
Il ne fait que iangler et braire.

IV

John Gower, *Confessio Amantis*, Book 3

(from *The Complete Works of John Gower*, ed. George C. Macaulay, vol. 2 [Oxford: Clarendon Press, 1901], pp. 246–8, lines 768–817, 831–5)

Mi Sone, be thou war ther by,
And hold thi tunge stille clos:
For who that hath his word desclos
Er that he wite what he mene
He is fulofte nyh* his tene*   near, pain
And lest* ful many time grace,   loses
Wher that he wolde his thonk* pourchace.   thanks
And over this, my Sone diere,
Of othre men, if thou miht hiere
In privete what thei have wroght,
Hold conseil and descoevere it noght,
For Cheste* can no conseil hele,   strife
Or be it wo or be it wele:
And tak a tale into thi mynde,
The which of olde ensample I finde.
Phebus, which makth the daies lihte,
A love he hadde, which tho hihte*   was called
Cornide, whom aboven alle
He pleseth: bot what schal befalle

Of love ther is noman knoweth,
Bot as fortune hire happes throweth.
So it befell upon a chaunce,
A yong kniht tok hire aqueintance
And hadde of hire al that he wolde:
Bot a fals bridd, which sche hath holde
And kept in chambre of pure yowthe,
Discoevereth all that evere he cowthe.* knew
This briddes name was as tho
Corvus, the which was thanne also
Welmore whyt than eny Swan,
And he, that schrewe* al that he can rogue
Of his ladi to Phebus seide;
And he for wraththe his swerd outbreide,* drew
With which Cornide anon he slowh.
Bot after him was wo ynowh,
And tok a full gret repentance,
Wherof in tokne and remembrance
Of hem whiche usen wicke speche,
Upon this bridd he tok this wreche,* vengeance
That ther he was snow whyt tofore,
Evere afterward colblak therfore
He was transformed, as it scheweth,
And many a man yit him beschreweth,
And clepen him into this day
A Raven, be whom yit men mai
Take evidence, whan he crieth,
That som mishapp it signefieth.
Be war therfore and sei the beste,
If thou wolt be thiself in reste,
Mi goode Sone, as I the rede. . . .

[*Gower includes here a brief retelling of the story of the nymph Laar, who divulged one of Jupiter's affairs to Juno. Jupiter cut out Laar's tongue and sent her to hell.*]

Mi Sone, be thou non of tho,
To jangle and telle tales so,
And namely that thou ne chyde,
For Cheste can no conseil hide,
For Wraththe seide nevere wel.

V

The Seven Sages of Rome

(ed. Karl Brunner, EETS OS 191 [London, 1933], pp. 100–4, lines 2193–2292)[1]

A burgeis was in Rome toun,
A riche man of gret renoun.
Marchaunt he was of gret auoir* — property
And had a wif was queint* and fair. — elegant (?)
But sche was fikel vnder hir lok,
And hadde a parti of Eue smok.
And manie ben yit of hire* kinne, — her
That ben al bilapped* ther inne! — wrapped up
The burgeis hadde a pie* in his halle, — magpie
That couthe telle tales alle
Apertlich, in freinch langage,
And heng in a fair cage
And seth lemmans comen and gon,
And teld hire louerd sone anon.
And for that the pie hadde isaid,
The wif was ofte iuel ipaid.
And the burgeis louede his pie,
For he wiste he couthe nowt lie.
So hit bifil, vpon a dai,
The burgeis fram home tok his wai,
And wente aboute his marchaundise,
The wif waited anon hire prise,* — advantage
And sente here copiner* fore; — lover
And whanne he com to the halle dore,
He no dorste nowt in hie
For the wreiing* of the pie. — betrayal
The wif him bi the hond hent,
And in to chaumbre anon thai went.
The pie bigan to grede* anon, — cry out
"Ya, now mi louerd is out igon,
Thou comest hider for no gode,
I schal you wraie* bi the rode!"* — betray, Cross
The wif thought schent* she was, — disgraced
A wrenche* she thoughte nathelas, — trick
And clepede a maide to make here bed,
And after, bi hir bother red,* — counsel
A laddre thai sette the halle to,
And vndede a tile or two.
Ouer the pie thai gan handel
A cler bacyn and a candel.

[1] In this transcription of the text, *th* has replaced thorn (Þ, þ)and *y, s, g* and *gh* are used for yogh (ȝ).

A pot ful of water cler
Thai sschadde vpon the pies swer.*   neck
With bacyn beting and kandel light
Tha bobbed* the pie bi night   deceived
And water on him gan schenche:
This was on of wommannes wrenche.
Tho the dai dawen gan,
Awai stal the yongeman.
Men vnlek* dore and windowe   unlocked
The pie him sschok with mochel howe,*   care
For, ssche was fain that hit was dai
The copiner was went his wai.
The gode burgeis was him icome
In to the halle the wai he nome.
The pie saide "bi god almight
The copiner was her to night
And hath idon the mochel sschame,
Imad an hore of oure dame!
And yit hit had ben to night
Gret rain and thonder bright.
Sehthen ich was brid in mi nest
I ne hadde neuere so iuel rest."
The wif hath the tale iherd
And thoughte wel to ben amered,*   marred
And saide "Sire thou hast outrage
To leue a pie in a kage.
To night was the weder fair and cler
And the firmament wel fair,
And sche saith hit hath ben thonder.
Sche hath ilowe* mani a wonder   lied about
But ich be awreke of here swithe,
Ne schal i neuer ben womman blithe."
The godeman askede his neghebours
Of that night and of the ours
And thai saide that al that night
Was the weder cler and bright.
The burgeis saide the pie
Ne scholde him nammore lie.
Nammo wordes he thar spak,
But also swithe his nekke tobrak.
And whanne he sey his pie ded
For sorewe coude he no Red.
He segh* hir [wete] and his cage   saw
He thoughte of gile and of outrage.
He wente him out, the ladder he segh*   sees
And vp to the halle Rof he stegh*   mounts
The pot with the water he fond,
That he brak with his hond,
And manie other trecherie
That was idon to his pie.
He went him doun with outen oth

In his herte grim and wroth.
And with a god staf ful sket* quickly
His wif ate dore he bet,
And bad hir go that ilche* dai same
On alder twenti deuel wai.
Lo sire, he saide, for a foles red,
The pie that saide soht,* was ded. truth
Hadde he taken god conseil
His pie hadde ben hol and hail.

Chaucer's Retraction

ANITA OBERMEIER

CHAUCER'S LIST OF WORKS

No direct sources for Chaucer's *Retraction* have been identified, and my purpose here is not to identify any particular source but to present analogues to the literary *topoi* contained in it. Although no chapter on the *Retraction* appeared in Bryan and Dempster (1941), as early as 1913, John Tatlock established "a well-marked though slim literary tradition" for it.[1] Tatlock found evidence of Chaucer's indebtedness to this tradition by focusing on works featuring the Latin term *retractatio* in their titles, such as Augustine's *Retractationes*, Bede's *Retractatio*, and Gerald of Wales' *Retractationes*.

In 1971, Olive Sayce expanded on Tatlock's argument by examining the *Retraction* in relation to the medieval prologues and epilogues tradition in the works of other medieval European writers.[2] She broke down the *Retraction* line by line into its component parts and identified matching phrases and passages in the prologues and epilogues found in their works. My own study has yielded statements from some seventy authors, many of which can be viewed as analogues to Chaucer's work. Although my investigation has not been limited to the study of the beginnings and endings of these writers' works, many of these "new" analogues do appear in their prologues, fewer in epilogues.[3] It appears, then, that in his *Retraction*, Chaucer transplanted some of the conventions found in prologues into his epilogue to *The Canterbury Tales*.

Tatlock and Sayce regarded Augustine's *Retractationes* as the earliest example of what J. de Ghellinck called "un genre nouveau."[4] Augustine amended and corrected all of his former books, a practice which seems to recall the custom of Hellenistic authors, like Isocrates and Galen, to catalogue their works and comment on them (*de libris ac ratione studiorum*).[5] But Augustine attempted to make this practice of authorial self-commentary into both a literary and religious endeavor. He first mentioned the planned composition of his *Retractationes* in a letter to Marcellinus in the year 412; in a later letter (427–28) to Bishop Quodvultdeus, he asserted that he will censure anything in all of his accumulated writings that "offends [Augustine] or might offend others."[6]

I wish to express my gratitude to Robert E. Bjork and Henry Ansgar Kelly for reading drafts of this chapter and kindly steering me in the right direction. Many thanks also to the Institute for Medieval Studies at the University of New Mexico for its support in the form of student assistance, and to Spring Robbins for providing this help to me.

1 John S. P. Tatlock, "Chaucer's *Retractions*," *PMLA* 21 (1913): 528.

2 Olive Sayce, "Chaucer's 'Retractions': The Conclusion of *The Canterbury Tales* and its Place in Literary Tradition," *Medium Aevum* 40 (1971): 230–48.

3 Anita Obermeier, *The History and Anatomy of Auctorial Self-Criticism in the European Middle Ages* (Amsterdam and Atlanta, 1999). For further examples of prologue and epilogue conventions, see Käthe Iwand, *Die Schlüsse der mittelhochdeutschen Epen* (Berlin, 1922); Richard Ritter, *Die Einleitungen der deutschen Epen* (Bonn, 1908), as well as two works by Julius Schwietering, *Die Demutsformel mittelhochdeutscher Dichter* (Berlin, 1921) and "The Origins of the Medieval Humility Formula," *PMLA* 69 (1954): 1279–91.

4 J. de Ghellinck, "Les Rétractations de Saint Augustin: examen de conscience de l'ecrivain," *Nouvelle Revue Théologique* 57 (1930): 481.

5 Georg Misch, *Geschichte der Autobiographie*, 4 vols (Bern, 1949–69), vol. 1.1, p. 173, vol. 1.2, pp. 341, 344.

6 Augustine, *Retractationum Libri II*, ed. Almut Mutzenbecher, *Corpus Christianorum Series Latina* 57 (Turnhout, 1984), Prologue; Mary Inez Bogan, trans., *The Retractations*, The Fathers of the Church 60 (Washington, DC, 1968), pp. xiii, 3.

Augustine's main intention was to correct the erroneous things he had claimed in his writings so that no errors would mislead his friends or enemies; he insisted on correcting his works publicly before an audience as well as distributing these corrections to the people from whom he could not recall them. In the prologue to his *Retractationes*, he uses the verb *recensare* to censure what displeased him ("quod me offendit uelut censorio stilo denotem": "with the pen of a censor, I am indicating what dissatisfies me").[7] His intention to rewrite his texts and himself is further indicated by the title *De recensione librorum*, which his biographer Possodius chose for the *Retractationes.*[8] Adolf Harnack, who wrote the definitive study on that work, also endorses this opinion that the title does not mean "corrections in the sense of a palinode but review in the sense of second attention," for, as Meredith F. Eller argues, "it is seldom that Augustine is compelled to retract anything."[9] One can best consider Augustine's work, then, not as a "retraction" in the English meaning of the word, but rather as a "retreatment" or "revision." And Augustine had some like-minded imitators. Bede, who had composed his *Expositio Actus Apostolorum* as early as 709, returned to that work between 725 and 731 to find it wanting. But, instead of reworking it, he published a *Retractatio*, in which four types of changes to the *Expositio* have been made: correction of "a small number of errors"; defense of choices; additions; and more in-depth usage of Greek.[10]

I

Bede, *Retractatio in Actus Apostolorum*

(from Bede, *Retractatio in Actus Apostolorum*, ed. M. L. W. Laistner, The Medieval Academy of America Publication 35 [1939; rpt. New York, 1970], Praefatio lines 3:1–11; trans. W. F. Bolton, *History of Anglo-Latin Literature 597–1066* [Princeton, 1967], vol. 1, p. 109)

Scimus eximium doctorem ac pontificem Augustinum, cum esset senior, libros retractationum in quaedam sua opuscula quae iuvenis condiderat fecisse, ut quae ex tempore melius crebro ex lectionis usu ac munere supernae largitatis didicerat; non ut de prisca confusus imperitia, sed ut de suo magis profectu gavisus monumentis inderet litterarum ac posteris legenda relinqueret. Cuius industriam nobis quoque pro modulo nostro placuit imitari, ut post expositionem actuum apostolorum, quam ante annos plures rogatu venerabilis episcopi Accae quanta valuimus sollertia conscripsimus, nunc in idem

[7] Augustine, *Retractationum Libri II*, Prologue, lines 5–6, 40–1; Bogan, *The Retractations*, p. 3.

[8] Meredith F. Eller, "*The Retractationes* of Saint Augustine," *Church History* 18 (1949): 173.

[9] Adolf Harnack, "Die *Retractationen* Augustin's," *Sitzungsberichte der Königlichen preussischen Akademie der Wissenschaften* 53 (1905): 1097; Eller, "*The Retractationes* of Saint Augustine," 173. See also Rosemarie Potz McGerr, "Retraction and Memory: Retrospective Structure in *The Canterbury Tales*," *Comparative Literature* 37 (1985): 97–113.

[10] Lawrence T. Martin, trans., *Bede's Commentary on the Acts of the Apostles*, Cistercian Studies 117 (Kalamazoo, MI, 1989), p. xxiii.

volumen brevem retractationis libellum condamus, studio maxime vel addendi quae minus dicta vel emendandi quae secus quam placuit dicta videbantur.

[I know that, when he was old, the distinguished teacher and bishop Augustine wrote books of retractions on some of his works which he had written as a youth, as he learned things better in later time out of the practice of frequent reading and the gift of heavenly bounty; not as being embarrassed by his initial ignorance, but more as taking pleasure in his progress he should publish it in written monuments and leave it to be read by later ages. And it has pleased me to take his labor as a model for myself, so that after my exposition of the Acts of the Apostles, which I wrote as far as my skill enabled me to, many years before, at the request of the venerable Bishop Acca, now I may make a small volume of retraction upon the same book, either by adding what seems to be missing or by correcting what seems to be wrong, with the greatest diligence.]

Tatlock includes Gerald of Wales' *Retractationes* in his study, although its element of self-criticism is rather slight: it lacks the dimension of guilt often associated with apologies to deities and instead sounds combative and begrudging.[11]

AUTHORIAL HUMILITY: ANALOGUES TO LINES 1081–4

Chaucer's *Retraction* is usually divided into three sections: the initial prayer, the author's plea for intercession on his behalf (1081–4); the "retractatio" proper, his confession of his literary offenses and the list of works (1085–9); and the final prayer (1090–2).[12]

Now preye I to hem alle that herkne this litel tretys or rede, that if ther be any thyng in it that liketh hem, that therof they thanken oure Lord Jhesu Crist, of whom procedeth al wit and al goodnesse./ And if ther be any thyng that displese hem, I preye hem also that they arrette it to the defaute of myn unkonnynge and nat to my wyl, that wolde ful fayn have seyd bettre if I hadde had konnynge./ For oure book seith, "Al that is writen is writen for oure doctrine," and that is myn entente./ Wherfore I biseke yow mekely, for the mercy of God, that ye preye for me that Crist have mercy on me and foryeve me my giltes.[13]

[11] In his introductory statement, Gerald juxtaposes the general fallibility of man, of the writer, and even more of the reader: "ea quae in opusculis nostris retractanda decrevimus, quatinus et lector caveat et pro certis incerta non habeat, hic proponere dignum duximus" [We have thought it fitting to set forth here those things in our works that we have decided should be retracted so that the reader may both be on guard and not take uncertainties for certainties] (Gerald of Wales, *Retractationes*, in *Opera*, ed. J. S. Brewer, 6 vols [London, 1861], I.425; my translation).

[12] For further discussion on the possible genesis of the *Retraction* as well as the evidence for its authenticity, see Heinrich Spies, "Chaucers 'Retractatio,'" *Festschrift Adolf Dobler* (Geneva, 1978), pp. 386–92.

[13] *The Riverside Chaucer* (Boston, 1987), p. 328. Chaucer uses the phrase on doctrine – meaning instruction – several more times (see the prologue to *The Astrolabe* lines 63–4 and *The Nun's Priest's Tale* lines 3441–2).

The first four lines can be classified as an example of authorial humility – pleas for intercession and prayers that are very common in medieval literature.[14] Analogous expressions of authorial humility are found in Bede, Jean de Meun, John Bromyard, Don Juan Manuel, and Boccaccio.

Bede uses the same conditional sentence structure as Chaucer: "in quo utroque opere, si quid utilitatis inveneris, dei donis adscribe; si quid superflui, meae fragilitati compatere" ["If you should find anything useful in either of these works, attribute it to God's gifts; if you find anything useless, have compassion on my frailty"].[15] Bede provides a twist on this phrasing in *The Ecclesiastical History*: "Lectoremque suppliciter obsecro ut, siqua in his quae scripsimus aliter quam se ueritas habet posita reppererit, non hoc nobis inputet, qui, quod uera lex historiae est, simpliciter ea quae fama uulgante collegimus ad instructionem posteritatis litteris mandare studuimus" ["So I humbly beg the reader, if he finds anything other than the truth set down in what I have written, not to impute it to me. For, in accordance with the principles of true history, I have simply sought to commit to writing what I have collected from common report, for the instruction of posterity"].[16]

II

Jean de Meun, *Le Testament*

(from *Le Testament Maistre Jehan de Meun: Un Caso Letterario*, ed. Silvia Buzzetti Gallarati [Alessandria, 1989], p. 205, lines 2109–12; my translation)

Et s'il y a nuls biens, en la gloire Dieu aille,
Et au salut de m'ame et as escoutans vaille;
Et du mal, s'il y est, leur pri qu'il ne leur chaille,
Mais retiengnent le grain et soufflent hors la paille.

[And if there is any good, may it go to the glory of God, and to the salvation of my soul and may it be of worth to those who are listening, and of the evil, if it is there, I beg them not to be concerned but to retain the wheat and throw out the chaff.]

14 See the studies by Iwand, Ritter, Sayce, Schwietering cited above as well as Tore Janson, *Latin Prose Prefaces: Studies in Literary Conventions* (Stockholm, 1964).

15 Bede, *Expositio Actuum Apostolorum et Retractatio*, ed. M. L. W. Laistner, The Medieval Academy of America Publication 35 (1939; rpt. New York, 1970), Praefatio lines 5: 16–17; trans. Lawrence T. Martin, *Commentary on the Acts of the Apostles*, Cistercian Studies 117 (Kalamazoo, MI, 1989), p. 6.

16 *Bede's Ecclesiastical History of the English People*, ed. and trans. Bertram Colgrave and R. A. B. Mynors (Oxford, 1991), pp. 6–7.

III

John Bromyard, *Summa Praedicantium*

(from John Bromyard, *Summa Praedicantium* [Nuremberg, 1485], Prologue, p. 2; my translation)[17]

Ceterum quicquid in hoc opusculo reprehendendum estimatur/ mee asscribatur insufficientie, quicquid vero vtile/ saluatoris et perpetue virginis attribuatur clemencie.

[Moreover, whatever is deemed reprehensible in this work should be attributed to my inadequacy; whatever is truly useful should be attributed to the mercy of the Savior and the perpetual Virgin.][18]

IV

Don Juan Manuel, *El Conde Lucanor*

(from Don Juan Manuel, *El Conde Lucanor*, ed. Carlos Alvar and Pilar Palanco [Barcelona, 1984], Primer prólogo, p. 8; trans. John E. Keller, L. Clark Keating, and Barbara E. Gaddy, *The Book of Count Lucanor and Patronio: A Translation of Don Juan Manuel's* El Conde Lucanor [New York, 1993], First Prologue, p. 52)[19]

Et lo que y fallaren que non es tan bien dicho, non pongan culpa a la mi entençión, mas pónganla a la mengua del mio entendimiento. Et si alguna cosa fallaren bien dicha o aprovechosa, gradéscanlo a Dios, ca Él es aquél por quien todos los buenos dichos et fechos se dizen et se fazen.

[And whatever they find therein that is not well said, let it not be blamed upon my intent, but rather on the weakness of my understanding. And if they find something well said or profitable, let them thank God for it, as He is the One through Whom all good sayings and deeds are spoken and done.]

17 This text was brought to my attention by Jesús Serrano Reyes. The work dates from 1390; however, according to W. A. Pantin, the *Summa* has been erroneously attributed to the later Bromyard and belongs to an earlier fourteenth-century Dominican by the same name (*The English Church in the Fourteenth Century* [Bloomington, IN, 1963], p. 147 n. 2).

18 I am grateful to Henry Ansgar Kelly for assistance with this translation.

19 Serrano Reyes argues for Chaucer's indebtedness to Spanish author Don Juan Manuel for the first three lines of the *Retraction*, "Spanish Modesty in *The Canterbury Tales*: Chaucer and Don Juan Manuel," *Journal of the Spanish Society for Medieval English Language and Literature* 5 (1995): 29–43.

V

Giovanni Boccaccio, *Genealogia Deorum Gentilium*

(from Giovanni Boccaccio, *Genealogia Deorum Gentilium*, ed. Vincenzo Romano, vol. 2 [Bari, 1951], Book XV, Conclusio, p. 785, lines 8–13; my translation)

> si quid boni inest, si quid bene dictum, si quid votis tuis consonum, gaudeo et exulto, et exinde labori meo congratulator, verum scientie mee imputes nolo, nec lauros aut honores alios ob id postulo; Deo quippe, a quo omne datum optimum et omne donum perfectum est, attribuas queso, eique honores impendito et gratias agito.
>
> [If it contains anything good, if it is well said, if it is suitable for your wishes, I am delighted and happy; from that I derive joy for my labor. I do not want you to impute truth to my learning, nor do I ask laurels or other honors for it; certainly, give to God, from whom every good and every perfect gift comes, the honors and thanks.]

THE "RETRACTATIO PROPER"
"Worldly Vanitees": Analogues to lines 1085–8

Lines 1085–8 of Chaucer's *Retraction* contain what Heinrich Spieß termed the "retractatio proper" with its two key elements: his admission of literary guilt and the list of works he regrets having written:

> . . . and namely of my translacions and enditynges of worldly vanitees, the whiche I revoke in my retracciouns:/ as is the book of Troilus; the book also of Fame; the book of the XXV. Ladies; the book of the Duchesse; the book of Seint Valentynes day of the Parlement of Briddes; the tales of Caunterbury, thilke that sownen into synne;/ the book of the Leoun; and many another book, if they were in my remembrance, and many a song and many a leccherous lay, that Crist for his grete mercy foryeve me the synne.

Chaucer is in good company expressing his regret for writing "worldly vanitees" – especially youthful love poetry – since numerous classical and medieval authors employed the same strategy.

"Worldly Vanitees": Graeco-Roman Analogues

Stesichorus of Himera (c. 630–553 BCE), a Western Greek writer of choral odes, is the father of literary apologies. As several ancient writers indicate, he wrote an exceedingly unflattering poem about Helen of Troy.[20] After the gods had punished him with blindness, he wrote a fragmentary poem titled "Palinodia," in which he apologized and regained his sight, as Isocrates

[20] C. A. Trypanis, *Greek Poetry: From Homer to Seferis* (Chicago, 1981), p. 104.

reports,[21] though the "Palinodia" does not mention Stesichorus's reputed blindness. Furthermore, in the *Phaedrus*, Plato (428–347 BCE) deals with Socrates' recognition of his literary error; Socrates, while preaching against love and, therefore, offending Eros, the son of Aphrodite, realizes his transgression. Since a superhuman voice reveals to him that he "had been guilty of impiety," Socrates comes to the same conclusion as later Christian poets: "I had a certain feeling of unease, as Ibycus says (if I remember rightly), 'that for offences against the gods, I win renown from all my fellow men'. But now I realize my offence."[22] Because Socrates wants to atone for his sin of chasing after worldly poetic glory, he refers to both Homer and Stesichorus.

VI

Plato, *Phaedrus*

(from Plato, *Phaedrus*, trans. C. J. Rowe [Warminster, UK, 1986], pp. 53, 55)

> So I, my friend, must purify myself, and for those who offend in the telling of stories there is an ancient method of purification, which Homer did not understand, but Stesichorus did. For when he was deprived of his sight because of his libel against Helen, he did not fail to recognise the reason, like Homer; because he was a true follower of the Muses, he knew it, and immediately composed the verses
>
> "This tale I told is false. There is no doubt:
> You made no journey in the well-decked ships
> Nor voyaged to the citadel of Troy."
>
> And after composing the whole of the so-called *Palinode* he at once regained his sight. So I shall follow a wiser course than Stesichorus and Homer in just this respect: I shall try to render my palinode to Love before anything happens to me because of my libel against him, with my head bare, and not covered as it was before, for shame.

During the Graeco-Roman period, self-critical authors apologize mainly to divinities and women, primarily in *post-culpam* attempts to alleviate or avert punishment, as seen in Stesichorus and Ovid. Another convention in the apology tradition is the "youth versus old age" *topos* that apologizes for an author's youthful writings. There has been a strain of scholarly opinion, often based on Gascoigne's account of Chaucer's death, which classifies the *Retraction* as a deathbed confession and thus as a piece of his old age. Horace is the first author to use this "youth versus old age" *topos*.

[21] Isocrates X 64, quoted in J. A. Davison, "Stesichorus and Helen," *From Archilochus to Pindar* (New York, 1968), p. 202.

[22] Plato, *Phaedrus*, trans. C. J. Rowe, p. 53.

VII

Horace, *Epistula ad Florum*

(from Horace, *Epistula ad Florum*, in *Epistles Book II and Epistle to the Pisones*, ed. Niall Rudd [Cambridge, 1989], p. 56, lines 141–4; my translation)

nimirum sapere est abiectis utile nugis,
141 et tempestiuum pueris concedere ludum,
ac non uerba sequi fidibus modulanda Latinis,
sed uerae numerosque modosque ediscere uitae.

[It would of course be useful for me to stop the trifles, to be wise, to concede the game to the young people, to whose age it is more fitting, and not chase after words that should be sung to the Latin lyre but to learn the rhythm and harmony of a true way of life.]

Ovid (43 BCE to 17 or 18 CE) committed a twofold offense, his crime and his song, for which he was banished to the Black Sea by Emperor Augustus. His literary offense is the *Ars Amatoria*, while speculation abounds about his other crime. Ovid, struggling with self-doubt in exile, penned apologies in *Ex Ponto* and *Tristia*:[23] "est tamen his gravior noxa fatenda mihi./ neve roges, quae sit, stultam conscripsimus Artem" ["Yet I must confess a weightier sin. Ask not what it is. But I have composed a foolish 'Art' "].[24] These texts contain a further *topos* of the apology tradition in the form of metatextual discussion of authorial motives for writing and apologizing.

VIII

Ovid, *Tristia*

(from *Ovid: Tristia. Ex Ponto*, trans. Arthur Leslie Wheeler, 2nd edn, Loeb Classics [Cambridge, MA, 1988], *Tristia* pp. 78–9, II.313–16; pp. 200–1, IV.x.59–62; pp. 254–8, V.xii.59–63, 68)

at cur in nostra nimia est lascivia Musa,
curve meus cuiquam suadet amare liber?
nil nisi peccatum manifestaque culpa fatenda est
paenitet ingenii iudiciique mei.
. . .
moverat ingenium totam cantata per urbem
nomine non vero dicta Corinna mihi.

[23] Kathryn L. McKinley's study demonstrates that copies of *Ex Ponto* and *Tristia* existed in England during the Middle Ages: "Manuscripts of Ovid in England 1100 to 1500," *English Manuscript Studies 1100–1700*, vol. 7, ed. Peter Beal and Jeremy Griffiths (London, 1998), pp. 41–85.

[24] *Ovid: Tristia. Ex Ponto*, trans. Arthur Leslie Wheeler, 2nd edn (Cambridge, MA, 1988), *Ex Ponto*, II.ix.72–3. See also *Ex Ponto*, III.iii.9–40.

multa quidem scripsi, sed, quae vitiosa putavi,
emendaturis ignibus ipse dedi.
. . .
nec tamen, ut verum fatear tibi, nostra teneri
V.xii.60 a componendo carmine Musa potest.
scribimus et scriptos absumimus igne libellos:
exitus est studii parva favilla mei.
nec possum et cupio non nullos ducere versus:

68 … in cineres Ars mea versa foret!

[Yet why is my Muse so wanton? Why does my book advise anybody to love? (II.315) There is naught for me but confession of my error and my obvious fault: I repent of my talent and my tastes. . . . My genius had been stirred by her who was sung throughout the city (IV.x.60) whom I called, not by a real name, Corinna. Much did I write, but what I thought defective I gave in person to the flames for their revision. . . . And yet, to confess the truth to you (V.xii.60) my Muse cannot be restrained from composing verses. I write poems which once written I consume in the fire; a few ashes are the result of my toil. I cannot and yet I long to refrain from writing verse; . . . I would that my "Art" had been turned to ashes!][25]

"Worldly Vanitees": Early Christian Analogues

Another group of analogues is found in the works of early Christian writers beset by a great ambivalence toward their own writing, an ambivalence stemming from their understanding of and attitude toward pagan antiquity and the seven liberal arts, especially the *trivium*. These writers are often recent converts to Christianity rushing to disengage themselves from pagan literature. They, therefore, stylize their writing opposite pagan fables to emphasize the truth of Christianity.

[25] Apuleius's second-century *Metamorphosis* (*The Golden Ass*) features a structure that can stand as a precursor to framed-story collections in the Middle Ages. *The Metamorphosis* demonstrates similarities to *The Canterbury Tales*: both works feature a frame-story and loosely connected tales narrated by individuals on a journey and relayed through one central character; they both cope with a narrative center that cannot always be located very easily; and they both move from the lewd and secular to the spiritual. Apuleius's eleventh chapter can be compared to the *Retraction* (Lucius Apuleius, *Metamorphoses oder Der Goldene Esel*, ed. and trans. Rudolf Helm, 6th edn, Schriften und Quellen der Alten Welt 1 [Berlin, 1970]). For a newer English translation, see P. G. Walsh, *The Golden Ass* (Oxford, 1994). Furthermore, Apuleius's contemporary Lucian (c. 120–190) presents the dilemma of an author who has joined the ranks of those he sought to malign in a previous essay: "But now I am wondering to what defence I should turn. Is it best to play the coward, turn my back, and admit my wrong-doing, taking refuge in the universal defence, Fortune, Fate, Destiny? Shall I ask pardon from my critics, who know that we have no control and are driven by a mightier power, especially one of those just mentioned? Shall I say we do not wish it, but have no responsibility at all for what we say or do? . . . Perhaps I have still one anchor left on board, to complain of old age and disease and poverty as well" (Lucian, *Apology for the "Salaried Posts in Great Houses,"* trans. K. Kilburn [Cambridge, MA, 1959], vol. 6, pp. 203, 205).

IX

Proba, *Probae Cento*

(from Faltonia Betitia Proba, *Probae Cento*, ed. Elizabeth A. Clark and Diane F. Hatch, *The Golden Bough, The Oaken Cross: The Vergilian Cento of Faltonia Betitia Proba* [Chico, CA, 1981], Proem, p. 14, lines 3–9, 13–14)

diuersasque neces, regum crudelia bella
cognatasque acies, pollutos caede parentum
insignis clipeos nulloque ex hoste tropaea,
sanguine conspersos tulerat quos fama triumphos,
innumeris totiens uiduatas ciuibus urbes,
confiteor, scripsi: satis est meminisse malorum:
nunc, deus omnipotens, sacrum, precor, accipe carmen
. . .
13 non nunc ambrosium cura est mihi quaerere nectar,
nec libet Aonio de uertice ducere Musas.

[And I have catalogued/ The different slayings, monarchs' cruel wars,/ And battle lines made up of hostile/ Relatives. (5) I sang of famous shields,/ Their honor cheapened by a parent's blood,/ And trophies captured from no enemy;/ Bloodstained parades of triumph "fame" had won,/ And cities orphaned of so many citizens,/ So many times. I confess [that I wrote]. It is/ Enough to bring these errors back to mind. Now, God almighty, accept my sacred/ Song . . . (13) no longer do I care to seek the ambrosial/ Drink, nor does it please to lead the Muses/ From Aonian peak.]

X

Sedulius, *Paschale Carmen*

(from Sedulius, *Paschale Carmen*, *Sedulii opera omnia*, ed. Johannes Huemer, *Corpus Scriptorum Ecclesiasticorum Latinorum*, X [Vienna, 1885], p. 2; my translation)

Cum saecularibus igitur studiis occupatus vim inpatientis ingenii, quod divinitatis in me providentia generavit, non utilitati animae sed inani vitae dependerem, et litterariae sollertia disciplinae lusibus infructuosi operis, non auctori serviret: tandem misericors Deus, rerum conditor, clementius fabricam sui iuris aspexit et stultos in me mundanae sapientiae diutius haberi sensus indoluit ac fatuum prudentiae mortalis ingenium caelesti sale condivit.

[When, therefore, as I was involved in worldly studies, I was spending the force of an impatient intelligence that divine providence had generated in me not on the good of my soul but on an empty life, and the adroitness of literary training was serving not the author but the games of an unfruitful work; finally the merciful God, creator of the world, looked more clemently on the

fabric of his law and grieved to see the foolish senses of worldly wisdom be held in me any longer, and seasoned my fatuous genius of mortal prudence with heavenly salt.]

XI

Sidonius Apollinaris, Letter IX.xvi

(from Sidonius Apollinaris, "Letter IX.xvi," in *Poems and Letters*, trans. W. B. Anderson, vol. 2 [Cambridge, MA, 1965], pp. 602–5, lines 41–64)

Nec recordari queo, quanta quondam
scripserim primo iuvenis calore;
unde pars maior utinam taceri
possit et abdi!
Nam senectutis propriore meta
quicquid extremis sociamur annis,
plus pudet, si quid leve lusit aetas,
nunc reminisci.
Quod perhorrescens ad epistularum
transtuli cultum genus omne curae,
ne reus cantu petulantiore
sim reus actu;
Neu puter solvi per amoena dicta,
schema si chartis phalerasque iungam,
clerici ne quid maculet rigorem
fama poetae.
Denique ad quodvis epigramma posthac
non ferar pronus, teneroque metro
vel gravi nullum cito cogar exhinc
promere carmen:
Persecutorum nisi quaestiones
forsitan dicam meritosque caelum
martyras mortis pretio parasse
praemia vitae.

[Nor can I recall how many things I wrote in the first fervour of youth; I only wish that most of them might be buried in silence! (45) For as the bourn of old age draws nearer, the closer I get to my last years, the more I am ashamed to remember now the flippant frolics of my youth. Appalled by this memory (50) I have transferred my study in all forms to the cultivation of letter-writing, lest, guilty as I was of wanton song, I should be guilty of wanton deed; And lest I should be thought a voluptuary demoralised by prettiness of language if I added to my pages tropes and trappings (55) so that my fame as a poet might not cast a slur on my strictness as a cleric. Lastly I shall not henceforth plunge headlong into the writing of a trivial poem, nor from this time on shall I be easily induced (60) to produce a poem in either light or weighty measure – Unless perhaps I tell of the inquisitions of the persecutors and how the martyrs, earning a place in heaven, won the reward of life at the cost of death.]

XII

Dracontius, *Satisfactio*

(from Blossius Aemilius Dracontius, *Satisfactio*, ed. Felicianus Speranza [Rome, 1978], p. 16, lines 105–8); my translation

te coram primum me carminis ullius, ausu
quod male disposui, paenitet et fateor.
post te, summe deus, regi dominoque reus sum,
cuius ab imperio posco gemens ueniam.

[In Thy presence first of all, I repent of that poem which in my rashness I foolishly composed, and this do I confess. After Thee, God Supreme, I am answerable to my lord the king, whose sovereignty, sighing, I entreat mercy.]

Lastly, even though Chaucer does not count his *Boece* among the questionable works, in the prose section I.23, 25–6 of Boethius's (480–524) *Consolation of Philosophy*,[26] Philosophy needs to eliminate the "poeticas Musas . . . scenicas meretriculas" [Muses of poetry . . . whores from the theater].

"Worldly Vanitees": Early Medieval Latin Analogues

Early medieval writers are primarily motivated by their desire for salvation and their fear of damnation. The medieval Latin authors Wandalbert von Prüm, Marbod de Rennes, Guibert de Nogent, Peter of Blois, and Ramon Llull apologize to God for their literary guilt, often citing the "youth versus old age" *topos*. To prove themselves acceptable in a cosmos that rejects works amorous in content and pagan in origin, these authors contrast their former writing practices with their current religious projects.

XIII

Wandalbert von Prüm, *Martyrologium*

(from Wandalbert von Prüm, *Martyrologium*, in *Poetae Latini Aevi Carolini*, ed. Ernst Dümmler, vol. 2, Monumenta Germaniae Historica [Munich, 1978], p. 576, Propositio lines 1–7; my translation)

Carmine qui vacuas captavi saepius auras
Rumores vulgi quaerendo stultus inanes,
Adgrediar tandem veram de carmine laudem
Quaerere et aeternum mihi conciliare favorem.

[26] Boethius, *Philosophiae Consolatio*, ed. Ludwig Bieler (Turnhout, 1984). Translations are available from a number of publishers.

Spectandos breviter signans actusque virosque
Atque dies anni reditu volvente per orbem,
Ordine quae lustrent scribens sollemnia quaeque.

[I who often held the empty breezes with song, foolishly seeking the empty gossip of the common crowd, let me come at last to seek true praise concerning song and win for myself eternal favor (5) briefly pointing out the noteworthy acts and men and writing in order all the feasts that illuminate the days of the year through its rotation in revolving cycle.]

XIV

Marbod de Rennes, *Liber decem capitulorum*

(from Marbod de Rennes, *Liber decem capitulorum*, ed. Rosario Leotta [Rome, 1984], pp. 59–62, lines I.1–13; my translation)

Quae iuvenis scripsi, senior dum plura retracto,
Paenitet et quaedam vel scripta vel edita nollem,
Tum quia materies inhonesta levisque videtur,
Tum quia dicendi potuit modus aptior esse:
Unde nec inventu pretiosa nec arte loquendi
Vel delenda cito vel non edenda fuissent.
Sed quia missa semel vox irrevocabilis exit
Erroremque nefas est emendare priorem,
Restat ut in reliquum iam cautior esse laborem,
Ne quid inornate vel ne quid inutile promam,
Praecipue quia iam veniae locus esse nequibit,
Qui quondam fuerat, dum stulta rudisque iuventus
Et levis in culpam poterat toleranda videri.

[As an old man reconsidering the many things I wrote as a young man, I regret them, wish not to have written and published this or that: some because the contents seem too facile and appear without dignity; (5) some because the presentation could have been more suitable. Hence, what was lacking both in form and invention should have been immediately stricken or never published. Once the word is released, it is gone and cannot be recalled. It is also not possible to correct the former error; what is left for me is to be more careful in the future (10) in order not to present anything without finesse or profit, especially since now there is no more room for forgiveness, as was available earlier when it could have seemed that youth, stupid, inexperienced and careless in guilt, was to be tolerated.]

XV

Guibert de Nogent, *Autobiographie*

(from Guibert de Nogent, *Autobiographie*, ed. and trans. Edmond-René Labande [Paris, 1981], Book 1, section XVII, pp. 134, 136, 138; trans. Paul J. Archambault, *A Monk's Confession: The Memoirs of Guibert of Nogent* [University Park, 1996], Book 1, section XVII, pp. 58–60)

[(134) Interea cum versificandi studio ultra omnem modum meum animum immersissem, ita ut universa divinae paginae seria pro tam ridicula vanitate seponerem, ad hoc ipsum, duce mea levitate, jam veneram, ut ovidiana et bucolicorum dicta praesumerem, et lepores amatorios in specierum distributionibus epistolisque nexilibus affectarem. . . . Nimirum utrobique raptabar, dum non solum verborum dulcium, quae a poetis acceperam, sed et quae ego profuderam lasciviis irretirer, verum etiam per horum et his similium revolutiones immodica aliquotiens carnis meae titillatione tenerer . . . (136) Inde accidit, ut, effervescente interiori rabie, ad obscaenula quaedam verba devolverer, et aliquas literulas minus pensi ac moderati habentes, immo totius honestatis nescias dictitarem. . . . (138) quasi ex necessitate rejectis imaginationibus, spiritualitate recepta, ad exercitia commodiora perveni.]

[(58) Meanwhile, I had fully immersed my soul in the study of verse-making. Consequently I left aside all the seriousness of sacred Scripture for this vain and ludicrous activity. Sustained by my folly I had reached a point where I was competing with Ovid and the pastoral poets, and striving to achieve an amorous charm in my way of arranging images and in well-crafted letters. . . . (59) In point of fact, I was doubly chained for I was enmeshed not only by the sweet words I had taken from the poets but also by the lascivious ones I poured forth myself. Moreover, by repeating these poetic expressions, I was sometimes prone to immodest stirrings of my flesh. . . . My inner turmoil reached such a point that I began to use a few slightly obscene words and to compose little poems entirely bereft of any sense of weight and measure, indeed shorn of all decency. . . . (60) it was almost inevitable that I should reject vain fantasies, and, paying heed to spiritual things once again, I took up more appropriate exercises.][27]

[27] A slightly more literal translation for lines "dum non solum . . . lasciviis irretirer" is "I was enmeshed by the frivolities not only of the sweet words that I had taken from the poets but also of those that I had myself produced."

XVI

Peter of Blois, *Epistola LXXVI*

(from Peter of Blois, *Epistola LXXVI*, in *Opera Omnia*, PL 207, ed. J.-P. Migne [Turnhout, 1956], cols 234, 237; trans. Richard W. Southern, *Medieval Humanism and Other Studies* [Oxford, 1970], p. 120; italics indicate my translation)

Ego quidem nugis et cantibus venereis, quandoque operam dedi, sed per gratiam ejus qui me segregavit ab utero matris meae, rejeci haec omnia a primo limine iuventutis . . . Omitte penitus cantus inutiles, et aniles fabulas, et naenias pueriles.[28]

[I too at one time occupied myself in writing frivolities and amorous poems, but by the Grace of Him who set me apart from my mother's womb, I put away such things when I became a man . . . *omit entirely idle songs, old-wives' tales, and childish pranks.*]

XVII

Ramon Llull, *Vita Coetanea*

(from Ramon Llull, *Vita coetanea, in Das Leben des seligen Raimund Llull, dei Vita coetanea und ausgewählte Texte aus seinen Werken und Zeitdokumenten*, ed. Erhard W. Platzeck [Düsseldorf, 1964], pp. 145–7; my translation)

II. Raymundus senescallus mense regis Maioricarum, dum iuvenis adhuc in vanis cantillenis seu carminibus componendis et aliis lasciviis seculi deditus esset nimis, sedebat nocte quadam iuxta lectum suum paratus ad dictandum et scribendum in suo vulgari unam cantilenam de quadam domina, quam tunc amore fatuo diligebat. Dum igitur cantilenam predictam inciperet scribere, respiciens a dextris vidit dominum Iesum Christum tanquam pendentem in cruce; quo viso timuit, et relictis que habebat in manibus, lectum suum, ut dormiret, intravit. III. In crastino vero surgens, et ad vanitates solitas rediens, nichil de visione illa curabat, immo cito quasi per octo dies postea, in loco quo prius, et quasi hora eadem, iterum se aptavit ad scribendum et perficiendum cantilenam suam predictam; cui Dominus iterum in cruce apparuit, sicut ante; ipse vero tunc territus plus quam primo, lectum suum intrans, ut alias, obdormivit; sed adhuc crastino apparitionem negligens sibi factam, suam lasciviam non dimisit; immo post paululum suam cantilenam nitebatur

[28] In his chapter on "*Nugae*: The Trifles of Learned Latin Poets," Marc Wolterbeek classifies *nugae* as "school exercises, amatory verses, comic narratives" belonging to erudite clergymen. Wolterbeek concludes that "*nugae*, then, are documents of a most peculiar sense of humor at the dawn of the High Middle Ages. They are the pioneering efforts of somewhat isolated scholars struggling to find a medium for a secular impulse" (*Comic Tales of the Middle Ages: An Anthology and Commentary*, Contributions to the Study of World Literature 39 [New York, 1991], pp. 43, 97).

perficere incoatam, donec sibi tertio et quarto successive diebus interpositis aliquibus Salvator in forma semper, qua primitus, appareret. IV. In quarta ergo vel etiam quinta vice, sicut plus creditur, eadem apparitione sibi facta territus nimium lectum suum intravit, secum tota illa nocte cogitando tractans quidnam visiones iste tociens iterate significare deberent. Hinc sibi quandoque dictabat conscientia, quod apparitiones ille nichil aliud pretendebant, nisi, quod ipse mox relicto mundo domino Jesu Christo ex tunc integre deserviret; illinc vero sua conscientia ream se prius et indignam Christi servitio acclamat; sicque super hiis nunc secum disputans, nunc attentius Deum orans, laboriosam noctem illam duxit insompnem. Denique, dante Patre luminum, consideravit Christi mansuetudinem, patientiam ac misericordiam, quam habuit et habet circa quoslibet peccatores; et sic intellexit tandem certissime Deum velle quod Raymundus mundum relinqueret Christoque corde ex tunc integre deserviret.[29]

[Ramon had been seneschal of the king of Mallorca. He was still young and had been dedicating himself a lot to the writing of vain lays or love songs and other worldly frivolities. Thus one night he was sitting at his bed ready to compose and write a lay in his vernacular to a lady with whom he was then passionately in love. And as he started to write the lay, he looked to his right and saw the Lord as if hanging on the cross. At this sight he was afraid, and he left off what he was engaged in and went to bed to sleep. Next morning, however, he got up and went about his usual vain dealings without thinking further about the vision. Then eight days later, at the same spot as before, almost at the same hour, he attempted once more to write down and finish said lay. The Lord appeared again on the cross as before. Thus he went to bed again and fell asleep, but more scared than before. The day after that, he did not think about the vision that had been revealed to him anymore and did not let go of his lascivious intentions. But a little later he tried to finish the lay he had begun, until the Savior appeared a third and fourth time within a few days, in the same form as the first time. There, the fourth or more likely the fifth time that the apparition was given, he went to bed greatly frightened and mused the entire night about what these repeated visions could mean. On the one hand, his conscience was telling him loudly and clearly that these apparitions could not mean anything else but that he should soon leave this world behind in order to serve the Lord Jesus Christ entirely from now on. But on the other hand, his conscience proclaimed itself burdened with guilt and not worthy to serve Christ. And thus, now disputing these things with himself, now attentively praying to God, he spent this troublesome night sleepless. Finally, through the gift of the Father of lights, he considered the condescension, patience, and mercy Christ showed, and still shows toward each sinner, and eventually came to the conclusion that God wanted Raymond to forsake the world and serve Christ from now on with his whole heart and devotion.]

"Worldly Vanitees": An Arabic Analogue

Ibn Hazm (994–1064), who composed *The Ring of the Dove* in Moslem Spain, exhibits authorial concerns similar to the ones of the Graeco-Roman and

29 The *Vita coetanea* exists in two forms, Latin and Catalan. The Latin text of Baudouin de Gaiffier has been established as the original, with the Catalan a somewhat inept translation (Hillgarth, *Ramon Lull and Lullism in Fourteenth-Century France* [Oxford, 1971], p. 46 n. 2).

medieval Christian writers. Like his Christian counterparts, Hazm addresses comments to both an earthly and a divine audience to place and justify his composition on love in a Moslem society.

XVIII

Ibn Hazm, *The Ring of the Dove*

(from Ibn Hazm, *The Ring of the Dove: A Treatise on the Art and Practice of Arab Love*, trans. A. J. Arberry [London, 1953], p. 281)

> I beg Allah's forgiveness for whatever the recording angels may note down, and the guardian angels enumerate against me, of this and the like; and I entreat His pardon as one who knows that his words shall be reckoned even as his deeds. If what I have said is not mere idle talk, for which no man shall be taken to task, yet my observations, God willing, shall prove to be pardonable peccadilloes; in any case they are hardly likely to rank as grave offences and abominations incurring Divine chastisement, nor do they count among those deadly sins specified in Holy Writ.

"Worldly Vanitees": Medieval German Analogues

The analogues of German authors focus primarily on *contemptus mundi*. For the German medieval poet, the important dichotomy features God and the poet. But most authors utilizing apologies in their works appeal equally to an earthly audience, especially when their work is intended to fulfill a dual purpose and effect a spiritual uplift in their listeners or readers. The emphasis on *contemptus mundi* in German is the byproduct of a generic focus. For early Christian writers the enemy has been classical literature and to a degree amorous writings; German literature presents contemporary, vernacular foes in the form of the courtly epic, the *Minnelied*, and the *Spielmannslied*. German analogues appear in prologues to saints' legends as well as biblical and lyrical poetry.

XIX

Hartmann von Aue, *Gregorius*

(from Hartmann von Aue, *Gregorius*, ed. Hermann Paul, 13th edn [Tübingen, 1984], pp. 20–3, lines 1–16, 35–42; my translation)

Mîn herze hât betwungen
dicke mîne zungen
daz si des vil gesprochen hât
daz nâch der werlde lône stât:
daz rieten im diu tumben jâr.

nû weiz ich daz wol vür wâr:
swer durch des helleschergen rât
den trôst ze sîner jugent hât
daz er dar ûf sündet,
als in diu jugent schündet,
und er gedenket dar an:
'dû bist noch ein junger man,
aller dîner missetât
der wirt noch vil guot rât:
du gebüezest si in dem alter wol',
der gedenket anders danne er sol
. . .
Durch daz waere ich gerne bereit
ze sprechenne die wârheit
daz gotes wille waere
und daz diu grôze swaere
der süntlîchen bürde
ein teil ringer würde
die ich durch mîne unmüezikeit
ûf mich mit worten hân geleit.

[My heart has often overcome my tongue, so that it has often spoken of that which inclines toward the reward of the world: (5) that is what the naive years advised it to do. Now I truly know this: anyone who has sinned, through the advice of the devil, the consolation in his youth (10) when youth pressed hard on him, and thinks: "You are still a young man, all your misdeeds will still be taken care of eventually; (15) you can still do penance for them in your old age" is not thinking as he should. . . . (35) Therefore, I am gladly willing to speak the truth of God's will so that the great heaviness of the sinful burden (40) I have heaped upon myself with my idle words, would be somewhat relieved.]

XX

Walther von der Vogelweide, "Mîn sêle müeze wol gevarn!"

(from Walther von der Vogelweide, "*Mîn sêle müeze wol gevarn!*" in *Walther von der Vogelweide: Leich, Lieder, Sangsprüch*e, ed. Karl Lachmann and Christoph Cormeau, 14th edn [Berlin, 1996], p. 149, lines 1–10; my translation)

Mîn sêle müeze wol gevarn!
ich hân zer welte manegen lîp
gemachet frô, man unde wîp:
künd ich dar under mich bewarn!
Lobe ich des lîbes minne, daz der sêle leit,
und giht, ez sî ein lüge, ich tobe.
der wâren minne giht si ganzer staetekeit,
wie guot si sî, wie sie iemer wer.
Lîp, lâ die minne, diu dich lât,
und habe die stæten minne wert.

[I wish my soul would find joyous salvation! I have brought joy with my song to many in the world, men and women. If only I could have saved myself from it! (5) If I praise the love of the body, my soul suffers. The soul says it is a lie; I am mad. It speaks of the complete reliability of true love, of how good it is, of how it always was. Body, leave the love that leaves you (10) and appreciate eternal love.]

XXI

Rudolf von Ems, *Barlaam und Josaphat*

(from Rudolf von Ems, *Barlaam und Josaphat*, ed. Franz Pfeiffer [Berlin, 1965], pp. 5, 404–5, lines 150–6, 16105–14, 16129–43; my translation)

ich hân dâ her in mînen tagen
leider dicke vil gelogen
und die liute betrogen
mit trügelîchen maeren:
ze trôste uns sündaeren
wil ich diz maere tihten,
durch got in tiusche berihten
…
diz maere ist niht von ritterschaft,
noch von minnen, diu mit kraft
an zwein gelieben geschiht;
es ist von âventiure niht,
noch von der liehten sumerzît:
ez ist der welte widerstrît
mit ganzer wârheit, âne lüge;
sunder spot und âne trüge
ist ez an tiuscher lêre
der kristenheit ein êre.
…
Nû lât mich vürbaz sprechen mê.
ich hâte mich vermezzen ê,
dô ich daz maere enbarte
von dem guoten Gêrharte,
haet ich mich dran versûmet iht
daz lîhte tumbem man geschiht,
daz ich ze buoze wolde stân,
ob mir würde kunt getân
ein ander maere: dêst geschehen.
nû kann ich des niht verjehen,
ob ich hân iht gebezzert mich:
dez weiz ich niht. noch wil ich
mit dirre buoze mich bewarn,
mîn sprechen an ein anderz sparn,
swes ich mich hie versûmet hân.

[I have, therefore, lied a lot in my days and cheated people with deceitful fables; as a consolation to us sinners, I will compose this story in German with God's help. . . . (16105) This tale deals neither with knights nor love, which happens with force to two lovers; it is neither about adventure nor about the light summertime: it is about the fight against the world, in all truth, without a lie, without mocking and without illusion; it is a German teaching, an honor for Christendom. . . . Let me still speak. (16130) I erred previously in putting forth the story of the good Gerhard; I wasted my time with that, which easily happens to a naive man; I wanted to bear my atonement if another story were revealed to me: this has happened. (16140) I cannot say now whether I improved: I do not know that. But I still want to protect myself with this penance and save my speaking for something else, something I have missed so far.]

"Worldly Vanitees": Medieval French Analogues

In medieval French literature, apologies to God for profane literature are found in both saints' legends and didactic poetry. Like the *Spielmann* in German literature, the medieval French *jongleur* was equally condemned and prosecuted by the Church for his amorous tales and stories of *aventure*, especially *fabliaux*, *dits*, and other works.[30]

XXII

Denis Piramus, *La Vie Seint Edmund le rei*

(from Denis Piramus, *La Vie Seint Edmund le rei: Poème anglo-normand du XIIe siècle*, ed. Hilding Kjellman [Geneva, 1974], pp. 3–41, lines 1–8, 13–21; trans. Dominica M. Legge, *Anglo-Norman Literature and its Background* [Oxford, 1963], p. 81; italics indicate my translation)

Mult ai usé cume pechere
Ma vie en trop fole manere,
E trop ai usée ma vie
E en peché e en folie.
Kant court hanteie of les curteis,
Si feseie les serventeis,
Chanceunettes, rimes, saluz
Entre les drues e les druz
. . .
Ceo me fist fere l'enemi,
Si me tinc ore a malbaili;
Jamés ne me burdera plus.
Jeo ai noun Denis Piramus;
Les jurs jolifs de ma jeofnesce

[30] Paul John Jones, *Prologue and Epilogue in Old French Lives of Saints before 1400* (Philadelphia, 1933), p. 43. See also John W. Baldwin, "The Image of the *Jongleur* in Northern France around 1200," *Speculum* 72 (1997): 635–63.

S'en vunt, si trei jeo a veilesce,
Si est bien dreit ke me repente.
En autre ovre mettrai m'entente,
Ke mult mieldre est e plus nutable.

[I have spent much of my life like a sinner, in a very foolish manner, and I have spent my life much in sin and folly. (5) When I frequented the court with the courtly, I made sirventes, songs, rhymes, and messages between lovers and their beloveds. . . . The Enemy made me do this, and I now consider myself in an evil plight. (15) Never will I jest again. My name is Denis Pyramus, my gay days of youth are passing and I approach old age. So it is fitting that I should repent; (20) I shall turn my mind to other things *that are much better and more notable.*]

XXIII

Guillaume le Clerc, *Le Besant de Dieu*

(from Guillaume le Clerc de Normandie, *Le Besant de Dieu*, ed. Pierre Ruelle, Université Libre de Bruxelles 54 [Bruxelles, 1973], p. 75, lines 79–86; my translation)

Guillame, uns clers qui fu normanz,
Qui versefia en romanz
Fablels e contes soleit dire.
En fole e en vaine matire
Peccha sovent: Deus li pardont!
Mult ama les desliz del mond
E mult servi ses enemis
Qui le guerreeint tut dis.

[Guillaume, a clerk from Normandy, wrote poetry in the vernacular and narrated *fabliaux* and tales. (80) In foolish and futile matters he often committed sins: God forgive him! He loved the delights of the world greatly and served his enemies, who fought him constantly.]

XXIV

Rutebeuf, *La Repentance de Rutebeuf*

(from Rutebeuf, *La Repentance de Rutebeuf*, in *Rutebeuf: Oeuvres complètes*, ed. Michel Zink [Paris, 1989], pp. 298–301; lines 1–8, 13–16, 38–40; my translation)

Laissier m'estuet le rimoier,
Car je me doi moult esmaier
Quant tenu l'ai si longuement.
Bien me doit li cuers larmoier,

C'onques ne me soi amoier
A Deu servir parfaitement,
Ainz ai mis mon entendement
En geu et en esbatement
...
Tart serai mais au repentir,
Las moi, c'onques ne sot sentir
Mes soz cuers que c'est repentance
N'a bien faire lui assentir
...
J'ai fait rimes et s'ai chantei
Sus les uns por aux autres plaire,
Dont Anemis m'a enchantei.

[I have to quit making verse, because I have reason to trouble myself about having cultivated it that long! My heart has great reason to weep: (5) never have I applied myself to serve God completely. I have put all my efforts to jest and amusements . . . It is pretty late for me to repent now, poor me: I will never remedy, for my stupid heart (15) never could feel what repentance is, nor be reconciled to doing good. . . . I have made poetry and I have sung at the expense of some in order to please others: (40) thus the devil has seduced me.]

XXV

Jean de Meun, *Le Testament*

(from *Le Testament Maistre Jehan de Meun: Un Caso Letterario*, ed. Silvia Buzzetti Gallarati [Alessandria, 1989], p. 121, lines 5–8; my translation)

J'ai fait en ma jeunesce maint dit par vanité,
Ou maintes gens se sont plusieurs foiz delité.
Or m'en doint Diex un faire par vraie charité
Pour amender les autres qui poi m'ont proufité.

[In my youth I have made many dits because of vanity, in which many people have been delighted several times. Now may God grant me to make one out of true charity so that I can make amends for the ones that have profited me little.]

"Worldly Vanitees": Medieval Italian Analogues

Chaucer's indebtedness to medieval Italian authors is well established, and analogues to the *Retraction* can be found in Dante, Boccaccio, and Petrarch. For instance, Dante's *Vita Nuova* delineates the poet's path from inept to successful poetry.[31] Giovanni Boccaccio's (1313–75) *Decameron* and

[31] Dante Alighieri, *Vita Nuova*, ed. Vittorio Cozzoli (Milan, 1995) and *Dante's Vita Nuova: A Translation and an Essay*, trans. Mark Musa (Bloomington, 1973).

Corbaccio[32] contain elements dealing with repenting of poetry. Boccaccio's most pronounced statement can be found in his letter to Mainardo Cavalcanti: "Sane, quod inclitas mulieres tuas domesticas nugas meas legere permiseris non laudo, quin immo queso per fidem tuam ne feceris"[33] [Indeed, I do not approve that you allow the renowned women of your household to read my trifles but rather implore you by your faith not to do so].

Several letters from Petrarch (1304–74) are important for the illumination of his attitudes towards poetry and his repenting of it: *Epistle to Posterity*, *He Turns from Profane to Religious Literature*, *Pleasures of Writing in Old Age*, and *Reproof of Boccaccio for Threatening to Burn His Poems*.[34] While the *Canzioniere* collection alternates between Petrarch's self-criticism and self-accolades, specifically the beginning and ending poems are most dismissive of earthly poetry.

XXVI

Francesco Petrarch, "Poem 1"

(from Francesco Petrarch, "Poem 1," in *Canzoniere*, ed. Gianfranco Contini [Turin, 1964], p. 1; trans. Robert M. Durling, *Petrarch's Lyric Poems. The Rime Sparse and Other Lyrics* [Cambridge, MA, 1976], "Poem 1," pp. 36–7)

Voi ch' ascoltate in rime sparse il suono
di quei sospiri ond'io nudriva 'l core
in sul mio primo giovenile errore,
quand'era in parte altr'uom da quel ch'i' sono:
del vario stile in ch' io piango et ragiono
fra le vane speranze e 'l van dolore,
ove sia chi per prova intenda amore
spero trovar pietà, non che perdono.
Ma ben veggio or sì come al popol tutto
favola fui gran tempo, onde sovente
di me medesmo meco mi vergogno;
et del mio vaneggiar vergogna è 'l frutto.
e 'l pentersi, e 'l conoscer chiaramente
che quanto piace al mondo è breve sogno.

[You who hear in scattered rhymes the sounds of those sighs with which I nourished my heart during my first youthful error, when I was in part another man from what I am now: (5) for the varied style in which I weep and speak

32 Giovanni Boccaccio, *Corbaccio*, ed. Pier Giorgio Ricci (Turin, 1977); *The Corbaccio or the Labyrinth of Love*, trans. and ed. Anthony K. Cassell, 2nd rev. edn (Binghamton, NY, 1993); *Decameron*, ed. Vittore Branca (Turin: Guilio Einaudi Editore, 1980); *The Decameron*, trans. Mark Musa and Peter Bondanella (New York, 1982).

33 Giovanni Boccaccio, *A Mainardo Cavalcanti (1373)*, in *Opere latine minori*, ed. Aldo Francesco Massèra (Bari, 1928), p. 211.

34 Latin originals can be found in *Epistole*, ed. Ugo Dotti (Turin, 1978) and the translated versions in Morris Bishop, *Letters from Petrarch* (Bloomington, 1966).

between vain hopes and vain sorrow, where there is anyone who understands love through experience, I hope to find pity, not only pardon. But now I see well how for a long time I was the talk of the crowd (10) for which often I am ashamed of myself within; and of my raving, shame is the fruit, and repentance, and the clear knowledge that whatever pleases in the world is a brief dream.]

Furthermore, in "Poem 366," Petrarch declares that "Medusa et l'error mio m'àn fatto un sasso/ d'umor vano stillante" [Medusa and my error have made me a stone dripping vain moisture].[35]

"Worldly Vanitees": Medieval British Analogues

Analogues to the *Retraction* also exist in English and Welsh medieval texts. A number of passages in William Langland's *Piers Plowman* attack goliardic poets and singers as reprehensible (see prologue to the A text and the C text, as well as Passus XII and XIII in the B text).[36] Llywelyn Goch's (1360–90) confession of sins in the Welsh poem, "I Dduw," includes both general offenses and specific literary crimes, the latter referring to the offending previous text.

XXVII

Llywelyn Goch, *I Dduw*

(from Llywelyn Goch, "I Dduw," *The Myvyrian Archaiology of Wales*, ed. Owen Jones et al. [Denbigh, 1870], p. 354, lines 23–8; trans. Rachel Bromwich, "The Earlier *Cywyddwyr:* Poets Contemporary with Dafydd ap Gwilym," ed. A. O. H. Jarman and Gwilym Rees Hughes, *A Guide to Welsh Literature*, vol. 2 [Swansea, 1979], p. 164)

Gwnaethum ar draethawd geuwawd gywydd
Lleucu yn eilfar lliw caen elfydd
Gwnaethum odineb nag ednebydd
Gwnaethost lynn Ebron ai afonydd
Cyffessaf wrthyd byd wybedydd
Cammau a wnaethum cymmen ieithydd.

[I made in writing a *cywydd* of false praise, comparing Lleucu of the snow's hue to the like of Mary; (25) I performed hidden adultery. I confess to Thee, who knowest all things, the wrongs that I did, skillful in words.]

35 Francesco Petrarch, "Poem 366" in *Canzoniere*, ed. Gianfranco Contini (Turin, 1964), pp. 396–7; trans. Robert M. Durling, *Petrarch's Lyric Poems. The Rime Sparse and Other Lyrics* (Cambridge, MA, 1976), "Poem 366," pp. 582–3, lines 111–12.

36 William Langland, *Piers Plowman: The A Version*, ed. George Kane, rev. edn, vol. 1 (London, 1988); *Piers Plowman: The B Version*, ed. George Kane and E. Talbot Donaldson, rev. edn, vol. 2 (London, 1988); *Piers Plowman: An Edition of the C-text*, ed. Derek Pearsall (Berkeley, 1978).

"Worldly Vanitees": Post-Chaucerian Analogues

There are a few interesting medieval but post-Chaucerian analogues, the most notable one by Pope Pius II Piccolomini (1405–64).

XXVIII

Pope Pius II, *Bulla Retractationum*

(from Aeneas Sylvius Piccolomini [Pope Pius II], *Bulla Retractationum*, in *Opera Omnia* [rpt. Frankfurt, 1967], pp. 1, 2, 3, 4, 8; my translation)

Delicta juventutis meae et ignorantias ne memineris etc. Pudet erroris, poenitet male fecisse et male dictorum scriptorumque, vehementer poenitet: plus scripto quam facto nocuimus. Sed quid agamus? Scriptum et semel emissum volat irrevocabile verbum. Non sunt in potestate nostra scripta, quae in multas inciderunt manus et vulgo leguntur. utinam latuissent quae sunt edita. nam si futuro in seculo manserint et aut malignas mentes inciderint, aut incautas fortasse scandalum parientur. . . . (2) Cogimur igitur, dilecti filii, beatum Augustinum imitari, qui, cum aliqua in suis voluminibus erronea inseruisset, retractationes edidit. Humilis et probatissimi vir ingenii, qui suas ineptias verecunde confiteri, ac corrigere, quam impudenter defendere maluit. Idem et nos faciemus: confitebimur ingenue ignorantias nostras, ne per ea, quae scripsimus, juvenes error irrepat, qui possit in futurum Apostolicam sanctam sedem oppugnare. . . . Si quid adversus hanc doctrinam inveneritis aut in dialogis, aut in epistolis nostris, quae plures a nobis sunt editae, aut in aliis opusculis nostris (multa enim scripsimus adhuc juvenes) respuite atque contemnite. Sequimini quae nunc dicimus (3) et seni magis, quam juveni credite, nec privatum hominem pluris facite, quam Pontificem. Aeneam rejicite, Pium recipite. . . . Dicent fortasse aliqui cum Pontificatu hanc nobis opinionem advenisse, et cum dignitate mutatam esse sententiam. . . . (4) scripsimus epistolas, et opuscula. hoc omnibus passim datur: docti et indocti scribunt: et quae scripsit ipse, nemo contemnit, nisi editionis fervorem tempus extinxerit. nobis placebant scripta nostra more poetarum, qui poemata sua tanquam filios amant. Nec in Basilea quenquam inveniebamus qui ea damnaret: probant enim similia similes: applaudebamus nobis ipsis et in editionibus nostris gloriabamur. . . . (8) Si qua vel vobis, vel aliis conscripsimus aliquando, quae huic doctrinae repugnent, illa, tanquam erronea, et juvenilis animi parum pensata judicia, revocamus, atque omnino respuimus.

[O Lord, do not think about the misdemeanors of my youth and my ignorance. I am ashamed of my error, I regret my bad words and writings, I regret them immensely; I have sinned more through my writings than my actions. But what should we do? One cannot recall the written and sent-out word. Those writings that have fallen into many hands and are widely read are not under my control. I wish that what has appeared had remained hidden, for if it should remain in the future and meet with evil or uncautious minds (2) it may bring forth scandal. . . . We are compelled, dear sons, to imitate St. Augustine, who, since he had inserted some erroneous material in his volumes, produced

retractations. Being a humble man and of upright mind, he preferred to confess with shame his ineptitudes and to correct them than to defend them brazenly. And we will do likewise: We will ingenuously confess our ignorances, lest through what we wrote as a youth, an error may creep in that could harm the holy apostolic see in the future. . . . If you should find anything against this teaching either in my dialogues or in my many published letters, or in other works of ours – for we wrote a lot as a youth – reject and despise it; heed what we say now (3) and give more credit to the old man than the young man; do not esteem the private person higher than the pope. Reject Aeneas and accept Pius. . . . Some will maybe say that we assimilated this opinion with the papacy and changed our opinion with the office. . . . (4) We wrote letters and small compositions, as anyone can do. Scholars and uneducated people alike write and no one despises what he himself has written, unless time dampens his fervor to publish. We delighted in our works, in the manner of poets who love their poems like their own children. At Basle we did not encouter anyone who would have rejected them because birds of a feather flock together. Therefore, we applauded ourselves and triumphed at the appearance of our works. . . . (8) If we have ever written anything to you (the faculty at the University of Cologne) or to others that goes against this teaching, we revoke and reject it as entirely erroneous and the ill-considered judgements of a juvenile mind.]

CHAUCER'S LIST OF WORKS

In lines 1088–9 of the *Retraction*, Chaucer continues the list of works in the chiastic pattern with compositions that he considers to be his worthy works, however undifferentiated they may be in that list: "But of the translacion of Boece de Consolacione, and othere bookes of legendes of seintes, and omelies, and moralitee, and devocioun,/ that thanke I oure Lord Jhesu Crist and his blisful Mooder, and alle seintes of hevene . . ." The rest of the *Retraction* is intercessory prayer (see note 3 above for further information). Chaucer's list divides his writings into the categories of valid and invalid writings in the Middle Ages. Furthermore, Chaucer lets some of his characters recite lists of his works both in *The Introduction to the Man of Law's Tale* and in the Prologue to *The Legend of Good Women*. The Man of Law expounds on Chaucer's prolific poetic output, especially listing the catalogue of the Seintes Legende of Cupide.[37] Both the God of Love and Alceste, provide lists of Chaucer's works in the *Legend*. The God of Love mentions the *Romaunt of the Rose* and *Troilus and Criseyde*. Alceste offers the following list:[38]

[37] In *The Riverside Chaucer*, p. 88, lines 61–76. For a discussion of the literary context of *The Introduction to the Man of Law's Tale*, see *The Riverside Chaucer*, pp. 854–6.

[38] *Prologue (G) to The Legend of Good Women*, lines 255, 265, in *The Riverside Chaucer*, p. 597.

XXIX

Chaucer, *Prologue to the Legend of Good Women*

(from *The Legend of Good Women, Prologue* (G), in *The Riverside Chaucer*, ed. Larry Benson [Boston, 1987], p. 600, lines 403–20)

"He hath maked lewed folk to delyte
To serven yow, in preysynge of youre name.
He made the bok that highte the Hous of Fame,
And ek the Deth of Blaunche the Duchesse,
And the Parlement of Foules, as I gesse,
And al the love of Palamon and Arcite
Of Thebes, thogh the storye is knowen lite;
And many an ympne for your halydayes,
That highten balades, roundeles, vyrelayes;
And, for to speke of other besynesse,
He hath in prose translated Boece,
And Of the Wreched Engendrynge of Mankynde,
As man may in Pope Innocent yfynde;
And mad the lyf also of Seynt Cecile.
He made also, gon is a gret while,
Orygenes upon the Maudeleyne.
Hym oughte now to have the lesse peyne;
He hath mad many a lay and many a thyng."

This list contains many of the same works the *Retraction* does (as well as some not mentioned and considered lost), but uses them for a completely different purpose. In the *Legend*, the author has to curry favor with Cupid for lack of amorous conduct; in the *Retraction*, he apologizes to the Christian God and the audience for the very same works (including *Troilus*; the *Romaunt* is missing) because of that content. Only the first half of the list, however, demonstrates Chaucer's service to the God of Love. The second half includes works that do not further the cause championed by the God of Love, such as the *Boece*, with which Chaucer tries to placate the Christian God in the *Retraction*. The list concludes with a phrase similar to the one rounding out the list in the Retraction: "many a lay and many a thyng."

Chaucer's lists of works have precursors in the custom of Hellenistic authors cataloging their works and commenting on them (*de libris ac ratione studiorum*), exemplified by Isocrates and Galen.[39] For instance, the famous physician Galen of Pergamum includes in his works sections titled, "On the Series of my Books" and "On My Books," along with three lists of his works.[40] The lists by other authors are not generally dichotomous like Chaucer's but often much more extensive. These lists seem to serve the purpose of establishing and

39 See note 5, p. 777

40 Georg Misch, *A History of Autobiography in Antiquity*, trans. E. W. Dickes (Westport, CT, 1973), vol. 1, p. 328.

authenticating an author's canon. After Augustine, whose list encompasses his entire book of *Retractationes*, we have Bede's *Retractatio*, already discussed above, as well as the list at the end of his *Ecclesiastical History*. Bede's work encompasses primarily scriptural exegesis, history, hagiography, and stylistics. The introduction to the list lacks any self-critical elements and ends with a grateful prayer about the mercy of God. Lists can also be found in works by Gerald of Wales, Chrétien de Troyes' *Cligés*, and Don Juan Manuel's *El Conde Lucanor*.

XXX

Bede, *Ecclesiastical History of the English People*

(trans. B. Colgrave and R. A. B. Mynors)

From the time I became a priest until the fifty-ninth year of my life I have made it my business, for my own benefit and that of my brothers, to make brief extracts from the works of the venerable fathers on the holy Scriptures, or to add notes of my own to clarify their sense and interpretation. These are the books:

The beginning of Genesis up to the birth of Isaac and the casting out of Ishmael: four books.

The tabernacle, its vessels, and the priestly vestments: three books.

The First Book of Samuel, to the death of Saul: four books.

On the building of the temple, an allegorical interpretation like the others: two books.

On the book of Kings: thirty questions.

On the Proverbs of Solomon: three books.

On the Song of Songs: seven books.

On Isaiah, Daniel, the twelve prophets, and part of Jeremiah: chapter divisions taken from the treatise of St Jerome.

On Ezra and Nehemiah: three books.

On the Song of Habakkuk: one book.

On the book of the blessed father Tobias, an allegorical explanation concerning Christ and the Church: one book.

Also, summaries of lessons on the Pentateuch of Moses, on Joshua and Judges, on the books of the Kings and Chronicles, on the book of the blessed father Job, on Proverbs, Ecclesiastes, and the Song of Songs, on the prophets Isaiah, Ezra, and Nehemiah.

On the Gospel of Mark: four books.

On the Gospel of Luke: six books.

Homilies on the Gospels, two books.

On the Apostle (Paul), I have transcribed in order whatever I found in the works of St Augustine.

On the Acts of the Apostles: two books.

On the seven catholic Epistles: one book each.

On the Apocalypse of St John: three books.

Also summaries of lessons on the whole of the New Testament except the Gospels.

XXX

Bede, *Historia Ecclesiastica Gentis Anglorum*

(from Bede's *Ecclesiastical History of the English People*, ed. and trans. Bertram Colgrave and R. A. B. Mynors [Oxford, 1991], pp. 566–71)

Ex quo tempore accepti presbyteratus usque ad annum aetatis meae LVIIII haec in Scripturam sanctam meae meorumque necessitati ex opusculis uenerabilium patrum breuiter adnotare, siue etiam ad formam sensus et interpretationis eorum superadicere curaui:

In principium Genesis, usque ad natiuitatem Isaac et eiectionem Ismahelis, libros IIII.

De tabernaculo et uasis eius ac vestibus sacerdotum, libros III.

In primam partem Samuhelis, idest usque ad mortem Saulis, libros IIII.

De aedificatione templi allegoricae expositionis, sicut et cetera, libros II.

Item in Regum librum XXX quaestionum.

In Prouerbia Salomonis libros III.

In Cantica Canticorum libros VII.

In Isaiam, Danihelem, XII prophetas et partem Hieremiae distinctiones capitulorum ex tractatu beati Hieronimi excerptas.

In Ezram et Neemiam libros III

In Canticum Habacum librum I.

In librum beati patris Tobiae explanationis allegoricae de Christo et ecclesia, librum I.

Item capitula lectionum in Pentateucum Mosi, Iosue, Iudicum; in libros Regum et Verba Dierum; in librum beati patris Iob; in Parabolas, Ecclesiasten et Cantica Canticorum; in Isaiam prophetam, Ezram quoque et Neemiam.

In euangelium Marci libros IIII.

In euangelium Lucae libros VI.

Omelarium euangeli libros II.

In Apostolum quaecumque in opusculis sancti Augustini exposita inueni, cuncta per ordinem transcribere curaui.

In Actus Apostolorum libros II.

In epistulas VII catholicas libros singulos.

In Apocalypsin sancti Iohannis libros III.

Item capitula lectionum in totum Nouum Testamentum, excepto euangelio.

Item librum epistularum ad diuersos: quarum de sex aetatibus saeculi una est, de

Also a book of letters to various people: one of these is on the six ages of the world; one on the resting-places of the children of Israel; one on the words of Isaiah, 'And they shall be shut up in prison and after many days shall they be visited'; one on the reason for leap year; and one on the equinox, after Anatolius.

Also of the histories of the saints: a book on the life and passion of St Felix the confessor, which I put into prose from the metrical version of Paulines; a book on the life and passion of St Anastasius which was badly translated from the Greek by some ignorant person, which I have corrected as best I could, to clarify the meaning. I have also described the life of the holy father Cuthbert, monk and bishop, first in heroic verse and then in prose.

A history of the abbots of the monastery in which it is my joy to serve God, namely Benedict, Ceolfrith, and Hwaetberht, in two books.

The history of the Church of our island and race, in five books.

A martyrology of the festivals of the holy martyrs, in which I have diligently tried to note down all that I could find about them, not only on what day, but also by what sort of combat and under what judge they overcame the world.

A book of hymns in various metres and rhythms.

A book of epigrams in heroic and elegiac metre.

Two books, one on the nature of things and the other on chronology: also a longer book on chronology.

A book about orthography, arranged according to the order of the alphabet.

A book on the art of metre, and to this is added another small book on the figures of speech or tropes, that is conerning the figures and modes of speech with which the holy Scriptures are adorned.

Gerald of Wales wrote a number of lists of his works, mostly as ammunition against his critics. In his *Libellus Invectionum* (*Book of Invective*), he describes the vision of a pious man who enumerates Gerald's works and relates their glory.[41] This is followed by the *Epistola ad Capitulum Herefordense de Libris a se Scriptis* (*Epistle to the Chapter of Hereford and Concerning Books Written by Himself*), a lengthy discussion of several of Gerald's works and the periods of their composition and publication in answer to Gerald's detractors.[42] A shorter piece lists most of the works Gerald has written: *Catalogus Brevior Librorum Suorum* (*Lesser Catalogue of his Books*).[43] Finally, in the *Retractationes*, he lists *Topographia Hybernica* (*The History and Topography of Ireland*), *Symbolum Electorum* (*Mark of the Chosen*), *Libellus Invectionum* (*Book of Invective*), and *Gesta Giraldi* (*Deeds of Gerald*) to answer charges against him.[44]

Chrétien de Troyes establishes his canon in his *Cligés* without any implication of guilt.

[41] Gerald of Wales, *Libellus Invectionum*, in *Opera*, ed. J. S. Brewer, 6 vols. (London, 1861), vol. 1, p. 159.

[42] Gerald of Wales, *Epistola ad Capitulum Herefordense de Libris a se Scriptis*, in *Opera*, ed. J. S. Brewer, vol. 1, pp. 409–19.

[43] Gerald of Wales, *Catalogus Brevior Librorum Suorum*, in *Opera*, ed. J. S. Brewer, vol. 1, pp. 421–3.

[44] Gerald of Wales, *Retractationes*, pp. 425–7. Furthermore, Rory McTurk argues that Gerald's "*Topographia Hibernie* may have been a source for Chaucer's House of Fame" ("Chaucer and Giraldus Cambrensis," *Leeds Studies in English* 29 [1998]: 173–83).

mansionibus filiorum Israel una, una de eo quod ait Isaias 'Et claudentur/ ibi in carcerem et post multos dies uisitabuntur', de ratione bissexti una, de aequinoctio iuxta Anatolium una.

Item de historiis sanctorum: librum uitae et passionis sancti Felicis confessoris de metrico Paulini opere in prosam transtuli; librum uitae et passionis sancti Anastasii male de Greco translatum et peius a quodam inperito emendatum, prout potui, ad sensum correxi; uitam sancti patris monachi simul et antistitis Cudbercti et prius heroico metro et postmodum plano sermone descripsi.

Historiam abbatum monasterii huius, in quo supernae pietati deseruire gaudeo, Benedicti, Ceolfridi, et Huaetbercti, in libellis duobus.

Historiam ecclesiasticam nostrae insulae ac gentis in libris V.

Martyrologium de nataliciis sanctorum martyrum diebus, in quo omnes, quos inuenire potui, non solum qua die uerum etiam quo genere certaminis uel sub quo iudice mundum uicerint, diligenter adnotare studui.

Librum hymnorum diuerso metro siue rythmo.

Librum epigrammatum heroico metro siue elegiaco.

De natura rerum, et de temporibus, libros singulos; item de temporibus librum unum maiorem.

Librum de orthographia alphabeti ordine distinctum.

Item librum de metrica arte, et huic adiectum alium de schematibus siue tropis libellum, hoc est de figuris/ modisque locutionum, quibus scriptura sancta contexta est.

XXXI

Chrétien de Troyes, *Cligés*

(from Chrétien de Troyes, *Cligés*, trans. Burton Raffel [New Haven, 1997], p. 1, lines 1–9)

Cil qui fist d'Érec et d'Énide,
Et les commandemanz d'Ovide
Et l'Art d'amors an romans mist,
Et le Mors de l'espaule fist,
Del roi Marc et d'Ysalt la blonde,
Et de la hupe et de l'aronde
Et del rossignol la muance,
Un novel conte rancommance.

[The poet who wrote of Erec
and Enide, and turned Ovid's
Remedies and his Art of Love [*sic*]
Into French, who wrote *The Shoulder*
Bite and "The Tale of King Mark
And Iseult," and "The Transformation
Of the Swallow, the Nightingale,
And the Hoopoe Bird," now starts
Another tale.]

In the introduction to *El Conde Lucanor*, Don Juan Manuel lists his works and their location. His list primarily attempts to protect his literary output from poor copies of his manuscripts: "*La crónica abreviada, El libro de los sabios, El libro de la cavallería, El libro del infante, El libro del cavallero et del escudero, El libro del Conde, El libro de la caça, El libro de los engeños, El libro de los cantares*" [*The Shortened Chronicle, The Book of the Sages, The Book of Chivalry, The Book of the Prince, The Book of the Knight and the Squire, The Book of the Count, The Book of Hunting, The Book of Siege Engines, and The Book of Songs*].[45]

[45] Don Juan Manuel, *El Conde Lucanor*, ed. Carlos Alvar and Pilar Palanco (Barcelona, 1984), p. 7; trans. John E. Keller, L. Clark Keating, and Barbara E. Gaddy, *The Book of Count Lucanor and Patronio: A Translation of Don Juan Manuel's* El Conde Lucanor (New York, 1993), p. 50.

Contributors and Editors

PETER G. BEIDLER, Lucy G. Moses Distinguished Professor of English, Lehigh University

KENNETH BLEETH, Professor of English and Director of Medieval Studies Program, Connecticut College

LAUREL BROUGHTON, Lecturer in English, University of Vermont

JOANNE A. CHARBONNEAU, Professor in Liberal Studies, University of Montana

WILLIAM E. COLEMAN, Professor of English and Comparative Literature, John Jay College and the Graduate Center, City University of New York

CAROLYN P. COLLETTE, Professor of English Language and Literature on the Alumnae Foundation at Mount Holyoke College

ROBERT M. CORREALE, Professor of English Emeritus, Wright State University, Ohio

VINCENT DIMARCO, Professor of English Emeritus, University of Massachusetts (Amherst)

PETER J. C. FIELD, Professor of English, University of Wales, Bangor

MARY HAMEL, Professor of English, Mt St Mary's University, Maryland

RALPH HANNA, Professor of Palaeography and Tutorial Fellow in English, Keble College, Oxford

TRAUGOTT LAWLER, Professor of English Emeritus, Yale University

ANITA OBERMEIER, Associate Professor of English, University of New Mexico

ROBERT R. RAYMO, Professor of English Emeritus, New York University

CHRISTINE RICHARDSON-HAY, University of Auckland

JOHN SCATTERGOOD, Professor of Medieval and Renaissance English, Trinity College, Dublin

N. S. THOMPSON, Freelance author and tutor

EDWARD WHEATLEY, Edward L. Surtz, S.J., Professor of Medieval Literature, Loyola University, Chicago

JOHN WITHRINGTON, Honorary Research Fellow in the School of English and Director of Student Recruitment and Admissions for the University of Exeter

General Index

Index of Manuscripts

(For a complete listing of the MSS of Boccaccio's *Teseida*, see pp. 121–4)

Corrigenda to Volume I

Publisher's note

In the case of *The Reeve's Tale*, readers may wish to consult the version of 'Le meunier et les .II. clers' in Larry D. Benson and Theodore M. Anderson, *The Literary Context of Chaucer's Fabliaux*, New York 1971.

In the case of the translated Latin extracts from Albertano in the analogues to *The Tale of Melibee*, we hope that corrections will appear in a future reprint; however, these extracts are not directly related to Chaucer's text, and there are no problems with the immediate source, namely the French text.

Clerk's Tale

p. 109, line 9 For "scepter" read "staff"

p. 109, lines 10–11 For "I know that such people have proved arrogant and despicable" read "I know from experience that the human race is both arrogant and base"

p. 111, line 35 For "as I was saying" read "as I might say"

p. 113, line 67 For "to hunting and pleasure" read "to hunting and hawking"

p. 113, line 81 For "before all else," read "as soon as possible"

p. 115, line 112 For "farmer" read "inhabitant"

p. 115, line 121 For "lying down on her hard bed" read "arranging her hard bed"

p. 115, lines 124–5 For "His keen insight had penetrated the obscurity in which her commonness hid her" read "With keen insight, he had perceived that virtue which the obscurity of her condition had hidden from the eyes of the common people"

p. 115, line 139 For "she could prepare for" read "she might hasten"

p. 117, lines 154–5 For "in any thing which concerns you and me" read "so that there may be agreement between you and me in everything"

p. 117, line 172 For "making the day most joyful" read " and that most happy day was passed"

p. 117, line 173 Read "such divine favour had shone on the poor bride"

p. 121, line 253 – p. 123, line 254 Read "if I knew beforehand your will, I would likewise begin to wish and desire whatever it was before you wished it."

p. 123, line 256 Read "nor shall death itself be equal to our love"

p. 123, line 264 For "See that you do what you are commanded" read " Take him, do what you are commanded"

p. 123, line 271 For "by the same man who . . ." read "the same place where he"

p. 123, line 280 For “humiliated by remorse and shame of his wife” read “out of remorse and shame at his humble marriage”

p. 125, line 315 For “it [the dowry] was not lost” read “it was not forgotten”

p. 127, line 347 For “enough women for this work” read “women suitable for this work”

p. 127, line 354 “of the next day” is omitted.

p. 129, line 385 For “His words produced almost unbearable joy and frantic devotion” read “[Griselda], hearing these things, almost senseless with joy and frantic with devotion”

p. 129, line 400 For “God is the appropriate tester of evils, as the Apostle James said; but he tempts no one himself.” read “As the Apostle James said, God is not a tempter of evils, and he tempts no-one himself.”

p. 140, line 9 For “loyal towns” read “good towns”

p. 141, line 22 For “see here that I wish to speak to you” read “ see what I want to say to you”

p. 143, line 42 For “I delight” read “I delighted”

p. 145, line 69 For “a mature and ancient courage” read “a mature and old spirit”

p. 145, lines 79–80 For “her great virtue, which could not be surpassed in a woman of such youth” read “her great virtue, more than is usually present in a woman of such an age”

p. 149, line 138 For “Then everyone believed that God had sent such grace to this woman” read “Then God increased and bestowed such grace in this woman”

p. 161, line 343 For “but rather was always uncertain about what would happen in the future” read “rather he always feared that it would turn out like this”

p. 163, lines 386–7 For “as if making fun of her [Griselda]” read “as if playfully”

p. 165, line 393 For “will not be able” read “would not be able”

Franklin’s Tale

p. 247, line 12 For “and for Rome to have no more trouble” read “provided that Rome might keep her honour”

p. 255 (passage 1), lines 17–18 For “as if we had such affection for stones in this kingdom” read “as if we had a scarcity of stones in this kingdom”

p. 255 (passage 2), lines 23-4 For “Not in the least could they make it turn by force” read “They could not, despite all their efforts, make even the smallest stone turn over”

Monk’s Tale

p. 423, line 32/ p. 425, line 22 For “which faced the Romans” read “belonging to the Romans”

p. 423, line 14/ p. 425, line 47 For “drollery” read “good manners, polished behaviour”

p. 436, line 6379/ p. 441 For "you will want to" read "you will be able to"

p. 437, lines 6403–4/ p. 441 For ". . . for it might not be suitable for a man to make his intelligence and prowess widely known" read "for this [i.e. weeping] does not befit a man known for intelligence and prowess"

p. 438, line 6442/ p. 441 For "he could give no advice" read "he could not do anything about it"

p. 443, lines 6513–15/ p. 446 For "His daughter Phania, who was very wise and subtle, told him indeed that she knew how to explain the dreams" read "His daughter Phania, who was so wise and subtle that she knew how to interpret dreams"

p. 444, lines 6534–5/ p. 446 For ". . . and when you make your way there" read "and when she hangs you on the gibbet . . ."

Nun's Priest's Tale

Marie de France

p. 455, line 19 For "Thus the fox who holds the cock; he will fare badly if he comes near them" read "See the fox, holding the cock!"

Roman de Renart

p. 459, lines 89–91 For "Pinte . . . answered from her perch to the cock's right" read "who slept at the cock's right side"

p. 461, line 151 "almost" is omitted.

p. 463, line 197 For "a good fit no need for scissors to be used on it" read "well made, without scissors or shears"

p. 471, line 365 "Renard has hold of you and is carrying you off' is omitted.

Renart le Contrefait

p. 477, line 31317 For "even if women quote the gospels" read "even if they [women] spoke gospel-truth"

p. 481, line 31370 For "in spite of himself a coward can see clearly" read "with difficulty [i.e. not at all] can a coward see clearly"

p. 481, line 31372 The same mistake is made with the parallel construction as above.

p. 481, lines 31377–8 For "Do you plan to be held by your fear in time to come?" read "Do you think you can hold back the future by your fear?"

p. 481, lines 31383-8 For "No man yet has been able to have so much or acquire sense or knowledge if he has so fearful a heart that he is unhappy" read "No man can be so wealthy or acquire so much sense or knowledge that he is not unhappy if his heart is overfearful"

p. 481, line 31387 For "He has never gone into any company" read "He will never be in any company"

p. 481, line 31394 The end of the quotation is signalled by an inverted comma in the translation but not the text.

p. 481, line 31478 For “but may bad luck not take me” read “provided that bad luck does not overcome me”

p. 483, line 31491 For “Here” read “Get out”

p. 485, line 33211 For “I’m looking for” read “I was seeking,”

p. 485, line 33243 For “he has” read “there is”

p. 487, line 33250 For “To Lord Renard it appeared good there” read “this was very evident in Lord Renard’s case”

Holkot

p. 487 “his friend begging that he would help him, *who had been betrayed by the snares of the innkeeper*” The italicized words are represented in the translation by an ellipsis.

p. 487 For “his friend’s most human proposal” read “his (own) most humane intention/plan [to help his friend]”

Parson’s Tale

p. 543, lines 3–5 Read “hasten anxiously to the calm haven and eternal security, seeking the proper, necessary, and unerring path, which indeed is penitence.”

p. 545, line 22 For “at the height of Lent” read “at the beginning of Lent”

p. 553, line 9 For “by whom” read “about what (things)”

p. 563, lines 25–6 For “I want the sinner to be thrown into a state of confusion by this disorder, not by an eternal disorder, from which I, a sinner, want to be set free.” read “I want to be confounded by this type of disorder, not by eternal [disorder], from which I, a sinner, want to be set free”

p. 565, line 88 For “The more He [God] is abandoned by a sinner, the more He loves him.” read “The more he is forgiven, the more he loves”

p. 581, line 104 For “. . . would he be wretched” read “would he not be wretched”